The Common Law Library

CLERK & LINDSELL ON TORTS

VOLUMES IN THE COMMON LAW LIBRARY

Arlidge, Eady & Smith on Contempt
Benjamin's Sale of Goods
Bowstead & Reynolds on Agency
Bullen & Leake & Jacob's Precedents of Pleadings
Charlesworth & Percy on Negligence
Chitty on Contracts
Clerk & Lindsell on Torts
Gatley on Libel and Slander
Goff & Jones, The Law of Restitution
Jackson & Powell on Professional Negligence
McGregor on Damages
Phipson on Evidence

THE COMMON LAW LIBRARY

CLERK & LINDSELL ON TORTS

SECOND SUPPLEMENT TO THE TWENTY-SECOND EDITION

Up to date to May 2019 with some additional developments incorporated

SWEET & MAXWELL

THOMSON REUTERS

Published in 2019 by Thomson Reuters, trading as Sweet & Maxwell.
Thomson Reuters is registered in England & Wales. Company number 1679046.
Registered Office and address for service: 5 Canada Square, Canary Wharf, London, E14 5AQ.

For further information on our products and services, visit *http://www.sweetandmaxwell.co.uk.*

Computerset by Sweet & Maxwell.
Printed and bound by CPI Group (UK) Ltd, Croydon, CR0 4YY.
No natural forests were destroyed to make this product: only farmed timber was used and re-planted.
A CIP catalogue record for this book is available from the British Library.

ISBN: 978-0-414-07260-2

GENERAL EDITOR

MICHAEL A. JONES, BA, LLM, PhD
Solicitor; Emeritus Professor of Law, University of Liverpool

CONSULTANT EDITOR

ANTHONY M. DUGDALE, BA, BCL
Emeritus Professor, Keele University

EDITORS

RODERICK BAGSHAW, BCL, MA (OXON)
Fellow of Magdalen College and Associate Professor of Law, University of Oxford

RICHARD A. BUCKLEY, MA, DPhil, DCL
Of Lincoln's Inn, Barrister; Emeritus Professor of Law, University of Reading

ANDREW S. BURROWS, QC, FBA, MA, DCL, LLM
Honorary Bencher of the Middle Temple, Barrister; Fellow of All Souls College and Professor of the Law of England, University of Oxford

HAZEL F. CARTY, MA
Of the Middle Temple, Barrister; Reader in Law, University of Manchester

KORIEH DUODU, BA
Of Lincoln's Inn, Barrister

PAULA GILIKER, BA, MA, BCL, PhD
Professor of Comparative Law, University of Bristol

GWILYM HARBOTTLE, BA
Of Lincoln's Inn, Barrister

BEN LONGSTAFF, BA
Of Gray's Inn, Barrister

FELICITY MCMAHON, LLB, LLM
Of the Middle Temple, Barrister

JOHN MURPHY, LLB, LLM
Professor of Common Law, University of Lancaster

JENNY STEELE, BA, LLM
Solicitor; Professor of Law, University of York

ANDREW TETTENBORN, MA, LLB
Of Lincoln's Inn, Barrister; Professor of Private and Commercial Law, University of Swansea

First Edition	(1889)	J.F. Clerk and W.H.B. Lindsell
Second Edition	(1896)	" " " "
Third Edition	(1904)	Wyatt Paine
Fourth Edition	(1906)	" " " "
Fifth Edition	(1909)	" " " "
Sixth Edition	(1912)	" " " "
Seventh Edition	(1921)	" " " "
Eighth Edition	(1929)	W.A. Macfarlane and G.W. Wrangham
Ninth Edition	(1937)	Under the General Editorship of Harold Potter
Tenth Edition	(1947)	" " " "
Eleventh Edition	(1954)	Under the General Editorship of John Burke and Peter Allsop
Twelfth Edition	(1961)	General Editor: A.L. Armitage
Thirteenth Edition	(1969)	" " " "
Fourteenth Edition	(1975)	General Editor: Sir A.L. Armitage and R.W.M. Dias
Fifteenth Edition	(1982)	General Editor: R.W.M. Dias
Sixteenth Edition	(1989)	" " " "
Seventeenth Edition	(1995)	General Editor: M.R. Brazier
Second Impression	(1996)	" " " "
Third Impression	(1998)	" " " "
Eighteenth Edition	(2000)	General Editor: A.M. Dugdale
Second Impression	(2003)	" " " "
Nineteenth Edition	(2006)	General Editors: A.M. Dugdale and M.A. Jones
Twentieth Edition	(2010)	General Editor: M.A. Jones
Twenty-First Edition	(2014)	General Editor: M.A. Jones
Twenty-Second Edition	(2017)	General Editor: M.A. Jones Consultant Editor: A.M. Dugdale

HOW TO USE THIS SUPPLEMENT

This is the Second Supplement to the Twenty-Second Edition of *Clerk & Lindsell on Torts*, and has been compiled according to the structure of the main volume.

At the beginning of each chapter of this Supplement, a mini table of contents of the sections in the main volume has been included. Where a heading in this table of contents has been marked with a square pointer, this indicates that there is relevant information in this Supplement to which the reader should refer. Material that is new to the Cumulative Supplement is indicated by the symbol □. Material that has been included from the previous supplements is indicated by the symbol ■.

Within each chapter, updating information is referenced to the relevant paragraph in the main volume.

TABLE OF CONTENTS

TABLE OF CASES

TABLE OF STATUTES

TABLE OF STATUTORY INSTRUMENTS

TABLE OF CIVIL PROCEDURE RULES

TABLE OF EUROPEAN SECONDARY LEGISLATION

REGULATIONS

DIRECTIVES

TABLE OF INTERNATIONAL TREATIES AND CONVENTIONS

CHAPTER 1

PRINCIPLES OF LIABILITY IN TORT

TABLE OF CONTENTS

2. THE FUNCTIONS AND DEVELOPMENT OF TORT LIABILITY

Distributive justice

Replace footnote 65 with:

[65] Whether that policy would look as rational if the claimants in *McFarlane* had received treatment at a private clinic operating for profit, and covered by insurance, is another matter, but it remains a policy judgment rather than a principle of distributive justice. See now *ARB v IVF Hammersmith Ltd* [2018] EWCA Civ 2803; [2019] 2 W.L.R. 1094 where the Court of Appeal confirmed that the legal policy issues that underpinned *McFarlane* also apply to breach of a strict contractual obligation. **1-16**

Retributive justice

Replace footnote 74 with:

[74] Lord Slynn argued similarly that it would not be reasonable to impose such liability on the doctor as he "does not assume responsibility for those economic losses" and that if the client "wants to be able to recover such costs he or she must do so by an appropriate contract". However, it would seem that the economic costs of raising a healthy child cannot be recovered even for breach of a strict contractual obligation: see *ARB v IVF Hammersmith Ltd* [2018] EWCA Civ 2803; [2019] 2 W.L.R. 1094. In *McFarlane*, the House of Lords allowed the mother's claim for the discomfort and inconvenience of the unwanted pregnancy and childbirth. In its subsequent decision in *Rees v Darlington Memorial Hospital NHS Trust* [2003] UKHL 52; [2004] 1 A.C. 309 at [8] (see further paras 1-39 and 8-95) Lord Bingham, leading the majority, considered that the discomfort award did not give adequate recognition to the parents' loss and added a further conventional award of £15,000 to reflect the claimants' loss of autonomy. The majority Law Lords all regarded this as a modest award and concerns about disproportionate recovery were not raised. **1-19**

3. THE FRAMEWORK OF TORT LIABILITY

(a) Interests protected by the law of torts

(i) Personal interests

Bodily integrity

Replace footnote 95 with:

1-26 [95] See *F v West Berkshire HA* [1990] 2 A.C. 1, per Lord Goff. But there is no free-standing cause of action for interference with a patient's autonomy: *Shaw v Kovac* [2017] EWCA Civ 1028; [2017] 1 W.L.R. 4773 at [48].

Trivial injury

Replace footnote 101 with:

1-29 [101] [2007] UKHL 39; [2008] 1 A.C. 281 at [7]. In *Yearworth v North Bristol NHS Trust* [2009] EWCA Civ 37; [2010] Q.B. 1 the Court of Appeal held that the negligent destruction of the claimants' sperm which had been stored for possible future use in fertility treatment did not constitute "personal injury", though the Court concluded that the stored sperm was capable of being owned by the men who had provided it and that this could give rise to an action in bailment. See also *A v A Health and Social Services Trust* [2011] NICA 28; [2012] N.I. 77 holding that the claimants, who had been born with a different skin colour from that of their parents as a result of negligence in the selection of gametes during the process of *in vitro* fertilisation carried out by the defendants, had not suffered compensatable damage. They could not point to "any physical or mental defect as a result of the process which led to their existence. As the judge correctly pointed out, they have no claim under the [Congenital Disabilities (Civil Liability) Act 1976] because they are healthy and normal children. Having a different skin colour from the majority of the surrounding population and their parents' cannot sensibly be regarded as damage or disability ... " (at [9]). The case is discussed by S. Sheldon, "Only skin deep? The harm of being born a different colour to one's parents" (2011) 19 Med. L. Rev. 657. *Rothwell* should be contrasted with *Dryden v Johnson Matthey Plc* [2018] UKSC 18; [2018] 2 W.L.R. 1109, where employees became sensitised to platinum salts without developing any symptoms and would not develop symptoms unless they were further exposed to platinum salts. The Court of Appeal held that they had not suffered compensatable personal injury, and the financial loss they sustained as a result of no longer being able to work with platinum salts constituted pure economic loss which fell beyond the scope of the employers' duty. The Supreme Court disagreed. In *Rothwell* the pleural plaques were symptomless and had no effect on the claimants' ability to lead their lives or to work, whereas in *Dryden* the claimants' capacity for work had been impaired and they were therefore significantly worse off. This constituted actionable personal injury which was more than negligible (ibid. at [40]).

No tort of invasion of privacy

Replace footnote 137 with:

1-37 [137] [2003] UKHL 53; [2004] 2 A.C. 406 at [18]. See now the Data Protection Act 2018.

Autonomy

Replace paragraph with:

1-39 In *Rees v Darlington Memorial Hospital NHS Trust*[145] a majority of a seven judge House of Lords recognised autonomy as an interest that could be protected by the law of tort. A sterilisation operation for which the defendant was responsible, was carried out negligently and its failure led to the claimant giving birth to an unwanted, but healthy child. Following its earlier decision in *McFarlane v Tayside Health Board*,[146] the House of Lords held that no damages could be awarded for the cost of bringing up such a child but the majority held that a conventional award of £15,000 should be made. Lord Bingham said that it "would not be intended to be compensatory ... but ... would afford some measure of recognition of the wrong done".[147] Lord Millett explained more fully that the award was "not for the birth of the child but for the denial of an important aspect of [the parents] personal autonomy, viz the right to limit the size of their family". He continued: "This is an important aspect of human dignity, which is increasingly being regarded as an important human right which should be protected by the law. The loss of this right is not an abstract or theoretical one. ...the parents have lost the opportunity to live their lives in the way that they wished and planned to do. The loss of this opportunity, whether characterised as a right or a freedom, is a proper subject for compensation by way of damages."[148] The award is made without proof of financial loss. Dissenting, Lord Steyn argued that it was for Parliament to create such a novel remedy and that the "Law Commissions and Parliament ought in any event, to consider the impact of the creation of a power to make a conventional award ... for the coherence of the tort system".[149] There may be other situations where autonomy could be recognised as an interest to be protected. In *Chester v Afshar*[150] Lord Steyn justified providing a remedy for a doctor's negligent failure to warn a patient of risks associated with surgery, on the basis of the need to "give due respect to the autonomy and dignity of each patient". However, he and the majority of the Lords chose to recognise this wrong by awarding the patient damages for the disability resulting from the surgery rather than for the loss of the opportunity to choose.[151] In *Rees*, autonomy was protected against negligent conduct but this raises the possibility that it might be protected against intentional conduct, for example, by the developing tort of misfeasance in a public office. However, there is no free-standing cause of action for interference with a claimant's autonomy. An action by a patient against a doctor for non-disclosure of the risks of treatment must be an action in negligence, albeit that the claim can be characterised as an interference with the patient's autonomous choices about whether to accept a particular medical treatment.[151A]

[145] [2003] UKHL 52; [2004] 1 A.C. 309.

[146] [2000] 2 A.C. 59.

[147] [2003] UKHL 52; [2004] 1 A.C. 309 at [8].

[148] [2003] UKHL 52; [2004] 1 A.C. 309 at [123].

[149] [2003] UKHL 52; [2004] 1 A.C. 309 at [46]. See also the similar views of Lord Hope at [77].

[150] [2004] UKHL 41; [2005] 1 A.C. 134 at [18].

[151] It is not surprising that Lord Steyn did not consider a conventional award for loss of opportunity to choose given his view in *Rees*. Lord Hoffmann in his dissent did suggest that there was "a case for a modest solatium" but felt that the cost of litigation made the "law of torts an unsuitable vehicle for distributing the modest compensation which might be payable": [2004] UKHL 41; [2005] 1 A.C. 134 at [34]. However, claims for a modest solatium are likely to be less costly than those for a substantial disability award.

[151A] See *Shaw v Kovac* [2017] EWCA Civ 1028; [2017] 1 W.L.R. 4773 at [48].

(c) Impact of the Human Rights Act 1998

Impact on existing principles

Replace paragraph with:

D v East Berkshire Community Health NHS Trust represents, perhaps, the high water mark of the Human Rights Act being relied upon to modify existing tort principles, involving as it did a stark departure from what would otherwise have been binding House of Lords' authority. Subsequent decisions have tended to suggest that their Lordships are content to leave claimants to their Human Rights Act remedies rather than adapt the common law to fill a perceived gap. So in *Smith v* 1-82

Chief Constable of Sussex[290] the claimant complained that the police had failed to act to prevent his former partner from attacking him, despite having been informed of previous attacks and death threats to the claimant. The Court of Appeal declined to strike out the claim as inconsistent with previous House of Lords authority.[291] Pill LJ commented that: "there is a strong case for developing the common law action for negligence in the light of Convention rights",[292] and considered that it was "unacceptable that a court, bound by section 6 of the 1998 Act, should judge a case such as the present by different standards depending on whether or not the claim is specifically brought under the Convention. The decision whether a duty of care exists in a particular situation should in a common law claim require a consideration of Article 2 rights."[293] The House of Lords[294] reversed the Court of Appeal, holding that no duty of care in negligence was owed by the police to the claimant. On the question of the interaction between the common law and Convention rights, Lord Bingham (again in a dissenting speech) agreed with the comments of Pill LJ and Rimer LJ in the Court of Appeal: although the existence of a Convention right could not call for the "instant manufacture of a corresponding common law right where none exists" nonetheless "one would be surprised if conduct which violated a fundamental right or freedom of the individual did not find a reflection in a body of law ordinarily as sensitive to human needs as the common law, and it is demonstrable that the common law in some areas has evolved in a direction signalled by the Convention".[295] On the other hand, Lord Hope considered that "the common law, with its own system of limitation periods and remedies, should be allowed to stand on its own feet side by side with the alternative remedy".[296] If there were gaps in the common law, they could be dealt with in domestic law under the Human Rights Act. Lord Brown also rejected the argument that, in a case such as *Smith*, the common law should develop "to reflect the Strasbourg jurisprudence". Given that the Human Rights Act provided for claims to be brought, it was "quite simply unnecessary now to develop the common law to provide a parallel cause of action".[297] Convention claims had "very different objectives from civil actions". Whereas civil actions were designed to compensate claimants for their losses, Convention claims were intended to uphold minimum human rights standards and to vindicate those rights.[298]

[290] [2008] EWCA Civ 39; [2008] P.I.Q.R. P12.

[291] *Hill v Chief Constable of West Yorkshire* [1989] A.C. 53 and *Brooks v Commissioner of Police of the Metropolis* [2005] UKHL 24; [2005] 1 W.L.R. 1495.

[292] [2008] EWCA Civ 39; [2008] P.I.Q.R. P12 at [53].

[293] [2008] EWCA Civ 39; [2008] P.I.Q.R. P12 at [57]. See also per Rimer LJ at [45]: "where a common law duty covers the same ground as a Convention right, it should, so far as practicable, develop in harmony with it; if so, the common law may well require a re-visiting of the *Hill* policy considerations, at least in the context of cases raising considerations of the right to life. It appears to me odd that, in that particular context, our jurisprudence can apparently acknowledge two parallel, but potentially inconsistent, approaches to the same factual situation."

[294] [2008] UKHL 50; [2009] 1 A.C. 225.

[295] [2008] UKHL 50; [2009] 1 A.C. 225 at [58], citing *D v East Berkshire Community NHS Trust.*

[296] [2008] UKHL 50; [2009] 1 A.C. 225 at [82].

[297] [2008] UKHL 50; [2009] 1 A.C. 225 at [136]. See also the comments of Lord Toulson in *Michael v Chief Constable of South Wales* [2015] UKSC 2; [2015] A.C. 1732 at [125] rejecting the claimant's argument that where there was a breach of Convention rights the common law should reflect that by providing an additional remedy in the tort of negligence. If there was no basis, applying orthodox common law principles, for a claimed duty of care then there was no rationale "for gold plating the claimant's Convention rights by providing compensation on a different basis from the claim under the Human Rights Act 1998".

[298] [2008] UKHL 50; [2009] 1 A.C. 225 at [138]. The converse argument, that in considering claims under the ECHR the courts should take into account the policy issues that have resulted in a conclusion that no duty of care at common law was owed by the defendant and so hold that there has been no breach of Convention rights, was rejected by the majority of the Supreme Court in *Commissioner of Police of the Metropolis v DSD* [2018] UKSC 11; [2019] A.C. 196 (risk of defensive policing and the diversion of resources from police work to compensation claims not relevant to whether the police owe an operational duty under ECHR art.3 when investigating criminal offences). Lord Neuberger commented, at [97], that: "Just as the majority of this Court accepted in *Michael v Chief Constable of South Wales* [2015] UKSC 2; [2015] A.C. 1732 at [123]–[128] that the domestic tortious test for liability should not be widened to achieve consistency with the human rights test, so should the human rights test for liability not be narrowed to achieve consistency with the domestic, tortious test." See also per Lord Kerr at [68]. See further para.14-93.

Chapter 2

CAUSATION IN TORT: GENERAL PRINCIPLES

Table of Contents

2. FACTUAL CAUSATION

(b) The uncertainty of hypothetical human conduct

(ii) Claimant's response to advice about risks of medical treatment

Negligent advice about the risks of medical treatment

Replace paragraph with:

2-15 Similarly, a patient who alleges that a doctor negligently failed to advise her about the risks of an operative procedure must prove that had she been informed about the risks she would have declined the treatment, thereby avoiding the risk that has now materialised.[44] This is a subjective test, i.e. it is a question of what *this claimant* would have done had the correct advice been given, not what a hypothetical reasonable claimant would have done.[45] In many cases resolution of the hypothetical question of what the claimant would have done had the defendant discharged his duty to advise about the risks, although dependent upon the credibility of evidence, is relatively straightforward. If the claimant would have proceeded with medical treatment even if given a warning, the defendant's breach of duty is not a cause of the damage (i.e. the physical harm which results from the materialisation of the non-disclosed risk). If, on the other hand, the claimant would never have accepted the treatment had she known about the risks the non-disclosure has caused the claimant's damage. The claimant would not have had that particular treatment and therefore the risk associated with the procedure would not have had an opportunity to materialise. There is, however, a third category of case where the claimant says that she would have postponed the decision, possibly in order to obtain further medical advice about the options, but she cannot in all honesty say what her ultimate decision would have been.[46] On one view, if the claimant would have undergone the procedure at some stage in the future, then she would have faced the same inherent risks associated with it, and so the defendant's negligent failure to inform her of those risks would have been of no causative effect. The alternative view is that the materialisation of a small random risk inherent in a particular medical treatment which produces injury to the claimant is the result of the particular time and circumstances in which the treatment was given (assuming that there is nothing which predisposes the particular patient to this risk), and therefore if treatment had been delayed to another occasion the probability is that the small inherent risk would not have materialised *on that occasion*, and so the materialisation of the risk is causally linked to the defendant's non-disclosure of the risk. In *Chester v Afshar*,[47] by a bare majority, the House of Lords held that the latter approach was correct.

44 See *Smith v Barking, Havering and Brentwood HA* (1988), [1994] 5 Med. L.R. 285; *McAllister v Lewisham and North Southwark HA* [1994] 5 Med. L.R. 343; *Lybert v Warrington HA* [1996] 7 Med. L.R. 71, CA; *Thompson v Blake-James* [1998] Lloyd's Rep. Med. 187 CA. There is no rule of law that a patient must give evidence personally about what would or would not have happened if she had been properly informed of the facts before making a decision: *Webb v Barclays Bank Plc and Portsmouth Hospitals NHS Trust* [2001] EWCA Civ 1141; [2002] P.I.Q.R. P8; [2001] Lloyd's Rep. Med. 500 at [42]. For more detailed discussion see M.A. Jones, *Medical Negligence*, 5th edn (Sweet & Maxwell, 2018), paras 7-081 to 7-114.

45 Cf. the Canadian approach in *Reibl v Hughes* (1980) 114 D.L.R. (3d) 1 Supreme Court of Canada, applying an objective test. The subjective test is, however, moderated by objective considerations which go to the credibility of the claimant's evidence that she would have done something different: see *Smith v Barking, Havering and Brentwood HA* [1994] 5 Med. L.R. 285. So, to say that the claimant would have acted rationally if given the appropriate advice is not to apply an objective "reasonable patient" test to causation, provided that there has been a scrupulous assessment of the claimant and her evidence and the judge has taken into account the personal and social considerations particular to the claimant: *Diamond v Royal Devon and Exeter NHS Foundation Trust* [2019] EWCA Civ 585 at [21]. If the evidence from the defendant doctor is that it is her practice not to disclose particular risks because if she did so most patients would choose to avoid the option that she considers to be the best, the claimant will have little difficulty in persuading the court that she would probably not have gone ahead with the option recommended by the doctor: see *Montgomery v Lanarkshire Health Board* [2015] UKSC 11; [2015] A.C. 1430, at [101]–[104].

46 Though the court may be able to conclude, from other evidence, what the claimant would probably have done, ultimately: see, e.g. *McAllister v Lewisham and North Southwark HA* [1994] 5 Med. L.R. 343. There is a further factual variant where there are multiple risk factors, and the claimant is warned about some, but not all, of the risks. If, say, the evidence is that the claimant was informed about risk A but not about risk B, and risk A materialises but the claimant states that had he been informed about *both* risk A and B he would have declined the procedure and so avoided the risk that has materialised, does the claim succeed on causation? In *Wallace v Kam* [2013] HCA 19; (2013) 87 A.L.J.R. 648 the High Court of Australia held that in these circumstances the claim will fail. The fact that the claimant would have declined treatment had he been informed about the risk that has not materialised is irrelevant. This is because: "the policy that underlies requiring the exercise of reasonable care and skill in the giving of that warning is neither to protect that right to choose nor to protect the patient from exposure to all unacceptable risks. The underlying policy is rather to protect the patient from the occurrence of physical injury the risk of which is unacceptable to the patient. It is appropriate that the scope of liability for breach of the duty reflect that underlying policy" (at [36]). The position might have been different if there was a "risk of a single physical injury to which there are several contributing factors the combination of which operate to increase the risk of that physical injury occurring. To fail to warn the patient of one factor while informing the patient of another may in a particular case be to fail to warn the patient of the extent of the risk and thereby to expose the patient to a level of risk of the physical injury occurring that is unacceptable to the patient" (at [34], discussing the reasoning of Lord Caplan in *Moyes v Lothian Health Board* 1990 S.L.T. 444).

47 [2004] UKHL 41; [2005] 1 A.C. 134, applying the majority decision of the High Court of Australia in *Chappell v Hart* [1998] HCA 55; (1998) 156 A.L.R. 517; commented on by Cane (1999) 115 L.Q.R. 21. For comment on *Chester v Afshar* see Jones (2005) 13 Tort. L.R. 40; Stapleton, "Occam's Razor Reveals an Orthodox Basis for *Chester v Afshar*" (2006) 122 L.Q.R. 426; Maskrey and Edis, "*Chester v Afshar* and *Gregg v Scott*: Mixed Messages for Lawyers" [2005] J.P.I.L. 205.

Chester v Afshar limited to cases of negligent medical advice

Replace paragraph with:

The Court of Appeal has treated the majority ruling in *Chester v Afshar* as applying an exceptional rule to cases of negligent failure to warn patients about the risks of medical treatment.[56] For claims in respect negligent advice by other professionals the traditional causation rules apply, and the claimant must normally demonstrate what advice should have been given, and that he would probably have acted on that advice thereby avoiding the loss. In *White v Paul Davidson & Taylor*[57] Arden LJ said that *Chester v Afshar* did not establish a new general rule on causation, but was an application of the principle in *Fairchild v Glenhaven Funeral Services Ltd*[58] that, in exceptional circumstances, rules of causation may be modified on policy grounds. The principle of informed consent to medical procedures had special importance in the law, but there were no particular policy reasons for departing from traditional principles of causation in an ordinary case of solicitors' 2-19 negligence.[59] In *Beary v Pall Mall Investments (A Firm)*[60] Dyson LJ rejected a submission that *Chester v Afshar* should be applied generally in claims for negligent financial advice. *Chester* was exceptional and constituted a departure from established principles of causation, justified by the particular policy considerations involved in patients giving informed consent to medical treatment.

[56] *Chester v Afshar* does not apply to cases of negligent medical *treatment*: *Correia v University Hospital of North Staffordshire NHS Trust* [2017] EWCA Civ 356; [2017] Med. L.R. 292 (patient consented to three-stage operation, but surgeon negligently performed only the first two stages; it did not follow that the patient had not made an informed choice to have the surgery, and the injury was not "intimately linked" with the duty to warn). *Chester v Afshar* requires the claimant to prove that she would at least have deferred the treatment if she had been warned about the risk. It cannot apply where the court concludes, on the facts, that it is probable that even if warned about the risks the claimant would have proceeded with the operation as and when she did: *Duce v Worcestershire Acute Hospitals NHS Trust* [2018] EWCA Civ 1307; [2018] P.I.Q.R. P18 (a proposition for which, it might be thought, no Court of Appeal pronouncement was necessary).

[57] [2004] EWCA Civ 1511; [2005] P.N.L.R. 15 at [40].

[58] [2002] UKHL 22; [2003] 1 A.C. 32; see para.2-52.

[59] [2004] EWCA Civ 1511 at [41]–[42].

[60] [2005] EWCA Civ 415; [2005] P.N.L.R. 35 at [38].

(v) Third party's hypothetical conduct

Replace footnote 81 with:

2-26 [81] [1995] 1 W.L.R. 1602; approved by the Supreme Court in *Perry v Raleys Solicitors* [2019] UKSC 5; [2019] 2 W.L.R. 636.

(c) Scientific uncertainty about causal mechanisms

(ii) Material contribution to the damage

Material contribution to psychiatric damage

Add new paragraph:

2-43A These issues were considered again in *BAE Systems (Operations) Ltd v Konczak*.[145A] Underhill LJ noted that the difference between the view expressed in *Hatton v Sutherland* and that of Smith LJ in *Dickins* was that Smith LJ appeared to suggest that psychiatric harm could never be divisible, whereas in *Hatton* the court had said that where there were multiple extrinsic causes, a "sensible attempt" should be made to apportion the harm between what is and is not attributable to the defendant's wrong. *Hatton* recognised that there may be cases where the harm was "truly indivisible" and that in such cases apportionment would be wrong, but there may be some cases where the harm would be divisible.[145B] Whether it is possible to make a "sensible attempt" to apportion the damage will depend on the facts and the medical evidence.[145C] Although the guidance given on apportionment in *Hatton* had been obiter, if there were differences between the views expressed in *Hatton* and *Dickins*, *Hatton* should be followed.[145D] The tribunal or court should:

> "try to identify a rational basis on which the harm suffered can be apportioned between a part caused by the employer's wrong and a part which is not so caused. I would emphasise, because the distinction is easily overlooked, that the exercise is concerned not with the divisibility of the causative contribution but with the divisibility of the harm. In other words, the question is whether the tribunal can identify, however broadly, a particular part

> of the suffering which is due to the wrong; not whether it can assess the degree to which the wrong caused the harm."[145E]

Moreover, if the claimant had a pre-existing mental disorder or vulnerability to psychiatric harm the court should take that into account in the assessment of damages by discounting the award to reflect the risk that the claimant would have developed the mental health condition in the future in any event, just as it would if the claimant had a vulnerability to developing a physical condition in the future. This principle applies whenever the claimant had a predisposition to develop the mental health problem in the future, whether the psychiatric harm is divisible or not (i.e. it is quite separate from the process of deciding whether the harm is capable of being apportioned for the purpose of determining causation).

[145A] [2017] EWCA Civ 1188; [2018] I.C.R. 1. For further discussion of *BAE Systems (Operations) Ltd v Konczak* see S. Bailey, "Apportionment and psychiatric injury" (2018) 34 P.N. 42.

[145B] [2017] EWCA Civ 1188; [2018] I.C.R. 1, per Underhill LJ at [67].

[145C] *Rahman v Arearose Ltd* [2001] Q.B. 351 provides an example where the medical evidence did distinguish between different causes of different aspects of the claimant's mental state: see para.2-122.

[145D] [2017] EWCA Civ 1188; [2018] I.C.R. 1 at [70] and [92], per Underhill and Irwin LJJ respectively.

[145E] [2017] EWCA Civ 1188; [2018] I.C.R. 1 at [71], per Underhill LJ.

(iii) Material contribution to the risk of damage

Defendant's negligence more than doubles existing risk

Replace footnote 157 with:

[157] [2007] EWCA Civ 1261 at [74]. See also *Jones v Secretary of State for Energy and Climate Change* [2012] EWHC 2936 (QB) where Swift J used a "doubling of the risk" approach to the determination of causation of both lung and bladder cancers where the claimants had been exposed to carcinogenic fumes and dust. See further *Heneghan v Manchester Dry Docks Ltd* [2016] EWCA Civ 86; [2016] 1 W.L.R. 2036 at [8] per Lord Dyson MR, where epidemiological evidence showed a more than doubling of the risk that it was asbestos rather than smoking which caused the deceased's lung cancer. This provided the answer to the "what" question, i.e. what toxin probably caused the lung cancer? It was not sufficient, however, to answer the "who" question, which arises in a multiple contributor case, where the issue is which contributor's asbestos caused the claimant's indivisible damage, i.e. lung cancer? In order to attribute causation to each of the multiple tortfeasors the court had to rely on *Fairchild v Glenhaven Funeral Services Ltd* [2002] UKHL 22; [2003] 1 A.C. 32 (para.2-52). *Heneghan* is discussed by R. Geraghty [2016] J.P.I.L. C83. See also *Magill v Panel Systems (DB Ltd)* [2017] EWHC 1517 (QB); [2017] Med. L.R. 440—deceased due to have heart surgery, but diagnosed with mesothelioma attributable to defendants' negligence and surgery was postponed; he died from a heart attack; the failure to have surgery doubled the risk of death; defendants were held liable for the death on basis that they had caused or contributed to an indivisible injury, i.e. a heart arrhythmia, which caused the death. 2-47

Replace paragraph with:

In *Sienkiewicz v Greif (UK) Ltd*[158] Lord Phillips agreed with Smith LJ's proposition: "as a matter of logic, if a defendant is responsible for a tortious exposure that has more than doubled the risk of the victim's disease, it follows on the balance of probability that he has caused the disease." However, where *Fairchild v Glenhaven Funeral Services Ltd*[159] applies to determine causation it is not appropriate to apply such a statistical approach, and accordingly the claimant cannot be *required* to prove that the defendant's breach of duty had more than doubled the risk. Lord Phillips said that where two agents have operated cumulatively and simultaneously in causing the onset of a disease there was "no scope for the application of the 'doubles the risk' test". In that situation *Bonnington Castings v Wardlaw*[160] would apply, with the consequence that where the disease was indivisible (as with lung cancer) a defendant who had tortiously contributed to the cause 2-48 of the disease would be liable in full; and where the disease was divisible (as with asbestosis) the tortfeasor would be liable for the share of the disease for which he was responsible.[161] On the other hand:

> "Where the initiation of the disease is dose related, and there have been consecutive exposures to an agent or agents that cause the disease, one innocent and one tortious, the position will depend upon which exposure came first in time. Where it was the tortious exposure, it is axiomatic that this will have contributed to causing the disease, even if it is not the sole cause. Where the innocent exposure came first, there may be an issue as to whether this was sufficient to trigger the disease or whether the subsequent, tortious, exposure contributed to the cause. I can see no reason in principle why the 'doubles the risk' test should not be applied in such circumstances, but the court must be astute to see that the epidemiological evidence provides a really sound basis for determining the statistical probability of the cause or causes of the disease."[162]

Finally, where there were competing alternative (as opposed to cumulative) potential causes of a disease or injury there was no reason in principle why epidemiological evidence should not be used to show that one of the causes was more than twice as likely as all the others put together to have caused the disease or injury.[163]

[158] [2011] UKSC 10; [2011] 2 A.C. 229 at [78].

[159] [2002] UKHL 22; [2003] 1 A.C. 32; see para.2-52.

[160] [1956] A.C. 613; see para.2-32.

[161] [2011] UKSC 10; [2011] 2 A.C. 229 at [90].

[162] [2011] UKSC 10; [2011] 2 A.C. 229 at [91].

[163] [2011] UKSC 10; [2011] 2 A.C. 229 at [93]. But the "doubling of risk" test should be used with caution. In *Williams v The Bermuda Hospitals Board* [2016] UKPC 4; [2016] A.C. 888 at [48] Lord Toulson said that: "If it is a known fact that a particular type of act (or omission) is likely to have a particular effect, proof that the defendant was responsible for such an act (or omission) and that the claimant had what is the usual effect will be powerful evidence from which to infer causation, without necessarily requiring a detailed scientific explanation for the link. But inferring causation from proof of heightened risk is never an exercise to apply mechanistically. A doubled tiny risk will still be very small."

(iv) Multiple tortfeasors and contribution to the risk

(3) Applying Fairchild

Limits to Fairchild

Replace footnote 185 with:

2-55 [185] [2002] UKHL 22; [2003] 1 A.C. 32 at [43], per Lord Nicholls. See also *Clough v First Choice Holidays and Flights Ltd* [2006] EWCA Civ 15; [2006] P.I.Q.R. P22; [2006] N.P.C. 8 (ordinary accident in which claimant slipped and fell; *Fairchild* did not apply). Note also that, conversely, proof of causation is not proof of breach of duty. So where a claimant has been exposed to asbestos in a number of employments, although the *Fairchild* principle may assist in establishing causation against an individual defendant, the fact that the claimant has developed mesothelioma does not, of itself, give rise to an inference that that defendant was also in breach of duty: *Brett v Reading University* [2007] EWCA Civ 88 at [21] and [24]. For the test of breach of duty in a case of mesothelioma see *Williams v University of Birmingham* [2011] EWCA Civ 1242; [2012] P.I.Q.R P4 at [40]; *Bussey v 00654701 Ltd (formerly Anglia Heating Ltd)* [2018] EWCA Civ 243; [2018] 3 All E.R. 354; [2018] I.C.R. 1242; para.13-29.

3. LOSS OF A CHANCE

(a) Loss of a chance of financial benefit

Delete footnote 270. 2-78

Replace paragraph with:

Allied Maples has frequently been followed[271] and in *Perry v Raleys Solicitors*[272] the Supreme Court approved the "sensible, fair and practicable dividing line" laid down in *Allied Maples*. In an action for professional negligence, where the question whether the client would have been better off depends upon what the client would have done upon receipt of competent advice, this must be proved by the claimant on the balance of probabilities. Where the claimed beneficial outcome depends upon what others would have done, the court must adopt the loss of chance approach.[273] The defendants had failed to advise the client to make a claim for a "services award" under a compensation scheme for former miners who had developed vibration white finger. The services award was intended to compensate for tasks that the claimant was no longer able to perform, due to his medical condition, such as gardening and DIY. In the action against the solicitors for the lost opportunity to claim for a services award, the trial judge concluded that the claimant had given dishonest evidence about his ability to perform the tasks, and held that he had not proved that he would have made an honest claim, if competently advised. The Court of Appeal held, inter alia, that the judge had been in error in conducting a trial within a trial on the causation issue as to whether the claimant would have brought an honest claim if competently advised. The issue, said the Court, was if the claimant had made a services claim, what would have been his chances of success? The Supreme Court disagreed. The taking of some positive step by the client is an essential, though not necessarily sufficient, element in the chain of causation, and the client is best-placed to assist the court with that question. This should be dealt with on the balance of probabilities. If the client proves, even on the narrowest balance, that he would have brought the claim, there is no discount in the value of the claim to take account of the substantial possibility that he might not have brought the claim. Conversely, if he fails to prove on the balance of probabilities that he would have initiated the action the client gets nothing. There was no reason in principle or in justice why either party to the professional negligence proceedings should be deprived of the full benefit of an adversarial trial of that issue.[273A] The mere fact that in determining the issue of what the claimant would have done involves consideration of facts that would have been relevant to the underlying claim is not a good reason not to subject them to the forensic rigour of a trial.[273B] Moreover, the claimant had to prove that, properly advised, his claim for a services award would have been an honest claim. Given that the loss of "nuisance value" claims cannot be the subject of an action in negligence against professional advisors,[273C] "then so, a fortiori, must dishonest claims." [273D] 2-79

[271] See, e.g. *Stovold v Barlows* [1996] P.N.L.R. 91; *First Interstate Bank of California v Cohen Arnold & Co* [1996] P.N.L.R. 17; *Motor Crown Petroleum Ltd v SJ Berwin & Co (A Firm)* [2000] Lloyd's Rep. P.N. 438; *Charles v Hugh James Jones & Jenkins (A Firm)* [2000] 1 W.L.R. 1278, CA; *Perkin v Lupton Fawcett (A Firm)* [2008] EWCA Civ 418; [2008] P.N.L.R. 30 (claimants succeeded in respect of 20% chance of being better off financially); *Wellesley Partners LLP v Withers LLP* [2015] EWCA Civ 1146; [2016] Ch. 529; *McGill v Sports and Entertainment Media Group* [2016] EWCA Civ 1063; [2017] 1 W.L.R. 989. See further paras 10-158 and 10-159; and for detailed discussion see *Jackson & Powell on Professional Liability*, 8th edn (London: Sweet & Maxwell, 2017), para.11–268 onwards. It is possible, though the matter remains unresolved, that in a claim by a disappointed beneficiary in a "negligent will" case (see para.10-113) the question of what the deceased testator would have done had there been

no breach of duty should be assessed on the basis of a lost chance, rather than the balance of probabilities (treating the testator as a third party in the action between the disappointed beneficiary and the negligent solicitor): *Feltham v Freer Bouskell* [2013] EWHC 1952 (Ch); [2014] P.N.L.R. 2 at [96]–[112].

272 [2019] UKSC 5; [2019] 2 W.L.R. 636 at [21].

273 [2019] UKSC 5; [2019] 2 W.L.R. 636 at [20]. The claimant does not have an option to choose whether to base a claim on a lost chance or to prove a claim on a balance of probabilities: *Assetco Plc v Grant Thornton UK LLP* [2019] EWHC 150 (Comm); [2019] 1 WLUK 344 at [406]–[415], per Bryan J. Of course, on a particular set of facts the evidence may be that the chance of the third party acting in a particular way was almost certain, such that in assessing the claimant's chance of obtaining a benefit or avoiding a loss the chance will be virtually 100% and there will be no reduction of the damages award (ibid. at [416]). Alternatively, the chance of a successful outcome may be almost zero, with the result that it is assessed as merely speculative, not substantial, so that causation will not be proved, as e.g. in *Mount v Barker Austin (A Firm)* [1998] P.N.L.R. 493 and *Hatswell v Goldbergs (A Firm)* [2001] EWCA Civ 2084; [2002] Lloyd's Rep. P.N. 359. See also *Hanif v Middleweeks* [2000] Lloyd's Rep. P.N. 920 at [14] per Mance LJ: "the court only assesses prospects and awards damages on a percentage basis—unless it is overwhelmingly clear on the material before the court that the claimant was almost bound to succeed or had, conversely, only a negligible prospect of success, in which case the court may move to a 100% or nil award".

273A [2019] UKSC 5; [2019] 2 W.L.R. 636 at [22]–[24].

273B [2019] UKSC 5; [2019] 2 W.L.R. 636 at [24], [37] and [41]. On the other hand, where the question is one which turns on the assessment of a lost chance, rather than upon proof on the balance of probabilities, it is generally inappropriate to conduct a trial within a trial: ibid. at [31].

273C *Kitchen v Royal Air Force Association* [1958] 1 W.L.R. 563 at 575.

273D [2019] UKSC 5; [2019] 2 W.L.R. 636 at [26]. The court "simply has no business rewarding dishonest claimants": ibid. at [27].

Assessing the chance of success

Replace paragraph with:

2-80 Where the original claim was struck out because a fair trial of the issues was no longer possible as a result of delay by the solicitors, the judge should not attempt to try the original claim in the action against the negligent solicitors, but should make a realistic assessment of the claimant's prospects of success in the original claim.[274] In *Mount v Barker Austin (A Firm)*[275] Simon Brown LJ set out four principles governing this type of claim: (1) the claimant has the legal burden of proving that he had a real and substantial rather than a negligible prospect of success; (2) the defendants have an evidential burden to show that despite having acted for the claimant in the litigation and charged for their services, that litigation was of no value, that burden being heavier in a case where the solicitors have failed to advise the client of the hopelessness of his prospects; (3) if it is more difficult now for the court to assess the strength of the claimant's original case than it would have been at the time of the original action this should not count against the claimant, but rather against the negligent solicitor; and (4) when assessing the claimant's chances of success the court should tend towards a generous assessment, given that it was the defendant's negligence which lost the claimant the opportunity of succeeding in full or in fuller measure.[276] Clearly, the court must be satisfied that the claimant has lost something of value. An action which was bound to fail or had no substantial prospect of success and was merely speculative was not something of value. It is only if the claim passes that test that the court should evaluate in percentage terms the full value of the lost claim.[277]

274 *Sharif v Garrett & Co (A Firm)* [2001] EWCA Civ 1269; [2002] 1 W.L.R. 3118 at [18]–[22]. The Supreme Court did not disagree with this proposition in *Perry v Raleys Solicitors* [2019] UKSC 5; [2019] 2 W.L.R. 636 at [38]. Lord Briggs simply pointed out that in *Sharif* the client had already started his claim, which was struck out for want of prosecution, and did not need to prove anything about what he would have done, on the balance of probabilities. This will be the situation in any case where proceed-

ings have already been issued and the claim has been lost through a negligent procedural error or delay by the claimant's solicitors: [2019] UKSC 5; [2019] 2 W.L.R. 636 at [33]. See also *Sharpe v Addison* [2003] EWCA Civ 1189; [2004] P.N.L.R. 23 and *Pearson v Sanders Witherspoon* [2000] P.N.L.R. 110 at 126–135 (CA) for discussion of how the court should assess the lost chance of successful litigation. For discussion of how to approach the assessment where there are multiple contingencies, each with its own probability see *Langford v Hebran* [2001] EWCA Civ 361; [2001] P.I.Q.R. Q13; *Assetco Plc v Grant Thornton UK LLP* [2019] EWHC 150 (Comm); [2019] 1 WLUK 344 at [418]–[449], per Bryan J.

[275] [1998] P.N.L.R. 493 at 510–511; apparently approved by the Supreme Court in *Perry v Raleys Solicitors* [2019] UKSC 5; [2019] 2 W.L.R. 636 at [34], though *Perry* was not concerned with assessing the value of the lost chance, except to say that the loss of what would have been a dishonest claim involves no loss at all.

[276] In *Phillips & Co v Whatley* [2007] UKPC 28; [2007] P.N.L.R. 27 at [45] the Privy Council confirmed that where there is doubt in assessing the lost chance, the court should err in favour of the claimant, since it is the defendant's negligence that has created the uncertainty.

[277] *Hatswell v Goldbergs (A Firm)* [2001] EWCA Civ 2084; [2002] Lloyd's Rep. P.N. 359 at [48], per Sir Murray Stuart-Smith (claimant's action in negligence against a firm of solicitors in respect of allowing a claim for medical negligence to become statute barred under the Limitation Act 1980 held to have no value, because the medical negligence claim was bound to fail). On the other hand, a decision that the claim was bound to fail does raise the question of what the solicitors were doing running the litigation in the first place. In *Dixon v Clement Jones Solicitors (A Firm)* [2004] EWCA Civ 1005; [2005] P.N.L.R. 6 at [30] Rix LJ described *Hatswell* as a "rare case" where the loss of the underlying litigation was worthless. In *Mount v Barker Austin (A Firm)* [1998] P.N.L.R. 493 the defendants also managed to prove that the original litigation had been bound to fail. For discussion of different ways of calculating lost chances see Evans, "Lies, damn lies and loss of a chance" (2006) 22 P.N. 99.

Add new paragraph:

In *Dixon v Clement Jones Solicitors (A Firm)*[278] the Court of Appeal said that in assessing the chance of success the court's job is not to find what the original decision in the underlying litigation would have been if that litigation had been fought out, but to assess the claimant's prospects of success. Thus, where the outcome in the underlying litigation would have depended on what the claimant would have done, hypothetically, if she had received appropriate information or advice from the original defendant, the claimant does not have to prove that causation issue on a balance of probabilities in order to show that the original claim had some prospects of success.[279] She merely has to prove that the original action had some value which was not negligible. The causation issue in the original action is merely one of a number of issues that are relevant to the prospect of success (which could include the prospects of settling the claim, as well as succeeding at a trial).[280] In *Perry v Raleys Solicitors*,[280A] Lord Briggs clearly had some reservations about this reasoning, since it appears to proceed on the basis that the claimant only had to prove what she would have done in the underlying litigation (where the issue was whether she would have entered a financially disastrous transaction had she been given competent advice by her accountants) on the basis of the chances of her entering the transaction rather than the balance of probabilities: **2-80A**

> "A rigid application of the *Allied Maples* test, namely whether the fact in issue was something that the claimant rather than a third party would have done, might lead to the opposite conclusion."

[278] [2004] EWCA Civ 1005; [2005] P.N.L.R. 6 at [27], per Rix LJ

[279] [2004] EWCA Civ 1005; [2005] P.N.L.R. 6 at [42].

[280] Rix LJ at [31] and [41] distinguished between cases where the claim against negligent solicitors is based on the loss of litigation due to the original action being struck out (as in *Dixon*) and cases involving loss of a transaction (as in *Allied Maples*), where the claimant would have to prove what she would have done, hypothetically, on a balance of probabilities.

[280A] [2019] UKSC 5; [2019] 2 W.L.R. 636 at [40].

Assessing the chance of success in light of subsequent events

Replace paragraph with:

2-81 Where new evidence becomes available or events occur after the date of the notional trial which would have changed the court's approach to the claim or the assessment of the damage, the issue arises as to whether the court should take this into account or whether it should proceed to make an assessment of the claimant's prospects on the basis of the information that would have been available at the date of the notional trial. In *Dudarec v Andrews*[281] liability was admitted in the initial claim against a negligent motorist for an accident in 1982, but there was an outstanding issue as to whether the claimant had failed to mitigate his loss by refusing to undergo surgery for a medical condition that was then believed to affect the claimant. The claim against the motorist was struck out in 1996 for want of prosecution, and in the subsequent action against the claimant's negligent solicitors the question of the claimant's alleged failure to mitigate arose in assessing the loss. However, in 2004, following further medical investigations, it was discovered that the claimant did not have the medical condition, and there was no need for surgery to correct it. The Court of Appeal held that, in assessing the loss in the action against the solicitors, where evidence becomes available for the first time after the date of the notional original trial, the facts as they had turned out should be taken into account.[282] The position may be different, however, if evidence emerges of an entirely new matter which could not possibly have been discovered at the date of the notional trial. The situation may depend on the circumstances. So, if a claimant had died of unrelated causes between the date of the notional trial and the assessment of damages, this should be taken into account because otherwise the claimant's estate would receive an unjustified windfall.[283] This issue was considered again in *Edwards v Hugh James Ford Simey (A Firm)*[283A] where the Court of Appeal emphasised that the question is what has the claimant lost as at the date of the original trial or settlement (applying the principles set out in *Mount v Barker Austin (A Firm).*[283B] The court should not simply assess "the strength of the case as at the date of the professional negligence trial, asking the claimant what he can now prove, on the basis of expert evidence which would not have been in existence had the original matter proceeded with competent representation".[283C] Only in exceptional cases should the court take into account after-coming evidence. In both *Dudarec v Andrews*[283D] and *Charles v Hugh James Jones & Jenkins*[283E] the relevant after-coming evidence would and should have been available at the notional trial date, had the litigation been competently conducted. What would constitute exceptional circumstances in which after-coming evidence should be taken into account? There

> "is no established threshold over which a party must step before such an after-coming event, which could not and would not have been known, should alter the outcome ... [But] there must be a requirement for a significant or serious scale to the consequences of the supervening event, before it should be permitted to establish an exception to the normal principle".[283F]

An example would be the subsequent death of the claimant where the original claim included future losses, such as loss of earnings. In *Edwards v Hugh James Ford Simey* itself, where the after-coming evidence would not have been available at the notional date of settlement, the evidence had an element of uncertainty, and the value of the claim was relatively small, the case did not fall within the exception.

[281] [2006] EWCA Civ 256; [2006] 1 W.L.R. 3002.

282 Applying *Charles v Hugh James Jones & Jenkins (A Firm)* [2000] 1 W.L.R. 1278.

283 [2006] EWCA Civ 256; [2006] 1 W.L.R. 3002 at [64], per Smith LJ On this point see *Whitehead v Hibbert Pownall & Newton* [2008] EWCA Civ 285; [2009] 1 W.L.R. 549 (action against solicitors in respect of negligent conduct of claim against hospital for damages for "wrongful birth" relating to the cost to the mother of raising a disabled child limited to the period between the child's birth and the mother's later death by suicide).

283A [2018] EWCA Civ 1299; [2018] P.N.L.R. 30.

283B [1998] P.N.L.R. 493, see para.2-80.

283C [2018] EWCA Civ 1299; [2018] P.N.L.R. 30 at [69].

283D [2006] EWCA Civ 256; [2006] 1 W.L.R. 3002.

283E [2000] 1 W.L.R. 1278.

283F [2018] EWCA Civ 1299; [2018] P.N.L.R. 30 at [73].

4. CAUSATION IN LAW

(b) Intervening acts

(iii) Intervening conduct of the claimant

Replace paragraph with:

2-128 In the 19th edn of this text it was suggested that "for the claimant's subsequent conduct to be regarded as a novus actus interveniens it should be such as can be characterised as reckless or deliberate" and that "unreasonable conduct can be dealt with by a finding of contributory negligence." However, in *Spencer v Wincanton Holdings Ltd* the Court of Appeal did not accept that this formulation provided a helpful test. Sedley LJ was "uneasy about the importation of a formula ('recklessly or deliberately') from the field of criminal law, where recklessness is commonly equated with intent. Intent has no obvious bearing on contributory fault: an intentional act may be anything from a fault-free act to a novus actus interveniens, and between those poles anything from an act of gross recklessness to one of forgivable inadvertence."[439] Aikens LJ considered that: "The line between a set of facts which results in a finding of contributory negligence and a set of facts which results in a finding that the 'unreasonable conduct' of the claimant constitutes a novus actus interveniens is not, in my view, capable of precise definition. … [E]ach case will depend on the facts and … the court will have to apply a value judgment to the facts as found."[439A] Mr Spencer's decision to attempt to put petrol in his car without using a prosthesis or his walking sticks could, of course, be variously described as "intentional", "deliberate", "unreasonable", "negligent" or (as Sedley LJ put it) a "misjudgment". Arguably, none of these terms provides much assistance in deciding whether it was "fair" to hold the defendants responsible for the consequences of his fall. On the other hand, the way in which the court chooses to characterise the claimant's conduct, the value judgment that is brought to bear on the issue, is not unimportant in reaching a conclusion.[440] On this basis, it is suggested that where a defendant has been negligent and the claimant has also been negligent (or has made a "misjudgement") the power to apportion damages for contributory negligence provides a better solution in reaching a "fair" outcome than finding that the claimant's mistake breaks the chain of causation.[441]

439 [2009] EWCA Civ 1404; [2010] P.I.Q.R. P8 at [19].

439A Commenting on this in *Clay v TUI UK Ltd* [2018] EWCA Civ 1177; [2018] 4 All E.R. 672 at [28] Hamblen LJ said that: "Various considerations may, however, commonly be relevant. In a case involving intervening conduct, these may include: (1) The extent to which the conduct was reasonably foreseeable in general, the more foreseeable it is, the less likely it is to be a novus actus interveniens. (2) The degree of unreasonableness of the conduct in general, the more unreasonable the conduct, the more likely it is to be a novus actus interveniens and a number of cases have stressed the need for a high degree of unreasonableness. (3) The extent to which it was voluntary and independent conduct in general, the more deliberate the act, the more informed it is and the greater the free choice involved, the more likely it is to be a novus actus interveniens." Contrasting the case with *Sayers v Harlow Urban DC* [1958] 1 W.L.R. 623, where the claimant, trapped in a public lavatory due to a faulty lock, was injured in attempting to escape from the toilet cubicle, Hamblen LJ observed, at [35], that in *Sayers* the court "considered it to be a case where the inconvenience was great and the danger slight; hence no novus actus interveniens. On the judge's findings, the present case was one of some inconvenience and the danger obvious and life threatening; hence a novus actus interveniens". The claimant in *Clay*, trapped on a balcony outside his hotel room due to a faulty lock, had attempted to climb to the balcony of an adjoining room and fell from the second storey. The Court of Appeal, Moylan LJ dissenting, upheld the judge's conclusion that the claimant's conduct was so unreasonable as to constitute a novus actus interveniens.

[440] So, e.g. it is hardly surprising when a court holds that the defendant is not responsible for a claimant's voluntary, deliberate and informed decision to use heroin. In *Wilson v Coulson* [2002] P.I.Q.R. P22, QBD, the claimant alleged that brain damage sustained in a road traffic accident, for which the defendant was responsible, had produced a personality change, which led to him becoming addicted to heroin. Harrison J held that the defendant was not liable for further brain damage caused by a heroin overdose, because the claimant's decision to use heroin was voluntary, deliberate and informed, and he had not lost the capacity or the power to say no: "He was the author of his own misfortune and what followed was caused by his own conduct". Cf. *Dalling v R J Heale & Co Ltd* [2011] EWCA Civ 365, para.2-127 fn.438.

[441] See Millner (1971) 22 N.I.L.Q. 168, 176–179, commenting on *McKew v Holland & Hannen & Cubitts (Scotland) Ltd* [1969] 3 All E.R. 1621; *Sayers v Harlow Urban DC* [1958] 1 W.L.R. 623. In *Spencer v Wincanton Holdings Ltd* [2009] EWCA Civ 1404; [2010] P.I.Q.R. P8 at [22] it was pointed out that contributory negligence had not been pleaded in *McKew*. In *Hicks v Young* [2015] EWHC 1144 (QB) at [44] Edis J came to the conclusion that, applying the test of fairness, novus actus interveniens should be applied differently in the tort of negligence as compared to trespass to the person on precisely the same facts (claimant's unreasonable actions did not break the chain of causation in negligence, resulting instead in a finding of contributory negligence, although the same unreasonable actions constituted novus actus interveniens in trespass to the person, where the defence of contributory negligence does not apply).

Failed sterilisation cases

Add new paragraph:

2-135A Both *Parkinson* and *Groom v Selby* were distinguished by the Court of Appeal in *Khan v Meadows*.[462A] The claimant consulted the defendant doctor for advice about whether she carried the gene for haemophilia. Following a blood test the claimant was given advice that led her to believe that any child she had would not have haemophilia. Subsequently she conceived and gave birth to a son who had both haemophilia and autism. In a "wrongful birth" claim for the additional costs associated with haemophilia and autism, the defendant accepted that but for causation was established since, if the claimant had known that she was at risk of having a child with haemophilia she would have had tests conducted during the pregnancy and would have had a termination of the pregnancy. The defendant also accepted that she was liable for the additional costs associated with the condition of haemophilia, but argued that she was not liable for the costs associated with the child's autism. The Court of Appeal agreed that, given the claimant's specific enquiry about the haemophilia gene, the scope of the defendant's duty was limited to the consequences of negligent advice about haemophilia (applying the *SAAMCO*[462B] test). The risk of autism is a risk that exists with every pregnancy; it is not a risk that increases if the child has haemophilia. The risk to the claimant of having a child with autism was not increased by the defendant's advice. The scope of the defendant's duty was to advise in relation to haemophilia in order to provide the claimant with an opportunity to avoid the risk of having a child with haemophilia. It was not to protect her from all the risks associated with pregnancy and continuing with the pregnancy.[462C]

[462A] [2019] EWCA Civ 152; [2019] 4 W.L.R. 26; J. McQuater [2019] J.P.I.L. C6.

[462B] *South Australia Asset Management Corp v York Montague Ltd* [1997] A.C. 191; see para.2-182.

[462C] *Parkinson* and *Groom v Selby* were different because: "In each the doctor had undertaken the task of protecting a patient from an unwanted pregnancy, in *Groom* the pregnancy itself, in *Parkinson* the continuation of the pregnancy. In both, the disability arose from genetic causes or foreseeable events during the course of the pregnancy which were not due to a new intervening cause": [2019] EWCA Civ 152; [2019] 4 W.L.R. 26 at [11].

5. REMOTENESS OF DAMAGE

(b) Remoteness and liability in negligence for physical damage

(iii) Type of damage

The answer depends on the question

Replace paragraph with:

The decision as to whether a particular type harm is foreseeable often depends on how the court chooses to frame the question. In *Hughes v Lord Advocate* the claimant suffered burns due to an unforeseeable explosion. The question asked by the House of Lords was whether burning was foreseeable, to which the answer was yes, because it was foreseeable that a paraffin lamp might overturn and burn the claimant. If, however, the question had been was burning by an explosion foreseeable, the answer would have been negative.[523] *Hughes* suggests that the courts should take a broad approach to categorising the "kind of damage" in a personal injury context.[524] In the case of an occupational disease, foreseeability of the risk of injury of the same type is sufficient. The defendant does not have to foresee the precise disease that the employee is likely to contract. Thus, if it was known that exposure to asbestos dust could produce lung disease (such as asbestosis) it is irrelevant that the causal link between asbestos and mesothelioma was not established until a later date.[525] In *Royal Opera House Covent Garden Foundation v Goldscheider*,[525A] a case of occupational deafness sustained by a musician in an orchestra, the Court of Appeal concluded that "the fact that the foreseeable risk was of long term rather than traumatic injury is ... neither here nor there", applying *Hughes v Lord Advocate*. 2-160

[523] Contrast *Doughty v Turner Manufacturing Co Ltd* where the question asked by the Court of Appeal was whether burning *as a result of* a chemical eruption was foreseeable (answer: no), rather than "was burning foreseeable?" (answer: yes).

[524] Such an approach was taken at first instance in *Bradford v Robinson Rentals Ltd* [1967] 1 W.L.R. 337. The claimant suffered frostbite as a result of being sent by his employer on a journey in a van not equipped with a heater. Rees J held that although the consequences of prolonged exposure to cold would be commonly thought to include colds, chilblains or even pneumonia, "frostbite which is admittedly unusual is nevertheless of the type and kind of injury which was reasonably foreseeable": [1967] 1 W.L.R. 337 at 344. A much narrower categorisation was employed in *Tremain v Pike* [1969] 1 W.L.R. 1556, in which the claimant, a herdsman employed by the defendants, contracted a rare disease, which was the result of coming into contact with rats' urine. He alleged that the defendants had been negligent in allowing rats to infest the farm buildings. They were held not liable on the ground that they had not been negligent. Payne J added however that even though injury through rat-bites or even illness through food contamination was foreseeable, this unforeseeable rare disease was a "different kind" of injury. It seems likely, however, that this narrow approach would not survive the reasoning in *Jolley v Sutton LBC* [2000] 1 W.L.R. 1082, see para.2-157.

[525] *Jeromson v Shell Tankers (UK) Ltd* [2001] EWCA Civ 101; [2001] I.C.R. 1223.

[525A] [2019] EWCA Civ 711 at [46].

(vi) *Claimant's impecuniosity*

Claimant's impecuniosity may be relevant where foreseeable

Replace paragraph with:

2-176 In *Lagden v O'Connor*[564] the House of Lords held that the rule in the *Liesbosch* that a defendant is not responsible for damage attributable to the claimant's impecuniosity could no longer be regarded as good law. It was not necessary to say that the *Liesbosch* case was wrongly decided. But the law had "moved on" and the correct test today is whether the loss was reasonably foreseeable. Lord Hope said that:

> "The wrongdoer must take his victim as he finds him ... This rule applies to the economic state of the victim in the same way as it applies to his physical and mental vulnerability. It requires the wrongdoer to bear the consequences if it was reasonably foreseeable that the injured party would have to borrow money or incur some other kind of expenditure to mitigate his damages."[565]

The effect is that the defendant must take the claimant as he finds him, not only with respect to his physical constitution but also with respect to his means. In practical terms this means that a motorist whose vehicle is off the road for repairs as a result of damage caused by a negligent defendant is entitled to enter into a credit hire agreement for the purpose of hiring an alternative vehicle while the vehicle is off the road and recover the additional cost of credit from the defendant (in practice the defendant's insurers), provided the claimant's impecuniosity is such that he would have been unable to obtain a replacement vehicle had he not used a credit hire company.[566]

564 [2003] UKHL 64; [2004] 1 A.C. 1067.

565 [2003] UKHL 64; [2004] 1 A.C. 1067 at [61]. Lord Nicholls commented, at [6], that it was not acceptable that a financially well-placed claimant would be able to hire a replacement vehicle, and obtain re-imbursement from the defendant's insurers, but an impecunious claimant would not. *Lagden* was applied in *Haxton v Philips Electronics UK Ltd* [2014] EWCA Civ 4; [2014] 1 W.L.R. 2721 (widow whose life expectancy had been reduced by defendant's negligence entitled to recover the diminution in the value of her existing claim for loss of dependency under the Fatal Accidents Act 1976 arising out of the death of her husband; it was "reasonably foreseeable that a curtailment of life may lead to a diminution in the value of a litigation claim and if a claimant has such a claim, the wrongdoer must take the victim as he finds him", per Elias LJ at [23]).

566 See *Stevens v Equity Syndicate Management Ltd* [2015] EWCA Civ 93; [2015] 4 All E.R. 458 (claimant entitled only to the basic hire rate, not the costs of any additional services received under the credit hire agreement); *McBride v UK Insurance Ltd* [2017] EWCA Civ 144; [2017] R.T.R. 27.

(c) Remoteness and liability in negligence for pure economic loss

(i) *Conceptual issues*

SAAMCO and the scope of the duty

Replace footnote 583 with:

2-182 583 [1997] A.C. 191 at 213, per Lord Hoffmann. See also *Hughes-Holland v BPE Solicitors* (also known as *Gabriel v Little*) [2017] UKSC 21; [2018] A.C. 599 at para.2-188, discussing and applying *South Australia Asset Management Corp v York Montague Ltd*. Where the defendant has been fraudulent then the whole risk of loss, including the risk of falls in the market, will be imposed upon the defendant: ibid. On the distinction between an "informer" and an "adviser" see *Dugdale* (1996) 12 P.N. 71 at 75, and generally on *SAAMCO, Stapleton* (1997) 113 L.Q.R. 1. Lord Hoffmann subsequently conceded that the restriction on the valuer's liability in *SAAMCO* was not best described by some limitation on the scope of his duty. In "Causation" (2005) 121 L.Q.R. 592, at 596 Lord Hoffmann said: "The scope of the duty of care is to take reasonable care to get the valuation right. It has nothing to do with the extent of the consequences for which the valuer is liable. When one considers what causal relationship is required, one is really speaking about extent of the liability and not about the scope of the duty. Professor Stapleton is right. I shall try to mend my language in future. But I will say this. There is a close link between the nature of the duty and the extent of liability for breach of that duty." See further Kinsky, "*SAAMCO* 10 years on: causation and scope of duty in professional negligence cases" (2006) 22 P.N. 86.

(ii) Impact of SAAMCO

Distinction between advice and information

Replace paragraph with:

In *Hughes-Holland v BPE Solicitors*[600] Lord Sumption had reservations about drawing accurate distinctions between giving advice and passing on information. Confusion had arisen because of: **2-188**

> "the descriptive inadequacy of these labels. On the face of it they are neither distinct nor mutually exclusive categories. Information given by a professional man to his client is usually a specific form of advice, and most advice will involve conveying information. Neither label really corresponds to the contents of the bottle."

Cases will fall into the "information" category where a professional adviser contributes a limited part of the material on which the client relies in deciding whether to enter into a transaction, but there are other considerations, and the assessment of the commercial merits of the transaction is exclusively a matter for the client.[601] In such cases the defendant's responsibility does not extend to the decision itself even where the material which the defendant supplied is known to be critical to the decision to enter into the transaction. The fact that the information provided was critical to the claimant's decision did not itself turn it into an "advice" case, otherwise the defendant would become the underwriter of the financial fortunes of the whole transaction by assuming a duty of care in relation to only one element of someone else's decision. Lord Sumption added that, in classifying the material as information or advice, every case was likely to depend on the range of matters for which the defendant assumed responsibility and no more exact rule could be stated.[602] *Aneco Reinsurance* was not authority for any general proposition of law beyond the particular factual context of that case.

[600] *Hughes-Holland v BPE Solicitors* (also known as *Gabriel v Little*) [2017] UKSC 21; [2018] A.C. 599 at [39].

[601] [2017] UKSC 21; [2018] A.C. 599 at [41].

[602] [2017] UKSC 21; [2018] A.C. 599 at [44]. On the facts of *Hughes-Holland v BPE Solicitors*, where the defendant solicitors had drawn up a loan facility agreement and charge over a property for the claimant, the solicitors had not assumed responsibility for the claimant's decision to lend money for the purpose of a property development scheme. They were unaware of the nature of the proposed development, its likely cost, the financial capacity of the borrower to fund it without the loan or the value of the property in its developed or undeveloped state. Their negligence had the effect of confirming one of a number of factors in the lender's assessment of the viability of the project, but even if that assumption had been correct the lender would still have lost the money because the project was not commercially viable.

CHAPTER 3

GENERAL DEFENCES

TABLE OF CONTENTS

2. Claimant's wrongdoing (ex turpi causa)

(a) Conceptual foundation of ex turpi causa

(iii) Claimant's reliance on his own illegality

Replace footnote 35 with:

3-10 [35] [1998] Q.B. 978 at 987; applied in *Henderson v Dorset Healthcare University NHS Foundation Trust* [2018] EWCA Civ 1841; [2018] 3 W.L.R. 1651 on very similar facts, *O v Ministry of Defence, West v Ministry of Defence* [2006] EWHC 19 (QB). See also *Hunter Area Health Service v Presland* [2005] NSWCA 33; (2005) 63 N.S.W.L.R. 22, where a majority of the Court of Appeal of New South Wales reached a similar conclusion to *Clunis* on similar facts (although the claimant had been found not guilty by reason of insanity rather than guilty of manslaughter due to diminished responsibility, as occurred in *Clunis*).

(v) The integrity of the legal system: rules or judicial discretion?

Reliance test rejected

Replace paragraph with:

3-25 These differing views were evident in *Patel v Mirza*.[67] The claimant paid £620,000 to the defendant under an illegal agreement between them to use the money for the purpose of "insider dealing". However, the insider information from a third party was not forthcoming, so the money was never used to place a bet on the movement of a company's share price. The defendant refused to hand the money back to the claimant who then brought a claim for breach of contract and unjust enrichment. The defendant's argument that because the contract was tainted by illegality[68] and therefore ex turpi causa applied to the claimant's action was unanimously rejected by the Supreme Court. There was no unanimity, however, as to the correct approach to the illegality defence. A nine judge Court divided sharply, yet again, on the correct basis underpinning the application ex turpi causa, with the majority taking the view that a range of factors should be taken into account, while the minority considered that this would confer too much discretion on the courts, requiring value judgments to be made about the respective claims of the public interest and those of the parties.

[67] [2016] UKSC 42; [2017] A.C. 467. For discussion see J. Goudkamp, "The end of an era? Illegality in private law in the Supreme Court" (2017) 133 L.Q.R. 14; E. Lim, "Ex Turpi Causa: Reformation not Revolution" (2017) 80 M.L.R. 927; and S. Green and A. Bogg (eds), *Illegality after Patel v Mirza* (Oxford: Hart Publishing, 2018).

[68] It amounted to a conspiracy to commit the offence of insider dealing under s.52 of the Criminal Justice Act 1993.

Replace paragraph with:

The consequence of this analysis for the majority in *Patel* was that *Tinsley v Milligan* should no longer be followed. A requirement that the claimant had to rely on the illegal contract or plead its illegality before the defence applied made "the question whether the court will refuse its assistance to the claimant to enforce his title to his property depend on a procedural question and it has led to uncertain case law about what constitutes reliance."[78] Moreover, although *Patel v Mirza* was a case in contract and unjust enrichment, there was no suggestion in the majority judgments that the same approach should not be applied to tort actions, and in *Henderson v Dorset Healthcare University NHS Foundation Trust* the Court of Appeal confirmed that *Patel* is not confined to contract cases.[78A] **3-28**

[78] [2016] UKSC 42; [2017] A.C. 467 at [110]–[111]. In response to the argument of the minority in *Patel v Mirza* that Lord Toulson's approach confers too much discretion on the court and will lead to uncertainty Lord Kerr said that since the preservation of the integrity of the legal system is *par excellence* a public policy consideration "the taking into account of countervailing policy considerations, in order to decide whether to give effect to it in a particular instance, is the only logical way to proceed" ([2016] UKSC 42; [2017] A.C. 467 at [129]). His Lordship added that: "Certainty or predictability of outcome may be a laudable aim for those who seek the law's resolution of genuine, honest disputes. It is not a premium to which those engaged in disreputable conduct can claim automatic entitlement" ([2016] UKSC 42; [2017] A.C. 467 at [137]).

[78A] [2018] EWCA Civ 1841; [2018] 3 W.L.R. 1651; [2019] P.I.Q.R. P3 at [81]. See also *XX v Whittington Hospital NHS Trust* [2018] EWCA Civ 2832; [2019] P.I.Q.R. Q4 at [65] per McCombe LJ. See further *Gujra v Roath* [2018] EWHC 854 (QB); [2018] 1 W.L.R. 3208 at [25] where Martin Spencer J said that: "it seems to me that Lord Toulson was, in *Patel*, laying down a test that was intended to cover all cases where the common law doctrine of illegality is pleaded as a defence to a civil claim." In that case, the defence was applied to a claim for malicious prosecution.

(vi) Relationship to duty of care in negligence

After "There are some cases where the", replace "courts' refusal to impose a duty of care in negligence has nothing to do with the difficulty of setting a standard of care, though everything to do with" with:

courts refuse to impose a duty of care in negligence because of **3-29**

(b) Applying ex turpi causa

After "There was no criticism of Gray in Patel v Mirza,", add new footnote 87A:

[87A] "It is impossible to discern in the majority judgments in *Patel* any suggestion that *Clunis* or *Gray* were wrongly decided or to discern that they cannot stand with the reasoning in *Patel*": *Henderson v Dorset Healthcare University NHS Foundation Trust* [2018] EWCA Civ 1841; [2018] 3 W.L.R. 1651 at [88]. **3-31**

Replace paragraph with:

However, even if there is a causal connection between the claimant's loss and the criminal activity the court must be satisfied that it would be "offensive to public notions of the fair distribution of resources" to allow the claimant to be compensated for the consequences of his criminal conduct. *Patel v Mirza* indicates that in reaching a judgment on this issue the court should take into account: (a) the underlying purpose of the prohibition which has been transgressed and whether that purpose will be enhanced by denial of the claim; (b) any other relevant public policies which may be rendered ineffective or less effective by denial of the claim; and (c) whether denial of the claim would be a proportionate response to the illegality.[91] Lord Toulson did not set out a prescriptive list of potentially relevant factors for consider- **3-32** ing whether it would be disproportionate to refuse a remedy to the claimant, but they included the seriousness of the offence, its centrality to the contract,[92] whether it was intentional and whether there was a marked disparity in the parties' respective culpability. There was no guidance as to the respective weights to be given to each of these factors.[92A] Cases pre-dating *Gray v Thames Trains Ltd* and particularly *Patel v Mirza* discussed below should be considered in the context of these decisions of the House of Lords and Supreme Court.[93]

[91] [2016] UKSC 42; [2017] A.C. 467 at [101] and [120]. His Lordship considered that "that trio of necessary considerations can be found in the case law": ibid. at [101]. They were applied in *Singularis Holdings (In Official Liquidation) v Daiwa Capital Markets Europe Ltd* [2017] EWHC 257 (Ch); [2017] P.N.L.R. 24 at [216]–[220], where Rose J held that ex turpi causa did not apply to a liquidator's claim against a stockbroker who had transferred money out of the insolvent company's account at the behest of the company's sole owner and director. An appeal in *Singularis Holdings Ltd (In Official Liquidation) v Daiwa Capital Markets Europe Ltd* was dismissed: [2018] EWCA Civ 84; [2018] 1 W.L.R. 2777. See also *Stoffel & Co v Grondona* [2018] EWCA Civ 2031; [2018] P.N.L.R. 36 where the Court of Appeal applied Lord Toulson's three factors in a claim against a firm of solicitors for negligence in failing to register the claimant's title to property. The claimant had participated in a mortgage fraud with a third party in order to obtain loan funds from a lender for the benefit of the third party, but this illegality was not a reason to bar her claim against the negligent solicitors. There was "no public interest in allowing negligent conveyancing solicitors ..., who are not party to, and know nothing about, the illegality, to avoid their professional obligations simply because of the happenstance that two of the clients for whom they act are involved in making misrepresentations to the mortgagee financier" but there was "a genuine public interest in ensuring that clients who use the services of solicitors are entitled to seek civil remedies for negligence/breach of contract" in circumstances where the client was not seeking to profit from the mortgage fraud (at [37]–[38] per Gloster LJ). It would have been entirely disproportionate to deny the claim (at [39]).

[92] In tort cases where there is no contract this may be interpreted as the centrality of the criminal behaviour to the claimant's loss, which may possibly be just another way of specifying the importance of the causal link.

[92A] An appellate court should not interfere in a trial judge's application of the test in *Patel v Mirza* "merely because it would have taken a different view had it been undertaking the evaluation. The test involves balancing multiple policy considerations and applying a proportionality approach. Accordingly, an appellate court should only interfere if the first instance judge has proceeded on an erroneous legal basis, taken into account matters that were legally irrelevant, or failed to take into account matters that were legally relevant": *Singularis Holdings Ltd (In Official Liquidation) v Daiwa Capital Markets Europe Ltd* [2018] EWCA Civ 84; [2018] 1 W.L.R. 2777 at [65] per Sir Geoffrey Vos C.

[93] At this point it may be worth recalling Lord Hoffmann's observation in *Gray v Thames Trains Ltd* [2009] UKHL 33; [2009] 1 A.C. 1339 at [30] that the policy underpinning ex turpi causa "is not based upon a single justification but on a group of reasons, which vary in different situations." This suggests that the factors relevant to the outcome will carry different weights depending on the context in which the issue arises.

(i) Seriousness of the claimant's conduct

Replace paragraph with:

3-34 It is clear that the seriousness of the claimant's offence was an important factor in both *Clunis*,[97] and *Gray*.[98] In *Murphy v Culhane*,[99] a widow sued in respect of her husband's death in the course of a violent affray. Lord Denning ruled that consideration be given to a defence of ex turpi as well as to questions of volenti and contributory negligence. In *Pitts v Hunt*,[100] the claimant was seriously injured in a motorcycle accident. He was a pillion passenger on a motor cycle involved in a collision which killed the rider. Both he and the rider had been drinking heavily prior to the accident. The claimant knew that the rider was uninsured and did not hold a licence. He had actively and forcefully encouraged the rider to drive in a reckless and dangerous manner. The Court of Appeal unanimously held that the claimant's own criminal conduct precluded him from recovering damages from the deceased rider's estate. *Pitts v Hunt* is not authority for the proposition that driving a vehicle whilst uninsured, or having drunk excessive amounts of alcohol, or driving or encouraging someone to drive recklessly will necessarily give rise to the defence of ex turpi causa. It was the combination of all of these factors that persuaded the court, whatever the theoretical basis for the defence, that the claimant's action should not succeed. Anti-competitive acts in breach of the Competition Act 1998 are of sufficiently serious turpitude to engage ex turpi causa, with the result that a party to such an agreement cannot claim damages for loss caused by being a party to that illegal agreement[101]; an attempted civil law bribe (intending to induce a breach of fiduciary duty) could be sufficient to engage the principle of ex turpi causa[102]; and an allegation of tax evasion may possibly give rise to the defence.[103] The misuse of illegal drugs is sufficiently serious to engage the illegality defence[104] as is making off without paying a taxi fare, contrary to s.3 of the Theft Act 1968 (an offence punishable by up to two years' imprisonment)[105]; and participating in a joint criminal enterprise with the rider of a bike to ride the bike dangerously (an offence also punishable by up to two years' imprisonment).[106] The potential severity of the sentence for a criminal offence is not in itself an indication that the defence will apply. In *Wallett v Vickers*,[106A] it was held that ex turpi causa did not apply where a motorist had been driving his vehicle dangerously (punishable by up to two years' imprisonment) lost control, crashed and was killed. He had been driving alongside the defendant's vehicle on a dual carriageway at up to twice the speed limit, with each driver trying to get to the point where the road narrowed to a single lane ahead of the other. The defendant was convicted of dangerous driving and sentenced to six months imprisonment. Males J concluded that there was no criminal joint enterprise, which required an intention to assist or encourage the commission of the crime:

> "In the absence of a criminal joint enterprise between the claimant and the defendant, dangerous driving by the claimant will not bar a claim pursuant to the ex turpi causa principle."[106B]

Infringement of a foreign patent does not cross the threshold of "turpitude"; only criminal acts and quasi-criminal acts would sufficiently engage the public interest.[107]

97 [1998] Q.B. 978.

98 See also *Worrall v British Railways Board* unreported 1999, CA, where the claimant alleged that an accident caused by the defendant's negligence brought about personality changes which led him to commit two serious criminal offences, and he claimed damages for the losses flowing from his imprisonment. The Court of Appeal, applying *Clunis*, held that public policy meant that the court should not assist a claimant who pleads and relies on his own criminal conduct to establish his claim. He was fully responsible for his actions (and had not claimed otherwise in the criminal proceedings—his defence had been an alibi, and he had not relied on any psychiatric evidence). See further *Wilson v Coulson* [2002] P.I.Q.R. P22; para.2-128, fn.420.

99 [1977] Q.B. 94.

100 [1991] 1 Q.B. 24.

101 *Safeway Stores Ltd v Twigger* [2010] EWCA Civ 1472; [2011] 2 All E.R. 841.

102 *Nayyar v Denton Wilde Sapte* [2009] EWHC 3218 (QB); [2010] P.N.L.R. 15 (an appeal on a different point was refused: *Nayyar v Denton Wilde Sapte* [2010] EWCA Civ 815).

103 *K/S Lincoln v CB Richard Ellis Hotels Ltd* [2009] EWHC 2344 (TCC); [2010] P.N.L.R. 5.

104 *B v Chief Constable of X* [2015] EWHC 13 (QB); [2015] I.R.L.R. 284.

105 *Beaumont v Ferrer* [2016] EWCA Civ 768; [2017] P.I.Q.R. P1.

106 *McCracken v Smith* [2015] EWCA Civ 380; [2015] P.I.Q.R. P19; but where the claimant pillion passenger did not encourage or assist the rider to ride dangerously there is no criminal joint enterprise, and mere foreseeability of dangerous riding is not enough: *Clark v Farley* [2018] EWHC 1007 (QB); [2018] P.I.Q.R. P15. Engaging in a conspiracy to defraud an insurance company by setting fire to vehicles at

the owner's instigation is not a "minor transgression": *Gujra v Roath* [2018] EWHC 854 (QB); [2018] 1 W.L.R. 3208 at [30].

[106A] [2018] EWHC 3088 (QB); [2019] P.I.Q.R. P6.

[106B] [2018] EWHC 3088 (QB); [2019] P.I.Q.R. P6 at [43], applying *McCracken v Smith* [2015] EWCA Civ 380; [2015] P.I.Q.R. P19. In passing, Males J noted, at [38], that careless driving is at the low end of the spectrum of turpitude: "careless driving is a criminal offence but nobody would suggest that careless driving by the claimant prevents the recovery of damages (reduced as appropriate on account of contributory negligence) in a road traffic case where both drivers are partly to blame. In such a case the recovery of damages does not offend public notions of the fair distribution of resources and poses no threat to the integrity of the law."

[107] *Les Laboratoires Servier v Apotex Inc* [2014] UKSC 55; [2015] A.C. 430. Lord Sumption, at [25], identified as examples of acts which would engage the ex turpi causa defence: cases of dishonesty or corruption; some anomalous categories of misconduct such as prostitution (which without being criminal was contrary to public policy); and the infringement of statutory rules enacted for the protection of the public interest and attracting civil sanctions of a penal character, such as competition law. Torts (other than those involving dishonesty), breaches of contract, statutory and other civil wrongs offended interests which are essentially private, not public, did not engage ex turpi causa.

(ii) Causal connection with the claimant's loss

Replace footnote 114 with:

3-36 [114] [2011] EWCA Civ 1532; [2012] 1 W.L.R. 2149 at [37]. See also per Tomlinson LJ at [73]: "there was no relevant nexus between the illegality upon which the claimant was engaged and the tortious conduct of [the defendant] which gave rise to his injuries". Cf. *Smith v Stratton* [2015] EWCA Civ 1413 where the occupants of a vehicle had been dealing drugs and the claimant passenger was injured in an accident during an attempt to escape the pursuit of a police vehicle. The use of the car was integral to the supply of drugs because it facilitated the sale of drugs and provided a means of rapid escape if escape was called for; ex turpi causa applied. Similarly, in *Blake v Croasdale* [2018] EWHC 1919 (QB); [2019] R.T.R. 8 ex turpi was applied where a vehicle being used to facilitate the supply of drugs crashed, having been driven at speed to escape from the police.

Where claimant cannot lawfully take advantage of lost opportunity

Replace footnote 121 with:

3-39 [121] So in *Rance v Mid-Downs HA* [1991] 1 Q.B. 587 the claimant alleged that as a result of the defendants' negligence a foetal abnormality was not detected during the course of a pregnancy, and she was therefore deprived of the opportunity of terminating the pregnancy. Due to the length of the gestation, however, an abortion on the ground of serious foetal handicap would not have been lawful under the Abortion Act 1967 (as it then stood). Brooke J held that on the facts there had been no negligence, but that in any event on the ground of public policy the court would not award compensation in circumstances where the claimant could not have turned her lost opportunity to value without breaking the law. In *Briody v St Helens and Knowsley AHA* [2001] EWCA Civ 1010; [2002] Q.B. 856 it was held that a claim for damages in respect of rendering the claimant infertile could not include the cost of procedures connected with surrogate motherhood if those procedures would be in breach of the Surrogacy Arrangements Act 1985. However, in *XX v Whittington Hospital NHS Trust* [2018] EWCA Civ 2832; [2019] P.I.Q.R. Q4, the Court of Appeal concluded that due to changes in the law on surrogacy, and in social values, public policy no longer supported this proposition. Public policy was "well-recognised to be variable and is not ossified for all time, once identified in any particular context" (at [64]). The claimant was entitled to recover the costs of entering commercial surrogacy arrangements in California, even though commercial surrogacy remains unlawful in the UK.

(iii) Proportionality

Proportionality between claimant's turpitude and claimant's loss

Replace paragraph with:

3-44 In *Patel v Mirza* Lord Toulson had indicated that the issue was "whether denial of the claim would be a proportionate response to the illegality, bearing in mind that punishment is a matter for the criminal courts",[141] which on one view suggests some comparison between the *extent* of the claimant's loss and the seriousness of the offence (given that in sentencing offenders the criminal law seeks to balance punishment with the seriousness of the offence). This could produce the odd result that where a claimant has suffered serious injury the outcome might be different from that where he had sustained minor injury. But none of the cases pre-dating *Patel* have taken this view. The issue of proportionality has been seen as linked to the seriousness of the claimant's criminal conduct rather than the seriousness of the damage sustained (and so the value of any damages that would be lost if ex turpi causa is applied). Thus, ex turpi causa may apply more extensive "punishment" (by refusing an award of damages) than would be considered appropriate in the context of a criminal offence.

[141] [2016] UKSC 42; [2017] A.C. 467 at [101] and [120]. See also *Gujra v Roath* [2018] EWHC 854 (QB); [2018] 1 W.L.R. 3208 at [30] where Martin Spencer J considered that the loss of damages claimed in an action for malicious prosecution (in respect of being remanded in custody for a few weeks and then being electronically tagged for a few months) was not "in any way disproportionate to the unlawfulness of the claimant's conduct in associating himself with a serious attempted fraud upon an insurance company." See further *Stoffel & Co v Grondona* [2018] EWCA Civ 2031; [2018] P.N.L.R. 36 at [39] where Gloster LJ set out a list of factors taken into account in concluding that, on the facts of that case, it would be "entirely disproportionate" to deny a claim against negligent solicitors for failing to register the claimant's title to property where the claimant had participated in a mortgage fraud. There was no risk that enforcement of the claim would undermine the integrity of the justice system.

(vi) Property rights

Replace footnote 170 with:

[170] See *R. (on the application of Best) v Chief Land Registrar* [2015] EWCA Civ 17; [2016] Q.B. 23 where the Court of Appeal held that a trespasser could apply to be the registered proprietor even though part of the period of adverse possession involved the commission of a criminal offence (since the coming into force of s.144(1) of the Legal Aid, Sentencing and Punishment of Offenders Act 2012 which criminalised squatting in a residential building having entered it as a trespasser where the trespasser is living or intending to live in the building). In *Rashid v Nasrullah* [2018] EWCA Civ 2685 at [69] Lewison LJ commented that *Patel v Mirza* [2016] UKSC 42; [2017] A.C. 467 was not a warrant for the rewriting of history. The Supreme Court in *Patel* had approved the balance struck in *Best*. Applying the doctrine of illegality on the facts of *Rashid* (the defendant was registered as the proprietor of the claimant's land following a fraud perpetrated by the defendant's father and the defendant had been in adverse possession for over 20 years) would undermine the law of adverse possession and the law of limitation more generally (at [75]). King LJ and Peter Jackson LJ agreed (at [83]) that "the scope for the doctrine of illegality is greatly reduced by the fact that the whole point of limitation is to limit the time for bringing claims, including good claims". The "careful statutory framework" of the Limitation Act 1980 would "in almost every case incorporate all the considerations mentioned in *Patel v Mirza*." **3-52**

(ix) Fraudulent claims

Replace paragraph with:

The fact that, during the course of litigation, a claimant has made fraudulent claims in respect of particular heads of loss does not prevent him from succeeding in respect of other heads of loss which were clearly proved, though the fraudulent exaggeration of a claim is an abuse of process and the court has jurisdiction to strike out such a claim at any stage of proceedings.[179] The power to strike out should only be exercised where it is just and proportionate to do so, and after a trial it will be exercised only in very exceptional circumstances. The court may also set aside a compromise agreement where the amount of the settlement has been based on the claimant's fraudulent representations as to the severity of his injuries.[180] The Criminal Justice and Courts Act 2015 s.57 provides that where the claimant has been "fundamentally dishonest" in a claim for damages for personal injuries the court *must* dismiss the claim entirely unless the court is satisfied that the claimant would suffer substantial injustice.[181] The Act does not define "fundamentally dishonest", though the Explanatory Notes to the Bill referred to gross exaggeration of the claim or collusion in a fraudulent claim brought by another person in connection **3-55** with the same incident or series of incidents.[181A] The intention of s.57 is to reverse *Summers v Fairclough Homes Ltd* by creating a presumption that a fraudulent claim or a fraudulent head of claim will result in the whole claim being struck out, though the court retains a discretion not to do so if the claimant would suffer "substantial injustice".

[179] *Summers v Fairclough Homes Ltd* [2012] UKSC 26; [2012] 1 W.L.R. 2004.

[180] See *Hayward v Zurich Insurance Co Plc* [2016] UKSC 48; [2017] A.C. 142; see para.2-22 for consideration of the causation issues where a defendant's insurer suspects that the claim is fraudulent but nonetheless settles the claim for substantial damages. Note that a fraudulent claim may result in an award of exemplary damages in the tort of deceit against the persons responsible for the fraud: *Hassan v Cooper* [2015] EWHC 540 (QB); [2015] R.T.R. 26; *Axa Insurance UK Plc v Financial Claims Solutions Ltd* [2018] EWCA Civ 1330; [2019] R.T.R. 1. Fraudulent claims can also lead to proceedings for contempt of court: *Aviva Insurance Ltd v Randive* [2016] EWHC 3152 (QB)); [2017] R.T.R. 16; *Aviva Insurance Ltd v Kovacic* [2017] EWHC 2772 (QB); [2017] 11 WLUK 117; *Aviva Insurance Ltd v Nazir* [2018] EWHC 1296 (QB); *Calderdale and Huddersfield NHS Foundation Trust v Atwal* [2018] EWHC 961 (QB); (2018) 162 B.M.L.R. 169. This includes contempt committed by dishonest lawyers or expert witnesses: *Liverpool Victoria Insurance Co Ltd v Khan* [2018] EWHC 2581 (QB); [2018] 10 WLUK 126 and [2019] EWCA Civ 392; [2019] 3 WLUK 290 (on the question of appropriate sentence).

[181] This includes dishonesty by the claimant in relation to a related claim by another person in connection with the same incident giving rise to the claimant's primary claim. See further B. Dixon, "Fundamental Dishonesty and the Criminal Justice and Courts Act 2015" [2015] J.P.I.L. 108; B. Dixon and J. McQuater, "Fundamental Dishonesty: Guidance for Practitioners" [2016] J.P.I.L. 121.

[181A] For consideration of the meaning of the term "fundamentally dishonest" see *London Organising Committee of the Olympic and Paralympic Games (In Liquidation) v Sinfield* [2018] EWHC 51 (QB); [2018] P.I.Q.R. P8; *Razumas v Ministry of Justice* [2018] EWHC 215 (QB); [2018] P.I.Q.R. P10; *Molodi v Cambridge Vibration Maintenance Service* [2018] EWHC 1288 (QB); [2018] R.T.R. 25; *Pinkus v Direct Line* [2018] EWHC 1671 (QB); [2018] P.I.Q.R. P20; *Howlett v Davies* [2017] EWCA Civ 1696; [2018] 1 W.L.R. 948; [2018] P.I.Q.R. Q3 (where the issue was addressed in the context of CPR r.44.16).

3. Contributory Negligence

(b) Contribution to damage

"Last opportunity" as a test of causation

After "that negligence should", add:

3-60 not

(d) The standard of care

Contributory negligence of children

Replace paragraph with:

3-82 In considering whether a child has taken reasonable care for his own safety regard must be had to the age of the child, the circumstances of the case and the knowledge by the particular child of the dangers to which the defendant's negligence has exposed him. In *Gough v Thorne*,[290] Lord Denning MR said that a very young child cannot be guilty of contributory negligence; an older child may be, but it depends on the circumstances. A judge should only find a child guilty of contributory negligence if he or she is of such an age as reasonably to be expected to take precautions for his or her own safety. This is not an entirely subjective test, because the question is whether an "ordinary child" of the claimant's age could be expected to have done any more than the claimant, and an ordinary child is neither a "paragon of prudence" nor "scatter-brained".[291] Theoretically, there is no age below which, as a matter of law, it can be said that a child cannot be guilty of contributory negligence, but in practice it is unreasonable to exact a high standard.[292] On the other hand, with older children there may be no good reason to apply a different standard from that applied to an adult.[293]

[290] [1966] 1 W.L.R. 1387; *Gardner v Grace* (1858) 1 F. & F. 359 (contributory negligence does not apply to an infant "of tender age", in this case 3¼ years).

[291] [1966] 1 W.L.R. 1387 at 1391, per Salmon LJ See also *Mullin v Richards* [1998] 1 W.L.R. 1304 where the Court of Appeal held that the standard of care to be applied to a *defendant* 15-year-old schoolgirl was whether an "ordinarily prudent and reasonable 15-year-old schoolgirl" would have appreciated the risk of harm to the claimant (applying the decision of the High Court of Australia in *McHale v Watson* (1966) 115 C.L.R. 199).

[292] The decision in *McKinnell v White*, 1971 S.L.T. 61 in which a child aged five, who was hit by a car on running across a road, was held equally to blame with the driver, looks particularly harsh; *Morales v Eccleston* [1991] R.T.R. 151 CA (11-year-old boy held to be 75% contributorily negligent when he was injured after he ran out on to a busy road without looking); *Paramasivan v Wicks* [2013] EWCA Civ 262 (13-year-old boy held 75% contributorily negligent when he ran into the road without looking); *Jackson v Murray* [2015] UKSC 5; [2015] 2 All E.R. 805 (13-year-old 50% contributorily negligent in crossing a rural road from behind a school minibus without looking); *Ellis v Kelly* [2018] EWHC 2031 (QB); [2018] 4 W.L.R. 124 (no finding of contributory negligence against an eight-year-old child who ran into the road—it was a case of "momentary misjudgment" by the child set against reckless conduct on the part of the defendant motorist. Yip J considered that a finding of contributory negligence against an eight-year-old is uncommon; contrast *AB v Main* [2015] EWHC 3183 (QB), which Yip J appeared to accept was an "outlier"). See L. Macfarlane, "Rethinking childhood contributory negligence: 'blame', 'fault'—but what about children's rights?" 2018 Jur. Rev. 75, contrasting the courts' approach to children's contributory negligence with the rights-based approach applied to determining children's interests in other areas of the law.

[293] *Phethean-Hubble v Coles* [2012] EWCA Civ 349; [2012] R.T.R. 31 (16-year-old cyclist who turned from the pavement into the road in front of defendant's car held to be 50% contributorily negligent; the judge had not been justified in reducing an initial assessment of 50% contributory negligence to 33% by reason of the claimant's age). One study has found, perhaps counter-intuitively, that in practice children falling within the 10–19 years age range were more likely to have a finding of contributory negligence made against them than adults: J. Goudkamp and D. Nolan "Contributory Negligence in the Twenty-First Century: An Empirical Study of First Instance Decisions" (2016) 79 M.L.R. 575. See further J. Goudkamp and D. Nolan, "Contributory Negligence in the Court of Appeal: An Empirical Study" (2017) 37 L.S. 437.

Contributory negligence of disabled persons

Replace paragraph with:

Ordinarily, the standard of care expected of a defendant is based on the assumption that others possess normal faculties,[294] but when it is known that a person to whom the duty is owed has some physical disability, for example only one eye,[295] a higher standard of care is required of the defendant. It is a different question, however, whether, assuming there is a breach of duty, the claimant's physical or mental disability can be taken into account in deciding whether there has been contributory negligence on his part. On principle, it would seem that when it has to be decided whether a person has taken reasonable care for his own safety, "reasonable" must have reference to his individual circumstances and infirmities. Although a motor vehicle is being driven negligently, an active man might get out of the way and avoid an accident, but if an elderly person cannot do so and is run down he was not, even under the old law, prevented from recovering.[296] It would seem that his damages should not be reduced, provided he exercised such care as was reasonable having regard to his age and physical condition.[297] In *Spearman v Royal United Bath Hospitals NHS Foundation Trust*,[297A] it was held that a claimant who had had a prior brain injury that had produced a change of personality and a strong phobia of hospitals, and also suffered from Type 1 diabetes which resulted in frequent hypoglycaemic attacks, during which he became single-minded and stubborn, had not been contributorily negligent when, in attempting to leave a 3-83 hospital he climbed five flights of stairs to the roof and fell from the roof. He had a history of acting unpredictably, without regard for his own safety, and was suffering from the effects of a hypoglycaemic attack which could also result in a patient acting unpredictably, irrationally and out of character. Martin Spencer J commented that:

> "Just as a young child is not guilty of contributory negligence in running out into a road where the child is so young as not to appreciate the danger of so doing, so too where a person's state of mind is such that, whether temporarily or permanently, they do not appreciate that they are putting themselves in danger and it cannot be said that they should have so appreciated. Otherwise, that would be to penalise a person for being ill or of unsound mind, and the law does not do that."[297B]

[294] per Lord Wright in *Bourhill v Young* [1943] A.C. 92 at 109.

[295] *Paris v Stepney BC* [1951] A.C. 367. Totally blind: *Haley v London Electricity Board* [1965] A.C. 778; cf. *Pritchard v PO* [1950] W.N. 310.

[296] *Daly v Liverpool Corp* [1939] 2 All E.R. 142 at 143 per Stable J: "I cannot believe that the law is quite so absurd as to say that, if a pedestrian happens to be old and slow and a little stupid, and does not possess the skill of the hypothetical pedestrian, he or she can only walk about his or her native country at his or her own risk." See also *M'Kibbin v Glasgow Corp*, 1920 S.C. 590.

[297] Contrast the standard of care applied to defendants with disabilities: see *Dunnage v Randall* [2015] EWCA Civ 673; [2016] Q.B. 639, para.8-161.

[297A] [2017] EWHC 3027 (QB); [2018] Med. L.R. 244.

[297B] [2017] EWHC 3027 (QB); [2018] Med. L.R. 244 at [74]. Contrast *Bright v Bourn* [2018] EWHC 1948 (QB); [2018] 7 WLUK 670, where a claimant who had suffered a brain injury and a stroke, and was unable to live on his own, was held to have been contributorily negligent when struck by a motorcycle while crossing the road. The judge cited *Dunnage v Randall* [2015] EWCA Civ 673; [2016] Q.B. 639 for the proposition that "a duty to take reasonable care for his own safety" was "not, in the circumstances of this case, reduced or any way diminished because of his disability" (at [21]). Despite the brain injury the claimant "was very independent, able to go out on his own and travelled widely on his own".

Collisions with pedestrians

Replace footnote 303 with:

3-86 [303] [2003] EWCA Civ 1107; [2004] R.T.R. 9 at [16]. In *Lunt v Khelifa* the Court of Appeal had upheld a finding of 30% contributory negligence in the case of a drunken pedestrian who stepped out in front of an oncoming vehicle. In *Jackson v Murray* [2015] UKSC 5; [2015] 2 All E.R. 805, [26], [38], and [50] the Supreme Court approved the approach taken in *Eagle v Chambers* to the assessment of contributory negligence in cases involving collisions between pedestrians and motor vehicles. See also *Sabir v Osei-Kwabena* [2015] EWCA Civ 1213; [2016] P.I.Q.R. Q4, applying *Jackson v Murray* and *Eagle v Chambers* in emphasising the higher causative potency of a motor vehicle in comparison to a pedestrian who steps in front of an approaching vehicle (claimant assessed as 25% contributorily negligent). On the other hand, foolhardy behaviour by pedestrians is likely to result in higher assessments of contributory negligence: *Belka v Prosperini* [2011] EWCA Civ 623 (pedestrian's contributory negligence assessed at two-thirds where he took take a deliberate risk in running across the road in front of a vehicle which had the right of way); *Lightfoot v Go-Ahead Group Plc* [2011] EWHC 89 (QB); [2011] R.T.R. 27 (40% reduction for contributory negligence in the case of a drunken pedestrian on the road). See further D. Dyal, "Contributory negligence in pedestrian road traffic accidents" [2018] J.P.I.L. 23.

Seat-belts and crash-helmets

Replace footnote 319 with:

3-90 [319] In *J (A Child) v Wilkins* [2001] R.T.R. 19; [2001] P.I.Q.R. P12 the Court of Appeal held that the same principles of apportionment as apply to contributory negligence should also apply to a case involving contribution under the Civil Liability (Contribution) Act 1978 when there was a failure to wear a seat-belt. The claimant was a two-year-old child who was held on her mother's knee in the front passenger seat of a car being driven by her aunt. The defendant negligently collided with the car, causing serious injuries to the claimant which could have been wholly avoided if she had been restrained in an approved child seat. The defendant joined the claimant's mother and aunt as CPR Pt 20 defendants. The

Court of Appeal upheld the judge's assessment that liability should be apportioned 75% to the defendant and 25% to the Pt 20 defendants, applying the approach adopted in *Froom v Butcher*. See also *Hughes v Williams* [2013] EWCA Civ 455; [2013] P.I.Q.R. P17 (mother negligent in restraining three-year-old child on a booster seat, for which the child did not meet the height or age criteria, rather than a forward facing child seat with a 5-point harness; mother held liable to 25% contribution under the Civil Liability (Contribution) Act 1978). See also *EMS (A Minor) v ES* [2018] NIQB 36.

(g) Apportionment

Replace paragraph with:

The discretion implicit in a test based on what is "just and equitable" allows the court to take an ad hoc approach to apportionment, treating the issue as essentially a question of fact. The court's disapproval of the claimant's conduct may be reflected in a large reduction for contributory negligence.[354] Where a particular type of accident is common it may be sensible to have guidelines for the appropriate deduction in order to produce both a reasonable level of consistency and certainty.[355] It is not simply a case of assessing the comparative blameworthiness of the parties, but of their respective "responsibility for the damage". So, for example, in the case of breach of strict statutory duty the defendant may not have been particularly careless, but may still bear a substantial responsibility for the damage.[356] In assessing the respective responsibilities of the parties the court should take into account the scope of the defendant's duty and the extent to which that duty involved taking precautions against the claimant's own negligence. That should then be weighed against the question of whether the claimant's fault was causative of the damage and "if it was, what the relative blameworthiness and causative potency of the parties' respective faults were".[357] **3-99**

[354] See *Barrett v Ministry of Defence* [1995] 1 W.L.R. 1217 CA where a naval airman died when he fell unconscious and choked to death on his own vomit, having consumed a large amount of extremely cheap alcohol supplied at a Norwegian naval base. The defendants had assumed a duty of care as to how he was treated once he fell unconscious. Damages were reduced by two thirds for the deceased's contributory negligence. See also *Jebson v Ministry of Defence* [2000] 1 W.L.R. 2055 (soldier injured when, in a drunken state, he fell off an army truck after a night out organised by the defendants held 75% contributorily negligent).

[355] See, e.g. *Froom v Butcher* [1976] Q.B. 286, para.3-90 in the context of the failure of passengers in a vehicle to wear a seat-belt. The fact that a standard reduction for contributory negligence of 25% can apply to the failure to wear a seatbelt, and a reduction of 20% will normally apply to accepting a lift from a drunken driver (*Owens v Brimmell* [1977] Q.B. 859, para.3-91) does not mean that a claimant who both accepted a lift from a drunken driver and failed to wear a seatbelt will be subject to a 45% deduction for contributory negligence: *Best v Smyth* [2010] EWHC 1541 (QB)—maximum reduction of 30% on the facts. See also *Clark v Farley* [2018] EWHC 1007 (QB); [2018] P.I.Q.R. P15 at [77] per Yip J: "the correct approach is to look at relative blameworthiness and causative potency as a whole, rather than assessing elements of contributory negligence separately and adding the percentages together." For an argument there should be more fixed apportionment rules see J. Goudkamp, "Apportionment of damages for contributory negligence: a fixed or discretionary approach?" (2015) 35 L.S. 621.

[356] per Lord Hoffmann in *Reeves v Commissioner of Police for the Metropolis* [2000] 1 A.C. 360 at 371: " ... what section 1 requires the court to apportion is not merely degrees of carelessness but 'responsibility' and ... an assessment of responsibility must take into account the policy of the rule, such as the Factories Acts, by which liability is imposed. A person may be responsible although he has not been careless at all, as in the case of breach of an absolute statutory duty. And he may have been careless without being responsible, as in the case of 'acts of inattention' by workmen."

[357] *Sahib Foods Ltd v Paskin Kyriakides Sands (A Firm)* [2003] EWCA Civ 1832; [2004] P.N.L.R. 22 at [66]—fire started as a result of claimants' negligence, but the rapid spread of the fire was the result of failing to install fire-resistant panels, which was attributable both to the defendant architects' negligence and the claimants' negligence in giving the defendants incorrect information as to the activities that would be carried out in the area. Claimants held responsible for the immediate fire damage, and two-thirds responsible for the spread of the fire. See also *St George v Home Office* [2008] EWCA Civ 1068; [2009] 1 W.L.R. 1670; para.3-63 (claimant's pre-accident lifestyle choices in becoming addicted to drugs and alcohol not of sufficient causative potency, looking at the comparative blameworthiness of the parties, to make it just and equitable to reduce damages for contributory negligence); and

Blackmore v Department for Communities and Local Government [2017] EWCA Civ 1136; [2018] Q.B. 471; [2018] P.I.Q.R. P1.

6. Miscellaneous defences

(b) Self-defence

Self-defence and injury to third parties

Replace paragraph with:

3-156 What would be the position if the defendant injured a bystander when defending himself against an attack? Self-defence cannot avail against the bystander, who was not attacking. In the early common law, when liability was strict, subject only to specific defences, the defendant was liable. Self-defence would have been a defence against the attacker had he been injured, but not against the bystander.[585] Today liability for personal injury is based on fault, so the defence might be absence of fault as long as the act in self-defence was itself reasonable, i.e. the defence of inevitable accident,[586] or possibly necessity. In *Scott v Shepherd*,[587] the defendant threw a lighted squib into a crowded marketplace. It landed on the stall of X, who to save himself and his goods, threw it aside. It fell on the stall of Y, who to save his goods, did the same; and the squib exploded in the claimant's face. The defendant was held liable to the claimant; but two judges said, obiter, that X and Y would not have been liable because they acted "under a compulsive necessity for their own safety and self-preservation". In *Mohmed v Barnes*,[587A] Turner J noted that *Scott* had been decided long before the emergence of the tort of negligence in its modern form, and that caution should be exercised in applying the dicta in *Scott* as though the law has stood still. Where the claimant was an innocent bystander and it was not the defendant's intention to inflict harm, the availability of a remedy should be gauged by the application of the usual tests for breach of duty and causation in negligence. The use of descriptive terms such as "self-defence" or "emergency" was apt to mislead by implying that some special and different test of liability should be applied:

> "The better modern view is that the stallholders X and Y in *Scott* would have escaped liability because their conduct was objectively reasonable, without the need to demonstrate a 'compulsive necessity for their own safety and self-preservation'."[587B]

If a defendant was acting in circumstances involving elements of self-defence or emergency these were factors to be taken into account in the overall judgment as to what courses of action were objectively reasonable at the time.

[585] Brian CJ in *The Case of Thorns* (1466) Y.B. 6 Ed. 4, f. 7 pl. 18; *Lambert v Bessey* (1681) T. Ray. 421 at 423.

[586] See para.3-171.

[587] (1773) 2 W. Bl. 892.

[587A] [2019] EWHC 87 (QB); [2019] 1 WLUK 242 at [22].

[587B] [2019] EWHC 87 (QB); [2019] 1 WLUK 242 at [23].

CHAPTER 4

JOINT LIABILITY AND CONTRIBUTION

TABLE OF CONTENTS

2. JOINT AND SEVERAL TORTS

Definition of joint tortfeasors

Replace paragraph with:

Thus, the agent who commits a tort on behalf of his principal and the principal himself are joint tortfeasors; so are the employee who commits a tort in the course of his employment and his employer (even if the employer became insolvent before the time of the trial[6]); so are an independent contractor who commits a tort and his employer, in those cases in which the employer is liable for his independent contractor.[7] Equally, a parent company and its subsidiary may be regarded as joint tortfeasors in respect of loss or injury suffered by employees of the subsidiary *so long as* a supervisory duty is borne by the parent company.[8] But the mere fact that a parent company appoints a director of the subsidiary who holds responsibility for health and safety matters in that company is not enough to attach liability to the parent company. He would need to be acting not just as a director of the subsidiary, but also on behalf of the parent in order for this to be the case.[9] Finally, a company director and the company itself may be regarded as joint tortfeasors where the director "is sufficiently bound up in [the company's] acts" to make him personally liable.[10] This will certainly occur where the wrongful acts complained of arise from a director's participation in a manner that goes beyond the mere exercise of his power of control through the constitutional organs of the company. An example is where he facilitates the breach of a design right with a view to enabling a breach of that right to occur.[11] Apart from these instances, concerted action is required. Where one person instigates another to commit a tort[12] they are joint tortfeasors; so are persons whose respective shares in the commission of a tort are done in furtherance of a common design.[13] However, it is important to appreciate that although mere facilitation of the commission of a tort will not suffice, a sufficient common design may nonetheless be held to exist where D1 makes a more than *de minimis* contribution to the commission of a tort by D2. The Supreme Court in *Fish & Fish Ltd v Sea Shepherd UK*[14] found that while a common design would normally be expressly communicated between the principal and the accessory, it could be inferred. The assistance, however, had to be more than de minimis or trivial. Lord Neuberger advised that "once the assistance is shown to be *more than trivial*, the proper way of reflecting the defendant's relatively unimportant contribution to the 4-04 tort is through the court's power to apportion liability, and then order contribution, as between the defendant and the primary tortfeasor."[15] For this reason, any case of unlawful means conspiracy could be explained in terms of joint tortfeasance where the unlawful means used constitute the commission of a tort. However, since the unlawful means in this tort can also include other wrongs, such as the commission of a common law crime,[16] it cannot be said that unlawful means conspiracy is an otiose cause of action.[17] "All persons in trespass who aid or counsel, direct, or join, are joint trespassers."[18] Similarly, according to the decision of Mackay J in *Daniels v Commissioner of Police for the Metropolis*,[19] there may be joint tortfeasance under the Protection from Harassment Act 1997 where the harassment on at least two occasions has been perpetrated by more than one person, each acting on separate occasions, in furtherance of some joint design. And anyone complicit in the commission of a deceit may likewise be regarded as a joint-tortfeasor so long as there is a common design.[20] However, an alleged joint tortfeasor cannot have actively co-operated to bring about the relevant act of the primary tortfeasor if he (the alleged joint tortfeasor) did not know about that act.[20A]

6 *Catanzano v Studio London Ltd* UKEAT/0487/11/DM (7 March 2012).

7 See, e.g. *Clark v Hosier Dickson Ltd* [2003] EWCA Civ 1467. For further instances in which an employer will be liable for the torts of an independent contractor, see para.6-62 onwards.

8 *Chandler v Cape Plc* [2012] EWCA Civ 525; [2012] 1 W.L.R. 3111. As Arden LJ explained, at [80]: "[T]his case demonstrates that in appropriate circumstances the law may impose on a parent company responsibility for the health and safety of its subsidiary's employees. Those circumstances include a situation where, as in this case, (1) the business of the parent and subsidiary are in a relevant respect the same; (2) the parent has, or ought to have, superior knowledge on some relevant aspect of health and safety in the particular industry; (3) the subsidiary's system of work is unsafe as the parent company knew, or ought to have known; and (4) the parent knew or ought to have foreseen that the subsidiary or its employees would rely on its using that superior knowledge for the employees' protection." Contrast *AAA v Unilever Plc* [2018] EWCA Civ 1532; [2018] B.C.C. 959: parent company owed no duty of care to those affected by acts or omissions of its subsidiary which had been responsible for its own decision-making and had not sought advice from the parent company. See also para.13-08 onwards.

9 *Thompson v Renwick Group Plc* [2014] EWCA Civ 635; [2014] P.I.Q.R. P18 at [25], per Tomlinson LJ.

10 *Koninklijke Philips Electronics NV v Princo Digital Disc GmbH* [2003] EWHC 2588 (Pat); [2004] 2 B.C.L.C. 5. See also *Contex Drouzhba v Wiseman* [2006] EWHC 2708 (QB); [2007] 1 B.C.L.C. 758 and *Global Crossing Ltd v Global Crossing Ltd* [2006] EWHC 2043 (Ch) where it was held that even where a company is dormant when the action is brought, a director and anyone else personally bound up in the commission of a tort (such as the company secretary who helped incorporate the defendant company in this passing off case) will be joint tortfeasors.

11 *Societa Esplosivi Industriali SpA v Ordnance Technologies (UK) Ltd (formerly SEI (UK) Ltd)* [2007] EWHC 2875 (Ch); [2008] 2 All E.R. 622 at [103], per Lindsay J.

12 *Brooke v Bool* [1928] 2 K.B. 578; *MCA Records Inc v Charly Records Ltd (No.5)* [2001] EWCA Civ 1441; [2002] E.M.L.R. 1; *White v Withers LLP* [2009] EWCA Civ 1122; [2010] 1 F.L.R. 859.

13 This statement of the law was approved in *The Koursk* [1924] P. 140 at 151, 156 and 159; and see *Brooke v Bool* [1928] 2 K.B. 578 at 585; *Mahesan v Malaysia Government Officers' Co-operative Housing Society Ltd* [1978] A.C. 374; *MCA Records Inc v Charly Records Ltd (No.5)* [2001] EWCA Civ 1441; [2002] E.M.L.R. 1.

14 [2015] UKSC 10; [2015] A.C. 1229 (Lords Sumption and Mance dissenting on the question of whether the charity's assistance could properly be regarded as de minimis and not from a difference about legal principles). Applied in *Vertical Leisure Ltd v Poleplus Ltd* [2015] EWHC 841 (IPEC) and *Glaxo Wellcome UK Ltd (t/a Allen & Hanburys) v Sandoz Ltd* [2017] EWCA Civ 227; [2017] F.S.R. 32. The Supreme Court also advised that there was no formula for determining whether that had happened and establishing liability was so fact-sensitive that it would be unwise for a court to produce such a formula.

15 [2015] UKSC 10; [2015] A.C. 1229 at [57] (emphasis added).

16 See *Customs and Excise Commissioners v Total Network SL* [2008] UKHL 19; [2008] 1 A.C. 1174. (The common law crime involved was that of cheating the Inland Revenue.)

[17] cf. Stevens, *Torts and Rights* (Oxford: OUP, 2006), p.249.

[18] *Petrie v Lamont* (1842) Car. Marsh. 93 at 96, per Tindal CJ.

[19] [2006] EWHC 1622 (QB).

[20] *Dadourian Group International Inc v Simms* [2009] EWCA Civ 169; [2009] 1 Lloyd's Rep. 601, *Clydesdale Bank Plc v Stoke Place Hotel Ltd (In Administration)* [2017] EWHC 181 (Ch).

[20A] *National Guild of Removers and Storers Ltd v Luckes* [2017] EWHC 3176 (IPEC): while a company could be held liable for an act of passing off arising from information on its website which neither the company nor its directors knew was there (the information had been reintroduced inadvertently by the website operator without their knowledge), the directors could not be liable as joint tortfeasors in respect of an act about which they knew nothing. They had only become aware of the reintroduction of the information on receiving a letter of complaint.

Add new paragraph:

The Court reiterated in *Federation International de L'Automobile v Gator Sports Ltd*[20B] that mere assistance or facilitation was not enough to make a defendant liable as a joint tortfeasor. It is clear that a common design is required as well. Where the defendant companies were not "one-man companies", the burden remained on the claimant to show that the directors were personally liable; a director was not to be automatically identified with the company, however much he controlled its affairs. **4-04A**

[20B] [2017] EWHC 3620 (Ch)). See also *Kalma v African Minerals Ltd* [2018] EWHC 3506 (QB).

At the start of the paragraph, replace "Mere" with:

Equally, mere **4-05**

3. CONTRIBUTION

Who may claim contribution?

Replace paragraph with:

Any person liable to another whether in tort, contract, breach of trust or otherwise,[55] may now recover contribution from any other person liable in respect of the same damage, regardless of the basis of the latter's liability.[56] Liability in respect of any damage means liability which has been or could be established in an action brought in England and Wales, even though the rules of private international law require the application of foreign law to determine any issue in dispute.[57] But a foreign judgment, it seems, gives no right to seek contribution from others liable in respect of the same damage. By s.1(2), even if, on the date when a claim for contribution is made, the claimant has ceased to be liable in respect of the damage in question—for example, if he has discharged his liability by payment or by compromise or the period of limitation has expired—he is still entitled to contribution providing that he was liable in respect of the relevant damage at the time when he was ordered to make the payment in respect of which contribution is sought, or when he made or agreed to make the payment. If D1 is sued for negligence in respect of personal injuries within three years of the damage being caused, he may recover contribution from D2 even if when he makes his claim three years have elapsed and the injured person could no longer sue D2.[58] But if D1 and D2 are jointly or concurrently liable for a tort created by virtue of anti-discrimination legislation, claims in respect of contribution are almost certainly only justiciable in the ordinary courts since an employment tribunal does not have jurisdiction to determine such matters.[59] **4-14**

[55] Civil Liability (Contribution) Act 1978 s.6(1).

[56] The right to claim contribution (which may be a payment in kind: *Baker & Davies Plc v Leslie Wilks* [2005] EWHC 1179 (TCC); [2005] 3 All E.R. 603) passes on the defendant's death to his personal representatives whether or not his liability had been established/admitted before his death: *Ronex Ltd v John Laing Construction Ltd* [1983] Q.B. 398. The defence of *ex turpi causa non oritur actio* cannot be relied upon in an answer to a claim for contribution under the 1978 Act: *K v P* [1993] Ch. 140, per Ferris J. The reason is that this would be inconsistent with the scheme of the Act: *Patel v Mirza* [2016] UKSC 42; [2017] A.C. 476 at [244], per Lord Sumption. S.6(1) of the Act is "deliberately wide" and should not be subjected to a condition precedent which is not to be found in the Act. Moreover, the Act gives the court ample power to fix the amount of contribution at a level, including zero, which takes into account all the factors which are relevant to *ex turpi causa non oritur actio*.

[57] Civil Liability (Contribution) Act 1978 s.1(6). See also *RA Lister Co Ltd v EG Thomson (Shipping) Ltd* [1987] 1 W.L.R. 1614; *Virgo S.S. Co SA v Skaarup Shipping Corp (The Kapetan Georgis)* [1988] 1 Lloyd's Rep. 352, per Hirst J: "nothing in the 1978 Act limits its scope to liabilities incurred in England and Wales."

[58] But D1 must bring his claim within two years of being ordered, agreeing to make or making a payment in respect of the damage: Limitation Act 1980 s.10. Note that where D1's agreement to settle requires embodiment in a consent order before the agreement becomes effective, there is authority that the two-year period runs from the date on which the consent order is made rather than the earlier date on which the agreement is reached: *Knight v Rochdale Healthcare NHS Trust* [2003] EWHC 1831 (QB); [2004] 1 W.L.R. 371. For the treatment of Pt 36 offers, see *Chief Constable of Hampshire v Southampton City Council* [2014] EWCA Civ 1541; [2015] P.I.Q.R. P5 (distinguishing *Knight*). A voluntary interim payment does not trigger the start of the two-year period for commencing contribution proceedings: *Spire Healthcare Ltd v Brooke* [2016] EWHC 2828 (QB); [2017] 1 W.L.R. 1177. Nor does an agreement in principle "subject to contract": *RG Carter Building Ltd v Kier Business Services Ltd* [2018] EWHC 729 (TCC); [2018] 1 W.L.R. 4598.

[59] *Beresford v Sovereign House Estates Ltd* [2012] I.C.R. D9 (EAT) at [12] per Underhill J.

Liability to contribution after settlement with claimant

Replace footnote 71 with:

4-19 [71] See, e.g. *Vanden Recycling Ltd v Kras Recycling BV* [2017] EWCA Civ 354; [2017] C.P. Rep. 33: satisfaction of the consent judgment against one tortfeasor in full and final settlement of the claims against it would bar claims against the concurrent tortfeasors for the same damage. Satisfaction of a settlement agreement as opposed to a judgment will only have this effect if the sum agreed and paid was intended to fix the full measure of the claimant's loss.

"Same damage"

Replace footnote 87 with:

4-22 [87] *Howkins & Harrison v Tyler* [2001] P.N.L.R. 27; [2001] Lloyd's Rep. P.N. 1 CA. See also *Dingles Building (NI) Ltd v Brooks* [2003] P.N.L.R. 8 (loss caused by a failure to obtain a contract for C was not the same as depriving C of the chance to obtain seven necessary signatures on that contract); *Webb v Barclays Bank Plc* [2001] EWCA Civ 1141; [2002] P.I.Q.R. P8; [2001] Lloyd's Rep. Med. 500 (D2's negligent medical advice that compounds the problems caused to C by D1 does amount to a contribution to the "same damage"); *Cohen v Davis* [2006] EWHC 768 (Ch); [2006] P.N.L.R. 33 (D2's negligent advice possibly contributed to depletion of company assets when it should have been wound up). Cf. *Luke v Kingsley Smith* [2003] EWHC 1559 (QB); [2004] P.N.L.R. 12).

Procedure

Replace footnote 101 with:

4-28 [101] *Stott v West Yorkshire Car Co Ltd* [1971] 2 Q.B. 651, not following *Calvert v Pick* [1954] 1 W.L.R. 456.

4. APPORTIONMENT

Apportionment of damages

Replace footnote 109 with:

4-29 [109] [1989] A.C. 328.

Replace footnote 112 with:

[112] [1997] 1 W.L.R. 426. In similar vein see *Madden v Quirk* [1989] 1 W.L.R. 702; *West London Pipeline & Storage Ltd v Total UK Ltd* [2008] EWHC 1296 (Comm); [2008] Lloyd's Rep. I.R. 688. See also *Brian Warwicker Partnership Plc v HOK International Ltd* [2005] EWCA Civ 962; [2006] P.N.L.R. 5, where it was said that non-causative factors that also involve a breach of duty are relevant considerations. **4-30**

5. INDEMNITY

Indemnity: mesothelioma cases

After "resect of any period where there was no such insurer, from IEG itself as a self-insurer.", add new footnote 158:

[158] On the operation on the broad equitable approach, see *RSA Insurance Plc v Assicurazioni Generali Spa* [2018] EWHC 1237 (QB); [2019] 1 All E.R. (Comm) 115. **4-41**

CHAPTER 5

CAPACITY AND PARTIES

TABLE OF CONTENTS

2. THE CROWN

(a) Crown Proceedings Act 1947

Torts "committed by servants or agents"

Replace paragraph with:

By s.2(1)(a), the Crown is made vicariously liable also for torts committed by its employees in the course of their employment, and for the torts of its independent contractors if committed in circumstances which would render a private **5-04** employer liable.[7] A proviso adds that the Crown shall not be liable unless the act or omission in question would, apart from the Act, have given rise to a cause of action in tort against "the servant or agent". So, for example, where servants of the Crown did not act in the knowledge that their acts were illegal—as is required for the tort of misfeasance in public office—there could be no vicarious liability for this tort on the part of the Crown.[8] The proviso also preserves such defences as act of state[9] and the exercise of statutory or prerogative powers.[10]

[7] The word "agent" in s.2(1)(a) includes an independent contractor employed by the Crown (s.38(2)), but the Crown is not subject to any greater liabilities in respect of acts or omissions of its independent contractors than it would be if it were a private person: s.40(2)(d). For an example of Crown liability for an independent contractor: see *Darling v Att Gen* [1950] 2 All E.R. 793. Note also the increased willingness of the courts to find non-delegable duties: *GB v Home Office* [2015] EWHC 819 (QB). *GB v Home Office* was not followed, however, in *Razumas v Ministry of Justice* [2018] EWHC 215 (QB); [2018] Med. L.R. 212; [2018] P.I.Q.R. P10 due to its entirely different legislative backdrop. The provision of healthcare was not part of a prison's mainstream or essential function, and formed no part of its statutory or common law duty.

[8] *Chagos Islanders v Att Gen* [2004] EWCA Civ 997. See also paras 14-120 to 14-135.

[9] See paras 5-16 to 5-18.

[10] See para.5-15.

Scope of the Act

Replace footnote 19 with:

5-07 [19] *Cooper v Hawkins* [1904] 2 K.B. 164; *Bombay Province v Bombay Municipal Corp* [1947] A.C. 58; *Secretary of State for Justice v Black* [2016] EWCA Civ 125; [2016] Q.B. 1060 (Crown not bound by the Health Act 2006 Pt 1 Ch.1—confirmed by *R. (on the Application of Black) v Secretary of State for Justice* [2017] UKSC 81, [2018] A.C. 215, Lady Hale classifying this as a principle of statutory interpretation as opposed to a presumption of Crown immunity). See Young (2018) 77 C.L.J. 237.

(c) Judicial and prerogative powers

Judicial acts

Replace paragraph with:

5-14 Section 2(5) excludes proceedings against the Crown for acts done by any person "while discharging or purporting to discharge any responsibilities of a judicial nature vested in him or any responsibilities which he has in connection with the execution of the judicial process".[42] The phrase "execution of the judicial process" receives a wide interpretation so that the purely administrative errors of a Registrar will also be caught.[43] The exception may well also extend to Crown employees such as members of administrative tribunals and inspectors at public inquiries carrying out duties which, at least for the purpose of conferring absolute privilege in defamation proceedings, have been classified as judicial.[44] *Mazhar v Lord Chancellor*[44A] confirmed that the Human Rights Act 1998 had not modified the constitutional principle of judicial immunity. Likewise, the Crown was not to be held vicariously liable for the acts of the judiciary.

[42] For a full discussion of judicial acts, see paras 5-100 to 5-119. In *Begraj v Secretary of State for Justice* [2015] EWHC 250 (QB), the court noted that the purpose of s.9(3) of the Human Rights Act 1998 was to preserve the s.2(5) of the Crown Proceedings Act 1947 position in the context of human rights damages claims. Where, therefore, a judge would benefit from judicial immunity in respect of a particular act, the state would equally not be liable under s.9(3) of the Human Rights Act 1998 (at [20]).

[43] *Quinland v Governor of Belmarsh Prison* [2002] EWCA Civ 174; [2003] Q.B. 306.

[44] *Jones v Department of Employment* [1989] 1 Q.B. 1 (a social security adjudicating officer does not perform judicial duties).

[44A] [2017] EWHC 2536 (Fam); [2018] Fam. 257.

(d) Acts of state

Acts of state

Replace paragraph with:

In *Rahmatullah v Ministry of Defence*,[56] the Supreme Court reviewed the defence of Crown act of state and held that the claims in tort would be barred if they related to acts which were: sovereign acts by their nature (that is, inherently governmental in nature), committed abroad, with the prior authority or subsequent ratification of the Crown, and in the conduct of foreign relations of the Crown. The class of acts must be so closely connected to that policy to be necessary in pursuing it.[57] In this case, the claimants alleged that they had been wrongfully detained or mistreated by UK and US troops during conflicts in Iraq and Afghanistan. The Supreme Court held that the doctrine extended at least to the conduct of military operations which were themselves lawful in international law,[58] but would not apply to torture or maltreatment in that such acts are not inherently governmental. It would also not generally apply to the expropriation of property.[59] On the assumed facts, therefore, the doctrine of Crown act of state would apply. In that Crown act of state would only arise when there were overriding reasons of public policy not to apply foreign tort law, it did not conflict with art.6 ECHR. The English doctrine of act of state will in any event not operate to preclude the courts from hearing proceedings between private litigants simply because those proceedings would incidentally raise questions as to the acts of foreign sovereign powers. The doctrine is also not a defence to claims made under the Human Rights Act 1998.[60] Any further extension of the defence of act of state is unlikely.[61] *Rahmatullah* was followed in *Alseran v Ministry of Defence*,[61A] which held that in principle an act can only be a Crown act of state if it has been authorised, or ratified, by a government policy or decision which is a lawful exercise of the Crown's powers as a matter of English domestic law. 5-18

[56] [2017] UKSC 1; [2017] A.C. 649 (allowing appeal against [2015] EWCA Civ 843; [2016] 2 W.L.R. 247).

[57] Lady Hale (with whom Lord Wilson and Lord Hughes agreed) [2017] UKSC 1; [2017] A.C. 649 at [37].

[58] This is not, however, the same as saying that the acts themselves were necessarily authorised in international law: Lady Hale [2017] UKSC 1; [2017] A.C. 649 at [37].

[59] But see Lord Sumption [2017] UKSC 1; [2017] A.C. 649 at [94].

[60] Lady Hale (with whom Lord Wilson and Lord Hughes agreed) in *Rahmatullah* [2017] UKSC 1; [2017] A.C. 649 at [14]. See, e.g. *Mohammed v Secretary of State for Defence* [2017] UKSC 2; [2017] A.C. 649.

[61] For the distinction between Crown act of state and foreign act of state, see Lord Mance in *Rahmatullah* [2017] UKSC 1; [2017] A.C. 649 at [50]–[52] and Lord Sumption at [89]. For foreign act of state and its relationship with state immunity, see now *Belhaj v Straw* [2017] UKSC 3; [2017] A.C. 964.

[61A] [2017] EWHC 3289 (QB)); [2018] 3 W.L.R. 95. See also Smith, "Acts of state in *Belhaj* and *Rahmatullah*" (2018) 134 L.Q.R. 20 who comments that while the three reasoned judgments in *Rahmatullah* disagreed on the nature and scope of the doctrine of Crown act of state and about whether it is a defence, a principle of abstention or both, this decision, combined with *Belhaj v Straw* [2017] UKSC 3; [2017] A.C. 964, marks a modest step forward for the separation of powers in foreign affairs, and for the judicial oversight of foreign policy.

4. FOREIGN STATES AND AMBASSADORS

(a) Foreign states

State Immunity Act 1978

Replace paragraph with:

5-28 The once controversial common law in this area has now been replaced by the State Immunity Act 1978. That Act seeks to restrict the immunity of foreign states from the jurisdiction of UK courts where the essence of the action against the state relates to commercial transactions undertaken by that state, or to a wrong committed in the UK in circumstances that make it appropriate for the obligations of the foreign government to be determined by UK courts.[73] Importantly, individual states within the USA do not constitute states for the purposes of the State Immunity Act. Rather, they are to be regarded as mere "constituent territories" within the federal state of the USA.[74] To a large extent the Act embodies the provisions of the European Convention on State Immunity of 1972. It also enabled the Government to ratify the Brussels Convention of 1926[75] relating to state-owned vessels.[76]

[73] In *Benkharbouche v Secretary of State for Foreign and Commonwealth Affairs* [2017] UKSC 62; [2017] I.C.R. 1327 at [51]–[52], Lord Sumption examined the historical background to state immunity, noting the progressive adoption of the restrictive doctrine of state immunity in the past 70 years due to the growing significance of state trading organisations in international trade. The case itself concerned state immunity with respect to employment claims brought by embassy staff and held that there would only be state immunity in an employment claim if the claim arose from an inherently sovereign act. It is clear that the state immunity principle is not inconsistent with the right to a fair trial contained in art.6 of the European Convention on Human Rights: see *McElhinney v Ireland* (31253/96) (2002) 34 E.H.R.R. 13.

[74] *Pocket Kings Ltd v Safenames Ltd* [2009] EWHC 2529 (Ch); [2010] Ch. 438.

[75] International Convention for the Unification of Certain Rules relating to the Immunity of State-owned Vessels (Cmd.5672) and Protocol (Cmd.5763).

[76] See *Hispano Americana Mercantil SA v Central Bank of Nigeria* [1979] 2 Lloyd's Rep. 277.

Procedural and remedial immunity

Replace paragraph with:

5-35 Proceedings against states must be initiated and conducted in the manner provided for by s.12[97] of the Act, and s.13 confers wide privileges on states in respect of refusal to grant disclosure of documents, and exempts states from certain remedies generally available in English courts. Briefly, foreign states are immune from the remedy by injunction, or any execution against state property movable or immovable save with their consent, and save in respect of property in use or intended for use for commercial purposes.

[97] See *Westminster CC v Government of the Islamic Republic of Iran* [1986] 1 W.L.R. 979, per Peter Gibson J; *PCL v Y* [2015] EWHC 68 (Comm); [2015] 1 W.L.R. 3948. Note that service of proceedings on a state under the State Immunity Act 1978 s.12(1) can only be served at the Ministry of Foreign Affairs in the country concerned: *Kuwait v Iraqi Airways Co* [1995] 1 W.L.R. 1147. It would suffice that the courier proffered it to the consignee at the ministry, even though the consignee refused to take the package: *Certain Underwriters at Lloyd's London v Syrian Arab Republic* [2018] EWHC 385 (Comm). See, generally, *General Dynamics UK Ltd v Libya* [2019] EWHC 64 (Comm); [2019] 1 All E.R. (Comm) 825.

(b) Ambassadors

Ambassadors

Replace paragraph with:

The law governing diplomatic immunity is contained in the Diplomatic Privileges Act 1964[108] which gives the force of law to the Vienna Convention on Diplomatic Relations of 1961, as set out in Sch.1 to the Act. The immunity granted is from suit and not from liability;[109] but this does not constitute an abrogation of the right to a fair trial under art.6 of the European Convention on Human Rights since the immunity's purpose—complying with a state's international law obligations to prevent hindrance to facilitate the diplomat in the fulfilment of his mission—has been held to be a proportionate interference with a tort victim's right under that provision.[110] Thus, if proceedings are begun at a stage when the defendant is no longer protected by his diplomatic status, and do not relate to his performance of functions as a member of the diplomatic mission, no immunity exists.[111] **5-39**

[108] See s.1. See also *Empson v Smith* [1966] 1 Q.B. 426; International Organisations Act 1981; Commonwealth Secretariat Act 1966; Consular Relations Act 1968. Individuals carrying out inspections for international arms control purposes have similar immunities: Arms Control and Disarmament (Privileges and Immunities) Act 1988 s.1; Arms Control and Disarmament (Inspections) Act 1991 s.5; Chemical Weapons Act 1996 s.27; Landmines Act 1998 s.15; Nuclear Explosions (Prohibition and Inspections) Act 1998 s.8 (not yet in force).

[109] *Dickinson v Del Solar* [1930] 1 K.B. 376 (insurance company liable even though diplomat defendant could not be sued).

[110] *Al-Malki v Reyes* [2015] EWCA Civ 32; [2016] 1 W.L.R. 1785. To the extent that diplomatic immunity is an aspect of state immunity, see now *Benkharbouche v Secretary of State for Foreign and Commonwealth Affairs* [2017] UKSC 62; [2017] I.C.R. 1327 which provides that, in so far as s.16(1)(a) of the State Immunity Act 1978 bars employment-related claims against a foreign state derived from EU law, the subsection should be disapplied and that, in so far as it bars other such claims, it is incompatible with art.6 of the European Convention on Human Rights.

[111] *Empson v Smith* [1966] 1 Q.B. 426; *Shaw v Shaw* [1979] Fam. 62.

Immunity

Replace footnote 113 with:

[113] Convention art.31(1). The exceptions are: (a) an action relating to private immovable property not held on behalf of the sending state for the purposes of the mission (the private residences of diplomats other than the head of a mission do not constitute premises held on behalf of the sending state for the purposes of the mission: *Intpro Properties (UK) Ltd v Sauvel* [1983] 2 W.L.R. 908); (b) an action relating to succession in which the diplomatic agent is involved as executor, administrator, heir or legatee as a private person and not on behalf of the sending state; and (c) an action relating to any professional or commercial activity exercised by the diplomatic agent outside his official functions (See now *Reyes v Al-Malki* [2017] UKSC 61; [2017] 3 W.L.R. 923; [2017] I.C.R. 1417). The immunity conferred by the Commonwealth Secretariat Act 1966 upon the Secretariat itself and upon certain members of its staff does not extend to actions for damage caused by motor vehicles. See the Schedule to the Act, paras 1 and 6, and cf. para.5. **5-40**

Duration of immunity

After "when he leaves the country (or upon the expiry of a reasonable time to do so", add new footnote 121A:

[121A] What constitutes a reasonable period is a matter for the court to determine in the context of inter-state diplomatic relations: *A Local Authority v X* [2018] EWHC 874 (Fam); [2019] 2 W.L.R. 202. **5-41**

6. BANKRUPTS

Liability insurance

Replace paragraph with:

5-51 With the coming into force of the Third Parties (Rights against Insurers) Act 2010,[155] Section 1(3) now permits the claimant to bring proceedings to enforce the rights against the insurer without having established the bankrupt's liability, although the claimant cannot enforce those rights without having established that liability.[155A] Where the insured person is a dissolved body corporate, s.6A now permits the claimant to recover damages from an insurer of that company without needing to restore the company to the register as a preliminary step.[155B] This addresses the problem highlighted by *Bradley v Eagle Star Insurance* and avoids the need for a claimant to bring preliminary proceedings against the insured.[156] Section 2 of the Act provides a new mechanism to enable a third party to bring proceedings against an insurer without first establishing the fact and amount of the insured's liability.[156A] On this basis, the claimant need only issue one set of proceedings against the insurer and may ask the court to make declarations both on the insured's liability to the claimant and the insurer's liability under the policy. If, in an action by the bankrupt, the insurer would have had a defence according to the terms of the policy, that defence will prevail against the injured person.[157] On the other hand, the insurer has no right to set off against the sums payable to the injured person the amount of any premiums due but unpaid when the liability accrued.[158] The action against the insurers, pursuant to the Act, must be commenced within the ordinary limitation period (i.e. proceedings have to be issued within six years of the cause of action arising, not the date of the bankruptcy).[159]Section 12 does provide, however, that if the claimant has issued proceedings against the insured in time, the claimant will not be time-barred from issuing fresh proceedings against the insurer for a declaration under s.2(2)(a).

[155] The Third Parties (Rights against Insurers) Act 2010 gives effect, with minor modifications, to the recommendations set out in the Law Commission and the Scottish Law Commission's 2001 joint report *Third Parties – Rights against Insurers* (Law Com No.272; Scot Law Com No.184) which was accepted by the Government in 2002. For transition provisions, see Third Parties (Rights against Insurers) Act 2010 Sch.3(3). The Act does not apply to reinsurance liabilities: see s.15.

[155A] On the operation of s.1 of the Third Parties (Rights against Insurers) Act 2010 and the transitional provisions, see *Redman v Zurich Insurance Plc* [2017] EWHC 1919 (QB); [2018] 1 W.L.R. 280. Schedule 3 to the 2010 Act expressly made it clear that the 1930 Act continued to apply where, before 1 August 2016, someone had become insolvent for the purposes of the 2010 Act and had incurred a liability against which they were insured. As liability was incurred when damage was caused, not when a claimant had established a right to compensation, in this case the 1930 Act applied. The transitional provisions did not provide for the 2010 regime to be applied retrospectively, so as to run in parallel with the regime under the 1930 Act.

[155B] Inserted by the Third Parties (Rights Against Insurers) Regulations 2016 (SI 2016/570). Note also the Third Parties (Rights Against Insurers) Act 2010 (Consequential Amendment of Companies Act 2006) Regulations 2018 (SI 2018/1162) which deals with a situation where the company has been dissolved many years before the claim is made and an application to restore the company to the register is out of time under s.1030(4) of the Companies Act 2006. By enabling the insurer to restore the company to the register, it facilitates the instigation of proceedings against other potential co-defendants in personal injury actions, e.g. asbestos claims.

[156] The new procedure removes the need to restore a dissolved company to the register of companies solely for the purpose of bringing an action against the company in order to establish the insured company's liability to the claimant so that the claimant could rely on the Third Parties (Rights against Insurers) Act in order to claim against the insurer.

[156A] The operation of s.2 of the Third Parties (Rights against Insurers) Act 2010 was explained in *BAE Systems Pension Funds Trustees Ltd v Royal & Sun Alliance Insurance Plc* [2017] EWHC 2082 (TCC); [2018] 1 W.L.R 1165.

[157] *Farrell v Federated Employers Insurance Association Ltd* [1970] 1 W.L.R. 1400; *Firma C-Trade SA v Newcastle Protection and Indemnity Association* [1991] 2 A.C. 1.

[158] *Murray v Legal and General Assurance Society Ltd* [1970] 2 Q.B. 495 See now s.10 of the 2010 Act (insurer's right of set off).

[159] *Lefevre v White* [1990] 1 Lloyd's Rep. 569.

8. Persons of unsound mind

Capacity to sue of persons of unsound mind

Replace paragraph with:

Normally no special rules apply to the bringing of actions by persons of unsound mind except that a person who (by reason of mental disorder within the meaning of the Mental Health Act 1983[209]) is incapable of managing his affairs, must have a litigation friend to conduct proceedings on his behalf.[210] No action in respect of acts done in pursuance of the Mental Health Act, however, may be brought without the leave of the High Court.[211] Time will not run under the Limitation Act 1980 until the claimant ceases to be under the disability, provided that he was under a disability when the cause of action accrued.[212] Where X commits a tort against Y causing Y to suffer unsoundness of mind, and Y thereafter commits a crime against Z (as a result of his diminished mental capacities) for which Y is convicted and subsequently detained in hospital, a question arises as to whether Y can pursue an action for damages against X. In *Gray v Thames Trains*,[213] the House of Lords held that the defence of ex turpi causa can be invoked to defeat any claims based on (i) the fact that Y was sentenced by a criminal court (and therefore lost earnings because of his conviction), or (ii) losses that were simply a consequence of his crime (rather than the sentence), such as damages payable to Z (or Z's dependants) as a result of the wrong done to Z. However, if the claimant is so profoundly mentally disturbed that he or she is completely unable to appreciate the unlawful nature of his act (and thus immune from conviction), or if he or she does not have the mental capacity to make a real choice, the defence of ex turpi cannot be raised.[214] **5-65**

[209] Mental Health Act 1983 s.1(2), where mental disorder is defined as "any disorder or disability of the mind; and 'mentally disordered' shall be construed accordingly".

[210] CPR r.21.2. See *S(FG) (Mental Health Patient), Re* [1973] 1 W.L.R. 178.

[211] Mental Health Act 1983 s.139(2). In *Winch v Jones* [1986] Q.B. 296, the Court of Appeal held that the correct test for leave to sue is whether on the material before the court the complaint appears to deserve fuller investigation, not whether the applicant has a prima facie case; cf. *James v London Borough of Havering* (1992) 15 B.M.L.R. 1. See further para.15-116.

[212] Limitation Act 1980 s.28(1). See generally para.32-21.

[213] [2009] UKHL 33; [2009] 1 A.C. 1339.

[214] In *Gray v Thames Trains* [2009] UKHL 33; [2009] 1 A.C. 1339, Lord Hoffmann adverted (at [27]) to the fact that the PTSD from which C was suffering diminished, but did not extinguish, his criminal responsibility. For discussion of the scope of this exception, see *Henderson v Dorset Healthcare University NHS Foundation Trust* [2018] EWCA Civ 1841; [2018] 3 W.L.R. 1651. See also paras 3-31 to 3-32.

10. ASSIGNEES

Transfers of undertakings

Replace paragraph with:

5-73 Where there is a transfer of an undertaking within the meaning of the Transfer of Undertakings (Protection of Employment) Regulations 2006 then on the transfer of an employee's contract of employment as part of the transfer of that undertaking, liability to pay the employee compensation for personal injuries sustained as a result of the transferor's negligence or breach of statutory duty passes to the new employer.[237] Similarly, where the transferor had effected an employer's liability insurance policy, the right to indemnity under the policy in respect of liability to an employee also transfers to the new employer under the Regulations.[238]

[237] *Bernadone v Pall Mall Services Group* [2000] 3 All E.R. 544.

[238] *Bernadone v Pall Mall Services Group* [2000] 3 All E.R. 544 (but note that the decision was made in relation to the former regulations: i.e., the Transfer of Undertakings (Protection of Employment) Regulations 1981).

11. CORPORATIONS

Liability of directors of limited company

Replace paragraph with:

5-82 In cases of deceit, however, things are different. In *Standard Chartered Bank v Pakistan National Shipping Corp (No.2)*,[265] a company director wrote a letter in which false representations were made on company notepaper. Notwithstanding the fact that the representation had all the appearance of being made on behalf of the company, their Lordships were adamant that the director could not escape personal liability. The approach in *Williams v Natural Life Health Foods* was distinguished on the basis that in that case the action had been for negligent misrepresentation. As Lord Hoffmann explained:

> "[*Williams* involved] an action for damages for negligent misrepresentation [and] in such a case liability depended upon an assumption of responsibility by the defendant... just as an agent can contract on behalf of another without incurring personal liability, so an agent can assume responsibility on behalf of another ... without assuming personal responsibility ... [But] [t]his reasoning cannot in my opinion apply to liability for fraud. No one can escape liability for his fraud by saying, 'I wish to make it clear that I am committing this fraud on behalf of someone else and I am not to be personally liable'."[266]

In the wake of this decision, it was arguably unclear which of negligent and fraudulent misrepresentations attracted the application of a special rule. However, in the light of both *Contex Drouzhba Ltd v Wiseman*[267] and *Renault UK Ltd v Fleetpro Technical Services*,[268] it has since become clear that it is cases of fraud that attract the special treatment. And it has elsewhere been held that the *Williams* principle is a rule of general application in tort.[269] That said, the objective test associated with determining whether a company director has assumed a personal responsibility is by no means an easy one to apply. Each case will turn on its own facts, for, as Walker J noted in *Macquarie Internationale Investments Ltd v Glencore UK Ltd*, there is a "lack of any principled or practical basis for distinguishing between assuming tortious responsibility in the course of acting as a director and doing so when not in the course of so acting".[270]

265 [2002] UKHL 43; [2003] 1 A.C. 959. *Standard Chartered* was applied in *Inter Export LLC v Townley* [2017] EWHC 530 (Ch) holding a company director liable in deceit for the value of a consignment of oil after the supplier had relied upon various misrepresentations she had made about the company's ability to pay for the oil (affirmed [2018] EWCA Civ 2068).

266 [2002] UKHL 43; [2003] 1 A.C. 959 at [21]–[22]. Lords Mustill, Slynn, Hobhouse and Rodger all concurred.

267 [2007] EWCA Civ 1201; [2008] B.C.C. 301.

268 [2007] EWHC 2541 (QB); [2008] Bus. L.R. D17.

269 See, e.g. *Koninklijke Philips Electronics NV v Princo Digital Disc GmbH* [2003] EWHC 2588 (Pat); [2004] 2 B.C.L.C. 50 (patent infringement).

270 [2008] EWHC 1716 (Comm); [2008] 2 B.C.L.C. 565 at [63].

Add new paragraph:

Once the personal liability in deceit of a sole director (who embodies the mind and will of the company), has been established, the courts will readily treat the company's liability as primary rather than vicarious[271] even though the director's wrongdoing constitutes fraud, and therefore entails wrongdoing of a kind that the courts are not usually willing to attribute to a company on the basis that "it is contrary to common sense and justice to attribute to a principal knowledge of something that his agent would be anxious to conceal from him".[272] On the other hand, it makes no sense to talk of such concealments in cases of companies with a sole director.[273] Furthermore, where the fraudulent conduct of a director causes loss, not only to some third party, but also to the company itself, the courts will again be unwilling to attribute the fraudulent conduct to the company which will be treated in law as a victim in its own right.[274] The recent case of *Singularis Holdings Ltd (in liquidation) v Daiwa Capital Markets Europe Ltd*[274A] confirms that the courts will be guided by the factual context and the purpose in dealing with any question of attribution, and that the fraudulent acts of a dominant director would not necessarily be attributed to the company. Here, in the light of the legitimate purpose for which the company had been established, and the context in which the defendant bank's duty and breach had arisen, the Court of Appeal held that it would have been wrong to attribute the conduct and knowledge of the sole shareholder and dominant director, Al Sanea, to the company, even when Al Sanea could be regarded as its directing mind and will. **5-82A**

271 *Stone & Rolls Ltd v Moore Stephens* [2009] UKHL 39; [2009] 1 A.C. 1391.

272 *Meridian Global Funds Management Asia Ltd v Securities Commission* [1995] 2 A.C. 500 at 511.

273 *Stone & Rolls Ltd v Moore Stephens* [2009] UKHL 39; [2009] 1 A.C. 1391 at [51].

274 *Bilta (UK) Ltd v Nazir (No.2)* [2015] UKSC 23; [2016] A.C. 1.

274A [2018] EWCA Civ 84; [2018] 1 W.L.R. 2777.

Liability of parent companies

Replace paragraph with:

If a parent company can be shown to be in breach of a personal duty owed to employees of a subsidiary company, that parent company may be held liable for a breach of that duty, even if the subsidiary company has ceased to exist. So, where a parent company was under an ongoing duty to provide health and safety advice to the employees of its subsidiary, the fact that its subsidiary had ceased to trade did not absolve the parent company of its joint and several liability towards the former employees.[275] The scope of *Chandler v Cape Plc*[275A] is being tested in a number of cases.[275B] **5-83**

[275] *Chandler v Cape Plc* [2012] EWCA Civ 525; [2012] 1 W.L.R. 3111. For the limitations on when a parent company will owe such a duty, see *Thompson v Renwick Group Plc* [2014] EWCA Civ 635; [2015] B.C.C. 855 and *AAA v Unilever Plc* [2017] EWHC 371 (QB) and paras 4-04 and 13-08. *AAA v Unilever Plc* [2017] EWHC 371 (QB) was affirmed on appeal: [2018] EWCA Civ 1532; [2018] B.C.C. 959.

[275A] [2012] EWCA Civ 525; [2012] 1 W.L.R. 3111.

[275B] See, most recently, *His Royal Highness Okpabi v Royal Dutch Shell Plc* [2018] EWCA Civ 191; [2018] B.C.C. 668 and *Lungowe v Vedanta Resources Plc* [2017] EWCA Civ 1528; [2018] 1 W.L.R. 3575. In *Vedanta Resources Plc v Lungowe* [2019] UKSC 20; [2019] 2 W.L.R. 1051, the Supreme Court clarified that the liability of parent companies in relation to the activities of their subsidiaries is not, in itself, a distinct category of negligence unsuited to summary determination, but may easily be traced back as far as the decision of the House of Lords in *Dorset Yacht Co Ltd v Home Office* [1970] A.C. 1004. The duty, then, could arise if there was a sufficiently high level of supervision and control of the activities at the mine with sufficient knowledge of the propensity of those activities to cause toxic escapes into the surrounding watercourses. These cases are discussed in more detail at para.13-09.

12. UNINCORPORATED ASSOCIATIONS AND TRADE UNIONS

Vicarious liability

Replace paragraph with:

5-93 As for vicarious liability for other torts—for example, negligence[305] and nuisance—apparently ordinary common law principles apply (whether or not the tort was committed in furtherance of a trade dispute). Exactly how vicarious liability principles apply to a trade union is unclear, especially in the case of non-employees, such as shop stewards. In *Heatons Transport v Transport and General Workers' Union*,[306] the House of Lords found, on the facts of the case, "general implied authority" ("emanating from the bottom", i.e. the members) for the shop stewards to take the unofficial action that they had undertaken. Although Lord Wilberforce was careful to restrict the decision in the *Heatons* case to vicarious liability under the now defunct Industrial Relations Act 1971 and its concept of "unfair industrial practices", and although the subsequent House of Lords' decision in *General Aviation Services (UK) Ltd v TGWU*,[307] stressed that each case had to be decided on its own facts, Scott J in *Thomas v National Union of Mineworkers (South Wales Area)*[308] established vicarious liability by applying the principle of the *Heatons* case, namely: "was the servant or agent acting on behalf of, and within the scope of the authority conferred by, the master or principal."

[305] A trade union owes a duty of care to use reasonable skill and care in advising or acting for a member in an employment dispute, though once the union engages solicitors to act on behalf of the member that duty ceases and any failings in the advice rendered is the responsibility of the solicitors: see *Friend v Institution of Professional Managers Specialists* [1999] I.R.L.R. 173.

[306] [1972] I.C.R. 308. *Heatons* was applied in *Unite the Union v Nailard* [2017] I.C.R. 121 (EAT) in relation to a claim that the union was vicariously liable for the sexual harassment of the claimant by elected branch officials. Affirmed on appeal: [2018] EWCA Civ 1203; [2019] I.C.R. 28.

[307] [1985] I.C.R. 615.

[308] [1985] I.C.R. 886.

After "to other unincorporated", replace "asscoiations." with:

5-94 associations.

18. CONSTABLES

Torts by constables

Replace footnote 399 with:

5-126 [399] *Mohidin v Commissioner of Police of the Metropolis* [2016] EWHC 105 (QB); [2016] 1 Costs L.R. 71. As Lord Lloyd-Jones commented in *James-Bowen v Commissioner of Police of the Metropolis*

[2018] UKSC 40; [2018] I.C.R. 1353 at [31], the possibility of such a claim is not fanciful, at least in cases where deliberate misconduct is alleged.

Protection of constable by warrant

Replace paragraph with:

At one time persons executing the warrants of justices were exposed to a double danger. If the warrant was issued without jurisdiction it was a nullity, and they could not plead its protection for any interference with the person or property of others. If it was issued with jurisdiction, they were still liable for anything they did which was not covered by its authority. They were thus endangered not only by their own mistakes, but by the mistakes of the justices. This situation was remedied by the Constables' Protection Act 1750 s.6. The object of this statute is that a constable who has obeyed a warrant may be protected,[406] and yet a party who has suffered a wrong may be under no difficulty as to his remedy. On inspection of the warrant the injured party can see whether it directed the act of which he complains. (Notably, a constable is not required to inform a man when he is actually arrested whether the arrest is by virtue of a warrant or otherwise.[407]) If it did direct the act, the claimant has no remedy against the constable, but may possibly sue the justice. If it did not, then the constable is liable.[408] More recently, the court in *Khan v Chief Constable of West Midlands*[408A] examined the application of s.6 of the Constables Protection Act 1750 in relation to a claim for damage to property caused during a search of premises under a magistrate's warrant. In ruling that what was done during the search was reasonably calculated to achieve the purpose of the warrant and so there was nothing to undermine the protection of the 1750 Act, Eady J also acknowledged that while it was regrettable that a search taking more than 12 hours would almost inevitably lead to distress, but that police officers have to carry out their responsibilities, while no doubt attempting to minimise the stress and inconvenience, in so far as they are able to do so consistently with those duties. The section does not apply where the cause of action is against the constable in respect of something which the warrant did not authorise.[408B] There are thus two issues that arise in connection with warrants: first, whether a valid warrant was properly executed; and secondly whether the warrant had the scope to confer the authority claimed by the constable. **5-128**

406 Although the warrant protects the constable, a person who maliciously and without reasonable cause instituted the process which induced the court to order the arrest may be liable in damages to the person arrested: *Roy v Prior* [1971] A.C. 470.

407 *R. v Kulynycz* [1971] 1 Q.B. 367.

408 In *Mouncher v Chief Constable of South Wales* [2016] EWHC 1367 (QB) at [453], Wyn Williams J accepted that the quashing of the warrant is a necessary pre-requisite to the bringing of a civil action under s.6.

408A [2017] EWHC 2185 (QB).

408B *Hoye v Bush* (1840) 1 Man. & G. 775.

CHAPTER 6

VICARIOUS LIABILITY

TABLE OF CONTENTS

1. INTRODUCTION

Scope of chapter

Replace paragraph with:

A person is liable not only for torts committed by himself,[1] but also, classically for those torts he has authorised or subsequently ratified. Authorising a tort involves instigating or procuring another to commit a tort. While this classical understanding of vicarious liability tends to relate simply to the commission of a common law tort by an employee, it is clear that vicarious liability is neither limited to the commission of common law torts, nor the commission of torts by those who are employees in the strict sense. According to Lord Phillips JSC in *Various Claimants v Catholic Child Welfare Society*,[2] the question of whether D2 can be held liable for the torts of D1 involves a two-stage test. The first stage involves considering "the relationship of D1 and D2 to see whether it is one that is capable of giving rise to vicarious liability".[3] And in the background there is the "policy objective underlying vicarious liability ... to ensure, in so far as it is fair, just and reasonable, that liability for tortious wrong is borne by a defendant with the means to compensate the victim".[4] The question of whether it is fair, just and reasonable to impose such liability was said by Lord Phillips to be illuminated by reference to five factors, namely, **6-01** "(i) the employer is more likely to have the means to compensate the victim than the employee and can be expected to have insured against that liability; (ii) the tort will have been committed as a result of activity being taken by the employee on behalf of the employer; (iii) the employee's activity is likely to be part of the business activity of the employer; (iv) the employer, by employing the employee to carry on the activity will have created the risk of the tort committed by the employee; (v) the employee will, to a greater or lesser degree, have been under the control of the employer."

[1] But note that liability may result from negligence in the selection of his servants: *Williams v Curzon Syndicate* (1919) 35 T.L.R. 475; *Adams (Durham) v Trust Houses* [1960] 1 Lloyd's Rep. 380.

[2] [2012] UKSC 56; [2013] 2 A.C. 1.

[3] [2012] UKSC 56; [2013] 2 A.C. 1 at [21].

[4] [2012] UKSC 56; [2013] 2 A.C. 1 at [34].

Add new paragraph:

6-01A The second stage requires there to be a sufficient "connection that links the relationship between D1 and D2 and the act or omission of D1".[4A] The first matter is to be determined by asking "whether the workman was working on behalf of an enterprise or on his own behalf and, if the former, how central the workman's activities were to the enterprise and whether these activities were integrated into the organisational structure of the enterprise".[4B] In this connection, the relationship between D1 and D2 need not be one of employer-employee in the strict sense since vicarious liability may well be imposed where there is merely a relationship "akin to that between an employer and an employee".[4C] Nor is the vicarious liability principle confined to D1's commission of a tort in the strict sense. In *Majrowski v Guy's and St Thomas' NHS Trust*[4D] the House of Lords held that it can also be invoked in connection with equitable wrongs as well as breaches of statutory obligations which ground awards of damages.[4F]

[4A] [2012] UKSC 56; [2013] 2 A.C. 1 at [21].

[4B] [2012] UKSC 56; [2013] 2 A.C. 1 at [49].

[4C] [2012] UKSC 56; [2013] 2 A.C. 1, at [47]. See further para.6-33.

[4D] [2006] UKHL 34; [2007] 1 W.L.R. 398.

[4F] [2006] UKHL 34; [2007] 1 W.L.R. 398 at [10] and [57], per Lords Nicholls and Hope respectively.

Employees and independent contractors

After "As the principles of liability generally differ according to the class to which the actual wrongdoer belongs, it is", replace "ormally" with:

6-03 normally

2. LIABILITY FOR EMPLOYEES

(a) Relationship of employer and employee

(i) Control test

Limitations of the control test

Replace paragraph with:

6-10 The inadequacy of the control test was most forcibly brought out in a series of cases concerning negligent hospital treatment. But even in the case of persons with no professional qualifications, it is often unrealistic to hold that the employer has any effective control. Recognising this, Lord Phillips has since set out a much more limited conception of the control test in the modern era. In his view, "the significance of control today is that the employer can direct what the employee does, not how he does it".[31] The more limited conception of the control test enunciated by Lord Phillips in *Various Claimants v Catholic Child Welfare Society*[32] was applied by the Court of Appeal in *NA v Nottinghamshire CC*[33] in the context of deciding that a local authority was not vicariously liable for the abusive way in which a foster child had been treated by his foster parents. The local authority, it was held, could not be made vicariously liable since it lacked the requisite degree of control over what foster parents do in relation to the quotidian provision of care for a foster child. However, on appeal, the Supreme Court reversed the decision of the Court of Appeal on the issue of vicarious liability, taking into account a number of factors: the torts were committed in the course of an activity carried out for the benefit of the local authority; the placement of children with foster parents created a relationship of authority and trust which rendered the children particularly vulnerable to abuse; the local authority's powers of approval, inspection, supervision and removal did not have any parallel in ordinary family life and the local authority exercised a significant degree of control over both what the foster parents did and how they did it; and local authorities could more easily compensate the victims of abuse.[34]

[31] *Various Claimants v Catholic Child Welfare Society* [2012] UKSC 56; [2013] 2 A.C. 1 at [36]. It has also been hinted that the absence of control in this watered-down sense may be fatal to the attempt by C to rely on D's vicarious liability: *Cox v Ministry of Justice* [2016] UKSC 10, [2016] A.C. 660 at [22]; *Kafagi v JBW Group Ltd* [2018] EWCA Civ 1157. Equally, the complete absence of integration into defendant's enterprise (the third of Lord Phillips' criteria concerning the fairness of imposing vicarious liability in the *Catholic Child Welfare Society* case (see para.6-01)) might also be fatal to the imposition of vicarious liability: *Davis v Fessey* [2018] 4 WLUK 29 at [17].

[32] [2012] UKSC 56; [2013] 2 A.C. 1, [36].

[33] [2015] EWCA Civ 1139; [2016] Q.B. 739.

[34] *Armes v Nottinghamshire CC* [2017] UKSC 60; [2018] A.C. 355, applying *Cox v Ministry of Justice* [2016] UKSC 10, [2016] A.C. 660; see para.6-33.

3. LIABILITY OF THE EMPLOYER

(a) Course of employment

Close connection test

Replace paragraph with:

The question whether a wrongful act is within the course of employment is a mixed question of fact and law,[112] and no simple test is appropriate to cover all cases.[113] The hitherto most frequently adopted test was that propounded by Salmond,[114] namely, that a wrongful act is deemed to be done in the course of the employment: **6-28**

> "if it is either (1) a wrongful act authorised by the master, or (2) a wrongful and unauthorised mode of doing some act authorised by the master. It is clear that the master is responsible for acts actually authorised by him: for liability would exist in this case, even if the relation between the parties was merely one of agency, and not one of service at all. But a master, as opposed to the employer of an independent contractor, is liable even for acts which he has not authorised, provided they are so connected with acts which he has authorised that they may rightly be regarded as modes—although improper modes—of doing them."

Adopting this test, the courts historically sought to distinguish between those acts of an employee which constitute an improper mode of carrying out his duties and those acts which fall outside the scope of his employment. However, in the light of the leading case, *Lister v Hesley Hall Ltd*,[115] that test is now inadequate in cases involving an employee's intentional wrongdoing. There, the issue for the House of Lords was whether the employers of a warden of a school boarding house could be vicariously liable for the acts of sexual abuse perpetrated by that warden on boys in his care. Their Lordships held that the Salmond test was unhelpful in cases of intentional wrongdoing, particularly where the employee sets out to benefit himself. Instead, they looked to the close connection between the acts in question and the employment. As Lord Steyn put it, the test for whether an employee has acted in the course of his employment was whether the tort was "so closely connected with his employment that it would be fair and just to hold the [employer] vicariously liable".[116] Applying this test to the facts of *Lister* it was held that, rather than the employment merely furnishing an opportunity to commit the sexual abuse, the connection between the employment and the torts was very strong. Lord Steyn noted that, "the reality was that the County Council were responsible for the care of the vulnerable children and employed [the warden] ... to carry out that duty on its behalf. And the sexual abuse took place while the employee was engaged in duties at the very time and place demanded by his employment."[117] Thus, he concluded, the sexual abuse was "inextricably interwoven with the carrying out by the warden of his duties".[118] In similar vein, the Court of Appeal held in *Gravil v Carroll*[119] that a punch thrown by the defendant club's player in the mêlée that followed the final whistle in a professional rugby match could be regarded as a sufficiently ordinary incident of a rugby match to engage the defendant's vicarious liability.[120] Likewise, a managing director who assaulted an employee at a private drinking session that followed a work's party, triggered the vicarious liability of the company for whom both he and the assaulted employee worked, given that he had attended the post-party drinking session in his capacity as managing director.[120A] Where, however, an employee returns to his place of work, while drunk, in order to assault a fellow employee who is working a night shift there, there will not be a sufficiently close connection for vicarious liability to be imposed: this would be "an independent venture of [the employee's] own, separate and distinct from [his] employment as a Senior Health Assistant at a care home".[121] By contrast, where a petrol station employee conducts an unprovoked, racially-motivated attack against a customer, there will be vicarious liability on the part of his employer because there is a sufficiently close connection. There is no close connection in such circumstances, for the nature of the employee's work is not such as to carry with it an inherent risk of "friction, confrontation or intimacy" with the victim.[122]

[112] In *HSBC Bank Plc v 5th Avenue Partners Ltd* [2009] EWCA Civ 296; [2009] 1 C.L.C. 503, Etherton LJ held (at [56]) that, ultimately, the decision as to whether there is vicarious liability "is a conclusion of law, based on primary facts, rather than a simple question of fact".

[113] Not only are there the two major tests considered below but also a separate test applicable to cases of deceit. As Lord Keith explained in *Armagas Ltd v Mundogas SA* [1986] 1 A.C. 717 at 780: "[d]ishonest conduct perpetrated with no intention of benefiting the employer but solely with that of procuring a personal gain or advantage to the employee is governed, in the field of vicarious liability, by a set of principles and a line of authority of peculiar application." In such cases the court must enquire whether the claimant was justified in relying on the false statement made by the employee. But note that no such question of reasonable reliance is to be posed in cases of negligent misstatement: *HSBC Bank Plc v 5th Avenue Partners Ltd* [2009] EWCA Civ 296; [2009] 1 C.L.C. 503.

[114] Now contained in *Salmond and Heuston on the Law of Torts*, 21st edn (1996), p.443.

[115] [2001] UKHL 22; [2002] 1 A.C. 215.

[116] [2001] UKHL 22; [2002] 1 A.C. 215 at [28]. Lord Millett also held, at [70], that the critical issue was "the closeness of the connection between the employee's duties and his wrongdoing". This test has its origins in two decisions of the Supreme Court of Canada: *Bazely v Curry* [1999] 2 S.C.R. 534 and *Jacobi v Griffiths* [1999] 2 S.C.R. 570.

[117] [2001] UKHL 22; [2002] 1 A.C. 215 at [25].

[118] [2001] UKHL 22; [2002] 1 A.C. 215 at [28]. See also *B v Nugent Care Society* [2009] EWCA Civ 827; [2010] 1 W.L.R. 516.

[119] [2008] EWCA Civ 689; [2008] I.C.R. 1222.

[120] [2008] EWCA Civ 689; [2008] I.C.R. 1222 at [23]; cf. *Bellman v Northampton* [2016] EWHC 3104 (QB); [2017] I.R.L.R. 124 (employer not liable for an assault committed by an employee after a Christmas party, even the though assault arose from a work-related discussion).

[120A] *Bellman v Northampton Recruitment Ltd* [2018] EWCA Civ 2214; [2019] 1 All E.R. 1133. Notably, the assault arose out of a work-related discussion between the claimant and the managing director which became (according to Irwin LJ, at [38]) "an exercise in laying down the law by [the managing director] ... an explicit assertion of his authority, vehemently and crudely expressed".

[121] *Weddall v Barchester Healthcare Ltd* [2012] EWCA Civ 25; [2012] I.R.L.R. 307, at [45] per Pill LJ; cf. *Wallbank v Wallbank Fox Designs Ltd* [2012] EWCA Civ 25; [2012] I.R.L.R. 307.

[122] *Mohamud v WM Morrison Supermarkets Plc* [2016] UKSC 11; [2016] A.C. 677. See further para.6-29.

After "Then against the background", replace "to" with:

of **6-29**

Replace paragraph with:

Another case in which all the circumstances of the case made it fair and just to conclude that the tort committed had a sufficiently close connection with the employment contract was *Brink's Global Services Inc v Igrox Ltd.*[130] There, an employee, engaged to fumigate containers prior to their being shipped, returned after work to one such container and stole several silver bars that were never recovered. Nonetheless, Moore–Bick LJ noted that by virtue of his job, the thief, Renwick, "was authorised to enter the secure compound where the container was stored and ... allowed to enter the container and thus have access to its contents". As such, it was held that there was a "sufficiently close connection between Renwick's theft of the silver and the purpose of his employment to make it fair and just that Igrox [his employer] should be held vicariously liable".[131] In the light of this decision, it is somewhat easier to see how certain earlier cases—such as *Morris v CW Martin and Sons Ltd*[132] and *Lloyd v Grace Smith & Co Ltd*[133] (which have widely been thought to turn upon the defendant's breach of a non–delegable duty of care)[134]—came to be presented in *Lister* as involving vicarious liability. On the other hand, the courts ought not to speculate about whether an employee is working late when he commits a tort on or near works premises after usual working hours have finished. The mere fact that someone is still wearing their work clothes is not conclusive evidence that they were still at work.[135] The courts may hold that a sufficiently close connection exists between the position held by the employee and the tort that he commits even if the tort is committed well beyond ordinary working hours. So, for example, vicarious liability was imposed in one case involving the misuse of private information, where the wrong in question was committed by an employee data controller using a personal computer at home to disseminate on the Internet personal data concerning fellow employees of their common employer.[135A] **6-31**

[130] [2010] EWCA Civ 1207; [2011] I.R.L.R. 343.

[131] [2010] EWCA Civ 1207; [2011] I.R.L.R. 343 at [30].

[132] [1966] 1 Q.B. 716.

[133] [1912] A.C. 716.

[134] In the light of such confusion, Lord Nicholls deliberately left these two cases to one side in *Dubai Aluminium*: see [2002] UKHL 48; [2003] 2 A.C. 366 at [27]–[28].

[135] *Fletcher v Chancery Supplies Ltd* [2016] EWCA Civ 1112.

[135A] *William Morrisons Supermarket Plc v Various Claimants* [2018] EWCA Civ 2339; [2019] 2 W.L.R. 99 at [79]. (It was also held (at [60]) that nothing under the Data Protection Act 1998 could be taken to exclude the vicarious liability of the employer in this case for the employee's commission of the common law tort of misuse of private information. The Act, in this regard, could only conceivably apply to this effect if the employee in question was "a data controller" for the purposes of the Act. The employee here did not fall within that definition.)

Broad approach

Replace paragraph with:

6-32 In similar claimant-friendly vein to *Lister* is the decision in *Kooragang Investment Pty Ltd v Richardson and Wrench Ltd*[136] where it was held that in establishing a particular employee's "course of employment", the court should not dissect the employee's tasks into component parts but should ask in a general sense: "what was the job at which he was engaged for his employer?"[137] Indeed, the idea that the courts may look more broadly to the question of whether what the employee was doing was in the furtherance of the employer's interests was made clear in the *Dubai Aluminium* case.[138] However, it is not vital that the employee's conduct be for the benefit of his employer. For even when the employee's conduct is not of benefit to the employer, this "does not mean that his conduct was not within the nature of his job viewed broadly and that there was not sufficient connection between the position in which he was employed and his wrongful conduct to make it right for [an employer]... to be held liable" according to the vicarious liability principle.[139]

[136] [1982] A.C. 462 at 471.

[137] See *Ilkiw v Samuels* [1963] W.L.R. 991 at 1004 (a case concerning a prohibition); *McPherson v Devon AHA* [1986] 7 C.L. 3.

[138] [2002] UKHL 48; [2003] 2 A.C. 366.

[139] *Group Seven Ltd v Notable Services LLP* [2019] EWCA Civ 614 at [153].

Relationship akin to employment

Replace paragraph with:

6-33 The most recent type of extension of the vicarious liability principle has occurred in cases in which the immediate tortfeasor can be said to be in a relationship with the defendant which is "akin to employment". So, for example, the relationship between a Roman Catholic priest and a bishop is regarded as close enough in character to an employer–employee relationship so as to make it fair and just that the diocese should be held vicariously liable in respect of acts of child abuse perpetrated by the priest.[140] The same is true of the relationship between lay brothers of the Catholic Church and the particular religious, unincorporated association to which they belong.[141] That the work arrangements between prisoners and the prison authorities for whom they perform remunerated tasks can also be held to fall within the present extension to the vicarious liability principle was confirmed by the Supreme Court in *Cox v Ministry of Justice*.[142] Their Lordships confirmed that, although the relationship in issue could be distinguished from a true contract of employment on the basis that it was not one voluntarily entered into, it was nonetheless sufficiently akin to an employment contract for vicarious liability to be imposed. As Lord Reed JSC explained, the fact that the prison service was obliged by statute to provide useful work for inmates was "not incompatible with the imposition of vicarious liability".[143] Equally, the present relationship was held not to be fundamentally different from an employer/employee relationship in so far as the prison service was a *not* a business whose primary purpose was to make a profit. It was enough, said Lord Reed JSC, that the tortfeasor was engaged in furthering the defendant's interests in a broad sense, regardless of whether those interests are commercial in nature.[144] Where, however, an agent makes unauthorised use of a facility that has only been made available to him by virtue of his being the agent of the defendant, and he does so for entirely personal reasons, there will be no vicarious liability on the part of the defendant. In such circumstances, the agent may be said to have engaged in an enterprise that is recognisably distinct from that of the defendant and as such will not have met the test applied at the second stage of the vicarious liability enquiry[144A]: "[t]o describe ... [the agent's] activity as in any sense an integral part of the business activities of ... [the defendant] would be a complete distortion of the true position or facts".[114B] Similarly, there was no vicarious liability for the negligence of a locum GP who caused harm to a patient by negligently advising her to stop taking conventional medicine for her pre-existing mental health problems and instead find healing through God.[144C] The locum's indoctrination of the claimant was no part of the business activity of the surgery that engaged him. Whereas the surgery was in the business of providing medical assistance, the relevant activities of the doctor which caused the claimant's suffering were religious, not medical, in nature. Accordingly, it could not be said that, by engaging the locum, the owners of the surgery had created or enhanced the risk of the tort's commission; and the case could be distinguished from the activity of the warden in *Lister*'s case. Whereas the warden in *Lister* had been endowed with particular pastoral duties towards the children he abused (the abuse being closely connected with his exercise of those pastoral duties), the locum was not engaged to evangelise or indoctrinate anyone.[144D]

[140] *JGE v English Province of Our Lady of Charity* [2012] EWCA Civ 938; [2013] Q.B. 722.

[141] *Various Claimants v Catholic Child Welfare Society* [2012] UKSC 56; [2013] 2 A.C. 1 at [47] per Lord Phillips J.S.C.

[142] [2016] UKSC 10; [2016] A.C. 660.

[143] [2016] UKSC 10; [2016] A.C. 660 at [38].

[144] [2016] UKSC 10; [2016] A.C. 660 at [30].

[144A] *Frederick v Positive Solutions (Financial Services) Ltd* [2018] EWCA Civ 431. On the first and second stages of the vicarious liability enquiry, see para.6-01.

[114B] [2018] EWCA Civ 431 at [67].

[144C] *Brayshaw v Partners of Apsley Surgery* [2018] EWHC 3286 (QB); (2018) 166 B.M.L.R. 76.

[144D] [2018] EWHC 3286 (QB); (2018) 166 B.M.L.R. 76 at [68].

Add new paragraph:

In relation to the third aspect of the appeal in *Cox*—premised on what had been said in a previous case[145] about vicarious liability only ever being imposed where it is fair, just and reasonable to do so—their Lordships were unpersuaded by the Ministry's contention that it would not be fair, just and reasonable to impose vicarious liability in the prison context. They took the view that the prospect of fraudulent claims arising out of alleged torts committed by prisoners against one another was a risk of entirely quotidian proportions against which the courts are sufficiently experienced in guarding.[146] There was, therefore, no especial risk that the recogni- **6-33A** tion of vicarious liability in this context would lead to an undesirable drain on scarce public resources. In any event, their Lordships were clear that it is plainly fair, just and reasonable to hold the prison service "liable to compensate a victim of negligence ... whether the negligent member of the team is a civilian or a prisoner".[147]

[145] *Various Claimants v Catholic Child Welfare Society* [2012] UKSC 56; [2013] 2 A.C. 1.

[146] [2016] UKSC 10; [2016] A.C. 660 at [44].

[147] [2016] UKSC 10; [2016] A.C. 660 at [42]. See also *Armes v Nottinghamshire CC* [2017] UKSC 60, holding a local authority vicariously liable for abuse of children by foster parents, the authority having placed the children with the foster parents.

(b) Examples of the modern broad approach

Employee acting on his own initiative

Replace paragraph with:

6-44 An employee acting on his own initiative (rather than his employer's) may be acting within the course of his employment. This will be the case where the employer either expressly or by implication has given the employee a discretion which he must exercise in the course of his employment. The employer will be liable for a wrongful exercise of such discretion. So, where D2 has given D1 actual authority to negotiate with a claimant on his behalf, and has expressly authorised D1 to do whatever he considers necessary to secure a loan from the claimant, D2 will be vicariously liable for any actionable misrepresentation made by D1 to the claimant which results in loss to the latter.[177A] All employees are deemed to have a discretion to act for the protection of the employer's property. Thus in *Poland v Parr*,[178] an off-duty employee gave a boy a cuff on the neck when he thought the boy was stealing sugar from his employer's cart. The boy fell and injured his leg and the employers were held liable, even though the employee was not employed to look after the sugar. The act complained of must, however, be such that it is reasonably necessary for the protection of the employer's property, or at least it must be such that it would have been reasonably necessary had the circumstances in fact been as the employee supposed them to be. An employee has no discretion in the course of his employment to punish or to give into custody one whom he supposes to have made an attempt upon his employer's property and so, if he acts after all danger to the property is over, or where no danger could be supposed to exist, his act will not be done in the course of his employment.[179]

[177A] *Khakshouri v Jimenez* [2017] EWHC 3392 (QB) at [124]–[125], per Green J.

[178] *Poland v Parr* [1927] 1 K.B. 366; cf. *Rees v Thomas* [1899] 1 Q.B. 1015; *Lowe v Pearson* [1899] 1 Q.B. 261; *Jones v Tarr* [1926] 1 K.B. 25 (cases decided under the Workmen's Compensation Acts).

[179] See, e.g. *Allen v London and SW Ry* (1870) L.R. 6 Q.B. 65 at 72, per Lush J; *Hanson v Walker* [1901] 1 K.B. 390.

Fraud of employee

Replace paragraph with:

6-52 In *Armagas Ltd v Mundogas (The Ocean Frost)*[202] the House of Lords endorsed a line of authority indicating that vicarious liability for fraud is governed by "a set of principles and a line of authority of peculiar application"[202A] so that "it is unnecessary to consider the development of the basis of vicarious liability in relation to torts such as negligence or trespass, which have followed a somewhat different line". And this remains the case notwithstanding the considerable development this area of the law has otherwise undergone in recent years.[202B] The principal will still be vicariously liable "if, but only if, the deceitful conduct of the agent was within his or her actual or ostensible authority".[202C] Of its very nature, fraud involves the deception of the victim and by that deception his persuasion to part with his property or do some other act to his own detriment and to the benefit of the person practising the fraud. For this reason the decision whether an employee committed fraud in the course of his employment can only be made after the authority, actual or ostensible, with which the employee is clothed has been ascertained. Thus in *Uxbridge Permanent Benefit Building Society v Pickard*,[203] a case of fraud committed by a solicitor's clerk, counsel for the defendant solicitor argued that the case should be treated as analogous to those cases in which an employee had been held to be on a "frolic of his own", but the argument was rejected.[204] The liability of an employer for fraud committed by his employee, though part of the law of employer and employee, has, in fact, a close connection with the law of principal and agent in contract, for there, too, the liability of the principal depends upon the authority, actual or ostensible, with which the agent is clothed.

[202] [1986] 1 A.C. 717.

[202A] [1986] 1 A.C. 717 at 780.

[202B] See para.6-01.

[202C] *Winter v Hockley Mint Ltd* [2018] EWCA Civ 2480; [2019] 1 W.L.R. 1617 at [48].

[203] [1939] 2 K.B. 248.

[204] [1939] 2 K.B. 248 at 254.

Employee's breach of statutory duty

Insert new sentence at end of paragraph:

The fact that the relevant statute speaks in terms of an employee's rights (rather than the duty of his or her fellow employee) constitutes no obstacle.[232A] **6-61**

[232A] *Timis v Osipov* [2018] EWCA Civ 2321; [2019] I.R.L.R 52.

4. INDEPENDENT CONTRACTORS

(a) General

Introduction

Replace paragraph with:

If the employer has employed an independent contractor to do work on his behalf, **6-62** the general rule is that the employer cannot be held vicariously liable for any tort committed by the contractor in the course of the execution of the work. One apparent exception to this general rule was espoused in *Barclays Bank v Various Claimants*[232B] In that case, Barclays had engaged a doctor to provide medical assessments of certain existing employees as well as of potential employees as part of the bank's recruitment process. Strictly speaking, the doctor was engaged as an independent contractor. Various claimants alleged that the doctor had assaulted them sexually in the course of the medical assessments and the question for the Court of Appeal was whether the bank could be held vicariously liable for those assaults. In a judgment (with which McCombe LJ and Sir Brian Leveson P agreed) Irwin LJ began by saying that "the law now requires answers to the specified questions laid down in *Cox* and *Mohamud*, and affirmed in *Armes*, rather than an answer to the question was the alleged tortfeasor an independent contractor".[232C] He went on to add that, in "adopting the approach of the Supreme Court, there will indeed be cases of independent contractors where vicarious liability will be established".[232D] This, he held, was just such a case. He felt unable to flaw the reasoning of the first instance judge, Davies J, who had held that the doctor's activity could properly be seen as part of the business activity of the bank for which reason it was capable of triggering the vicarious liability of the bank.[232E] The employees of a contractor, whilst acting as such, stand in the same position as their employer. But the employer of the contractor is not automatically liable for the torts committed by the contractor's employees.[233] Of course, even though the damage complained of may have been caused by the wrongful act or omission of an independent contractor or his employee, it may also be attributable to the negligence or other personal fault of the employer. If, for example, he has negligently selected an incompetent contractor, or if he has employed an insufficient number of men,[234] or has himself so interfered with the manner of carrying out the work that damage results,[235] he will himself have committed a tort for which he can be held liable. Also, if the employer has authorised or ratified the independent contractor's tort, then on normal principles he will be jointly liable for that tort.[236]

[232B] [2018] EWCA Civ 1670; [2018] I.R.L.R. 947.

[232C] [2018] EWCA Civ 1670; [2018] I.R.L.R. 947 at [44].

[232D] [2018] EWCA Civ 1670; [2018] I.R.L.R. 947 at [45].

[232E] [2017] EWHC 1929; [2017] I.R.L.R. 1103 at [30]. Cf. *Razumas v Ministry of Justice* [2018] EWHC 215 (QB); [2018] P.I.Q.R. P10.

[233] *Milligan v Wedge* (1840) 12 A. & E. 737; *Salsbury v Woodland* [1970] 1 Q.B. 324; *D & F Estates Ltd v Church Commissioners for England* [1989] A.C. 177. The position might, of course, be affected by contract: see, e.g. *National Trust v Haden Young* (1994) 72 B.L.R. 1. Equally, the employer may now, presumably, be liable in these circumstances if the situation is one of those envisaged in *Barclays Bank Plc v Various Claimants* [2018] EWCA Civ 1670; [2018] I.R.L.R. 947 in which an employer can be held vicariously liable for the torts of an independent contractor.

[234] *Pinn v Rew* (1916) 32 T.L.R. 451.

[235] *McLaughlin v Pryor* (1842) 4 M. G. 48; *Burgess v Gray* (1845) 1 C.B. 578.

[236] See, e.g. *Ellis v Sheffield Gas Consumer's Co* (1853) 2 E. & B. 767.

(c) Common law non-delegable duties

Common law duties

Replace paragraph with:

6-66 If a non-delegable duty is found to exist at common law, then the employer of an independent contractor is as much liable for its breach as if the duty had been created by statute. A particular difficulty that has beset this area of law is that of knowing when such a duty exists at common law.[248] In the past, it has been impossible to state general principles with any degree of confidence since the English courts have generally failed to identify or adhere to any such principles. That said, a telling feature of the leading cases on non-delegable duties is the fact that there is nearly always an *affirmative duty* for which the defendant has assumed responsibility.[249] This aspect of the cases was certainly stressed in the now leading case of *Woodland v Swimming Teachers Association*.[250] There, the Supreme Court was faced with a case in which the claimant had suffered severe brain injury during a school swimming lesson held at a local authority swimming pool. The lesson in question was organised and provided by an independent contractor. In relation to the action against the local education authority, the claimant alleged breach of a non-delegable duty. In finding for the claimant, the Supreme Court offered the following guidance on the imposition of non-delegable duties to exercise reasonable care. Specifically side-lining those cases concerning highways and hazards (considered below), Lord Sumption—with whom Lords Clarke, Toulson and Wilson agreed—opined as follows:

> "[T]he remaining cases are characterised by the following defining features: (1) The claimant is a patient or a child, or for some other reason is especially vulnerable or dependent on the protection of the defendant against the risk of injury ... (2) There is an antecedent relationship between the claimant and the defendant, independent of the negligent act or omission itself, (i) which places the claimant in the actual custody, charge or care of the defendant, and (ii) from which it is possible to impute to the defendant the assumption of a positive duty to protect the claimant from harm, and not just a duty to refrain from conduct which will foreseeably damage the claimant ... (3) The claimant has no control over how the defendant chooses to perform those obligations, i.e. whether personally or through employees or through third parties. (4) The defendant has delegated to a third party some function which is an integral part of the positive duty which he has assumed towards the claimant; and the third party is exercising, for the purpose of the function thus delegated to him, the defendant's custody or care of the claimant and the element of control that goes with it. (5) The third party has been negligent not in some collateral respect but in the performance of the very function assumed by the defendant and delegated by the defendant to him."[251]

Mindful of the emphasis in *Woodland* on the presence of especial claimant vulnerability or dependency in typical non-delegable duty cases, Coulson J in *GB v Home Office*[252] held that a non-delegable duty is owed by the Home Office to immigration detainees in respect of the provision of medical care while being held in an immigration removal centre. He noted the vulnerability of such persons and held there to be "a positive duty to protect GB from harm" which included a duty to provide medical care.[253] By contrast, despite the admitted vulnerability of children in local authority care, the Court of Appeal in *NA v Nottinghamshire CC*[254] did not feel that it was appropriate to regard a local authority as having been in breach of a non-delegable duty to take reasonable steps to protect a young girl in its care from harm when she was abused at the hands of foster parents with whom the defendant authority had placed her. According to Tomlinson LJ, "[i]n order to be non-delegable a duty must relate to a function which the purported delegator ... has assumed for itself a duty to perform".[255] The Supreme Court agreed that a local authority does not come under a non-delegable duty owed to children placed with foster parents.[256] Such a duty would create a potential conflict between the local authority's duty towards a child under s.18 of the Child Care Act 1980 and the authority's interests in avoiding exposure to liability. A non-delegable duty would also amount to a form of state insurance for the actions of the child's family members.[257]

[248] For an attempt to explain such duties see Murphy, "Juridical Foundations of Common Law Non-Delegable Duties" in Neyers et al (eds.), *Emerging Issues in Tort Law* (2007).

[249] For endorsement of the assumption of responsibility criterion, see *S v Lothian Health Board* [2009] CSOH 97; 2009 S.L.T. 689.

[250] [2013] UKSC 66; [2014] A.C. 537.

[251] [2013] UKSC 66; [2014] A.C. 537 at [23]. In a separate judgment, Baroness Hale also signalled (at [38]) her approval of this five-point summary of the law.

[252] [2015] EWHC 819 (QB).

[253] [2015] EWHC 819 (QB) at [28]–[34].

[254] [2015] EWCA Civ 1139; [2016] Q.B. 739.

[255] [2015] EWCA Civ 1139; [2016] Q.B. 739 at [25]. Similarly, although the Ministry of Justice owes prison inmates a non-delegable duty to arrange the provision of healthcare, that duty does not extend to the actual delivery of such care since delivering "[h]ealthcare is not… part of the prison institution's mainstream (or essential) function": *Razumas v Ministry of Justice* [2018] EWHC 215 (QB); [2018] P.I.Q.R. P10 at [151], per Cockerill J.

[256] *Armes v Nottinghamshire CC* [2017] UKSC 60; [2018] A.C. 355.

[257] Note, however, that the Supreme Court did come to the conclusion that the local authority could be vicariously liable for the abuse of children placed in the care of foster parents. See para.6-10.

Extra hazardous activities

At end of quotation, after "principal employer's peril.", add footnote:

6-73 [283A] [1934] 1 KB 191 at 200.

CHAPTER 7

FOREIGN TORTS

TABLE OF CONTENTS

2. JURISDICTION

Jurisdiction: three international instruments

Replace paragraph with:

Where the defendant is domiciled[3] in a state within the European Union, and the proceedings were commenced before 10 January 2015, the rules governing jurisdiction are to be found in the European Regulation on Jurisdiction and the Recognition and Enforcement of Judgments in Civil and Commercial Matters (Brussels I). Where the defendant is domiciled in a country party to the "parallel" Lugano Convention on Jurisdiction and Judgments (i.e. those of the former EFTA states that remain outside the EU, like Iceland, Switzerland and Norway), the question of jurisdiction is governed by the Civil Jurisdiction and Judgments Act 1991. The material provisions of Brussels I and the Convention are more or less identical. Thus, according to art.5(3) of both instruments, in all "matters relating to tort, delict or quasi-delict",[3A] the defendant may be sued either where he is domiciled or in the country where the "harmful event" occurred.[4] And if the place where the harmful event occured is relied upon, there is no requirement that the claimant be the immediate victim of the tort.[5] Also, if, in an action that is brought principally against D1 (domiciled in state A), it is prudent to add D2 (domiciled in state B) as a second defendant, such joining of D2 to the proceedings will be permissible provided that "the claims are so closely connected that it is expedient to hear and determine them together to avoid the risk of irreconcilable judgments resulting from separate proceedings".[6] That said, matters may be complicated where D1 is domiciled in this country while D2 is domiciled abroad and D2 has already indicated its willingness to submit to the jurisdiction of the foreign court. This is what happened in *Vedanta Resources Plc v Lungowe*.[6A] In that case, the Supreme Court began by recognising that art.4 of the Recast Brussels Regulation[6B] granted jurisdiction to the English courts in respect of the tort action against D1 (which was D2's parent company).[6C] It then noted that D2 had signalled its willingness to be sued before the Zambian courts (Zambia being the place of the harmful even). But the Supreme Court stopped short of saying that, in such circumstances, the English courts would be required to decline jurisdiction under art.4, since art.4 is not designed to prevent the risk of irreconcilable judgments. The true position, the court said, was this: the risk of irreconcilable judgments was a relevant consideration, but not a trump card. 7-03

Any risk of irreconcilable judgements lay with the claimants, and it was their choice whether they wanted to run this risk by suing D1 in England and D2 in Zambia (when in fact both defendants could be sued in Zambia).[6D]

[3] Domicile for the purposes of the Regulation and the Civil Jurisdiction and Judgments Act 1991 is defined in the case of an individual as residence of a more than transient or temporary nature, and in the case of a company as the "seat of the business": see arts 41–46 of Brussels I and the Lugano Convention. See art.63 of the Recast Regulation. It has been held that if C can advance a "good arguable case" that D was domiciled in England, this will suffice for the purposes of establishing D's domicile in England: *Tugushev v Orlov* [2019] EWHC 645 (Comm) at [44].

[3A] As the CJEU put it: "[t]he decisive criterion ... to identify the area within which an action fell was not the procedural context of which that action was part, but the legal basis of the action": *NK v BNP Paribas Fortis NV* (C-535/17) EU:C:2019:96; [2019] I.L.Pr. 10. So, as was held in this case, if money is wrongfully appropriated in the context of bankruptcy proceedings, the relevant cause of action will lie in tort (and thus within the tort jurisdiction rules). It will not come within the rules applicable to Bankruptcy located in another Regulation (i.e. Council Regulation (EC) No.1346/2000).

[4] Commonly termed "the alternative jurisdiction". Note, too, that art.5(3) (and now also art.7(2) of the Recast Regulation, we may suppose) "must be interpreted as meaning that an action for a negative declaration seeking to establish the absence of liability in tort, delict, or quasi-delict falls within the scope of that provision": *Folien Fischer AG v Ritrama SpA* (C-133/11) [2013] Q.B. 523.

[5] *Deutsche Bahn AG v Morgan Advanced Materials Plc* [2013] EWCA Civ 1484; [2014] C.P. Rep. 10.

[6] Council Regulation art.6(1) (now art.8(1) of the Recast Regulation). On the way in which the question of whether there exists a risk of irreconcilable judgments should be determined, see *Alfa Laval Tumba AB v Separator Spares International Ltd* [2012] EWCA Civ 1569; [2013] 1 W.L.R. 1110 at [36]; *OJSC VTB Bank v Parline Ltd* [2013] EWHC 3538 (Comm).

[6A] [2019] UKSC 20; [2019] 2 W.L.R. 1051.

[6B] See para.7-04.

[6C] Note that art.4 can be invoked in order to sue a defendant in the Member State in which that defendant is domiciled regardless of whether the claimant is also domiciled in a Member State.

[6D] [2019] UKSC 20; [2019] 2 W.L.R. 1051 at [75].

Add new paragraph:

7-03A Where damage results from C's reliance, in country X, on false information contained in a prospectus issued in country Y, the fact that C's reliance occurs in country X, and the fact that C's money payments are made out of bank accounts in country X, will be indicative of the harm having occurred in country X, even though the defective prospectus was published in country Y.[6E]

[6E] *Löber v Barclays Bank Plc* (C-304/17) [2019] 4 W.L.R. 5.

Tort, delict and quasi-delict

Replace paragraph with:

7-05 The special jurisdiction rule governing tort cases is, as noted above, actually expressed in terms of cases of "tort, delict and quasi-delict".[8] This somewhat wordy phrase was construed by Jackson J in *Hewden Tower Cranes Ltd v Wolfkram GmbH*[9] in the light of the decision of the European Court of Justice in *Kalfelis v Schröder, Münchmeyer, Hengst & Co*[10] as "an autonomous concept, which is to be interpreted, for the application of the Convention, principally by reference to the scheme and objectives of the Convention".[10A] It was further held in that case that the phrase was capable of embracing a claim for contribution from a joint-tortfeasor under the Civil Liability (Contribution) Act 1978. It did not matter, said Jackson J, that the proceedings under the 1978 Act could not be said to fit the English notion of a tort. All that mattered was that those proceedings fell within the convention's autonomous concept of a "tort, delict or quasi-delict". A similar ruling was made in the first instance case of *Iveco SpA, Iveco Ltd v Magna Electronics Srl*.[11] But in *XL Insurance Co SE v AXA Corporate Solutions Assurance*[12] Judge Waksman QC expressed some doubts about the correctness of the Hewden Tower Cranes decision in this respect. He observed, correctly it is submitted, that a claim for contribution made by D1 against D2 arises by virtue of a rule of law and not because D1 has been the victim of D2's tort, delict or quasi-delict. In other words, even though contribution claims only arise after the commission of a tort, they are not in themselves claims in tort, delict or quasi-delict. In the case before him, Judge Waksman was content to advert to a distinction between the instant case and Hewden Tower Cranes, namely, that "the contribution claim here is not between tortfeasors but joint insurers". On this basis he felt perfectly at liberty to hold that the instant case did not fall within the relevant words of the Recast Regulation.[13] While the matter of whether contribution claims should be regarded as claims in tort, delict or quasi-delict clearly requires final resolution, it has certainly been held that a claim for repayment of a wrongly levied fine—a claim for unjust enrichment—is a purely administrative issue and thus falls beyond the scope of the "civil and commercial matters" that delimit the scope of the Regulation.[14] On the other hand, it has been held that an action based on predatory pricing (so as to constitute a breach of competition law) does fall within the definition of a tort, delict or quasi-delict.[14A]

[8] This does not mean, however, that the default rule—granting jurisdiction to the courts of the country in which the defendant is domiciled (art.2 of Brussels I, and art.4 of the Recast Regulation)—cannot be invoked: *Lungowe v Vendetta Resources Plc* [2016] EWHC 975 (TCC); [2016] B.C.C. 774.

[9] [2007] EWHC 857 (TCC); [2007] 2 Lloyd's Rep. 138.

[10] [1988] E.C.R. 5565.

[10A] It certainly covers cases of misrepresentation: *Aspen Underwriting Ltd v Credit Europe Bank NV* [2018] EWCA Civ 2590; [2019] 1 Lloyd's Rep. 221; *Ashley v Jimenez* [2019] EWHC 17 (Ch).

[11] [2015] EWHC 2887 (TCC); [2015] 2 C.L.C. 963 at [48]. See also *Arcadia Petroleum Ltd v Bosworth* [2016] EWCA Civ 818; [2016] C.P. Rep. 48 (conspiracies to breach contracts of employment are matters of tort law for these purposes).

[12] [2015] EWHC 3431 (Comm); [2016] Lloyd's Rep. I.R. 420.

[13] [2015] EWHC 3431 (Comm); [2016] Lloyd's Rep. I.R. 420 at [62].

[14] *Gazdasagi Versenyhivatal v Siemens Aktiengesellschaft Österreich* [2016] 5 C.M.L.R. 14; [2016] I.L. Pr 33.

[14A] *AB flyLAL-Lithuanian Airlines (in liquidation) v Starptautiskā lidosta "Rīga" VAS* (C-27/17) EU:C:2018:533; [2019] 1 W.L.R. 669 (ECJ).

Actions for breach of confidence.

Replace paragraph with:

The key concept of "harmful event" has been interpreted by the European Court of Justice to mean either the place where the wrongdoing occurred, or the place where resulting damage ensued.[21] Thus, in *Shevill v Presse Alliance SA*,[22] the ECJ ruled that in defamation cases, claimants have the option of suing either in the place where a libel originates, or in *any* place where damage occurs, albeit only to the extent that the claimant suffers damage in that place.[23] The same is true of internet-based misuse of private information[23A] and negligent misstatements made in one country, but relied upon detrimentally by the claimant, in another.[24] Likewise, it has been held by the ECJ that where a trade mark is registered in Member State A, but infringed in Member State B, the courts of either state will be entitled to hear the case.[25] By contrast, in *Anton Durbeck GmbH v Den Norske Bank ASA*[26] it was held **7-07** that the "harmful event" took place in London where the London Branch of a Norwegian Bank instigated the wrongful interference with a contract of carriage of goods by sea by causing the ship carrying the goods to be wrongly arrested and detained in Panamanian waters. Similarly, in *AMT Futures Ltd v Marzillier, Dr Meier & Dr Guntner Rechtsanwaltsgesellschaft mbH*,[27] where A induced B to commence litigation against C in Germany in breach of an exclusive jurisdiction clause in a contract between B and C (stating that any litigation involving B and C should be heard in England), the Supreme Court said that the place of the harmful event was Germany and not England. This was so despite the fact that C had been deprived of the benefit of having any litigation occur in England where C was based. The place of the harmful event was held to be Germany partly because this was where the wrongdoing occurred (i.e. the inducement to breach the contract) and partly because this was where the direct harm occurred (i.e. the cost of litigating in Germany). The idea that the place of the harmful event should be the place in which harm originates was continued in *JSC BTA Bank v Khrapunov*.[27A] That case concerned a conspiracy to injure by unlawful means. The relevant conspiracy agreement was made in England although the harmful acts done pursuant to that agreement were committed outside England. One question for the Supreme Court was whether the English court had jurisdiction under art.5(3) of the Lugano Convention on the basis that this creates a facility to claim jurisdiction based on the place where the harmful event occurred. (Notably, this provision contains identical words to those found in the Recast Brussels Regulation.) In a joint speech prepared by Lord Sumption and Lord Lloyd-Jones JJSC (with which the remaining members of the Supreme Court agreed) it was held (at [41]) that it was right to treat "the place where the conspiratorial agreement was made as the place of the event which gives rise to and is at the origin of the damage".[27B] The case is noteworthy not just because it offers Supreme Court authority on the meaning of "place of the harmful event" but also because it adds to the body of previous jurisprudence that has only hitherto recognised physical events as being the kinds of events that might be regarded as the origin of the damage.

[21] (21/76) *Bier v Mines Potasse d'Alsace* [1976] E.C.R. 1735; *Minister Investments v Hyundai* [1988] 2 Lloyd's Rep. 621; *Saïd v Groupe L'Express* [2018] EWHC 3593 (QB); [2019] E.M.L.R. 9. The place where the harmful event occurs will also cover sufficiently closely related contingent damage: *Cronos Containers NV v Palatin* [2002] EWHC 2819 (Comm); [2003] 2 Lloyd's Rep. 489.

[22] [1995] 2 A.C. 18 ECJ. But note that where the loss is purely financial, the court will not treat a mere loss of funds from a claimant's bank account as, per se, a sufficient connecting factor. It will look for some other connecting factor to justify a derogation from the default rule governing jurisdiction: *Universal Music International Holding BV v Schilling* [2016] Q.B. 967; [2016] 3 W.L.R. 1139.

[23] The same approach is taken in conversion cases where D wrongfully retains in state X property belonging to C (where C is located in state Y): *Mazur Media Ltd v Mazur Media GmbH* [2004] EWHC 1566 (Ch); [2004] 1 W.L.R. 2966 at [45], per Lawrence Collins J.

[23A] *BVC v EWF* [2018] EWHC 2674 (QB); [2019] I.L.Pr. 7.

[24] *Barclay-Watt v Alpha Panereti Public Ltd* (unreported, November 23, 2012). On the other hand, it has also been held that the place where the harmful event occurs covers the place where the misstatement was made: *London Helicopters Ltd v Heliportugal LDA-INAC* [2006] EWHC 108 (QB); [2006] 1 All E.R. (Comm) 595; *Newstat Holdings Ltd v Zani* [2006] EWHC 342 (Comm); [2006] 1 All E.R. (Comm) 607.

[25] *Wintersteiger AG v Products 4U Sondermaschinenbau GmbH* (C–523/10) [2012] E.T.M.R. 31. The difficulties that arise in connection with the use of the internet to infringe the sui generis rights that exist with respect to electronic databases were considered by the ECJ in *Football Dataco Ltd v Sportradar GmbH* (C-173/11) [2013] 1 C.M.L.R. 29. There, data protected by such a right was uploaded from a database onto a computer in Member State A. It was later forwarded, upon request, to a website user in Member State B. It was held that in such circumstances, an infringement may be said to have occurred "at least, in Member State B, where there is evidence from which it may be concluded that the act

discloses an intention on the part of the person performing the act to target members of the public in Member State B": at [47]. Note however, the different rules that apply in the case of EU Trade Marks: *AMS Neve Ltd v Heritage Audio SL* [2016] EWHC 2563 (IPEC); [2017] F.S.R. 16.

[26] [2003] EWCA Civ 147; [2003] Q.B. 1160.

[27] [2017] UKSC 13; [2018] A.C. 439.

[27A] [2018] UKSC 19; [2018] 2 W.L.R. 1125.

[27B] [2018] UKSC 19; [2018] 2 W.L.R. 1125 at [41]. Strictly, the decision concerned jurisdiction under art.5(3) of the Lugano Convention; but this contains identical words to those found in the Recast Brussels Regulation.

Replace footnote 29 with:

[29] To like effect see *Mazur Media Ltd v Mazur Media GmbH* [2004] EWHC 1566 (Ch); [2004] 1 W.L.R. 2966; *Actial Farmaceutica LDA v De Simone* [2016] EWCA Civ 1311; [2016] 2 C.L.C. 1020. Compare the interpretation of CPR PD 6B para.3.9(a) in cases falling beyond Regulation 44/2001 art.5(3) in *Wink v Croatia Osiguranje* [2013] EWHC 1118 (QB) (which does embrace a deterioration in the claimant's health after he has returned to his country of domicile for the purposes of determining whether C will be entitled to service out of the jurisdiction). See also paras 7-10 to 7-12. **7-08**

Jurisdiction: common law

Replace paragraph with:

Where the defendant is domiciled in a country which is not bound by the Regulation or party to the Lugano Convention, he may be served with a claim form if he is simply present in England. However, if the claim has little or no substantive connection with England, the defendant can apply for a stay of proceedings on grounds of forum non conveniens.[34] Exceptionally, the availability of legal aid (or some other form of financial aid in bringing proceedings) may be a factor in determining issues of forum non conveniens.[35] Where a tort is committed in England, leave may be sought to serve the claim form abroad in accordance with CPR r.6.36.[36] For these purposes, a tort is committed in England if either damage was sustained within the jurisdiction or resulted from an act committed within the jurisdiction. But it is not necessary to establish that all the relevant damage was sustained in England,[37] nor that all the relevant acts were committed in England.[38] Similarly, additional claims and parties can be added because it makes sense that multiple "claims arising out of the same or closely related facts should be tried together, whether by adding defendants to an existing claim or adding claims to an action against an existing defendant".[38A] A judge should "look at the tort alleged in a common-sense way and ask whether the damage has resulted from substantial and efficacious acts committed within the jurisdiction".[39] In an application under CPR r.6.36 the claimant must satisfy the court that England is a proper and appropriate forum for resolution of the dispute between the parties,[40] and that there is a serious issue to be tried.[41] As a general matter, it has been held that in relation to service out that: **7-10**

> "First, the claimant must satisfy the court that, in relation to the foreign defendant to be served with the proceedings, there is a serious issue to be tried on the merits of the claim, i.e. a substantial question of fact or law or both. This means that there has to be a real, as opposed to a fanciful, prospect of success on the claim. Secondly, the claimant must satisfy the court that there is a good arguable case that the claim against the foreign defendant falls within one or more of the classes of case for which leave to serve out of the jurisdiction may be given (often referred to as 'the gateways') which are set out in paragraph 3.1 of Practice Direction 6B. Thirdly, the claimant must satisfy the court that in all the circumstances England is clearly or distinctly the appropriate forum for the trial of the dispute and that in all the circumstances the court ought to exercise its discretion to permit service of the proceedings out of the jurisdiction."[41A]

34 *Spiliada Maritime Corp v Cansulex Ltd* [1987] A.C. 460; *Connelly v RTZ Coren Plc* [1998] A.C. 854.

35 *Connelly v RTZ Coren Plc* [1998] A.C. 854 at 873, per Lord Goff; *Carlson v Rio Tinto Plc* [1999] C.L.C. 551. A lack of financial assistance in the appropriate forum which means that the claimant will be unable to afford not only professional legal representation but also necessary expert evidence does amount to a denial of justice that justifies refusing a stay of proceedings: *Lubbe v Cape Plc* [2000] 1 W.L.R. 1545.

36 In order to do this, the claimant must show one of the grounds in CPR PD 6B para.3.1.

37 *Booth v Phillips* [2004] EWHC 1437 (Comm); [2004] 1 W.L.R. 3292 at [36]. See also *Wink v Croatia Osiguranje* [2013] EWHC 1118 (QB) where "any damage flowing from the tort" was considered enough to meet the requirement of "damage ... sustained within the jurisdiction" for the purposes of CPR PD 6B para.3.9(a).

38 *Metall and Rohstoff AG v Donaldson Lufkin & Jenrett Inc* [1990] 1 Q.B. 391.

38A *Eurasia Sports Ltd v Tsai* [2018] EWCA Civ 1742; [2018] 1 W.L.R. 6089 at [46].

39 *Metall and Rohstoff AG v Donaldson Lufkin & Jenrett Inc* [1990] 1 Q.B. 391 at 437.

40 See *Spiliada Maritime Corp v Cansulex Ltd* [1987] A.C. 460; *Arab Monetary Fund v Hashim (No.3)* [1991] 2 A.C. 114.

41 *Iiyama (UK) Ltd v Samsung Electronics Co Ltd* [2018] EWCA Civ 220; [2018] 4 C.M.L.R. 23 at [41].

41A *EasyGroup Ltd v Easy Fly Express Ltd* [2018] EWHC 3155 (Ch); [2019] E.T.M.R. 13 at [7] per Arnold J. Note also, that in cases involving the infringement of intellectual property rights, it may be that the case can only be resolved properly in this country because technical questions about the validity and infringement of intellectual property rights are governed by a domestic registration regime in relation to which local knowledge is key: *Huawei Technologies Co Ltd v Conversant Wireless Licensing SARL* [2019] EWCA Civ 38.

Add new paragraph:

7-10A In cases of internet libel, the Court of Appeal has stressed the fact that the need for a common-sense approach in determining questions of *forum conveniens* and service out of the jurisdiction is particularly strong.[42] However, since then, the ECJ has suggested that "[g]iven that the impact which material placed online is liable to have on an individual's personality rights might best be assessed by the court of the place where the alleged victim has his centre of interests, the attribution of jurisdiction to that court corresponds to the objective of the sound administration of justice".[43]

42 *King v Lewis* [2004] EWCA Civ 1329; [2005] E.M.L.R. 4.

43 *eDate Advertising GmbH v X; Martinez v MGN Ltd* [2012] Q.B. 654. Note that actions for misuse of private information count as tort actions for these purposes: *Vidal-Hall v Google Inc* [2015] EWCA Civ; [2016] Q.B. 1003, at [43].

Replace paragraph with:

7-12 In relation to torts committed abroad by foreign states or their agents, the doctrine of state immunity will, so long as it is enlivened, provide an absolute bar to jurisdiction,[47] Equally, the common law doctrine of act of state will apply if the act was either committed within the sovereign territory of the state concerned or, on foreign soil in circumstances where the acts complained of, though ostensibly tortious, are not in breach of any clearly defined rules of international law, for in such circumstances the acts complained of "are done on the plane of international law, and their lawfulness can be judged only by that law"[48] (and not, therfore, by the domestic courts).

47 *Belhaj v Straw; Rahmatullah v Ministry of Defence* [2017] UKSC 3; [2017] A.C. 964. See also para.5-28 onwards.

48 *Belhaj v Straw; Rahmatullah v Ministry of Defence* [2017] UKSC 3; [2017] A.C. 964 at [234], per Lord Sumption JSC.

Jurisdiction in the case of cross-border torts within the UK

Add new paragraph:

When the 1982 Act is in play (because a jurisdiction dispute concerning courts in two different parts of the UK exists), the Brussels Recast Regulation is completely inapplicable. Thus, when in one case the English court sought to stay proceedings under s.49 of the 1982 Act (on the basis of *forum non conveniens*), it was entitled to do so.[49A] It was not precluded from so doing under the Brussels Recast Regulation since Scotland and England belong to the same jurisdiction for the purposes of the Regulation. The dispute was (from a Regulation point of view) a purely internal one, and therefore beyond the scope of the Regulation (which only applies to jurisdictional conflicts between the courts of two different Member States). **7-13A**

49A *Kennedy v National Trust for Scotland* [2019] EWCA Civ 648.

3. CHOICE OF LAW

Rome II

Replace paragraph with:

Since 11 January 2009, questions of choice of law in matters of tort and delict within the European Community have been governed by a directly applicable instrument: Regulation (EC) No.864/2007 on the Law Applicable to Non-Contractual Obligations.[50] The Regulation is generally referred to as Rome II and that name is adopted here. The scope of the Regulation is limited to civil and commercial matters. Certain issues, therefore, fall beyond its purview. These include matters of evidence and procedure[51] and matters relating to violations of privacy and personality rights (such as defamation).[52] Prior to the entry into force of Rome II, a distinction could be drawn between the question of which body of law—the *lex loci delicti* or the *lex fori*—governs the question of liability and which governs the question of quantum. However, in *Moreno v Motor Insurers Bureau*,[53] the Supreme Court put this beyond doubt, holding that Rome II applies the *lex loci delicti* both to questions of liability and those of quantum. Since Rome II has no retrospective effect,[53A] there continues to be, for the present at least, three sets of choice of law rules in play. This will continue until all actions within the scope of the Private International Law (Miscellaneous Provisions) Act 1995[54] have either been heard or exceeded their respective limitation periods. **7-14**

50 art.2(1). Although Rome II draws a distinction between entry into force and the date from which the instrument becomes applicable, it has been confirmed that the date from which its provisions are to apply is 11 January 2009: *Homawoo v GMF Assurances SA* (C–412/10) [2012] I.L.Pr. 2.

51 art.1(3). *PJSC Tatneft v Bogolyubov* [2017] EWCA Civ 1581; [2018] 4 W.L.R. 14 at [33].

52 art.1(1)(g).

53 [2016] UKSC 52; [2016] 1 W.L.R. 3194.

53A *Iiyama (UK) Ltd v Samsung Electronics Co Ltd* [2018] EWCA Civ 220; [2018] 4 C.M.L.R. 23; *Sophocleous v Secretary of State for the Foreign and Commonwealth Office* [2018] EWCA Civ 2167; [2019] 2 W.L.R. 956 at [1], per Longmore LJ.

54 See para.7-19 onwards.

Exceptions to the general rule

Replace footnote 63 with:

7-17 [63] *Marshall (Deceased) v Motor Insurers Bureau* [2015] EWHC 3421 (QB); [2016] P.I.Q.R. Q5 at [19] (permission to appeal refused: [2017] EWCA Civ 17; [2017] R.T.R. 20).

Add new paragraph:

7-17A A third (possible) exception to the general rule in art.4(1) is contained in art.12 which provides that "[t]he law applicable to a non-contractual obligation arising out of dealings prior to the conclusion of a contract, regardless of whether the contract was actually concluded or not, shall be the law that applies to the contract or that would have been applicable to it had it been entered into". It therefore covers fraudulent misrepresentations. So, if D makes fraudulent representations to C in one country, and those misrepresentations induce C to enter into a contract with D that is to be performed in a different country, then the governing law will be the law of the country in which the contract was (to be) performed. However, it has been suggested, obiter, that art.12 has no purchase where D1 and D2 have conspired to defraud C and C subsequently wishes to bring an action against D1 if the only parties to the (would-be) contract induced by the fraudulent misrepresentation are D2 and C. [64A] Article 12 is restricted to non-contractual obligations between the actual parties to the (putative) contract.[64B] So, in a case where D1 is not a party to the contract, the relevant choice of law rule must be determined by reference to art.4.

[64A] *Republic of Angola v Perfectbit Ltd* [2018] EWHC 965 (Comm).

[64B] *Republic of Angola v Perfectbit Ltd* [2018] EWHC 965 (Comm) at [200].

Choice of law under the 1995 Act

Replace paragraph with:

7-20 Section 10 of the 1995 Act abolished the rules of common law on choice of law except in relation to defamation and analogous claims where the common law rules survive. Section 11(1) provides that: "The general rule is that the applicable law is the law of the country in which the events constituting the tort or delict in question occur."[67] The *lex loci delicti* thus becomes prima facie the governing law. Where elements of the relevant events occur in different countries, s.11(2) provides that in cases relating to personal injury or death, the applicable law under the general rule is taken as being the country where the individual was when he sustained the injury; in cases relating to damage to property, it shall be the country where the property was when it was damaged; and in any other case it shall be "the law of the country in which the most significant element or elements of those events occurred". Thus, for example, where a misstatement generated in England was read and acted upon to the claimant's detriment in Monaco, the applicable law was Monégasque law.[68] Where Iraqi citizens sought compensation from the MOD for alleged unlawful imprisonment and ill-treatment at the hands of British armed forces during the UK's military action in Iraq between 2003 and 2009 it was held that Iraqi law was the relevant law given that Iraq was the country in which the events constituting the tort had occurred.[68A]

[67] But note that for these purposes, the notion of a tort or delict has a meaning particular to the 1995 Act: see *OJSC Oil Co Yugraneft v Abramovich* [2008] EWHC 2613 (Comm) at [221].

[68] *Morin v Bonhams Brooks Ltd* [2003] EWCA Civ 1802; [2003] 2 All E.R. (Comm) 36. See in similar vein *Constantin Medien AG v Ecclestone* [2014] EWHC 387 (Ch) (conspiracy formulated in London, but harm caused in Germany).

[68A] *Alseran v Ministry of Defence* [2017] EWHC 3289 (QB); [2018] 3 W.L.R. 95 at [36]).

4. PARTICULAR TYPES OF TORT

Intellectual property rights

After "exclusive jurisdiction as those cases will inevitably involve a question of validity of registration.", add new footnote: **7-31**

[106A] Nor does it matter that the validity of the patent is only, arguably, an incidental matter because what is centrally in issue is the scope of a licence granted by the patent holder: *Ablynx NV v VHsquared Ltd* [2019] EWHC 792 (Pat).

CHAPTER 8

NEGLIGENCE

TABLE OF CONTENTS

1. THE TORT OF NEGLIGENCE

Requirement for actionable damage

Replace paragraph with:

8-05 Damage is the gist of the tort of negligence. Without damage there is no tort. Negligence does not impose a duty to act carefully; it is a duty not to inflict damage carelessly.[9] But the damage that has been caused must be recognised by the court as "actionable damage". Damage in this sense is "an abstract concept of being worse off, physically or economically, so that compensation is an appropriate remedy."[10] In the context of personal injury, actionable damage does not mean simply a physiological change. The damage must have some perceptible effect on the claimant's health or capability. Thus, symptomless pleural plaques on the lungs developed as a result of inhaling asbestos fibres do not constitute actionable damage; nor does this become actionable damage when combined with the anxiety of the claimants due to their knowledge of the risk of developing serious disease in the future as a result of their exposure to asbestos.[11] The harm must also exceed a minimum threshold of severity in order to qualify as actionable damage. Thus, a "transient, trifling, self-limiting, reversible reaction to an irritant is not 'actionable injury' for the purposes of the law of tort."[12] Moreover, the type of damage must also be recognised by the court as actionable in the particular circumstances in which it occurred. *Greenway v Johnson Matthey Plc*[13] employees who had been sensitised to platinum salts without developing any symptoms, and who would not develop symptoms unless they were further exposed to platinum salts, had not suffered compensatable personal injury. They had suffered financial loss because they were no longer able to work with platinum salts, but this constituted pure economic loss which did not fall within the scope of an employers' duty of care for the health and safety of employees.[14] *Greenway v Johnson Matthey Plc* was reversed on appeal. In *Dryden v Johnson Matthey Plc*[14A] the Supreme Court held that the sensitisation to platinum salts which prevented the claimants from working with platinum salts constituted actionable personal injury. The claimants' bodily capacity for work had been impaired and they were therefore significantly worse off. This amounted to actionable bodily damage which was more than negligible. This distinguished the case from *Rothwell v Chemical & Insulating Co* where the pleural plaques were "nothing more than a marker of exposure to asbestos dust, being symptomless in themselves and not leading to or contributing to any condition which would produce symptoms, even if the sufferer were to be exposed to further asbestos dust." But the sensitisation of the claimants to platinum salts in *Dryden* constituted "a change to their physiological make-up which means that further exposure now carries with it the risk of an allergic reaction, and for that reason they must change their everyday lives so as to avoid such exposure."[14B] The loss of part of their capacity to work was a loss of bodily function.

[9] See the quotation from Viscount Simonds speech in *Overseas Tankship (UK) Ltd v Morts Dock & Engineering Co Ltd (The Wagon Mound)* [1961] A.C. 388 at 425. See further, para.2-152.

[10] *Rothwell v Chemical & Insulating Co* [2007] UKHL 39; [2008] 1 A.C. 281 at [7].

[11] *Rothwell v Chemical & Insulating Co* [2007] UKHL 39; [2008] 1 A.C. 281.

[12] *Saunderson v Sonae Industria (UK) Ltd* [2015] EWHC 2264 (QB) at [179] per Jay J.

[13] [2016] EWCA Civ 408; [2016] 1 W.L.R. 4487.

[14] See also *A v A Health and Social Services Trust* [2011] NICA 28; [2012] N.I. 77 (claimants born with a different skin colour from that of their parents due to negligence in the selection of gametes for *in vitro*

fertilisation had not suffered actionable damage: "Having a different skin colour from the majority of the surrounding population and their parents' cannot sensibly be regarded as damage or disability...", at [9]).

14A [2018] UKSC 18; [2018] 2 W.L.R. 1109.

14B [2018] UKSC 18; [2018] 2 W.L.R. 1109 at [47] per Lady Black).

2. DUTY OF CARE

(b) The test for notional duty

Fairness and the three stage test

Replace paragraph with:

8-16 After a period during which the courts had debated both the relationship of foreseeability and proximity and the relevance of policy considerations,[45] the outcome was summarised by Lord Bridge in *Caparo Industries Plc v Dickman*[46]:

> "What emerges is that, in addition to the foreseeability of damage, necessary ingredients in any situation giving rise to a duty of care are that there should exist between the party owing the duty and the party to whom it is owed a relationship characterised by the law as one of 'proximity' or 'neighbourhood' and that the situation should be one in which the court considers it fair, just and reasonable that the law should impose a duty of a given scope on the one party for the benefit of the other."[47]

This passage has been cited in numerous subsequent decisions[48] and is now the accepted test for the existence of a notional duty. Commenting on the role of the three criteria in *Caparo*, Lord Oliver said:

> "... it is difficult to resist the conclusion that what have been treated as three separate requirements are, at least in most cases, in fact merely facets of the same thing, for in some cases the degree of foreseeability is such that it is from that alone the requisite proximity can be deduced, whilst in others the absence of the essential relationship can most rationally be attributed simply to the court's view that it would not be fair and reasonable to hold the defendant responsible."[49]

Clearly, the criteria can be viewed as overlapping.[50] It has been said that "that the two headings (proximity and justice) are no more than two labels under which the court examines the pros and cons of imposing liability in negligence in a particular type of case".[51] To an extent, this is true of whatever formula is used to determine duty. As Sir Robin Cooke has observed:

> "Ultimately the exercise can only be a balancing one and the important object is that all relevant factors be weighed. There is no escape from the truth that, whatever formula be used, the outcome in a grey area case has to be determined by judicial judgment. Formulae can help organise thinking but they cannot provide answers."[52]

The last point is significant, for although the factors which are relevant to one criterion may also be relevant to another, the criteria help organise thinking because they direct the court to the different questions with reference to which the balancing exercise is conducted.[53] In *Robinson v Chief Constable of West Yorkshire*[53A] Lord Reed said that the proposition that *Caparo* had established a test that applies to all claims in negligence, and that as a result the court will only impose a duty of care where it considers it fair, just and reasonable to do so, is mistaken.[53B] *Caparo* had repudiated the idea that there is a single test which can be applied in all cases. Novel cases should be considered using the incremental approach.[53C] Where claims are not novel, but fall within an existing category of duty, *Caparo* is not relevant and the court simply has to apply established principles to the particular circumstances of the case. It is not appropriate in such cases for the court to resort to what it considers to be fair, just and reasonable, discarding established principles, in order to achieve a result that the court thinks better fits the broader merits.[53D] In a novel case the court has to exercise judgment when deciding whether a new duty of care should be imposed, and it is the exercise of this judgment that involves consideration of what is "fair, just and reasonable".[53E]

[45] The debate centred on the so-called "two-stage test" of Lord Wilberforce in *Anns v Merton LBC* [1978] A.C. 728 at 751–752, a case concerning local authority liability for omission. However, the test seemed to equate proximity with contemplation or foreseeability. The lack of a proximity requirement in the sense of a "close and direct relationship" led to criticism of the Wilberforce test and its eventual replacement by the three stage test in *Caparo*.

[46] [1990] 2 A.C. 605 at 617–618.

[47] Lord Oliver also referred to this three stage, foreseeability, proximity, justice and reasonableness test, [1990] 2 A.C. 605 at 633 and Lord Jauncey at 658 cited Lord Griffiths' speech in *Smith v Eric S Bush* [1990] 1 A.C. 831 at 865, as authority for "the three criteria ... foreseeability of damage, proximity of relationship and reasonableness".

[48] See for example in the House of Lords: *Spring v Guardian Assurance Plc* [1995] 2 A.C. 296 at 333, per Lord Slynn; *Marc Rich & Co v Bishop Rock Marine* [1996] A.C. 211 at 235, per Lord Steyn.

[49] [1990] 2 A.C. 605 at 618.

[50] "These considerations inevitably shade into each other": *Elguzouli-Daf v Commissioner of Police of the Metropolis* [1995] Q.B. 335 at 349, per Steyn LJ.

[51] *White v Jones* [1995] 2 A.C. 207 at 221, per Nicholls VC; *Caparo Industries Plc v Dickman* [1990] 2 A.C. 605 at 628, per Lord Roskill: " ... they are but labels descriptive of the very different factual situations which can exist in particular cases and ... must be carefully examined ... before it can be pragmatically determined whether a duty of care exists ...".

[52] *South Pacific Manufacturing Co Ltd v New Zealand Security Consultants & Investigations Ltd* [1992] 2 N.Z.L.R. 282 at 294. As Lord Pearce said in *Hedley Byrne & Co Ltd v Heller & Partners Ltd* [1964] A.C. 465 at 536, the answer "depends ultimately on the courts' assessment of the demands of society for protection from the carelessness of others".

[53] In *Perre v Apand Pty Ltd* (1999) 164 A.L.R. 606 at 684, Kirby J noted the value of the labels in the threefold test in helping to "steer the mind through the task in hand" by providing the "headings to which considerations may be assigned". However, the majority of the High Court preferred to address the considerations directly, albeit without consensus as to which considerations were crucial.

[53A] [2018] UKSC 4; [2018] 2 W.L.R. 595 at [21]–[29].

[53B] Citing Lord Toulson in *Michael v Chief Constable of South Wales Police* [2015] UKSC 2; [2015] A.C. 1732 at [106].

[53C] See para.8-23.

[53D] See the quotation at para.8-25.

[53E] [2018] UKSC 4; [2018] 2 W.L.R. 595 at [27] per Lord Reed.

Public policy

Replace paragraph with:

8-21 More general considerations of the "public good" have been invoked by the courts. Thus a duty has been denied on the grounds that it would lead to defensive decision making in policing,[83] social services,[84] social housing,[85] regulatory activity[86] or inhibit the work of advocates.[87] But assessments of public policy can change as is shown by the conclusion that the policy reasons supporting social service[88] or advocates immunity[89] are no longer applicable. On occasion, broader consequential arguments are invoked[90] but judges are rightly hesitant to pursue such arguments when they have neither the full information nor the basis on which to evaluate the information that is presented. In *McLoughlin v O'Brian*[91] Lord Scarman commented that "considerations ... of social, economic and financial policy, are not such as to be capable of being handled within the limits of the forensic process".[92] In *Spring v Guardian Assurance Plc*[93] Lord Lowry warned against the use of speculative policy reasons, commenting that "public policy should be invoked only in clear cases in which the potential harm to the public is incontestable, ... whether the anticipated harm to the public will be likely to occur must be determined on tangible grounds instead of on mere generalities and ... the burden of proof lies on those who assert that the court should not enforce a liability which prima facie exists." Thus, in *Capital and Counties Plc v Hampshire CC*[94] Stuart-Smith LJ dismissed a range of consequential arguments against the liability of the fire brigades as unsubstantiated, and in *Rothwell v Chemical & Insulating Co*[95] Lord Hoffmann, whilst agreeing with the decision of the Court of Appeal to reject claims for anxiety caused by harmless pleural plaques, rejected the policy reasons given by the Court on the ground that they were "consequentialist in nature" and "speculative".[96] In *Barrett v Enfield LBC*,[97] the House of Lords was equally dismissive of the "policy" argument that imposition of a duty might lead to defensive conduct or diversion of resources to record keeping or self-justification. In the Australian High Court, McHugh J has warned against basing a duty on assumptions that insurance may be readily available and that consequently a duty would have the effect of "loss spreading".[98] However, where imposition of a duty would undermine an established insurance framework, then it will be a legitimate consideration.[99] The current attitude of the appellate courts is seen clearly in *McFarlane v Tayside Health Board*[100] where Lord Steyn expressly sought to avoid the "quick sands" of public policy and Lord Millett drew a distinction between relevant "legal policy" and irrelevant "public policy". In *Robinson v Chief Constable of West Yorkshire*[100A] Lord Reed emphasised that where there is an existing category of duty, as where liability would arise at common law for a positive act of negligence by a private individual, concerns about public policy cannot override that liability simply because the defendant is performing a statutory function (an obvious example of this would be driving a motor vehicle on a public road). The true question, said his Lordship, is whether, properly construed, the statute excludes the liability which would otherwise arise. The circumstances of *Robinson*, where the police had been negligent in knocking over a 76-year-old frail lady in the street whilst attempting to arrest a suspected offender, constituted a positive act of negligence for which there was no "immunity" in the form of an absence of a duty of care, such as where the claimant's injury is caused by a third party whom the police have failed to apprehend (which would constitute an omission to act). A private individual who had negligently knocked the claimant over causing injury would have owed a duty of care, and there was no reason why the police would not come under a similar duty (though the question of what constitutes a breach of that duty might be more nuanced, given that the police have to take into account the risk of a suspect resisting arrest).[100B]

[83] *Hill v Chief Constable of West Yorkshire* [1989] A.C. 53; *Smith v Chief Constable of Sussex Police* [2008] UKHL 50; [2009] 1 A.C. 225. See also the difference of view expressed in *Michael v Chief Constable of South Wales* [2015] UKSC 2; [2015] A.C. 1732 as to whether imposing a duty of care on the police would lead to defensive practices between Lord Toulson (at [121]–[122]) and Lord Kerr (at [179], who considered that it was arguable that the risk of litigation improves professional standards). Note that arguments about the risk of defensive practice arising from imposing liability on the police in respect of the manner in which they investigate criminal offences do not apply to claims based on art.3 of the ECHR: *Commissioner of Police of the Metropolis v DSD* [2018] UKSC 11; [2019] A.C. 196 at [71] per Lord Kerr: "Carrying out police investigations efficiently should not give rise to a diversion

of resources. On the contrary, it should lead to more effective investigation of crime, the enhancement of standards and the saving of resources. There is no reason to suppose that the existence of a right under article 3 to call to account egregious errors on the part of the police in the investigation of serious crime would do other than act as an incentive to avoid those errors and to deter, indeed eliminate, the making of such grievous mistakes." See also per Lord Neuberger at [97]; cf. Lord Hughes (dissenting). For a critique of the resort to "policy" without supporting evidence to justify the conclusion see Smith (2009) 125 L.Q.R. 215. In *Robinson v Chief Constable of West Yorkshire* [2018] UKSC 4; [2018] A.C. 736 at [112] Lord Hughes acknowledged that "the danger of defensive policing lacks hard evidence" but nonetheless considered that the risk of defensive practice was inevitable, since "we see the consequences of defensive behaviour daily in the actions of a great many public authorities. I do not see that it can seriously be doubted that the threat of litigation frequently influences the behaviour of both public and private bodies and individuals." Of course, whether the threat of litigation influences potential defendants to exercise reasonable care (as it should) or produces an over-reaction is another matter.

84 *X v Bedfordshire CC* [1995] 2 A.C. 633.

85 A duty of care on a social landlord to warn tenants about the risk of violence from another tenant "would deter social landlords from intervening to reduce the incidence of anti-social behaviour": *Mitchell v Glasgow CC* [2009] UKHL 11; [2009] 1 A.C. 874 at [28], per Lord Hope; see also per Baroness Hale at [77]. See Mullender (2009) 125 L.Q.R. 384.

86 *Yuen Kun-Yeu v Att Gen of Hong Kong* [1988] A.C. 175; *Harris v Evans* [1998] 1 W.L.R. 1285.

87 *Rondel v Worsley* [1969] 1 A.C. 191.

88 *D v East Berkshire NHS Trust* [2003] EWCA Civ 1151; [2004] Q.B. 558; affirmed [2005] UKHL 23; [2005] 2 A.C. 373. See para.14-18.

89 *Arthur JS Hall & Co v Simons* [2002] 1 A.C. 615. See also *Jones v Kaney* [2011] UKSC 13; [2011] 2 A.C. 398, holding that the immunity that formerly applied to expert witnesses in respect of claims for negligence should be abolished (see paras 10-39 and 14-41); *Smith v Ministry of Defence* [2013] UKSC 41; [2014] A.C. 52 narrowing the scope of "combat immunity" (see para.14-45).

90 See for example Lord Keith's assertion in *Rowling v Takaro Properties Ltd* [1988] A.C. 473 at 502, that imposing a duty of care on local authorities in relation to building inspection might lead inspectors to increase "unnecessarily, the requisite depth of foundations, thereby imposing a very substantial and unnecessary financial burden on members of the community". In *Gregg v Scott* [2005] UKHL 2; [2005] 2 A.C. 176 at [90], Lord Hoffmann invoked the financial consequences to the NHS as a reason for rejecting the loss of chance claim, whilst Lord Nicholls at [54], argued that it was for Parliament to introduce legislation if it felt that the financial consequences were not acceptable.

91 [1983] 1 A.C. 410 at 430. See also the comment of Hoffmann J in *Morgan Crucible Co Plc v Hill Samuel Bank Ltd* [1991] Ch. 295 at 303: " ... courts do not have the information on which to form anything more than a very broad view of the economic consequences of their decisions. For this reason they are more concerned with what appears to be fair and reasonable than with wider utilitarian calculations."

92 Note that in *X (Minors) v Bedfordshire CC* [1995] 2 A.C. 633 at 737, Lord Browne-Wilkinson held that a duty could not be imposed on public authorities in respect of their policy decisions because matters of "social policy, the allocation of finite resources ... the balance between pursuing desirable social aims as against the risk to the public inherent in so doing" were not justiciable by the courts. This lack of justiciability should be a general restraint upon courts considering such matters when a duty question arises: see the divergence of view in *Gregg v Scott*, at fn.90.

93 [1995] 2 A.C. 296 at 326.

94 [1997] Q.B. 1004 at 1044. The arguments included the fear that imposition of a duty would open the floodgates of litigation, distract fire brigades from fire-fighting, lead to massive claims against the taxpayer and have an adverse effect on insurance practice. The court did restrict the scope of the duty owed by fire brigades but on grounds of proximity rather than policy and fairness. See para.14-38. See also *Wembridge Claimants v Winter* [2013] EWHC 2331 (QB), para.13-07, rejecting the contention that the employers of fire officers should have an immunity from claims by their employees.

95 [2007] UKHL 39; [2008] 1 A.C. 281 at [17]. See also per Lord Hope at [50]. See further para.8-91.

96 The Court of Appeal [2006] EWCA Civ 27; [2006] 4 All E.R. 1161 had cited the stress of medical litigation on the claimants and the disproportionate costs of such litigation as reasons for rejecting the claims.

97 [2001] 2 A.C. 550 at 568 and 589, per Lords Slynn and Hutton. See also the rejection of the "defensive practice" argument by Lord Nicholls in *Gregg v Scott* [2005] UKHL 2; [2005] 2 A.C. 176 at [55]–[56], and by Lord Lloyd-Jones in *Darnley v Croydon Health Services NHS Trust* [2018] UKSC 50; [2018] 3 W.L.R. 1153 at [22].

98 *Perre v Apand Pty Ltd* (1999) 164 A.L.R. 606 at 640. He said that these considerations "do not assist but rather impede the relevant inquiry". See further *Lambert v Barratt Homes Ltd* [2010] EWCA

Civ 681; [2010] B.L.R. 527 and *Vernon Knight Associates v Cornwall Council* [2013] EWCA Civ 950; [2013] B.L.R. 519 (below para.8-175) where there was a marked difference of opinion as to the relevance of the insurance position of the parties when considering an occupier's "measured duty of care" in respect of naturally occurring hazards.

[99] See *Marc Rich & Co v Bishop Rock Marine Co Ltd* [1996] 1 A.C. 211, where Lord Steyn rejected a duty partly on the ground that it would undermine the existing insurance practice which was based on the Hague Rules.

[100] [2000] 2 A.C. 59 at 83 and 108.

[100A] [2018] UKSC 4; [2018] 2 W.L.R. 595 at [41].

[100B] For criticism of the substitution of the positive act/omission distinction for consideration of policy issues see para.14-37 to para.14-37C.

Incrementalism

Replace paragraph with:

In his speech in *Caparo*, Lord Bridge described the criteria for duty of care as "little more than convenient labels to attach to the features of different specific situations which the law recognises pragmatically as giving rise to a duty of care of a given scope" and continued: **8-23**

> "Whilst recognising, of course, the importance of the underlying general principles common to the whole field of negligence, I think the law has now moved in the direction of attaching greater significance to the more traditional categorisation of distinct recognisable situations as guides to the existence, the scope and the limits of the varied duties of care which the law imposes."[102]

Phillips LJ explained the essence of incrementalism thus:

> "When confronted with a novel situation the court does not ... consider these matters [foreseeability, proximity and fairness] in isolation. It does so by comparison with established categories of negligence to see whether the facts amount to no more than a small extension of a situation already covered by authority, or whether a finding of the existence of a duty of care would effect a significant extension to the law of negligence. Only in exceptional cases will the court accept that the interests of justice justify such an extension."[103]

The greater the step forward required to impose liability, the more courts will need to evaluate the consequences and be assured that it is what justice requires. He went on to cite as an example of such an exceptional case, *White v Jones*,[104] where a majority of the House of Lords recognised that a solicitor could be liable to an intended beneficiary of his client's will. Lord Goff was prepared to impose a duty going beyond the accepted principles and limits because there was no other way to produce practical justice for the beneficiary and because in the 15 years since Megarry J had taken this step at first instance, it appeared that such liability had created no problems in practice. The importance of taking an incremental approach to decisions about novel negligence claims which go beyond the existing categories of duty was emphasised by Lord Reed in *Robinson v Chief Constable of West Yorkshire*.[104A]

[102] [1990] 2 A.C. 605 at 618. He went on to refer to the wisdom of the dictum of Brennan J in *Sutherland Shire Council v Heyman* (1985) 60 A.L.R. 1 at 43–44.

[103] *Reeman v Department of Transport* [1997] P.N.L.R. 618 at 625.

[104] [1995] 2 A.C. 287.

[104A] [2018] UKSC 4; [2018] 2 W.L.R. 595 at [21], [27].

Application of the three-stage test

Replace paragraph with:

8-25 The three-stage approach has been largely established in cases concerned with economic loss or public services. In *Marc Rich & Co AG v Bishop Rock Marine Co Ltd*[115] the House of Lords rejected the suggestion that in cases of physical damage the only requirement was foreseeability and the threefold test had no application. Rather, it was held that the test was universal in its application. However, in *Perrett v Collins*[116] Hobhouse LJ stressed that where a case fell within the established categories of liability, "a defendant should not be allowed to seek to escape from liability by appealing to some vaguer concept of justice or fairness" as the previous authorities "have by necessary implication held that it is just, fair and reasonable that the claimant should recover". In *Perrett* the claimant had suffered personal injury in the crash of an aircraft which the defendant had negligently certified as being in airworthy condition. Hobhouse LJ considered that as the case fell within the recognised category of liability for personal injury, the only question was whether there was sufficient foreseeability and proximity. This latter requirement was satisfied by the fact that the defendant had an involvement in the activity which gave him a "measure of control over and responsibility for a situation, which if dangerous, will be liable to injure the claimant". He concluded: "Once this proximity exists, it ceases to be material what form the unreasonable conduct takes. The distinction between negligent misstatement and other forms of careless conduct ceases to be legally relevant." Thus, the fact that the negligence of the defendant:

> "did not involve the direct infliction of physical damage did not exclude the existence of a duty of care … . The highest that the point could be put is that where the conduct would amount to a direct invasion … a special justification is required to negative liability. But where on general principle in the context of foreseeable risk of personal injury, a duty of care exists, lack of directness, unless it destroys the causative link, provides the defendant with no answer."[117]

He distinguished the application of the threefold test in *Marc Rich* on the ground that that case was not concerned with an established category of liability for personal injury but rather with a novel question raising broad policy considerations analogous to those relevant in economic loss cases.

115 [1996] A.C. 211.

116 [1999] P.N.L.R. 77. In *Robinson v Chief Constable of West Yorkshire* [2018] UKSC 4; [2018] A.C. 736 at [26] Lord Reed expressly endorsed the approach of Hobhouse LJ, observing that: "Where the existence or non-existence of a duty of care has been established, a consideration of justice and reasonableness forms part of the basis on which the law has arrived at the relevant principles. It is therefore unnecessary and inappropriate to reconsider whether the existence of the duty is fair, just and reasonable (subject to the possibility that this court may be invited to depart from an established line of authority). Nor, a fortiori, can justice and reasonableness constitute a basis for discarding established principles and deciding each case according to what the court may regard as its broader merits. Such an approach would be a recipe for inconsistency and uncertainty…".

117 [1999] P.N.L.R. 77 at 91.

(d) Defendant's status

Conflicts of interest

Replace paragraph with:

8-44 The Court of Appeal in *Phelps v Hillingdon LBC*[191] applied the same reasoning to deny a duty on the part of an educational psychologist but the House of Lords[192] reversed this decision, concluding that the fact that the psychologist owed a duty to the employing authority was no reason for holding that no duty was owed to the child being assessed. In *D v East Berkshire NHS Trust*[193] the Court of Appeal, following *Phelps*, held that the defendant could be vicariously liable for the alleged negligence of its doctors when making a diagnosis of non-accidental injury to a child. A duty could be owed by the doctor to the child when making such a diagnosis or recommending that the child should be taken into care.[194] This conclusion was accepted by the House of Lords. However, it was held that no duty was owed to the parents of a child who was suspected to be the victim of abuse because the child's interests were in potential conflict with the interests of the parents if the professionals involved in the investigation were to owe a duty both to the victim of suspected abuse and the suspected perpetrator of that abuse.[195] The appropriate level of protection for a parent suspected of abusing his child was that the clinical and other investigations had to be conducted in good faith. Lord Nicholls said that:

> "A doctor is obliged to act in the best interests of his patient. In these cases the child is his patient. The doctor is charged with the protection of the child, not with the protection of the parent. The best interests of a child and his parent normally march hand-in-hand. But when considering whether something does not feel 'quite right', a doctor must be able to act single-mindedly in the interests of the child. He ought not to have at the back of his mind an awareness that if his doubts about intentional injury or sexual abuse prove unfounded he may be exposed to claims by a distressed parent."[196]

In *Jain v Trent Strategic HA*[197] it was held that a public authority exercising a statutory power, the purpose of which was the protection of the residents of a nursing home, owed no duty of care to the owners of the home as to the manner in which it exercised that power. The authority might owe a duty to the residents but could not also owe a duty to the proprietors, whose interests could conflict with those of the residents (applying *D v East Berkshire Community Health NHS Trust*).[198] Similarly, in *James-Bowen v Commissioner of Police of the Metropolis*[198A] the Supreme Court held that an employer does not owe a duty to employees to defend a civil action brought against the employer, based on vicarious liability for the alleged misconduct of those employees, in a manner that protects the employees from economic or reputational harm. The interests of the employer and the employees were fundamentally different. The employees' interests were in protecting their reputation and the potential financial consequences of an adverse outcome, whereas the employer's interests involved weighing a number of factors: the prospects of successfully defending the action (involving an assessment of the reliability and veracity of the employees), the importance attached to successfully defending the claim, what resources should be devoted to its defence, and whether the cost and effort of defending the claim was justified. In addition, the Commissioner of Police, as a holder of public office, has a public duty to act as she considers appropriate in the interests of the police service, and this duty was totally inconsistent with her owing a duty of care to protect the reputational interests of her employees in such circumstances.[198B] **8-44A**

[191] [1999] 1 W.L.R. 500.

[192] [2001] 2 A.C. 619. If the no duty reasoning had been upheld, it is difficult to see how any employed professional could owe a duty to a client/patient. See further para.14-14.

[193] [2003] EWCA Civ 1151; [2004] Q.B. 558; affirmed [2005] UKHL 23; [2005] 2 A.C. 373. See further para.14-21.

[194] Effectively departing from the view of the House of Lords in *X (Minors) v Bedfordshire CC*. In *CN*

v Poole BC [2017] EWCA Civ 2185; [2018] 2 W.L.R. 1693 the Court of Appeal had suggested that the decision of the Court of Appeal in *D v East Berkshire NHS Trust* [2003] EWCA Civ 1151; [2004] Q.B. 558 that medical professionals and social workers could owe a duty of care to children when making decisions about their welfare, had been impliedly overruled because it was inconsistent with the decision of the House of Lords and Supreme Court. However, when *CN v Poole BC* reached the Supreme Court this view was rejected (at [2019] UKSC 25; [2019] 2 W.L.R. 1478). *D v East Berkshire NHS Trust* is still good law, though the Supreme Court upheld the decision in *CN v Poole BC* that a local authority did not owe a duty of care arising out of the authority's responsibilities under the Children Act 1989 to the claimant children who were being subjected to harassment and abuse by neighbours.

[195] Note, however, *Merthyr Tydfil CBC v C* [2010] EWHC 62 (QB); [2010] P.I.Q.R. P9, where Hickinbottom J, whilst accepting that a local authority does not owe a duty of care to those who are suspected of abusing a child, concluded that there is no general principle that where a local authority owe a duty of care to a child, it cannot as a matter of law at the same time owe a duty of care to the parents of that child. The fact that there was "some conceivable potential for such a conflict in the future is insufficient to make an authority immune from a suit in negligence at that hands of a parent" (at [36]). (The claimant's action against the local authority was in respect of psychiatric harm that she suffered due to the alleged failure of the local authority properly to investigate her concerns that her children had been abused by an older child). It may be that the decision in *Merthyr Tydfil CBC v C* turned on its "quite exceptional facts": *F-D v Children and Family Court Advisory Service* [2014] EWHC 1619 (QB); [2015] 1 F.C.R. 98 (CAFCASS did not owe a duty of care to the parent of a child when giving advice to the court about a child's welfare due to potential conflict with the statutory duty imposed on CAFCASS.)

[196] [2005] UKHL 23; [2005] 2 A.C. 373 at [85]; see also per Lord Rodger at [110] and Lord Brown at [129]. Cf. Lord Bingham's dissenting speech at [37] arguing that the potential conflict of duties was more apparent than real. See also *West Bromwich Albion FC Ltd v El-Safty* [2006] EWCA Civ 1299; [2007] P.I.Q.R. P7; [2007] L.S. Law Med. 50 at [25] where (in a claim by a professional football club against a doctor in respect of its financial loss arising out of the negligent treatment of one of its players) Rix LJ considered that there was a potential conflict of interest between the club and the player: "the danger of a conflict of interest between a sports employer and a sportsman, all the more important where the sportsman may think that his principal interest is tied up in his soonest possible availability to his employer, must loom large. It militates against implying a contract with the employer rather than with the patient, or with the employer as well as with the patient."

[197] [2009] UKHL 4; [2009] 1 A.C. 853. See also *Desmond v Chief Constable of Nottinghamshire* [2011] EWCA Civ 3; [2011] 1 F.L.R. 1361 where the Court of Appeal held that no duty of care is owed by the police to a person applying for an enhanced criminal record certificate, even though errors in the information provided affected the claimant's ability to obtain employment, partly on the basis that if such a duty were held to exist "there would be a plain conflict between the … putative duty to [the claimant] and the statutory purpose of protecting vulnerable young people" (at [49]). See further *C v T Borough Council* [2014] EWHC 2482 (QB); [2015] E.L.R. 1 (no duty owed when providing information to the police for the purpose of an enhanced criminal record certificate); *Jowhari v NHS England* [2014] EWHC 4197 (QB) (no duty owed to dentist arising out of removal from a dental performers list since statutory scheme was designed to protect the public from unsuitable dentists and a private law duty owed to the dentist would conflict with the statutory scheme).

[198] See further para.14-43. In a rather different context, see *Hilton v Barker Booth & Eastwood* [2005] UKHL 8; [2005] 1 W.L.R. 567, where the House of Lords held a solicitor under a duty to disclose to a client relevant but confidential information about another client. In effect, the solicitor had to break its duty to one or other client and should not have got itself into that position. See paras 10-121, 10-143 and 10-146.

[198A] [2018] UKSC 40; [2018] 1 W.L.R. 4021.

[198B] In addition, Lord Lloyd-Jones noted that a duty to the employees would inevitably inhibit the conduct of the defence, and would also be "inconsistent with the important legal policy which encourages the settlement of civil claims and seeks to promote out of court settlement. The resulting risk of exposure to consequential claims would, in many situations, operate as a powerful disincentive to settlement": [2018] UKSC 40; [2018] 1 W.L.R. 4021 at [35]–[36].

(e) Omissions

The principle

Replace paragraph with:

8-47 In *Smith v Littlewoods Organisation Ltd*[204] Lord Goff stated the fundamental principle that "the common law does not impose liability for what are called pure omissions". As authority he cited the speech of Lord Diplock in *Home Office v Dorset Yacht Co Ltd*[205]:

> "The parable of the good Samaritan which was evoked by Lord Atkin in *Donoghue v Stevenson* illustrates, in the conduct of the priest and Levite who passed by on the other side, an omission which was likely to have as its reasonable and probable consequence damage to the health of the victim of the thieves, but for which the priest and Levite would have incurred no civil liability in English Law. Examples could be multiplied ... you need not warn (your neighbour) of a risk of physical danger to which he is about to expose himself ...; you may watch your neighbour's goods being ruined by a thunderstorm though the slightest effort on your part could protect them from the rain ... ."[206]

The principle only applies to pure omissions. A person who creates a danger, however blamelessly, may come under a consequential duty to take precautions to prevent injury resulting. Thus, a motorist who has to leave his vehicle unlit, may be under a duty to warn other motorists of the obstruction.[207] A manufacturer aware of a dangerous feature in its product may be under a duty to warn users[208] and this may apply where the dangerous defect is discovered subsequent to the sale of the product.[209] It was said that "a manufacturer who realises that omitting to warn customers about something which might result in injury to them must take reasonable steps to attempt to warn them, however lacking in negligence he may have been when the goods were sold". In such cases, the omission is not considered in isolation but as part of the activity as a whole. It is simply the element which makes the activity negligent. The whole activity amounts to a "misfeasance". The pure omission principle applies only where the failure to act can be viewed in isolation from other aspects of the defendant's activity and classed as "nonfeasance". Thus, a negligent failure by the police to apprehend an offender, with the result that he goes on to commit further offences, injuring the claimant, constitutes an omission for which the police will not be responsible, but negligence in the course of arresting a suspect with the result that police officers cause injury to the claimant constitutes a positive act falling into an existing category of the duty of care.[209A]

[204] [1987] A.C. 241 at 247.

[205] [1970] A.C. 1004 at 1060.

[206] In similar vein Viscount Dilhorne said that a person would not be liable if "he fails to warn a person nearby whom he sees about to step off the pavement into the path of an oncoming vehicle or if he fails to rescue a child in difficulties in a pond": [1970] A.C. 1004 at 1027.

[207] *Lee v Lever* [1974] R.T.R. 35. See para.8-208.

[208] *Vacwell Engineering Co Ltd v BDH Chemicals Ltd* [1971] 1 Q.B. 111.

[209] *E Hobbs Farms Ltd v Baxendale Chemical Co Ltd* [1992] 1 Lloyd's Rep. 54 at 65, per Deputy Judge Ogden QC: "a manufacturer who realises that omitting to warn customers about something which might result in injury to them must take reasonable steps to attempt to warn them, however lacking in negligence he may have been when the goods were sold." There, a product advertised as "self-extinguishing" caused extensive fire damage to a customer. The manufacturer was held liable in negligence for failing to correct its advertising once it became clear that the product might not be "self-extinguishing". See further para.11-32.

[209A] *Robinson v Chief Constable of West Yorkshire* [2018] UKSC 4; [2018] 2 W.L.R. 595. See also *Rigby v Chief Constable of Northamptonshire* [1985] 1 W.L.R. 1242.

(i) Special relationship

Protective relationships

Replace footnote 229 with: 8-52

[229] *ABC v St George's Healthcare NHS Foundation Trust* [2017] EWCA Civ 336; [2017] P.I.Q.R. P15; sed quaere, and contrast *Smith v University of Leicester NHS Trust* [2016] EWHC 817.

(iii) *Specific responsibility for protection from third parties*

Assumption of responsibility by public authorities

Replace paragraph with:

8-57 Such cases are extremely fact-sensitive, but as a general rule it will be rare for a public authority to be found to have assumed responsibility to a claimant to protect them from harm caused by a third party. In *Smith v Chief Constable of Sussex Police*[251] the claimant complained that the police had failed to act to prevent his former partner from attacking him, despite having been informed of previous attacks and death threats to the claimant. The House of Lords held that no duty of care in negligence was owed by the police to the claimant.[252] The same conclusion was reached by the Supreme Court in *Michael v Chief Constable of South Wales*[253] where a majority of the justices held that the police did not owe a duty of care to a woman killed by her ex-partner when she had made an earlier 999 phone call to the police complaining that her ex-partner had assaulted her and had threatened to kill her. There had been no assumption of responsibility to the deceased arising from what had been said to her when she phoned the emergency number requesting assistance.[254] Similarly, in *Mitchell v Glasgow CC*[255] the House of Lords held that a social landlord did not owe a duty of care to a tenant to warn him that another tenant, about whom he had made a number of complaints, had threatened to kill him.[256] In *X v Hounslow LBC*[257] the Court of Appeal commented that: "a public authority will not be held to have assumed a common law duty merely by doing what the statute requires or what it has power to do under a statute, at any rate unless the duty arises out of the relationship created as a result, such as in Lord Hoffmann's example of the doctor patient relationship".

[251] [2008] UKHL 50; [2009] 1 A.C. 225; see para.14-31; Burton, "Failing to Protect: Victims' Rights and Police Liability" (2009) 72 M.L.R. 283.

[252] Applying *Hill v Chief Constable of West Yorkshire* [1989] A.C. 53 and *Brooks v Commissioner of Police of the Metropolis* [2005] UKHL 24; [2005] 1 W.L.R. 1495. See also *Rathband v Chief Constable of Northumbria* [2016] EWHC 181 (QB), both of which are discussed at para.14-37. On the liability of the police generally see paras 14-28 to 14-37. Contrast *Robinson v Chief Constable of West Yorkshire* [2018] UKSC 4; [2018] A.C. 736 where the claimant's injury was caused by a positive act of negligence by the police, rather than an omission to prevent harm to the claimant by a third party. See paras 8-21 and para.14-37.

[253] [2015] UKSC 2; [2015] A.C. 1732; see paras 14-32 and 14-33.

[254] [2015] UKSC 2; [2015] A.C. 1732 at [138] per Lord Toulson, distinguishing *Kent v Griffiths* [2001] Q.B. 36 on the basis that the call handler in that case gave misleading assurances that an ambulance would be arriving shortly. Though as Lord Kerr noted in a dissenting judgment, at [165], the possibility that the police could be found to have undertaken responsibility to someone who called for emergency assistance, depending on what the call handler happened to say to the caller, creates the risk of arbitrary distinctions being drawn. So, for example, in *Sherratt v Chief Constable of Greater Manchester* [2018] EWHC 1746 (QB); [2019] P.I.Q.R. P1 it was held that the police had assumed responsibility to the deceased (who committed suicide) on the basis of the information given by the call handler to the deceased's mother when she telephoned 999 to express her concerns about her daughter's mental state. The call handler gave specific assurances that police officers would be despatched as a priority to the daughter's house to check on her wellbeing and that, if necessary, the police would arrange for her daughter's transfer to hospital. The clear assurance to the mother, combined with detrimental reliance by the mother on that assurance, distinguished the case from *Michael v Chief Constable of South Wales* (given the lack of assurances in Michael). The circumstances, said King J, were closer to Kent v Griffiths where a general practitioner and the claimant's husband had relied on assurances that an ambulance would arrive promptly.

[255] [2009] UKHL 11; [2009] 1 A.C. 874. See further paras 14-56, 14-62, 14-64 and 14-86 for comment on *Mitchell*.

[256] Lord Hope commented that: "as a general rule, ... a duty to warn another person that he is at risk of loss, injury or damage as the result of the criminal act of a third party will arise only where the person who is said to be under that duty has by his words or conduct assumed responsibility for the safety of the person who is at risk": [2009] UKHL 11; [2009] 1 A.C. 874 at [29]. See also *Thomson v Scottish Ministers* [2013] CSIH 63; 2013 S.C. 628—no duty of care owed by the Prison Service to a member of the public killed by a prisoner on short term leave, where the risk to the general public, even if grave, was not enough to satisfy the requirement of proximity; there had to be a special risk of harm to the claimant greater than that to which the general public were exposed; *Furnell v Flaherty* [2013] EWHC 377 (QB)—no duty owed by local authority or Health Protection Agency to defendant to notify outbreak of E.coli at defendant's petting farm, or to take steps to limit visitors' exposure to infection; mere knowledge on the part of the local authority or Health Protection Agency fell far short of giving rise to an assumption of responsibility.

[257] [2009] EWCA Civ 286; [2010] H.L.R. 4 at [60]; see para.14-64.

Replace paragraph with:

On the other hand, there are some situations where it can be said that a public authority has expressly assumed responsibility to provide assistance. For example, an Accident and Emergency department of a NHS hospital holds itself out to the public as willing to accept patients for treatment following accidental injury or in emergency situations, and so will be taken to owe a duty of care to those presenting themselves for treatment.[257A] This duty applies to the actions of healthcare professionals and, in some circumstances, the actions of non-medical staff. In *Darnley v Croydon Health Services NHS Trust*[257B] the Supreme Court held that the duty applied to an Accident and Emergency department receptionist who, it was alleged, had given the claimant incorrect information about how long he would have to wait to be seen by the medical staff, as a result of which he left the hospital and subsequently suffered a serious deterioration in his medical condition. Once he had presented himself to the receptionist, provided any requested information and been booked in, the claimant was accepted into the system and entered into a relationship of patient and healthcare provider with the defendants. The standard of care expected of non-medical staff may be different from that applied to healthcare professionals, depending on the circumstances, but in the context of providing misleading information to a patient it was not appropriate to distinguish between medical and non-medical staff.[257C] **8-58**

[257A] *Barnett v Chelsea and Kensington Hospital Management Committee* [1969] 1 Q.B. 428.

[257B] [2018] UKSC 50; [2018] 3 W.L.R. 1153.

[257C] "The respondent had charged its non-medically qualified staff with the role of being the first point of contact with persons seeking medical assistance and, as a result, with the responsibility for providing accurate information as to its availability": [2018] UKSC 50; [2018] 3 W.L.R. 1153 at [17] per Lord Lloyd-Jones. His Lordship considered that this was an established category of duty of care, by analogy with the decision of the Court of Appeal in *Kent v Griffiths, Roberts and London Ambulance Service* [2001] Q.B. 36: "In both cases, as a result of the provision of inaccurate information by non-medically qualified staff, there was a delay in the provision of urgently required medical attention with the result that serious physical injury was suffered" (at [20]).

Add new paragraph:

There may also be situations where the claimant is in a particularly close relationship with a public authority, such that no express assumption of responsibility is required to establish a duty of care. In *Selwood v Durham CC*[258] the Court of Appeal held that it was at least arguable that two NHS Trusts had assumed responsibility to a social worker employed by a local authority who was attacked and seriously injured by a mental health patient. The social worker worked closely with the two NHS Trusts to provide integrated health and social care. The working relation- **8-58A** ship between the three defendants (the Trusts and the local authority) was set out in a lengthy policy document governing working arrangements. The patient was known to have a history of violent behaviour and posed a risk of harm to others. Employees of the Trusts became aware that he had expressed his intention to kill the claimant if he saw her, but the claimant was not warned. Smith LJ considered that it was possible to infer an assumption of responsibility from the circumstances, and in particular the close working relationship, "to do what was reasonable in the circumstances to reduce or avoid any foreseeable risk of harm to which an employee of a co-signatory was exposed in the course of their joint operations."[259] Given that the defendants, in their capacity as employers, would owe a duty of care to their employees, it was not a big step to suggest that they could owe a duty of care in respect of the actions of a third party to someone in the claimant's position, since "the force of some of the policy considerations which render a wider duty undesirable is much less than if the duty is said to be owed to the world at large."[260C]

[258] [2012] EWCA Civ 979; [2012] P.I.Q.R. P20.

[259] [2012] EWCA Civ 979; [2012] P.I.Q.R. P20 at [52].

[260C] [2012] EWCA Civ 979; [2012] P.I.Q.R. P20 at [53].

Responsibility for danger

Replace paragraph with:

8-60 The third situation identified by Lord Goff in *Smith v Littlewoods Organisation Ltd*[268] as giving rise to a duty is where the defendant "negligently causes or permits to be created a source of danger, and it is reasonably foreseeable that third parties may interfere with it and, sparking off the danger, thereby cause damage to persons in the position of the [claimant]". He cited as an example of such a case, *Haynes v Harwood*[269] where the defendant's employee was responsible for creating a source of danger by leaving a horse-drawn van unattended in a busy street, the danger was sparked off by a mischievous child throwing a stone at the horses causing them to bolt and the defendant was held liable for the resulting injuries. Lord Goff held that the principle had no application to the facts of *Smith*, as "the empty cinema could (not) be properly described as an unusual danger in the nature of a fire hazard". Indeed, Lord Goff stressed that liability under this principle would be very rare for otherwise the ordinary householders could "be held liable for acting in a socially acceptable manner".[270] This restrictive approach was confirmed in *Topp v London Country Bus Ltd.*[271] The defendant had carelessly left a minibus unlocked, with keys in the ignition, outside a pub for some nine hours until it was stolen by a third party who, minutes later, negligently drove the bus into the claimant. May J held that although it was foreseeable that the bus might be stolen and the thief might injure other road users, there could be no liability under the danger principle as a "parked minibus is no more a source of danger than every other vehicle on the road".[272]

[268] [1987] A.C. 241 at 272.

[269] [1935] 1 K.B. 146. He gave a further example of a person who stored a large quantity of fireworks in an unlocked shed when it was foreseeable that mischievous boys might trespass into the shed and set off the fireworks. See also *Holian v United Grain Growers Ltd* (1980) 112 D.L.R. (3d) 611, where there was theft of a poisonous chemical by young children.

[270] Lord Goff noted that "there are nowadays many things which might be described as possible sources of fire if interfered with by third parties, ranging from matches to firelighters to electric irons and gas cookers and even oil-fired central heating systems". Leaving these commonplaces of modern life unprotected from third party intervention could not give rise to liability.

[271] [1993] 1 W.L.R 926 CA.

[272] [1993] 3 All E.R. 448 at 459; affirmed by the Court of Appeal: [1993] 1 W.L.R 926; [1993] 3 All E.R. 464. May J suggested that a duty might have been improperly conceded in *Hayman v London Transport Executive* [1982] CA transcript 74, where a bus company was found liable for damage caused by a stolen bus following previous complaints of buses being stolen. He distinguished *Hayman* as decided on its own special facts. The rejection of *Hayman* and policy reasons given for denying a duty, the lack of inherent danger and the unfairness of holding motorists liable for the damage done by their stolen cars, suggest that even a high degree of foreseeability of theft would be insufficient to ground a duty. See further *Rankin (Rankin's Garage & Sales) v J.J.* 2018 SCC 19; (2018) 422 D.L.R. (4th) 317, where a majority of the Supreme Court of Canada reached the same outcome as *Topp v London Country Bus Ltd*, but on the basis that the theft of an unlocked vehicle, with keys left in the ashtray, by two youths was unforeseeable. In the absence of an evidentiary basis the risk of theft in general did not necessarily include the risk of theft by minors (who were more likely to drive a stolen vehicle in a dangerous manner). *Sed quaere*.

(f) Psychiatric injury and distress

Psychiatric injury

Replace paragraph with:

A claimant can recover in respect of a recognised psychiatric illness[284] suffered as a result of his own physical injury or imperilment or as a result of the physical injury or imperilment of another caused by the defendant. Any recognised psychiatric illness will suffice. There has been recovery for morbid depression,[285] hysterical personality disorder,[286] post-traumatic stress disorder,[287] pathological grief disorder[288] and chronic fatigue syndrome.[289] In the case of illness suffered as a result of the trauma of being endangered or physically injured, the claimant is referred to as a "primary victim" and will recover provided that *physical injury* was reasonably foreseeable as a result the defendant's negligence. It is possible that a claimant who was in some other way a direct participant in the incident may also be treated as a primary victim and be able to recover if *psychiatric illness* was foreseeable, even if they were not in danger of physical injury. In the case of illness suffered solely as a result of the injury or endangerment of another, the claimant is referred to as a "secondary victim" and recovery is subject to a number of policy restrictions. In addition, there are a number of special cases where illness results from factors other than personal injury or imperilment. The result is a "patchwork quilt of distinctions which are quite difficult to justify".[290] The whole area of law was reviewed in 1998 by the Law Commission[291] which recommended reform of the law by both legislation and the courts. Since the report there has been no legislation but the courts seem to have adopted a more flexible approach to the distinction between primary and secondary victims and a less restrictive approach to recovery by secondary victims. In the light of this, legislative reform seems unnecessary.[292] **8-63**

[284] *McLoughlin v O'Brian* [1983] 1 A.C. 410 at 431 per Lord Bridge; *Alcock v Chief Constable of the South Yorkshire Police* [1992] 1 A.C. 310 at 409 per Lord Oliver. This excludes ordinary grief, distress or any other normal human emotion. In *Saadati v Moorhead* 2017 SCC 28; (2017) 409 D.L.R. (4th) 395 the Supreme Court of Canada held that, in Canadian law, there was no requirement that a claimant seeking to establish liability for mental injury was required to prove, by expert evidence, that he was suffering from a condition that would be diagnosed as a psychiatric illness by the medical profession. The claimant did not have to prove that he was suffering from a particular psychiatric illness to which the medical profession had attached a "label"; it was sufficient that the defendant could have foreseen mental injury. There was no necessary relationship between reasonably foreseeable mental injury and a diagnostic classification scheme. Moreover, said the Supreme Court, there should be no difference between claims for mental injury and claims for physical injury, and there was no requirement for claimants alleging physical injury to show that their condition carried a particular classificatory label. *Saadati* is discussed by M. McInnes, "Negligent infliction of mental harm in the Supreme Court of Canada" (2018) 134 L.Q.R. 1. For concern about using the shifting diagnostic criteria for psychiatric conditions in the legal context see J. Ahuja, "Liability for psychological and psychiatric harm: the road to recovery"

(2015) 23 Med. L. Rev. 27 at 39–40, and R. Orr, "Speaking with different voices: the problems with English law and psychiatric injury" (2016) 36 L.S. 547.

[285] *Hinz v Berry* [1970] 2 Q.B. 40.

[286] *Brice v Brown* [1984] 1 All E.R. 997.

[287] The illness in question in *White v Chief Constable of the South Yorkshire Police* [1999] 2 A.C. 455. The claim failed on other grounds.

[288] *Vernon v Bosley (No.1)* [1997] 1 All E.R. 577.

[289] *Page v Smith* [1996] A.C. 155.

[290] *White v Chief Constable of the South Yorkshire Police* [1999] 2 A.C. 455 at 500, per Lord Steyn.

[291] *Liability for Psychiatric Illness*, Law Com No.249.

[292] In its Response to a Consultation on Damages the Ministry of Justice concluded that: "The arguments in this complex and sensitive area are finely balanced. On balance the Government continues to take the view that it is preferable for the courts to have the flexibility to continue to develop the law rather than attempt to impose a statutory solution": *The Law on Damages*, CP(R) 9/07, July 2009, p.51.

(i) Primary victims

The foreseeability test

Replace footnote 298 with:

8-64 [298] [1996] A.C. 155 at 189. It follows that there is "no requirement for a primary victim who brings a claim for 'pure' psychiatric injury to show that the injury was caused by shock": *YAH v Medway NHS Foundation Trust* [2018] EWHC 2964 (QB); [2019] 1 W.L.R. 1413 per Whipple J at [34].

Participation

8-68 *After "following the alleged negligence of the defendant solicitor, as a", delete "being a".*

(ii) Secondary victims

Close tie of love and affection

Replace footnote 347 with:

8-71 [347] Contrast *Shorter v Surrey and Sussex Healthcare NHS Trust* [2015] EWHC 614 (QB); (2015) 144 B.M.L.R. 136 where the defendants conceded that a relationship between sisters which, on the evidence, was almost like mother and daughter was sufficiently close and loving to satisfy this element of the test for a "secondary" victim. In *RE (A Minor) v Calderdale and Huddersfield NHS Foundation Trust* [2017] EWHC 824 (QB); [2017] Med. L.R. 390 at [48], the defendants conceded that a grandmother who was present at the traumatic birth of her grandchild was in a sufficiently close relationship. See also *King v Philcox* [2015] HCA 19; (2015) 320 A.L.R. 398 where the High Court of Australia held that at common law a motorist could owe a duty of care to the brother of a passenger killed in an accident caused by the motorist's negligence, where the brother did not witness the accident but came upon the aftermath (the action failed due to statutory restrictions on the category of claimants where the claimant was not present at the accident itself).

Sudden shock

Replace footnote 389 with:

8-79 [389] *Ronayne* was applied in *Owers v Medway NHS Foundation Trust* [2015] EWHC 2363 (QB); [2015] Med. L.R. 561 where a husband had witnessed the effects of his wife suffering a stroke which the defendants had negligently failed to diagnose and treat. Stewart J concluded that although the events were "very distressing" they were not "horrifying" or "wholly exceptional" by objective standards and by reference to persons of ordinary susceptibility. See also *Wild v Southend University Hospital NHS Foundation Trust* [2014] EWHC 4053 (QB); [2016] P.I.Q.R. P3 where it was held that a father present in the delivery room when it was discovered that the baby had already died in utero had not witnessed a horrific event leading to death or serious injury and so was not a "secondary" victim. To similar effect are:

Less v Hussain [2012] EWHC 3513 (QB); [2013] Med. L.R. 383 and *Wells v University Hospital Southampton NHS Foundation Trust* [2015] EWHC 2376 (QB); [2015] Med. L.R. 477 at [86] (obiter). Contrast *RE (A Minor) v Calderdale and Huddersfield NHS Foundation Trust* [2017] EWHC 824 (QB); [2017] Med. L.R. 390 where during the delivery the child became "stuck" due to shoulder dystocia, which one of the defendants' expert witnesses described as "one of the most frightening of medical emergencies". Goss J held (at [47] and [48]) that both the mother and the child's grandmother (who was present throughout) had experienced a sudden, shocking event "that was exceptional in nature and horrifying as judged by objective standards and by reference to persons of ordinary susceptibility". The judge (at [40]) considered that, in any event, the mother qualified as a "primary" victim on the basis that the baby's head "had crowned but her body remained in the birth canal. At this point she was not a separate legal entity from her mother and, in law, they are to be treated as one." See also *YAH v Medway NHS Foundation Trust* [2018] EWHC 2964 (QB); [2019] 1 W.L.R. 1413 per Whipple J at [22]: "settled law" that a "mother is a primary victim in so far as she suffers personal injury consequent on negligence which occurs before the baby is born". Nor does the mother cease to be a primary victim at the moment the child is born: "The fact that the claimant's psychiatric damage became manifest later in time, after [the baby] was born, does not change the claimant's status" (at [24]); and *Zeromska-Smith v United Lincolnshire Hospitals NHS Trust* [2019] EWHC 980 (QB) at [96].

(iii) Psychiatric illness resulting from factors other than personal injury or imperilment

Psychiatric harm following disciplinary proceedings

Replace paragraph with:

In *French v Sussex CC*[413] the Court of Appeal held that where employees suffered stress and consequent psychiatric illness as a result of criminal and disciplinary charges which followed an allegedly negligently organised police operation this was not, and was not analogous to, a "stress at work" case. The employees had to satisfy the *Alcock* criteria for psychiatric illness following a traumatic event (which they could not do). On the other hand, in *Yapp v Foreign and Commonwealth Office*[414] the Court of Appeal accepted that the approach adopted in the stress at work cases (and the analysis developed by Hale LJ in *Hatton v Sutherland*) could be applied to a one-off event such as the unfair imposition of a disciplinary sanction by the employer.[415] However, it would not usually be foreseeable that even seriously unfair disciplinary action would lead the employee to develop a psychiatric illness (as opposed to distress and anger) unless there were signs, of which the employer was or should have been aware, of some pre-existing vulnerability to psychiatric harm. It would be exceptional that an apparently robust employee, with no history of any psychiatric ill-health, would develop a depressive illness as a result even of a very serious setback at work and the employer would be entitled to assume that an employee is of "reasonable fortitude" in the absence of actual or constructive knowledge to the contrary.[416] **8-87**

[413] [2006] EWCA Civ 312.

[414] [2014] EWCA Civ 1512; [2015] I.R.L.R. 112.

[415] Applying *Croft v Broadstairs & St Peter's Town Council* [2003] EWCA Civ 676. See also *K v Chief Constable of the Police Service of Scotland* [2019] CSOH 9; [2019] 1 WLUK 300.

[416] See also *Coventry University v Mian* [2014] EWCA Civ 1275; [2014] E.L.R. 455; [2014] Med. L.R. 502 (employer not in breach of duty because, in the circumstances, instituting disciplinary procedures was within the range of reasonable responses by an employer); *Piepenbrock v The London School of Economics and Political Science* [2018] EWHC 2572 (QB); [2018] E.L.R. 596 (claimant's psychiatric reaction to defendants' handling of complaint against the claimant not reasonably foreseeable).

(g) Unwanted childbirth and loss of autonomy

No duty in respect of cost of unwanted child

Replace footnote 441 with:

8-92 [441] [2000] 2 A.C. 59 at 114. Lord Slynn said at 76, that if a client wanted to be able to recover the costs of raising a healthy child he or she must do so "by an appropriate contract", but in *Rees v Darlington Memorial Hospital NHS Trust* [2003] UKHL 52; [2004] 1 A.C. 309 at [133] Lord Scott considered that the "same result must be reached whether the claimant was a private patient or an NHS patient", i.e. whether the claim was brought in contract or tort. In *ARB v IVF Hammersmith Ltd* [2018] EWCA Civ 2803; [2019] 2 W.L.R. 1094 the Court of Appeal confirmed that whether the action was based in tort or on breach of a strict contractual obligation, the same policy objections to awarding compensation for the costs of raising a healthy child applied.

Loss of autonomy claims

Replace paragraph with:

8-96 In *Rees* Lord Millett described autonomy as "an important aspect of human dignity which is increasingly being regarded as an important human right which should be protected by law".[452] There may be other situations where the purpose of a duty of care could be seen as the protection of the claimant's autonomy. For example, the doctor's duty of care to warn a patient of risks associated with a treatment has as its purpose the protection of the patient's right to choose. In *Chester v Afshar*[453] Lord Steyn justified providing a remedy for a doctor's failure to warn on the basis of the need to give "due respect to the autonomy and dignity of each patient".[454] In *Chester* the majority of the House of Lords gave effect to the patient's right to autonomy by adopting a somewhat controversial approach to causation to enable the patient to claim compensation for the physical damage resulting from the risk of which she was not warned.[455] An alternative approach would have been recognition the importance of the right to autonomy with a conventional award along the lines of that given in *Rees*.[456] However, in *Shaw v Kovac*[456A] the Court of Appeal held that there is no free-standing cause of action for interference with a claimant's autonomy. An action by a patient against a doctor for non-disclosure of the risks of treatment will be an action in negligence, which requires proof of damage over and above an interference with autonomy per se.[456B]

[452] [2003] UKHL 52; [2004] 1 A.C. 309 at [123].

[453] [2004] UKHL 41; [2005] 1 A.C. 134.

[454] [2004] UKHL 41; [2005] 1 A.C. 134 at [18]. He quoted Dworkin's explanation in *Life's Dominion* (1993), p.224:

> "The value of autonomy derives from the capacity it protects: the capacity to express one's own character—values, commitments, convictions, and critical as well as experiential interests—in the life one leads. Recognising an individual right of autonomy makes self-creation possible. It allows each of us to be responsible for the shaping of our lives according to our own coherent or incoherent—but in any case, distinctive—personality. It allows us to lead our own lives rather than being led along them."

[455] See para.2-16 onwards for a full analysis of the causation argument in *Chester*.

[456] Dissenting in *Chester* [2004] UKHL 41; [2005] 1 A.C. 134, Lord Hoffmann mooted the idea of "a modest solatium" (at [34]) and Lord Bingham pointed to the problem of "reinforcing the right by providing for the payment of potentially very large damages" as compensation for the unwarned risk (at [9]). Lord Steyn, giving the leading majority speech, was perhaps unlikely to have argued for a conventional solatium because in *Rees* he had described such a conventional award as "contrary to principle" and a matter for Parliament and the Law Commissions to consider: [2003] UKHL 52; [2004] 1 A.C. 309 at [46]. See para.1-39.

[456A] [2017] EWCA Civ 1028; [2017] 1 W.L.R. 4773 at [48].

[456B] See paras 8-191 and 8-192.

(h) Financial loss resulting from reliance or dependence

Replace footnote 459 with:

459 *Perre v Apand Pty Ltd* (1999) 164 A.L.R. 606 at 623. **8-97**

(i) The need for a special relationship

Multi-test approach

Replace footnote 488 with:

488 For examples of this cross-checking approach, see Owen J in *Heritage Joinery v Krasner* [1999] P.N.L.R. 906 at 917; *McFarlane v Tayside Health Board* [2000] 2 A.C. 59 at 83, where Lord Slynn considered the nature of the assumption of responsibility by the defendant when coming to the conclusion that it would not be fair, just and reasonable for him to bear the economic losses claimed; *HSBC Bank Plc v 5th Avenue Partners Ltd* [2009] EWCA Civ 296; [2009] 1 C.L.C. 503; and *Playboy Club London Ltd v Banca Nazionale Del Lavoro SpA* [2016] EWCA Civ 457; [2016] 1 W.L.R. 3169 at [17] (no duty owed by bank to casino in respect of credit reference on a customer given to casino's agent, an arrangement designed to preserve the confidentiality of customers; there was no assumption of responsibility by the bank since the casino was not identified as the recipient of the reference, nor any special relationship between the bank and the casino, nor was it fair, just and reasonable to impose liability when the casino had deliberately concealed its existence. The decision was affirmed on appeal: [2018] UKSC 43; [2018] 1 W.L.R. 4041, see further, para.8-107); *Seddon v Driver and Vehicle Licensing Agency* [2019] EWCA Civ 14 at [56]–[87] (no duty of care owed to prospective purchaser of a motor vehicle by the DVLA as to the accuracy of the information contained in the vehicle registration document). **8-104**

(ii) Relevant factors

(1) The purpose of the statement or service

Purpose of statement

Replace paragraph with:

Where the statement is provided in response to the claimant's request, its purpose may be identified from the nature of the request. In other cases, the purpose may be clear from instructions given to the professional by a third party. Thus in *Hedley Byrne*, where the bank responded to a request to supply information about its customer's creditworthiness, it was clear that the purpose was to enable the person to whom it was directed, i.e. a client of the requesting bank, to advance credit to the customer. But where the existence of the person who will actually rely on the statement is unknown to the defendant, then the defendant will not have the relevant knowledge of the purpose of the transaction, and so will not assume responsibility to that unknown person. In *Banca Nazionale del Lavoro SPA v Playboy Club London Ltd*[496A] a bank responded to a request for a credit reference on a customer made by a casino's agent. The bank had no knowledge of the casino, an arrangement designed to preserve the confidentiality of the casino's customers. When the casino sued the bank in respect of the negligent reference the Supreme Court held that no duty of care had arisen between bank and casino. Lord Sumption said that it was fundamental to such a duty that the defendant is assuming a responsibility to an identifiable (although not necessarily identified) person or group of persons. The representor "must not only know that the statement is likely to be communicated to and relied upon by [the claimant].[496B] It must also be part of the statement's known purpose that it should be communicated and relied upon by [the claimant], if the representor is to be taken to assume responsibility to [the **8-107** claimant]." There was no evidence that the bank knew that its reference would be communicated to or relied upon by anyone other than the agent.

[496A] [2018] UKSC 43; [2018] 1 W.L.R. 4041.

[496B] [2018] UKSC 43; [2018] 1 W.L.R. 4041 at [11]. Lord Mance pointed out, at [25], that had the representation been made, expressly or impliedly, for the benefit of an unnamed (rather than an entirely undisclosed) principal or client of the agent, the case would have paralleled *Hedley Byrne & Co Ltd v Heller & Partners Ltd* and the claim should then have succeeded.

Add new paragraph:

8-107A In other cases, the context of the professional's retainer will identify the purpose. Thus, in *Caparo*[497] the House of Lords held that in its statutory context, the purpose of an audit report was restricted to enabling shareholders to exercise their proprietary interests in the management of the company and did not extend to enabling shareholders or anyone else to make informed investment decisions. It followed that no duty was owed to shareholders or investors suffering investment losses as a result of relying on a negligent audit report. Similarly in the absence of special knowledge, auditors owe a duty neither to creditors who rely on the audit report when advancing credit[498] nor to guarantors relying on the report in deciding whether to continue with a guarantee on behalf of the company.[499] However, where auditors give audit-related advice to directors or shareholders of the client the purpose of that information may be sufficiently clear to give rise to a duty to the recipients.[500] The circumstances of the communication may indicate the purpose. In *Peach Publishing Ltd v Slater & Co*[501] it was held that accountants owed no duty of care to purchasers of their client who had relied on the accountants' statement that the management accounts were "essentially reliable, subject to not having been audited" which was communicated to both them and the client at the acquisition meeting prior to the purchase. The circumstances of the meeting led to the conclusion that the purpose for which the statement was communicated was to indicate to the client that it might give a qualified warranty as to the accounts. The accountants were present at the meeting as adviser to the client and not as an independent expert "on whom those on both sides of the transaction might be expected to rely". The purpose may not always be clear as is illustrated by the difference of opinion in relation to the listing particulars and prospectuses issued in connection with the sale of shares or other securities.[502] Where, however, "a company actively invites potential investors to make use of information originally produced for a different purpose, it can hardly complain if they do so."[503]

[497] [1990] 2 A.C. 605.

[498] *Al-Saudi Bank v Clarke Pixley (A Firm)* [1990] Ch. 313; *Esanda Finance Corp v Peat Marwick Hungerfords* (1997) 142 A.L.R. 750; [2000] Lloyd's Rep. P.N. 684. Similarly, an actuary producing a report on a client's pension fund does not owe a duty of care to a third party who relied on that report when purchasing the client even though the actuary was aware that its report had been passed to the third party: *Precis (521) v William Mercer Ltd* [2005] EWCA Civ 114; [2005] P.N.L.R. 28. See also *Man Nutzfahrzeuge AG v Freightliner Ltd* [2007] EWCA Civ 910; [2008] P.N.L.R. 6.

[499] *Ikumene v Leong* (1993) 9 P.N. 181.

[500] Thus in *Coulthard v Neville Russell* [1998] P.N.L.R. 276, *Siddell v Smith Cooper & Partners* [1999] P.N.L.R. 511, and *The Law Society v KPMG Peat Marwick* [2000] 1 W.L.R. 1921; [2000] P.N.L.R. 831, the Court of Appeal refused to strike out claims brought by directors, shareholders, and the Law Society, respectively. See further paras 10-215 to 10-218.

[501] [1998] P.N.L.R. 364.

[502] Contrast *Al Nakib Investments (Jersey) Ltd v Longcroft* [1990] 1 W.L.R. 1390, where it was held that the purpose of the prospectus was to guide those subscribing to shares and not those purchasing on the market, with *Possfund Custodian Trustees v Diamond* [1996] 1 W.L.R. 1351, where it was suggested

that changes in the legislation governing the issue of securities meant that listing particulars and prospectuses should now be regarded as intended to protect "after market" purchases.

[503] *Taberna Europe CDO II Plc v Selskabet (formerly Roskilde Bank A/S) (In Bankruptcy)* [2016] EWCA Civ 1262; [2017] Q.B. 633 at [11] per Moore-Bick LJ ("investor presentation" placed on defendants' website intended to be relied upon by potential investors for the purpose of deciding whether to invest in its subordinated securities; however, no duty of care because defendants were entitled to rely on a disclaimer in the document).

After "Citing Caparo, the court rejected the claim on the ground that the purpose of the certificate was to promote safety at sea and not to enable purchasers to make sound investments.", add new footnote 503A:

[503A] See also *Seddon v Driver and Vehicle Licensing Agency* [2019] EWCA Civ 14, applying *Reeman* (no duty of care owed by DVLA to a prospective purchaser of a motor vehicle as to the accuracy of the information contained in the vehicle registration document). **8-108**

Purpose of service

Replace footnote 508 with:

[508] [2015] EWHC 115 (QB); [2016] 1 W.L.R. 2499. See also *Schubert Murphy v The Law Society* [2014] EWHC 4561 (QB); [2015] P.N.L.R. 15; affirmed [2017] EWCA Civ 1295; [2017] 4 W.L.R. 200 (arguable that the Law Society could owe a duty of care if it negligently listed a fraudster as a solicitor on the official Roll of solicitors published on its website because solicitors and members of the public relied on the accuracy of the Roll). **8-109**

Replace paragraph with:

The purpose of the service was also an element in the House of Lords' decision in *White v Jones* that a solicitor retained by a testator owed a duty of care to the intended beneficiary of the will. Lord Browne-Wilkinson stated that "the solicitor by accepting the instructions has entered upon, and therefore assumed responsibility for, the task of procuring the execution of a skilfully drawn will knowing that the beneficiary is wholly dependent upon his careful carrying out or his function".[510] As in the case of statements, questions arise as to the purpose of a service. An example is provided by the Court of Appeal decision in *Carr-Glynn v Frearsons (A Firm)*[511] where it was held that a solicitor's duty of care to an intended beneficiary extended to serving a notice of severance of the joint tenancy over the bequeathed property. The fact that the testator's estate would also have a claim against the solicitor did not bar the claim of the intended beneficiary. Chadwick LJ explained that: **8-110**

> "the key ... is to recognise that ... the duties owed by the solicitors are limited by reference to the kind of loss from which they must take care to save harmless the persons to whom those duties were owed.... The loss from which the testator and his estate are to be saved harmless is the loss which those interested in the estate ... will suffer if effect is not given to the testator's testamentary intentions.... The duty owed ... to the specific legatee ... is, also, a duty to take care to ensure that effect was given to the testator's testamentary intentions."

Hence, the claims of the estate and the legatee could be regarded as complementary. Both followed from the purpose of the service.

[510] [1995] 2 A.C. 207 at 275. The *White* principle was applied in *Gorham v British Telecommunications Plc* [2000] 1 W.L.R. 2129, to impose a duty on a pension adviser to the dependants of its client, and both *White* and *Gorham* were followed in *Dean v Allin & Watts (A Firm)* [2001] EWCA Civ 758; [2001] 2 Lloyd's Rep. 249; [2001] P.N.L.R. 39, to impose a duty on a solicitor to a party on the other side of his client's transaction. However, it will be rare for a solicitor to be found to have assumed responsibility to a party on the other side of an arms' length transaction. Reliance by the other party in such circumstances "is presumptively inappropriate", given that it will not normally be reasonable for the other party to rely on what the solicitor said and it would be unusual for the solicitor reasonably to

foresee such reliance: *Steel v NRAM Ltd (formerly NRAM Plc)* [2018] UKSC 13; [2018] 1 W.L.R. 1190 at [32], per Lord Wilson. For detailed discussion of the will and related cases, see paras 10-113 to 10-118.

[511] [1999] Ch. 326 at 337.

Replace footnote 513 with:

8-111 [513] [2006] EWCA Civ 1299; [2007] P.I.Q.R. P7; [2007] L.S. Law Med. 50. See also *Harrison v Technical Sign Co Ltd* [2013] EWCA Civ 1569; [2014] P.N.L.R. 15—surveyor owed no duty to a tenant or to members of the public when asked by the tenant to inspect an awning over the tenant's shop front for damage because the surveyor was acting as an agent of the landlord of the property, and the request from the tenant was one of complaint; the surveyor was not asked to advise the tenant or to inspect the shop front on its behalf. In *Seddon v Driver and Vehicle Licensing Agency* [2019] EWCA Civ 14 at [66] the Court of Appeal noted that motor vehicle registration documents are provided by the DVLA for the statutory purpose of collecting tax and ensuring vehicles operating on the roads are registered not "for the private purpose of informing the commercial decisions of those who may choose to purchase registered vehicles."

(2) Knowledge of the defendant

Knowledge of reliance

Replace paragraph with:

8-113 Knowledge that the advisee will rely on the statement without obtaining independent advice will also be relevant. In *James McNaughton Paper Group Ltd v Hicks Anderson & Co*[523] the defendant accountants had shown the draft accounts of their client to the claimants who were proposing a takeover of the client. The defendants were held to owe no duty of care as they had no knowledge that the claimants would rely on accounts marked "draft" or on their oral statements about the accounts "*without any further inquiry or advice* for the purpose of reaching a concluded agreement with [the client]".[524] The same principles apply where the defendant has provided a service. The case for imposing a duty will be strongest where the defendant knows that his service is likely to impact directly upon the claimant without there being any independent check on the quality of that service. Thus, in the case of a building employer suffering loss as a result of the negligent work of a subcontractor or local authority inspector, one reason for the reluctance to impose a duty on the negligent defendant has been that the employer will be likely to have engaged his own professionals to check on the quality of the work.[525] Moreover, where the incorrect information provided by the defendant could have readily been checked by the claimant it will neither be reasonable for the claimant to have relied on the information, nor foreseeable to the defendant that the claimant would rely on the information. In *Steel v NRAM Ltd (formerly NRAM Plc)*.[525A] the defendant was a solicitor, acting for a borrower, who carelessly drew up documents releasing all the properties on which the loan was secured instead of the intended partial release. The lender executed the release, with the consequence that they had no security over the properties when the borrower became insolvent, and then sued the solicitor in negligence for the loss of the money loaned to the borrower. The Supreme Court held that there had been no assumption of responsibility by the solicitor to the lender. It was not reasonable for the lender to have relied on the solicitor's representations and it was not reasonably foreseeable to the solicitor that the lender would so rely since it had failed to check the accuracy of the representations. Any prudent bank taking basic precautions would have checked the accuracy of the representations by reference to its file or by asking for further clarification. Thus, Lord Wilson commented:

"a commercial lender about to implement an agreement with its borrower referable to its security does not act reasonably if it proceeds upon no more than a description of its terms put forward by or on behalf of the borrower. The lender knows the terms of the agreement and indeed, as in this case, is likely to have evolved and proposed them. ... No authority has been cited to the court, nor discovered by me in preparing this judgment, in which it has been held that there was an assumption of responsibility for a careless misrepresentation about a fact wholly within the knowledge of the representee. The explanation is, no doubt, that in such circumstances it is not reasonable for the representee to rely on the representation without checking its accuracy and that it is, by contrast, reasonable for the representor not to foresee that he would do so."[525B]

[523] [1991] 2 Q.B. 113.

[524] [1991] 2 Q.B. 113 at 145, Neill LJ's emphasis. Similarly, in *Scullion v Bank of Scotland Plc* [2011] EWCA Civ 693; [2011] 1 W.L.R. 3212 the Court of Appeal held that a valuer preparing a valuation report for a mortgagee did not owe a duty of care to the purchaser for a buy-to let transaction. That was a commercial transaction (in contrast with *Smith v Eric S Bush* [1990] 1 A.C. 831 where the purchaser was buying his own home) and a valuer was entitled to conclude that the purchaser was commercially astute and more likely to obtain, and afford, an independent valuation or survey. See also *McCullagh v Lane Fox & Partners* [1996] P.N.L.R. 205, where it was held that an estate agent owed no duty of care to a prospective purchaser of a property in respect of a statement about the area of the plot as he was entitled to assume that his statements would be independently checked by the purchaser or his advisers. *McCullagh* was distinguished in *Duncan Investments Ltd v Underwoods* [1997] P.N.L.R. 521 at 538, on the ground that the estate agent advising a purchaser as to the resale price of property "ought to have realised, that he was, and was to be, the only source of advice". The defendant's appeal in *Duncan* was allowed but only in relation to damages and not liability: [1998] P.N.L.R. 754.

[525] See for example, *Investors in Industry Ltd v South Bedfordshire DC* [1986] Q.B. 1034 at 1062, per Slade LJ. See also *Patchett v Swimming Pool & Allied Trades Association Ltd* [2009] EWCA Civ 717; [2010] 2 All E.R. (Comm) 138—no assumption of responsibility from statements made on trade association's website because potential customers were advised to obtain an information pack which would have revealed that a swimming pool installer with whom the claimants had entered into a contract, but who had become insolvent, was only an affiliate member of the trade association, and so was not subject to the same vetting as a full member and was not subject to the trade association's bond and warranty scheme.

[525A] [2018] UKSC 13; [2018] 1 W.L.R 1190.

[525B] [2018] UKSC 13; [2018] 1 W.L.R. 1190 at [38].

Knowledge of the class to which the advisee belongs

After "The defendant may know of the claimant only as a member of a class of persons likely to be relying on his work.", add new footnote 531A:

[531A] If the defendant is unaware of the existence of the claimant, even as an unidentified member of an identifiable class, then he will not have the required knowledge for a duty of care to arise: see *Banca Nazionale del Lavoro SPA v Playboy Club London Ltd* [2018] UKSC 43; [2018] 1 W.L.R. 4041, see further, para.8-107. **8-116**

(3) Reasonable reliance or dependence

Reasonable reliance or dependence

Replace footnote 537 with:

[537] The danger in using the term "reasonable reliance" in relation to a fact situation like that in *Spring* is apparent from the dissent of Lord Keith on the ground that the claimant had not factually relied on the defendant's statement. In *Gatt v Barclays Bank Plc* [2013] EWHC 2 (QB) at [34]–[35], Judge Moloney QC was prepared to apply *Spring* to the provision of information by a bank to a credit reference agency, the duty being owed not solely to the customer about whom the reference was provided, but also the spouse of that customer where she was a joint account holder and co-director of a family business that was dependent on her husband's credit. The judge noted "the importance of credit rating in the modern world and the analogies (more than just semantic) between job references and credit references". The action failed on the facts. In *Durkin v DSG Retail Ltd* [2014] UKSC 21; [2014] 1 W.L.R. 1148 a bank that had provided credit for a consumer transaction (the purchase by the claimant of a **8-117**

computer) conceded that it was under a duty of care not to make untrue statements about the claimant to credit reference agencies. The Supreme Court held that it was in breach of that duty by notifying the credit reference agencies that the claimant had defaulted on the credit agreement without first checking the claimant's assertion that the contract of sale had been rescinded. On the other hand, a credit reference agency does not owe a duty of care in negligence to members of the public about whom it collects data: *Smeaton v Equifax Plc* [2013] EWCA Civ 108; [2013] 2 All E.R. 959 (credit reference agency's responsibilities governed by the Data Protection Act 1998 (see now the Data Protection Act 2018) and the Consumer Credit Act 1974; there was no scope for imposing a co-extensive duty in tort). Similarly, there is no duty of care owed by the police to a person applying for an enhanced criminal record certificate, even though errors in the information provided affect the claimant's ability to obtain employment: *Desmond v Chief Constable of Nottinghamshire* [2011] EWCA Civ 3; [2011] 1 F.L.R. 1361. There was no assumption of responsibility by the police beyond that required by the proper performance of the statutory duty to provide a certificate, and there was no sufficient relationship between the police and the claimant (distinguishing *Spring*). See further para.14-36.

Dependence and vulnerability

Replace footnote 544 with:

8-118 [544] Contrast the position where the purchase is of a buy-to let property by a purchaser who is effectively making a commercial investment decision: *Scullion v Bank of Scotland Plc* [2011] EWCA Civ 693; [2011] 1 W.L.R. 3212 (no duty owed by valuer to purchaser in respect of report provided to mortgagee). See also *Seddon v Driver and Vehicle Licensing Agency* [2019] EWCA Civ 14 (no duty owed by DVLA to purchaser of "historic vehicle" as to the accuracy of information contained in the vehicle registration document; the claimant "could have arranged for his own expert inspection of the vehicle. The substantial price he was paying for the vehicle [£250,000] called for all precautions to be taken", at [81](5) per Hamblen LJ).

Scope of contract between parties

Replace footnote 570 with:

8-125 [570] [1995] 2 A.C. 145 at 186. See also Lord Bridge in *Scally v Southern Health and Social Services Board* [1992] 1 A.C. 294 at 303: "If a duty of the kind in question was not inherent in the contractual relationship, I do not see how it could possibly be derived from the tort of negligence." It is also of note that Lord Woolf in *Spring v Guardian Assurance Plc* [1995] 2 A.C. 296 at 353, cited Lord Bridge and was concerned to show that the tortious duty owed by an employer when giving a reference was no wider than that which could be implied as a term of the employment contract.

Opportunity to secure contractual safeguards

After "that the contractor was safeguarded by the terms of its contract with the employer.", add new footnote 573A:

8-126 [573A] See also *Seddon v Driver and Vehicle Licensing Agency* [2019] EWCA Civ 14 where the Court of Appeal concluded that the DVLA did not owe a duty of care to the purchaser of a "historic vehicle" as to the accuracy of information contained in the vehicle registration document because the purchaser could have stipulated for contractual warranties by the vendor and/or he could have arranged for his own expert inspection of the vehicle.

Informal or social context

Replace footnote 592 with:

8-129 [592] As occurred in *Burgess v Lejonvarn* [2017] EWCA Civ 254; [2017] B.L.R. 277 (architect who agreed to help friends with a garden landscape project had undertaken responsibility and, though not under a duty to provide professional services (in the absence of a contract), she owed a duty of care in respect of the services she actually provided; she had provided the services in the expectation that this would lead to paid work. At a subsequent trial it was found that there had been no breach of duty by the architect: *Burgess v Lejonvarn* [2018] EWHC 3166 (TCC); (2018) 181 Con. L.R. 204). This same policy is applied in contractual actions. See *Balfour v Balfour* [1919] 2 K.B. 571. A party to a social or family arrangement will not be held liable in contract unless there is positive evidence that the party intended to enter into a contractual relationship.

3. BREACH OF DUTY

(b) The criteria of reasonableness

(i) Objectivity

Test related to activity not actor

Replace footnote 701 with:

701 [1987] Q.B. 730 at 750–751. See also *FB v Princess Alexandra Hospital NHS Trust* [2017] EWCA Civ 334; [2017] P.I.Q.R. P17 (senior house officer in hospital Accident & Emergency department held to the same standard as a consultant doctor in taking a history. History taking was "a basic skill which hospital doctors at all levels are expected to possess", per Jackson LJ at [64]). **8-152**

Acting in an emergency

Replace paragraph with:

Where the defendant's conduct has occurred in the course of responding to an emergency this will be regarded as relevant to the objective standard of care required. All that is necessary in such a circumstance is that the conduct should not have been unreasonable, taking the exigencies of the particular situation into account.[717] Thus in *Ng Chun Pui v Lee Chuen Tat*[718] the Privy Council held that the driver of a coach, who had braked, swerved and skidded when another car had cut in front of him without warning, had acted reasonably in the emergency. Hospital, police and fire services may all be faced with emergency situations. In the hospital context it has been said that "full allowance must be made for the fact that certain aspects of treatment may have to be carried out in … battle conditions".[719] But some emergencies can be anticipated and planned for, especially in a professional context, and it may be negligent to fail to make appropriate arrangements to deal with an emergency.[720] Chasing a suspected criminal may count as an emergency situation. So in *Marshall v Osmond*[721] the claimant, a suspect, was injured when a police car drew up alongside the car from which he was starting to run away. It was held that in such circumstances the police action should not be judged by the same standard of care as would apply when there is time for reflection. But the extent to which the emergency justifies the risk taken will be a matter of degree. It may not absolve an emergency vehicle driver of responsibility for going through red traffic lights,[722] and the speed at which an emergency vehicle may travel when responding to an emergency must take account of the prevailing road conditions.[723] Again, in *Rigby v Chief Constable of Northamptonshire*[724] the police fired a canister of CS gas into the claimant's shop to flush out a dangerous psychopath. The shop caught fire. The police were found to be negligent in not having fire-fighting equipment to hand when there was a substantial risk of fire. Where the situation allows time for reflection but still presents a dilemma, the courts may still make allowances.[725] It is arguable that although a person's failings are not ordinarily taken into account in determining the reasonableness of conduct, the contrary should be the case where such a person is placed in an emergency, which is not of his making. Any judgment on the reasonableness of his reaction should take account of his limitations. **8-157**

717 This is sometimes referred to as the rule in *The Bywell Castle* (1879) 4 P. & D. 219. It used to be thought that the principle was limited to fear of personal injury, not danger to property; but this is not so. See per Lord Sumner in *S.S. Singleton Abbey v S.S. Paludina* [1927] A.C. 16 at 28.

718 [1988] R.T.R. 298 PC. See also *Parkinson v Liverpool Corp* [1950] 1 All E.R. 367, where the driver of a bus braked suddenly to avoid a dog which appeared suddenly in front of him and a passenger was

thrown to the floor of the bus. The driver was held to have acted reasonably in the emergency. *Parkinson* was applied in a similar set of circumstances in *Wooller v LTB* [1976] R.T.R. 206.

[719] *Wilsher v Essex AHA* [1987] Q.B. 730 at 749, per Mustill LJ who continued: "An emergency may overburden the available resources, and, if an individual is forced by circumstances to do too many things at once, the fact that he does one of them incorrectly should not lightly be taken as negligence." On the facts of the case, he held this consideration to be irrelevant as there was no evidence that the defendant's "attention had been distracted" or that they had "to take a difficult decision on the spur of the moment". See also *Darnley v Croydon Health Services NHS Trust* [2018] UKSC 50; [2018] 3 W.L.R. 1153 at [22] per Lord Lloyd-Jones: "It is undoubtedly the fact that Hospital A&E departments operate in very difficult circumstances and under colossal pressure. This is a consideration which may well prove highly influential in many cases when assessing whether there has been a negligent breach of duty."

[720] See *Bull v Devon AHA* [1993] 4 Med. L.R. 117, CA (inadequate system for calling consultant obstetrician to emergency delivery). But this may depend on how rare the foreseeable emergency is and the resources available to deal with it: *Garcia v St Mary's NHS Trust* [2006] EWHC 2314 (QB) at [95]–[96].

[721] [1983] Q.B. 1034; cf. *Henry v Chief Constable of Thames Valley* [2010] EWCA Civ 5; [2010] R.T.R. 14—reasonable for police officer to use his vehicle as a means of impeding a suspect's escape but in the circumstances (claimant was dismounting from his motorcycle at his home) not in such a manner as would create any foreseeable risk of injury. In some circumstances, e.g. where a dangerous suspect was at large, a police officer might be justified in using a car as a trap or barrier even if that created a risk of injuring the suspect.

[722] See *Griffin v Mersey Regional Ambulance* [1998] P.I.Q.R. P34. See para.8-176.

[723] *Armsden v Kent Police* [2009] EWCA Civ 631; [2009] R.T.R. 31 (speed of police vehicle using flashing blue warning light, but not its siren, excessive when approaching a junction round a bend); *Smith v Chief Constable of Nottinghamshire Police* [2012] EWCA Civ 161; [2012] R.T.R. 23 (police vehicle responding to an emergency, with flashing blue lights, being driven at 40–50mph in a busy town centre on a Friday night hit pedestrian in the middle of the road; police driver found negligent).

[724] [1985] 1 W.L.R. 1242.

[725] An example is *The Ketch Frances v The Highland Loch* [1912] A.C. 312. Very shortly before the Highland Loch was due to be launched, the Frances fouled her anchor in the path of the launching. Preparations for launching having already been made, it would have been dangerous to workmen and property to have left the Highland Loch as she was. In the circumstances the defendants decided to proceed with the launching and so run the risk of colliding with the Frances. A collision did result with extensive damage to the Frances. It was held that the defendants were not liable as they had acted reasonably in the dilemma.

(ii) Balancing cost and benefit

The Compensation Act 2006

Replace footnote 828 with:

8-181 [828] [2009] EWHC 1881 (QB) at [93]. See also *Humphrey v Aegis Defence Services Ltd* [2014] EWHC 989 (QB) (defendants justified in employing interpreters who were not as physically fit as other employees engaged as private defence contractors in Iraq, even though this increased the risk of injury to others, because interpreters were a "scarce commodity" and the defendants were engaged in the socially valuable activity of reconstruction work which would be prevented without interpreters; Compensation Act 2006 s.1 applied, although it "add[ed] nothing to *Tomlinson*" (at [112]). The Court of Appeal dismissed the claimant's appeal without referring to the Compensation Act 2006: [2016] EWCA Civ 11; [2017] 1 W.L.R. 2937.

Replace footnote 834 with:

8-184 [834] See paras 8-49 and 8-50. The ambulance service does have a duty to respond to an emergency call, since once the call has been accepted they have undertaken responsibility: *Kent v Griffiths, Roberts and London Ambulance Service* [2001] Q.B. 36.

(iii) *Common practice and expectations*

Common practice, expectations and risk warnings to patients

Replace paragraph with:

This is the "prudent patient" test of information disclosure adopted in Canada and Australia[882] which puts the court in the position of deciding what a prudent patient would have wanted to know about a proposed treatment, rather than leaving it to the medical profession to decide what the patient should be told.[883] Alternatively, even if the objective "reasonable patient" would not have attached significance to the risk, if the doctor knew or ought to have known that the individual patient would attach significance to the risk it will be a breach of duty to fail to disclose it. This more subjective element of the test allows for differences in the patient's circumstances from those of the hypothetical reasonable patient, though in practice it may more frequently be an issue where the patient manifests concern through asking questions about risks or alternative treatments.[884] In applying the test, the assessment of what constitutes a "material risk" does not depend simply on percentages or the magnitude of the risk. The court should also take into account the nature of the risk, the potential effects on the life of the patient, the importance to the patient of the potential benefits of the treatment, the alternative treatments available, and the risks involved in those alternatives.[885] The information must also be presented to the patient in a comprehensible manner. **8-192**

[882] *Reibl v Hughes* (1980) 114 D.L.R. (3d) 1 (SCC); *Rogers v Whitaker* (1992) 175 C.L.R. 479 (HCA).

[883] [2015] UKSC 11; [2015] A.C. 1430 at [83]: "Responsibility for determining the nature and extent of a person's rights rests with the courts, not with the medical professions."

[884] There are two exceptions to the prudent patient test: (1) information may be withheld if the doctor reasonably considers that disclosure would be seriously detrimental to the patient's health (but this is a limited exception and should not be used to subvert the general principle, preventing the patient from making an informed choice because the doctor considers that the patient will make a choice contrary to her best interests: [2015] UKSC 11; [2015] A.C. 1430 at [91]); and (2) circumstances of necessity, e.g. where the patient is unconscious or otherwise unable to make a decision.

[885] [2015] UKSC 11; [2015] A.C. 1430 at [89]. On the facts of *Montgomery* the Supreme Court concluded that the pursuer should have been informed of the risks of proceeding to a vaginal delivery and that there should have been a discussion about the alternative of Caesarean section. The contrast between the risks of the two forms of delivery was "stark". The therapeutic exception did not apply, though the consultant obstetrician considered that it was not generally in the maternal interest to have a Caesarean section. The doctor's duty was to explain to the patient why she considered one of the available treatment options to be medically preferable to the others, whilst taking care to see that the patient was aware of the considerations for and against each option ([2015] UKSC 11; [2015] A.C. 1430 at [95]). *Montgomery* was applied in *Webster v Burton Hospitals NHS Foundation Trust* [2017] EWCA Civ 62; [2017] Med. L.R. 113; *Thefaut v Johnston* [2017] EWHC 497 (QB), [2017] Med. L.R. 319; and *KR v Lanarkshire Health Board* [2016] CSOH 133; *Gallardo v Imperial College Healthcare NHS Trust* [2017] EWHC 3147 (QB); [2018] P.I.Q.R. P6 (failure to inform about outcome of surgery, prognosis, and the follow-up care and treatment options); *Hassell v Hillingdon Hospitals NHS Foundation Trust* [2018] EWHC 164 (QB); (2018) 162 B.M.L.R. 120 (claimant not told about risk of paralysis as a result of spinal cord injury and not advised about conservative treatment options); *Mills v Oxford University Hospitals NHS Trust* [2019] EWHC 936 (QB) (claimant not informed about alternative surgical technique and the comparative risks and benefits). In *Duce v Worcestershire Acute Hospitals NHS Trust* [2018] EWCA Civ 1307, [2018] P.I.Q.R. P18 the Court of Appeal held that *Montgomery* involves a two-stage test: (1) what risks associated with an operation were or should have been known to the medical professional in question; and (2) were the risks material? The second limb is a matter for the court, but the first falls within the expertise of medical professionals. If the risk was not known the question of its materiality does not arise: "a clinician is not required to warn of a risk of which he cannot reasonably be taken to be aware" (at [43]).

(d) Particular instances of breach

(i) Road accidents

Pedestrian accidents

Replace footnote 979 with:

8-206 [979] See paras 3-86 and 3-87. See also D. Dyal, "Contributory negligence in pedestrian road traffic accidents" [2018] J.P.I.L. 23.

Dangers on the road

Replace paragraph with:

8-208 A person who negligently creates a danger on the road will be liable for any resulting accident. Thus, a local authority which planted trees adjacent to the road and failed to cut them back was held liable when a branch broke a bus window and injured a passenger,[984] but where the defendant's tree fell on the road causing an accident and there was nothing to indicate this was likely to happen, there was no liability.[985] Construction work on the road can lead to liability, so where a local authority put in a drainage pipe and reinstated the surface, it was held liable for negligently failing to discover that the surface had subsided. The successful claimant was thrown off his cycle by the uneven road surface.[986] Even the marker studs in the middle of the road can constitute a danger if they become loose and so a highway authority has been held liable for injury to a cyclist knocked over by a loose stud.[987] The authority's failure to take reasonable care to maintain the road led to its liability. In *Levine v Morris*[988] an authority was held liable for positioning the leg of a road sign so close to the edge of the carriageway as to endanger road users.[989] In *Cassin v Bexley LBC*[990] the police and the council had an agreement that the council would clear the road of bollards which might be used as missiles in a protest march. The council removed the bollards before the march and the claimant, a motorcyclist hit one of the plinths left behind. The council argued that it had discharged its duty to take reasonable care by doing as the police requested. The Court of Appeal held that the authority had a duty to keep the road safe until it was closed, that they had a duty not to remove the bollards until that occurred and as it had not ensured this it had failed in its duty and so was liable. The House of Lords' decision in *Stovin v Wise*[991] established that there is no liability for an omission to remove a dangerous obstruction adjacent to a highway but where the authority has created the danger the position is different. In *Kane v New Forest DC*,[992] *Stovin* was distinguished on the ground that the defendant planning authority in *Kane* had created the source of danger since it had required the construction of the footpath and knew that the sightlines to the road made it dangerous to use. Private individuals may also be liable. Leaving a vehicle without lights in a dark road may be evidence of negligence.[993] Parking on a bend may also be negligent.

[984] *Hale v Hants and Dorset Motor Service Ltd* [1947] 2 All E.R. 628.

[985] *Caminer v Northern and London Investment Trust* [1951] A.C. 88.

[986] *Newsome v Darton Urban DC* [1938] 3 All E.R. 93.

[987] *Skilton v Epsom Urban DC* [1937] 1 K.B. 112.

[988] [1970] 1 W.L.R. 71.

[989] See also *Bird v Pearce & Somerset CC (Third Party)* [1978] R.T.R. 290 where a highway authority was held to owe motorists a duty of care not to create dangers by obliterating markings, though in *Gorringe v Calderdale MBC* [2004] UKHL 15; [2004] 1 W.L.R. 1057 some doubt was cast on the correct-

ness of the decision in *Bird v Pearce*. See further *Foulds v Devon CC* [2015] EWHC 40 (QB) (inspection and maintenance of railings by the local authority with a view to protecting pedestrians from falling down a drop onto a road below, did not amount to an undertaking of responsibility by the authority to a cyclist who crashed into the railings and fell over the drop. The railings were not intended to act as a crash barrier).

[990] (1999) 1 L.G.L.R. 810; [1999] B.L.G.R. 694.

[991] [1996] A.C. 923. Applied in *Sumner v Colborne* [2018] EWCA Civ 1006; [2018] 3 All E.R. 1049; [2019] Q.B. 430 (no duty in respect of vegetation on land adjacent to the highway which obstructed visibility of road users, distinguishing *Yetkin v Newham LBC* [2010] EWCA Civ 776; [2011] Q.B. 827 where the defendants had planted vegetation on the central reservation of a highway).

[992] [2001] EWCA Civ 878; [2002] 1 W.L.R. 312. See also *Yetkin v Newham LBC* [2010] EWCA Civ 776; [2011] Q.B. 827—planting shrubbery in a central reservation such as to obscure the view of pedestrians attempting to cross the road created a foreseeable danger to users of the highway, and it did not have to be established that the authority had created a "trap".

[993] per Edmund Davies J in *Parish v Judd* [1960] 1 W.L.R. 867 at 870–871. It was held to be plain and obvious negligence to leave a lorry on the wrong side of the road at night with its lights on: *Chisman v Electromation (Export) Ltd* (1969) 6 K.I.R. 456; *Watson v Heslop* [1971] R.T.R. 308. In *Wagner v Grant* [2016] CSIH 34; 2016 S.L.T. 699 the driver of a large milk tanker that was "lit up better than a Christmas tree" was held to have been negligent in obstructing both lanes of the road while reversing into a farm entrance, though the motorcycle rider who rode into it was held to have been 60% contributorily negligent. A motorist, who has to leave his vehicle unlit, may be negligent if he fails to display a warning sign, but this does not absolve other drivers. See *Lee v Lever* [1974] R.T.R. 35. A vehicle parked on the highway in a manner that creates a dangerous obstruction may also constitute a public nuisance: *Dymond v Pearce* [1972] 1 Q.B. 496, CA (though on the facts the collision with the lorry on this case was held to be entirely due to the fault of the motorcyclist who ran into the back of the lorry).

(ii) The liability of carriers

Ships and aircraft

After "imposes strict liability for damage caused to person or property on land or water,", add new footnote 1048A:

[1048A] Though note that s.76(1) excludes liability for trespass or nuisance by reason only of the flight of an aircraft over any property at a reasonable height. On this see *Peires v Bickerton's Aerodromes Ltd* [2017] EWCA Civ 273; [2017] 1 W.L.R. 2865. **8-214**

(iii) Care for children

Parental duty to child

Add new paragraph:

Similar policy issues arise where a third party alleges that a parent has been negligent in supervising a child. This is most likely to arise in the context of road traffic accidents where a child has run into the road and been struck by a vehicle. If the child is too young to be found contributorily negligent, the defendant motorist may seek contribution from the parent under the Civil Liability (Contribution) Act 1978 on the basis that the parent did not provide appropriate supervision and so was negligent in allowing the child to run into traffic. In *Ellis v Kelly*,[1054A] Yip J rejected an argument that either the child or the parent must be negligent if a child runs into the road in circumstances where an older child or adult would be held contributorily negligent. The responsibility of the child and the parent should be considered separately by reference to the appropriate standard of care.[1054B] Moreover, there could be serious implications of finding parents liable in such circumstances: "Parents are not reasonably able to secure insurance to guard against the risk of claims arising out of their parenting generally. ... In a case in which the parent owns assets such as the family home, the family may face fears that action **8-215A** will be taken to enforce against the property. The potential to interfere with family life, including the rights of siblings, is significant."[1054C] Routinely joining parents in such litigation would also create a risk of encouraging an over-cautious approach, "interfering with parents' assessments of when it is appropriate to allow children some freedom to foster growth and independence."[1054D] It followed, said Yip J, that caution should be exercised by courts considering claims against parents in such cases.

[1054A] [2018] EWHC 2031 (QB); [2018] 4 W.L.R. 124.

[1054B] [2018] EWHC 2031 (QB); [2018] 4 W.L.R. 124 at [72]. On the evidence, holding the child's mother responsible would "impose far too high a standard on an ordinary parent making ordinary decisions in the course of parenting as to how to keep her child reasonably safe while gradually being allowed more responsibilities and freedoms" (at [71]).

[1054C] [2018] EWHC 2031 (QB); [2018] 4 W.L.R. 124 at [77].

[1054D] [2018] EWHC 2031 (QB); [2018] 4 W.L.R. 124 at [78].

School's non-delegable duty

Replace footnote 1088 with:

8-222 [1088] *Armes v Nottinghamshire CC* [2017] UKSC 60, [2018] A.C. 355; although the Supreme Court went on to hold that the local authority could be vicariously liable for the abuse of children placed in the care of foster parents; see para.6-10.

Sports supervision

Replace paragraph with:

8-224 Misuse of gymnasium equipment may lead to liability[1093] and common practice may be no defence if risks remain. In *Cassidy v City of Manchester*[1094] a 13-year-old playing goalkeeper in an indoor hockey game was injured when she tripped on the leg of a bench being used as the goal. The teacher's evidence was that the positioning of the bench had been adopted in his teaching training college and by other local schools. It was conceded that it was not universal practice, but the education authority argued, by analogy with medical cases, that it had followed a "respected body of opinion in the gymnastic field which recognised the propriety of such practice". Hutchison LJ upheld the finding of liability by the trial judge, commenting that the picture would have been different if the practice had been universal. He also rejected the claim that the girl had been contributorily negligent, saying what she did was "the sort of thing that an enthusiastic child may do in the heat of a game of hockey". Failure adequately to supervise contact sports such as rugby may also give rise to liability.[1095] The same is true of potentially dangerous activities such as swimming.[1096] However, there are limits to what can be expected of a school. In *Chittock v Woodbridge School*[1097] it was held that issuing a reprimand to a school student who had skied off piste contrary to instructions was within the reasonable range of responses for the teacher to have adopted. Failure to prevent the student skiing or requiring him to ski subject to supervision did not amount to negligence. The school was not liable for a subsequent injury to the student caused by his careless skiing. In any case, supervision would not have prevented the second accident. The Court of Appeal has held that a school's responsibility to its pupils does not extend to taking out insurance on their behalf against sporting injuries, nor to advising their parents to take out such insurance.[1098] Where facilities or activities are offered to adults, a school may expect more foresight of risk to be shown.[1099]

[1093] *Fowles v Bedfordshire CC* [1995] P.I.Q.R. P380 where lack of supervision and mispositioning of a safety mat led to injury and liability.

[1094] Unreported 12 July 1995.

[1095] *Smoldon v Whitworth* [1997] P.I.Q.R. P133. See para.8-159.

[1096] *O'Shea v Royal Borough of Kingston on Thames* [1995] P.I.Q.R. P208 (local authority pool but the principle is the same: prohibition of diving was the only safe system).

[1097] [2002] EWCA Civ 915; [2003] P.I.Q.R. P6. See also *Hammsersley-Gonsalves v Redcar and Cleveland BC* [2012] EWCA Civ 1135; [2012] E.L.R. 431 (claimant pupil struck by golf club swung by another pupil; teacher could not be expected to see every action of each of 22 boys and so held not negligent in supervising the group); *Porter v Barking & Dagenham LBC, The Times,* 9 April 1990 (QBD) (allowing two 14-year-old boys to practise putting the shot unsupervised not negligent); *Murray v McCullough* [2016] NIQB 52 (school discharged its duty of care to 15-year-old pupil who suffered dental injuries when hit in the mouth by a hockey stick by highly recommending the use of a mouth guard; no obligation to make the wearing of mouth guards mandatory); *Pook v Rossall School* [2018] EWHC 522 (QB); [2018] E.L.R. 402 (no breach of duty in allowing 10-year-old child to run from changing rooms to hockey pitch).

[1098] *Van Oppen v Trustees of the Bedford Charity* [1990] 1 W.L.R. 235.

[1099] In *Comer v St Patrick's RC School* Unreported 1997, Buxton LJ rejected a claim by a parent injured in a fathers' day race, saying: "It was not reasonably foreseeable that in these circumstances any adult in the situation in which this race took place would so run as to expose himself to injury."

CHAPTER 9

BREACH OF STATUTORY DUTY

TABLE OF CONTENTS

2. CATEGORISING BREACHES OF STATUTORY DUTY

Relationship between the parties

Delete footnote 34. **9-10**

3. IS THE BREACH ACTIONABLE?

Express provision

Replace paragraph with:

9-11 Simply because the damage suffered by the claimant appears to fall within the terms of the statute, it does not necessarily follow that an action for breach of statutory duty simpliciter will lie. If, of course, the statute in question or some other statute[35] expressly provides that a civil remedy does[36] or does not[37] lie for breach of the duty there is less difficulty. On the other hand, even where the statute expressly provides for a civil remedy for its breach there can still be questions as to the extent of its application.[38] For example, in *Merlin v British Nuclear Fuels Plc*,[39] it was held that the term "damage to property" in s.7(1) of the Nuclear Installations Act 1965 meant physical damage to tangible property and did not extend to economic loss. Contamination by ionising radiation which did not damage the fabric of the property but increased the risk of injury to the health of occupants in the future, and reduced the value of the property, was not actionable. *Merlin* was distinguished by the Court of Appeal in *Blue Circle Industries Plc v Ministry of Defence*,[40] where it was held that contamination of land by radioactive material constitutes physical damage to the land, even though the consequence was economic in that the property was worth less and expenditure was incurred in removing the contaminated top soil. The extensive cleansing operations and restrictions on the use of the land was sufficient to demonstrate physical damage and thus enable the claimants to recover for the consequent diminution in the value of their property.[41] In *No.1 West India Quay (Residential) Ltd v East Tower Apartments Ltd*[41A] the Court of Appeal drew attention to the reasoning underlying the legislative provision in s.4 of the Landlord and Tenant Act 1988 that "A claim that a person has broken any duty under this Act may be made the subject of civil proceedings in like manner as any other claim in tort for breach of statutory duty." By adding a remedy which was not available at common law a less draconian and more precise approach to relief for breach of the Act was afforded to the court.[41B]

[35] s.71 of the Health and Safety at Work Act 1974 provided for civil liability for breach of the Building Regulations, now repealed and replaced by s.38 of the Building Act 1984 but still not in force. It has been suggested that there is liability for breach of the Building Regulations even without s.38: *Anns v London Borough of Merton* [1978] A.C. 728 at 759, per Lord Wilberforce. Cf. *Peabody Donation Fund (Governors) v Sir Lindsay Parkinson & Co Ltd* [1985] A.C. 210 HL.

[36] For examples of express provisions in a statute that a civil remedy will lie for a breach of the duty created see: Nuclear Installations Act 1965 s.12 and the Nuclear Installations Act 1969; Gas Act 1965 s.14(1); Health and Safety at Work Act 1974 s.47(2); Highways Act 1980 s.41; Consumer Protection Act 1987 s.41; Water Resources Act 1991 s.48A (added by the Water Act 2003 s.24). The Protection from Harassment Act 1997 expressly creates both a criminal offence and a civil remedy for breach of the Act.

[37] e.g. Health and Safety at Work Act 1974 s.47(1)(a), which negatives civil liability for breach of ss.2–8 of the Act.

[38] In addition to showing that the statute imposes a liability to civil action the claimant must of course show that this liability attaches to the particular defendant sued: see *Smith v George Wimpey & Co Ltd* [1972] 2 Q.B. 329.

[39] [1990] 2 Q.B. 557.

[40] [1999] Ch. 289 CA.

[41] See also the Highways Act 1980 s.41, which imposes a duty on highway authorities to maintain the highway (subject to the defence in s.58 for the highway authority to prove that it exercised reasonable care) and s.41(1A) (inserted by the Railways and Transport Safety Act 2003 s.111) which provides that "a highway authority are under a duty to ensure, so far as is reasonably practicable, that safe passage along a highway is not endangered by snow or ice" (reversing *Goodes v East Sussex CC* [2000] 1 W.L.R. 1356). The duty to maintain the highway under s.41 does not include a duty to provide appropriate warning signs of hazards on the highway, since this does not involve repair of the physical or structural condition of the highway or render it more or less passable for ordinary traffic: *Gorringe v Calderdale MBC* [2004] UKHL 15; [2004] 1 W.L.R. 1057. See also *Valentine v Transport for London* [2010] EWCA Civ 1358; [2011] P.I.Q.R. P7; cf. *Wilkinson v York CC* [2011] EWCA Civ 207. The expression "maintain and keep in good condition and repair" in s.28 of the Tramways Act 1870 involves the same duty as that imposed on a highway authority by the Highways Act 1980 s.41. This is an absolute duty, but it does not require perfection. The standard of maintenance is measured by considerations of safety: *Roe v Sheffield CC* [2003] EWCA Civ 1; [2004] Q.B. 653, per Pill LJ at [61] and [62] (cf. Sedley LJ at [91] to [96]). The duty applies to a dangerous accumulation of water on the surface of the highway, caused by a longstanding blockage of the highway drainage system: *Mott MacDonald Ltd v Department of Transport* [2006] EWCA Civ 1089; [2006] 1 W.L.R. 3356. Cf. *Ali v City of Bradford* [2010] EWCA Civ 1282; [2012] 1 W.L.R. 161 (no civil action for breach of statutory duty against a highway authority for failing to prevent obstruction of the highway contrary to the Highways Act 1980 s.130(3)).

[41A] [2018] EWCA Civ 250; [2018] 1 W.L.R. 5682.

[41B] See per Lewison LJ in [2018] EWCA Civ 250; [2018] 1 W.L.R. 5682 at [21].

(a) Duty imposed for the protection of a particular class of individuals

Protection of a limited class of the public

Replace paragraph with:

The fact that a statutory provision was designed to protect a particular class of individuals may, but not necessarily will, lead to the conclusion that breach of the duty gives rise to a common law action for damages.[56] In some instances the existence of an action for breach of statutory duty is clear and longstanding. Thus, industrial safety legislation designed to protect workers from injury at work has long been treated as conferring a common law action.[57] On the other hand, legislation creating administrative mechanisms for the protection of children at risk of neglect or abuse, though clearly intended to protect a particular class of the public, does not confer such an action.[58] Similarly, s.117 of the Mental Health Act 1983, which imposes a duty to provide after-care services for patients discharged from mental hospitals, while undoubtedly designed to promote the social welfare of such individuals does not give rise to an action for breach of statutory duty.[59] The claimant must establish that Parliament intended that the statute should confer a private law right of action "sounding in damages".[60] In *R. v Deputy Governor of Parkhurst Prison Ex p. Hague*,[61] the House of Lords reiterated that the primary question in relation to an action for breach of statutory duty is always whether the legislature intended to create a civil remedy for aggrieved individuals. 9-14

> "The fact that a particular provision was intended to protect certain individuals is not of itself sufficient to create a private law right of action upon them, something more is required to show that the legislature intended such conferment."[62]

So the fact that one of the purposes of the Prison Rules is to protect the welfare of prisoners was insufficient to create a right to sue for breach of those rules relating to the discipline and segregation of prisoners. Similarly, the fact that the safety provisions in Ch.II of Pt V of the Merchant Shipping Act 1995 and the Fishing Vessel (Safety Provisions) Rules 1975[63] were enacted for the protection of those who go to sea in fishing vessels does not create a right of action in damages for their breach.[64] In *Cullen v Chief Constable of the Royal Ulster Constabulary*[65] Lord Millett considered that the right of detained persons to consult in private with a solicitor, and to be informed of the reasons for delaying access to a solicitor, contained in s.15 of the Northern Ireland (Temporary Provisions) Act 1987 and s.58 of the Police and Criminal Evidence Act 1984 was not for the protection of a limited class. It was a:

> "quasi-constitutional right of fundamental importance in a free society—indeed its existence may be said to be one of the tests of a free society—and like *habeas corpus* and the right to a fair trial it is available to everyone. It is for the benefit of the public at large. We can all of us, the innocent as well as the guilty, sleep more securely in our beds for the knowledge that we cannot be detained at any moment at the hands of the state and denied access to a lawyer."[66]

This dictum must however now be read, along with the majority decision of the House of Lords in the case itself to the effect that breach of a detained person's right to consult a solicitor does not give right to an action for damages for breach of statutory duty, alongside the unanimous decision of a seven member Supreme Court that the failure of Scottish criminal law to afford such a right to detained persons constituted a breach of art.6 of the European Convention on Human Rights.[67]

[56] In *Trustee in Bankruptcy of St John Poulton's Trustee in Bankruptcy v Ministry of Justice* [2010] EWCA Civ 392; [2011] Ch. 1 the Court of Appeal held that the Insolvency Rules 1986 r.6.13, intended to protect creditors in an insolvency, cannot give rise to an action for breach of statutory duty in the event of failure by a court to comply with a requirement in the Rules to notify the Chief Land Registrar of the filing of a petition against the bankrupt.

[57] See para.9-17.

[58] *X (Minors) v Bedfordshire CC* [1995] 2 A.C. 633. Though see now *Z v UK* [2001] 2 F.L.R. 612; [2001] 2 F.C.R. 246 (ECtHR) granting compensation to the claimants in *X (Minors) v Bedfordshire CC* for breach of art.3 of the European Convention for the Protection of Human Rights. The failure of a social services authority to intervene to prevent serious, long-term neglect and abuse of children amounted to inhuman and degrading treatment within the meaning of art.3. The UK was also found to have been in breach of art.13 of the Convention in that the applicants did not have available to them an appropriate means of determining their allegations that the authority had failed to protect them from inhuman or degrading treatment or the possibility of obtaining an appropriate award of compensation for the damage suffered as a consequence. On *Z v UK* see Gearty (2002) 65 M.L.R. 87; Davies (2001) 117 L.Q.R. 521. Note that if similar facts to *X (Minors) v Bedfordshire CC* were to recur, the children would now be owed a duty of care in the tort of negligence: *JD v East Berkshire Community Health NHS Trust* [2005] UKHL 23; [2005] 2 A.C. 373, affirming the Court of Appeal decision ([2003] EWCA Civ 1151; [2004] Q.B. 558) to depart from *X (Minors) v Bedfordshire CC* on this point.

[59] *Clunis v Camden and Islington HA* [1998] Q.B. 978 CA. The wording of the section fell short of the "exceptionally clear statutory language" required by Lord Browne-Wilkinson in *X v Bedfordshire CC* in order to create a claim for breach of statutory duty arising out of social welfare legislation. Cf. *AK v Central and North West London Mental Health NHS Trust* [2008] EWHC 1217 (QB); [2008] P.I.Q.R. P19; [2008] L.S. Law Med. 428. In *Richards v Worcestershire CC* [2017] EWCA Civ 1998; [2018] Med. L.R. 131 at [80] Jackson LJ expressed agreement, obiter, with the proposition in *Clunis v Camden and Islington HA* that inadequate after-care services, contrary to s.117 of the Mental Health Act 1983, do not give rise to an action for damages for breach of statutory duty.

[60] *Pickering v Liverpool Daily Post and Echo Newspapers Ltd* [1991] 2 A.C. 370.

[61] [1992] 1 A.C. 58 HL.

[62] [1992] 1 A.C. 58 at 170–171, per Lord Jauncey.

[63] SI 1975/330.

[64] *Todd v Adams and Chope (t/a Trelawney Fishing Co) (The "Margaretha Maria")* [2002] EWCA Civ 509; [2002] 2 Lloyd's Rep. 293.

[65] [2003] UKHL 39; [2003] 1 W.L.R. 1763.

[66] [2003] UKHL 39; [2003] 1 W.L.R. 1763 at [67]. Unfortunately, the facts of *Cullen* demonstrated precisely the opposite of this assertion. Mr Cullen was detained at the hands of the state and denied access to a lawyer, and then denied compensation for this breach of the law. Query how easily any of us should sleep, whether guilty or innocent. Cf. the dissenting speeches of Lord Bingham and Lord Steyn taking the view that s.15 protected the rights of a limited and specific class, i.e. detained persons.

[67] See *Cadder v HM Advocate* [2010] UKSC 43; [2010] 1 W.L.R. 2601.

(c) Actions against public authorities

Replace paragraph with:

9-33 *X v Bedfordshire CC*[159] is symptomatic of a general trend against finding that a private law remedy lies against public authorities charged with the protection of the public welfare. Lord Browne-Wilkinson suggested that only exceptionally will "... an administrative system designed to promote the social welfare of the community" give rise to private rights enforceable by an action for breach of statutory duty. This is partly because enforcement by the civil law is seen as unlikely to be Parliament's choice of an effective means of enforcing public protection measures. More significant, perhaps, is the courts' perception of the economic consequences of the potentially large number of cases against public authorities that might ensue, both in terms of the impact upon a local authority's resources and its consequent effect on the ability of the authority to carry out its statutory functions.[160] This was certainly expressed to be an important factor in denying that social services authorities owed a common law duty of care in the tort of negligence, and cannot have been far from their Lordships minds when addressing the issue of breach of statutory duty. Notwithstanding the fact that the child protection legislation (the Children and Young Persons Act 1969, the Child Care Act 1980, and the Children Act 1989) was clearly for the protection of a limited class, namely children at risk, and that until 1991 the legislation contained only limited machinery for enforcing those statutory duties, the House of Lords held that a social services authority were not liable for breach of statutory duty in respect of the manner in which they conducted an investigation or made a decision whether or not to remove a child into care. The legislation established an administrative system designed to promote the social welfare of the community. The judgments to be made were of "peculiar sensitivity", involving striking a difficult balance between protecting a child from the risk of harm and harm created by disrupting the relationship between the child and its parents in being removed into care. Decisions would often have to be taken on the basis of inadequate and disputed facts. All the statutory provisions were dependent upon the subjective judgment of the local authority. Lord Browne-Wilkinson doubted whether a claim for breach of statutory duty could ever arise where the relevant duty was dependent on the defendant first having formed a subjective belief. The language and structure of the legislation was inconsistent with any intention to create private law rights. In such a context it required exceptionally clear statutory language to show a Parliamentary intention that social services authorities should be liable in damages for an erroneous judgment.[161] Accordingly, it was impossible to treat such duties as being more than public law duties. In *Poole BC v GN*[161A] the Supreme Court held that without more, such as an assumption of responsibility in the specific case, the provisions of the Children Act 1989 are not capable of generating a common law duty of care on social workers to protect children from abuse by third parties wholly unrelated to the children's own families.

159 [1995] 2 A.C. 633.

160 See the comments of Lord Bridge in *Murphy v Brentwood DC* [1991] 1 A.C. 398 at 482, in the context of a negligence action.

161 [1995] 2 A.C. 633 at 747.

161A [2019] UKSC 25; [2019] 2 W.L.R. 1478.

A human rights perspective

Replace paragraph with:

In the case of *X (Minors) v Bedfordshire CC* the European Court of Human Rights found that the failure of the social services authority to intervene to prevent serious, long-term neglect and abuse of children constituted inhuman and degrading treatment and found the UK to be in breach of art.3 of the Convention.[163] As in *TP and KM v UK* the UK was also found to have been in breach of art.13 of the Convention in that the applicants did not have available to them an appropriate means of determining their allegations that the authority had failed to protect them from inhuman or degrading treatment or the possibility of obtaining an appropriate award of compensation for the damage suffered as a consequence. In both cases the court awarded substantial compensation. It was emphasised that the abuse in *Z v UK* was both serious and had been occurring for some considerable time, and it seems likely, therefore, that not all failures to intervene to protect children at risk of harm will meet the requirements of "inhuman and degrading treatment" under 9-35 art.3. Subsequently, in *JD v East Berkshire Community Health NHS Trust*[164] the Court of Appeal held that *X (Minors) v Bedfordshire CC; M (A Minor) v Newham London BC* could not survive the Human Rights Act 1998. Accordingly, it was no longer "legitimate to rule that, as a matter of law, no common law duty of care is owed to a child in relation to the investigation of suspected child abuse and the initiation and pursuit of care proceedings".[165] Although it was possible that there could be factual situations where it was not fair, just or reasonable to impose a duty of care each case would fall to be determined on its individual facts. This remarkable decision (effectively the Court of Appeal overruled the House of Lords' decision in *X v Bedfordshire* on the basis of the human rights jurisprudence) was upheld by the House of Lords,[166] who also agreed with the Court of Appeal's conclusion that, though a duty of care could be owed to the child when making such a decision, no such duty was owed to the parents or the person suspected of abuse.

[163] *Z v UK* [2001] 2 F.L.R. 612; [2001] 2 F.C.R. 246. For discussion of *Z v UK* see Gearty (2002) 65 M.L.R. 87; Davies (2001) 117 L.Q.R. 521.

[164] [2003] EWCA Civ 1151; [2004] Q.B. 558.

[165] [2003] EWCA Civ 1151; [2004] Q.B. 558 at [84]. See also *Poole BC v GN* [2019] UKSC 25; [2019] 2 W.L.R. 1478 in which the Supreme Court confirmed that the decision of the Court of Appeal in *JD v East Berkshire Community Health NHS Trust* remained good law despite doubts expressed by the Court of Appeal itself in the *Poole* case (see [2017] EWCA Civ 2185; [2018] 2 W.L.R. 1693).

[166] [2005] UKHL 23; [2005] 2 A.C. 373.

Replace paragraph with:

9-36 In *Phelps v Hillingdon LBC*[167] a seven-judge House of Lords held that such policy factors, such as those canvassed in *X (Minors) v Bedfordshire CC*, should not be conclusive against the possibility of a common law duty of care in negligence owed by an educational psychologist or a teacher when making an assessment of a pupil's educational needs. Clearly, there is no authority for the proposition that such claims will in future give rise to an action for breach of statutory duty. Indeed, *Phelps* is clear authority that there is no private law action for breach of statutory duty based on breach of the Education Acts 1944 or 1981 in respect of the failure to provide suitable education for an individual pupil.[168] On the other hand an action based in common law negligence, arising out of the public authority's performance of its statutory duties, or a claim based on a breach of the European Convention for the Protection of Human Rights, though not necessarily coterminous with breach of a statutory provision, might go a significant way towards filling the gap for claimants.

[167] [2001] 2 A.C. 619.

[168] See para.9-38.

Negligence actions against public authorities

Replace footnote 182 with:

9-40 [182] See *Yetkin v Newham LBC* [2010] EWCA Civ 776; [2011] Q.B. 827. Cf. *Sumner v Colborne and Denbighshire CC* [2018] EWCA Civ 1006; [2019] Q.B. 430.

(e) Kind of damage sustained by the claimant

Replace paragraph with:

9-43 The alleged breach of statutory duty must give rise to the kind of damage generally remediable in tort. In *Pickering v Liverpool Daily Post and Echo Newspapers Ltd*,[194] the House of Lords found that the unauthorised publication of information concerning the claimant in breach of the Mental Health Tribunal Rules, though adverse to the patient's interests, did not give rise to a claim for breach of statutory duty. Such a violation of privacy was not a loss or injury of a kind for which the law awards damages. The breach of the statute must result in personal injury, damage to property or recognised economic loss. It will become apparent that in general the courts are much more ready to infer a right of action for breach of statutory provisions designed to ensure personal safety, particularly of employees. They are cautious about inferring the existence of such an action where the harm suffered is economic loss.[195]

[194] [1991] 2 A.C. 370 HL.

[195] See *R. v Deputy Governor of Parkhurst Prison Ex p. Hague* [1992] 1 A.C. 58 at 160–161, per Lord Bridge. See also *Greenway v Johnson Matthey Plc* [2014] EWHC 3957 (QB); [2015] P.I.Q.R. P10, at [34] per Jay J (aff'd [2016] EWCA Civ 408; [2016] 1 W.L.R. 4487): "interests of an economic nature" not normally included in the concept of "welfare" in the Health and Safety at Work etc Act 1974). The decision of the Court of Appeal in *Greenway v Johnson Matthey Plc* (affirming Jay J) was subsequently reversed by the Supreme Court, but without affecting the point in the text, i.e. the Court held that, correctly interpreted, the facts indicated that the claimants *had* suffered physical damage (so the question of the irrecoverability of economic loss in breach of statutory duty and negligence did not arise): see *Dryden v Johnson Matthey Plc* [2018] UKSC 18; [2018] 2 W.L.R. 1109. Note the availability of actions for economic loss occasioned by violation of European Community legislation: see para.9-46.

(g) Breach of European legislation

Replace paragraph with:

In *Kirklees MBC v Wickes Building Supplies Ltd*,[215] the House of Lords questioned whether *Bourgoin* was correct to require proof of abuse of power in light of the decision of the European Court of Justice in *Francovich v Italian Republic*.[216] The European Court of Justice has now held that an individual is entitled to damages for the failure of a Member State properly to implement EU legislation. In *R. v Secretary of State for Transport Ex p. Factortame Ltd (No.4)*,[217] it was held that European Community law confers a right to damages when three conditions are satisfied: 9-48

(1) the rule of Community law breached was intended to confer rights on individuals;
(2) the breach was sufficiently serious[218]; and
(3) there is a direct causal link between the breach and the damage sustained.[219]

Bourgoin can no longer be regarded as correct, in so far as it required proof of abuse of power by the Member State in failing to implement European legislation. It remains unclear whether the right to damages is properly to be categorised as an action for breach of statutory duty, but what is highly unlikely is that the principles applied to determine when an individual has such a right will develop in the same haphazard manner as the common law "rules" on breach of statutory duty. Moreover, if statutory regulations are introduced to implement a EU Directive, it does not follow that a claimant can fortuitously take advantage of those "rules" in an action for breach of the regulations, instead of the relevant criteria of European Union law, where those criteria happen to be less favourable to his claim than the common law approach.[220]

[215] [1993] A.C. 227 at 280–282.

[216] (C–6 and 9/90) [1993] 2 C.M.L.R. 66.

[217] [1996] Q.B. 404 at 499 ECJ.

[218] As to what constitutes a serious breach, see *R. v HM Treasury Ex p. British Telecommunications Plc* [1996] Q.B. 615; *Dillenkofer v Federal Republic of Germany* [1997] Q.B. 259 ECJ; *R. v Secretary of State for Transport Ex p. Factortame Ltd (No.5)* [2000] 1 A.C. 524 HL; *Byrne v Motor Insurers Bureau*

[2008] EWCA Civ 574; [2009] Q.B. 66; *Test Claimants in the Franked Investment Group Litigation v Inland Revenue Commissioners* [2010] EWCA Civ 103; [2010] S.T.C. 1251; [2010] B.T.C. 265; reversed in part at [2012] UKSC 19; [2012] 2 A.C. 337; *Delaney v Secretary of State for Transport* [2015] EWCA Civ 172; [2015] 1 W.L.R. 5177.

[219] For an unsuccessful attempt to obtain damages for breach of the three conditions see *AB v Home Office* [2012] EWHC 226; [2012] 4 All E.R. 276 in which the claimant sought compensation for alleged breach of an EC Directive (the "Citizens Directive") relating to residence. For a successful attempt see *Barco De Vapor BV v Thanet DC* [2014] EWHC 490 (Ch); [2015] Bus. L.R. 593.

[220] See *EnergySolutions EU Ltd v Nuclear Decommissioning Authority* [2017] UKSC 34; [2017] 1 W.L.R. 1373. Cf. *Lancashire Care NHS Foundation Trust v Lancashire CC* [2018] EWHC 200 (TCC)); (2018) 177 Con. L.R. 246.

4. DAMAGE WITHIN THE AMBIT OF THE STATUTE

Injury not contemplated by the statute

After "unless the injury was of the type which the statute was passed to prevent.", add new footnote 229A:

9-50 [229A] "When seeking to articulate what constitutes actionable harm, it is necessary to have regard to the object and scope of the statutory duty imposed": per Marcus Smith J in *Britned Development Ltd v ABB* [2018] EWHC 2616 (Ch); [2019] Bus. L.R. 718 at [427].

Chapter 10

PROFESSIONAL LIABILITY

Table of Contents

1. GENERAL CONSIDERATIONS

(a) Professional liability in general

Professional liability

Replace footnote 7 with:

[7] See, e.g. *Pantelli Associates Ltd v Corporate City Developments Number Two Ltd* [2010] EWHC 3189 (TCC); [2011] P.N.L.R. 12; *Caribbean Steel Co Ltd v Price Waterhouse* [2013] UKPC 18; [2013] 4 All E.R. 338; *Wattret v Thomas Sands Consulting Ltd* [2015] EWHC 3455 (TCC); [2016] P.N.L.R. 15. But the rule is not immutable: *ACD (Landscape Architects) Ltd v Overall* [2012] EWHC 100 (TCC); [2012] P.N.L.R. 19 at [16] (Mann J). Indeed, it has been held in England not to apply to most cases of lawyers' negligence, apparently on the basis that judges know about legal practice: *Bown v Gould & Swayne* [1996] P.N.L.R. 130. On the general admissibility of expert evidence in professional negligence cases, see *Devon Commercial Property Ltd v Barnett* [2019] EWHC 700 (Ch) at [117]–[123]. **10-03**

(b) Duties of care to clients, patients and others

Clients and patients: statements and advice

Replace footnote 27 with:

[27] As in, e.g. *Hedley Byrne & Co Ltd v Heller & Partners Ltd* [1964] A.C. 465. A more recent instance is *Burgess v Lejonvarn* [2017] EWCA Civ 254; [2017] P.N.L.R. 25 (free advice to homeowner by architect at start of project: project later abandoned). **10-05**

Clients and patients: concurrent liability in contract and tort

Replace paragraph with:

Most professional services in England, other than medical treatment within the NHS, are provided pursuant to a contract between the professional and the client. Since s.13 of the Supply of Goods and Services Act 1982,[29] like the common law, implies a term that services supplied in the course of a business will be rendered with reasonable care and skill, it follows that professional negligence will normally constitute a breach of contract. Nevertheless it is now clear that this does not bar **10-06** concurrent liability in tort: a matter of some little importance, since in a few cases the existence of a duty in tort may have considerable advantages for the claimant, notably in terms of limitation.[30] Earlier authority having been mixed,[31] the matter of concurrent liability was put beyond doubt in 1994 by the House of Lords in *Henderson v Merrett Syndicates Ltd.*[32] Certain Names at Lloyd's sued their underwriting agents, with whom they were in contractual relation, for negligence. An issue of limitation arose,[33] and the Names alleged the agents were concurrently liable in tort so as to have the benefit of a longer period of limitation. Lord Goff, delivering the leading judgment, held that the Names could sue in tort, and that the existence of a contractual relationship was no objection. As a matter of principle, he said,

> "it is difficult to see why concurrent remedies in tort and contract, if available against the medical profession, should not also be available against members of other professions, whatever form the relevant damage may take."[34]

Since *Henderson*, it has been accepted that any professional is prima facie liable to his client in both contract and tort.

[29] Or, in the case of services provided to a consumer, s.49 of the Consumer Rights Act 2015. Note, however, that courts are unwilling, though not unpersuadable, to regard a professional as contracting with anyone other than his client. This is particularly true in areas such as medicine, where there might otherwise arise an awkward conflict of duties: see *Bot v Barnick* [2018] EWHC 3132 (QB) (private hospital owed no contractual duty to patient's partner).

[30] In particular, because (i) time runs in contract from the time of breach, but in the tort of negligence from the time when damage is suffered, which may be a good deal later (the point at issue in *Midland Bank v Hett, Stubbs & Kemp* [1979] Ch. 384 and *Henderson v Merrett Syndicates Ltd* [1995] 2 A.C. 145); and (ii) a contract claimant cannot claim the benefit of the "latent damage" provision in s.14A of the Limitation Act 1980 (see *Iron Trades Mutual Insurance Ltd v Buckenham* [1990] 1 All E.R. 808, approved in *Société Commerciale de Réassurance v ERAS Ltd* [1992] 2 All E.R. 82). On the other hand, tort also has its disadvantages. Whatever the position in contract, where professional advice is provided to X the courts will not allow Y to sue in tort under the rule in *Hedley Byrne & Co Ltd v Heller & Partners Ltd* [1964] A.C. 465 on the basis that he was acting as X's undisclosed principal. See *Playboy Club London Ltd v Banca Nazionale del Lavoro SpA* [2018] UKSC 43; [2018] 1 W.L.R. 4041.

[31] Until the 1970s, it was generally thought that while liability for physical damage or personal injury was concurrent (e.g. *Edwards v Mallan* [1908] 1 K.B. 1002), liability for economic loss lay only in contract (see *Bagot v Stevens Scanlon & Co Ltd* [1966] 1 Q.B. 197). However, following *Hedley Byrne & Co Ltd v Heller & Partners Ltd* [1964] A.C. 465 a series of decisions had accepted the possibility of concurrent liability (see, e.g. *Midland Bank Trust Co Ltd v Hett, Stubbs & Kemp* [1979] Ch.384; *Ross v Caunters* [1980] 1 Ch. 297, 308 and *Nitrigin Eireann Teoranta v Inco Alloys* [1992] 1 W.L.R. 498, 503).

[32] [1995] 2 A.C. 145. Followed in the Commonwealth generally: see *Astley v Austrust Ltd* (1999) 197 C.L.R. 1; *Central Trust Co v Rafuse* [1986] 2 S.C.R. 147; *Riddell v Porteous* [1999] 1 N.Z.L.R. 9.

[33] i.e. proceedings had been started within six years of loss suffered, but not of the acts alleged to have constituted negligence.

[34] [1995] 2 A.C. 145, 190. See too *Equitas Ltd v Walsham Bros & Co Ltd* [2013] EWHC 3264 (Comm): [2014] P.N.L.R. 8 at [41]–[52] (Males J).

Duties to third parties: physical damage

Replace paragraph with:

10-10 Matters are less straightforward, however, where the alleged negligence amounts to simple omission to take steps to protect the third party from injury. Here there is normally no liability. So, for example, health professionals in diagnosing illness generally owe a duty to the patient, but not to others such as relatives, even where their interests may be vitally affected.[51] Again, there is no case in England[52] making a professional liable for failing to inform the authorities that a client may amount to a public danger; for example where a doctor or solicitor knows that his client is mentally ill and making threats against an ex-girlfriend, or is an alcoholic who regularly drives when drunk, or is HIV positive but continues to indulge in unprotected intercourse. Thus in *Palmer v Tees NHS Trust*[53] an unstable outpatient attached to the defendant hospital brutalised and murdered a little girl. Her estate sued the hospital for failing to confine, supervise or otherwise control the patient concerned; but the hospital was held to have owed her no duty of care in the circumstances.[54] However, liability cannot be ruled out. Although delicate issues of confidentiality may cloud the issue here, professional regulation increasingly allows, and sometimes even requires, this to be overridden in cases of severe danger; and where it is there is no obvious reason not to impose liability.[55]

[51] *Smith v University of Leicester NHS Trust* [2016] EWHC 817 (QB) (inherited disease likely to affect not only patient but relatives). See too *Child & Family Agency v A* [2018] IEHC 112 at [15]–[17], where Twomey J, in the Irish High Court, could not rule out liability in the event of failure to disclose a boyfriend's HIV status to a girlfriend with whom he was having regular unprotected sex.

[52] But see in the US context, *Tarasoff v Regents of the University of California*, 551 P. 2d 334 (1976); *Semler v Psychiatrics Institute of Washington*, 538 F. 2d 121 (1976); and *Durtlinger v Artiles*, 673 P. 2d 86 (1983); also the Canadian decision in *Brown v University of Alberta Hospital* (1997) 145 D.L.R. (4th) 63.

[53] [1998] Lloyd's Law Rep. Med. 447; [2000] P.N.L.R. 87.

[54] Note, however, that if the victim were another inmate it must be arguable, since *Rabone v Pennine Care NHS Foundation Trust* [2012] UKSC 2; [2012] 2 A.C. 72 and *Reynolds v UK* (2012) 55 E.H.R.R. 35, that there would be a claim for the infringement of the right to life under art.2 of the ECHR.

[55] For example, the GMC imposes a professional duty on doctors to inform the DVLA of incapacitated drivers who insist on continuing behind the wheel: see its publication *Confidentiality: reporting concerns about patients to the DVLA or the DVA*. If such a failure were to result in a severe accident, the imposition of liability cannot be excluded. And see *ABC v St George's Healthcare NHS Trust* [2017] EWCA Civ 336; [2017] P.I.Q.R. P15 (patient known to be suffering from inherited Huntington's disease: refusal to strike out claim by relative for failing to pass this information on).

Duties to third parties: economic loss

Replace list with:

(1) There must be a fairly close degree of proximity between the parties.[57] 10-11

(2) There will generally not be liability to an indeterminate class of persons, or in respect of an indeterminate class of transactions.[58]

(3) Where a professional undertakes to provide advice or information for a client knowing that the client intends to use that information or advice to induce a third party to act in a manner which will be to his detriment if the professional is negligent, the professional may owe a duty to the third party.[59] The key question will often[60] be whether the third party can reasonably, and may foreseeably,[61] rely on the advice or information provided by the professional.[62]

(4) There will generally be no duty imposed where the duty owed to the client would conflict with the suggested duty to the third party,[63] or where there is a chain of contractual relationships between the professional and his client, and the client and the third party, which would be subverted by the imposition of a direct duty in tort.[64]

(5) Where the object of the duty undertaken to the client is to confer a benefit on the third party, a duty may be owed concurrently to that person so as to allow him to recover for loss of any expected benefit,[65] but this is not invariable. The tendency is to limit such recovery to cases where, if unable to sue the professional, the third party could not recover against anyone and

would thus be left without a remedy.[66] Where there would be double liability, the third party claimant will almost invariably fail.[67]

(6) There is, in general, no duty to persons other than clients in respect of breaches of professional duties affecting the quality (as against the safety) of goods or buildings.[68]

[57] A feature repeatedly stressed in discussing the extent of liability. See, e.g. *Ross v Caunters* [1980] Ch. 297, 308 (Megarry VC); *White v Jones* [1995] 2 A.C. 207, 269 (Lord Goff), 271 (Lord Browne-Wilkinson); *Clarke v Bruce Lance & Co* [1988] 1 W.L.R. 881, 888 (Balcombe LJ); *Caparo Industries plc v Dickman* [1990] 2 A.C. 605, 621 (Lord Bridge), 658 (Lord Jauncey); *Seymour v Ockwell* [2005] EWHC 1137 (QB); [2005] P.N.L.R. 39 at [126].

[58] Thus in relation to statements, the House of Lords in *Caparo Industries Plc v Dickman* [1991] 2 A.C. said that in general a duty would be owed only if the defendant knew that (i) his statement would foreseeably reach the claimant or a class of which he was a member, and (ii) it was intended to be used and relied on in respect of the particular transactions in which the claimant in fact used it. So while shareholders were a foreseeable class of claimants, auditors' reports were not sent to them in order for them to make up their mind about whether they wanted to take over the company. See also *Al Nakib Investments v Longcroft* [1990] 1 W.L.R. 1390; *The Morning Watch* [1990] 1 Lloyd's Rep. 547; and *The Nicholas H.* [1994] 1 Lloyd's Rep. 492.

[59] *JEB Fasteners Ltd v Marks Bloom & Co* [1981] 3 All E.R. 289 (upheld on appeal on the causation issue: [1983] 1 All E.R. 583). See too *Royal Bank of Scotland Plc v Bannerman Johnstone Maclay* [2005] CSIH 39; 2005 S.C. 437; [2005] P.N.L.R. 43. But this will depend on the circumstances. Where provision is made in a contract with a professional for assignment of its benefit to a third party, this is likely to preclude a direct duty to the third party in the absence of such an assignment: *BDW Trading Ltd v Integral Geotechnique (Wales) Ltd* [2018] EWHC 1915 (TCC); [2018] P.N.L.R. 34.

[60] But not invariably. In *White v Jones* [1995] 2 A.C. 207 a disappointed legatee recovered from negligent solicitors despite the lack of any reliance. But the House of Lords realised that this was a somewhat unusual situation.

[61] See *Ta Ho Ma Pty Ltd v Allen* (1999) 47 N.S.W.L.R. 1 (mortgagee's claim against valuer fails since reliance unforeseeable).

[62] See, e.g. *Raja v Austin Gray* [2002] EWCA Civ 1965; [2003] Lloyd's Rep. P.N. 126 (valuer employed by receiver who undervalues property to be sold by the latter owes no direct duty to property owner: lack of reliance an important feature).

[63] *Clarke v Bruce Lance & Co*, above at 370; *Connolly-Martin v Davis* [1999] P.N.L.R 826; *Huxford v Stoy, Hayward and Co* (1989) 5 B.C.C. 421; *Kamahap Investments v Chu's Central Market* (1989) 64 D.L.R. (4th) 167. But this is not so, of course, if the defendant professed to be acting for both parties concerned: see *Mortgage Express v Bowerman (No 2)* [1996] 2 All E.R. 836 (solicitor acting for mortgagor and mortgagee obtained suspicious information from mortgagor; liable for failing to pass on to mortgagee).

[64] See *Henderson v Merrett Syndicates Ltd* [1995] 2 A.C. 145, 534 (Lord Goff).

[65] *Ross v Caunters* [1980] Ch. 297; *White v Jones* [1995] 2 A.C. 207; *Richards v Hughes* [2004] EWCA Civ 266; [2004] P.N.L.R. 35 (accountants allegedly botched school fees tax saving scheme: CA refused to strike out claim by children whose fees were to be paid, though sceptical as to prospects of success). cf. *Al-Kandari v Brown (J.R.) and Co* [1987] Q.B. 514; *Arbuthnott v Fagan & Feltrim Underwriting Agencies Ltd, The Times,* 26 July 1994. Note that where professional advice is provided to X, the courts will not allow Y to sue under the rule in *Hedley Byrne & Co Ltd v Heller & Partners Ltd* [1964] A.C. 465 on the basis that he was acting as X's undisclosed principal: see *Playboy Club London Ltd v Banca Nazionale del Lavoro SpA* [2018] UKSC 43; [2018] 1 W.L.R. 4041, criticised in J. Grower and O. Sherman, "Equivalent to contract? Confronting the nature of the duty arising under Hedley Byrne v Heller" (2019) 135 L.Q.R. 177.

[66] Compare *White v Jones* [1995] 2 A.C. 207 (solicitor liable to disappointed legatee, since no other remedy for claimant) with *Raja v Austin Gray* [2002] EWCA Civ 1965; [2003] Lloyd's Rep. P.N. 126 (receiver liable to owner for sale at undervalue: hence no need for additional liability of valuer who undervalued property). See too *Mortensen v Laing* [1992] 2 N.Z.L.R. 282 (insurance assessor owes no duty to insured, who has adequate remedy against insurer).

[67] See, e.g. *Carr-Glyn v Frearsons* [1999] Ch. 326 (*White v Jones* duty owed to legatee only because of finding that estate could not have sued in own name); and cf. *Corbett v Bond Pearce* [2001] EWCA Civ 531; [2001] 3 All E.R. 769.

[68] See *Dept of the Environment v Thomas Bates & Sons Ltd* [1991] 1 A.C. 499 and *Murphy v Brentwood DC* [1991] 1 A.C. 398 (realty); cf. *Simaan General Contracting v Pilkington Glass Ltd (No.2)* [1988] Q.B. 758 (personalty).

Duties of care and assignment

Replace footnote 69 with:

[69] *Offer-Hoar v Larkstore Ltd* [2006] EWCA Civ 1079; [2006] 1 W.L.R. 2926. Sometimes there is express provision for assignment; compare the facts of *BDW Trading Ltd v Integral Geotechnique (Wales) Ltd* [2018] EWHC 1915 (TCC); [2018] P.N.L.R. 34. **10-12**

Duties to clients and others: the impact of company law

Replace paragraph with:

10-13 Even though a professional may owe a duty of care to a given claimant and be in breach of it, the claimant's loss may nevertheless be irrecoverable in so far as (a) he holds shares in a company, (b) his loss reflects a mere diminution in the value of those shares, and (c) the company would have had a similar action for breach of duty against the defendant. In such a situation the company, and the company alone, is entitled to sue.[73] Thus in *Johnson v Gore Wood & Co*[74] a property company controlled by the claimant was allegedly misadvised by a firm of solicitors and suffered a loss: as a result the claimant's holding in it underwent a proportionate devaluation. Despite a finding that the solicitors had owed a duty of care to the claimant as well as to the company, the House of Lords held that the claimant could claim nothing in respect of that devaluation. However, the limits of this rule must be noted. It does not apply where the company has no claim and hence the only duty is that owed to the shareholder;[75] nor where the loss to the shareholder is a loss over and above that due to the diminution of the company's assets,[76] for example where accountants' negligence in respect of a subsidiary company affects the stability or reputation of the relevant holding company.[77] And even where there is an overlapping liability to the company it does not apply where that liability is merely technical or ancillary: thus it cannot be prayed in aid to bar an action by a secured creditor against its own receiver for wasting the assets of a corporate debtor on the ground that the receiver, as technical agent to the debtor, could in strict law have been sued by the latter.[78]

[73] See *Prudential Assurance Co Ltd v Newman Industries Ltd (No 2)* [1982] Ch. 204. See also *Breeze v Norfolk Chief Constable* [2018] EWHC 485 (QB); [2018] 2 B.C.L.C. 638 at [24]–[25].

[74] [2002] 2 A.C. 1. See too *Day v Cook* [2001] EWCA Civ 592; [2001] P.N.L.R. 32; *Barings Plc v Coopers & Lybrand* [2002] P.N.L.R. 16 (parent company could not sue accountants for negligence causing loss to Singapore subsidiary by facilitating unauthorised trades: this was merely reflective loss).

[75] *George Fischer (G.B.) Ltd v Multi Construction Ltd* [1995] 1 B.C.L.C. 260; *Johnson v Gore Wood & Co* [1999] P.N.L.R. 426, 456.

[76] cf. *Heron International v Grade (Lord)* [1983] B.C.L.C. 244.

[77] *Barings Plc (in admin) v Coopers & Lybrand* [1997] 1 B.C.L.C. 427; [1997] P.N.L.R. 179 (*semble*) (Note that these were different proceedings from those at [2002] P.N.L.R. 16, above).

[78] *International Leisure Ltd v First National Trustee Co UK Ltd* [2012] EWHC 1971 (Ch); [2013] Ch. 346.

Duties of care: illegality

Replace paragraph with:

10-14 There is no doubt that a professional may be liable for negligently failing to prevent a client from being illegally defrauded by employees,[79] or from inadvertently falling foul of the criminal law.[80] But issues of illegality may nevertheless affect liability in two ways. First, relief may be refused to a claimant guilty of underlying illegality. For example, a client of an accountant has been held disentitled to sue for negligence in connection with a transaction intended all along to be combined with a substantial tax fraud.[81] Secondly, there may be a limited exception where a fraudster is sole owner, and in sole control, of a company which later sues its professional advisers for failing to prevent the fraud concerned. Thus in *Stone & Rolls Ltd (in liquidation) v Moore Stephens (A Firm)*[82] a company acting as the catspaw of S, a confidence trickster, defrauded a bank of some $100 million. The House of Lords, by a majority, struck out the company's claim against its auditors for failing to stop the fraud, citing the maxim ex turpi causa non oritur actio. But the *Stone & Rolls* exception is highly limited[83]; it applies only where (i) the fraudster was the directing mind of the company and not a mere employee,[84] (ii) there are no other innocent directors or shareholders,[85] and (iii) there is a very close connection between the fraud and the claim.[86] In all other cases professional liability remains unaffected.

[79] See, e.g. *Barings Plc v Coopers & Lybrand (No 7)* [2003] EWHC 1319 (Ch); [2003] P.N.L.R. 34 (accountants); *Singularis Holdings Ltd (In Official Liquidation) (A Company Incorporated in the Cayman Islands) v Daiwa Capital Markets Europe Ltd* [2018] EWCA Civ 84; [2018] 1 W.L.R. 2777 (stockbrokers).

[80] See, e.g. *Coulthard v Neville Russell* [1998] P.N.L.R. 276 (technical company assistance in purchasing own shares); and *Griffin v UHY Hacker Young & Partners* [2010] EWHC 146 (Ch); [2010] P.N.L.R. 20 (breach of "phoenix" provisions of Companies Acts); *Osman v Ralph Moss Ltd* [1970] 1 Lloyd's Rep. 313 (insurance brokers liable for negligently leaving motorist uncovered so that he was fined).

[81] See the Irish decision in *English v O'Driscoll* [2016] IEHC 584; [2017] P.N.L.R. 9. There is some doubt, however, whether this result would apply in England since the narrowing of the illegality defence in *Patel v Mirza* [2016] UKSC 42; [2017] A.C. 467. See the decision in *Stoffel & Co v Grondona* [2018] EWCA Civ 2031; [2018] P.N.L.R. 36 (negligence claim by mortgagor against solicitors not barred by fact that claimant had been "fronting" for a different party in fraud of the lender).

[82] [2009] UKHL 39; [2009] 1 A.C. 1391. The effective claimant, of course, was the bank victim of the fraud, who had put the company into liquidation and then persuaded the liquidator to sue for its benefit. For an approving note, see P. Watts, "Audit Contracts and Turpitude" (2010) 126 L.Q.R. 14; for a less approving one, E. Ferran, "Corporate Attribution and the Directing Mind and Will" (2011) 127 L.Q.R. 239.

[83] Indeed, it was referred to in *Jetivia SA v Bilta (UK) Ltd* [2014] UKSC 23; [2016] A.C. 1 at [30] as a case to be put "on one side in a pile and marked 'not to be looked at again'". Similarly, the Ontario Court of Appeal found it of "limited assistance" in *Livent Inc v Deloitte & Touche* 2016 ONCA 11; (2016) 393 DLR (4th) 1. It is also worth noting, more generally, that in *Patel v Mirza* [2016] UKSC 42; [2017] A.C. 467 the Supreme Court, while not commenting directly on *Stone & Rolls*, emphasised the need to tailor the application of the ex turpi causa maxim to those cases where public policy genuinely demands the dismissal of a suit.

[84] This was accepted in *Stone & Rolls*: see [2009] UKHL 39; [2009] 1 A.C. 1391 at [28] (Lord Phillips). Admittedly it was left open in *Jetivia SA v Bilta (UK) Ltd* [2014] UKSC 23; [2016] A.C. 1 at [29]; but the position seems logical.

[85] See *Jetivia SA v Bilta (UK) Ltd* [2014] UKSC 23; [2016] A.C. 1 at [80]–[81] (Lord Sumption) and [24]–[27] (Lords Neuberger, Clarke and Carnwath). This had been suggested in *Stone & Rolls* itself: see [2009] UKHL 39; [2009] 1 A.C. 1391 at [173]–[174] (Lord Walker); [201] (Lord Brown) (though not by the third member of the majority, Lord Phillips: see [55]–[56]). On this cf. further *Madoff Securities International Ltd v Raven* [2013] EWHC 3147 (Comm); [2014] Lloyd's Rep. F.C. 95 at [314]–[320] (Popplewell J) and *Singularis Holdings Ltd (In Official Liquidation) (A Company Incorporated in the Cayman Islands) v Daiwa Capital Markets Europe Ltd* [2017] EWHC 257 (Ch); [2017] 1 Lloyd's Rep. 226 at [188] (Rose J). *Singularis Holdings Ltd (In Official Liquidation) v Daiwa Capital Markets Europe Ltd* has been upheld in the Court of Appeal: see [2018] EWCA Civ 84; [2018] 1 W.L.R. 2777.

[86] Cf. *Sharma (former Liquidator of Mama Milla Ltd) v Top Brands Ltd* [2015] EWCA Civ 1140; [2017] 1 All E.R. 854.

(d) Liability as trustee

Professional holding property as trustee

Replace paragraph with:

10-19 In many cases where a professional handles money or property on behalf of others, he becomes a trustee of it, either because required to do so by law (as in the case of client funds held by solicitors, stockbrokers and insurance brokers[114]) or because of ad hoc arrangements (notably in conveyancing transactions[115]). If such a trust arises, then his duty is to employ the funds strictly in accordance with his authority: any disbursement of them other than in accordance with the terms of the trust[116] is a breach of trust. For this the trustee is in general strictly liable without proof of fault[117] (and, importantly, without the possibility of reduction of liability for contributory negligence[118]), his duty being not so much to compensate for the beneficiary's net loss, as with damages in contract or tort,[119] as to put the beneficiary in the position he would have occupied had the terms of thc trust been observed.[120] However, even where such strict liability exists it may be possible for the defendant to claim the protection of s.61 of the Trustee Act 1925, which gives the court a discretion to exonerate a trustee from liability if he has acted honestly and reasonably, and ought fairly to be excused for his breach of trust.[121]

[114] Solicitors: see the SRA Accounts Rules 2017, made by the Solicitors Regulation Authority under the Solicitors Act 1974. Insurance brokers: see the CASS 5 rules, made under the Financial Services and Markets Act 2000 by the Financial Services Authority (now the Financial Conduct Authority). Stockbrokers: CASS 8, from the same source.

[115] For example, in a mortgage transaction solicitors regularly hold the mortgage funds on trust for the lender pending disbursement. In an ordinary property sale they may or may not hold the completion monies on trust for the purchaser before completion: compare *Purrunsing v A'Court & Co* [2016] EWHC 789 (Ch); [2016] 4 W.L.R. 81 and *P&P Property Ltd v Owen White & Catlin LLP* [2018] EWCA Civ 1082; [2018] 3 W.L.R. 1244.

[116] But note that the terms of any trust are likely to be far from coterminous with the general obligations of the professional. It is thus entirely possible for the professional to be in breach of retainer but not in breach of trust, as where a solicitor for a lender fails to reveal relevant information to the lender before disbursing mortgage monies. Here his only liability is in negligence. See *Bristol & West Building Society v Mothew* [1998] Ch. 1, 24 (Millett LJ); *Target Holdings Ltd v Redferns* [1996] A.C. 421, 436 (Lord Browne-Wilkinson); *AIB Group (UK) Plc v Mark Redler & Co Solicitors* [2013] EWCA Civ 45; [2013] P.N.L.R. 19 at [13] (Patten L.J.); also *Gabriel v Little* [2013] EWCA Civ 1513 (a point not raised on appeal in *BPE Solicitors v Hughes-Holland* [2017] UKSC 21; [2018] A.C. 599).

[117] See *Target Holdings Ltd v Redferns* [1996] A.C. 421. So there is automatic breach of trust where solicitors part with mortgage lenders' monies against either a bogus solicitors' undertaking engineered by fraudsters (*Lloyds TSB Bank Plc v Markandan & Uddin* [2012] EWCA Civ 65; [2012] 2 All E.R. 884) or a forged transfer (*Nationwide Building Society v Davisons Solicitors* [2012] EWCA Civ 1626; [2013] P.N.L.R. 12). Conversely the same may apply to solicitors paying property purchase monies to fraudsters: e.g. *Purrunsing v A'Court & Co* [2016] EWHC 789 (Ch); [2016] 4 W.L.R. 81 and *Dreamvar (UK) Ltd v Mishcon De Reya (A Firm)* [2016] EWHC 3316 (Ch). On the latter see R. Kennedy, "Conveyancing fraudsters— who picks up the bill after P&P and Dreamvar?" (2018) 34 P.N. 205. Note that the new Law Society Code for Completion, effective 1 May 2019, allows solicitors held liable here to pass on the bill to the seller's solicitors by providing for the latter to warrant that they are acting for the true owners of the property to be sold.

[118] Whether under the Law Reform (Contributory Negligence) Act 1945 or under s.61 of the Trustee Act 1925: see *Lloyds TSB Bank Plc v Markandan & Uddin (A Firm)* [2012] EWCA Civ 65; [2012] 2 All E.R. 884.

[119] "[T]he common law rules of remoteness of damage and causation do not apply' (Lord Browne-Wilkinson in *Target Holdings Ltd v Redferns* [1996] A.C. 421, 434); *AIB Group (UK) Plc v Mark Redler & Co Solicitors* [2013] EWCA Civ 45; [2013] P.N.L.R. 19 at [47] (Patten LJ).

[120] See, e.g. *Target Holdings Ltd v Redferns* [1996] A.C. 421, 434–435 (Lord Browne-Wilkinson); *AIB Group (UK) Plc v Mark Redler & Co* [2014] UKSC 58; [2015] A.C. 1503. In such cases some care may have to be taken, in the absence of express agreement as to the terms of any trust, in determining whom the monies are actually held in trust for. See, e.g. *Bellis v Challinor* [2015] EWCA Civ 59; [2016] W.T.L.R. 43 (monies paid into solicitor's client account disbursed to fraudsters: no claim by payers, since on the facts the trust was in favour of the fraudsters from the beginning); also *Chang v Mishcon de Reya* [2015] EWHC 164 (Ch) (similar).

[121] A point first made by Rimer J in *Lloyds TSB Bank Plc v Markandan & Uddin (A Firm)* [2012] EWCA Civ 65; [2012] 2 All E.R. 884 at [61]; for an example see see *Nationwide Building Society v Davisons Solicitors* [2012] EWCA Civ 1626; [2013] P.N.L.R. 12 (solicitors entirely innocently duped into releasing loan monies to bogus solicitors in league with fraudsters). But s.61 sets a high hurdle and most such applications fail: for a recent instance see *Purrunsing v A'Court & Co* [2016] EWHC 789 (Ch); [2016]

4 W.L.R. 81 (solicitor duped into acting for fraudster in property transaction too credulous when faced with evasive answers). See too, on the application of s.61 to professionals such as solicitors, M. Haley, "Section 61 of the Trustee Act 1925: a judicious breach of trust?" [2017] C.L.J. 537, 557 et seq.

(e) Liability for breach of fiduciary duty

(i) *Fiduciary duties generally*

Incidence of fiduciary duties

Replace footnote 125 with:

10-21 [125] J. Shepherd, "Towards a Unifying Concept of Fiduciary Relationships" (1981) 97 L.Q.R. 51; see also *Hospital Products v United States Surgical Corporation* (1984) 156 C.L.R. 41, 97 (Mason J); *White v Jones* [1995] 2 A.C. 206, 271 (Lord Browne-Wilkinson); *Brewer v Iqbal* [2019] EWHC 182 (Ch); [2019] P.N.L.R. 15 at [36]–[42].

Fiduciary duties: content

Replace footnote 143 with:

10-22 [143] Note that service here may include a past relationship: *Longstaff v Birtles* [2001] EWCA Civ 1219; [2002] 1 W.L.R. 470. These are not the only equitable duties in question; for example, a professional fiduciary may also owe a duty, when exercising a discretion, not to fail to take account of relevant matters (see *Brewer v Iqbal* [2019] EWHC 182 (Ch); [2019] P.N.L.R. 15 at [44]–[48]). But they are the most important in the context of professional liability.

Conflict of interest

Replace footnote 165 with:

10-27 [165] *Kelly v Cooper* [1993] 1 A.C. 205, above (where estate agent properly acting for competing sellers A and B, no duty to pass on to A information received in confidence from B); see too *Medsted Associates Ltd v Canaccord Genuity Wealth (International) Ltd* [2019] EWCA Civ 83 (effect of knowledge of client that fiduciary remunerated by other party, though not at what level).

(f) Breach of confidence

The duty of confidence

Replace paragraph with:

10-32 The duty of confidence is not, of course, absolute. It may be excluded by agreement.[190] More importantly, disclosure may be justified in the public interest,[191] or where there is a statutory duty to disclose information,[192] or on order of the court (only lawyers being protected by privilege against disclosure in England).[193] The courts will, however, define public interest fairly narrowly, weighing the primary public interest in maintaining confidentiality against the merits of access to particular information. Thus disclosure of the identities of two doctors found to be HIV positive,[194] and of information of the adverse effects of a pregnancy testing device after the product had been withdrawn,[195] were both held not to be justified. In contrast, in *W v Egdell*[196] a consultant psychiatrist engaged by a prisoner to report on his suitability for parole was held justified in sending a report on his patient to the Home Office. The report suggested that the prisoner could not be safely released, and, the court held, the interest in protecting the public clearly outweighed any argument in favour of confidentiality. In similar vein, the Canadian Supreme Court has stated that medical confidentiality may be displaced where there is a clear risk of serious and imminent harm to a specific person or closely-defined group of possible victims.[197] It is not necessary to demonstrate that there has been wrongdoing on the part of the client or patient to justify a breach of confidence,[198] but the onus is on the defendant to establish that the conduct of the claimant, or the public policy arguments in favour of disclosure, are such that the duty of confidence should exceptionally be displaced.[199] It is possible that there might even be a common law duty to break confidence, for example where a patient is known to be suffering from a genetically-transmissible disease and there is a clear danger that unless warning is given his grandchildren may be born affected by it.[200]

[190] See, e.g. *Mortgage Express Ltd v Sawali* [2010] EWHC 3054 (Ch); [2011] P.N.L.R. 11 (solicitors acting for purchasers and mortgage lenders: purchasers' common-form authorisation to share files with lenders: no right to object to disclosure to lenders in course of litigation by latter).

[191] The jurisprudence on what amounts to a "public interest" defence is enormous. See, e.g. *Initial Services v Putterill* [1968] 1 Q.B. 396; *Fraser v Evans* [1969] 1 Q.B. 349; *Lion Laboratories Ltd v Evans* [1985] Q.B. 526. Professional standards laid down by the appropriate bodies may of course be relevant here: see, e.g., the Accounting Standards laid down by the Financial Reporting Council, or the guidance for doctors from the GMC on matters such as the reporting of patients who insist on driving while incapacitated. See too *ABC v St George's Healthcare NHS Trust* [2017] EWCA Civ 336; [2017] P.I.Q.R. P15 (refusal to strike out claim against hospital for failing to break medical confidence and warn family member about inherited disease). In *Child & Family Agency v A* [2018] IEHC 112 Twomey J in the Irish High Court declined to order a breach of medical confidentiality to allow disclosure of the HIV status of a man to his girlfriend; but this was largely on the ground of lack of proof of sexual relations, and also because HIV is no longer a deadly or very dangerous disease.

[192] e.g. the Proceeds of Crime Act 2002, s.330 (duty to report suspicions of money laundering, matters of particular relevance to lawyers and accountants); and the Public Health (Control of Disease) Act 1984, ss.13, 45C, 45F and 45P and SI 2010/659 (duty of doctors to pass on details of those suffering from notifiable diseases or other conditions threatening public health).

[193] See P. Matthews, "Breach of Confidence and Legal Privilege" (1984) 1 L.S. 77. And see *Robertson v Canadian Imperial Bank of Commerce* [1994] 1 W.L.R. 1493.

[194] *X v Y* [1988] 2 All E.R. 648.

[195] *Schering Chemicals Ltd v Falkman Ltd* [1982] Q.B. 1.

[196] [1990] Ch. 359. This is in accordance with the demands of ECHR art.8: *Z v Finland* (1998) 25 E.H.R.R. 371.

[197] See *Smith v Jones* (1999) 169 D.L.R. (4th) 385 (patient unburdens himself to psychiatrist about disconcerting sado-masochistic fantasies concerning prostitutes: medical confidence displaced to allow psychiatrist to tell authorities). Indeed, in the European context this exception may be mandated by art.10 of the European Convention on Human Rights: see *Juppala v Finland* [2009] 1 F.L.R. 617 (infringement of art.10 to make discloser of suspicions of child abuse liable to defamation proceedings). See too *Child & Family Agency v A* [2018] IEHC 112 at [4], where Twomey J expressed the test as whether "on the balance of probabilities, the failure to breach patient confidentiality creates a significant risk of death or very serious harm to an innocent third party." In that case the mere prospect of contracting HIV was held not serious enough.

[198] *Lion Laboratories Ltd v Evans* [1985] Q.B. 526, 550 (Griffiths LJ); *Attorney-General v Guardian Newspapers Ltd (No.2)* [1990] 1 A.C. 109, 268–269 (Lord Griffiths).

[199] *X v Y* [1988] 2 All E.R. 648.

[200] *ABC v St George's Healthcare NHS Foundation Trust* [2017] EWCA Civ 336; [2017] P.I.Q.R. P15 (refusal to strike out such a claim as unarguable). Compare, however, *C v Cairns* [2003] Lloyd's Rep. Med. 90, exonerating a doctor for having failed in 1975 to pass on to the police suspicions of sexual interference with a child. See too R. Gilbar, "It's Arrived! Relational Autonomy Comes to Court: ABC v St George's Healthcare NHS Trust" (2018) 26 Med. L. Rev. 125.

(g) Professional liability: exclusion of duty

Excluding professional liability

Replace footnote 202 with:

[202] The interpretation of the clause can be a matter of some complexity: see, e.g. *University of Keele v Price Waterhouse* [2004] EWCA Civ 583; [2004] P.N.L.R. 43 (clause held not to cover liability in question). Note that as between commercially sophisticated parties, the previous tendency of judges to construe clauses against the person seeking to exclude liability is much reduced, with the emphasis lying now on a businesslike reading of the clause concerned. See the consulting engineers' case of *Persimmon Homes Ltd v Ove Arup & Partners Ltd* [2017] EWCA Civ 373; [2017] P.N.L.R. 29 at [56]–[59] **10-33**

(Jackson LJ); also G. McMeel, "The Impact of Exemption Clauses and Disclaimers: Construction, Contractual Estoppel and Public Policy", in A. Dyson, J. Gondkamp and F. Wilmot-Smith (eds), *Defences in Contract* (Oxford: Hart, 2017), p.234.

(h) Immunities from suit

(ii) Witness immunity and collateral attack on previous decisions

Testimony and connected matters

Replace footnote 245 with:

10-39 [245] [2011] UKSC 13; [2011] 2 A.C. 398. See too *Ridgeland Properties Ltd v Bristol CC* [2011] EWCA Civ 649; [2011] R.V.R. 232 at [47] (Sullivan LJ); K. Hughes [2011] C.L.J. 516, and S. Carr and H. Evans, "The Removal of Immunity for Expert Witnesses" (2011) 27 P.N. 128. *Jones v Kaney* seems to have had a cautious welcome in New Zealand: see *EBR Holdings Ltd (In Liq) v McLaren Guise Associates Ltd* [2016] NZCA 622; [2017] 3 N.Z.L.R. 589, refusing to strike out such a claim.

2. Medicine and allied professions

(a) Duties in general

Liability for refusal to provide treatment

Replace footnote 286 with:

10-46 [286] In *Barnett v Chelsea & Kensington HMC* [1969] 1 Q.B. 428, 435, where Nield J clearly suggested that a hospital casualty department would not be liable if it closed its doors and refused to see anyone. But in *Kent v Griffiths* [2001] Q.B. 36 it was held that ambulance crews owed at least some duty to arrive with due expedition, and it would seem difficult to distinguish the position of health authorities. In addition there might well be scope for liability under s.8 of the Human Rights Act, especially if the patient died and art.2 (the right to life) were engaged: cf. *Rabone v Pennine Care NHS Foundation Trust* [2012] UKSC 2; [2012] 2 A.C. 72, and more recently the decision of the ECtHR in *Fernandes v Portugal* (2018) 66 E.H.R.R. 28, accepting at [201] that where failure to provide treatment resulted from a "systemic or structural dysfunction" there might be a breach of art.2.

Liability to those other than patients

Replace paragraph with:

10-47 There is no reason why a doctor should not be liable in tort to someone other than his patient if the requirements of foreseeability and proximity are satisfied. Thus in *Evans v Liverpool Corp*[288] a hospital prematurely discharged a small boy with scarlet fever. The child went home and infected his family. The hospital escaped liability, but only on the basis that no negligence could be attributed to it.[289] Similarly, in *McFarlane v Tayside Health Board*[290] it was not disputed that where a hospital negligently advised that a father's vasectomy had been effective, it could be liable to the mother for the pangs of unnecessary childbirth. In addition, there is no reason why there should not be liability for psychiatric injuries to non-patients caused by various forms of medical malpractice.[291] However, the general rules applicable to such injuries[292] apply equally here, notably the requirement that the claim arise from witnessing a particular traumatic incident.[293] In practice this greatly reduces the scope for such claims in the medical context.[293A]

[288] [1906] 1 K.B. 160. This head of liability could be significant where, for example, negligent non-diagnosis of a STD causes the patient to infect his wife.

[289] Having employed an apparently competent doctor as an independent contractor.

[290] [2000] 2 A.C. 59, overruling *Emeh v Kensington & Chelsea & Westminster AHA* [1985] Q.B. 1012 on this point: see too *Kealey v Berezowski* (1996) 30 O.R. (3d) 37. Note that the case was pointedly not followed by the High Court of Australia: *Cattanach v Melchior* [2003] HCA 38; (2003) 215 C.L.R. 1.

New Brunswick similarly allows claims for upbringing costs: *Stockford v Johnston* (2008) 335 N.B.R. (2d) 74.

[291] *Farrell v Avon HA* [2001] Lloyd's Rep. Med. 458 (father has claim for psychiatric injury as primary victim on being falsely told baby dead and given wrong deceased infant to cuddle); *Froggatt v Chesterfield & North Derbyshire Royal Hospital NHS Trust* [2002] All E.R. (D) 218 (Dec) (unnecessary mastectomy: husband and son recover for psychiatric injury caused as a result); also *North Glamorgan NHS Trust v Walters* [2002] EWCA Civ 1792; [2003] P.I.Q.R. P16 and *RE (A Minor) v Calderdale NHS Foundation Trust* [2017] EWHC 824 (QB); (2017) 156 B.M.L.R. 204.

[292] See para.8-63 onwards.

[293] *Liverpool Women's Hospital NHS Foundation Trust v Ronayne* [2015] EWCA Civ 588; [2015] P.I.Q.R. P20; *Shorter v Surrey & Sussex Healthcare NHS Trust* [2015] EWHC 614 (QB); (2015) 144 B.M.L.R. 136; *Owers v Medway NHS Foundation Trust* [2015] EWHC 2363 (QB); [2015] Med. L.R. 561. For criticism, see A. Burrows & J. Burrows, "A Shocking Requirement in The Law on Negligence Liability for Psychiatric Illness" (2016) 24 Med. L. Rev. 278. See too *RE (a child) v Calderdale and Huddersfield NHS Foundation Trust* [2017] EWHC 824 (QB); (2017) 156 B.M.L.R. 204 (perinatal negligence leading to injury to baby and psychiatric injury to mother: mother can sue as primary victim since child not yet separate person at time of negligence).

[293A] Though it does not eliminate them. See, e.g. *YAH v Medway NHS Foundation Trust* [2018] EWHC 2964 (QB); [2019] 1 W.L.R. 1413 (psychiatric injury suffered by mother at seeing result of obstetric negligence on baby shortly after birth: mother primary victim within *Page v Smith* [1996] A.C. 155 and hence able to sue).

Replace paragraph with:

However, the limits of such liability need to be noted. For one thing, it seems difficult to make a medical practitioner liable for a pure omission under this head. Thus although there is some authority that a doctor or medical authority that knows a patient is dangerous owes a duty to take steps to restrain or otherwise prevent him from causing harm to a third party,[294] and that a health authority may have to take steps to test family members for inherited diseases where it knows from having treated a patient that they are likely to be suffering from them,[295] the courts have stopped short of saying that a doctor in diagnosing a patient owes a general duty to third parties who might be affected by the diagnosis.[296] Secondly, any duty tends to be limited to protecting third parties from actual illness or injury. With other losses, although it is certainly possible that there may be a duty,[297] in practice it is unlikely. Thus where an applicant for a job is required to be examined by his prospective employer's company doctor and the latter negligently reports him seriously unhealthy, it has been held that no duty of care is owed: the mere fact that negligence may foreseeably harm the applicant is insufficient to allow the court to infer an undertaking of responsibility towards him.[298] And similarly, where a consultant examining an injured footballer allegedly misdiagnosed his injuries and thereby unnecessarily deprived his club of his highly profitable services, it was held that no duty was owed to the club.[299] **10-48**

[294] A possibility apparently accepted in Australia (*Hunter & New England Local Health District v McKenna* [2014] HCA 44; (2014) 314 A.L.R. 505 at [31]. But there may be strong countervailing arguments in a particular case, notably the need strictly to circumscribe powers to constrain a patient against his will, which may make it appropriate to deny a duty. That was held to be the case in *Hunter* itself.

[295] *ABC v St George's Healthcare NHS Trust* [2017] EWCA Civ 336; [2017] P.I.Q.R. P15 (omission by father's doctor to inform daughter that father had Huntington's disease, allegedly resulting in possible defects in daughter's own child: strikeout refused). See also R. Gilbar, "It's Arrived! Relational Autonomy Comes to Court: ABC v St George's Healthcare NHS Trust" (2018) 26 Med. L. Rev. 125.

[296] *Smith v University of Leicester NHS Trust* [2016] EWHC 817 (QB) (late diagnosis of congenital disease: no duty owed to family of patient, even though latter would have been invited to be tested as a result of timeous diagnosis).

[297] e.g. if an employee wishing to move jobs requires a clean bill of health from his existing company doctor and the latter negligently misreports the state of his health: cf. *Spring v Guardian Assurance plc* [1995] 2 A.C. 296.

[298] *Kapfunde v Abbey National plc* [1998] I.R.L.R. 583.

[299] *West Bromwich Albion Football Club Ltd v El-Safty* [2006] EWCA Civ 1299; [2007] P.I.Q.R. P7 (criticised, J. O'Sullivan, "Negligent medical advice and financial loss: 'sick as a parrot'?" [2007] C.L.J. 14). See too *Bot v Barnick* [2018] EWHC 3132 (QB) (no liability to partner of patient for incautious remarks on patient's sanity which allegedly caused relationship problems).

(b) Consent to treatment

(ii) Children

Younger children

Replace paragraph with:

10-60 In the case of younger children who clearly have not yet reached the level of maturity and understanding to consent to treatment on their own behalf (i.e. *Gillick*-incompetent children), parental consent authorises any treatment clearly for the benefit of the child, and thus protects the doctor from a claim in battery. Parents do not however have a converse right to veto treatment. In cases of emergency, abandonment or neglect it is clear that doctors can lawfully act to safeguard a child's life or health without parental agreement on the basis of necessity.[389] Furthermore, even where parents honestly believe that they are acting in the child's best interests, their judgment may be overruled by the court. So in *Re B (A Minor) (Wardship: Medical Treatment)*[390] parents of a Downs syndrome baby refused consent to an operation necessary to save her life believing it would be kinder to let her die. The Court of Appeal ordered that surgery go ahead; it was not for parents—or courts—to say a child should die unless the quality of life confronting that child was "demonstrably awful".[391] On a similar principle, where parents refuse blood transfusions for religious reasons so as to endanger the child's life, an order is almost certain to be made to disregard the parental veto.[391A] Conversely, while parents' wishes that a child be given a chance to live are in account and likely to be given great weight, they too are not conclusive if, on the whole, it is in the child's best interests that further treatment be withheld.[392]

[389] *Gillick v West Norfolk AHA* [1986] A.C. 112 at 189 (Lord Scarman) and 205 (Lord Templeman). And see too the even more extreme *Re A (Children) (Conjoined Twins: Surgical Separation)* [2001] Fam. 147 (necessity justifies surgical separation of Siamese twins even though death of one certain to result).

[390] [1981] 1 W.L.R. 1421.

[391] As was held to be the case in *Re C (A Minor) (Wardship: Medical Treatment)* [1990] Fam. 26; *Re J (A Minor) (Wardship: Medical Treatment)* [1991] Fam. 33. On the other hand, this is not an absolute rule: see *Re T (A Minor)(Wardship: Medical Treatment)* [1997] 1 W.L.R. 242, where a mother's decision to refuse consent to a liver transplant for a baby was upheld in exceptional circumstances. See too *X (Baby) v An NHS Trust* [2012] EWHC 2188 (Fam); (2012) 127 B.M.L.R. 188.

[391A] See, for example, *Re O (A Minor) (Medical Treatment)* [1993] 2 F.L.R. 149.

[392] *Portsmouth NHS Trust v Wyatt* [2004] EWHC 2247 (Fam); [2005] 1 F.L.R. 21. See too two tragic cases of very young children in a close to vegetative state through irreversible brain damage: *Great Ormond Street Hospital for Children NHS Foundation Trust v Yates* [2017] EWCA Civ 410; [2018] 4 W.L.R. 5, especially at [112], and *Re E (A Child)* [2018] EWCA Civ 550; [2019] 1 W.L.R. 594. In both orders were made authorising withdrawal of treatment. Note that in *Gard v UK* (2017) 65 E.H.R.R. SE9 (a follow-on from *Yates*, above, following the refusal on 8 June 2017 of leave to appeal), the position in English law with regard withdrawal of life support from a seriously ill baby was held in to be accordance with art.8 of the ECHR. Generally note E. Cave, "Who Knows Best (Interests)? The Case of Charlie Gard" (2018) 26 Med. L. Rev. 500.

(iii) Persons suffering from mental incapacity

Non-detainable mentally incapacitated patients

Replace paragraph with:

10-63 At common law,[401] a mentally incapacitated person over the age of 18 could not validly consent to, or refuse, treatment. Nor could his relatives consent on his behalf, or for that matter the court[402] (though there could be a declaration as to lawfulness on the basis that medical treatment was in the patient's best interests[403] if carried out to save life or prevent deterioration in physical or mental health).[404] Today, however, the matter is governed by the Mental Capacity Act 2005,[405] providing as follows. Where a person lacks capacity to decide,[406] then under s.5(2) any treatment is justified if reasonably believed by the person giving it to be in that person's best interests.[407] A number of safeguards apply. The doctor[408] must try to encourage the patient to participate in the decision;[409] consider his past wishes, beliefs and values, if known;[410] and furthermore consider the views of anyone the patient wishes to be consulted, and those of anyone else caring for him or interested in his welfare.[411] In addition, forcible treatment is justified only where the person providing it reasonably believes it is necessary to prevent harm to the patient,[412] and where that treatment is in fact a proportionate response.[413] It should be noted that the defence under s.5 applies not only where the patient is in fact incapable, but where the doctor reasonably believes him to be so.[414] In addition, the court now has an explicit statutory jurisdiction to make a declaration as to the lawfulness or otherwise of treatment,[415] a power which will normally be exercised in favour of treatment,[416] though obviously not invariably so.[417] In addition there is a power to make a decision on behalf of the patient[418] or appoint a person (known as a "deputy") to decide on his behalf.[419] Pending an application to the court, there is a general immunity in respect of treatment to preserve the patient's life.[420] Where a person is already in a hospital or care home, there is an additional power in the administration of the organisation to detain that person and provide compulsory treatment to sustain life or prevent serious deterioration pending a court order,[421] unless a valid advance direction or other authorised decision to refuse treatment is in force.[422]

[401] The common law position remains relevant for events before 1 October 2007 (when the relevant provisions of the Mental Capacity Act 2005 came into force), and after that date for any matters not pre-empted by the 2005 Act.

[402] Since the disappearance of the former *parens patriae* jurisdiction of the High Court: see *Re F (Mental Patient: Sterilisation)* [1990] 2 A.C. 1, 59 onwards Lord Bridge in *Re F* lamented the lack of a specific jurisdiction to consent for the patient: ibid. at 52.

[403] Including an interim declaration: see *NHS Trust v T (adult patient: refusal of medical treatment)* [2004] EWHC 1279 (Fam); [2005] 1 All E.R. 387, applying CPR 25.1(1)(b).

[404] See *Re F (Mental Patient: Sterilisation)* [1990] 2 A.C. 1, especially at 55 (Lord Brandon). See too *Airedale NHS Trust v Bland* [1993] A.C. 789.

[405] An Act based largely on Law Commission Report No.231, *Mental Incapacity* (1995). See O. Ward, "The Mental Capacity Act 2005" [2005] N.I.L.Q. 275; J. Coggon, "Ignoring the Moral and Intellectual Shape of the Law after Bland: The Unintended Side-Effect of a Sorry Compromise" (2007) 27 L.S. 110. It has been in force since 1 October 2007. A Code of Practice as to the application of the Act is issued by the Ministry of Justice pursuant to ss.42 and 43, the current version dating from 2007.

[406] i.e. where he cannot understand or weigh relevant information, or communicate a decision, owing to impairment of, or a disturbance in the functioning of, the mind or brain: 2005 Act s.2(1). An important feature of the legislation is that a person may well have capacity to take some decisions but not others: see *Masterman-Lister v Jewell* [2002] EWCA Civ 1889; [2003] 1 W.L.R. 1511 and *Re W (medical treatment: anorexia)* [2016] EWCOP 13; (2016) 151 B.M.L.R. 220.

[407] A concept which, it should be noted, does not encompass anything motivated by a desire to bring about the patient's death: s.4(5). On this see J. Coggon, "Ignoring the Moral and Intellectual Shape of the Law after Bland: The Unintended Side-Effect of a Sorry Compromise" (2007) 27 L.S. 110. Best interests may where appropriate include the promotion of altruistic aims: see *Home Secretary v Skripal* [2018] EWCOP 6; [2018] Med. L.R. 276 (taking of blood sample from unconscious victim of alleged poison attack by foreign agents for purposes of analysis to determine origin of poison).

[408] Or, mutatis mutandis, any other medical personnel involved.

[409] s.4(4).

[410] s.4(6). Presumably this means that it would be hard, though not necessarily impossible, to justify administering a blood transfusion to a known Jehovah's Witness.

[411] s.4(7). Failure to do this may render an action unlawful and possibly trigger a breach of the patient's right to private and family life under art.8 of the ECHR: *Winspear v City Hospitals Sunderland NHS Foundation Trust* [2015] EWHC 3250 (QB); [2016] Q.B. 691.

[412] s.6(2).

[413] s.6(3).

[414] See s.5(1). The point was confirmed at *An NHS Trust v Y* [2018] UKSC 46; [2018] 3 W.L.R. 751 at [92].

[415] s.15. Nevertheless the intervention of the court is not necessary, even where what is in the patient's best interests is withdrawal of CANH leading to certain death. This was confirmed not to be contrary to art.2 of the EHCR in *An NHS Trust v Y* [2018] UKSC 46; [2018] 3 W.L.R. 751. Earlier authorities had suggested that at common law such consent might be necessary: e.g. *Airedale NHS Trust v Bland* [1993] A.C. 789 at 859, 873, 875, 885.

[416] See *Aintree University Hospitals NHS Foundation Trust v James* [2013] UKSC 67; [2014] A.C. 591 (only appropriate not to allow treatment if ineffective and of no benefit at all); also the earlier *DH NHS Foundation Trust v PS* [2010] EWHC 1217 (Fam); [2010] 2 F.L.R. 1236, on which R. Mullender, "Involuntary medical treatment, incapacity, and respect" (2011) 127 L.Q.R. 167; and also *W v M* [2011] EWHC 2443 (CoP); [2012] 1 W.L.R. 1653.

[417] See *A NHS Foundation Trust v X* [2014] EWCOP 35; (2014) 140 B.M.L.R. 41 (anorexic and alcohol-dependent patient who maintained habits despite repeated force-feeding in hospital: although highest regard due to the preservation of life, declaration granted that in the circumstances, lawful not to force-feed). Provided that a suitable legal framework is provided, a court jurisdiction to authorise non-treatment is likely to survive a challenge under art.2 of the ECHR: see the decision of the ECtHR in *Lambert v France* (2016) 62 E.H.R.R. 2; (2015) 145 B.M.L.R. 28; An *NHS Trust v Y* [2018] UKSC 46; [2018] 3 W.L.R. 751. Note too *Gard v UK* (2017) 65 E.H.R.R. SE9, confirming the position in *Lambert*.

[418] See ss.16(1)(a), 17(1)(d). There was no such power at common law: *Re F (Mental Patient: Sterilisation)* [1990] 2 A.C. 1, 59 onwards.

[419] s.16(2)(b). It would seem that the "treatment" to which the deputy must consent does not include the withdrawal of life-support: see *Aintree University Hospitals NHS Foundation Trust v James* [2013] UKSC 67; [2014] A.C. 591 at [18]–[19] (Lady Hale) (though contra in Canada, it would seem: see *Rasouli (Litigation Guardian) v Sunnybrook Health Sciences Centre* [2013] SCC 53; (2013) 364 D.L.R. (4th) 195).

[420] See ss.6(6), 6(7).

[421] Mental Capacity Act 2005 s.4A (in force from 1 April 2009). In certain cases, however, such detention may fall foul of art.5 or art.8 of the ECHR, as in *Hillingdon LBC v Neary* [2011] EWHC 1377 (CoP); [2011] 4 All E.R. 584 (detention of autistic patient in support unit without proper regard to whether better off there, or to his own clearly-expressed desire to be at home).

[422] Mental Capacity Act 2005 Sch.A1 para.12(1)(f).

(c) What amounts to medical negligence

(i) In general

What amounts to medical negligence: general

Replace paragraph with:

10-65 To amount to medical negligence, any alleged error in diagnosis and/or treatment must be shown to derive from a failure to attain the required degree of skill and competence of a reasonable practitioner.[428] This question falls to be answered, of course, in the light of the practitioner's specialisation[429] and the post that he holds.[430] Thus a general practitioner is not expected to attain the standard of a consultant obstetrician when delivering a baby. However if he elects to practise obstetrics he must attain the skill of a general practitioner undertaking obstetric care of his own patients,[431] and in all cases general practitioners and other doctors must exercise care in determining when to refer a patient for a consultant's or other second opinion.[432] In determining the standard of competence to be achieved, the normal negligence rule applies that no allowance is made for inexperience or personal lack of competence.[433] A practitioner faced with a matter beyond his competence must refer the patient to a consultant or other expert;[434] by doing so he will discharge his duty.[435] Similarly, all hospitals are on principle judged by the same standard: a prisoner, for example, is entitled to the same standard of care in a prison hospital (subject to those constraints necessitated by his incarceration itself) as any other patient.[436] In *Wilsher*, Mustill LJ left open the question of whether the standard of care might be affected by "battle conditions".[437] It is now clear, however, that this is a very relevant factor, and a doctor should not be harshly judged when faced with a life-threatening condition where immediate measures are required.[438] In a suitable case a practitioner may be held liable for unprofessional conduct not of itself amounting to medical fault.[438A]

[428] "The test is the standard of the ordinary skilled man exercising and professing to have that special skill. A man need not profess the highest expert skill, it is well established law that it is sufficient if he exercises the ordinary skill of a competent man exercising that particular art." See *Bolam v Friern HMC* [1957] 1 W.L.R. 582, 586 (McNair J). This was approved by the Privy Council in *Chin Keow v Government of Malaysia* [1967] 1 W.L.R. 813 and by the House of Lords in *Whitehouse v Jordan* [1981] 1 W.L.R. 246. See too *Maynard v West Midlands RHA* [1984] 1 W.L.R. 634 and *Sidaway v Bethlem Royal Hospital* [1985] A.C. 871. On the other hand, there may be a tendency to avoid over-strict standards where this might discourage innovative or adventurous treatment: cf. the cautious approach in the New Zealand decision in *Ellis v Counties Manukau District Health Board* [2007] 1 N.Z.L.R. 196.

[429] *Maynard v West Midlands RHA* [1984] 1 W.L.R. 634, 638 (Lord Scarman); cf. *Shakoor v Kang Situ* [2001] 1 W.L.R. 410 (Chinese traditional healing).

[430] *Wilsher v Essex AHA* [1987] Q.B. 730, 751 (Mustill LJ) (reversed on a different point at [1988] A.C. 1074). See too *FB v Princess Alexandra Hospital NHS Trust* [2017] EWCA Civ 334; [2017] P.I.Q.R. P17 at [57]–[60] (Jackson LJ: standard reckoned by post held or then being fulfilled, e.g. in the case of "acting up"). Note that his Lordship left it open whether a higher duty might be owed in contract: see [61]–[62].

[431] *Hucks v Cole, The Times,* 9 May 1968; [1993] 4 Med. L.R. 393.

[432] *Payne v St Helier Group HMC* [1952] C.L.Y. 2442.

[433] *Wilsher v Essex Area Health Authority* [1987] Q.B. 730: reversed on another point [1988] A.C. 1074. See also *Djemal v Bexley HA* [1995] 6 Med. L.R. 269. The same goes for any other incapacity personal to the practitioner, such as his own illness: *Nickolls v Ministry of Health, The Times,* 4 February 1955, CA. See also *FB v Princess Alexandra Hospital NHS Trust* [2017] EWCA Civ 334; [2017] P.I.Q.R. P17 at [59] (Jackson LJ).

[434] *Payne v St Helier Group HMC* [1952] C.L.Y. 2992. See also *Poole v Morgan* [1987] 3 W.W.R. 217 (newly trained ophthalmologist liable for not referring complicated case to consultant).

[435] *Wilsher v Essex AHA* [1987] Q.B. 730, 774 (Glidewell LJ).

[436] *Brooks v Home Office* [1999] 2 F.L.R. 33. Pill J's contrary suggestion in *Knight v Home Office* [1990] 3 All E.R. 237, 243 now seems discredited.

[437] See [1987] Q.B. 730, 749.

[438] *Vernon v Bloomsbury HA* [1995] 6 Med. L.R. 297 (not negligent considerably to exceed recommended dose of gentamicin in emergency brought on by endocarditis); *Mulholland v Medway NHS Foundation Trust* [2015] EWHC 268 (QB); (2015) 144 B.M.L.R. 50 (busy hospital doctor entitled to rely on advice from A&E team without carrying out exhaustive analysis of his own). cf. *Hardaker v Newcastle HA* [2002] Lloyd's Rep. Med. 512 (re duty owed by the police as surrogate providers of emergency medical attention).

[438A] *Brayshaw v Partners of Apsley Surgery* [2018] EWHC 3286 (QB); (2018) 166 B.M.L.R. 76 (wholly inappropriate religious proselytism causing disturbed patient to suffer further mental health problems).

Effect of departure from accepted practice

Replace footnote 443 with:

[443] [2007] EWHC 487 (QB); (2007) 96 B.M.L.R. 180. But the departure must be relatively substantial: 10-67

see *Darnley v Croydon Health Services NHS Trust* [2017] EWCA Civ 151; [2017] Med. L.R. 245 (15-minute officially-recommended A&E waiting time extensible at least to 30 minutes without a finding of negligence. The case was successfully appealed on other grounds: see *Darnley v Croydon Health Services NHS Trust* [2018] UKSC 50; [2018] 3 W.L.R. 1153). The importance of guidelines and protocols in this connection is touched on in M. Brazier and E. Cave, *Medicine, Patients & the Law*, 6th edn (2016) para.7.11.

Negligence: the Bolam test and professional practice

Replace paragraph with:

10-68 The standard of care demanded of medical practitioners is that required of any professional person. However, the vital decision in *Bolam v Friern H.M.C.*[447] makes it clear that, in determining whether a defendant has fallen below the required standard of care, great regard must be shown to responsible medical opinion, and to the fact that reasonable doctors may differ. As McNair J put it, a practitioner who acts in conformity with an accepted current practice is not negligent "merely because there is a body of opinion which would take a contrary view".[448] The point is neatly illustrated by *Maynard v West Midlands Regional Health Authority*.[449] The defendants subjected the claimant to a diagnostic procedure, mediastinoscopy. This carried a risk of damage to the vocal chords, which unfortunately materialised. Having heard experts on both sides, the trial judge held for the claimant. His judgment was overruled in the Court of Appeal and the House of Lords. As Lord Scarman said, "a judge's 'preference' for one body of distinguished professional opinion to another also professionally distinguished is not sufficient to establish negligence in a practitioner."[450] Again, in *Whitehouse v Jordan*[451] the allegation was that the defendant persisted too long in an attempt to deliver a baby by use of forceps and should have proceeded more speedily to Caesarean section. Despite damning evidence from expert witnesses of the dangers of pulling so many times with forceps, the House of Lords reversed the judge's finding of negligence. The defendant's equally eminent experts had testified that they would have followed the practice. It followed that the claimant failed the *Bolam* test. As with individual practitioners, so with organisations: a general hospital policy will not generally be held to amount to negligence if supported by a respectable, if minority, body of opinion.[452] The practical result is that proving fault in a doctor on the basis of his choice of a particular technique or method can be very difficult. Since even a relatively small body of supportive medical opinion may be effective to satisfy the *Bolam* test,[453] the claimant effectively has to show that no body of respectable medical opinion would have supported what the doctor did.

[447] [1957] 1 W.L.R. 582.

[448] *Bolam v Friern HMC* [1957] 1 W.L.R. 582, 587–588. This statement formed part of a jury direction in a case where the administration of ECT had disastrous side-effects. The jury took the hint and found for the defendants. In *Hii Chii Kok v Ooi Peng Jin London Lucien* [2017] SGCA 38; (2017) 162 B.M.L.R. 28 at [79]–[83], Sundaresh Menon CJ in the Singapore Court of Appeal resisted an invitation to move away from the *Bolam* test, made on the basis that it was too favourable to the medical profession.

[449] [1984] 1 W.L.R. 582. Other examples are legion. See, e.g. *Hughes v Waltham Forest AHA* [1991] 2 Med.L.R. 155; *Rance v Mid-Downs HA* [1991] 1 Q.B. 587; and *Buxton v Abertawe Bro Morgannwg University Local Health Board* [2010] EWHC 1187 (QB); (2010) 115 B.M.L.R. 62; *Baker v Cambridgeshire and Peterborough NHS Foundation Trust* [2015] EWHC 609 (QB), [2], [29] (application of *Bolam* test to psychiatrist). Note also *D v South Tyneside NHS Trust* [2003] EWCA Civ 878; [2004] P.I.Q.R. P12 (choice of healthcare trust not to observe disturbed patient hourly is within *Bolam* and hence no liability for self-harm that such observation would have prevented).

[450] See [1984] 1 W.L.R. 582, 587–588. See too *Lane v Worcestershire Acute Hospitals NHS Trust* [2017] EWHC 1900 (QB) (priority between two urgent treatments, both necessary; not for judge to select). But note *Smith v Tunbridge Wells HA* [1994] 5 Med. L.R. 334.

[451] [1981] 1 W.L.R. 246; see M. Brazier and E. Cave, *Medicine Patients & The Law*, 6th edn (2016), paras 8.13 to 8.14.

[452] *Cowley v Cheshire & Merseyside Strategic HA* [2007] EWHC 48 (QB); (2007) 94 B.M.L.R. 29 (hospital policy of denying certain drugs to pregnant women until onset of labour professionally defensible, and hence not negligent).

[453] *De Freitas v O'Brien* [1995] 6 Med. L.R. 108 (11 spinal surgeons). See too *Sharpe v Southend HA* [1997] 8 Med. L.R. 299, where Cresswell J emphasised that a medical expert testifying as to his preferred practice should indicate as a matter of course whether he thought a responsible body of medical opinion might disagree with him.

Replace footnote 456 with:

[456] [1998] A.C. 232; also *C v North Cumbria University Hospitals NHS Trust* [2014] EWHC 61 (QB); [2014] Med. L.R. 189 at [23]–[25] (Green J). See generally R. Mulheron, "Trumping Bolam: a critical legal analysis of Bolitho's 'gloss'" [2010] C.L.J. 609. See too *E v Australian Red Cross Society* (1991) 99 A.L.R. 601 (warning against too ready acceptance of common medical practice). In *Hii Chii Kok v Ooi Peng Jin London Lucien* [2017] SGCA 38; (2017) 162 B.M.L.R. 28 at [63]–[64], Sundaresh Menon CJ in the Singapore Court of Appeal pointed out that the *Bolitho* proposition was not inconsistent with *Bolam* but was actually inherent in it: the fact that the courts should not take sides between legitimate expert views meant that views that for some reason were clearly illegitimate should not receive credit. **10-69**

(ii) Diagnosis

Negligence in diagnosis

Replace footnote 466 with:

[466] *Langley v Campbell, The Times,* 6 November 1975. See too the decision of the Supreme Court of Ireland in *Collins v Mid-Western Health Board* [2000] 1 I.R. 154 (failure to spot potential seriousness of respiratory problems: patient later died from brain haemorrhage), and the Scottish decision in *Brown v Craig Nevis Surgery* [2018] CSOH 84 (tell-tale signs of angina). **10-71**

Replace footnote 472 with:

[472] *R v Croydon HA* [1998] Lloyd's Rep. Med. 44; cf. the criminal law decision in *R. v Rose* [2017] EWCA Crim 1168; [2018] Q.B. 328 (optometrist failing to spot obvious signs of deadly hydrocephalus not guilty of manslaughter). **10-72**

(iii) Treatment and prescribing

Errors in treatment

Replace footnote 490 with:

[490] *Voller v Portsmouth Corp* (1947) 203 L.T.J. 264. The same goes for other professionals: see *Darnley v Croydon Health Services NHS Trust* [2018] UKSC 50; [2018] 3 W.L.R. 1153 at [22] (constant pressure on A&E departments likely to be highly influential in assessing whether fault shown). **10-75**

(iv) Failure to inform

Negligent failure to inform

Replace paragraph with:

10-78 It was long assumed that the *Bolam* test referred to above applied to this duty as to any other:[507] provided that the practitioner followed respectable practice in deciding on the information to be given, he was protected.[508] But in 2015 the Supreme Court in *Montgomery v Lanarkshire Health Board,*[509] following the lead of several other common law jurisdictions,[510] departed from earlier House of Lords authority[511] and took the view that such an approach was inappropriate in respect of a duty whose raison d'être was the protection of a patient's personal autonomy and right to self-determination. Under the view taken by a majority of the court,[512] the duty on doctors is now simply one to take reasonable care to ensure that a patient is aware of all material risks of injury inherent in a given treatment.[513] Unlike decisions as to what treatment is appropriate, rightly left largely up to medical judgment,[513A] this is a matter for the court to determine. The relevant test is whether a reasonable person in the patient's position[514] would be likely to attach significance to the risk,[515] since only thus can the patient's right to autonomy be given effect.[516] Unless the patient makes it clear that he does not wish to discuss the matter and wants to consent in any case, he must be apprised of any material risks involved in any recommended treatment and of any reasonable alternative or variant treatments.[517] In deciding whether an alternative treatment is reasonable, it seems that the *Bolam* criterion applies: but in advising of the risks associated with such treatments, *Montgomery* rules.[517A] The only qualifications are these: (i) a doctor may withhold information seriously detrimental to the patient's health,[518] and (ii) the requirement does not apply in circumstances of necessity, for example where an unconscious patient requires urgent treatment.[519] To satisfy the *Montgomery* requirements, any information given must be comprehensible and such as to enable a patient to make an informed decision:[520] a blizzard of technicality followed by a formulaic signature on a consent form is not enough.[521]

[507] Indeed, it applies "to every aspect of the duty of care owed by a doctor to his patient in the exercise of his healing functions as respects that patient:"—Lord Diplock in *Sidaway v Bethlem Royal Hospital* [1985] A.C. 871, 893–894.

[508] See *Sidaway v Bethlem Royal Hospital* [1985] A.C. 871, and *Blyth v Bloomsbury AHA* (1987) [1993] 4 Med. L.R. 151 CA. There was some justification for this: an over-propensity to warn may be self-defeating, as observed by Lord Templeman in *Sidaway* ([1985] A.C. 871, 904) and in R. Heywood, "Excessive Risk Disclosure: the Effects of the Law on Medical Practice" (2005) 7 Med. Law Int. 93.

[509] [2015] UKSC 11; [2015] A.C. 1430; on which, see R. Heywood and J. Miola, "The changing face of pre-operative medical disclosure: placing the patient at the heart of the matter" (2017) 133 L.Q.R. 296. See too *Healy v Buckley* [2015] IECA 251; *Hii Chii Kok v Ooi Peng Jin London Lucien* [2017] SGCA 38; (2017) 162 B.M.L.R. 28.

[510] Notably Australia (*Rogers v Whittaker* (1992) 110 C.L.R. 625), Canada (*Reibl v Hughes* (1980) 114 D.L.R. (3d) 1) and Ireland (*Fitzpatrick v White* [2007] IESC 51; [2008] 3 I.R. 551).

[511] i.e. *Sidaway v Bethlem Royal Hospital* [1985] A.C. 871, above.

[512] Lord Neuberger PSC and Lords Kerr, Clarke, Wilson, Reed and Hodge.

[513] [2015] UKSC 11; [2015] A.C. 1430 at [82]. See C.P. McGrath, "'Trust me, I'm a patient . . .': disclosure standards and the patient's right to decide" [2015] C.L.J. 211; R. Heywood, "R.I.P. Sidaway: patient-oriented disclosure—a standard worth waiting for?" (2015) 23 Med. L. Rev. 455. As to what it is reasonable to expect disclosure of, this is a function of likelihood and severity: *Hii Chii Kok v Ooi Peng Jin London Lucien* [2017] SGCA 38; (2017) 162 B.M.L.R. 28 at [140].

[513A] A point confirmed in the Scottish case of *Taylor v Dailly Health Centre* [2018] CSOH 91; 2018 S.L.T. 1324 (failure to diagnose ACS and advise accordingly). The determination of whether the relevant risk of injury exists in the first place is, it seems, likewise regarded as a matter of medical judgment subject to *Bolam*: see *Duce v Worcestershire Acute Hospitals NHS Trust* [2018] EWCA Civ 1307; [2018] P.I.Q.R. P18, especially at [42]–[44].

[514] Unless the practitioner knows, or should know, that this specific patient attaches significance to it: in that case the matter has to be disclosed (see [2015] UKSC 11; [2015] A.C. 1430 at [87]). The characteristics of the actual patient may be of some little importance, for example where it is known that he attaches importance to a given sport or pastime: *Thefaut v Johnston* [2017] EWHC 497 (QB); [2017] Med. L.R. 319 at [56] (Green J).

[515] [2015] UKSC 11; [2015] A.C. 1430 at [87]-[88]. It follows that genuinely negligible risks can still be ignored: see *Tasmin v Barts Health NHS Trust* [2015] EWHC 3135 (QB) (tiny risks inherent in foetal blood sampling), and *also A v East Kent Hospital University NHS Foundation Trust* [2015] EWHC 1038 (QB); [2015] Med. L.R. 262 at [84]. The same has been said in Singapore: *Hii Chii Kok v Ooi Peng Jin London Lucien* [2017] SGCA 38; (2017) 162 B.M.L.R. 28 at [140]–[141]. In the same case it was said that entirely obvious risks need not be disclosed.

[516] [2015] UKSC 11; [2015] A.C. 1430 at [75]-[81]. See too at [108] (Lady Hale). For discussion see J. Laing, "Delivering informed consent post-*Montgomery*: Implications for medical practice and professionalism" (2017) 33 P.N. 128; J. Herring, "Elbow Room for Best Practice? Montgomery, Patients' Values, and Balanced Decision-Making in Person-Centred Clinical Care" (2017) 25 Med. L. Rev. 582.

[517] [2015] UKSC 11; [2015] A.C. 1430 at [87]. The result is that even if the patient is treated impeccably, if any injury in fact results he can sue for it. A straightforward example is *Hassell v Hillingdon*

Hospitals NHS Foundation Trust [2018] EWHC 164 (QB); (2018) 162 B.M.L.R. 120 (spinal operation for degenerate disc carried out with all care leaves patient paralysed: hospital liable because perceptible risk not disclosed, and, had it been, patient would have opted for conservative treatment). Note too *AH v Greater Glasgow Health Board* [2018] CSOH 57; 2018 S.L.T. 535 at [87], doubting whether the limitations in *Hughes-Holland v BPE Solicitors* [2017] UKSC 21; [2018] A.C. 589 apply in such cases. That the patient can decline further information is made clear in *Hii Chii Kok v Ooi Peng Jin London Lucien* [2017] SGCA 38; (2017) 162 B.M.L.R. 28 at [150].

517A See the carefully-argued Scottish decision in *AH v Greater Glasgow Health Board* [2018] CSOH 57; 2018 S.L.T. 535 at [43]–[45] (Lord Boyd).

518 [2015] UKSC 11; [2015] A.C. 1430 at [88]. On this see E. Cave, "The ill-informed: Consent to medical treatments and the thrapeutic exception" (2017) 46 C.L.W.R. 140.

519 [2015] UKSC 11; [2015] A.C. 1430 at [88].

520 But if it is, the presence of a minor inaccuracy is not fatal: *Connolly v Croydon Health Services NHS Trust* [2015] EWHC 1339 (QB). See too *Ollosson v Lee* [2019] EWHC 784 (QB) (oral warning of "small" risk of testicular pain following vasectomy sufficient without going into further detail).

521 [2015] UKSC 11; [2015] A.C. 1430 at [90]; see too *Thefaut v Johnston* [2017] EWHC 497 (QB); [2017] Med. L.R. 319 at [59] (Green J).

Replace paragraph with:

The principle in *Montgomery*, moreover, applies not only to therapy proper but to all medical advice, so that it covers (for example) advice whether to continue with labour or submit to a Caesarian birth.[522] No doubt it also covers warnings as to the risks inherent in medical experimentation.[523] Indeed, despite the lack of any potential interference with the patient's autonomy in deciding whether to submit to treatment, it now seems that it will be applied to all cases turning on advice or the lack of it. Thus in *Spencer v Hillingdon Hospital NHS Trust*[524] it was equally held to apply to failure to advise post-operative treatment; and in *Webster v Burton Hospitals NHS Foundation Trust*[525] the Court of Appeal applied *Montgomery* rather than *Bolam* to a failure to advise early inducement in a troublesome pregnancy. Indeed, these developments seem to indicate that in many medical contexts, *Montgomery* is increasingly becoming the rule and *Bolam* the exception. On the other hand, the limits of *Montgomery* need to be noted. In particular, while injury suffered as a result of treatment given without informed consent can form the subject of an action, the mere fact of failure to inform the patient properly is not of itself actionable.[525A] **10-79**

522 *Tasmin v Barts Health NHS Trust* [2015] EWHC 3135 (QB).

523 So held in Canada: *Halushka v University of Saskatchewan* (1965) 53 D.L.R. (2d) 436.

524 *Spencer v Hillingdon Hostpital NHS Trust* [2015] EWHC 1058 (QB): see especially at [32].

525 [2017] EWCA Civ 62; [2017] Med. L.R. 113. See also *Hii Chii Kok v Ooi Peng Jin London Lucien* [2017] SGCA 38; (2017) 162 B.M.L.R. 28 at [121].

525A A point put beyond doubt by the Court of Appeal in *Shaw v Kovac* [2017] EWCA Civ 1028; [2017] 1 W.L.R. 4773. Similarly it is always open to a defendant to plead that the claimant would have opted for the relevant procedure in any case: e.g. *Diamond v Royal Devon & Exeter NHS Foundation Trust* [2019] EWCA Civ 585.

(d) Medical negligence: particular issues

(i) Self-harm

Self-harm: vulnerable victims

Replace paragraph with:

Whatever the position with a sane and unconstrained adult, it is clear that where a person is particularly vulnerable, as with a child, prisoner or mental patient, matters are different and there may here be a duty of care.[528] This applies to medical **10-81** professionals as to any other defendant.[529] Moreover, human rights jurisprudence makes it clear that in such cases art.2[530] and possibly art.8[531] of the Convention are engaged. In *Savage v South Essex Partnership NHS Foundation Trust*[532] the House of Lords accordingly held potentially liable a mental hospital which failed to take steps to prevent the suicide of a detained mental patient. If, they said, a hospital either failed to take general measures to guard against suicide by mental patients, or knowing of a particular risk of suicide failed to take reasonable steps to stop it, they would be liable.[533] In the later *Rabone v Pennine Care NHS Foundation Trust*[534] the Supreme Court set its seal on this development by applying it to an informal, non-detained patient negligently allowed leave in the course of which she hanged herself. The principle, it was said, applied not simply to those under state constraint, but to anyone "especially vulnerable by reason of their physical or mental condition".[535] It follows from this that health professionals dealing with vulnerable patients, be they in prison hospitals,[536] mental hospitals or possibly even in the hands of ordinary doctors or other professionals,[536A] will owe this limited duty to prevent actual or attempted suicide. In a suitable case where the patient retains a degree of autonomy, a deduction for contributory negligence will be appropriate,[536B] as it is elsewhere where suicide is made the subject of a wrongful death claim.[536C]

[528] *Reeves v Metropolitan Police Comm'r* [2000] 1 A.C. 360 (duty to guard against suicide by prisoner).

[529] e.g. *Baker v Cambridgeshire and Peterborough NHS Foundation Trust* [2015] EWHC 609 (QB) at [27] (indication by GP of possible suicidal tendencies in person with bipolar affective disorder: duty in psychiatrist to whom referred to take steps). This is also implicit in cases such as *Rabone v Pennine Care NHS Foundation Trust* [2012] UKSC 2; [2012] 2 A.C. 72.

[530] e.g. *Keenan v UK* (2001) 33 E.H.R.R. 913; cf. *Kilinĉ v Turkey* (Application No 40145/98) (unreported) ECtHR, 7 June 2005.

[531] e.g. *K v Central & North West London Mental Health NHS Trust* [2008] EWHC 1217 (QB); [2008] P.I.Q.R. P19 at [73]. The argument is that an unsuccessful suicide attempt or other self-harm may compromise a person's later private life.

[532] [2008] UKHL 74; [2009] 1 A.C. 681.

[533] Strictly speaking, *Savage* was a claim not at common law but for damages for breach of art.2 of the Convention. But it is suggested that the same result would follow at common law.

[534] [2012] UKSC 2; [2012] 2 A.C. 72. This development was approved wholeheartedly by the ECtHR in *Reynolds v UK* (2012) 55 E.H.R.R. 35.

[535] [2012] UKSC 2; [2012] 2 A.C. 72 at [22] (Lord Dyson). This again was decided under s.8 of the Human Rights Act 1998, the claimants being the suicide's parents, who were barred from claiming under domestic law by the limited provisions of the Fatal Accidents Act 1976 as to who could claim for wrongful death. See generally A. Tettenborn, "Wrongful Death, Human Rights and the Fatal Accidents Act" (2012) 128 L.Q.R. 327.

[536] Cf. *Nyang v G4S Care & Justice Services Ltd* [2013] EWHC 3946 (QB) (person detained pending deportation: accepted, duty to prevent self-harm).

[536A] See *PPX v Aulakh* [2019] EWHC 717 (QB), where a GP in charge of a troubled patient was regarded as being under a duty to refer him to a crisis mental health team if he had given indications of a present suicidal intention (which on the facts he had not).

[536B] In *PPX v Aulakh* [2019] EWHC 717 (QB), above, it was held that if liability had been established a 25% reduction would have been appropriate.

[536C] See generally *Corr v IBC Vehicles Ltd* [2008] UKHL 13; [2008] 1 A.C. 884; see para.3-69.

(iii) Failed sterilisation

Failed sterilisation: limitations on recovery

Replace footnote 566 with:

10-87 [566] Lord Steyn specifically left it open whether contractual claims might be treated differently: [2000] 2 A.C. 59, 76. He also left it open whether a different rule would apply to a disabled child. See [2000]

2 A.C. 59, 84. On the former point, in *ARB v IVF Hammersmith Ltd* [2018] EWCA Civ 2803; [2019] Med. L.R. 119 the Court of Appeal decided, in another context, that the bar applied equally to contractual claims.

Replace paragraph with:

However, after *McFarlane* there were a number of developments. In *Parkinson v St James & Seacroft University NHS Trust*[569] the Court of Appeal distinguished *McFarlane* and held that where the child was born disabled there could be a claim for the extra costs incurred over and above normal child-rearing expenses. After this, the matter came again before a seven-judge House of Lords in *Rees v Darlington Memorial Hospital NHS Trust*,[570] where the issue was whether *McFarlane* should be departed from, and if not whether it applied to claims by a parent who was herself disabled. The House was unanimous in upholding *McFarlane* and declining to give damages for child-rearing expenses; and a bare majority[571] decided that it made no difference that the parent was disabled. However, the majority also put a gloss on the *McFarlane* bar and decided that where it applied there should nevertheless be a conventional award of £15,000 to mark the wrong done to the parents.[572] What was not finally decided was whether an award could still be made for the extra costs of bringing up a disabled child,[573] but the better position[574] seems to be that it can.[575] *McFarlane* and *Rees* were tort cases, and did not decide in terms whether the cost of bringing up an unwanted child could be recovered in a contract action; indeed in *McFarlane* Lords Slynn at 76, Steyn at 76 and Clyde at 99 left the point open. However, a minority in *McFarlane* (Lords Millett and Hope) also thought that the loss was inherently unquantifiable, since the joy of parenthood could not be disregarded, from which it would follow that even a contract claim would be barred. In *ARB v IVF Hammersmith Ltd*,[575A] a contract claim based on a broken agreement not to use frozen sperm for procreation without the donor's consent, Nicola Davies LJ regarded the refusal to award the costs of upbringing as a matter of legal policy and applied it there too. She took into account the inherent difficulty of measuring the loss, and also unhappiness with the notion that a private patient could succeed in such a claim while an NHS patient could not. Although none of these reasons is entirely convincing the matter must now be regarded as settled. **10-88**

[569] [2001] EWCA Civ 530; [2002] Q.B. 266. There seems to be no need for disability as such. In *Khan v Meadows* [2019] EWCA Civ 152; [2019] 4 W.L.R. 26 it was admitted that a claim would lie for the extra cost of raising a haemophiliac child.

[570] [2003] UKHL 52; [2004] 1 A.C. 309 (criticised, V. Chico, "Wrongful Conception; Policy, Inconsistency and the Conventional Award" (2007) 8 Med. Law Int. 139 and C. Purshouse, "Liability for lost autonomy in negligence: Undermining the coherence of tort law?" (2015) 22 Torts L.J. 226).

[571] Lords Bingham, Nicholls, Millett and Scott.

[572] Following a suggestion put out by Lord Millett in *McFarlane*: [2000] 2 A.C. 59, 114. See too para.8-82 onwards. But this artificial measure is not available where the unwanted child is stillborn: see *Less v Hussain* [2012] EWHC 3513 (QB); (2013) 130 B.M.L.R. 51. The solution in *McFarlane* and *Rees* has been rejected in Singapore: see *ACB v Thomson Medical Pte Ltd* [2017] SGCA 38, providing for limited damages on a different basis, and K. Amirthalingam, "Reproductive negligence: unwanted child or unwanted parenthood?" (2018) 134 L.Q.R. 15. The point has been left open in New Zealand: see *J v Accident Compensation Corporation* [2017] NZCA 441; [2017] 3 N.Z.L.R. 804 at [39]–[41].

[573] Logically it could be argued that such a claim would be anomalous. Having decided over 20 years ago that the disabled child cannot itself sue for "wrongful birth" (see *McKay v Essex AHA* [1982] Q.B. 1116), it would be somewhat curious if the law were now to admit a claim for damages of a similar sort through the medium of an action by the parents for the extra costs of upbringing.

[574] On the basis that the three dissentients in *Rees* (Lords Steyn, Hope and Hutton) regarded *Parkinson* as correct. Of the majority, Lords Bingham and Nicholls thought no claim should lie. But Lord Millett left the point open, as did Lord Scott: though the latter thought a distinction might have to be drawn between cases where the failed sterilisation was with a view to preventing the birth of a disabled child

and those where it was not. Thus only two out of seven Law Lords clearly disapproved of *Parkinson*, and even then what they said was obiter.

575 Such is generally accepted in the profession. For instance, in *Farraj v King's Healthcare NHS Trust* [2008] EWHC 2468 (QB) at [2] (appealed on other grounds: [2009] EWCA Civ 1203; [2010] 1 W.L.R. 2139) and in *P v Taunton & Somerset NHS Trust* [2009] EWHC 1965 (QB); [2009] LS Law Medical 598; (2009) 110 B.M.L.R. 164 at [7] it was admitted that *Parkinson* remained binding pending further developments. A claim for the costs of raising a disabled child was allowed by the Canadian Supreme Court in *Krangle (Guardian ad litem) v Brisco* [2002] 1 S.C.R. 205, and seems to have been permitted in England in *McGuinn v Lewisham & Greenwich NHS Trust* [2017] EWHC 88 (QB). In *Khan v Meadows* [2019] EWCA Civ 152; [2019] 4 W.L.R. 26 the ability to recover for such extra costs was admitted. It was decided in the same case, however, that the only relevant disability was that in respect of which negligence had been shown. So where a doctor failed to spot a haemophilia gene and as it happened a child was born with both haemophilia and autism, the mother recovered in respect of the former but not the latter. The autism was, said the court, outside the scope of any duty owed by the doctor.

575A [2018] EWCA Civ 2803; [2019] Med. L.R. 119 at [34]–[39].

(iv) Liability of other medical and quasi-medical professionals

Other allied professions

Replace paragraph with:

10-92 Similar principles to those relating to the liability of medical practitioners govern that of other allied professions too, such as physiotherapists,[590] ambulance crews and paramedics,[591] A&E receptionists[592] and others.[593] Thus in *X (Minors) v Bedfordshire CC*[594] a local authority educational psychologist allegedly provided misleading advice to parents over their children's schooling. The House of Lords declined to strike out a claim in negligence by the children; and in *D v East Berkshire Community NHS Trust*[595] the Court of Appeal held that medical and other experts employed by a local authority owed a duty of care to children in respect of decisions about whether or not they should be taken into care.[596] However, it must be remembered that considerations of public policy may well impinge here to a greater extent than elsewhere.[597] Thus in *D v East Berkshire Community NHS Trust*[598] it was held that local authority experts advising on whether children should be (or not be) taken into care owed a duty to the children, but not to the parents: recognition of a duty to the latter, it was pointed out, would cut across the principle that such decisions had to be taken in the interests of the children concerned and no-one else.

590 *Clarke v Adams* (1950) 94 S.J. 599.

591 *Taaffe v East of England Ambulance Service NHS Trust* [2012] EWHC 1335 (QB); (2012) 128 B.M.L.R. 71; *Hayes v South East Coast Ambulance Service NHS Foundation Trust* [2015] EWHC 18 (QB); *Welds v Yorkshire Ambulance Service NHS Trust* [2016] EWHC 3325 (QB).

592 *Darnley v Croydon Health Services NHS Trust* [2018] UKSC 50; [2018] 3 W.L.R. 1153 (A&E receptionists expected to act as an averagely competent and well-informed person performing the function of a receptionist at a department providing emergency medical care: liable when, owing to receptionist's alleged overestimate of waiting time, the patient left prematurely and suffered complications as a result).

593 e.g. police administering emergency aid (see *Hardaker v Newcastle HA* [2002] Lloyd's Rep. Med. 512), and specialist laboratories to whom hospitals send samples to analyse (*Farraj v King's Healthcare NHS Trust* [2009] EWCA Civ 1203; [2010] 1 W.L.R. 2139).

594 [1995] 2 A.C. 633. For another case concerning psychiatrists, see *Landau v Werner* (1961) 105 S.J. 1008.

595 [2003] EWCA Civ 1151; [2004] Q.B. 558; appealed on another point at [2005] UKHL 23; [2005] 2 A.C. 373.

596 Similarly, *S v Gloucestershire CC* [2001] Fam. 313 had earlier held that such experts were liable for failing to look after children already in council care.

597 See para.10-42.

598 [2005] UKHL 23; [2005] 2 A.C. 373. See para.10-44.

(e) Liability of hospitals, health authorities and other bodies

Medical negligence: liability for independent contractors

Replace paragraph with:

A series of judgments from the 1950s onwards, in England[612] and elsewhere,[613] suggested that since the central function of a hospital or health authority was to ensure the provision of healthcare to patients, it ought to be directly liable to those patients for any negligence in thc performance of that function, without reference to whether the person actually responsible for the negligence was an employee or an independent contractor. These suggestions were emphatically endorsed as correct by the Supreme Court in *Woodland v Swimming Teachers Association*,[614] where it was said that such direct liability was appropriate where (as in the case of a patient) the claimant was dependent on the care or protection of the defendant, there was some antecedent relationship between the parties, and the person at fault had been negligent in the performance of the function assumed by the defendant and delegated to him.[615] It should be emphasised, however, that liability of this kind is limited to negligence in the actual provision of healthcare,[616] and also applies only to organisations that actually undertake the provision of healthcare rather than merely arranging incidentally for its provision by someone else.[617] Nor, it is submitted, does it apply to negligence on the part of a consultant or physician specifically chosen by the patient.[618] **10-95**

[612] Notably *Cassidy v Ministry of Health* [1951] 2 K.B. 343, 360–362 (Denning LJ's minority judgment); *Roe v Minister of Health* [1954] 2 Q.B. 66, 82 (ditto); *X (Minors) v Bedfordshire CC* [1995] 2 A.C. 633 at 740 (Lord Browne-Wilkinson); *Robertson v Nottingham HA* [1997] 8 Med. L.R. 1, 13 (Brooke LJ); also *M v Calderdale HA* [1998] Lloyd's Rep. Med. 157.

[613] See *Commonwealth v Introvigne* (1982) 150 C.L.R. 258, 270, 275 (Gibbs and Murphy LJJ); also *Ellis v Wallsend District Hospital* (1989) 17 N.S.W.L.R. 553 (though cf. the Canadian *Yepremian v Scarborough General Hospital* (1980) 110 D.L.R. (3d) 513).

[614] [2013] UKSC 66; [2014] A.C. 537. The case did not concern medical negligence, but this does not affect its authority.

[615] See [2013] UKSC 66; [2014] A.C. 537 at [22]–[23] (Lord Sumption); also [34]–[38] (Baroness Hale). For a discussion of the application of these principles to medical negligence see P. Giliker, "Non-delegable duties and institutional liability for the negligence of hospital staff: fair, just and reasonable?" (2017) 33 P.N. 109. See, however, for a sceptical view of Lord Sumption's dicta, C. Beuermann, "Do Hospitals Owe a So-Called 'Non-Delegable' Duty of Care to Their Patients?" (2018) 26 Med. L. Rev. 1.

[616] See Lord Sumption at [2013] UKSC 66; [2014] A.C. 537 at [24], approving *Farraj v King's Healthcare NHS Trust* [2009] EWCA Civ 1203; [2010] 1 W.L.R. 2139 (hospital not liable for negligence of independent analytical laboratory).

[617] [2013] UKSC 66; [2014] A.C. 537 at [19], approving the result in *A v Ministry of Defence* [2004] EWCA Civ 641; [2005] Q.B. 183 (Ministry not liable for negligence of hospital subcontracted to treat Service families). But the line can be difficult to draw. In so far as prisons and similar institutions undertake, or are required, to provide healthcare to inmates, they are liable for the fault of independent contractors to whom they delegate: *GB v Home Office* [2015] EWHC 819 (QB). However, this is generally not the case today; and as a result prisons are not, it seems, liable for the negligence of independent medical personnel or organisations entrusted by them with prisoner healthcare. See *Razumas v Ministry of Justice* [2018] EWHC 215 (QB); [2018] P.I.Q.R. P10, following the earlier *Morgan v Ministry of Justice* [2010] EWHC 2248 (QB) and distinguishing *GB v Home Office*, above.

[618] See Lord Sumption at [2013] UKSC 66; [2014] A.C. 537 at [23], limiting liability to cases where the claimant had no substantial say in the selection of the subcontractor. See too *Ellis v Wallsend District Hospital* (1989) 17 N.S.W.L.R. 553.

(g) Medical negligence: causation

(iv) Causation and failure to warn

Causation: "failure to warn" cases

Replace paragraph with:

10-106 A patient alleging injury by way of the materialisation of a risk of which he was not and should have been warned must prove that his injury results from that breach of duty. He must thus prove that, had he been warned of the risk, he would not have consented to the treatment.[678] Although there is room for some argument as to whether the criterion here is objective or subjective, it is suggested that the better view is that the sole question is whether *this* patient would have consented; the reaction of the hypothetical "reasonable patient" being out of account.[679] A problem may arise where no adequate warning was given of the risks of a given treatment and it is clear that had one been forthcoming the patient would have refused it, but on the evidence he would later have changed his mind and undergone the same treatment, carrying the identical risk. If the risk eventuates, is the injury caused by the failure to warn? In *Chester v Afshar*[680] the House of Lords held that it was. Even if this involved some departure from the normal rules of causation (since the claimant could not argue that, but for the defendant's negligent failure to warn, she would not have incurred the risk[681]), the importance attached to the claimant's right to make an informed decision justified applying a special rule.[682] In addition, it is suggested that a doctor guilty of failure to warn will be liable only for the eventuation of the risk he ought to have warned about. If a doctor causes a patient to undergo treatment by negligently failing to warn him of the risk of laryngeal damage, he should hardly be liable if the patient in fact succumbs to an adverse reaction to the anaesthetic.[683]

[678] *Ferguson v Hamilton Civic Hospitals* (1983) 144 D.L.R. (3d) 219; *White v Turner* (1981) 120 D.L.R. (3d) 269. But note that a court may be fairly ready to infer this in a suitable case: *McAllister v Lewisham HA* [1994] 5 Med. L.R. 343, noted [1995] C.L.J. 30.

[679] This is consistently assumed in the cases. See, e.g. *Smith v Barking, Havering & Brentwood HA* [1994] 5 Med. L.R. 285; *Smith v Salford HA* [1994] 5 Med. L.R. 321. The point has been specifically decided in this way, after careful canvassing of the arguments, in Australia: *Ellis v Wallsend District Hospital* (1989) 17 N.S.W.L.R. 553. *Contra*, however, in Canada: *Reibl v Hughes* (1980) 114 D.L.R. (3d) 1, and cf. *Smith v Arndt* (1997) 148 D.L.R. (4th) 448.

[680] [2004] UKHL 41; [2005] 1 A.C. 134, R. Heywood, "Informed Consent through the Back Door" [2005] N.I.L.Q. 266. See para.2-15. Note, however, that courts are alert to keep *Chester v Afshar* within reasonable bounds. Where a doctor explains treatment in detail but then negligently fails to carry out part of it, causation must be proved in the ordinary way. It is not open to the claimant to dress this up as a case of failure to warn and thus avoid the burden of proving causation: see *Correia v University Hospital of North Staffordshire NHS Trust* [2017] EWCA Civ 356; [2017] E.C.C. 37.

[681] Which may be doubtful. It is hard to see why the claimant should not have succeeded on orthodox causation grounds. She was claiming for injury, not for loss of the chance of avoiding it: cf. *Gregg v Scott* [2005] UKHL 2; [2005] 2 A.C. 176. But for the defendant's failure to warn her she would not have been injured when she was. If she had had the same operation later, there was a 99% chance that she would not have suffered the same injury then. She had therefore proved "but-for" causation on an overwhelming balance of probabilities. See *Marshall v Hull & East Yorkshire Hospitals NHS Trust* [2014] EWHC 4326 (QB) at [79]; also *Crossman v St George's Healthcare NHS Trust* [2016] EWHC 2878 (QB); (2017) 154 B.M.L.R. 204. In an identical Australian case, *Chappell v Hart (1998) 72 A.L.J.R. 1344*, a majority of the High Court seemingly accepted this point: see at p.1347–1348 (Gaudron J), 1359 (Gummow J) and 1370 (Kirby J); see P. Cane, "A Warning About Causation" (1999) 115 L.Q.R. 21 and M. Stauch, "Taking the Consequences for Failure to Warn of Medical Risks: Chappel v Hart" (2000) 63 M.L.R. 261. See too C. Purshouse, "Causation, coincidences and Chester v Afshar" (2017) 33 P.N. 220. For a further suggestion that the claimant in *Chester v Afshar* should have succeeded on ordinary causation grounds see *Meadows v Khan* [2017] EWHC 2990 (QB); [2018] 4 W.L.R. 8 at [52]–[55] (Yip J).

[682] [2004] UKHL 41; [2005] 1 A.C. 134, at [24] (Lord Steyn), [86]–[87] (Lord Hope), [101] (Lord Walker). But the patient bears the burden of proving that he would indeed have put off the treatment: *Duce v Worcestershire Acute Hospitals NHS Trust* [2018] EWCA Civ 1307; [2018] P.I.Q.R. P18. There has been notable reluctance since to extend the case outside medical malpractice: e.g. *White v Paul Davidson & Taylor* [2004] EWCA Civ 1511; [2005] P.N.L.R. 15 at [30]–[35] (Arden LJ).

[683] So held in Australia: *Wallace v Kam* [2013] HCA 19; (2013) 297 A.L.R. 383 (see too Gummow J in *Chappell v Hart* (1998) 72 A.L.J.R. 1344, 1357). cf. the non-medical decision in *Darby v National Trust* [2001] EWCA Civ 189; [2001] P.I.Q.R. P27.

3. LAW

(b) Duties owed by lawyers

(i) Duties to clients

Duties owed to clients

Replace footnote 699 with:

[699] A point made abundantly clear by Lord Neuberger MR in *Padden v Bevan Ashford Solicitors* [2011] EWCA Civ 1616; [2012] 1 W.L.R. 1759 at [41] (inadequate advice to wife called upon to charge her property for husband's liability; fact that solicitors advised free of charge did not lighten onerous duty placed on them). Note, however, that there can be no duty to advise unless and until a retainer, or some similar arrangements, exists between the solicitor and the "client": see *Aroca Seiquer y Asociados v Adams* [2018] EWCA Civ 1589; [2018] P.N.L.R. 32, where the point was accepted (though a contract of retainer was in the event found). **10-109**

(ii) Duties to third parties

Duties to non-clients

Replace footnote 714 with:

[714] *Yeatman v Yeatman* (1887) 7 Ch D. 210; *White v Jones* [1995] 2 A.C. 207, 256 (Lord Goff). See also *Roberts v Gill & Co* [2010] UKSC 22; [2011] 1 A.C. 240 and *Whitehead v Hibbert Pownall & Newton (a firm)* [2008] EWCA Civ 285; [2009] 1 W.L.R. 549 (solicitor instructed specifically by mother to bring proceedings in respect of birth of handicapped child: mother unexpectedly dies: solicitor owes no duty to child's father to advise as to the possibility of continuing the claim); also *Connaught Income Fund, Series 1 (In liquidation) v Hewetts* [2016] EWHC 2286 (solicitors instructed by buyer of commercial property owed no general duty to investment scheme providing funds to buyer). See also, *Joseph v Farrer & Co LLP* [2017] EWHC 2072 (Ch); [2018] P.N.L.R. 1 at [36]. **10-112**

Duties to third parties: will and gift cases

Replace footnote 739 with:

[739] *Hemmens v Wilson Browne & Co* [1995] Ch. 223, following suggestions by Lord Goff in *White v Jones* [1995] 2 A.C. 207, 262; J. O'Sullivan, "Professional liability to third parties for inter vivos transactions" (2005) 21 P.N. 142. The ostensible reason is that the would-be donor could always have changed his mind, and hence causation was not established. *Sed quaere*. If the evidence was that the donor would not have changed his mind, why logically should this make any difference? Compare the Scots decision in *Steven v Hewats* [2013] CSOH 61; [2013] P.N.L.R. 22 refusing despite *Hemmens* to dismiss a claim by a donee *inter vivos* in respect of misdrafting by a solicitor which caused the gift to be chargeable to IHT on the donor's subsequent death. Compare *Joseph v Farrer & Co LLP* [2017] EWHC 2072 (Ch); [2018] P.N.L.R. 1 (rich man instructs solicitors to make arrangements for regular munificent gifts by trustees to lover: no duty to take steps to make promise irrevocable or guard against trustees terminating gifts). **10-114**

Duties to third parties: conveyancing transactions

Replace paragraph with:

There is no doubt that a solicitor undertaking conveyancing may owe a duty to some third parties, especially those whose interests are not opposed to his client's.[740] **10-115**

However, owing to the opposed interests of the parties to a conveyancing transaction, it is not very common for duties to be owed by one party's solicitor to the other party himself.[741] It is true that in some such cases there may still be a duty of care, in particular in respect of the giving of specific information;[742] but even here the law is not straightforward. In the difficult case of *Gran Gelato Ltd v Richcliff (Group) Ltd*[743] it was held that in answering enquiries before contract, conveyancing solicitors owed no duty to the potential purchasers. This, with respect, seems too restrictive. Later dicta suggest that the decision in *Gran Gelato* may be open to reconsideration;[744] and in *First National Commercial Bank Plc v Loxleys*[745] the Court of Appeal refused to strike out a claim on very similar facts.

740 See, e.g. *Dean v Allin & Watts* [2001] EWCA Civ 758; [2001] P.N.L.R. 39 (duty to client's lender to ensure lender's security not affected by invalidity).

741 *Gran Gelato Ltd v Richcliff (Group) Ltd* [1992] Ch. 560, 570 (Nicholls VC; see too *P&P Property Ltd v Owen White & Catlin LLP* [2018] EWCA Civ 1082; [2018] 3 W.L.R. 1244 at [82] (solicitor for fraudulent seller owed no duty to defrauded buyer). That a solicitor will not readily be held to owe a duty to the other party to the transaction was trenchantly confirmed by the Supreme Court in the Scottish decision in *Steel v NRAM Ltd* [2018] UKSC 13; [2018] 1 W.L.R. 1190. A borrower owned a number of industrial units subject to standard securities in favour of NRAM; as each unit was sold off, NRAM would release its security over that unit against payment of a given sum. On one sale the borrower's solicitors mistakenly enclosed a release of all NRAM's security; NRAM equally inadvertently executed it. Later the borrower became insolvent, and NRAM, having become unsecured, lost the monies advanced by it. NRAM's action against the solicitors failed, partly because its reliance on the solicitors' description of the release had been unreasonable and unforeseeable, and partly also because the claim represented an illegitimate attempt to extend the duties of a solicitor for one party further than was justified (see especially at [25]–[32]). On the *NRAM* case generally, see E. Gordon, "Out with the old, in with the older? *Hedley Byrne* reliance takes centre stage" [2018] C.L.J. 251.

742 See, e.g. the Scottish decision in *NRAM Plc v Steel* [2016] CSIH 11; [2016] P.N.L.R. 20 (borrower's solicitor sends lender release for security never intended to be released; lender signs it; solicitor liable to lender). And cf. *Edwards v Lee*, *The Times,* 5 November 1991 (solicitor gave clean reference to other party on client he knew to have 13 fraud charges outstanding). *Steel v NRAM* has been reversed by the Supreme Court: see [2018] UKSC 13; [2018] 1 W.L.R. 1190.

743 [1992] Ch. 560. cf. *Wilson v Bloomfield* (1979) 123 S.J. 860.

744 See *McCullagh v Lane Fox & Partners Ltd* [1996] P.N.L.R. 205, 227 onwards (Hobhouse LJ). However, despite the fact that *Gran Gelato Ltd v Richcliff (Group) Ltd* has been doubted, it should be noted that it was cited without adverse comment by Lord Wilson JSC in *Steel v NRAM Ltd* [2018] UKSC 13; [2018] 1 W.L.R. 1190 at [29].

745 [1997] P.N.L.R. 211. Significantly, *Gran Gelato* has been disowned in Ireland (*Doran v Delaney* [1998] 2 I.L.R.M. 1) and strongly doubted in Australia (*Bebonis v Angelos* [2003] NSWCA 13; (2003) 56 N.S.W.L.R. 12).

Duties to third parties: other cases

Replace footnote 749 with:

10-116 749 *Edenwest Ltd v CMS Cameron McKenna (A Firm)* [2012] EWHC 1258 (Ch); [2013] B.C.C. 152 (solicitors to receiver owe no duty to company); see too *Lee v Abedian* [2016] QSC 92; [2017] 1 Qd.R. 549 (solicitor for one side in property deal preparing report suggesting fraud by other party: no duty of care).

(iii) Duties as trustee or under the law of trusts

Liability under the law of trusts

Replace paragraph with:

10-119 In addition to any duties in contract or tort, a lawyer may owe a duty to a client as trustee of the latter's funds. This arises particularly[760] where the solicitor for a purchaser or mortgage lender is entrusted with the price or mortgage monies for transmission to the vendor.[761] In such a case the solicitor's duty is to disburse the monies according to his instructions or account for them to the client: if he fails to do this, he is presumptively liable for breach of trust,[762] whether he disburses the funds at the wrong time,[763] omits to apply them to pay off prior charges,[764] transfers them to impostors not entitled to receive them,[765] or pays them over against a forged transfer.[766] Where such a breach is committed his duty is not strictly to compensate the beneficiary for his net loss, as in tort,[767] as to restore the trust monies so as to put the trust fund in the position it would have occupied had the terms of the trust been observed.[768] However, in practice the measure of compensation is much the same, and indeed the House of Lords and the Supreme Court have both criticised the idea that a technical change in the cause of action should make a large difference in the measure of recovery.[769]

760 But not exclusively. The same position can equally arise with a straightforward express trust (e.g.*Daniel v Tee* [2016] EWHC 1538 (Ch); [2016] 4 W.L.R. 115 and *Levack v Philip Ross & Co (a firm)* [2019] EWHC 762 (Comm)) or with monies held pending a loan to any other borrower against security over its assets. See, e.g. *Gabriel v Little* [2013] EWCA Civ 1513; (2013) 16 I.T.E.L.R. 567 (though no such trust was found on the facts) (the point did not feature on appeal in *BPE Solicitors v Hughes-Holland* [2017] UKSC 21; [2018] A.C. 599).

761 This is not the only case. The same position can equally arise with, for instance, monies held for loan to a company against security over the company's assets (e.g. *Bellis v Challinor* [2015] EWCA Civ 59; [2016] W.T.L.R. 43; or held against payment for services (*Chang v Mishcon de Reya* [2015] EWHC 164 (Ch)) (though in neither case was a trust found to exist on the facts).

762 See para.10-19; *Target Holdings Ltd v Redferns* [1996] A.C. 421; *Lloyds TSB Bank Plc v Markandan & Uddin* [2012] EWCA Civ 65; [2012] 2 All E.R. 884); *Nationwide Building Society v Davisons Solicitors* [2012] EWCA Civ 1626; [2013] P.N.L.R. 12). It should be noted, however, that mere negligence in protecting the client's interest, for instance by failing to notice matters that might raise suspicions and warn the client of them, is not covered: here liability is simply for negligence. See *Bristol & West Building Society v Mothew* [1998] Ch. 1, and *Birmingham Midshires Building Society v Infields* (1999) 66 Con. L.R. 20.

763 *Target Holdings Ltd v Redferns* [1996] A.C. 421.

764 *AIB Group (UK) Plc v Mark Redler & Co* [2014] UKSC 58; [2015] A.C. 1503.

765 *Mortgage Express Ltd v Iqbal Hafeez Solicitors* [2011] EWHC 3037 (Ch); *Lloyds TSB Bank Plc v Markandan & Uddin* [2012] EWCA Civ 65; [2012] 2 All E.R. 884; *Purrunsing v A'Court & Co* [2016] EWHC 789 (Ch); [2016] 4 W.L.R. 81.

766 *Nationwide Building Society v Davisons Solicitors* [2012] EWCA Civ 1626; [2013] P.N.L.R. 12.

767 "[T]he common law rules of remoteness of damage and causation do not apply" (Lord Browne-Wilkinson in *Target Holdings Ltd v Redferns* [1996] A.C. 421, 434); *AIB Group (UK) Plc v Mark Redler & Co Solicitors* [2014] UKSC 58; [2015] A.C. 1503 at [98] (Lord Reed). Equally there is no scope for reduction of any award for contributory negligence, whether under the Law Reform (Contributory Negligence) Act 1945 or otherwise: *Lloyds TSB Bank Plc v Markandan & Uddin* [2012] EWCA Civ 65; [2012] 2 All E.R. 884.

768 See, e.g. *Target Holdings Ltd v Redferns* [1996] A.C. 421, 434-435 (Lord Browne-Wilkinson); *AIB Group (UK) Plc v Mark Redler & Co* [2014] UKSC 58; [2015] A.C. 1503 at [92]–[93] (Lord Reed). One case where this made a difference was *Various Claimants v Giambrone & Law (A Firm)* [2017] EWCA Civ 1193; [2018] P.N.L.R. 2 (lawyers liable for releasing buyers' deposits on Calabrian properties without obtaining stipulated guarantees, without reference to whether guarantees would have been worth anything). For a critical comment see P. Davies, "Equitable compensation and the SAAMCO principle" (2018) 134 L.Q.R. 165.

769 See Lord Browne-Wilkinson in *Target Holdings Ltd v Redferns* [1996] A.C. 421, 436–439; *AIB Group (UK) Plc v Mark Redler & Co* [2014] UKSC 58; [2015] A.C. 1503 at [64]–[66] (Lord Toulson). On this see A. Shaw-Mellors, "Equitable compensation for breach of trust: still missing the target?" [2015] J.B.L. 165.

Replace paragraph with:

Liability for breach of trust is not dependent on fault. However, it may be possible for the solicitor to invoke s.61 of the Trustee Act 1925, which gives the court a discretion to exonerate a trustee from liability if he proves that he has acted honestly and reasonably, and ought fairly to be excused for his breach of trust.[770] But the standard under s.61 is an exacting one, and in practice it can be difficult for a solicitor to invoke it in order to extricate himself from liability.[771] It should also **10-120** be noted that where funds are held on trust, the duties arising under the trust are generally narrower than those under the solicitor's retainer:[772] thus even in respect of the disbursement of funds the solicitor may well be guilty of negligence without in addition being in breach of trust.[773]

[770] See Rimer LJ in *Lloyds TSB Bank Plc v Markandan & Uddin (A Firm)* [2012] EWCA Civ 65; [2012] 2 All E.R. 884 at [61]. For cases where solicitors in breach of trust benefited from the section, see *Nationwide Building Society v Davisons Solicitors* [2012] EWCA Civ 1626; [2013] P.N.L.R. 12 (solicitors entirely innocently duped into releasing loan monies to bogus solicitors in league with fraudsters); *Ikbal v Sterling Law* [2013] EWHC 3291 (Ch); [2014] P.N.L.R. 9 (release against forged transfer). The cases are discussed in J. Lowry & R.Edmunds, "Relieving the trustee-solicitor: a modern perspective on section 61 of the Trustee Act 1925?" (2017) 133 L.Q.R. 223.

[771] See, e.g. *Purrunsing v A'Court & Co* [2016] EWHC 789 (Ch); [2016] 4 W.L.R. 81 at [38]; also *P&P Property Ltd v Owen White & Catlin LLP* [2018] EWCA Civ 1082; [2018] 3 W.L.R. 1244 especially at [111]. Note that if the solicitor cannot disprove negligence of a kind related to the loss suffered, the jurisdiction to relieve falls away, even if the fault was in fact non-causative: *Santander UK v RA Legal Solicitors* [2014] EWCA Civ 183; [2014] P.N.L.R. 20. Furthermore, s.61 cannot be invoked so as to reduce any award on account of contributory negligence: *Lloyds TSB Bank Plc v Markandan & Uddin (A Firm)* [2012] EWCA Civ 65; [2012] 2 All E.R. 884. See too, on the application of s.61 to solicitors, M. Haley, "Section 61 of the Trustee Act 1925: a judicious breach of trust?" [2017] C.L.J. 537, 557 et seq.

[772] See *Bristol & West Building Society v Mothew* [1998] Ch. 1, 24 (Millett LJ); *Target Holdings Ltd v Redferns* [1996] A.C. 421, 436 (Lord Browne-Wilkinson).

[773] e.g. *Bristol & West Building Society v Mothew* [1998] Ch. 1 (failing to pass on relevant information to lender); also *Lloyds TSB Bank Plc v Markandan & Uddin (A Firm)* [2012] EWCA Civ 65; [2012] 2 All E.R. 884 at [42]–[46] and *DB UK Bank Ltd v Edmunds & Co* [2014] P.N.L.R. 12 (Ch) (failure to register lender's interest after completion). For a non-conveyancing case of the same type see *BPE Solicitors v Hughes-Holland* [2017] UKSC 21; [2018] A.C. 599 (solicitors for lender at fault, but not in breach of trust, in failing to mention suspicious features).

(iv) Fiduciary duties

Fiduciary liabilities

Replace paragraph with:

10-121 In addition to possible liability for breach of contract or tort, or breach of trust, a lawyer owes certain fiduciary duties to his client, for breach of which he may be liable to pay compensation.[774] Thus solicitors are guilty of breach of fiduciary duty if they disclose information received from a client which is confidential, or which (even if it is technically public) would harm the client's interests[775]; if they enter into a business in partnership with a client without disclosing the full facts so as to enable the clients to make a properly informed decision[776]; if they pay away client's monies to a borrower in the knowledge that certain conditions of the loan have not been satisfied[777]; and if, when acting for both lender and borrower, they deliberately fail to pass on to the lender relevant information obtained from the borrower while acting for him.[778] Similarly, too, with a solicitor who acts for two parties in circumstances where his ability to provide full loyalty to either is compromised.[779] In practice, it should be noted, many of these duties can equally be expressed as implied terms of any contract between lawyer and client.[780] Besides duties owed as fiduciaries, lawyers may also of course be liable to other remedies in the law of trusts, such as dishonest assistance in a breach of trust[781] or knowing receipt of trust property.[782]

[774] See generally para.10-20.

[775] e.g. information that a client for whom they are acting in a commercial conveyancing transaction is a convicted fraudster: see *Hilton v Barker Booth & Eastwood* [2005] UKHL 8; [2005] 1 W.L.R. 567 at [34] (Lord Walker).

[776] *Longstaff v Birtles* [2001] EWCA Civ 1219; [2002] 1 W.L.R. 470. See too *Swindle v Harrison* [1997] 4 All E.R. 705 (undisclosed profits from loan to client).

[777] e.g. *Bristol & West Building Society v May, May & Merrimans* [1996] 2 All E.R. 801. Inadvertent wrongdoing will, however, generally not suffice: see *Bristol & West Building Society v Mothew* [1998] Ch. 1, and *Birmingham Midshires Building Society v Infields* (1999) 66 Con. L.R. 20.

[778] *Nationwide Building Society v Balmer Radmore (A Firm)* [1999] P.N.L.R. 606.

[779] See, e.g. *Hilton v Barker Booth & Eastwood* [2005] UKHL 8; [2005] 1 W.L.R. 567; *Ball v Druces & Attlee (No 2)* [2004] EWHC 1402 (QB); [2004] P.N.L.R. 39. And cf. *Clark Boyce v Mouat* [1994] 1 A.C. 428 (same principle accepted, though claim failed on the facts). The question of conflict of interest is dealt with in more detail below: see para.10-143.

[780] Thus in *Hilton v Barker Booth & Eastwood* [2005] UKHL 8; [2005] 1 W.L.R. 567, where solicitors improperly compromised their loyalty to a conveyancing client, all parties were content to treat the duty as a contractual one.

[781] See, e.g. *Underhill & Hayton's Law of Trusts and Trustees*, 19th edn (2016), Ch 24 and *Lewin on Trusts*, 19th edn (2016), Ch.40. For examples, see *Pulvers (A Firm) v Chan* [2007] EWHC 2406 (Ch); [2008] P.N.L.R. 9 (solicitors handling mortgage money knowingly paid it away to mortgage fraudsters); *Clydesdale Bank Plc v Workman* [2013] EWHC B38 (Ch); [2014] P.N.L.R. 18 (appeal allowed on the facts, [2016] EWCA Civ 73; [2016] P.N.L.R. 18) (knowingly helping property owner pay away purchase monies in defiance of unregistered charge); also *Nolan v Minerva Trust Co Ltd* [2014] JRC 78A (Jersey Royal Court). See too *Group Seven Ltd v Notable Services LLP* [2019] EWCA Civ 614, a case of stolen funds laundered through a solicitor's client account. The claim succeeded on the basis that the defendant had known facts which indicated that what he was doing was regarded as dishonest by reasonable people. Morgan J at first instance had held (see [2017] EWHC 2466 (Ch); [2018] P.N.L.R. 6 at [454]–[472]) that, while knowledge that funds were not at the free disposal of the person providing them sufficed, as would knowledge of some specific illegality such as money-laundering, it was not enough merely to show that a defendant had knowingly breached the relevant solicitors' accounts rules. This point was left open by the Court of Appeal at [102].

[782] For details of this liability, see, e.g. *Underhill & Hayton's Law of Trusts and Trustees*, 19th edn (2016), Ch.24 and *Lewin on Trusts*, 19th edn (2016), Ch.42. For examples, see *Pulvers (A Firm) v Chan* [2007] EWHC 2406 (Ch); [2008] P.N.L.R. 9, above (solicitors also liable for knowing receipt).

(c) Wasted costs orders

Liability under the Senior Courts Act 1981, s.51: "wasted costs orders"

Replace paragraph with:

Under s.51 of the Senior Courts Act 1981,[783] where a legal representative has been guilty of any "improper, unreasonable, or negligent act or omission", the court may order him to pay any costs wasted as a result. This jurisdiction, which extends somewhat vague powers previously available at common law,[784] covers solicitors and barristers (though not in-house lawyers, except when they are exercising rights of audience[785]) in any case where they are exercising a "right to conduct litigation",[786] a phrase apt to cover not only actual proceedings in court but any act in connection with litigation.[787] Orders may be obtained by a party against either his own or his opponent's lawyers.[788] It is a summary jurisdiction applying at any stage in the proceedings up to and including the proceedings relating to the detailed assessment of costs,[789] normally exercised by the trial judge, though only after giving the representative a chance to be heard.[790] **10-122**

[783] As rewritten by s.4 of the Courts and Legal Services Act 1990. Note that this provision also covers the unified Family Court, and in addition the County Court. In addition, ss.111 and 112 of the 1990 Act inserted a new s.19A into the Prosecution of Offences Act 1985 to provide an analogous jurisdiction in the case of criminal courts. See generally CPR, 48.7 (civil cases) and in criminal cases the Costs in Criminal Cases (General) Regulations 1986 (SI 1986/1335) regs 3A–3D (as amended) and the *Practice Direction (Costs in Criminal Proceedings)* [2015] EWCA Crim 1568 (as amended by the *Practice Direction (Costs in Criminal Proceedings) 2015 Amendment No.1* [2016] EWCA Crim 98), para.4.2.

[784] On which see *Myers v Elman* [1940] A.C. 282 and *Orchard v S.E. Electricity Board* [1987] Q.B. 565.

[785] See *R v Lambeth BC, Ex p. Wilson* (1998) 30 H.L.R. 64 and Senior Courts Act 1981 s.51(13). See generally *Lloyd & Son Ltd (In Administration) v PPC International Ltd* [2016] EWHC 2162 (QB); [2017] P.N.L.R. 1. Note that in immigration cases Home Office Presenting Officers (HOPOs) are not amenable to wasted costs orders: they are not regarded as professional advocates owing a duty as such

to the court. See *Re Awuah (Wasted Costs Orders)* [2017] UKFTT 555 (IAC); [2018] P.N.L.R. 7 at [22]–[23].

786 1981 Act, s.51(13). Thus dilatory solicitors who had come off the record well before proceedings were started were not amenable (*Byrne v Sefton Health Authority* [2001] EWCA Civ 1904; [2002] 1 W.L.R. 775); nor is a solicitor liable for merely failing to bring a timeous appeal (*Radford & Co v Charles* [2003] EWHC 3180 (Ch); [2004] P.N.L.R. 25).

787 *Medcalf v Mardell* [2002] UKHL 27; [2003] 1 A.C. 120 at [18]–[20] (Lord Bingham).

788 *Medcalf v Mardell* [2002] UKHL 27; [2003] 1 A.C. 120 at [18]–[19] (Lord Bingham).

789 CPR, 53.1PD. There is no jurisdiction to make such an order at a later stage: *Sharma v Hunters (Wasted Costs)* [2011] EWHC 2546 (CoP); [2012] P.N.L.R. 6.

790 1981 Act s.51(6); CPR, r.48.7(2); *S v M* [1998] 3 F.C.R. 665.

(d) Immunities

Collateral challenge and abuse of process

Replace paragraph with:

10-126 An action for negligence against a lawyer may, like any other action,[829] be struck out if it amounts to an impermissible collateral challenge to the previous decision of a court of competent jurisdiction. Thus in *Smith v Linskills*[830] a convicted burglar attempted to sue his solicitor for negligence, alleging that had his defence been properly conducted he would have been acquitted. The Court of Appeal struck out the action as an abuse of process: unless compelling new evidence was produced which "entirely change[d] the aspect of the case",[831] it was contrary to public policy to allow the conviction to be effectively re-litigated in the civil courts. A similar principle may apply to attempts to impugn a final judgment in contested civil proceedings,[832] though here the jurisdiction is much more sparingly exercised.[833] But the limits of this rule must be noted. It applies only to proceedings where the claimant has had a reasonable opportunity to present his case, and not (for example) to cases where the defendants' negligence deprives the claimant of the chance of a successful appeal,[834] or of the services of a suitable expert to support his story.[835] Furthermore, the bar on collateral attack is much less stringently applied in the case of consent orders,[836] even where those orders embody a settlement which has by law to be approved by the court.[837] Although in such a case subsequent proceedings in negligence are prima facie abusive, they will normally be allowed to proceed if (a) good reason is shown why steps were not taken to challenge the original decision by appeal or otherwise;[838] and (b) the claimant has been deprived of either a reasonable opportunity to appreciate that substantially better terms could have been obtained, or has been placed in the position of having to accept a settlement significantly less advantageous than he should have had.

829 e.g. actions against the police for assault aimed at impugning confessions on the basis of which the claimant has been convicted of a criminal offence: *Hunter v Chief Constable of West Midlands* [1982] A.C. 529. For its application to professional negligence proceedings, albeit against non-lawyers, see *Arts & Antiques Ltd v Richards* [2013] EWHC 3361 (Comm); [2014] P.N.L.R. 10 (insurance brokers).

830 [1996] 1 W.L.R. 763. See too *Somasundaram v M. Julius Melchior* [1988] 1 W.L.R. 1394 and *Workman v Deansgate 123 LLP* [2019] EWHC 360 (QB). If the proceedings were ultimately favourable to the claimant, his action for damages will of course be allowed to proceed, since then it does not impugn anything: *Acton v Graham Pearce* [1997] 3 All E.R. 909.

831 [1996] 1 W.L.R. 763, 771; see too *Hunter v Chief Constable of West Midlands* [1982] A.C. 529, 545 (Lord Diplock).

832 See, e.g. *Laing v Taylor Walton (A Firm)* [2007] EWCA Civ 1146; [2008] P.N.L.R. 11 (simple attack on otherwise impeccable finding of fact in previous proceedings); *Ahmad v Wood* [2018] EWHC 996 (QB); [2018] P.N.L.R. 28 (previous matrimonial proceedings: attack on amount awarded); also L. Haller, "Abuse of process, collateral attack and claims against lawyers" (2015) 34 C.J.Q. 377.

[833] See *Nesbitt v Holt* [2007] EWCA Civ 249; [2007] P.N.L.R. 24 (client's allegation that claim had been settled without authority not abusive, despite previous decision by employment tribunal that settlement had been with authority: allegation only abuse of process if advancement manifestly unfair to other side). See too Lord Bingham CJ's judgment in the Court of Appeal in *Hall (Arthur JS) & Co v Simons* [2002] 1 A.C. 615. In the House of Lords, however, Lord Hoffmann doubted whether the principle could apply where a lawyer was sued for negligence in conducting civil proceedings (see [2002] 1 A.C. 615, 701). Lord Steyn said: "It would not ordinarily be necessary to rely on the *Hunter* principle in the civil context but I would accept that the policy underlying it should still stand guard against unforeseen gaps." ([2002] 1 A.C. 615, 680).

[834] *Walpole v Partridge & Wilson* [1994] Q.B. 106.

[835] A contrary decision in *Palmer v Durnford Ford* [1992] Q.B. 483 was discountenanced in *Walpole v Partridge & Wilson* [1994] Q.B. 106.

[836] See *Hall (Arthur JS) & Co v Simons* [2002] 1 A.C. 615, 647 (Lord Bingham CJ in the Court of Appeal).

[837] For example, settlements of claims by minors, or for ancillary relief in matrimonial cases. Where the consent order embodies a settlement that does not have to be approved, it is indeed doubtful whether the "collateral attack" principle applies at all: see *Saif Ali v Sydney Mitchell* [1980] A.C. 198, 223 (Lord Diplock).

[838] For a neat example see *R(L) v Witherspoon* [1999] P.N.L.R. 766 (action against solicitors for delay in prosecuting contact proceedings; because of delay, decision against claimant since not in best interests of child to upset established arrangements: no strike-out on basis of "collateral attack" rule).

(e) What amounts to breach of duty

Proving negligence

Replace footnote 870 with:

[870] See *McFarlane v Wilkinson* [1997] P.N.L.R. 578 (solicitors); *Matrix Securities Ltd v Theodore Goddard* [1998] P.N.L.R. 290 and *Bark v Hawley* [2004] EWHC 144 (QB); [2005] P.N.L.R. 3 (barristers); and the Northern Ireland decision in *McIlgorm v Bell Lamb & Joynson* [2001] P.N.L.R. 28 (both). Other instances are *Football League Ltd v Edge Ellison* [2006] EWHC 1462 (Ch); [2007] P.N.L.R. 2 and *Barker v Baxendale Walker Solicitors* [2016] EWHC 664 (Ch); [2016] S.T.I. 1266. An appeal to the Court of Appeal in *Barker v Baxendale Walker Solicitors (a Firm)* [2016] EWHC 664 (Ch); [2016] S.T.I. 1266 was allowed on other grounds: see [2017] EWCA Civ 2056; [2018] 1 W.L.R. 1905. **10-131**

Solicitor acting on counsel's advice

Replace footnote 883 with:

[883] The phrase is Taylor LJ's: *Locke v Camberwell HA* [1991] 2 Med. L.R. 249, 254 (If solicitor "reasonably thinks counsel's advice is obviously or glaringly wrong, it is his duty to reject it."). See too *Firstcity Insurance Ltd v Orchard* [2003] P.N.L.R. 9 at [82] (Forbes J). See too *Dunhill v Brook & Co* [2018] EWCA Civ 505 at [49] (Leveson P). **10-133**

(f) Specific duties

(i) The duty to advise

The duty to advise

Replace paragraph with:

10-134 A lawyer owes a duty to give his client reasonably careful, competent and comprehensive[886] advice concerning any transaction in respect of which he is instructed. Thus he must keep the client informed of the progress of the transaction,[887] and warn of any specific risks inherent in it,[888] such as a possible ultra vires problem with municipal lending,[889] the possibility that a borrower offering shares as security does not in fact own them,[890] the risk of liability for breach of fiduciary duty in a property deal,[891] or the dangers inherent where a wife contemplates burdening her share in the matrimonial home to support her husband's business indebtedness.[892] In a conveyancing transaction he must bring to his notice matters such as the risk of exchanging contracts before a purchaser has paid a deposit,[893] a defect in the title to, or adverse right of way over, a property to be bought,[894] a recent sale at a much lower price[895] or an absence of relevant planning permission for prior works[896] or a known future proposed use.[897] When acting for a lender he must advise the lender of any matters specifically mentioned in the latter's instructions, together with other matters raising serious suspicions as to the behaviour of the borrower,[898] such as unusual features in the transaction[899] or a recent sale at a price much less than the valuation.[900] In advising employers on the drafting of employment contracts he must warn of matters that might be unexpectedly favourable to the employee[901]; conversely, in advising employers on dismissing a senior employee he must apprise them of contractual terms favourable to their position.[902] In litigation, he must advise properly on the prospects of success.[903] Depending on the circumstances, the duty to advise may include a duty to take account of the fact that the law is uncertain,[904] or indeed that it may be changed by judicial decision.[905]

886 e.g. where a wife contemplates charging her share in the matrimonial home for her husband there must be more than formulaic advice not to enter into the transaction at all: *Padden v Bevan Ashford Solicitors* [2011] EWCA Civ 1616; [2012] 1 W.L.R. 1759; and cf. another formulaic advice case, *Procter v Raleys Solicitors* [2015] EWCA Civ 400; [2015] P.N.L.R. 24. See too *Padden v Bevan Ashford Solicitors (No 2)* [2013] EWCA Civ 824; [2013] P.N.L.R. 34 (wife thought burdening her property would prevent husband's prosecution for fraud: solicitors ought to have advised that this was unlikely). So too with commercial clients: see *Redstone Mortgages Ltd v B Legal Ltd* [2014] EWHC 3398 (Ch) (need for advice as to effect of shared ownership lease on value of security).

887 *Groom v Crocker* [1939] 1 K.B. 194 at 222. Cf. *Jenmain Builders Ltd v Steed & Steed* [2000] P.N.L.R. 616 (duty to warn purchaser client that he was in "contract race").

888 *Boyce v Rendells* (1983) 268 E.G. 268 at 272; *Ohna v Goldberg* [2014] EWHC 4693 (Ch).

889 *Haugesund Kommune v Depfa ACS Bank (No 2)* [2010] EWHC 227 (Comm); [2010] P.N.L.R. 21 (reversed, but not on this point, in *Haugesund Kommune v Depfa ACS Bank* [2011] EWCA Civ 33; [2011] 3 All E.R. 655).

890 *Clack v Wrigleys Solicitors LLP* [2013] EWHC 413 (Ch) (in fact no damage suffered, since shares worthless anyway).

891 See the Scots decision in *Keith v Davidson Chalmers* 2004 S.C. 287.

892 *Etridge v Pritchard Englefield* [1999] P.N.L.R. 839; *McGregor v Michael Taylor & Co* [2002] 2 Lloyd's Rep. 468; *Padden v Bevan Ashford Solicitors* [2011] EWCA Civ 1616; [2012] 1 W.L.R. 1759. See too the Irish Supreme Court's decision in *O'Carroll v Diamond* [2005] IESC 21; [2005] P.N.L.R. 34.

893 *Morris v Duke-Cohan & Co* (1975) 119 S.J. 821. However, at least where a client is of some sophistication there is no duty to advise not to buy one property without being assured of the sale of a previous one whose proceeds are to finance the purchase: *Flynn v King* [2017] IEHC 735; [2018] P.N.L.R. 15.

894 See, e.g. *Pilkington v Wood* [1953] Ch. 770; *Piper v Daybell Court & Cooper & Co* (1969) 210 E.G. 1047. So too with major development plans affecting it: *Orientfield Holdings Ltd v Bird & Bird LLP* [2015] EWHC 1963 (Ch); [2015] P.N.L.R. 33.

895 *Eden (NI) Ltd v Mills Selig (A Firm)* [2016] NIQB 71; [2017] P.N.L.R. 2 (though there the claim failed on causation grounds).

896 *Oates v Pitman* [1998] P.N.L.R. 683 (liability admitted); *G. P. & B. v Bulcraig & Davies* (1988) 12 E.G. 103. Similarly with the lack of a NHBC guarantee on a recently-built house: *Rickards v Jones (No 2)* [2002] EWCA Civ 1344; [2003] P.N.L.R. 13. See too *Various Claimants v Giambrone and Law (A Firm)* [2017] EWCA Civ 1193; [2018] P.N.L.R. 2 (duty to warn unsophisticated buyers of Calabrian properties of possible building permit problems). In the same case the Court of Appeal upheld a finding that on the facts the lawyers had also been at fault in failing to warn about the criminality endemic to Calabria. The point mattered because as it transpired the whole scheme was fraudulent.

897 *AW Group Ltd v Taylor Walton (A Firm)* [2014] EWCA Civ 592.

898 e.g. *Bristol & West Building Society v Mothew* [1998] Ch. 1 (second charge throwing doubt on mortgagors' ability to repay); *Swindle v Harrison* [1997] 4 All E.R. 705; [1997] P.N.L.R. 641 (hidden arrangements for borrower to profit from loan); *Mortgage Express Ltd v Abensons Solicitors* [2012] EWHC 1000 (Ch); [2012] 2 E.G.L.R. 83 (mortgagor buying from company he himself owned); *Godiva*

Mortgages Ltd v Keepers Legal LLP [2012] EWHC 1757 (Ch) (no control over deposit and seller paying buyer's costs).

899 *Capital Home Loans Ltd v Hewit & Gilpin Solicitors Ltd* [2016] NIQB 13; [2016] P.N.L.R. 24 (price paid partly in shares in vendor, and advance used to pay solicitors' fees).

900 *E. Surv Ltd v Goldsmith Williams Solicitors* [2015] EWCA Civ 1147; [2016] 4 W.L.R. 44 (remarkable discrepancy between valuation and recent purchase price).

901 *Newcastle International Airport Ltd v Eversheds LLP* [2013] EWCA Civ 1514; [2014] 1 W.L.R. 3073 (drafting glitch gave employee disproportionately bloated bonus: in fact action failed on causation grounds).

902 *Commodities Research Unit International (Holdings) Ltd v King & Wood Mallesons LLP* [2016] EWHC 727 (QB); [2016] P.N.L.R. 29 (appeal dismissed, [2017] EWCA Civ 1197; [2018] P.N.L.R. 3).

903 e.g. the Scottish decision in *Campbell (or Pearson) v Imray* [2004] P.N.L.R. 1 (solicitors negligent in advising that action statute-barred without adverting to the possibility of an application to lift the bar).

904 *Herrmann v Withers LLP* [2012] EWHC 1492 (Ch); [2012] P.N.L.R. 28 (negligent to fail to warn of uncertainty of purchaser's right to use communal garden, despite eminent conveyancing counsel's advice that all was well).

905 *Williams v Thompson Leatherdale* [2008] EWHC 2574 (QB); [2009] P.N.L.R. 15 (barrister—but not solicitor—advising on ancillary relief negligent in not advising delay pending decision in *White v White* [2001] 1 A.C. 596). But obviously not with unforeseeable changes: *Schumann v Veale Wasbrough* [2015] EWCA Civ 441; [2015] P.N.L.R. 25.

Extent of duty to advise

Replace footnote 911 with:

911 e.g. *Griffiths v Evans* [1953] 1 W.L.R. 1424 (if instructed to advise with regard to statutory industrial injury payments, no duty to advise about potential claim in negligence at common law). See too *Lyons v Fox Williams LLP* [2018] EWCA Civ 2347; [2019] P.N.L.R. 9 (solicitors engaged to advise on insurance claim owe no duty to advise of other policies that might have responded). **10-136**

Replace footnote 923 with:

923 [2004] UKPC 14; [2004] P.N.L.R. 31. See also, *John Mowlem Construction Ltd v Neil F. Jones & Co* [2004] EWCA Civ 768; [2004] P.N.L.R. 45 (no duty in solicitors acting for defendant to professional negligence claim to remind defendants to renew indemnity insurance cover); *Football League Ltd v Edge Ellison (a firm)* [2006] EWHC 1462 (Ch); [2007] P.N.L.R. 2 (no duty to warn highly professional League that counterparty to contract might become insolvent owing them money; *Kandola v Mirza Solicitors LLP* [2015] EWHC 460 (Ch); [2015] P.N.L.R. 19 (uncreditworthiness of real estate seller). See also the Irish decision in *Flynn v King* [2017] IEHC 735; [2018] P.N.L.R. 15 (no duty to warn of risks of buying one property without being assured of the sale of, and payment for, a different one whose proceeds were to be used to finance the acquisition). **10-137**

(ii) The duty to explain documents

Duty to explain documents

Replace footnote 926 with:

926 Including advising on the possibility of a dispute arising from those documents: *Balogun v Boyes Sutton & Perry* [2017] EWCA Civ 75; [2017] P.N.L.R. 20 (discrepancy between headlease and sublease). **10-138**

(iv) The duty to take care in carrying through a transaction

Replace paragraph with:

Solicitors instructed to carry out a particular transaction owe a duty to ensure that, **10-140** as far as possible, the affair proceeds according to plan. Thus care must be taken to read documents thoroughly,[935] to draft documentation effectively[936] and properly,[937] with where necessary suitable co-ordination between the members of the firm involved[938]; and to obtain, and where necessary check, relevant information from the counterparty.[939] Similarly, solicitors acting for purchasers must take steps to register any title obtained[940]; and those acting for mortgagees must take proper steps to ensure that the mortgage documents are valid, and that the signatures on them are genuine.[941]

[935] See the Hong Kong decision in *Hondon Development Ltd v Powerise Investments Ltd* [2005] 3 HKLRD 605; [2006] P.N.L.R. 1 (solicitors negligent in not spotting discrepancy in size of shop unit apparent from conveyancing documents).

[936] *UCB Corporate Services Ltd v Clyde & Co* [2000] P.N.L.R. 841 (lenders' security as drafted ineffective under Statute of Frauds 1677: City solicitors who advised them on it understandably held negligent).

[937] This means to draft not only as instructed (*Wellesley Partners LLP v Withers LLP* [2015] EWCA Civ 1146; [2016] Ch. 529), but also as unambiguously as possible: see *Queen Elizabeth's School Blackburn Ltd v Banks Wilson* [2001] EWCA Civ 1360; [2002] P.N.L.R. 14 (imprecise drafting caused legal expenses of establishing true position). The case is criticised in S. Gee, "The Solicitor's duty to warn that a court might take a different view" (2003) 19 P.N. 362, but (it is suggested) not particularly convincingly. On the duty to avoid potential arguments, see too *Balogun v Boyes Sutton & Perry* [2017] EWCA Civ 75; [2017] P.N.L.R. 20 (solicitors in breach in failing to ensure underlease of restaurant gave unambiguous access to communal ventilation, though case failed on causation grounds); also *Barker v Baxendale Walker Solicitors (a Firm)* [2017] EWCA Civ 2056; [2018] 1 W.L.R. 1905 (aggressive tax scheme likely to be challenged by Revenue; although not negligent to advise that it was effective, duty to advise of uncertainties; successful claim following Revenue attack and settlement with Revenue).

[938] *Swain Mason v Mills & Reeve* [2011] EWHC 410 (Ch); [2011] S.T.C. 1177 at [150] (Arnold J) (appeal dismissed, save as to costs, [2012] EWCA Civ 498; [2012] S.T.C. 1760). See too *Summit Financial Group Ltd v Slaughter & May, The Times,* 2 April 1999.

[939] See *Cottingham v Attey Bower* [2000] P.N.L.R. 557 (vendor provides no evidence of planning consent for extension: in fact none granted: purchaser's solicitor negligent not to enquire further).

[940] See the Irish case of *Rosbeg Partners Ltd v L.K. Shields (A Firm)* [2018] IESC 23; [2018] P.N.L.R. 26.

[941] *Zwebner v Mortgage Corp'n Ltd* [1998] P.N.L.R. 769.

(v) The duty to take care in conduct of litigation

Replace paragraph with:

10-141 A lawyer is under a duty to take care at all stages during litigation, whether in court or out of it.[942] A solicitor who delays issuing proceedings so that his client's action becomes statute-barred will almost certainly[943] be held to be negligent.[944] Similarly he will be liable if he issues proceedings against the wrong parties,[945] save in exceptional circumstances.[946] Delay in prosecuting litigation once started so that the action is struck out for want of prosecution,[947] or even if not struck out, is to the detriment of the client in other respects,[948] are other common examples of negligence in the conduct of litigation. The duty to conduct litigation with care also includes a duty to collate evidence and ensure it is available to the court,[949] and not to withdraw without adequate notice.[950] Similarly a solicitor or barrister is under a duty to exercise care in settlement negotiations and may be liable if he advises his client to settle for a sum that is too high or low, as the case may be.[951] The client's financial interests must be properly protected, for example by obtaining proper security for costs,[952] or taking proper steps to safeguard any sums recovered.[953] But advice, while it must be sufficient to inform the client's decision as to how to proceed, need not be exhaustive: as Baroness Hale has put it, "there is still a respectable body of professional opinion that the client pays for the advocate's opinion, not her doubts."[954]

[942] Since *Hall (Arthur JS) & Co v Simons* [2002] 1 A.C. 615; above, para.10-125.

[943] Though not absolutely invariably, e.g. where limitation law is unexpectedly changed by judicial decision.

[944] *Fletcher & Jon v Jubb Booth & Helliwell* [1920] 1 K.B. 275.

[945] *Losner v Michael Cohen & Co* (1975) 119 S.J. 340. See too *Gill v Lougher* (1830) 1 In. & J. 170 (wrong court).

[946] *Martin Boston v Roberts* [1996] P.N.L.R. 45.

[947] *Fitzpatrick v Batger & Co Ltd* [1967] 1 W.L.R. 706. This may require very forceful advice to the client: see the Irish decision in *Emerald Isle Assurances & Investments Ltd v Dorgan* [2016] IECA 12.

[948] e.g. *Stewart v Patterson Donnelly Solicitors* [2014] NIQB 103; [2015] P.N.L.R. 7 (intervening insolvency of other party); *Emerald Isle Assurances & Investments Ltd v Dorgan* [2016] IECA 12 (indolent lawyers: strikepout more likely, thus affecting settlement value).

[949] *Browning v Brachers* [2004] EWHC 16 (QB); [2004] P.N.L.R. 28 (liability in solicitors for failing to assemble evidence on time, with result that client prevented from relying on it at trial) (appealed on other grounds, [2005] EWCA Civ 753; [2005] P.N.L.R. 44).

[950] *Kim v Oh* [2013] NZHC 925; [2013] 2 N.Z.L.R. 825.

[951] e.g. *Hall (Arthur JS) & Co v Simons* [2002] 1 A.C. 615; see too *McNamara v Martin Mears & Co* (1983) 126 S.J. 69; *Perry v Raleys Solicitors* [2019] UKSC 5; [2019] 2 W.L.R. 636 (negligent advice not to pursue one head of claim). See too *Dunhill v Brook & Co* [2018] EWCA Civ 505 at [45]–[46] (Leveson P).

[952] *Martin Boston v Roberts* [1996] P.N.L.R. 45.

[953] *Agouman v Leigh Day (A Firm)* [2016] EWHC 1324 (QB); [2016] P.N.L.R. 32 (recoveries obtained for Ivorian claimants left in Ivorian bank, where swiftly annexed by local strongmen manipulating judicial system).

[954] *Moy v Pettman Smith* [2005] UKHL 7; [2005] 1 W.L.R. 581 at [28].

Replace footnote 958 with:

[958] *Hall (Arthur JS) & Co v Simons* [2002] 1 A.C. 615, 681–682 (Lord Steyn); *Moy v Pettman Smith* [2005] UKHL 7; [2005] 1 W.L.R. 581 at [59]–[60] (Lord Carswell). See too, for similar comments, *Dunhill v Brook & Co* [2018] EWCA Civ 505 at [45]–[48] (Leveson P). **10-142**

(vi) The duty to avoid a conflict of interest

Replace footnote 961 with:

[961] *Morkot v Watson & Brown Solicitors* [2014] EWHC 3439 (QB); [2015] P.N.L.R. 9 (purchasers' solicitor hand-in-glove with vendors: liable in damages to purchasers who lost money); see too *Ball v Druces & Attlee (No 2)* [2004] EWHC 1402 (QB); [2004] P.N.L.R. 39. Cf. *Longstaff v Birtles* [2001] EWCA Civ 1219; [2002] 1 W.L.R. 470 and *Day v Mead* [1987] 2 N.Z.L.R. 443 (both cases of advice by solicitors to invest in businesses in which firm interested). See too, confirming the points made here, *Western Avenue Properties Ltd v Soni* [2017] EWHC 2650 (QB); [2018] P.N.L.R. 10. A solicitor who had acted for the claimant was restrained from acting for an opponent in the absence of clear proof that they were not in possession of relevant confidential information. The fact that the new client had signed a waiver was given little if any weight; so too the argument that the new opponent might thereby be deprived of their lawyer of choice. **10-143**

(g) Damages

(ii) Measure of recovery

Net loss only recoverable

Replace footnote 1014 with:

[1014] *Portman Building Society v Bevan Ashford* [2000] P.N.L.R. 336 CA (mortgage lender retains right to sue negligent solicitors, despite having already claimed under mortgage indemnity policy). Less defensibly, this remains the case even if the underwriters have waived any right to subrogation: *Bristol & West Building Society v May, May & Merrimans (No.2)* [1998] 1 W.L.R. 336. The *Portman* case was overruled on another point in *BPE Solicitors v Hughes-Holland* [2017] UKSC 21; [2018] A.C. 599, but not so as to affect the issue here. **10-152**

Non-pecuniary loss

Replace footnote 1024 with:

[1024] See *Shaw v Leigh Day* [2017] EWHC 825 (QB); [2017] P.N.L.R. 26 (refusal to strike claim). **10-153**

The "SAAMCO limitation"

Replace paragraph with:

10-155 The important surveyors' case of *South Australia Asset Management Co v York Montague Ltd*[1031] (often abbreviated to *SAAMCO*) establishes that a claimant relying on a failure to advise him properly on some matter of fact will recover only the damage he has suffered as a specific result of the advice having been wrong: even though his total loss stemming from reliance on the advice may be greater, and entirely foreseeable, the excess is irrecoverable.[1032] There is no doubt that this principle applies equally to lawyers.[1033] Hence where, through a solicitor's negligent advice, the claimant purchases a property he would not otherwise have bought, his damages will not normally include any sum in respect of either a subsequent decline in property values generally, or any other unconnected factor depreciating the particular property.[1034] Again, a lender misadvised as to the legal enforceability of a loan agreement cannot recover where the loan is lost through the borrower's inability to repay it[1035]; and a lender misled as to the purpose of a loan cannot recover in so far as he would still have lost his money even if he had known the facts.[1036] Yet again, solicitors who negligently fail to warn lenders that the necessary security is not in place before releasing loan monies,[1037] or that there are suspicious features indicating a possible overvaluation which suggest that any lender should steer clear,[1038] are liable only for the loss flowing from the deficiency in the security.

1031 [1997] A.C. 191. See also para.10-191.

1032 *South Australia Asset Management Corporation v York Montague Ltd* [1997] A.C. 191, 241 (Lord Hoffmann); *BPE Solicitors v Hughes-Holland* [2017] UKSC 21; [2018] A.C. 599 at [25]–[45] (Lord Sumption). See also J. Thomson, "SAAMCO revisited" [2017] C.L.J. 476; H. Evans, "Solicitors and the scope of duty in the Supreme Court" (2017) 33 P.N. 193.

1033 See, e.g. *Lloyds Bank Plc v Crosse & Crosse* [2001] EWCA Civ 366; [2001] P.N.L.R. 34; *BPE Solicitors v Hughes-Holland* [2017] UKSC 21; [2018] A.C. 599.

1034 e.g. *Lloyds Bank Plc v Crosse & Crosse* [2001] EWCA Civ 366; [2001] P.N.L.R. 34 (failure to spot troublesome restrictive covenant: solicitors liable only for depreciation due to the covenant, not whole loss); *Cottingham v Attey Bower* [2000] P.N.L.R. 557 (failure to advise that extension illegally built: damages limited to the loss due specifically to lack of planning consent); *Credit & Mercantile Plc v Nabarro* [2014] EWHC 2819 (Ch); [2015] P.N.L.R. 14 (undevelopable land). See too *Trust Co of Australia v Perpetual Trustee Co* (1997) 42 N.S.W.L.R. 237; and cf. *Bank of Scotland plc v Edwards* (1995) 44 Con. L.R. 77. Note too the Irish decision in *Rosbeg Partners v L.K. Shields (A Firm)* [2018] IESC 23; [2018] P.N.L.R. 26 (solicitors who negligently failed to register title, thus rendering land unsaleable, liable only for costs of doing so, plus any diminution in value before matter could be put right).

1035 *Haugesund Kommune v Depfa ACS Bank* [2011] EWCA Civ 33; [2011] 3 All E.R. 655. Cf. *Broker House Insurance Services Ltd v OJS Law* [2010] EWHC 3816 (Ch); [2011] P.N.L.R. 23. Compare *BPE Solicitors v Hughes-Holland* [2017] UKSC 21; [2018] A.C. 599 (failure to advise of possible misuse of loan funds: no liability where non-repayment due simply to uncreditworthiness of borrower).

1036 *BPE Solicitors v Hughes-Holland* [2017] UKSC 21; [2018] A.C. 599.

1037 *AIB Group (UK) Plc v Mark Redler & Co* [2013] EWCA Civ 45; [2013] P.N.L.R. 19 at [10] (Patten LJ); also the Irish decision in *KBC Bank Ireland Plc v BCM Hanby Wallace (A Firm)* [2012] IEHC 120; [2013] P.N.L.R. 7 (reversed on other grounds, [2013] IESC 32; [2013] P.N.L.R. 33).

1038 As in *Portman Building Society v Bevan Ashford* [2000] P.N.L.R. 344. In that case there was held to be full liability, but this result was stated to be wrong by Lord Sumption in *BPE Solicitors v Hughes-Holland* [2017] UKSC 21; [2018] A.C. 599 at [52]. The same, it is suggested, goes for a series of other cases on similar facts, such as of *Leeds & Holbeck Building Society v Alex Morison & Co*, 2001 S.C.L.R. 41; [2001] P.N.L.R. 346, *Newcastle Building Society v Paterson Robertson & Graham*, 2001 S.C. 734; [2001] P.N.L.R. 870, and *Michael Gerson Investments Ltd v Haines Watts* [2002] P.N.L.R. 34.

Replace paragraph with:

10-156 Although the *SAAMCO* limitation began as a limitation of liability for negligent advice, it reflects a more general rule: namely, that a wrongdoer is not liable except for the kind of loss which the duty breached was designed to prevent.[1039] So failing to warn a joint tenant that a devise of his share is ineffective in the absence of prior severance engenders liability to the disappointed beneficiary but not to the estate thus diminished;[1040] and it has been held that if a solicitor fails to prosecute proceedings with due expedition, he may be liable if the action is struck out for delay, but not generally if the defendant becomes bankrupt in the meantime.[1041]

[1039] *South Australia Asset Management Corporation v York Montague Ltd* [1997] A.C. 191, 210 (Lord Hoffmann).

[1040] *Carr-Glyn v Frearsons* [1999] Ch. 326, 337 (Chadwick LJ).

[1041] *Pearson v Sanders Witherspoon* [2000] P.N.L.R. 110. Query, however, whether this is necessarily correct. It could equally be argued, on the basis of *BPE Solicitors v Hughes-Holland* [2017] UKSC 21; [2018] A.C. 599, that a solicitor was accepting a more general responsibility for the loss of the ability to recover. A different result was reached by the New South Wales Court of Appeal in *Mal Owen Consulting Pty Ltd v Ashcroft* [2018] NSWCA 135.

Qualification to the "SAAMCO limitation"

Replace footnote 1042 with:

[1042] The phrase is Lord Sumption's: *BPE Solicitors v Hughes-Holland* [2017] UKSC 21; [2018] A.C. 599 at [40]. In such a case he regarded it as "pragmatic justice" that the solicitor should be liable for the whole loss. **10-157**

Replace footnote 1044 with: **10-158**

Loss of a chance

[1044] N. Jansen, "The Idea of a Lost Chance" (1999) 19 O.J.L.S. 271. For extensive discussion of the rules relating to loss of a chance, including how multiple contingencies are to be treated, see *Assetco Plc v Grant Thornton UK LLP* [2019] EWHC 150 (Comm) at [428]–[455].

Replace paragraph with:

Prima facie the burden is on the claimant to prove, on a balance of probabilities, that the defendant lawyer's negligence was a cause of his loss: if he can do so, he recovers in full, while otherwise he receives nothing.[1045] In certain cases, however, the claimant, whether he sues in contract or tort,[1046] may recover damages based on the loss of the chance of making a gain or avoiding a loss. One such instance concerns bungled litigation, referred to below.[1047] But in *Allied Maples Ltd v Simmons & Simmons*[1048] the Court of Appeal made it clear that the principle was wider than this, and that wherever the chance of making a gain or avoiding a loss depended substantially on the hypothetical actions of a third party, *prima facie* a "loss of chance" award was appropriate. Solicitors advising the purchasers of a company negligently failed to warn them that the sellers' warranties against contingent liabilities were inadequate. Although the purchasers could not prove on a balance of probabilities that the sellers would have agreed to an extended warranty if asked, it was held that they were entitled to an award based on the chance that such an agreement would have been forthcoming. For these purposes there must be a real and substantial chance: a fanciful or speculative one will generally be ignored.[1049] **10-158**

[1045] e.g. *Sykes v Midland Bank Executor and Trustee Co Ltd* [1971] 1 Q.B. 113.

[1046] Most cases allowing such recovery have been in contract, but not all: for a case where it was accepted that the same rule applied in tort, see *Khan v R.M. Falvey* [2002] EWCA Civ 400; [2002] P.N.L.R. 28.

[1047] See para.10-160.

[1048] [1995] 1 W.L.R. 1602; see too Lord Briggs in *Perry v Raleys Solicitors* [2019] UKSC 5; [2019] 2 W.L.R. 636 at [17]–[22]. For a virtual carbon copy of *Allied Maples*, see the later *Perkin v Lupton Fawcett* [2008] EWCA Civ 418; [2008] P.N.L.R. 30. See too *McGregor v Michael Taylor & Co* [2002]

2 Lloyd's Rep. 468 (solicitors at fault in failing to advise wife of possibility of setting aside charge over her share of shared home: 75% loss of chance award); *Magical Marking Ltd v Ware & Kay LLP* [2013] EWHC 59 (Ch) (misadvice to company about right to remove director: loss of chance of amicable arrangement for departure); *Wellesley Partners LLP v Withers LLP* [2015] EWCA Civ 1146; [2016] Ch. 529 (loss of chance of profitable business in New York). And cf. the earlier cases of *Hall v Meyrick* [1957] 2 Q.B. 455 and *Dunbar v A & B Painters Ltd* [1986] 2 Lloyd's Rep. 38.

1049 As a rule of thumb Proudman J has expressed the view that any chance less than 10 per cent should be disregarded: *Harding Homes (East Street) Ltd v Bircham Dyson Bell* [2015] EWHC 3329 (Ch) at [167]. (Note that the actual result in that case was doubted by Bryan J in *Assetco Plc v Grant Thornton UK LLP* [2019] EWHC 150 (Comm) at [447]; he opined that there should have been a simple multiplication exercise.)

Replace paragraph with:

10-159 The "loss of chance" principle applies as much in favour of the defendant as the claimant. Thus in *Stovold v Barlows*,[1050] vendors' solicitors negligently failed to transmit the documentation to prospective purchasers on time; the purchasers withdrew, and the property was sold later for a great deal less. Even though the vendors proved on the balance of probabilities that had the documents arrived on time the purchasers would not have withdrawn, it was held that the vendors' damages fell to be discounted by the probability that they might have declined to proceed in any case. This can be significant where a claim against lawyers includes a claim for consequential loss of a profitable business opportunity: even if the opportunity would more likely than not have materialised, there should it seems be a discount for the chance that it would not have done so.[1051] Where several contingencies would have affected the likelihood of the claimant gaining a particular benefit, the practice is to multiply them together.[1051A] But this is only justified if they are truly independent of each other: if they are interdependent, then a more nuanced approach than the purely mathematical one is called for.[1051B]

1050 [1996] P.N.L.R. 19. In the earlier *Martin Boston & Co v Roberts* [1996] P.N.L.R. 45 solicitors who failed to advise clients to insist on a guarantee from X were held liable in full, with no discount to reflect the possibility that X would not have given it. But *Allied Maples* was not referred to, and it is submitted that this case is of doubtful authority on the point. That the *Allied Maples* principle could be invoked as much by the defendant as the claimant was confirmed by Bryan J, after extensive discussion, in the accounting case of *Assetco Plc v Grant Thornton UK LLP* [2019] EWHC 150 (Comm) at [411]–[417].

1051 *Wellesley Partners LLP v Withers LLP* [2015] EWCA Civ 1146; [2016] Ch. 529, especially at [44] (Floyd LJ). By contrast general claims for loss of profits over a period of time seem to be decided on a balance of probabilities basis (e.g. *Vasiliou v Hajigeorgiou* [2010] EWCA Civ 1475). This is a difficult distinction to draw or understand: see A. Tettenborn, "Professional Liability and Remoteness" (2016) 32 P.N. 66, 67–68.

1051A *Assetco Plc v Grant Thornton UK LLP* [2019] EWHC 150 (Comm) at [447]–[448].

1051B See Bryan J in *Assetco Plc v Grant Thornton UK LLP* [2019] EWHC 150 (Comm) at [422], following cases such as *Tom Hoskins Plc v EMW Law (A Firm)* [2010] EWHC 479 (Ch); [2010] 3 WLUK 336; [2010] E.C.C. 20.

Bungled litigation: measure of damages

Replace paragraph with:

10-160 The best-established instance of a "loss of chance" award arises where a lawyer negligently causes a client to lose in litigation: in such a case the measure of recovery is the client's loss of the chance of winning. Hence if the client had a 40 per cent chance of recovering £10,000, the measure of loss will be £4,000. The leading case is *Kitchen v R.A.F.A.*[1053] The claimant's husband was electrocuted at home; his widow's solicitors then negligently allowed her claim against the electricity suppliers to become statute-barred. She was awarded £2,000 in her professional negligence action, on the basis that, had she succeeded in a Fatal Accidents Act action, she would have recovered £3,000, and that her chances of success would have been two-thirds. Lord Evershed MR said:

"[A]ssuming that the plaintiff has established negligence, what the court has to do in such a case as the present is to determine what the plaintiff has lost by that negligence. The question is: Has the plaintiff lost some rights of value, some chose in action of reality and substance? In such a case it may be that its value is not easy to determine, but it is the duty of the courts to determine that value as best as it can."[1054]

For these purposes, the claimant must demonstrate an appreciable chance that he would have won on the merits. The mere "nuisance-value" of a demonstrably bad claim will not suffice.[1055] But once the claimant has leapt this hurdle the court must do its best to assess the value of the claim[1056] and the chance of success.[1057] In addition to the value of the claim, the client may of course recover any costs he has had to pay, or has been prevented from recovering from the other side, as a result of his lawyers' incompetence,[1058] plus any other foreseeable consequential loss.[1059] It should be noted that, before a claimant can invoke the rule in *Kitchen's* case, he must demonstrate on a balance of probabilities that he would in fact have prosecuted the action.[1060] In addition the claimant must prove that the claim was honest: whatever a claim's actual prospects of success, as Lord Briggs pithily put it in *Perry v Raleys Solicitors Ltd*,[1060A] the court "simply has no business rewarding dishonest claimants".

[1053] [1958] 1 W.L.R. 563.

[1054] At 274–275; and see *Gregory v Tarlo* (1964) 108 S.J. 219; *Maylon v Lawrence Messer and Co* [1968] 2 Lloyd's Rep. 539.

[1055] See *McFarlane v Wilkinson* [1997] P.N.L.R. 578, 606; *Harrison v Bloom Camillin* [2001] P.N.L.R. 7 at [87].

[1056] Which means a sober assessment of the chances of recovery and emphatically not a re-trial of the putative proceedings: *Haithwaite v Thomson Snell & Passmore (A Firm)* [2009] EWHC 647 (QB); [2009] P.N.L.R. 27 and *Perry v Raleys Solicitors* [2017] EWCA Civ 314; [2017] P.N.L.R. 27 at [38] (Gloster LJ). An appeal was allowed by the Supreme Court (see *Perry v Raleys Solicitors* [2019] UKSC 5; [2019] 2 W.L.R. 636), but the point made by her Ladyship remains sound.

[1057] Including the chances of success where causation was in issue in the original proceedings: *Dixon v Clement Jones* [2004] EWCA Civ 1005; [2005] P.N.L.R. 6.

[1058] A straightforward example is *Brinn v Russell Jones & Walker* [2002] EWHC 2727 (QB); [2003] P.N.L.R. 16 (solicitors bungle libel proceedings against X; claimant thereby forced to sue Y, another publisher, to clear his name: award of unrecovered costs in proceedings against Y). See too *Adrian Alan Ltd v Fuglers* [2002] EWCA Civ 1655; [2003] P.N.L.R. 14; *Browning v Brachers* [2004] EWHC 16 (QB); [2004] P.N.L.R. 28 (reversed on factual grounds, [2005] EWCA Civ 753; [2005] P.N.L.R. 44).

[1059] So decided in Northern Ireland: *Macmahon v Doran & Co* [2001] P.N.L.R. 35 (upheld on other grounds in the NI Court of Appeal: [2002] P.N.L.R. 33) (cash flow losses stemming from failure to collect on putative judgment).

[1060] *Harrison v Bloom Camillin* [2001] P.N.L.R. 7 at [83] (Neuberger J); *Perry v Raleys Solicitors* [2019] UKSC 5; [2019] 2 W.L.R. 636 at [20], [27] (Lord Briggs).

[1060A] [2019] UKSC 5; [2019] 2 W.L.R. 636 at [27].

Replace footnote 1061 with:

[1061] [2007] EWHC 1628 (Comm); [2008] P.N.L.R. 2; see too *Commodities Research Unit International (Holdings) Ltd v King & Wood Mallesons LLP* [2016] EWHC 727 (QB); [2016] P.N.L.R. 29 (appeal dismissed, [2017] EWCA Civ 1197; [2018] P.N.L.R. 3). **10-161**

Replace paragraph with:

In assessing the amount of any putative recovery, the amount of any likely settlement is taken into account,[1064] taking due notice of the circumstances, including those of the parties themselves.[1065] Where the claim is inflated, the court should decide what, on the whole, was likely to have been awarded.[1066] If there are claims and counterclaims, each should be evaluated and a percentage deduction determined, and then the sums set-off against each other.[1067] Where any recovery **10-162** would have been reduced by the amount of any social security benefits received by the claimant, it seems the net recoverable amount should be taken, with any percentage discount being applied to that sum.[1068] The value of the claim should generally be taken as at the time of the putative decision, since it is that value of which the claimant has been deprived.[1069] It seems, therefore, that where some new event occurs subsequent to that date which goes to augment or reduce the claimant's original loss, that event is out of account in the action against the solicitor.[1070] However, there is an important qualification to this principle. Where, at the time of the notional trial, a question of prognosis would have arisen (for example, as to whether a personal injury claimant's condition was likely to deteriorate), then it seems that any subsequent events which make that prognosis unnecessary are in account.[1071] The assessment of the chances of success is in its nature a matter of informed impression. In a suitable case where the claimant would almost certainly have won, a figure of 100 per cent may be appropriate.[1072] Where the chances of success under different heads of loss are appreciably different, a separate computation should be made for each.[1073] Furthermore, there is an evidential burden on a defendant to show that the action would have failed; in the event of doubt, the issue should be decided in favour of the claimant.[1074] In so far as a point of law would have arisen, there is no necessary objection to assessing the chances of success. However, it will generally be assumed that the putative court deciding the case would have got the law right.[1075]

[1064] *Harrison v Bloom Camillin* [2001] P.N.L.R. 7 at [82] onwards (Neuberger J). But where there is no indication that a settlement would have yielded a substantially different sum from that which would have been awarded by the court, then little if any account should be taken of it: *Charles v Hugh James Jones & Jenkins* [2000] 1 W.L.R. 1278 at 1294 (Swinton Thomas LJ).

[1065] *Brinn v Russell Jones & Walker* [2002] EWHC 2727 (QB); [2003] P.N.L.R. 16 (loss of chance of libel settlement from the *Oldie*, a small and cash-strapped monthly magazine: small likelihood of substantial offer highly relevant).

[1066] See *Browning v Brachers* [2004] EWHC 16 (QB); [2004] P.N.L.R. 28.

[1067] *Browning v Brachers* [2004] EWHC 16 (QB); [2004] P.N.L.R. 28. But it is not normally appropriate to perform a separate calculation for each part of a claimant's claim: *Dudarec v Andrews* [2006] EWCA Civ 256; [2006] 1 W.L.R. 3002 at [54] (Sedley LJ).

[1068] So decided in Australia: *Green v Berry* [2001] Qd. R. 605.

[1069] *Charles v Hugh James Jones & Jenkins* [2000] 1 W.L.R. 1278 at 1290 (Swinton Thomas LJ); *Hunter v Earnshaw* [2001] P.N.L.R. 42; *Edwards v Hugh James Ford Simey (A Firm)* [2018] EWCA Civ 1299; [2018] P.N.L.R. 30 at [67]. See H. Evans, "Valuing bungled litigation and later facts" (2019) 35 P.N. 71.

[1070] A conclusion provisionally accepted by Swinton Thomas LJ in *Charles v Hugh James Jones & Jenkins* [2000] 1 W.L.R. 1278, 1290, and applied in the Scots decision in *Campbell (or Pearson) v Imray* [2004] P.N.L.R. 1 (claimant's condition deteriorated between putative hearing and trial of professional negligence action, vastly increasing her loss: nevertheless, subsequent increase out of account). See too *Hunter v Earnshaw* [2001] P.N.L.R. 42; *Nikolaou v Papasavas, Phillips & Co* (1988) 82 A.L.R. 617.

[1071] See *Charles v Hugh James Jones & Jenkins* [2000] 1 W.L.R. 1278; *Dudarec v Andrews* [2006] EWCA Civ 256; [2006] 1 W.L.R. 3002; *Whitehead v Hibbert Pownall & Newton (a firm)* [2008] EWCA Civ 285; [2009] 1 W.L.R. 549. Sed quaere: as was pointed out in *Campbell (or Pearson) v Imray* [2004] P.N.L.R. 1 at [21], the result may be that the claimant recovers more (or less) from his solicitor than he could have recovered from the original defendant. Hence in *Edwards v Hugh James Ford Simey* [2018] EWCA Civ 1299; [2018] P.N.L.R. 30 at [69] Irwin LJ accepted that subsequent events which could have been foreseen at the notional trial date should be in account, despite the general rule that the relevant time was that of the notional trial date.

[1072] *Harrison v Bloom Camillin* [2001] P.N.L.R. 7 at [87] (Neuberger J). See too *Somatra v Sinclair Roche & Temperley (No 2)* [2003] EWCA Civ 1474; [2003] 2 Lloyd's Rep. 855 (solicitors' bad advice to insurance claimant led to settlement of claim at two-thirds, whereas it otherwise would have settled at 75%: award of total difference upheld).

[1073] *Harrison v Bloom Camillin* [2001] P.N.L.R. 7 at [88] (Neuberger J).

[1074] *Mount v Barker Austin* [1998] P.N.L.R. 493, 511 (Simon Brown LJ).

[1075] *Harrison v Bloom Camillin* [2001] P.N.L.R. 7 at [101] (Neuberger J).

4. SURVEYORS AND VALUERS

(b) Negligence

(ii) Valuation

Breach of duty: valuation

Replace footnote 1148 with:

[1148] e.g. *John D. Wood (Residential) Ltd v Knatchbull* [2002] EWHC 2822 (QB); [2003] P.N.L.R. 17 (negligence in estate agent and valuer acting for seller not to draw seller's attention to comparable house that sold for £60,000 more than seller's price); also see *Helm Housing Ltd v Myles Danker Associates Ltd* [2015] NIQB 73; [2016] P.N.L.R. 4. But the surveyor must take account of the limitations of such comparable figures, for example where owing to deep discounting in a new development they do not reflect actual prices paid: see *Platform Funding Ltd v Anderson & Associates Ltd* [2012] EWHC 1853 (QB) and *Webb Resolutions Ltd v E.Surv Ltd* [2012] EWHC 3653 (TCC); [2013] P.N.L.R. 15. The Red Book issued by the RICS now specifically makes this clear. For how far comparables should take account of market movements, see *Dunfermline Building Society v CBRE Ltd* [2017] EWHC 2745 (Ch); [2018] P.N.L.R. 13. **10-178**

Valuation: the "bracket"

Replace footnote 1164 with:

[1164] See *Titan Europe 2006–3 Plc v Colliers International UK Plc (In Liquidation)* [2015] EWCA Civ 1083; [2016] P.N.L.R. 7 approving earlier authority such as *K/S Lincoln v CB Richard Ellis Hotels Ltd* [2010] EWHC 1156 (TCC); [2010] P.N.L.R. 31. Note too the share valuation case of *Goldstein v Levy Gee* [2003] EWHC 1574 (Ch); [2003] P.N.L.R. 35. Whether the rule is sensible is another matter. If a valuer negligently misses the fact that a £1 million house suffers from death-watch beetle and as a result overvalues it at £1.09 million, why should he escape scot-free? Further confirmation that a valuation within the "bracket" pre-empts the issue of negligence comes in *Dunfermline Building Society v CBRE Ltd* [2017] EWHC 2745 (Ch); [2018] P.N.L.R. 13 at [33]. **10-180**

(c) Damages

(ii) Measure of recovery

Replace paragraph with:

Just as the value of the property in the condition wrongly attributed to it by the defendant is out of account, so is the cost of putting it into such condition, even if the claimant, having bought the house, proceeds reasonably to incur it,[1207] and apparently even if the surveyor was specifically instructed to advise on the costs of repair.[1208] Such cost may, however, be some guide as to the difference in value.[1209] It should be noted that, as in the law of damages generally, the fact that the purchaser has recouped his loss from another source is generally left out of account: thus in *Gardner v Marsh & Parsons (A Firm)*[1210] the purchaser of a leasehold flat recovered in full for defects overlooked by his surveyor, even though they were later remedied by the landlord at his own expense. **10-189**

[1207] *Watts v Morrow* [1991] 1 W.L.R. 1421; *Holder v Countrywide Surveyors Ltd* [2002] EWHC 856 (TCC); [2003] P.N.L.R. 3. Any contrary inference from *Perry v Sidney Phillips* [1982] 1 W.L.R. 1297 must now be discounted. But if the cost of repair was substantially lower than the difference in value, *quaere* if the claimant would be expected to incur it to mitigate his loss. cf. *Daisley v B. S. Hall & Co* (1972) 225 E.G. 1553. See too the contract case of *Moore v National Westminster Bank Plc* [2018] EWHC 1805 (TCC); [2018] P.N.L.R. 33 (same measure where no report provided at all).

[1208] *Smith v Peter North & Partners* [2001] EWCA Civ 1553; [2002] P.N.L.R. 12 (surveyors asked to value equestrian property, and estimate cost of repairs necessary to bring it up to scratch: expenses underestimated, but no recovery because property worth more than price paid). Sed quaere: if the surveyors had not been negligent purchasers would doubtless have bought another property not needing exorbitant expenditure). Note, however, that in the absence of acceptable evidence of diminution in value, for example with seriously defective properties, it may be legitimate to take the costs of repair, *faute de mieux*, as the correct figure for diminution: *Moore v National Westminster Bank Plc* [2018] EWHC 1805 (TCC); [2018] P.N.L.R. 33.

1209 *Steward v Rapley* [1989] 1 E.G.L.R. 159; *Oswald v Countrywide Surveyors Ltd* (1996) 50 Const. L.R. 1.

1210 [1997] 1 W.L.R. 489.

Measure of damages available to mortgagees

Replace paragraph with:

10-191 Where money is advanced by a mortgagee on the basis of a negligent valuation, the House of Lords in *South Australia Asset Management Co (SAAMCO) v York Montague Ltd*[1213] made it clear that in principle the lender can recover the losses suffered by him as a result of the valuation being inaccurate, but no more. This sum[1214] is computed by first taking the capital sum advanced,[1215] less what was (or, if greater, what should have been) recovered by realising the security and/or suing the debtor. There is then added to it (i) any expenses incurred in enforcing the security; and (ii) the interest (if any) that would otherwise have been earned by the claimant on the capital sum advanced against the inadequate security[1216] (but not the interest that should have been paid by the mortgagor himself[1217]). However, the amount by which the security has been over-valued generally forms a cap for any such award. This is largely on the basis that any loss over and above this figure cannot result from the over-valuation. However, Lord Hoffmann also gave a further reason: namely, that since a valuer did not make any statement about the possible future value of the security, it would be unfair to impose on him an open-ended liability for all loss suffered owing, for example, to a general decline in property values, even if such a loss might have been foreseeable.[1218] The result is that, while there is no bar on the lender being compensated for losses due to a collapse in property values,[1219] such loss can only be claimed up to the amount of the over-valuation.[1220] The principles in the *SAAMCO* case are not limited to over-valuation case. In any case where the defendant's negligent misrepresentation leads the claimant to lend on the security of property, the claimant is generally limited to the amount, if any, by which the lender has been misled as to the value of the security he is getting.[1221]

1213 [1997] A.C. 191; also *Bank of Ireland v Faithful & Gould Ltd* [2014] EWHC 2217 (TCC); [2014] P.N.L.R. 28; and generally *BPE Solicitors v Hughes-Holland* [2017] UKSC 21; [2018] A.C. 599. See J. Stapleton, "Negligent valuers and falls in the property market" (1997) 113 L.Q.R. 1; J. O'Sullivan, "Negligent Professional Advice and Market Movements" [1997] C.L.J. 19. See also para.2-182 onwards. See also J. Thomson, "SAAMCO revisited" [2017] C.L.J. 476. For the scope of application of the "SAAMCO cap" to mortgagees' advisers acting as project managers, see *Lloyds Bank Plc v McBains Cooper Consulting Ltd* [2018] EWCA Civ 452; [2018] P.N.L.R. 23.

1214 Which is available to the lender even though it has personally suffered less, or no, loss, because (for example) it has syndicated the loan (see *Paratus AMC Ltd v Countrywide Surveyors Ltd* [2011] EWHC 3307 (Ch); [2012] P.N.L.R. 12 at [54] et seq and *Titan Europe 2006-3 Plc v Colliers International UK Plc* [2015] EWCA Civ 1083; [2016] P.N.L.R. 7), or it is a mere subsidiary put in funds by a parent corporation (*Legal & General Mortgage Services Ltd v Underwoods* [1997] P.N.L.R. 567). These developments are criticised, though ultimately unconvincingly, in N. Goh, "Syndicated Loans, Recovery of Third-Party Loss and the Res Inter Alios Acta Principle" [2016] L.M.C.L.Q. 368.

1215 Seemingly the whole capital sum, even if a refinancing transaction was involved and part of it went to pay off previous indebtedness to the same lender. In *Tiuta International Ltd (In Liquidation) v De Villiers Chartered Surveyors Ltd* [2016] EWCA Civ 661; [2016] P.N.L.R. 34 the Court of Appeal by a majority rejected a submission that damages were limited to the amount of the lender's new exposure. This difficult decision has now been reversed by the Supreme Court, to much relief: see *Tiuta International Ltd (In Liquidation) v De Villiers Chartered Surveyors Ltd* [2017] UKSC 77; [2017] 1

W.L.R. 4627; [2018] P.N.L.R. 12. Where a lender advances monies against over-valued security and part of those monies goes to pay off old indebtedness to the same lender, the valuer is liable only in respect of any increased exposure.

1216 But such sums must be proved: *Mortgage Express v Countrywide Surveyors Ltd* [2016] EWHC 1830 (Ch); [2016] P.N.L.R. 35. In a suitable case, the lender may alternatively recover extra interest charges incurred from having had to borrow the money: *Birmingham Midshires Building Society v Phillips* [1998] P.N.L.R. 468. It seems that the right to claim the cost to the lender of the funds is a general one not limited to interest costs as such: thus a lender who has hedged by entering into an interest rate swap is not barred from claiming the costs associated with the swap. See *Mortgage Agency Services Number One Ltd v Edward Symmons LLP* [2013] EWCA Civ 1590.

1217 Since had the surveyor acted properly there would have been no loan in the first place, and hence no interest paid: see *Swingcastle Ltd v Alastair Gibson* [1991] 2 A.C. 223.

1218 Thus in Australia the *South Australia* case has not been followed where the valuers expressed the view that their valuation was good for three to five years: *Kenny & Good Pty Ltd v MGICA* (1999) 73 A.L.J.R. 901. Two judges (McHugh and Gummow JJ) thought *South Australia* correct but distinguishable: the other three (Gaudron, Kirby and Callinan JJ) inclined to the view that it was wrong. The case has been accepted as correct in New Zealand: *Bank of New Zealand v N.Z. Guardian Trust Co* [1999] 1 N.Z.L.R. 664, 682–683.

1219 As the Court of Appeal had held: [1995] Q.B. 375.

1220 Where the claimant has already recovered a sum from a third party, he may set that sum against that portion of his loss that is irrecoverable under the *South Australia* case, thus preserving full recovery from the surveyor: see *Law Debenture Trust Corp'n plc v Hereward Phillips* [1999] P.N.L.R. 725.

1221 *Bristol & West Building Society v Mothew* [1998] Ch. 1 (statement to prospective first mortgagee that no second charges contemplated). See too *Scullion v Bank of Scotland Plc (t/a Colleys)* [2011] EWCA Civ 693; [2011] 1 W.L.R. 3212 at [62]–[68] (Lord Neuberger MR).

5. Architects and Consulting Engineers

(a) Duties

(i) Duties to clients

Duties to clients

Replace footnote 1257 with:

1257 *Sutcliffe v Thackrah* [1974] A.C. 727 (deciding that no quasi-arbitral immunity applied); see too *Lloyds Bank Plc v McBains Cooper Consulting Ltd (No.2)* [2016] EWHC 2045 (TCC); [2017] P.N.L.R. 11. That liability here is based on negligence and not on any stricter duty was confirmed without hesitation by Coulson J in *Dhamija v Sunningdale Joineries Ltd* [2010] EWHC 2396 (TCC); [2011] P.N.L.R. 9. The decision in *Lloyds Bank Plc v McBains Cooper Consulting Ltd* was varied on appeal, but not on this point: see [2018] EWCA Civ 452; [2018] P.N.L.R. 23. **10-198**

(ii) Duties to others

Economic loss—liability to purchasers, etc

Replace footnote 1272 with:

1272 [1991] 1 A.C. 499. See too *Murphy v Brentwood DC* [1991] 1 A.C. 398; I. Duncan Wallace, "Anns beyond repair" (1991) 107 L.Q.R. 228. Suggestions by Lord Bridge in the latter case (at 475), that there might be an exception where negligent construction or design caused danger to third parties and expense was incurred averting it, were comprehensively discountenanced in *Thomas v Taylor Wimpey Developments Ltd* [2019] EWHC 1134 (TCC). Irish courts, by contrast, seem to be more generous here: e.g. *McGhee v Alcorn* [2016] IEHC 59; [2016] P.N.L.R. 25. **10-201**

Economic loss—other cases

Replace footnote 1277 with:

1277 *Galliford Try Infrastructure Ltd v Mott MacDonald Ltd* [2008] EWHC 1570 (TCC); [2009] P.N.L.R. 9. See too *Turton & Co Ltd v Kerslake & Partners* [2000] 3 N.Z.L.R. 406. So too with architects, where **10-202** courts will not readily infer that an architect who contracts with a client X Ltd will also accept responsibility to associated companies Y and Z: see *Riva Properties Ltd v Foster + Partners Ltd* [2017] EWHC 2574 (TCC); (2017) 175 Con. L.R. 45 at [135]–[151] (Fraser J). An additional feature in that case militating against such duties was that provision had been made for specific third party warranties.

(b) Breach of duty

(i) *Design and supervision*

Design and supervision

Replace footnote 1290 with:

10-206 [1290] *George Hawkins v Chrysler U.K. Ltd* (1986) 38 Build. L.R. 36. For an example of a higher duty being accepted by a consulting engineer, see *Greaves v Baynham Meikle* [1975] 1 W.L.R. 1095. In practice the engagement of an architect or consulting engineer is likely to be on the basis of a standard agreement such as *RIBA's Standard Agreement 2010* (2012 Revision); and many of the details of the obligations undertaken will be found in that agreement. An architect will normally be expected to be familiar with the RIBA Job Book: see *Riva Properties Ltd v Foster + Partners Ltd* [2017] EWHC 2574 (TCC); (2017) 175 Con. L.R. 45 at [154] (Fraser J).

(ii) *Advice*

Breach of duty: advice

Replace paragraph with:

10-208 An architect may be liable in negligence if he offers misleading advice on matters pertinent to his engagement. Thus an architect who provides misleading estimates of likely cost,[1316] or fails to take account of the probable impact of inflation,[1317] may be liable in negligence to the client. An architect who negligently recommended a firm of builders as "very reliable" was found liable on evidence that the builders were in no sense either financially or professionally responsible.[1318] There can equally be liability for failure to advise on important matters.[1319] Architects may be expected, like surveyors, to have at least a limited knowledge of the law.[1320] It has been held that an engineer cannot be liable for giving negligent advice on a subject which the recipient of the advice knows as much about as he does,[1321] but this may be regarded as doubtful. An architect will not be expected to advise a sophisticated client on matters the client is likely to be already familiar with, unless specifically instructed.[1321A]

[1316] *Moneypenny v Hartland* (1826) 2 C. & P. 278. cf. *Gable House Estates v Halpern Partnership* (1995) 48 Con. L.R. 1 (negligent estimate of profitability of project).

[1317] *Nye Saunders & Partners v AE Bristow* (1987) 37 Build. L.R. 92, CA.

[1318] *Pratt v George J. Hill Associates (a firm)* (1987) 38 Build. L.R. 25.

[1319] e.g. the likelihood of cost overruns: see *Plymouth & South West Co-operative Society v Architecture Structure & Management Ltd* [2006] EWHC 5 (TCC); 108 Con. L.R. 77; [2006] C.I.L.L. 2366.

[1320] *B. L. Holdings Ltd v Wood* (1978) 10 Build. L.R. 48 (no negligence on the facts): see Dugdale & Stanton, *Professional Negligence* (3rd edn, 1998), para.17–15.

[1321] *G. Percy Trentham v Beattie Wilkinson*, 1987 S.L.T. 449. But note that in a suitable case damages may be reduced on account of contributory negligence: *Crédit Agricole SA v Murray* [1995] N.P.C. 33 (semble).

[1321A] See *Riva Properties Ltd v Foster + Partners Ltd* [2017] EWHC 2574 (TCC); (2017) 175 Con. L.R. 45 at [130]–132] (Fraser J).

(c) Damages

Damages

Replace paragraph with:

10-209 The measure of damages for personal injury and property damage need not concern us here. In the case of bad design of a building, the measure of recovery is prima facie the reasonable cost of correcting the defects.[1322] However, the claimant will be limited to any diminution in value if either he does not intend to do the work,[1323] or the coat of doing so is wholly unreasonable.[1324] Provided the claimant acts reasonably, he is not prevented from claiming the costs of correction at a later stage, even if substantially greater than at the time the works were carried out.[1325] For other breaches of duty, such as bad advice, it is suggested that the claimant is entitled to be put in the position he would have occupied if the duty to advise had been properly performed.[1326] Consequential damages, for instance, wasted expenditure or loss of profits, are also available.[1327] Similarly, where as a result of an architect's negligence the claimant finds himself liable to a third party, he can claim the amount of that liability, or where appropriate a sum paid in reasonable settlement of a third party's claim.[1328] Where an architect is guilty of negligence in design, advice or similar work, he will generally remain liable to the client even though the latter has since disposed of the property for full value.[1329]

[1322] *McGlinn v Waltham Contractors Ltd (No 3)* (2007) 111 Con. L.R. 1 at [787]; also *West v Ian Finlay & Associates (A Firm)* [2013] EWHC 868 (TCC) at [250] (Edwards-Stuart J) (decision reversed on unconnected grounds, [2014] EWCA Civ 316; [2014] B.L.R. 324); compare the construction decision in *East Ham BC v Bernard Sunley & Sons Ltd* [1966] A.C. 406. The claimant must of course mitigate his loss (*George Fischer Holding Ltd v Multi Design Consultants Ltd* (1998) 61 Con. L.R. 85): but where works have already been carried out on professional advice, the defendant will have some difficulty in repelling an inference that the expenditure was reasonable: cf. the property damage case of *Skandia Property UK Ltd v Thames Water Plc* [1999] B.L.R. 338.

[1323] See *Nordic Holdings Ltd v Mott McDonald Ltd* (2001) 77 Con. L.R. 88 and *London Fire & Emergency Planning Authority v Halcrow Gilbert Associates Ltd* [2007] EWHC 2546 (TCC); and cf. generally the builders' case of *Ruxley Electronics & Construction Ltd v Forsyth* [1996] A.C. 344.

[1324] So held in the construction case of *Ruxley Electronics & Construction Ltd v Forsyth* [1996] A.C. 344. That there is no reason to treat architects any differently is suggested by Ramsey J in *Cooperative Group Ltd v John Allen Associates Ltd* [2010] EWHC 2300 (TCC); (2010) 28 Const. L.J. 27 at [369]–[370].

[1325] *London Congregational Union v Harriss & Harriss* [1985] 1 All E.R. 335; see too *Catlin Estates Ltd v Carter Jonas (a firm)* [2005] EWHC 2315 (TCC); [2006] P.N.L.R. 15, and cf. *Dodd Properties Ltd v Canterbury CC* [1980] 1 W.L.R. 433.

[1326] e.g. *Ampleforth Abbey Trust v Turner & Townsend Management Ltd* [2012] EWHC 2137 (TCC); (2012) 144 Con. L.R. 115. See too *Riva Properties Ltd v Foster + Partners Ltd* [2017] EWHC 2574 (TCC); (2017) 175 Con. L.R. 45 at [207]–[214] (Fraser J) (losses caused by economic downturn not within scope of architects' duty to advise).

[1327] See, e.g. *Earl's Terrace Properties Ltd v Nilsson Design Ltd* [2004] EWHC 136 (TCC) (negligent architect: loss of use of funds while defects sorted out); *John Grimes Partnership Ltd v Gubbins* [2013] EWCA Civ 37; [2013] P.N.L.R. 17 (property development designs provided late: consulting engineer liable for foreseeable loss in development value of land due to delay).

[1328] cf. *Biggin v Permanite Ltd* [1951] 2 K.B. 314 and McGregor, *Damages*, 20th edn (2017), para.21–038; also *P & O Developments Ltd v Guys & St Thomas's Hospital* [1999] B.L.R. 1.

[1329] On the principle in *Alfred McAlpine Construction Ltd v Panatown Ltd* [2001] 1 A.C. 518: see *Catlin Estates Ltd v Carter Jonas (a firm)* [2005] EWHC 2315 (TCC); [2006] P.N.L.R. 15.

6. FINANCE PROFESSIONALS

(a) Accountants and auditors

(v) Breach of duty: advice

Advice

Replace paragraph with:

Accountants provide advice on all kinds of matters, from share valuations[1403] to **10-225** tax[1404] to advice on tendering for work[1405] to company administration to advice on how to administer the financial side of a business. Such advice can also include information as to how particular transactions should be treated for accounting purposes.[1405A] In giving such advice, an accountant must show a reasonable level of care, including where necessary a knowledge of the law.[1406] Although it seems that in general the duty owed by an accountant advising on a course of action ceases to apply after the time of reliance but no further, circumstances may indicate a continuing duty.[1407] It is suggested that a rule analogous to the *Bolam* rule[1408] applies here: even if the advice is wrong,[1409] the accountant will not be liable if a respectable body of opinion would have supported it.[1410]

[1403] On share valuations by accountants see, e.g. *Goldstein v Levy Gee* [2003] EWHC 1574 (Ch); [2003] P.N.L.R. 35. Analogous principles often apply here to those obtaining in relation to valuations of land, for example as to the permissible "bracket" of error: see *Goldstein v Levy Gee* [2003] EWHC 1574 (Ch); [2003] P.N.L.R. 35; *Dennard v PricewaterhouseCoopers LLP* [2010] EWHC 812 (Ch); and above, para.10-176.

[1404] See Reed, "Professional Negligence and the Tax Adviser" [2004] *Private Client Business* 318. Also cases such as *Mehjoo v Harben Barker (A Firm)* [2014] EWCA Civ 358; [2014] 4 All E.R. 806 (extent of tax adviser's duty to engage in general tax planning activities for client: no breach in the circumstances).

[1405] *Whiteleys (a firm) v Trafalgar Consultancy Ltd* [2006] EWCA Civ 503; [2006] All E.R. (D) 75 (May).

[1405A] For an example, see *Manchester Building Society v Grant Thornton UK LLP* [2019] EWCA Civ 40; [2019] P.N.L.R. 12.

[1406] e.g. *Coulthard v Neville Russell* [1998] P.N.L.R. 276 (misadvice about impact of company law).

[1407] So held in Australia: *Swan & Baker Pty Ltd v Marando* [2013] NSWCA 233 (duty to warn of impending collapse of investment fund while investor had benefit of cooling-off period).

[1408] *Bolam v Friern HMC* [1957] 1 W.L.R. 582, above, para.10-67.

[1409] If it is correct there will be no liability, even if the client is put to expense because the Revenue disagree: *Grimm v Newman* [2002] EWCA Civ 1621; [2003] 1 All E.R. 67.

[1410] cf. the lawyer's tax advice case of *Matrix Securities Ltd v Theodore Goddard* [1998] P.N.L.R. 290. In *Halsall v Champion Consulting Ltd* [2017] EWHC 1079 (QB); [2017] P.N.L.R. 32 it was seemingly assumed that *Bolam* applied in the accounting context.

(viii) Damages: measure of recovery

Replace paragraph with:

10-228 Assuming the claimant can show reliance and loss, the measure of damages is the sum that will put the claimant in the position he would have been in had the accountant performed his duty. In the common case of negligent advice, the measure of damages is generally the amount by which he is out of pocket[1419] as a result of relying on the advice in question, plus any consequential loss.[1420] So where assets to be sold by a client are undervalued, the client recovers that part of the price foregone.[1421] Where a client takes over a company on the basis of audited figures that are wrong, he prima facie recovers the difference, if any, between what he paid for the company and what it was in fact worth at that time.[1422] Again, where tax accountants misadvise clients over their tax affairs, the measure of damages is the extra tax unnecessarily payable.[1423] In a suitable case there may be an award for loss of a chance.[1424] But as with valuers' negligence,[1425] the scope of the duty broken is vital to the computation of damages. An accountant providing negligent advice (or negligently failing to provide advice at all) is liable only for the consequences of the advice being negligent (or lacking). Thus auditors failing to spot that a company is insolvent may be liable for the amount of a dividend unlawfully declared,[1426] but will not be liable for the consequences of further loans being made to that company by others in the same group: this is a question of an ordinary business risk, on which it is not their function to advise.[1427] Similarly, even if accountants fail to spot that a company is in fact insolvent such that it ought to be put into liquidation, they are not liable for ordinary trading losses incurred merely as a result of the company continuing in existence,[1427A] though they may be liable in so far as the company's method of trading is affected by failure to spot (for example) widespread fraud.[1427B] In a suitable case damages may, of course, fall to be reduced where the claimant has been contributorily negligent.[1428]

[1419] The mere fact that the claimant is a corporate vehicle wholly financed by a third party and thus personally may have lost nothing is, it is suggested, generally to be disregarded: compare the surveyor cases of *Titan Europe 2006-3 Plc v Colliers International UK Plc* [2015] EWCA Civ 1083; [2016] P.N.L.R. 7 and *Legal & General Mortgage Services Ltd v Underwoods* [1997] P.N.L.R. 567. But where the claimant sues on the basis that the negligence of the defendant has caused it to make an irrecoverable loan to a borrower, account must be taken of any refinancing by the third party which involves repayment of that loan, since this causes the alleged loss to disappear: see *Swynson Ltd v Lowick Rose LLP (in liquidation)* [2017] UKSC 32; [2018] A.C. 313. See, on *Swynson v Lowick Rose* in the Supreme Court, P. Watts, "Lucky escapes" (2017) 133 L.Q.R. 542.

[1420] For example, any loss resulting from bankruptcy caused by accountants' negligence: see *Demarco v Bulley Davey* [2006] EWCA Civ 188; [2006] P.N.L.R. 27. Subsequent events may, of course, equally go to reduce damages. See, e.g. *Murfin v Ford Campbell* [2011] EWHC 1475 (Ch); [2011] P.N.L.R. 28 (accountants' negligence allegedly causes claimant to incur liability: liability later eliminated for other reasons), and *Swynson Ltd v Lowick Rose LLP* [2017] UKSC 32; [2018] A.C. 313 (irrecoverable loan later paid off by third party in refinancing transaction).

[1421] *Dennard v PricewaterhouseCoopers LLP* [2010] EWHC 812 (Ch) (reduced there to represent the element of chance).

[1422] *West Coast Finance v Gunderson, Stokes, Walton* (1975) 56 D.L.R. (3d) 460; *Scott Group v Macfarlane* [1978] 1 N.Z.L.R. 553, 585, et seq. (Cooke J). (*Contra*, however, at 576 onwards, per Woodhouse J). But in a suitable case, where a claimant cannot be expected to liquidate his investment immediately, a later time may be taken: see *Twomax Ltd v Dickson M'Farlane & Robinson*, 1982 S.C. 113. In any event it seems that the claimant can recover the costs of a re-audit; *Tormont Holdings v Thorne Gunn & Helliwell* (1975) 62 D.L.R. (3d) 465.

[1423] e.g. *Midland Packaging Ltd v HW Accountants Ltd* [2010] EWHC 1975 (QB); [2011] P.N.L.R. 1.

[1424] *Dennard v PricewaterhouseCoopers LLP* [2010] EWHC 812 (Ch); also *Altus Group (UK) Ltd v Baker Tilly Tax & Advisory Services LLP* [2015] EWHC 12 (Ch); [2015] S.T.I. 158.

[1425] See *South Australia Asset Management Co v York Montague Ltd* [1997] A.C. 191, above, para.10-187.

[1426] *Sasea Finance Ltd v KPMG* [2000] 1 All E.R. 676. See too *Assetco Plc v Grant Thornton UK LLP* [2019] EWHC 150 (Comm) at [967]–[969] (Bryan J).

[1427] See *Bank of Credit & Commerce International (in liq) v Price Waterhouse (No.4)* [1999] B.C.C. 351. For another instance, cf. the actuaries' case of *Andrews v Barnett Waddingham (a firm)* [2006] EWCA Civ 93; [2006] P.N.L.R. 24 (misadvice as to whether annuity protected under Policyholders Protection Act 1975 irrelevant where underwriter of annuity not insolvent anyway). More recently, see *Manchester Building Society v Grant Thornton UK LLP* [2019] EWCA Civ 40; [2019] P.N.L.R. 12 (advice as to accounting treatment of swaps is information rather than advice and does not, within SAAMCO and *Hughes-Holland v BPE Solicitors* [2017] UKSC 21; [2018] A.C. 599, carry with it potential liability for costs of closing out swaps entered into as a result of that advice).

[1427A] *Assetco Plc v Grant Thornton UK LLP* [2019] EWHC 150 (Comm) at [932]–[934], following dicta of Langley J in *Equitable Life Assurance Society v Ernst & Young* [2003] EWHC 112 (Comm); [2003] P.N.L.R. 23 at [85].

[1427B] See *Assetco Plc v Grant Thornton UK LLP* [2019] EWHC 150 (Comm), especially at [919]–[966].

[1428] e.g. *Barings Plc (In Liq) v Coopers & Lybrand* [2003] EWHC 1319 (Ch); [2003] P.N.L.R. 34 (accountants negligently failed to draw attention to suspicious signs of unauthorised trading: damages reduced to take account of failings in claimants' own internal procedures). See too *Slattery v Moore Stephens* [2003] EWHC 1869 (Ch); [2004] P.N.L.R. 14 (tax adviser negligently failed to shelter earnings from UK tax: taxpayer's claim reduced by 50 per cent for his failure to act on the Revenue's pointed suggestion that earnings in fact taxable).

(b) Accountants as receivers

Accountants and receivers

Replace paragraph with:

10-230 The appointment of a receiver[1430] is a very general remedy available in equity.[1431] Strictly speaking the liability of a receiver to the owner of the property concerned is of no interest to a tort lawyer, since it is now clear that it is a liability in equity and not in tort.[1432] Nevertheless, receivers are in practice nearly always accountants or similar financial professionals, and their liability as such it is an important aspect of their liability which deserves brief coverage here. It matters in particular in one case, namely, where a mortgagee or chargee,[1433] acting under a power contained in the relevant instrument, appoints a receiver to realise his security.

[1430] Who is almost invariably an accountant. Note that this is a specific reference to a receiver. The duties of a person acting as a statutory officer in insolvency, such as an administrator, are different and derived from a separate legislative framework, beyond the scope of this work. See *Davey v Money* [2018] EWHC 766 (Ch); [2018] Bus. L.R. 1903 at [252]–[254].

[1431] See generally *Kerr & Hunter on Receivers and Administrators*, 19th edn (2009).

[1432] *Downsview Nominees Ltd v First City Corp.* [1993] A.C. 295; *Medforth v Blake* [2000] Ch. 86, 97 (Scott VC).

[1433] Including a company debenture-holder-cum-floating chargee, the commonest situation where the problem arises.

Replace paragraph with:

10-231 A receiver appointed in these circumstances, while theoretically an agent of the debtor, acts under the general direction of the chargee. It is to the chargee that his first duty is owed. Thus, where he takes over a business he may close it down forthwith and sell the assets for what they will fetch, even if this is disastrous to the chargor.[1434] Similarly, if he decides to sell assets, he owes the chargor no duty of care with regard to the actual timing of the realisation of those assets (since this would unduly hamper the chargee's right to realise his security[1435]). The receiver's only duty in this respect is one of good faith: that is, not to act fraudulently or for an improper motive.[1436] Put another way, breach of this duty necessarily involves intentional conduct amounting to more than mere negligence, and encompassing either an improper motive or an element of bad faith, but it need not amount to dishonesty.[1436A] It is not enough for these purposes to show that the sale was to an associate of the mortgagee appointing the receiver.[1436B] However, once a receiver has determined on a course of action, such as sale of the assets or the continuing of the business, he must normally carry this out with due care. This duty of care operates on analogous principles to the duty owed by a mortgagee to his mortgagor.[1437] Thus if he chooses to realise the security forthwith, he owes a duty,[1438] certainly to the chargor himself[1439] and possibly to any surety of his,[1440] to get a reasonable amount for it.[1441] Similarly, a receiver must show proper diligence in carrying on a business. Thus in *Medforth v Blake*[1442] it was held that receivers managing a pig-farming business owed the chargor at least some duty to do so in a commercial manner and keep costs under control. In so far as the receiver acts as the chargee's agent or on his orders, the chargee will be liable equally with him,[1443] but not otherwise.[1444] The receiver's duty of care, however, is not owed to anyone other than the debtor, a co-mortgagor or incumbrancer interested in the mortgaged property,[1445] or possibly the debtor's guarantor. Thus it cannot be invoked by a shareholder,[1446] creditor,[1447] subsequent incumbrancer[1448] or (it would seem) the beneficiary of property held on trust by the debtor.[1449]

[1434] *Re B. Johnson & Co* [1955] Ch.634, 661 (Jenkins LJ).

[1435] *Tse Kwong Lam v Won Chit Sen* [1983] 1 W.L.R. 1394, 1434. See also the *Standard Chartered* case at 1417. The creditor, not surprisingly, has the same immunity: *China & South Sea Bank v Tan* [1990] A.C. 536. *A fortiori*, the creditor owes no duty to the debtor or any guarantor in deciding when to appoint a receiver: *Shamji v Johnson Matthey Bankers Ltd* [1991] B.C.L.C. 36. Whether this is entirely fair to the debtor is open to some doubt: compare the New Zealand Receiverships Act 1993 s.18, requiring the receiver to have reasonable regard to the interests of the debtor and his unsecured creditors, subject to his overriding duty to the creditor.

[1436] For example, where (as in *Downsview Nominees Ltd v First City Corp'n* [1993] A.C. 295) the receiver refuses an offer by a subsequent incumbrancer to purchase his interest for the full amount owing, thus showing an intention to do something other than simply realise his security as advantageously as possible. Note that the burden of proof of bad faith or improper motive is on the claimant: *Devon Commercial Property Ltd v Barnett* [2019] EWHC 700 (Ch) at [28]–[29].

[1436A] *Devon Commercial Property Ltd v Barnett* [2019] EWHC 700 (Ch) at [188].

[1436B] *Devon Commercial Property Ltd v Barnett* [2019] EWHC 700 (Ch) at [194].

[1437] Lord Denning MR implied as much in *Standard Chartered Bank Ltd v Walker* [1982] 1 W.L.R. 1410, 1414. For the principle as between mortgagor and mortgagee, see *Cuckmere Brick Ltd v Mutual Finance Ltd* [1971] Ch. 949.

[1438] Which seems to include liability for independent contractors, such as valuers, employed by him: see *Cuckmere Brick Co Ltd v Mutual Finance Ltd* [1971] Ch. 949 at 973 (Cross LJ), *Raja v Austin Gray* [2002] EWCA Civ 1965; [2003] Lloyd's Rep. P.N. 126, and G. Lightman and G. Moss, *The Law of Receivers and Administrators of Companies* (5th edn, 2011), para.13-042 onwards. But the independent contractor is not himself liable directly to the claimant: see *Raja*, above.

[1439] Including someone whose property stands charged with the debt, even if not personally liable to pay it: *Knight v Lawrence* [1993] B.C.L.C. 215.

[1440] In *Standard Chartered Bank Ltd v Walker* [1982] 1 W.L.R. 1410 and *American Express International Banking Corp'n v Hurley* [1985] 3 All E.R. 564, the duty was held to be owed to guarantors; and in *Raja v Austin Gray EWCA* [2002] EWCA Civ 1965; [2003] Lloyd's Rep. P.N. 126 the CA thought it was also person whose property was mortgaged to support the debt. But the correctness of this was doubted by Lightman J in *Burgess v Auger* [1998] B.C.L.C. 478.

[1441] *Standard Chartered Bank Ltd v Walker* [1982] 1 W.L.R. 1410; also *American Express International Banking Corp'n v Hurley* [1985] 3 All E.R. 564. See too the administrator's case of *Brewer v Iqbal* [2019] EWHC 182 (Ch); [2019] P.N.L.R. 15 at [79]–[89].

[1442] [2000] Ch. 86; see too A. Kenny, "Equity, commercial sense and the borrower" [1999] Conv. 434.

[1443] As in *Standard Chartered Bank v Walker* [1982] 1 W.L.R. 1410, where the bank was liable for the acts of the receiver, since it had largely directed its operations.

[1444] Thus in *American Express v Hurley* [1985] 3 All E.R. 564 it was held that the receiver had acted purely as agent for the debtor until it went into liquidation, and thereafter for the bank. But it was stressed in that case that the question whether the receiver is an agent for the creditor is a question of fact in all cases. See generally the CA decision in *National Bank of Greece v Pinios Shipping Co (The Maira)* [1990] 1 A.C. 637 (reversed on other grounds in the House of Lords: *ibid.*). Just conceivably a chargee who appoints a receiver it ought to know to be incompetent may be liable to the debtor: *Shamji v Johnson Matthey Bankers Ltd* [1991] B.C.L.C. 36, 42.

[1445] *Downsview Nominees Ltd v First City Corp Ltd* [1993] A.C. 295; *Alpstream AG v PK Airfinance SàRL* [2015] EWCA Civ 1318; [2016] 2 P. & C.R. 2.

[1446] *Burgess v Auger* [1998] B.C.L.C. 478.

[1447] *Latchford v Beirne* [1981] 3 All E.R. 705, per Milmo J (semble); *Hague v Nam Tai Electronics Inc* [2008] UKPC 13; [2008] P.N.L.R. 27; [2008] B.C.C. 295.

[1448] *Downsview Nominees Ltd v First City Corp* [1993] A.C. 295.

[1449] This seems to follow from the analogy of *Parker-Tweedale v Dunbar Bank Plc* [1991] Ch. 26.

(c) Stockbrokers

Stockbrokers

Replace footnote 1450 with:

[1450] An example of a case not concerning execution of commissions was *Singularis Holdings Ltd v Daiwa Capital Markets Europe Ltd* [2017] EWHC 257 (Ch); [2017] 1 Lloyd's Rep. 226 (negligently **10-232** allowing cash on deposit for client to be fraudulently spirited away). *Singularis Holdings Ltd (In Official Liquidation) v Daiwa Capital Markets Europe Ltd* has been upheld in the Court of Appeal: see [2018] EWCA Civ 84; [2018] P.N.L.R. 19.

(d) Financial professionals and advisers

Liability to clients

Replace footnote 1465 with:

10-234 [1465] See, e.g. *Seymour v Ockwell* [2005] EWHC 1137; [2005] P.N.L.R. 39; also *Medsted Associates Ltd v Canaccord Genuity Wealth (International) Ltd* [2019] EWCA Civ 83 (though there the court doubted whether on the facts the relation was fiduciary).

Scope of duty

Replace paragraph with:

10-236 Where positive financial advice is provided which it is clear is likely to be relied on by a client or customer, there is presumptively a duty of care to make sure it is considered and correct.[1470] Thus in a series of cases banks have been held liable where they have misadvised customers on particular investments.[1471] On the other hand, a positive duty to give advice will not be inferred from the mere fact that a financial organisation enters into a transaction with a customer.[1472] But the extent of any duty owed depends ultimately on the terms of a financial adviser's retainer.[1473] Thus while an adviser will readily be held to owe a duty to advise on matters directly pertinent to the transaction in question,[1474] he will not generally come under any duty to advise about collateral matters.[1475]

[1470] *Cornish v Midland Bank Plc* [1985] 3 All E.R. 513, especially at 516–517 (Croom-Johnson LJ), 520 (Glidewell LJ).

[1471] e.g. *Woods v Martins Bank Ltd* [1959] 1 Q.B. 55; *Cornish v Midland Bank Plc* [1985] 3 All E.R. 513; *Verity v Lloyds Bank Plc* [1995] CLC 1557; *Rubenstein v HSBC Bank Plc* [2012] EWCA Civ 1184; [2012] 2 C.L.C. 747.

[1472] e.g. *Barclays Bank Plc v Khaira* [1992] 1 W.L.R. 623 and *Bankers Trust International Plc v PT Dharmala Sakti Sejahtera* [1996] C.L.C. 518; see too *JP Morgan Bank v Springwell Navigation Corp* [2008] EWHC 1186 (Comm) (appealed on other grounds at [2010] EWCA Civ 1221; [2010] 2 C.L.C. 705).

[1473] *Denning v Greenhalgh Financial Services Ltd* [2017] EWHC 143 (QB); [2017] P.N.L.R. 19 at [47] (Green J). This will very often be co-extensive with the adviser's regulatory duties: see *Seymour v Ockwell* [2005] EWHC 1137; [2005] P.N.L.R. 39, and cf. *Lloyd Cheyham & Co Ltd v Eversheds* (1985) 2 Lloyds P.N. 154.

[1474] e.g. *Bateson v Savills Private Finance Ltd* [2013] EWHC 719 (QB); [2013] P.N.L.R. 20 (mortgage adviser: duty to warn of redemption penalties and fact that where several properties mortgaged, all were cross-charged).

[1475] e.g. *Denning v Greenhalgh Financial Services Ltd* [2017] EWHC 143 (QB); [2017] P.N.L.R. 19 (pension adviser: no duty to advise client that might have claim against previous adviser).

7. INSURANCE BROKERS

(c) Damages

Other claims against brokers

Replace footnote 1559 with:

10-251 [1559] See [2001] UKHL 51; [2002] 1 Lloyd's Rep. 157 at 180, 181, 186–187; also *BPE Solicitors v Hughes-Holland* [2017] UKSC 21; [2018] A.C. 599 at [43] (Lord Sumption).

(d) Causation of loss

Causation

Replace paragraph with:

It is not enough for the claimant to show that the broker was negligent: he must in addition show that the broker's negligence caused the loss he is complaining of. So a client cannot complain if the insurance that should have been obtained would not in fact have covered him in the events that happened,[1576] and a fortiori if he would have been uninsurable even if the broker had acted properly.[1577] Again, if it is plain that, even assuming the broker had placed the risk properly, the underwriters would have rightly refused to pay anything for some unconnected reason, then there will be no substantial damages.[1578] But this is a difficult plea to sustain: in the absence of convincing evidence that the claim would not in fact have been paid, the claimant is likely to succeed.[1579] **10-255**

[1576] *Channon v Ward* [2017] EWCA Civ 13; [2018] Lloyd's Rep. I.R. 239.

[1577] *Jones v Environcom Ltd* [2011] EWCA Civ 1152; [2012] P.N.L.R. 5 (failure to warn about warranty which client would never have satisfied).

[1578] e.g. *Newbury International Ltd v Reliance National Insurance Co (UK) Ltd* [1994] 1 Lloyd's Rep. 83 (non-disclosure by brokers, but insurers could, and would, have declined to pay for the separate reason of lack of any insurable interest). See too *Gunns v Par Insurance Brokers* [1997] 1 Lloyd's Rep. 173; also *Fraser v Furman Productions Ltd* [1967] 3 All E.R. 57 (though there it was found that the underwriters could not have repudiated liability, and even if they could they would have paid ex gratia); also *Dalamd Ltd v Butterworth Spengler Commercial Ltd* [2018] EWHC 2558 (Comm); [2019] P.N.L.R. 6. See generally D.C. Jess, *Insurance of Commercial Risks: Law and Practice* (4th ed, 2011), paras 4-40 to 4-42.

[1579] *Quaere* where the burden of proof lies here. Diplock LJ in *Fraser v Furman Productions Ltd* [1967] 3 All E.R. 57 at 63-64, thought it was on the defendant, but this may be going too far. The better view, it is suggested, is that it is always up to the claimant to prove his loss, though no doubt with an evidential burden on the defendant to in regard to certain defences. cf. *Toikan Insurance Broking Pty Ltd v Plasteel Windows (Australia) Pty Ltd* (1988) 15 N.S.W.L.R. 641.

Replace footnote 1583 with:

[1583] *Unity Insurance Brokers Pty Ltd v Rocco Pezzano Pty Ltd* (1998) 72 A.L.J.R. 937; see too *Mander v Commercial Union Assurance Co Ltd* [1998] Lloyd's Rep. I.R. 93, especially at 1410–149 and *Dalamd Ltd v Butterworth Spengler Commercial Ltd* [2018] EWHC 2558 (Comm); [2019] P.N.L.R. 6 at [133], plus the authorities cited there. But according to the latter case at [130]–[132] the assured must actually pursue the underwriter: if the cover is in fact good, he cannot proceed directly against the broker without even attempting to recover from the insurer. **10-256**

CHAPTER 11

PRODUCT LIABILITY AND CONSUMER PROTECTION

TABLE OF CONTENTS

1. PRODUCT LIABILITY IN GENERAL

Replace footnote 6 with:

[6] Directive 85/374. For coverage of the 1987 Act, see para.11-45 onwards. Another example is the Employer's Liability (Defective Equipment) Act 1969, making employers strictly liable in certain cases for faulty work equipment (see Ch.13). Yet another is the Vaccine Damage Payments Act 1979, providing for fixed-sum payments to those suffering severe disablement as a result of certain vaccinations. More recently, see s.2 of the Automated and Electric Vehicles Act 2018 (not yet in force), imposing an element of strict liability on the insurers of automated vehicles that cause accidents when driving themselves. **11-01**

3. NEGLIGENCE

(a) Generally

Distributors, etc.

Replace footnote 62 with:

11-12 [62] *Kubach v Hollands* [1937] 3 All E.R. 907 (seller of chemicals failed to test them before sale as instructed; liable for injuries suffered by third party user). See also *Holmes v Ashford* [1950] 2 All E.R. 76; and also more recently *Faisal v Younis* [2018] EWHC 1111 (QB) (negligence of shopkeeper in displaying caustic soda with non-childproof cap within easy reach of small boy who ate some: liability apportioned two-thirds to manufacturer and one-third to retailer). Cf. *Prendergast v Sam & Dee* [1989] 1 Med. L.R. 36 (doctor writes illegible prescription; chemist misreads it and supplies wrong medicine; chemist and doctor both liable to poisoned patient).

(b) Damage

"Other property": components fitted by manufacturer, etc.

Replace footnote 116 with:

11-24 [116] [1987] 1 W.L.R. 1. See too *Muirhead v Industrial Tank Specialities Ltd* [1986] Q.B. 507 (manufacturers of motors not liable for repairs to pumps to which they were fitted, and which were damaged when motors cut out); and the Singapore decision in *Man B&W Diesel SE Asia Pte Ltd v PT Bumi International Tankers* [2004] 2 S.L.R. 300 (ship grounded owing to failure of engines: engines negligently manufactured by subcontractors engaged by builders: no tort action by shipowners against subcontractors). Canadian courts, by contrast, on occasion allow recovery in such cases: see *Plas-Tex Canada Ltd v Dow Chemicals of Canada Ltd* (2005) D.L.R. (4th) 650 (pipes shatter because of defective resin used in manufacture; owners of pipes can sue). In *Bahamasair Holdings Ltd v Messier Dowty Inc* [2018] UKPC 25; [2019] 1 All E.R. 285 this principle may have been lost sight of. Where a part of the landing gear of an aircraft failed, making the machine a total loss, the manufacturer of the relevant part was held liable to the aircraft owner for failure to warn. There is no indication, however, that the part that failed was a replacement, rather than an original, part.

(c) Liability

(iii) Failure to warn

The duty to warn

Replace footnote 145 with:

11-30 [145] Compare the US Supreme Court decision in *Air & Liquid Systems Corp v DeVries*, 586 U.S. (19 March 2019) (equipment that required asbestos add-ons to work: duty to warn of danger emanating from the latter). One California court has, perhaps worryingly, held a proprietary drug producer potentially liable for failing to warn a user of generics based on it. See *Conte v Wyeth, Inc*, 85 Cal.Rptr. 3d 299 (2008); (2009) 105 B.M.L.R. 122.

4. THE CONSUMER PROTECTION ACT 1987 PART I

(a) Generally

Interpretation

Replace paragraph with:

11-47 Section 1(1) provides as follows:

> "This Part shall have effect for the purpose of making such provision as is necessary in order to comply with the product liability Directive and shall be construed accordingly."

The subsection enables judges to pay heed to the Directive and decisions of the European Court when interpreting the Act.[208] In any case it is clear that where English legislation aims to give effect to EU law, the courts will strain to resolve any ambiguities in favour of the latter. Occasionally there seems to be a conflict between the Directive and the 1987 Act.[209] Here it is arguable that as a matter of strict law the wording of the Act ought to prevail.[210] Nevertheless, in *A v National Blood Authority*[211] it was accepted without argument on the point that, if there was a conflict, the wording of the Directive ought to be applied.[212] The aim of the Directive is, among other things, to provide a high degree of protection to consumers, and it should be interpreted accordingly;[212A] on the other hand, it has been said that this does not entail that such protection be regarded as an overriding objective in all cases.[212B]

[208] And also, at least in practice, to decisions of the courts of other EU members. A number of such decisions were referred to in the leading decision in *A v National Blood Authority* [2001] 3 All E.R. 289.

[209] Notably in relation to s.4(1)(e) (the "development risks defence") (though the ECJ was not convinced on this point: *Commission v UK* (C-300/95) [1997] 3 C.M.L.R. 923). See para.11-71.

[210] Despite s.2(1) of the European Communities Act 1972. This is because Directives do not generally have horizontal direct effect except as against governmental and analogous bodies (see *Faccini Dori v Recreb Srl* [1995] 1 C.M.L.R. 665).

[211] [2001] 3 All E.R. 289 at 308. See too *Gee v DePuy International Ltd* [2018] EWHC 1208 (QB); [2018] Med. L.R. 347 at [67] (Andrews J).

[212] If the national law were to be applied and later found to be in manifest conflict with the Directive, then it seems the relevant government would be liable to the party prejudiced for any loss suffered: see the principle adumbrated by the ECJ in *R. v Secretary of State for Transport Ex p. Factortame Ltd (No.3)* (C-221/89) [1991] 3 C.M.L.R. 589 and *Köbler v Austria* (C-224/01) [2003] 3 C.M.L.R. 28.

[212A] The recitals to the Directive refer, among other things, to the need for a "fair apportionment of the risks inherent in modern technological production" and repeatedly to the "protection of the consumer"; and in *Boston Scientific Medizintechnik GmbH v AOK Sachsen-Anhalt-Die Gesundheitskasse* (C-503/13) [2015] 3 C.M.L.R. 6; (2015) 144 B.M.L.R. 225 at AG40 it was suggested that in interpreting it account "must be taken of art.168(1) TFEU and the second sentence of art.35 of the Charter of Fundamental Rights of the European Union, which require a high level of human health protection in the definition and implementation of all Union policies and activities".

[212B] *Gee v DePuy International Ltd* [2018] EWHC 1208 (QB); [2018] Med. L.R. 347 at [73] (Andrews J).

(c) When is a product "defective"?

"Defect"

Replace paragraph with:

Section 3(1) states that there is a defect in a product for the purposes of the Act: **11-54**

> "if the safety of the product is not such as persons generally are entitled to expect[232]; and for those purposes "safety", in relation to a product, shall include safety with respect to products comprised in that product and safety in the context of risks of damage to property, as well as in the context of risks of death or personal injury."

For the purpose of determining this, s.3(2) lays down guidelines and provides that "all the circumstances" are in account, including the manner and purposes of marketing, get-up, the use of any mark in relation to the product, instructions and warnings, and what might reasonably be expected to be done with or in relation to the product. It should be noted, however, that a defect must affect safety: a defect regarding mere usability is not within the Act.[232A]

[232] The wording of the Directive is: "which a person is entitled to expect."

[232A] *Busby v Berkshire Bed Co Ltd* [2018] EWHC 2976 (QB) at [142] (fall from bed during energetic activity on it: although bed missing casters, not defective within s.3).

Proof of defectiveness

Replace paragraph with:

11-55 Although the Act pointedly dispenses with the need to prove fault, the claimant must still prove defectiveness.[233] It is not enough merely to show that the product failed and caused damage;[234] nor that a product is defective and that damage occurred, if that damage might equally have had some other cause.[235] On the other hand, the court may on occasion accept proof by inference: thus in a suitable case it has been said to be open to a judge to find a product defective if it failed in use and no other plausible explanation is available.[236]

[233] What is the position where the claimant cannot prove an actual inadequacy, but can show that identical products have failed and thus that there is an appreciable chance that this item was not properly functional? In *Boston Scientific Medizintechnik GmbH v AOK Sachsen-Anhalt-Die Gesundheitskasse* (C-503/13) [2015] 3 C.M.L.R. 6; (2015) 144 B.M.L.R. 225, a case concerning pacemakers, the ECJ decided that, at least in the medical context where safety was a primary consideration, "where it is found that such products belonging to the same group or forming part of the same production series have a potential defect, it is possible to classify as defective all the products in that group or series, without there being any need to show that the product in question is defective" (see [41]). In addition it decided that the proper protection of consumers against damage caused by defective products required that the costs of surgery to replace the pacemaker should also be recoverable: see [47]–[50]. For proceedings following this holding see the German decision in *BGH* 09.06.2015, Az. *VI ZR 284/12 & VI ZR 327/12* (four failures in pacemakers out of 46,000, some 17–20 times the normal risk, suffices to create liability). See generally B. van Leeuwen and P. Verbruggen, "Resuscitating EU Product Liability Law?" (2015) 23 Eur. Rev. Priv. L. 899.

[234] *Foster v Biosil Ltd* (2000) 59 B.M.L.R. 178 (unexplained rupture of breast implant: no liability in absence of proof of what went wrong); *Richardson v London Rubber Co Ltd* [2000] Lloyd's Rep. Med. 280 (unexplained failure of condom); *Love v Halfords Ltd* [2014] EWHC 1057 (QB); [2014] P.I.Q.R. P20 (defect in cycle could have been due to mishandling). Indeed, it has been said that such presumptions would be contrary to EU law: see *W v Sanofi Pasteur* (C-621/15) [2017] 4 W.L.R. 171; [2018] 1 C.M.L.R. 16 at [36]–[37] and *Gee v DePuy International Ltd* [2018] EWHC 1208 (QB); [2018] Med. L.R. 347 at [79]–[80] (Andrews J). But courts elsewhere in Europe do not necessarily accept this: see the French decision in *Aix-en-Provence*, October 2, 2001, 2001 D. (IR) 3092.

[235] *Hufford v Samsung Electronics (UK) Ltd* [2014] EWHC 2956 (TCC); [2014] B.L.R. 633 (house fire might have originated either in a refrigerator or in material strewn around it: claimant lost); see also *Gee v DePuy International Ltd* [2018] EWHC 1208 (QB); [2018] Med. L.R. 347 at [98].

[236] *Ide v ATB Sales Ltd* [2008] EWCA Civ 424; [2008] P.I.Q.R. P13 (mountain bicycle handlebars broke, throwing rider: decision in favour of rider upheld, even though no specific evidence of particular defect). To similar effect is the German decision in *OLG Koblenz* 12.02.2014, 5 U 762/14 (deep fat fryer caught fire: burden of proof on defendant to show that no defect). American authority on strict product liability shows a similar tendency: see, e.g. *Moores v Sunbeam Products, Inc*, 425 F.Supp.2d 151 (Me 2003). In *W v Sanofi Pasteur* (C-621/15) [2017] 4 W.L.R. 171; [2018] 1 C.M.L.R. 16 the ECJ held that there was no inconsistency between such practices and art.4 of the Directive, since this was a matter of national (procedural) law, and besides it was right to construe the Directive generously in favour of victims. See too, for other cases where a defect was inferred, *Baker v KTM Sportmotorcycle UK Ltd* [2017] EWCA Civ 378; [2018] E.C.C. 35 (brakes on two-year-old fully-maintained motorcycle inexplicably seized, throwing and injuring its rider) and *Al-Iqra v DSG Retail Ltd* [2019] EWHC 429 (QB) (electric heater ignited, causing house fire).

Manufacturing and design defects

Replace footnote 242 with:

11-56 [242] [2001] 3 All E.R. 289, 317–318. See too *Gee v DePuy International Ltd* [2018] EWHC 1208 (QB); [2018] Med. L.R. 347 at [93] (Andrews J); and V. Westphalen, *Produkthaftungshandbuch* (1990), paras 23–24 (discussing the Directive in the German context).

Defects: safety "such as persons generally are entitled to expect"

Replace paragraph with:

The phrase "such as persons generally are entitled to expect" involves an objectively reasonable expectation, rather than any actual belief:[244] as such it is clearly meant to introduce some flexibility.[245] A person cannot legitimately expect a car to have armour-plating even if this would reduce the chances of injury in an accident: again, merely because some cars have special safety features such as anti-lock brakes, this does not necessarily mean that cheaper models without such features are therefore defective.[246] Similarly, if a product is reasonably safe it may be non-defective even if as a result of a manufacturing error it is not up to normal standards.[247] However, it should be noted that the criterion of what is defective remains a stringent one. Thus in *A v National Blood Authority*,[248] concerning transfused blood containing the hepatitis C virus, it was held that concept referred to the public's legitimate expectation, not its actual expectation. Hence the fact that the public knew that there was an inevitable risk that some blood would be contaminated despite all possible precautions did not prevent liability arising in respect of that which was contaminated: a recipient had a right to expect that the blood he got would be safe.[249] The relevant time for such expectation to be measured has been said to be when the product is first marketed, though hindsight may be employed to determine whether that standard was in fact met.[249A] **11-58**

[244] *A v National Blood Authority* [2001] 3 All E.R. 289, 311 (Burton J); *Wilkes v Depuy International Ltd* [2016] EWHC 3096 (QB); (2017) 153 B.M.L.R. 91 at [69] (Hickinbottom J).

[245] It has thus been said in Germany (rightly, it is suggested) that "a manufacturer can be expected to take more far-reaching measures where there is serious danger to human life or health than in the case where what is to be feared is only damage to property or possessions or slight injury": see *BGH* 5.2.2013, *VI ZR 1/12* at [13].

[246] In *Gee v DePuy International Ltd* [2018] EWHC 1208 (QB); [2018] Med. L.R. 347 at [96] Andrews J denied, in a case concerning artificial hips, that the Directive or the 1987 Act imposed a warranty of performance on a producer. Compare the German decisions in *OLG Düsseldorf* 20.12.2002, 14 U 99/02 at [58] (under the Directive, food manufacturers are "not bound to formulate edible products from the beginning so as to promote the highest degree of health", and hence no liability merely for producing confectionery very unhealthily high in sugar); and *BGH* 5.2.2013, *VI ZR 1/12* at [15] ("absolute safety cannot be expected of every product in every situation"). There is a similar move in the US: see the New York decision in *Pigliavento v Tyler*, 669 N.Y.S.2d (1998) (safety rail available as optional extra for cement mixer: mixer not defective within American strict liability law merely because purchaser chose to forgo safety feature). See too Hickinbottom J in *Wilkes v Depuy International Ltd* [2016] EWHC 3096 (QB); (2017) 153 B.M.L.R. 91, especially at [65] (hip replacement cannot be expected to be foolproof, especially where implanted in overweight and very active patient).

[247] So held in *Tesco Stores Ltd v Pollard* [2006] EWCA Civ 393 (not defective, even though manufacturing glitch made container of dishwasher powder less childproof than it should have been, with result that child ate contents: nevertheless, held reasonably safe and not defective).

[248] [2001] 3 All E.R. 289, 334 onwards.

[249] See too the German Supreme Court decision in *BGHZ 181, 253; BGH VI ZR 107/08*, 16.6.2009, especially at [16] (liability for airbag which unexpectedly deployed on rough road: question is not subjective but objective, whether product "offers degree of safety regarded as obligatory by prevailing public opinion in the area concerned"). Note, however, that this interpretation is not entirely uncontroversial. The Austrian Supreme Court, interpreting "defect," held in 1997 that an electrical voltage surge did not amount to a "defect" since this was an unavoidable risk that everyone knew about. See *OGH* 16.04.1997, 7 OB 2414/96t, (noted P. Kolba [1998] Cons. L.J. 81).

[249A] *Gee v DePuy International Ltd* [2018] EWHC 1208 (QB); [2018] Med. L.R. 347 at [84] (Andrews J). With respect, this may be open to question. If legitimate expectations change over the time a product is on the market (for example on poisonous pollution from cars), a producer should clearly escape in respect of an early product; but should he be exonerated if he continues to produce it after the change in expectations? A better criterion might be the time the particular product of which complaint is made left the producer's control.

"All the circumstances"

Add to end of paragraph:

11-59 The fact that a product satisfied, or did not satisfy, an official or industry standard is relevant to whether it was defective, but not conclusive either way.[250A]

[250A] *Gee v DePuy International Ltd* [2018] EWHC 1208 (QB); [2018] Med. L.R. 347 at [170]–[178], following *Pollard v Tesco Stores Ltd* [2006] EWCA Civ 393, in which a product had been held non-defective despite non-compliance.

Replace paragraph with:

11-60 Apart from specific instances, s.3(2) of the 1987 Act says that "all the circumstances" are in account in deciding whether a product is defective. Nevertheless, it seems that this phrase cannot be taken quite *au pied de la lettre*. In *A v National Blood Authority*[251] Burton J. expressed the view that it was improper to take into account at least two matters, namely (a) the practicality and cost of possible measures to avoid the defect, and (b) the social benefits of the product as compared to its risks. To do otherwise, he said, would subvert the intention of the Act and the Directive and frustrate the ex post facto strict liability it was meant to impose.[252] However, it may well be that these remarks may have to be modified, at least with regard to (a), in cases involving standard products. Even if there is no difference in principle between standard and non-standard products, it seems unlikely that, say, a car or chain-saw produced as designed would be regarded as defective merely because some fantastically expensive or awkward addition might have increased its safety: the legitimate expectation of the public cannot extend that far.[253]

[251] [2001] 3 All E.R. 289, 334 onwards.

[252] [2001] 3 All E.R. 289, 335–336. Compare *Wilkes v Depuy International Ltd* [2016] EWHC 3096 (QB); (2017) 153 B.M.L.R. 91 at [66]–[67], where Hickinbottom J expressed some doubts as to whether this was so. In *AH v Greater Glasgow Health Board* [2018] CSOH 57; 2018 S.L.T. 535 at [114], a Scottish court discussing the defectiveness of vaginal mesh inserts was inclined to accept the view expressed in *Wilkes*, as was Andrews J in *Gee v DePuy International Ltd* [2018] EWHC 1208 (QB); [2018] Med. L.R. 347 at [143].

[253] Compare *Wilkes v Depuy International Ltd* [2016] EWHC 3096 (QB); (2017) 153 B.M.L.R. 91 at [66]–[67], where Hickinbottom J expressed some scepticism as to the irrelevance of risk-benefit generally. So too did Andrews J in *Gee v DePuy International Ltd* [2018] EWHC 1208 (QB); [2018] Med. L.R. 347 at [144]–[167]. On the *Wilkes* decision, see J. Eisler, "One step forward and two steps back in product liability: the search for clarity in the identification of defects" [2017] C.L.J. 230 and D. Nolan, "Strict product liability for design defects" (2018) 134 L.Q.R. 176.

Inherently dangerous products

Add new footnote 263A to end of paragraph:

11-61 [263A] Hence Andrews J's interesting suggestion in *Gee v Depuy International Ltd* [2018] EWHC 1208 (QB); [2018] Med. L.R. 347 at [112] that in such cases one should ask whether such products were abnormally hazardous.

Warnings and instructions

Replace paragraph with:

11-62 Among the relevant criteria for defectiveness in s.3 of the Act are "any instructions for, or warnings with respect to, doing or refraining from doing, anything with or in relation to the product".[264] In many cases, especially of "standard products",[265] the adequacy of warnings and instructions may make all the difference.[266] A chain-saw is not defective as such: without adequate safety instructions, it probably is.[267] With regard to warnings, where the danger is a known one, presumably the standard will bear some similarity to that in negligence, despite the strict liability thrust of the Act[268]; was it reasonable to require the manufacturer to provide a warning in the circumstances? Dangers obvious to the user do not need to be warned against[269]; presumably the same would apply to very remote possibilities. But if the danger is entirely unknown, then the position may be different. Suppose a new drug is highly effective but, unknown to anyone, has the propensity to produce horrendous side-effects when given to a small class of patients. It is submitted that, in line with the strict liability approach in the Act, it would be regarded as defective in the absence of some clear warning as to the side-effects.[270] In some cases a warning to an intermediary might suffice,[271] for example with pharmaceuticals, where a warning to the prescribing physician might well be enough. In others, it is suggested that a manufacturer may be entitled to expect the intermediary to provide it.[272] A warning may be required of the nature of a product where this is necessary to avoid danger.[273] There seems, however, to be no duty under the Act (unlike the common law[274]) to warn of dangers that subsequently become apparent.

[264] See s.3(2)(a). For a case of a sufficient warning, see *Worsley v Tambrands Ltd* [2000] P.I.Q.R. 95 (explicit warning on tampons with regard to toxic shock syndrome).

[265] See para.11-56.

[266] Compare *OGH* 22.2.2011, 8 Ob 14/11h (Austrian Supreme Court), reported as *Re Defective Instructions on Oven Cleaner* [2012] E.C.C. 10 (instructions on corrosive product must include instructions on emergency procedures when skin affected).

[267] Cf. the Sale of Goods Act case of *Wormell v RHM* [1986] 1 W.L.R. 336 (reversed on the facts, [1987] 1 W.L.R. 1091).

[268] "When the factual issue is not whether the product itself is defective but whether the manufacturer has provided adequate warnings, the existence of a product defect and a breach of duty are defined by the same standard-reasonable care under the circumstances": *Smith v ER Squibb*, 273 N.W. 2d 476 at 480 (1979), decided under American strict liability law.

[269] Cf. *B (A Child) v McDonald's Restaurants Ltd* [2002] EWHC 490 (QB) (no duty to warn in relation to hot coffee).

[270] The producer might, of course, have a defence under the "development risks" provision in s.4(1)(e). But this is irrelevant to the question of defectiveness. Note, however, in this context the French decision in Cass.Civ. 26.09.2018, No 17-21271, also reported as *Consorts X v Office National d'Indemnisation des Accidents Médicaux, des Affections Iatrogènes et des Infections Nosocomiales* [2018] E.C.C. 36, suggesting that some products are so dangerous within the Directive that they remain defective even with a warning.

[271] See *AH v Greater Glasgow Health Board* [2018] CSOH 57; 2018 S.L.T. 535 at [125], and *Gee v DePuy International Ltd* [2018] EWHC 1208 (QB); [2018] Med. L.R. 347 at [169]; and also cf. the negligence case of *Holmes v Ashford* [1950] 2 All E.R. 76. See generally P. Ferguson, "Liability for pharmaceutical products: a critique of the 'learned intermediary' rule" (1992) 12 O.J.L.S. 60.

[272] e.g. where A supplies B with chemicals for B to make up into children's chemistry sets. The chemicals no doubt require precise instructions and warnings as to use: but this is clearly something for B to provide, and the chemicals could hardly be said to be "defective" when they left A's factory because at that stage no warning was included.

[273] For example, a statement on bottled gas canisters as to whether they contain butane or more volatile propane: see the French decision in *Cass Civ 1ère*, 04.02.2015, 13-19781.

[274] See para.11-32.

(d) What defences are available?

Compliance with a legal requirement

Replace footnote 279 with:

[279] A point confirmed by Andrews J in *Gee v DePuy International Ltd* [2018] EWHC 1208 (QB); [2018] Med. L.R. 347 at [170]–[178]. The same is true with negligence and compliance with statutory duties **11-66**

as to health and safety; see *Bux v Slough Metals Ltd* [1973] 1 W.L.R. 1358, and *Best v Wellcome Foundation* [1983] 3 I.R. 421.

Uncirculated products

Replace footnote 283 with:

11-67 [283] Under the ECJ's decision in *Veedfald v Arhus Amtskommune* [2003] 1 C.M.L.R. 41 (injury to hospital patient from contaminated cleansing fluid made in-house: held, the fluid had nevertheless been "put into circulation" within intent of the Directive). On the meaning of "put into circulation" under the Directive and its potential wide application, see the German decision in OLG Hamm, 02.11.2016 – 21 U 14/16 (farmer agisting horse on own farm fed it with his own silage, which turned out defective: liable under Directive when horse fell ill as a result).

(e) Defendants

Those who hold themselves out as producers

Replace footnote 312 with:

11-76 [312] For an example of potential liability arising from such outsourcing see *Busby v Berkshire Bed Co Ltd* [2018] EWHC 2976 (QB) especially at [21]. If the other firm is abroad, e.g. in South Korea, the European firm will in addition be liable as an importer; see para.11-77.

5. BREACH OF STATUTORY DUTY: THE CONSUMER PROTECTION ACT 1987 PART II

Unsafe products

Replace footnote 368 with:

11-90 [368] For an example of such a claim (though unsuccessful on the facts), see *Howmet Ltd v Economy Devices Ltd* [2016] EWCA Civ 847; 168 Con. L.R. 27 (dangerous electric fire-safety probe). An example of a successful statutory duty claim under the predecessor of the Electrical Equipment (Safety) Regulations 2016 was *Stoke-on-Trent College v Pelican Rouge Coffee Solutions Group Ltd* [2017] EWHC 2829 (TCC) (defective drinks vending machine set fire to building).

CHAPTER 12

OCCUPIERS' LIABILITY AND DEFECTIVE PREMISES

TABLE OF CONTENTS

2. THE OCCUPIERS' LIABILITY ACT 1957

(a) Scope of the 1957 Act

Scope of occupier's liability: "occupancy duty" and "activity duty"

Replace paragraph with:

The Act is not entirely clear on this point, s.1(1) providing that the rules in it: **12-04**

> "shall have effect in place of the rules of the common law, to regulate the duty which an occupier of premises owes to his visitors in respect of dangers due to the state of the premises or to things done or omitted to be done on them."

It could be argued that these words are wide enough for the Act to apply to all injuries on land due to the negligence of the occupier, thus erasing the common law distinction. But while there may of course be statutory liability for dangers in the state of land due to activities on it,[6] it now seems clear that the specific reference to the "state of the premises" limits the effect of the Act to occupancy duties.[7] As Lord Hoffmann has observed, the mere fact that a person may get into danger on a given piece of land is not itself a peril due to the state of the premises, and even if the occupier's acts or omissions may concurrently affect his safety this does not widen the ambit of the subsection.[8] Furthermore, this seems right in principle; if A's activity hurts B, the regime governing it should be the same whether or not B happens to have been on A's land at the time. Thus injuries due to the occupier shooting a person on his land,[9] inadequately controlling thugs in a nightclub,[10] failing to teach a visitor to use sports equipment,[11] or failing to ensure safe working conditions for a contractor,[12] have been held to fall outside the occupier's liability regime and within that of general negligence.[13] In any case, where the claimant's status is not in issue there is often little practical difference between his remedy under the Act and that at common law. The issue in many cases will be one of fact: was the claimant foreseeable,[14] and has the duty to take reasonable care been broken?[15] Indeed, even in clear "occupancy duty" cases the courts have on occasion simply ignored the Act.[16]

[6] e.g. *Lear v Hickstead Ltd* [2016] EWHC 528 (QB); [2016] 4 W.L.R. 73 (parking arrangements alleged (unsuccessfully) to create danger for which defendants liable).

[7] See *Fowles v Bedfordshire CC* [1995] P.I.Q.R. P380; *Revill v Newberry* [1996] Q.B. 567 at 574 onwards; *Bottomley v Todmorden Cricket Club* [2003] EWCA Civ 1575; [2004] P.I.Q.R. P18 at [31], per Brooke LJ; *Kolasa v Ealing Hospital NHS Trust* [2015] EWHC 289 (QB) at [44]–[47]. For earlier expressions of the same view see F. Odgers, "Occupiers' Liability: A Further Comment" [1957] C.L.J. 39; P. North, *Occupiers' Liability* (1971), pp.80–82. The text here was approved by Martin Spencer J in *Spearman v Royal United Bath Hospitals NHS Foundation Trust* [2017] EWHC 3027 (QB); [2018] Med. L.R. 244 at [58]-[59]. See also *Bosworth Water Trust v SSR* [2018] EWHC 444 (QB) (failure to give proper warnings about dangers of crazy golf does not involve occupiers' liability). In the Scottish case of *Anderson v Imrie* [2018] CSIH 14; 2018 S.C. 328 Lords Brodie and Drummond Young, at [28] and [53], thought a case of injury to a child on a dangerous farm gate was better viewed as involving child supervision rather than occupiers' liability. *Sed quaere*. In this particular case, why not both?

[8] *Tomlinson v Congleton BC* [2003] UKHL 47; [2004] 1 A.C. 46 at [26]–[27]. Strictly speaking this case concerned the interpretation of the Occupiers' Liability Act 1984: but the wording interpreted is the same, and hence its reasoning clearly applies to the 1957 Act. Similar cases are *Keown v Coventry NHS Trust* [2006] EWCA Civ 39; [2006] 1 W.L.R. 953 (when a child climbed on, and fell off, a fire escape, not within 1984 Act since no complaint as to the dangerous state of the premises); *Baldacchino v West Wittering Estate Plc* [2008] EWHC 3386 (QB) (similarly with regard to injuries suffered from diving off impeccably maintained navigation beacon); and *Hatcher v ASW Ltd* [2010] EWCA Civ 1325, a case under the Occupiers' Liability Act 1984 (child injured while climbing on buildings in abandoned Cardiff steelworks equipped with formidable anti-trespasser defences: held, no danger *due to state of premises*). See too *Donoghue v Folkestone Properties Ltd* [2003] EWCA Civ 231; [2003] Q.B. 1008 at [53], per Lord Phillips; and *Siddorn v Patel* [2007] EWHC 1248 (QB). On the other hand, a danger at a tourist attraction due to the presence of embedded railway tracks was held to be a danger due to the state of the premises in *Liddle v Bristol CC* [2018] EWHC 3673 (QB) (though there was no liability on the facts).

[9] *Revill v Newberry* [1996] Q.B. 567 (see Neill LJ at 574 onwards).

[10] *Everett v Comojo (UK) Ltd* [2011] EWCA Civ 13; [2012] 1 W.L.R. 150.

[11] *Fowles v Bedfordshire CC* [1995] P.I.Q.R. P380; *Poppleton v Trustees of the Portsmouth Youth Activities Committee* [2007] EWHC 1567 (QB) (the question was not discussed on appeal: [2008] EWCA Civ 646; [2009] P.I.Q.R. P1); *Pinchbeck v Craggy Island Ltd* [2012] EWHC 2745 (QB), especially at [42] (bad supervision of adult adventure playground). So also with an occupier whose negligence consists in knowingly allowing contractors to work on his land without proper regard for the safety of their own employees: *Tafa v Matsim Properties Ltd* [2011] EWHC 1302 (QB). See too *Pook v Rossall School* [2018] EWHC 522 (QB); [2018] E.L.R. 402 (supervision of schoolgirls running enthusiastically to hockey match).

[12] *Yates v National Trust* [2014] EWHC 222 (QB); [2014] P.I.Q.R. P16, esp. at [37] (tree surgeon); also *McCarthy v Marks & Spencer Plc* [2014] EWHC 3183 (QB), especially at [61] and [81] (building contractors dealing with asbestos).

[13] Or as often as not, in the case of a business occupier, health and safety legislation such as the Provision and Use of Work Equipment Regulations 1998 (SI 1998/2306). In practice the majority of claims for accidents at work tend to be brought under such provisions with the 1957 Act used as a mere fallback. Normally these duties do not affect private residential occupiers, though this is not entirely true: see generally *Kmiecic v Isaacs* [2011] EWCA Civ 451; [2011] I.C.R. 1269.

[14] On which the claimant's status may well be relevant de facto. Trespassers are, one hopes, generally less foreseeable than lawful visitors.

[15] But the question might conceivably be relevant in other ways. For example, it may be important with regard to the construction of an occupier's liability insurance policy, which will often cover him for liability as occupier but not otherwise. Thus in *New Zealand Ins Co v Prudential Ins Co* [1976] 1 N.Z.L.R.

84, a court was asked (and declined) to decide the source of the liability of a deceased occupier who committed suicide leaving poison in the kitchen which a visitor later accidentally drank. See P. North, *Occupiers' Liability* (1971), pp.79–87.

[16] See, e.g. *Davies v Borough of Tenby* [1974] 2 Lloyd's Rep. 469; *Ward v Tesco Stores Ltd* [1976] 1 W.L.R. 810.

(b) Who is an occupier?

Who is an occupier?

Replace paragraph with:

12-08 The Act does not define an "occupier". The rules of the common law, therefore, continue to determine this question.[34] Furthermore, little guidance as to who is an occupier for the purpose of occupiers' liability is to be obtained from the use of the word "occupier" in other branches of the law. There may be more than one occupier of the same premises, each under a duty to use care dependent on his degree of control, and each liable to a visitor (with a claim to contribution over).[35] So where a householder hands over his premises to builders, each may well be an occupier as against a visitor who is injured, with liability in one, or other, or both.[36]

[34] See, e.g. *Greenhalgh v British Railways Board* [1969] 2 Q.B. 286; *Shtern v Cummings* [2014] UKPC 18 at [17].

[35] *Wheat v E Lacon & Co Ltd* [1966] A.C. 552 at 577–579, 581, 585–586, 587, 589; *Fisher v CHT Ltd (No.2)* [1966] 2 Q.B. 475; *AMF International Ltd v Magnet Bowling Ltd* [1968] 1 W.L.R. 1028 at 1052; *Couch v McCann* (1977) 77 D.L.R. (3d) 387; *Ferguson v Welsh* [1987] 1 W.L.R. 1553.

[36] That one of two occupiers could be liable to the exclusion of the other was confirmed by the Scots decision in *Anderson v Imrie* [2016] CSOH 171; 2017 Rep. L.R. 21 (a case concerned with the Occupiers' Liability (Scotland) Act 1960, but there is no reason to think it inapplicable to the 1957 Act). *Anderson v Imrie* was unsuccessfully appealed to the Inner House: see [2018] CSIH 14; 2018 S.C. 328. Lords Brodie and Drummond Young, at [28] and [53], thought the case better viewed as involving child supervision rather than occupiers' liability: *sed quaere*. There is no reason why it should not be both.

(c) Who is a visitor?

Limited permission

Replace footnote 86 with:

12-18 [86] *Gould v McAuliffe* [1941] 2 All E.R. 527. See too *Spearman v Royal United Bath Hospitals NHS Foundation Trust* [2017] EWHC 3027 (QB); [2018] Med. L.R. 244, especially at [56] (confused visitor to hospital climbed five staircases, went into non-public part and fell off flat roof: held, a lawful visitor). It was suggested here that a mere honest mistake should suffice, but this arguably goes too far: it seems unacceptable to a landowner to burden him with the consequences of unreasonable errors.

Highway users

Replace footnote 104 with:

12-21 [104] See *Greenhalgh v BRB* [1969] 2 Q.B. 286 (where a counter-argument based on s.2(6) of the Act was rejected); *McGeown v NI Housing Executive* [1995] 1 A.C. 233. Cf. *Whiting v Hillingdon LBC* (1970) 68 L.G.R. 437; *Brady v Dept of the Environment (NI)* [1990] 5 N.I.J.B. 9. Ironically, although a landowner escapes liability to people *on* a path over his land, he faces more hazard as soon as they stray *off* it, since then he owes a duty under the 1984 Act, or if the straying is tolerated, under the 1957 Act. See, e.g. *McKaskie v Cameron* (HHJ Howarth, Blackpool County Court, 1 July 2009) (farmer liable under 1957 Act where cattle mauled walker who strayed off path to use a tolerated shortcut). But this may not be the case in Ireland: see *O'Shaughnessy v Dublin CC* [2017] IEHC 774 at [41] where the contrary was assumed.

(d) The common duty of care

The common duty of care

Replace footnote 119 with:

12-26 [119] See *Berryman v Hounslow LBC* (1998) 30 H.L.R. 567 CA (non-functioning of lift in block of flats not within s.2 even though claimant foreseeably injured through having to carry heavy shopping up the stairs). See also the Irish decision in *Byrne v Ardenheath Co Ltd* [2017] IECA 293 (not negligent to fail to provide pedestrian-only exits from car park).

Examples of liability

Replace paragraph with:

12-28 An occupier has, on the facts, been held liable: for creating dangers, for example by polishing a floor so highly as to be dangerous,[126] providing an unstable deck-chair[127] or a lift apt to ensnare the fingers of unwary users,[128] or switching on electricity when a decorator is working near exposed live cables[129]; for failure to alleviate hazards by leaving asbestos unremoved,[130] an icy driveway unsalted,[131] a hole in a garden unfilled,[132] a builder's trench unguarded[133] or a known rickety balcony accessible to partygoers[133A]; for leaving a trolley in a supermarket aisle so as to trip a shopper engrossed in eye-level merchandise[134]; for omitting to light stairs adequately,[135] stack cargo properly,[136] or remove potential hazards likely to injure playing children[137]; and for failure to warn of hazards such as shallow water under a diving-board.[138] Occupiers have equally been held liable for failure to anticipate problems caused by human agency, as where a supermarket allowed uncontrolled children to career into customers,[139] or no notices were posted to forewarn golfers on a fairway of flying balls.[140] This may even cover deliberate wrongdoing, as where a spectator was trampled at a football match when hooligans forced their way into the ground through an inadequately-maintained exit barrier.[141]

[126] *Adams v SJ Watson & Co* (1967) 117 N.L.J. 130. See too *Appleton v Cunard S.S. Co* [1969] 1 Lloyd's Rep. 150. Standards may be getting stricter here. In the Irish decision in *Jedruch v Tesco Ireland Ltd* [2018] IEHC 205 a worker recovered after slipping on a wet lavatory floor. It was suggested that in industrial premises non-slip tiles were likely to be required in such places to satisfy the duty of care.

[127] *Hollingworth v Southern Ferries Ltd* [1977] 2 Lloyd's Rep. 70.

[128] *Sandford v Eugene* (1970) 115 S.J. 33, per Hinchliffe J.

[129] *Fisher v CHT Ltd (No.2)* [1966] 2 Q.B. 475. See too *Lough v Intruder Detention & Surveillance Fire & Security Ltd* [2008] EWCA Civ 1009 (householder 25% responsible for letting repairman doing non-urgent work use temporarily unbanistered staircase rather than telling him to come back later). The latter decision, with respect, seems somewhat generous to the claimant.

[130] *Amaca Pty Ltd v King* (2011) 35 V.R. 280.

[131] *Waldick v Malcolm* [1991] 2 S.C.R. 456. For other slipping cases see *Jennings v British Railways Board* (1984) 134 N.L.J. 584 (not clearing litter); *Garner v Walsall Hospitals NHS Trust* [2004] EWCA Civ 702 (not cleaning slimy manhole cover).

[132] *Butcher v Southend-on-Sea BC* [2014] EWCA Civ 1556.

[133] *Moon v Garrett* [2006] EWCA Civ 1121; [2007] P.I.Q.R. P3. See too *Hall v Holker Estate Co Ltd* [2008] EWCA Civ 1422; [2008] N.P.C. 143 (goalpost that fell on footballer).

[133A] *Libra Collaroy Pty Ltd v Bhide* [2017] NSWCA 196.

[134] *Palfrey v Morrisons Supermarkets Plc* [2012] EWCA Civ 1917.

[135] *Stone v Taffe* [1974] 1 W.L.R. 1575.

[136] *The Vladimir Timofeyev* [1983] 1 Lloyd's Rep. 378 (stevedore fell into unexpected chasm in badly-loaded cargo of timber).

[137] *Jolley v Sutton LBC* [2000] 1 W.L.R. 1082 (derelict boat left ready to fall onto children playing with it).

[138] *Davies v Borough of Tenby* [1974] 2 Lloyd's Rep. 469. See too *McCarrick v Park Resorts Ltd* [2012] EWHC B27 (QB) (unguarded and deceptively shallow pool). But not so where the danger is obvious: *Risk v Rose Bruford College* [2013] EWHC 3869 (QB); [2014] E.L.R. 157 (dive into paddling-pool by foolish youth).

[139] *Beardmore v Franklins Management Services Pty Ltd* [2003] 1 Qd R. 1.

[140] *Phee v Gordon* [2013] CSIH 18; 2013 S.C. 379.

[141] *Hosie v Arbroath Football Club*, 1978 S.L.T. 122. See too *Bluett v Suffolk CC* [2004] EWHC 378 (QB) (inadequate security leading to drug-fuelled attack on claimant in authority home). But the disinclination of courts to make A liable for the criminal acts of B make successful claims rare (cf. *Modbury Triangle Shopping Centre Pty Ltd v Anzil* (2000) 205 C.L.R. 254, denying recovery on this basis for a brutal attack in an unlit car-park). Furthermore, in England occupiers' liability claims for the direct result of a deliberate attack are unlikely, save in recourse proceedings, because the criminal injuries compensation scheme gives the claimant access to no-fault compensation from the taxpayer in any case.

Examples of non-liability

Replace paragraph with:

An occupier has, on the facts, been held not liable: to a motel customer who climbed onto a log and fell off it,[142] a walker in a park who fell off a rustic bridge with a low parapet,[143] or a hotel guest who leaned out of a second-floor window and fell out[144]; to a walker in a cathedral close who tripped over a small concrete protuberance;[145] to a supermarket customer who fell over a pile of cartons in a gangway[146]; to a shopper who fell down a few stone stairs unequipped with a hand-rail outside a Georgian shop[147]; to an unsteady reveller who toppled over a low balustrade at the Ritz Hotel[148]; to a child of eight falling against a brick and flint wall in a school playground[149]; and to a footballer breaking his leg against a concrete wall near the touch-line.[150] Domestic occupiers have escaped liability where a domestic visitor tripped over a lowered washing-line,[151] and where a party-goer dived into a shallow paddling-pool[152] or suffered injury in horse-play on a bouncy castle.[153] Employers were held not liable where a lightly-used approach road in their occupation included no footpath, with the result that an employee walking to work was knocked down by a car.[153A] **12-29**

[142] *Phillis v Daly* (1988) 15 N.S.W.L.R. 65.

[143] *Sutton LBC v Edwards* [2016] EWCA Civ 1005; [2017] P.I.Q.R. P2. See too *Singh v Cardiff CC* [2017] EWHC 1499 (QB) (no liability when tipsy pedestrian strayed from footpath and fell from unfenced open land into stream).

[144] *Lewis v Six Continents Plc (formerly Bass Plc)* [2005] EWCA Civ 1805.

[145] *Rochester Cathedral v Debell* [2016] EWCA Civ 1094.

[146] *Doherty v London Co-operative Society* (1966) 110 S.J. 74; 116 N.L.J. 388; cf. *Ward v Tesco Stores Ltd* [1976] 1 W.L.R. 810.

[147] *Brown v Lakeland Ltd* [2012] CSOH 105; 2012 Rep. L.R. 140. See too *Wheat v E Lacon & Co Ltd* [1966] A.C. 552 (visitor killed owing to the inadequacy of a handrail and the absence of a bulb in a light at the top of stairs). Cf. *Martin v Greater Glasgow Health Board*, 1977 S.L.T. 66 and *Green v Building Scene Ltd* [1994] P.I.Q.R. P259 CA.

[148] *Ward v Ritz Hotel (London) Ltd* [1992] P.I.Q.R. P315.

[149] *Ward v Hertfordshire CC* [1970] 1 W.L.R. 356. Cf. *Comer v St Patrick's School* Unreported November 13, 1997 (participant in sports day fathers' race in similar predicament).

[150] *Simms v Leigh Rugby Football Club* [1969] 2 All E.R. 923. See too *Wheeler v Trustees of St Mary's Hall, Chislehurst, The Times,* 10 October 1989.

[151] *Breen v Newbury* [2003] EWHC 2959 (QB).

[152] *Cockbill v Riley* [2013] EWHC 656 (QB).

[153] *Perry v Harris (a Minor)* [2008] EWCA Civ 907; [2009] 1 W.L.R. 19.

[153A] *Mullen v Kerr* [2017] NIQB 69.

Factors in account

Replace paragraph with:

12-30 In determining whether what was done or not done by the occupier was in fact reasonable, and whether in the particular circumstances of the case the visitor was reasonably safe, the court is free to consider all the circumstances,[154] such as the foreseeability of injury,[155] how obvious the danger is,[156] the age or infirmity of the visitor,[157] the purpose of his visit, the conduct to be expected of him, and the state of knowledge of the occupier.[158] The difficulty and expense of removing the danger is a relevant factor,[159] as is the time in which a reasonable occupier may be expected to spot and deal with a hazard,[160] the practice of occupiers generally,[161] and any relevant official or semi-official safety rules.[162] The presence of a reasonable system for dealing with possible dangers, such as regular patrols, is a powerful indicator that any duty of care has been satisfied.[162A] Thus it has been held unreasonable to expect a local authority to supervise a municipal swing at all times, or otherwise disable it, in case a child falls off it.[163] Similarly the court is entitled to take into account the likelihood of the danger materialising[164]: if one allows a reputable organisation to use land, one may well justifiably assume that it will act responsibly.[165] Again, the precautions expected of a householder are likely to be less than those of a professional.[166] With amenity or wilderness land, the desirability of keeping it in an unaltered state is relevant.[167] Furthermore, it seems the occupier is entitled to take at least some account of aesthetic matters,[168] and to leave his premises in their original condition even though particular safety features may later become available.[169] An occupier who reasonably acts on professional or semi-professional advice is also likely to escape liability.[170] Conversely, failure to obtain or follow such advice, or to perform an adequate risk assessment, may well tip the balance in favour of liability.[171] It should also be noted that s.1 of the Compensation Act 2006[172] may be relevant here. This requires a court in any negligence action to have regard to whether requiring steps to avoid an accident might prevent, limit or discourage desirable activity. This may well incline a court to be indulgent to the occupiers of amenity land, cycle paths and the like faced with a claim that demanding precautions ought to have been taken[173] (though in practice this seems to have been the approach anyway[174]).

[154] In *Butcher v Southend-on-Sea BC* [2014] EWCA Civ 1556 at [11] Bean LJ unsurprisingly held that the list of factors appearing in this paragraph should in no way be regarded as a simple check-list.

[155] *West Sussex CC v Pierce* [2013] EWCA Civ 1230; [2014] P.I.Q.R. P5 (freak accident from sharp projection underneath school water-fountain: no liability); see too *Sutton LBC v Edwards* [2016] EWCA Civ 1005; [2017] P.I.Q.R. P2. Hindsight clearly needs to be avoided in this connection: *McCarthy v Marks & Spencer* [2014] EWHC 3183 (QB) at [94] (asbestos in roof void).

[156] Examples of obvious dangers carrying no liability were *Sutton LBC v Edwards* [2016] EWCA Civ 1005; [2017] P.I.Q.R. P2, esp at [42]–[43] (bridge in park with low parapet) and *Singh v Cardiff CC* [2017] EWHC 1499 (QB) (unfenced open land leading down to stream). A case on the other side o the line was *Ireland v David Lloyd Leisure Ltd* [2013] EWCA Civ 665 (barbell in rack in gym severed weightlifter's finger: liability for lack of warning of this). See too *Cook v Swansea CC* [2017] EWCA Civ 2142, especially at [34].

[157] For a neat example, see *Pollock v Cahill* [2015] EWHC 2260 (QB) (open casement window in bedroom occupied by blind man).

[158] In a suitable case, as in the rest of the law of negligence, res ipsa loquitur may apply. See, e.g. *Ward v Tesco Stores Ltd* [1976] 1 W.L.R. 810; *Kealey v Heard* [1983] 1 W.L.R. 573; *Hassan v Gill* [2012] EWCA Civ 1291; [2013] P.I.Q.R. P1 (slipping on grape at fruit stall: evidentiary burden not discharged by two-hourly sweep of area); *Dawkins v Carnival Plc (t/a P & O Cruises)* [2011] EWCA Civ 1237; [2012] 1 Lloyd's Rep. 1 (slippage on pool of liquid in popular walk-through location on cruise ship; inference drawn, in absence of clear evidence, that puddle had probably been there long enough to attract a duty to mop it up).

[159] e.g. *Tedstone v Bourne Leisure Ltd (t/a Thoresby Hall Hotel & Spa)* [2008] EWCA Civ 654 (occupier of jacuzzi not bound to mop up all spills immediately); *Sutton v Syston Rugby Football Club Ltd* [2011] EWCA Civ 1182 (no need for minute inspection of rugby pitch for debris). A fortiori where removal of the danger would itself be unsafe: see *Hughes (A Minor) v Newry & Mourne DC* [2012] NIQB 54 (child injured by firework abandoned in park: no liability in council for failure to remove, since operatives sent to tidy up likely to be set upon by thugs who frequented park). In Australia it has been held that the threat to employment caused by demanding extensive precautions is a relevant factor: *Hennessy v Patrick Stevedores Operations* [2014] NSWSC 1716 (reversed on other grounds: [2015] NSWCA 253). See too *Cook v Swansea CC* [2017] EWCA Civ 2142, especially at [35] (cost of regular gritting of car parks); also the Scots decision in *Cairns v Dundee CC* [2017] CSOH 86; [2017] Rep. L.R. 96.

[160] *Shepherd v Travelodge Hotels Ltd* [2014] CSOH 162; 2015 Rep. L.R. 2 (not negligent to fail to clear up spilt oil for 30 minutes); see too *Knight v Rentokil Initial Facilities Services Ltd* [2008] EWCA Civ 1219 (very transient hazard at airport). Cf. however *Ward v Tesco Stores Ltd* [1976] 1 W.L.R. 810 (fault in failure to mop up spill in supermarket for 15 minutes).

[161] *Waldick v Malcolm* [1991] 2 S.C.R. 456 (custom of not salting driveways even in extreme weather, though there this was overridden by other factors in favour of liability).

[162] See *AB (a protected party by his litigation friend, CD) v Pro-Nation Ltd* [2016] EWHC 1022 (QB) (building regulations); *McCarrick v Park Resorts Ltd* [2012] EWHC B27 (QB) (HSE guidance); *Wilson v Haden (t/a Clyne Farm Centre)* [2013] EWHC 229 (QB) (British Standards).

[162A] *Beaton v Ocean Terminal Ltd* [2018] CSOH 74; 2018 Rep. L.R. 110 (system to deal with wet floor due to roof leak); *Walker v Lyons* [2018] IEHC 21 (system for cleaning hospital pantry: no breach of duty under equivalent Irish legislation).

[163] *Simonds v Isle of Wight CC* [2003] EWHC 2303 (QB); [2004] E.L.R. 59.

[164] *Perry v Harris (a Minor)* [2008] EWCA Civ 907; [2009] 1 W.L.R. 19 (see para.8-205) (insufficient likelihood of injury on bouncy castle to justify extensive safety measures); *Tacagni v Penwith DC* [2013] EWCA Civ 702 (no sufficient likelihood of falls to justify making occupier fence off six-foot drop onto road).

[165] See *Cole v Davis-Gilbert* [2007] EWCA Civ 396; [2007] All E.R. (D) 20 (March) (occupier of village green entitled to assume British Legion, having set up temporary maypole, will plug hole so passer-by does not step into it).

[166] *Perry v Harris (A Minor)* [2008] EWCA Civ 907; [2009] 1 W.L.R. 19 (householder not liable for failure to observe detailed health and safety instructions accompanying bouncy castle hired by him for party).

[167] *Cowan v The Hopetoun House Preservation Trust* [2013] CSOH 9; 2013 Rep. L.R. 62 (no need to fence ha-ha at stately home, though duty to warn visitors at night). See too the Australian decision in *Department of Natural Resources v Harper* [2000] 1 V.R. 1 (no duty to warn about danger of falling trees in national park).

[168] Cf. *Phillis v Daly* (1988) 15 N.S.W.L.R. 65 (no liability to motel customer who fell off a log acting as a rustic boundary to a car-park; it could have been replaced with a foolproof but unsightly fence, but the occupier acted reasonably in not doing so).

[169] See *McGivney v Golderslea* (2001) 17 Const. L.J. 454 (ordinary glass in door shattered on impact and cut visitor: CA deny liability, since such glass acceptable when building put up even though building regulations today require toughened glass). Presumably, however, this would not apply in extreme cases. Could an industrialist escape liability under the 1957 Act to his employees if he continued to operate a factory replete with blue asbestos, merely because the premises were built in 1850 when such materials were acceptable? It seems unlikely.

[170] *Wattleworth v Goodwood Road Racing Co Ltd* [2004] EWHC 140 (QB); [2004] P.I.Q.R. P25 (motor racetrack proprietors not liable for hazard when took advice of sport's governing body); also *Browning v Odyssey Trust Co Ltd* [2014] NIQB 39 (precautions in ice-hockey stadium in accordance with governing body rules, so no liability when spectator hit by puck). Similar cases are *Hufton v Somerset CC* [2011] EWCA Civ 789; [2011] E.L.R. 482 (school pupil slipped on a puddle of water in a school hall: school exonerated, on basis that it had an adequate system in place for preventing such hazards). Similarly, the National Trust was exonerated in *Bowen v National Trust* [2011] EWHC 1992 (QB) when despite impeccable risk-assessment a tree branch on an amenity property fell, killing a child.

[171] See *Bailey v Command Security Ltd* Unreported 25 October 2001 QBD (security guard fell off unfenced lift aperture; occupiers liable together with employers, subject to 25% contributory negligence); *Phee v Gordon* [2013] CSIH 18; 2013 S.C. 379 (golfer struck by ball negligently mishit from another tee; course owners 80 per cent liable, partly on basis of lack of proper formal assessment of danger); also *Corbett v Cumbria Kart Racing Club* [2013] EWHC 1362 (QB). But note Sharp J's comment in *West Sussex CC v Pierce* [2013] EWCA Civ 1230; [2014] P.I.Q.R. P5 at [12]: in all cases the question is whether reasonable care was taken, and simply asking whether a proper risk assessment was

undertaken is an unacceptable judicial shortcut. See too the decision under the Occupiers' Liability (Scotland) Act 1960 in *C v City of Edinburgh Council* 2018 S.L.T. (Sh Ct) 34 (large sign at school fell on parent's head in high wind after screws rusted: liability for not conducting risk assessment and regular checks).

[172] See para.8-180. See also the Social Action, Responsibility and Heroism Act 2015, under s.2 of which the court in an action for negligence or breach of statutory duty "must have regard to whether the alleged negligence or breach of statutory duty occurred when the person was acting for the benefit of society or any of its members." This Act (applicable to events after 13 April 2015) might well be relevant in the case of amenity land, playgrounds, etc.

[173] Thus the 2006 Act was invoked in *Sutton v Syston Rugby Football Club Ltd* [2011] EWCA Civ 1182 as one reason for not holding a rugby club liable for failing to inspect its pitch minutely before every match in case it might contain debris.

[174] See cases such as *Simonds v Isle of Wight CC* [2003] EWHC 2303 (QB); [2004] E.L.R. 59. In *Wilkin-Shaw v Fuller* [2012] EWHC 1777 (QB); [2012] E.L.R. 575 at [42] (not an occupier's case), Owen J. suggested that the 2006 Act added nothing to the common law. See too *Cook v Swansea CC* [2017] EWCA Civ 2142, especially at [35] (possible need to close car parks on cold nights, argument against a duty to grit against ice).

Obvious dangers and ordinary risks

Replace paragraph with:

12-31 No duty is owed as occupier[175] in respect of dangers which are entirely obvious to a reasonable visitor, such as the fact that a sea wall covered with seaweed may be slippery,[176] that a rustic path may trip,[177] that a concrete drive in front of a house may be uneven,[178] that one can fall off an escalator,[179] or that piping hot coffee may scald if spilt.[180] Nor is there any duty to protect visitors in respect of the ordinary risks of activities which they elect to engage in on land: to say otherwise would elevate paternalism over ordinary freedom. In *Tomlinson v Congleton BC*[181] the House of Lords trenchantly affirmed this principle. It accordingly denied recovery to a swimmer injured by swimming in a lake who argued that his injury had been foreseeable and that he would not have suffered it had he been prevented from swimming at all. Lord Hoffmann put the point thus:

> "I think it will be extremely rare for an occupier of land to be under a duty to prevent people from taking risks which are inherent in the activities they freely choose to undertake upon the land. If people want to climb mountains, go hang gliding or swim or dive in ponds or lakes, that is their affair. Of course the landowner may for his own reasons wish to prohibit such activities. He may think that they are a danger or inconvenience to himself or others. Or he may take a paternalist view and prefer people not to undertake risky activities on his land. He is entitled to impose such conditions ... But the law does not require him to do so."[182]

Thus children who choose to mountaineer on fire-escapes,[183] holidaymakers and revellers who dive into obviously shallow pools,[184] skiers who elect to ski near a precipice,[185] and others acting in clearly dangerous ways,[186] are likely to obtain little sympathy. Furthermore, where the claimant's injuries are caused by his own perverse or unpredictable conduct, this may well in a suitable case be regarded as breaking the chain of causation.[187] On the other hand, this exoneration of the occupier is, it seems, premised on the avoidability of the danger: thus in *Liddle v Bristol CC*[187A] it was said that while obvious hazards on an unfenced quayside would not give rise to liability to a lone cyclist suffering injury, it might be different were large crowds to be present at the same spot.

[175] But a duty may be owed in some other respect: for instance, if an occupier lends his aid to someone carrying out an obviously dangerous activity and then in doing so fails to take proper care. See *Biddick v Morcom* [2014] EWCA Civ 182 (undertaking by householder to support trap door under workman).

[176] *Staples v West Dorset DC* [1995] P.I.Q.R. P439 (holidaymaker slipping on the Cobb at Lyme Regis). See too *Darby v National Trust* [2001] EWCA Civ 189; [2001] P.I.Q.R. P27 (ill-advised visitor drowned while swimming in pond outside stately home); *Department of Natural Resources v Harper* [2000] 1 V.R. 1 (no duty to warn about danger of falling trees in national park). However, in *English Heritage v Taylor* [2016] EWCA Civ 448; [2016] P.I.Q.R. P14 the Court of Appeal refused to interfere with a finding that a sheer drop on the ramparts of a castle was not obvious. With respect this seems over-generous to the claimant (though he was held 50% to blame). See too *Cook v Swansea CC* [2017] EWCA Civ 2142 especially at [34] (ice in car park on very cold day).

[177] See the Scots decision in *Leonard v Loch Lomond & Trossachs National Park Authority* [2015] CSIH 44; 2016 S.C.L.R. 102.

[178] See the Australian decision in *Neindorf v Junkovic* [2005] HCA 75; (2006) 222 A.L.R. 631.

[179] *Lavin v Dublin Airport Authority Plc* [2016] IECA 268 (decided under the Irish occupiers' liability legislation).

[180] *B (A Child) v McDonald's Restaurants Ltd* [2002] EWHC 490 (QB).

[181] [2003] UKHL 47; [2004] 1 A.C. 46.

[182] [2003] UKHL 47; [2004] 1 A.C. 46 at [45]. See too [59], per Lord Hutton) and [81], per Lord Hobhouse. Strictly speaking this was a case under the Occupiers' Liability Act 1984: but the reasoning applies equally to liability under the 1957 Act.

[183] *Keown v Coventry NHS Trust* [2006] EWCA Civ 39; [2006] 1 W.L.R. 953 (a case under the 1984 Act, but still in point).

[184] See *Grimes v Hawkins* [2011] EWHC 2004 (QB) (teenage visitor disabled after misjudging dive into entirely ordinary domestic swimming pool; householder understandably held not liable); also *Risk v Rose Bruford College* [2013] EWHC 3869 (QB); [2014] E.L.R. 157 (dive into paddling-pool at student union event); also *Evans v Kosmar Villa Holiday Plc* [2007] EWCA Civ 1003; [2008] 1 W.L.R. 297 (action against tour operator under Package Travel, Package Holidays and Package Tours Regulations 1992, but raising the same issues). See too *Unger v City of Ottawa* (1989) 58 D.L.R. (4th) 98 (no liability when drunken swimmer dived off a life-guard's chair into three feet of water).

[185] See the Scots decision in *Struthers-Wright v Nevis Range Development Co Plc* [2006] CSOH 68.

[186] See, e.g. *Clark v Bourne Leisure Ltd* [2011] EWCA Civ 753 (no negligence where disabled bar patron tried to steer wheelchair down a flight of stairs obvious as such to a casual glance, in the belief that they constituted a wheelchair ramp).

[187] *Jolley v Sutton LBC* [1998] 1 W.L.R. 1546, 1555 (Woolf and Roch LJJ) (reversed for other reasons at [2000] 1 W.L.R. 1082). Cf. *Unger v City of Ottawa* (1989) 58 D.L.R. (4th) 98 (no liability when drunken swimmer dived off a life-guard's chair into three feet of water).

[187A] [2018] EWHC 3673 (QB) at [109]–[110].

5. LIABILITY OF LANDLORD

Defective Premises Act 1972 s.4

Replace paragraph with:

Unlike s.3, s.4 of the Act[433] deals with defects arising during the currency of the lease.[434] Its effect is to impose on the landlord a statutory duty of care (which is not the same as the occupier's common duty of care) in respect of defects arising in leased premises where either he has the duty to repair under the lease,[435] or (even where he is under no duty to repair) the premises are let under a tenancy giving him "the right to enter the premises to carry out any description of maintenance or repair of the premises".[436] In the latter case, however, the landlord is under no duty to the tenant in respect of defects which the lease expressly requires the latter to repair.[437] The landlord's duty under s.4 is simply to take such care as is reasonable in the circumstances to see that those likely to be affected by the defect are reasonably safe.[438] It should be noted that liability is not dependent on actual knowledge,[439] but merely the means of knowledge.[440] Thus the landlord can be liable for general failure to repair or maintain even if not given actual notice of the defect.[441] On the other hand, s.4 is based on the duty of the landlord to keep premises in repair, which 12-85 means that it does not cover defects, even dangerous ones, that are inherent in the building and cannot be categorised as "disrepair".[442] By s.6(3), the duty under s.4 cannot be excluded or restricted, and is in addition to any other duty owed by the landlord.[443] It is in practice a highly important duty in the context of council and housing association lettings, since the duty to repair in such cases will very often be on the landlord.[444]

[433] Which replaces a narrower provision in the Occupiers' Liability Act 1957 s.4. Note that in Wales a more generous regime will apply as from the activation of the Renting Homes (Wales) Act 2016 ss.91 to 99. This applies to both leases and licences, and puts the landlord under a general duty to maintain the premises in repair and fit for habitation throughout the relevant period, with repairs to be done as soon as the landlord has notice of their necessity.

[434] See s.4(3). It applies mutatis mutandis to licences: s.4(6).

[435] s.4(1).

[436] s.4(4). The duty would seem to apply where the landlord has any duty to repair and/or right of entry, whether or not the duty or right concerned the particular defect complained of. On the definition of a right of entry for repairs under s.4, see *McAuley v Bristol CC* [1992] Q.B. 134 (includes obligation to afford "reasonable facilities" to landlord's workmen).

[437] s.4(4). Note, however, that this immunity applies only to actions by the tenant himself. The landlord's duty to third parties other than the tenant is unaffected: *Boldack v East Lindsey DC* (1999) 31 H.L.R. 41.

[438] For an example of liability under the section, see *Stockley v Knowsley MBC* (1986) 279 E.G. 677 CA (landlord liable for not doing anything about frozen pipes and subsequent flood, despite having been asked to): *Smith v Bradford Corp* (1982) 44 P. & C.R. 171 (landlord liable for state of patio). An argument that the section created any stricter liability was decisively rejected by Jay J in *Lafferty v Newark & Sherwood DC* [2016] EWHC 320 (QB); [2016] H.L.R. 13, and also by the Northern Ireland Court of Appeal in *Argue v Northern Ireland Housing Executive* [2016] NICA 18.

[439] Defective Premises Act 1972 s.4(2). This reversed the position under the erstwhile s.4 of the Occupiers' Liability Act 1957, on which see *O'Brien v Robinson* [1973] A.C. 912.

[440] In *Pritchard v Caerphilly CBC* (Cardiff County Court, 26 November 2013), 2013 WL 6980728, it was confirmed that the means of knowledge necessary to impose liability was the same whether based on a duty to repair under s.4(1) or a right to carry out repairs under s.4(4).

[441] *Sykes v Harry* [2001] EWCA Civ 167; [2001] Q.B. 1014 (landlord liable to tenant poisoned by improperly maintained gas fire despite lack of formal notice, though tenant contributorily negligent for not letting him know); *Rogerson v Bolsover DC* [2019] EWCA Civ 226 (unsafe manhole cover in garden).

[442] *Dodd v Raebarn Estates Ltd* [2017] EWCA Civ 439; [2017] 2 P. & C.R. 14. (staircase built without rail). See too *Alker v Collingwood Housing Association* [2007] EWCA Civ 343; [2007] 1 W.L.R. 2230 and *Sternbaum v Dhesi* [2016] EWCA Civ 155; [2016] H.L.R. 16.

[443] s.6(2). Outside this section a landlord could be liable for an omission (a) in contract, for breach of a covenant to repair or (in some cases) a condition that the premises be fit for habitation, or (b) for breach of the duty imposed on builders by s.1 of the Defective Premises Act. For s.1, see North, 36 M.L.R. 628; J. Spencer, "The Defective Premises Act 1972 – Defective Law and Defective Law Reform: Part I" [1974] C.L.J. 307.

[444] See, e.g. Landlord and Tenant Act 1985 ss.8 and 9 (implied undertaking by landlord to keep certain small houses fit for human habitation) ss.11 and 12 (implied covenant by lessor to repair structure and exterior of dwelling-house and certain installations in it, where the lease is for less than seven years: no exclusion or limitation of this obligation except on authority of county court). On the scope of s.11, see the Court of Appeal decisions in *Wainwright v Leeds CC* (1984) 82 L.G.R. 657 and *Quick v Taff-Ely BC* [1986] Q.B. 809, and that of the Supreme Court in *Edwards v Kumarasamy* [2016] UKSC 40; [2016] A.C. 1334. These provisions are replaced in England by ss.9A–9C (introduced by s.1 of the Homes (Fitness for Human Habitation) Act 2018), in force from 20 March 2019, which extends the duty effectively to all dwellings. However, s.9B provides that s.9A does not apply to a lease granted before the commencement date, except as provided in s.9B(4), (5), (6). In Wales these provisions will be replaced by ss.91–92 of the Renting Homes (Wales) Act 2016, when in force.

Chapter 13

EMPLOYERS' LIABILITY

Table of Contents

1. Introduction

Breach of statutory duty—post 1 October 2013

Replace paragraph with:

A major change to civil liability for breach of statutory duty, including liability under the many health and safety regulations, was made by s.69 of the Enterprise and Regulatory Reform Act 2013, which came into force on 1 October 2013. Section 69 amended s.47 of the Health and Safety at Work etc. Act 1974 so far as it relates to civil liability. Section 47 now provides that breach of a duty imposed by a statutory instrument "containing health and safety regulations" made under s.15, or breach of a duty imposed by an existing statutory provision,[7] shall not be actionable except so far as regulations under s.47 so provide.[8] The government's rationale for this change was to ensure that a claim for damages for breach of health and safety duties could only succeed where an injured employee can prove that the employer has been negligent. This was part of its drive to reduce the "burden of health and safety", and the perception that there is unfairness when regulations impose a strict duty on employers rendering them liable to pay compensation despite reasonable care having been taken to protect employees from harm. Whether the imposition of a stricter form of liability than negligence on employers truly does give rise to unfairness is highly debateable, given that: (1) employers are already under a duty to comply with health and safety legislation, since breach will normally constitute a criminal offence; (2) liability to employees is (or should be) covered by insurance, which has been compulsory since 1972[9]; and (3) there is a strong economic argument in favour of strict liability combined with compulsory insurance for harm to employees, in that it "internalises" the real cost of production of goods and services into the price charged to the employer's customers.[10] The change applies to breaches of duty occurring on or after 1 October 2013,[11] and so the previous law continues to apply to claims arising from breaches of duty which oc- 13-02 curred before that date. Moreover, it is arguable that even for claims arising on or after that date the measure of what constitutes reasonable care for the safety of employees in the tort of negligence should be mediated by reference to the health and safety legislation. After all, if it is a criminal offence to fail to comply with the relevant statutory duty it is difficult to see how the employer can argue that it was *reasonable* to breach the duty.[12] A pursuer's argument to this effect was accepted in *Gilchrist v Asda Stores Ltd*,[13] although here, the defender offered no substantial argument to the contrary. In *Kennedy v Cordia (Services) LLP*,[14] Lord Reed and Lord Hodge (with whom Lady Hale, Lord Wilson and Lord Toulson agreed) said: "the expansion of the statutory duties imposed on employers in the field of health and safety has given rise to a body of knowledge and experience in this field, which ... creates the context in which the court has to assess an employer's performance of its common law duty of care". In the same case, the Supreme Court determined that employers' duties at common law have themselves evolved to encompass duties to conduct risk assessments and therefore, to some extent, to anticipate risks. It is to be expected that cases interpreting the Regulations will continue to be referred to, but their precise future influence in actions brought in negligence and under unaffected legislation is difficult to predict. In *Cockerill v CKX*,[14A] a case stemming from an accident which occurred on 1 October 2013, it was common ground that in assessing the nature of the common law employer's duty, it is permissible to have regard to the statutory duties, "in order to understand in more detail what steps reasonable and conscientious employers can be expected to take to provide a reasonably safe workplace and system of work".[14B] However, it should also be remembered that Parliament had intended to make a "perceptible change" to the legal relationship between employer and employee: it would not be the case that all breaches of the regulations would be regarded as negligent.[14C]

[7] The list of relevant existing statutory provisions (as defined in s.53 of the Act) is set out in Sch.1 of the Health and Safety at Work etc. Act 1974. The actionability of legislation which is not made under HSWA 1974 s.15 nor by the primary legislation specified in Sch.1 of the Enterprise and Regulatory Reform Act 2013 is not affected by s.69. This includes regulations made under the European Communities Act 1972 s.2(2) and/or under the Merchant Shipping Acts 1979 and 1995.

[8] Limited exceptions have been made in relation to risk assessments in respect of new or expectant mothers and working during compulsory maternity leave: Health and Safety at Work etc. Act 1974 (Civil Liability) (Exceptions) Regulations 2013 (SI 2013/1667).

[9] The Employers' Liability (Compulsory Insurance) Act 1969 came into force on 1 January 1972.

[10] See *Cairns v Northern Lighthouse Board* [2013] CSOH 22; 2013 S.L.T. 645 at [37], [38] and [43] per Lord Drummond Young (see para.1-74).

[11] Enterprise and Regulatory Reform Act 2013 s.69(10); SI 2013/2227 art.2(f).

[12] See N. Tomkins, "Civil health and safety law after the Enterprise and Regulatory Reform Act 2013" [2013] J.P.I.L. 203; and P. Limb and J. Cox, "Section 69 of the Enterprise and Regulatory Reform Act 2013 - plus ca change?" [2014] J.P.I.L. 1. The difference between strict liability and negligence will tend to come into clearer focus where the damage was unforeseeable (for which there can be no liability in negligence), rather than where the issue is whether the precautions taken by the employer in the face of foreseeable harm were reasonable. In the latter case it is arguable that the statutory duty will set the standard of what was reasonable. See also A. Roy, "Without a safety net: litigating employers' liability claims after the Enterprise Act" [2015] J.P.I.L. 15.

[13] [2015] CSOH 77; 2015 Rep. L.R. 95. Equally, in another case in which the alleged breach occurred after 1 October 2013, *Jones v Scottish Opera* [2015] CSOH 64; 2015 S.L.T. 401, at [19], counsel proposed that the content of the negligence duty was "informed by" the applicable Regulations. Without commenting on this proposal, the court found that a common law duty of care was owed on *Caparo* principles, and that it had been breached.

[14] *Kennedy v Cordia (Services) LLP* [2016] UKSC 6; [2016] 1 W.L.R. 597 at [64]; see para.13-32.

[14A] [2018] EWHC 1155 (QB).

[14B] [2018] EWHC 1155 (QB) at [17].

[14C] [2018] EWHC 1155 (QB) at [18].

2. LIABILITY FOR BREACH OF PERSONAL DUTY OF CARE

(a) Nature of the employer's duty

Financial losses

Replace paragraph with:

Without a specific assumption of responsibility, the duty will not extend to protecting the property of the employee[26] or his financial interests. Thus, in *Reid v Rush & Tompkins Group Plc*[27] the Court of Appeal held that an employer posting an employee overseas owes no duty either to provide him with insurance or advise him to take out such insurance himself. But in *Spring v Guardian Assurance*[28] the House of Lords held that an employer providing a reference for an employee may be subject to a duty of care and liable for economic loss suffered by the employee as a result of a negative reference compiled on the basis of careless research,[29] and in *Lennon v Commissioner of Police of the Metropolis*[30] the Court of Appeal held that a specific assumption of responsibility stemming from an undertaking about housing allowances, did give rise to a duty of care and liability in respect of financial losses suffered by the employee. The court in *Lennon* noted that this was an example of a tortious duty of care going beyond the concurrent contractual duty owed by the employer.[31] Where the duty arises from the relationship rather than a specific undertaking, it will mirror the implied duty arising under the contract of employment and the employee may claim under both contract and tort concurrently.[32] In *Greenway v Johnson Matthey Plc*[33] the Court of Appeal held that the purpose of the employer's duty to employees is to safeguard the health, safety and welfare of employees, and this is true both of tort law and of implied contractual duties between employer and employee. The Court of Appeal considered that sensitisation to chlorinated or halogenated platinum salts, caused by exposure, was not a personal injury. Thus, the consequences of these physiological changes were categorised as unrecoverable economic losses. On appeal, the Supreme Court reversed the judgment of the Court of Appeal.[33A] Actionable personal injury for the purposes of a claim in negligence or breach of statutory duty included a physical change which made a person appreciably worse off in respect of health, capability, or physical capacity to enjoy life. Since the sensitisation affected their capacity to work, the claimants were appreciably worse off as a result of the physical changes. This, it was suggested, made the case clearly distinguishable from *Rothwell v Chemical and Insulating Co Ltd*,[33B] where the claimants suffered from asymptomatic pleural plaques. Since the physical changes were classified as personal injury in its own right, the company's argument that the claimants were in reality claiming for loss of earnings, and therefore for pure economic loss, fell away. 13-05

[26] *Deyong v Shenburn* [1946] K.B. 227.

[27] [1990] 1 W.L.R. 212. See also *Outram v Academy Plastics Ltd* [2001] I.C.R. 367, where it was held that the duty of care did not extend to advising the employee to join a pension scheme.

[28] [1995] 2 A.C. 296.

[29] Unfavourable comments about an employee should be confined to matters into which reasonable investigation has been made and there must be reasonable grounds for believing the statements to be

true. Thus, a suspicion of dishonesty by the employee should not be raised in the reference if the charges of dishonesty have never been put to him, and have never been the subject of proper investigation or formal disciplinary proceedings: *Cox v Sun Alliance Life Ltd* [2001] EWCA Civ 649; [2001] I.R.L.R. 448. *Spring* does not apply where no reference has ever been provided by the employer: *Legal & General Assurance Ltd v Kirk* [2001] EWCA Civ 1803; [2002] I.R.L.R. 124 (no liability where, due to a dispute about a claim for the return of £7,500 in commission, the employee did not apply for another job in the financial services industry because the dispute would have been referred to in any reference and would have prevented another employer offering him a job). See also *Aspin v Metric Group Ltd* [2004] EWHC 1265 (QB): no duty owed by an employer to an employee in giving reasons for dismissing the employee or in disseminating those reasons. The duty of care owed in respect of the giving of references was specific to the giving of references, and does not apply more generally to the reasons surrounding the dismissal.

[30] [2004] EWCA Civ 130; [2004] 1 W.L.R. 2594; [2004] 2 All E.R. 266. *Outram* was distinguished on the ground that the duty arose from a specific assumption of responsibility rather than the general relationship.

[31] In *Crossley v Faithful & Gould Holdings Ltd* [2004] EWCA Civ 293; [2004] I.C.R. 1615; [2004] 4 All E.R. 447, the Court of Appeal held that a general duty on the employer to take reasonable care for the economic well-being of an employee could not be implied as a term of the employment contract as it would impose an unfair burden on employers. It was not the function of an employer to act as an employee's financial adviser and it was not fair to require the employer to consider the employee's financial circumstances when it took lawful business decisions which might affect the employee's economic welfare. Cf. *Scally v Southern Health and Social Services Board* [1992] 1 A.C. 294 where the House of Lords was prepared to imply a term into a contract of employment requiring an employer to take reasonable steps to bring the existence of a contingent right to the notice of an employee, even though the effect was to sustain a claim for purely economic loss. See also *Hagen v ICI Chemicals and Polymers Ltd* [2002] I.R.L.R. 31 QBD, where it was held that employers can owe a duty of care that statements made to employees about the terms of a transfer of an undertaking in which they were employed to another employer were made with reasonable care. Elias J found that there was an implied contractual duty to take reasonable care in making such statements (which related to the terms of the employees' pension rights with the new employer) where the transfer would have an impact on the future economic interests of the employees, the transfer was unlikely to take place if a significant body of the employees objected, the employer had access to information that was unavailable to the employees, and the employer knew that its information or advice would carry significant weight with the employees. There was also a corresponding duty in the tort of negligence.

[32] *Matthews v Kuwait Bechtel Corp* [1959] 2 Q.B. 57.

[33] [2016] EWCA Civ 408; [2016] 1 W.L.R. 4487.

[33A] *Dryden v Johnson Matthey Plc* [2018] UKSC 18; [2018] 2 W.L.R. 1109.

[33B] [2007] UKHL 39; [2008] A.C. 281.

Duty owed by parent company

Replace paragraph with:

13-09 Some subsequent cases have distinguished *Chandler v Cape*, finding some or all of the factors set out by the Court of Appeal to be lacking. There are also signs, however, that courts will continue to build on *Chandler* to find duties owed directly by parent companies in a wider range of instances. *Thompson v Renwick Group Plc*,[60] falls into the former category. Here, the Court of Appeal concluded that a holding company had not assumed a duty of care to employees of its subsidiary in health and safety matters simply because the parent company had appointed an individual as a director of the subsidiary company with responsibility for health and safety matters. That individual was not acting on behalf of the parent company, but acting pursuant to his fiduciary duty to the subsidiary as a director. Moreover, on the facts of *Thompson*, there was no evidence that the parent holding company carried on any business at all, other than holding shares in other companies. It was not a situation where the parent company was better placed, because of its superior knowledge or expertise, to protect the employees of subsidiary companies against the risk of injury and where, because of that, it was fair to infer that the subsidiary would rely on the parent deploying its superior knowledge in order to protect its employees from the risk of injury.[61]

[60] [2014] EWCA Civ 635; [2014] P.I.Q.R. P18.

[61] [2014] EWCA Civ 635; [2014] P.I.Q.R. P18 at [37].

Add new paragraph:

The approach in *Chandler v Cape* has been further considered in claims brought, not by employees, but by those living in the vicinity of mining and other operations, and affected by pollution. In *Vedanta Resources Plc v Lungowe*,[62] a claim alleging personal injury, damage to property, and loss of income, amenity and enjoyment of land, was brought in the English courts in relation to the activities in Zambia of a mining company, "KCM". The claimants were not employees, but the duty to employees by a parent company in *Chandler v Cape*[63] was influential in the decision. The actions were brought not only against KCM, but also against its UK parent company, "Vedanta". Hearing preliminary issues, the Supreme Court upheld the Court of Appeal's decision both that the claims were within the jurisdiction of the English courts, and that there was a real issue to be tried between the claimants and Vedanta, the parent company. Lord Briggs, with whom all the other Justices agreed, concluded that there was no special category of negligence case involving the liability of parent companies for the activities of their subsidiaries. Applying the approach of Sales LJ in *AAA v Unilever Plc*,[64] a duty will be owed by the parent if ordinary principles of the law of tort regarding the imposition of a duty toward the claimant are satisfied in the particular case: the indicia in *Chandler* are merely helpful guidelines. In *AAA v Unilever Plc*, Sales LJ proposed two basic types of case in which a parent may owe duties in respect of the activities of their subsidiaries. These are: (i) where the parent has effectively taken over the management of the relevant activity of the subsidiary either in place of or jointly with the subsidiary; and (ii) where the parent has advised the subsidiary on how it should manage the particular risk concerned.[65] The Supreme Court in *Lungowe* was reluctant, however, to restrict the potential duty to these categories, and appeared to set out a much broader set of factors which would point towards a duty. Lord Briggs pointed to three routes to the imposition of a duty.[65A] First, there may be a general group-wide policy in place, which has inherent flaws. Secondly, the parent may go beyond proclaiming policies for the group and may take active steps (by training, supervision, or enforcement) to see that they are implemented. Thirdly, and perhaps most controversially, the parent may incur the relevant duty to third parties if "it holds itself out as exercising that degree of supervision and control of its subsidiaries",[65B] even if it does not do so in fact. This is not necessarily an issue of reliance: rather, its omission appears to be an abdication of a "responsibility which has been publicly undertaken". There was no reason to doubt the judge's view that there was sufficient material available to the court to demonstrate that the claimants had an arguable case. It should be noted that both the judge, and the Supreme Court, recognised that the final resolution of the question whether a duty was owed would depend on material that would be available only should the trial proceed. 13-09A

[62] [2019] UKSC 20; [2019] 2 W.L.R. 1051.

[63] [2012] EWCA Civ 525; [2012] 1 W.L.R. 3111; see para.13-08.

[64] [2018] EWCA Civ 1532; [2018] B.C.C. 959 at [36].

[65] In *AAA* itself, [2018] EWCA Civ 1532; [2018] B.C.C. 959, it was concluded that no duty of care was owed by the parent company to the claimant employees of a Kenyan subsidiary. There had been violent unrest following an election, and this led to murders, rapes and assaults of employees. In this case, a

duty was not arguable so that there was no "anchor" defendant justifying service of proceedings in the UK. The evidence showed that the subsidiary did not receive relevant advice from Unilever in relation to violent unrest and crisis management; and that the subsidiary understood that it was responsible for devising its own risk management policy and for handling the severe crisis that unfolded.

[65A] [2019] UKSC 20; [2019] 2 W.L.R. 1051 at [52]–[53].

[65B] [2019] UKSC 20; [2019] 2 W.L.R. 1051 at [53].

Add new paragraph:

13-09B Before the Supreme Court's decision in *Vedanta Resources Plc v Lungowe*,[65C] in *His Royal Highness Okpabi v Royal Dutch Shell Plc*,[65D] the Court of Appeal decided a case in which the claimants had been affected by the consequences of Shell's polluting activities in Nigeria. The first defendant ("RDS") was the parent company of the Shell group; the second defendant was a subsidiary of the first defendant, incorporated in Nigeria, and an exploration and production company. The question of whether RDS could owe a duty of care to the claimants was essential to the question of the court's jurisdiction. By a majority, the Court of Appeal held that the claimants could not demonstrate a properly arguable case that RDS owed them a duty of care on the basis of an assumed responsibility for devising a material policy which was the subject of the claim, or on the basis that it controlled or shared control of the operations which were the subject of the claim. The issuing of mandatory policies for a group could not, it was suggested, mean that a parent has taken control of the operation of a subsidiary such as to give rise to a duty of care in favour of all of those affected by the policies.[65E] Dissenting, Sales LJ suggested that the claimants' argument was that RDS had taken control of management of the operation and security of the pipeline and facilities to a material degree; and that if this factual allegation were to be established, this would be "a true *Chandler v Cape* type case". Taking a different view of the likelihood that sufficient new evidence would be produced by the claimants, Sir Geoffrey Vos in a concurring judgment warned of "the unlikelihood ... of an international parent like RDS undertaking a duty of care to all those affected by the operations of all its subsidiaries".[65F] In *Vedanta Resources Plc v Lungowe*, the Supreme Court referred to *Okpabi* and made clear that the issuing of mandatory policies may, in some circumstances, be the basis for a duty on the part of the parent company, if that policy contained inherent flaws. This was essentially similar to the position in *Chandler v Cape* itself, where the subsidiary had inherited an unsafe system of work from its parent company; and the same result might be expected whether it was an employee of the subsidiary, or a third party, whose safety was affected.[65G] Whatever the correct interpretation of *Okpabi* on its facts, the approach of the majority would therefore appear to have been disapproved by the Supreme Court.

[65C] [2019] UKSC 20; [2019] 2 W.L.R. 1051; see para.13-09A.

[65D] [2018] EWCA Civ 191; [2018] Bus. L.R. 1022.

[65E] [2018] EWCA Civ 191; [2018] Bus. L.R. 1022 at [89].

[65F] [2018] EWCA Civ 191; [2018] Bus. L.R. 1022 at [206].

[65G] *Vedanta Resources Plc v Lungowe* [2019] UKSC 20; [2019] 2 W.L.R. 1051 at [52].

Secondary exposure to risk

Replace paragraph with:

13-10 An employer's failure to take reasonable steps to protect employees from exposure to risk, for example from toxic substances such as asbestos dust, may also result in the exposure of family members or, indeed, members of the public to such a risk. The fact that there would have been liability to an employee does not mean there must also be liability to those suffering as a result of secondary exposure. Whether there is liability will depend upon the foreseeability of damage to the particular claimant. In *Maguire v Harland & Wolff Plc*[66] the majority of the Court of Appeal rejected a claim by the wife of an employee who had developed mesothelioma as a result of exposure to asbestos dust when washing her husband's dusty work clothes. The majority of the Court held that at the time when the exposure occurred, in the early 1960s, the risks of familial exposure were not recognised by the industry or the medical profession.[67] Judge LJ said:

> "It does not necessarily follow that an employer who should have appreciated the risk of harm to his employees, and taken precautions for their safety, should simultaneously have appreciated, and addressed, a familial risk arising from secondary exposure."[68]

More recently, courts have been required to consider the relevant date at which it can be said that at least some employers should have become aware that there was no safe level of exposure to asbestos, and that a risk was therefore posed to family members by "secondary" exposure to asbestos dust, whether on overalls or other clothing, or on the employee's hair, for example. In *Maguire*, the majority had determined that this knowledge could not reasonably be expected before the publication, in 1965, of a major study into the effects of low-level exposure to asbestos, by Newhouse and Thomson.[68A] In *Gibson v Babcock International Ltd*,[68B] the deceased's husband (who had himself died from mesothelioma) had been employed by the defenders from 1962–74. Adopting the majority's approach in *Maguire*, Lady Carmichael reached the conclusion that from at latest October 1965, when the Newhouse and Thomson article was given wide currency through an article in the *Sunday Times*, a large employer such as the defenders ought reasonably to have been aware than even lower levels of exposure would pose a risk not only to employees, but also to their families. There was a duty to reduce exposure to the lowest level practicable; and there were simple, effective ways of doing so. Before 1965, it was not appreciated that such risks were posed to family members; from 1965, the position was different. A compatible conclusion was reached in the English High Court in *Carey v Vauxhall Motors*,[68C] where the deceased's husband had been employed by the defendants from 1976–79. It was concluded that by 1965, it had become common knowledge that there could be no safe or permissible level of exposure, direct or indirect, to asbestos dust. The defendant's liability was not affected by the existence of exposure during an earlier period, from 1961-62. Before these recent decisions, it had already been recognised that, where the exposure of family members or the public to dangerous pollutants from a workplace can be foreseen, the employer's liability will not be limited to its own workforce. In *Margereson and Hancock v JW Roberts Ltd*,[69] the Court of Appeal held the employer liable for the mesothelioma suffered by members of the public who, as children, had been exposed to asbestos dust which had escaped from the workplace in vast quantities. Russell LJ approved the observation of Holland J at first instance that:

> "There is nothing in the law that circumscribes the duty of care by reference to the factory wall … . If the evidence shows with respect to a person outside the factory that he or she was exposed to the knowledge of the defendants, actual or constructive, to conditions of dust emissions no materially different to those giving rise within the factory to a

duty of care, then I can see no reason not to extend to that extra-mural neighbour a comparable duty of care."[70]

[66] [2005] EWCA Civ 1; [2005] P.I.Q.R. P21.

[67] Contrast the settlement of a claim by the Ministry of Defence in 2007, in favour of a daughter (Deborah Brewer) who used to hug her father when he returned from work in his dusty overalls. The date of exposure—including the period from 1966—was vital.

[68] [2005] EWCA Civ 1; [2005] P.I.Q.R. P21 at [51]. Mance LJ noting that it would be a "particularly hard case" if the claimant's case failed when the defendant was "admittedly in substantial breach of its duty to [the employee]", took a different view of the facts and held that there was sufficient foreseeability of familial risk to ground liability. His approach essentially required employers to review the evidence and draw their own conclusions about the existence of familial risk. It was considered, but not followed, by the Outer House of the Court of Session in *Gibson v Babcock International* [2018] CSOH 78; 2018 S.L.T. 886. However, it was noted that some studies referred to by Mance LJ had not been made available to the court.

[68A] M.L. Newhouse and H. Thompson, "Mesothelioma of pleura and peritoneum following exposure to asbestos in the London area", *British Journal of Industrial Medicine* (1965) 22, 261–296 (6/50).

[68B] [2018] CSOH 78; 2018 S.L.T. 886.

[68C] [2019] EWHC 238 (QB).

[69] [1996] P.I.Q.R. P358.

[70] [1996] P.I.Q.R. P154 at P182.

(b) Aspects of the employer's personal duty

Safe system of work

Replace paragraph with:

13-21 This is an over-arching obligation, supporting and supplementing the other aspects of the personal duty. At its lowest, it requires appropriate instruction of the workforce as to the safe performance of the task.[136] But with a task of any complexity, it requires the use of a safe system of work. This may involve the organisation of the work, the procedure to be followed in carrying it out, the sequence of the work, the taking of safety precautions and the stage at which they are to be taken, the number of workers to be employed and the parts to be taken by them, and the provision of any necessary supervision.[137] It can, however, be applied to a single operation. In *Winter v Cardiff RDC*[138] Lord Oaksey said that where "the mode of operation is complicated or highly dangerous or prolonged or involves a number of men performing different functions", or where it is "of a complicated or unusual character", a system should be prescribed, but "where the operation is simple and the decision how it shall be done has to be taken frequently, it is natural and reasonable that it should be left to the … workman on the spot". When there is an obligation to prescribe a system, the obligation is "to take reasonable steps to provide a system which will be reasonably safe, having regard to the dangers necessarily inherent in the operation".[139] Thus, it is a question of fact whether a system should be prescribed, and in deciding this question regard must be had to the nature of the operation, and whether it is one which requires proper organisation and supervision in the interests of safety. When the operation is one regulated by statute or statutory regulations, compliance with those provisions is evidence, but not conclusive evidence, that the common law duty has been fulfilled[140] because "the reasonable employer is entitled to assume prima facie, that the dangers which occur to a reasonable man have occurred to Parliament or the framers of the regulations",[141] but in exceptional cases or where some special peril is anticipated the common law duty is not restricted by the statutory requirements.[142] A safe system of work will often require that the employer has undertaken an adequate risk assessment.[143] The significance of the duty to undertake an adequate risk assessment, and to act on it accordingly, has become increasingly plain since the decision of the Supreme Court in *Kennedy v Cordia (Services) LLP*.[143A] *Kennedy* has been discussed and followed in a range of negligence cases since liability was removed from all but negligent breaches of industrial safety legislation by the Enterprise and Regulatory Reform Act 2013 s.69, for example: *Chisholm v D & R Hankins (Menea) Ltd*[143B]; *Cassells v Allan*[143C]; and *Cockerill v CXK Ltd*.[143D]

136 *General Cleaning Contractors Ltd v Christmas* [1953] A.C. 180 at 189, per Lord Oaksey.

137 See *Speed v Thomas Swift & Co Ltd* [1943] K.B. 557, especially, per Lord Greene at 563.

138 [1950] 1 All E.R. 819 at 823.

139 per Lord Tucker in *General Cleaning Contractors Ltd v Christmas* [1953] A.C. 180 at 195.

140 *Franklin v Gramophone Co Ltd* [1948] 1 K.B. 542, per Somervell LJ at 558; *Chipchase v British Titan Products Co Ltd* [1956] 1 Q.B. 545.

141 *England v NCB* [1953] 1 Q.B. 724 at 732, per Somervell LJ (the decision of the Court of Appeal was varied by the House of Lords: [1954] A.C. 403).

142 *NCB v England* [1954] A.C. 403; *Bux v Slough Metals Ltd* [1973] 1 W.L.R. 1358 (breach of common law duty but not of statutory duty). But note that even where failure to give instructions does not amount to negligence at common law, there may still be a breach of statutory duty: *Boyle v Kodak Ltd* [1969] 1 W.L.R. 661.

143 See *Vaile v London Borough of Havering* [2011] EWCA Civ 246; [2011] E.L.R. 274 where an education authority was held liable to a teacher injured in an attack by a 14-year-old autistic pupil. Although the claimant could not identify what precise steps should have been taken in order to prevent the attack, this was the result of a failure to assess the risks posed by the pupil in light of his behaviour, and a proper risk assessment would have led to the identification of steps which would have avoided the injuries. See further para.13-50 in relation to an employer's statutory duty to undertake risk assessments under the Management of Health and Safety at Work Regulations.

143A [2016] UKSC 6; [2016] 1 W.L.R. 597; discussed in para.13-32.

143B [2018] EWHC 3407 (QB).

143C [2019] CSOH 14.

143D [2018] EWHC 1155 (QB).

(c) Standard of care expected of an employer

Application to cases of mesothelioma

Replace paragraph with:

13-29 With cases of low level exposure to asbestos, liability has been defeated on the basis that there has been no breach of duty either at common law or in the case of those statutory duties interpreted as akin to negligence. The general approach to breach of duty, as elaborated in *Baker v Quantum Clothing*, remains applicable to mesothelioma cases, notwithstanding the modification of the test for causation in such cases.[180] In *Williams v University of Birmingham*[181] the Court of Appeal held that the correct test in relation to breach of duty in mesothelioma cases was not whether the defendant exercised reasonable care to avoid exposing the claimant to a *material increase of the risk* of developing mesothelioma, but whether the defendant exercised reasonable care to ensure that the claimant was not exposed to a foreseeable risk of asbestos-related injury (with the question of foreseeability to be judged by reference to the state of knowledge and practice at the time). The test for establishing causation may have been modified by the House of Lords in *Fairchild*, but there was nothing to suggest that the test for breach of duty in mesothelioma cases had been altered so that a claimant only had to demonstrate that the defendant failed to take reasonable steps to ensure that the claimant or victim was not exposed to a "material increase in the risk of mesothelioma".[182] In *Bussey v 00654701 Ltd (formerly Anglia Heating)*[182A] the Court of Appeal provided important clarification of an issue raised by the decision in *Williams*, without questioning the result of the decision itself nor other aspects of its reasoning. In *Bussey*, the first instance judge had felt bound by *Williams* to decide that the claimant could not succeed if his exposure by the defendant, which took place between 1965 and 1968, was at a level below that provided in Technical Data Note 13 ("TDN13"), which was published by HM Factory Inspectorate in 1970. It appeared that the Court in *Williams* had referred to this as establishing what was considered to be an "acceptable level" of exposure at the relevant time. In *Bussey* the Court of Appeal considered that TDN13 did not set such a definitive level for exposure either in 1970, or before that time. Rather, the test for the content of the employer's duty where knowledge was developing continued to be that set out by Swanwick J in *Stokes v Guest Keen and Nettlefold*.[182B] Applying the general foreseeability test to the circumstances of *Bussey* itself, the question was whether the employer ought to have foreseen, during the period 1965–1968, that if Mr Bussey cut and caulked pipes in the manner he did, he would be exposed to an unacceptable risk of asbestos-related injury? TDN13 did not set out a bright line and when he treated it as significant, Aikens LJ in *Williams* had not been setting out a principle of law. A more nuanced approach was required, asking what knowledge an employer ought to have acquired at the relevant time and determining what risks the employer should have foreseen. TDN13 should not be seen as a universal test of foreseeability in mesothelioma cases. By 1965, it had begun to be realised that there was no safe level of exposure, and that exposure to "relatively small quantities" of asbestos dust was associated with the risk of mesothelioma. Rather, TDN13 set out the levels that would trigger a prosecution by the Factory Inspectorate. The issue of foreseeability needs to be considered in light of what the employer knew or ought to know at the relevant time. In *Bussey* itself, this question had not been considered at trial, and the case was returned to the trial judge for redetermination.[182C]

[180] See *Fairchild v Glenhaven Funeral Services Ltd* [2002] UKHL 22; [2003] 1 A.C. 32, para.2-52 onwards.

[181] [2011] EWCA Civ 1242; [2012] P.I.Q.R P4.

[182] [2011] EWCA Civ 1242; [2012] P.I.Q.R P4 at [40]. See also *Asmussen v Filtrona United Kingdom Ltd* [2011] EWHC 1734 (QB) at [55] (approved by Aikens LJ in *Williams v University of Birmingham* [2011] EWCA Civ 1242; [2012] P.I.Q.R P4 at [37]); *McDonald v Department for Communities and Local Government* [2014] UKSC 53; [2015] A.C. 1128 (on the state of knowledge at the time injury was not foreseeable from the level of exposure to asbestos experienced by the claimant); *McGregor v Genco (FC) Ltd* [2014] EWHC 1376 (QB) (to similar effect); *Hill v John Barnsley & Sons Ltd* [2013] EWHC 520 (QB) (claimant succeeded on the basis of the levels of exposure to asbestos established, and the employers' failure to take adequate precautions); *McCarthy v Marks and Spencer Plc* [2014] EWHC 3183 (QB) (where mesothelioma had not been foreseeable by the standards of the time); *Woodward v Secretary of State for Energy and Climate Change* [2015] EWHC 3604 (QB) (where the employer had acted reasonably in following guidance set out at the time by the Health and Safety Executive); *Smith v Portswood House Ltd* [2016] EWHC 939 (QB) (where foreseeability at the time of the alleged exposure was to be judged according to the requirements of a *Factories Inspectorate Technical Note* issued in 1970). These decisions must now be read subject to the decision in *Bussey v 00654701 Ltd (formerly Anglia Heating)* [2018] EWCA Civ 243; [2018] 3 All E.R. 354, which calls into question the reasoning in some first instance decisions. In particular, it clarifies that the Technical Note referred to in *Smith v Portswood House* does not set a definitive "acceptable level" for exposure. See the main text of this paragraph.

[182A] [2018] EWCA Civ 243; [2018] 3 All E.R. 354.

[182B] [1968] 1 W.L.R. 1776; see para.13-27.

[182C] See also *Hawkes v Warmex Ltd* [2018] EWHC 205 (QB): an employer would be liable if any form of asbestos-related disease was foreseeable, and it had failed to reduce exposure to the greatest extent practicable; if read correctly, there was no conflict between the approach in *Jeromson v Shell Tankers Ltd* [2001] EWCA Civ 101; [2001] I.C.R. 1223 (see para.13-28) and *Williams v University of Birmingham*.

Duty to conduct risk assessments

Add new paragraph:

In *Cockerill v CXK Ltd*,[198A] it was again emphasised, relying on *Kennedy v Cordia Services LLP*,[198B] that risk assessments play a significant role in the content and discharge of an employer's duty of care. It remained relevant to consider reg.3(1) of the Management of Health and Safety at Work Regulations 1999, requiring a suitable and sufficient risk assessment. While this no longer creates an actionable duty to carry out a risk assessment, making such a risk assessment "is an obvious measure for an employer to take in discharge of its duty of care". The decision in *Cockerill* illustrates both the continued relevance of some of the Regulations and the change in the law brought about by the Enterprise and Regulatory Reform Act 2013 s.69.[198C] The employer had not conducted its own risk assessment, but on the evidence had considered an existing risk assessment in relation to premises which it had hired on a short-term basis. Whether or not this omission was capable of being a technical breach of the Regulations (a point which was not decided), it would not be considered negligent. Reliance on the existing risk assessment was reasonable and a new assessment was unlikely to have made any difference to the precautions taken. The risk (posed by an uneven step) was not one which would be appreciated only by application of expertise or special knowledge, and the employee was not in a particularly vulnerable position in relation to the risk.[198D] The existing precautions—marking the step with hazard tape—amounted to a reasonable response. The significance of risk assessment for the analysis of breach of the duty of care at common law is also illustrated by the decision in *Cassells v Allan*.[198E] Here, the deceased had been run down by a coach while "greeting" the vehicle in the car park in the course of her employment. The second defendant's risk assessment did not consider the risk involved in this practice, and this was a negligent omission. Consideration of the risk would have led to the practice being discontinued so that the omission was a cause of the injury. The fact that, after an incident, a risk assessment is broadened to include the risk that has now eventuated, does not imply that the original omission of the risk was negligent: this would be to judge the issue with hindsight. In *Shelbourne v Cancer Research UK*,[198F] an employer had not been negligent in failing to include in their risk assessment the possibility that an inebriated employee would act dangerously on the dance floor at an office party. Context was all-important, and previous parties had not given rise to any similar behaviour. **13-32A**

[198A] [2018] EWHC 1155 (QB).

[198B] [2016] UKSC 6; [2016] 1 W.L.R. 597; see para.13-32.

[198C] See paras 13-02 and 13-41.

[198D] [2018] EWHC 1155 (QB) at [82].

[198E] [2019] CSOH 14.

[198F] [2019] EWHC 842 (QB).

Occupational stress

Replace paragraph with:

13-34 In *Yapp v Foreign and Commonwealth Office*[205] the Court of Appeal reviewed *Barber* and subsequent cases in relation to occupational stress and arrived at a summary of how questions of foreseeability and remoteness should be applied:

(1) In considering, in the context of the common law duty of care, whether it is reasonably foreseeable that the acts or omissions of the employer may cause an employee to suffer a psychiatric injury, such an injury will not usually be foreseeable unless there were indications, of which the employer was or should have been aware, of some problem or psychological vulnerability on the part of the employee (derived from *Barber v Somerset*).

(2) That approach extends to cases where the employer has committed a one-off act of unfairness such as the imposition of a disciplinary sanction.

(3) In neither kind of case should that be regarded as an absolute rule: *Barber* contains no more than guidance and each case must turn on its own facts.

(4) In claims for breach of the common law duty of care it is immaterial that the duty arises in contract as well as tort: they are in substance treated as covered by tortious rules. In order to establish whether the duty is broken, it will be necessary to establish whether psychiatric injury was reasonably foreseeable; and if that is established, no issue as to remoteness can arise when such injury eventuates.

(5) In claims for breach of express contractual term, the contractual test of remoteness will be applicable.

In *Yapp* itself, the claimant had been suddenly withdrawn from his post in response to allegations of misconduct which proved to be untrue. He later developed a depressive illness. There were no prior signs of vulnerability to stress. The Court pointed out that, in principle, an employer's conduct in a particular case may be so devastating that it is foreseeable that even a person of ordinary robustness might develop a depressive illness as a result. In this particular case, however, it was concluded that it was not reasonably foreseeable that the defendant's action in withdrawing the claimant from his post without giving him the opportunity to state his case might lead him to develop psychiatric illness.[206] A contrasting case which similarly concerned the conduct of an investigation into the pursuer's conduct is *K v Chief Constable of the Police Service of Scotland*.[206A] There were breaches of the employer's duty of care in moving the pursuer from her existing role without objective evaluation or scrutiny and without presenting them to the pursuer, and (further) in wrongfully informing her that her move was temporary; and she had experienced previous incidents of stress. A case where the psychological harm to the claimant was found to be unforeseeable is *Piepenbrock v London School of Economics and Political Science*.[206B] It was held that the defendant employer had no relevant prior information as to the claimant's personality or medical issues which should have put it on notice of his vulnerability to mental ill-health. Although it should have resolved the complaints against him expeditiously, its breaches did not create a foreseeable risk of psychiatric injury.

[205] [2014] EWCA Civ 1512; [2015] I.R.L.R. 112 at [119].

[206] [2014] EWCA Civ 1512; [2015] I.R.L.R. 112 at [124].

[206A] [2019] CSOH 9.

[206B] [2018] EWHC 2572 (QB); [2018] E.L.R. 596.

Material contribution

Replace paragraph with:

On the other hand, the employee does not have to prove that the breach of duty was the sole cause, merely that it made a material contribution to his mental illness.[227] The difficulty has been in determining whether and when damages fall to be apportioned where there are other potential causes. Equally, the existence of one or more other potential causes has also been distinguished from the situation where damages fall to be reduced because of the likelihood of future harm irrespective of the tort, where there is a susceptible claimant. In *Garrod v North Devon NHS Primary Care Trust*,[228] Henriques J reduced damages to reflect the vulnerability of a particular claimant to stress, relying on Hale LJ's suggestion in *Hatton* that where: **13-39**

> "it is established that the constellation of symptoms suffered by the claimant stems from a number of different extrinsic causes then a sensible attempt should be made to apportion liability accordingly."[229]

The Court of Appeal in *Dickins v O2 Plc*[230] unanimously declared (albeit obiter) that this was no longer the right approach. In *Dickins*, the trial judge had reduced the claimant's damages to reflect the fact that other non-tortious factors, including her vulnerable personality and relationship with her partner, had interacted with her employer's negligence in bringing about the harm. The claimant did not appeal against this reduction in damages. But Smith LJ (with the agreement of Wall LJ and Sedley LJ) was of the view that the approach, based as it was on dicta of Hale LJ which were incompatible with the decision of the Court of Appeal in *Bailey v Ministry of Defence*,[231] was not appropriate to a stress case of this type. In *Bailey*, the Court of Appeal allowed recovery in full where the claimant could establish that the defendant's breach made a "material contribution to" an indivisible injury, which is to say that its causal potency was more than negligible. Smith LJ stated the position as follows:

> ". . . apportionment of the whole of the damages is usually carried out only in cases where the injury is divisible. In such cases the seriousness of the medical condition in question is often related to the degree of exposure to the agent causing it; in other words the condition is 'dose-related'. The true nature of such cases is that the tort has caused only part of the overall injury."[232]

It follows that although Hale LJ in *Hatton* treated *Rahman v Arearose*[233] as a case where damage for mental injury was apportioned even though the injury was not divisible, *Rahman* should be seen as a case where the court (rightly or wrongly) accepted expert evidence that the claimant was suffering from more than one distinct psychiatric condition, and that each of these was attributable to a different cause. As such, it fell within the definition of cases where "the tort has caused only part of the overall injury", and therefore of divisible injury. In a case in which the claimant has been "tipped over the edge" into a breakdown by a series of factors, the Court of Appeal in *Dickins v O2* considered that the analysis in *Rahman* is not appropriate. Essentially, the Court of Appeal in *Dickins* took the view that such damage generally is indivisible. Although Hale LJ's observations were qualified by the caveat that damage should not be apportioned where the injury was to be regarded as genuinely indivisible, there was a tension between the dicta in *Hatton*, and in *Dickins v O2*. As Sedley LJ observed, the decision in *Bailey v Ministry of Defence*[234] will now be binding on lower courts in these circumstances, rather than the obiter observations of Hale LJ in *Hatton*.

227 [2002] EWCA Civ 76; [2002] 2 All E.R. 1 applying *Bonnington Castings Ltd v Wardlaw* [1956] A.C. 613. *Bonnington* is now understood to be a case in which contribution to a progressive disease would lead to apportionment of damages to reflect the causative influence of the tort. That does not reflect all cases of mental harm, as this paragraph explains.

228 [2006] EWHC 850 (QB); [2007] P.I.Q.R. Q1.

229 [2006] EWHC 850 (QB); [2007] P.I.Q.R. Q1 at [71].

230 [2008] EWCA Civ 1144; [2009] I.R.L.R. 58.

231 [2008] EWCA Civ 883; [2009] 1 W.L.R. 1052.

232 ibid. at [44].

233 [2001] Q.B. 351.

234 [2008] EWCA Civ 883; [2009] 1 W.L.R. 1052.

Add new paragraph:

13-39A In *BAE Systems (Operations) v Konczak*,[235] a later Court of Appeal has resolved this tension in favour of the remarks of Hale LJ: to the extent that there is a difference, *Hatton* should be followed. They did so without reference to the decision in *Bailey v Ministry of Defence*, which has remained controversial and open to interpretation.[235A] In *Konczak*, the Court of Appeal distinguished between two remarks of Hale LJ in *Hatton*. Among Hale LJ's "practical propositions" were proposition 15:

> "Where the harm suffered has more than one cause, the employer should only pay for the proportion of the harm suffered which is attributable to his wrongdoing, unless the harm is truly indivisible …";

and proposition 16:

> "The assessment of damages will take account of any pre-existing disorder or vulnerability and of the chance that the claimant would have succumbed to a stress-related disorder in any event".

Proposition 16 looks to the future, in light of the claimant's vulnerability, and may lead to a reduction in damages to reflect the likelihood that harm would have occurred in any event. Proposition 15, however, relates to competing causes of harm already suffered. Underhill LJ declared that "both propositions are tools which enable a tribunal to avoid over-compensation in these difficult cases".[235B] Underhill LJ suggested that the court in *Dickins* had overstated the difference between its own approach, and that of Hale LJ in *Hatton*: Hale LJ recognised the existence of "truly indivisible" injuries and agreed that in such cases, there was no basis for apportionment under proposition 15. The difference lay in an assumption on the part of the Court in *Dickins v O2* that such injuries generally were indivisible. However, the Court of Appeal in *BAE Systems* appears to have added an important gloss to Hale LJ's proposition 15. According to Underhill LJ,[235C] in any case of this type "the tribunal should try to identify a rational basis on which the harm suffered can be apportioned between a part caused by the employer's wrong and a part which is not so caused". This exercise, it was emphasised, was concerned with the divisibility of the harm, and not the divisibility of the cause. This approach takes as its starting point that there should be an attempt to divide the injury, pointing to a preference for apportionment where this can be consistent with the injury suffered. Underhill LJ added that on his reading of *Rahman* and *Hatton*, in the "difficult" case where an employee is "tipped over the edge" by a particular incident, the tribunal "should seek to find a rational basis for distinguishing between a part of the illness which is due to the employer's wrong and a part which is due to other causes".[235D]

This did not assist the defendant in *BAE* itself, since no such rational basis had been identified. Plainly, however, future defendants will seek to establish through expert evidence that there is a rational basis that tribunals may use in following the emphasis placed on apportionment in *BAE Systems*. As Irwin LJ added in a concurring judgment, the difficulty may be seen as one of medicine or science, rather than legal principle.[235E] Nonetheless, the instruction to future courts to try to find a rational basis for apportionment is a matter of legal emphasis, and no doubt reflects Irwin LJ's further observation that "compensation should never become windfall".[235F]

[235] [2017] EWCA Civ 1188; [2018] I.C.R. 1 at [70].

[235A] See para.2-33.

[235B] [2017] EWCA Civ 1188; [2018] I.C.R. 1 at [62].

[235C] [2017] EWCA Civ 1188; [2018] I.C.R. 1 at [71].

[235D] [2017] EWCA Civ 1188; [2018] I.C.R. 1 at [72].

[235E] [2017] EWCA Civ 1188; [2018] I.C.R. 1 at [93].

[235F] [2017] EWCA Civ 1188; [2018] I.C.R. 1 at [92].

3. BREACH OF STATUTORY DUTY

Enterprise and Regulatory Reform Act 2013 s.69

After "as from 1 October 2013,", add new footnote 242A:

[242A] In *Johnson v University of Bristol* [2017] EWCA Civ 2115, a claim framed in terms of the Provision and Use of Work Equipment Regulations 1998 and the Workplace (Health, Safety and Welfare) Regulations 1992, was said to give rise to no significant matters of law, because whatever was said in the judgment about the civil consequences of the regulations no longer had any applicability to the circumstances of contemporaneous or future events. Therefore, the Court would not embark upon a full judgment, and offered a short form judgment in its place. **13-41**

Industrial safety legislation

Replace paragraph with:

It has been established since *Groves v Lord Wimborne*[247] that breach of penal legislation designed to promote industrial safety can give rise to an action for breach of statutory duty by an injured worker. The action for breach of statutory duty provided a means of avoiding the doctrine of common employment, and the legislation was often stricter in the standards applied than the tort of negligence. For many years the two actions have been routinely combined in claims by injured employees against their employers. The degree of protection conferred by an action for breach of statutory duty varies considerably with the wording of the particular provision. Sometimes legislation has been treated as imposing an absolute obligation on the employer. For example, in *John Summers & Sons Ltd v Frost*[248] it was held that s.14(1) of the Factories Act 1937, which provided that every dangerous part of any machinery must be securely fenced, created an absolute obligation, in the sense that it was not a defence to show that it was impracticable to fence, even though fencing would make the machine unusable. Some statutory duties are qualified by the phrase "so far as is reasonably practicable", and the assessment of what is reasonably practicable can involve a calculation somewhat similar to that in deciding what constitutes reasonable care for the tort of negligence. However, it is important not to be drawn into treating statutory provisions as creating something equivalent to negligence standards, just because they include a reference to reasonableness. In *Edwards v National Coal Board*[249] Asquith LJ suggested that where there is "gross **13-42** disproportion" between the risk and the measures necessary to avoid the risk, the risk being "insignificant" in relation to the cost, then the measures were not reasonably practicable. In *Baker v Quantum Clothing*,[250] a case requiring interpretation of s.29 of the Factories Act 1961,[251] the Court of Appeal underlined that there is a difference between a "gross disproportion" test as set out by Asquith LJ in *Edwards v National Coal Board*, and the test for negligence at common law. Smith LJ emphasised that for an employer to avoid liability:

> "... he has to show that the burden of eliminating the risk substantially outweighed the 'quantum of risk'. When that forensic process is compared and contrasted with the process by which liability at common law is established, it is hard to understand how lawyers and judges have so often fallen into the error of thinking that there is no significant difference between the two."[252]

The Supreme Court[253] reversed the judgment of the Court of Appeal. Lord Mance, in the majority, said that the point did not need to be resolved given his approach to "safety",[254] but nonetheless he considered that the "gross disproportion" test was an "unjustified gloss" on the statutory wording.[255] His Lordship did not refer expressly to *Edwards v National Coal Board*, but took the view that: "The criteria relevant to reasonable practicability must on any view very largely reflect the criteria relevant to satisfaction of the common law duty of care. Both require consideration of the nature, gravity and imminence of the risk and its consequences, as well as of the nature and proportionality of the steps by which it might be addressed, and a balancing of the one against the other."[256] Lord Mance rejected any assumption that the statutory duties must necessarily be intended to be stricter than the common law, arguing that the imposition of criminal liabilities implied that the duties should not be interpreted too broadly. Lord Dyson, also in the majority, did not comment on the "gross disproportion" test, but referred to *Edwards v National Coal Board* as the leading authority on the meaning of "reasonably practicable" in industrial safety legislation. Since Lord Mance's comments on "gross disproportion" were not necessary to his decision, and he did not mention *Edwards* expressly, it is suggested that the authority of that decision is unaffected. There is some difficulty describing the gross disproportion test as a "gloss" on the statutory language given that the interpretation was well established long before the Factories Act 1961 was drafted. In *Goldscheider v Royal Opera House Covent Garden Foundation*[256A] a case of serious hearing impairment caused by exposure to noise during orchestral rehearsals, the Court of Appeal made the point that it will be very difficult for a defendant to establish that all "reasonably practicable" steps have been taken, if it has subsequently made adaptations that avoid the risk.[256B] Reasonable practicability is in this sense different from foreseeability, which is not to be judged with hindsight.

[247] [1898] 2 Q.B. 402.

[248] [1955] A.C. 740. For discussion of *Groves v Lord Wimborne* and points of distinction between claims based on breach of the Factory Acts and a claim based on breach of safety regulations under the Merchant Shipping Act 1995 s.121, and the Fishing Vessel (Safety Provisions) Rules 1975 (SI 1975/330) see *Todd v Adams and Chope (t/a Trelawney Fishing Co) (The "Margaretha Maria")* [2002] EWCA Civ 509; [2002] 2 Lloyd's Rep. 293 at [33]–[35]. The Court of Appeal concluded that Parliament had not intended that breach of these provisions should give rise to a civil action for breach of statutory duty. Cf. *Cairns v Northern Lighthouse Board* [2013] CSOH 22; 2013 S.L.T. 645, where Lord Drummond Young distinguished *Todd*, holding that breach of reg.5 of the Merchant Shipping and Fishing Vessels (Health and Safety at Work) Regulations 1997 (SI 1997/2962), made under s.85 of the Merchant Shipping Act 1995, did confer a right to a civil remedy. Regulations made under the Merchant Shipping Act 1995 retain civil liability as they are not within the terms of s.69 Enterprise and Regulatory Reform Act 2013.

[249] [1949] 1 All E.R. 743 at 747.

[250] [2009] EWCA Civ 499; [2009] P.I.Q.R. P19.

[251] The majority of the Factories Act 1961 was repealed by the Workplace (Health, Safety and Welfare) Regulations 1992 (SI 1992/3004), including s.29, which therefore applies only to pre-1993 events and is to this extent unaffected by s.69 Enterprise and Regulatory Reform Act 2013, para.13-41.

[252] [2009] EWCA Civ 499; [2009] P.I.Q.R. P19 at [87].

[253] *Baker v Quantum Clothing Ltd* [2011] UKSC 17; [2011] 1 W.L.R. 1003.

[254] See paras 13-44 and 13-45.

[255] [2011] UKSC 17; [2011] 1 W.L.R. 1003 at [84].

[256] [2011] UKSC 17; [2011] 1 W.L.R. 1003 at [82].

[256A] [2019] EWCA Civ 711 at [42].

[256B] Here, the orchestra pit had been reconfigured to reduce exposure to noise on the part of musicians. The claim was for breaches of duty under the Control of Noise Regulations 2005. In relation to "safety" of the workplace in this claim, and particularly foreseeability, see para.13-45.

Safety

Replace paragraph with:

"Safety" was considered in *Larner v British Steel Plc*.[264] Here, the Court of Appeal held that in determining whether a place of work had been kept "safe" (for the purposes of the Factories Act 1961 s.29(1)) for any person working there, it would be wrong to import a test of "reasonable foreseeability" of danger. The obligation imposed by the section was strict, with no reference to foreseeability, reasonable or otherwise, and such a requirement would have the effect of limiting successful claims for breach of statutory duty to circumstances where the worker would also succeed in a parallel claim for negligence. *Larner v British Steel* was accepted by the Court of Appeal as not only binding, but also correct in principle, in *Baker v Quantum Clothing*.[265] The "safety" of a place of work was to be judged objectively without reference to reasonable foresight of injury, though if the risk in question was one which the employer cannot reasonably have been expected to have known about, then the employer should be able to show that no steps to avoid the risk were "reasonably practicable",[266] thus avoiding liability. On appeal to the Supreme Court, the approach of the Court of Appeal to "safety" was disapproved and *Larner v British Steel* was overruled.[267] The majority concluded that the interpretation of "safety" should reflect reasonable foreseeability judged in accordance with the standards of the time, in line with cases interpreting s.14 of the same Act.[268] There was no such thing as an unchanging notion of "safety". Although it was not disputed that the burden of showing that it was not reasonably practicable to make the workplace "safe" lay with the employer, the employee must do more than show that an injury occurred and was likely with hindsight. The employee must also show that there was a reasonable foreseeability of harm and that the risk of harm was not acceptable, before the workplace could be shown not to have been "safe". Safety, according to the majority, was a matter of opinion. The minority rejected this view, emphasising that the section did not refer to reasonable safety, and arguing that a workplace which was believed (even reasonably) to be safe at the time of exposure was not necessarily safe for the purposes of the statute. The question, rather, should be whether there were reasonably practicable steps that could have been taken in view of the knowledge existing at the time of exposure. In line with the approach of the Court of Appeal, the minority would therefore have dealt with issues of reasonableness largely in connection with "reasonable practicability", where the burden is on the employer. Lord Clarke, in the minority, emphasised that the 13-45 purpose of the statutory duty was first and foremost to protect employees, not employers, and that a balance between these interests was established through the qualification that employers may show they have taken all steps that are "reasonably practicable". His Lordship suggested that s.29 was different from common law duties in that it was "results-oriented": there was a duty to achieve a particular result (that the workplace should be safe, not reasonably safe or believed to be safe), but the content of the duty was only to do what was reasonably practicable to this end.[269] In *Goldscheider v Royal Opera House Covent Garden Foundation*,[269A] it was emphasised that the precise injury suffered does not need to be foreseen, and perhaps does not need to be reasonably foreseeable, for the claimant to show that it was "unsafe". Here, the Regulations were enacted to protect employees from exposure to excessive noise at work. It was not foreseen that exposure at the levels shown would cause "sudden" injury; but exposure at these levels was considered likely to cause long-term injury. Once the defendant had failed to show reduction of exposure to the lowest level that was reasonably practicable, the fact that the foreseeable risk was of long-term injury was irrelevant. Notably, the Court cited common law authority on remoteness to damage to support this contention.[269B] In *D v Amec Group Ltd*,[269C] it was accepted by the Inner House of the Court of Session that "safety" for the purposes of the Fire (Scotland) Act 2005 s.53 extended to protection of mental as well as physical integrity. The content of the applicable duty was to ensure safety as far as "reasonably practicable". Although "safety" encompassed mental integrity, the employee had failed to identify any fire safety measure which would have prevented him from suffering harm, and therefore had not established any breach on the part of the employer when he suffered post-traumatic stress disorder following a fire in a factory.

[264] [1993] I.C.R. 551; [1993] 4 All E.R. 102.

[265] [2009] EWCA Civ 499; [2009] P.I.Q.R. P19.

[266] See para.13-42.

[267] *Baker v Quantum Clothing Group Ltd* [2011] UKSC 17; [2011] 1 W.L.R. 1003.

[268] See para.13-44.

[269] Lord Kerr agreed, at [177], that "a place is safe or it is not. A place which is not safe cannot be said to be safe merely because it is believed to be, however justified the belief." The effect of applying the s.14 authorities on "dangerousness" to the s.29 duty is that claimants encounter more obstacles to a claim under s.29 than under s.14. First they must show that the workplace was not "safe" according to the standards of the time (effectively importing a foreseeability requirement), and the employer then has the opportunity to show that steps to make the workplace safe would not be reasonably practicable. The majority's approach therefore significantly increases the protection of employers where s.29 is concerned.

[269A] [2019] EWCA Civ 711 at [46].

[269B] *Hughes v Lord Advocate* [1963] A.C. 837; *Page v Smith* [1996] 1 A.C. 155.

[269C] [2017] CSIH 75; 2018 S.C. 247.

Health and Safety at Work, etc. Act 1974

After "Reform Act 2013.", at the end of the paragraph add:

13-47 The status of the Regulations in the event of the UK's withdrawal from the EU is maintained as a result of the European Union (Withdrawal) Act 2018 s.2(1), which states that: "EU-derived domestic legislation, as it has effect in domestic law immediately before exit day, continues to have effect in domestic law on and after exit day" (with a date for coming into force not yet determined). "EU-derived legislation" includes regulations passed in order to give effect to EU Directives

Duty to conduct risk assessment

Replace paragraph with:

The content of the Regulations made under the Health and Safety at Work, etc. Act 1974 in some respects resembles the older statutory provisions. A mixture of duties is imposed on employers. Some are absolute[303] and safety must be guaranteed. Others require that employers do what is reasonably practicable.[304] The number of Regulations is large and it is not possible here to do more than provide an outline of what have been the most significant Regulations in terms of civil litigation by employees.[305] It has been suggested that the Regulations should not be construed so as to overlap.[306] **13-52**

[303] Reg.6(1) of the Provision and Use of Work Equipment Regulations 1992 (SI 1992/2932), requiring every employer to ensure that work equipment is maintained in an efficient state, an efficient working order and in good repair, imposed an absolute duty: *Stark v Post Office* [2000] P.I.Q.R. P105. See now the Provision and Use of Work Equipment Regulations 1998 (SI 1998/2306).

[304] See the Manual Handling Operations Regulations 1992 (SI 1992/2793); on which see *Koonjul v ThamesLink Healthcare Services* [2000] P.I.Q.R. P123, CA; *Swain v Denso Marston Ltd* [2000] I.C.R. 1079; [2000] P.I.Q.R. P129 CA. See also J. Hendy, "Industrial Accident Claims: Reasonable Practicability" [2001] J.P.I.L. 209. Even where avoidance is not reasonably practicable, the employer is under a duty to conduct a risk assessment and take steps to reduce risks. The dangers for employers of treating risk assessment as a "tick box" exercise are well illustrated by *Denton Hall Legal Services v Fifield* [2006] EWCA Civ 169; [2006] Lloyd's Rep. Med. 251 (a case involving the Management of Health and Safety at Work Regulations 1992 and the Health and Safety (Display Screen Equipment) Regulations 1992).

[305] Regulations include the Management of Health and Safety at Work Regulations 1999 (SI 1999/3242); Provision and Use of Work Equipment Regulations 1998 (SI 1998/2306); Personal Protective Equipment at Work Regulations 1992 (SI 1992/2966); Workplace (Health, Safety and Welfare) Regulations 1992 (SI 1992/3004); Manual Handling Operations Regulations 1992 (SI 1992/2793); Control of Noise at Work Regulations 2005 (SI 2005/1643); Control of Substances Hazardous to Health Regulations 2002 (SI 2002/2677; as amended by SI 2003/978 and SI 2004/3386); Control of Lead at Work Regulations 2002 (SI 2002/2676); Control of Asbestos Regulations 2012 (SI 2012/632, which consolidate the Asbestos Regulations); Ionising Radiations Regulations 2017 (SI 2017/1075); Ionising Radiation (Medical Exposure) Regulations 2017 (SI 2017/1322); Justification of Practices Involving Ionising Radiation Regulations 2004 (SI 2004/1769); Control of Artificial Optical Radiation at Work Regulations 2010 (SI 2010/1140); Health and Safety (Display Screen Equipment) Regulations 1992 (SI 1992/2792); Work at Height Regulations 2005 (SI 2005/735; as amended by SI 2007/114); Supply of Machinery (Safety) Regulations 2008 (SI 2008/1597); Merchant Shipping and Fishing Vessels (Health and Safety at Work) Regulations 1997 (SI 1997/2962); Merchant Shipping and Fishing Vessels (Manual Handling Operations) Regulations 1998 (SI 1998/2857); Merchant Shipping and Fishing Vessels (Provision and Use of Work Equipment) Regulations 2006 (SI 2006/2183; as amended by SI 2008/2165); Merchant Shipping and Fishing Vessels (Lifting Operations and Lifting Equipment) Regulations 2006 (SI 2006/2184; as amended by 2008/2166); Merchant Shipping and Fishing Vessels (Control of Noise at Work) Regulations 2007 (SI 2007/3075); Merchant Shipping and Fishing Vessels (Control of Vibration at Work) Regulations 2007 (SI 2007/3077 as amended by SI 2010/1110); Construction (Design and Management) Regulations 2015 (SI 2015/51); Control of Electromagnetic Fields at Work Regulations 2016 (SI 2016/588). See also the Health and Safety (Miscellaneous Provisions and Revocation) Regulations 2017 (SI 2017/304); and the Health and Safety (Amendment) (EU Exit) Regulations 2018 (SI 2018/1370) (not yet in force).

[306] *Mason v Satelcom Ltd, East Potential Ltd* [2008] EWCA Civ 494; [2008] I.C.R. 971 at [21], per Longmore LJ, and at [54], per Ward LJ. This was applied in *Heeds v Chief Constable of Cleveland* [2018] EWHC 810 (QB); [2018] P.I.Q.R. P13 to exclude the operation of the Provision and Use of Work Equipment Regulations 1998, where there would have been liability, and to apply instead the Workplace (Health, Safety and Welfare) Regulations 1992, where there was no liability.

(a) Provision and Use of Work Equipment Regulations

Work equipment and the coverage of the Regulations

Replace paragraph with:

The Provision and Use of Work Equipment Regulations 1998[319] reg.4(1) provides **13-55** that every employer[320] shall ensure that work equipment[321] is so constructed or adapted as to be suitable for the purpose for which it is used or provided. The duty in reg.4 is strict, and the definition of "work equipment" (reg.2(1)) which is "provided for use or used by an employee at his work" (reg.3(2)) will therefore be vital in defining the ambit and limits of the strict liability thereby created. The meaning of these provisions has been subject to close analysis by the House of Lords in *Spencer-Franks v Kellogg Brown & Root*,[322] and *Smith v Northamptonshire CC*,[323] and the Court of Appeal in (amongst others) *Mason v Satelcom*.[324] Earlier, in *Hammond v Commissioner of Police for the Metropolis*,[325] the Court of Appeal had taken a more restrictive approach, now disapproved by the House of Lords, in which "work equipment" applied only to the "tools of the trade" provided by an employer for use by his employees when they are at work, but not other objects provided by others or on which the employee was working. So a mechanic employed by the Commissioner of Police who was working on a van owned by the Metropolitan Police Authority was not covered by the Regulations when a bolt on the van sheared off. The van could have been the work equipment of a police officer driving it, but not of the police mechanic repairing it, at least when the van was not the property of the employer of the mechanic. Regulation 3(2) provides that: "The requirements imposed by these Regulations on an employer in respect of work equipment shall apply to such equipment provided for use or used by an employee of his at work." In *PRP Architects v Reid*,[326] the Court of Appeal distinguished *Hammond* and held that an employee leaving at the end of a day's work who used a lift located in the lobby of the building where the employee worked (the lift being situated in the common parts of the building and not leased to the employer) was using it at work within the meaning of reg.3(2). Although as with the wheel bolt in *Hammond* the lift was the property of a third party, it was "a facility used in the course of work, which is different from an object worked on".[327] In *Rooney v Western Education and Library Board*,[328] a canteen assistant suffered personal injury from a broken cup or mug while drying staff crockery. It was held that a staff mug or cup was "work equipment" for the purposes of the Provision and Use of Work Equipment Regulations (Northern Ireland) 1999. Though not supplied by her employers, it had become part of the generally used crockery in the canteen, and in drying it, she was using it at work: "use" in reg.2(1) expressly included cleaning, and drying is part of cleaning.

[319] SI 1998/2306. The Regulations revoked and replaced the Provision and Use of Work Equipment Regulations 1992 (SI 1992/2392). See also the Personal Protective Equipment at Work Regulations 1992 (SI 1992/2966), on which see *Fytche v Wincanton Logistics Plc* [2004] UKHL 31; [2004] I.C.R. 975; [2004] 4 All E.R. 221, see para.13-54, and *Threlfall v Kingston-upon-Hull CC* [2010] EWCA Civ 1147; [2011] I.C.R. 209, para.13-51.

[320] Note that by reg.3(3) the Provision and Use of Work Equipment Regulations 1998 also apply to any person who has control to any extent (and to the extent of his control) over (i) work equipment; (ii) a person at work who uses or supervises or manages the use of work equipment; or (iii) the way in which work equipment is used at work. In *Casson v Hudson* [2017] EWCA Civ 125; [2017] P.I.Q.R. P12, a prisoner on day release was injured falling from a ladder while carrying out decorating work at a church, and claimed against the church for his injuries. His claim failed. The ladder was in good condition; he had been required not to use ladders when taking his placement; and the church did not supervise his work or offer him instruction. Within the terms of reg.3(3), even if the ladder was "work equipment" (which the court below had held it was not, given the prohibition on use of ladders), the church would only have control of "(i) work equipment", and not of "(ii) a person at work who uses or supervises … work equipment; or (iii) the way in which work equipment is used at work". Thus, the only duty that would be brought into play would be the duty of maintenance under reg.5. Duties to provide training and to ensure the suitability of the equipment would not be triggered. In *Mason v Satelcom* [2008] EWCA Civ 494; [2008] I.C.R. 971, a service engineer fell from a ladder that was too short for the job he was undertaking, having found the ladder in the room where the equipment was to be serviced. His employers were found to have been negligent and in breach of the Work Equipment Regulations in fail-

ing to provide a suitable ladder. Relying on reg.3(3), the employers brought proceedings against the occupier of the room in question on the basis that although the occupier did not supply the ladder, they could have removed it or placed a notice on it. The Court of Appeal reversed the judge's decision that the occupier should contribute 25% of the claimant's damages. The occupier did not have control of the ladder to a relevant extent; or, if they did have control of the ladder, the extent of their control did not justify liability on their part. See also *Hyndman v Brown and Bradley* [2012] NICA 3, where the Court of Appeal in Northern Ireland held that the second defendant, who had loaned a harvester to the claimant's employer, did not have control of the harvester at the time of the accident. It was appropriate for the work and well-maintained, and the claimant's employer was an experienced contractor. The second defendant had no control over the staff selected to operate the machinery and no control over how they operated it.

[321] reg.2(1) provides that work equipment is "any machinery, appliance, apparatus, tool or installation for use at work (whether exclusively or not)".

[322] [2008] UKHL 46; [2008] I.C.R. 863; [2009] 1 All E.R. 269.

[323] [2009] UKHL 27; [2009] 4 All E.R. 557; [2009] I.C.R. 734. This case concerned reg.5 of the Provision and Use of Work Equipment Regulations 1998 (see para.13-64), but the case turned upon the definition of "work equipment". It is explored in para.13-60.

[324] [2008] EWCA Civ 494; [2008] I.C.R. 971.

[325] [2004] EWCA Civ 830; [2004] I.C.R. 1467; [2005] P.I.Q.R. P1. This was a decision on the Provision and Use of Work Equipment Regulations 1992. The Court of Appeal held in *Hammond* that a mechanic employed by the Metropolitan Police Authority was not covered by the Regulations when a bolt on the van sheared off. The van was not the work equipment of the employee repairing it. *Hammond* was disapproved by the House of Lords in *Spencer-Franks v Kellogg Brown & Root* [2008] UKHL 46; [2008] I.C.R. 863; [2009] 1 All E.R. 269.

[326] [2006] EWCA Civ 1119; [2007] I.C.R. 78; [2007] P.I.Q.R. P4. Contrast *Heeds v Chief Constable of Cleveland* [2018] EWHC 810 (QB); [2018] P.I.Q.R. P13, where a door was held not to be work equipment. Though a specialist door, it was "nevertheless a door". The case was approached instead under the Workplace (Health, Safety and Welfare) Regulations 1992 reg.18, where liability was less strict, and for this reason the claim failed.

[327] [2006] EWCA Civ 1119; [2007] I.C.R. 78; [2007] P.I.Q.R. P4 at [19], per Pill LJ.

[328] [2015] NIQB 87.

Absolute duty in regulation 5

Replace paragraph with:

Regulation 5(1) of the 1998 Regulations provides that every employer shall ensure that work equipment is maintained in an efficient state, in efficient working order and in good repair.[352] In *Ball v Street*[353] the Court of Appeal held that this imposed an absolute duty, and that it was irrelevant that the type of accident which occurred was unforeseeable. The regulation was designed to make it easier for an injured workman to bring a claim by simply requiring him to prove that the mechanism of the machine failed to work efficiently or was not in good repair and that this failure caused the accident. However, the claimant is required to show on the balance of probabilities that it was a defect in the equipment that caused the accident. In *Bond v Tom Croft (Bolton) Ltd*,[353A] the employer suggested that operator misuse was an alternative cause of the accident. The claimant failed to show that there was a defect in the ladder from which he fell, the judge preferring, on the basis of expert evidence, the suggestion that the claimant had fallen because he was "overreaching" (stretching beyond the safe limit while working on the ladder). The burden did not pass to the employer to show that the injury was not caused by a defect. The fact that work equipment was required to be "suitable" for the purposes of reg.4 did not affect the nature and level of the absolute obligation of maintenance in reg.5.[354] In *Johnstone v AMEC Construction Ltd*[355] the Inner House of the Court of Session accepted that the very fact that a barrier fence failed to remain in position and was blown over by the wind meant that it was not maintained in an efficient state, in efficient working order and in good repair, as required by reg.5.[356] 13-64

[352] In *Yorkshire Traction Co Ltd v Searby* [2003] EWCA Civ 1856; (2004) 148 S.J.L.B. 61 the Court

of Appeal concluded that a failure to provide a screen to protect the driver of a bus from attack by passengers did not constitute a breach of the Provision and Use of Work Equipment Regulations 1992 reg.5.

353 [2005] EWCA Civ 76; [2005] P.I.Q.R. P22.

353A [2018] EWHC 1290 (QB).

354 The strictness of the reg.5 duty was also emphasised by the House of Lords in *Smith v Northamptonshire CC* [2009] UKHL 27; [2009] 4 All E.R. 557; [2009] I.C.R. 734. The reg.5 duty was described by Lord Hope as "absolute" although in this instance, for the reasons explored in para.13-60, the defective ramp did not fall within the definition of "work equipment". Cf. *Horton v Taplin Contracts Ltd* [2002] EWCA Civ 1604; [2003] I.C.R. 179; [2003] P.I.Q.R. P12 at [10] where the Court of Appeal indicated that reg.20 of the Provision and Use of Work Equipment Regulations 1992 (which provided that "every employer shall ensure that work equipment or any part of work equipment is stabilised by clamping or otherwise where necessary for the purposes of health or safety"), though suggestive of absolute liability actually required foreseeability because "a step is realistically only 'necessary' when the mischief to be guarded against can be reasonably foreseen." For discussion of *Horton* see Fetto and Karseras (2003) 153 N.L.J. 53. On the general relationship between assessment of risks and duties under Health and Safety Regulations to provide suitable equipment, training, etc. see para.13-50.

355 [2010] CSIH 57; 2011 S.C.L.R. 178; 2010 Rep. L.R. 96.

356 Applying the dictum of Lord Reid in *Millar v Galashiels Gas Company* [1949] A.C. 275, 290: "If the duty is proper maintenance and maintenance is defined as maintenance in efficient working order, then, once it is established that the duty goes beyond a duty to exercise care the fact that on a particular occasion the mechanism was not in working order shows that there had not been proper maintenance." There was also a breach of reg.4 on the facts of *Johnstone*. The fence was treated as work equipment which was used by the appellant, a security guard who was patrolling the perimeter and was injured when he first tried to replace the fence, and then to step over it. See also *Swilas v Clyde Pumps Ltd*, 2012 S.L.T. (Sh Ct) 146 where perimeter gates were held to be "work equipment" so far as a security guard was concerned. The fact that they were also part of the fabric of the premises was irrelevant; *Hodgkinson v Renfrewshire Council* [2011] CSOH 142.

(b) Workplace (Health, Safety and Welfare) Regulations

Replace paragraph with:

13-76 In *Lewis v Avidan Ltd*[390] the claimant slipped on a patch of water which had leaked from a concealed pipe just before the accident. The Court of Appeal found that there was no breach of reg.5 since, given that the defendants had not been negligent, the floor was maintained in an efficient state. Even if the pipe itself constituted equipment for the purposes of reg.5, it was not equipment a fault in which was liable to result in a failure to comply with the regulations. A fault in the pipe would be liable to produce a flood which would render the floor slippery, but that in itself would not result in a breach of reg.12(3) which is qualified by reasonable practicality. The mere fact of an unexpected flood did not mean that a floor was not in an efficient state for the purposes of reg.5(1). *Lewis v Avidan Ltd* should be contrasted with *Ellis v Bristol CC*,[391] where the Court of Appeal concluded that the employers were in breach of reg.12 when a care assistant at a home for the elderly slipped in a pool of urine left by one of the residents on a floor of the home. The surface was smooth vinyl and was slippery when wet. The evidence indicated that the majority of the residents were incontinent and they urinated on the floor several times a week. Regulation 12(1) and (2) required the court to consider the suitability of the floor in the context of the circumstances of its use. This included not only the temporary nature of the hazard but also the frequency and regularity of the occurrence. In *Aldenham v Deacon*,[392] a school nurse sustained injuries when she slipped on a wet floor on her return from lunch. Eady J. held that liability under reg.12(3) was established because the corridor could have been cleaned in the evenings when it was less frequented. This would have reduced the risk of injury, and the essence of reg.12(3) was reduction of risk. The known risk should be balanced against the effort and expense of eliminating it. Similarly, in *McLeish v Lothian NHS Board*,[392A] a nurse who fell on the wet floor of a ward succeeded in a claim. The positioning of a cleaning trolley in the doorway did not amount to a warning. On this basis, she had received no warning, either verbal or visible, that the floor was wet; the wet floor sign was not deployed and no alternative wet floor warning was given; and the wet floor sign was a reasonably practicable measure.

[390] [2005] EWCA Civ 670; [2006] P.I.Q.R. P6.

[391] [2007] EWCA Civ 685; [2007] I.C.R. 1614; [2007] P.I.Q.R. P26; applied in *Cheung v Zhu* [2011] EWHC 2913 (QB).

[392] [2008] EWHC 2343 (QB).

[392A] [2017] CSOH 71; 2017 Rep. L.R. 90

(c) Manual Handling Operations Regulations

Distinct duties

Replace paragraph with:

The test for whether manual handling operations involve a risk of being injured is that "there must be a real risk, a foreseeable possibility of injury; certainly nothing approaching a probability".[400] Moreover, the employer is not entitled to assume that all his employees will on all occasions behave with full and proper concern for their own safety.[401] There may be a duty to provide training for manual handling even where the attendant risks might appear obvious. In *Smith v S Notaro Ltd*,[402] the defendants were in breach of reg.4 in failing to provide training for manual handling over uneven ground.[403] On the other hand, the court must also consider the background against which the incident took place and assess the alleged obligation in its real context. So there was no breach of the Regulations where a care assistant had injured her back when pulling a low wooden bed from against a wall.[404] The court was entitled to take account of the size of the employer (a small residential home with a small number of staff), that the claimant was an experienced member of staff and had received prior training in bending and lifting techniques. It would be impracticable to require the employer to assess each task and provide guidance as to how those tasks were to be carried out where innumerable everyday domestic tasks were involved. But where an employer had failed to take appropriate steps to reduce the risk by failing to give the training necessary to increase awareness of the risk of back injury from twisting while carrying a load there was a breach of reg.4.[405] Where the accident arose from a wholly unforeseen risk, where, for example, the employee had created that risk by acting contrary to normal procedures for the task, the claim may fail on the basis that any breach of the regulations was not the cause of the injury.[406] The need for proof of a causal link between a failure to conduct a proper risk assessment and injury sustained by the employee is emphasised by the Court of Appeal's decision in *West Sussex CC v Fuller*.[407] The burden of proving this causal link is on the claimant. It was remarked that in many workplace situations, a failure by the employer to assess the risks of injury involved in a manual handling operation and to take appropriate steps to reduce the risk of injury to the lowest level practicable, would effectively cast on to the employer the evidential burden of showing that its failure was not at least a cause of the accident. However, that was because there would be an obvious connection between the injury and the risks associated with the activity being undertaken. Here, the cause of the accident was unconnected with the risk generated by the operation in question and the incident leading to injury did not fall within the ambit of the risk that the local authority had been required to assess. 13-79

[400] *Koonjul v ThamesLink Healthcare Services* [2000] P.I.Q.R. P123 at 126, per Hale LJ. See also *Bennetts v Ministry of Defence* [2004] EWCA Civ 486 at [39], per Carnwath LJ: "even a 'slight' risk may

be a relevant risk in the sense that it brings Regulation 4 into play", citing *Hawkes v London Borough of Southwark*, unreported, 1998, CA. The requirement in *Koonjul* for a "real risk" was applied in *Stuart v Lewisham and Greenwich NHS Trust* [2017] EWCA Civ 2091; (2018) 160 B.M.L.R. 180. The recorder had effectively found that there was no "real risk" where a midwife lifted an oxygen box weighing no more than 8kg. This would not have posed a risk to most people, and as such the duty to conduct a risk assessment did not apply.

401 *Koonjul v ThamesLink Healthcare Services* [2000] P.I.Q.R. P123.

402 [2006] EWCA Civ 775.

403 See also *Walsh v TNT UK Ltd* [2006] CSOH 149; 2006 S.L.T. 1100 (employer in breach of reg.4(1)(b)(ii) of the 1992 Regulations in failing to send the employee on refresher courses on manual handling).

404 *Koonjul v ThamesLink Healthcare Services* [2000] P.I.Q.R. P123 CA, referred to for guidance in relation to breach of the employer's common law duty of care in *Cockerill v CXK Ltd* [2018] EWHC 1155 (QB); see further, para.13-32.

405 *O'Neill v DSG Retail Ltd* [2002] EWCA Civ 1139; [2003] I.C.R. 222. See also *Skinner v Aberdeen CC*, 2001 Rep. L.R. 118 (Court of Session, OH): employer's failure to train or instruct the claimant on how to approach the task of lifting some broken slabs, in order to reduce the risk of injury to the lowest possible level, amounted to a breach of reg.4(1)(b)(i) and reg.4(1)(b)(ii). In *Costa v Imperial London Hotels Ltd* [2012] EWCA Civ 672 it was held that an absence of refresher training is capable of constituting a breach of reg.4, on the basis of a failure to take appropriate steps to reduce the risks to the lowest level reasonably practicable, but it must still be shown that the absence of refresher training caused the injury (i.e. that the training would have led the claimant to alter their practice, and that it would have avoided the particular injury).

406 *Bennetts v Ministry of Defence* [2004] EWCA Civ 486, where the claimant's back injury was caused not by the weight of the postal bag she was attempting to move, nor the height to which the bag was lifted, but as a result of her pulling at a bag that had snagged on a trolley. This (the claimant's decision to proceed in this way) was an event that was unforeseen, and therefore would not have been identified by a risk assessment by the employers.

407 [2015] EWCA Civ 189.

(d) Control of Substances Hazardous to Health Regulations

Replace paragraph with:

13-80 Regulation 7(1) of the Control of Substances Hazardous to Health Regulations 2002[408] requires every employer to ensure that the exposure of his employees to substances hazardous to health is either prevented or, where this is not reasonably practicable, adequately controlled. It is in the nature of these Regulations that they may be invoked in relation to exposure over a number of years, and with delayed effects, so that their applicability may be less immediately truncated by the commencement of the Enterprise and Regulatory Reform Act s.69 than some of the other regulations.[408A] The regulations apply between an employer and employee. Although by reg.3 they are owed to third parties who are affected by substances used at work, it has been concluded that they are not imposed on a hospital trust for the benefit of a patient in a case of infection, where there is no relevant substance being used at work: MRSA is not a "substance arising out of or in connection with work at the work place".[409] Contrast, however, *Miller v Greater Glasgow Health Board*,[410] where it was found at least arguable that a patient who contracts MRSA may be able to rely on the Regulations. Regulation 7(3) provides that where it is not reasonably practicable to prevent exposure to a substance hazardous to health, the employer must apply protection measures appropriate to the activity and consistent with the risk assessment. In *Dugmore v Swansea NHS Trust*[411] the Court of Appeal considered the meaning of the words "reasonably practicable" in a previous version of the Regulations.[412] The claimant was a nurse who developed a latex allergy as a result of using powdered latex gloves. The Court of Appeal held that the duty to ensure that exposure was prevented or adequately controlled under reg.7(1) was absolute. The defence of reasonable practicability qualified only the duty of total prevention, not the requirement to see that exposure is adequately controlled.

It was for the employers to prove that it was not reasonably practicable to replace latex gloves with vinyl gloves (it "was not rocket science waiting to be invented"). With a simple step of this nature questions of the degree and magnitude of the risk did not arise, but even if they did the onus was on the employers to go out and find out about them. The regulation does not refer to the foreseeability of the risk:

> "To import into the defence of reasonable practicability the same approach to foreseeability of risk as is contained in the common law of negligence would be to reduce the absolute duty to something much closer to the common law, albeit with a different burden of proof."[413]

Moreover, it could not be adequate control to require the employee to wear powdered latex gloves when other barriers were available. The purpose of the Regulations is protective and preventive, and they involve positive obligations to seek out the risks and take precautions against them. Thus:

> "It is by no means incompatible with their purpose that an employer who fails to discover a risk or rates it so low that he takes no precautions against it should nevertheless be liable to the employee who suffers as a result."[414]

This approach was affirmed and applied by the Court of Appeal in *Allison v London Underground Ltd*,[415] a case applying reg.9 of the Provision and Use of Work Equipment Regulations 1998.[416]

[408] SI 2002/2677 (as frequently amended).

[408A] See, for example, *Cotton v Helphire Ltd* [2019] EWHC 508 (QB), a claim for breach of reg.11, requiring health surveillance under certain circumstances. In this instance, however, it had not been established that the claimant's condition was work-related, nor that the employer should have understood his symptoms to be those of a work-related disease triggering the health surveillance duty.

[409] *Billington v South Tees Hospitals NHS Foundation Trust*, County Court (Bristol), 6 January 2015.

[410] [2010] CSIH 40; 2011 S.L.T. 131 at [52]–[56].

[411] [2002] EWCA Civ 1689; [2003] I.C.R. 574; [2003] 1 All E.R. 333; discussed by Fetto and Karseras (2003) 153 N.L.J. 53.

[412] The Control of Substances Hazardous to Health Regulations 1988 (SI 1988/1657). The employer's duty was expressed in similar terms to that required by the 2002 Regulations.

[413] [2002] EWCA Civ 1689; [2003] 1 All E.R. 333 at [23], per Hale LJ (relied on in the context of the Workplace (Health, Safety and Welfare) Regulations 1992 in *Cruz v Chief Constable of Lancashire Police* [2016] EWCA Civ 402, para.13-69). See also the discussion of the advantages offered to claimants by the Control of Substances Hazardous to Health Regulations in comparison to common law in respect of MRSA in D. Bennett, "Litigating hospital acquired MRSA as a disease" [2004] J.P.I.L. 197.

[414] [2002] EWCA Civ 1689; [2003] 1 All E.R. 333 at [27].

[415] [2008] EWCA Civ 71; [2008] I.C.R. 719; see para.13-50.

[416] Contrast the approach taken to the words "reasonably practicable" in *R. v HTM Ltd* [2006] EWCA Crim 1156; [2006] I.C.R. 1383; [2007] 2 All E.R. 665, where the issue was whether they modified an employer's duties under s.2 of the Health and Safety at Work, etc Act 1974 for the purposes of criminal liability. The Court of Appeal (at [23]) did not disagree with the approach taken to reg.7 in *Dugmore v NHS Trust*.

4. DEFENCES

Contributory negligence

Replace paragraph with:

Contributory negligence is a defence both to an action in negligence and breach of statutory duty. In general, however, the carelessness of employees as claimants is treated more leniently than the negligence of employers, even where liability rests 13-86 upon the vicarious responsibility of the employer for the negligence of another employee. So, "[i]t is not for every risky thing which a workman in a factory may do in his familiarity with the machinery that a [claimant] ought to be held guilty of contributory negligence".[437] The House of Lords has accepted that precisely the same conduct by an employee might lead to a different conclusion on negligence, depending upon whether the employee is suing as a claimant or whether a third party (possibly another employee) is suing the employer as vicariously liable for the employee's conduct.[438] The fact that the deceased was carrying out her duties as an employee with attendant risks, albeit carelessly, was also considered a relevant factor in *Cassells v Allan*,[438A] where Mrs Cassells had died as a result of a collision with a coach: "Mrs Cassells did not create a sudden hazard, by running in front of the bus. She was a person on foot, vulnerable to injury by a large vehicle, and acting in the course of her employment." Although she had approached a moving vehicle, the driver and the employer should bear the greater part of the responsibility. Where the employee's claim is based on the employer's breach of statutory duty, the underlying policy of the legislation is also a factor in setting the standard of care for contributory negligence. Thus, in *Staveley Iron and Chemical Company Ltd v Jones*[439] Lord Tucker commented that:

> "In Factory Act cases the purpose of imposing the absolute obligation is to protect the workmen against those very acts of inattention which are sometimes relied upon as constituting contributory negligence so that too strict a standard would defeat the object of the statute."

In some instances an allegation of contributory negligence simply points to a breach of the employer's duty to take reasonable care to protect employees from their own carelessness or inadvertence.[440]

[437] *Flower v Ebbw Vale Steel Iron & Coal Ltd* [1934] 2 K.B. 132 at 140, per Lawrence J, approved by Lord Wright at [1936] A.C. 206 at 214. See also *Caswell v Powell Duffryn Associated Collieries Ltd* [1940] A.C. 152, para.9-64. See also *Casson v Spotmix Ltd (in Liquidation)* [2017] EWCA Civ 1994, where the claimant's hand was trapped in machinery he had been cleaning while it was in operation. Too much emphasis had been placed by the trial judge on the fact that the claimant, with hindsight, acknowledged that this was a dangerous procedure; and more attention should have been paid to the fact that other employees cleaned the machinery in the same way. There should have been no finding of contributory negligence. The employers in this case were in breach for failing to provide adequate training in how to clean the machinery.

[438] *Staveley Iron & Chemical Co Ltd v Jones* [1956] A.C. 627 at 642, 648.

[438A] [2019] CSOH 14; see also para.13-32.

[439] [1956] A.C. 627 at 648; *Sherlock v Chester CC* [2004] EWCA Civ 201 at [30] and [32], per Latham LJ. See also para.9-64.

[440] *General Cleaning Contractors Ltd v Christmas* [1953] A.C. 180. In *Bhatt v Fountain Motors Ltd* [2010] EWCA Civ 863; [2010] P.I.Q.R. P17 where breaches of the Work at Height Regulations 2005 exposed an employee to unnecessary risk of injury Richards LJ observed, at [34], that an employee's "failure to follow the prescribed procedure when doing work he should not have been required to do at all, and when using equipment that he should not have been required to use if the work was to be done, does not mean that the accident was caused by him alone. It goes only to contributory negligence"; applied in *Sharp v Top Flight Scaffolding* [2013] EWHC 479 (QB) (where breach of the same Regulations arose from a failure to ensure that the claimant was properly trained or supervised).

Chapter 14

PUBLIC SERVICE LIABILITY

Table of Contents

2. Negligence Liability

(a) Justiciability

Crown act of state and non-justiciability

Replace paragraph with:

Non-justiciability is recognised as underpinning some, and perhaps all, aspects of the doctrine of "Crown act of state". The doctrine precludes tort actions in relation to "acts which are by their nature sovereign acts, acts which are inherently **14-10** governmental, committed in the conduct of the foreign relations of the Crown",[39] and is therefore a separate application of "non-justiciability", and is not confined to the tort of negligence. It does not apply to actions under the Human Rights Act 1998. In *Rahmatullah*, there was divergence between Justices of the Supreme Court as to whether "Crown act of State" could be entirely explained in terms of "non-justiciability or abstention",[40] or whether there are in fact two aspects to the doctrine: a relatively narrow principle of non-justiciability, and a "tort defence".[41] Baroness Hale DPSC offered the solution of a non-justiciability principle, which was nevertheless wider than the one espoused in the courts below. On this basis, the non-justiciability principle extended to "aspects of the conduct of military operations abroad as well as the high policy decision to engage in them",[42] and the questions raised could be seen as non-justiciable "even though their subject matter was entirely suitable for determination by a court".[43] Crown act of state relates to sovereign acts; committed abroad; in the conduct of the foreign policy of the state; so closely connected to that policy to be necessary in pursuing it; and at least extending to the conduct of military operations which are themselves lawful in international law.[44] The interpretation of Crown act of state fell to be further considered in *Alseran v Ministry of Defence*,[44A] which continued the claims by Iraqi civilians under both the law of tort, and the HRA[44B] The claimants contended that by implication, given the statement of Baroness Hale in the Supreme Court, the defence did not apply in the context of military operations which were not lawful in international law. Leggatt J rejected this argument. The order provided by the Supreme Court had made plain that "the conduct and/or policy in question do not have to be lawful in international law". As he read it, "conduct" is broader than "act", and encompasses not just the particular act complained of by the claimant, such as the act of detaining him, but the conduct of the military operation in the course of which that act occurred. Thus, the Supreme Court was understood to have declared that the application of the Crown act of state doctrine does not depend on establishing that either the allegedly wrongful act or the wider military operation of which the act formed part, or the policy decision to engage in that operation, was lawful in international law.

[39] *Rahmatullah v Ministry of Defence* [2017] UKSC 1; [2017] A.C. 649 at [33] per Baroness Hale.

[40] This was the view of Lord Mance JSC, with whom Lord Hughes JSC agreed. Non-justiciability was also identified as the basis of the related doctrine of foreign act of state in the judgments of Lord Mance JSC, and of Lord Neuberger JSC, in *Belhaj v Straw* [2017] UKSC 3; [2017] A.C. 964. In that case however, the doctrine was not effective and the claims proceeded to trial.

[41] This was the view of Lord Sumption JSC.

[42] [2017] UKSC 1; [2017] A.C. 649 at [33].

[43] [2017] UKSC 1; [2017] A.C. 649 at [33].

[44] [2017] UKSC 1; [2017] A.C. 649 at [37]. It was accepted that the doctrine would not extend to acts of torture, for example.

[44A] [2017] EWHC 3289 (QB); [2018] 3 W.L.R. 95.

[44B] See further para.14-118.

(b) Fair just and reasonable

(i) Child welfare

Duty to the child

Replace paragraph with:

Following *Barrett v Enfield LBC*[70] it is clear that a duty of care is owed to a child who has been taken into care by an authority. *Barrett* limited the authority of *Bedfordshire* to the proposition that decisions about taking a child into care did not give rise to a duty. However, in *D v East Berkshire Community NHS Trust*[71] the Court of Appeal held that this proposition was no longer applicable. In *East Berkshire* the claims stemmed from the accusations of medical authorities that parents had been abusing their children. These accusations proved unfounded but resulted in the temporary removal of the children from their parents. Both parents and children claimed to be owed a duty of care by the medical authorities. Although not involving a claim against social services as in *Bedfordshire*, the claim did arise from the investigation of child abuse. Lord Phillips MR giving the judgment of the Court of Appeal held that the policy reasons justifying denial of a duty in *Bedfordshire* could no longer apply because of the Human Rights Act 1998. This enabled parents and children to claim that an authority which negligently removed children into care, was in breach of s.6 of the Act. Section 6 required a public body to comply with the articles of the European Convention for the Protection of Human Rights including art.8 which required respect for family life.[72] As, subsequent to the Act coming into force in October 2000, parents and children could make a claim based on breach of the duty in s.6 against a public service, there was no point in protecting the service from a common law negligence claim. To the extent that such a claim might upset the process of taking a discretionary decision or might lead to defensive conduct and diversion of resources, this would happen anyway as a result of the s.6 claim. Thus, Lord Phillips concluded: "the decision in *Bedfordshire* cannot survive the 1998 Act."[73] The events in *Berkshire* occurred before 2000 and hence a Human Rights Act claim was not available to the claimants but Lord Phillips reasoned: 14-18

> "This cannot constitute a valid reason of policy for preserving a limitation of the common law duty of care which is not otherwise justified. On the contrary, the absence of an alternative remedy for children who were the victims of abuse before October 2000 militates in favour of the recognition of a common law duty of care once the public policy reasons against this have lost their force."

Consequently, he said:

> "it will no longer be legitimate to rule that, as a matter of law, no common law duty of care is owed to a child in relation to the investigation of suspected child abuse and the initiation and pursuit of care proceedings. It is possible that there will be factual situations where it is not fair, just or reasonable to impose a duty of care but each case will fall to be determined on its own individual facts."[74]

However, he held that no duty would be owed to the parents as: "It will always be in the parents' interest that the child should not be removed" and hence "the child's interests are in potential conflict with the interests of the parents" with the result that there were "cogent reasons of public policy for concluding that, where child care decisions are being taken, no common law duty of care should be owed to the parents".[75] The decision in respect of the duty to the children was not appealed but that in respect of the denial of a duty to the parents was taken to the House of Lords.[76] A suggestion by the Court of Appeal in *CN v Poole BC*[76A] that the Court of Appeal in *D v East Berkshire Community NHS Trust* had been impliedly overruled by subsequent decisions and should no longer be followed has been roundly rejected by the Supreme Court.[76B] *D v East Berkshire Community NHS Trust* remains good law.

[70] [2001] 2 A.C. 550. See also *S v Gloucestershire CC* [2001] Fam. 313, where the Court of Appeal followed the approach in *Barrett* and refused to strike out claims that a social work authority was liable to children for negligently failing to prevent their abuse by foster parents.

[71] [2003] EWCA Civ 1151; [2004] Q.B. 558.

[72] For the application of art.8 to this situation, see para.14-108.

[73] [2003] EWCA Civ 1151; [2004] Q.B. 558 at [83]. Wright, "Immunity no more" (2004) 20 P.N. 58 at 63, criticised *D v East Berkshire* as an "illegitimate attempt to overrule a House of Lords' decision [*Bedfordshire*]" and argued that the same result could have been achieved legitimately on the basis of the undermining of *Bedfordshire* in *Barrett* and *Phelps*. In the House of Lords in *D v East Berkshire* [2005] UKHL 23; [2005] 2 A.C. 373, the Court of Appeal's decision in relation to the duty to the child was not in question but Lord Bingham, at [21], noted Wright's criticism. In *Leeds CC v Price* [2005] EWCA Civ 289; [2005] 1 W.L.R. 1825, shortly after *D v East Berkshire* in the Court of Appeal and before the judgment of the House of Lords, a Court of Appeal including Lord Phillips declined to depart from a House of Lords authority and to follow a subsequent judgment of the European Court of Human Rights instead, suggesting that this would be "iconoclasm of a different dimension" from their decision in *D v East Berkshire* (at [33]). The implication that *East Berkshire* involved a degree of iconoclasm, together with more recent trends sketched in the following paragraphs of this chapter, suggest that this sort of move will not be repeated.

[74] [2003] EWCA Civ 1151; [2004] Q.B. 558 at [84].

[75] [2003] EWCA Civ 1151; [2004] Q.B. 558 at [86].

[76] See para.14-21.

[76A] [2017] EWCA Civ 2185; [2018] 2 W.L.R. 1693.

[76B] *Poole BC v GN* [2019] UKSC 25; [2019] 2 W.L.R. 1478 at [75].

Abuse by foster parents

Replace paragraph with:

14-19 In *NA v Nottinghamshire CC*[77] the Court of Appeal held that a local authority was not vicariously liable for abuse perpetrated by foster carers on children placed in their care by the authority, nor did the authority owe a non-delegable duty of care to children in these circumstances.[78] On appeal, the Supreme Court agreed[79] that a local authority does not come under a non-delegable duty, since such a duty could create a conflict with the authority's statutory duty to the child under the Child Care Act 1980 and the local authority's interests in avoiding potential liability. A non-delegable duty would also amount to a form of state insurance for the actions of the child's family members. However, the Supreme Court reversed the Court of Appeal on the issue of vicarious liability, concluding that the local authority could be vicariously liable for the actions of foster carers. Applying *Cox v Ministry of Justice*,[80] several factors were considered to be relevant to this conclusion; the torts were committed in the court of an activity carried out for the benefit of the local authority; the placement of children with foster parents rendered the children particularly vulnerable to abuse; the local authority exercised a significant degree of control over both what the foster parents did and how they did it; and local authorities could more easily compensate the victims of abuse.[81]

[77] [2015] EWCA Civ 1139; [2016] Q.B. 739.

[78] On which see *Woodland v Swimming Teachers Association* [2013] UKSC 66; [2014] A.C. 537; see also, para.6-63.

[79] *Armes v Nottinghamshire CC* [2017] UKSC 60; [2018] A.C. 355. *Armes* was applied in *Razumas v Ministry of Justice* [2018] EWHC 215 (QB); [2018] Med L.R. 212, concluding that no non-delegable duty was owed by the Ministry of Justice to serving prisoners that would extend to responsibility for negligent medical care provided by a healthcare trust. There was also no vicarious liability in this situation.

[80] [2016] UKSC 10; [2016] A.C. 660; see para.6-33.

[81] *Armes v Nottinghamshire CC* [2017] UKSC 60; [2018] A.C. 355 at [59]–[64]. Though as Lord Hughes pointed out (at [77]) in his dissenting judgment "(deep pockets or insurance) ... cannot by itself be a principled ground for vicariousl liability and tends to be circular."

Child welfare and child support

Replace paragraph with:

In *Rowley v Secretary of State for Work and Pensions*,[82] claims were brought by three children and their mother alleging that negligent enforcement of maintenance payments by the Child Support Agency ("CSA") had resulted in economic losses, as well as psychological injury to the first child claimant, who suffered from cerebral palsy. All of the claims were struck out for a variety of reasons. There was no voluntary assumption of responsibility since the Secretary of State was statutorily obliged under the Child Support Act 1991 to make a maintenance assessment; and the relationship between the CSA and the claimants was not sufficiently similar to a solicitor-client relationship to be treated as analogous to that established duty category. These are essentially issues of proximity. Dyson LJ giving the judgment of the Court further held however that such a duty would not be "fair, just and reasonable". The Child Support Act 1991 "provided a sufficiently comprehensive remedy" to conclude "that a duty of care would be inconsistent with the statutory scheme".[83] Claims could also be referred to the ombudsman, and the cost of litigation "might well be out of proportion to the sums likely to be realistically at stake". *Rowley* is part of a series of decisions rejecting claims for civil remedies framed in tort or in terms of Convention rights, and brought against the Child Support Agency and the Secretary of State in respect of the Child Support Act 1991.[84] However the reasoning deployed is plainly of much broader application. For example in *Murdoch v Department for Work and Pensions*,[85] Walker J applied *Rowley* and ruled that an action in negligence would be inconsistent with the statutory scheme relating to the payment of incapacity benefit and income support. The relevant statute made plain the intended finality of the determination of entitlement under the Act. There would also have been no duty in any event following the approach in *Customs and Excise Commissioners v Barclays Bank Plc*.[86] In particular, action in discharge of a statutory duty does not in itself amount to an "assumption of responsibility", for it is not voluntary; there was no special degree of proximity; any such development would be more than incremental; and it would not be "fair, just and reasonable" to offer a common law remedy where other remedies existed.[87] 14-20

[82] [2007] EWCA Civ 598; [2007] 1 W.L.R. 2861.

[83] [2007] EWCA Civ 598; [2007] 1 W.L.R. 2861 at [74]. Remedies to the parent included a right of appeal, right to receive interest on payments on arrears, and the right to seek judicial review.

[84] See also *R. (Kehoe) v Secretary of State for Work and Pensions* [2005] UKHL 48; [2006] 1 A.C. 42; para.14-101: the absence of a direct enforcement mechanism for parents did not engage art.6(1); and *Kehoe v UK* (2010/06) [2008] 2 F.L.R. 1014; (2009) 48 E.H.R.R. 2, where an application in respect of this claim was dismissed by the European Court of Human Rights: para.14-101. See also *Treharne v*

Secretary of State for Work and Pensions [2008] EWHC 3222 (QB); [2009] 1 F.L.R. 853 (a Human Rights Act claim based on art.8 of the ECHR); para.14-106.

[85] [2010] EWHC 1988 (QB); [2011] P.T.S.R. D3.

[86] [2006] UKHL 28; [2007] 1 A.C. 181.

[87] On this last point see also for example *Home Office v Mohammed* [2011] EWCA Civ 351; [2011] 1 W.L.R. 2862, discussed in para.14-61. See also *Seddon v Driver and Vehicle Licensing Agency* [2019] EWCA Civ 14; para.14-66.

No duty to suspect parent

Replace footnote 93 with:

14-21 [93] See [2005] UKHL 23; [2005] 2 A.C. 373 at [47], [44] and [50]. Damages under the Human Rights Act were awarded at first instance to parents whose children had been placed in foster care without their consent in *Williams v Hackney LBC* [2015] EWHC 2629 (QB); on appeal however, it was concluded that the placement had not been in breach of art.8: *Williams v Hackney LBC* [2017] EWCA Civ 26; [2017] 3 W.L.R. 59. Damages were awarded under the Human Rights Act against both police and social services in *D (Children) v Wakefield MDC* [2016] EWHC 3312 (Fam); [2017] 2 F.L.R. 1353. The injury was directly that of the parent, who was wrongly accused and had her children removed despite the availability of exonerating evidence: see para.14-105.

(iii) Police services

Police services

Replace paragraph with:

14-28 In *Hill v Chief Constable of West Yorkshire*[124] where the claimant had alleged that the police had been negligent in failing to apprehend a mass murderer and were liable for the death of her daughter who was the murderer's last victim, it was held that there was insufficient proximity between the police and a member of the general public to give rise to a duty of care in relation to the apprehension of the criminal. But in addition the House of Lords held that on public interest grounds, no duty would be owed in relation to the investigation of crime.[125] The reasons bore some similarity to those justifying denial of a duty in *Bedfordshire*. First, the fear of liability might lead to the police function "being carried on in a detrimentally defensive frame of mind". Secondly, defending litigation would lead to "a significant diversion of police manpower and attention from their most important function, the suppression of crime" and thirdly, the court was not an appropriate body to determine the reasonableness of a discretionary policing decision. In *Hughes v National Union of Mineworkers*[126] it was held that the same policy denying a duty also applied to "on the spot operational decisions" in the course of policing serious public disorder. *Hill* was followed by the Court of Appeal in *Osman v Ferguson*[127] which concerned the alleged negligent failure of the police to arrest a known suspect in time to prevent harm to the claimant and where, in distinction to *Hill's* case, the relationship of the police and the claimant might have been close enough to support a finding of proximity. McCowan LJ held that the policy reasons for denying a duty applied even where there was a relationship of proximity and where the police function concerned prevention of crime rather than an investigation.[128] In *Ancell v McDermott*[129] the Court of Appeal held that a duty should be denied in respect of the police function of maintaining the safety of highways. In *Ancell* it was alleged that the police had acted negligently in failing to warn road users of a dangerous oil spillage on the road. Beldam LJ stressed the "formidable diversion of police manpower" that would result from having to defend such cases were a duty to be owed.[130] In *Elguzouli-Daf v Commissioner of Police*[131] the Court of Appeal applied the reasoning in *Hill* to hold that the Crown Prosecution Service owed no duty of care to those it was prosecuting. The broader "conflict of interest" argument[132] would also presumably lead to the same conclusion. A further application of the reasoning in *Hill*, before *Osman v UK*, was the decision of the House of Lords in *Calveley v Chief Constable of Merseyside Police.*[133] Here police officers claimed against a Chief Constable on the ground that disciplinary proceedings had been negligently conducted. Giving the opinion of a unanimous House of Lords, Lord Bridge rejected the negligence claim on the ground that it would be contrary to public policy to impose a duty of care on investigating police officers to those suspected of crime and "[i]f no duty of care is owed by a police officer investigating a suspected crime to a civilian suspect, it is difficult to see why a police officer who is subject to [a disciplinary] investigation should be in any better position".[134] The decision in *Calveley* was in turn influential in the Supreme Court's decision in *James-Bowen v Commissioner of Police of the Metropolis.*[134A] No duty of care was owed to police officers when a decision was made to settle a claim for the Chief Constable's vicarious liability for the alleged torts of the officers. If there was no duty of care when disciplinary investigations had been initiated by the police in *Calveley*, then no such duty could be owed where an action was initiated by a third party, since the Chief Constable's role was less proactive. In addition, the defendant Chief Constable, in her particular role, should be enabled to make decisions freely in light of her public duty. For these and other reasons (for example, the likelihood that the interests of the employer and employee would be at odds where settlement of vicarious liability claims was in issue), it would not be "fair, just and reasonable" to impose a duty.

[124] [1989] A.C. 53.

[125] [1989] A.C. 53 at 63.

[126] [1991] 4 All E.R. 278.

[127] [1993] 4 All E.R. 344.

[128] Notice that the manner in which the *Hill* policy reasons were applied to this case—as though they created a "blanket immunity"—led to a finding that the UK had been in breach of EHCR art.6, in *Osman v UK* [1999] 1 F.L.R. 193 (European Court of Human Rights). The courts' response to this has helped to shape many areas of public authority liability, as noted in para.14-15. Where the police are concerned however the policy reasons appear to have been reasserted in something close to their general form: para.14-31.

[129] [1993] 4 All E.R. 355.

[130] [1993] 4 All E.R. 355 at 366.

[131] [1995] Q.B. 335. See also *Kumar v Commissioner of Police* unreported 31 January 1995 where the Court of Appeal upheld the striking out of an allegation that the police were negligent in pursuing a hopeless prosecution against the claimant.

[132] Explored in connection with child welfare decisions in para.14-21.

[133] [1989] A.C. 1228. Claims brought for breach of statutory duty and misfeasance in public office were also rejected: see paras 9-30 and 14-121.

[134] [1989] A.C. 1228 at 1238.

[134A] [2018] UKSC 40; [2018] 1 W.L.R. 4021.

Developments since Osman v UK

Replace paragraph with:

Leaving aside cases where there is an assumption of responsibility,[146] such "exceptional cases" have not so far been recognised, and their existence now appears unlikely given not only the outcomes but also the reasoning by the majority **14-31** justices in *Smith v Chief Constable of Sussex Police*,[147] and *Michael v Chief Constable of South Wales Police*,[148] though in *Robinson v Chief Constable of West Yorkshire Police*,[148A] the Supreme Court held that a case where a positive act resulted in physical injury did not fall within the *Hill* principle, which was concerned with cases of failure to protect from harm.[148B] In *Smith*, the House of Lords struck out a claim by the victim of a savage assault by his former partner, the claimant arguing that the police had failed to protect him from the assailant despite repeated warnings of the danger. Lord Bingham, dissenting, would have recognised that this case fell within a narrow "liability principle", which would arise in circumstances falling short of an assumption of responsibility (although he also would have found such an assumption on the facts). According to Lord Bingham, "if a member of the public (A) furnishes a police officer (B) with apparently credible evidence that a third party whose identity and whereabouts are known presents a specific and imminent threat to his life or physical safety, B owes A a duty to take reasonable steps to assess such threat and, if appropriate, take reasonable steps to prevent it being executed".[149] The other members of the House of Lords differed from Lord Bingham in their approach as well as in the outcome, Lord Hope concluding clearly that within the core of the *Hill* "principle", the policy goals served by that case could not be secured if the duty of care depended on a case by case analysis. Rather, a "robust approach" was needed to avoid wasteful diversion of police time. Lord Brown argued that there was no need for common law to develop in order to cover such cases, which he thought were much better ruled out "on a class basis". This looks very much like the *Hill* immunity, though it is subject to an exception for assumption of responsibility, and in theory at least there may be a duty of care outside the "core" application of *Hill*, justifying the assertion that the principle does not amount to an "immunity" by a different name. The existence of a remedy under the Human Rights Act 1998 was an important link in Lord Brown's reasoning, since he considered extension of the common law to be "simply unnecessary" given the existence of an alternative remedy in domestic law. Lord Phillips' approach was more balanced. He agreed in the result with the majority, but thought it "hard to judge" whether the policy concerns in *Brooks* really justified the rule against a duty in such cases. The broad reach of the Hill principle is illustrated by *B v Reading BC*.[150] A father who had been wrongly accused of sexually assaulting his three-year-old daughter brought actions in negligence against an investigating police officer, and in misfeasance in a public office against the police officer and a social worker. Mackay J noted the comments of Lord Nicholls in *Brooks* concerning the possibility of exceptional cases falling outside the core principle in *Hill* but added that "No decided case has been put before me in which such an exceptional circumstance has been found to fall outside the *Hill* principle".[151] Nor could there be said to be an "assumption of responsibility" to a suspected parent. Claims in misfeasance and conspiracy also failed because there was no evidence of bad faith. Despite a series of grossly leading questions being put to the child in interview, and despite the fact that the most damning remarks alleged to have been made by the child proved, on examination of interview recordings, never to have been said at all, neither the claim in negligence nor misfeasance succeeded. The reasoning against police liability in the UK case law has not been accepted in Canada, where the Supreme Court has recognised that the police may owe a duty in the manner of their investigation not just to potential victims of crime in circumstances of close proximity,[152] but also to *suspects*.[153] This directly contrasts with the core application of the *Hill* policy reasoning.

[146] See para.14-35.

[147] Reported together with *Van Colle v Chief Constable of Hertfordshire* [2008] UKHL 50; [2009] 1 A.C. 225 (for discussion of *Van Colle*, which was a claim under the Human Rights Act, see para.14-83).

[148] [2015] UKSC 2; [2015] A.C. 1732.

[148A] [2018] UKSC 4; [2018] 2 W.L.R. 595.

[148B] See para.14-37.

[149] Reported together with *Van Colle v Chief Constable of Hertfordshire* [2008] UKHL 50; [2009] 1 A.C. 225 at [44]: this defines the content of Lord Bingham's proposed "liability principle".

[150] [2009] EWHC 998 (QB); [2009] 2 F.L.R. 1273.

[151] [2009] EWHC 998 (QB); [2009] 2 F.L.R. 1273 at [30].

[152] Such a duty had already been recognised by Canadian courts in cases of close proximity: *Jane Doe v Metropolitan Toronto (Municipality) Commissioners of Police* (1998) 160 D.L.R. (4th) 697.

[153] *Hill v Hamilton-Wentworth Regional Police Services Board* [2007] 3 S.C.R. 129; (2007) 285 D.L.R. (4th) 620 (SCC). For comment see N. Rafferty (2008) 24 P.N. 78; E. Chamberlain (2008) 124 L.Q.R. 205.

Replace paragraph with:

Both the courts' continued commitment to the *Hill* principle, and the potential significance of the alternative remedy under HRA, referred to in the previous paragraph, are illustrated by the decision of the Supreme Court in *Michael v Chief Constable of South Wales Police*.[155] The claim concerned the murder of a woman after she had placed two 999 calls to police. Due to an alleged failure to transcribe her words accurately, her initial call was downgraded to a lower priority level requiring a response within 60 minutes, rather than the highest priority requiring a response within five minutes. During this time, her former partner returned and fatally attacked her. It was argued by the claimants that the call handler had failed to appreciate the urgency of the call, and it appears that she did not hear the deceased say that her former partner had threatened to return and "kill" (rather than "hit") her. A negligence claim was struck out by the Supreme Court but a claim based on art.2 ECHR and the Human Rights Act was allowed to proceed to trial. Evidently the case bears comparison with *Smith*. For the majority, Lord Toulson urged that in this instance, the question was not whether the police should benefit from a special "immunity" from actions in negligence but whether they should be liable in circumstances where ordinarily no duty of care would be owed.[156] The refusal of the courts to impose a private law duty on the police to exercise reasonable care to safeguard potential victims of crime, except where there is a "representation and reliance",[156A] did not involve giving special treatment to the police.[157] Rather, they reflected the law's general approach to omissions.[158] These features of the majority judgment were doubted by Baroness Hale, pointing out that there would have been little need to create and maintain the *Hill* principle through cases such as *Smith* and *Brooks* if the cases merely turned on the ordinary principles of negligence: the absence of omissions liability, in particular, is not generally complete but subject to exceptions.[159] The majority agreed with counsel for the claimants that the likely effects of liability on the actions of the police, which had been part of the justification for the decision in *Hill*, were hard to predict, but argued that any alleged positive impact on policing was also to be discounted for the same reason (namely, lack of evidence). On the other hand the court could be sure that the existence of such a duty would have "potentially significant financial implications" for the police.[160] In relation to the argument that common law should develop in harmony with the positive duties of the state under arts 2 and 3, Lord Toulson argued that tort should not be used to remedy interferences with Convention rights, 14-32 partly because of its higher damages awards: he saw no reason "for gold plating the claimant's Convention rights by providing compensation on a different basis from the claim under the Human Rights Act 1998".[161] He was also concerned that the common law duty urged by the claimants would be wider than the positive duty recognised by the Convention.[162]

[155] [2015] UKSC 2; [2015] A.C. 1732.

[156] [2015] UKSC 2; [2015] A.C. 1732 at [116].

[156A] For a successful argument that such a representation and reliance was arguable, on facts somewhat similar to *Michael* itself, see *Sherratt v Chief Constable of Greater Manchester* [2018] EWHC 1746 (QB); [2019] P.I.Q.R. P1; see para.14-35. Here, it was arguable that the Chief Constable had assumed responsibility for the welfare of a woman who committed suicide, when a call handler assured the woman's mother that officers would arrive and ensure her daughter was taken to hospital, should this be necessary. There was, arguably, both an assurance, and reliance on the part of the mother.

[157] [2015] UKSC 2; [2015] A.C. 1732 at [115].

[158] On liability for omissions, see para.8-47 onwards. Note also the decision in *Griffiths v Chief Constable of Suffolk* [2018] EWHC 2538 (QB); [2019] Med. L.R. 1, where an NHS trust was not liable in negligence for the death of a woman (G) who was murdered by her former partner, where it was argued that in light of the danger he posed to G, he should have been admitted to hospital against his wishes. There was no sufficient basis on which the Trust should have known he posed a risk to G's life. Claims under the HRA against both the Trust and the police also failed: see further para.14-83.

[159] [2015] UKSC 2; [2015] A.C. 1732 at [190].

[160] [2015] UKSC 2; [2015] A.C. 1732 at [122].

[161] [2015] UKSC 2; [2015] A.C. 1732 at [125].

[162] [2015] UKSC 2; [2015] A.C. 1732 On the breadth of the positive Convention duty, see para.14-82 et seq.

Replace paragraph with:

14-34 Before the decision of the Supreme Court in *Michael*, in *DSD v Commissioner of Police for the Metropolis*,[165] Green J found the defendant liable under the HRA for violations of positive duties arising under art.3 ECHR. He identified a series of systemic failings which caused the police to fail to apprehend a serial rapist and to cut short the series of attacks that he perpetrated on women, including the claimants. The circumstances are very similar to those in *Hill* itself. Although Lord Toulson in *Michael* referred to *DSD*, he said that he would not wish to influence the Court of Appeal's consideration of the case.[166] Subsequently, the Court of Appeal affirmed Green J's decision, as did the Supreme Court.[167] In relation to the law of negligence, both *Michael* and *DSD* raise the question of how far the policy reasons underlying the *Hill* decision can ultimately be retained if the same issues are capable of founding an HRA claim. While the absence of a duty in respect of investigation of crime is no longer referred to as an "immunity", it is still worth noting that immunities are now regarded by the courts as to be retained only to the extent that they serve a clear purpose. If the same issues are to be litigated in any event, this plainly weakens the argument for an immunity.[168] In the same way, the possibility of litigation in an HRA action might be thought to undermine the objectives of the *Hill* "principle". However, in *D v Commissioner of the Metropolis*,[168A] the Supreme Court argued that the goals of the two areas of law were different: just as the law of tort did not need to be reinterpreted in order to fall into line with the HRA, so also the HRA action did not need to be narrowed to reflect the ambit of the law of tort.

[165] [2014] EWHC 436 (QB).

[166] [2015] UKSC 2; [2015] A.C. 1732 at [128].

[167] *DSD v Commissioner of Police for the Metropolis* [2015] EWCA Civ 646; [2016] Q.B. 161 and [2018] UKSC 11; [2019] A.C. 196, see para.14-37A.

[168] As recognised in *Smart v Forensic Science Service Ltd* [2013] EWCA Civ 783; [2013] P.N.L.R. 32, para.14-49.

[168A] [2018] UKSC 11; [2019] A.C. 196 at [97].

Assumption of responsibility by the police

Replace paragraph with:

Situations where responsibility is assumed by the police are recognised as constituting an exception to the *Hill* principle at common law, and as a category of liability in the absence of a positive act. Although "voluntary assumption of responsibility" is best seen as a special variation of proximity, it has also been said that where such an assumption exists, the further condition that imposition of a duty is "fair, just and reasonable" no longer applies.[169] On this logic, cases where there is such an assumption therefore fall outside the general policy reasoning. The defendant in *Brooks*[170] accepted that cases of assumption of responsibility by the police fell outside the *Hill* principle. The leading example of this is *Swinney v Chief Constable of Northumbria Police*[171] where the Court of Appeal held it arguable that the police owed a duty of care to an informant to whom they had assumed a responsibility by giving him an undertaking of confidentiality. The court also considered that the public interest in the encouragement of the free flow of information to the police could outweigh the interest in the police carrying out the function of investigating and suppressing crime uninhibited by the spectre of negligence litigation.[172] In *An Informer v A Chief Constable*,[173] the Court of Appeal declined to extend this reasoning to recognise a duty to protect the economic interests of a police informer, deciding that the case fell within the *Hill* principle. Two members of the Court, Arden LJ and Pill LJ, focused on the particular circumstances of the alleged duty, acknowledging that stronger cases may arise in future.[174] In *CLG v Chief Constable of Merseyside*,[175] the Court of Appeal also declined to extend the reasoning in *Swinney* to protect witnesses, rather than informants. The claimant witnesses were forced to move house when their address was inadvertently revealed to those who might reasonably be expected to do them harm, partly through the actions of both the police and the CPS. Applying the reasoning in *Brooks*, whilst there might be an ethical case for arguing that the claimant witnesses were entitled to expect the same support from the police as an informant, this did not convert into a duty of care, and there was no assumption of responsibility comparable to that in *Swinney*.[176] Routine statements had been taken, and witness summonses were eventually served; there was nothing to suggest that the addresses were disclosed on a confidential basis. An assumption of responsibility was however found to be arguably present in *Sherratt v Chief Constable of Greater Manchester*,[176A] a case whose facts are relatively close to those in *Michael v Chief Constable of South Wales*.[176B] Here, a woman had committed suicide. Her mother had placed an emergency call requesting assistance because she feared the deceased would take an overdose. A duty of care was arguable because there was sufficient evidence that the call handler had assured the mother that police would attend and take steps to ensure her daughter's safety, taking her to hospital should this be necessary. Therefore, the mother took no further steps of her own, for example by calling for an ambulance. The call handler appears to have downgraded the call from "emergency" to "priority", and the officers did not attend until over three hours later. It did not matter that the assurance was made to the mother, while it was her **14-35** daughter who was owed the claimed duty; nor was it relevant that the duty was to prevent the daughter from harming herself.

[169] *Henderson v Merrett Syndicates* [1995] 2 A.C. 145; *Customs and Excise Commissioners v Barclays Bank Plc* [2006] UKHL 28; [2007] 1 A.C. 181.

[170] [2005] UKHL 24; [2005] 1 W.L.R. 1495; para.14-30.

[171] [1997] Q.B. 464. The claimant lost at the subsequent trial on the ground that the police were not in breach of the duty: *Swinney v Chief Constable of Northumbria Police (No.2)* (1999) 11 Admin L.R. 811.

[172] Note also the case of *Costello v Chief Constable of Northumbria Police* [1999] 1 All E.R. 550; [1999] I.C.R. 752, in which a police officer was assaulted by a prisoner while another officer who was present specifically for the claimant's protection did nothing to help. The second officer admitted that he was under a "police duty" to assist his colleague, and the Court of Appeal held that he had assumed a responsibility which could also give rise to a duty of care in negligence. The policy issues which would preclude a duty either to a member of the public or to a fellow officer outside such extraordinary facts were noted by the Court of Appeal.

[173] [2012] EWCA Civ 197; [2013] Q.B. 579.

[174] See also *PBD v Chief Constable of Greater Manchester* [2013] EWHC 3559 (QB), Silber J concluding that neither duty, nor breach had been established . The claimants alleged negligence causing psychiatric damage and economic loss where they had been forced to enter the witness protection programme, the first claimant's name having been revealed to his former criminal associates during the course of a new prosecution. The relationship here was considered less proximate than the relationship in *An Informer*.

[175] [2015] EWCA Civ 836.

[176] [2015] EWCA Civ 836 at [24].

[176A] [2018] EWHC 1746 (QB); [2019] P.I.Q.R. P1.

[176B] [2015] UKSC 2; [2015] A.C. 1732; see para.14-31.

Replace paragraph with:

14-36 Even in a case which falls outside the *Hill* principle, it still must be established that a duty of care is owed, and here too a voluntary assumption of responsibility may be required as an aspect of applying the usual *Caparo* principles. In *Desmond v Chief Constable of Nottinghamshire Police*,[177] the claimant had been questioned after an allegation of sexual assault but it proved that he had not been involved in the incident and no prosecution was pursued. When the claimant later sought employment as a teacher, he applied for an enhanced criminal record certificate. The Chief Constable authorised release of information about the suspicion of sexual assault, but no information was supplied concerning its resolution. No attempt was made by the police disclosure unit to contact the investigating officer nor to locate his pocket book. The Court of Appeal struck out the action as disclosing no arguable duty of care. The officers were performing statutory duties and if the policy of the statute was not to create a liability, the same policy should "ordinarily exclude" a common law duty of care.[178] There would need to be particular circumstances, such as the assumption of responsibilities or carrying out of acts, to justify such a duty. In this instance, there could not be said to be a voluntary assumption of responsibility, because the defendant acted under a statutory duty. To be voluntarily assumed, a duty must not be identical to a duty imposed by statute.[179] It was also considered relevant that the claimant might have other remedies, albeit of a different type. This included the potential for a remedy under HRA for interference with art.8 rights, a claim for which was still continuing in *Desmond* itself. Policy reasoning said to be similar to that in *Desmond* was used in *C v T BC*,[180] to deny a duty of care on the part of a local authority providing information to the police for use in the creation of an Enhanced Criminal Record Certificate; there were other remedies available and a duty would deter those who would otherwise provide information to the police which would assist in safeguarding. In *Desmond* *v Foreman*,[181] Tugendhat J held that the claimant had a real prospect of succeeding in an argument based on art.8 ECHR and the Data Protection Act 1998, and also had a real prospect of defeating a defence of qualified privilege in defamation.

[177] [2011] EWCA Civ 3; [2011] 1 F.L.R. 1361; [2011] Fam. Law 358. In *Robinson v Chief Constable of South Yorkshire Police* [2018] UKSC 4; [2018] A.C. 736, Lord Reed stopped short of questioning the correctness of *Desmond*, but did suggest that some of its broader statements were incorrect.

[178] [2011] EWCA Civ 3; [2011] 1 F.L.R. 1361; [2011] Fam. Law 358 at [39].

[179] See also para.14-66.

[180] [2014] EWHC 2482 (QB); [2015] E.L.R. 1.

[181] [2012] EWHC 1900 (QB).

Scope of the Hill principle

Replace paragraph with:

In *Robinson v Chief Constable of West Yorkshire Police*,[182] three members of the Supreme Court determined that the *Hill* principle was confined to cases of omission, and did not apply to positive acts causing personal injury on the part of the police. There were no dissents as to the outcome of the case, but two members of the Court, Lord Mance and Lord Hughes, adopted a very different analysis of the nature of the *Hill* principle and its applicability. In *Robinson*, officers had attempted to arrest a suspect on a busy shopping street, and three men had collided with the claimant, who suffered injuries as a result. The Court of Appeal had applied *Hill* and its policy reasoning to deny liability. Lord Reed (with whom Baroness Hale and Lord Hodge agreed) concluded, however, that where positive actions by the police caused physical injury, the police would be liable in the same way as any other person, and there would be no need to apply the *Caparo* test, which was described as applying only to "novel claims". Moreover, the central point of *Caparo* was said to be not that it set out a "tripartite" test, since the decision had denied the possibility of a general test for negligence. Rather, its central point was that development of the law should be "incremental" and based upon the starting point of established categories. The policy reasons expressed in *Hill* would have no application to such a claim, which fell within an established duty category, namely positive acts causing physical injury. However, Lord Reed went further, suggesting that the *Hill* case was concerned with policy considerations chiefly because it was decided in the era of *Anns v Merton*, and seeking to explain more recent decisions applying *Hill* not in terms of policy, but in terms of their concern with omissions rather than positive acts, and in terms of other established, general reasons for denying a duty. For example, *Brooks v Commissioner of Police of the Metropolis*[183] was explained as involving actions which were "merely insensitive": such actions "are not normally actionable", even if they result in psychiatric illness.[184] Policy discussion in the leading cases should not be "consigned to history"; but the fact that the police did not owe positive duties was not merely a result of policy reasoning by a "recent generation of judges". Rather it built on long-established principles. **14-37**

[182] [2018] UKSC 4; [2018] 2 W.L.R. 595.

[183] [2005] UKHL 24; [2005] 1 W.L.R. 1495; see para.14-30.

[184] [2018] UKSC 4; [2018] A.C. 736 at [60].

Add new paragraph:

Lord Reed's opinion further develops the logic of *Michael v Chief Constable of* **14-37A**
South Wales,[185] which had held that the police were not liable because their ac-

tions fell within the category of omissions, and not because the police are specially protected through the application of policy reasoning. It applies that logic to a case of commission, arguing that the case should not be seen as a novel one simply because the tortfeasors were police officers acting in the restraint of crime. It is suggested that there are some difficulties with the reasoning of Lord Reed, considered in this and the following paragraph. First, his approach depends upon the definition of a particular case as falling within an "established duty category", and would appear to include in a single, unproblematic category any case where a positive act causes physical injury. But why is this the appropriate definition of the relevant "or the nature of the established duty category"? Why is it not possible for the nature of the defendant's activities, to take a case into the realms of the "novel", or indeed, into the realms of a category which has previously been considered, and treated as problematic? Less than two weeks after the decision in *Robinson*, in *D v Commissioner of Police for the Metropolis*,[186] all five members of a differently constituted Supreme Court seemed to treat duties in the investigation and suppression of crime in precisely these terms. They described the police as being exempt from a duty of care in cases where they are engaged in the investigation of crime, without reference to any distinction between acts and omissions, and explained that exemption in policy terms. While *D* is centrally concerned with duties under art.3 ECHR and was a claim under the HRA,[186A] the distinction with common law was essential to the decision. Lord Kerr, with whom Baroness Hale and Lord Neuberger both agreed, said that "no assumption should be made that an exemption of police from liability at common law apply mutatis mutandis to liability for breach of Convention rights".[186B] Lord Neuberger, with whom Baroness Hale also agreed, referred to the line of cases from *Hill* to *Michael*, and said that

> "Those cases establish that, absent special factors, our domestic law adopts the view that, when investigating crime, the police owe no duty of care in tort to individual citizens. That is because courts in this country consider that the imposition of such a duty would, as Lord Hughes JSC puts it, at [132], 'inhibit the robust operation of police work, and divert resources from current inquiries; it would be detrimental, not a spur, to law enforcement'."[186C]

This appears to present the investigation of crime as belonging to a separate and problematic category, irrespective of whether the negligence consists of acts, omissions, or both. Lord Reed's approach in *Robinson* appears to treat the distinction between positive acts and omissions, and between physical harm and other types as loss, as uniquely definitive. Notably, he dismissed the House of Lords decision in *Marc Rich v Bishop Rock Marine*[186D] as a case "in which the reasoning was essentially directed to considerations relevant to economic loss", despite the fact that it was a case of physical damage and loss in which the relevance of *Caparo* was precisely in issue. In *Robinson*, Lord Mance argued, it is suggested correctly, that it is unrealistic to suppose that courts will not take account of policy considerations when developing an "established category" of case. Such considerations are likely to be especially pertinent in deciding which category a case should be said to fall within.

[185] [2015] UKSC 2; [2015] A.C. 1732; see para.14-32.

[186] [2018] UKSC 11; [2019] A.C. 196.

[186A] See para.14-93.

[186B] [2018] UKSC 11; [2019] A.C. 196 at [69].

[186C] [2018] UKSC 11; [2019] A.C. 196 at [97].

[186D] [1996] A.C. 211.

Add new paragraph:

Second, as demonstrated by Lord Mance and Lord Hughes in their separate judgments, to treat more recent decisions applying as though they do not proceed on the basis of policy considerations would be inconsistent with the reasoning of those cases, including many decided long after *Caparo* and the demise of *Anns*, and requires a considerable degree of rewriting. This point was also made by Baroness Hale in her dissenting opinion in *Michael*. Such a reinterpretation of earlier decisions may have considerable repercussions. Third, Lord Reed's attempt to describe some cases in terms of established principle, rather than policy concerns, is at times unconvincing for other reasons. For example, *Brooks* was treated by the House of Lords which decided the case as involving positive and direct negligence by the police, not as a case where their actions were merely "inconsiderate", and the applicability of the *Hill* policy reasoning was expressly debated (and accepted) by the House. In summary, an attempt to marginalise policy reasoning in an area previously dominated by policy considerations both where there is a positive act resulting in injury (where it now appears there will be a duty), and where there is a mere omission (leading to no liability, except where relevant exceptions, principally an assumption of responsibility, apply), would be both ambitious, and potentially problematic. While accepting that the breadth of application of the policy reasoning from *Hill* has been open to valid criticism, to divide the cases too starkly into those concerning positive acts, which will succeed, and those concerning omissions, which will fail, even with recognised exceptions such as "assumption of responsibility" cases, would be to resort to a formulaic solution in an area currently filled with policy concerns. If this position is to be taken in cases beyond the realm of personal injury, it would at least need much more refinement. For example, it would become necessary to deal with issues such as the notion of conflicting public and private duties, exemplified by *Elguzouli-Daf v Commissioner of Police of the Metropolis*,[186E] as recently discussed by the Supreme Court in *SXH v Crown Prosecution Service*,[186F] but also represented in many other cases involving public authorities. **14-37B**

[186E] [1995] QB 335; [1995] 2 W.L.R. 173.

[186F] [2017] UKSC 30; [2017] 1 W.L.R. 1401; see para.14-106.

Add new paragraph:

The decision in *Robinson* also casts some further doubt on the decision, and at least the approach, in *Rathband v Chief Constable of Northumbria Police*.[186G] Here, the *Hill* principle operated to defeat a claim by a police officer against his Chief Constable as quasi-employer. Males J recognised that the "starting point" was different in a claim brought by a police officer, since a Chief Constable owes to officers within his force a non-delegable duty to provide a safe system of work (as recognised in *Mullaney v Chief Constable of West Midlands*[186H]). He reasoned however that this duty may be excluded by reason of the public policy arguments encapsulated in the *Hill* principle, and that at least in some such cases, these policy arguments would outweigh those underpinning the non-delegable duty. Males J also suggested that there was no "assumption of responsibility" in the particular case, so that the *Hill* principle could be decisive in relation to what was "fair, just and reasonable". No HRA claim based on ECHR art.2 was made in this case. It is sug- **14-37C** gested that the relationship between the non-delegable duty owed to quasi employees, and the presence of an "assumption of responsibility", merits further reflection, irrespective of the potential impact of the decision in *Robinson*.

186G [2016] EWHC 181 (QB).

186H [2001] EWCA Civ 700; [2001] Po. L.R. 150.

(iv) Rescue services

Rescue services

Replace footnote 190 with:

14-38 190 [2013] EWHC 2331 (QB).

(c) Proximity

(i) Regulatory agencies

Regulatory agencies

Replace paragraph with:

14-51 Where a regulatory agency has sufficient control over an activity and the purpose of the scheme is to protect the class to which the claimant belongs, then there may be sufficient proximity to justify a duty. On the no duty side of the line is *Yuen Kun-yeu v Att Gen of Hong Kong*[257] where depositors who lost money on the collapse of a regulated financial institution, claimed against the regulatory authority alleging that it had negligently failed to deregister the institution. Giving judgment of the Privy Council, Lord Keith concluded that the applicable legislation "placed a duty on the (regulator) to supervise companies in the general public interest, but no special responsibility towards individual members of the public". Two factors led to that conclusion. First, that rather than acting in the interests of just one particular group, the regulator had to balance the interests of different groups, potential depositors whose loss might be averted by de-registration and existing depositors for whom de-registration would have a disastrous effect. Secondly, the regulator had no power to control the day-to-day activities of the regulated financial institutions, so that depositors were not entitled to rely on the fact of registration as a guarantee of the soundness of a particular company.[258] On the other side of the line is *Perrett v Collins*[259] where the Court of Appeal held that an agency responsible for inspecting the construction of light aircraft did owe a duty of care to those injured in a crash resulting from faulty construction by the builder. Hobhouse LJ found proximity on the ground that the defendant had a "measure of control over and responsibility for a situation, which if dangerous, will be liable to injure the [claimant]". He distinguished two other inspection cases, *Philcox v Civil Aviation Authority*[260] and *Reeman v Department of Transport*,[261] on the ground that the claims had been brought by the owner of the plane and boat respectively whereas the purpose of the inspection scheme was to protect those being carried against personal injury and not the owners against damage to their property. Although the *Perrett* decision was based on proximity, the control and purpose factors could also be viewed as relevant to the reasonableness of any duty and hence, in the regulatory agency cases as in others, the criteria of proximity and reasonableness have a tendency to overlap. Another successful action against a regulatory authority was *Watson v British Box-*

ing Board of Control.[262] The claimant, a boxer, succeeded in his argument that the regulatory body with responsibility for the sport owed him a duty to provide immediate ringside medical attention. There was sufficient proximity between the parties, since a limited number of individuals made up the membership of the defendants, and injuries of the sort incurred were almost inevitable. In *Wattleworth v Goodwood Road Racing Co Ltd*,[263] the claimant's husband had died during an amateur track day at Goodwood, when his car collided three times with a tyre wall. The action was brought against the occupiers on the basis of their occupancy duty, and also against the RAC (the national body with power to licence motor racing vehicles) and the FIA (the body governing international competitive motor racing), both of which had previously inspected the track. The RAC was held to owe a duty to the deceased, which it had however discharged (there was no breach); the FIA did not have sufficient involvement with the safety of individuals in the position of the deceased to owe a duty at all.[264]

[257] [1988] A.C. 175.

[258] [1988] A.C. 175 at 196–197.See also *Davis v Radcliffe* [1990] 1 W.L.R. 821 PC; and *Curran v Northern Ireland Co-Ownership Housing Association Ltd* [1987] A.C. 718, where the agency, which was responsible for administering grants for home improvement work, was held not liable to a claimant who discovered that such work on the house he had purchased had been carried out defectively. The House of Lords noted that the agency had no powers of control: "Once approval has been given for a grant, the executive has no powers to control the building owner, still less the builder whom he chooses to employ, in the execution of the work." It had a power to withhold the grant if it discovered that the work was defective but Lord Bridge considered that the purpose of this power was the protection of the "public revenue" and not the subsequent purchasers of the property.

[259] [1999] P.N.L.R. 77. In *Thames Trains Ltd v Health & Safety Executive* [2003] EWCA Civ 720, the Court of Appeal cited *Perrett*, dismissing the Executive's application to strike out the claims of victims of the Ladbroke Grove rail crash. It could be reasonably argued that the Executive should be made liable, not for failing to use statutory powers involving expenditure of money, but for the negligent exercise, or failure to exercise, its statutory powers through the Railway Inspectorate, if its action or inaction was plainly wrong.

[260] (1995) L.S. Gaz. 33; *The Times*, 8 June 1995.

[261] [1997] P.N.L.R. 618. Hobhouse LJ followed *Swanson Estate v Canada* (1991) 80 D.L.R. (4th) 741, where Transport Canada which had responsibility for regulating the safety of commercial airlines was held liable to the victims of a plane crash caused after it had negligently allowed the airline to continue unsafe flying practices which led to the crash. Transport Canada had extensive control including powers to interview pilots, revoke the appointment of airline management and suspend the operating licence. See also *Seddon v Driver and Vehicle Licensing Agency* [2019] EWCA Civ 14: no duty of care owed by the DVLA to the purchaser of a classic car who had relied upon a vehicle registration certificate. The purchaser's reliance was outside the statutory purpose of the certificate.

[262] [2001] Q.B. 1134.

[263] [2004] EWHC 140 (QB); [2004] P.I.Q.R. P25.

[264] An analogous case brought not against a regulatory agency but a surveyor, who had inspected a shopfront shortly before pedestrians were severely injured by detached fascia falling from the building, is *Harrison v Technical Sign Co Ltd* [2013] EWCA Civ 1569; [2014] P.N.L.R. 15. *Perrett v Collins* was distinguished since there, the purpose of the inspection was to assess the aircraft's fitness to fly and the risk to the public in case of negligence was obvious; while in *Harrison* itself, proximity was lacking because the purpose of the inspection was in no sense to secure the safety of members of the public.

(iii) Police

Replace paragraph with:

In *Hill v Chief Constable of West Yorkshire*[269] a duty was denied on policy grounds but it was also rejected for lack of proximity. The claim had been brought on behalf of the last victim of a murderer who, it was alleged, the defendant had negligently failed to catch. The likely victim was not identifiable but merely one **14-53** of a very large number of women at risk and for that reason the House of Lords held that there was insufficient proximity to found a duty. Similarly, in *Alexandrou v Oxford*[270] the Court of Appeal held that there was no special relationship sufficient to found a duty between the police and a member of the public making an emergency call to the police. Glidewell LJ considered that if a duty arose in response to such a call, it would also be "owed to all members of the public who gave information of a suspected crime against themselves or their property".[271] There could not be a special relationship, that is, proximity, with such a wide class. As in *Hill*, the alternative ground of the decision was that of general policy. With the suggestion in *Brooks*[272] that the application of the policy principle in *Hill* might have to be reconsidered in cases on the margins, it seemed possible that the issue of proximity would take on more significance. However, *Smith v Chief Constable of Sussex Police* appears to be one where proximity was established, yet did not suffice to dispel the general policy factors. Within the "core" of the *Hill* principle it seems necessary to show something stronger than proximity per se, namely an assumption of responsibility. In *Michael v Chief Constable of South Wales*[273] direct discussion with the victim of crime through a "999" call was insufficient, on the facts, to give rise to an assumption of responsibility, and it therefore appears that such an assumption will not easily be established. In *Smith* Lord Brown said that the question was whether a duty of care "should be found to exist when the police, without having assumed any particular responsibility towards the eventual victim, are engaged rather in discharging their more general duty of combating and investigating crime".[274] However, in *Robinson v Chief Constable of West Yorkshire Police*,[275] the Supreme Court determined that where the alleged negligence of the police consists in a positive act causing physical injury, even if sustained in the course of combating and investigating crime, the *Caparo* test does not apply, as the case will fall within a recognised duty situation.[275A]

269 [1989] A.C. 53.

270 [1993] 4 All E.R. 328.

271 [1993] 4 All E.R. 328 at 338.

272 *Brooks v Commissioner of Police for the Metropolis* [2005] UKHL 24; [2005] 1 W.L.R. 1495. See para.14-30.

273 [2015] UKSC 2; [2015] A.C. 1732.

274 [2008] UKHL 50; [2009] 1 A.C. 225 at [122].

275 [2018] UKSC 4; [2018] A.C. 736.

275A See para.14-37.

(d) Omissions

(ii) Common law basis for duty

Voluntary assumption

Replace paragraph with:

14-66 The second requirement identified in para.14-63 (responsibility must be voluntarily assumed and not simply imposed by statute) was clearly stated by the Court of Appeal in *Rowley v Secretary of State for Work and Pensions*,[327] giving effect to statements in *Gorringe v Calderdale*[328]: if a statutory duty which is not itself actionable gives rise to a duty at common law, that would be surprising. The need for a voluntary assumption independent of statutory duties formed the basis of the decision in *Sandford v London Borough of Waltham Forest*,[329] that the defendant council did not owe a duty at common law to provide aids and equipment which it had assessed should be provided. The provision of these items fell, in effect, within the statutory duty owed under the National Health Service and Community Care Act 1990, to undertake the assessment in question. Similarly in *St John Poulton's Trustee in Bankruptcy v Ministry of Justice*,[330] the duty of the court under the Insolvency Rules 1986, to send notice of a bankruptcy petition to the Chief Land Registrar, did not give rise to a private right of action. The duty arose through the operation of the Rules and not through anything said or done by the court or its officers. This was no more voluntary than the position of the bank served with a freezing order in *Customs and Excise Commissioners v Barclays Bank*,[331] and could not be interpreted as a voluntary assumption of responsibility. Similarly in *Seddon v Driver and Vehicle Licensing Agency*,[331A] no duty was found to be owed by the DVLA to the purchaser of a classic car, who had relied on the vehicle registration certificate which stated that the car was a classic. The defendant was under a statutory obligation to issue registration certificates to collect the correct taxes and ensure all vehicles were registered. This obligation did not extend to a duty of care to prospective purchasers. Amongst other reasons, as the issue of certificates was not voluntary there was no voluntary assumption of responsibility, and the purchaser was seeking to rely on the document for purposes other than its statutory purpose (namely the collection of tax, the raising of revenue for the government and ensuring vehicles operating on the roads in the UK are registered).[331B]

[327] [2007] EWCA Civ 598; [2007] 1 W.L.R. 2861. See also *Darby v Richmond Upon Thames LBC* [2015] EWHC 909 (QB).

[328] [2004] UKHL 15; [2004] 1 W.L.R. 1057.

[329] [2008] EWHC 1106 (QB); [2008] B.L.G.R. 816.

[330] [2010] EWCA Civ 392; [2011] Ch. 1.

[331] [2006] UKHL 28; [2007] 1 A.C. 181.

[331A] [2019] EWCA Civ 14.

[331B] [2019] EWCA Civ 14 at [58].

3. LIABILITY UNDER THE HUMAN RIGHTS ACT 1998

(a) Article 6 and common law liability

The substantive/procedural distinction

Replace footnote 385 with:

[385] [2017] UKSC 1; [2017] A.C. 649. See the discussion in para.14-10. **14-77**

(b) Public authority liability under the Human Rights Act 1998

Jurisdictional extent of the HRA: Article 1

Replace paragraph with:

14-80 Article 1 of the Convention provides that contracting states will secure the rights and freedoms defined in the Convention to everyone within their jurisdiction. Prior to *Al-Skeini v UK*,[396] it was thought that the application of the Convention was essentially territorial, with defined exceptions. In *R. (Smith) v Oxfordshire Assistant Deputy Coroner*,[397] the majority of the Supreme Court also interpreted the

Strasbourg jurisprudence existing at that time as stating that the rights and freedoms in the Convention could not be divided and tailored to particular circumstances. In both respects, the decision of the Grand Chamber in *Al-Skeini* has had a significant impact on this understanding, as was carefully explained in the judgment of Lord Hope (with the agreement on this point of all members of the Supreme Court) in *Smith v Ministry of Defence*.[398] In particular, three points were made by Lord Hope in relation to the current interpretation of art.1. In *Smith* itself, these points together led the Supreme Court to conclude that the state's armed forces overseas are capable of being within its jurisdiction for the purposes of art.1. First, the Strasbourg Court in *Al-Skeini* formulated a general principle with respect to state authority and control, designed to ensure that domestic courts would apply the general principle. The principle could therefore apply to circumstances which the Strasbourg Court itself had not considered, rather than simply explaining a range of exceptional situations. Secondly, the extent of the Convention is not necessarily "essentially territorial". Rather, the general principle is concerned with circumstances where the state had authority and control over the individuals concerned. Thirdly, the Grand Chamber departed from its earlier statements, to the effect that the package of rights in the Convention is indivisible. As a consequence, the court when considering an alleged breach of a Convention right, need not concern itself with the question whether the state is in a position to guarantee other Convention rights to that individual under the circumstances.[399] The decision in *R. (Smith) v Oxford Assistant Deputy Coroner*[400] was therefore departed from. Whilst unanimous on this point, members of the Supreme Court were divided on the question of how art.2 applied to the claims in hand.[401] In addition to claims brought by military personnel, the expanded jurisdictional extent of the HRA has enabled a series of cases to be brought by foreign citizens in respect of British military operations overseas.[402] In *R. (on the application of Hoareau) v Secretary of State for Foreign and Commonwealth Affairs*,[402A] it was held that the decision in *Al-Skeini v UK* had not affected the position in respect of dependent territories. Here, the European Court of Human Rights had not found that the Convention extended to such territories in the absence of a declaration under art.56 by the contracting state. The court therefore applied the approach in *R. (on the application of Bancoult) v Secretary of State for Foreign and Commonwealth Affairs*,[402B] holding that neither the Convention, nor the HRA 1998, extended to the Chagos Islands.

396 (2011) 53 E.H.R.R. 18.

397 [2010] UKSC 29; [2011] 1 A.C. 1.

398 [2013] UKSC 41; [2014] A.C. 52.

399 [2013] UKSC 41; [2014] A.C. 52 at [49].

400 [2010] UKSC 29; [2011] 1 A.C. 1.

401 See para.14-85. For application of *Al-Skeini v UK and Smith* on this point, see *Kontic v Ministry of Defence* [2016] EWHC 2034 (QB): actions of UK troops in Kosovo were attributable to the U.N., not the Ministry of Defence, but irrespective of this, jurisdiction did not arise from effective control where troops were not in a position to secure the Convention rights, other than arts 2 and 3; and *Al-Saadoon v Secretary of State for Defence* [2016] EWCA Civ 811; [2017] Q.B. 1015: exception to territorial control founded on physical power and control did not extend to every situation in which a Convention party used physical force, but did cover a range of situations where there was an element of control over an individual prior to use of lethal force. During the post-occupation period in Iraq, the UK was exercising some of the public powers normally exercised by the Iraqi government and during this period, fell into the exception to territorial jurisdiction based on exercise of public powers.

402 See the decisions of the Court of Appeal in *R. (Al-Saadoon) v Secretary of State for Defence* [2016] EWCA Civ 811; [2017] Q.B. 1015; see para.14-92, and of the Supreme Court in *Mohammed v Ministry of Defence (No 2)* [2017] UKSC 2; [2017] A.C. 821; see para.14-95.

[402A] [2019] EWHC 221 (Admin).

[402B] [2016] UKSC 35; [2017] A.C. 300.

Positive operational duty to protect life

Replace paragraph with:

Where the operational duty to protect life under art.2 is concerned, *Osman v UK* remains authoritative.[416] The operational duty of the police under art.2 was the subject of detailed consideration by the House of Lords in *Van Colle v Chief Constable of the Hertfordshire Police*.[417] The allegation in this case was that the defendant police authority was aware that a prosecution witness was being intimidated by the accused but failed to take action to protect him. He was murdered by the accused. The House of Lords accepted that a positive obligation to protect the life of a particular individual arises from art.2 where it is established that the authorities knew or ought to have known at the time of the existence of a real and immediate risk to the life of that person. The duty that would then arise is a duty to take measures which, judged reasonably, might be expected to avoid the risk. The claim was rejected, however, on the ground that it could not reasonably be said that the police officer involved should have apprehended the imminent threat of violence against the witness. No lower threshold of knowledge would be applied in circumstances where the conduct of the authorities had exposed the individual to the risk: the *Osman* test for the existence of the positive operational duty was invariable. In *Van Colle v UK*,[418] the European Court of Human Rights also concluded that there had been no violation of art.2, applying the test in *Osman*. It could not be said that the facts involved higher risk factors than in *Osman* itself. Two members of the Court, though concurring in the result, implied that *Osman* set too demanding a test and should be revisited.Although *Osman* has been said to set a high threshold for the existence of the positive duty,[419] it was stated in both *Van Colle* and *Savage v South Essex Partnership NHS Trust* that this should not be taken to refine the test in any way.[420] A similar conclusion in relation to both an NHS Trust, and a police force, where a woman (G) was murdered by her former partner, was reached in *Griffiths v Chief Constable of Suffolk*.[420A] The NHS Trust, when considering whether to admit the former partner to hospital, did not know, nor ought it to have known, of any real or immediate threat to G's life; and there was not a sufficient basis for concluding that there was a risk to the general public. Equally, there was nothing to suggest to the police that there was an imminent risk to G. This was a weaker case than either *Osman* or *Van Colle*. An additional argument for the claimants, G's children, was that there was a protective duty under art.8, to protect G from harassment, and that such harassment was foreseeable. This claim was also dismissed: the Strasbourg jurisprudence did not permit a breach of the positive duties under arts 2 and 3 to be based on a failure to take steps required by art.8; and the police did not breach their duty under art.8.[420B] In *Savage v South Essex Partnership NHS Foundation Trust*,[421] the approach of the House of Lords in *Savage* and *Van Colle* was taken to provide helpful guidance to a lower court; but the general method was to apply the approach of the Strasbourg court, described by Mackay J as: "to set out the facts of the case fairly fully, … state the test and then simply state its finding that violation of the article is or is not established". As with other claims based on Convention rights, if a breach of art.2 is shown then there is no need to prove causation in the English law sense: loss of substantial chance of survival is **14-83** sufficient.[422] Indeed, art.2 may be violated where the person at risk survives. This too distinguishes the Human Rights Act claim, from the claim in tort.

[416] The *Osman* approach was also applied to a claim arguing positive duties under art.8 in *Bedford v Bedfordshire CC* [2013] EWHC 1717 (QB); [2013] H.R.L.R. 33; [2014] B.L.G.R. 44.

[417] [2008] UKHL 50; [2009] 1 A.C. 225.

[418] (7678/09) (2013) 56 E.H.R.R. 23.

[419] *Officer L, Re* [2007] UKHL 36; [2007] 1 W.L.R. 2135 at [20], per Lord Carswell.

[420] *Van Colle v Chief Constable of the Hertfordshire Police* [2008] UKHL 50; [2009] 1 A.C. 225 at [30], per Lord Bingham; *Savage v South Essex Partnership NHS Trust* [2008] UKHL 74; [2009] 1 A.C. 681 at [78], per Baroness Hale.

[420A] [2018] EWHC 2538 (QB); [2019] Med. L.R. 1.

[420B] For discussion of liability for breach of art.8, see paras 14-102 to 14-109.

[421] [2010] EWHC 865 (QB); [2010] P.I.Q.R. P14; [2010] Med. L.R. 292.

[422] [2010] EWHC 865 (QB); [2010] P.I.Q.R. P14; [2010] Med. L.R. 292 at [82].

Replace paragraph with:

14-84 The existence of two different types of obligation to protect life under art.2 was noted by the House of Lords in *Savage v South Essex Partnership NHS Trust*.[423] In light of the decision of the European Court of Human Rights in *Powell v UK*,[424] it was accepted in *Savage* that the operational duty to protect life in individual circumstances does not generally extend to ordinary negligence alleged to have been committed in the course of treatment in hospital. Such negligence is not sufficient to amount to a violation of art.2. But the situation in *Savage* was different because the deceased was suffering from paranoid schizophrenia and was being treated as a detained patient in an open acute psychiatric ward. She absconded from hospital and committed suicide by throwing herself in front of a train. The House of Lords concluded that the status of the deceased as a *detained* patient made the difference, as she was to be regarded as akin to a prisoner in custody in terms of her vulnerability and dependence. Her circumstances were similar to those in *Keenan v UK*,[425] where a positive operational duty to prevent suicide was recognised to exist. The claim should proceed to trial,[426] and the decisions in *Powell* and *Osman* were not incompatible: they simply dealt with different aspects of the positive duty to protect life. Subsequently, in *Rabone v Pennine Care NHS Foundation Trust*,[427] the Supreme Court found that the operational duty to protect life was owed to a psychiatric patient who was not formally detained. In this instance, the reality of the patient's situation was not markedly different from that of a detained patient. Given the control exercised by the defendant over the deceased, the difference between her situation and that of a detained patient was "one of form, not of substance".[428] In taking this route, the Supreme Court was extending the positive operational duty further than any decision of the Strasbourg Court at that time. Lord Brown, however, was at pains to point out that this was not a reversal of the general approach taken by the House of Lords and later the Supreme Court, most notably in *R. (Ullah) v Special Adjudicator*,[429] namely that the English courts should offer no greater protection of Convention rights through the HRA than was offered by the Strasbourg Court. Rather, this was a case where the Strasbourg Court had yet to rule on the relevant issues in the particular form in which they arose. Lord Dyson concluded, indeed, that the European Court of Human Rights would hold that the operational duty existed in this case. Notably, in *D v Commissioner of Police of the Metropolis*,[429A] Lord Kerr regarded *Rabone* as a case signalling retreat from the Ullah approach, and as recognising that where there is no directly relevant decision of the ECtHR, domestic courts must reach their own conclusions. With this, he agreed: "Reticence by the courts of the UK to decide whether a Convention right has been violated would be an abegnation of our statutory obligation under section 6 of the HRA".[429B] Several of the judges referred to the developing nature of the positive operational duty under art.2, and its gradual extension since it was first recognised in *Osman v UK*.[430] Nevertheless, it remains the case that in the "generality of cases" involving medical negligence, there is no operational duty under art.2.[431] It is increasingly difficult to be certain of where the boundary between *Powell* type cases, governed by negligence law principles, and *Osman* or *Rabone* type cases will lie, given rejection by the Supreme Court of a bright line based on formal detention in this case. Subsequently, in *Reynolds v UK*,[432] the European Court of Human Rights found a violation of art.13, in conjunction with art.2, where the applicant's domestic claim in relation to the death of her son while in the care of a NHS Trust had been struck out. He had been a voluntary patient suffering with schizophrenia. There was little discussion of the applicable principles, other than by reference to the Supreme Court's decision in *Rabone*. The UK courts have therefore been at the forefront of developing Convention jurisprudence on this point.

[423] [2008] UKHL 74; [2009] 1 A.C. 681.

[424] (2000) 30 E.H.R.R. CD362.

[425] (2001) 33 E.H.R.R. 38.

[426] See *Savage v South Essex Partnership NHS Foundation Trust* [2010] EWHC 865 (QB); [2010] P.I.Q.R. P14 where Mackay J held that there had been a breach of art.2, on the facts.

[427] [2012] UKSC 2; [2012] 2 A.C. 72.

[428] [2012] UKSC 2; [2012] 2 A.C. 72 at [34].

[429] [2004] UKHL 26; [2004] 2 A.C. 323.

[429A] [2018] UKSC 11; [2018] A.C. 196; see para.14-93.

[429B] [2018] UKSC 11; [2019] A.C. 196 at [78].

[430] The "incremental" development of the positive duty was also referred to in *Daniel v St George's Healthcare Trust* [2016] EWHC 23 (QB); [2016] 4 W.L.R. 32. Following the Strasbourg jurisprudence, Lang J concluded that where detainees are concerned, medical practitioners, both inside and outside a prison setting, are subject to the art.2 duty, as well as prison officers and police officers. Equally, since it is the state which is subject to the operational duty, "it can apply not only to the detaining authority but also to other public authorities who from time to time may have responsibility for the detainee, such as a hospital or ambulance service" (at [29]). Here, however, there was no breach of the duty.

[431] [2012] UKSC 2; [2012] 2 A.C. 72 at [33].

[432] (2694/08) (2012) 55 E.H.R.R. 35.

Duties to investigate derived from art.2

Add new paragraph:

There is also a requirement that investigation into a death should begin promptly. **14-87A** In *Re Jordan's Application for Judicial Review*,[443A] a claim was based on delay in beginning an inquest into a fatal shooting by the police in Northern Ireland in 1992. In 2001, the European Court of Human Rights had found a failure to carry out a prompt investigation, resulting in a breach of art.2. The victim's father sought a declaration and damages. The Court of Appeal in Northern Ireland appeared to hold as a general rule that a claim for damages should be dealt with once the inquest had fully concluded. The Supreme Court explained that there were countervailing reasons why, in a particular case, there should be no stay of a damages action based on delay. ECHR rights had to be applied in a way which rendered them practical and effective; the right conferred by HRA s.7 was a civil right within art.6, so that a claimant was entitled to have the claim determined within a reasonable time; and any stay of an action had to pursue a legitimate aim, bearing in mind its proportionality, to satisfy the art.6 guarantee of effective access to a court. There needed to be a balancing exercise, rather than a general rule, especially where claimants were elderly or infirm. It was unclear what decision the Court of Appeal would have reached if it had assessed proportionality and individual circumstances.

[443A] [2019] UKSC 9.

Positive duty to investigate

Replace footnote 459 with:

14-92 [459] [2016] EWCA Civ 811; [2017] Q.B. 1015.

Article 3 and failure to investigate

Replace paragraph with:

14-93 In *Ruddy v Chief Constable of Strathclyde*,[460] the Supreme Court considered and rejected procedural objections to a damages claim based on violations of art.3, both in relation to an alleged assault by police officers and in relation to an alleged failure to investigate. The Courts below in Scotland had rejected the claims as irrelevant, on the basis that they involved a disguised attempt to challenge decisions through a claim for damages, whereas a judicial review action would be the appropriate course. The Supreme Court drew attention to the fact that the allegations were all of completed acts or failures to act. The applicant was not seeking to have decisions corrected, but was seeking just satisfaction for breach of art.3 rights.[461] Notably, these features also resemble an action in tort. The capacity of the positive duty under art.3, modelled on *Osman v UK*, to allow claimants to by-pass the limitations on claims for police negligence outlined in earlier paragraphs is underlined by the case of *D v Commissioner of Police for the Metropolis*.[462] The police in this instance were held to have breached their duties to investigate a series of violent crimes against women. Rapes and sexual assaults were crimes which fell within the protection of art.3. The Human Rights Act 1998 imposed on the state a duty rigorously to enforce laws which prohibited conduct constituting a violation of art.3, and this required that complaints of ill-treatment amounting to a violation of art.3 be properly investigated. This duty arose even where non-state agents were responsible for the infliction of harm. Further, this would not only be breached by failures which were at a systemic level; serious failures which were merely operational could suffice to breach the positive duty, provided those failures were "egregious" and significant. As Lord Neuberger put it, if there is a duty to investigate, this should be understood to be a duty to investigate effectively.[463] Here, both structural and systemic, and operational failures could be identified, and the judge had correctly identified that an award of damages under the HRA was justified. The considerations which militated against police liability in negligence for failures in investigation did not apply to a claim under the HRA, since the basis of liability was in each case different. Given that it had been decided that the common law duty should not be adapted to harmonise with the ECHR, "so should the latter duty rem ain free from the influence of the pre-HRA domestic law".[464] Further, there was no room in relation to the HRA for such complexities as the notion of "proximity", which were relevant to negligence actions at common law, nor for the notion of what was "fair, just and reasonable". The issue was simpler: did the state fail to comply with its protective obligation under art.3? Either the police had a protective duty under art.3, or they did not.[464A] Thus, the Supreme Court was undeterred by the fact that a duty was here recognised in circumstances very close to the core of the *Hill* principle.[464B] The decision maintains the potential for actions under the HRA to provide remedies in circumstances where the common law will not, and which would traditionally be pursued through the common law of tort.

[460] [2012] UKSC 57; 2013 S.C. (U.K.S.C.) 126; [2013] H.R.L.R. 10.

[461] [2012] UKSC 57; 2013 S.C. (U.K.S.C.) 126; [2013] H.R.L.R. 10 at [15].

[462] [2018] UKSC 11; [2019] A.C. 196.

[463] [2018] UKSC 11; [2019] A.C. 196 at [92].

[464] [2018] UKSC 11; [2019] A.C. 196 per Lord Kerr at [68].

[464A] [2018] UKSC 11; [2019] A.C. 196 per Lord Kerr at [69] and [70].

[464B] See para.14-28 onwards.

Art.5(1) and military operations

Replace paragraph with:

The extension of the territorial application of the ECHR in *Al-Skeini v UK*[474] raised the question of whether art.5 of the Convention was well suited to the circumstances of military intervention, including peace-keeping operations. In *Hassan v United Kingdom*,[475] the detention of a civilian in Iraq for a period of nine days did not fall within any of the six exhaustive permitted grounds of detention under art.5(1). Nevertheless, the Grand Chamber of the European Court of Human Rights held that the detention did not violate art.5. Article 5(1) had to be adapted to circumstances in which international humanitarian law provided relevant safeguards against arbitrary detention. In *Mohammed v Ministry of Defence (No 2)*[476] the Supreme Court applied *Hassan* to a case where the military operation was not international in nature, arguing that the reasoning in *Hassan* applied in the same way. In this instance, authority for the detention was derived from relevant Security Council Resolutions, and art.5(1) had to adapt to these Resolutions: detention was justified when it was required for imperative reasons of security. Following *Hassan*, the "fundamental purpose" of art.5(1) was to guard against arbitrariness.[477] As detention was subject to the terms of the Security Council Resolutions, it was not arbitrary. The exhaustive list of cases in art.5(1) had to yield to these different circumstances, if Convention states are to play a part in peace-keeping operations. *Hassan* is not to be read as adding a seventh permitted ground for detention, namely military detention in armed conflict. Rather, "[i]ts effect is … to recognise that sub-paragraphs (a) to (f) cannot necessarily be regarded as exhaustive when the Convention is being applied to such a conflict, because their exhaustive character reflects peacetime conditions".[478] There had been no breach of art.5(1) in the case of *Al-Waheed*, and the lawfulness of detention would be ascertained at trial in the case of *Mohammed*.[479] The majority Justices were divided on the question of whether a breach of the procedural requirement in art.5(4) had been established, or whether this could only be determined at trial. Lord Sumption argued that breach had been established, but that this need not necessarily lead to an award of damages.[480] 14-95

[474] (2011) 53 E.H.R.R. 18; see para.14-80.

[475] (2014) 38 B.H.R.C. 358.

[476] [2017] UKSC 2; [2017] 2 A.C. 821. The decision included the leapfrog appeal from *Al-Waheed v Ministry of Defence* [2014] EWHC 2714 (QB).

[477] [2017] UKSC 2; [2017] A.C. 821 at [63] (Lord Sumption). This has strong echoes of the reasoning of the House of Lords in *Austin v Commissioner of Metropolitan Police* [2009] UKHL 5; [2009] 1 A.C. 564, para.14-94.

[478] [2017] UKSC 2; [2017] A.C. 821 at [68].

[479] Lords Reed and Kerr JJSC dissented.

[480] See further para.14-98.

Ancillary rights under art.5

Replace paragraph with:

14-98 Article 5(4) ECHR specifies a right for those arrested or detained to have the lawfulness of their detention "decided speedily by a court", and release ordered if the detention is unlawful. Article 5(4) may be violated by delayed reviews by the Parole Board, even where release would not have been ordered. Equally, art.5(1) may clearly be breached in circumstances which fall short of a false imprisonment, where an applicant has been deprived of "conditional liberty" through delay in the hearing. Significant questions have surrounded the approach to awarding damages in such cases given the general reluctance to create tort-like remedies in respect of maladministration, and the Supreme Court in *R. (Faulkner) v Secretary of State for Justice*; *R. (Sturnham) v Parole Board*[489] has provided guidance.[490] The decision of the Supreme Court in *R. (on the application of Kaiyam) v Secretary of State for Justice*[491] identified a distinction between unlawful detention in breach of art.5(1), and detention which remains lawful but which nevertheless breaches an ancillary right under art.5. In the latter case, the appropriate remedy is not a declaration of unlawfulness but damages to reflect frustration and anxiety. The Supreme Court therefore declined to follow the judgment of the European Court of Human Rights in *James v UK*.[492] There was a duty to provide rehabilitative courses and opportunities which were required for an offender to show that he was no longer a danger to the public and could be released. However, failure to comply with this duty could not be grounds for the continued detention to be unlawful, since safety of release had not been demonstrated. This was an ancillary duty not specifically set out in art.5 and an award of damages similar to those made for delay in parole hearings was the appropriate remedy. These would not be at a level previously awarded by the European Court of Human Rights, since they would be solely aimed at compensating for frustration and anxiety; the detention itself continued to be lawful. However, in *Brown v Parole Board for Scotland*,[492A] the Supreme Court departed from its earlier decision in *Kaiyam*, considering that the decision in *James v UK* could now be perceived to be part of a clear and constant line of decisions, so that it should be followed. It was also now clear that the Supreme Court in *Kaiyam* had misunderstood the implications of locating the obligation to provide an opportunity for rehabilitation in art.5(1), rather than understanding it as an ancillary duty inherent in art.5 as a whole. In particular, the European Court of Human Rights had made clear in *James v UK* itself that the result of finding a breach of art.5(1)(a) in these circumstances would not be that an order would be made for the release of the prisoner, but that this aspect of the decision was not brought to the attention of the Supreme Court. Rather, through a combination of judicial review and subsequent action to ameliorate the prisoner's position, the cause of unlawfulness could itself be removed, while detention continued. UK courts would now follow *James v UK*, recognising that the hurdle for establishing a breach of art.5(1) is a high one. Indeed, the European Court of Human Rights had applied a higher hurdle than the one outlined by the Supreme Court in *Kaiyam*, applying a test of "arbitrariness" rather than reasonableness; and had made clear that this was to be assessed by reference to the history of custody as a whole, rather than in relation to particular decisions. In *Kaiyam v UK*,[492B] the Court had found no violation on this basis and the claims were ruled inadmissible. Inadvertently, the Supreme Court in *Kaiyam* had imposed a more onerous duty on prison authorities than the duties recognised in *James*, and this was not the usual situation. *James* would now be followed. In *R. (on the application of Lee-Hirons) v Justice Secretary*[493] a claimant who had been conditionally discharged from a secure hospital was recalled by the Secretary of State. Adequate reasons were given orally at the time of the recall, and there was no breach of duty at common law, nor under art.5(2) of the Convention. The Secretary of State conceded that there had been subsequent breaches of both the common law duty, and art.5(2), when written reasons were not then supplied until 15 days after the recall. There was no connection between this failure, and the lawfulness of detention, and the failure did not mean the detention was unlawful under art.5(1), nor at common law. The claimant had not shown that the violation of his art.5(2) rights was sufficiently serious to warrant the payment of damages under the HRA. The application of ancillary rights under art.5(4) was also in issue in *Mohammed v Ministry of Defence (No 2)*.[494] The majority Justices were divided on the question whether it had been shown that art.5(4) was breached, given the nature of the review processes in place. Lord Sumption, concluding that there had been a breach, pointed out that such a breach does not necessarily render detention unlawful under art.5(1) (applying *Kaiyam*); and that the question of whether a fair review process would have resulted in earlier release would be answered at trial.[495] Neither *Mohammed*, nor *Lee-Hirons*, was referred to in the decision of the Supreme Court in *Brown v Parole Board for Scotland*.

489 [2013] UKSC 23; [2013] 2 A.C. 254.

490 See further para.14-116.

491 [2014] UKSC 66; [2015] A.C. 1344; [2015] 2 All E.R. 822.

492 (2012) 56 E.H.R.R.

492A [2017] UKSC 69; [2018] A.C. 1.

492B (2016) 62 E.H.R.R. SE13.

493 [2016] UKSC 46; [2017] A.C. 52.

494 [2017] UKSC 2; [2017] A.C. 821, para.14-95.

495 [2017] UKSC 2; [2017] A.C. 821 at [110].

Article 8 Right to respect for private and family life

Replace paragraph with:

In a range of cases relating to personal information and photographs, public authorities may also be defendants to Human Rights Act actions invoking art.8. In **14-103**
S v UK,[511] the European Court of Human Rights held that the UK had violated the art.8 rights of the applicants, who had not been convicted of any crime, by keeping cellular (DNA) samples and fingerprints pursuant to a blanket and indiscriminate policy. Subsequently, the Supreme Court has declared that the applicable guidelines, rather than the governing legislation, were incompatible with the Convention[512]; and new legislative provisions allowing a more limited scheme of retention has been brought into force.[513] In *Wood v Chief of Police for the Metropolis*,[514] the Court of Appeal referred to *S v UK* and held that the defendant had violated the claimant's rights under art.8 in taking and retaining a photograph

of the claimant. The claimant was a member of an organisation called "campaign against the arms trade", who attended a general meeting of a corporation which had been involved in organising arms fairs. Police officers (who had been led to expect that trouble might be caused at the meeting) spoke to the claimant afterwards, and took his photograph, which they retained but did not add to a database. The Court of Appeal held that the mere fact that a photograph was taken would not itself engage art.8, and in this respect the outcome would be similar whether the photograph was taken by the state (a "vertical" case or instance of the negative duty not to violate art.8), or by a private media corporation (a "horizontal" case or instance of the state's positive duty to protect art.8, through providing a remedy at law). "Aggravating circumstances" in the form of harassment during the taking of the photograph could make the difference, but these were not present in this case. Rather, unnecessary retention of the photographs and the anxiety instilled in the claimant were sufficient to engage art.8 in this case. It should be noted that since the purpose of taking and retaining the photographs was potentially a legitimate one, a question of proportionality therefore arose before there could be a finding of a violation. Here the Court of Appeal was divided (Laws LJ dissenting), but the majority held that the police action was disproportionate in the circumstances of the case. A different conclusion was reached by the Supreme Court in the case of *R. (on the application of Catt) v Association of Chief Police Officers of England, Wales and Northern Ireland.*[515] The claimant had a long history of political protest and attended many public demonstrations. Also, intelligence had been overtly compiled and retained over a long period. The Supreme Court held that the art.8 rights of the claimant were engaged but that the interferences were in each case prescribed by law and proportionate, since they pursued legitimate policing goals. In the case of the retention of information, there was sufficient flexibility in the policy adopted to allow for destruction of the records at an earlier stage if they no longer served a policing purpose. Notably however, the European Court of Human Rights in *Catt v UK* has ruled that the Supreme Court's conclusion that the interferences were proportionate was incorrect and an art.8 violation was established.[515A] While a pressing need to collect the personal data had been demonstrated, there was no such need to *retain* the data. The applicant was dependent on diligent application of highly flexible safeguards, whose effectiveness in permitting deletion of any of the data had not been evidenced. Further, the personal data revealed political viewpoints, which were particularly protected through art.11 ECHR.

[511] (2009) 48 E.H.R.R. 50.

[512] *R. (on the application of GC) v Commissioner of Police of the Metropolis* [2011] UKSC 21; [2011] 1 W.L.R. 1230.

[513] Protection of Freedoms Act 2012 s.1, inserting a new s.63D on the destruction of fingerprints and DNA profiles into the Police and Criminal Evidence Act 1984: in force 31 October 2013.

[514] [2009] EWCA Civ 414; [2010] 1 W.L.R. 123.

[515] [2015] UKSC 9; [2015] A.C. 1065.

[515A] *Catt v UK* (Application no. 43514/15), published 24 January 2019.

Add new paragraph:

14-103A Subsequently, in *R. (on the application of Butt) v Secretary of State for the Home Department,*[515B] the Court of Appeal sought to apply the Supreme Court's decisions in *R. (on the application of Catt) v Association of Chief Police Officers of England, Wales and Northern Ireland,*[515C] and in *JR38's Application for Judicial Review,*[515D] in light of the Strasbourg jurisprudence, to a very different case. The claim concerned the Prevent Duty Guidance for England and Wales and the Higher Education Prevent Duty Guidance, and the gathering of data about a public speaker by the Government's Extremism Analysis Unit. As Etherton LJ framed it, this was a claim for privacy in respect of information publicly available by search of the internet and social media, "being views the claimant has expressed publicly and which he wishes to continue to promote to students and others in order to encourage them to follow his way of thinking and details as to where and how he has promoted those views."[515E] In his view, unless precluded by authority, the natural conclusion was that Dr Butt could not have had any legitimate or objectively reasonable expectation of privacy in relation to the information about him recorded and retained by the E.A.U. After consideration of a range of decisions of the Strasbourg court, it was concluded that there was an overarching principle that there could not be a violation unless there was a legitimate expectation of privacy in the subject matter of the complaint, notwithstanding Lord Sumption's remarks about the possibility of a violation through "systematic retention and storage" in *R. (Catt)*, and still more demanding statements from the Strasbourg Court in *Catt v UK*.[515F] In *Butt*, the Court of Appeal concluded that the claimant had no objectively reasonable expectation of privacy in the information collected, and thus his claim could not succeed. The Court also held that if art.8 had been engaged, the interference would have been justified within art.8(2) and his case was distinguishable from that of *Catt*. His data was collected and had been retained by the E.A.U. for a relatively short period before he commenced proceedings. Furthermore, unlike the situation for Mr Catt, Dr Butt's personal information was not of a particularly sensitive nature (indeed, he was publicising and promoting it). Nor was there any evidence that Dr Butt had ceased to be of any interest in relation to the *Prevent* strategy, whereas Mr Catt's information was kept beyond the point at which he was considered in any sense a potential danger. In *R. (on the application of CL) v Chief Constable of Greater Manchester Police*,[515G] the court rejected a suggestion that a separate regime was required for consideration of data retention concerning minors: here, the retention of data in relation to alleged "sexting" incidents involving the claimant was argued to be proportionate and the regime adequately protected the claimant's rights. Though decided before the decision in *Catt v UK*, there are significant differences in the kind of information retained in this case and the rationale for its retention.

[515B] [2019] EWCA Civ 256.

[515C] [2015] UKSC 9; [2015] A.C. 1065; see para.14-103.

[515D] [2015] UKSC 42; [2016] A.C. 1131. This claim concerned photographs of the claimant taken whilst rioting: art.8 was held not to be engaged as there was no reasonable expectation of privacy in the claimant's public and unlawful activities.

[515E] [2019] EWCA Civ 256 at [67].

[515F] [2019] EWCA Civ 256 at [75] and [76].

[515G] [2018] EWHC 3333 (Admin); [2019] A.C.D. 20.

Replace paragraph with:

The exercise in proportionality and balancing which is familiar in the context of "horizontal" claims is also exercised in claims against public authorities where art.8 rights are engaged but information about individuals is released for legitimate reasons. In *R. (L) v Commissioner of Police of the Metropolis*,[516] the defendant police authority had released information in connection with an "enhanced criminal record certificate", to the effect that the claimant's son had been placed on the Child **14-104**

Protection Register for reasons of neglect. The information was correct, and potentially relevant given that the claimant was seeking employment in a school. The Supreme Court held that art.8 was engaged and that the public interest justification for the disclosure must be weighed in the balance against the claimant's art.8 right. Referring to *Campbell v MGN*,[517] the public interest should not be given presumptive priority over the art.8 rights of the applicant for such a certificate,[518] and the previous approach had been wrong in seeming to invite such priority.[519] Here, however, the decision to release the information would not be quashed, because the risk to children was properly held to outweigh the prejudicial effects of disclosure in this particular case. In *R. (on the application of R) v Chief Constable of Greater Manchester*,[519A] the Supreme Court held that disclosure of an acquittal on a charge of rape in an enhanced criminal record certificate was a proportionate interference with art.8 rights. It noted, however, the absence of guidance to employers in how to assess information about an acquittal, and proposed that careful thought should be given to inclusion of details about acquittals. The absence of any presumptive priority between art.8 and art.10 was emphasised by the Supreme Court in *Re Guardian News and Media Ltd*,[520] a case concerned with reporting restrictions rather than a claim for damages. However, the Supreme Court also noted the decision of the European Court of Human Rights in *Petrina v Romania*,[521] and particularly its assertion that in cases where publication raises a matter "of general interest", art.10(2) "scarcely leaves any room for restrictions on freedom of expression".[522] The anonymity orders were discharged.

516 [2009] UKSC 3; [2010] 1 A.C. 410.

517 [2004] UKHL 22; [2004] 2 A.C. 457.

518 It is important to note that the information disclosed did not relate to a criminal conviction, but was included as "other" potentially relevant information.

519 Lord Scott disagreed with this approach, suggesting that the entire point of the ECRC was to protect the vulnerable, and that there was an inherent decision to prioritise this over the art.8 rights of applicants.

519A [2018] UKSC 47; [2018] 1 W.L.R. 4079; [2019] 1 All E.R. 391.

520 [2010] UKSC 1; [2010] 2 A.C. 697. See also *Re BBC* [2014] UKSC 25; [2015] A.C. 588, upholding the anonymity of an asylum seeker convicted of an offence against children, where that anonymity was designed to protect him from violence once deported, so that open justice was departed from in the interests of justice and in order to protect X. In the event of any conflict between common law values and Convention values, the Convention values will take priority.

521 (78060/01), 14 October 2008.

522 [2010] UKSC 1; [2010] 2 A.C. 697 at [51].

Replace footnote 523 with:

14-105 523 For a successful claim see *D (Children) v Wakefield MDC* [2016] EWHC 3312 (Fam); [2017] 2 F.L.R. 1353.

Replace paragraph with:

14-106 Some limits have, however, been placed on the extension of the art.8 right. In *Anufrijeva v Southwark LBC*[528] the claimant alleged that the authority's failure to provide housing suitable for an elderly family member prevented the family from living together and was in breach of art.8. Family life is not an interest protected by the law of tort[529] and hence this claim went beyond any possible liability in tort. The Court of Appeal rejected the art.8 claim. Lord Woolf said that for there to be a breach of art.8 there had to be an element of culpability at least involving knowledge that family life was at risk. A breach of domestic law would be evidence of culpability. He also considered that art.8 would apply more readily where the family unit and children were involved, and that in the context of welfare support it was hard to conceive of it applying unless the art.3 prohibition on inhuman and degrading treatment was also engaged.[529A] Finally, he noted that where the problem was one of the dilatory conduct of the authorities, it would have to be shown that the consequences were serious before there would be an infringement. In *A v Essex CC*,[530] the Court of Appeal held that the burdens placed upon a family when a gravely disabled child was excluded from his school (in this case, for valid reasons) could not give rise to a claim for breach of art.8. Sedley LJ said that "[t]he applicability of art.8 has grown since the inception of the Convention, but the contention that the denial by the state of legal rights, engages art.8 by disrupting the individual's or the family's well-being is an argument too far".[531] It was important to emphasise that although the family's predicament was not to be underestimated, the Convention was not "a panacea for every ill". Sedley LJ also referred to Lord Woolf's remarks in *Anufrijeva*, reiterating that in a case of failure to alleviate need, it was hard to envisage that an art.8 claim would succeed unless the family's suffering was sufficiently severe to engage art.3. In *Treharne v Secretary of State for Work and Pensions*,[532] the claim was for damages in relation to failure by the Child Support Agency to enforce a maintenance assessment. A claim framed in negligence inevitably could not succeed after the decision in *Rowley v Secretary of State for Work and Pensions*,[533] so the claim for damages proceeded on the basis that there had been a violation of the claimants' art.8 rights. This claim was comprehensively dismissed by Cranston J. Article 8 did not confer a right to welfare benefits on individuals, and to the extent that it imposed a positive duty on the state to provide such support (particularly in respect of the upbringing of children), this was at a minimal level. More analogously to tort claims and with specific reference to *Marcic v Thames Water Utilities*,[534] the scheme as a whole complied with the requirements of art.8 and its malfunctioning in particular cases was not sufficient to ground a claim under art.8.

[528] [2003] EWCA Civ 1406; [2004] Q.B. 1124.

[529] See *F v Wirral MBC* [1991] Fam. 69.

[529A] This observation was also relied upon in denying an art.8 claim in *R. (on the application of McDonagh) v Enfield LBC* [2018] 1287 (Admin); [2018] H.L.R. 43. Other factors were also taken into account, including that the Housing Authority's culpability was not great, lack of availability of other suitable options, and that the family was not separated. A breach of statutory duty was, however, established.

[530] [2008] EWCA Civ 364; [2008] H.R.L.R. 31.

[531] [2008] EWCA Civ 364; [2008] H.R.L.R. 31 at [23].A claim under First Protocol, art.2 also failed. On this point, there was an appeal to the Supreme Court, but the appeal was rejected: *A v Essex CC* [2010] UKSC 33; [2011] 1 A.C. 280, para.14-113.

[532] [2008] EWHC 3222 (QB); [2009] 1 F.L.R. 853.

[533] [2007] EWCA Civ 598; [2007] 1 W.L.R. 2861; see para.14-20.

[534] [2003] UKHL 66; [2004] 2 A.C. 42.

Add new paragraph:

A further limit to the extent of art.8 was recognised by the Supreme Court in *SXH v Crown Prosecution Service (United Nations High Commissioner for Refugees Intervening)*.[534A] The claimant was a Somali national. She had come to the UK using false travel documents, was arrested, and on arrest immediately claimed asylum. She was remanded in custody, charged with possessing a false identity document. Nearly six months later, she was granted asylum, and sought damages from the CPS on the basis that the decision to prosecute her was an unlawful interference with her **14-106A** art.8 rights, given the high likelihood of success in her claim to asylum. The Supreme Court concluded that if the criminalisation of conduct did not violate art.8, neither did the decision to prosecute. Given that the relevant legislation was Convention-compliant, art.8 was not applicable to the decision to prosecute. It is unclear whether this is dependent on the decision to prosecute being reasonable, in the sense that the evidential test is satisfied. In *SXH* there was a concession that this was the case, a factor considered important in the subsequent decision of the Outer House of the Court of Session in *Whitehouse v Gormley*.[534B] In *Whitehouse*, by contrast, there was a claim that the prosecution was not based on sufficient evidence. Distinguishing *SXH*, it was held that a decision to prosecute may in some circumstances involve a violation of art.8, so that the case should proceed to trial. However, in *SXH* itself, the Supreme Court added the broad point that the duty of the CPS is to the public, so that recognition of a duty of care towards victims or suspects would put the service in a position of potential conflict. According to Lord Toulson, similar considerations are applicable when considering the applicability of art.8 in the context of a decision to prosecute. That decision places the question of determining guilt before a court; and the court is also responsible for decisions as to bail or remand in custody.[534C] This appears to be in contrast with the approach in *D v Commissioner of Police for the Metropolis*,[534D] in which the positive duty to investigate was said to be free from considerations of proximity, justice and fairness which arise in relation to negligence actions against the police.[534E] Lord Toulson expressed no conclusion on a question which was raised at a late stage in proceedings, namely whether the continuation of a prosecution which had not violated art.8 when initiated could nevertheless become a violation of art.8. No argument had been heard on the question. However, Lord Kerr in a concurring judgment pointed to the decision in *Zenati v Commr of Police of the Metropolis*,[534F] where art.5 was considered capable of being breached when a prosecution was unjustifiably prolonged. The same need to keep a prosecution under review could apply to violations of art.8.

[534A] [2017] UKSC 30; [2017] 1 W.L.R. 1401.

[534B] [2018] CSOH 93.

[534C] [2017] UKSC 30; [2017] 1 W.L.R. 1401 at [38].

[534D] [2018] UKSC 11; [2019] A.C. 196.

[534E] See para.14-93.

[534F] [2015] EWCA Civ 80; [2015] Q.B. 758; see para.14-97.

Relationship between common law and art.8

Replace paragraph with:

14-109 In *Watkins v Secretary of State for the Home Department*[550] Lord Rodger noted that although the tort of misfeasance in public office could not be extended to cover interference with the constitutional right to unimpeded communication with a legal advisor, it might now be possible for the claimant to bring proceedings under s.8 of the Human Rights Act for damages for breach of certain of the guarantees in arts 6 and 8 of the Convention. But this was a reason why the common law does not need to develop to protect the rights; there is a remedy suited to that purpose. *Watkins* is one of a series of decisions in the House of Lords in which the common law and Human Rights Act actions were separated in this way. It is a corollary of the separation of tort duties and remedies, and their counterparts under the Human

Rights Act, that there may in principle be liability under the statute where no claim in tort is available. This is illustrated by *Jain v Trent Strategic HA*.[551] Here, the House of Lords thought that a claim for violation of Convention rights on similar facts to this would be at least arguable. Even so, no duty of care would be recognised, as it would not be "fair, just and reasonable" to impose liability. Therefore, it was clear that even tort principles which are overtly premised on policy considerations would be maintained in circumstances where a violation of Convention rights is arguable. This illustrates clearly that the immediate influence of the art.6 elements of the decision in *Osman v UK* had been left behind. It remains to be seen whether a new phase has been reached in which a negative reaction to *Osman* no longer influences the law, but there are signs that this is the case. An important indication is the willingness of the Supreme Court to extend "tort-like" duties to protect life under the Human Rights Act, beyond the point already reached by the European Court of Human Rights, in *Rabone v Pennine Care NHS Foundation Trust*,[552] *Smith v Ministry of Defence*,[553] and *D v Commissioner of Police for the Metropolis*,[553A] thus outflanking settled policy reasons against liability in tort. Since positive duties also arise under other articles, including art.8, these developments have potentially broader reach.

[550] [2006] UKHL 17; [2006] 2 A.C. 395 at [64].

[551] [2009] UKHL 4; [2009] 1 A.C. 853; para.14-43.

[552] [2012] UKSC 2; [2012] 2 A.C. 72. See para.14-81.

[553] [2013] UKSC 41; [2014] A.C. 52. See para.14-85.

[553A] [2018] UKSC 11; [2019] A.C. 196; see para.14-93.

Article 14 Prohibition of discrimination

Replace paragraph with:

States are required by art.14 of the ECHR to protect the Convention rights of everyone without discrimination. In *E v Chief Constable of the Royal Ulster Constabulary*,[562] the claimant argued that the passive approach of the police was in breach of ECHR art.14. The art.14 claim, like the art.3 claim explored above, failed. The House of Lords held that there was no evidence that the police would have handled the situation any differently had the claimant been a Protestant encountering a Catholic protest. As such, there was no evidence that the police had been motivated by sectarian bias. The key test, according to Lord Carswell, is whether there has been a "failure to treat like cases alike".[563] In *A v Essex CC*,[564] Sedley LJ emphasised that *unlawful* discrimination might take the form of treating unalike cases as though they were alike. In other words, it is right to discriminate between cases which are different, and this does not breach art.14. In that case, it was right for the education authority to treat a gravely disabled child differently and therefore to discriminate in his favour. The removal of the child from a school which could not cope with him, pending a more appropriate placement, could not be seen as unlawful discrimination. In *R. (on the application of Johnson) v Secretary of State for the Home Department*[565] the Supreme Court held that there was an arguable claim that art.14 rights, read with art.8, had been violated. The claimant, a Jamaican national born out of wedlock, was subject to deportation but would not have been had his parents been married. This was an accident of birth which was not his fault, and use of this to impose a character test had to be justified. In *Smith v Lancashire Teaching Hospitals NHS Foundation Trust*,[565A] the Court of Appeal dealt with a claim that there had been a violation of art.14 in conjunction with art.8, holding that **14-111** art.14 may be violated even in the absence of violation of art.8, provided the measure complained of had a more than tenuous connection with the values protected by art.8, and was discriminatory and not justified. The claimant had lived with a man in the same household as husband and wife for 11 years until his death resulting from admitted negligence of the defendant. A claim for dependency damages under Fatal Accidents Act 1976 s.1 was settled and the claimant argued that denial of bereavement damages to her as a cohabiting partner was discriminatory. Section 1A(2)(a) of the Fatal Accidents Act 1976 had not extended bereavement damages to cohabitees. The court found that in all the circumstances of this claim, discrimination between the claimant and a surviving spouse required to be justified in order to avoid infringing art.14 in conjunction with art.8, and there was no evidence of any such justification since dependency damages had been extended to cohabitees of over two years. There was no scope for interpretation of the statutory language as extending to such a cohabitee, and so the appropriate remedy was a declaration of incompatibility with art.14 in conjunction with art.8.

[562] [2008] UKHL 66; [2009] 1 A.C. 536; para.14-91.

[563] [2008] UKHL 66; [2009] 1 A.C. 536 at [64], quoting from the speech of Lord Hoffmann in *R. (Carson) v Chief Constable of the Royal Ulster Constabulary* [2005] UKHL 37; [2006] 1 A.C. 173 at [14].

[564] [2008] EWCA Civ 364; [2009] B.L.G.R. 182; [2008] E.L.R. 321.

[565] [2016] UKSC 56; [2017] A.C. 365.

[565A] [2017] EWCA Civ 1916; [2018] Q.B. 804.

First Protocol, article 1 Right to peaceful enjoyment of possessions

Replace paragraph with:

14-112 The right to peaceful enjoyment of possessions was argued to be engaged alongside art.8 in the unsuccessful claim for nuisance and breach of Convention rights, in *Marcic v Thames Water Utilities Ltd.*[566] This was a claim brought by a property owner, and it seems that in most such cases the tort of private nuisance will provide a better remedy than an action under the Human Rights Act. Article 1 of the First Protocol may also be relevant to public service liability in a range of other circumstances. In *R. (K) v HM Treasury*,[567] K applied for restrictions on her access to funds to be set aside. Her husband's assets had been frozen world-wide on the basis of his involvement in an organisation linked to Al-Qaeda. K was given a licence to withdraw funds for basic family expenses, subject to a monthly reporting requirement. Burton J. held that the public interest was wide and that the reporting requirement did not breach art.8 or art.1 of the First Protocol, since it was proportionate under the circumstances.[568] It has been held that deprivation of one's passport does not amount to a violation of art.1 Protocol 1. The fact that a passport is a tangible object is not sufficient to constitute it as a "possession", and its significance or essence is that it represents an intangible privilege or entitlement, which was not "marketable".[569] Nevertheless, in *Atapattu*, a claim at common law for conversion was successful, indicating that some possessions may be protected by conversion though not suitable for protection under art.1 Protocol 1. However, it appears that a legitimate expectation based on a judicial ruling or statutory provision is capable of protection under art.1 Protocol 1. In *The Gas and Electricity Markets Authority v Infinis Plc*[570] the respondents were deprived of a pecuniary benefit when they were refused accreditation for Renewables Obligations Certificates under two Orders in respect of their electricity generating stations. As the damage suffered was pecuniary and could be clearly calculated, "just satisfaction" required that it should be fully compensated, permitting compensation in respect of pecuniary loss where tort would not provide a remedy. In *Breyer Group Plc v Department of Energy and Climate Change*[571] the Court of Appeal determined that there had been unjustified interference with the possessions of the claimants, even where loss of goodwill was created by a mere proposal which was therefore not itself unlawful, though the proposed course of action would have been unlawful if implemented. Following clear and consistent Strasbourg and domestic jurisprudence, "possessions" in art.1 of the First Protocol ECHR could take the form of goodwill which had already been established by a company but could not be applied to a future income stream.[572] Thus, where existing contracts were abandoned through an unjustified interference, the claimants were entitled to damages. In *Bank Mellat v HM Treasury (No 2)*,[573] the Supreme Court also referred to goodwill as amounting to a "possession" for the purposes of art.1 of the First Protocol ECHR. In *Bank Mellat v HM Treasury*,[574] the Court of Appeal determined that, in accordance with the principles applied in Strasbourg, it was the company and not its shareholders which had the status to recover losses suffered as a consequence of a breach of Convention rights. The bank argued that a wide range of economic interests was protected by Protocol 1 art.1, including tangible and intangible interests; on this point, the Court of Appeal determined that the recoverability of the full range of losses argued for should be considered at trial. In *R. (Mott) v Environment Agency*,[574A] the Supreme Court held that a fisherman's rights under Protocol 1 art.1 had been breached by conditions attached to his licence to catch salmon by the statutory regulator. Although the restrictions imposed were a proper exercise of the defendant's powers to control fishing activity in the interests of protection of the environment, a fair balance nevertheless had to be struck between public and private interests. The conditions amounted to a reduction of 95 per cent of the benefit of the claimant's fishing right and there had been no consideration of the particular impact on the claimant's livelihood, nor of the relative severity of the impact on him, as compared to those whose interest was recreational. Given the severity and disproportion of the impact on him, his Convention rights had been breached, and damages were an appropriate remedy. However, in future cases where the authorities had given appropriate consideration to issues of fair balance, courts should give weight to their assessment. In *R v M*,[574B] the claimant's rights under Protocol 1 art.1 had not been violated by the threat of prosecution for trade mark infringement. He was free to sell his goods provided the misleading trade marks were removed, and there was no unjustified interference with his possessions.

[566] [2003] UKHL 66; [2004] 2 A.C. 42.

[567] [2009] EWHC 1643 (Admin); [2009] Lloyd's Rep. F.C. 533.

[568] Applying the test for proportionality as required in *Huang v Secretary of State for the Home Department* [2007] UKHL 11; [2007] 2 A.C. 167.

[569] *R. (on the application of Atapattu) v Secretary of State for the Home Department* [2011] EWHC 1388 (Admin); followed in *Young v Young* [2012] EWHC 138 (Fam); [2012] Fam. 198 where it was also held that confinement to the UK was not confinement to a sufficiently limited place to engage art.5. A claim under art.8 also failed in each case.

[570] [2013] EWCA Civ 70; [2013] J.P.L. 1037.

[571] [2015] EWCA Civ 408; [2015] 1 W.L.R. 4559

[572] [2015] EWCA Civ 408; [2015] 1 W.L.R. 4559 at [43], [45].

[573] [2013] UKSC 39; [2014] A.C. 700.

[574] [2016] EWCA Civ 452; [2017] Q.B. 67.

574A [2018] UKSC 10; [2018] 1 W.L.R. 1022.

574B [2017] UKSC 58; [2017] 1 W.L.R. 3006.

First Protocol, article 2 Right to education

Replace paragraph with:

14-113 Protocol 1 art.2 of the ECHR provides that "[n]o person shall be denied the right to education". The applicability of this article to school exclusions was considered by the House of Lords in *Ali v Lord Grey School Governors*.[575] The exclusion from school in that case (pending investigation of an allegation of arson) was found to be incapable of amounting to a breach of Protocol 1 art.2. There was a difference of approach within the House of Lords, Lord Bingham asking[576] whether there was a denial of effective access to such educational facilities as the state provides, and Lord Hoffmann asking whether there had been a systemic failure of the education system as a whole. In *A v Essex CC*,[577] Protocol 1 art.2 was considered in connection with facts somewhat closer to educational negligence cases such as *Phelps v Hillingdon LBC*.[578] The case concerned a gravely disabled child, who had been placed in a special school by the local education authority, but whose behaviour was considered too challenging for the school to cope with, posing a danger both to other students and to staff. He was therefore excluded from the school, and it was a period of several months before a more appropriate setting could be found, during which period the child was educated at home. The Court of Appeal found that this interlude amounted to neither a failure of the education system, nor an exclusion from it (the two tests in *Ali v Lord Grey*),[579] and as such it could not amount to a breach of the Convention right to education. Claims under arts 3, 8, and 14 also failed. The Supreme Court dismissed an appeal, but was divided on a number of significant issues. On the appellant's key argument that exclusion from state education at school for a period of 18 months was capable of amounting to a violation of art.2 of the first Protocol, a majority of the Court (Baroness Hale and Lord Kerr dissenting) agreed that this was not the case: only "systemic failure" in the education system could amount to a violation of the right. There would not be a violation of the right simply because a state failed to cater "for the special needs of a small, if significant, portion of the population which is unable to profit from mainstream education".[580] Rather, the article "guarantees fair and non-discriminatory access for [a child with special needs] to the limited resources actually available to deal with his special needs". Thus the appellant's primary contention, that there was a positive obligation on the state to make provision for children with special needs, in these circumstances at enormous cost, was rejected. Equally, the appellant could not rely on a breach of domestic law as constituting a violation of the art.2 right: this was established by the *Lord Grey School* case. However, a different majority of the Court (Lords Phillips and Kerr, and Baroness Hale) also concluded that there was an arguable case that during the 18 months during which the appellant was excluded from school, he did not in fact have access to the educational resources that were, or might have been made, available. Essentially, he did not receive any education at all. However, both Lord Phillips and Lord Kerr nevertheless concluded that the existence of an arguable case did not justify an extension of time to bring the claim outside the one year limitation period applied to claims under the Human Rights Act 1998. The issues that arose would turn on the facts of the individual case, and would not be matters of principle; nor was it likely that substantial damages would be awarded. The claim, though arguable, was time barred. A successful claim for violation of this right, applying *A v Essex CC*, was made in *R. (on the application of E) v Islington LBC*.[580A] Through repeated changes in where the family was housed, without reference to her need for education, E had missed 50 per cent of her schooling for a particular school year. The impact of the periods of absence was particularly difficult for her, given the problems she faced as a result of her mother's disabilities. This amounted in E's particular case to a denial of the essence of her right to education for that year, and she would be awarded both a declaration, and damages.

[575] [2006] UKHL 14; [2006] 2 A.C. 363.

[576] [2006] UKHL 14; [2006] 2 A.C. 363 at [24].

[577] [2008] EWCA Civ 364; [2009] B.L.G.R. 182; [2008] E.L.R. 321; [2010] UKSC 33; [2011] 1 A.C. 280.

[578] [2001] 2 A.C. 619.

[579] Sedley LJ pointed out that in *DH v Czech Republic* (2008) 47 E.H.R.R. 3, the European Court of Human Rights found that Protocol 1, art.2 could be breached where the education system remained intact but failed a specific child. This was a case concerning the diversion of Roma children to "special schools".

[580] [2010] UKSC 33; [2011] 1 A.C. 280 at [75] per Lord Phillips.

[580A] [2017] EWHC 1440 (Admin); [2018] P.T.S.R. 349.

(c) Damages under the Human Rights Act 1998

Discretionary damages

Replace paragraph with:

An award of damages is at the discretion of the court and s.8(3) of the 1998 Act provides that it should only be made if in the light of any other relief it is necessary to "afford just satisfaction". Section 8(2) specifies that damages may be awarded by a court which is able to award damages in civil proceedings.[580B] Section 8(4) of the Act provides that in determining whether to award damages or the amount of damages a domestic court must take into account the principles adopted by the ECHR in awarding compensation. This is to ensure consistency between domestic and European awards. In *Anufrijeva v Southwark LBC*,[581] Lord Woolf delivering the judgment of the Court of Appeal, said: **14-114**

> "In considering whether to award compensation ... there is a balance to be drawn between the interests of the victim and those of the public as a whole ... . The court has a wide discretion in respect of the award of damages for breach of human rights ... . Damages are not an automatic entitlement but ... a remedy of 'last resort'."

He went on to say that an equitable approach should be taken to whether it was "just and appropriate" to award damages and this would involve considering the scale and manner of the violation and whether other remedies were sufficient to vindicate the infringed right. Thus, the onus is on the victim and if, say, he is already entitled to common law damages, an award would not be necessary. The same might be the case if the common law remedy was injunctive relief. The ECHR does not award punitive or exemplary damages and in *R. (KB) v Mental Health Review Tribunal*[582] Burnton J held that: "s.9(3) of the 1998 Act, by prohibiting any award of damages otherwise than by way of compensation, expressly prohibits the award of exemplary damages." In *Watkins v Secretary of State for the Home Department*[583] the House of Lords emphasised that exemplary damages are generally not awarded by the

European Court of Human Rights, and since damages under s.8 are modelled on Strasbourg awards, they should not be recoverable under the Human Rights Act. The claimant's argument that the tort of misfeasance in a public office extended to cases where there was no "material damage" provided there was a violation of constitutional rights was seen as an attempt to circumvent the non-availability of exemplary damages under the Human Rights Act. The ECHR has also refused to make awards to wrongdoers and it is likely that an award would be reduced to reflect the contribution of the victim to the harm.

[580B] Thus in *O.B. (Ukraine) v Entry Clearance Officer* EWCA Civ 1216, the Court of Appeal refused to award damages in proceedings which had been commenced at the Upper-Tier Tribunal (though damages would also have been refused because the refusal of a visitor visa complained of had in any event been reversed). If damages were sought under s.8, different proceedings would need to be commenced.

[581] [2003] EWCA Civ 1406; [2004] Q.B. 1124 at [56].

[582] [2003] EWHC 193 (Admin); [2004] Q.B. 936 at [60].

[583] [2006] UKHL 17; [2006] 2 A.C. 395.

Article 5 and damages

Replace footnote 588 with:

14-116 [588] [2013] UKSC 23; [2013] 2 A.C. 254 at [24]. See, however, the decision of the Supreme Court in *R. (on the application of Kaiyam) v Secretary of State for Justice* [2014] UKSC 66; [2015] A.C. 1344, not following *James v UK*. Rather, where there was a failure to provide access to relevant courses and opportunities, damages would be awarded on the same basis as in a case of delay (discussed in this paragraph). However, since the decision of the Supreme Court in *Brown v Parole Board for Scotland* [2017] UKSC 69; [2018] A.C. 1, *Kaiyam* is not to be followed. See further, para.14-98.

Assessment of damages

Replace paragraph with:

14-118 Reference in the courts to the quantum awarded in Strasbourg has now become routine and domestic courts have had the opportunity to deal with a range of issues arising in respect of quantum. In *Van Colle v Chief Constable of the Hertfordshire Police*,[604] the Court of Appeal left open for future consideration the question whether compensation under the HRA could be awarded for the distress suffered by the parents of a potential police witness who had been murdered following the failure of the police to take proper steps to protect his right to life under art.2. Sir Anthony Clarke MR noted the defendant's argument that "no Strasbourg award includes compensation for the applicant's own suffering except where the applicant was also a direct victim"[605] but as the defendants had not contended that no award should be made to the parents personally, he simply reduced the trial award to each parent from £17,500 to £7,500. The House of Lords reversed the decision of the Court of Appeal on liability without commenting on the assessment of damages.[606] In *R. (B) v DPP*,[607] Toulson LJ simply said that the amount awarded by way of "just satisfaction" in respect of a failure to prosecute, which thereby violated the art.3 rights of the victim, "should be in line with the customary level of Strasbourg awards in this area, which tend to be relatively modest", and awarded £8,000. In *R. (on the application of Waxman) v Crown Prosecution Service*,[608] Moore-Bick LJ awarded £3,500 in relation to a failure to prosecute an individual who was harassing the claimant, thus violating the claimant's art.8 rights. This was a less severe case than some of those considered by the European Court of Human Rights, in which applicants had been left vulnerable to serious physical abuse through failures to prosecute; but the failure did substantially affect the claimant's well-being. In *Savage v South Essex Partnership NHS Foundation Trust*,[609] Mackay

J said that it was hard to discern the principles on which Strasbourg awards were determined, but was referred to a table of awards made by the European Court of Human Rights. Taking into account that there had already been a full inquest into the death, he awarded £10,000, stating that this could only be "a symbolic acknowledgement that the defendant ought properly to give her some compensation to reflect her loss".[610] That award was discussed without dispute by the Supreme Court in *Rabone v Pennine Care NHS Foundation Trust.*[611] Here, the Court of Appeal's proposed award of £5,000 to each of the bereaved parents (had it found a violation) was not the subject of an appeal. Lord Dyson thought there was force in the argument that it was too low, but in the absence of an appeal by the claimants on quantum, the award was approved. Relevant factors in determining such an award in the context of breach of the operational duty to protect life included the closeness of family ties, and the serious nature of the breach in this instance. In *OOO v The Commissioner of Police for the Metropolis*,[612] Wyn Williams J identified substantial distress and frustration to be recognised by the European Court of Human Rights as justifying an award of damages for failure to investigate. In assessing damages, he took into account that the violation was in respect of failure to investigate rather than perpetration of the inhuman treatment, and referred to the restricted period of time during which the failure could be said to have extended the suffering of the claimants. This allowed him to position the case relative to others determined in Strasbourg, and he awarded £5,000 to each claimant. The decision in *Alseran v Ministry of Defence*,[612A] dealing with test cases for over 600 similar claims (the "Iraqi civilian litigation") incorporates some important statements of principle for approaching damages awards under the HRA, which may be particularly attuned to test cases. Leggatt J suggested that despite the fact that HRA awards do not require application of the domestic scale of damages, it may sometimes be important to consider domestic awards. In assessing damages, three considerations were described as paramount: (a) transparency: the parties and the public were entitled to a reasoned judgment from which it could be seen how the sum awarded in each case had been arrived at; (b) objectivity: although the assessment of damages inescapably involved an exercise of judgment, justice required the adoption of an approach which was based on external standards and not simply on the intuition of the individual judge; and (c) predictability: that was of vital importance in test cases, since there was a very strong public interest in facilitating the settlement of similar claims. In quantifying the claimants' human rights damages claims, the first stage was to identify the injuries which the claimant had suffered as a result of the relevant breach of his Convention rights and assess the amount of compensation that would be awarded for those injuries in accordance with English tort law. The court had then to consider whether to depart from or adjust that sum having regard to wider considerations of what was just and equitable in all the circumstances. The court was entitled to take account of the fact that the country where the claimants resided and suffered harm had a lower cost and standard of living than the UK. Damages would be assessed at around half the amount that would be recoverable on a claim in tort to which English law applied. Each of the claimants were awarded sums of around £10,000 to £15,000 in relation to ill-treatment, in addition to sums of between £2,700 and £3,300 for unlawful detention and additional damages for personal injury and the costs of medical treatment.

[604] [2007] EWCA Civ 325; [2007] 1 W.L.R. 1821.

[605] [2007] EWCA Civ 325; [2007] 1 W.L.R. 1821 at [114].

[606] [2008] UKHL 50; [2009] 1 A.C. 225.

[607] [2009] EWHC 106 (Admin); [2009] 1 W.L.R. 2072; see para.14-90.

[608] [2012] EWHC 133 (Admin); [2012] A.C.D. 48.

[609] [2010] EWHC 865 (QB); [2010] P.I.Q.R. P14; [2010] Med. L.R. 292.

[610] [2010] EWHC 865 (QB); [2010] P.I.Q.R. P14; [2010] Med. L.R. 292 at [97].

[611] [2012] UKSC 2; [2012] 2 A.C. 72.

[612] [2011] EWHC 1246 (QB); [2011] H.R.L.R. 29.

[612A] [2017] EWHC 3289 (QB); [2018] 3 W.L.R. 95.

Replace paragraph with:

14-119 In *Dobson v Thames Water*,[613] the Court of Appeal followed *Hunter v Canary Wharf* and held that the assessment of damages for nuisance should not include an amount representing loss of amenity and interference suffered by members of the household other than the party with the rights required to pursue the action. Rather, damages would reflect the value of the property and diminution in amenity value. A member of the household whose loss was therefore not directly taken into account in the award of damages might have a claim under art.8 provided the nuisance affected their home, the Human Rights Act providing the sort of action which nuisance has not been extended to encompass. Having said that, the award of damages to the household in nuisance would be relevant to the Human Rights Act remedy and (given the modest levels of such awards) the tort award may well be thought to suffice in providing just satisfaction to other occupants in most circumstances. The Court of Appeal also thought it clear that the person with the relevant proprietary right would be unable to expect an additional award to reflect the violation of art.8. Given the modesty of Strasbourg awards, and the relative generosity of tort damages, it was inconceivable that such a "top up" would be found appropriate. Applying these principles, Ramsey J concluded at the trial of the actions that although there had been violations of the art.8 rights of the claimants, no damages under the HRA were "necessary" to afford just satisfaction in addition to the awards made for amenity nuisance.[614] In the case of those without a proprietary interest living in family homes, all the circumstances of the case were to be taken into account. These circumstances included the award of damages in nuisance to those with proprietary interests, which would reflect the actual impact of the nuisance on the amenity of those living in the property. Even where the claimant was not a family member and/or not a minor, so that there was no guarantee that they would receive a share of the damages, it was not established that the award of damages was "necessary". This reflected the fact that "the principal objective of the Convention is to declare any infringement and put a stop to it", and that "the interests of an individual, rather than the wider public, are only part of the matters for consideration".[615] Other relevant circumstances in this case included the fact that the court made declarations in respect of violations of art.8 rights, and that remedies were available under ss.80 and 82 of the Environmental Protection Act 1990 by abatement notices and by way of a complaint to OFWAT under s.94 of the Water Industry Act 1991. The very different case of *D v Commissioner of Police for the Metropolis*[615A] provides something of a contrast. Here, awards of damages under the Human Rights Act were made to two claimants who had already been awarded compensation in a civil action against the rapist who had attacked them, and through the Criminal Injuries Compensation Fund. The police were liable for a breach of positive duties under art.3.[616] Green J reasoned that the earlier awards must be taken into account according to s.8(3) HRA but that these awards did not remove the justification for an award of damages for violation of the claimants' rights by the defendant police authority. The violation by the defendants was not vindicated by the earlier awards, since these related to the rapes themselves, not to the additional harm and rights violations involved in the failure to investigate. While it was not possible to be entirely clear about which aspects of the harm suffered by the claimants was caused by the police handling of their claims, (for example, the failure to believe their accounts and failure to take them seriously), nevertheless there was additional harm flowing from those breaches and therefore an award of damages should be made to each of the two claimants. These awards were set at £22,250 and £19,000, respectively.

[613] [2009] EWCA Civ 28; [2009] 3 All E.R. 319.

[614] *Dobson v Thames Water Utilities Ltd* [2011] EWHC 3253 (TCC); (2011) 140 Con. L.R. 135.

[615] *Dobson v Thames Water Utilities Ltd* [2011] EWHC 3253 (TCC); (2011) 140 Con. L.R. 135 at [1099].

[615A] [2014] EWHC 2493 (QB); [2015] 1 W.L.R. 1833.

[616] The Supreme Court, confirming the outcome ([2018] UKSC 11; [2019] A.C. 196), could see no flaw in the reasoning of Green J in relation to the assessment of damages.

4. MISFEASANCE IN PUBLIC OFFICE

(a) Nature of the tort

Untargeted malice

Replace paragraph with:

The basis of liability for untargeted malice was reviewed in *Three Rivers DC v Bank of England (No.3).*[628] Here some 6,000 investors who lost deposits when the fraudulently run Bank of Credit and Commerce International ("BCCI") collapsed, claimed that the senior officials of the Bank of England acted in bad faith in: (a) licensing BCCI in 1979 when they knew it was unlawful to do so; (b) shutting their eyes to what was happening at BCCI after the license was granted; and (c) failing to close BCCI when the known facts cried out for action in the mid-1980s. The question was whether these allegations were sufficient to ground liability for misfeasance in public office on the part of the Bank of England. The Bank argued that for liability under the second limb it must be shown that the officials knew of the illegality of their acts and of the probability of resulting injury and that recklessness as to the illegality and probable injury was not sufficient. The claimant argued that objective recklessness in the sense of there being an obvious risk to which the defendant had failed to give any thought, was sufficient. The House of Lords held that recklessness was sufficient but only in its subjective sense. Lord Steyn commented that to impose liability where the defendant had acted with reckless indifference to the illegality of his act and the probability of its causing injury, was "an organic development, which fits into the structure of our law governing intentional torts" and that "the policy underlying it is sound: reckless indifference to consequences is as blameworthy as deliberately seeking such consequences".[629] But he also said that the difficulty with a test of objective recklessness was that "it could not be squared with a meaningful requirement of bad faith in the exercise of public powers which is the *raison d'etre* of the tort". Hence, the claimant has to prove that the public officer acted with a state of mind of reckless indifference to the illegal- 14-122 ity of his act and its consequences. The nature of untargeted malice sufficient for the tort was considered by Nicol J in *TBS v Metropolitan Police Commissioner*.[629A] Here, the claimant's father had been an undercover police officer who had embarked on a relationship with his mother, an animal rights activist, while assuming a false identity. The claimant was born in 1985, and his father's true identity as a police officer was revealed only in 2012. The claim related to the psychological consequences of these events. Nicol J declined to strike out actions framed in misfeasance, and in negligence. So far as misfeasance was concerned, the claimant asserted that the tortfeasor knew that the claimant "was likely to suffer psychiatric damage or was recklessly indifferent to this consequence". A submission that this was insufficient, and that the claimant needed to show that psychiatric injury was known to be a probable consequence, was rejected. Language used by the House of Lords in *Three Rivers* had varied, but Lord Steyn had used the expression "likely to cause damage" as a test of liability; and Lord Hope had referred to a "serious risk that the plaintiff would suffer loss". The point was too uncertain for striking out to be an appropriate course.

[628] [2001] UKHL 16; [2003] 2 A.C. 1.

[629] [2003] 2 A.C. 1 at 192. Note that Lord Millett at 235, took a different view, considering that knowledge was not a substitute for the relevant intention. See also *Douglas v Hello! Ltd* [2005] EWCA Civ 595; [2006] Q.B. 125 at [222], where Lord Phillips said that the element of intention required for the economic torts could not be applied to misfeasance where the gist of the tort is deliberate abuse of power.

[629A] [2017] EWHC 3094 (QB).

(b) Scope of the tort

Public officer

Replace paragraph with:

14-131 The alleged tortfeasor must be a public officer, though it has been said that ordinarily the individual should not be the defendant. Rather, the ordinary approach is to bring an action against an institution or body on the basis that it will be vicariously liable for the misfeasance of its officers, rather than proceeding directly against individuals. This is for the protection of individuals going about their public duty who may be the subject of ill-founded claims, and should be the direct subject of a claim only where "absolutely necessary".[665] In *Three Rivers*[666] Lord Steyn said that the office had to be understood in a "relatively wide sense" and thus, citing *Jones*,[667] would extend to "a local authority exercising private law functions as a landlord". In *AA v Southwark LBC*,[668] three of the defendant council's officers were found to have exercised their powers as public officers in relation to a local authority secure tenancy for an improper motive, with the intention of harming the claimant by evicting him when there were no reasonable grounds for doing so and arranging for his possessions to be seized and destroyed unlawfully. Each was liable for misfeasance in a public office and the local authority was also vicariously liable. Other actions in tort and under the HRA (for actions inconsistent with art.8 ECHR) were also established. It is the nature of the office exercising power and not the nature of the power which is crucial. As *Jones* illustrates, a collective public body such as a council can be liable although there is some uncertainty as to the extent to which it must have been infected with malice. In *Rawlinson v Rice*[669] the New Zealand Court of Appeal resolved doubts in the lower court by holding that public office extended to judicial office and that a District Court judge could be sued for misfeasance in public office. *Three Rivers* and *Bourgoin SA v Ministry of Agriculture Fisheries and Food*[670] illustrates the potential importance of the tort in the regulatory context but its major impact may be in the law enforcement area. In *Brent LBC v Davies*,[670A] Zacaroli J held that governors of a grant-maintained school were "public officers" for the purpose of an action in misfeasance in a public office. They were said to fulfil one of the responsibilities of government, while the public had a significant interest in the discharge of their duties.

[665] *Adams v Law Society of England and Wales* [2012] EWHC 980 (QB) at [160]–[162].

[666] [2003] 2 A.C. 1 at 191.

[667] *Jones v Swansea CC* [1990] 1 W.L.R. 1453.

[668] [2014] EWHC 500 (QB).

[669] [1998] 1 N.Z.L.R. 454.

[670] [1986] Q.B. 716. The case concerned the revocation of an import license for French turkeys by the defendant ministry.

[670A] [2018] EWHC 2214 (Ch).

Officers with law enforcement responsibility

Replace list with:

(a) *Police officers.* The alleged collusion in the improper release of a violent criminal in *Akenzua*[671] is one example of the kind of situation that can give rise to misfeasance liability. There is obvious scope for the tort in relation to the more extreme instances of police malpractice such as the fabrication of evidence. In *Rees v Commissioner of Police for the Metropolis*, the actions of a police officer who had perverted the course of justice by directly encouraging testimony from an unreliable "witness", also amounted to misfeasance in public office.[671A] A different example is provided by *Elliott v Chief Constable of Wiltshire*[672] where the court refused to strike out a misfeasance claim against a police officer alleged to have got a troublesome journalist dismissed from his newspaper by improperly revealing his past criminal convictions to the editor of the paper. In *DIL v Commissioner of Police of the Metropolis*[673] the court considered a claim that officers engaged in covert surveillance operations had developed long-term sexual relationships with the claimants as part of those operations, under the supervision of superior officers. This behaviour amounted to deceit, assault, misfeasance in public office and negligence. The court concluded that it was not open to the police to offer a "neither confirm nor deny" response. Again, it has been suggested that a wilful refusal by a police officer to intervene to stop a violent attack on an individual, could constitute misfeasance.[674] Similarly in *Amin v Imran Khan & Partners*,[675] a claim in negligence, a failure to add a claim for misfeasance where the claimants' son, a young offender of Asian origin, had been killed by a cellmate who was known to be both racist and dangerous, was (amongst other failings) held to be in breach of the defendant solicitor's duty of care: this suggests that the misfeasance claim was thought to have some prospect of success. The police immunity which bars negligence claims in respect of the investigation of crime, has no application to misfeasance claims.[676] **14-132**

(b) *Crown prosecutors.* In *Elguzouli-Daf v Commissioner of Police of the Metropolis*[677] Steyn LJ recognised that liability for misfeasance in public office "might attach to the decision of a C.P.S prosecutor" and that "a citizen who is aggrieved by a prosecutor's decision, has in our system potentially extensive private law remedies for a deliberate abuse of power".

(c) *Prison officers.* In *Racz v Home Office*[678] the House of Lords recognised that prison officers who were alleged to have deliberately exceeded their powers under the Prison Rules by maliciously moving the claimant to a strip cell, could be liable for misfeasance in public office. There is a considerable potential for claims in this context and also an overlap with claims under the Human Rights Act 1998.

(d) *Social workers.* In *F v Wirral BC*[679] Stuart-Smith LJ commented that where social workers consciously exceeded their powers in relation to children, they and the responsible authority might be liable for misfeasance in public office. As in *Elguzouli-Daf*, this suggestion was made in part as justification for denial of a duty of care in negligence.[680]

[671] [2002] EWCA Civ 1470; [2003] 1 W.L.R. 741, see para.14-126.

[671A] [2018] EWCA Civ 1587: the claimants succeeded in showing damage sufficient for the actions in misfeasance and malicious prosecution. On the malicious prosecution elements, see paras 16-24; 16-50; 16-55; and 16-58.

[672] *The Times,* 5 December 1996.

[673] [2014] EWHC 2184 (QB).

[674] *R. v Dytham* [1979] Q.B. 722.

[675] [2011] EWHC 2958 (QB).

[676] See *Bennett v Commissioner of the Police for the Metropolis* (1998) 10 Admin. L.R. 245, where the claimant claimed that the defendant had tricked him into flying to the UK where he was arrested on theft charges. The court dismissed the defendant's application to strike out on the basis of the public policy immunity. The claimant's claim was also struck out on the ground that he had failed to establish malice against the defendant. His earlier claim of misfeasance against the Secretary of State in relation to his certificate of public interest immunity for documents relating to the case, also failed for lack of malice: [1995] 1 W.L.R. 488.

[677] [1995] Q.B. 335 at 347.

[678] [1994] 2 A.C. 45.

[679] [1991] Fam. 69 at 107.

[680] See also *B v Reading BC* [2009] EWHC 998 (QB); [2009] 2 F.L.R. 1273; para.14-123, where a misfeasance action based on wrongdoing by a social worker failed on the facts for lack of subjective recklessness and lack of knowing excess of powers.

CHAPTER 15

TRESPASS TO THE PERSON

TABLE OF CONTENTS

4. INTENTIONAL INFLICTION OF INJURY

(a) Liability based on defendant's intention to cause harm

The mental element: intention to cause at least mental or emotional distress

Replace paragraph with:

15-16 In *Wong v Parkside Health NHS Trust*[68] the Court of Appeal held that in order to be categorised as an act "calculated to cause harm" to the claimant the defendant must have intended to violate the claimant's interest in her freedom from such harm, namely physical injury or a recognised psychiatric illness. The defendant's conduct must be such that that degree of harm was so likely to result that the defendant cannot be heard to say that he did not mean it to do so. He will be taken to have meant it to do so by the combination of the likelihood of such harm being suffered as a result of his behaviour and his deliberately engaging in that behaviour.[69] It has been debated whether this will include objective recklessness (Court of Appeal in *Wainwright*)[70] or subjective recklessness (House of Lords in *Wainwright*).[71] The Supreme Court in *Rhodes* stated that where a recognised psychiatric illness is the product of severe mental or emotional distress, it is sufficient for the tort that the defendant intended to cause severe distress which in fact results in recognisable illness.[72] It was not necessary to prove that the defendant intended to cause the illness in question. Recklessness would not, however, be included in the definition of the mental element: "to hold that the necessary mental element is intention to cause physical harm or severe mental or emotional distress strikes a just balance".[73] The line is therefore drawn at intentionality. In *Brayshaw v Partners of Apsley Surgery*[73A] the court found it very unlikely that the defendant had the requisite intention to cause harm - the intention of the defendant, misguided as it may have been, was the claimant's well-being and the improvement of her spiritual (and therefore mental) health and, in the view of the judge, a long way from the type of conduct which this tort is intended to catch.

[68] [2001] EWCA Civ 1721; [2003] 3 All E.R. 932.

[69] [2001] EWCA Civ 1721; [2003] 3 All E.R. 932 at [12].

[70] [2001] EWCA Civ 2081; [2002] Q.B. 1334 at [79] per Buxton LJ.

[71] *Wainwright v Home Office* [2003] UKHL 53; [2004] 2 A.C. 406 at [45] per Lord Hoffmann.

[72] See also (also known as *ABC v West Heath 2000 Ltd*) [2015] EWHC 2687 (QB); [2016] P.I.Q.R. Q2 (sexting of vulnerable pupil in special school—perpetrator could not realistically say that the obvious consequences of his actions were unintended).

[73] [2015] UKSC 32; [2016] A.C. 219 at [89]. Lord Neuberger (Lord Wilson agreeing) also suggested (obiter) at [119] that there was a powerful case for stating that where an intent to cause distress was an essential ingredient of the tort, it should be enough for the claimant to establish that he suffered sufficient distress as a result of the defendant's statement.

[73A] [2018] EWHC 3286 (QB); (2018) 166 B.M.L.R. 76 (allegation of psychiatric harm as a result of religious practices and religious doctrines imposed on claimant by a locum doctor she had consulted).

(c) Protection from Harassment Act 1997

Replace footnote 84 with:

15-19 [84] The Protection from Harassment Act 1997 s.3(A). See, e.g. *AMP v Persons Unknown* [2011] EWHC 3454 (TCC); [2011] Info. T.L.R. 25 at [44]–[45] per Ramsey J; *Triad Group plc v Makar* [2019] EWHC 423 (QB) at [44]–[49].

Replace paragraph with:

"Harassment" is not defined in the 1997 Act, though s.7(2) states that it "includes alarming the person or causing the person distress" and "conduct" includes speech.[88] It has also been held that the conduct in question "must be grave" since the only difference between the crime and the tort of harassment is the standard of proof; and in any event, "in life one has to put up with a certain amount of annoyance: things have got to be fairly severe before the law, civil or criminal, will intervene".[89] Thus, where a newspaper publishes a series of articles concerning a press officer who has had an affair with a prominent MP, it will not amount to harassment to publish those articles since "discussion or criticism of sexual relations which arose within a pre-existing professional relationship, or of sexual relationships which involved the deception of a spouse, or a civil partner, or others with a right not to be deceived, were matters which a reasonable person would not think was conduct amounting to harassment and would think was reasonable, unless there were some other circumstances which made it unreasonable".[90] On the other hand, the relationship between the gravity of the crime and its tortious equivalent is not a precise one since a tort action may lie even though the facts would not persuade a prosecuting authority to pursue the case criminally.[91] Breach of s.1(1) of the Act does not, however, catch a single act of harassment because there must be "a course of conduct".[92] In relation to a breach of s.1(1) the harassment must occur at least twice to be actionable.[93] A series of articles in a newspaper can constitute a course of conduct for this purpose.[94] Sinister and alarming emails which went beyond the "acceptably brusque", and anonymous threatening telephone calls, in the course of a dispute about a commercial debt, have been held to constitute harassment.[95] So too have repeated, groundless demands by a local authority to a council house tenant to pay rent at an alternative (and, for the claimant, inconvenient) location.[96] More recently, the Court of Appeal in *Worthington v Metropolitan Housing Trust Ltd*[96A] found that a number of letters and e-mails over a period of time from a housing association to the claimants (assured tenants) stating, among other things, that the defendant was taking immediate action to expel the claimants from their homes crossed the boundary between that which was unattractive and even unreasonable, and that which was oppressive and unacceptable. The law did not require that each particular item of correspondence had been oppressive and unreasonable – the question was the correspondence as a whole. But for breach of s.1(1A) (involving harassment of more than one person) a course of conduct can be established if it involves a course of conduct on at least one occasion in relation to each of those persons.[97] The Act does not protect a corporate entity.[98] **15-20**

[88] Protection from Harassment Act 1997 s.7(4). In *Thomas v News Group Newspapers Ltd* [2001] EWCA Civ 1233; [2002] E.M.L.R. 78 at [30] Lord Phillips MR said that: "'Harassment' is, however, a word which has a meaning which is generally understood. It describes conduct targeted at an individual which is calculated to produce the consequences described in s.7 and which is oppressive and unreasonable". This approach was endorsed by the Court of Appeal in *Banks v Ablex Ltd* [2005] EWCA Civ 173; [2005] I.C.R. 819 at [20].

[89] *Ferguson v British Gas Trading Ltd* [2009] EWCA Civ 46; [2010] 1 W.L.R. 785 at [18]; *Majrowski v Guy's and St Thomas' NHS Trust* [2006] UKHL 34; [2007] 1 A.C. 224 at [30].

[90] *Trimmingham v Associated Newspapers Ltd* [2012] EWHC 1296 (QB); [2012] 4 All E.R. 717 at [262] per Tugendhat J.

[91] *Veakins v Kier Islington Ltd* [2009] EWCA Civ 1288; [2010] I.R.L.R. 132 at [12], per Maurice Kay LJ; Rimer and Waller LJJ concurred.

[92] *Lau v DPP* [2000] 1 F.L.R. 799—gap of four months between two incidents; insufficient to amount to a "course of conduct"; cf. *Jones v Hipgrave* [2004] EWHC 2901 (QB); [2005] 2 F.L.R. 174—two incidents, eight months apart, could constitute a "course of conduct". For the purposes of the Act, the issue is whether the course of conduct, looked at as a whole, is harassing not whether the incidents

individually could be regarded as harassing: *Iqbal v Dean Manson Solicitors* [2011] EWCA Civ 123; [2011] I.R.L.R. 428. A single act of harassment might still fall within the principle of *Wilkinson v Downton*, but following the decision of the House of Lords in *Wainwright v Home Office* [2003] UKHL 53; [2004] 2 A.C. 406 the claimant would have to prove physical or psychiatric damage.

[93] Protection from Harassment Act 1997 s.7(3)(a) provides that in the case of conduct in relation to a single person (i.e. involving a breach of s.1(1)), a "course of conduct" must involve conduct on at least two occasions in relation to that person. Furthermore, for conduct to count, it must cross "the boundary between unattractive and even unreasonable conduct and conduct which is oppressive and unacceptable": *Conn v Sunderland CC* [2007] EWCA Civ 1492; [2008] I.R.L.R. 324 at [12], per Gage LJ.

[94] *Thomas v News Group Newspapers Ltd* [2001] EWCA Civ 1233; [2002] E.M.L.R. 78.

[95] *Potter v Price* [2004] EWHC 781 (QB).

[96] *Allen v Southwark LBC* [2008] EWCA Civ 1478. Similarly, hundreds of automatic calls from a call centre to a bank customer have been held to amount to harassment: *Roberts v Bank of Scotland* [2013] EWCA Civ 882.

[96A] [2018] EWCA Civ 1125; [2018] H.L.R. 523. For its impact on drafting letters threatening legal action, see Shmilovits (2019) 135 L.Q.R. 27.

[97] Protection from Harassment Act 1997 s.7(3)(b).

[98] Protection from Harassment Act 1997 s.7(5) provides that: "References to a person, in the context of the harassment of a person, are references to a person who is an individual". See also *Daiichi Pharmaceuticals UK Ltd v Stop Huntingdon Animal Cruelty* [2003] EWHC 2337 (QB); [2004] 1 W.L.R. 1503. Cf. *Bayer Plc v Shook* [2004] EWHC 332 (QB). It is clear, however, that whilst only an individual can be a victim of harassment, a perpetrator can be a corporate body (see *Kosar v Bank of Scotland Plc (t/a Halifax)* [2011] EWHC 1050 (Admin); [2011] B.C.C. 500) or an unincorporated body, such as a partnership (see *Iqbal v Dean Manson Solicitors* [2011] EWCA Civ 123; [2011] I.R.L.R. 428—at least for the purposes of civil liability).

Replace paragraph with:

15-21 There are defences for conduct pursued for the purpose of preventing or detecting crime; conduct pursued under any enactment or rule of law or to comply with a condition or requirement imposed by any person under any enactment; or for conduct that was reasonable in the particular circumstances.[99] There is no guidance in the Act as to what constitutes reasonable conduct. However, the Supreme Court has made clear that, "[b]efore an alleged harasser can be said to have had the purpose of preventing or detecting crime… he must have thought rationally about the material suggesting the possibility of criminality and formed the view that the conduct said to constitute harassment was appropriate for the purpose of preventing or detecting it".[100] In addition, it has also been said that the Act was not intended to be used to prevent individuals from exercising a right to protest about issues of public interest and the courts will seek to exercise caution in drawing the line between the legitimate exercise of the right to freedom of expression and unlawful interference with the rights of others.[101] On the other hand, unless there are exceptional circumstances, it will not be reasonable, for the purposes of the defence, to pursue a course of conduct which is clearly in breach of an injunction.[102] Moreover, conduct amounting to harassment for the purposes of the Act is not justified merely because the defendant believes it to be reasonable.[103] Helpfully, in *Dowson v Chief Constable of Northumbria* Simon J offered a summary of what must be proved in order for a claim in harassment to succeed:

> "(1) There must be conduct which occurs on at least two occasions,
> (2) which is targeted at the claimant,
> (3) which is calculated in an objective sense to cause alarm or distress, and
> (4) which is objectively judged to be oppressive and unacceptable.
> (5) What is oppressive and unacceptable may depend on the social or working context in which the conduct occurs.

(6) A line is to be drawn between conduct which is unattractive and unreasonable, and conduct which has been described in various ways: 'torment' of the victim, 'of an order which would sustain criminal liability'."[104]

In *Levi v Bates*,[105] the Court of Appeal clarified that while in most harassment cases the claimant will be the intended target of the perpetrator's course of conduct (as suggested by Simon J above), it may infrequently happen that a course of conduct which, because it is targeted at him, is clearly harassment as against A, causes just as much alarm and distress to B, even though B is not the intended target of the perpetrator's misconduct, although *foreseeably* likely to be harmed by it. In this case, harassment of the claimant's husband had foreseeably affected his wife. There was no reason why Parliament, in the absence of express words, should by implication be found to have deliberately excluded from the protection of the Act persons who are foreseeably alarmed and distressed by a course of conduct of the targeted type contemplated by the word "harassment".[106] It followed that (2) above should be read as "conduct which is targeted at an individual".

[99] Protection from Harassment Act 1997 s.1(3). For these purposes a subjective test of reasonableness is applied; and although an actual crime need not have been committed, the crime that D was intending to prevent must have been specific both in the sense that a particular victim and a particular, imminent danger could be identified: *EDO Technology Ltd v Campaign to Smash EDO* [2005] EWHC 2490 (QB). These qualifications mean that the defence cannot be lightly invoked by the police in relation to harassment that is purely incidental to crime prevention: see, e.g. *Dowson v Chief Constable of Northumbria* [2009] EWHC 907 (QB). The "particular circumstances" referred to in s.1(3)(c) must be those prevailing at the time at which reasonableness is to be assessed: *Hourani v Thomson* [2017] EWHC 432 (QB) at [208] (here not reasonable where the defendants had formed their beliefs about the subject too readily and without sufficient critical analysis and research).

[100] *Hayes v Willoughby* [2013] UKSC 17; [2013] 1 W.L.R. 935 at [15] per Lord Sumption JSC. *Chief Constable of Surrey v Godfrey* [2017] EWHC 2014 (QB) follows *Hayes* in its treatment of the requirement of rationality test under s.1(3).

[101] *EDO Technology Ltd v Campaign to Smash EDO* [2005] EWHC 2490 (QB) at [26] per Walker J.

[102] *DPP v Moseley (Joanna), The Times,* 23 June 1999.

[103] *DPP v Moseley (Joanna), The Times,* 23 June 1999.

[104] [2010] EWHC 2612 (QB) at [142].

[105] [2015] EWCA Civ 206; [2016] Q.B. 91.

[106] [2015] EWCA Civ 206; [2016] Q.B. 91 at [29].

5. FALSE IMPRISONMENT

(a) What constitutes false imprisonment?

Imprisonment

Replace paragraph with:

False imprisonment is "the unlawful imposition of constraint on another's freedom of movement from a particular place".[110] The tort is established on proof of: (1) the fact of imprisonment; and (2) the absence of lawful authority to justify that imprisonment. For these purposes, imprisonment is complete deprivation of liberty for any time, however short, without lawful cause.[111] Even confining an individual in a doorway for a few seconds without lawful authority would amount to a false imprisonment.[112] In the context of someone who is mentally ill, the Supreme Court has ruled that the question of whether that person has been deprived of his or her liberty for the purposes of s.64(5) of the Mental Capacity Act 2005, means that he or she "was under continuous supervision and control and was not free to leave".[113] Whether the same test for "deprivation of liberty" will be applied **15-23** to the common law on false imprisonment remains to be seen. The Court of Appeal recently acknowledged that it would extend to constructive imprisonment, not involving any physical force, but "overbearing compulsion, connoting restraint within some limits defined by a will or power exterior to our own".[113A] But what at least is certain is that a prisoner need not be placed under lock and key for the purposes of this tort. It is enough that his movements are simply constrained at the will of another.[114] The constraint may be actual physical force, amounting to a battery, or merely the apprehension of such force, or it may be submission to a legal process.[115] A mere partial interference with freedom of movement does not amount to an imprisonment. If a road is blocked so that a man is prevented from exercising a right of way and he is compelled to turn back, he has not been imprisoned.[116] Nor is making a charge against a person without actual arrest an imprisonment.[117] But where the claimant was invited to enter a waiting-room by two fellow-employees who waited outside in the immediate neighbourhood while a third man called the police, it was held that there was evidence of an intention to restrict the liberty of the claimant and therefore of an imprisonment.[118] Any restraint within defined bounds which is a restraint in fact may be an imprisonment.[119]

[110] *Collins v Wilcock* [1984] 1 W.L.R. 1172 at 1178.

[111] *Bird v Jones* (1845) 7 Q.B. 742; *Meering v Grahame-White Aviation Co* (1919) 112 L.T. 44. But note that bail relieves the prisoner from imprisonment: *Syed Mahamud Yusuf-ud-Din v Secretary of State for India* (1903) 19 T.L.R. 496; L.R. 30 Ind. App. 154.

[112] *Walker v Commissioner of Police of the Metropolis* [2014] EWCA Civ 897; [2015] 1 W.L.R. 312. See Tomlinson LJ at [46]: "a fundamental constitutional principle is at stake. The detention was indeed trivial, but that can and should be reflected in the measure of damages and does not render lawful that which was unlawful."

[113] *P v Cheshire West and Chester Council* [2014] UKSC 19; [2014] A.C. 896 at [47] per Lady Hale.

[113A] *R. (on the application of Jollah) v Secretary of State for the Home Department* [2018] EWCA Civ 1260; [2019] 1 W.L.R. 394 at [57] per Davis LJ (in this case a curfew subsequently found to be unlawful amounted to false imprisonment, the court noting that the notice of restriction had contained a warning as to the criminal consequences of breaching the curfew. *Jollah* is currently on appeal to Supreme Court). However, a residence condition that required the claimant to live at a specified address, to seek the permission of the Secretary of State to change that address and not spend more than three consecutive nights away from the address without prior written consent from the Secretary of State did not amount to "imprisonment": *R. (on the application of W) v Secretary of State for the Home Department* [2019] EWHC 254 (Admin).

[114] *Bird v Jones* (1845) 7 Q.B. 742, at 744 per Coleridge J.

[115] *Warner v Riddiford* (1858) 4 C.B. (N.S.) 180.

[116] *Bird v Jones* (1845) 7 Q.B. 742. In similar vein see *Robinson v Balmain New Ferry Co* [1910] A.C. 295.

[117] *Simpson v Hill* (1795) 1 Esp. 431.

[118] *Meering v Grahame-White Aviation Co* (1919) 122 L.T. 44.

[119] *Meering v Grahame-White Aviation Co* (1919) 122 L.T. 44 at 53–54, per Atkin LJ.

Placing reasonable conditions on the claimant's exit

At end of paragraph add:

15-28 In contrast, an unlawful curfew by which the claimant could only leave his house during the curfew hours (absent a reasonable excuse) in circumstances which could attract a criminal sanction did not amount to reasonable conditions on the claimant's exit.[134A]

[134A] *R. (on the application of Jollah) v Secretary of State for the Home Department* [2018] EWCA Civ 1260; [2019] 1 W.L.R. 394.

(d) Imprisonment in unauthorised places or conditions

Intolerable conditions

Replace footnote 163 with:

15-38

[163] e.g. *Middleweek v Chief Constable of Merseyside* (Note) [1992] 1 A.C. 179; *Weldon v Home Office* [1992] 1 A.C. 58.

(f) Responsibility for imprisonment committed through the instrumentality of officers of justice

Arrests by ministerial officers

Replace paragraph with:

If the arrest or other trespass is effected by a purely ministerial officer and not under the authority of any court, the defendant must clearly be answerable if he in fact authorised the act in question. It is not necessary that he should in terms have made a request or demand; it is enough if he makes a charge on which it becomes the duty of the constable to act.[180] But it is quite a different thing if a party simply gives information, and the constable thereupon acts according to his own judgment. In such a case the informer incurs no responsibility in the tort of false imprisonment.[181] The critical test is whether the defendant was "responsible for the claimant's arrest by directing or requesting, or directly encouraging the officers to arrest the claimant; and in that respect did they go beyond laying information before police officers for them to take such action as they saw fit".[182] In *Ali v Heart of England NHS Foundation Trust*,[182A] the court applied the distinction in *Davidson v Chief Constable of North Wales*[182B] between a mere witness (a member of hospital security staff) who simply gave information to the proper authority (here the police) on which it could act or not, and someone who procured or directly requested or encouraged the police to arrest the claimant. The former would not be liable for false imprisonment even if the information provided was incorrect. If a person signs the charge-sheet after an arrest has been made, this may be evidence that he has authorised the arrest by a ministerial officer, but it is only evidence and not conclusive.[183] Thus where a constable having taken the claimant into custody on his own judgment, requested the defendant to sign the charge-sheet and the defendant did so, it was held that there was no evidence to make him liable for the imprisonment.[184] But where the officer stated that he would not detain the claimant unless the defendant made a charge and signed the charge-sheet and the defendant thereupon signed the charge-sheet, this was held to be evidence of an imprisonment by the defendant.[185] 15-43

[180] *Hopkins v Crowe* (1836) 4 A. & E. 774; *Roberts v Buster's Auto Towing Service Ltd* (1976) 70 D.L.R. (3d) 716 (BCSC).

[181] *Gosden v Elphick* (1849) 4 Ex. 445; *Grinham v Willey* (1859) 4 H. & N. 496 at 499, per Pollock CB.

[182] *Ahmed v Shafique* [2009] EWHC 618 (QB) at [87], per Sharp J. See also *Davidson v Chief Constable of North Wales* [1994] 2 All E.R. 597 (store detective not liable when she gave erroneous information causing police to arrest claimant).

[182A] [2018] EWHC 591 (Ch).

[182B] [1994] 2 All E.R. 597.

[183] In *Sewell v National Telephone Co* [1907] 1 K.B. 557, Collins MR said (at 560): "The act that was done (signing the charge-sheet) was merely to provide a prosecutor and that does not let in liability to an action for false imprisonment unless the person who takes that step has taken on himself the responsibility of directing the imprisonment".

[184] *Grinham v Willey* (1859) 4 H. & N. 496.

[185] *Austin v Dowling* (1870) L.R. 5 C. & P. 534.

6. DEFENCES TO TRESPASS TO THE PERSON

Trespass ab initio

Replace footnote 210 with:

15-50 [210] Lord Denning MR suggested that the doctrine was obsolete in *Chic Fashions (West Wales) Ltd v Jones* [1968] 2 Q.B. 299 though he appeared to change his mind in *Cinnamond v British Airports Authority* [1980] 1 W.L.R. 582 at 588.

(b) Preventing crime

Replace footnote 215 with:

15-52 [215] *R. v Morris* [2013] EWCA Crim 436; [2014] 1 W.L.R. 16 at [19] per Leveson LJ (s.3 relied on in relation to the offence of dangerous driving). Rejected in *R. v Wilkinson* [2018] EWCA Crim 2154; [2019] R.T.R. 20 as "entirely fanciful".

(c) Preventing a breach of the peace

Statutory powers in relation to disorderly or offensive behaviour

Replace paragraph with:

15-61 Section 5 of the Public Order Act 1986 creates an additional and complementary offence of using threatening or abusive words or behaviour or disorderly behaviour, or displaying any writing, sign or other visible representation which is threatening or abusive, within the hearing or sight of a person likely to be caused harassment, alarm or distress thereby.[268] As with the offence created by s.4, an offence under s.5 may be committed in a public or private place subject to the same exception as regards dwellings. A general power of arrest in relation to the commission of these offences exists under s.24 of the Police and Criminal Evidence Act 1984. Unlike the Public Order Act 1986 s.4A, under s.5 the prosecution does not have to prove any intention to cause harassment, alarm or distress.[268A] The relevant mental element set out in s.6(4), namely either an intention that the words or behaviour should be threatening or abusive, or an awareness that they may be threatening or abusive.

[268] As amended by the Crime and Courts Act 2013 s.57(2) which removed the "insulting" limb from s.5(1). See *DPP v Orum* [1989] 1 W.L.R. 88 (a constable may be the person subjected to alarm); and alarm may be on behalf of a third party and not necessarily personal alarm (*Lodge v DPP* [1989] C.O.D. 179).

[268A] *DPP v Smith* [2017] EWHC 3193 (Admin).

(d) Lawful arrest

(i) When is arrest justified?

Statutory powers of summary arrest

Replace footnote 281 with:

15-65 [281] Note that the Police Reform Act 2002 s.38 (police powers for civilian staff) provides that the chief officer of police of any police force may designate a relevant employee as a community support officer, investigating officer, detention officer or escort officer. These civilian officers then have certain powers of a police officer, as set out in Sch.4 to the Act. This includes the power to use reasonable force if a police officer would be entitled to use reasonable force in carrying out those functions. See also s.39 conferring powers on contracted-out staff, where a police authority has entered into a contract with a private organisation for services relating to the detention or escort of persons who have been arrested or who are otherwise in custody. Note that Police Reform Act 2002, s.38 (as amended by the Policing and Crime Act 2017 Pt 3 with effect from 15 December 2017) now reads:

> *38 Police powers for civilian staff and volunteers*
> (1) The chief officer of police of any police force may designate a relevant employee as either or both of the following—
> (a) a community support officer;
> (b) a policing support officer.
> (1A) The chief officer of police of any police force may designate a police volunteer as either or both of the following—
> (a) a community support volunteer;
> (b) a policing support volunteer.

Section 38(6B) provides that the powers and duties that may be conferred or imposed on a person designated under this section include any power or duty of a constable, other than a power or duty specified in Pt 1 of Sch.3B (excluded powers and duties). Schedule 4 has been repealed by the 2017 Act.

Arrest by a constable

Replace paragraph with:

Section 24(1) of the Police and Criminal Evidence Act provides that a constable may arrest without a warrant: **15-67**

> "(a) anyone who is about to commit an offence;
> (b) anyone who is in the act of committing an offence;
> (c) anyone whom he has reasonable grounds for suspecting to be about to commit an offence;
> (d) anyone whom he has reasonable grounds for suspecting to be committing an offence."

If a constable has reasonable grounds for suspecting that an offence has been committed (even though it turns out that no such offence has been committed), he may arrest without a warrant anyone whom he has reasonable grounds to suspect of being guilty of it.[284] And if an offence has been committed, a constable may arrest without a warrant: (a) anyone who is guilty of the offence, and (b) anyone whom he has reasonable grounds for suspecting to be guilty of it.[285] These powers of summary arrest can only be exercised if the constable has reasonable grounds for believing that for any of the reasons mentioned in s.24(5) it is necessary to arrest the person in question.[286] The reasons are:

> "(a) to enable the name of the person in question to be ascertained (in the case where the constable does not know, and cannot readily ascertain, the person's name, or has reasonable grounds for doubting whether a name given by the person as his name is his real name);
> (b) correspondingly as regards the person's address;
> (c) to prevent the person in question—
> (i) causing physical injury to himself or any other person;
> (ii) suffering physical injury;
> (iii) causing loss of or damage to property;
> (iv) committing an offence against public decency[287]; or
> (v) causing an unlawful obstruction of the highway;
> (d) to protect a child or other vulnerable person from the person in question;
> (e) to allow the prompt and effective investigation of the offence or of the conduct of the person in question;
> (f) to prevent any prosecution for the offence from being hindered by the disappearance of the person in question."

[284] s.24(2).

[285] s.24(3).

[286] s.24(4). The fact that the arrest must be necessary impliedly requires a police officer to consider measures short of arrest for "if he does not do so he is open to challenge". On the other hand, "[t]o require of a policeman that he pass through particular thought processes each time he considers an arrest, and in all circumstances no matter what urgency or danger … is to impose an unrealistic and unattainable burden": *Hayes v Chief Constable of Merseyside Police* [2011] EWCA Civ 911; [2012] 1 W.L.R. 517 at [40], applied in *Kandawala v Cambridgeshire Constabulary CBS* [2017] EWCA Civ 391.

[287] This provision applies only where members of the public going about their normal business cannot reasonably be expected to avoid the person in question: s.24(6).

Reasonable grounds for suspicion

Replace footnote 297 with:

15-69 [297] *Alanov v Chief Constable of Sussex* [2012] EWCA Civ 234 at [25] per Aikens LJ. See also *Mouncher v Chief Constable of South Wales* [2016] EWHC 1367 (QB) at [434], expressing doubt, however, at the treatment of the omission of relevant material in the briefing of the arresting officer in *Alford* fn.294 above (see [431]–[433]). The court in *Commissioner of Police of the Metropolis v MR* [2019] EWHC 888 (QB) confirmed at [31] that the test for establishing that there are reasonable grounds for suspicion is well established and the threshold for suspicion is low.

Replace footnote 298 with:

15-70 [298] *O'Hara v Chief Constable of the Royal Ulster Constabulary* [1997] A.C. 286: not enough that the arresting officer was instructed to arrest C by a superior officer. See also *Parker v Chief Constable of Essex* [2018] EWCA Civ 2788; [2019] 1 W.L.R. 2238.

Acting on reasonable suspicion

Replace footnote 309 with:

15-72 [309] *Plange v Chief Constable of South Humberside Police* (1992) 156 L.G. Rev. 1024. On the question whether it is lawful to arrest a suspect solely in order to impose bail conditions when the police have reasonable grounds to believe that bail conditions were necessary to protect a witness from intimidation which might make the investigation substantially less effective, see *R. (on the application of L) v Chief Constable of Surrey* [2017] EWHC 129 (Admin); [2017] 1 W.L.R. 2047.

(iii) Duty after arrest complete

Constables and private persons

Replace paragraph with:

15-79 In *Dallison v Caffery*,[343] it was held that at common law what amounts to reasonable conduct subsequent to arrest differed according to whether the arrestor was a private citizen or a constable. While a private citizen had no right to initiate an investigation by, for example, taking the person arrested on a detour to effect an identification,[344] constables' powers should be more liberally interpreted. Thus, a constable might reasonably take an arrested person back to his home to see if stolen property is there, or to some place where the arrested person alleges that there is evidence of an alibi.[345] This distinction is preserved by s.30 of the Police and Criminal Evidence Act 1984. Sections 30(1) and (1A) provide that whenever a person is arrested by a constable at a place other than a police station or taken into custody by a constable after arrest by some other person "the person must be taken by a constable to a police station as soon as practicable after the arrest". But s.30(10) preserves the common law rule from *Dallison v Caffery* to allow some latitude for preliminary inquiries by constables by providing that "[n]othing in subsection (1A) … prevents a constable delaying taking a person to a police station or releasing him under section 30A if the condition in subsection (10A) is satisfied". In turn, subsection (10A) makes clear that the condition is that "the presence of a person at a place (other than a police station) is necessary in order to carry out such investigations as it is reasonable to carry out immediately". In addition, specific statutory powers of arrest may prescribe a time period within which the arrested person must be brought before a magistrate.[346] Note that s.30(10) of the Police and Criminal Evidence Act 1984, as amended by Policing and Crime Act 2017 Pt 4 s.53(3)(c), now reads: "(10) Nothing in subsection (1A) or in section 30A prevents a constable delaying taking a person to a police station or releasing him under section 30A if the condition in subsection (10A) is satisfied."

[343] [1965] 1 Q.B. 348.

[344] *Hall v Booth* (1834) 3 N. & M. 316.

[345] *Dallison v Caffery* [1965] 1 Q.B. 348. A refusal by a constable to make such a detour to confirm or deny an arrested person's alibi does not render the arrest and detention unlawful. He has discretion in the matter: *McCarrick v Oxford* [1983] R.T.R. 117.

[346] *Wheeldon v Wheeldon* [1997] 3 F.C.R. 769.

(h) Consent by the claimant

The limits of consent

Replace paragraph with:

The victim's consent alone does not constitute a defence to a criminal charge of assault "if actual bodily harm is intended and/or caused".[413] Some lawful justification for the permission to do, or risk, harm must be present, as is the case where a person participates in a lawful game or sport or consents to surgery. It is not in the public interest that "people should try to cause, or should cause each other actual bodily harm, for no good reason"[414] and hence such conduct is prohibited by the criminal law. The House of Lords in *R. v Brown*,[415] holding that consensual sadomasochism could constitute criminal assault, found that it was irrelevant that the ensuing bodily harm was trifling or transient. Any degree of ascertainable bodily harm is justifiable only if "good reason" justifies the accused's conduct.[416] In *R v BM*[416A] the Court of Appeal ruled that body modification, such as the removal of an ear or nipple, or tongue splitting, performed on a consenting adult by a practitioner with no medical training or qualification, could not form an exception to the general rule in *R v Brown* that consent was no defence to causing actual bodily harm or wounding. The Court held that whilst there were exceptions, two features underpinned almost all of them: 15-94

> "First, they may produce discernible social benefit. That is true of the sporting exceptions and may even be true of boxing or 'dangerous exhibitions' as entertainment ... [T]he second is that it would simply be regarded as unreasonable for the common law to criminalise the activity if engaged in with consent by (on behalf of) the injured party. That would apply to tattooing and piercing ... New exceptions should not be recognised on a case by case basis, save perhaps where there is a close analogy with an existing exception to the general rule established in the *Brown* case."[416B]

Nonetheless, even though consent may not bar a prosecution, it is submitted that consent will constitute a good defence to a civil action in battery.[417] The claimant cannot claim compensation for the consequences of an act which he has freely invited, or in respect of which he has consented. The footballer cannot allege that a legitimate tackle is a battery:[418] consent to physical contact within the rules of the game may be implied.[419] Thus, when the defendant maintains that the claimant consented to the force used against him, the key question becomes whether that consent extended to the degree or type of force employed against him. The claimant's consent need not be specific to the alleged act of battery. He may consent to the general contact envisaged in a fight or in sport.[420] Moreover, when the act consented to constitutes a crime and the claimant is a participant in mutual criminal activity, a civil action between the parties may be barred on the grounds of ex turpi causa.[421] Contributory negligence is not a defence to trespass to the person, and therefore the claimant's conduct is relevant only in so far as it constitutes consent or the principle of ex turpi causa applies.[422]

[413] *Att Gen's Reference (No.6 of 1980)* [1981] Q.B. 715 at 719; *R. v Coney* (1882) 8 Q.B.D. 534 (prize fighters were held guilty of assault despite mutual consent).

[414] *Att Gen's Reference (No.6 of 1980)* [1981] Q.B. 715 at 719; *R. v Coney* (1882) 8 Q.B.D. 534.

[415] [1994] 1 A.C. 212. The European Court of Human Rights has ruled that the judgment in *R. v Brown* did not constitute a violation of art.8 of the Convention (respect for private life): *Jassard and Brown v UK* (1997) 24 E.H.R.R. 39.

[416] *R. v Brown* was distinguished in *R. v Wilson (Alan Thomas)* [1997] Q.B. 47. In *R. v Dica* [2004] EWCA Crim 1103; [2004] Q.B. 1257 the Court of Appeal held that it was possible to consent to the risk of contracting a potentially fatal disease (HIV) through "ordinary" sexual intercourse (although if the defendant deliberately caused infection or spread HIV with intent to cause grievous bodily harm, the agreement of the participants provides no defence: [2004] EWCA Crim 1103; [2004] Q.B. 1257 at [58]).

[416A] [2018] EWCA Crim 560; [2019] Q.B. 1.

[416B] [2018] EWCA Crim 560; [2019] Q.B. 1 at [40]–[41].

[417] *Murphy v Culhane* [1977] Q.B. 94.

[418] Although this is sometimes referred to as the defence of volenti non fit injuria, volenti is not appropriate. The players in a contact sport have consented to the contacts that, in a different context, would otherwise amount to a battery. They have not, however, assumed the risk of injury attributable to negligence by participants in the sport. See para.3-131.

[419] Cf. the position of those who work with children with special needs, who display violent tendencies, who do not impliedly consent to violence against them: *H v Crown Prosecution Service* [2010] EWHC 1374 (Admin); [2012] Q.B. 257.

[420] *Blake v Galloway* [2004] EWCA Civ 814; [2004] 1 W.L.R. 2844 at [20].

[421] *Murphy v Culhane* [1977] Q.B. 94. See further para.3-02 et seq.

[422] *Co–operative Group (CWS) Ltd v Pritchard* [2011] EWCA Civ 329; [2012] Q.B. 320; see para.3-67.

Consent and fraud in the context of medical treatment

Replace paragraph with:

15-97 It has been said that if a patient's consent to medical treatment has been obtained by fraud or misrepresentation then it is not a valid consent,[426] though in *Sidaway v Bethlem Royal Hospital Governors*[427] Sir John Donaldson MR limited this to situations where there has been fraud or misrepresentation as to the nature of what is proposed to be done.[428] However, in the light of *R. v Dica* the position may have to be reconsidered. In *Appleton v Garrett*[429] a dentist was held liable in trespass to the person for carrying out unnecessary dental treatment, on a large scale, for profit. He withheld the information that the treatment was unnecessary because he knew that the claimants would not have consented had they known the true position. In such cases, arguably, what occurs is not strictly "medical treatment", so the consent must go not simply to the defendant's act (e.g. drilling a tooth), but also to the context in which the act takes place (i.e. providing bona fide, medical treatment that is appropriate). On the other hand, the failure by a dentist to tell patients that she had been struck off the dental register did not vitiate the patient's consent and thus render the accused criminally liable for assault as there was still bona fide treatment supplied and it merely related to the dentist's qualifications or attributes.[430] However, a fraudulent misrepresentation that the person administering Botox injections was a medical practitioner where administration by a medically qualified practitioner was for each woman a condition of giving consent would be regarded as deception capable of vitiating consent.[430A]

[426] "Of course, if information is withheld in bad faith, the consent will be vitiated by fraud": *Chatterton v Gerson* [1981] Q.B. 432 at 443, per Bristow J.

[427] [1984] Q.B. 493 at 511.

[428] This approach is reflected in *Chatterton v Gerson* [1981] Q.B. 432 at 443 where Bristow J said: "once the patient is informed in broad terms of the nature of the procedure which is intended, and gives her consent, that consent is real". See also *Hills v Potter* [1984] 1 W.L.R. 641 at 653; [1983] 3 All E.R. 716 at 728; *Freeman v Home Office (No.2)* [1984] Q.B. 524 at 556, per Sir John Donaldson MR.

[429] [1996] P.I.Q.R. P1; [1997] 8 Med. L.R. 75.

[430] *R. v Richardson (Diane)* [1999] Q.B. 444. Cf. *R. v Tabassum* [2000] Lloyd's Rep. Med. 404.

[430A] *R v Melin (Ozan)* [2019] EWCA Crim 557.

(i) Confinement and treatment for mental disorder under the Mental Health Act 1983

Detention under the Mental Health Act 1983

Replace paragraph with:

The detention, care and treatment of mentally disordered patients for their mental disorder[437] is governed by the Mental Health Act 1983 (based on the philosophy that, whenever possible, the admission to hospital and treatment of mentally disordered patients should be on a voluntary basis[438]). Part II of the Act makes provision for the compulsory admission to, and detention in, hospital of certain mentally disordered patients. It constitutes the sole ground on which mentally incapacitated persons may be compulsorily admitted to hospital for the purpose of assessment and treatment of their disorder.[439] The common law doctrine of necessity cannot be used as an alternative.[440] The key provisions here are s.2 providing for admission for assessment, s.3 providing for admission for treatment, and s.4 providing for "an emergency application". An application for admission for assessment must be founded on the written recommendation of two medical practitioners and must be made on the grounds that the patient: **15-100**

(a) is suffering from mental disorder of a nature or degree which warrants detention in hospital for assessment (or for assessment followed by medical treatment) for at least a limited period; and
(b) ought to be so detained in the interests of his own health or safety or with a view to the protection of others.

Admission for assessment authorises the patient's detention for 28 days.[441] In cases of urgent necessity an emergency application for admission for assessment may be founded on the recommendation of one medical practitioner alone and will authorise the patient's detention for 72 hours.[442] Applications for admission for treatment must be made under s.3 of the Act on the grounds that:

> "(a) he [the patient] is suffering from mental disorder of a nature or degree which makes it appropriate for him to receive medical treatment in a hospital; *and*
> (c) it is necessary for the health or safety of the patient or for the protection of other persons that he should receive such treatment and it cannot be provided unless he is detained under this section; and
> (d) appropriate medical treatment is available for him."

Part IVA of the 1983 Act makes special provision for the treatment of community patients.[443] Of particular note is the fact that such patients may have their liberty curtailed to the extent that they may have to comply with certain conditions attached to the community treatment order, such as those requiring attendance at a certain place for treatment or periodic examination.[444] In *Welsh Ministers v PJ*[444A] the Supreme Court warned that imposing conditions in a community treatment order which would amount to a deprivation of the patient's liberty would, however, breach art.5 ECHR. The fact that the purpose of the deprivation was to enhance rather than curtail the patient's freedom did not affect this assessment.

[437] The Mental Health Act 1983 does apply to treatment for physical ailments, even in respect of patients who are detained under the Act: *F v West Berkshire HA* [1990] 2 A.C. 1.

[438] See Mental Health Act 1983 s.131(1). On the other hand, compulsory detention is possible, and although there is a Code of Practice dealing with seclusion of detained patients, it is not per se unlawful to depart from the Code. Properly used, seclusion does not violate arts 3, 5 or 8 of the European Convention on Human Rights: *R. (on the application of Munjaz) v Mersey Care NHS Trust* [2005] UKHL 58; [2006] 2 A.C. 148.

[439] Note the concept of mental disorder is *not* synonymous with that of incapacity. As such, non-consensual treatment of a *competent* patient's disorder is possible under the 1983 Act.

[440] *R. (on the application of Sessay) v South London and Maudsley NHS Foundation Trust* [2011] EWHC 2617 (QB); [2012] Q.B. 760.

[441] Mental Health Act 1983 s.2(4).

[442] s.4(4).

[443] "Community patients" are those in respect of whom a community treatment order has been made under s.17A(7). These are patients who have been detained under the Mental Health Act 1983 but discharged by the responsible clinician under s.17A(1) subject to being liable to recall under s.17E.

[444] s.17B(2), (3).

[444A] [2018] UKSC 66; [2019] 2 W.L.R. 82.

Conditional discharge

Replace paragraph with:

15-114 It is not uncommon for tribunals to impose conditions (e.g. as to appropriate supervision or accommodation) when ordering the discharge of a detained patient.[489A] If conditions are imposed, it may be difficult for a social services authority or health authority to meet those conditions, given limitations on their resources. But the failure of a social services authority or health authority to make the necessary arrangements to comply with the conditions attached to a conditional discharge, with the result that the patient remains detained, does not render the tribunal's decision unlawful, nor does it amount to a breach of art.5(1).[490] Section 117 of the Mental Health Act 1983 imposes a duty on the clinical commissioning group or local health board and the local social services authority to provide or arrange the provision of after-care services for patients who have ceased to be detained, but this is not an absolute obligation and there is no contravention of art.5 if, as a consequence of the failure to meet this statutory duty, the discharge cannot be put into effect.[491] Section 117 does not apply, however, to a patient on escorted leave of absence from a hospital.[491A] In *R. (on the application of H) v Secretary of State for the Home Department*[492] Lord Bingham said that the duty of the health authority was simply to use its best endeavours to procure compliance with conditions laid down by a mental health review tribunal for the conditional discharge of a patient. Where a tribunal considers that a patient can be satisfactorily treated and supervised in the community, if its conditions for discharge were met, the patient is not unlawfully detained if it proves impossible to meet those conditions with the result that the patient remains detained in hospital. Where the alternative, should the conditions prove impossible to meet, is not discharge, either absolutely or subject only to a condition of recall, but continued detention, the failure to meet the conditions does not render the patient's continued detention unlawful. It is only where there are no longer any grounds for detention that continued detention would be unlawful.[493]

[489A] Note that in relation to a conditionally discharged restricted patient, the Supreme Court has ruled that neither the tribunal nor the Secretary of State are permitted to impose conditions amounting to detention or a deprivation of liberty, even if the patient consents: *Secretary of State for Justice v MM* [2018] UKSC 60; [2018] 3 W.L.R. 1784.

[490] *R. v Mental Health Review Tribunal Ex p. Hall* [2000] 1 W.L.R. 1323.

[491] *R. (on the application of K) v Camden and Islington HA* [2001] EWCA Civ 240; [2002] Q.B. 198.

[491A] *R. (on the application of CXF) v Central Bedfordshire Council* [2018] EWCA Civ 2852; [2019] 1 W.L.R. 1862.

[492] [2003] UKHL 59; [2004] 2 A.C. 253; [2004] 1 All E.R. 412 at [29]; applied in *R. (on the application of W) v Doncaster MBC* [2004] EWCA Civ 378; [2004] B.L.G.R. 743.

[493] [2003] UKHL 59; [2004] 2 A.C. 253; [2004] 1 All E.R. 412 at [28], per Lord Bingham.

Protection against civil or criminal proceedings

Replace footnote 498 with:

[498] A failure to obtain the leave of the High Court under s.139(2) renders the proceedings a nullity: *Seal v Chief Constable of South Wales Police* [2007] UKHL 31; [2007] 1 W.L.R. 1910. Since the failure renders the proceedings a nullity, it follows that if, by the time the procedural error has been discovered, the limitation period has expired the claimant cannot issue fresh proceedings with a view to obtaining leave. In *Seal v UK* (50330/07) (2012) 54 E.H.R.R. 6; [2011] M.H.L.R. 1 the European Court of Human Rights held that the requirement to obtain leave under s.139(2) did not involve a breach of the claimant's right of access to the court under art.6. As to the criteria governing an application for leave under s.139, see *Winch v Jones* [1986] Q.B. 296; *Johnston v Chief Constable of Merseyside* [2009] EWHC 2969 (QB); [2009] M.H.L.R. 343 and, more recently, *Hewlett v Chief Constable of Hampshire* [2018] EWHC 3927 (QB) (permission to issue claim under s.139(2)). **15-116**

(j) Treatment and care of patients lacking mental capacity (other than under the Mental Health Act 1983)

(i) Common law

Restraint at common law

Replace paragraph with:

Subsequently, in *HL v UK*[522] the European Court of Human Rights held that although the common law defence of necessity could provide a legal basis for detention of a patient lacking capacity, it must be shown that the detention was not arbitrary. Necessity did not provide a set of procedural rules, so there was no provision for a review of the patient's detention. The contrast between the lack of any fixed procedural rules by which the admission and detention of compliant incapacitated persons was conducted, and the extensive procedural safeguards contained in the Mental Health Act 1983 was "striking".[523] This resulted in the patient's liberty being removed by the hospital's health care professionals solely on the basis of their own clinical assessments, completed as and when they considered fit. Neither habeas corpus nor any remedies available via judicial review were adequate as they did not allow for the resolution of complaints on the basis of incorrect diagnoses and judgments. Thus, L's detention contravened arts 5(1) and 5(4) of the European Convention on Human Rights, and it was irrelevant that he had not **15-122** resisted his detention.[524] The court's decision in *HL v UK* would appear to undermine the common law defence of necessity, at least in so far as it relates to detention of a mentally ill claimant.[525] So, even if a mentally ill person is housed otherwise than in a care home or hospital pursuant to the Mental Health Act, and that person's living arrangements are relatively normal, those arrangements (insofar as they involve constant supervision and control) must be subject to periodic, independent checks in order not to comprise a deprivation of their liberty.[526] Procedural safeguards of this kind are contained in the amended Mental Capacity Act 2005.[527] The Court of Appeal has held, however, that in general there is no art.5 deprivation of liberty in the case of life-saving treatment of a person of unsound mind in the urgent or intensive care context where the mentally ill patient was receiving materially the same medical treatment as a person of sound mind.[528]

[522] (Application No.45508/99) (2005) 40 E.H.R.R. 32; (2005) 17 B.H.R.C. 418.

[523] (Application No.45508/99) (2005) 40 E.H.R.R. 32; (2005) 17 B.H.R.C. 418 at [120].

[524] This point has been subsequently endorsed by the Supreme Court in *P v West Cheshire and Chester Council* [2014] UKSC 19; [2014] A.C. 896 at [55] per Lady Hale.

[525] There is nothing, however, in the decision to suggest that the necessity principle cannot be invoked in connection with other forms of treatment.

[526] *P v West Cheshire and Chester Council* [2014] UKSC 19; [2014] A.C. 896.

[527] See Mental Capacity Act 2005 ss.4A, 4B and Sch.A1 (in relation to those detained in hospitals or care homes and the power of a court to authorise deprivations of liberty). In *P v West Cheshire and Chester Council* [2014] UKSC 19; [2014] A.C. 896, Lady Hale seemed to think (at [8]) that these amendments were a satisfactory response to the concerns raised in *HL v UK*.

[528] *R. (on the application of Ferreira) v HM Senior Coroner for Inner South London* [2017] EWCA Civ 31; [2018] Q.B. 487, the Court of Appeal confining the *West Cheshire* case to the question of living arrangements for persons of unsound mind. The patient was, in the view of the Court, physically restricted by her illness and the treatment she received (which included sedation), but the root cause of any loss of liberty was her physical condition, not any restrictions imposed by the hospital.

Replace footnote 531 with:

15-123 [531] s.136 of the Mental Health Act 1983 empowers a constable, who finds in a place to which the public have access, a person who appears to him to be suffering from mental disorder, and to be in immediate need of care or control, to remove that person to a place of safety (as defined in s.135(6) of the Act) if the constable thinks it necessary to do so in the interests of the mentally disordered person, or for the protection of other persons. Section 136(1) of the Mental Health Act 1983 has been amended by the Policing and Crime Act 2017 Pt 4, ss.80(4),(5) and now reads as follows:

> (1) If a person appears to a constable to be suffering from mental disorder and to be in immediate need of care or control, the constable may, if he thinks it necessary to do so in the interests of that person or for the protection of other persons—
> (a) remove the person to a place of safety within the meaning of section 135, or
> (b) if the person is already at a place of safety within the meaning of that section, keep the person at that place or remove the person to another place of safety.
> (1A) The power of a constable under subsection (1) may be exercised where the mentally disordered person is at any place, other than—
> (a) any house, flat or room where that person, or any other person, is living, or
> (b) any yard, garden, garage or outhouse that is used in connection with the house, flat or room, other than one that is also used in connection with one or more other houses, flats or rooms.
> (1B) For the purpose of exercising the power under subsection (1), a constable may enter any place where the power may be exercised, if need be by force.
> (1C) Before deciding to remove a person to, or to keep a person at, a place of safety under subsection (1), the constable must, if it is practicable to do so, consult—
> (a) a registered medical practitioner,
> (b) a registered nurse,
> (c) an approved mental health professional, or
> (d) a person of a description specified in regulations made by the Secretary of State.

The new subsection (1C) thus requires police officers to obtain advice from a doctor, nurse, approved mental health professional (or other person specified in any regulations which may be made) before exercising their powers under s.136, unless in the officer's judgment it would not be practicable to do so. An officer might decide it is not practicable to consult if, for example, he or she needs to act without delay in order to keep a person safe from immediate danger.

(n) Detection of persons prior to deportation

Detention of persons prior to deportation

Replace paragraph with:

The Immigration Act 1971 Sch.3 para.2, provides that where a recommendation for deportation of an illegal immigrant has been made, and that person is not detained in pursuance of the sentence or order of any court, the immigrant shall be detained pending the making of a deportation order, unless (a) the court by which the recommendation is made grants bail to the person, or (b) the person is released on immigration bail under Sch.10 of the Immigration Act 2016.[583A] Nonetheless, in such instances, there is an implied duty to undertake ongoing reviews of a detainee, so the Secretary of State will be liable for false imprisonment or a breach of art.5 of the European Convention on Human Rights if he fails to undertake such reviews while the making of a deportation order is still pending.[584] Equally, there are important limits on the power to recommend deportation in the first place. The leading case is *Lumba v Secretary of State for the Home Department*.[585] There, the claimants were foreign nationals who had been detained after completing sentences of imprisonment for various offences, pending deportation under the Immigration Act 1971. They alleged that they had been unlawfully detained because, although the Home Office had a published policy on the circumstances in which detention would be used, the Secretary of State had applied an unpublished policy involving almost blanket detention of all foreign national prisoners pending deportation. The claimants sought judicial review and damages for false imprisonment on the basis that the unpublished policy was unlawful in that it involved a breach of public law rendering their detention under that policy illegal. The defendant argued, inter alia, that the claimants would have been detained even if the decision to detain had been made in accordance with the published policy. The Supreme Court, by a majority, held that the unpublished policy was unlawful and that consequently the claimants had been falsely imprisoned by virtue of an unlawful exercise of the Secretary of State's power to detain.[586] It was no defence to prove that a lawful decision to detain the claimants could and would otherwise have been made.[587] On the other hand, a different majority of the Supreme Court also held that the causation test was relevant to the question of whether the claimants should be awarded substantive, as opposed to nominal, damages for the false imprisonment. Since the claimants were entitled to be placed in the position that they would have been in had the tort not been committed, and if the Secretary of State had applied the published policy the claimants would still have been detained, they had suffered no loss or damage from the false imprisonment and were entitled only to nominal damages to reflect the fact that they had been the victim of a tort.[588] In addition, the Secretary of State's decision to detain prior to deportation will be subject to judicial review if there is no prospect of effecting a deportation for reasons other than that the detainee is thwarting the process by failing to declare important personal information required by the authorities in the country to which he is due to be deported.[589] Nor may the Secretary of State issue a cessation order—bringing to an end a detainee's refugee status—as a mere device in order to give the semblance of legitimacy to a deportation order (which in turn would legitimate the detention).[590] And a claim for false imprisonment will similarly be available where the Secretary of State either unreasonably prolongs a detention in the face of either serious mental health **15-136** problems caused to the detainee by virtue of the detention where no immediate prospect of resolving the deportation issue exists,[591] or where there is a telling absence of any real chance of effecting a deportation.[592]

[583A] As amended by the Immigration Act 2016.

[584] *Kambadzi v Secretary of State for the Home Department* [2011] UKSC 23; [2011] 1 W.L.R. 1299.

[585] [2011] UKSC 12; [2012] 1 A.C. 245. See also *R. (on the application of O) v Secretary of State for the Home Department* [2016] UKSC 19; [2016] 1 W.L.R. 1717. Note also *Onos v Secretary of State for the Home Department* [2016] EWHC 59 (Admin) and *R. (on the application of FK) v Secretary of State for the Home Department* [2016] EWHC 56 (Admin) (Secretary of State not following own published policy). Cf. *R. (on the application of Lee-Hirons) v Secretary of State for Justice* [2016] UKSC 46; [2017] A.C. 52.

[586] Note, however, that not every breach of public law will give rise to a cause of action in false imprisonment. According to Lord Dyson ([2011] UKSC 12; [2012] 1 A.C. 245 at [68]), public law errors that do not bear upon the decision to detain will not do so.

[587] [2011] UKSC 12; [2012] 1 A.C. 245 at [62], [175], [221] and [239] per Lords Dyson, Hope, Collins and Kerr respectively.

[588] In similar vein, see also *OM (Nigeria) v Secretary of State for the Home Department* [2011] EWCA Civ 909 and *R. (on the application of Moussaoui) v Secretary of State for the Home Department* [2012] EWHC 126 (Admin); [2012] A.C.D. 55. See further para.1-13.

[589] *R. (on the application of MH) v Secretary of State for the Home Department* [2010] EWCA Civ 1112. See *R. (on the application of Z (Eritrea)) v Secretary of State for the Home Department* [2017] EWCA Civ 14: detention of a failed asylum seeker for 43 months pending deportation lawful where asylum seeker had caused his detention to be prolonged by his persistent failure to co-operate in obtaining an emergency travel document and by his repeated issue of judicial review proceedings.

[590] *R. (on the application of Draga) v Secretary of State for the Home Department* [2012] EWCA Civ 842 at [71] per Sullivan LJ.

[591] *R. (on the application of Lamari) v Secretary of State for the Home Department* [2012] EWHC 1630 (Admin). Cf. *R. (on the application of LE (Jamaica)) v Secretary of State for the Home Department* [2012] EWCA Civ 597 (the detainee's schizophrenia was capable of being satisfactorily managed within detention) and *R. (on the application of Moussaoui) v Secretary of State for the Home Department* [2012] EWHC 126 (Admin); [2012] A.C.D. 55 (the detainee's mental health was merely one, non-determinative consideration along with his conviction for many prior thefts). More recently in *R. (on the application of Adegun) v Secretary of State for the Home Department* [2019] EWHC 22 (Admin), the court held that when the Secretary of State was on notice that the claimant was suffering from a serious mental health condition, he should not have continued the claimant's detention without first seeking to obtain the views of the detention centre's healthcare staff on the manageability of his condition in detention.

[592] *R. (on the application of Murad) v Secretary of State for the Home Department* [2012] EWHC 1112 (Admin); *R. (on the application of ZA (Iraq)) v Secretary of State for the Home Department* [2015] EWCA Civ 168.

7. DAMAGES

Damages in trespass

Replace paragraph with:

15-139 Any trespass to the person, however slight, gives a right of action to recover at least nominal damages. The defendant may still be liable in trespass for all the consequences flowing from the tort whether or not those consequences are foreseeable.[598] Even where there has been no physical injury, substantial damages may be awarded for indignity, discomfort or inconvenience. Where liberty has been interfered with, damages are given to vindicate the claimant's rights even though no pecuniary damage has been suffered.[599] However, where a claimant has been falsely imprisoned by virtue of a breach by the defendant of public law principles, the claimant will be able to recover only nominal damages if, on the facts, proper compliance with public law would have resulted in the claimant's detention. In such circumstances, the claimant will have suffered no loss or damage as a result of the defendant's unlawful exercise of the power to detain.[600] Equally, in *Parker v Chief*

Constable of Essex,[600A] substantial damages would not be awarded for false imprisonment where the police could establish that, had the defendant acted lawfully (here the claimant had been falsely imprisoned because the arresting officer had not personally had reasonable grounds for suspecting that the claimant was guilty of an offence, as required by PACE 1984 s.24(2)), the claimant would have been detained in any event, because no harm would ultimately have been caused. The test is what would have happened had it been appreciated what the law required. The Court held that "[l]ying behind the decision in *Lumba* therefore is the principle that although procedural failings are lamentable and render detention unlawful, they do not, of themselves, merit substantial damages ... That is not to encourage sloppy practice but, rather, to reflect actual loss."[600B]

[598] *Wilson v Pringle* [1987] Q.B. 237 at 247; *Williams v Humphrey, The Times*, 20 February 1975.

[599] cf. *Kuchenmeister v Home Office* [1958] 1 Q.B. 496. See *Beckett v Walker* [1985] C.L.Y. 129 (£200 for 53 hours after negligent issue of warrant).

[600] *Lumba v Secretary of State for the Home Department* [2011] UKSC 12; [2012] 1 A.C. 245; *Bostridge v Oxleas NHS Foundation Trust* [2015] EWCA Civ 79; [2015] Med L.R. 113 (in the context of detention under the Mental Health Act 1983).

[600A] [2018] EWCA Civ 2788; [2019] 1 W.L.R. 2238, allowing appeal against [2017] EWHC 2140 (QB).

[600B] [2018] EWCA Civ 2788; [2019] 1 W.L.R. 2238 at [104] and [108] per Sir Brian Leveson P.

Add new paragraph:

Apart from any special damages alleged and proved, such as medical expenses, **15-139A** the damages are at large. The time, place and manner of the trespass and the conduct of the defendant may be taken into account and the court may award aggravated damages on these grounds.[601] In *W v Meah*,[602] an award of damages was made in respect of rape and vicious sexual assault. The issue of quantum in such cases had not previously been considered in England. Woolf J held that aggravated damages could be awarded. Since then, however, the appropriateness of aggravated damages has been questioned in *Richardson v Howie*.[603] There, the Court of Appeal considered that where the claimant was the subject of an attack constituting trespass to the person, compensatory damages should be awarded for injury to feelings, including the indignity, mental suffering, humiliation or distress as well as anger or indignation arising from the circumstances, but that the award should not be characterised as aggravated damages. Their Lordships felt it was no longer appropriate to describe the damages awarded for injury to feelings as aggravated damages. On the other hand, where the claimant has sustained psychiatric harm as a result of an assault or harassment, it may be better for the judge to make an assessment of damages in respect of that psychiatric harm separately from the damages awarded in respect of injury to feelings.[604] Certainly, the point was made in *Rowlands v Chief Constable of Merseyside* that there is a difference between psychiatric harm and "the humiliation and injury to pride and dignity that may follow from the particular circumstances of the [wrongful] arrest".[605] In such circumstances, the claimant is entitled to compensation for this, over and above any established psychiatric harm. By contrast, where the claimant is disabled and receives an award of damages for injury to feelings under the Disability Discrimination Act 1995, "the risk of overlap is such that an award of aggravated damages is inappropriate".[606] The division between basic damages (reflecting injury to the claimant's feelings caused by the wrong itself) and aggravated damages (reflecting the manner in which it was committed) was examined in *R. (on the application of Diop) v Secretary of State for the Home Department*[606A] where the judge held that drawing a sharp distinction when dealing with a claim for injury to feelings was inevitably arbitrary and that, in such circumstances, it would be better to make one global award of general damages which would reduce the risk of double counting.[606B]

[601] *Rookes v Barnard* [1964] A.C. 1129 at 1221–1233; *Broome v Cassell & Co Ltd* [1972] A.C. 1027. For consideration of the principles relevant to breach of the European Convention on Human Rights when patients detained under the Mental Health Act 1983 were denied speedy hearings to review their detention, contrary to art.5(4) of the Convention, see *R. (on the application of KB) v Mental Health Review Tribunal, Secretary of State for Health* [2003] EWHC 193 (Admin); [2004] Q.B. 936.

[602] [1986] 1 All E.R. 935. See also *R. (on the application of Jollah) v Secretary of State for the Home Department (No. 2)* [2017] EWHC 2821 (Admin), approved [2018] EWCA Civ 1260; [2019] 1 W.L.R. 394, where the court awarded compensatory damages, but rejected a claim for aggravated damages on the basis that there were no aggravating features—the errors made by the Secretary of State and the Home Office throughout did not amount to that kind of conduct—and more significantly, there were no aggravating features present such as would suggest that the amount of compensatory damages was insufficient.

[603] [2004] EWCA Civ 1127; [2005] P.I.Q.R. Q3. See also *CD v Catholic Child Welfare Society* [2016] EWHC 3335 (QB). Aggravated damages were, however, awarded in *Mohidin v Commissioner of Police of the Metropolis* [2015] EWHC 2740 (QB): basic award did not provide adequate compensation for the racist humiliation inflicted on Mohidin.

[604] *Martins v Choudhary* [2007] EWCA Civ 1379; [2008] 1 W.L.R. 617.

[605] [2006] EWCA Civ 1773; [2007] 1 W.L.R. 1065 at [28].

[606] *ZH v Commissioner of Police for the Metropolis* [2012] EWHC 604 (QB); [2012] Eq. L.R. 425 at [156] per Sir Robert Nelson (quantum of damages not challenged when unsuccessfully appealed: [2013] EWCA Civ 69; [2013] 1 W.L.R. 3021).

[606A] [2018] EWHC 3420 (Admin).

[606B] [2018] EWHC 3420 (Admin) at [44] and [46].

Criminal injuries compensation

Replace footnote 624 with:

15-143 [624] See the Criminal Injuries Compensation Act 1995. Details of the scheme are available at the Criminal Injuries Compensation Authority website: *https://www.gov.uk/government/organisations/criminal-injuries-compensation-authority* [Accessed 1 May 2019].

Damages for related human rights breaches

Replace paragraph with:

15-144 As noted at various points in this chapter, there is considerable overlap between the various torts involving trespass to the person and the European Convention on Human Rights. But cases involving detention by state authorities are worthy of special note from the perspective of damages since it is possible that the tort of false imprisonment may not have been committed, even though there has been a violation of the art.5(4) right to a speedy review of the continuing need for a prisoner's detention. Such was the case in *R. (on the application of Sturnham) v Parole Board*.[625] In that case, a prisoner was serving an indeterminate sentence. His imprisonment was prolonged because of delay on the part of the Parole Board in reviewing his case following the expiry of his tariff. Since his incarceration remained grounded in law until such time as the Board reviewed his case and sanctioned his release, he was unable to sue on the basis of either the tort of false imprisonment or under the Human Rights Act 1998 in respect of a violation of his art.5(1) right to liberty. On the other hand, there was a violation of his art.5(4) right to a speedy review of his case. In respect of such delays, the Supreme Court held that where, on the balance of probabilities, the prisoner would have enjoyed an earlier release but for the delay, he should be awarded compensatory damages. As to quantum in such cases, Lord Reed JSC. said that "the most reliable guidance as to the quantum of awards under section 8 will ... be awards made by the European Court [of Human Rights] in comparable cases brought by applicants from the UK or other countries with a similar cost of living".[626] Modest damages were also said to be payable in cases where, even though it could not be shown that an earlier review would have resulted in an earlier release, the breach of art.5(4) had demonstrably or presumptively caused the prisoner to suffer feelings of frustration and anxiety about his continued detention.[627] In *R. (on the application of Kaiyam) v Secretary of State for Justice*,[628] the Supreme Court also found a duty under art.5 ECHR to facilitate the rehabilitation and release of prisoners serving indeterminate sentences when in the post-tariff stage. This would be implied as an ancillary duty: "a duty not affecting the lawfulness of the detention, but sounding in damages if breached. Such a duty can readily be implied as part of the overall scheme of article 5, read as a whole".[629] In *Brown v Parole Board for Scotland*,[630] the Supreme Court (unanimously) took the opportunity to reconsider the approach adopted in *R (on the application of Kaiyam) v Secretary of State for Justice* in the light of more recent case law of the European Court of Human Rights which indicated that the approach in that case had been significantly different from, and more demanding than, the duty imposed by the Convention. In particular, in rejecting the appeals of the prisoners in *Kaiyam v UK*[631] and finding on the facts of *Kaiyam* that a real opportunity for rehabilitation had been provided to the applicants, the European Court of Human Rights had indicated that cases on breach of art.5.1(a) on account of a delay in access to rehabilitative courses would be rare and declined to adopt the Supreme Court's analysis of an ancillary duty. In particular, the ECtHR's approach does not entail an obligation under the Convention to secure the applicant's immediate release, as other remedies exist which can remedy the lack of opportunity for rehabilitation. The Supreme Court commented that, on this basis, the courts should now:

> "adopt the same approach to the interpretation of article 5(1)(a) as has been followed by the European court ... and cease to treat the obligation in question as an ancillary obligation implicit in article 5 as a whole. Emphasis should however be placed on the high threshold which has to be surmounted in order to establish a violation of the obligation".[632]

625 [2013] UKSC 23; [2013] 2 A.C. 254. See further paras 14-116 and 14-117.

626 [2013] UKSC 23; [2013] 2 A.C. 254 at [39].

627 [2013] UKSC 23; [2013] 2 A.C. 254 at [13].

628 [2014] UKSC 66; [2015] A.C. 1344. See also *Kaiyam v UK Application No.28160/15* (2016) 62 E.H.R.R. SE13: no appearance of a violation of art.5(1) ECHR—application inadmissible.

629 [2014] UKSC 66; [2015] A.C. 1344 at [38].

630 [2017] UKSC 69; [2018] A.C. 1, *R. (on the application of Kaiyam)* superseded.

631 (2016) 62 E.H.R.R. SE 13.

632 [2017] UKSC 69; [2018] A.C. 1 at [44]–[45].

[illegible]

[illegible]

[illegible]

[illegible]

CHAPTER 16

MALICIOUS PROSECUTION

TABLE OF CONTENTS

1. INTRODUCTION

Extension to civil claims

Replace paragraph with:

In *Crawford Adjusters (Cayman) Ltd v Sagicor General Insurance (Cayman) Ltd*,[6] the Privy Council chose by a majority of 3–2 to depart from the position stated by the House of Lords in *Gregory v Portsmouth CC*,[7] arguing that the rationale for excluding a tort of malicious prosecution of civil proceedings was no longer valid. The status of the decision in *Crawford* was somewhat uncertain until the decision of the Supreme Court in *Willers v Joyce*.[8] As a decision of the Privy Council, *Crawford Adjusters* appeared to be of only persuasive authority, particularly given that it was subject to two strong dissenting judgments.[9] On the other hand, it was clearly based upon analysis of English law. In *Willers v Joyce*,[10] a panel of nine justices decided (again by a bare majority, of 5–4) that the tort of malicious prosecution extends in English law to civil actions generally. As noted by Lord Wilson, a member of the majority in both cases, it seems likely there will be more claims for malicious civil prosecution, than for malicious criminal prosecution, in modern conditions.[11] Indeed, Lord Sumption, dissenting in both decisions, regarded the tort of malicious prosecution as it applies to criminal proceedings, as virtually extinct, and saw it as ironic that the well-established restriction on the tort should be swept away and a potentially very wide tort created which would offer litigants an occasion for prolonging disputes by way of secondary litigation.[12] Making the same point in the minority in *Willers v Joyce*, Lord Mance referred to the creation of an action for malicious civil prosecution as "necromancy".[13] It is suggested that it is an exaggeration to see the tort as applied to criminal proceedings as extinct, though 16-02 the era of public prosecutions has certainly ensured that it is less widely used than it its heyday; but that it remains the case that the tort as it applies to civil proceedings has the potential to become much broader.

[6] [2013] UKPC 17; [2014] A.C. 366. Commented on by T.K.C. Ng (2014) 130 L.Q.R. 43.

[7] [2000] 1 A.C. 419 HL.

[8] [2016] UKSC 43; [2018] A.C. 779.

[9] Lords Neuberger and Sumption dissented.

[10] [2016] UKSC 43; [2018] A.C. 779.

[11] "... in England and Wales, there is much less chance of being a victim of a criminal prosecution brought maliciously and without reasonable cause than of a civil action so brought. For most criminal prosecutions are brought at the direction of the Crown Prosecution Service, which, by its code, must first be satisfied that the evidence in support of it is such as to render the chance of a conviction greater than even": [2013] UKPC 17; [2014] A.C. 366 at [68].

[12] [2013] UKPC 17; [2014] A.C. 366 at [144]–[148]. It is also ironic perhaps that after taking the litigation to the Supreme Court and establishing the general availability of an action for malicious civil prosecution, the claimant failed at trial: *Willers v Joyce* [2018] EWHC 3424 (Ch). The defendant could not be regarded as the prosecutor of the civil action against the claimant; there was clear reasonable and probable cause for the action; and it had not been established that the defendant's sense of embitterment toward the claimant was sufficient to constitute malice. Equally, there was no evidence of collateral or improper purpose sufficient for a claim in abuse of process (see para.16-66 et seq). See further, paras 16-24A and 16-56.

[13] [2016] UKSC 43; [2018] A.C. 779 at [131].

Policy balance

Replace footnote 16 with:

16-03 [16] See the decision of the Supreme Court of Canada, dismissing an action against a Crown prosecutor, in *Kvello v Miazga* [2009] SCC 51; [2010] 1 W.W.R. 45. In England and Wales malicious prosecution has not been successfully argued against Crown prosecutors as it has in exceptional cases in Canada: *Nelles v Ontario* [1989] 2 S.C.R. 170; *Proulx v Quebec* [2001] SCC 66; [2001] 3 S.C.R. 9. Note, however, the unsuccessful action against an officer of HM Customs and Excise in *Coudrat v Commissioners of Her Majesty's Revenue and Customs* [2005] EWCA Civ 616; [2005] S.T.C. 1006and against the CPS in *Rudall v CPS* [2018] EWHC 3287 (QB); [2019] Lloyd's Rep. F.C. 115. Similar issues may arise in actions against police officers.

2. Kinds of damage caused And meaning of "malicious prosecution"

Nature of damage caused

Replace paragraph with:

16-07 In *Manley v Commissioner of Police for the Metropolis*,[34] the Court of Appeal endorsed the following statement by Roch LJ in *Clark v Chief Constable of Cleveland Police*,[35] setting out the three heads of compensation for malicious prosecution, but advised caution in the balance between them.

> "Compensation for malicious prosecution has three aspects. First, there is the damage to a person's reputation. The extent of that damage will depend upon the claimant's actual reputation and upon the gravity of the offence for which he has been maliciously prosecuted. The second aspect is the damage suffered by being put in danger of losing one's liberty or of losing property. Compensation is recoverable in respect of the risk of conviction. *McGregor on Damages* 16th Edition paragraph 1862 considers that an award under this head is basically for injury to feelings, unless there has been a conviction followed by imprisonment. The third aspect is pecuniary loss caused by the cost of defending the charge."

In *Manley*, it was pointed out that although a claimant of bad character[36] may not suffer damage to reputation to the same extent if prosecuted for an additional offence, there may be greater risk of punishment, and a risk of more severe punishment, should the prosecution succeed, all of which will cause stress and anxiety. In *Breeze v Chief Constable of Norfolk Constabulary*,[36A] it was held that two directors who had been unsuccessfully prosecuted and expressly vindicated at trial could not succeed in their claim for the total loss of the share value in the company which resulted from their prosecution: the principle in *Johnson v Gore Wood*[36B] applied, so that the appropriate claimant was the company itself. The directors' claim was framed in both malicious prosecution, and misfeasance in a public office. The company could not have pursued the claim in malicious prosecution, since it had not itself been prosecuted. However, it could in principle pursue the claim in misfeasance and thus was the appropriate party to seek to recover damages. However, the claimants were given the opportunity to plead that they fell within an exception to the *Johnson v Gore Wood* principle, in that the tort had deprived the company of all its value, effectively preventing it from pursuing its claim. This was a broad, but potentially arguable interpretation of the exception in *Giles v Rhind*.[36C]

[34] [2006] EWCA Civ 879; (2006) 150 S.J.L.B. 889 at [26].

[35] [1999] EWCA Civ 1357; [2000] C.P. Rep 22.

[36] Bad character should not be confused with living an "unconventional" lifestyle such as choosing to live away from society in squalid and unsanitary conditions which leads to a low level of social standing: *Calix v Attorney General of Trinidad and Tobago* [2013] UKPC 15; [2013] 1 W.L.R. 3283 at [10], "reputation has an objective value".

[36A] [2018] EWHC 485 (QB).

[36B] [2002] 2 A.C. 1.

[36C] [2002] EWCA Civ 1428; [2003] Ch. 618.

Replace footnote 48 with:

[48] [2016] UKSC 43; [2018] A.C. 779. **16-09**

"Malicious prosecution"

Replace footnote 51 with:

[51] The impact on reputation of certain civil proceedings was part of the rationale for extension to civil claims. In *Willers v Joyce* [2016] UKSC 43; [2018] A.C. 779 at [38], Lord Wilson referred to the proceedings as part of "determined campaign to destroy a person's reputation". **16-10**

Malicious institution of other proceedings

Replace paragraph with:

16-11 Prior to the recent extension to civil proceedings in general, it was recognised that in addition to a remedy for malicious prosecution, a claim in tort would lie in a "few special cases of abuse of legal process".[53] These included malicious presentation of a winding up order or bankruptcy petition,[54] maliciously procuring a bench warrant[55] or search warrant,[56] and the malicious arrest of a ship.[57] The common feature of such claims was that the very institution of proceedings resting on an ex parte legal process may cause immediate and irreversible damage to the claimants. Lord Steyn in *Gregory v Portsmouth CC*[58] suggested that such claims did not constitute a separate tort of malicious abuse of process but rather they resembled the parent tort of malicious prosecution too closely to warrant separate treatment.[59] The majority of the Privy Council in *Crawford Adjusters*, and of the Supreme Court in *Willers v Joyce*,[60] argued that these cases supported the existence of a general tort of malicious prosecution applying to both criminal and civil proceedings, as part of a rationalisation of the field. The majority justices, and particularly Lord Wilson JSC, regarded this as a return to a broader principle. In the minority however, Lord Neuberger pointed out that no case had been identified where a civil prosecution was the basis of a successful claim in malicious prosecution beyond those identified here;[61] and Lord Sumption considered it coherent to limit the tort to civil claims where a power is invoked ex parte and without adjudication.[62]

[53] *Gregory v Portsmouth CC* [2000] 1 A.C. 419 HL at 427, per Lord Steyn. These special cases are discussed more fully at para.16-64 onwards. and were described by Baroness Hale in the *Crawford Adjusters case* [2013] UKPC 17; [2014] A.C. 366 at [86] as a "rag bag" list of ex parte processes which do damage before they can be challenged.

[54] *Quartz Hill Consolidated Gold Mining Co v Eyre* (1883) 11 Q.B.D. 674. In this case, the court made it clear that in no case can a person, who has maliciously and unreasonably set the law in motion, absolve himself from the consequences which he invited and brought to pass, by the suggestion that their immediate cause was a mistake on the part of the judge: (1883) 11 Q.B.D. 674 at 684, per Brett MR cf. *Farley v Danks* (1855) 4 E. & B. 493 at 499; 119 E.R. 180 at 182. See also *Pike v Waldrum* [1952] 1 Lloyd's Rep. 431.

[55] *Roy v Prior* [1971] A.C. 470 HL.

[56] *Gibbs v Rea* [1998] A.C. 786 PC.

[57] *The Walter D Wallet* [1893] P. 202. In *Congentra AG v Sixteen Thirteen Marine SA (The Nicholas M)* [2008] EWHC 1615 (Comm); [2009] 1 All E.R. (Comm) 479; [2008] 2 Lloyd's Rep. 602, Flaux J concluded that the facts could arguably fall within the category of "wrongful arrest" (of a ship) recognised in *Gregory v Portsmouth CC* and that this case may be an example of its application in a modern context. Here the ship had been detained for repairs while chartered by the defendant, and the claimant argued that the delay (which had caused them to lose their next charter) was the product of a conspiracy. An action in respect of wrongful arrest of a ship requires the claimant to prove that the arrest has been made in bad faith or with "crass negligence": *The Evangelismos* (1858) 12 Moo P.C. 352; 14 E.R. 945; *The Volant* (1864) Br. & L. 321; 167 E.R. 385. A mere error of judgment in arresting the ship, in the absence of bad faith, is not sufficient: *The Strathnaver* (1875) L.R. 1 App. Cas. 58. A failure to exercise reasonable care to ascertain entitlement to arrest the vessel does not amount to "crass negligence". Rather this refers to those "cases in which objectively there is so little basis for the arrest that it may be inferred that the arresting party did not believe in his entitlement to arrest the vessel or acted without any serious regard to whether there were adequate grounds for the arrest of the vessel": *Centro Latino Americano de Commercio Exterior SA v Owners of the Kommunar (The Kommunar) (No.3)* [1997] 1 Lloyd's Rep. 22 at 30, per Colman J. Query whether art.1 of the First Protocol to the ECHR would now permit a ship owner to recover compensation for the wrongful arrest of a ship in the absence of bad faith or "crass negligence" by the defendant.

[58] [2000] 1 A.C. 419 at 427.

[59] This is distinct from the tort of "abuse of process" which originated in *Grainger v Hill* (1838) 4 Bing. N.C. 212; 132 E.R. 769, and which is not dependent on absence of reasonable and probable cause and malice: see para.16-67.

[60] [2016] UKSC 43; [2018] A.C. 779.

[61] [2016] UKSC 43; [2018] A.C. 779 at [152].

[62] [2016] UKSC 43; [2018] A.C. 779 at [174].

3. MALICIOUS PROSECUTION

Essentials of the tort of malicious prosecution

Replace paragraph with:

16-12 In an action for malicious prosecution the claimant must show first that he was prosecuted by the defendant, that is to say, that the law was set in motion against him by the defendant on a criminal charge or, now, via civil proceedings[63]; secondly, that the prosecution was determined in his favour[64]; thirdly, that it was without reasonable and probable cause; and fourthly, that it was malicious. The onus of proving every one of these is on the claimant. Evidence of malice of whatever degree cannot be invoked to dispense with or diminish the need to establish separately each of the first three elements of the tort.[65] Nor does the presence of malice affect the operation of the defence of illegality, which may apply to defeat an action for malicious prosecution.[65A]

[63] *Crawford Adjusters (Cayman) Ltd v Sagicor General Insurance (Cayman) Ltd* [2013] UKPC 17; [2014] A.C. 366; *Willers v Joyce* [2016] UKSC 43; [2018] A.C. 779. Note that these decisions did not imply that any change was needed to the other three requirements for the tort.

[64] *Bynoe v Bank of England* [1902] 1 K.B. 467; cf. per Crompton J in *Castrique v Behrens* (1861) 3 E. & E. 709 at 721; 121 E.R. 608 at 613; and per Byles J in *Basebé v Matthews* (1867) L.R. 2 C.P. 684 at 689; *Everett v Ribbands* [1952] 2 Q.B. 198 CA; *Dunlop v Customs & Excise Commissioners*, *The Times*, 17 March 1998; (1998) 142 S.J.L.B. 135 (limitation period runs from acquittal).

[65] *Martin v Watson* [1994] Q.B. 425 CA.

[65A] *Gujra v Roath* [2018] EWHC 854 (QB); [2018] 1 W.L.R. 3208.

(a) Prosecution

What is a prosecution?

Replace footnote 77 with:

[77] [2016] UKSC 43; [2018] A.C. 779 at [51]; Lord Mance thought that "logically", the extension to civil claims should also apply to "any individual application or step in the course of a civil action" (at [133]); but it is doubtful that this is the case given the need to "set the law in motion". Prior to *Willers v Joyce*, in *Energy Venture Partners v Malabu Oil & Gas Ltd* [2014] EWHC 1390 (Comm), Males J felt unable to rule out the existence of a tort of malicious defence of civil proceedings following the decision in *Sagicor*; but thought that the requirement of an extraneous motive was not, in any case, present in the case (at [15]). It is suggested that the comments of Lord Toulson make the existence of such a tort less likely. **16-14**

Application of Martin v Watson

After "the professional prosecutor is able to exercise an independent judgment in the matter.", add new footnote 112A:

[112A] An illustrative decision at first instance, applying the test in *Martin v Watson*, is *Kalma v African Minerals Ltd* [2018] EWHC 3506 (QB). The claim related to the potential liability of the defendant company where several forms of injury, loss, and damage were inflicted by the police during and after a protest at the company's site in Sierra Leone in 2010, and a strike in 2012. In respect of the claims for malicious prosecution, it was held that it was not in this instance "virtually impossible for the police to have exercised any independent discretion or judgment on the matter". Indeed, the police appeared in some instances to be willing to proceed without evidence from any source. **16-21**

Replace paragraph with:

In contrast, in *Ministry of Justice (Sued as Home Office) v Scott*,[125] the Court of Appeal declined to strike out an action for malicious prosecution brought by S, a serving prisoner, where the initial complainants had been prison officers. An incident had occurred in which S alleged that he had been assaulted by a prison guard, H. Following the incident, S had been prosecuted on charges of assaulting H and for affray, but had been acquitted on both charges. In an action for malicious prosecution, he claimed that five prison guards had given false evidence against him in a malicious prosecution. The Court of Appeal thought it arguable that the prison officers could be said to have "procured" the prosecution. While the role of the CPS in modern law would make it rare for individual complainants to be found to be the prosecutor where the CPS made a decision to proceed,[126] nevertheless in this case it was "unrealistic" to think that the CPS could make any decision other than to go forward with the prosecution where five prison guards gave evidence. It was arguably virtually impossible for the CPS to exercise any independent discretion in such a case. Notably, this was the case even though other potential evidence might be available,[127] but the strong terms in which five officers gave **16-24** evidence was always likely to be decisive in the independent prosecutors' decision. It is suggested that this case is far removed from the typical case of an individual complainant as in *H v AB*, and that it is therefore not inconsistent with the approach to such cases taken there. Longmore LJ, in particular, emphasised in *Scott* that he could not be sure, for the purposes of striking out, that the CPS had been able to reach a judgment to prosecute which was independent of the "mere assertion of the potential witnesses for the prosecution".[128] He also implied that the ability to weigh the credibility of witness statements in the light of other evidence would make a difference to the conclusion about independent judgment. Also applying the approach of the authorities examined here is the decision of the Court of Appeal in *Rees v Commissioner of Police for the Metropolis*.[129] Here, a police officer had prompted evidence from an unreliable witness, and had concealed this fact from the CPS. The Court of Appeal concluded that the officer's conduct was such that the CPS "were deprived of their ability to exercise a truly independent judgment".[129A] It should be asked what effect it would have had on their judgment if they had been told that the evidence of the eyewitness—who suffered from a personality disorder and was highly suggestible—had been improperly procured. It was accepted that the cases are "fact specific". Here, however, the investigating officer had presented to the independent prosecutor a case which he knew included an important feature procured through his own criminality. Applying the words of Wall LJ in *H v AB*, "There is nothing more likely to have 'overborne or perverted' the decision to prosecute".[130] A less nuanced approach appears to have been expressed in *Commissioner of Police for the Metropolis v Copeland*,[131] where a police officer who alleged he had been assaulted by the claimant was held to be the prosecutor, though he was not the prosecuting officer. Although there were other witnesses and other sources of evidence, the Court of Appeal held that the bad faith of the officer, as found by the civil jury, had vitiated the discretion of the prosecutors. It is suggested that the Court of Appeal's description of the authorities considered in this and the preceding paragraphs in terms of a "simple quest" to determine who was in substance responsible for the prosecution does not capture the restricted approach to defining witnesses as prosecutors to be found in those cases.

[125] [2009] EWCA Civ 1215. See also *The Commissioner of the Police of the Metropolis v Copeland* [2014] EWCA Civ 1014; [2015] 3 All E.R. 391.

[126] Pill LJ [2009] EWCA Civ 1215 at [41], expressly endorsing comments to this effect in *H v AB* [2009] EWCA Civ 1092; *The Times*, 28 October 2009 at [58].

[127] Pill LJ [2009] EWCA Civ 1215 at [41], with whom the other judges agreed, did not accept that "the right to bring an action for malicious prosecution is confined to cases in which there is a single prosecution witness with exclusive knowledge of the facts".

[128] [2009] EWCA Civ 1215 at [50].

[129] [2018] EWCA Civ 1587.

[129A] [2018] EWCA Civ 1587 at [57].

[130] [2018] EWCA Civ 1587 at [59].

[131] [2014] EWCA Civ 1014; [2015] 3 All E.R. 391.

Add new paragraph:

16-24A **Application to prosecution of civil claims** In *Willers v Joyce*,[131A] Rose J observed that the question of who is the prosecutor may be more difficult to answer in relation to a malicious civil prosecution. As she explained, "There is clearly a difficulty ... in transposing the test set out in the authorities arising from criminal prosecutions into a situation where the previous prosecution is of a civil claim .... When the CPS brings a prosecution, it is relatively straightforward to identify who, outside the organisation, has provided the information which results in the decision to prosecute. Where a company decides to embark on a major piece of litigation there are many different individuals inside and outside the corporate structure who will have contributed their information and opinions."[131B] Nevertheless, the approach set out in *Martin v Watson* and later cases could be applied. In doing this, it was not enough to attempt to attribute the company's acts to its director, on the basis that he was the dominant personality and controlling mind behind the company. A more detailed approach to the decision to prosecute the action would be required: "in deciding whether an individual who generally has a position of influence within the company should have the company's actions attributed to him, I consider it is necessary to examine in detail his role in the particular decision taken, not simply to move from generalised expressions of his dominant—even terrifying—personality to an assumption that he took the decision in question, at least where there is evidence about how the particular decision was actually taken." Applying the approach in the case law derived from *Martin v Watson*, Rose J accepted that Mr Gubay probably expressed his strong view that the Langstone Action should be commenced but did not accept that the directors did not exercise their independent judgement in coming to the conclusion that it was a proper case to bring. Mr Gubay was not the prosecutor of the Langstone Action on that basis.[131C]

[131A] [2018] EWHC 3424 (Ch).

[131B] [2018] EWHC 3424 (Ch), [192].

[131C] [2018] EWHC 3424 (Ch), [219].

Maliciously continuing proceedings

Add new footnote 151A at end of paragraph:

[151A] This point was not considered on appeal: [2018] EWCA Civ 1587; see further paras 16-50 and 16-55. **16-30**

(c) Reasonable and probable cause

Reasonable and probable cause

Replace footnote 167 with:

[167] See however *Rudall v CPS* [2016] EWHC 2884 (QB), where a claim against both CPS and police was considered arguable. The claimant alleged that the aim of pursuing a prosecution was to prevent him from practising as a solicitor. At trial, the claim failed on the facts since there was reasonable and probable cause for the prosecution, and no malice was established: *Rudall v CPS* [2018] EWHC 3287 (QB); [2019] Lloyd's Rep. F.C. 115; see paras 16-50 and 16-60. **16-35**

(ii) Factors relevant to reasonable and probable cause

Absence of belief in merits of prosecution

Replace paragraph with:

Certain older authorities suggest that a prosecutor ought to be convinced, if not of the guilt of the accused, at least of the probability of his guilt. However, it has also been said that when the question of honest belief arises it is sufficient for the prosecutor to believe in his right to prosecute, or that the prosecution is justifiable, **16-50** and it is not necessary that he should have a positive belief in the guilt of the accused.[226] This may be summarised as belief in the merits of the cause rather than belief in guilt, and this test seems more appropriate in an era of public prosecutions. This approach is also broadly compatible with the approach of the Supreme Court of Canada in *Kvello v Miazga*,[227] where it was suggested that a Crown prosecutor, at least, should set aside personal views and not allow these to substitute for those of the judge and jury. The question arises of whether others involved in the administration of justice are subject to a similar test, including the police in respect of some of their functions. The key English authority of *Glinski v McIver*[228] also provides some support but includes conflicting opinions on this point. The opinions of Lord Denning (a public prosecutor need not be convinced of the guilt of the accused; he need only be satisfied that there is a proper case to go before the court),[229] and Lord Devlin (the prosecutor is only concerned with the question whether there is a case fit to be tried) are broadly compatible with the approach in *Kvello*. The opinion of Lord Radcliffe (the test is honest belief in the truth of the charge) and to some extent the opinion of Viscount Simonds (the defendant's belief is relevant, though it is hard to say there is lack of reasonable and probable cause where the defendant has acted on competent advice), are less compatible with it. Lord Reid concurred with the less easily categorised conclusions of Viscount Simonds. In *Coudrat v Commissioners of Her Majesty's Revenue and Customs*,[230] the Court of Appeal referred to *Glinski v McIver* and derived from it a test based on whether a charging officer believed there was a case fit to be tried; and whether there was, objectively, evidence sufficient to justify such a belief. In *Rees v Commissioner of Police for the Metropolis*[230A] McCombe LJ referred to the judgments of Lords Denning and Devlin in *Glinski v McIver* when addressing the question whether a prosecutor (in this case, a police officer) has subjective reasonable and probable cause for the prosecution where he presents a case heavily reliant on evidence which is highly likely to be ruled inadmissible because of his own misconduct. McCombe LJ concluded that the case presented by the officer to the CPS was not a "proper" one; nor was it "fit to be tried". There was no evidence that he had given any thought to the question whether there was a case fit to be laid before the court without the tainted evidence, and the officer could not be found to have "honestly believed" that there was a proper case to be laid before the court. Here, there may have been objectively sufficient evidence, without the witness whose evidence was likely to be inadmissible, to provide reasonable and probable cause to prosecute; but the officer could not be said to have *believed* that he had reasonable and probable cause.[230B] In *Rudall v CPS*[230C] the court emphasised that absence of subjective belief in the charge, in the sense above, was conclusive of absence of reasonable and probable cause even if objectively, such a cause existed. On the facts however, the prosecutor had a genuine belief in the charge.

[226] *Turner v Ambler* (1847) 10 Q.B. 252; 116 E.R. 98; *Haddrick v Heslop* (1848) 12 Q.B. 267; 116 E.R. 869; *Tempest v Snowden* [1952] 1 K.B. 130 at 139, per Denning LJ; *Leibo v Buckman* [1952] 2 All E.R. 1057 at 1069; *Hicks v Faulkner* (1878) 8 Q.B.D. 167 at 171; and where it is laid down that the defendant must have believed in the guilt of the accused, must now be read in the light of the above cases. And see *Glinski v McIver* [1962] A.C. 726, where Lord Denning at 759 expressed it as an honest belief that there is a case proper to be laid before the court, and Lord Devlin at 766-767 as cause for thinking that the claimant was probably guilty and that he had a good enough case to warrant a prosecution.

[227] [2009] SCC 51; [2010] 1 W.W.R. 45.

[228] [1962] A.C. 726. The defendant was a police detective.

[229] See particularly at 758, "Guilt or innocence is for the tribunal and not for him [the prosecutor]".

[230] [2005] EWCA Civ 616; [2005] S.T.C. 1006.

[230A] [2018] EWCA Civ 1587, at [69]–[75].

[230B] [2018] EWCA Civ 1587 at [76].

[230C] [2018] EWHC 3287 (QB); [2019] Lloyd's Rep. F.C. 115.

Replace footnote 232 with:

[232] *The Code for Crown Prosecutors* (2018) at [5.1] et seq. 16-51

(d) Malice

Improper motives

Replace paragraph with:

The Privy Council in *Williamson v Attorney General of Trinidad and Tobago*[250] made it clear that "[a]n improper and wrongful motive lies at the heart of the tort" and "must be the driving force behind the prosecution". "Malice in this context has the special meaning common to other torts and covers not only spite or ill-will but also improper motive."[251] The proper motive for a prosecution is, of course, a desire to secure the ends of justice.[252] If a claimant satisfies a jury, either negatively that this was not the true or predominant[253] motive of the defendant or affirmatively that something else was, he proves his case on the point. Mere absence of proper motive is generally evidenced by the absence of reasonable and probable cause.[254] The jury, however, are not bound to infer malice from unreasonableness[255]; and in considering what is unreasonable they are not bound to take the ruling of the judge. 16-55

> "Absence of reasonable cause, to be evidence of malice, must be absence of such cause in the opinion of the jury themselves, and I do not think they could be properly told to consider the opinion of the judge on this point if it differed from their own—as it possibly might and in some cases probably would—as evidence for their consideration in determining whether there was malice or not."[256]

The Privy Council in *Williamson*[257] confirmed that malice, though a separate requirement, "can be inferred from a lack of reasonable and probable cause". However, it was emphasised that the finding of malice is always dependent on the facts of the individual case. It may be concluded that lack of reasonable and probable cause is not always sufficient to show malice. The absence of belief in the defendant's mind as to the merits of the case (appropriately adjusted in light of the discussion of reasonable and probable cause, above) will probably afford strong evidence of malice[258]; so also any lack of good faith in his proceedings, any indication of a desire to concoct evidence or procure a conviction at any cost.[259] In *Rees v Commissioner of Police for the Metropolis*[260] it was concluded that honest belief in the guilt of the claimant does not negate the existence of malice. The judge had ruled that the senior investigating officer's preparation of the prosecution case was tainted by illegality of a serious kind (an intention to pervert the course of justice). This finding was sufficient to render him malicious: "He knowingly put before the decision-maker a case which he knew was significantly tainted by his own wrongdoing and which he knew could not be properly presented in that form to a court." To find that there was no malice in such a case would be "a negation of the rule of law". If someone, in spite of a warning that his action towards the claimant was illegal, takes legal advice and persists in his proceeding, his action may be not so much malicious as ignorant. He thought he was acting under good advice and relied on bad law.[261] A claimant may sometimes be able to show what the exact motive was, as by proving expressions of spite or ill-will on the defendant's part[262]; or by showing that he had some collateral object to secure.[263] Thus, where the defendant had said that by indicting the claimant he would close his mouth in another legal proceeding then pending, it was held that this was good evidence of malice.[264] In *A v State of New South Wales*,[264A] the police officer who charged the claimant with sexually abusing two young children said that if it was up to him he would not have charged the claimant, but that he had been under "pressure" to do so from superior officers who told him to lay the charges if there was a prima facie case, because the claimant was an employee of the Police Service. The High Court of Australia held that this "pressure" could constitute evidence of an improper motive, and therefore of malice, on the basis that the dominant purpose of the police officer was not to bring a wrongdoer to justice but to avoid criticism by, or perhaps even secure the favour of, his superiors.

[250] [2014] UKPC 29 at [12].

[251] *Gibbs v Rea* [1998] A.C. 786 at 797 PC, and see *Mitchell v Jenkins* (1833) 5 B. & Ad. 588 at 595; 110 E.R. 908 at 910 (see also para.22-207 onwards).

[252] per Alderson B. in *Stevens v Midland Counties Ry* (1854) 10 Ex. 352 at 356; 156 E.R. 480 at 482. See also *Wershof v Commissioner of Police for the Metropolis* [1978] 3 All E.R. 540.

[253] cf. *Winfield and Jolowicz on Tort*, 19th edn (2014) at [20-016], pointing out that motives are frequently mixed.

[254] See *Gibbs v Rea* [1998] A.C. 786.

[255] *Mitchell v Jenkins* (1833) 5 B. & Ad. 588; 110 E.R. 908; *Brown v Hawkes* [1891] 2 Q.B. 718; *Wershof v Commissioner of Police for the Metropolis* [1978] 3 All E.R. 540. However, the relationship between the absence of reasonable and probable cause for the prosecution and proof of malice can be difficult. "In particular, attempts to reduce that relationship to an aphorism—like, absence of reasonable cause is evidence of malice, but malice is never evidence of want of reasonable cause—may very well mislead. Proof of particular facts may supply evidence of both elements. For example, if the plaintiff demonstrates that a prosecution was launched on obviously insufficient material, the insufficiency of the material may support an inference of malice as well as demonstrate the absence of reasonable and probable cause. No universal rule relating proof of the separate elements can or should be stated": *A v State of New South Wales* [2007] HCA 10; (2007) 81 A.L.J.R. 763 at [90] (citations omitted).

[256] *Hicks v Faulkner* (1878) 8 Q.B.D. 167 at 175; approved by Brett MR in *Quartz Hill Consolidated Gold Mining Co v Eyre* (1883) 11 Q.B.D. 674 at 687.

[257] [2014] UKPC 29.

[258] *Haddrick v Heslop* (1848) 12 Q.B. 267; 116 E.R. 869; cf. *Leibo v Buckman* [1952] 2 All E.R. 1057 at 1064, per Denning LJ (dissenting).

[259] *Clarke v Postan* (1834) 6 C. & P. 423; 172 E.R. 1304; *Stevens v Midland Counties Ry* (1854) 10 Ex. 352; 156 E.R. 480; *Heath v Heape* (1856) 1 H. & N. 478; 156 E.R. 1289; *Busst v Gibbons* (1861) 30 L.J. Ex. 75.

[260] [2018] EWCA Civ 1587.

[261] *Snow v Allen* (1816) 1 Stark, 502; 171 E.R. 543; cf. *Pike v Waldrum* [1952] 1 Lloyd's Rep. 431 at 452.

[262] See *Michell v Williams* (1843) 11 M. & W. 205; 152 E.R. 777.

[263] *Stevens v Midland Counties Ry* (1854) 10 Ex. 352; 156 E.R. 480, but it is not malice when the defendant's motive was to recover his money and he had at that time first to prosecute, i.e. not malice to do something which the law said must be done before civil proceedings could be brought: *Abbott v Refuge Assurance Co Ltd* [1962] 1 Q.B. 432 CA.

[264] *Haddrick v Heslop* (1848) 12 Q.B. 267; 116 E.R. 869.

[264A] [2007] HCA 10; (2007) 81 A.L.J.R. 763.

Application to civil proceedings

Replace paragraph with:

16-56 The meaning of malice should in principle be the same whether the proceedings in issue are civil or criminal. It was made clear in *Willers v Joyce*[265] that malice, and absence of reasonable and probable cause, are two separate requirements. No submissions were made to the Supreme Court in relation to malice in this case, but Lord Mance in the minority expressed concern that the test for malice as it stands could be too inclusive. In particular, Lord Mance thought it clear from the facts of *Crawford Adjusters* that malice can be established where the defendant's "dominant motive" is to injure, even if he also believes the claim to be well founded and intends to "injure" the claimant by pursuing it to judgment.[266] He would have preferred to confine malice to cases where there is actual appreciation on the part of the defendant that the original claim was unfounded. This however does not fit the existing authorities; and it may be added that the need to show absence of reasonable and probable cause provides an extra safeguard. Thus, a civil claimant who is motivated by ill-will, but whose genuine belief in the truth of the allegations is also reasonable, would not be the subject of a successful claim. In determining the trial of the claim in *Willers v Joyce*,[267] Rose J pointed out that,

> "It is difficult to transpose the element of malice or improper motive from the criminal case law to the civil context. Criminal prosecutions are brought in the public interest by an impartial Government agency which has no private interest in the outcome of the proceedings. In contrast, a claimant in a civil action does not need to show any reason why he is bringing the claim other than the desire to recover money to which he is entitled as a matter of law. The court does not generally inquire into whether the motive of a claimant bringing an action is proper or improper. Every judge of the Business & Property Courts has experience of presiding over cases arising out of the unreasoning hatred that is generated when former close friends and business partners fall out. Indeed, part of the function of the judicial process is to provide a non-violent course through which such bitter enmity can be channelled and, one hopes, resolved to some extent by the cathartic process of the trial and judgment. Another difference is that the CPS has only a limited discretion not to pursue a prosecution where there is a good prospect of a conviction. An individual claimant in a civil case (subject to any fiduciary duties as a director, liquidator or executor) has an unfettered discretion to forbear from pursuing a valuable civil claim if he does not want to upset a continuing good relationship with the potential defendant or simply if he does not want the hassle of court proceedings."

Rose J concluded that the question of what will constitute malice for the purpose of prosecution of a civil claim had not been resolved by the Supreme Court in *Willers v Joyce*[268]; and that it is even more entwined with the issue of lack of reasonable and probable cause than where the bringing of a criminal case is in issue. As she had found that Mr Gubay was not in fact the prosecutor of the action in question, and that there was reasonable and probable cause for that claim, she did not need to decide whether Mr Gubay's state of mind amounted to malice.

[265] [2016] UKSC 43; [2018] A.C. 779 at [54].

[266] [2016] UKSC 43; [2018] A.C. 779 at [139].

[267] [2018] EWHC 3424 (Ch) at [280].

[268] [2016] UKSC 43; [2018] A.C. 779.

Replace paragraph with:

Given that in *Martin v Watson*[271] the House of Lords ruled that where it is essentially the evidence of a private person which procures a prosecution by the police that person is to be considered a prosecutor, police whose information motivates the decision to proceed with a prosecution by the Crown Prosecution Service, as well as those who proceed with charges themselves, should be capable of being regarded **16-58** as prosecutors for the purpose of this tort. Indeed it is arguable that they should be more likely to be regarded as prosecutors, since prosecutorial experience is less likely to permit the effective weighing of credibility of the police officers providing information and evidence, than the weighing of credibility of lay witnesses or complainants. However, even if police officers are still held to be prosecutors, when the evidence has been reviewed by lawyers in the Crown Prosecution Service and found sufficient to proceed, proof of absence of reasonable and probable cause may be exceptionally difficult.[272] But it seems it is not impossible. In *Clifford v Chief Constable of Hertfordshire Constabulary*,[273] at first instance, Cranston J accepted the claimant's argument that having launched the prosecution, the police in that case retained a duty to inform the CPS of matters that became known and that were relevant to the prosecution. As such, the police may still be regarded as "prosecuting" the offence for the purposes of tort liability even if the prosecution is transferred to an independent prosecutor. This applies whether it is the police, or the prosecutor, who lays the charges. The question will be whether the conduct of the police, in terms of what they have done or omitted to do in relation to the independent prosecutor, satisfies the components of the tort.[274] These aspects of the decision in *Clifford* were not followed by Mitting J in *Rees v Commissioner of Police of the Metropolis*,[275] on the basis that they were not consistent with decisions regarding witnesses and whether they could be treated as "the prosecutor".[276] Mitting J suggested that "it cannot be that the police become a prosecutor ... merely because after charge they fail to forward some non-trivial information to the CPS relevant to the prosecution".[277] It was possible that if the police deliberately suppress information which would reveal to the CPS that the prosecution had become baseless, that may suffice for the police to be treated as prosecutor; but that would need to be tested in a case where it arose. An appeal from the decision of Mitting J was upheld, but did not consider this point, since the police officer was considered to be "the prosecutor".[277A] Nevertheless, absence of evidence as to subjective belief in the fitness of the case for trial on the part of the officer was sufficient to show absence of reasonable and probable cause. The decision of Mitting J in *Rees* was applied in *Coghlan v Chief Constable of Cheshire Police*,[277B] expressing caution about the comments in *Clifford* and striking out a claim for malicious prosecution against police officers on the basis that they were not prosecutors.[277C]

[271] [1996] 1 A.C. 74. For a recent example concerning the police, see *The Commissioner of the Police of the Metropolis v Copeland* [2014] EWCA Civ 1014; [2015] 3 All E.R. 391 (correct question was whether the policeman was instrumental in bringing the prosecution or was, in substance, the person, or at the very least, a person responsible for the prosecution being brought).

[272] See *Reynolds v Commissioner of Police for the Metropolis* [1985] Q.B. 881 CA.

[273] [2008] EWHC 3154 (QB).

[274] [2008] EWHC 3154 (QB) at [48]-[50]. The decision of Cranston J was reversed on appeal, but not on this point: *Clifford v Chief Constable of Hertfordshire* [2009] EWCA Civ 1259 (the judge had rejected one account of events for reasons which were flawed). The claim of malicious prosecution was ultimately held to be made out at trial: [2011] EWHC 815 (QB).

[275] [2017] EWHC 273 (QB).

[276] See para.16-19 onwards.

[277] [2017] EWHC 273 (QB) at [154].

[277A] [2018] EWCA Civ 1587.

[277B] [2018] EWHC 34 (QB).

[277C] Further, separate claims for malicious prosecution were also struck out in *Coghlan v Chief Constable of Greater Manchester* [2018] EWHC 1784 (QB).

Add to end of paragraph:

At trial, however, Lambert J concluded that there was no evidence to undermine the honesty and integrity of the prosecutor, nor to suggest lack of honest belief in the charge.[283A] **16-60**

[283A] *Rudall v CPS* [2018] EWHC 3287 (QB); [2019] Lloyd's Rep. F.C. 115.

4. MALICIOUS PROCEEDINGS IN BANKRUPTCY AND LIQUIDATION

Malicious proceedings in bankruptcy and liquidation

Replace footnote 300 with:

[300] [2016] UKSC 43; [2018] A.C. 779. **16-64**

5. ABUSE OF CIVIL PROCESS

Scope of the tort: extortion under colour of process

Replace footnote 313 with:

[313] [2016] UKSC 43; [2018] A.C. 779, at [25]. **16-67**

6. VEXATIOUS USE OF PROCESS

No civil action for perjury

Replace footnote 357 with:

[357] *Silcott v Commissioners of Police for the Metropolis* (1996) 8 Admin. L.R. 633 CA; *Gizzonio v Chief Constable of Derbyshire*, *The Times*, 29 April 1998 (no action for malicious denial of bail). The application of the defence to an action in misfeasance was also confirmed in *Hersi & Co v Lord Chancellor* [2018] EWHC 946 (QB). **16-76**

Replace paragraph with:

The immunity of witnesses in court is treated as necessary in the interests of the administration of justice and is based on public policy.[359] This immunity will extend to a prospective witness in giving proof of evidence before the commencement of the trial, since if the witness could be sued on the basis of his witness statement made before the trial this would undermine the basic immunity given to a witness for evidence given in court.[360] The immunity also extends to statements made out of court which could fairly be said to be part of the process of investigating a crime or a possible crime with a view to prosecution.[361] On the other hand, in *Darker v Chief Constable of West Midlands Police*[362] the House of Lords held that the immunity does not extend to the fabrication of evidence which was to be referred to in a statement of evidence. Although, said Lord Hope, there was force in the argument that for the purpose of the immunity there was no logical distinction between making witness statements and investigation and other preparatory conduct with a view to making the witness statements, the predominant requirement of public policy was that claimants who had suffered a wrong should have a right to a remedy. There was a distinction between what a witness says in court (including what a prospective witness states in a witness statement that he will say in court) and the fabrication of evidence. So, for example, the immunity would apply to a witness who falsely stated in the witness box that a suspect had made an oral confession to him, but would not apply to a witness who, in order to support the evidence he would give in court, fabricated a written note containing an admission that the **16-77** suspect had not made.[363] The Court of Appeal in *Singh v Reading BC*[364] also indicated that the immunity would only extend to that necessary to prevent the core immunity in relation to the giving of evidence from being outflanked. Similarly, in *Daniels v Chief Constable of South Wales*[365] it was said that concealment and withholding of evidence would be treated in the same way as fabrication of evidence, and that the immunity was essentially a witness immunity which had been subject to certain "limited but necessary extensions".[366] In *Crawford v Jenkins*[367] the Court of Appeal said that there was a fundamental distinction between claims which involved an abuse of the process of a court, including both malicious prosecution and malicious procurement of a bench warrant[368]; and claims which involved no such abuse of process. It was right as a matter of both principle and policy that in the former category, where the court itself could not be the subject of an action, a claim should be available against the person who procures the misuse of the court's process. However, in a case in the latter category, where a complainant has procured an arrest without invoking a process of the court and where no prosecution follows, in principle the police who carry out the arrest may be liable and thus there is no reason to depart from the usual witness immunity rule. Thus, the defendant in this case, who made a complaint to the police against her former husband leading to his arrest, was protected by the witness immunity rule. In *Hersi & Co v Lord Chancellor*,[368A] it was determined that withholding information in evidence is equivalent to giving misleading evidence, so that any such allegation also falls within the ambit of witness immunity.

[359] *Darker v Chief Constable of West Midlands Police* [2001] 1 A.C. 435 at 445–446, per Lord Hope.

[360] *Watson v M'Ewan* [1905] A.C. 480 at 487. It is irrelevant whether the witness actually gives evidence based on the witness statement: *Darker v Chief Constable of West Midlands Police* [2001] 1 A.C. 435 at 458.

[361] *Taylor v Serious Fraud Office* [1999] 2 A.C. 177.

[362] [2001] 1 A.C. 435.

[363] [2001] 1 A.C. 435 at 469, per Lord Hutton. "The purpose of the immunity is to protect witnesses against claims made against them for something said or done in the course of giving or preparing to give evidence. It is not to be used to shield the police from action for things done while they are acting as law enforcers or investigators", per Lord Hope at [2001] 1 A.C. 435 at 448.

[364] [2013] EWCA Civ 909; [2013] 1 W.L.R. 3052. In this case, it did not apply where the complaint related not to the content of the witness statement (which, it was alleged, had been obtained under pressure by the defendants), but the means by which it had been procured in an action for breach of the claimant's employment contract with the defendants. See also *Smart v The Forensic Science Service Ltd* [2013] EWCA Civ 783; [2013] P.N.L.R. 32 (allegations of deceit and negligence in handling and preparation of exhibits for use in criminal trial not struck out).

[365] [2015] EWCA Civ 680.

[366] [2015] EWCA Civ 680 at [42].

[367] [2014] EWCA Civ 1035; [2016] Q.B. 231; [2015] 1 All E.R. 476.

[368] *Roy v Prior* [1971] A.C. 470.

[368A] [2018] EWHC 946 (QB) at [115].

CHAPTER 17

WRONGFUL INTERFERENCE WITH GOODS

TABLE OF CONTENTS

2. CONVERSION

(a) Forms of conversion

(i) Conversion by taking or receiving property

Taking and using or interfering with goods

Replace paragraph with:

17-11 A mere transitory exercise of dominion, such as unlawfully "borrowing" or using goods, may still amount to conversion. "If a man takes my horse and rides it and then redelivers it to me nevertheless I may have an action against him, for this is a conversion, and the redelivery is no bar to the action but shall be merely a mitigation of damages."[45] Thus in *Kuwait Airways Corp v Iraqi Airways Co*[46] Iraqi forces unlawfully expropriated a number of Kuwaiti airliners and the defendants' pilots then ferried them from Kuwait to Iraq. This ferrying was assumed all along to amount to a conversion of the aircraft involved.[47] And again, in New Zealand it has been held that unlawfully taking a car for a joy-ride is equally a conversion of it[48]; and in England that the same goes for an estranged partner who takes papers and sends them to her solicitors to be copied for use in divorce proceedings.[49] In short, any taking of a chattel for the use of the defendant or a third party potentially amounts to a conversion,[50] and the fact that the defendant did not intend permanently to deprive the owner of his property is of itself not conclusive.[51] It follows that, if a defendant wrongfully takes and uses the chattel of another, and without further default on his part it is lost or damaged before it can be returned to the owner, he is potentially liable for the whole damage.[52] In *384238 Ontario Ltd v R.*[53] the Canadian Federal Court of Appeal held that when the Crown detained stock under the mistaken belief that they had a lien over it, but gave it back three days later when they realised their mistake, they were not liable in conversion. It is submitted, with respect, that this is wrong.[54] The essence of conversion lies in the exercise of dominion contrary to the owner's interest, and the fact that the defendant does not use what he keeps should be irrelevant.[55]

[45] *Rolle* Ab.tit. Action sur Case, p.5; *Lord Petrie v Heneage* (1701) 12 Mod. 519 at 520, per Holt CJ (unauthorised wearing of another's pearl); *Model Dairy Co Ltd v White* (1935) 41 Arg. L.R. 432; and *Milk Bottles Recovery Ltd v Camillo* [1948] V.L.R. 344 (use by defendants of others' milk bottles for delivery of their own milk). Cf. *Penfolds Wines Pty Ltd v Elliot* (1946) 74 C.L.R. 204 and S. Douglas, "The Nature of Conversion" [2009] C.L.J. 189, 203. American authority may be different here, with

frequent suggestions that a very transitory use is often said not to be conversion: see *Prosser on Torts*, 5th edn (West Group, 1984), 101 and, e.g. *Jeffries v Pankow*, 229 P. 963 (Ore 1928).

[46] [1995] 1 W.L.R. 1147, appealed to the House of Lords on other grounds: [2002] UKHL 19; [2002] 2 A.C. 883.

[47] In the event the defendants' acts in so doing were held protected by sovereign immunity. But subsequent acts done in relation to the aircraft, not cloaked by sovereign immunity, were held to amount to actionable conversion: *Kuwait Airways Corp v Iraqi Airways Co* [2002] UKHL 19; [2002] 2 A.C. 883.

[48] *Aitken Agencies Ltd v Richardson* [1967] N.Z.L.R. 65, approved by Allsop J in *Bunnings Group Ltd v CHEP Australia Ltd* [2011] NSWCA 342; (2012) 82 N.S.W.L.R. 420 at [138]. See too *Tongue v RSPCA* [2017] EWHC 2508 (Ch); [2018] B.P.I.R. 229, especially at [93] (removing cattle from claimant's farm to another with no right to do so).

[49] See *White v Withers LLP* [2009] EWCA Civ 1122; [2009] 3 F.C.R. 435. In the Court of Appeal Wilson and Sedley LJJ at [73] and [84] suggested that if the evidence was ultimately admissible in the matrimonial proceedings this should equally immunise the defendant against liability in tort; Ward LJ at [57]–[58] doubted whether this was so. In *Imerman v Tchenguiz* [2010] EWCA Civ 908; [2011] Fam. 116 at [36]–[53], [116]–[117], the Court of Appeal trenchantly, and it is suggested rightly, upheld Ward LJ's minority view.

[50] per Alderson B in *Fouldes v Willoughby* (1841) 8 M. & W. 540 at 548. See too, per Holt CJ in *Petre v Heneage* (1701) 12 Mod. 519 at 520; *Mulgrave v Ogden* (1590) Cro. Eliz. 219.

[51] *The Playa Larga* [1983] 2 Lloyd's Rep. 171 (person causing ship to sail away with claimant's sugar on board liable even though he took no part in subsequent sale of sugar to third party). The passage in the text (para.21-12 of the 15th edn) was quoted at p.181. See too *Brandeis Goldschmidt Ltd v Western Transport Ltd* [1981] Q.B. 864. See too *Tongue v RSPCA* [2017] EWHC 2508 (Ch); [2018] B.P.I.R. 229, especially at [92]–[93] (conversion for RSPCA to move cattle from absent farmer's land to another farm where they could be better cared for).

[52] This paragraph was approved by Mance J in *Kuwait Airways v Iraqi Airways Co* [1999] C.L.C. 31 (upheld without discussion of the point: [2002] UKHL 19; [2002] 2 A.C. 883).

[53] (1984) 8 D.L.R. (4th) 676. Note that this decision can be supported on an alternative ground: i.e. that the claimant was estopped from asserting his rights.

[54] This passage was cited by Mance J, without disapproval, in *Kuwait Airways v Iraqi Airways* [1999] C.L.C. 31 (appealed on other grounds: [2002] UKHL 19; [2002] 2 A.C. 883).

[55] cf. the position where goods are wrongfully retained after a demand for their return; here the question whether the defendant uses them is irrelevant. See, e.g. *Brandeis Goldschmidt Ltd v Western Transport Ltd* [1981] Q.B. 864.

Replace footnote 56 with:

[56] Conversion must be "an interference with the property which would not, as against the true owner, be justified, or at least excused, in one who came lawfully into the possession of the goods" (Lord Blackburn in *Hollins v Fowler* (1875) L.R. 7 H.L. 757, 766, followed by Allsop P in *Bunnings Group Ltd v CHEP Australia Ltd* [2011] NSWCA 342; (2012) 82 N.S.W.L.R. 420 at [149]). Thus it has been said that mistakenly and momentarily taking the wrong hat from a rack is not conversion: J. Fleming, *The Law of Torts*, 10th edn (Thomson Reuters, 2011), para.4.100. See too *ACN 116746859 v Lunapas Pty Ltd* [2017] NSWSC 1583 at [111] ("The mere detention or the mere handling of a plaintiff's goods will not necessarily amount to conversion by a defendant. But once the degree of use amounts to employing the goods as if they were owned, then a conversion is established. That point can be reached without any subjective intention to convert the goods"). **17-12**

(ii) Conversion by transfer of property

Misdelivery by bailee

Replace footnote 88 with:

[88] *Motis Exports Ltd v Dampskibsselskabet AF 1912, Aktieselskab* [1999] 1 Lloyd's Rep. 837 (affirmed on other grounds, [2001] 1 Lloyd's Rep. 211). For a more up-to-date example involving electronic delivery and the use of a hacked PIN number, see *Glencore International AG v MSC Mediterranean Shipping Co SA* [2017] EWCA Civ 365; [2017] 2 Lloyd's Rep. 186. **17-19**

(iii) *Conversion by loss: the case of the bailee*

Goods lost or destroyed

Replace footnote 102 with:

17-21 [102] *Ross v Johnson* (1772) 5 Burr. 2825; see *Heald v Carey* (1852) 11 C.B. 977. See also *Newman v Bourne & Hollingsworth Ltd* (1915) 31 T.L.R. 209, *Volcafe Ltd v Cia Sud Americana de Vapores* [2018] UKSC 61; [2019] A.C. 358 at [9]–[10] (Lord Sumption). Before 1978 the bailee was also liable in detinue: see para.17-03.

(b) Subject matter of conversion

Tangible and intangible property

Replace footnote 175 with:

17-36 [175] *Thunder Air Ltd v Hilmarsson* [2008] EWHC 355 (Ch). See too *Your Response Ltd v Datateam Business Media Ltd* [2014] EWCA Civ 281; [2015] Q.B. 41 (partly on basis that intangible material in database not subject to conversion, no possibility of having a lien over it). See too *Capita Plc v Darch* [2017] EWHC 1248 (Ch); [2017] I.R.L.R. 718 at [67]–[74] (emails).

Realty when severed

Replace paragraph 17-39 with:

17-39 There can be no conversion of land.[193] But if a portion of realty is severed and taken away, the owner, instead of suing in respect of the injury to be realty, may elect to treat the severed portion as his chattel and sue for its conversion. In this way a remedy may be obtained for coal wrongfully worked, timber wrongfully cut, or fixtures wrongfully removed.[194] However, there must be severance; while chattels remain fixed to the realty no action in conversion lies, even if (as in the case of tenant's fixtures) they are chattels which the claimant has a right to take away.[195]

[193] However, title-deeds, though by a quirk of the law not regarded as personalty, can form the subject-matter of conversion: see *Plant v Cotterill* (1860) 5 H. & N. 430. But today, now that such deeds are of relatively minor importance in establishing rights, this is not of great significance. See too, following the text here, *Plantation Holdings (FZ) LLC v Dubai Islamic Bank PJSC* [2017] EWHC 520 (Comm) at [252] (no conversion of a leasehold interest).

[194] *Berry v Heard* (1637) Cro. Car. 242; *Wood v Morewood* (1841) 3 Q.B. 440n; *Mills v Brooker* [1919] 1 K.B. 555; *Belgrave Nominees P/L v Berlin-Scott Air Conditioning P/L* [1984] V.R. 947. For a colourful contemporary instance, see the outré decision in *Creative Foundation v Dreamland Leisure Ltd* [2015] EWHC 2556 (Ch); [2016] Ch. 253 (valuable graffiti by modish street artist peeled off). See also *Gibson v. F.K. Developments Ltd* 2017 BCSC 2153 (cutting down a tree).

[195] *Mackintosh v Trotter* (1838) 3 M. & W. 184. But there may, however, be a special action on the case if there be an interference with the exercise of the right of removal; see *London and Westminster Loan and Discount Co v Drake* (1859) 6 C. & B. (N.S.) 798.

17-41 *Replace footnote 203:*

Dead bodies

[203] R. Atherton, "Who owns your body?" (2003) 77 A.L.J. 178; J. Wall, "The legal status of body parts: a framework" (2011) 31 O.J.L.S. 783; N. Palmer and E. McKendrick (eds), *Interests in Goods*, 2nd edn (Informa Law, Routledge, 1998), Ch.2; S. Green and J. Randall, *The Tort of Conversion* (Oxford: Hart, 2009), p.115 onwards; S. Douglas and I. Goold, "Property in human biomaterials: a new methodology" [2016] C.L.J. 478; S. Walpole, "Property in human bodily products" (2019) 135 L.Q.R. 31.

Replace paragraph with:

17-41 It has been said that there is no property in a corpse.[204] However, it now seems clear that this exception, in so far as it remains at all, is a very narrow one. To begin with, there is venerable authority that once a body has undergone a process or other application of human skill, such as stuffing or embalming, it can be the subject of property in the ordinary way.[205] And the same goes for body parts: thus in the grisly case of *R. v Kelly*[206] robbers who abstracted and sold preserved anatomical specimens from the Royal College of Surgeons' collection were held rightly convicted of theft. Furthermore, in *Yearworth v North Bristol NHS Trust*[207] the Court of Appeal doubted whether there was even a need for the application of a process of human skill. It is suggested that these doubts were well-founded. Take the case of bodies and body parts which have not been subject to any such process, but are legitimately wanted for some other purpose, such as accident investigation or use as an exhibit in court. Despite the earlier suggestions to the contrary,[208] there seems no reason in principle why they should not be subject to property rights: it would certainly be odd if they could be purloined by any passer-by with impunity.[209] In so far as there can be property in corpses or parts thereof, presumably it will vest initially in the first possessor.[210] It should also be noted that, even if there is no property in a corpse, personal representatives or other persons charged with the duty of burying a body have certain rights to its custody and possession in the interim,[211] infringements of which are actionable.[212] But this right does not include a right to the return of organs lawfully removed for post-mortem or similar purposes.[213] Also, by statute[214] relatives also have certain powers in relation to the use of a body for medical purposes.

[204] See Blackstone, *Commentaries*, 15th edn (1809), Bk II, Ch.28, 429; *Handyside's case* (1749) 2 East P.C. 652 (unsuccessful claim in trover against doctor for bodies of Siamese twins); *R. v Sharpe* (1857) Dears. & B. 160 at 163; *Williams v Williams* (1882) 20 Ch D. 659, 665; see too *Takamore v Clarke* [2012] NZSC 116; [2013] 2 N.Z.L.R. 733 at [70] (Elias CJ: no action in conversion by next-of-kin). In *Dobson v North Tyneside Health Authority* [1997] 1 W.L.R. 596 it was held that the next-of-kin had no property in a corpse or part of it: but that is a slightly different matter, and leaves open the issue of property as such.

[205] *Doodeward v Spence* (1908) 6 C.L.R. 406 (grisly museum exhibit consisting of stillborn child with two heads: action in detinue succeeded). Hence it is submitted that conversion would lie for a skeleton or cadaver, or part of it, used for research or exhibition: cf. *Re Organ Retention Group Litigation* [2004] EWHC 644 (QB); [2005] Q.B. 506 at [148]; [2004] Fam. Law 501. And compare *Masson v Westside Cemeteries Ltd* (1996) 135 D.L.R. (4th) 361 (ashes deposited in vault: next-of-kin successfully sued cemetery as bailees when it lost them).

[206] [1999] Q.B. 621.

[207] [2009] EWCA Civ 37; [2010] Q.B. 1. See particularly at [45], per Lord Judge CJ. Also note the British Columbia case of *JCM v ANA* 2012 BCSC 584; (2012) 349 D.L.R. (4th) 471.

[208] *Dobson v North Tyneside AHA* [1997] 1 W.L.R. 596 (deceased's brain pickled in paraffin for use at inquest, then disposed of: next-of-kin sue for conversion. Held: not equivalent to stuffing or embalming, and no property arose); see too *Re Cresswell* [2018] QSC 142 at [152]–[161]. But the case could equally well be decided on the basis that if property did arise, it was not vested in the next-of-kin anyway.

[209] Cf. *R. v Kelly* [1999] Q.B. 621 at 631, where Rose LJ thought it not unarguable that property would inhere. See generally S. Douglas and I. Goold, "Property in human biomaterials: a new methodology" [2016] C.L.J. 478. Cf., however, *Re Lee* [2018] 2 N.Z.L.R. 731, where Heath J in the New Zealand High Court denied that there could as a matter of law be property in sperm taken from a dead man.

[210] The statement in the text was accepted by Gage J in *Re Organ Retention Group Litigation* [2004] EWHC 644 (QB); [2005] Q.B. 506 at [156] (parents have no right to sue in conversion or any analogous tort where organs removed for post-mortem purposes and then kept). Compare *Dobson v North Tyneside AHA* [1997] 1 W.L.R. 596.

[211] *Takamore v Clarke* [2012] NZSC 116; [2013] 2 N.Z.L.R. 733 at [73] (Elias CJ). As to who has the right to bury, it seems that in the case of a child it is the parents (e.g. *R. v Vann* (1851) 2 Den. 325), and in the case of anyone else the executor or administrator: cf. *Smith v Tamworth City* (1997) 41 N.S.W.L.R. 680. If there is no such person it is the person with the best right to a grant of administration: *Burrows v HM Coroner for Preston* [2008] EWHC 1387; [2008] 2 F.L.R. 1225 (QB) at [13] (Cranston J). If matters are unclear it is the person in good faith de facto possession, but the decision of the person concerned is challengeable in court if wholly unreasonable: *Grandison v Nembhard* (1989) 4 B.M.L.R. 140, 143 (Vinelott J). See too H. Conway, "Frozen Corpses and Feuding Parents: Re JS (Disposal of Body)" (2018) 81 M.L.R. 132.

[212] So held in Canada: *Edmunds v Armstrong Funeral Home Ltd* [1931] 1 D.L.R. 676. Similarly a New Zealand court has held the right enforceable by injunction: *Murdoch v Rhind* [1945] N.Z.L.R. 425 (prevention of burial outside family plot). Cf. *Pollok v Workman* (1900) 2 F. 354 and *Hughes v Robertson*, 1913 S.C. 394. All these cases concerned unauthorised post-mortems. US authority is largely to the same effect: e.g. *Torres v State of New York*, 228 N.Y.S. 2d 1005 (1962). In *Re Organ Retention Group Litigation* [2004] EWHC 644 (QB); [2005] Q.B. 506, Gage J seemed willing provisionally to accept this conclusion.

[213] *Re Organ Retention Group Litigation* [2004] EWHC 644 (QB); [2005] Q.B. 506. Note however *MacKenzie v Att-Gen* [2015] NZHC 191 at [68]–[75], where the holding in the *Organ Retention* case was doubted in New Zealand.

[214] See Human Tissue Act 2004 Pt I.

Human tissue

Replace paragraph with:

17-42 A living person, and organs within him, cannot be owned or possessed.[216] It follows that the proper cause of action for unlawful removal of an organ is assault, rather than conversion.[217] However, substances produced by a living person are on principle subject to the ordinary rules of property. After some doubt, this was made clear by the Court of Appeal in *Yearworth v North Bristol NHS Trust*,[218] where donors of sperm samples were allowed to bring proceedings in breach of bailment against a hospital which negligently allowed them to spoil, thus causing them distress. On the other hand, it should be remembered that, even if there are rights of property in sensitive human productions such as sperm or organs, the owner's rights to deal with such material are severely limited under the Human Fertilisation and Embryology Act 1990 and the Human Tissue Act 2004. The removal of tissue from a dead person without relatives' consent may also raise issues of art.8 and on occasion art.3 of the ECHR.[218A]

[216] See *R. v Bentham* [2005] UKHL 18; [2005] 1 W.L.R. 1057 (person using fingers as make-believe gun could not be convicted of "possessing" imitation firearm); *Yearworth v North Bristol NHS Trust* [2009] EWCA Civ 37; [2010] Q.B. 1 at [30]; *Re Cresswell* [2018] QSC 142 at [126]. This is salutary, since otherwise the recipient of a transplanted organ would potentially be liable as a converter. See generally N. Palmer and E. McKendrick (eds), *Interests in Goods*, 2nd edn, Ch.2. It is also arguable that s.32 of the Human Tissue Act 2004, prohibiting commercial dealings in organs for transplant, shows a legislative intent to preclude claims for damages reckoned by their value.

[217] Cf. *Moore v Regents of the University of California*, 793 P.2d 479 (1990) (not conversion to use patient's excised spleen for profitable biotechnology development, though it was a breach of physician's fiduciary duty).

[218] [2009] EWCA Civ 37; [2010] Q.B. 1; also *Bazley v Wesley Monash IVF Pty Ltd* [2010] QSC 118; [2011] 2 Qd R. 207 (though cf. *Re Edwards* [2011] NSWSC 478; (2011) 4 A.S.T.L.R. 392, where the court was regarded as having a discretion to allot the substance to whoever it thought just). See too *R. v Welsh* [1974] R.T.R. 478 and *R. v Rothery* [1976] R.T.R. 550 (alleged drunk drivers properly convicted of theft of samples of own urine); and generally L. Skene, "Property Interests in Human Bodily Material" (2012) 20 Med. L. Rev. 227.

[218A] See *Elberte v Latvia* (2015) 61 E.H.R.R. 7 and R. Neethu, "Elberte v Latvia: The to be or Not to be Question of Consent" (2017) 25 Med. L. Rev 484.

(c) Persons entitled to sue

(i) Generally

Claimant must have possession or immediate right to possession

Add to end of paragraph:

17-43 The holder of a bill of lading has for these purposes a right to immediate possession of the goods it relates to, and this remains the case (it seems) even if it is an order bill and there has been no endorsement of it to him.[223A]

[223A] *Cro Travel Pty Ltd v Australia Capital Financial Management Pty Ltd* [2018] NSWCA 153 at [232]–[256], following the antique authority of *Meyer v Sharpe* (1813) 5 Taunt 79.

(iii) Title to sue by virtue of immediate right to possession

Immediate right to possession

After "Just as mere possession will found an action in conversion, so also will an immediate right to possession.", add new footnote 288A:

[288A] So in *Jeddi v Sotheby's* [2018] EWHC 1491 (Comm) the bailor of a valuable pot was held able to sue without reference to whether he was in fact the true owner. **17-59**

Bailment at will

Replace footnote 311 with:

[311] (1849) 4 Ex. 339; and see *Jelks v Hayward* [1905] 2 K.B. 460 and *Jeddi v Sotheby's* [2018] EWHC 1491 (Comm) (jar merely bailed to acquaintance: bailor can recover it from auctioneer). In *East West Corp v DKBS 1912* [2003] EWCA Civ 83; [2003] Q.B. 1509, Mance LJ doubted whether a person who delivered a bill of lading relating to goods to a bank to be held to his order could sue for conversion of the goods it represented. Sed quaere: this seems contrary to principle. See Baughen [2003] L.M.C.L.Q. 413. **17-63**

(d) Position of defendant

(ii) Conversion wrongful unless excused

Replace footnote 338 with:

[338] *R. (Coleman) v Governor of Wayland Prison* [2009] EWHC 1005 (Admin); *The Times*, 23 April 2009. The general principle remains, but the actual decision has been reversed by statute: see the Prison Act 1952 s.42A, inserted by the Prisons (Property) Act 2013. Similarly the fact that the defendant acted from good motives is irrelevant. See *Tongue v RSPCA* [2017] EWHC 2508 (Ch); [2018] B.P.I.R. 229, especially at [92]–[93] (conversion for RSPCA to move cattle without permission from absent farmer's land to another farm where they could be better cared for); also *Maitland Hudson v Solicitors Regulation Authority* [2017] EWHC 1249 (Ch) (arguable case of conversion where SRA handed over claimant's HDDs to partner with whom in dispute, in order to help latter prepare defence). **17-70**

(iii) Defendant's ignorance of claimant's right generally no defence

Defendant's ignorance of claimant's right generally irrelevant

After "is likely to find himself with no defence. Nevertheless, two", add:

qualifications need noting. First, the fact that he has acted in good **17-71**

(iv) Exceptional cases where ignorance of claimant's title a defence

Agent not intending to alter property

Replace footnote 356 with:

[356] See the case put by Bramwell LJ in *Cochrane v Rymill* (1879) 40 L.T. 744, 746. If he knows that the sale he is procuring is wrongful and infringes the claimant's possessory rights, he may however be liable for procuring a conversion. Compare *Wolff v Trinity Logistics USA Inc* [2018] EWCA Civ 2765 at [28]. **17-75**

Miscellaneous statutory protections

Replace paragraph with:

17-79 Commercial considerations necessitate some statutory mitigation of the normally strict liability of the converter. Four instances are particularly worth noting. First, in the case of cheques, a bank is strictly liable at common law if it collects a cheque for payment into its customer's account to which the customer in fact has no title.[373] However, s.4 of the Cheques Act 1957[374] now protects the bank provided it can show it acted in good faith and without negligence. The authorities on this section are legion and complex, and the reader is referred to specialist works on banking law for details.[375] Secondly, protection is now available in certain cases of insolvency. Thus ss.307(4) and 346(7) of the Insolvency Act 1986 shield a person who deals for value with a bankrupt's property not knowing of the bankruptcy, and hence in ignorance of the fact that property concerned will have ipso facto vested in the trustee in bankruptcy. And, perhaps more significantly, s.234(3) of the same Act provides that a liquidator, receiver or administrator who seizes what appears to be the company's property[376] is not liable in damages[377] to the true owner unless he had reasonable grounds for believing he was not entitled to act as he did.[377A] Thirdly, s.117 of the Consumer Credit Act 1974 now protects a pawnbroker from liability provided he hands over the pledge to someone producing the pawn receipt.[378] He need not concern himself with whether that person is in fact the true owner of the goods. Fourthly, under the Tribunals, Courts and Enforcement Act 2007 Pt 3, (which replaces the previous process of execution with a statutory procedure), the enforcement agent who replaces the sheriff is given extensive protection from liability in respect of seizure of goods that seem to, but in fact do not, belong to the debtor.[379]

[373] e.g. *Capital & Counties Bank Ltd v Gordon* [1903] A.C. 240.

[374] Replacing the slightly narrower s.82 of the Bills of Exchange Act 1882; see also s.80 of the same Act.

[375] e.g. *Ellinger's Modern Banking Law*, 5th edn (2011), Chs.10–11.

[376] But apparently only tangible property: see *Welsh Development Agency v Export Finance* [1992] B.C.L.C. 148 at 171, 190.

[377] A significant limitation. If the liquidator, etc. sells the property, presumably his liability to account for the sale proceeds—whether by way of an action for money had and received or a tracing action—remains. Such a liability is not a liability in damages.

[377A] Note that he is similarly protected from later misfeasance proceedings: see s.304(3) of the 1986 Act, and the decision in *Birdi v Price* [2018] EWHC 2943 (Ch); [2019] Bus. L.R. 489 (technicalities of the tools of trade exception in bankruptcy: no negligence shown).

[378] Even, apparently, if the pawnbroker knows of the lack of title. Presumably, however, the section refers to the actual receipt: a pawnbroker handing over the goods against a forgery, however undetectable, seemingly falls outside the umbrella of s.117 and is therefore strictly liable.

[379] See Sch.12 paras 63–68. Many of the protections depend on reasonable belief, on which see *Rooftops South West Ltd v Ash Interiors (UK) Ltd* [2018] EWHC 2799 (QB).

3. REMEDIES FOR CONVERSION

(a) Orders for delivery

(i) Judgment for specific delivery

Judgment for specific delivery and consequential damages

Replace footnote 433 with:

[433] See, e.g. *Blue Sky One Ltd v Blue Airways LLC* [2009] EWHC 3314 (Comm) (jumbo jets accepted to be commercially unique; but specific delivery still refused, since no undue prejudice would be suffered by the claimants who held them largely with a view to leasing) (see [314]–[316]); *Dawsonrentals Bus and Coaches Ltd v Geldards Coaches Ltd* [2015] EWHC 2596 (QB) (specific return of leased buses used for school transport delayed for a week, to allow school authorities to find alternative transport). See too *Sharma v Plumridge*, unreported 22 May 1991 CA (no specific delivery of pet dogs owing to passage of time). Another instance is the county court case of *Probert v Society for the Welfare of Horses*, Pontypool County Court, reported in the *Daily Telegraph* for 1 February 1997. The owner of a horse was convicted of mistreating it and fined; the animal was later removed and unlawfully kept by the defendant charity. The judge refused an order for specific delivery against the charity, despite the claimant's impeccable title. Human rights considerations may also militate against the grant of the remedy, it seems: see *Capita Plc v Darch* [2017] EWHC 1248 (Ch); [2017] I.R.L.R. 718 at [67]–[74] (demand for handover of emails, even if sounding in conversion—which it did not—might well be met with an art.8 defence concerning privacy). **17-89**

(b) Damages

Replace footnote 447: **17-93**

General rule: value of the goods

[447] See generally Edelman, *McGregor on Damages*, 20th edn (London: Sweet & Maxwell, 2017), para.38-006 onwards; A. Tettenborn, "Damages in Conversion—The Exception or the Anomaly?" [1993] C.L.J. 128.

Damages for deprivation of goods

Replace paragraph with:

In theory, conversion is no different from any other tort: the measure of damages is simply the loss suffered by the claimant.[448] In practice, however, the measure of damages for deprivation of his goods is nearly always their market value.[449] To some extent this is an arbitrary rule, not dependent on the claimant's loss. Thus, for example, an owner of goods is entitled to recover their value even if the defendant proves that the claimant would have been deprived of his goods in any event, and hence that the claimant has, in some sense, suffered no loss at all—a rule which doubtless reflects considerations of simplicity and public policy as anything else.[450] So in *Kuwait Airways Corp v Iraqi Airways Co*[451] aircraft forcibly removed by Iraqi forces invading Kuwait were converted by the defendant airline. The House of Lords rebuffed a plea by the defendants that the claimants would in any case have been kept out of their property as a result of the activities of the Iraqi army. In addition the claimant is entitled to recover any special loss which flows naturally and directly from the wrong.[452] Where goods are repeatedly converted, prima facie each conversion is a separate tort carrying a separate liability.[453] **17-93**

[448] "The aim of the law, in respect of the wrongful interference with goods, is to provide a just remedy. Despite its proprietary base, this tort does not stand apart and command awards of damages measured by some special and artificial standard of its own … . The fundamental object of an award of damages in respect of this tort, as with all wrongs, is to award just compensation for loss suffered." (Lord Nicholls in *Kuwait Airways v Iraq Airways Co* [2002] UKHL 19; [2002] 2 A.C. 883 at [67]). See too *Brandeis*

Goldschmidt & Co Ltd v Western Transport Ltd [1981] Q.B. 864 at 870, per Brandon LJ; *VFS Financial Services Ltd v Euro Auctions Ltd* [2007] EWHC 1492 (QB) at [102]; *Checkprice (UK) Ltd (in administration) v Revenue & Customs Commissioners* [2010] EWHC 682 (Admin); [2010] S.T.C. 1153 at [56] (Sales J). Also *Plantation Holdings (FZ) LLC v Dubai Islamic Bank PJSC* [2017] EWHC 520 (Comm) at [256] (Picken J).

[449] "Normally ("prima facie") the measure of damages is the market value of the goods at the time the defendant expropriated them. This is the general rule, because generally this measure represents the amount of the basic loss suffered by the claimant owner. He has been dispossessed of his goods by the defendant." (Lord Nicholls in *Kuwait Airways v Iraq Airways Co* [2002] UKHL 19; [2002] 2 A.C. 883 at [67].). It has been said that departures from the value of the goods as the measure of damages, while entirely permissible, are rare: see *Blue Sky One Ltd v Mahan Air* [2010] EWHC 631 (Comm) at [114] (Beatson J). See too, also suggesting a strong predilection for the value of the goods, *Al-Khyami v El-Muderris* [2018] EWHC 24 (QB) at [75].

[450] S. Douglas, "The Nature of Conversion" [2009] C.L.J. 198, 220, perceptively suggests as much. In any case the disregard of what would otherwise have happened to the goods applies only to value claims, and not (for example) to consequential losses, where causation must be proved in the ordinary way: see *Glenmorgan Farm Ltd v New Zealand Bloodstock Leasing Ltd* [2011] NZCA 672; [2012] 1 N.Z.L.R. 555.

[451] [2002] UKHL 19; [2002] 2 A.C. 883. See too *Kuwait Airways Corp v Iraqi Airways Co (No.10)* [2002] EWHC 1626 (Comm).

[452] *Re Simms* [1934] 1 Ch.1 CA. See para.17-108 onwards, for consequential damages.

[453] cf. *RB Policies* at Lloyds v Butler [1950] 1 K.B. 76 (a limitation case). In *Middle Temple v Lloyds Bank Plc* [1999] All E.R. (Comm) 193 and *Linklaters v HSBC Bank Plc* [2003] EWHC 1113 (Comm); [2003] 2 Lloyd's Rep. 545 it was suggested, obiter, that there might be contribution between serial converters under s.1 of the Civil Liability (Contribution) Act 1978. *Sed quaere*. If the two conversions took place on different occasions, were both defendants liable for the "same damage" as required by s.1(1) of that Act? It seems doubtful.

Presumption of value against wrongdoer?

Replace paragraph with:

17-99 Where there is a doubt about the value of a chattel which has passed wrongfully into the possession of a defendant, there is some authority that he must either produce it or account for its non-production, or otherwise it will be assumed against him that it was of the highest possible value.[483] But the authority is somewhat dated, and it is suggested that the courts today are more likely to insist on proper proof of value by the claimant.[484] Thus where a Hatton Garden jeweller lost diamonds entrusted to him, but there was no clear evidence of their quality, Field J understandably declined to give the claimant an almost certain windfall by awarding damages on the assumption that all the diamonds had been "finest quality" (the highest grade in the diamond trade).[485] On the other hand, where miscellaneous items of relatively low value are involved, courts may in practice award a fairly rough-and-ready figure without demanding meticulous proof.[485A]

[483] *Armory v Delamirie* (1721) 1 Stra. 505.

[484] In the British Columbia decision in *Bangle v Lafreniere* 2012 BCSC 256; 214 A.C.W.S. (3d) 309 at [39], Sewell J said that the "maximum value" presumption applied "only in situations in which the wrongful conduct of the defendant makes it impracticable for the plaintiff to value the loss." Cf. *Williamson v Phillips, Son & Neale*, unreported 29 July 1998 (presumption referred to in *Armory v Delamirie*, above, only applies, if at all, where other evidence entirely lacking).

[485] *Colbeck v Diamanta (UK) Ltd* [2002] EWHC 616 (QB).

[485A] See the trespass to goods case of *Diaz v Karim* [2017] EWHC 595 (QB) (unlawful eviction of student from lodging: items of personal property thrown out and lost: round figure of £5,000 awarded).

(ii) Damages beyond value of goods: special damages

Aggravated and exemplary damages

Replace footnote 509 with:

509 *Owen & Smith v Reo Motors (Britain) Ltd* [1934] All E.R. Rep. 734 (high-handed deprivation of car). See too *King v Gross* (2008) 443 A.R. 214 (obsessive dog-lover kidnapping, secreting and spaying breeder's prize Shih-Tzu). See also *Al-Khyami v El-Muderris* [2018] EWHC 24 (QB) at [77]. **17-107**

Consequential damage

Replace paragraph with:

The claimant may recover all such damages as are the natural and direct result of the conversion, for example the cost of seeking out the chattel converted,[513] or hiring a replacement for it,[514] litigation costs against third parties,[515] or (where appropriate) a rise in value between the time of conversion and the time of judgment.[516] In the case of conversion by refusal to hand over goods there may be a claim for deterioration and accruing storage charges.[517] In the case of conversion amounting to a public aspersion on the claimant's ownership or business integrity, damages may reflect that fact.[518] A defendant may, it seems, be liable for specific profits lost owing to the claimant being deprived of the chattel,[519] or for the loss of a contract for the purchase of it.[520] However, the mere abstract capacity for profitable use is normally reckoned as included in the capital value; where it is, the loss of such use is not a separate head of damage, since otherwise there would be double recovery.[521] In *Maitland Hudson v Solicitors Regulation Authority*[521A] it was said that consequential damages could never be barred under the rules of novus actus interveniens. This may, with respect, go too far. True, a convertor cannot plead that goods would have been lost anyway through third-party action,[521B] but an extension of this to all consequential losses might lead to bizarre results and must remain open to doubt. **17-108**

513 *Aziz v Lim* [2012] EWHC 915 (QB) at [117] (diamonds wrongfully sold, ending up in the hands of Swiss buyers: owner can claim cost of seeking out, and attempting to recover possession of, diamonds in Geneva)

514 On which, see the negligence case of *Lagden v O'Connor* [2003] UKHL 64; [2004] 1 A.C. 1067 (if claimant's financial position such that he has to pay an increased rate of hire, he can claim the full amount).

515 As in *Trafigura Beheer BV v Mediterranean Shipping Co SA* [2007] EWHC 944 (Comm); [2007] 2 All E.R. (Comm) 149 (copper converted by carrier; costs of litigation with third parties recoverable). The point was not raised on appeal (see [2007] EWCA Civ 794; [2008] 1 All E.R. (Comm) 385).

516 See *The Playa Larga* [1983] 2 Lloyd's Rep. 171; para.17-95.

517 *Uzinterimpex JSC v Standard Bank Plc* [2008] EWCA Civ 819; [2008] 2 Lloyd's Rep. 456 (though the claim there failed on mitigation grounds).

518 *Ecclestone v Khyami* [2014] EWHC 29 (QB) at [152]-[160] (Dingemans J) (though the claim failed on the facts).

519 *Bodley v Reynolds* (1846) 8 Q.B. 779 (carpenter's tools: loss of employment).

520 *Williams v Peel River Land Co* (1886) 55 L.T. 689; *Oakley v Lyster* [1931] 1 K.B. 148. And see *Michael v Hart* [1901] 2 K.B. 867

521 *Reid v Fairbanks* (1853) 13 C.B. 692; cf. *The Llanover* [1947] P. 80.

521A [2017] EWHC 1249 (Ch).

521B See *Kuwait Airways Corp v Iraqi Airways Co (No.6)* [2002] UKHL 19; [2002] 2 A.C. 883 at [546]; [609]–[615]

Loss of hire or use-value

Replace footnote 532 with:

17-111 [532] *Strand Electric and Engineering Co Ltd v Brisford Entertainments Ltd* [1952] 2 Q.B. 246. See too *Inverugie Investments Ltd v Hackett* [1995] 1 W.L.R. 713, per Lord Lloyd; *Ministry of Defence v Ashman* [1993] 2 E.G.L.R. 102 (applying a similar principle to land). For a discussion of the nature of use-value damages, and confirmation that they are in essence compensatory, see *Morris-Garner v One Step (Support) Ltd* [2018] UKSC 20; [2018] 2 W.L.R. 1353 at [26] and [95] (Lord Reed) and [115]–[123] (Lord Sumption).

Replace footnote 540 with:

17-113 [540] So held in *Tanks and Vessels Industries Ltd v Devon Cider Co Ltd* [2009] EWHC 1360 (Ch); see especially at [62]–[67]. See also *Al-Khyami v El-Muderris* [2018] EWHC 24 (QB) at [76].

(iii) Nature of claimant's interest

Claimants with limited interest and similar cases in relation to reduction of damages

Replace footnote 549 with:

17-116 [549] *The Charlotte* [1908] P. 206 (strictly speaking a negligence case; but the principle is the same). Compare more recently *The Baltic Strait* [2018] EWHC 629 (Comm); [2018] 2 Lloyd's Rep. 33 at [31]–[33] (Andrew Baker J).

4. Trespass to Goods

(a) The nature of trespass to goods

The nature of trespass to goods

Replace footnote 602 with:

17-130 [602] "The act of handling a man's goods without his permission is prima facie tortious."—Lord Diplock in *Inland Revenue Commissioners v Rossminster Ltd* [1980] A.C. 952 at 1011. Similarly with boarding a bus other than as a bona fide passenger: *Rugby Football Union v Viagogo Ltd* [2011] EWHC 764 (QB); [2011] N.P.C. 37 at [10] (Tugendhat J) (upheld on other grounds, [2012] UKSC 55; [2012] 1 W.L.R. 3333); physically manhandling horses and foxhounds as part of an anti-hunting protest (*Fitzwilliam Land Co v Cheesman* [2018] EWHC 3139 (QB)), or climbing on trucks in the course of a demonstration against fracking (*UK Oil and Gas Investments Plc v Persons Unknown* [2018] EWHC 2252 (Ch); [2019] J.P.L. 161). A novel example might be where a defendant sends a voluminous fax message to the claimant's fax number knowing that the recipient does not wish to receive it. In *Chair King Inc v GTE Mobilnet, Inc*, 135 S.W.2d 365 (2004) a Texas court seems to have accepted that the sending of "junk faxes" might be a trespass, but in the event denied liability on the basis that trespass required physical harm and no harm had been done.

Chapter 18

DECEIT

Table of Contents

1. Introduction

Definition

Replace footnote 5 with:

[5] See, e.g. *Derry v Peek* (1889) 14 App. Cas. 337, 374 (Lord Herschell); *Standard Chartered Bank v Pakistan National Shipping Corp* [1998] 1 Lloyd's Rep. 684, 704 (Cresswell J); *AIC Ltd v ITS Testing Services (UK) Ltd* [2006] EWCA Civ 1601; [2007] 1 Lloyd's Rep. 555 at [251] (Rix LJ); *Parna v G & S Properties Ltd* [1971] S.C.R. 306, 316 (Spence J); *McBride v Christie's Australia Pty Ltd* [2014] NSWSC 1729 at [335]. For a recent esoteric application see *A v Att-Gen* [2018] 3 N.Z.L.R. 439 (police search under fake warrant: liability for loss caused). **18-01**

Deceit and other liability for misrepresentation

Replace footnote 8 with:

[8] "Charges of fraud should not be lightly made or considered"—*Mason v Clarke* [1955] A.C. 778, 794 (Viscount Simonds). See too Sales LJ in *Playboy Club London Ltd v Banca Nazionale Del Lavoro SpA (No 2)* [2018] EWCA Civ 2025 at [46]: "The pleading of fraud or deceit is a serious step, with significance and reputational ramifications going well beyond the pleading of a claim in negligence". It is unethical for a member of the Bar to allege fraud without clear instructions and reasonably credible evidence: Bar Standards Board's Code of Conduct, D.11.2(c). But note that this evidence need not necessarily be admissible in court: thus in the wasted costs decision in *Medcalf v Mardell* [2002] UKHL 27; [2003] 1 A.C. 120 the House of Lords declined to castigate as improper the pleading of fraud on the basis of documents subject to legal professional privilege. **18-02**

Ambit of liability

Replace paragraph with:

In a few cases liability in deceit is curtailed for public policy reasons; for example, privilege in court proceedings extends as much to deceit as to any other **18-03** liability.[16] But these exceptions are narrow. Thus the courts have declined to introduce a qualification for statements made within the family,[17] and the House of Lords have emphatically held that it is no defence that the defendant told lies merely in his capacity as the servant or agent of someone else.[18]

[16] *Walsh v Staines* [2008] EWCA Civ 1324; [2009] C.P. Rep. 16. But the immunity is strictly limited. So the mere fact that a payment has been embodied in a consent order is no bar to proceedings in deceit to recover it: *Zurich Insurance Co Plc v Hayward* [2011] EWCA Civ 641; [2011] C.P. Rep. 39 (insurance payout to person now alleged to have been malingering; appealed on other grounds, [2016] UKSC 48; [2017] A.C. 142). In *Smart v Forensic Science Service Ltd* [2013] EWCA Civ 783; [2013] P.N.L.R. 32 the Court of Appeal refused to strike out a deceit claim by a criminal defendant against a laboratory said to have deliberately falsified evidence against him: sed quaere. An action in deceit can equally be given even though the now defendant has previously obtained judgment in default against the current claimant: see *Gentry v Miller* [2016] EWCA Civ 141; [2016] 1 W.L.R. 2696 and its sequel, *UK Insurance Ltd v Gentry* [2018] EWHC 37 (QB) (recovery in respect of insurance fraud arising out of bogus collision).

[17] See *P v B (Paternity: Damages for Deceit)* [2001] 1 F.L.R. 1041 (action by cohabitee against girlfriend for duping him into thinking a child was his and hence paying for its upkeep) and the similar *A v B* [2007] EWHC 1246 (QB); [2007] 2 F.L.R. 1051. The existence of liability, it was said, would not tend to subvert intimate relationships, particularly since a claimant was unlikely to sue while the relationship was still on foot. But this is not uncontroversial: in *Magill v Magill* [2006] HCA 51; (2006) 81 A.L.J.R. 254 a majority in the High Court of Australia (Gummow, Kirby, Crennan, and Hayne JJ) seems to have thought that the tort of deceit should have little or no part to play in interspousal relations, and in *PP v DD* 2017 ONCA 180; (2017) 409 D.L.R. (4th) 691 the Ontario Court of Appeal regarded this as a reason to strike out a claim for deceit where a girlfriend, having falsely assured the plaintiff she was using contraception, fell pregnant by him. See generally N. Wikeley & L. Young, "Secrets and lies: no deceit down under for paternity fraud" (2008) 20 Child & Fam. L.Q. 81. In *AXB v BXA* [2018] EWHC 588 (QB) Eady J followed *P v B* and *A v B*, and awarded damages for sums paid out by a besotted lover to a girlfriend who affected falsely to be pregnant by him.

[18] *Standard Chartered Bank v Pakistan National Shipping Corp (No.2)* [2002] UKHL 43; [2003] 1 A.C. 959 (on which, see Parker [2003] L.M.C.L.Q. 1). But there may be some incidental protection for a mere mouthpiece in this connection: see *GE Commercial Finance Ltd v Gee* [2005] EWHC 2056 (QB); [2006] 1 Lloyd's Rep. 337, referred to below at para.18-21 fn.112.

Standard of proof in deceit claims

Replace footnote 22 with:

18-04 [22] See *Re H (Minors)* [1996] A.C. 563, 586-587, as explained in *Re S-B (Children)* [2009] UKSC 17; [2010] A.C. 678 at [13]–[18] (Lady Hale). See too, to the same effect, *UK Insurance Ltd v Gentry* [2018] EWHC 37 (QB) at [19]–[21] (Teare J).

2. REQUIREMENTS

(a) Representation

Misrepresentation or misleading conduct required for liability

Replace paragraph with:

18-05 To found an action in deceit the claimant must show a misrepresentation of present fact or law (or, at the very least, something done which was aimed at inducing action on the basis of false information).[25] However, a representation may be either express or implied from conduct[26]; furthermore, adopting the representation of a third party can be sufficient.[27] Where an issue arises as to whether a representation is true or not, the reasonable meaning of what the defendant said is often decisive.[28] Nevertheless, in strict law the issue in a deceit case is the meaning the representee was intended to put on what was said, even if this differs from the literal meaning of the words used:

"If a person makes a representation of that which is true, if he intends that the party to whom the representation is made should not believe it to be true, that is a false representation."[29]

Conversely, if a statement is in terms untrue, but is not intended to be interpreted in its literal sense, it cannot be charged as a deceit.[30]

[25] For example, the deceit may be practised, not on a person, but on a machine such as a computer: *Renault UK Ltd v Fleetpro Technical Services* [2007] EWHC 2541 (QB); [2008] Bus. L.R. D17 at [122]. In *IG Index Plc v Colley* [2013] EWHC 478 (QB) at [746]–[763] Stadlen J held defendants liable for fraud where, aided by a dishonest employee, they placed false bets with a spread-betting company; in addition, he explicitly stated that there was no requirement for any misrepresentation at all. But this is problematical, since if it is true it is not clear where the boundaries of fraud fall to be drawn. Furthermore, it must be arguable that there was at least an implicit (and untrue) representation there by the defendants that the bets placed by them represented bona fide transactions.

[26] See para.18-06 onwards. See too *Whyfe v Michael Cullen & Partners* [1993] E.G.C.S. 193 (business lease very obscurely worded, with rent inevitably uneconomic and surrender an inevitability: Court of Appeal refuse to strike out action by lessees for deceit on basis that lease deliberately dressed up to look unremarkable when in fact not).

[27] *Bradford Third Equitable Benefit Building Society v Borders* [1941] 2 All E.R. 204 at 211 (Lord Maugham). (In fact fraud was held not established on the facts of the case.)

[28] *Property Alliance Group Ltd v Royal Bank of Scotland Plc* [2016] EWHC 3342 (Ch), especially at [230]–[231] (meaning of "hedge" in financial context). The meaning of a given statement may very well depend on the wider context: see *Copthall Ltd v Scorched Earth Services Ltd* [2017] EWHC 1341 (QB) at [36]-[47] (representation that $1.4 million advanced by third party to business in which claimant asked to invest; clear from previous negotiations that this did not mean a pure cash injection). See also *Barley v Muir* [2018] EWHC 619 (QB) at [177] (Soole J). So too with highly imprecise words: if it is clear that a reasonable representee would understand them in a particular way, they remain perfectly capable of being deceitful. See, e.g. *Burki v Seventy Thirty Ltd* [2018] EWHC 2151 (QB) (statement that dating agency had a "substantial" number of unattached available men held to be false when in fact it had at best 100).

[29] See Alderson B. in *Moens v Heyworth* (1842) 10 M. & W. 147 at 158.

[30] See para.18-25.

Active conduct or concealment

Replace paragraph with:

Active non-verbal conduct can amount to misrepresentation, and hence deceit, just as much as words can.[38] So, for instance, pledging goods knowing one has no title to them is deceit,[39] as is ordering goods on credit for someone known to be insolvent[40] or presenting company accounts to a buyer in the knowledge that they have been doctored.[41] No doubt the same would apply to an agent knowingly contracting without authority to do so. Indeed, it seems that in a suitable case the mere doing of business with another may in itself carry a representation that the business is bona fide and in accordance with established practice.[42] Another straightforward example is positive steps taken to conceal defects in something being sold (as against merely keeping silent about them). So in *Gordon v Selico Ltd*,[43] the Court of Appeal awarded damages for deceit where a defendant fraudulently arranged to cover up infestations of dry rot in a flat before letting it. Similarly, in the antique case of *Schneider v Heath*[44] a seller of a ship was held liable when he deliberately floated it so as to hide sub-waterline defects when the buyer came to inspect it. **18-08**

[38] See the old criminal case of *R. v Barnard* (1837) 7 C. & P. 784 (buyer donned university garb to which not entitled and thus induced seller to give him credit: held, rightly convicted of obtaining by false pretences). A more modern instance (in a claim brought under s.2(1) of the Misrepresentation Act 1967) is *Spice Girls Ltd v Aprilia World Service BV* [2002] EWCA Civ 15; [2002] E.M.L.R. 27 (representation by conduct: participating jointly in the filming of advertisements for the claimant constituted a representation that pop group did not contemplate breaking up during the term of the advertising contract).

[39] *Advanced Industrial Technology Corp Ltd v Bond Street Jewellers Ltd* [2006] EWCA Civ 923; *FundingSecure Ltd v Green* [2019] EWHC 208 (Ch). See too the Canadian decision in *HSBC Bank Canada v Lourenco* 2012 ABQB 380; (2012) Alta. L.R. (5th) 1.

[40] *Contex Drouzhba Ltd v Wiseman* [2007] EWCA Civ 1201; [2008] B.C.C. 301 (though complications may arise under the Statute of Frauds Amendment Act 1828: see para.18-52).

[41] *Man Nützfahrzeuge AG v Freightliner Ltd* [2005] EWHC 2347 (Comm), especially at [79] onwards. The point was not argued on appeal at [2007] EWCA Civ 910; [2008] P.N.L.R. 6. See too *Bennett Gould & Partners Ltd v O'Sullivan* [2018] EWHC 2450 (QB) at [91] (supply of insurance broking profit figures to proposed joint venturer carries implication that those profits were honestly earned).

[42] *Lindsay v O'Loughnane* [2010] EWHC 529 (QB); [2012] B.C.C. 153 (controller of foreign exchange dealers booked deals knowing that, contrary to previous practice and business ethics, clients' sums not segregated but used immediately to pay pressing creditors; liable for deceit when dealers collapsed owing claimant over £500,000). Flaux J referred specifically to an implicit representation that the company was trading "properly and legitimately": see [100]–[119]). Presenting a loan proposal based on the EURIBOR rates index is similarly a representation that the lender is not itself fraudulently manipulating the index (though it does not imply that someone else is not doing so): *Marme Inversiones 2007 SL v NatWest Markets Plc* [2019] EWHC 366 (Comm) at [142]. On the other hand, since charges for work done are often the subject of negotiation, the mere submission of an invoice is not necessarily a representation that the sum claimed is actually owing: see *Browne (J) Construction Co Ltd v Chapman Construction Services Ltd* [2016] EWHC 152 (QB); (2016) 165 Con. L.R. 175 at [70].

[43] (1986) 18 H.L.R. 219.

[44] (1813) 3 Camp 506. Cf. *Reynell v Sprye* (1852) 1 De G.M. & G. 660; *Walters v Morgan* (1861) 3 De G.F. & J. 718 at 723; and see too *Abel v McDonald* (1964) 45 D.L.R. (2d) 198.

Misrepresentation: promises and statements of intention

Replace footnote 59 with:

18-11 [59] The prospectus said the money was wanted for further investment in the business: in fact it was needed to pay off existing debts. See too *Al Khudairi v Abbey Brokers Ltd* [2010] EWHC 1486 (Ch); [2010] P.N.L.R. 32, especially at [124]–[126] (Newey J) (claimants' money deposited with company, misused and lost: fraudulent statements by company controller as to how he intended to handle claimants' money held to amount to deceit, thus allowing personal claim against controller on company's insolvency). See also *Khakshouri v Jimenez* [2017] EWHC 3392 (QB) (representation of intent not to sell asset unless with the benefit of a collateral land deal).

Continuing representations

After "Whereas this inference will be readily drawn if the representation seeks to induce the claimant to enter into some transaction,", add new footnote 93A:

18-18 [93A] As, for example, in *Inter Export LLC v Townley* [2018] EWCA Civ 2068; see especially at [30]–[32] (representation by director that buyer had funds to pay for commodity).

(b) State of mind

(i) The belief of the defendant

Timing: statement becoming untrue ex post facto

Replace footnote 115 with:

18-24 [115] *Incledon v Watson* (1862) 2 F. & F. 841; *With v O'Flanagan* [1936] Ch. 575, 584; *Bradford Third Benefit Building Society v Borders* [1941] 2 All E.R. 205 at 220, per Lord Wright; R. Bigwood, "Pre-Contractual Misrepresentation and the Limits of the Principle in With v O'Flanagan" [2005] C.L.J. 94. This includes the case where a misrepresentation is made by one agent and it is another agent who fails to correct it: *Marme Inversiones 2007 SL v NatWest Markets Plc* [2019] EWHC 366 (Comm) at [260]–[261]. Compare the reasoning in *Briess v Woolley* [1954] A.C. 333 (see para.18-18) on continuing representations.

(ii) State of mind: vicarious liability

Knowledge: vicarious liability of employer

Replace paragraph with:

There is no doubt that a blameless employer may be vicariously liable for a deceit committed by a dishonest employee in the course of his employment,[121] in the same way as he can be liable for any other deliberate tort.[122] In general the normal rules of vicarious liability apply.[123] However, there are two important limitations on the employer's potential liability in this connection. First, it has to be shown that the employee in the course of his employment not only acted dishonestly, but actually committed the principal act amounting to the tort of deceit. The point was neatly illustrated by *Crédit Lyonnais Nederland NV v Export Credits Guarantee Department*.[124] As part of a scheme to induce a bank to buy forged bills of exchange relating to bogus export transactions, a fraudster obtained certain guarantees from the defendants, which he had suborned X, a dishonest employee of theirs, to authorise on their behalf. The bank sued the defendants in deceit, arguing (correctly) that the employee was liable to them as an accessory of the fraudster, and that in issuing the guarantees to aid the fraudster he had acted within the scope of his employment. The House of Lords nevertheless held that the action failed. The essential elements of the tort of deceit had been committed by the fraudster and not by X, and the mere fact that X had abetted a tort in the course of his employment did not make the defendants liable for it as his employers. Secondly, the rule that an act may be done in the course of employment even if entirely unauthorised[125] is modified in the case of deceit. An employer will be vicariously liable for a statement made by his employee only if the employee had actual or ostensible authority to make it.[126] So in *Armagas Ltd v Mundogas SA*[127] an employee of the defendant shipping company, while negotiating on their behalf but without their authority, defrauded the claimants into thinking that the defendants were contracting to charter a ship for three years. The claimant's action for breach of contract having failed because the employee had no authority to contract on their behalf, the House of Lords held that their action in deceit on the basis of vicarious liability for their employee's deception was equally doomed: absent authority to make representations, there could be no liability in tort for unauthorised statements.[128] In *Frederick v Positive Solutions (Financial Services) Ltd*[128A] it was argued that the limitation of vicarious liability to statements made with actual or ostensible authority had been overtaken by the new approach taken in *Various Claimants v Institute of the Brothers of the Christian Schools*[128B] and *Cox v Ministry of Justice*.[128C] Flaux LJ, with whom the other members of the Court of Appeal agreed, declined to decide the point, since on either score the claimants had to fail; but pointedly observed[128D] that cases such as *Kooragang Investment Pty Ltd v Richardson & Wrench*[128E] and *Armagas Ltd v Mundogas SA*[128F] had never been disapproved. In the later decision in *Winter v Hockley Mint Ltd*,[128G] however, the Court of Appeal determined the point and decided that scope of authority remained the test for vicarious liability for an agent's fraud. **18-26**

[121] e.g. *Lloyd v Grace, Smith and Co* [1912] A.C. 716 (solicitor's clerk defrauding client); *Barings Plc (In Liquidation) v Coopers & Lybrand (Issues Re Liability)* [2003] EWHC 1319 (Ch); [2003] P.N.L.R. 34 (lies told by unauthorised traders to company's auditors to cover up their trail: held, employers liable on principle to auditors on basis of vicarious liability). Cf. *Barwick v English Joint Stock Bank* (1867) L.R. 2 Ex. 259, 265, per Willes J. Equally it does not matter for these purposes that the fraud was as much against the employer as the claimant: cf. *Kwei Tek Chao v British Traders & Shippers Ltd* [1954] 2 Q.B. 459, 470 (per Devlin J).

[122] See, e.g. *Morris v Martin* [1966] 1 Q.B. 716 (conversion by theft). For what amounts to "course of employment" in this connection, see generally *Lister v Hesley Hall Ltd* [2001] UKHL 22; [2002] 1 A.C. 215 and para.6-29 onwards. See too *Frederick v Positive Solutions (Financial Services) Ltd* [2018] EWCA Civ 431 (financial adviser persuaded claimants to remortgage homes to invest in fraudulent scheme of his own; submitted fraudulent mortgage applications through Web portal of defendants, with whom associated; no liability in defendants, since they had done no more than provide the opportunity for the fraud, and in any case fraudster's activity had been a "recognisably independent business" from the defendants' and thus outside the scope of any employment).

[123] For example, as to seconded servants: see the Scots decision in *Royal Bank of Scotland Plc v Bannerman Johnstone MacLay* [2005] CSIH 39; 2005 1 S.C. 437; [2005] P.N.L.R. 43 (accountant seconded to company by firm tells lies to its bankers: arguable that still employed by firm and hence latter liable). Similarly, a representor may act for two people at the same time. See *Man Nützfahrzeuge AG v Freightliner Ltd* [2005] EWHC 2347 (Comm), especially at [92], et seq. (financial manager of company presents falsified accounts to potential buyer of company: acting for both company and seller). The point was not argued on appeal: [2007] EWCA Civ 910; [2008] P.N.L.R. 6.

[124] [2000] 1 A.C. 486.

[125] e.g. *Limpus v London General Omnibus Co* (1862) 1 H. & C. 862.

[126] See *Lloyd v Grace, Smith & Co* [1912] A.C. 716, especially at 736 (Lord Macnaghten); *Armagas Ltd v Mundogas SA* [1986] A.C. 717, below. For a case of actual authority giving rise to liability see *Khakshouri v Jimenez* [2017] EWHC 3392 (QB), esp at [124]–[125] (one director giving other director carte blanche to negotiate on his behalf for loan to a struggling Charlton Athletic FC). But there are dicta in *Group Seven Ltd v Notable Services LLC* [2019] EWCA Civ 614 at [145] that vicarious liability, even for deceit, may possibly extend beyond statements made with authority.

[127] [1986] A.C. 717.

[128] A rule which seemingly applies to negligent misstatement as well: *Kooragang Investment Pty Ltd v Richardson & Wrench* [1982] A.C. 462.

[128A] [2018] EWCA Civ 431.

[128B] [2012] UKSC 56; [2013] 2 A.C. 1

[128C] [2016] UKSC 10; [2016] A.C. 660.

[128D] [2018] EWCA Civ 431 at [77].

[128E] [1982] A.C. 462.

[128F] [1986] A.C. 717.

[128G] [2018] EWCA Civ 2480; [2019] 1 W.L.R. 1617.

Knowledge and agency: the fraudulent agent

Replace footnote 134 with:

18-27 [134] *Barings Plc (In Liquidation) v Coopers & Lybrand (A Firm) (Issues Re Liability)* [2003] EWHC 1319 (Ch); [2003] P.N.L.R. 34, especially at [728]. See too *Singularis Holdings Ltd (In Official Liquidation) (A Company Incorporated in the Cayman Islands) v Daiwa Capital Markets Europe Ltd* [2017] EWHC 257 (Ch); [2017] 1 Lloyd's Rep. 226 at [221]–[227] (Rose J), a case of negligence leading to the abstraction of client funds from a stockbroker. The *Singularis* case ([2017] EWHC 257 (Ch); [2017] 1 Lloyd's Rep. 226) was unsuccessfully appealed on this point: see [2018] EWCA Civ 84; [2018] P.N.L.R. 19 at [73]–[80] (Rose LJ).

Knowledge and agency: other cases

Replace footnote 137 with:

18-28 [137] It was once doubted whether an agent who knowingly lied on the orders of a guilty principal was personally liable at all: but this heresy was scotched by the House of Lords in *Standard Chartered Bank v Pakistan National Shipping Corp (No.2)* [2002] UKHL 43; [2003] 1 A.C. 959 (on which see B. Parker, "Fraudulent Bills of Lading and Bankers' Commercial Credits" [2003] L.M.C.L.Q. 1). See also *International Media Advertising Ltd v Ministry of Culture and Tourism of the Republic of Turkey* [2018] EWHC 3285 (QB) at [275]–[283].

(c) Representation intended to be acted on by the claimant

Representation must be intended to be acted on by claimant

Replace paragraph with:

In order to give a cause of action in deceit, not only must the statement complained of be untrue to the defendant's knowledge, but it must in addition be made with intent to deceive the claimant: with intent, that is to say, that it shall be acted upon by him.[146] It seems that intent, for these purposes, includes not only the case where the defendant actually desires the claimant to rely on what he says, but also where he appreciates that in the absence of some unforeseen intervention he will actually do so.[147] But if intent of one or other kind is not shown, then the claimant will fail. So where the defendant, a director of an oil company, untruly stated to a broker that the company had received no news of a major find, intending by this untruth to protect the company's interests and not to induce shareholders to sell their holdings, it was held that no action for fraud lay at the suit of a shareholder.[148] However, provided the defendant intended the claimant to act on the representation, it is immaterial whether he intended him so to act in the precise way in which he did.[149] **18-30**

[146] *Peek v Gurney* (1873) L.R. 6 H.L. at 377, 411–413 (Lord Cairns); *Bradford Third Benefit Building Society v Borders* [1941] 2 All E.R. 205 at 211; *Kitcher v Fordham* [1955] 2 Lloyd's Rep. 705 at 707.

[147] *Shinhan Bank Ltd v Sea Containers Ltd* [2000] 2 Lloyd's Rep. 406 (buyer signing receipts for undelivered goods knowing seller would use then to obtain bank finance: liable to bank in deceit when seller collapsed). This criterion of "intent" is borrowed from criminal law: see *R. v Woollin* [1999] 1 A.C. 82. The passage at this footnote was approved in *Zagora Management Ltd v Zurich Insurance Plc* [2019] EWHC 140 (TCC); (2019) 182 Con. L.R. 180 at [743]–[745].

[148] *Tackey v McBain* [1912] A.C. 186. See too *Goose v Wilson Sandford & Co (No.2)* [2001] Lloyd's Rep. P.N. 189. More recently, see *Zagora Management Ltd v Zurich Insurance Plc* [2019] EWHC 140 (TCC); (2019) 182 Con. L.R. 180 (producer of fraudulent building regulations certificate for apartment block did not intend reliance by later buyer of freehold).

[149] *Goose v Wilson Sandford & Co (No.2)* [2001] Lloyd's Rep. P.N. 189.

Representation not made to claimant directly

Replace footnote 158 with:

[158] (1873) L.R. 6 H.L. 377. See also, *Tackey v McBain* [1912] A.C. 186 (untrue denial of major find by oil company made to protect company's interests generally, not to influence market: no liability to shareholder who sold on faith of it); and also *Wetherspoon (JD) Plc v Van De Berg & Co Ltd* [2007] EWHC 1044; [2007] P.N.L.R. 28; *Group Seven Ltd v Nasir* [2017] EWHC 2466 (Ch); [2018] P.N.L.R. 6 at [516]–[521] (Morgan J) (varied on appeal on other grounds: *Group Seven Ltd v Notable Services LLC* [2019] EWCA Civ 614). **18-32**

(d) Claimant must have been influenced by the misrepresentation

The claimant must have been influenced by the misrepresentation

Replace footnote 166 with:

[166] See, e.g. *Holmes v Jones* (1907) 4 C.L.R. 1692; see too *Zagora Management Ltd v Zurich Insurance Plc* [2019] EWHC 140 (TCC); (2019) 182 Con. L.R. 180. The statement in this paragraph was approved by Lewison J in *Mellor v Partridge* [2013] EWCA Civ 477 at [20]. **18-34**

Joint inducement suffices

Replace paragraph with:

Although the claimant must show that he was induced to act as he did by the **18-35** misrepresentation, it need not have been the sole cause. Provided it substantially contributed to deceiving him, that will be enough.[173] If the claimant's mind was partly influenced by the defendant's misstatements the defendant will not be any the less liable because the claimant was also partly influenced by a mistake of his own.[174] In such cases, moreover, the claimant has the benefit of a presumption that he was influenced at least to some extent by the deceptive statement.[175] *Hayward v Zurich Insurance Co Plc*[175A] establishes that influence on the claimant's mind suffices, and that the mere fact that the claimant held strong suspicions that what had been said to him might be false will not of itself bar his claim if in fact it was.[175B] But the limits of this must be noted. It has been held that if the claimant not only suspects, but actually knows, that what he hears is false, this pre-empts the matter. Here he cannot sue, for the simple reason that he was never taken in and hence cannot have been induced.[175C] One comment is in order. The distinction introduced in this case between knowledge and strong suspicion may not in practice be clear-cut or easy to draw, and may well engender further litigation.

[173] *Parabola Investments Ltd v Browallia CAL Ltd* [2009] EWHC 901 (Comm); [2009] 2 All E.R. (Comm) 589 (unsuccessfully appealed on other grounds, [2010] EWCA Civ 486; [2011] Q.B. 477); *Leni Gas & Oil Investments Ltd v Malta Oil Pty Ltd* [2014] EWHC 893 (Comm) at [16] (Males J). See too *Australian Steel & Mining Corp Pty Ltd v Corben* [1974] 2 N.S.W.L.R. 202; *Paul & Vincent v O'Reilly* (1913) 49 Ir. L.T. 89. Cf. the negligent misrepresentation case of *JEB Fasteners Ltd v Marks Bloom & Co* [1983] 1 All E.R. 583 at 589, per Stephenson LJ, and the compromise case of *Hayward v Zurich Insurance Co Plc* [2016] UKSC 48; [2017] A.C. 142. See too *Khakshouri v Jimenez* [2017] EWHC 3392 (QB) at [20] (Green J); *BV Nederlandse Industrie Van Eiprodukten v Rembrandt Enterprises, Inc* [2019] EWCA Civ 596 at [26]–[43]. On the *Zurich* case, see K. Lindeman, "Unravelling settlements made with 'eyes wide open'" (2017) 36 C.J.Q. 273; R. Lee, "Proof of Inducement in the Law on Misrepresentation" (2017) L.M.C.L.Q. 151; and K. Loi, "Pre-contractual misrepresentations: mistaken belief induced by mis-statements" [2017] J.B.L. 598.

[174] See *Edgington v Fitzmaurice* (1885) 29 Ch. 459 at 483, per Bowen LJ; also *Peek v Derry* (1887) 37 Ch D. 541. Cf. *Tatton v Wade* (1856) 18 C.B. 371.

[175] See *Dadourian Group International Inc v Simms* [2009] EWCA Civ 169; [2009] 1 Lloyd's Rep. 601 at [95]–[108] following dicta in *Goose v Wilson Sandford & Co (No.2)* [2001] Lloyd's Rep. P.N. 189 at 200–201); *OMV Petrom SA v Glencore International AG* [2015] EWHC 666 (Comm) at [133]–[158] (Flaux J). See also *Khakshouri v Jimenez* [2017] EWHC 3392 (QB) at [20] (Green J); also *BV Nederlandse Industrie Van Eiprodukten v Rembrandt Enterprises, Inc.* [2019] EWCA Civ 596 at [25], where it is made clear that the presumption is a rebuttable inference of fact, not a preumption of law.

[175A] [2016] UKSC 48; [2017] A.C. 142

[175B] See also, E. Bant, "Unravelling Fraud in the Wake of *Hayward v Zurich Insurance*" [2019] L.M.C.L.Q. 91.

[175C] See *Holyoake v Candy* [2017] EWHC 3397 (Ch) especially at [386]–[395] (Nugee J).

3. DAMAGES

Measure of damages

Replace paragraph with:

18-41 The measure of damages in deceit is the loss directly flowing from the claimant's reliance on the defendant's statement[188]; that is, generally speaking, the sum that will put him in the same position as if he had not relied on it.[189] Credit must of course be given for any gains made by the claimant,[190] though such gains must unsurprisingly be tangible rather than emotional or fleeting.[190A]

[188] "The defendant is bound to make reparation for all the actual damages directly flowing from the fraudulent inducement."—Lord Denning MR in *Doyle v Olby* (Ironmongers) Ltd [1969] 2 Q.B. 158, 167. See too *Clark v Urquhart* [1930] A.C. 28, 67–68 (per Lord Atkin).

[189] See *Doyle v Olby* (Ironmongers) Ltd [1969] 2 Q.B. 158, 167 (Lord Denning MR); *GE Commercial Finance Ltd v Gee* [2005] EWHC 2056 (QB); [2006] 1 Lloyd's Rep. 337 at [335], per Tugendhat J.

[190] *Smith New Court Securities Ltd v Citibank NA* [1997] A.C. 254 at 267, per Lord Browne-Wilkinson. See, e.g. *Komerçni Banka AS v Stone & Rolls Ltd* [2002] EWHC 2263 (Comm); [2003] 1 Lloyd's Rep. 383 (bank deceived into paying out on fraudulent letter of credit: credit for fee received for issuing it). The defendant bears the burden of proving such benefits: see *Midco Holdings Ltd v Piper* [2004] EWCA Civ 476; [2004] N.P.C. 59 and *Barker v Winter* [2018] EWHC 1785 (QB) at [28]. In *Burki v Seventy Thirty Ltd* [2018] EWHC 2151 (QB) at [174]–[175] it was said that no credit fell to be given for the value of services received: thus a claimant duped into paying for computer dating services recovered her entire membership fee without reference to what was actually provided in return. It is suggested, however, that this must be limited to cases where what was supplied was of little or no value to the claimant. If A dupes B into buying, say, electricity from him at more thaen the going rate for a year, is it really open to B to sue A for all his money back and get, in effect, a year's free power? One hopes not.

[190A] *Barker v Winter* [2018] EWHC 1785 (QB) at [28] (munificent transfers of money obtained from besotted lover: no credit for sensual pleasures of lavish lifestyle derived partly from monies given).

Position if representation true irrelevant

Replace paragraph with:

Since the claimant's entitlement is to be put in the position he would have occupied had he not relied on the defendant's representation, it follows that no account is taken of what his position would have been had that representation been true.[191] Two consequences follow from this. First, if the claimant is duped into buying an asset, he is generally entitled to recover the difference between the price paid and the market value of the property he received in exchange, and not the difference between the market value and the amount the defendant said the property was worth.[192] Thus in *Doyle v Olby (Ironmongers) Ltd*,[193] where the claimant was deceived into buying a run-down and infructuous business, an award of the latter sum was overturned by the Court of Appeal. Conversely, a seller deceived into delivering goods by a representation that payment is forthcoming recovers the market value of those goods.[193A] Secondly, if the claimant is deceived into entering into a transaction by a statement as to the gains to be made from it, he can recover only the amount he loses as a result of relying on the representation and not the profit the defendant said he would make. So in *East v Maurer*,[194] where the seller of a business fraudulently overstated the profits available, the Court of Appeal reversed a judgment at first instance awarding the buyer the amount of those extra profits.[195] However, the loss flowing from reliance on the defendant's representation may, in an exceptional case, approximate to restoring his position had the statement been true. Thus in *BHP Billiton Petroleum Ltd v Dalmine SpA*[196] quality control employees of a subcontractor supplying pipes for an offshore oil project certified pipes as sound which they knew to be substandard. In due course the pipes leaked. The project owner sued the subcontractor in deceit. It was accepted that it was entitled to be put in the position it would have occupied had the pipes in fact been up to standard: the reason being that, had the subcontractor's employees not mis-certified the pipes concerned, they would have been rejected and sound pipes supplied in their stead without further charge. **18-42**

[191] See, e.g. *McConnell v Wright* [1903] 1 Ch. 546 at 554 (Collins MR); *Doyle v Olby (Ironmongers) Ltd* [1969] 2 Q.B. 158, 166 (Lord Denning MR); *East v Maurer* [1991] 1 W.L.R. 461, 465 (Beldam LJ); *Smith New Court Securities Ltd v Citibank NA* [1997] A.C. 254 at 281–282 (Lord Steyn); *Inter Export LLC v Townley* [2017] EWHC 530 (Ch) at [6]–[8] (Proudman J) (upheld on appeal at [2018] EWCA Civ 2068). The position in many American jurisdictions is different: e.g. *Midwest Home Distributor, Inc v Domco Industries, Ltd*, 585 NW.2d 735 at 738–742 (Iowa 1998).

[192] Thus if a defendant fraudulently says the asset is worth £120 when it is in fact worth £90, and the claimant buys it for £110, damages in deceit are £20 and not £30. For statements of this principle, see, e.g. *Pearson v Wheeler* (1825) Ry. & M. 303 at 304; *Doyle v Olby (Ironmongers) Ltd* [1969] 2 Q.B. 158 at 166, per Lord Denning MR; *Saunders v Edwards* [1987] 1 W.L.R. 1116 at 1121, per Kerr LJ; *Smith New Court Securities Ltd v Citibank NA* [1997] A.C. 254 at 281–282, per Lord Steyn.

[193] [1969] 2 Q.B. 158.

[193A] *Inter Export LLC v Townley* [2018] EWCA Civ 2068, especially at [58]–[68], upholding the earlier *Smith Kline & French Laboratories Ltd v Long* [1989] 1 W.L.R. 1.

[194] [1991] 1 W.L.R. 461. See also the negligence case of *Swingcastle Ltd v Alastair Gibson* [1991] 2 A.C. 223 (valuers misvalue property for mortgagees: mortgagors insolvent: no recovery for interest that mortgagors should have paid and which would have been recoupable from property if valuation correct).

[195] Though it did award the claimant the profits she would have made had she bought another similar business.

[196] [2003] EWCA Civ 170; [2003] B.L.R. 271.

Claims for would-be profits

Replace footnote 197 with:

18-43 [197] See, e.g. *East v Maurer* [1991] 1 W.L.R. 461 (purchaser duped into buying business by overstated profits: recovers profits she would have made from alternative business she would have bought); *Parabola Investments Ltd v Browallia Cal Ltd* [2010] EWCA Civ 486; [2011] Q.B. 477. See too *Clef Aquitaine SàrL v Laporte Minerals (Barrow) Ltd* [2001] Q.B. 488, and *4Eng Ltd v Harper* [2008] EWHC 915 (Ch); [2009] Ch. 91 (fraudster's victim can claim in respect of chance that he would have made other, highly profitable, investment of money he was swindled out of) (commented on in C. Mitchell, "Loss of chance in deceit" (2009) 125 L.Q.R. 12). So too where a claimant is induced to withdraw funds from a potentially profitable investment already made. See *Khakshouri v Jimenez* [2017] EWHC 3392 (QB) (investor induced to withdraw money from profitable US property deal and lend it to ailing football club; although repaid his loan, investor recovered would-be US profits).

Timing

Replace footnote 209 with:

18-44 [209] *Parabola Investments Ltd v Browallia Cal Ltd* [2010] EWCA Civ 486; [2011] Q.B. 477 at [32] onwards. See also *Khakshouri v Jimenez* [2017] EWHC 3392 (QB).

Consequential losses

Replace footnote 225 with:

18-46 [225] £500 was given for distress in *Saunders v Edwards* [1987] 1 W.L.R. 1116, and also in *Shelley v Paddock* [1979] Q.B. 120 (affirmed [1980] Q.B. 348), and again in *Burki v Seventy Thirty Ltd* [2018] EWHC 2151 (QB) (lovelorn lady duped into joining computer dating club: see especially at [175]–[181]). See too *Shaw v Sequence (UK) Ltd* [2004] EWHC 3249 (QB); [2004] All E.R. (D) 232 (Nov) (annoyance of clients deceived by their estate agent: £1,000 basic award plus £1,500 aggravated damages); *Kinch v Rosling* [2009] EWHC 286 (QB) (£10,000 for distress of victim bankrupted owing to fraud); and the colourful Canadian decision in *Beaulne v Ricketts* (1979) 96 D.L.R. (3d) 550 (claimant deceived into bigamous marriage). But one Canadian decision goes the other way: in *PP v DD* 2017 ONCA 180; (2017) 409 D.L.R. (4th) 691 a boyfriend failed to recover for distress at his girlfriend's falling pregnant following false statements as to her use of contraceptives.

Aggravated and exemplary damages

Replace paragraph with:

18-48 There is little doubt that aggravated damages may be awarded to compensate the claimant for injury to his feelings arising from a blatant or callous exercise in deceit.[232] As for exemplary damages, since the decision in *Kuddus v Chief Constable of Leicestershire*[233] they are clearly available in principle, at least where the deceit was by a public authority or was calculated to make a profit over and above any damages received.[234] An instance where they were awarded was *Axa Insurance UK Plc v Financial Claims Solutions Ltd*,[235] where fraudulent claims arising out of bogus road accidents were made against motor insurers. The Court of Appeal awarded £20,000 against the company responsible, and an additional £20,000 against each of the moving spirits behind it. The requirement that the tort be committed with a view to gains outstripping losses it held satisfied, perhaps surprisingly, by the fact that the defendants had hoped not to be caught and hence to keep their gains for themselves. In addition the court held that the existence of criminal proceedings or confiscation proceedings, or the availability of contempt of court proceedings, should not adversely affect an award of exemplary damages if otherwise appropriate.

[232] *Archer v Brown* [1985] Q.B. 401. See also *Mafo v Adams* [1970] 1 Q.B. 548 at 558; *Saunders v Edwards* [1987] 1 W.L.R. 1116; *Shaw v Sequence (UK) Ltd* [2004] EWHC 3249 (QB); [2004] All E.R. (D) 232 (Nov) (deceit by estate agent: damages of £1,000 for vexation increased to £2,500 for over-contentious attitude and non-apology). But account may be taken of the fact that conduct that seems heartless was the result of some affliction affecting the defendant. See *Barker v Winter* [2018] EWHC 1785 (QB) at [28] (large cash gifts obtained by deceitful lover: account taken of fact that lover pathologically addicted to obtaining and spending money). With respect this seems remarkably generous to the defendant, and more appropriate to criminal than civil proceedings.

[233] [2001] UKHL 29; [2002] 2 A.C. 122: see para.28-142.

[234] i.e. Lord Devlin's categories in *Rookes v Barnard* [1964] A.C. 1129; see para.28-135 onwards. For an example of an award of punitive damages for a deceit aimed at profit, see *Hassan v Cooper* [2015] EWHC 540 (QB); [2015] R.T.R. 26 (attempt to make a fraudulent claim arising out of a genuine car accident: award against the claims agents responsible related to the amount which they had attempted to extract from the defendant's insurers; smaller award against individual claimant).

[235] [2018] EWCA Civ 1330; [2019] R.T.R. 1.

7. THE ACTION FOR FRAUD ARISING OUT OF BRIBERY

Fraud and bribery

Replace paragraph with:

When an agent is bribed to persuade his principal to enter into a transaction on terms disadvantageous to the latter, he may of course make himself liable in deceit: for example, if he untruthfully tells his principal that the terms are the best that can be obtained. But even if he does not, and merely deals on the principal's behalf, this event itself gives rise to a tortious liability[270] in both himself and the briber to the principal for loss suffered by the latter.[271] This head of claim is somewhat confusingly known as "fraud",[272] and shares some,[273] though not all,[274] of the elements of the tort of deceit.[275] **18-55**

[270] There is a parallel compensatory claim in equity against the agent for breaking his fiduciary duty, and against the briber for helping him break it (see *Royal Brunei Airlines Sdn Bhd v Tan* [1995] 2 A.C. 378). But in *Fyffes Group Ltd v Templeman* [2000] 2 Lloyd's Rep. 643 at 660 Toulson J pointed out that the measure of damages was the same under either head (save possibly for the availability of compound interest in an equitable claim).

[271] Examples are numerous. See, e.g. *Salford Corp v Lever* [1891] 1 Q.B. 168 CA; *Grant v Gold Exploration and Development Syndicate Ltd* [1900] 1 Q.B. 233; *Hovendon & Sons v Millhoff* (1900) 83 L.T. 41; *Arab Monetary Fund v Hashim* [1993] 1 Lloyd's Rep. 543 (employer paid contractor the full amount due under a contract which was induced by a bribe paid to the employer's agent: employer entitled to recover amount of the bribe from contractor on the basis that contractor received a greater sum than what was the true price).

[272] "Bribery is ... a specialist variety of fraud": HHJ Pelling in *Chancery Client Partners Ltd v MRC 957 Ltd* [2016] EWHC 2142 (Ch); [2016] Lloyd's Rep. F.C. 578 at [23]. See too, for similar statements, *Conway v Prince Eze* [2019] EWCA Civ 88 at [106], and *Motortrak Ltd v FCA Australia Pty Ltd (No 2)* [2018] EWHC 1464 (Comm) at [15] (Moulder J).

[273] For example, the exacting standard of proof (see *Fyffes Group Ltd v Templeman* [2000] 2 Lloyd's Rep. 643 at 656), and the inapplicability of contributory negligence (see below).

[274] For example, an employer can be vicariously liable under this head even for an act that was not within his employee's actual or ostensible authority, thus marking off this head of liability from deceit proper.

[275] "[T]he claim based on bribery is not a species of deceit but a special form of fraud where there is no representation made to the principal of the agent let alone reliance."-Steel J in *Petrotrade Inc v Smith* [2000] 1 Lloyd's Rep. 486 at 490. For a useful summary of the ingredients of the cause of action, see

Otkritie International Investment Management Ltd v Urumov [2014] EWHC 191 (Comm) at [66]–[73] (Eder J). On the other hand, a dishonest agent may also commit deceit by lying to his principal, in which case he is liable in the ordinary way: see, e.g. *Mahesan v Malaysia Government Officers Co-operative Housing Society Ltd* [1979] A.C. 374 and *Daraydan Holdings Ltd v Solland International Ltd* [2004] EWHC 622 (Ch); [2005] Ch. 119.

Replace paragraph with:

18-56 The measure of damages under this head is the loss actually suffered by the principal.[276] There is a strong, though not conclusive,[277] presumption that the amount of the bribe represents a loss to the principal, on the pragmatic basis that he would otherwise have benefited from it by way of discount or otherwise.[278] In addition the principal can claim any further losses he may have suffered.[279] As with deceit properly so called, contributory negligence is no defence.[280] In addition to being liable in damages, both the errant agent and, it seems, the briber himself are liable to pay over the amount of the bribe to the principal[281] on the basis that they are regarded as having been unjustly enriched by the amount of it.[282] But the claims for damages and for recoupment of the amount of the bribe are alternative: the principal must elect which to exercise.[283]

[276] See *Mahesan v Malaysia Government Officers Co-operative Housing Society Ltd* [1979] A.C. 374 at 381. If none, for example if the attempt to bribe is unsuccessful, there is therefore no liability: *Chancery Client Partners Ltd v MRC 957 Ltd* [2016] EWHC 2142 (Ch); [2016] Lloyd's Rep. F.C. 578.

[277] *Mahesan v Malaysia Government Officers Co-operative Housing Society Ltd* [1979] A.C. 374 at 383, per Lord Diplock. The statements in *Novoship (UK) Ltd v Mikhaylyuk* [2012] EWHC 3586 (Comm) at [108] and *Motortrak Ltd v FCA Australia Pty Ltd* [2018] EWHC 990 (Comm) at [134]–[136] that there is an "irrebuttable" presumption of loss in the amount of the bribe should be taken with some scepticism.

[278] *Industries & General Mortgage Co Ltd v Lewis* [1949] 2 All E.R. 573; *Petrotrade Inc v Smith* [2000] 1 Lloyd's Rep. 486; *Fyffes Group Ltd v Templeman* [2000] 2 Lloyd's Rep. 643.

[279] For example, if he can show a specific way in which the agreement negotiated by the corrupt agent is less advantageous to him than a contract negotiated at arm's length. See, e.g. *Fyffes Group Ltd v Templeman* [2000] 2 Lloyd's Rep. 643.

[280] *Corporación National del Cobre de Chile v Sogemin Metals Ltd* [1997] 1 W.L.R. 1396.

[281] Agent: see, e.g. *Boston Deep Sea Fishing Co v Ansell* (1888) 39 Ch D. 339 and Briber: see *Fyffes Group Ltd v Templeman* [2000] 2 Lloyd's Rep. 643.

[282] The agent because he should not have taken the bribe in the first place: the briber because he presumably gained at least to the extent of the bribe.

[283] *Mahesan v Malaysia Government Officers Co-operative Housing Society Ltd* [1979] A.C. 374; also *Motortrak Ltd v FCA Australia Pty Ltd* [2018] EWHC 990 (Comm) at [138] (Moulder J). See A. Tettenborn, "Bribery, Corruption and Restitution-The Strange Case of Mr Mahesan" (1979) 95 L.Q.R. 68 and C. Needham, "Recovering the Profits of Bribery" (1979) 95 L.Q.R. 532.

CHAPTER 19

TRESPASS TO LAND AND DISPOSSESSION

TABLE OF CONTENTS

1. THE NATURE OF TRESPASS

Examples of trespass

Replace paragraph with:

It is a trespass to remove any part of the land in the possession of another or any part of a building or other erection which is attached to the soil so as to form part of the realty. So a landlord who removes the doors and windows of a house in the possession of his tenant commits a trespass,[3] but there is no trespass if he has the supply of gas and electricity cut off so as to compel the tenant to leave the house.[4] It is also a trespass to place anything on or in land in the possession of another, such as fixing air conditioning equipment into his wall,[5] entering land below the surface by mining or otherwise,[6] or growing a creeper up his wall.[7] While dumping rubbish on another's land is trespass, causing land to become fouled by a discharge of oil into a navigable river is not.[8] Equally, one who has a right of entry upon another's land and acts in excess of his right (such as unreasonable user of a public highway[8A]) or after his right has expired, is a trespasser.[9] And a person who, without authorisation, enters an area that has been designated a safety zone by a public authority, is also a trespasser.[9A] Every continuance of a trespass is a fresh trespass in respect of which a new cause of action arises from day to day as long as the trespass continues. So one who built on the claimant's land some buttresses to support a road and paid damages in an action for trespass was held liable in damages in a second action for not removing the buttresses after notice.[10] **19-02**

[3] *Lavender v Betts* [1942] 2 All E.R. 72.

[4] *Perera v Vandiyar* [1953] 1 W.L.R. 672. By the Protection from Eviction Act 1977 s.1 it is an offence unlawfully to evict or harass residential occupiers or to re-enter leasehold premises without court order. But breach of duty under the Act does not give rise to an action for compensation: *McCall v Abelesz* [1976] Q.B. 585. Criminal compensation may be available: *R. v Bokhari* (1974) 59 Cr. App. R. 303. An injunction is available for breach of s.3 of the Act as a tort: *Warder v Cooper* [1970] Ch. 495. The Housing Act 1988 ss.27–29, gives a prescribed measure of damages for unlawful eviction and extends the offence of harassment.

[5] *Eaton Mansions (Westminster) Ltd v Stinger Compania de Inversion SA* [2011] EWCA Civ 607; [2011] H.L.R. 42.

[6] See paras 19-16 and 19-70.

[7] *Simpson v Weber* (1925) 41 T.L.R. 302.

[8] *British Waterways Board v Severn Trent Water Ltd* [2001] EWCA Civ 276; [2002] Ch. 25. See paras 19-08 and 20-02 for the difference between trespass and nuisance.

[8A] *Cambridge CC v Traditional Cambridge Tours Ltd* [2018] EWHC 1304 (QB); [2018] L.L.R. 458.

[9] *Hillen v ICI (Alkali) Ltd* [1936] A.C. 65.

[9A] *Sheffield CC v Fairhall* [2017] EWHC 2121 (QB); [2018] R.T.R. 11; [2018] Env. L.R. 12 at [68].

[10] *Holmes v Wilson* (1839) 10 A. & E. 503; *Konskier v Goodman Ltd* [1928] 1 K.B. 421.

Aircraft

Replace paragraph with:

19-05 Section 76(1) of the Civil Aviation Act 1982 provides that no action shall lie in respect of trespass by reason only of the flight of aircraft over any property at a height above the ground which, having regard to wind, weather and all the circumstances of the case, is reasonable, or of the ordinary incidents of such flight. Section 76(2) further provides that where material loss or damage[19] is caused to any person or property on land or water by, or by a person in, or an article or person falling from, an aircraft while in flight,[19A] taking off[20] or landing, then unless the loss or damage was caused or contributed to by the negligence of the person by whom it was suffered, damages in respect of the loss or damage shall be recoverable without proof of negligence or intention or other cause of action as if the loss or damage had been caused by the wilful act, neglect or default of the owner of the aircraft. This part of the Act applies only to liability for civil (not military) aircraft.[21]

[19] Which includes, in relation to persons, loss of life and personal injury: s.105.

[19A] "Flight" is not confined to lateral travel from one fixed point to another. It may refer to an aircraft that takes off, flies to a certain point (for, say, reconnaissance) and then returns to the same place from which it took off: *Peires v Bickerton's Aerodromes Ltd* [2017] EWCA Civ 273; [2017] 1 W.L.R. 2865 at [48]–[49].

[20] This seems only to include that period after the aircraft has come to its take-off position: *Blankley v Godley* [1952] 1 All E.R. 436.

[21] Civil Aviation Act 1982 Pt III.

Trespass lies without damage

Replace paragraph with:

19-09 To support an action of trespass it is not necessary that there should have been any actual damage.[33] The fact that trespass is actionable per se has enabled the action of trespass to be used for the purpose of settling title through actions of ejectment, though today such questions may also be decided by a declaratory judgment. The reason for this principle seems to be that acts of direct interference with another's possession are likely to lead to breaches of the peace and the policy of the law therefore demands that the claimant be relieved from the requirement of proving damage. So where the owners of an industrial enterprise anticipate the commission of trespass by environmental protestors they can be granted an interim injunction to prevent such trespass.[34] Where entry is merely threatened, a quia timet injunction is the appropriate remedy,[35] though in cases where the would-be protestors are persons unknown, such injunctions can only be granted with extreme caution on the part of the courts. Thus, in one case in which various fracking companies reasonably anticipated that various protest groups would seek to disrupt their activities, the Court of Appeal was insistent that a *quia timet* injunction could only be obtained within strict limits.[35A] Equally, where a potential threat is posed by something growing on the claimant's land which was planted there by the defendant, the claimant may seek a mandatory injunction to have the defendant remove it.[36] It is reasonable to anticipate a future trespass where protestors who have trespassed in the past have only modified the nature of their protests. Accordingly, injunctive relief for a prolonged period of time may be granted in such circumstances.[37]

[33] See, e.g. *Anchor Brewhouse Developments v Berkley House (Docklands Developments) Ltd* (1987) 2 E.G.L.R. 173. Nor is the trifling nature of the trespass any defence: *Yelloly v Morley* (1910) 27 T.L.R. 20.

[34] *Hampshire Waste Services Ltd v Intending Trespassers upon Chineham Incinerator* [2003] EWHC 1738 (Ch); [2004] Env. L.R. 9.

[35] *Hampshire Waste Services Ltd v Intending Trespassers upon Chineham Incinerator* [2003] EWHC 1738 (Ch); [2004] Env. L.R. 9.

[35A] *Boyd v Ineos Upstream Ltd* [2019] EWCA Civ 515. The agreed judgment of Court of Appeal (at [34]) set out six requirements: (i) a sufficiently real and imminent risk of trespass would have to exist; (2) it would have to be impossible to name the persons likely to commit the tort; (3) there would have to be the ability to give effective notice of the injunction (and for the method of such notice to be set out in the order); (4) the terms of the injunction would have to correspond to the threatened tort and not be so wide as to prohibit lawful conduct; (5) its terms would also have to be sufficiently clear and precise so as to enable persons potentially affected to know what they had not to do; and (6) the injunction would have to have clear geographical and temporal limits.

[36] *Nelson v Nicholson, The Independent,* 22 January 2001.

[37] See *Wensley v Persons Unknown* [2014] EWHC 3702 (Ch) (granting a two-year injunction to restrain anti-fracking protestors from trespassing on rural land in Lancashire).

4. JUSTIFICATION OF TRESPASS

(b) Justification under right of way and easement

Water

Replace paragraph with:

There is no general right in the public to pass over the foreshore for the purpose of bathing in the sea.[192] There may however be an exception in relation to fishing and navigation in the sea that covers the foreshore at high tide.[193] Furthermore, an exclusive right to gather shellfish from the foreshore may be acquired by prescription, but that exclusive right will not extend to sandbanks that subsequently (and fairly suddenly) become attached to the foreshore when channels that had formerly separated those sandbanks from the foreshore silt up.[194] To allow the established prescriptive right to be extended over the sandbanks in this way would be tantamount to conferring an exclusive right over new territory by prescription without there being the requisite long-use that characterises such rights. It would, without proper legal foundation, eclipse overnight the right held by members of the public to take shellfish from those sandbanks.[195] There is no public right to enter the foreshore for the collection of sea-coal cast there from submarine outcrops.[196] 19-44

There is no right to put down permanent moorings in tidal waters where the bed soil is privately owned.[197] Though public rights of navigation have been established from time immemorial over many navigable rivers, there is no public right at common law to tow on the banks of a navigable river,[198] and the public cannot acquire, by prescription, the statutory right to navigate a river.[199]

[192] *Blundell v Catterall* (1821) 5 B. & A. 268.

[193] *Llandudno Urban DC v Woods* [1899] 2 Ch. 705.

[194] *Loose v Lynn Shellfish Ltd* [2016] UKSC 14; [2017] A.C. 599.

[195] *Loose v Lynn Shellfish Ltd* [2016] UKSC 14; [2017] A.C. 599 at [73].

[196] *Alfred F Beckett v Lyons* [1967] Ch. 449.

[197] *Fowley Marine (Emsworth) Ltd v Gafford* [1968] 2 Q.B. 618 (though there is a right to navigate and anchor temporarily). The same rules apply to tidal stretches of canals: see *Moore v British Waterways Board* [2013] EWCA Civ 73; [2013] Ch. 488.

[198] *Ball v Herbert* (1789) 3 T.R. 253.

[199] *Att Gen (ex rel. Yorkshire Derwent Trust Ltd) v Brotherton* [1992] 1 A.C. 425, construing s.31(1) of the Highways Act 1980.

(d) Justification by licence

Effect of revocation

Replace footnote 237 with:

19-50 [237] *Cardiff CC v Lee* [2016] EWCA Civ 1034; [2017] 1 W.L.R. 1751.

(f) Police powers of entry and search

Search warrants

Replace paragraph with:

19-64 Section 8 of the Police and Criminal Evidence Act 1984 provides that a magistrate may issue a search warrant to enter and search premises on the application of a constable, when he (the magistrate) is satisfied that there are reasonable grounds for believing that the following conditions are met:

(1) an indictable offence has been committed;
(2) there is material on the premises likely to be of substantial value[307] to the investigation of the offence;
(3) that material is likely to be relevant[308] evidence;
(4) the material does not consist of items subject to legal privilege[309] or excluded material[310] or special procedure[311] material; and
(5) access to the material cannot practicably be obtained without a warrant or the purpose of the search will be frustrated unless the constable gains immediate entry to the premises.[312]

A constable entering premises under the authority of a search warrant granted under s.8 may seize and retain any evidence in respect of which the search was authorised.[313] The general power to issue search warrants to facilitate the investigation of crime granted by s.8 of the 1984 Act is without prejudice to, and additional to, other statutory powers to grant such warrants.[314] There is no general rule that a constable must first exhaust all other means of obtaining access to the relevant material before seeking the issue of a search warrant.[315] Nor is there any obligation to disclose to the party affected by the warrant the material upon which the magistrates had relied when deciding to grant the warrant. Instead, "all that is required is that ... [the magistrate] be satisfied, from the information contained in the constable's application and from the constable's answers on oath to any questions put, 'there are reasonable grounds for believing' the matters set out in section 8(1)(a) to (e)".[315A] And such warrants, according to the Supreme Court, can perfectly well be obtained on an ex parte basis.[315B]

[307] Whether by itself or together with other material: see s.8(1)(b).

[308] Evidence admissible at a trial for the offence: see s.8(4).

[309] As defined in s.10.

[310] Defined by ss.11–13. Excluded material basically consists of confidential personal records of a trade, business or profession, human tissue, etc. taken for medical purposes and "journalistic material" held in confidence.

[311] Defined by s.14. Confidential material not falling within the ambit of excluded material.

[312] s.8(1)(e), (3).

[313] s.8(2). But note the wider powers of seizure under s.19: see also para.17-129 onwards.

[314] s.8(5). Several such powers continue to be relevant, e.g. Theft Act 1968 s.26(1) and (3) (to enter and search for stolen goods); Misuse of Drugs Act 1971 s.23(3) (to search for controlled drugs); Obscene Publications Act 1959 s.3.

[315] *R. v Billericay JJ and Dobbyn Ex p. Frank Harris (Coaches)* [1991] Crim. L.R. 472.

[315A] *R. (on the application of Haralambous) v St Albans Crown Court* [2018] UKSC 1; [2018] A.C. 236 at [15].

[315B] *R. (on the application of Haralambous) v St Albans Crown Court* [2018] UKSC 1; [2018] A.C. 236 at [27].

Add new paragraph:

On the other hand, police officers are under a duty to disclose all material facts when making a without-notice application for a search warrant, including information which might undermine the application. And the duty to make such disclosure extends to disclosing facts which were not actually known, but which would have been known had the officer made proper inquiries.[315C] A warrant to search premises does not of itself authorise the search of persons found there.[316] Moreover, it seems arguable that a warrant procured out of malice will not be valid.[317] Equally, even in the absence of bad faith, a warrant will be invalid if those responsible for drafting it "acted with patent and egregious disregard for, or indifference to, the constitutional safeguards within the statutory scheme".[318] And a search will not be lawful if the copy of the warrant the officer concerned is obliged to give to the occupier[319] fails to specify all those particulars contained in s.15(6) of the 1984 Act.[320] **19-64A**

[315C] *R. (on the application of Brook) v Preston Crown Court* [2018] EWHC 2024 (Admin); [2018] A.C.D. 95 at [16].

[316] *Herman King v The Queen* [1969] 1 A.C. 304. But it may permit an officer executing the search warrant to detain someone, to prevent them walking around their own home, while it is being searched. The authority given by the warrant has to enable the search to be effective: *DPP v Meaden* [2003] EWHC 3005 (Admin); [2004] 1 W.L.R. 945.

[317] See *Fitzpatrick v Commissioner of Police of the Metropolis* [2012] EWHC 12 (Admin); [2012] Lloyd's Rep. F.C. 361 at [144].

[318] *R. (on the application of Chatwani) v National Crime Agency* [2015] EWHC 1283 (Admin); [2015] A.C.D. 110, at [141], per Hickinbottom J.

[319] Police and Criminal Evidence Act 1984, s.16(5).

[320] *R. (on the application of Bhatti) v Croydon Magistrates' Court* [2010] EWHC 522 (Admin); [2011] 1 W.L.R. 948.

Replace paragraph with:

19-65 Section 16 enacts rules relating to the execution of search warrants and applies whether the relevant warrant is issued under s.8 of the 1984 Act or by virtue of some other statutory power.[321] It provides inter alia that a warrant to enter and search premises may be executed by any constable, and may authorise persons to accompany any constable who is executing it. Entry and search under a warrant must be within one month from its date of issue and at a reasonable hour unless it appears to the constable executing it that the purposes of the search will be frustrated by entry at a reasonable hour. Provision is made for the constable to identify himself to the occupier if he is present and for the production of the warrant.[322] A search under warrant is limited to a search for the purposes for which the warrant is issued. Accordingly, searches conducted under warrants that are drawn too widely are unlawful. This may occur where the warrant fails to comply with the requirement in s.15(6)(b) to specify, "so far as practicable", the articles sought.[323] But the qualification "so far as practicable" is an important one since it will allow for some measure of latitude in the terms in which a warrant is constructed where a search of various different types of electronic devices may be necessary,[324] or where it is impossible to specify in advance the type of property sought because the property in question is bound up with, and likely to shed light on, money laundering activities.[325] On the other hand, a warrant will certainly be regarded as having been drawn too widely where it purports to permit seizure of material "deemed relevant" by the searching officers.[325A] This is because such wording would effectively delegate to the officers concerned a task that, under the statute, falls to the justices. Any officer who seized material that turned out to be irrelevant could (inappropriately) seek subsequently to legitimise his entry and seizure simply by saying that he had deemed the seizure relevant at the time. The application for a search warrant must also specify which part of the premises is to be searched where police are aware that the premises comprise a number of individual dwellings.

[321] e.g. Protection from Harassment Act 1997, s.2B. See also s.15 of the 1984 Act in relation to procedural safeguards in this context; *R. v Reading JJ Ex p. South West Meats Ltd* [1992] Crim. L.R. 672. Note, however, that the safeguards contained in s.16 (as well as those contained in s.15) do not apply to post-arrest powers of search under s.18 or s.32 of PACE: *R. (on the application of Singh) v National Crime Agency* [2018] EWHC 1119 (Admin); [2018] 1 W.L.R. 5073.

[322] If there is a dispute about whether there has been compliance with these requirements, the onus is on the police officer to show on the balance of probabilities that he identified himself and that he produced the warrant: *Alleyne v Commissioner of Police of the Metropolis* [2012] EWHC 3955 (QB) at [96]. See s.16(6)–(7) for the duty of a constable executing a warrant on premises in the absence of the occupier. *R. v Chief Constable of Lancashire Ex p. Parker* [1993] Q.B. 577.

[323] *Van der Pijl v Kingston Crown Court* [2012] EWHC 2989 (Admin); [2013] 1 W.L.R. 2706.

[324] *R. (on the application of Cabot Global Ltd) v Barkingside Magistrates' Court* [2015] EWHC 1458 (Admin); [2015] 2 Cr. App. R. 26.

[325] *R. (on the application of Atwal) v Lewes Crown Court* [2015] EWHC 1783 (Admin).

[325A] *R. (on the application of Superior Import/Export Ltd) v Revenue and Customs Commissioners* [2017] EWHC 3172 (Admin); [2018] Lloyd's Rep. F.C. 115.

5. MEASURE OF DAMAGES

(a) General

Replace paragraph with:

19-66 A claimant in trespass is entitled to recover damages, even though he has sustained no actual loss.[326] To recover substantial damages the claimant must show an interest in the land beyond an interest for a day or two, otherwise the damages will usually be nominal.[327] But whether the measure of damages must correspond precisely with the claimant's interest is not clear. According to a number of recent cases, one method of quantifying the damages is by reference to a hypothetical negotiation between the parties. The damages are fixed in accordance with the price the defendant would have had to pay to do the acts complained of had he negotiated for permission to do them. However, the licence fee will be computed in line with the actual duration of the trespass rather than by reference to any longer period of time for which the defendant would probably have sought permission to do the thing complained of had the parties actually negotiated a licence.[328] The use of hypothetical contracts now rests on Supreme Court authority. In *Bocardo SA v Star Energy UK Onshore Ltd*,[329] the court used the hypothetical contract device, but was careful to be attentive to the background statutory (compulsory aquistion) scheme that would have impinged upon any negotiations between the parties.[330] Where the claimant has altogether been deprived of his land through a trespass, damages will amount at least to the value of his interest, but there appears to be no authority for the proposition that the value of his interest generally limits the measure of damages.[331] Indeed, it has been held that in wrongful eviction cases, the claimant may recover damages not merely for the letting value of the property for the full length of time that the right of occupation had existed, but also for the anxiety, inconvenience and stress involved in the loss of the home.[331A] In cases of unauthorised parking, the court retains the freedom to compute for itself the damages payable where the defendant refuses to pay a penalty imposed by a private parking enforcement company. But, in deciding the quantum, where the parking enforcement company is a member of an accredited trade association ("ATA"), the court is likely to "be influenced ... [on] quantum by the fact that the charges [levied by the company] had been approved in advance by the ATA".[332] When substantial damage has been caused, the measure of damages varies according to whether the trespass belongs to one or other of the three following classes.

[326] Such damages are likely to be nominal only: *Hanina v Morland* (2000) 97(47) L.S. Gaz. 41. Injunctions may also be obtained in such cases: *Patel v WH Smith (Eziot) Ltd* [1987] 1 W.L.R. 853.

[327] *Twyman v Knowles* (1853) 13 C.B. 222; *Rust v Victoria Graving Dock* (1887) 36 Ch D. 113 at 119.

[328] *Eaton Mansions (Westminster) Ltd v Stinger Compania de Inversion SA* [2013] EWCA Civ 1308; [2014] H.L.R. 4.

[329] [2010] UKSC 35; [2011] 1 A.C. 380.

[330] [2010] UKSC 35; [2011] 1 A.C. 380 at [91], per Lord Brown.

[331] cf. the rule for bailee of goods in *The Winkfield* [1902] P. 42. See also para.17-83.

[331A] *Smith v Khan* [2018] EWCA Civ 1137; [2018] H.L.R. 31 at [39] and [45].

[332] *R. (on the application of Duff) v Secretary of State for Transport* [2015] EWHC 1605 (Admin); [2015] R.T.R. 28 at [41], per Edis J.

6. ACTION FOR THE RECOVERY OF LAND

Recovery of land and correction of Land Register

Replace paragraph with:

In the action for the recovery of land (sometimes called ejectment), the claimant is out of possession and claims immediate possession of the land. To do this he must recover "by the strength of his own title and not by the weakness of the defendant's".[361] He must therefore prove the links in his own title.[362] He may, for example, prove his title as a mortgagee and claim for possession if the mortgagor is in default.[363] The defendant, on the other hand, need only prove that he is in possession and need not prove any title.[364] Proof that the claimant was in possession 19-73 before the defendant,[365] no matter for how short a time, is prima facie evidence of his having title, for such prior possession raises a presumption that he was seised in fee; and such presumption cannot be rebutted merely by showing that the claimant did not derive his possession from any person who had title.[366] Whether or not it may be rebutted by showing that the title is in fact in a third person is doubtful, though *Doe (dec'd) Carter v Barnard*[367] and *Nagle v Shea*[368] suggest that *jus tertii* is a defence. An important point to note in this context is that where A has defrauded B out of his title to land, and subsequently registered title in his own name, B will be able to seek rectification of the register. But B must do this within twelve years since the effluxion of time from the moment that A took possession will count towards A's claiming adverse possession (and thereby being in a position to defeat a rectification of the register).[369]

361 *Martin v Strachan* (1744) 5 T.R. 107n.

362 *Philips v Philips* (1878) 4 Q.B.D. 127.

363 *West Penwith Rural DC v Gunnell* [1968] 1 W.L.R. 1153.

364 *Danford v McAnulty* (1883) 8 App. Cas. 456 at 462, per Lord Blackburn.

365 For these purposes, a local authority is deemed to have possession of a public highway so that a possession order can be obtained against protestors occupying it and causing a public nuisance: *City of London Corp v Samede* [2012] EWHC 34 (QB); (2012) 109(5) L.S.G. 21.

366 *Doe (dec'd) Smith v Webber* (1834) 1 A. & E. 119; *Doe (dec'd) Hughes v Dyeball* (1829) Moo. M. 346.

367 (1849) 13 Q.B. 945.

368 (1874) Ir. Rep. 8 C.L. 224.

369 *Rashid v Nasrullah* [2018] EWCA Civ 2685. The previous Court of Appeal decision in *Parshall v Bryans* [2013] EWCA Civ 240; [2013] Ch. 568 was held to be inconsistent with the House of Lords' decision in *JA Pye (Oxford) Ltd v Graham* [2002] UKHL 30; [2003] 1 A.C. 419.

Mesne profits

Replace paragraph with:

19-76 In an action for the recovery of possession of land the claimant may join a claim for mesne profits (i.e. damages for wrongful occupancy),[381] but he is entitled, too, to pursue an award of mesne profits in a subsequent action.[382] When the claimant sues for mesne profits alone, he must first enter to gain possession, and then the principle of trespass by relation[383] enables him to sue for former profits. But if recovery of land is time-barred by adverse possession, the right to recover mesne profits and rent is lost.[384] Mesne profits include compensation for the value of the use and occupation of the premises,[385] and also any damage which has been caused to the premises themselves,[386] for the term "mesne profits" is not confined to the profits which have accrued to the defendant, but extends to all loss that the claimant has sustained.[387] In considering the value of the use and occupation the net annual value must be taken.[388] In *Inverugie Investments Ltd v Hackett* the wrongfully dispossessed owner of a block of hotel apartments, which he had acquired for investment purposes, was able to recover a "reasonable rent" for each apartment for 365 days a year, notwithstanding that for much of the year partial occupancy at discounted prices was apparently all that could have been achieved in practice.[389] In similar vein is the decision of the Court of Appeal in *Shepherd v Collect Investments Ltd.*[389A] There, the court had to grapple with the difficult question of quantifying the rental value of industrial land upon which the trespasser had tipped a certain amount of waste matter. The appellant had been a trespasser on the respondent's land for 51 months and had been ordered to pay damages equating to lost rent valued at £78,000 per annum. The appellant argued that this figure was too high because the expert valuation from which this figure was derived was not a genuine estimate of what would have been a reasonable rent for the land concerned. Instead, the expert valuer had based the amount on the average rental value of industrial land in that part of the country. The appellant's argument that the figure arrived at was too high was based on the fact that it failed to take account of the waste that he himself had tipped there and which would have reduced significantly the amount that could have been obtained by way of rent for that land. In a judgment with which the other members of the Court of Appeal signalled their agreement, David Richards LJ held that the valuation was a legitimate one and that the trespasser "could not rely on the poor condition of the land to justify a lower figure".[389B]

[381] See para.19-28. On the measure of damages see *Ministry of Defence v Ashman* (1993) 66 P.C.R. 195, and *Ministry of Defence v Thompson* (1993) 66 P. & C.R. 195.

[382] The subsequent action for mesne profits is not prevented by the doctrine of res judicata: *Farrar v Leongreen Ltd* [2017] EWCA Civ 2211; [2018] 1 P. & C.R. 17. This is because that doctrine "only operates where the claimant seeks to sue again upon the same cause of action". Yet, if "the respondent sought to rely in the second action upon causes of action [for mesne profits] which are distinct from the cause of action upon which it had relied in the first action [i.e. the action for possession]", then "the respondent remained entitled to seek to bring a claim... [for mesne profits] on which its second action was based" ([2017] EWCA Civ 2211; [2018] 1 P. & C.R. 17 at [26], per Sales LJ).

[383] See para.19-28. But no entry is required after C's land interest ceases: *Southport Tramways v Gandy* [1897] 2 Q.B. 66.

[384] *Mount Carmel Investments Ltd v Thurlow (Ltd)* [1988] 1 W.L.R. 1078; *Jolly, Re* [1900] 2 Ch. 616.

[385] This is whether occupied by the defendant himself or by a tenant holding under him: *Doe v Harlow* (1840) 12 A. & E. 40.

[386] *Dunn v Large* (1783) 3 Doug. 335.

[387] *Goodtitle v Tombs* (1770) 3 Wils. 118 at 121. Note that mesne profits contain a combination of compensatory and restitutionary elements: *Inverugie Investments Ltd v Hackett* [1995] 1 W.L.R. 713 at 718, per Lord Lloyd.

[388] Tax to which a claimant receiving rent would have been liable is to be deducted: *Hall & Co Ltd v Pearlberg* [1956] 1 W.L.R. 244.

[389] *Inverugie Investments Ltd v Hackett* [1995] 1 W.L.R. 713 at 718, per Lord Lloyd.

[389A] [2018] EWCA Civ 162.

[389B] [2018] EWCA Civ 162 at [29] (David Richards LJ).

7. STATUTES OF LIMITATION

Adverse possession and licensed possession

Replace paragraph with:

Adverse possession for a period of 12 continuous years extinguishes title[399] and in effect produces an involuntary loss of property by a proprietor who fails to challenge a squatter (or other adverse possessor),[400] within the period of time allowed by statute. Also, to interrupt the adverse possession, the title owner must meaningfully bring the adverse possessor's possession to an end.[401] Since the law on adverse possession (which has been held not to be undermined by the doctrine of illegality[401A]) permits a successful squatter, even with knowledge of the true title, to expropriate without compensation, it is necessary to define closely the limits of his ability to acquire another's land by adverse possession. However, where there is no evidence as to who the true owner is, the Land Registry will be entitled to register the applicant squatter's possessory, not absolute, title based on his or her adverse possession.[402] The phrase "adverse possession" in the Limitation Act 1980,[403] means no more than that a person is in adverse possession in whose favour 19-79 time can run under the statute. By necessary implication, "time cannot run ... in favour of a licensee" whose possession has been granted or tolerated.[404] Happily the courts have elaborated upon the concept. The leading case is *JA Pye (Oxford) Ltd v Graham.*[405] There, the House of Lords insisted that the words of the Act were to be given their ordinary and plain meaning. Thus, upon satisfaction of the twin tests of factual possession and intention to possess, time would run against the true owner. Adverse possession, Lord Hope said, is not a complex notion but one "used as a convenient label only, in recognition simply of the fact that the possession is adverse to the interests of the paper owner".[406] On the other hand, the statutory provisions governing adverse possession have since been held by the European Court of Human Rights to support violations of art.1 of Protocol 1 of the ECHR which provides for the right to the peaceful enjoyment of one's property.[407] But the existing rules persist; and despite what Lord Hope said about the relative simplicity of the concept of adverse possession, it has since been established that the question of the requisite intention requires some clarification. In *Roberts v Swangrove Estates Ltd,*[408] the Court of Appeal held that intention to trespass had to be distinguished from intention to enter into possession and on this basis found that the defendants had been in adverse possession even though they never intended to trespass.[409] Since then, it has been further clarified that in order to satisfy the statutory requirement of having reasonable belief that the disputed land was actually owned by the person in adverse possession,[410] such belief is to be judged according to what the person in adverse possession believed *personally* rather than what it was (or would have been) reasonable for the solicitors acting on his behalf to believe.[411]

[399] Limitation Act 1980, ss.15 and 17 (subject to s.18 in the case of unregistered land; and subject to the Land Registration Act 2002 s.98(1) in the case of registered land). The same 12 year rule applies to loss of title by adverse possession in Northern Ireland by virtue of the Limitation (Northern Ireland) Order 1989, art.21(1): *O'Brien v Martin* [2017] NICh 20.

[400] It is possible to enter into adverse possession without being a squatter. For example, one might acquire title to an unregistered stretch of a tidal river bed: see *Port of London Authority v Ashmore* [2010] EWCA Civ 30; [2010] 1 All E.R. 1139 (acknowledged to be correct in *Moore v British Waterways Board* [2013] EWCA Civ 73; [2013] Ch. 488 at [57], per Lewison LJ). Equally, one may have been the tenant of a company registered abroad whose land in this country, when the company is wound up, passes to the Crown as bona vacantia. In principle, one may acquire rights of adverse possession against the Crown in such circumstances since one's occupation has never been with the consent of the Crown: *Everitt v Zeital* [2018] EWHC 1316 (Ch).

[401] *Zarb v Parry* [2011] EWCA Civ 1306; [2012] 1 W.L.R. 1240.

[401A] *Rashid v Nasrullah* [2018] EWCA Civ 2685 at [68]–[72].

[402] *R. (on the application of Truong Dia Diep) v Land Registry* [2010] EWHC 3315 (Admin).

[403] Sch.1 Pt I para.8.

[404] See, e.g. *Smart v Lambeth LBC* [2013] EWCA Civ 1375; [2014] H.L.R. 7; *Smith v Molyneaux* [2016] UKPC 35; [2017] 1 P. & C.R. 7.

[405] [2002] UKHL 30; [2003] 1 A.C. 419.

[406] [2002] UKHL 30; [2003] 1 A.C. 419 at [69].

[407] *JA Pye (Oxford) Ltd v UK* (2006) 43 E.H.R.R. 3.

[408] [2008] EWCA Civ 98; [2008] Ch. 439.

[409] [2008] EWCA Civ 98; [2008] Ch. 439 at [87]. However, where there has been a mistaken registration of both A and B as the registered owners of land, it is impossible for either party to enter into adverse possession vis-à-vis the other since anyone with registered title cannot possibly be in adverse possession relative to another. Adverse possession as between A and B only becomes possible after the mistake in the Register has been rectified: see *Parshall v Bryans* [2013] EWCA Civ 240; [2013] Ch. 568.

[410] Land Registration Act 2002 Sch.6 para.5(4)(c).

[411] *IAM Group Plc v Chowdrey* [2012] EWCA Civ 505; [2012] 2 P. & C.R. 13 at [27], per Etherington LJ.

Replace paragraph with:

So far as factual possession is concerned, the person claiming adverse possession will satisfy this requirement if he is able to provide evidence of his user of the land.[412] One established example is that of paving an area of land with a permanent surface.[412A] In deciding whether the defendant is entitled to mount a counterclaim based on his adverse possession, the judge is bound to take seriously the evidence of both parties, as the Court of Appeal made emphatically clear in *Weymont v Place*.[413] In *Best v Chief Land Registrar*,[414] the Court of Appeal also supplied some examples of the kinds of acts to which the claimant might advert in seeking to demonstrate his adverse possession. These included, not merely the act of squatting but also the act of maintaining the property itself, and even maintaining external structures, such as a boundary fence. In essence, as Morgan J put it in *Food Converters Ltd v Newell*,[414A] "the concept of possession of land does not require a person to be physically present on the land for every moment of the 12-year period... [for it is enough] if the person claiming to be in possession for 12 years, without interruption, has had the requisite degree of control of the land throughout the relevant period of 12 years". **19-80**

[412] *Akhtar v Brewster* [2012] EWHC 3521 (Ch).

[412A] *Thorpe v Frank* [2019] EWCA Civ 150.

[413] [2015] EWCA Civ 289; [2015] C.P. Rep. 29.

[414] [2015] EWCA Civ 17; [2016] Q.B. 23.

[414A] [2018] EWHC 926 (Ch) at [35].

[illegible]

So far as adverse possession is concerned, the person claiming adverse possession [illegible] the requirement [illegible] to provide evidence of his use of the land. [illegible] land with a [illegible] surface. In deciding whether the standard is satisfied [illegible] the adverse possessor, the [illegible] bound to take account [illegible] of both parties [illegible] the Court of Appeal made [illegible] clear [illegible]. In [illegible] the Court of Appeal [illegible] examples of the [illegible] the claimant [illegible] adverse possession [illegible]. [illegible] not merely the [illegible] the concept of possession of land [illegible] the land for [illegible] years [illegible] the person claiming [illegible] possession [illegible] without [illegible] control of the land throughout the [illegible] period. 19.86

[illegible]

CHAPTER 20

NUISANCE AND RYLANDS V FLETCHER

TABLE OF CONTENTS

1. THE NATURE OF NUISANCE

(b) Scope of private nuisance

Private nuisance

Replace paragraph with:

20-06 Just as in issues of public nuisance, modern statutory control has had an effect in diminishing the role of private nuisance as a regulation of duties between neighbours. Refusal of planning permission may prevent many activities which would otherwise be a nuisance, but the tort of nuisance still provides sanctions against excessive interferences from activities which are not in themselves unlawful or unpermitted by public control over the use of property. The acts which constitute public nuisances are all of them unlawful acts. In private nuisance, on the other hand, the conduct of the defendant which results in the nuisance is, of itself, not necessarily or usually unlawful. A private nuisance may be and usually is caused by a person doing, on his own land, something which he is lawfully entitled to do. His conduct only becomes a nuisance when the consequences of his act are not confined to his own land but extend to the land of his neighbour by:

(1) causing an encroachment on his neighbour's land, when it closely resembles trespass;

(2) causing physical damage to his neighbour's land or building or works or vegetation upon it; or
(3) unduly interfering with his neighbour in the comfortable and convenient enjoyment of his land.

It may be a nuisance when a person does something on his own property which interferes with his neighbour's ability to enjoy his property by putting it to profitable use. It is also a nuisance to interfere with some easement or profit or other right used or enjoyed with his neighbour's land. In referring to the breaking down of instances of private nuisance into the three categories referred to in this paragraph Sir Terence Etherton MR expressed himself as follows in *Network Rail Infrastructure Ltd v Williams*[25A]:

> "The difficulty with any rigid categorisation is that it may not easily accommodate possible examples of nuisance in new social conditions or may undermine a proper analysis of factual situations which have aspects of more than one category but do not fall squarely within any one category, having regard to existing case law".

The instant case concerned the notorious "bamboo-like perennial plant" Japanese knotweed which had spread from the defendant's land on to that of the claimants. It involved both category (1), encroachment, and category (3), interference with enjoyment.

[25A] See [2018] EWCA Civ 1514; [2018] 3 W.L.R. 1105 at [41].

(ii) Nuisance by interference with enjoyment

Examples

Add new footnote 53A to end of paragraph:

[53A] See also per Mann J in *Fearn v The Board of Trustees of the Tate Gallery* [2019] EWHC 246 (Ch) at [165]–[168]. **20-09**

Standard of comfort

Replace paragraph with:

A nuisance of this kind, to be actionable, must be such as to be a real interference with the comfort or convenience of living according to the standards of the average man. An interference which alone causes harm to something of abnormal sensitiveness does not of itself constitute a nuisance.[62] A man cannot increase the liabilities of his neighbour by applying his own property to special uses, whether for business or for pleasure.[63] In practice the general application of the concepts of foreseeability and reasonable user may have rendered the notion of abnormal sensitivity less significant in modern law,[64] although it is submitted that it remains useful as a guideline when applying those broad concepts in particular cases.[64A] But once the nuisance is established, the remedies by way of damages or an injunction will extend to delicate and sensitive operations such as the growing of orchids.[65] When it is said that a householder is entitled to have the air in his house untainted and unpolluted by any acts of his neighbour, that means that he is entitled to have "not necessarily air as fresh, free and pure as at the time of building the plaintiff's house the atmosphere then was, but air not rendered to an important degree less compatible, or at least not rendered incompatible, with the physical comfort of human existence".[66] Moreover, the discomfort must be substantial not merely with reference to the claimant; it must be of such a degree that it would be substantial **20-11** to any person occupying the claimant's premises, irrespective of his position in life, age, or state of health; it must be "an inconvenience materially interfering with the ordinary comfort physically of human existence, not merely according to elegant or dainty modes and habits of living, but according to plain and sober and simple notions among the English people".[67] Where a social practice is sufficiently general and widely practised, there is no reason why it should not be protected, though pursued for pleasure and not profit. Thus, to send regularly large volumes of heavy smoke over a field habitually used for sporting activities may well be accounted a nuisance. And normal horticulture is certainly protected. It is not necessary to prove injury to health.[68] Indeed, it seems that no regard should be had to the needs of insomniacs or invalids.[69]

[62] *Robinson v Kilvert* (1889) 41 Ch D. 88 (ordinary heating damaging brown paper—"exceptionally delicate trade"); *Bridlington Relay Ltd v Yorkshire Electricity Board* [1965] Ch. 436 (interference with special radio and television relay system); *Fearn v The Board of Trustees of the Tate Gallery* [2019] EWHC 246 (Ch) at [211] ("a particularly sensitive property").

[63] *Eastern and South African Telegraph Co v Cape Town Tramways* [1902] A.C. 381 at 383; *Hoare & Co v McAlpine* [1923] 1 Ch. 167; *Whycer v Urry* [1956] J.P.L. 365 (Court of Appeal held practice of ophthalmic optician in a business area too specially delicate for protection); *Cooke v Forbes* (1867) L.R. 5 Eq. 166 (sulphuretted hydrogen damaged coconut matting by reason of delicate nature of its manufacture, injunction refused without prejudice to claim in damages).

[64] See *National Rail Infrastructure Ltd v CJ Morris* [2004] EWCA Civ 172; [2004] Env. L.R. 41 at [33]–[35], per Buxton LJ.

[64A] See also per Mann J in *Fearn v The Board of Trustees of the Tate Gallery* [2019] EWHC 246 (Ch) at [228]–[230].

[65] See per Lord Simonds in *McKinnon Industries Ltd v Walker* [1951] 3 D.L.R. 577 at 581.

[66] per Knight Bruce VC in *Walter v Selfe* (1851) 4 De G. & Sm. 315 at 322; affirmed 19 L.T. 308; *Polsue and Alfieri v Rushmer* [1907] A.C. 121.

[67] *Walter v Selfe* (1851) 4 De G. & Sm. 315 at 322.

[68] *Crump v Lambert* (1867) L.R. 3 Eq. 409.

[69] *Bloodworth v Cormack* [1949] N.Z.L.R. 1058 at 1064, per Callan J; *Murray v Laus* [1960] N.Z.L.R. 126 (noise).

(iv) Natural nuisances

Development of liability

Replace paragraph with:

20-21 The development of liability for natural nuisances was taken a large step further by the Court of Appeal in *Leakey v National Trust*.[118] The National Trust owed a natural hill in Somerset which by natural forces slipped so as to damage the claimant's contiguous property. It was argued for the Trust that there could be no liability for such accidents of nature, and also that if there was any liability it sounded only in negligence and not in nuisance. The statement of claim did not refer to "negligence" as such but alleged breach of duty to take reasonable care to prevent the defendant's land from falling onto the claimant's. Megaw LJ was prepared to regard that "as being properly described as a claim in nuisance".[119] On the issue of substance the court followed *Goldman v Hargrave* both as to the existence of the duty and as to its scope and content.[120] In *Bybrook Barn Centre v Kent CC*[121] the Court of Appeal applied *Leakey v National Trust* to hold a highway authority liable for flooding caused when a naturally occurring stream overflowed as it passed through a culvert owned by the defendant highway authority. The authority was aware that the culvert had become inadequate to carry the stream, but had failed to take remedial measures. *Goldman v Hargrave* and *Leakey v National Trust* were referred to in *Network Rail Infrastructure Ltd v Williams*[121A] in which the Court of Appeal imposed liability on Network Rail for failing to prevent the spread of Japanese knotweed from their land.

[118] [1980] Q.B. 485 CA, noted by Markesinis in [1980] C.L.J. 259. See also Markesinis, "Negligence, Nuisance and Affirmative Duties of Action" (1989) 105 L.Q.R. 104 at 118–119, where *Sedleigh-Denfield v O'Callaghan*, *Goldman v Hargrave* and *Leakey v National Trust* are related to the House of Lords' judgments in *Smith v Littlewoods Ltd* [1987] 1 A.C. 241.

[119] [1980] Q.B. 485 at 514.

[120] See also *Holbeck Hall Hotel Ltd v Scarborough BC* [2000] Q.B. 836 CA (no liability for land slip which could not have been foreseen without extensive geological investigations).

[121] [2001] B.L.R. 55; [2001] Env. L.R. 30.

[121A] [2018] EWCA Civ 1514; [2018] 3 W.L.R. 1105.

(vi) Necessity for damage

Necessity for damage

Replace paragraph with:

In nuisances of the second kind,[144] namely, those causing physical damage to land, actual, not merely prospective, damage is essential to a cause of action. Until damage is caused no nuisance exists, only the potentiality of a nuisance.[145] But an injunction of a *quia timet* nature can be obtained in the face of impending harm, though no actual damage has as yet occurred. If the impending damage is not imminent or at least very likely to occur in the near future, the court will not usually exercise its discretion in the issue of an injunction.[146] In *Network Rail Infrastructure Ltd v Williams*,[146A] which concerned the potential of Japanese knotweed for causing harm, Sir Terence Etherton MR said, obiter: **20-26**

> "It is usually said that there must be proof of imminent physical injury or harm for a quia timet injunction to be granted… . It is possible, however, that that is too prescriptive and that what matters is the probability and likely gravity of damage rather than simply its imminence… . Although the point has not been considered before in the cases I see no reason why, in appropriate circumstances, as in the present case, a claimant should not be able to obtain a final mandatory injunction where the amenity value of the land is diminished by the presence of roots even though there has not yet been any physical damage".

[144] See para.20-06.

[145] *Sedleigh-Denfield v O'Callaghan* [1940] A.C. 880 at 896 and 919–920.

[146] *Salvin v North Brancepeth Coal Co* (1874) L.R. 9 Ch. 705. "If some picturesque haven opens its arms to invite the commerce of the world, it is not for this court to forbid the embrace, although the fruit of it should be the sights, and sounds, and smells of a common seaport and shipbuilding town, which would drive the Dryads and their masters from their ancient solitude", per James LJ at 709–710.

[146A] See [2018] EWCA Civ 1514; [2018] 3 W.L.R. 1105 at [71]–[72].

Other cases

Replace paragraph with:

In other cases of nuisance, no actual financial or physical damage need be proved. **20-27**
Where the nuisance consists of an encroachment, the law will presume damage.[146B] In a case where rain-water was caused to fall on the claimant's land by a cornice projecting from the defendant's building, it was said, "the mere fact of the defendant's cornice overhanging the plaintiff's land may be considered as a nuisance to him, importing a damage which the law can estimate".[147] Similarly, if the nuisance consists of interference with the amenities of living, such as is

produced by noise or smells, no actual financial loss or injury to health[148] need be proved. The damage in such a case consists in the annoyance and discomfort caused to the occupier of the premises. The same rule applies to nuisances which consist of interference with easements.

> "Disturbance of easements and the like, as completely existing rights of use and enjoyment, is a wrong in the nature of trespass, and remediable by action without any allegation or proof of specific damage."[149]

A public nuisance is only actionable at the suit of a private person on proof of special damage.[150]

[146B] This proposition was confirmed by Sir Terence Etherton MR in *Network Rail Infrastructure Ltd v Williams* [2018] EWCA Civ 1514; [2018] 3 W.L.R. 1105 at [42] (encroachment by Japanese knotweed).

[147] *Fay v Prentice* (1845) 1 C.B. 828, per Coltman J. But where there is no original encroachment, damage must be proved, as for roots and branches of trees: *Lemmon v Webb* [1894] 3 Ch. 1 at 11, per Lindley LJ.

[148] *Crump v Lambert* (1867) L.R. 3 Eq. 409.

[149] per Lord Wright MR in *Nicholls v Ely Beet Sugar Factory Ltd* [1936] Ch. 343 at 349 (not necessary to prove damage in action by owner of a several fishery against a person who had discharged refuse into a stream).

[150] See para.20-181.

Intangible loss

Replace paragraph with:

20-29 Where an actionable nuisance interferes with the claimant's property and in addition damages his chattels, it seems that the claimant can recover such consequential damages.[157] Damages for personal injury, however, do not appear as such[158] to be recoverable in private nuisance.[159] It has always seemed unlikely that such damages could be recovered, given the focus of the tort upon property and its enjoyment. No reported English case appears to have given such an award, and dicta in the House of Lords now support the view that such recovery is not possible.[160] In cases involving interference with amenity and enjoyment of property the court must place a value on an intangible loss which "cannot be assessed mathematically".[161] The Court of Appeal once suggested that such damages could be assessed by analogy with damages for personal injury,[162] but this was disapproved by the House of Lords in *Hunter v Canary Wharf Ltd.*[163] Since only the owner, or the occupier with the right to exclusive possession, is entitled to sue for interference with enjoyment each member of a family does not have a separate cause of action, and "the quantum of damages does not depend on the number of those enjoying the land in question".[164] If, however, the defendant is a public authority an individual family member may have a cause of action under art.8 of the European Convention for the Protection of Human Rights, for interference with his private and family life.[165] If interference with amenity has been so great as to reduce the value of the claimant's property, a substantial award of damages for the reduction in value will normally be taken to include compensation for the loss of amenity itself: the claimant will therefore be unlikely to receive a separate award under that head.[166] In *Network Rail Infrastructure Ltd v Williams*[166A] claimants on to whose land Japanese knotweed had spread were awarded substantial sums, based on the reduction in value of their properties, for the loss of enjoyment of their land.

[157] See *Hunter v Canary Wharf Ltd* [1997] A.C. 655 at 706, per Lord Hoffmann. See also *Midwood Co Ltd v Manchester Corp* [1905] 2 K.B. 597; *Halsey v Esso Petroleum Co Ltd* [1961] 1 W.L.R. 683.

[158] Evidence of illness, for example, can no doubt be invoked to prove the gravity of a nuisance, provided the claimant is not hypersensitive.

[159] Such damages are, however, still recoverable in public nuisance until the Supreme Court rules otherwise: see *The Claimants appearing on the Register of the Corby Group Litigation v Corby BC* [2008] EWCA Civ 463; [2009] Q.B. 335. Cf. doubts expressed obiter by Lord Goff in *Hunter v Canary Wharf Ltd* who was inclined to the view that the appropriate remedy for personal injuries should now only "lie in our fully developed law of negligence, and that personal injury claims should be altogether excluded from the law of nuisance": see [1997] A.C. 655 at 692.

[160] See especially per Lord Lloyd in [1997] A.C. 655 at 696 and per Lord Goff (previous note). But cf., per Lord Cooke (dissenting) in [1997] A.C. 655 at 718–719.

[161] per Lord Lloyd in *Hunter v Canary Wharf Ltd* [1997] A.C. 655 at 696, citing *Ruxley Electronics and Construction Ltd v Forsyth* [1996] A.C. 344. See also per Lord Hoffmann in the *Hunter* case [1997] A.C. 655 at 706 (and per Lord Cooke at 712); *Jan de Nul (UK) v NV Royal Belge* [2000] 2 Lloyd's Rep. 700 at 716 (the decision in this case was subsequently affirmed: see [2002] EWCA Civ 209; [2002] 1 Lloyd's Rep. 583).

[162] See *Bone v Seale* [1975] 1 W.L.R. 797.

[163] See per Lord Hoffmann in [1997] A.C. 655 at 706. The multiplicand/multiplier *method* of assessing general damages can nevertheless be conveniently deployed in nuisance cases where there is a loss of amenity: see *Anslow v Norton Aluminium Ltd* [2012] EWHC 2610 (QB) at [474].

[164] per Lord Lloyd in *Hunter v Canary Wharf Ltd* [1997] A.C. 655 at 696.

[165] See *Dobson v Thames Water Utilities* [2009] EWCA Civ 28; [2009] 3 All E.R. 319. For subsequent proceedings see [2011] EWHC 3253 (TCC); (2011) 140 Con. L.R. 135 (liability for breach of the Convention established but, on the facts, damages unnecessary to achieve "just satisfaction"). For a case in which the European Court of Human Rights imposed liability under art.8 for illness caused by pollution in the water supplied to the claimant's home see *Otgon v Moldova (22743/07)* (2016) 19 C.C.L. Rep. 618.

[166] See *Raymond v Young* [2015] EWCA Civ 456; [2015] H.L.R. 41.

[166A] [2018] EWCA Civ 1514; [2018] 3 W.L.R. 1105.

4. WHO CAN SUE FOR NUISANCE?

Occupiers and residents

Replace footnote 318 with:

[318] See *Regency Villas Ltd v Diamond Resorts (Europe) Ltd* [2015] EWHC 3564 (Ch); [2016] 4 W.L.R. 61 (subsequent proceedings in the Court of Appeal at [2017] EWCA Civ 238; [2017] Ch. 516, and the Supreme Court at [2018] UKSC 57; [2018] 3 W.L.R. 1603, did not affect the point in the text). **20-63**

Reversioner

Replace paragraph with:

A reversioner can sue for injury done to the reversion, but not otherwise. It follows from this that the injury must be of a permanent nature, and not a mere temporary annoyance. Permanent in this connection means: **20-65**

> "such as will continue indefinitely unless something is done to remove it. Thus, a building which infringes ancient lights is permanent within the rule, for, though it can be removed before the reversion falls into possession, still it will continue until it be removed. On the other hand, a noisy trade, and the exercise of an alleged right of way, are not in their nature permanent within the rule, for they cease of themselves, unless there be someone to continue them."[335]

Accordingly, a reversioner can sue for acts which tend either to destroy evidence of the fact that the adjoining land is burdened with a servitude in his favour, or to establish evidence against him that his land is burdened with a corresponding servitude in favour of the adjoining land. For example, he can sue in respect of the erection of a hoarding against his ancient lights,[336] the locking of a gate across a way to which he is entitled for his tenants,[337] the erection by the adjoining owner of a house with projecting eaves so that rain-water is discharged upon his land,[338] and the discharge of sewage from a drain.[339] So, too, where the claimant was entitled for his tenants to a right of access to his wharf and siding from the railway of the defendants, and the defendants, with the intention of preventing such access, left large quantities of rolling stock lying continually across the mouth of the siding, the obstruction thereby caused was considered sufficiently permanent to enable the claimant to sue for an injury to his reversionary interest.[340] Keeping vans an unreasonable time in the highway is not actionable at the suit of a reversioner, because the defendant cannot acquire a prescriptive right to commit a public nuisance.[341] Physical injury to the reversion, such as is caused by vibration calculated to destroy buildings on the land, gives a right of action to the reversioner.[342] In *Metropolitan Housing Trust Ltd v RMC FH Co Ltd*[342A] Morgan J noted, in the context of *potential* loss of a right to light, that it was clear that a "reversioner can sue in relation to a nuisance where the nuisance will, or even might, continue to a time when the reversion falls into possession".

[335] *Jones v Llanrwst Urban DC (No.2)* [1911] 1 Ch. 393 at 404, per Parker J.

[336] *Shadwell v Hutchinson* (1829) M. & M. 350; *Metropolitan Association v Petch* (1858) 5 C.B. (N.S.) 504.

[337] *Kidgill v Moor* (1850) 9 C.B. 364.

[338] *Tucker v Newman* (1839) 11 A. & E. 40.

[339] *Jones v Llanrwst Urban DC (No.2)* [1911] 1 Ch. 393.

[340] *Bell v Midland Ry* (1861) 10 C.B. (N.S.) 287. See also *John Smith & Co (Edinburgh) Ltd v Hill* [2010] EWHC 1016 (Ch); [2010] 2 B.C.L.C. 556 at [29] per Briggs J and para.20-66.

[341] *Mott v Shoolbred* (1875) L.R. 20 Eq. 22.

[342] *Meux's Brewery Co v City of London Electric Lighting Co* [1895] 1 Ch. 287 at 317; *Colwell v St Pancras BC* [1904] 1 Ch. 707.

[342A] See [2017] EWHC 2609 (Ch); [2018] Ch. 195 at [54].

5. WHO CAN BE SUED FOR NUISANCE?

(b) Occupier

Statutory undertakers

Replace paragraph with:

20-77 The principle that an occupier of land can be liable for continuing a nuisance, which he has not created, cannot be applied without qualification to occupiers who are statutory undertakers. In such cases it will be necessary to consider whether the imposition of liability would be consistent with the statutory scheme. In *Marcic v Thames Water Utilities*[394] the House of Lords, reversing the Court of Appeal, held that the authorities favouring the imposition of liability for the "continuance" or "adoption" of nuisances had not impliedly overruled a separate line of authority relating to flooding caused by overloaded sewers. It is therefore still the law that water companies, which are obliged to permit all in their area to have access to the drainage system, will not be liable in nuisance simply because the sewers are no longer able to cope with the increased demand and flooding results. Where the underlying problem is the need for more resources to be allocated to improvement of the infrastructure, the statutory scheme contained in the Water Industry Act 1991 provided for that need to be evaluated by a Director General of Water Services; and the imposition of common law nuisance liability would be inconsistent with his role.[395] Lord Nicholls said that it was "abundantly clear that one important purpose of the enforcement scheme in the 1991 Act is that individual householders should not be able to launch proceedings in respect of failure to build sufficient sewers".[396] The principle in the *Marcic* case will not protect the defendants from liability at common law if the nuisance resulted not from a mere lack of capacity in the sewerage system but from a negligent failure at operational level adequately to discharge their statutory responsibilities to clean and maintain the sewers.[397] Statutory undertakers in breach of a statutory obligation will not thereby incur liability for any nuisance allegedly resulting unless the statute in question gives rise to liability for breach of statutory duty under the usual principles applicable to such claims.[398]

394 [2003] UKHL 66; [2004] 2 A.C. 42; [2004] 1 All E.R. 135.

395 See now the Water Industry Act 1991 s.1A (inserted by the Water Resources Act 2003 s.34) which replaces the Director General of Water Services with the Water Services Regulation Authority, but this does not affect the point in the text.

396 [2003] UKHL 66; [2004] 2 A.C. 42; [2004] 1 All E.R. 135 at [35]. But cf. *Southern Gas Networks Plc v Thames Water Utilities Ltd* [2018] EWCA Civ 33; [2018] 1 W.L.R. 5977 at [81] per Hickinbottom LJ suggesting that the reasoning of Lord Nicholls on this point differed significantly from that of Lord Hoffmann, who apparently considered that the common law *itself* precluded an action when the sewers were inadequate because new ones had not been constructed.

397 See *Dobson v Thames Water Utilities* [2007] EWHC 2021 (TCC); [2008] 2 All E.R. 362, although this case was subsequently appealed (see [2009] EWCA Civ 28; [2009] 3 All E.R. 319) there was no appeal on this point. At the trial of the action liability for common law nuisance was imposed on the defendants: see *Dobson v Thames Water Utilities* [2011] EWHC 3253 (TCC); (2011) 140 Con. L.R. 135. Cf. *Bell v Northumbrian Water Ltd* [2016] EWHC 133 (TCC); *Oldcorn v Southern Water Services Ltd* [2017] EWHC 62 (TCC); [2017] Env. L.R. 25.

398 See *Dwr Cymru Cyfyngedig (Welsh Water) v Barratt Homes Ltd* [2013] EWCA Civ 233; [2013] 1 W.L.R. 3486 (no liability for failure to permit access to sewers contrary to s.106 of the Water Industry Act 1991). For the action for breach of statutory duty see Ch.9.

(c) Landlord and tenant

Landlord's liability in other cases

Replace paragraph with:

The owner is liable if he has let the premises to a tenant for the purpose of doing an act likely to cause a nuisance, for example burning lime,[413] if he has authorised his tenant to do an act which is likely to cause a nuisance,[414] or if he has let the premises with a nuisance on them.[415] On the other hand: 20-81

> "If a landlord lets premises, not in themselves a nuisance, but which may or may not be used by the tenant so as to become a nuisance, and it is entirely at the option of the tenant so to use them or not, and the landlord receives the same benefit whether they are used or not, the landlord cannot be made responsible for the acts of the tenant."[416]

The law was reviewed by the Supreme Court in *Coventry v Lawrence (No.2)*[417] which concerned the possible liability of landlords for a noise nuisance caused by their tenants while engaging in speedway racing and similar activities, at a stadium which the landlords had leased to them. Three points emerge from the leading judgment of Lord Neuberger.[418] First, the terms of the lease will not themselves give rise to liability unless they render the nuisance "inevitable, or nearly certain". Secondly, the presence or absence of generally worded covenants against nuisance will rarely be relevant in determining the scope of the substance of the lease. Thirdly, if the lease itself does not give rise to liability, the landlord can only be liable if he "actively" or "directly" participated in the commission of the nuisance.[419] This is inevitably a very fact-sensitive inquiry.[419A] The Court of Appeal once struck out a claim in nuisance against a landlord for failing to prevent his tenants from subjecting the claimant to racial harassment.[420] Nevertheless, a landlord can be liable in nuisance if he allows "troublemakers to occupy his land and to use it as a base for causing unlawful disturbance to his neighbours".[421] Thus in *Lippiatt v South Gloucestershire Council*,[422] in which the defendant failed to remove travellers who had encamped on its land and caused nuisances against neighbouring farmers, the Court of Appeal refused to strike out a claim against the defendant. Where the owner is liable, that does not relieve the occupier from liability.[423]

[413] *Harris v James* (1876) 45 L.J.Q.B. 545; *Sampson v Hodson-Pressinger* [1981] 3 All E.R. 710 CA; *Tetley v Chitty* [1986] 1 All E.R. 663. cf. *Southwark LBC v Mills* [2001] 1 A.C. 1.

[414] *Jenkins v Jackson* (1888) 40 Ch D. 71. See comment by McNeill J in *Tetley v Chitty* [1986] 1 All E.R. 663 at 671, preferring to place the landlord's responsibility on objective foreseeability. It is clear that negligence in the letting with regard to potential nuisance is actionable. On the facts the case was within the principle in *Harris v James* (1876) 45 L.J.Q.B. 545.

[415] *R. v Pedley* (1834) 1 A. & E. 822.

[416] *Rich v Basterfield* (1847) 4 C.B. 783.

[417] [2014] UKSC 46; [2015] A.C. 106.

[418] See [2014] UKSC 46; [2015] A.C. 106 at [15]–[18].

[419] This aspect of the case led to a division of opinion between the Justices as to the interpretation to be placed on the particular facts of the case (the majority exonerated the landlord whilst a minority would have imposed liability).

[419A] See, e.g. *Fouladi v Darout Ltd* [2018] EWHC 3501 (landlord not liable).

[420] See *Hussain v Lancaster CC* [2000] Q.B. 1. See also *Smith v Scott* [1973] Ch. 314 (local authority held not liable for nuisance created by their tenants in annoying neighbours by noise and vandalism).

[421] per Evans LJ in *Lippiatt v South Gloucestershire Council* [2000] Q.B. 51 at 61.

[422] [2000] Q.B. 51.

[423] *R. v Watts* (1703) 1 Salk. 357; *Att Gen v Roe* [1915] 1 Ch. 235.

6. DEFENCES TO AN ACTION FOR NUISANCE

(b) Authorisation by statute

Negligent exercise of statutory powers

Replace paragraph with:

20-89 A defendant who creates a nuisance through the exercise of statutory powers will therefore normally be liable if he exercises those powers negligently.[460] Difficult questions on the boundary between public and private law may occasionally arise if the defendant contends that the context in which the power was exercised rendered that exercise "non-justiciable", or immune from liability, on grounds of general public interest[461] or because it concerned a "policy" rather than an "operational" matter.[462] These issues do, however, more commonly arise in relation to negligence liability as such,[463] when an attempt is made to use the statute as the foundation for a liability which would not otherwise exist, than in the context of the tort of nuisance.

[460] See *Geddis v Proprietors of Bann Reservoir* (1878) 3 App. Cas. 430 at 455–456, per Lord Blackburn. But cf. per Lord Browne-Wilkinson in *X (Minors) v Bedfordshire CC* [1995] 2 A.C. 633 at 732–733. If the statute in question contains its own compensation scheme it will be a question of fact and construction whether even victims of negligence are confined to the statutory scheme or can bring a common law claim: see, e.g. *Hall v Environment Agency* [2017] EWHC 1309 (TCC); [2018] 1 W.L.R. 1433; see also *Southern Gas Networks Plc v Thames Water Utilities Ltd* [2018] EWCA Civ 33; [2018] 1 W.L.R. 5977.

[461] See *X (Minors) v Bedfordshire CC* [1995] 2 A.C. 633.

[462] See *Barrett v Enfield LBC* [2001] 2 A.C. 550 HL, in which the House of Lords showed revived inter-

est in the "policy/operational" distinction originally developed in *Anns v Merton LBC* [1978] A.C. 728 but questioned in *Rowling v Takaro Properties Ltd* [1988] A.C. 473.

[463] See Ch.8. See also Buckley, *The Law of Negligence and Nuisance*, 6th edn (2017), Ch.15.

(f) Ignorance of the nuisance

Trees

Replace footnote 522 with:

[522] [2014] EWHC 1891; [2014] 3 E.G.L.R. 59 at [73]. See, e.g. *Witley Parish Council v Cavanagh* [2018] EWCA Civ 2232 (liability imposed). **20-100**

7. PARTICULAR TYPES OF NUISANCE

(b) Liability in respect of damage caused by escaping water

(i) Common law

Diversion of natural stream

Replace footnote 625 with:

[625] per Lord Finlay LC in *Greenock Corp v Caledonian Ry* [1917] A.C. 566 at 572. Whether a diversion has actually caused any flooding alleged to have resulted from it can give rise to difficult questions of fact; see, e.g. *Davies v Campfield* [2017] EWHC 2746 (Ch). **20-126**

(ii) Statutory undertakers

Negligence and strict liability

Replace paragraph with:

Those bodies now concerned with water resources[646] operate under statutory powers, and at common law they are exempt from liability except on proof of negligence, unless the statute preserves their liability.[647] A very large exception to this general rule is now contained in the Water Industry Act 1991 s.209, which provides that "where an escape of water, however caused, from a pipe vested in a water undertaker causes loss or damage", then the undertaker is strictly liable.[647A] It is a defence that the escape was wholly due to the claimant's fault, or that of his servant, agent or contractor, but act of God or independent act of a third party is no defence, and the statutory liability is therefore "far stricter than under the rule in *Rylands v Fletcher*".[648] The words "loss or damage" are, however, apparently confined to those heads of damage normally recoverable in negligence, so that the "purely non-physical is excluded from recovery",[649] and interruption with the domestic gas supply has been held to be outside the section.[650] **20-132**

[646] See the Water Industry Acts 1991 and 1999, and the Water Resources Act 1991.

[647] *Green v Chelsea Waterworks Co* (1894) 70 L.T. 547; *Dunn v Birmingham Canal Co* (1872) L.R. 8 Q.B. 42. The Reservoirs Act 1975 s.28, Sch.2, preserves strict liability for the construction of reservoirs.

[647A] See also the related provision in s.82 of the New Roads and Street Works Act 1991 which similarly imposes strict liability upon statutory undertakers in certain circumstances, but apparently does not preclude the imposition of negligence liability if the particular nature of the claimants' loss causes it to fall outside the strict liability scheme: see *Southern Gas Networks Plc v Thames Water Utilities Ltd* [2018] EWCA Civ 33; [2018] 1 W.L.R. 5977.

[648] per Lord Hoffmann in *Transco v Stockport MBC* [2003] UKHL 61; [2004] 2 A.C. 1 at [42]. The Contributory Negligence Act 1945, the Fatal Accidents Act 1976, and the Limitation Act 1980 apply to the liability under the section.

[649] per Stanley Burnton J *Anglian Water Services Ltd v Crawshaw Robins & Co Ltd* [2001] B.L.R. 173 at [149].

[650] See *Anglian Water Services Ltd v Crawshaw Robins & Co Ltd* [2001] B.L.R. 173

(iii) Sewers and drains

Statutory provisions

Replace paragraph with:

20-134 When sewers are made or maintained under statutory provisions, an action will normally lie for damage caused by an overflow of the sewers, if the overflow was due to the original negligent construction of the sewers[656] or to a subsequent negligent act on the part of the sewage authority, as by sending sewage from one sewer into another already overcharged with sewage.[657] The omission to enlarge the capacity of the sewer to enable it to deal with an increase of population, so that a flood occurs, does not give rise to an action for negligence or nuisance at common law if the sewage authority has taken the sewers over from some predecessor.[658] This proposition was confirmed by the House of Lords in *Marcic v Thames Water Utilities*.[659] In a case of this nature, the appropriate remedy is instead complaint to the Water Services Regulation Authority pursuant to the Water Resources Act 2003.[660] If the sewage authority has itself constructed the sewers and has failed to enlarge them so as to meet the growing needs of their district, whether it is liable for the damage caused by an overflow depends on the true construction of the statute imposing the duty to sewer. The imposition of liability for negligent failure to operate a sewage works will not necessarily conflict with the statutory scheme for regulation by the Water Services Regulation Authority: whether it does so will depend upon the extent to which issues of policy or capital expenditure were involved.[661] Even if it is not liable in negligence the sewage authority may be liable in nuisance if it caused, continued or adopted the nuisance.[662] Liability for damages for breach of statutory duty will not, however, be imposed unless the usual requirements for such a claim are satisfied.[663] In *Dwr Cymru Cyfyngedig (Welsh Water) v Barratt Homes Ltd*[664] the Court of Appeal held that s.106 of the Water Industry Act 1991, which obliges water companies to permit access to its sewers, does not give rise to a claim for damages for breach of statutory duty if the company fails to comply with it. An occupier wrongfully denied access can, however, obtain redress in public law by an application to the court to compel it.[665]

[656] *Fleming v Manchester Corp* (1881) 44 L.T. 517; *Brown v Sargent* (1858) 1 F. & F. 112.

[657] *Dent v Bournemouth Corp* (1897) 66 L.J.Q.B. 395.

[658] *Pride of Derby and Derbyshire Angling Association v British Celanese Ltd* [1953] Ch. 149; *Smeaton v Ilford Corp* [1954] Ch. 450; *Lawrysyn v Town of Kipling* (1965) 48 D.L.R. (2d) 660, affirmed in (1966) 55 D.L.R. (2d) 471.

[659] [2003] UKHL 66; [2004] 2 A.C. 42. For an analysis of the relationship between statute and common law in the reasoning of the House of Lords in *Marcic v Thames Water Utilities* see *Southern Gas Networks Plc v Thames Water Utilities Ltd* [2018] EWCA Civ 33; [2018] 1 W.L.R. 5977 at [81] per Hickinbottom LJ. See also para.20-77.

[660] The Water Services Regulation Authority replaced the former Director General of Water Services (see the Water Industry Act 1991, s.1A, inserted by the Water Act 2003 s.34). For cases on equivalent earlier statutory provisions see *Stretton's Derby Brewery Co v Derby Corp* [1894] 1 Ch. 431; *Robinson v Workington Corp* [1897] 1 Q.B. 619; *Hesketh v Birmingham Corp* [1924] 1 K.B. 260.

[661] See *Dobson v Thames Water Utilities* [2007] EWHC 2021 (TCC); [2008] 2 All E.R. 362 (subsequently appealed: see [2009] EWCA Civ 28; [2009] 3 All E.R. 319, but there was no appeal on this point). For the trial of the action in this case see *Dobson v Thames Water Utilities* [2011] EWHC 3253 (TCC); (2011) 140 Con. L.R. 135 in which liability at common law for an odour nuisance was imposed.

[662] *Smeaton v Ilford Corp* [1954] Ch. 450.

[663] See Ch.9.

[664] [2013] EWCA Civ 233; [2013] 1 W.L.R. 3486.

[665] See *Barratt Homes Ltd v Dwr Cymru Cyfyngedig (Welsh Water)* [2009] UKSC 13; [2010] 1 All E.R. 965 (decided in earlier proceedings between the same parties).

(d) Nuisance to light

Prospects and privacy

Replace paragraph with:

It is not a nuisance to interfere with a view or prospect[746] where the act complained of is otherwise lawful.[747] Moreover, according to the older authorities, it is not a nuisance for a man to erect a building on his own land which enables him to invade the privacy of his neighbour by looking through his windows or otherwise.[748] Nevertheless, it now appears that "the law of nuisance is capable, in an appropriate case, of operating so as to protect the privacy of a home as against another landowner".[749] An extreme (and hypothetical) example might be the erection of a tower deliberately to facilitate viewing into the houses and gardens of neighbours.[749A] Although public law, in the field of public health and town and country planning, is clearly also relevant here, "the planning process is [not] by itself a sufficient mechanism for protecting against all infringement of property rights".[749B] The developing law in this area does not, however, undermine the old authorities which deny that loss of a view or prospect is actionable in nuisance. Their continuing vitality was reflected in the 1997 decision of the House of Lords in *Hunter v Canary Wharf Ltd*,[750] in which they were invoked by analogy to justify refusal of relief for interference with the path of television signals by the erection of a large building: **20-154**

> "The house owner who has a fine view of the South Downs may find that his neighbour has built so as to obscure his view. But there is no redress, unless, perchance, the neighbour's land was subject to a restrictive covenant in the house owner's favour. It would be a good example of what in law is called '*damnum absque injuria*': a loss which the house owner has undoubtedly suffered, but which gives rise to no infringement of his legal rights. In the absence of a restrictive covenant, there is no legal right to a view."[751]

[746] *William Aldred's Case* (1610) 9 Co. Rep. 57b at 58b; *Dalton v Angus* (1881) 6 App. Cas. 740 at 824, per Lord Blackburn.

[747] *Campbell v Paddington Corp* [1911] 1 K.B. 869.

[748] *Browne v Flower* [1911] 1 Ch. 219. See also *Victoria Park Racing Co v Taylor* (1937) 58 C.L.R. 479 (broadcasting horse-racing commentary from property adjacent to race-course).

[749] See *Fearn v The Board of Trustees of the Tate Gallery* [2019] EWHC 246 (Ch) at [169] per Mann J (claim failed on the facts).

[749A] See *Fearn v The Board of Trustees of the Tate Gallery* [2019] EWHC 246 (Ch) at [178]. The development of the common law in this area may reflect the influence of the Human Rights Act 1998 and art.8 of the European Convention on Human Rights ("respect for... private and family life"): see per Mann J in *Fearn v The Board of Trustees of the Tate Gallery* [2019] EWHC 246 (Ch) at [170]–[174].

[749B] See *Fearn v The Board of Trustees of the Tate Gallery* [2019] EWHC 246 (Ch) at [177] per Mann J.

[750] [1997] A.C. 655.

[751] [1997] A.C. 655 at 699, per Lord Lloyd. For criticism of this position see Pontin, "A room with a view in English Nuisance Law" (2018) 38 L.S. 644.

(e) Fire

(iii) Responsibility for fire

Vicarious liability for operations involving the creation of fire

Replace footnote 790 with:

20-163 [790] See [2008] EWHC 6 (TCC); [2008] B.L.R. 155. The decision is equally applicable to both negligence and nuisance: see *Tinseltime Ltd v Roberts* [2011] EWHC 1199 (TCC); [2011] B.L.R. 515 at [49] per Judge Stephen Davies. See also *Lindsay v Berkeley Homes (Capital) Plc* [2018] EWHC 2042.

8. OBSTRUCTION OF THE HIGHWAY

(a) Right of access

Right of access to highway

Replace paragraph with:

20-180 "The owner of land adjoining a highway has a right of access to the highway from any part of his premises. This is so … whether he is entitled to the whole or some interest in the ground subjacent to the highway or not. The rights of the public to pass along the highway are subject to this right of access: just as the right of access is subject to the rights of the public and must be exercised subject to the general obligations as to nuisance and the like imposed upon a person using the highway."[864]

This common law right of access remains in force, though nowadays qualified considerably by public law.[865] It is a private right, distinct from the right of the owner of that land to use the highway itself as one of the public.[866] It is not confined to access to the door of the house, but includes a right of access to the walls, for example for the purpose of displaying advertisements.[867] An interference with this right is actionable per se,[868] and, if it is such as to hinder customers from resorting to the house for business purposes, damages for loss of business can be obtained.[869] An owner of land adjoining a navigable river has a similar private right of access to the river.[870] This private right ceases as soon as the highway is reached and any subsequent interference, for example with the right to carry goods from the premises to a van standing in the roadway, is a public nuisance if it is a nuisance at all.[871]

[864] per Lord Atkin in *Marshall v Blackpool Corp* [1935] A.C. 16 at 22. Other cases to the same effect are: *St Mary, Newington v Jacobs* (1871) L.R. 7 Q.B. 47; *Tottenham Urban DC v Rowley* [1912] 2 Ch. 633, affirmed [1914] A.C. 95; cf. *Ching Garage Ltd v Chingford Corp* [1961] 1 W.L.R. 470 HL (Highways Act 1980 s.66); cf. *LCC v Cutts* [1961] 1 W.L.R. 292, DC.

[865] e.g. Highways Act 1980 ss.126–131.

[866] *Lyon v Fishmongers' Co* (1876) 1 App. Cas. 662; *Att Gen v Thames Conservators* (1862) 1 H. & M. 1; *Chaplin v Westminster Corp* [1901] 2 Ch. 329 at 333–335; *Ineos Upstream Ltd v Persons Unknown* [2017] EWHC 2945 (Ch) at [42].

[867] *Cobb v Saxby* [1914] 3 K.B. 822.

[868] *Walsh v Ervin* [1952] V.L.R. 361.

[869] *Fritz v Hobson* (1880) 14 Ch D. 542 at 554–556.

[870] *Lyon v Fishmongers' Co* (1876) 1 App. Cas. 662; *Chaplin v Westminster Corp* [1901] 2 Ch. 329.

[871] *Chaplin v Westminster Corp* [1901] 2 Ch. 329. See also *Hiscox Syndicates Ltd v The Pinnacle Ltd* [2008] EWHC 1386 (QB); [2008] N.P.C. 71 at [14] per Akenhead J.

(c) Non-repair of highway

Standard of care

Replace footnote 951 with:

[951] *Yetkin v Newham LBC* [2010] EWCA Civ 776; [2011] Q.B. 827. See also *Kane v New Forest DC* [2001] EWCA Civ 878; [2002] 1 W.L.R. 312. Cf. *Sumner v Colborne and Denbighshire CC* [2018] EWCA Civ 1006; [2019] Q.B. 430 (no liability for view-obscuring vegetation merely *adjacent* to the highway). **20-193**

CHAPTER 21

ANIMALS

TABLE OF CONTENTS

2. THE ANIMALS ACT 1971

(a) Strict liability for animals under section 2

Section 2(2)(a) Likelihood of damage or its severity

Replace footnote 26 with:

[26] Note that in *Mirvahedy v Henley* [2003] UKHL 16; [2003] 2 A.C. 491 at [97] and [98], Lord Scott in his dissenting speech, said that whilst he agreed with the rejection of a test of "probability" in *Smith*, he was "unable to agree that 'such as might happen', a phrase consistent with no more than possibility, can be right" and suggested a test of "reasonably to be expected". On the facts, he considered that the test was not satisfied as a horse loose on the highway does not usually result in damage to third parties, that if damage to third parties does result the damage is not usually severe, no more perhaps than a dent to a car, and that the cases in which serious injury or damage results are fortunately few and far between. He cited the Court of Appeal decision in *Jaundrill v Gillett, The Times,* 30 January 1996 in support of his conclusion but as the application of s.2(2)(a) had been conceded by the defendant, he proceeded on the assumption that the damage was likely. In *Williams v Hawkes* [2017] EWCA Civ 1846; [2018] R.T.R. 16 (see para.21-08) *Jaundrill v Gillett* was described as likely to be confined to its facts. Considerable caution should be given before citing it as an authority. **21-05**

Replace paragraph with:

For the most part, subsequent courts have found the test in s.2(2)(a) to be easily satisfied. Indeed in *Goldsmith v Patchcott*,[28] a case where the claimant suffered serious injury through being thrown from a horse, Jackson LJ expressly said that s.2(2)(a) "will only eliminate a small number of cases". He added that "[m]ost animal-related damage which someone wishes to sue about" would fall into one of the categories in the subsection.[29] By contrast, the meaning of s.2(2)(a) was raised as a significant issue in *Turnbull v Warrener*,[30] and the Court was divided on the proper approach to take. Maurice Kay LJ was of the view—consistent with *Smith v Ainger* and intervening authorities such as *Freeman v Higher Park Farm*[31]—that there was no need to show that severe injury was statistically probable in order to fall within s.2(2)(a). Where a rider is thrown from a horse, as in this instance, severe injury was "reasonably to be expected". Lewison LJ, by contrast, was prepared to say that authorities such as *Freeman* were, in respect of s.2(2)(a), decisions of fact rather than principle, and that the statute had never been intended to apply to an "ordinary riding accident". It was not, in his Lordship's view, self-evident that a **21-06** rider who falls from a rearing horse (or a cantering horse) "is likely to suffer severe injury", because many such accidents occur without severe injury being suffered, and was prepared to uphold the judge's decision that the test in s.2(2)(a) was not fulfilled. Since Stanley Burnton LJ agreed with the reasoning of Lewison LJ on this point, the likelihood is that a range of accidents treated in recent years as clearly within s.2, and particularly riding accidents, will in future be questioned much more closely. It is suggested however that there is clearly no need to demonstrate statistical likelihood for the terms of s.2(2)(a) to be satisfied.[32] Illustrating this, s.2(2)(a) was held not to be satisfied, in circumstances where s.2(2)(b) and s.2(2)(c) would be so satisfied, in *Lynch v Ed Walker Racing Ltd*.[32A] The claimant was a stable boy who had been thrown from a horse and rendered unconscious when the horse whipped around and fell. Following a trial of liability, the judge held that neither limb of s.2(2)(a) had been satisfied and dismissed the claim. On the basis of the witness evidence, which stated that injuries were rare as a result of a horse whipping around and that people rarely fell off a horse because it whipped, she held that it was unlikely that an injury would be caused (limb one) by a horse whipping around and that if an injury was caused, it was unlikely to be severe (limb two). Langstaff J conceded that, at first glance, it seemed that the judge might have erred. It appeared that she had looked at the first limb of s.2(2)(a) but not the second. But the evidence on the likelihood of injury and the severity of the injury overlapped. When the judge looked at the facts of the case and said that it was not common for a fall of the instant type, she might have been addressing the severity, as if an injury was unlikely at all then it was unlikely to be severe. The judge emphasised the speed, circumstances and seriousness; that went not only to the likelihood of an injury but its severity too. There was no basis for disturbing her decision.

28 [2012] EWCA Civ 183; [2012] P.I.Q.R. P11.

29 [2012] EWCA Civ 183; [2012] P.I.Q.R. P11 at [33].

30 [2012] EWCA Civ 412; [2012] P.I.Q.R. P16.

31 [2008] EWCA Civ 1185; [2009] P.I.Q.R. P6.

32 All three judges in *Turnbull v Warrener* agreed, in any event, that the claim failed because it fell within the defence in s.5(2) (see para.21-16). For comparison see *Tapp v Trustees of the Blue Cross Society* unreported 15 May 2013 (Northampton County Court): s.2(2)(a) was satisfied because a bite by a horse was inherently likely to be severe given the size of the animal; the defence under s.5(2) failed because the claimant had not engaged with the animal, but entered a field where it approached her.

32A [2017] EWHC 2484 (QB).

Section 2(2)(b) Characteristics of the animal

Replace paragraph with:

21-08 In *Mirvahedy v Henley*[38] the majority of the House of Lords approved the *Cummings* rather than the *Breedon* interpretation. In *Mirvahedy* the claimant motorist suffered personal injuries when the car he was driving collided with the defendants' horse which had panicked and escaped with several others from its field. It was not clear what had frightened the horses in this way. The House of Lords held, by a majority of three to two, that the defendants were liable under s.2(2) as the behaviour of the horse fulfilled the requirements of the subsection. To bolt was a characteristic of the species which was normal "in particular circumstances", the circumstances here being some sort of fright or other external stimulus.[39] Giving the leading speech, Lord Nicholls conceded that on this interpretation:

> "it [wa]s not easy to conceive of circumstances where dangerous behaviour which is characteristic of a species will not satisfy requirement (b) [as] a normal but dangerous characteristic of a species will usually be identifiable by reference to particular times or particular circumstances. [This] means that requirement (b) will be met in most cases where damage was caused by dangerous behaviour as described in requirement (a)."[40]

He justified the interpretation as according more easily with the statutory language. Lord Walker recognised that this interpretation would impose strict liability for behaviour which was entirely normal for that animal of his species and would make the keeper's liability depend on knowledge of something which was likely to be common knowledge among those who keep the animals. But as between the keeper, who could decide whether "to run the unavoidable risks involved in [keeping the animal and] whether or not to insure against those risks", and the entirely innocent victim of the animal's behaviour, he could see "nothing unjust or unreasonable in the [keeper] having to bear the loss".[41] The approach in *Mirvahedy v Henley* was followed in *Williams v Hawkes*.[41A] Here, a Charolais steer had escaped from its field and found its way onto a major road after being "spooked". It ran along the highway in a panic and collided with the claimant's car. The Court found that s.2(2)(b) was satisfied, since expert evidence suggested that the likelihood of damage was due to characteristics of the steer not normally found in animals of the same species except at particular times or in particular circumstances, and was not simply due to the size and weight of the steer. There were no grounds for differentiating between this case and *Mirvahedy* on the basis that the steer had run into the claimant's car while the horse in *Mirvahedy* had remained static. In *Estacio v Honigsbaum*,[41B] *Mirvahedy* was applied to a bite by a dog which had probably taken fright on being trapped in a tight space while its owner was seeking to get it into a car. As Deputy District Judge Tomlinson put it, biting is not something which dogs do ordinarily but it is something that dogs do at particular times and in particular circumstances and one of those particular times and circumstances is where a dog might feel itself threatened or a dog might find itself in a constrained space. Section 2(2)(b) was satisfied, as were the other limbs of s.2(2).

[38] [2003] UKHL 16; [2003] 2 A.C. 491.

[39] See also *Tapp v Trustees of the Blue Cross Society* 15 May 2013 (Northampton County Court) above fn.32, where a horse which bit the claimant had adopted a herd mentality which was normal in the circumstances for horses which had escaped from a field, and s.2(2)(a) was satisfied.

[40] [2003] UKHL 16; [2003] 2 A.C. 491 at [43]. Lord Nicholls at [46] argued that this did not empty requirement (b) of all content as it could operate to bar a claim in some cases of accidental damage:

> "Take a large and heavy domestic animal such as a mature cow. There is a real risk that if a cow happens to stumble and fall on someone, any damage will be severe. This would satisfy requirement (a). But a cow's dangerousness in this regard may not fall within requirement (b). This dangerousness is due to a characteristic normally found in cows at all times. The dangerousness results from their very size and weight. It is not due to a characteristic not normally found in cows except at particular times or in particular circumstances."

[41] [2003] UKHL 16; [2003] 2 A.C. 491 at [157]. This reasoning is, perhaps, less apposite in cases where the claimant has willingly participated in an activity with full knowledge of the usual risks inherent in it. Being bound by *Mirvahedy*, the Court of Appeal has turned toward restricting liability in such cases by means of the defence of assumption of risk: see para.21-16.

[41A] [2017] EWCA Civ 1846; [2018] R.T.R. 16.

[41B] (County Court, Clerkenwell) 18 May 2017.

4. COMMON LAW LIABILITIES

Common law liabilities

Replace paragraph with:

21-27 In *Whippey v Jones,*[135] the Court of Appeal emphasised in respect of liability in negligence that the duty of care will generally be breached only if a reasonable person in the defendant's position would "contemplate that injury is likely to follow" from his acts or omissions.[136] In this case, the defendant had acted as a reasonable dog-handler would do, and the judge had erred in finding the duty of care to have been breached where the injury was only foreseeable as a "possibility". The defendant, Mr Whippey, had taken his Great Dane, Hector, to a park for exercise. Hector was found by the judge to be "gentle". He did not jump up. However, he weighed around 12 and a half stone and was inclined to approach people in a manner that might appear to be aggressive. He was, therefore, intimidating. Mr Whippey unleashed Hector after satisfying himself that no other people were present. He did not see the claimant, Mr Jones, who was running along the footpath. Hector knocked the claimant causing him to slip towards a river and break his ankle. The judge found that the injury did not fall within s.2(2)(a) of the Animals Act 1971, since it had not been an injury the animal was *likely* to cause (nor that was likely to be severe). He did find, however, that the defendant was liable in negligence, since the injury was foreseeable "as a possibility". The Court of Appeal concluded that liability in negligence in these circumstances required foreseeability of injury as a likelihood, so that the "possibility" of injury as established on the facts was not enough. It should perhaps be noted that the relevant test was also explained by the Court in a more general and more orthodox way: "there must be a sufficient probability of injury to lead a reasonable person (in the position of the defendant) to anticipate it".[137] One approach is to regard *Whippey v Jones* as a case of reasonable risk-taking, like *Bolton v Stone.*[138] Consideration of likelihood is thus more easily understood as a relevant aspect of breach of duty. The defendant had (it was found) carefully checked for other adults, and Hector was not inclined to be aggressive rather than intimidating. As such, the defendant had acted reasonably in unleashing him. Although *Whippey v Jones* was cited in *Harris v Miller,*[139] the test applied appears more conventional. The claimant had, at the age of 14, been seriously injured falling from a horse owned by the defendant. It was found that the horse, a thoroughbred, was powerful and difficult to control. The defendant had limited experience of riding and the claimant had not previously ridden a horse, rather than a pony. The defendant's standard of care was to be assessed "by reference to that of the ordinary and reasonably prudent horse owner": such a person "would ensure that he or she is possessed of sufficient information about both horse and rider to be able to assess any risk from what is an inherently dangerous activity".[140] In this instance, the duty of care was breached.

135 [2009] EWCA Civ 452; (2009) 159 N.L.J. 598. See also *Addis v Campbell* [2011] EWCA Civ 906.

136 [2009] EWCA Civ 452; (2009) 159 N.L.J. 598 at [16].

137 [2009] EWCA Civ 452; (2009) 159 N.L.J. 598

138 [1951] A.C. 850; see para.8-168.

139 [2016] EWHC 2438 (QB) at [97].

140 [2016] EWHC 2438 (QB) at [150].

CHAPTER 22

DEFAMATION

TABLE OF CONTENTS

1. GENERALLY

Action of defamation

Replace footnote 4 with:

[4] For examples of causes of action, see conspiracy (*Lonrho v Fayed (No.5)* [1993] 1 W.L.R. 1489 CA); breach of an implied duty not to damage trust between an employer and employee (*Malik v BBCI* [1995] 3 All E.R. 545 CA; *BCCI v Ali* [1999] 4 All E.R. 83); negligence (*Spring v Guardian Assurance* [1995] 2 A.C. 296, where the House of Lords granted a remedy to the claimant who sued his former employer for negligence in writing a derogatory reference in relation to him, though an action for libel would not have lain since the occasion was one of qualified privilege and malice could not be shown); harassment (e.g. *Georgallides v Etzin* [2005] EWHC 1790 (QB)); misuse of private information (*McKennitt v Ash* [2006] EWCA Civ 1714; [2008] Q.B. 73); and breach of statutory duty under the Data Protection Act 2018 and Human Rights Act 1998. **22-01**

Costs

After "The provisions, which came into force", replace "are currently not applicable to defamation claims. It is anticipated that conditional fee agreements will be replaced and other cost-reducing measures are being considered by Government but at the time of writ- ing the position remains unclear.":

generally in April 2013, were brought into force in relation to defamation claims **22-06**
on 6 April 2019.[24A] Success fees are no longer recoverable from the losing party, although after the event insurance premiums remain recoverable.

[24A] Legal Aid, Sentencing and Parliament of Offenders Act 2012 (Commencement No.13) Order 2018 (SI 2018/1287).

3. WHAT IS DEFAMATORY?

(a) The test

The test at common law

Replace paragraph with:

A statement may be defamatory in relation to the claimant's personal character, **22-16**
office or vocation. In the former case the test usually applied was whether the matter complained of was calculated to hold the claimant up to "hatred, contempt, or ridicule".[81] This "ancient formula" was, however, insufficient in all cases, for a person's business reputation may be damaged in ways which nobody would connect with "hatred, ridicule or contempt", as, for instance, the imputation of a clever fraud which however much to be condemned morally and legally might yet not excite what a member of the jury might understand as hatred or contempt.[82] Lord Atkin in *Sim v Stretch*[83] applied the test, "would the words tend to lower the claimant in the estimation of right-thinking members of society generally". Or, in the words of Neill LJ in *Gillick v BBC*[84] would the words be "likely to affect a person adversely in the estimation of reasonable people generally". The alternative "or which would cause him to be shunned or avoided" must be added to cover such cases as an imputation of insanity.[85] What is defamatory in one era may not continue to be so in another. The most common direction given to juries in recent times was that a defamatory allegation is one that tends to make reasonable people think the worse of the claimant.[86] *Brown v Bower*[86A] is a recent example of the potential for changing social mores to affect what is and is not defamatory. The court found the meaning of the words complained of to be that there were grounds to suspect that

the claimant had paid young male prostitutes to subject him to consensual rough sex. The parties had agreed that the words complained of were defamatory at common law. Nicklin J was troubled by the possibility that they might not be, and considered whether, despite the parties' agreement, he ought to determine the issue, it being one of law.[86B] He took the view that he should only do so if the argument that the meaning was not defamatory was overwhelming, which it was not. The question was therefore adjourned to later in the proceedings.

[81] per Parke B in *Parmiter v Coupland* (1840) 6 M. & W. 105 at 108; cf. *Capital and Counties Bank v Henty* (1882) 7 App. Cas. 741 at 762. The test laid down by Parke B is not exhaustive.

[82] per Scrutton and Atkin LJJ in *Tournier v National Provincial Bank* [1924] 1 K.B. 461 at 477, 487.

[83] (1936) 52 T.L.R. 669 at 671; followed by Scott LJ in *Holdsworth v Associated Newspapers Ltd* [1937] 3 All E.R. 872 at 880; cf. *Sim v HJ Heinz Co Ltd* [1959] 1 W.L.R. 313, and see *Skuse v Granada Television Ltd* [1996] E.M.L.R. 278 CA.

[84] [1996] E.M.L.R. 267.

[85] *Youssoupoff v MGM Pictures Ltd* (1934) 50 T.L.R. 581 at 587. Scrutton LJ preferred "a false statement about a man to his discredit", (1934) 50 T.L.R. 581 at 584. The sound track in *Youssoupoff* was held to be libellous. There seems to be no reason in principle why a visual representation in a film should not also be libellous.

[86] *Sim v Stretch* [1936] 2 All E.R. 1237. Also see *Tolley v JS Fry & Sons Ltd* [1931] A.C. 333. Note that, under s.11 of the Defamation Act 2013 there is no presumptive right to a jury.

[86A] [2017] EWHC 2637 (QB); [2017] 4 W.L.R. 197.

[86B] Applying *Monroe v Hopkins* [2017] EWHC 433 (QB); [2017] 4 W.L.R. 68.

Serious Harm

Replace footnote 89 with:

22-19 [89] [2017] EWCA Civ. 1334; [2018] Q.B. 594; affirmed on appeal: [2019] UKSC 27; [2019] 3 W.L.R. 18.

Replace paragraph with:

22-20 Summarising the findings of the court, Davis LJ distilled the following points[92]:

(1) Section 1(1) of the 2013 Act has the effect of giving statutory status to *Thornton*, albeit also raising the threshold from one of substantiality to one of seriousness: no less, no more, but equally no more, no less. *Thornton* has thus itself been superseded by statute.

(2) The common law presumption as to damage in cases of libel, the common law principle that the cause of action accrues on the date of publication, the established position as to limitation and the common law objective single meaning rule are all unaffected by s.1(1).

(3) If there is an issue as to meaning (or any related issue as to reference) that can be resolved at a meaning hearing, applying the usual objective approach in the usual way. If there is a further issue as to serious harm, then there may be cases where such issue can also be appropriately dealt with at the meaning hearing. If the meaning so assessed is evaluated as seriously defamatory it will ordinarily then be proper to draw an inference of serious reputational harm. Once that threshold is reached further evidence will then be likely to be more relevant to quantum and any continuing dispute should ordinarily be left to trial.

(4) Courts should ordinarily be slow to direct a preliminary issue, involving substantial evidence, on a dispute as to whether serious reputational harm has been caused or is likely to be caused by the published statement.

(5) A defendant disputing the exisatence of serious harm may in an appropriate case, if the circumstances so warrant, issue a Part 24 summary judgment application or issue a a *Jameel* application: the Jameel jurisdiction continuing to be available after the 2013 Act as before (albeit in reality likely only relatively rarely to be appropriately used).

(6) All interlocutory process in such cases should be sought to be managed in a way that is proportionate and cost-effective and actively promotes the overriding objective.
(7) Finally, it may be that in some respects the position with regard to bodies trading for profit, under s.1(2), will be different.

Note that on appeal the Supreme Court dismissed the appeal in *Lachaux* and approved the decision of Warby J at first instance.[92A] The Supreme Court confirmed that the repetition rule (which has nothing to do with the seriousness threshold) and the rule in *Dingle* (evidence of damage to reputation by earlier publications of substantially the same statement are irrelevant to the assessment of damage caused by the publication complained of) survive.

[92] [2017] EWCA Civ 1334; [2018] Q.B. 594 at [82].

[92A] [2019] UKSC 27; [2019] 3 W.L.R. 18.

Add new paragraph:

The serious harm threshold cannot be overcome by aggregating the harm caused by two or more less serious defamatory imputations; multiple articles cannot be treated as a "statement" for the purposes of s.1.[92B] Reference (i.e. the extent to which the claimant is identifiable from the publication) may be relevant to serious harm: if only a small number of individuals would understand the defamatory statement to refer to the claimant it may not cause serious harm to reputation. In *Alexander-Theodotou v Kounis*[92C] the court found that only a small number of readers would have identified the claimants as those being referred to, and those individuals would already have formed an adverse opinion of the claimants' conduct in the relevant matter; as such no serious harm was caused, and the claim was dismissed. **22-20A**

[92B] *Sube v News Group Newspapers Ltd* [2018] EWHC 1961 (QB); [2018] 1 W.L.R. 5767.

[92C] [2019] EWHC 956 (QB).

Add new paragraph:

Although the Court of Appeal warned against lengthy interim proceedings on the issue of serious harm in *Lachaux v Independent Print Ltd*,[93] it may be appropriate to order the matter be tried as a preliminary issue where the particular circumstances warrant it,[93A] though in this case the circumstances were exceptional as the parties had agreed to having the issue determined as a preliminary issue before the ruling in *Lachaux* and the evidential investigation was likely to be modest. Allegations that imputed arrogance, greed and unreasonable behaviour in relation to the claimants' benefit claims were found to be defamatory at common law and statements of opinion, but did not to cross the serious harm threshold, in *Sube v News Group Newspapers Ltd (1) and Express Newspapers (2)*.[93B] Whilst such allegations could attract disapproval, the court found that they did not relate to the most important of societal norms and there were no allegations of dishonesty or unlawful behaviour. It was also found that where an imputation is an opinion that lessens its defamatory impact. The court did not hear argument on and therefore did not make a decision as to whether the serious harm test requires the court also to consider whether imputations taken together can collectively overcome the threshold. In *Morgan v Associated Newspapers Ltd*[93C] the court found a three-part meaning, with the first two limbs being factual, but not defamatory of themselves, whilst a third (which was based upon the first two) was defamatory and opinion. This defamatory meaning was found to have a tendency to cause serious harm to the claimant's reputation. Drawing some general principles from *Sube*, relevant considerations included: (i) the gravity of the defamatory meaning the court finds; (ii) the gravity of the opinion/criticism; (iii) context and presentation; (iv) where opinion is clearly presented to **22-20B** the reader as such it may well mitigate its defamatory impact; (v) whether the source of the criticism, if identified, is authoritative; and (vi) whether the publisher has adopted or "put its weight" behind the criticism. If the court cannot draw an inference of serious harm, in order to continue with the claim a claimant will have to demonstrate that the serious harm threshold at s.1 is overcome by way of evidence.[93D]

[93] [2017] EWCA Civ 1334; [2018] Q.B. 594.

[93A] *Hope Not Hate Ltd v Farage* [2017] EWHC 3275 (QB).

[93B] [2018] EWHC 1234 (QB).

[93C] [2018] EWHC 1725 (QB); [2018] E.M.L.R. 25.

[93D] *Tinkler v Ferguson* [2019] EWCA Civ 819 at [28].

Serious financial loss

Replace paragraph with:

22-21 In *Brett Wilson LLP v Persons Unknown*,[94] the court for the first time considered s.1(2) of the Defamation Act 2013, which requires a body which trades for profit to prove that the publication complained of has caused or is likely to cause serious financial loss. The claim was against persons unknown who had published accusations of misconduct against the firm on the "Solicitors from Hell" website. The claimant applied for default judgment. The claimant is a boutique law firm which attracted a considerable amount of work from the internet. It was able to show that one potential client had not instructed the firm because of the publication. It also relied on other factors such as the prominence of the publication complained of on an internet search for the firm's name, the inference that other individuals would have read the publication complained of but not notified the claimant and the claimant's belief that there had been a considerable drop-off in the conversion of enquiries to instructions since the publication complained of. On the basis of this the court found that there was sufficient evidence of serious financial loss. This suggests the court is taking a holistic approach to assessing whether serious financial loss has been or is likely to be caused. Once the serious harm threshold had been overcome, damages were considered to be at large.[95] On a summary disposal after judgment in default Warby J found that the claimant in *Pirtek (UK) Ltd v Jackson*[95A] had shown both that the words complained of had a tendency to cause serious financial loss, and that the uncontradicted evidence of actual financial loss occasioned by spending money on a public relations consultant was serious, and overcame the s.1(2) hurdle. Serious financial loss, like other forms of serious harm, is capable of inference from the evidence.[95B]

[94] [2015] EWHC 2628 (QB); [2016] 4 W.L.R. 69.

[95] See also *Undre v London Borough of Harrow* [2016] EWHC 931 (QB); [2017] E.M.L.R. 3, where the court again considered the s.1(2) Defamation Act 2013 serious financial loss threshold. The second claimant failed to meet the threshold since the evidence relied upon did not show any loss to have been caused by the publication complained of.

[95A] [2017] EWHC 2834 (QB).

[95B] *Euroeco Fuels (Poland) Ltd v Szczecin and Swinoujscie Seaports Authority SA* [2018] EWHC 1081 (QB), [2018] 4 W.L.R. 133 at [71]; *Burki v Seventy Thirty Ltd* [2018] EWHC 2151 (QB); *Gubarev v Orbis Business Intelligence Ltd* [2019] EWHC 162 (QB); in addition to the cases referred to earlier in para.22-21.

Defamatory meaning

Replace paragraph with:

22-22 In considering whether a statement has or is capable of having a defamatory meaning, the court should give to the material in question its "natural and ordinary meaning". Words are to be taken in the sense that is most natural and obvious, and in which those to whom they are spoken will be sure to understand them. The test of reasonableness guides and directs the court.[96] In *Gillick v BBC*[97] and *Skuse v Granada Television*[98] the Court of Appeal stated that the court should give to material in a television programme the natural and ordinary meaning which it would have conveyed to the ordinary reasonable viewer, bearing in mind that a television audience would not give the programme the analytical attention of a lawyer to the meaning of a document, an auditor to the interpretation of accounts or an academic to the content of a learned article. These days the reasonable reader or viewer is considered to have a stronger stomach and more discriminating judgment than traditionally recognised.[99] He must be credited with having achieved a level of education which was not widely accessible to earlier generations.[100] Whether the statement is defamatory or not depends not on the intention of the defendant but on the probabilities of the case and on the natural tendency of the publication having regard to the surrounding circumstances, subject to the serious harm threshold under s.1 of the Defamation Act 2013.[101] At common law, if the words published have a defamatory tendency it will suffice even though the imputation is not believed by the person to whom they are published.[102] The mere intention to vex and annoy will not make language defamatory, which is not so in its own nature. Words apparently defamatory may be proved by evidence of the circumstances, such as special background facts known to publishees, to have been understood in another and innocent meaning. However the defendant will remain liable in respect of any person unaware of such facts.[103] Under the Defamation Act 2013, the need to establish that the statement has caused or is likely to cause serious harm to reputation means that some of these well-established principles will have to be re-considered. Judicial determination of meaning as a preliminary issue does not necessarily establish the intensity of the sting, which may be a matter for trial. In some cases, the meaning of the words complained of and their defamatory sting will go together, but not always.[104] Whilst in the libel context there can be only one meaning that the court may find the words bear, it is worthy of note that in malicious falsehood[105] the single meaning rule does not apply, which could lead to a claimant failing in libel but succeeding in malicious falsehood. The Court of Appeal has considered such a potential outcome "bizarre".[106] The principles to be applied when determining the natural and ordinary meaning of words were recently re-stated in *Koutsogiannis v The Random House Group Ltd*,[106A] and the classic exposition of the principles in *Jeynes v News Magazines Ltd*,[106B] with the addition given in *Rufus v Elliott*,[106C] was cited with approval by the Supreme Court in *Stocker v Stocker*.[106D] Generally no evidence beyond the words themselves is admissible,[106E] although as in *Greenstein v Campaign Against Anti-Semitism*[106F] on occasion evidence proving the existence of contextual material can be admitted.[106G] The court may determine meaning without a hearing.[106H]

[96] These principles derive from a long list of authorities and are repeated whenever meaning is determined. See *Lewis v Daily Telegraph Ltd* [1964] A.C. 234; *Skuse v Granada Television Ltd* [1996] E.M.L.R. 278; *Gillick v Brook Advisory Centres (No.1)* [2001] EWCA Civ 1263; *Jeynes v News Magazines Ltd* [2008] EWCA Civ 130. For a discussion of the reasonable reader, see para.22-17.

[97] [1996] E.M.L.R. 267. Capability is likely to become a non-issue as a result of s.11 of the Defamation Act 2013 removing the presumption in favour of jury trial.

[98] [1996] E.M.L.R. 278.

[99] *Lukowiak v Unidad Editorial SA* [2001] E.M.L.R. 46 at [47] per Eady J.

[100] *Lennon v Scottish Daily Record and Sunday Mail Ltd* [2004] EWHC 359 (QB); [2004] E.M.L.R. 18 at [40].

[101] For the most recent re-iteration of this guidance see the judgment of Sir Anthony Clarke MR in *Jeynes v News Magazines Ltd* [2008] EWCA Civ 130 at [14].

[102] *Hough v London Express Newspaper Ltd* [1940] 2 K.B. 507 at 515; approved *Morgan v Odhams Press Ltd* [1971] 1 W.L.R. 1239 HL, per Lord Morris at 1252 and per Lord Reid at 1246, but disbelief of the defamatory statement may mitigate damages; see also *Slim v Daily Telegraph Ltd* [1968] 2 Q.B. 157 at 172, 173, per Diplock LJ; cf. *Theaker v Richardson* [1962] 1 W.L.R. 151. Of course in such a situation the serious harm threshold would now act as a bar to any action.

[103] *Hankinson v Bilby* (1847) 16 M. & W. 442 (slander).

[104] *Simpson v MGN Ltd* [2016] EWCA Civ 772; [2016] E.M.L.R. 26.

[105] See Ch.23.

[106] *Cruddas v Calvert* [2015] EWCA Civ 171; [2015] E.M.L.R. 16.

[106A] [2019] EWHC 48 (QB) at [11], [12].

[106B] [2008] EWCA Civ 130.

[106C] [2015] EWCA Civ 121; [2015] E.M.L.R. 17.

[106D] [2019] UKSC 17; [2019] 2 W.L.R. 1033 at [35], [36].

[106E] 123 *Koutsogiannis v The Random House Group Ltd* [2019] EWHC 48 (QB).

[106F] [2019] EWHC 281 (QB).

[106G] See also para.22-23 and *Yeo v Times Newspapers Ltd* [2014] EWHC 2853 (QB); [2015] 1 W.L.R. 971.

[106H] *Hewson v Times Newspapers Ltd* [2019] EWHC 650 (QB).

Add new paragraph:

22-22A Where one or both parties seek a ruling on meaning the parties must apply for an order for it to be heard as a preliminary issue so as to enable the court to use its case management and, where appropriate, costs budgeting powers.[106I] A ruling on meaning can be sought at any time after the Particulars of Claim. In *Morgan v Associated Newspapers Ltd*[106J] Nicklin J noted that significant complication and cost would have been avoided had the court been asked to determine meaning (and the issue of fact/opinion) before a defence was filed. However, ruling on meaning as a preliminary issue will not always be appropriate if doing so would not be likely to save time and cost, and if meaning is not easily separable from other issues.[106K] Once the court has determined the actual meaning of the words, it is not open to the defendant to seek to defend as true some other meaning.[106L]

[106I] *Bokova v Associated Newspapers Ltd* [2018] EWHC 320 (QB).

[106J] [2018] EWHC 3960 (QB).

[106K] *Reay v Beaumont* [2018] EWHC 2172 (QB).

[106L] *Bokova v Associated Newspapers Ltd* [2018] EWHC 2032 (QB); [2019] 2 W.L.R. 232.

Context

Replace paragraph with:

22-23 The context in which words are published is very important. In construing the meaning of an alleged libel, the whole publication is to be taken into account, provided that it all relates to the same defamatory allegation. This includes all of the text, even where spread across different pages, headlines, photographs and any text/insert boxes.[107] The claimant is not permitted to pick out this or that sentence which he may consider defamatory, for there may be other passages which will take away their sting. Bane and antidote may be found together. In the case of the internet, words may take on a different interpretation because of the way people treat and react to bulletin boards and blogs. It has been said that words published on bulletin boards and blogs may be more akin to slanders than libels.[108] Language which is not defamatory on its face may become so when the circumstances are taken into account. In *Lord McAlpine of West Green v Bercow*[109] an apparently innocuous question posted on Twitter was found to be defamatory to certain readers who would have been aware of specific facts. The tweet was: "Why is Lord McAlpine trending? *innocent face*". The judge observed that the tweet was not a publication to the world at large, such as a daily newspaper or broadcast. It was a publication on Twitter and the hypothetical reader must be taken to be a reasonable representative of users of Twitter who followed the defendant. The circumstances which would be known to such readers were that there was extensive speculation regarding the identity of an unnamed "senior Tory politician" who was said to be guilty of child abuse. The claimant would have been known to have been a senior conservative politician. The court concluded that the words "innocent face" would be regarded as insincere and ironical, giving rise to the defamatory imputation that the claimant was the abuser. Particular care needs to be taken where the words are published in a political context, especially during election time. Whilst the rules of meaning require no adaptation where the individual said to be defamed is a political or civil servant, it is necessary to avoid an over-elaborate analysis.[110] The Court of Appeal confirmed the importance of context in determining meaning in *Bukovsky v Crown Prosecution Service*,[110A] where the words complained of were contained in a charging announcement published by the Crown Prosecution Service. In that context, the court upheld the judge's finding that the ordinary reasonable reader would not have understood that the claimant, having been charged with "making" indecent photographs of children, was present at the scene of the abuse and took the photographs himself. Rather, they would understand that words have special meanings when used in statutes, and would understand that the claimant had been charged with making indecent photographs of children contrary to Protection of Children Act 1978 s.1. The Court of Appeal added that it would proceed cautiously when asked to substitute its view on meaning for that of the first instance judge and would only do so where it was satisfied that the judge was wrong. The Supreme Court confirmed the importance of context in *Stocker v Stocker*,[110B] in which the fact that publication was in a Facebook post was critical, as Facebook is a casual medium, where an ordinary reader would read a post quickly and move on. The first instance judge was wrong to consider the dictionary definition of words in determining meaning. The meaning of the words "He tried to strangle me" in a Facebook post was that the claimant had grasped the defendant by the throat and applied force to her neck rather than that he had tried to kill her; as such the defendant's justification defence succeeded. Context and presentation were also key to the determination of meaning in *Poroshenko v BBC*.[110C] The judge noted that the ordinary viewer would only watch a television report once; as such it is the overall impression that will be most important and over-analysis should be avoided. Whether any antidote in a piece will reduce the gravity of the meaning of a publication taken overall is highly dependent upon context.[110D]

[107] *Charleston v News Group Newspapers Ltd* [1995] 2 A.C. 65 HL. In *Dee v Telegraph Media Group Ltd* [2010] EWHC 924 (QB); [2010] E.M.L.R. 20 Sharp J ruled that in relation to newspaper articles on the same subject spread over a number of pages, the ordinary reasonable reader was to be taken to have turned over the pages and read what he was directed to on the continuation pages. In *Horan v Express Newspapers* [2015] EWHC 3550 (QB) the court considered the full context of the article complained of, including the text on both pages 1 and 5 of the newspaper, the photograph used, the headlines and insert box. But in *Telnikoff v Matusevitch* [1992] A.C. 343 the House of Lords decided that a letter, written by the defendant, had to be looked at on its own since the claimant's article, to which it was a response, would not necessarily have been read by those who read the letter.

[108] *Smith v ADVFN Plc* [2008] EWHC 1797 (QB).

[109] [2013] EWHC 1342 (QB).

[110] *Waterson v Lloyd* [2013] EWCA Civ 136; [2013] E.M.L.R. 17 at [66]; *Thompson v James* [2014] EWCA Civ 600; [2014] B.L.G.R. 664; *Mughal v Telegraph Media Group Ltd* [2014] EWHC 1371 (QB).

[110A] [2017] EWCA Civ 1529; [2018] 4 W.L.R. 13.

[110B] [2019] UKSC 17; [2019] 2 W.L.R. 1033.

[110C] [2019] EWHC 213 (QB).

[110D] See also *Zarb-Cousin v Association of British Bookmakers* [2018] EWHC 2240 (QB).

Add new paragraph at end:

22-23A Material behind a hyperlink in online words complained of may need to be taken into account as part of the context when determining meaning,[110E] although in *Falter v Atzmon*[110F] consideration of the hyperlinked video did not make any difference to the meaning found. Nicklin J did not purport to make a hard and fast rule about the approach the ordinary reasonable reader would take to hyperlinks. At one extreme there might be a publication which consisted of little more than a hyperlink such that it would be necessary to click the link to make sense of the publication, and at the other a publication with a large number of links might be such that it would be unrealistic to expect more than a small minority of readers to look at them all. In *Poulter v Times Newspapers Ltd*[110G] Nicklin J drew a distinction between the online and hard copy versions of articles in that in the hard copy the two articles complained of were on the same two pages separated by a photograph of the claimant, whereas the online articles were at separate URLs. Although one article was accessible from the other via a "related link", there was no exhortation or encouragement to readers to follow the link.

[110E] *Greenstein v Campaign Against Anti-Semitism* [2019] EWHC 281 (QB); see *Yeo v Times Newspapers Ltd* [2014] EWHC 2853 (QB); [2015] 1 W.L.R. 971 where an article elsewhere in the same edition of a newspaper was also treated as relevant contextual material.

[110F] [2018] EWHC 1728 (QB).

[110G] [2018] EWHC 3900 (QB).

Defamatory matter published as hearsay

Replace paragraph with:

22-24 Matter which is otherwise defamatory will not be the less actionable merely because it is rumour, hearsay, or supposition. If the rule were otherwise, every dealer in defamation would have free range provided that the libel or slander was preceded by some such preface to his libel as "I am informed", "I am of opinion".[111] In *Shah v Standard Chartered Bank*[112] the agent of the defendant had made statements to Bank of England representatives to the effect that the claimants' company had been guilty of money laundering. The claimants sued and the defendants alleged inter alia that they were merely repeating what had been rumoured. The Court of Appeal considered the cases of *Aspro Travel v Owners Abroad*[113] and *Stern v Piper*[114] and applied the "repetition rule" affirming that, in the words of Lord Devlin in *Lewis v Daily Telegraph Ltd*, "for the purposes of the law of libel a hearsay statement is the same as a direct statement and that is all there is to it". It is therefore not enough to justify the existence of a rumour; the publication of it would be justified only by showing objectively that the rumour was true. The court preferred *Stern v Piper* to *Aspro Travel v Owners Abroad* which, in their view, should be confined to its own facts and should not be treated as laying down a general principle.[115] The rule on repetition was discussed in *Al-Fagih v HH Saudi Research and Marketing*[116] and in *Lukowiak v Unidad Editorial SA*,[117] in both of which the allegations made by the defendants consisted of "reportage" of allegations made by others and merely reported by the newspaper in question. The rule established in *Stern v Piper* and

Shah v Standard Chartered Bank was confirmed, although the Court acknowledged the special difficulties connected with the duty of a free press to report disputes on matters of public interest. Eady J in *Lukowiak* also considered the effect of the 2001 Strasbourg decision in *Thoma v Luxembourg*[118] where it was held that "a general requirement for journalists systematically to distance themselves from the content of a quotation that might insult or provoke others or damage their reputation was not reconcilable with the press's role" and would be an infringement of art.10. However, in the event, Eady J decided the issue of the reported allegations in the overall context of qualified privilege. In *Al-Fagih* the Court of Appeal confirmed that the question of reported allegations in the defendant's newspaper was to be viewed overall in the light of the defence of qualified privilege as stated in *Reynolds.*[119] In *Chase v News Group Newspapers Ltd*[120] the Court of Appeal upheld the decision of Eady J, to the effect that the "repetition rule" approved in *Stern* and *Shah* was correct and was not inconsistent with the requirements of the Human Rights Act 1998, as it was not an undue restraint on the defendant's rights under art.10 of the Convention. Where part of the publication complained of consists of hearsay statements, when assessing meaning the court should take the usual approach and view the publication as a whole.[121] In *Lachaux v Independent Print Ltd*[122] it was confirmed that the repetition rule survives the coming into force of the Defamation Act 2013. In *Hewson v Times Newspapers Ltd*[122A] it was observed that words such as "alleged" or "claimed" are unlikely, of themselves, to shield a publisher from the effect of the repetition rule. Rather, it is the overall effect of the publication which matters.[122B]

[111] See *Harrison v Thornborough* (1713) 10 Mod. 196; *M'Pherson v Daniels* (1829) 10 B. & C. 263; *Watkin v Hall* (1868) L.R. 3 Q.B. 396; *Botterill v Whytehead* (1879) 41 L.T. 588; *Cadam v Beaverbrook Newspapers Ltd* [1959] 1 Q.B. 413; *Lewis v Daily Telegraph Ltd* [1964] A.C. 234; and see para.22-216; *Truth (NZ) Ltd v Holloway* [1960] 1 W.L.R. 997 PC.

[112] [1999] Q.B. 241.

[113] [1996] 1 W.L.R. 132.

[114] [1997] Q.B. 123.

[115] [1999] Q.B. 241.

[116] [2001] EWCA Civ 1634; [2002] E.M.L.R. 13.

[117] [2001] E.M.L.R. 46.

[118] (2003) 36 E.H.R.R. 21, ECtHR.

[119] *Reynolds v Times Newspapers Ltd* [2001] 2 A.C. 127. See also *Roberts v Gable* [2007] EWCA Civ 721; [2008] Q.B. 502.

[120] [2002] EWCA Civ 1772; [2003] E.M.L.R. 11. See also *Mark v Associated Newspapers* [2002] EWCA Civ 772; [2002] E.M.L.R. 38.

[121] *Hiranandani-Vandrevala v Times Newspapers Ltd* [2016] EWHC 250 (QB); [2016] E.M.L.R. 16: the court took into account the denials included, the repeated uses of the word "alleged" and that the publisher had not adopted the allegations, and found the piece bore a meaning of "cogent grounds to suspect" guilt rather than guilt.

[122] [2015] EWHC 620 (QB); confirmed by the Supreme Court: [2019] UKSC 27; [2019] 3 W.L.R. 18.

[122A] [2019] EWHC 650 (QB).

[122B] *Poulter v Times Newspapers Ltd* [2018] EWHC 3900 (QB) at [43], [44]; and *Poroshenko v BBC* [2019] EWHC 213 (QB) at [28].

4. SLANDER

Slander distinguished from libel

Replace footnote 227 with:

22-43 [227] [2016] EWHC 2858 (QB); [2018] Q.B. 1015 at [43].

(a) Imputing a criminal offence

The imputation of a criminal offence must be clear

Replace footnote 233 with:

22-44 [233] *Curtis v Curtis* (1834) 10 Bing. 477; see also *Francis v Roose* (1838) 3 M. & W. 191. Nor is it is necessary to plead any particular criminal offence, although doing so has been described as "helpful": *Barkhuysen v Hamilton* [2016] EWHC 2858 (QB); [2018] Q.B. 1015 at [149].

5. PUBLICATION

Publication by agent

Replace paragraph with:

22-57 The maxim of *respondeat superior*[303] applies, and if an employee acting within the scope of his employment publishes a libel the employer can be sued.[304] Section 1(4) of the Defamation Act 1996 provides that, for the purposes of the statutory defence under s.1:

> "Employees or agents of an author, editor or publisher are in the same position as their employer or principal to the extent that they are responsible for the content of the statement or the decision to publish it."

In *Regan v Taylor*[305] the defendant was a solicitor representing a police officer in several libel actions. In an interview he described the magazine "Scallywag", of which the claimant was editor, in deeply unfavourable terms, without having any specific authority from his client. He claimed that his statement was covered by qualified privilege and the Court of Appeal upheld the decision of the court at first instance to enter summary judgment for him since there was no reasonable prospect of this defence being rebutted. In *Monir v Wood*[305A] the defendant, chairman of the local UKIP political party branch, was liable for a tweet posted by the vice-chairman, given that the task of tweeting had been delegated to the vice-chairman, and the defendant retained control of the twitter account throughout. Having decided that the defendant was liable for publication by his agent, the court did not consider it necessary to decide whether he was vicariously liable for the tweet.

[303] "Let the superior answer."

[304] *Citizens' Life Assurance Co v Brown* [1904] A.C. 423; *Finburgh v Moss Empires*, 1908 S.C. 928 (slander); *Neville v C & A Modes*, 1945 S.C. 175 (slander). For cases where the publication was held outside the scope of the employment, see *Glasgow Corp v Lorimer* [1911] A.C. 209 at 214, per Lord Loreburn LC; *Aiken v Caledonian Ry*, 1913 S.C. 66; *Mandelston v NB Ry*, 1917 S.C. 442. As to master and servant and scope of employment see para.6-05 onwards.

[305] [2000] E.M.L.R. 549; (2000) 150 N.L.J. 392.

[305A] [2018] EWHC 3525 (QB).

Responsibility for publication on the Internet

Replace paragraph with:

22-63 The author of a publication online is liable as the publisher of the statement according to ordinary principles of liability. In *Bussey Law Firm PC v Page*[325] publication of a defamatory posting on Google Maps was found to have originated from the defendant's Google account. The court concluded that the account holder was responsible for publication, and that his argument that the account had been hacked was extremely improbable. Publication of tweets on Twitter have founded libel claims.[326] If a message on a publicly accessible website or social media page is intended to be private it is for the person writing to ensure it is sent privately. Taking part in an exchange on a public Facebook wall is akin to putting a comment on an office noticeboard accessible to anyone or sending a letter to a company and failing to mark it private.[327] However, the author may not be worth suing or may not be identifiable. The issue that has exercised the courts and legislators is to what extent those who facilitate publication online are liable and that depends upon what role they play and their state of knowledge.[328] The cases to date are not easy to reconcile and nor is it always easy to distinguish between liability for publication and the defences that are available for those who publish on the internet or allow material to remain online.[329] Broadly speaking, where an internet intermediary knows or ought reasonably to be aware of the content of the article complained of, though not necessarily of its defamatory nature as a matter of law, and has a realistic ability to control publication of such content, the intermediary is the main or primary publisher of such content.[330] Where an internet intermediary merely 'facilitates' access to websites provided by others by, for example, providing the computer systems through which communications happen to pass on their route from one computer to another, there is, no publication.[331] Where an internet intermediary hosts a website and has not received notification of the defamatory material then it is neither the primary or secondary publisher of the material complained of.[332] Where an internet intermediary that hosts a website is notified of the defamatory postings, it is to be treated as a publisher if it fails to disable access to, or take down, the material once it has had reasonable time to do so.[333] However, all these points address whether a host or facilitator is prima facie liable. In addition to being able to avail themselves of all the general defences to a defamation claim, internet service providers gain additional protection from the Electronic Commerce (EC Directive) Regulations 2002, implementing an EU Directive,[334] s.1 of the Defamation Act 1996[335] and ss.5 and 10 of the Defamation Act 2013.[336] Though the Defamation Act 1996 s.1 and the Electronic Commerce (EC Directive) Regulations 2002 may also apply to an "operator of a website", the Defamation Act 2013 s.5, read together with the Defamation (Operators of Website Regulations) 2013, provides an additional defence where the operator can show that it was not the operator who posted the statement on the website.[337] Not imposing liability on the host of an internet forum for anonymous comments is not a breach of art.8 of the European Convention on Human Rights.[337A] The author of comments on a person's Facebook "wall" was directly responsible for the publication of those comments to all of the person's Facebook "friends" who read them.[337B]

325 [2015] EWHC 563 (QB).

326 *Lord McAlpine of West Green v Bercow* [2013] EWHC 1342 (QB); *Monroe v Hopkins* [2017] EWHC 433 (QB); [2017] 4 W.L.R. 68.

327 *Stocker v Stocker* [2016] EWHC 474 (QB).

328 See *Gatley on Libel and Slander* (12th edn), Ch.6.

329 For defences see para.22-173.

330 *Tamiz v Google Inc* [2013] EWCA Civ 68; [2013] 1 W.L.R. 2151; but see *Oriental Press Group Ltd v Fevaworks Solutions Ltd* [2013] HKFCA 47 and *Gatley on Libel and Slander* (12th edn) at para.6.29 ("the applicable principles for internet publications"). The claimant in *Tamiz v Google* sought to chal-

lenge his inability to bring a claim against Google for comments on a blog post before the European Court of Human Rights, but the court rejected the claim as manifestly ill-founded: *Tamiz v UK*[2018] E.M.L.R. 6.

331 *Bunt v Tilley* [2006] EWHC 407 (QB); [2007] 1 W.L.R. 1243.

332 *Tamiz v Google Inc* [2013] EWCA Civ 68; [2013] 1 W.L.R. 2151. As the editors of *Gatley on Libel and Slander* (12th edn) point out that this would appear to sweep away the common law rule that liability is strict and was rejected in the HKFCA in *Oriental Press Group Ltd v Fevaworks Solutions Ltd* [2013] HKFCA 47.

333 *Tamiz v Google Inc* [2013] EWCA Civ 68; [2013] 1 W.L.R. 2151.

334 See paras 22-178 to 22-181.

335 See para.22-177.

336 See paras 22-182 to 22-183.

337 See paras 22-182 to 22-183.

337A *Høiness v Norway* (Application no. 43624/14), 19 March 2019.

337B *Stocker v Stocker* [2019] UKSC 17; [2019] 2 W.L.R. 1033, point on liability for Facebook posts directly addressed in the first instance judgment at [2016] EWHC 474 (QB).

6. DEFENCES

(a) Justification/Truth

(i) Justification under the common law

(1) Meaning to be proved true

"Grounds to suspect" meanings

Replace paragraph with:

22-68 In *Chase v News Group Newspapers Ltd*,[352] the claimant, a nurse, sued the defendants for allegations that health service officials had gone to the police and told them that she was suspected of having killed a number of seriously ill children in her care. The defendants pleaded justification and the court had to decide what was the "sting" of the words in question. The Court of Appeal gave a comprehensive summary of the rules relating to justification, especially where the allegation complained of amounts to a statement that a claimant is suspected of serious crime, namely: (1) "the conduct rule"[353]—that where the defendant states that there are reasonable grounds for the suspicion, there must be some conduct of the defendant to give rise to that suspicion; (2) the "repetition rule"—that a suspicion based on hearsay will not, as a rule, be enough;[354] and (3) that a defendant cannot rely, by way of justification, on events occurring subsequently to the occasion when the reasonable suspicion was alleged. The Court of Appeal held that these rules are not incompatible with art.10 of the ECHR. However, it did qualify the strictness of the rules in two material ways. First, strong circumstantial evidence implicating a claimant may afford reasonable grounds to suspect even if it does not directly focus on some conduct of the claimant. Secondly, the admissibility of hearsay is now generally permitted under the Civil Evidence Act 1995.[355] Provided the defendant complies with the rules for the admission of hearsay evidence,[356] such evidence may be relied upon to establish a primary fact. The rules make life difficult for defendants in terms of the evidence they are allowed to adduce and the matters that can be put to a claimant in cross-examination. This has meant that whilst there are a number of interim disputes about whether a publication carries a guilt or reasonable grounds to suspect meaning, few cases reach trial where the only issue is whether it is true that there were reasonable grounds to suspect the claimant of the conduct alleged.[357] Despite the conduct rule strong circumstantial evidence may be admissible to defend as true a "grounds to suspect meaning"[357A] but the opinions of those who carried out an investigation into the claimant are not "circumstantial evidence" and no conclusion about the claimant's conduct could be inferred from their opinions.[357B]

[352] [2002] EWCA Civ 1772; [2003] E.M.L.R. 11.

[353] On which see *King v Telegraph Group Ltd* [2003] EWHC 1312 (QB) (on appeal at [2004] EWCA Civ 613; [2005] 1 W.L.R. 2282), in which Eady J sets out what have become known as the "Musa King principles", and *Miller v Associated Newspapers Ltd* [2014] EWCA Civ 39 in which the Court of Appeal affirmed the Musa King principles.

[354] See para.22-69.

[355] For the use of hearsay evidence in the context of a reasonable grounds to suspect defence see *Miller v Associated Newspapers* [2014] EWCA Civ 39 at [31]–[40].

[356] See under CPR Pt 33.

[357] For a rare example of a "reasonable grounds to suspect" defence succeeding at trial, see *Rothschild v Associated Newspapers Ltd* [2013] EWCA Civ 197; [2013] E.M.L.R. 18. However, the defence was unsuccessful in *Miller v Associated Newspapers Ltd* [2014] EWCA Civ 39, which highlighted the evidential difficulties defendants may face in complying with the conduct rule.

[357A] *King v Telegraph Group Ltd* [2003] EWHC 1312 (QB).

[357B] *Miah v BBC* [2018] EWHC 1054 (QB).

(b) Absolute privilege

(i) Judicial proceedings

Judicial proceedings

Replace paragraph with:

With regard to judicial proceedings "neither party, witness, counsel, jury or judge, can be put to answer civilly, or criminally, for words spoken in office".[398] The rule is not confined to actions of defamation but applies whatever cause of action is sought to be derived from what was said or done in judicial proceedings,[399] unless perhaps the gist of the action is an abuse of the process of the court arising from some act or statement in the proceedings,[400] or where the antecedent act was not within the immunity.[401] The authorities are clear, uniform, and conclusive, that no action of slander or libel lies whether against judges, counsel, witnesses, or parties, for words written or spoken in the ordinary course of any proceedings before any court or tribunal recognised by law.[402] This immunity extends to all tribunals exercising functions equivalent to those of an established court of justice and "applies wherever there is an authorised inquiry, which, though not before a court of justice, is before a tribunal which has similar attributes".[403] This doctrine has never been extended further than to courts of justice and to tribunals acting in a similar manner. There is no single test which can conclusively determine whether a particular tribunal does act in a manner sufficiently similar to a court in order to be afforded absolute privilege in respect of its proceedings. Neither the fact that one tribunal is not empowered to take a final decision on the issue within its jurisdiction,[404] nor the fact that another tribunal is directed to conduct its hearing in private,[405] will necessarily prevent either tribunal being entitled to the protection of absolute privilege. The characteristics which the tribunal does share with courts of justice must be examined and a decision made whether the tribunal shows sufficient similarity in its functions and procedures for it to be said that it was "acting 22-82

... in a manner as nearly as possible similar to that in which a Court of justice acts in respect of an inquiry before it".[406] In *Huda v Wells*[406A] Nicklin J held that complaints to the General Osteopathic Council were protected by absolute privilege as that body is quasi-judicial in nature.

[398] per Lord Mansfield CJ in *R. v Skinner* (1772) Lofft 55 at 56. As to counsel, see *Munster v Lamb* (1883) 11 Q.B.D. 588; dissenting at 608 from Lord Denman CJ in *Kendillon v Maltby* (1842) Car. & M. 402 at 408, that judges are liable for slanderous language not relevant to the cases before them. As to witnesses, see *Seaman v Netherclift* (1876) 2 C.P.D. 53; cf. *Hargreaves v Bretherton* [1959] 1 Q.B. 45 (no liability in tort for perjury by a witness); the protection of a witness in the box extends to statements made by him in the preparation of a "proof"; *Watson v Jones* [1905] A.C. 480; *Beresford v White* (1914) 30 T.L.R. 591; *Lincoln v Daniels* [1962] 1 Q.B. 237 CA; *Marrinan v Vibart* [1963] 1 Q.B. 528 CA; *Thompson v Turbott* [1962] N.Z.L.R. 298; but see *Roy v Prior* [1971] A.C. 470 HL (action for maliciously procuring an arrest and status of evidence given ex parte). As to fair comment on a statement by a witness in the witness-box, see *Green v Odhams Press Ltd* [1958] 2 Q.B. 275 CA, and see 21 M.L.R. 517.

[399] *Marrinan v Vibart* [1963] 1 Q.B. 528 CA; *Hargreaves v Bretherton* [1959] 1 Q.B. 45. However, the immunity no longer applies to barristers *Hall v Simons* [2002] 1 A.C. 615 and expert witnesses: *Jones v Kaney* [2011] UKSC 13; [2011] 2 A.C. 398.

[400] See *Roy v Prior* [1971] A.C. 470; *Gregory v Portsmouth CC* [2000] 1 A.C. 419 at 427; *Iqbal v Mansoor* [2013] EWCA Civ 149; [2013] C.P. Rep. 27.

[401] *Singh v Reading BC* [2013] EWCA Civ 909; [2013] 1 W.L.R. 3052.

[402] per Kelly CB in *Dawkins v Lord Rokeby* (1873) L.R. 8 Q.B. 255 at 263. The privilege extends to superior and inferior courts, e.g. county court (*Scott v Standfield* (1868) L.R. 3 Ex. 230); bankruptcy registrar (*Ryalls v Leader* (1866) L.R. 1 Ex. 296); coroner (*Thomas v Churton* (1862) 2 B. & S. 475); magistrates in petty sessions (*Law v Llewellyn* [1906] 1 K.B. 487; *Primrose v Waterson* (1902) 4 F. 783, Ct of Sess). *White v Southampton University Hospitals NHS Trust* [2011] EWHC 825 (QB); [2011] Med. L.R. 296 found that the General Medical Council's Fitness to Practise Directorate is a quasi-judicial body; a letter sent by a medical director to the General Medical Council raising concerns about a doctor's probity and conduct was protected by absolute privilege. In *Mayer v Hoar* [2012] EWHC 1805 (QB) words that had been used in a letter written by a barrister in response to a request for comment by the Bar Standards Board were protected by absolute privilege.

[403] per Lord Esher in *Royal Aquarium Society Ltd v Parkinson* [1892] 1 Q.B. 431 at 442; approved *O'Connor v Waldron* [1935] A.C. 76 at 81; *Lincoln v Daniels* [1962] 1 Q.B. 237 (where the authorities are reviewed). Illustrations of such tribunals are: military courts of inquiry (*Dawkins v Lord Rokeby* (1873) L.R. 8 Q.B. 255; *Dawkins v Prince Edward of Saxe-Weimar* (1876) 1 Q.B.D. 499); the disciplinary committee constituted under s.46 of the Solicitors Act 1957 (*Addis v Crocker* [1961] 1 Q.B. 11; see also *Gray v Avadis* [2003] EWHC 1830 (QB); *The Times*, 19 August 2003—letters sent in connection with an investigation by the Office of Supervision of Solicitors); the General Medical Council under the Medical Act 1858 (*Leeson v General Council of Medical Education* (1889) 43 Ch D. 366 at 379, 383, 386); the Benchers of an Inn of Court (*Lincoln v Daniels* [1962] 1 Q.B. 237 CA; *Marrinan v Vibart* [1963] 1 Q.B. 528 CA); but not the Bar Council for it is the Benchers of the Inns (now the Senate on transfer by the Inns, cf. *S (A Barrister), Re* [1970] 1 Q.B. 160), who exercise the judicial functions of adjudicating on the complaint (*Lincoln v Daniels* [1962] 1 Q.B. 237 CA; *R. v West Yorkshire Coroner Ex p. Smith* [1985] Q.B. 1096 DC). And see *Report of the Committee on the Law of Defamation*, Cmd.7536, para.94.

[404] *Trapp v Mackie* [1979] 1 W.L.R. 377 HL (inquiry into the dismissal of a headmaster where the final decision lay not with the commissioner conducting the inquiry but the Secretary of State for Scotland. The House of Lords found that in practice the commissioner's decision would have a major influence on the final decision).

[405] *Addis v Crocker* [1961] 1 Q.B. 11; *Lincoln v Daniels* [1962] 1 Q.B. 237.

[406] *Royal Aquarium and Summer and Winter Garden Society Ltd v Parkinson* [1982] 1 Q.B. 431 at 432; and see *Trapp v Mackie* [1979] 1 W.L.R. 377 at 383, per Lord Diplock; and contrast *Att-Gen v BBC* [1981] A.C. 303 HL.

[406A] [2017] EWHC 2553 (QB); [2018] E.M.L.R. 7.

(iii) Official communications

Official communications

Replace paragraph with:

22-93 It is frequently the duty of public servants, both civil and military, to publish matter of a defamatory nature, especially in the confidential reports which in the ordinary course of affairs must be furnished to their superiors. The privilege attaching to such communications is absolute. It has been held that an official report on one of his subordinates, furnished by a general to his superiors, is privileged, though made maliciously.[446] There were two grounds for this, one applying only to military and naval affairs, the other to the public service generally: (1) no one serving in Her Majesty's forces can, in respect of any matter of discipline or question affecting his military status, appeal to any other jurisdiction than that which is created by the military law to which he has voluntarily submitted himself;[447] and (2) as a matter of public policy officers of the army, just as Ministers of the Crown, should make their official communications without any possible fear of consequences before them.[448] On this latter principle it has been held that communication made by a Secretary of State to his Parliamentary Under-Secretary in the course of his official duty cannot be made the subject of an action for libel.[449] The fact that a communication relates to commercial matters does not of itself preclude it from being one relating to state matters and therefore absolutely privileged.[450] It has been doubted whether absolute privilege for communications between officers of state extends below communications on the ministerial level.[451] In *Hasselblad (GB) Ltd v Orbinson*[452] the Court of Appeal held that communications with the European Commission relating to the enforcement of competition proceedings should be afforded absolute privilege. In *Mahon v Rahn (No.2)*[453] absolute privilege was held to apply to a report which the defendant bankers had provided to the TSA in the course of their investigations into fraud and also to the SFO which had initiated an unsuccessful prosecution against the claimants for fraud.[454] In *Lonsdale v National Westminster Bank Plc*[454A] Karen Steyn QC (sitting as a Deputy High Court Judge) held that absolute privilege did not to extend to a report by the defendant bank to the National Crime Agency, although qualified privilege was said to apply. This decision, however, appears not to have taken account of an earlier case which considered similar issues in respect of a complaint to police, and in respect of which absolute privilege was held to apply.[454B]

[446] *Dawkins v Lord Paulet* (1869) L.R. 5 Q.B. 94.

[447] See *Sutton v Johnstone* (1785) 1 T.R. 493; *Re Mansergh* (1861) 1 B. & S. 400; *Dawkins v Lord Rokeby* (1875) 7 H.L. 744.

[448] per Mellor J, in *Dawkins v Lord Paulet* (1869) L.R. 5 Q.B. 94 at 117; *Adam v Ward* [1917] A.C. 309.

[449] *Chatterton v Secretary of State for India* [1895] 2 Q.B. 189; *Grant v Secretary of State for India* (1877) 2 C.P.D. 445; *Fayed v Al-Tajir* [1988] Q.B. 712 CA.

[450] *Isaacs v Cook* [1925] 2 K.B. 391 (official report by High Commissioner for Australia in United Kingdom to Prime Minister of Australia); *Peerless Bakery Ltd v Watts* [1955] N.Z.L.R. 339.

[451] In first instance in *Szalatnay-Stacho v Fink* [1946] 1 All E.R. 303, per Henn Collins J (this point was not considered in the Court of Appeal. [1947] K.B. 1); and see *Richards v Naum* [1967] 1 Q.B. 620 CA; *Peerless Bakery Ltd v Watts* [1955] N.Z.L.R. 339. But see *Multigroup Bulgaria Holdings v Oxford Analytica Ltd* [2001] E.M.L.R. 28.

[452] [1985] Q.B. 475 CA.

[453] [2000] 1 W.L.R. 2150.

[454] See also *Taylor v Director of the Serious Fraud Office* [1999] 2 A.C. 177 and *Westcott v Westcott* [2008] EWCA Civ 818; [2009] Q.B. 407.

[454A] [2018] EWHC 1843 (QB); [2019] Lloyd's Rep. F.C. 94.

[454B] See *Westcott v Westcott* [2008] EWCA Civ 818; [2009] Q.B. 407 and the cases cited earlier in this paragraph.

(d) Publication on a matter of public interest

(i) Reynolds defence/defence under s.4 of the Defamation Act 2013

Responsible journalism under the Defamation Act 2013

Replace paragraph with:

22-155 Although the responsible journalism test and Lord Nicholls' 10 factors (or similar) were not (after debate in Parliament) included in s.4 of the Defamation Act 2013, the factors remain relevant to the defence, as the defendant must show that he or she "reasonably believed" that publication of the statement complained of was in the public interest. In determining whether the defendant's belief was "reasonable" the court will consider the same types of questions as were posed under *Reynolds*, such as the steps taken to verify the information, the status of the information and whether the allegations were put to the claimant. In interpreting the new statutory defence the courts will also need to balance the competing rights in play—art.8 right to reputation and art.10 right to freedom of expression.[686] Another important aspect of determining what is reasonable under the statutory defence is the allowance the court is required to give to editorial discretion by s.4(4).[687] This reflects the position as outlined in *Flood v Times Newspapers Ltd*,[688] and as made clear in the explanatory notes, applies to all defendants, not just those with traditional newsroom editorial set-ups. The defence has twice been considered by the Court of Appeal in *Economou v de Freitas*[689] and *Serafin v Malkiewicz*.[690]

[686] The balancing exercise to be undertaken by the court in such circumstances was set out by Lord Steyn in *Re S (A Child) (Identification: Restrictions on Publication)* [2004] UKHL 47; [2005] 1 A.C. 593 at [17].

[687] "... the court must make such allowance for editorial judgment as it considers appropriate."

[688] [2012] UKSC 11; [2012] 2 A.C. 273.

[689] [2018] EWCA Civ 2591; [2019] E.M.L.R. 7.

[690] [2019] EWCA Civ 852.

Replace paragraph with:

22-156 *Economou* was a case in which the defendant, Mr de Freitas, was a member of the public, and was sued personally, but media organisations who had published articles which were authored by or contained contributions from him were not sued. Mr de Freitas was the father of a woman who had made a complaint of rape against the claimant. The CPS did not charge the claimant, and he brought a private prosecution against Ms de Freitas for perverting the course of justice, which the CPS took over. Shortly before the trial Ms de Freitas, who suffered from bipolar affective disorder, killed herself. Mr de Freitas contributed to a number of publications relating to his daughter's death, criticising the CPS and calling for the coroner to investigate its role in her death. The court found two of the publications actionable with the most serious meaning being there were strong grounds to suspect that the claimant was guilty of rape and had falsely prosecuted Ms de Freitas for perverting the course of justice. There was no dispute that the subject matter of the articles was of public interest, so argument centred on whether the defendant reasonably believed that publication was in the public interest. The Court of Appeal confirmed that "the statement complained of" in s.4 means the actual words used, and that therefore the defendant's intended meaning could be relevant to whether his belief was objectively reasonable. As to whether Mr de Freitas was entitled to rely on the media organisations to carry out further checks and enquiries, Sharp LJ acknowledged that the issue raised difficulties for both free speech and reputation. She made clear that whether the s.4 defence applies will depend upon all the facts of the particular case. The Court of Appeal affirmed that the *Reynolds* factors could continue to be relevant to a s.4 defence. However, they are not the only factors to be taken into account and their relevance and weight will differ in accordance with the particular circumstances. In the present case, whether Mr de Freitas' conduct fell below the standard set out in the *Reynolds* factors was not the key to determining whether his belief was reasonable. Warby J at first instance had not found that the defendant had left verification all to the media, but that he had some information and had made what, for a person in his position, were reasonable and responsible investigations into the merits of the case against his daughter. Further, in the particular circumstances of the case Warby J made no error in concluding that in a story aimed at the CPS, including the claimant's side of the story would make little sense, and that the defendant had limited room for manoeuvre in expressing his criticisms of the CPS without risking implying something defamatory about the claimant.

Add new paragraph:

In *Serafin* the Court of Appeal took the view that the article complained of did not contribute to a debate of general interest, because it was not about broader public interest themes, such as the running of a charity for whom the claimant had been a contractor and supplier. Rather it was about the claimant's conduct as a private individual in those roles and in his personal life. Thus the s.4 defence failed on the first limb. The Court endorsed Lord Nicholls' check-list in *Reynolds* as relevant to both the issue of whether the journalist acted responsibly and to whether a public interest existed in the article at all.[691] It found that the test under s.4 was somewhat different from that in *Reynolds*: **22-156A**

> "First, under s.4(1)(a), the defendant has to show that the statement was, or formed part of, a statement on a matter of 'public interest'. Second, under s.4(1)(b), the defendant has to show that he 'reasonably believed' that publishing the statement was in the public interest. The two limbs of s.4 are clearly linked."[692]

The defence also failed on the second limb, in relation to which the defendants' failure to put matters to and seek comment from the claimant, and others with direct knowledge of events, was considered particularly important. There was no urgency in publication and the tone of the article was gratuitously offensive. There were other journalistic failures such as allegations for which the defendants had no evidential basis. Commenting on the decision in *Economou* the Court of Appeal observed that the facts of that case were exceptional and wholly distinguishable from those in *Serafin*. The Court said that the s.4 defence should be confined to that which is necessary to protect the art.10 right to freedom of expression, and that consideration must always also be given to a claimant's art.8 right to reputation, and to vindication where unproven allegations are published. This might be considered a tightening of the defence, at least where the defendant is a traditional journalist or media organisation. It thus appears that whilst the s.4 defence is flexible in terms of taking account of the particular circumstances in each case, the *Reynolds* factors relating to responsible journalism remain alive and well in determining whether the defence applies. Despite *Economou*, it seems it will be a rare case indeed where the s.4 defence succeeds without some attempt having been made to put allegations to, and seek comment from, the subject matter of the story. The distinction drawn between the public and private life of the claimant when determining whether the article was in the public interest at all is also worthy of note.

[691] [2019] EWCA Civ 852 at [48].

[692] [2019] EWCA Civ 852 at [46].

Add new paragraph:

22-156B The s.4 defence failed in *Hourani v Thomson*,[692A] where the court found that the defendants did not have a reasonable belief that publication was in the public interest and indeed had taken no steps to verify the material. The s.4 defence also failed in relation to an online article in *Burgon v News Group Newspapers Ltd*[692B] because the defendant failed to include in the article relevant information given by the claimant. When the matter was put to him, Mr Burgon told the journalist that the stylised "S" on an album cover was not a reference to Nazi iconography but to a Black Sabbath album cover. Dingemans J found that including a reference to Black Sabbath was necessary as a part of responsible journalism.

[692A] [2017] EWHC 432 (QB), in particular at [164]–[174].

[692B] [2019] EWHC 195 (QB).

(e) Honest comment/opinion

(i) *Comment not fact*

Fact or comment

Replace paragraph with:

22-162 Whether a statement is fact or comment can be a very difficult distinction, particularly because in many publications there is a mixture of both. There is no statutory definition of fact and comment, ultimately the question is how the words would strike the ordinary reasonable reader.[712] This requirement is continued under s.3(2) of the Defamation Act 2013. A convenient and succinct summary of the basic principles the court will apply when determining whether a statement is one of fact or of opinion can be found in *Koutsogiannis v Random House Group Ltd*.[712A] More broadly, the following principles can be derived from the decided cases:

(1) In *Branson v Bower (No.1)*[713] Latham LJ approved the judgment of Cussen J in *Clarke v Norton*[714] where he said:

> "More accurately it has been said that the sense of comment is something which is or can reasonably be inferred to be a deduction, inference, conclusion, criticism, remark, observation, etc."

(2) Where the statement is a pure value judgment, incapable of proof, it is likely to be regarded as a comment. For example, the suggestion that a critic is "completely out of touch with the tastes and entertainment requirements of the picture-going public" is a matter of judgment and is clearly a comment.[715] In *British Chiropractic Association v Singh*[716] the claimant sued over the claim in a newspaper article that the BCA "happily promote[d] bogus treatments" by chiropractors, even though there was "not a jot of evidence" to support claims that such treatments could be effective against a number of children's ailments. The Court of Appeal reversed the decision of the judge and concluded that such a statement, appearing on the "Comment and Debate" page of the newspaper, was a value judgment rather than an allegation of fact. The allegation amounted to an evaluation of published material as giving no evidential support to a claim, and

that was a matter for scientific opinion.

(3) Where the defendant refers to certain facts and makes it clear that the statement in question is an inference from the facts, it will generally be considered comment.[717] This technique is often utilised by the makers of documentaries, who might set out a number of facts from which they draw the conclusion that the claimant is, for example, unfit for public office. The conclusion will clearly be comment. However, it is vital to bear in mind that where the preceding matters are defamatory statements of fact in their own right, they will have to be justified, i.e. proved true or substantially true.[718]

(4) A bald statement with no supporting facts is unlikely to be considered a comment.[719] To say that "C is a disgrace to the profession of journalism" may sound like an opinion but, in the absence of any indication of the basis for the statement, it is likely to be treated as a statement of fact. To say that "C disclosed the identity of his source and is therefore a disgrace to the profession of journalism" clearly identifies the latter allegation as comment based on the fact that he has disclosed his source.[720]

(5) The defence is not limited to pure value judgments. A statement which appears to be factual and which is either true or false, may nevertheless be regarded as a comment where it is apparent that it is an inference drawn from other facts. This issue arises most commonly where the defendant has attributed an improper motive to the claimant. The traditional view, to use the words of Bowen LJ in *Edgington v Fitzmaurice*[721] is that "[t]he state of a man's mind is as much a fact as the state of his digestion". However, it is now clear that such allegations will often be regarded as statements of opinion. In *Branson v Bower (No.1)*[722] the meaning contended for by the claimant was that he was using his promise of a private charity fund to disguise his true intention to promote Virgin, and that he was a hypocrite, motivated by revenge and self-interest rather than charity. The defendant argued that the article was comment, and that the allegations made were value judgments or imputations of motive or intention which were akin to value judgments. It was contended that to require a defendant to have to prove the truth of value judgments would be an infringement of art.10 of the ECHR. Eady J agreed, concluding that the traditional English view in *Edgington* had been affected by recent developments in the law. He said:

> "More recently, however, the courts have been readier to treat the attribution of motive, in some cases, as matters of inference or comment. [...] In the end, however, any such classification must depend upon the words actually used and upon their context."

The Court of Appeal upheld the judge's finding and his reasons.[723] In *Keays v Guardian Newspapers Ltd*[724] the claimant, the former mistress of Lord Parkinson, complained about an article in the "Comment" section of *The Observer* which was entitled "The mother of all women scorned". There was a bold headline underneath stating "The vituperative Sara Keays has enlisted her damaged daughter to her cause." The article, a column, chronicled the "distasteful showing" of the previous week, in which the claimant and her daughter (by Lord Parkinson) had appeared in television and newspaper interviews. The claimant complained that the newspaper accused her of cynically using her daughter, Flora, to get back at Lord

Parkinson by allowing her to give interviews to which she could not properly consent. She also complained over the statement in the article that she had given a "kiss and tell" story to the *Sunday Times* in 1982, when she was pregnant with Flora. The defendants argued that the article was capable only of being comment. Eady J. agreed, stating that the article bore "the unmistakable badge of comment". He observed that the article was clearly in the comment section of the newspaper, and had the appearance of drawing inferences as to fact or motivation from the surrounding context. In the circumstances he had no hesitation in ruling that the article was comment.

(6) In contrast, a statement to the effect that a claimant has been guilty of a particular act is likely to be considered factual unless it is apparent that it is merely an inference drawn from other facts. To say of a composer that he organised the wrecking of concerts is a statement of fact which can only be justified.[725] Likewise, the allegation that the claimants have been party to a plot to force the end of a play is either true or false and is a statement of fact.[726] An allegation of dishonesty, fraud or attempted fraud, or of reasonable grounds to suspect the same, is likely to be an allegation of fact rather than one of comment.[727] Similarly an allegation of forgery was found to be one of fact rather than opinion.[728]

(7) The context in which the statement appears is relevant. Bold headlines and assertions in news stories are more likely to be considered statements of fact,[729] whereas criticisms in leader articles, letters or personal columns are more likely to be considered comment. The reader understands that the statements represent the personal views of the columnist. Prefacing statements with the words "in my opinion" or "in my judgment" may help, but is not necessary if it is clear from the context that they are comment.[730] A similar principle applies to reviews of products or literary, dramatic or musical works.[731] These inevitably involve the subjective evaluation of the reviewer. Humour is also more likely to be considered to be comment, albeit exaggerated and prejudiced. It is sometimes claimed by a claimant's advocate that mere "vituperation" or "invective" is not comment. Such a submission was advanced in relation to a newspaper review of the performance of an actress which included the suggestion that "her bum is too big". However, in cases of "vituperation" the closest alternative to comment is vulgar abuse which does not appear to get the claimant any further.[732] Moreover, both English and European cases recognise the right to use strong language which may shock and cause offence.[733]

(8) In *Cook v Telegraph Media Group Ltd*[734] the court concluded that the allegation that the claimant was a "low value MP" was unarguably a comment rather than a statement of fact. Also, an allegation that the claimant set out to exploit or abuse the expenses system for MPs was capable of being fact or comment. Political speech is more likely to be categorised as comment, following the Strasbourg jurisprudence.[735] That political speech is more likely to be categorised as opinion was confirmed in both *Yeo v Times Newspapers Ltd*[736] and *Barron v Collins*.[737] In *Yeo* it was stated that it is important to consider what the words in their political context indicate to the reader about the kind of statement the author intends to make.[738]

(9) The words which are alleged to be comment must be stated within the publication. This is in contrast to the supporting facts, which need not be directly stated. A comment cannot be an implication which the reader might

draw from the publication but which is not stated.[739] The reader should be able to point to specific words in the publication and recognise them as comment. A defendant in his defence should generally identify the particular words of the publication which he alleges to be comment.[740]

(10) In deciding whether a statement is comment, consideration may only be given to the publication which is the subject matter of the claim and not other publications to which it refers. In *Telnikoff v Matusevitch*[741] the claimant wrote an article in the Daily Telegraph following which the defendant wrote (and the newspaper published) a letter which was critical of the claimant's article. When read in the context of the original article the allegations in the letter were held to be clearly comment. However, the House of Lords held that the letter should be construed in isolation, on the ground that many readers of the letter would not have read or remembered the article.

(11) Where the defendant has failed to distinguish clearly between the facts on which he is commenting and the comment which he wishes to make, the statements may be regarded as factual.[742] Hence the importance of clearly identifying the comment.

(12) Whether a statement is fact or comment is to be determined by how it would be understood by the ordinary reader.[743] In contrast to determining defamatory meaning, it may be that there is less scope for attributing "loose thinking".[744]

(13) In addressing the principles to be applied when determining whether a statement is one of fact or opinion, Warby J summarised the position in *Yeo v Times Newspapers Ltd*[745] as follows:

> "The statement must be recognisable as comment, as distinct from an imputation of fact: *Gatley* para.12.7. Comment is 'something which is or can reasonably be inferred to be a deduction, inference, conclusion, criticism, remark, observation, etc.': *Branson v Bower* [2001] EWCA Civ 791; [2001] E.M.L.R. 15, [26]. The ultimate determinant is how the words would strike the ordinary reasonable reader: *Grech v Odhams Press* [1958] 2 Q.B. 275, 313. The subject-matter and context of the words may be an important indicator of whether they are fact or comment: *Singh* [26], [31]."

The judge stated[746] that he approached the issues of whether the statement is fact or opinion and meaning together, rather than one after the other. The Court of Appeal indicated in *Singh* that it would often be appropriate to consider meaning and then fact/opinion, but that it may not always be appropriate to do so. In *Donovan v Gibbons*[747] the judge also expressed the view that it mattered little in which order the issues of: (a) whether the publication was defamatory at all, (b) whether it was fact or comment, and (c) meaning, were addressed. Citing *Yeo*, HHJ Richard Parkes QC took account of the context (a video on YouTube) but was not convinced of the analogy counsel sought to draw with review websites such as Trip Advisor where the reader/viewer expects the statements to be comments. In *Butt v Secretary of State for the Home Department*[747A] Nicol J found that a meaning that the claimant was "an extremist hate speaker who legitimises terrorism and from whose pernicious and poisonous influence students should be protected" was an expression of opinion.

[712] *Grech v Odhams Press Ltd* [1958] 2 Q.B. 275 CA; *London Artists Ltd v Littler* [1969] 2 Q.B. 375 CA.

[712A] [2019] EWHC 48 (QB) at [16], [17].

[713] [2001] EWCA Civ 791; [2001] E.M.L.R. 32.

[714] [1910] V.L.R. 494 at 499.

[715] *Turner v MGM Pictures Ltd* [1950] 1 All E.R. 449. See also *Burstein v Associated Newspapers Ltd* [2007] EWCA Civ 600; [2007] 4 All E.R. 319.

[716] [2010] EWCA Civ 350; [2011] 1 W.L.R. 133.

[717] *Hunt v Star Newspapers Co Ltd* [1908] 2 K.B. 309.

[718] *Broadway Approvals Ltd v Odhams Press Ltd* [1964] 2 Q.B. 683.

[719] *O'Brien v Marquis of Salisbury* (1889) 54 J.P. 215; *Kemsley v Foot* [1952] A.C. 345.

[720] See, e.g. *Kemsley v Foot* [1952] A.C. 345.

[721] (1885) 29 Ch D. 459 at 483, a case on misrepresentation.

[722] Unreported 24 November 2000.

[723] *Branson v Bower (No.1)* [2001] EWCA Civ 791; [2001] E.M.L.R. 32.

[724] [2003] EWHC 1565 (QB).

[725] See *Burstein v Times Newspapers Ltd* [2001] 1 W.L.R. 579 CA.

[726] *London Artists Ltd v Littler* [1969] 2 Q.B. 375. See also *Thornton v Telegraph Media Group Ltd* [2009] EWHC 2863 (QB).

[727] *Wasserman v Freilich* [2016] EWHC 312 (QB).

[728] *Umeyor v Nwakamma* [2015] EWHC 2980 (QB).

[729] *Smith's Newspaper v Becker* (1932) 47 C.L.R. 279 at 303.

[730] See *Keays v Guardian Newspapers Ltd* [2003] EWHC 1565 (QB).

[731] *Merivale v Carsen* (1888) 20 Q.B.D. 275.

[732] See *Cornwell v Myskow* [1987] 1 W.L.R. 630. See para.22-24.

[733] See *Lingens v Austria* (1986) 8 E.H.R.R. 407; *De Haes & Gersils v Belgium* (1997) 25 E.H.R.R. 1; *Nilsen & Johnsen v Norway* (2000) 30 E.H.R.R. 878; *Thorgeirson v Iceland* (1992) 14 E.H.R.R. 843 and *Jerusalem v Austria* (2003) 37 E.H.R.R. 25; *Branson v Bower (No.1)* unreported 24 November 2000, per Eady J; *Branson v Bower (No.2)* [2002] Q.B. 737; *Keays v Guardian Newspapers Ltd* [2003] EWHC 1565 (QB).

[734] [2011] EWHC 763 (QB); see also in the same litigation at [2011] EWHC 1134 (QB).

[735] *Waterson v Lloyd* [2013] EWCA Civ 136; [2013] E.M.L.R. 17.

[736] [2014] EWHC 2853 (QB); [2015] 1 W.L.R. 971.

[737] [2015] EWHC 1125 (QB).

[738] [2014] EWHC 2853 (QB); [2015] 1 W.L.R. 971 at [97].

[739] *Hunt v Star Newspapers Co Ltd* [1908] 2 K.B. 309; *Tinkler v Ferguson* [2019] EWCA Civ 819.

[740] *Control Risks Ltd v New English Library Ltd* [1990] 1 W.L.R. 183.

[741] [1992] 2 A.C. 343.

[742] *Hunt v Star Newspapers Co Ltd* [1908] 2 K.B. 309.

[743] *Slim v Daily Telegraph Ltd* [1968] 1 Q.B. 157; *Barron v Collins* [2015] EWHC 1125 (QB).

[744] See *Keays v Guardian Newspapers Ltd* [2003] EWHC 1565 (QB).

[745] [2014] EWHC 2853 (QB); [2015] 1 W.L.R. 971 at [88].

[746] [2014] EWHC 2853 (QB); [2015] 1 W.L.R. 971 at [32].

[747] [2014] EWHC 3406 (QB).

[747A] [2017] EWHC 2619 (QB).

Add new paragraph:

22-162A Allegations that imputed arrogance, greed and unreasonable behaviour in relation to the claimants' benefit claims were found to be defamatory at common law and statements of opinion, but did not to cross the serious harm threshold, in *Sube v News Group Newspapers Ltd (1) and Express Newspapers (2)*.[747B] Whilst such allegations could attract disapproval, the court found that they did not relate to the most important of societal norms and there were no allegations of dishonesty or unlawful behaviour. None of the factual allegations in the article were found to be defamatory. The court also found that where an imputation is an opinion, that mitigates its defamatory impact. In *Morgan v Associated Newspapers Ltd*[747C] a defamatory opinion meaning was found to cross the serious harm threshold. The decision in *Sube* was described as "a most unusual case on the facts". Nicklin J analysed the case law on defamation and opinion, making clear that in order to avail of an honest opinion defence the statement of opinion must be based on true facts. In *Greenstein v Campaign Against Antisemitism*[747D] Nicklin J found allegations of anti-Semitism and of lying to be expression of opinion in the context in which they were published.

[747B] [2018] EWHC 1234 (QB).

[747C] [2018] EWHC 1725 (QB); [2018] E.M.L.R. 25.

[747D] [2019] EWHC 281 (QB).

(ii) Sufficient factual basis

Factual basis under the Defamation Act 2013 s.3

Replace paragraph with:

Section 3(4) recasts the requirement that the comment must be based on facts which are known to be true or protected by privilege. It requires the defendant to show that "an honest person could have held the opinion on the basis of (a) any fact which existed at the time the statement complained of was published; (b) anything asserted to be a fact in a privileged statement published before the statement complained of." Section 3(3) retains the requirement, as stated in *Joseph v Spiller*,[758] that the statement complained of indicated, whether in general or specific terms, the basis of the opinion. The extent to which s.3(4) changes the law remains to be interpreted by the courts. The Explanatory Notes state that the intention was to simplify the law whilst "retain[ing] the broad principles of the common law defence".[759] That the defence can be based on any facts existing at the time of publication, if interpreted widely, could be a far-reaching change to the law—a defendant who stated an opinion based on wholly false facts could succeed in his or her defence on the basis of facts of which he had no knowledge at the time of publication, potentially relating to a wholly different area of the claimant's life, provided that an honest person could have based the comment on those facts. However, the defendant would still need to give sufficient indication of the factual basis for the opinion. In *Morgan v Associated Newspapers Ltd*[759A] Nicklin J indicated (obiter) that s.3(4) means that there must be a nexus between the opinion and the subject upon which it is expressed.[759B] On a proper construction of s.3 a defence would not succeed if every fact set out in the publication was wrong, but some other fact existed upon which the opinion could be based. This would be a radical departure from the previous law, not indicated in the Explanatory Notes to the Act. Where an honest opinion defence is pleaded the particulars must be sufficient and pleaded with proper particularity.[759C] As the question under s.3 is whether an honest person could have held the opinion expressed based on facts existing at the time, other, potentially exculpatory facts, are not relevant to this objective as- 22-164 sessment under s.3(4)(a). If the defendant was said to have known the exculpatory facts it might be relevant to s.3(5) whether they honestly held the opinion.[759D]

[758] [2010] UKSC 53; [2011] 1 A.C. 852.

[759] Explanatory Notes to the Defamation Act 2013 at [22].

[759A] [2018] EWHC 3960 (QB).

[759B] See also *Burki v Seventy Thirty Ltd* [2018] EWHC 2151 (QB).

[759C] *Morgan v Associated Newspapers Ltd* [2018] EWHC 3960 (QB) referring to *Ashcroft v Foley* [2012] EWCA Civ 423; [2012] E.M.L.R. 25; *Higginbotham v Leech* (1842) 10 M. & W. 361.

[759D] *Carruthers v Associated Newspapers Ltd* [2019] EWHC 33 (QB).

(h) Miscellaneous defences

(i) Limitation

Limitation

Replace footnote 829 with:

22-197 [829] *Otuo v Watchtower Bible and Tract Society of Britain* [2017] EWCA Civ 136; [2017] E.M.L.R. 15.

Replace paragraph with:

22-198 The disapplication of the one-year limitation period is an exceptional step, the Court of Appeal held in *Bewry v Reed Elsevier (UK) Ltd*,[832] overturning the first instance decision to disapply the limitation period. The claimant had failed to provide a good reason for the delay which occurred both before and after the issue of proceedings. The first instance judge had found that the claimant was not aware of the limitation period for some time, although the Court of Appeal determined that there was not a sufficient evidential basis for this finding. In any event, ignorance of the limitation period will rarely, if ever, carry much weight given the sound policy reasons underlying the one-year period. In *Brady v Norman*[833] the Court of Appeal confirmed that, when considering the discretion to dis-apply the limitation period for defamation actions it was proper to take into account the respective prejudice to the parties which would be caused by a decision to dis-apply, or to refuse to dis-apply, the limitation period. The President accepted that, as noted in *Steedman v BBC*,[834] in a libel action, a direction under s.32A is always highly prejudicial to the defendant. In such a claim, brought to protect one's reputation, this ought to be pursued with vigour, given the ephemeral nature of most media publications. In *Lokhova v Tymula*[835] unexplained delay in progressing proceedings, coupled with a weak substantive case, meant the balance of prejudice did not favour disapplying the limitation period. The defendant would be substantially more prejudiced by the disapplication of the limitation period than the claimant would be by its application. In *Economou v de Freitas*[836] the court refused a claimant permission to amend his claim to add a new claim in respect of which the one-year limitation had expired. Warby J considered the appropriate course to take was to consider the general principles as to adding causes of action outside the limitation period in accordance with s.35(3) of the Limitation Act 1980. As the proposed new claim arose out of a different communication, albeit between the same parties, Warby J considered that since it did not arise out of the same or substantially the same facts as were already in issue, he had no power or discretion to permit the amendment. When considering s.32A of the Limitation Act, Warby J found that the application came too close to trial and the delay in raising the issue was not adequately explained, and so the defendant would suffer substantial prejudice if the limitation period were disapplied, whereas the claimant would suffer no serious prejudice given the claims he had already pleaded. He refused to disapply the limitation period. In *Nugent v Willers*[836A] when examining a provision of Isle of Man law almost identical in terms to s.32A of the Limitation Act, the Privy Council approved the principles in *Brady v Norman* and *Steedman v BBC*, summarising the position as follows[836B]:

(1) It is for the claimant to make out a case for the disapplication of the normal limitation rule.
(2) The court is required to have regard to all of the circumstances and in particular the length of and reasons for the delay; the date when all or any of the facts relevant to the cause of action became known to the claimant and the extent to which he acted promptly and reasonably; and the extent to which, having regard to the delay, relevant evidence is likely to be unavailable or less cogent than it would have been if the claim had been brought within time.
(3) Allowing an action to proceed will always be prejudicial to a defendant but, conversely, the expiry of the limitation period will always be in some degree prejudicial to the claimant. Accordingly, in exercising its discretion, the court must consider the degrees of prejudice to the claimant and the defendant, all of the other circumstances to which attention is directed by the section and any other relevant circumstances of the particular case in issue.
(4) It was plainly the intention of Parliament that a claimant should assert and pursue his need for vindication speedily.

The Privy Council stated that the court is entitled to treat some periods of delay as more relevant than others, and that it is reasonable for a court to take the view that the most relevant period of delay will be that after the relevant facts came to the claimant's attention.

832 [2014] EWCA Civ 1411; [2015] 1 W.L.R. 2565.

833 [2011] EWCA Civ 107; [2011] E.M.L.R. 16.

834 [2001] EWCA Civ 1534; [2002] E.M.L.R. 17.

835 [2016] EWHC 225 (QB).

836 [2016] EWHC 1218 (QB).

836A [2019] UKPC 1; [2019] E.M.L.R. 14.

836B [2019] UKPC 1; [2019] E.M.L.R. 14 at [17].

(iv) Abuse of process

Jameel **and** ***Thornton*** **grounds**

Replace paragraph with:

Attempts have been made to rely upon the Court of Appeal decision in *Jameel v Dow Jones & Co Inc*[849] to strike out cases as an abuse of process where "the game is not worth the candle." This will often be because there has been publication to a limited number of individuals, and/or because the publication does not constitute a real and substantial tort.[850] The defendant in such cases argues that the claim is trivial, and as such it would be disproportionate for the court to allow it to continue. The court will consider all the circumstances of the case, including the seriousness of the libel, the numbers to whom it was published, the potential damages likely to be awarded should the claimant succeed and the cost of continuing 22-203 proceedings. Applications of this nature have been made many times in recent years.[851] In assessing whether a libel claim is an abuse of process a court should consider what the claimant could achieve by way of vindication if the case went to trial, including matters which would go to the assessment of damages.[852] Where a claimant has been able to effectively restore their reputation through other means it may become an abuse of process on *Jameel* grounds to continue a libel claim.[853] Where a claimant has received vindication from one defendant but wishes to continue the case against another, the court should consider whether for practical purposes the claimant has obtained all he or she is going to obtain by way of redress such that continuing the case would be futile,[854] whereas just because a claim against one defendant would amount to *Jameel* abuse, does not automatically mean that a claim against a second defendant will also be an abuse.[854A]

[849] [2005] EWCA Civ 75; [2005] Q.B. 946.

[850] *Thornton v Telegraph Media Group Ltd* [2010] EWHC 1414 (QB); [2011] 1 W.L.R. 1985.

[851] For example, and in addition to *Jameel* and *Thornton* themselves: *Mardas v New York Times* [2008] EWHC 3135 (QB); [2009] E.M.L.R. 8; *Adelson v Associated Newspapers Ltd* [2008] EWHC 278 (QB); [2009] E.M.L.R. 10; *Haji-Ioannou v Dixon* [2009] EWHC 178 (QB); *Carrie v Tolkien* [2009] EWHC 29 (QB); [2009] E.M.L.R. 9; *Lonzim Plc v Sprague* [2009] EWHC 2838 (QB); *Baturina v Times Newspapers Ltd* [2011] EWCA Civ 308; [2011] 1 W.L.R. 1526; *Kaschke v Osler* [2010] EWHC 1075 (QB); *Hays Plc v Hartley* [2010] EWHC 1068 (QB); *Kordowski v Hudson* [2011] EWHC 2667 (QB); *Tamiz v Google* [2013] EWCA Civ 68; [2013] 1 W.L.R. 2151; *Euromoney Institutional Investor Plc v Aviation News Ltd* [2013] EWHC 1505 (QB); *Tamiz v Guardian News & Media Ltd* [2013] EWHC 2339 (QB); *Ansari v Knowles* [2013] EWCA Civ 1448; [2014] C.P. Rep. 9; *Liberty Fashion Wears Ltd v Primark Stores Ltd* [2015] EWHC 415 (QB); *Alsaifi v Trinity Mirror Plc* [2018] EWHC 1954 (QB), [2019] E.M.L.R. 1.

[852] *Weston v Bates and Leeds United Football Club* [2015] EWHC 3070 (QB).

[853] *Sobrinho v Impresa Publishing SA* [2016] EWHC 66 (QB); [2016] E.M.L.R. 12.

[854] *Ansari v Knowles* [2013] EWCA Civ 144, [2014] C.P. Rep. 9, where the Court of Appeal refused to strike out the claim.

[854A] *Alsaifi v Trinity Mirror Plc* [2018] EWHC 1954 (QB); [2019] E.M.L.R. 1.

Abuse of process—advancing matters already determined

Replace footnote 864 with:

22-206 [864] *Richardson v Trinity Mirror (Merseyside) Ltd* [2016] EWHC 1927 (QB) (available at: *www.5rb.com/wp-content/uploads/2016/07/Richardson-v-Trinity-Mirror-judgment.pdf*).

8. REPETITION

Injury by repetition

Replace footnote 907 with:

22-218 [907] *Lachaux v Independent Print Ltd* [2017] EWCA Civ 1334; [2018] Q.B. 594; confirmed on appeal: [2019] UKSC 27; [2019] 3 W.L.R. 18.

Where repetition authorised or intended

Replace footnote 914 with:

22-221 [914] *Slipper v BBC* [1991] 1 Q.B. 283 CA; *Economou v de Freitas* [2018] EWCA Civ 2591; [2019] E.M.L.R. 7.

9. REMEDIES

(e) Mitigation of damages

(iii) Conduct of the claimant

Conduct of the claimant

Replace paragraph with:

The conduct of the claimant is a relevant factor in the assessment of damages.[994] **22-240** Conduct in this context is limited to the claimant's acts and omissions at the time the material is published and in the course of the litigation. It follows from general principles that a claimant must take reasonable steps to minimise the loss from the unlawful act. Delay in making a complaint can contribute to the injury to reputation (and would also suggest that the claimant has not been injured by the publication). This is particularly a factor where the defendant agrees to apologise as soon as the matter is brought to his attention. There may be occasions where the claimant has to a certain extent provoked the defamatory statement but the strict requirements of the defence of consent are not met and the defendant cannot rely on a "reply to attack" qualified privilege. The claimant's conduct can nevertheless mitigate the damages. In *Gorman v Mudd*,[995] Russell LJ felt that the claimant took part of the blame for the "unseemly quarrel that developed between her and the defendant". In *Godfrey v Demon Internet Ltd*[996] the defendant sought to rely on allegedly inflammatory internet postings by the claimant which, it submitted, were intended to provoke people into libelling him. There must be a direct correlation between the provocation and the libel. In *Burstein*[997] the Court of Appeal rejected the defendant's primary submission that the claimant had provoked the libel. The claimant in *Trumm v Norman*[998] would have been awarded £15,000 in damages but for the fact that he had published on his website comments that were unnecessarily provocative and offensive and which led to the publication of the allegations of which he complained in the proceedings. Damages were reduced to £7,500. The fact that the allegations have been published previously and the claimant has not taken any action is not to be taken into account.[999] This rule, known as "the rule in *Dingle*" remains good law after the coming into force of the Defamation Act 2013.[999A] Nor may a court take into account any omission by the claimant to complain about other defamatory parts of the publication in question.[1000] In any event, the failure to complain may be the subject of cross-examination as to credit.[1001]

[994] See *Cassell v Broome* [1972] A.C. 1027 at 1071H and *John v MGN Ltd* [1997] Q.B. 586.

[995] *Independent,* 16 October 1992, CA.

[996] [2001] Q.B. 201.

[997] [2001] 1 W.L.R. 579 at [24].

[998] [2008] EWHC 116 (QB).

[999] *Associated Newspapers Ltd v Dingle* [1964] A.C. 371. This rule survives the coming into force of the Defamation Act 2013: *Lachaux v Independent Print Ltd* [2017] EWCA Civ 1334.

[999A] *Lachaux v Independent Print Ltd* [2017] EWCA Civ 1334; [2018] Q.B. 594; confirmed on appeal: [2019] UKSC 27; [2019] 3 W.L.R. 18.

[1000] *Plato Films Ltd v Speidel* [1961] A.C. 1090; although where properly pleaded as justification, they may mitigate damages under the principles set out above.

[1001] Following *Burstein* it is arguable that these matters should be considered as directly relevant background context.

(g) Relief under the Summary Procedure

Add to end of paragraph:

22-250 An application for summary disposal may be dealt with on the papers, as may an application for judgment in default: if such an application is made, the claimant should file a skeleton argument to assist the court.[1026A]

[1026A] *Charakida v Jackson* [2019] EWHC 858 (QB).

(h) Publication of a summary of the court's judgment

Defamation Act 2013 s.12

Replace paragraph with:

22-251 Section 12 allows the court to order the defendant to publish a summary of its judgment. This is a potentially important new discursive remedy for claimants. The wording of the summary and the time, form and manner of its publication are a matter for the parties to agree,[1027] but if they cannot agree, the court will settle the wording[1028] and give such directions as to time manner, form and place of publication as it considers reasonable and practicable in the circumstances.[1029] This provision builds on the (rarely used) power under the summary procedure[1030] to order that a summary of its judgment be published where the parties cannot agree a correction or apology. Exactly how far the court will go in terms of directions for placement, timing and manner of publication of the summary of its judgment remains to be seen.[1031] It is expected that claimants will now seek this remedy as standard. It may be that vindication in this manner will affect damages awards, however at present a reasoned judgment is treated as a fairly marginal factor in assessing damages.[1032] The power under s.12 was first used in *Rahman v ARY Network Ltd*[1033] where Sir David Eady ordered broadcaster ARY to broadcast a summary of his judgment. The court did not order this remedy in *Monir v Wood*[1033A] where the publication complained of was a tweet, and there was no method by which the defendant could publish a summary of the judgment such that it would come to the attention of a significant number of those to whom the defamatory statement had been published. Nicklin J considered that the publicity that would likely be given to the judgment by other means would provide sufficient vindication.

[1027] s.12(2).

[1028] s.12(3).

[1029] s.12(4).

[1030] Defamation Act 1996 ss.8–9.

[1031] For example, will the court order that a newspaper run the summary on its front page if the story complained of was on the front page?

[1032] *Purnell v Business Magazine Ltd* [2007] EWCA Civ 744; [2008] 1 W.L.R. 1.

[1033] [2016] EWHC 3570 (QB).

[1033A] [2018] EWHC 3525 (QB).

(i) Injunction

Final injunctions

Add to end of paragraph:

22-256 If the claimant seeks an injunction against an internet publisher, they must establish that England and Wales is the centre of their interests.[1052]

[1052] *Bolagsupplysningen OÜ v Svensk Handel AB* (C-194/16) [2018] Q.B. 963; *Said v Groupe L'Express* [2018] EWHC 3593 (QB); [2019] E.M.L.R. 9.

Chapter 23

MALICIOUS FALSEHOOD

Table of Contents

1. Malicious Falsehood

Malicious falsehood and defamation compared

Replace footnote 14 with:

[14] [2010] EWCA Civ 609; [2011] Q.B. 497, overturning [2009] EWHC 1717 (QB); [2010] Q.B. 204 (but not [2009] EWHC 781 (QB), see fn.10). In *Tinkler v Ferguson* [2019] EWCA Civ 819 at [29] Longmore LJ noted (of a malicious falsehood claim): "a claimant can seek to show that any reasonably available meaning of the statement in question was false and made maliciously". **23-03**

2. Essentials of the Action

Essentials of the action

Replace paragraph with:

In *Royal Baking Powder Co v Wright, Crossley & Co, Crossley & Co* the essentials of the action[49] were defined as: false words which are maliciously published and which are calculated to cause (and do cause) the claimant pecuniary loss. However the tort is often defined as applying to falsehoods "about" the claimant.[50] For example, in *Kaye v Robertson*, Glidewell LJ defined the essentials as "… that the defendant has published about the [claimant] words which are false, that they were published maliciously and that special damage has followed as the direct and natural result of their publication".[51] As this would include a falsehood, for example, about the claimant's product,[52] or indeed as in *Riding v Smith*, the claimant's wife,[53] it might be more appropriate to state that the words should concern the claimant or his property or otherwise refer to the claimant's pecuniary interests.[54] There appears to be a special case of malicious falsehood, where the defendant makes an untrue claim to a title of any kind or to be an inventor or designer—this falsehood may be actionable by the legitimate owner of the title in question, though the claimant is not referred to by the defendant. In *Customglass v Salthouse*[55] the false statement that the defendant had designed the claimant's boat was malicious falsehood, while in *Serville v Constance*[56] Harman J held that the defendant's false claim to a boxing title in fact held by the claimant was capable of amounting to malicious falsehood.[57] The claimant must in the first place strictly set out and prove the words complained of as in an action for defamation.[58] He must prove that they are **23-10** false,[59] and he must prove that they are malicious.[60] The falsehood must be published to persons other than the claimant. It would appear that republication which is the natural and probable consequence of the initial deliberate publication might render the defendant liable,[61] though Laws LJ in *McManus v Beckham*, preferred the test "it must ... be demonstrated that D foresaw that the further publication would probably take place or that D (or a reasonable person in D's position) should have so foreseen and that in consequence increased damage to C would ensue".[62] He found the root question to be whether "D, who has slandered C, should justly be held responsible for damage which has been occasioned ... by a further publication". Except in cases within s.3 of the Defamation Act 1952,[63] actual damage must be proved. An action for malicious falsehood, unlike an action for defamation, survives the death of the claimant.[64] In *Huda v Wells*[64A] Nicklin J held that in malicious falsehood "publication" (as with defamation claims) takes place where the statement complained of is heard or read by the publishee. In a malicious falsehood claim, that claim had to be limited to alleged publications within England and Wales.[64B]

49 *Royal Baking Powder Co v Wright, Crossley & Co, Crossley & Co* (1901) 18 R.P.C. 95 at 99 per Lord Davey: "To support such an action it is necessary for the [claimants] to prove (1) that the statements complained of were untrue; (2) that they were made maliciously—that is, without just cause or excuse; (3) that the [claimants] had suffered special damage thereby."

50 In *Marathon Mutual Ltd v Waters* [2009] EWHC 1931 (QB); [2010] E.M.L.R. 3 at [9], Judge Moloney QC accepted the defendants' argument that there must be some reference to the claimant or his business, to comply with art.10 ECHR that a restriction on free speech must be prescribed by law and not disproportionate.

51 *Kaye v Robertson* [1991] F.S.R. 62 at 67.

52 *Ajinomoto Sweeteners Europe SAS v Asda Stores Ltd* [2010] EWCA Civ 609; [2011] Q.B. 497.

53 (1876) 1 Ex. D. 91. The court also commented that malicious falsehood would lie where false allegations of infectious diseases affecting a claimant's workforce were made.

54 In *Niche Products Ltd v MacDermid Offshore Solutions LLC* [2013] EWHC 3540 (IPEC); [2014] E.M.L.R. 9 Birss J refused to strike out a claim for malicious falsehood. The parties were trade rivals and the claimant had issued a report that the defendant had changed the formulation of its product. The defendant published a letter stating that the claimant's report was "misleading and erroneous". Birss J stated "if a statement is likely to cause pecuniary damage then there is a nexus between the alleged falsehood and the claimant's economic interests" (at [32]; application to stay proceedings rejected by the Court of Appeal: [2014] EWCA Civ 379).

55 [1976] 1 N.Z.L.R. 36.

56 [1954] 1 All E.R. 662 at 665.

57 However, though these cases were referred to by Judge Maloney QC, sitting as a High Court Judge in *Marathon Mutual Ltd v Waters* [2009] EWHC 1931; [2010] E.M.L.R. 3 it is submitted that he was wrong not to strike out the claim in malicious falsehood from the claimant whose income was largely derived from the "target" of the alleged falsehood (cf. *Gatley on Libel and Slander*, 12th edn (London: |Sweet & Maxwell, 2013), para.21.4 and C. Wadlow, *The Law of Passing Off: Unfair Competition by Misrepresentation*, 5th edn (London: Sweet & Maxwell, 2016), para.6-16).

58 *Gutsole v Mathers* (1836) 1 M. & W. 495. In *Cornwall Gardens Ltd v Garrard & Co Ltd* [2001] EWCA Civ 699, the Court of Appeal endorsed Bar Council guidance on counsel's obligations before pleading fraud, and applied it to the tort of malicious falsehood. As to the meaning of "reasonably credible admissible evidence" before alleging fraud, see *Medcalf v Mardell* [2002] UKHL 27; [2003] 1 A.C. 120.

59 There is no presumption in favour of the goodness of a man's title to property or of the quality of his merchandise.

60 *Royal Baking Powder Co v Wright, Crossley & Co* (1901) 18 R.P.C. 95; *British Railway Traffic, etc. Co v CRC Co* [1922] 2 K.B. 260; *Shapiro v La Morta* (1924) 40 T.L.R. 39 at 201.

61 *Cellactite & British Uralite v HH Robertson Co* [1957] C.L.Y. 1989; *The Times,* 23 July 1957.

62 [2002] EWCA Civ 939; [2002] 1 W.L.R. 2982 at [43]. See also Waller LJ at [34].

[63] See para.23-16.

[64] *Hatchard v Mege* (1887) 18 Q.B.D. 771.

[64A] [2017] EWHC 2553 (QB); [2018] E.M.L.R. 7 at [10].

[64B] See *Berezovsky v Forbes Inc (No.1)* [2000] 1 W.L.R. 1004 HL, Lord Hope at 1032.

[illegible]

[illegible]

[illegible]

CHAPTER 24

ECONOMIC TORTS

TABLE OF CONTENTS

1. GENERAL

The core economic torts

Replace paragraph with:

24-01 The torts of procuring a breach of contract, intimidation, unlawful interference and conspiracy are generally described today as "economic torts".[1] They form the core of the liabilities for intentional torts in respect of economic interests and the principles governing them are closely interrelated. The description "economic torts" is useful, even if not strictly accurate when the liabilities involved can extend more widely than damage to "economic" interests. The general patterns of liability still contain "ramshackle" elements (for they have "lacked their Atkin")[2] and sometimes they are presented to the courts as "unidentified economic torts".[3] The term "economic tort" is also applied more widely to other torts, such as passing off, malicious falsehood, slander of title, and wrongs in respect of patents, trademarks or breach of copyright (often referred to as wrongs to "intellectual property")[4] with which the core economic torts are frequently contiguous.[5] The nature and enforcement of the economic torts increasingly raise new policy questions, not least their relationship to the rights of free speech and freedom of association, both rights which are recognised in the European Convention on Human Rights and given statutory recognition in the Human Rights Act 1998, or to EU law.[6]

[1] cf. Lord Neuberger in *Revenue & Customs Commissioners v Total Network SL* [2008] UKHL 19; [2008] 1 A.C. 1174 at [216]: "Unlawful means conspiracy is one of the so-called economic torts, which included procuring a breach of contract, unlawful interference, causing loss by unlawful means, intimidation and conspiracy to injure (or lawful means conspiracy). These torts present problems even if they are considered individually (and yet more problems if they are treated as a genus)." For a valuable critical analysis see H. Carty, *An Analysis of the Economic Torts*, 2nd edn (Oxford: OUP, 2010); see too S. Deakin, "Economic Relations", Ch.30 in C. Sappideen and P. Vines (eds), *Fleming's The Law of Torts*, 10th edn (Thomson Reuters: Australia, 2011) updating Fleming's own Ch.30 in the 9th edn (Thomson Reuters: Australia, 1998). Older but still valuable specialist texts are J. Heydon, *Economic Torts*, 2nd edn (London: Sweet & Maxwell, 1978), P. Cane, *Tort Law and Economic Interests*, 2nd edn (Oxford: OUP, 1996) and T. Weir, *Economic Torts* (1997). In general tort texts see D. Howarth, M. Matthews, J. Morgan, J. O'Sullivan and S. Tofaris, *Hepple and Matthews' Tort: Cases and Materials*, 7th edn (Oxford: OUP, 2015), Ch.15; S. Deakin, A. Johnston and B. Markesinis, *Markesinis and Deakin's Tort Law*, 7th edn (Oxford: OUP, 2013), Ch.15; E. Peel and J. Goudkamp (eds), *Winfield and Jolowicz on Tort*, 19th edn (London: Sweet & Maxwell, 2014), Ch.19; C. Witting, *Street on Torts*, 15th edn (Oxford: OUP, 2018), Ch.15. See too R. Smith, "The Economic Torts: Their Impact on Real Property" (1977) 41 Conv. (N.S.) 318; R. Heuston and R. Buckley (eds), *Salmond and Heuston on the Law of Torts*, 21st edn (1996), Ch.16.

[2] Wedderburn (1983) 46 M.L.R. 224 at 226. In *Revenue & Customs Commissioners v Total Network SL* [2008] UKHL 19; [2008] 1 A.C. 1174 at [224], Lord Neuberger observed that the notion of a single consistent approach to what constitutes unlawful means in relation to the economic torts (which the House of Lords rejected in that case) could be said to be inconsistent with this ramshackle nature. See generally H. Carty, "Intentional Violation of Economic Interests" (1988) 104 L.Q.R. 250; P. Sales and D. Stilitz, "Intentional Infliction of Harm by Unlawful Means" (1999) 115 L.Q.R. 411; Bagshaw (1998) 18 O.J.L.S. 729; H. Carty (1999) 19 L.S. 489 (joint tortfeasors and "accessory" liability for assistance); J. Eekalaar (1990) 106 L.Q.R. 223 (conspiracy); P. Loughlan (1989) 9 O.J.L.S. 260 (assisting breach of fiduciary duty); P. Sales [1990] C.L.J. 491 (conspiracy and secondary liability); P. Davies and P. Sales, "Intentional Harm, Accessories and Conspiracies" (2018) 134 L.Q.R. 69;A. Tettenborn [1982] C.L.J. 58; D. Freedman [1999] C.L.J. 288; cf. attitudes in USA: S. Perlman, "Interference with

Contract and Other Economic Expectations" (1982) 49 Univ. Chi. L.R. 61; and the classic article: F.P. Sayre, "Inducing Breach of Contract" (1923) 36 Harv. L.R. 663.

[3] McCarthy J, *Mantruck Services Ltd v Ballinlough Electrical Refrigerators Co* [1992] 1 I.R. 351 at 358 (Ir. Sup. Ct). For Commonwealth developments: on Australia: Barker, et al, *The Law of Torts in Australia*, 5th edn (2012), Ch.6; on New Zealand: S. Todd, et al, *Todd on Torts* (formerly, *Law of Torts in New Zealand*, 8th edn (2019), Ch 13; on Canada: L. Klar, *Tort Law*, 6th edn (2017), Ch.17.

[4] See Chs 23, 25 and 26.

[5] See *Microdata Information Services v Rivendale Clyne* [1991] F.S.R. 681. Both liability in tort for interference with a person's interests by unlawful means and clarifications of liability for breach of some equitable obligations, have opened a wider range of liability plus new difficulties of the relationship between the two: see *Indata Equipment Supplies Ltd v ACL Ltd* [1998] F.S.R. 248 CA, and para.24-81.

[6] See, per Neill LJ in *Middlebrook Mushrooms Ltd v TGWU* [1993] I.C.R. 612 CA at 620 (on the European Convention of Human Rights and free speech); compare Lord Denning MR in *Associated Newspapers Group v Wade* [1979] I.C.R. 664 at 690, who appears to go too far in treating interference with free speech and the freedom of the press as per se unlawful means. Quaere the effect of the Human Rights Act 1998. On European Union or EC law (as it is often still known), see *Barretts & Baird (Wholesale) Ltd v Institution of Professional Civil Servants* [1987] I.R.L.R. 3; *Three Rivers DC v Bank of England (No.3)* [2003] 2 A.C. 1 HL. *Francovich v Italy* (C-69/90) [1991] E.C.R. I-5357 ECJ; *Garden Cottage Foods v Milk Marketing Board* [1984] A.C. 130 HL (action for breach of European "statutory duty").

Replace footnote 14 with:

[14] *OBG Ltd v Allan* [2007] UKHL 21; [2008] 1 A.C. 1; *Revenue & Customs Commissioners v Total Network SL* [2008] UKHL 19; [2008] 1 A.C. 1174. See H. Carty, "The Economic Torts in the Twenty First Century" (2008) 124 L.Q.R. 641; S. Deakin and J. Randall "Rethinking the Economic Torts" (2009) 72 M.L.R. 519; P. Davies and P. Sales, "Intentional Harm, Accessories and Conspiracies" (2018) 134 L.Q.R. 69. **24-02**

Inducing or procuring breach of contract

Replace footnote 27 with:

[27] per Slade LJ in *RCA Corp v Pollard* [1983] Ch. 135 at 156. But on interference causing loss of "secondary" or remedial rights, see now *Law Debenture Trust Corp v Ural Caspian Oil Corp Ltd* [1995] Ch. 152 CA; *Marex Financial Ltd v Sevilleja* [2017] EWHC 918 (Comm), [2017] 4 W.L.R. 105 (limited on appeal as a result of "reflective loss", [2018] EWCA Civ 1468; [2019] Q.B. 173); see para.24-32. **24-04**

2. PROCURING A BREACH OF CONTRACT

Replace paragraph with:

Knowingly and intentionally to procure or, as it is often put, to induce a third party to break his contract to the damage of the other contracting party without reasonable justification or excuse is a tort. In *Quinn v Leathem* Lord Macnaghten said that "a violation of a legal right committed knowingly is a cause of action, and … . It is a violation of legal right to interfere with contractual relations recognised by law if there be no sufficient justification for the interference."[71] It had been so decided in *Lumley v Gye*[72] by a majority in the Queen's Bench with respect to contracts for personal services, and later by the Court of Appeal[73] when it was held to extend to other classes of contract. It has now been held to apply to contracts of all kinds.[74] But where A induces B to break his contract with C, it has been held that C can sue A, but B cannot (at any rate where the procurement is direct) because B "must resist A's effort by strength of will".[75] Thus, where cricket authorities imposed a ban aimed at persuading players who had entered into contracts with a promoter to withdraw from the contracts whether or not it was lawful so to do, the promoters (not the players) brought an action based on this tort.[76] The ingredients of the tort were restated by the House of Lords in *OBG Ltd v Allan* with a view to drawing a clear line between this, the *Lumley v Gye* tort, and the tort liability for unlawful interference.[77] **24-14**

71 [1901] A.C. 495 at 510. (Care is required: in *OBG Ltd v Allan* [2007] UKHL 21; [2008] 1 A.C. 1 at [16] Lord Hoffmann expressly identified this dictum as "capable of giving rise to confusion".) Cf. *Meretz Investments NV v ACP Ltd* [2006] EWHC 74 (Ch); [2007] Ch. 197 at [379] where Lewison J said that on the facts there it did not matter whether the absence of sufficient justification was part of the gist of the tort, as Lord Macnaghten's formulation might suggest, or whether sufficient justification was a defence to what would otherwise be tortious conduct. On justification see para.24-55. But the tort is "commonly described as the tort of procuring breaches of contract", per Evershed MR in *DC Thomson & Co Ltd v Deakin* [1952] Ch. 646 at 676; "persuasion or procurement or inducement", per Jenkins LJ at 694. See also per Neill LJ in *Middlebrook Mushrooms Ltd v TGWU* [1993] I.C.R. 612 at 618. In *JT Stratford & Son Ltd v Lindley* [1965] A.C. 269, Lord Upjohn at 338 and Lord Donovan at 342 spoke of "procuring"; Lords Radcliffe and Pearce at 328, 332 and 334 of "inducing"; and Lord Reid at 324 of "interference". There are "three essential elements in the tort of unlawful procurement of a breach of contract: the act, the intent and the resulting damage," per Diplock LJ in *Emerald Construction Co Ltd v Lowthian* [1966] 1 W.L.R. 691 at 703; compare Stuart-Smith LJ in *F v Wirral MBC* [1991] Fam. 69 at 114-115. Cf. Arden LJ summarising the elements of the tort after *OBG Ltd v Allan* [2007] UKHL 21; [2008] 1 A.C. 1 in *Meretz Investments NV v ACP Ltd* [2007] EWCA Civ 1303; [2008] Ch. 244 at [114]. In *Global Resources Group Ltd v Mackay* [2008] CSOH 148; 2009 S.L.T. 104 Lord Hodge having noted at [6] the parties' agreement that there were no material differences between the laws of Scotland and England in relation to this delict or tort, observed at [9] that Scots judges had drawn extensively on English law in defining this delict; but as he pointed out, cf. their views on recklessness, para.24-18. For a critique of the tort see Howarth (2005) 68 M.L.R. 195.

72 (1853) 2 E. & B. 216. Historically, the tort has grown out of the status relationship between master and servant but has been rationalised into one form of the "violation of a legal right committed knowingly", per Ralph Gibson LJ in *F v Wirral MBC* [1991] Fam. 69 at 107. In *Lumley v Gye* itself, the contract was for "services" rather than a contract of service.

73 *Bowen v Hall* (1881) 6 Q.B.D. 333 CA; *Temperton v Russell* [1893] 1 Q.B. 715, where the dicta must not be given a scope wider than the text indicates: *Allen v Flood* [1898] A.C. 1; *Crofter Hand Woven Harris Tweed Co v Veitch* [1942] A.C. 435 at 466. For example it is not tortious merely to induce one person not to contract with another; that wrong belonged to the early "master and servant" laws before 1867, as a crime. There is a "chasm" today between the legality of that action and the unlawfulness of procuring breach of an existing contract: *Allen v Flood*, above at 121, per Lord Herschell. See also *Midland Cold Storage Ltd v Steer* [1972] Ch. 630 at 644–645; *National Hockey League v Pepsi Cola Canada Ltd* (1995) 122 D.L.R. (4th) 412 (BCCA). Inducing one person not to contract with another may, however, become tortious if unlawful means are used or threatened: see para.24-74. So, too, if the defendant intends to procure a breach of any contract that will be made, an injunction may be granted: *Torquay Hotel Co Ltd v Cousins* [1969] 2 Ch. 106 CA, and para.24-23.

74 See *Jasperson v Dominion Tobacco Co* [1923] A.C. 709 at 713; *DC Thomson & Co Ltd v Deakin* [1952] Ch. 646 at 677, per Evershed MR, and at 693, per Jenkins LJ. As to its application to contracts affecting land, see *Pritchard v Briggs* [1980] Ch. 338 CA, discussed para.24-44.

75 per Upjohn LJ in *Boulting v Association of Cinematograph, Television and Allied Technicians* [1963] 2 Q.B. 606 at 639–640; *Williams v Hursey* (1959) 103 C.L.R. 30 at 77. But the party induced might sue for "unlawful interference" founding upon the unlawful inducement to have the contract broken; see para.24-72.

76 *Greig v Insole* [1978] 1 W.L.R. 302; but the players had locus standi to seek a declaration that the authorities' rules imposing the ban were in restraint of trade.

77 *OBG Ltd v Allan* [2007] UKHL 21; [2008] 1 A.C. 1, per Lord Hoffmann at [8] and [39]–[44]; per Lord Nicholls at [168]–[193]. Cf. the analysis of the tort in terms of eight essential elements in *Sar Petroleum Inc v Peace Hills Trust Co* 2010 NBCA 22; (2010) 318 D.L.R. (4th) 70 at [39]–[78]. Compare the summary of five essential elements in *TSG Franchise Management Pty Ltd v Cigarette & Gift Warehouse (Franchising) Pty Ltd (No.2)* [2016] FCA 674; (2017) 340 A.L.R. 230 at [57].

(a) Knowledge and intention

Replace paragraph with:

24-15 "An act of inducement is not by itself actionable."[78] The procurer must act with the requisite knowledge of the existence of the contract and intention to interfere with its performance: a "two-fold requirement".[79] The claimant must show that there was an intentional invasion of his contractual rights and not merely that the breach of contract was the natural consequence of the defendant's conduct;[80] he must show that the breach of contract was an end in itself or the means to an end.[81] The defendant must be shown to have knowledge[82] of the existence of a contract; but "in many cases a third party may be deemed to know of the almost certain existence of a contract and indeed of some of its likely terms".[83] The defendant need not know of the precise terms to be liable,[84] for given that he knew of the existence of the contract, the test of his intention is objective.[85] However, it has been accepted that an honest belief by the defendant that the outcomes sought by him would not involve any breach of contract was inconsistent with an intention to induce breach of contract even where the belief was mistaken in law, muddleheaded or illogical.[86] Good faith as such is no defence if knowledge and intention are proved.[87] If the defendant is in "honest doubt" about the contract, he may escape liability, unless he is found to have made a "conscious decision not to inquire".[88]

[78] per Lord Devlin in *Rookes v Barnard* [1964] A.C. 1129 at 1212. Nor is an act facilitating breach without more: *Credit Lyonnais Bank Nederland NV v Export Credits Guarantee Department* [2000] 1 A.C. 486 HL at 496 and 500.

[79] per Lord Diplock in *Merkur Island Shipping Corp v Laughton* [1983] 2 A.C. 570 at 608; per Neill LJ in *Middlebrook Mushrooms Ltd v TGWU* [1993] I.C.R. 612 at 621. See now *OBG Ltd v Allan* [2007] UKHL 21; [2008] 1 A.C. 1, per Lord Hoffmann at [39]-[41] and Lord Nicholls at [192]. Cf. *Qantas Airways v Transport Workers Union of Australia* [2011] FCA 470; (2011) 280 A.L.R. 503 at [442]–[444] noting the view that although the requirement of knowledge was sometimes expressed as separate, it was in fact an aspect of intention; sufficient knowledge meant sufficient to ground an intention to interfere with contractual rights: *Allstate Life Insurance Co v Australia and New Zealand Banking Group Ltd* (1995) 130 A.L.R. 469. The better view is that the two elements are distinct.

[80] *Stott v Gamble* [1916] 2 K.B. 504; *Rickless v United Artists Corp* [1986] F.S.R. 507 at 518-524; affirmed [1988] Q.B. 40 CA; *DC Thomson & Co Ltd v Deakin* [1952] Ch. 646 at 663 and 698; *Central Canada Potash Co Ltd v Govt of Saskatchewan* (1979) 88 D.L.R. (3d) 609 SCC at 641–642.

[81] *OBG Ltd v Allan* [2007] UKHL 21; [2008] 1 A.C. 1 at [42]–[43] per Lord Hoffmann; see too *Sar Petroleum Inc v Peace Hills Trust Co* 2010 NBCA 22; (2010) 318 D.L.R. (4th) 70 at [51]–[55] where it was said that the Supreme Court of Canada's decision in *Jones v Fabbi* [1973] S.C.R. 42 was to the same effect.

[82] Knowledge "is an essential ingredient of the cause of action", per Lord Russell of Killowen in *British Industrial Plastics Ltd v Ferguson* [1940] 1 All E.R. 479 at 483; *OBG Ltd v Allan* [2007] UKHL 21; [2008] 1 A.C. 1, per Lord Hoffmann at [39]–[41], and Lord Nicholls at [192].

[83] per Neill LJ in *Middlebrook Mushrooms Ltd v TGWU* [1993] I.C.R. 612 at 621, and per Hoffmann LJ at 622 (there may be "common knowledge that the trade involves contracts that would be disrupted by the defendant's acts", citing *Union Traffic Ltd v TGWU* [1989] I.C.R. 98 at 104); but there the claimant growers adduced not even a "shadowy case" that the defendants knew of their contracts with supermarkets when they distributed leaflets urging the public not to buy their produce: per Neill LJ at 621. The phrase "deemed to know" has caused some confusion in this context: the key question is whether the defendant knew of the contract or made a conscious decision not to inquire: *OBG Ltd v Allan* [2007] UKHL 21; [2008] 1 A.C.1 at [39]–[41] per Lord Hoffmann; *Wolff v Trinity Logistics USA Inc* [2018] EWCA Civ 2765 at [46]–[52]; cf. *Century 21 Canada Limited Partnership v Rogers* 2011 BCSC 1196; (2011) 338 D.L.R. (4th) 32 at [348]–[350]: knowledge included situations where the defendant had the means of knowledge.

[84] *Stratford & Son Ltd v Lindley* [1965] A.C. 269 HL; *Square Grip Reinforcement Ltd v Macdonald (No.2)* 1968 S.L.T. 65 at 72, per Lord Milligan; *Merkur Island Shipping Corp v Laughton* [1983] 2 A.C. 570 at 609, per Lord Diplock.

[85] *Greig v Insole* [1978] 1 W.L.R. 302 at 337-338; but ignorance of the precise terms may assist a defendant who denies any intention to cause a breach: per Slade J at 336. In claims for an interim injunction the claimant may (and often does) win this argument by producing the contract to the defendant in court.

[86] *OBG Ltd v Allan* [2007] UKHL 21; [2008] 1 A.C.1 per Lord Nicholls at [202]; *1044807 Alberta Ltd v Brae Centre Ltd* 2008 ABCA 397; (2008) 302 D.L.R. (4th) 70 at [47]–[50] citing the decision in *Mainstream Properties Ltd v Young* one of the cases decided by the House of Lords in *OBG Ltd v Allan* where the defendant financier honestly believed that two employees of the claimant company would not be breaking their employment contracts in pursuing a development opportunity for themselves rather than trying to secure it for their employer.

[87] *Pritchard v Briggs* [1980] Ch. 338 at 410-415, per Goff LJ, at 424, per Stephenson LJ; *Greig v Insole* [1978] 1 W.L.R. 302 at 337–338 and 343–344. On knowledge in corporate defendants see, per Hoffmann J in *Law Debenture Trust Corp v Ural Caspian Oil Corp Ltd* [1993] 1 W.L.R. 138 at 148 (reversed on other grounds: [1995] 2 Ch. 152 CA). *Meridian Global Funds Management Asia Ltd v Securities Commrs* [1995] 2 A.C. 500, PC; Grantham (1996) 59 M.L.R. 732; on how a corporation can forget: Wedderburn (1984) 47 M.L.R. 345.

[88] *OBG Ltd v Allan* [2007] UKHL 21; [2008] 1 A.C.1 per Lord Hoffmann at [40]–[41]. See too *Diver v Loktronic Industries Ltd* [2012] NZCA 131; [2012] 2 N.Z.L.R. 388 where it was held that since this was an intentional tort, a subjective rather than an objective inquiry was required to establish whether the defendant had sufficient knowledge of the contract. Where actual knowledge was not proved, it had to be shown that the defendant had a suspicion of sufficient strength that a contract existed and made a deliberate choice not to make inquiries. It was not sufficient that the existence of a contract must have been obvious.

Replace footnote 98 with:

24-17 [98] *Hill v First National Finance Corp* [1989] 1 W.L.R. 225 at 233–234, per Stuart-Smith L.J.; *DC Thomson & Co Ltd v Deakin* [1952] Ch. 646 at 696–697, per Jenkins LJ. See too *Walsh v Nicholls* (2004) 241 D.L.R. (4th) 643 (NBCA) at [58]; cf. *Meretz Investments NV v ACP Ltd* [2007] EWCA Civ 1303; [2008] Ch. 244 at [126]–[127], per Arden LJ: while "the mere fact that by injuring a third party a person intends to further his own business interests does not mean that he does not have the intent to injure that party", that proposition did not apply "where the causative act is something which the party believes he has a contractual right to do as against the relevant person, notwithstanding that the act would coincidentally cause that person detriment or loss". Thus no intention to induce breach of a leaseback option was established where the defendants believed on the basis of legal advice that the exercise of a power of sale would overreach this right. Cf. *Century 21 Canada Limited Partnership v Rogers Communications Inc* 2011 BCSC 1196; (2011) 338 D.L.R. (4th) 32 at [352] where it was said that it was necessary to prove that the defendant acted with the *desire to cause breach of contract* with the substantial certainty that breach of contract would result from the defendant's conduct or indifference to whether the contract would be breached. cf. *TSG Franchise Management Pty Ltd v Cigarette & Gift Warehouse (Franchising) Pty Ltd (No.2)* [2016] FCA 674; (2017) 340 A.L.R. 230 at [58] citing *Sanders v Snell* [1998] HCA 64; (1998) 196 C.L.R. 329: something more than an uncommunicated desire that the contract be breached had to be shown.

Recklessness

Replace footnote 106 with:

24-18 [106] [1966] 1 W.L.R. 691 at 700-701. Cf. *Torquay Hotel Co Ltd v Cousins* [1969] 2 Ch. 106 per Winn LJ at 146: "without regard to whether and without investigating whether" a contract existed. See too *Solihull MBC v NUT* [1985] I.R.L.R. 211 at 214 where Warner J. held that since there was a serious issue to be tried as to whether the non-teaching activities which the defendant union called on its members to boycott were contractual, a sufficient case had been made out for an interlocutory (interim) injunction. "Reckless indifference or wilful blindness could amount to knowledge": *TSG Franchise Management Pty Ltd v Cigarette & Gift Warehouse (Franchising) Pty Ltd (No.2)* [2016] FCA 674; (2017) 340 A.L.R. 230 at [59]. Cf. where there was no evidence of the existence or terms of the contracts of which the defendants were alleged to have induced breach: *Middlebrook Mushrooms Ltd v TGWU* [1993] I.C.R. 612 at 621 per Neill LJ allowing the defendants' appeal against an interlocutory injunction granted ex parte.

(b) Breach

(i) Breach of an existing contract

Replace paragraph with:

24-20 The tort consists in the intentional inducement of the breach of an existing and valid contractual obligation.[113] In *Allen v Flood* Lord Herschell declared "a breach of contract" to be "the essence" of the cause of action,[114] and in *OBG Ltd v Allan* both Lord Hoffmann and Lord Nicholls were explicit that breach of contract was an essential ingredient of this tort.[115] The court, however, is prepared to grant a remedy if that is proved, even if the evidence of the terms of the contract is "scanty",[116] though not where there is no such evidence at all.[117] Moreover, an injunction will lie even if no contract exists if the defendant has made it clear by his threats that he will, if one is concluded, procure its breach.[118] The mere fact that the party induced had an option to terminate the contract under its terms is of no avail to a defendant who has procured a breach.[119] It is enough if the breach is of the only remaining obligation of a contract otherwise fulfilled (such as a valid covenant not to compete by an employee who has long ago left the employment).[120]

The breach of the contract procured by the defendant is not required to be a breach of a "primary" obligation; the tort may be committed where the violation is of a "secondary" right, such as the right to a particular remedy under the contract which has ceased to be available by reason of the defendant's actions.[121] But it cannot be a tort to induce a party to abstain from performance of a contract that is "not a synallagmatic contract at all but a mere unilateral or 'if' contract without any obligations on the part of [the claimant] as to its duration,"[122] nor to induce a person *to* perform his contractual obligations.[123]

113 No tort is committed if the contract has not been formed: *McKernan v Fraser* (1931) 46 C.L.R. 343; *Nichol v Martyn* (1799) 2 Esp. 732 at 734; *Midland Cold Storage Ltd v Steer* [1972] Ch. 630 at 644-645; *National Hockey League v Pepsi Cola Canada* (1995) 122 D.L.R. (4th) 412 (BCCA); compare *Gershman v Manitoba Vegetable Producers Marketing Board* (1977) 69 D.L.R. (3d) 114 at 117-120. This proposition was briefly considered by the Court of Appeal in *Wolff v Trinity Logistics USA Inc* [2018] EWCA Civ 2765 at [38]: there is no reason why a defendant cannot be held liable for procuring someone to act in a way that will breach a contract that he has not yet made, provided that the encouragement or persuasion continues to operate at the time that the (now existing and valid) contract is breached.

114 [1898] A.C. 1 at 121: "an unlawful act—namely, a breach of contract—was regarded as the gist of the action", at 123.

115 [2007] UKHL 21; [2008] 1 A.C. 1 at [44] and [189] respectively. In *Canada Limited Partnership v Rogers Communications Inc* 2011 BCSC 1196; (2011) 338 D.L.R. (4th) 32 at [355] it was held that *DC Thomson & Co Ltd v Deakin* [1952] Ch. 646 CA at 686 was authority for holding that whether the defendant's actions in fact resulted in a breach of contract was a straightforward question of causation.

116 *Dimbleby & Sons v NUJ* [1984] 1 W.L.R. 427 at 434, per Lord Diplock; *Daily Mirror Newspapers Ltd v Gardner* [1968] 2 Q.B. 762 at 779–780 per Lord Denning and 782–783, per Davies LJ. So too "sketchy" evidence of contracts based on daily orders (in interlocutory proceedings): *Crazy Prices (Northern Ireland) Ltd v Hewitt* [1980] I.R.L.R. 396 NICA at 399–400.

117 *Middlebrook Mushrooms Ltd v TGWU* [1993] I.C.R. 612 CA (the court will not "invent hypothetical contracts": per Hoffmann LJ at 623).

118 See *Torquay Hotel Co Ltd v Cousins* [1969] 2 Ch. 106 CA (defendants intended to procure non-performance of "existing contracts by Esso and future contracts by Alternative Fuels so as to prevent those companies supplying oil to the Imperial Hotel": per Lord Denning MR at 141; no contract subsisted with Alternative Fuels; defendants liable to injunction in respect of both; see also Winn LJ at 146); and see *Union Traffic Ltd v TGWU* [1989] I.C.R. 98 at 105–106, per Bingham LJ and at 111–113, per Lloyd LJ.

119 *Emerald Construction Co Ltd v Lowthian* [1966] 1 W.L.R. 691 CA. But contrast *Cutsforth v Mansfield Inns* [1986] 1 W.L.R. 558 at 563, per Sir Neil Lawson.

120 Bingham LJ in *Rickless v United Artists Corp* [1988] Q.B. 40 CA at 58–59.

121 *Law Debenture Trust Corp v Ural Caspian Oil Corp Ltd* [1995] Ch. 152 CA at 170 (Beldam LJ dubitante); *Marex Financial Ltd v Sevilleja* [2017] EWHC 918 (Comm); [2017] 4 W.L.R. 105 (limited on appeal as a result of "reflective loss", [2018] EWCA Civ 1468; [2019] Q.B. 173); but it is not clear after these judgments precisely what are the "secondary rights" on which the claimant can rely where the remedy is discretionary and has not been obtained at the time of the defendant's act; semble no liability will arise in the absence of unlawful means; compare the case where the claimant complains of an interference rendering the contract less valuable and the other party to it has performed all of his obligations, as in *RCA Corp v Pollard* [1983] Ch. 135, where the claimant's right was not violated.

122 Lord Diplock in *Dimbleby & Sons v NUJ* [1984] 1 W.L.R. 427 at 434.

123 *Central Canada Potash Co Ltd v Government of Saskatchewan* (1979) 88 D.L.R. (3d) 609 SCC at 640. But the tort may be committed even if the obligations of one party are fully performed: *Rickless v United Artists Corp* [1988] Q.B. 40.

(iv) Breach of other obligations

Statutory duties

Replace paragraph with:

So, it is a tort knowingly and intentionally to induce a breach of statutory duty[150]—at least where the provision affords a right to the claimant because the 24-28 contravention is, on the true construction of the statute, actionable by him.[151] This tort of inducing a breach of statutory duty requires "a cause of action between obligor and obligee",[152] and the claimant still has to show "that on its true construction the statute which imposed the prohibition gave rise to a civil remedy".[153] This limitation, however, has been blurred by judgments which have accepted that a contravention of statute which does not afford such a right to the claimant may nonetheless still be a form of "unlawful means" on which he can rely in an action for intentional "unlawful interference".[154]

[150] *F v Wirrall MBC* [1991] Fam. 69 at 114–115, per Stuart-Smith LJ. This may severely restrict, if not effectively remove, the right to take industrial action from workers who are subject to statutory duties since it will generally be tortious for a trade union to call on its members to take such action as an inducement to breach these duties: see *Ministry of Justice v Prison Officers' Association* [2017] EWHC 1839 (QB); [2018] I.C.R. 181.

[151] *Lonrho Ltd v Shell Petroleum (No.2)* [1982] A.C. 173 HL; *Meade v Haringey LBC* [1979] 1 W.L.R. 637 CA; *Cutler v Wandsworth Stadium Ltd* [1949] A.C. 398 HL; *Lonrho Plc v Fayed* [1992] 2 Q.B. 479 at 488, per Dillon LJ (affirmed on different grounds [1992] 1 A.C. 448 HL); *BBC Enterprises v Hi-Tech Xtravision* [1991] 2 A.C. 327 HL.

[152] per Butler-Sloss LJ in *Associated British Ports v TGWU* [1989] 1 W.L.R. 939 at 959; *Lonrho Ltd v Shell Petroleum (No.2)* [1982] A.C. 173 HL.

[153] per Dillon LJ in *Lonrho Plc v Fayed* [1990] 2 Q.B. 479 at 488 (affirmed on other grounds [1992] 1 A.C. 448 HL).

[154] See *Associated British Ports v TGWU* [1989] 1 W.L.R. 939 CA at 959–961, per Butler-Sloss LJ, and at 965–966, per Stuart-Smith LJ (employers were not afforded a civil action for breach of statutory duty by dock workers induced by defendants, but claimants succeeded in claim based on unlawful interference; reversed on other grounds, [1989] 1 W.L.R. 939 HL); treated (it is submitted, per incuriam) as a case of "rights conferred by statute", per Hoffmann J in *Law Debenture Trust Corp v Ural Caspian Oil Corp* [1993] 1 W.L.R. 138 at 150 (reversed on other grounds [1995] Ch. 152 CA), and as "interference with a statutory duty imposed on a third party giving corresponding rights to the claimant", per Stuart-Smith LJ in *F v Wirral MBC* [1991] Fam. 69 at 114.

Equitable obligations

Replace footnote 155 with:

24-29 [155] See generally on the equitable principles: J. Glister and J. Lee, *Hanbury and Martin: Modern Equity*, 21st edn (2018), Ch.12, on fiduciaries, Ch.22; A.J. Oakley, *Parker and Mellows: The Modern Law of Trusts*, 9th edn (2008), Ch.10; and S. Worthington, *Equity*, 2nd edn (2006), Chs 5 and 6, especially pp.178–191. On constructive trusts and restitution: Lord Millett (1998) 114 L.Q.R. 398 and W. Cornish, R.C. Nolan, J. O'Sullivan, G.J. Virgo (eds), *Restitution: Past, Present and Future* (1998), pp.199–217 (Sir Peter Millett) and Ch.15 (Lord Nichols); cf. A. Tettenborn [1996] C.L.J. 36. On equitable compensation for breach of fiduciary duty see *Cia de Seguros Imperio v Heath (REBX) Ltd* [2001] 1 W.L.R. 112 CA.

Replace paragraph with:

24-31 An equally strange, if different, pattern emerges in respect of procuring breach of fiduciary and "trustee" duties. Such duties may arise from contractual obligations to act solely in the interests of another or from special relationships of the parties (director and company, for example, or trustee and beneficiary) when "different labels are stuck on different manifestations of the same duty",[166] or from facts which evince a special confidence placed by one party in the other (as when confidential information is imparted).[167] The principles governing the position of third parties divide between "recipients" and "accessories"; they have been authoritatively established by Lord Nicholls in the *Royal Brunei Airlines* decision,[168] where a company holding money on trust for the airline used it, as the defendant its managing director arranged, to relieve its own cash-flow problems. He was held liable as an "accessory" to the breach of trust (and the company was liable too, because his knowledge was the company's knowledge). "Knowing assistance" arises when the third party had, as here, assisted and procured the breach of duty; he was liable to account if he had acted dishonestly, i.e. not as an honest person would in all the circumstances (not quite the test of "knowingly and intentionally" in the parallel tort liability). Without a finding of dishonesty, this limb of liability cannot extend to a party who participates by releasing confidential information (which may be the "trust property").[169] But if "knowing receipt" is alleged, i.e. that he had "knowingly received" trust property or assets resulting from it, the claimant must prove that he knew or ought to have known that it was traceable to the breach of duty.[170] But, even if there are equitable remedies against those who knowingly receive the proceeds, or wrongfully assist in the breaches, of a trust, yet there appears still to be no general *tort* of "procuring a breach of trust", nor (it seems) of breach of "fiduciary duty".[171] In neither case is there necessarily a "constructive trust"; on the other hand, these are not necessarily cases where there is a "correspondence" in liability, even if not exact, with the principles of tort. Moreover, fiduciaries normally owe their duty only to the beneficiary (owed by a director to the company, for example) not to others, such as creditors or even shareholders; and the breach of duty can in principle even be set right by ratification, for example by shareholders acting as the company.[172] On the other hand, the concept of "privity" (for example in fiduciary duty between director and company) may not now be such a conclusive consideration when a third party can sue one of the parties to a contract who deliberately threatens a breach (or, it is submitted, actually acts in breach) to do him damage, even though he is not a party to the contract.[173] At present, it appears that a third party, who cannot be liable in tort for procuring breach of trust,[174] is unlikely to be liable in parallel for inducing breach of fiduciary duty unless the claimant can prove dishonesty.[175] The creation of a tort of procuring breaches of fiduciary duty, which at present appears not to fit well with the precedents, might be welcome; its creation would need, however, adjustments to fit with other areas such as company law, as well.[176]

[166] Lord Browne-Wilkinson in *Henderson v Merrett Syndicates Ltd* [1995] 2 A.C. 145 at 205. But not all fiduciary relationships give rise to constructive trusts, nor do duties to account or duties of "fidelity" necessarily involve fiduciary duties: per Millett LJ in *Paragon Finance v Thakerar* [1999] 1 All E.R. 400 at 412–416; *Nottingham University v Fishel* [2000] I.C.R. 1462. For a convenient typology of "constructive" and other "trusts" see *Terra Energy v Kilborn Energy Alberta* (1999) 170 D.L.R. (4th) 405 (Alta. CA).

[167] The termination of the duty may depend on the nature of the duty: *R. v Blake* [1988] Ch. 439 CA; cf. the exposition by Megarry VC in *Tito v Waddell (No.2)* [1977] Ch. 106, including the doctrines of "self dealing" and "fair dealing".

[168] *Royal Brunei Airlines v Tan* [1995] 2 A.C. 378 PC, reviewing the English and Commonwealth decisions and commentary, and settling the meaning of the leading authority *Barnes v Addy* (1874) L.R. 9 Ch. App. 244 at 251–252; liability for "knowing receipt" by a third party requires proof that he had such knowledge that his receipt was traceable to a breach of trust or fiduciary duty as to make it unconscionable for him to retain the benefit and must be distinguished from liability for "assisting breach" of trust or fiduciary duty, which requires proof of dishonesty.

[169] *Satnam Investments v Dunlop Haywood Ltd* [1999] 3 All E.R. 652 CA (trade competitor did not participate in others' breach of fiduciary duty owed to S by publishing confidential information; nor did it act dishonestly, even when it took advantage of the commercial opportunity for itself. On "knowing receipt" see Lord Nicholls Ch.15 in Cornish, et al., *Restitution: Past, Present and Future* and Harpum, also in Cornish, et al. Ch.16, pp.247–250.

[170] *Royal Brunei Airlines v Tan* [1995] 2 A.C. 378 PC; *El Ajou v Dollar Land Holdings* [1994] 2 All E.R. 685 at 700, Hoffmann J; *Bank of Credit and Commerce International SA v Ali (No.2)* [2001] UKHL 8; [2002] 1 A.C. 251; *Citadel General Assurance v Lloyd's Bank of Canada* (1998) 152 D.L.R. (4th) 411 (SCC: bank liable for knowing receipt, not procurement or assistance); *BCCI v Akindele* [2001] Ch. 437 CA; *Walker v Stones* [2001] Q.B. 902 CA; *Trustor AB v Smallbone (No.3)* [2001] 1 W.L.R. 1177; Nolan [2000] C.L.J. 447 (knowing receipt); *Casio Computer Co Ltd v Sayo* [2001] EWCA Civ 661 (knowing assistance).

[171] In *FM Capital Partners Ltd v Marino* [2018] EWHC 1768 (Comm) at [82], Cockerill J summarised the conditions for liability for dishonestly assisting a breach of fiduciary duty, noting that they were not seriously in issue in the case: this liability is potentially both broader than liability for procuring a breach of contract—in that it can cover acts that assist, induce or procure a breach—and narrower—in that the defendant must have acted dishonestly in providing the assistance. See also *Iranian Offshore Engineering & Construction Co v Dean Investment Holdings SA* [2019] EWHC 472 (Comm). In some circumstances it may be possible to formulate a claim as being one for the tort of conspiracy to cause harm by the use of unlawful means—those means being a breach of fiduciary duty—as a way of avoiding the need to prove dishonesty; but this approach will require proof that the conspirators shared a common intention of causing harm to the claimant.

[172] *Stein v Blake* [1998] 1 All E.R. 724 CA; *Brown v Bennett* [1998] 2 B.C.L.C. 97; *Boulting v ACCT* [1963] 2 Q.B. 606 CA; Smith (1998) 114 L.Q.R. 14. On the exceptions and uncertainties in directors' duties in company law and ratification, see Gower and Davies *Principles of Modern Company Law*, 10th edn (2016), Ch.16; also S. Worthington on fiduciaries and "self-denial" [1990] C.L.J. 500–508, and "Corporate Governance: Remedying and Ratifying Directors' Breaches" (2000) 116 L.Q.R. 638.

[173] *Rookes v Barnard* [1964] A.C. 1129 HL. See too Contracts (Rights of Third Parties) Act 1999, which modifies the doctrine of "privity of contracts": Treitel, *Law of Contract*, 14th edn (2015), Ch.14.

[174] *Metall und Rohstoff AG v Donaldson, Lufkin & Jenrette Inc* [1990] 1 Q.B. 391 CA (no tort is needed in the light of equitable remedies against third parties: *sed quaere*).

[175] But see Loughlan "Liability for Assistance in a Breach of Fiduciary Duty" (1989) 9 O.J.L.S. 260; also Carty (1999) 19 L.S. 489 at 510–514; cf. Sales [1990] C.L.J. 491.

[176] On the absence of a general principle of accessory liability, see Carty (1999) 19 L.S. 489; and for a stimulating discussion of problems in employment, contractual obligations, trust and fiduciary duties, see L. Clarke "Mutual Trust and Confidence, Fiduciary Relationships and the Duty of Disclosure" (1999) 28 I.L.J. 348. In Cornish, et al. (eds), *Restitution: Past, Present and Future* (1998) and P. Cane, J. Stapleton (eds), *The Law of Obligations* (1998) distinguished contributors do not examine in detail the problem of unlawful means in tort, showing the dominance of the equitable institutions in much of this field.

24-33 *Replace footnote 179:*

Breach of confidence

[179] See W. Cornish, D. Llewellyn and T. Aplin, *Intellectual Property: Patents, Copyright, Trade Marks and Allied Rights*, 9th edn (2019), Ch.8.

Replace footnote 181 with:

24-33 [181] See Ch.27; W. Cornish, D. Llewellyn and T. Aplin, *Intellectual Property: Patents, Copyright, Trade Marks and Allied Rights*, 9th edn (2019), Ch.8; cf. Meagher, Gummow, Lathane, *Equity: Doctrines and Remedies*, 5th edn (2014) Ch.41.

(c) The wrongful procurement

(i) Direct inducement

Replace footnote 190 with:

24-35 [190] *British Motor Trade Association v Salvadori* [1949] Ch. 556; *Sefton v Tophams Ltd* [1964] 1 W.L.R. 1408, per Stamp J; [1965] Ch. 1140, per Sellers and Harman LJJ (reversed on other grounds [1967] A.C. 50); *Wolff v Trinity Logistics USA Inc* [2018] EWCA Civ 2765 at [43].

Replace footnote 197 with:

24-36 [197] *Said v Butt* [1920] 3 K.B. 497; see per Evershed MR in *DC Thomson & Co Ltd v Deakin* [1952] Ch. 646 at 680–681. Contrary to the usual doctrine, any such servant of the company here counts as its alter ego: see [1960] C.L.J. 14 at 16. But if the servant or agent goes outside his authority, he can personally be an inducer, per Evershed MR in *DC Thomson & Co Ltd v Deakin*. See too *ADGA Systems International Ltd v Valcom Ltd* (1999) 168 D.L.R. (4th) 351 (Ont. CA); *Root Quality Pty Ltd v Root Control Technologies Pty Ltd* (2000) 177 A.L.R. 231 Fed. Ct of Aus; *Ontario Ltd v Magna International Inc* (2001) 200 D.L.R. (4th) 521 (Ont. CA); *Kay Aviation b.v. v Rofe* (2002) 202 D.L.R. (4th) 683 (Pr. Ed. Is. CA); *Walsh v Nicholls* (2004) 241 D.L.R. (4th) 643 (NBCA) at [66]. In *XY Inc v International Newtech Development Inc* 2013 BCCA 352; (2013) 366 D.L.R. (4th) 443, [58]–[66] it was emphasised that the "*Said v Butt* exception only applied where the individuals were performing their functions as corporate officers." The Singapore Court of Appeal carried out a detailed analysis of the rationale and limits of the *Said v Butt* exception in *PT Sandipala Arthaputra v ST Microelectronics Asia Pacific Pte Ltd* [2018] SGCA 17; [2018] 1 S.L.R. 818. This was cited and relied on by Lane J in *Antuzis v DJ Houghton Catching Services Ltd* [2019] EWHC 843 (QB), where he held that the question whether an employee or director had acted bona fide (so as to avoid liability for having induced a company to breach a contract) was one directed at the employee's or director's conduct and intention in relation to his duties towards the company—not towards the claimant (at [114]). On the facts, he concluded that two defendants, respectively the sole director of a company and its company secretary, were liable for having induced the company's breach of its contracts with the claimants, who were employed to catch chickens.

Inconsistent transactions

Replace paragraph with:

In his exposition of the elements of the tort in *Thomson v Deakin* Jenkins LJ said that, where a third person with knowledge of a contract "has dealings with the contract breaker which the third party knows to be inconsistent with the contract, he has committed an actionable interference".[240] So, where the claimants agreed with third parties not to resell cars except as provided in their covenants and the defendants induced those parties to resell the cars to them in breach of the covenants in order to make a profit for themselves they committed the tort.[241] But it has been held that merely accepting the benefit of an inconsistent contract at the proposal of the contractor did not amount to tortious conduct.[242] Nor was the acquisition of property from an associated company actionable as this tort even though that company was known to have procured breaches of covenants concerning the property and therefore to be at risk of an injunction at the suit of the claimant, and the transfer of the property to the defendant provided an "easy escape from the salutary remedy" of a mandatory injunction to retransfer the property.[243] Still less does liability arise for "facilitating" a breach without any common design or intentional procurement of a breach.[244] While it has been suggested that in *OBG Ltd v Allan* the House of Lords "reaffirmed that a positive act of inducement or procurement is essential to the wrong",[245] none of the speeches in that decision directly addressed the issue of whether inconsistent transactions should still be seen as a form of direct inducement of breach.[245A] **24-42**

[240] *DC Thomson & Co Ltd v Deakin* [1952] Ch. 646 at 694, citing *British Industrial Plastics Ltd v Ferguson* [1940] 1 All E.R. 479 HL; see too Neill LJ in *Middlebrook Mushrooms Ltd v TGWU* [1993] I.C.R. 612 at 618. The second contract is probably not void unless the parties know of its inconsistent effect: *British Homophone Ltd v Kunz* (1935) 152 L.T. 589 at 593. In *The Beans Group Ltd v Myunidays Ltd* [2019] EWHC 320 (Comm), the defendant accepted that the quoted dictum from Jenkins LJ remains the law, despite the suggestion that it is inconsistent with the House of Lords' definitive reconsideration of the tort in *OBG Ltd v Allan* [2007] UKHL 21; [2008] 1 A.C. 1, perhaps because of a preference for winning the "case at first instance, if at all, on the facts, rather than attempting an ambitious argument of law which might be more vulnerable to appeal" (at [100]).

[241] *British Motor Trade Association v Salvadori* [1949] Ch. 556; *Midland Bank Trust Co v Green* [1980] Ch. 590 at 598–604 (reversed on other grounds [1981] A.C. 513 HL; husband an inducer through wife). Cf. Weir's unhistorical objection to such decisions: *Economic Torts* (1997), 36n.

[242] *Batts Combe Quarry Ltd v Ford* [1943] Ch. 51 CA; cf. *Long v Smithson* (1918) 88 L.J.K.B. 223.

[243] *Law Debenture Trust Corp v Ural Caspian Oil Corp Ltd* [1995] Ch. 152 CA at 164, per Bingham MR.

[244] See *Credit Lyonnais Bank Nederland v Export Credits Guarantee Dept* [2000] 1 A.C. 486 HL at 499–500, per Lord Woolf MR (tort law does not follow the wider liabilities of the criminal law); *Paterson Zochonis Ltd v Merfarken Packaging Ltd* [1986] 3 All E.R. 522 CA at 530–534 and 539–542; *CBS Songs v Amstrad Consumer Electronics Plc* [1988] A.C. 1013 HL; *British Telecommunications Plc v One in a Million* [1999] 1 W.L.R. 903; [1998] 4 All E.R. 476 at 487. See too *Harry Winton Investments Ltd v CIBC Development Corp* (2001) 199 D.L.R. (4th) 709 (Ont CA).

[245] *Calor Gas Ltd v Express Fuels (Scotland) Ltd* [2008] CSOH 13; 2008 S.L.T 123 at [47]. In that case it was held that no liability arose for inducing breach of a contractual obligation to return empty gas

cylinders to a dealer authorised by the pursuer when cylinders were returned to dealers who had changed their suppliers from the pursuer to the defenders.

[245A] In *Palmer Birch (a partnership) v Lloyd* [2018] EWHC 2316 (TCC); [2018] 4 W.L.R. 164, the court held that a defendant had committed the tort by "diverting" funds away from a contracting party with the intention of inducing it to breach a building contract, even though he was not under a legal obligation to provide the party with further funds. HHJ Russen QC, explained, at [361]: "If the fine dividing line in this case between prevention and inducement turns upon the ability to categorise [the defendant's] actions as a diversion of funds away from [the contracting party] then, on the particular facts of this case and even in the absence of any unperformed contractual obligation to fund [the contracting party], he was guilty of that. Although those funds did not reach [the contracting party's] bank account, they could and should have done so. Whereas a simple finding that [the defendant] could have made the funds available to [the contracting party], but simply chose not to, might arguably leave [the claimants] on the wrong side of that fine line, my further conclusion that he should in the circumstances have done so sustains their claim ..." . That decision may appear surprising since refusing to provide a contracting party with the funds that it needs to perform a contract cannot be equated with persuading the party to breach its contract. But the court was satisfied that by altering his plans with regard to the funding of the contracting party, and doing so with the intention of bringing about a breach of contract at a particular point in time, the defendant had gone further than simply "preventing" further performance of the contract. Where a defendant's diversion of funds away from a company is a wrong to the company, a claim by a creditor of the company for inducing a breach by means of such diversion may fall foul of the principle against claims for "reflective loss": *Marex Financial Ltd v Sevilleja* [2018] EWCA Civ 1468; [2019] Q.B. 173 (reversing [2017] EWHC 918 (Comm); [2017] 4 W.L.R. 105).

Replace footnote 246 with:

24-43 [246] [1952] Ch. 646 at 694, citing *De Francesco v Barnum* (1890) 45 Ch D. 430. Many cases of this kind have concerned the old action for the "harbouring" of another's servant: *Fred Wilkins Ltd v Weaver* [1915] 2 Ch. 322. (The action was abolished by Administration of Justice Act 1982 s.2(c)(iii)). See Browne-Wilkinson J in *Swiss Bank Corp v Lloyds Bank Ltd* [1979] Ch. 548 at 572–574 (reversed on other grounds [1982] A.C. 584 HL). See Cohen-Grabelsky (1982) 45 M.L.R. 241; Tettenborn [1982] C.L.J. 58; Carty (1988) 104 L.Q.R. 250. In *The Beans Group Ltd v Myunidays Ltd* [2019] EWHC 320 (Comm), the defendant did not commit the tort when it initially entered a contract with a third party that was inconsistent with that party's contract with the claimant (which demanded exclusivity) because, at that time, the defendant honestly believed that the third party was at liberty to enter such a contract. The judge held, however, that the defendant commited the tort when it continued to supply services to the third party after being informed of the terms of the claimant's inconsistent contract, since the third party would have gone back to receiving such services from the claimant if the defendant had not continued its "inconsistent dealing".

(ii) Indirect procurement

Replace footnote 266 with:

24-47 [266] *OBG Ltd v Allan* [2007 UKHL 21; [2008] 1 A.C. 1 at [36]. See also, to similar effect, *Palmer Birch (a partnership) v Lloyd* [2018] EWHC 2316 (TCC); [2018] 4 W.L.R. 164 at [59]: "the necessary ingredient of a breach of contract in the inducement tort means that the liability of the alleged tortfeasor rests [...] upon a degree of participation in the breach of contract which satisfies the general requirements of accessory liability for the wrongful act of another person."

(d) Damage

Replace paragraph with:

24-51 The claimant must prove not only the wrongful interference but also that he has been damaged by the breach of contract.[274] If the breach, which has been procured by the defendant, has been such as must in the ordinary course of business inflict damage upon the claimant, it is unnecessary for him to prove particular damage.[275] Where the defendant continued to employ a servant after notice that he was still contractually bound to serve the claimants, no action was maintainable on proof that the servant would in no circumstances return to the claimants' service, and that therefore they had suffered no damage caused by the defendant.[276] When damage can be proved, or inferred, the claimant is entitled to recover in respect of that damage which was intended[277] or, whether intended or not, was a consequence of the tort which is not too remote.[278] Thus, the claimant may recover in respect of loss of business caused by non-performance of contracts other than that of which the defendant induced a breach, where such loss is foreseeable; but not for losses caused to his business which were not foreseeable or intended by the defendant.[279]

[274] *Exchange Telegraph Co v Gregory* [1896] 1 Q.B. 147; *Sefton v Tophams Ltd* [1965] Ch. 1140 (reversed on other grounds [1967] 1 A.C. 50); *British Industrial Plastics v Ferguson* [1938] 4 All E.R. 504; *Jones Bros (Hunstanton) Ltd v Stevens* [1955] 1 Q.B. 275. On the place where damage is suffered and service out of the jurisdiction: *Metall und Rohstoff AG v Donaldson, Lufkin & Jenrette Inc* [1990] 1 Q.B. 391 CA at 435–449 (overruled on other matters, *Lonrho Plc v Fayed* [1992] A.C. 448 HL); see also the Private International Law (Miscellaneous Provisions) Act 1995.

[275] *Exchange Telegraph Co v Gregory* [1896] 1 Q.B. 147; *Goldsoll v Goldman* [1914] 2 Ch. 603 at 615; *British Motor Trade Association v Salvadori* [1949] Ch. 556; *Nauru Local Govt Council v New Zealand Seamen's Union* [1986] 1 N.Z.L.R. 466 (NZCA): (loss of profit-making opportunity allowed); cf. *Lonrho Plc v Fayed (No.5)* [1993] 1 W.L.R. 1489 CA (no damages for loss of reputation); but see *Joyce v Sengupta* [1993] 1 W.L.R. 337 at 348–349 and 351.

[276] *Jones Bros (Hunstanton) Ltd v Stevens* [1955] 1 Q.B. 275.

[277] *Lumley v Gye* (1853) 2 E. & B. 216 at 233–234, per Erle J; *Quinn v Leathem* [1901] A.C. 495 at 537, per Lord Lindley.

[278] *British Motor Trade Association v Salvadori* [1949] Ch. 556 at 568–569; *Boxfoldia Ltd v N.G.A.* [1988] I.C.R. 752 (damage reasonably foreseeable). See, too, on measure of damages, *Posluns v Toronto Stock Exchange* (1964) 46 D.L.R. (2d) 210; affirmed (1968) 67 D.L.R. (2d) 165; Brodie (1998) 27 I.L.J. 79. *Quaere* whether *Pratt v BMA* [1919] 1 K.B. 244 is authority for allowing recovery for non-pecuniary loss; cf. *McGregor on Damages*, 20th edn (2017), para.48-008, or whether this is merely part of arriving at "a round sum based on the pecuniary loss proved", per Lord Devlin in *Rookes v Barnard* [1964] A.C. 1129 at 1221 ("leaving aside" aggravated damages). In *Walsh v Nicholls* (2004) 214 D.L.R. (4th) 643 (NBCA) at [84] it was said that punitive damages "are not excluded from the arsenal of proper judicial responses to intentional procurement of breach of contract"; cf. *Delphinium Ltée c 512842 NB Inc* 2008 NBCA 56; (2008) 296 D.L.R. (4th) 694 (NBCA) in which the defendant's appeal against punitive damages was allowed where the essence of the deliberate business decision to procure breach was "nothing more than what is referred to in the jurisprudence as an 'efficient breach'" which "exacted a sufficiently stiff price" in compensatory damages.

[279] *Jones v Fabbi* (1973) 37 D.L.R. (3d) 27, applying *The Wagon Mound (No.1)* [1961] A.C. 388 and *McGregor on Damages*, 20th edn (2017), para.48-006. See also, *Jones v Fabbi* (1975) 49 D.L.R. (3d) 316 (on mitigation of damage). On difficulties in restoring the claimant to his original position: *Lakefield v Black* (1999) 166 D.L.R. (4th) 96 (Ont CA). On loss of a chance caused by inducement of breach of contract see *McGill v Sports and Entertainment Media Group* [2016] EWCA Civ 1063; [2017] 1 W.L.R. 989 at [57] et seq.

3. INTIMIDATION

The tort of intimidation

Replace footnote 325 with:

[325] [2014] VSCA 348; (2015) 318 A.L.R. 107. The submission was made on the ground that as defined in *Sid Ross Agency Ltd v Actors and Announcers Equity Association of Australia* [1971] 1 N.S.W.L.R. 760 intimidation depended entirely on the decision in *Rookes v Barnard* [1964] A.C. 1129, and that the tort articulated there had been subsumed in the broader tort of interference with business by the House of Lords' decision in *OBG Ltd v Allan* 2007 UKHL 21; [2008] 1 A.C. 1. In the Victoria Supreme Court decision it was noted that in *Northern Territory v Mengel* (1995) 185 C.L.R. 307 the Australian High Court had overruled its earlier decision that a separate cause of action existed where a person suffered loss as a result of the unlawful and intentional or positive act of another, and in *Sanders v Snell* [1998] HCA 64; (1998) 196 C.L.R. 329 it had declined to rule on whether the broader tort of intentionally causing loss to the plaintiff's business by unlawful means was part of Australian law. **24-60**

(b) Unlawful act

Crimes and torts

Replace footnote 358 with:

[358] per Lord Evershed, in *Rookes v Barnard* [1964] A.C. 1129 at 1182. See also Lord Devlin at 1206: "It is not of course disputed that if the act threatened is a crime, the threat is unlawful". If, however, the **24-64**

definition of "unlawful means" in the tort of intimidation is to be aligned with the definition used in the interference tort after *OBG Ltd v Allan* [2007] UKHL 21; [2008] 1 A.C. 1, then threats to commit crimes will be insufficient as a foundation for the tort of intimidation (at least in its three-party form) unless the crime concerned, if committed, could give rise to a private law claim by the person threatened. And as to statutory criminal offences, see below para.24-69. See also *Hargreaves v Bretherton* [1959] 1 Q.B. 45 (use of perjury to damage claimant; no cause of action); *Roberts v Stone Ltd* (1945) 172 L.T. 240 at 242.

Other unlawful means

Replace paragraph with:

24-66 If the meaning of "unlawful acts" or "unlawful means" is to be consistent across the economic torts, it ought to follow that liability for intimidation, whether it is seen as a separate tort or as one form of the unlawful interference tort, should be limited to cases where the act threatened falls within the scope of "unlawful acts" or "unlawful means" as decided by authorities on any of the economic tort liabilities including unlawful means conspiracy and the now apparently superseded liability for indirectly procuring breach of, or interference with, contract by unlawful means. However, the current state of the authorities does not support a consistent definition of "unlawful means" across the economic torts. As the Supreme Court cautioned in *JSC BTA Bank v Ablyazov (No 14)*[367A] "Some of the elements of the torts, notably intention and unlawful means are common to more than one of them. But it is dangerous to assume that they have the same content in each context." The foundation for this comment was the decision of the House of Lords in *Revenue and Customs Commissioners v Total Network SL*[367B] not to apply to the tort of unlawful means conspiracy the limits on what could constitute "unlawful means" that they had previously recognised in the context of the tort of "intentionally harming the claimant by unlawful acts against third parties", namely that those acts should be actionable at the suit of the third party.[367C] Where a claim in intimidation is based on a threat made against a third party, as in *Rookes v Barnard*,[367D] it is strongly arguable that the narrower definition of "unlawful means"—requiring a threat of an act that would be actionable by that party if it were committed—is applicable.[367E] It should be noted, however, that a claimant may also be able to rely on a threat of an act which is potentially tortious against a third party but where the tort is not complete as for example where no damage has been suffered by that party.[368]

367A [2018] UKSC 19; [2018] 2 W.L.R. 1125 at [6].

367B [2008] UKHL 19; [2008] 1 A.C. 1174.

367C This sentence follows the terminology used in *JSC BTA Bank v Ablyazov (No 14)* [2018] UKSC 19; [2018] 2 W.L.R. 1125 at [12]. In this chapter, the tort of "intentionally harming the claimant by unlawful acts against third parties" is usually referred to more concisely as "the unlawful interference tort", but here the longer formulation is appropriate, since it has become orthodox for courts to link the adoption of a more limited definition of "unlawful means" in this context to the fact that the claims discussed in detail in *OBG Ltd v Allan* [2007] UKHL 21; [2008] 1 A.C. 1 involved the use of unlawful means against third parties with the intention of harming the claimant.

367D [1964] A.C. 1129.

367E In *OBG Ltd v Allan* [2007] UKHL 21; [2008] 1 A.C. 1 at [61] Lord Hoffmann expressly excluded cases of "two party intimidation", where a claimant was compelled by unlawful intimidation to act to his own detriment, from his discussion of "unlawful means", since he said that such cases raised "altogether different issues". For further discussion of "two-party intimidation", see para.24-69.

368 *Lonrho Plc v Fayed* [1990] 2 Q.B. 479 at 490, per Dillon LJ and at 492, per Ralph Gibson LJ (no need for official to whom fraudulent misrepresentation was directed to suffer damage); the principle laid down in this case of unlawful interference must a fortiori apply to a claim based on intimidation. It does not support a case where he has no right to sue, damage or no damage, as in *Associated British Ports v TGWU* [1989] 1 W.L.R. 939 CA (holding otherwise: reversed on other grounds: [1989] 1 W.L.R. 939 HL).

4. UNLAWFUL INTERFERENCE

Unlawful interference with economic and other interests

Replace paragraph with:

In *OBG Ltd v Allan* the House of Lords both confirmed the existence of a tort of hitherto uncertain ambit which consists of one person using unlawful means with the object and effect of causing damage to another and clarified some aspects of the liability.[406] While recognition of the existence of this tort can be traced back to *Allen v Flood*, nearly ninety years later it could still be described as "relatively undeveloped".[407] In *JT Stratford & Son Ltd v Lindley* two of the Law Lords gave as an alternative to procuring breach of contract as the ground for their decision, the fact that the respondents had used unlawful means to interfere with the business of the appellants.[408] While such "interference with business" does not require that existing contracts have been broken, the cause of action only exists where the claimant has suffered damage which the defendant has intentionally brought about by the use of unlawful means. The distinct identities of this unlawful interference tort and the tort of procuring breach of contract were one of the main points to emerge from the review of the ambit of both torts undertaken by the House of Lords in *OBG Ltd v Allan*. Earlier characterisations of the unlawful interference tort as a "genus" of which procuring breach of contract was a "species" were there rejected. In a commercial context it had been said that the tort of unlawful interference was based on the proposition: "a man who is carrying on a lawful trade or calling has a right to be protected from any unlawful interference with it"[409]; but this formulation is too wide. As in the other economic torts damage is essential to the cause of action and must be shown to have been, or be about to be, caused by the unlawful interference.[410] "The essence of the tort is deliberate interference with the [claimant's] interests by unlawful means" and the intention to injure must be a "contributing cause" of the claimant's loss.[411] While it has been said that the defence of justification which applies to the tort of procuring breach of contract is "not usually regarded as a defence to this tort",[412] the existence of such a defence has been suggested.[413] **24-72**

[406] *OBG Ltd v Allan* [2007] UKHL 21; [2008] 1 A.C. 1; see in particular Lord Hoffmann at [46]–[64] and Lord Nicholls at [141]–[167]. Where they disagreed Lady Hale at [302] and Lord Brown at [319] expressed agreement with Lord Hoffmann. One issue that remains unresolved is that of the appropriate name by which this tort should be known, as the Canadian Supreme Court observed in *Bram Enterprises Ltd v A.I. Enterprises Ltd* 2014 SCC 12; (2014) 266 D.L.R. (4th) 573, where the single judgment of Cromwell J refers variously to both Lord Hoffmann's terminology and—perhaps more helpfully—simply "the unlawful means tort": 2014 SCC 12; (2014) 266 D.L.R. (4th) 573 at [2]. In *OBG Ltd v Allan* Lord Hoffmann referred to it, at [6], as "the tort of causing loss by unlawful means", while Lord Nicholls, at [141], used the more familiar label of "interference with business by unlawful means"; in *JSC BTA Bank v Ablyazov (No 14)* [2018] UKSC 19; [2018] 2 W.L.R. 1125 Lord Lloyd-Jones and Lord Sumption referred to it, at [6], as "unlawful interference with economic and other interests (sometimes called the 'intentional harm' tort)" and, at [12], as "the tort of intentionally harming the claimant by unlawful acts against third parties"; cf. the earlier formulations by Lord Diplock delivering the only substantive speech in *Hadmor Productions Ltd v Hamilton* [1983] 1 A.C. 191 at 228–229; *Merkur Island Shipping Corp v Laughton* [1983] 2 A.C. 570 at 609 and *Dimbleby & Sons Ltd v NUJ* [1984] 1 W.L.R. 427 at 429–30. For post-*OBG Ltd v Allan* formulations see Arden LJ in *Meretz Investments NV v ACP Ltd* [2007] EWCA Civ 1303; [2008] Ch. 244 at [115]; *Global Resources Group Ltd v Mackay* [2008] CSOH 148; 2009 S.L.T. 104 at [17] and *Correia v Canac Kitchens* (2008) 294 D.L.R. (4th) 525 (Ont. CA) where the tort is referred to as both "the intentional interference action" at [95] and "causing loss by unlawful means" at [100]. In *Future Investments SA v Federation Internationale De Football Association* [2010] EWHC 1019 (Ch), where part of the claim was for "causing harm by unlawful means", Floyd J stated the law at [19]–[25] in the same terms as Lord Hoffmann in *OBG Ltd v Allan*. In *Qantas Airways v Transport Workers Union of Australia* [2011] FCA 470; (2011) 280 A.L.R. 503 at [425]–[426] Moore J concluded that since the High Court in *Sanders v Snell* [1998] HCA 64; (1998) 196 C.L.R. 329 at [35]–[36] had found it unnecessary to decide whether this tort should be recognised in Australia,

it had yet to be declared part of Australian law. On the recognition and development of the tort generally across common law jurisdictions see *Bram Enterprises Ltd v A.I. Enterprises Ltd* 2014 SCC 12; (2014) 366 D.L.R. (4th) 573 at [50]–[76], and H. Carty "The Modern Functions of the Economic Torts; Reviewing the English, Canadian, Australian and New Zealand positions" (2015) 74 C.L.J. 261.

[407] *Barretts & Baird (Wholesale) Ltd v IPCS* [1987] I.R.L.R. 3 at 10, per Henry J; cf. Lord Herschell in *Allen v Flood* [1898] A.C. 1 at 136–137.

[408] [1965] A.C. 269 at 324, per Lord Reid and 328–329, per Viscount Radcliffe: "the defendants have inflicted injury on the plaintiffs in the context of their business and have resorted to unlawful means to bring this about." The question whether the tort can extend to protect interests that are not associated with "business" has rarely been raised, but in *Chalfont St Peter Parish Council v Holy Cross Sisters Trustees Inc* [2019] EWHC 1128 (QB), Swift J stated, at [99], that there was "no authority for the proposition that a claimant's interests protected by the unlawful means tort extend beyond economic interests, and I can see no reason in principle which would justify such conclusion." With respect, it is suggested that one of the things that the tort protects claimants against is the use of unlawful means to prevent others from performing contracts with them, and in this context there is no good reason for confining the tort to protecting the benefit of "business" contracts.

[409] *Ex p. Island Records* [1978] Ch. 122 at 136, per Lord Denning MR, but see *Lonrho v Shell Petroleum (No.2)* [1982] A.C. 173 HL, rejecting this approach.

[410] In *Lonrho v Fayed* [1990] 2 Q.B. 479 CA, the court allowed an appeal against the decision striking out a claim which alleged that the defendant had made fraudulent misrepresentations about his own qualities to a Government Minister intending that his interests would gain (by the Minister not taking action in relation to a take-over bid that he had made by referring it to the Monopolies and Mergers Commission) and those of the plaintiff, Lonrho, a rival bidder whose bid was referred to the Commission, would suffer and that the latter had suffered damage through the loss of a business opportunity; affirmed on other grounds [1992] 1 A.C. 448 HL. Compare the different analysis by Millet J in *Lonrho v Fayed (No.2)* [1992] 1 W.L.R. 1. On the distinction between an award of damages in this tort and an award for defamation arising out of the same events see *Alleslev-Krofchak v Valcom Ltd* 2010 ONCA 557; (2010) 322 D.L.R. (4th) 193 at [92].

[411] *Barretts & Baird (Wholesale) Ltd v IPCS* [1987] I.R.L.R. 3 at 10, per Henry J, adopting Cooke CJ in *Van Camp Chocolates Ltd v Aulsebrooks Ltd* [1984] N.Z.L.R. 354 at 360; per Dillon LJ in *Lonrho v Fayed* [1990] 2 Q.B. 479 at 489.

[412] *Johnson v BFI Canada Inc* 2010 MBCA 101; (2010) 326 D.L.R. (4th) 497 at [55].

[413] *A.I. Enterprises Ltd v Bram Enterprises Ltd* 2012 NBCA 33; (2012) 350 D.L.R. (4th) 601 at [56] as one of the "essential tenets of the unlawful means tort"; (reversed on appeal without reference to this issue: 2014 SCC 12; (2014) 366 D.L.R. (4th) 573).

(a) Intention

Replace paragraph with:

24-73 In *OBG Ltd v Allan* the House of Lords confirmed that in this tort "the defendant must have intended to inflict the harm of which the complaint is made".[414] "Because damage to economic expectations is sufficient to found a claim, there need not have been any intention to cause a breach of contract or interfere with contractual rights."[415] So where A perpetrates deceit upon B intending B to act in a way which will cause damage to C, he is liable to C whether or not damage is also suffered by B since the unlawful means were in their nature actionable even if B's cause of action was not complete because he suffered no damage.[416] But where a defendant union brought its members out on strike in breach of employment contracts in a dispute with the employer who was consequently unable to fulfil functions under statute to the damage of the claimant abattoir owners, they could not sue the union because the damage, though an unavoidable by-product of the strike, was not the consequence of any intention to injure them.[417] But while the "purpose or intention of inflicting injury on the [claimant]" is an essential element of the tort,[418] it is not necessary to prove that this was the defendant's predominant purpose; it is sufficient that the unlawful act was "in some sense directed against ... or intended to harm the [claimant]".[419] A series of recent cases have raised the question whether a defendant can be held to have intended to harm a claimant if it used unlawful means to raise the prices that it could charge its customers, but was unsure and indifferent as to whether those customers would incur a loss as a result, or be able to pass the extra costs on.[420] On this point, the current position appears to be that a defendant who intends to make a gain by obtaining a higher price will only be held to have intended to cause loss to whoever pays the extra amount if it was "inherent in the nature of the arrangements" that the defendant's gain would be at the claimant's expense.[421] A defendant is not liable for this tort if he uses unlawful means with the intent to cause damage to X but his acts result in damage to Y even if that loss is foreseeable.[422]

[414] [2007] UKHL 21; [2008] 1 A.C. 1 per Lord Nicholls at [141]; cf. Lord Hoffmann at [62]: "One intends to cause loss even though it is the means by which one achieves the end of enriching oneself."

[415] [2007] UKHL 21; [2008] 1 A.C. 1, per Lord Hoffmann at [8].

[416] *Lonrho v Fayed* [1990] 2 Q.B. 479 CA, affirmed on other grounds [1992] 1 A.C. 448 HL; *National Phonograph Co Ltd v Edison Bell Consolidated Phonograph Co Ltd* [1908] 1 Ch. 355 CA.

[417] *Barretts & Baird* (Wholesale) Ltd v IPCS [1987] I.R.L.R 3 at 7 and 10.

[418] *Copyright Agency Ltd v Haines* (1982) 40 A.L.R. 264 at 275; *Pacific Western Airlines v British Columbia Federation of Labour* (1986) 26 D.L.R. (4th) 87 at 91–95.

[419] *Lonrho v Fayed* [1990] 2 Q.B. 479 at 488–489 per Dillon LJ and see Ralph Gibson LJ at 494 and Woolf LJ at 494 ("desire" to injure not required), affirmed on other grounds [1992] 1 A.C. 448 HL. See also *OBG Ltd v Allan* [2007] UKHL 21; [2008] 1 A.C. 1, per Lord Hoffmann at [62]: "In the unlawful means tort, there must be an intention to cause loss. ... [I]t is necessary to distinguish between ends, means and consequences. One intends to cause loss even though it is the means by which one achieved the end of enriching oneself. On the other hand, one is not liable for loss which is neither a desired end nor a means of attaining it but merely a foreseeable consequence of one's actions." See too *Reach MD Inc v Pharmaceutical Manufacturers Association of Canada* (2003) 227 D.L.R. (4th) 458 (Ont. CA) at 471–472: "The first element of this tort will be met so long as [the defendant's] unlawful act was in some measure directed against [the claimant]. That is so even if ... [the defendant's] predominant purpose was to advance its own interests and those of its members." Cf. *Print N'Promotion (Canada) Ltd v Kovachis* 2011 ONCA 23; (2011) 329 D.L.R. (4th) 421 where the landlord's termination of the head lease because of the tenant's failure to pay the rent was not actionable in tort by a sub-tenant who was thereby prevented from using a wall of the premises for advertising purposes as an "intentional interference with contractual relations and economic interests" inter alia because no intention to damage the sub-tenant was established.

[420] *W.H. Newson Holding Ltd v IMI Plc* [2013] EWCA Civ 1377, [2014] Bus LR 156; *Emerald Supplies Ltd v British Airways Plc (Nos 1 & 2)* [2015] EWCA Civ 1024, [2016] Bus.L.R. 145; *Media-Saturn Holding Gmbh v Toshiba Information Systems (UK) Ltd* [2019] EWHC 1095 (Ch).

[421] *Emerald Supplies Ltd v British Airways Plc (Nos 1 & 2)* [2015] EWCA Civ 1024, [2016] Bus.L.R. 145 at [170]; *Media-Saturn Holding Gmbh v Toshiba Information Systems (UK) Ltd* [2019] EWHC 1095 (Ch) at [235]. In the *Emerald Supplies Ltd* case (at [168]–[169]) the Court of Appeal was inclined to accept that a claimant could establish the requisite intention if the defendant's intended gain would necessarily be at the expense of a member of a limited and identifiable class, and it was a member of that class, but expressly rejected the suggestion that a claimant could establish an intention to injure it by relying on the fact that the defendant's gain would necessarily fall on someone linked to the defendant by a chain of contracts, since this would involve "an unknown and unknowable range of potential claimants".

[422] *Barretts & Baird (Wholesale) Ltd v IPCS* [1987] I.R.L.R. 3; expressly endorsed by Lord Hoffmann in *OBG Ltd v Allan* [2007] UKHL 21; [2008] 1 A.C. 1 at [64]: "The damage to the abattoir owners was neither the purpose of the strike nor the means of achieving that purpose which was to put pressure on the government." *Van Camp Chocolates Ltd v Aulsebrooks Ltd* [1984] N.Z.L.R. 354 (NZCA).

(b) Unlawful means

Interference with the administration of justice

Replace footnote 441 with:

[441] It has been said that proceedings for contempt of court are intended to uphold the authority of the courts and do not allow a claimant to bring an action for solace or compensation: *Johnson v Walton* [1990] 1 F.L.R. 350 at 353, per Lord Donaldson MR. It may be noted, however, that the *Acrow (Automation)* decision was relied on by the Court of Appeal in *Associated British Ports v TGWU* [1989] 1 W.L.R. **24-77**

939 at 960 and 965 in support of the conclusion that the unlawful means relied on did not have to be independently actionable by the claimant, a conclusion that must now be subject to the majority view in *OBG Ltd v Allan* [2007] UKHL 21; [2008] 1 A.C. 1 on what constitutes unlawful means (see para.24-75). Some forms of contempt of court may constitute "unlawful means" for the purposes of the separate tort of conspiracy to cause harm by the use of unlawful means: *JSC BTA Bank v Ablyazov (No 14)* [2018] UKSC 19; [2018] 2 W.L.R. 1125, see para.24-104.

Crimes and breaches of statutes

After "In the wise-ranging review of the scope and ingredients of the unlawful interference tort.", add new footnote 471A:

24-86 [471A] In *Bram Enterprises Ltd v A.I. Enterprises Ltd* 2014 SCC 12; (2014) 366 D.L.R. (4th) 573 at [74], Cromwell J identified one of the advantages of adopting the narrow definition of "unlawful means" for the interference tort as being that such an approach would "not risk 'tortifying' conduct rendered illegal by statute for reasons remote from civil liability."

Breach of contract as unlawful means

Add new footnote 490A to end of paragraph:

24-91 [490A] A parallel issue concerns whether breaches of contract can constitute "unlawful means" for the purposes of the tort of conspiracy to cause harm by the use of unlawful means. Authorities relevant to this issue were discussed in *Palmer Birch (a partnership) v Lloyd* [2018] EWHC 2316 (TCC), [2018] 4 W.L.R. 164 at [228]–[234], and Judge Russen QC decided to proceed on the basis that a conspiracy to breach contracts can be tortious: see para.24-107.

5. CONSPIRACY

(a) General

24-93 *Replace footnote 497:*

The nature of conspiracy

[497] See *Crofter Hand Woven Harris Tweed Co v Veitch* [1942] A.C. 435 at 439–445, per Viscount Simon LC; and at 461–472, per Lord Wright; the monumental judgment of Evatt J in Australia in *McKernan v Fraser* (1931) 46 C.L.R. 343 at 363-412; *Lonrho Plc v Fayed* [1992] 1 A.C. 448 at 463–466, per Lord Bridge; *Revenue & Customs Commissioners v Total Network SL* [2008] UKHL 19; [2008] 1 A.C. 1174 at [65]–[78], per Lord Walker; *Canada Cement La Farge v British Columbia Lightweight Aggregate Ltd* (1983) 145 D.L.R. (3d) 385 SCC at 396–400. For a critical appraisal see H. Carty, "The Tort of Conspiracy as a Can of Worms", Ch.13 in G.A. Pitel, et al., (eds) *Tort Law: Challenging Orthodoxy* (Oxford: Hart, 2013). For a critique of judicial development of tortious liability for conspiracy which argues that if Lord Nicholls' analysis of the "unlawful means" tort in *OBG Ltd v Allan* [2007] UKHL 21; [2008] 1 A.C. 1 is preferred to that of Lord Hoffmann (see para.24-75), there is neither a need nor any justification for a separate tort of conspiracy in either of its forms, see Paul S. Davies and Sir Philip Sales, "Intentional Harm, Accessories and Conspiracies" (2018) 134 L.Q.R. 69.

Replace paragraph with:

24-93 "A conspiracy consists ... in the agreement of two or more to do an unlawful act, or to do a lawful act by unlawful means."[498] The principles were developed largely in the course of the twentieth century.[499] Conspiracy may be a crime[500]; but the historical links between the crime and the tort have now been greatly weakened.[501] The crime inheres in the agreement to act unlawfully[502]; but the tort arises when damage is caused or threatened by the combination.[503] As a tort:

> "very little is heard of it until the nineteenth century, when it was brought into prominence as a result of the legislature having, in 1875, enacted that combination in furtherance of trade disputes should not be indictable as conspiracies in any case where the act, if committed by one person, would not be a crime."[504]

It is now clear that a "conspiracy to injure might give rise to civil liability even though the end were brought about by conduct and acts which by themselves, and apart from the element of combination or concerted action, could not be regarded as a legal wrong".[505]

[498] *Mulcahy v R.* (1868) L.R. 3 H.L. 306 at 317, per Wiles J; *Baxendale-Walker v Middleton* [2011] EWHC 998 (QB) at [59]–[60].

[499] *Crofter Hand Woven Harris Tweed Co v Veitch* [1942] A.C. 435 at 461, per Lord Wright. The tort is "a modern invention": per Lord Denning MR in *Midland Bank Trust Co Ltd v Green* (No.3) [1982] Ch. 529 at 539. Cf. *JSC BTA Bank v Khrapunov* [2018] UKSC 19; [2018] 2 W.L.R. 1125 at [6] per Lords Sumption and Lloyd-Jones: "of all the economic torts it is the one whose boundaries are perhaps the hardest to define in principled terms."

[500] See Criminal Law Act 1977 ss.1 and 5 abolishing the crime of conspiracy except for conspiracy to defraud (*Scott v Metropolitan Police Commissioner* [1975] A.C. 819 HL); conspiracy to corrupt public morals (*Shaw v DPP* [1962] A.C. 220 HL); conspiracy to outrage public decency (*R. v Knuller* [1973] A.C. 435 HL). The crime of conspiracy otherwise rests upon the agreement to pursue conduct which involves the commission of a criminal offence. See Smith and Hogan, *Criminal Law*, 15th edn (2018), ch.11.3.

[501] Although "both the crime and the tort grew from a common root" there is "no good logical or historical reason" for "slavishly applying in the law of tort" rules applicable to the crime: per Oliver J in *Midland Bank Trust Co Ltd v Green (No.3)* [1979] Ch. 496 at 522 and 525; affirmed [1982] Ch. 529 CA where Fox LJ said at 540 that although "the crime and the tort shared the same definition ... [which] suggests some considerable affinity between the two ... the affinity is not ... in fact very close at all". See too *JSC BTA Bank v Khrapunov* [2018] UKSC 19; [2018] 2 W.L.R. 1125 at [9] per Lords Sumption and Lloyd-Jones: while "the essence of the crime is the agreement or understanding that the parties will act unlawfully, whether or not it is implemented ... a tortious conspiracy, like most tortious acts, must have caused loss to the claimant or the cause of action will be incomplete. It follows that a conspiracy must necessarily have been acted on. But there is no more to it than that. The critical point is that the tort of conspiracy is not simply a particular form of joint tortfeasance." It is actionable as a distinct tort once it is established that a conspiracy has caused loss and it is not a form of secondary liability but a primary liability: per Lord Wright in *Crofter Handwoven Harris Tweed Co v Veitch* [1942] A.C. 435 at 462: "it is in the fact of conspiracy that the unlawfulness resides," reaffirmed by the House of Lords in *Revenue & Customs Commissioners v Total Network SL* [2008] UKHL 19; [2008] 1 A.C. 1174.

[502] *Mulcahy v R.* (1868) L.R. 3 H.L. 306 at 317. *Phillips v News Group Newspapers Ltd* [2012] UKSC 28; [2013] 1 A.C. 1 at [43]–[45] per Lord Walker; the offence of conspiracy was complete when the agreement was made and the conspirators could be prosecuted even though no performance had taken place.

[503] *Midland Bank Trust Co Ltd v Green (No.3)* [1979] Ch. 496 at 523–524, per Oliver J, affirmed [1982] Ch. 529 CA, per Fox LJ at 541. Intentional, not merely foreseeable, damage is essential to the tort: *Crofter Hand Woven Harris Tweed Co Ltd v Veitch* [1942] A.C. 435 at 461 per Lord Wright; it is "the gist" of the cause of action, per Lord Diplock in *Lonrho Ltd v Shell Petroleum Co Ltd (No.2)* [1982] A.C. 173 at 188. Parallels between the tort and the crime must now be drawn with great caution. See *Kuwait Oil Tanker Co SAK v Al-Bader* [2000] 2 All E.R. (Comm) 271 at 312.

[504] *Midland Bank Trust Co Ltd v Green (No.3)* [1979] Ch. 496 at 523, per Oliver J; the Conspiracy and Protection of Property Act 1875 s.3 gave this protection after *R. v Bunn* (1872) 12 Cox 316, had extended the crime of conspiracy in relation to organising strikes. That section was replaced by the Criminal Law Act 1977 ss.1 and 3. Similar protection against liability for the tort of conspiracy was provided by the Trade Disputes Act 1906 s.1; now TULRCA 1992 s.219(2); see para.24-140.

[505] *Quinn v Leathem* [1901] A.C. 495 at 510, per Lord Macnaghten, approved in *Crofter* [1942] A.C. 435, per Viscount Maugham at 448, per Lord Wright at 461. Cf. *JSC BTA Bank v Khrapunov* [2018] UKSC 19; [2018] 2 W.L.R. 1125 at [10] where "the absence of just cause or excuse" for the combination was said to be "a more useful concept" in explaining what made a conspiracy tortious than either "a predominant purpose of injuring the claimant" in the case of lawful means conspiracy or "the use of unlawful means" in the case of the other form of conspiracy. "In either case there is no just cause or excuse *for the combination*." (emphasis in the original).

The combination

Replace paragraph with:

The tort requires an agreement, combination, understanding, or concert to injure, involving two or more persons. Of the various words used to describe a conspiracy, "combination" has been preferred to "agreement" on the ground that "agreement" **24-95** might be thought to require some agreement of a contractual kind, whereas all that is needed is a combination and common intention.[513] Although judicial descriptions have referred to "concerted action taken pursuant to agreement", a party to a conspiracy need not understand the legal effect of it. But he must know the facts on the basis of which it is unlawful.[513A] Moreover there must be a combination; the absence of overt acts or an uncommunicated intention to join a conspiracy may show that there has not been an effective combination. Husband and wife were once thought to be one person in the eyes of the common law and, therefore, to be incapable of conspiring together.[514] This is still the case in criminal conspiracy although even in the criminal law spouses are liable for conspiracies begun before marriage.[515] But it has been held that, in the absence of binding authority, and of compelling rationale or public policy, the primitive maxim that spouses are one person should not be imported into the tort of conspiracy where liability is not complete until the agreement has been carried into effect and concerted action taken. The gravity of the injury sustained does not vary "according to whether those who inflict it are casual acquaintances or are indissolubly conjoined in wedded bliss".[516]

[513] *Belmont Finance Corp v Williams Furniture Ltd (No.2)* [1980] 1 All E.R. 393 at 404, per Buckley LJ; cf. *Crofter Hand Woven Harris Tweed Co Ltd v Veitch* [1942] A.C.435 at 439–440 and 461, per Viscount Simon and Lord Wright. Cf. *Douglas v Hello! Ltd (No.3)* [2003] EWHC 786; [2003] 3 All E.R. 996 where conspiracy allegations failed, inter alia, because there was "no common plan or intent" between those said to be involved. Cf. *Phillips v News Group Newspapers Ltd* [2010] UKSC 28; [2013] 1 A.C. 1 at [44] where Lord Walker said that the crime of conspiracy "involved an agreement, express or implied." See also *Energy Renewals Ltd v Borg* [2014] EWHC 2166 (Ch); [2014] I.R.L.R. 73 and *JSC BTA Bank v Khrapunov* [2018] UKSC 19; [2018] 2 W.L.R. 1125 at [9]: "the fact of combination may alter the legal character and consequences of overt acts".

[513A] This proposition, which corresponds to the view of Buckley LJ in *Belmont Finance Corp v Williams Furniture Ltd (No.2)* [1980] 1 All E.R. 393 at 404, has come under challenge: in some cases it has been submitted that a defendant should not be held liable for a conspiracy to cause harm by the use of unlawful means unless he knew that the means were unlawful. Support for such a submission can be gleaned from *Meretz Investments NV v ACP Ltd* [2007] EWCA Civ 1303; [2008] Ch. 244 (particularly at [124], [127], [146] and [174]) where a defendant who believed that his acts were lawful avoided liability, and in some cases it has been accepted without dispute, e.g. *Brent London BC v Davies* [2018] EWHC 2214 (Ch) at [284]. The submission was addressed, and the ratio of *Meretz* carefully analysed, in *Stobart Group Ltd v Tinkler* [2019] EWHC 258 (Comm), where HHJ Russen QC decided to treat himself as bound by *Belmont*. In support of the conclusion, he noted the practical difficulties with assessing conspirators' understandings of the state of the law, and that focusing on knowledge of the unlawfulness of the means used might detract from the notion that part of the reason why the behaviour is tortious is because the conspirators have combined with the intention of causing harm to the claimant: at [547]–[573]. This conclusion differed from that reached by Morgan J after an equally detailed discussion of the issue in *Digicel (St Lucia) Ltd v Cable & Wireless Plc* [2010] EWHC 774 (Ch) at Annex I, [93]–[118].

[514] *DPP v Blady* [1912] 2 K.B. 89 at 92 (Lush J, dissenting on other matters); *Mawji v R.* [1957] A.C. 126 (polygamous marriage; the point was conceded).

[515] s.2(2)(a) of the Criminal Law Act 1977.

[516] *Midland Bank Trust Co Ltd v Green (No.3)* [1979] Ch. 496 at 527, per Oliver J; affirmed [1982] Ch. 529 CA at 538, per Lord Denning MR, and at 541, per Fox LJ.

Replace footnote 520 with:

24-96 [520] *Belmont Finance Corp v Williams Furniture Ltd (No.2)* [1980] 1 All E.R. 393 CA; *Prudential Assurance Co Ltd v Newman Industries Ltd (No.2)* [1982] Ch. 204 CA (in both of which the knowledge of directors was imputed to their companies); *Digicel (St Lucia) Ltd v Cable & Wireless Plc* [2010] EWHC 774 (Ch) at Annex I, [77].

(b) Unlawful means conspiracy

(i) Intention

After "the economic tort liabilities that are based on the use of unlawful means.", add new footnote 536:

[536] Cases where it has been accepted that the necessary "intention" to cause loss to the claimant is the same in the unlawful interference tort and in unlawful means conspiracy include: *Meretz Investments NV v ACP Ltd* [2007] EWCA Civ 1303, [2008] Ch. 244 CA at [146]; *Digicel (St Lucia) Ltd v Cable & Wireless Plc* [2010] EWHC 774 (Ch) at Annex I, [84]; *Emerald Supplies Ltd v British Airways Plc (Nos 1 & 2)* [2015] EWCA Civ 1024, [2016] Bus.L.R. 145 at [133]; *Palmer Birch (a partnership) v Lloyd* [2018] EWHC 2316 (TCC), [2018] 4 W.L.R. 164 at [220]; *Media-Saturn Holding Gmbh v Toshiba Information Systems (UK) Ltd* [2019] EWHC 1095 (Ch) at [226]. Similarly, in *Recovery Partners GP Ltd v Rukhadze* [2018] EWHC 2918 (Comm); [2019] Bus.L.R. 1166 at [446](iv), Cockerill J applied dicta from *OBG Ltd v Allan* [2007] UKHL 21, [2008] 1 A.C. 1 on "intention" for the purposes of the interference tort in order to hold defendants liable for unlawful means conspiracy. 24-100

(ii) Unlawful means

Replace paragraph with:

There is no good reason why the ambit of "unlawful means" in this form of conspiracy should not be coterminous with its scope in the other economic torts, but this is currently not the law: a broader range of unlawful acts can constitute "unlawful means" for the purposes of the conspiracy tort as against the three-party interference tort.[538] It has been held that whenever an act is itself tortious, a combination to do that act is a tortious conspiracy.[539] Thus a combination which does damage to the claimant by means of intimidatory threats to break contracts[540] or by way of procurement of breaches of contracts[541] or by violence or fraud[542] is actionable. While not all equitable wrongs appear to be unlawful means, where a serious contravention occurs it is still open to the court to regard such wrongs as unlawful means for the purposes of conspiracy.[543] In some circumstances, a claim will fail not because any element of the cause of action is absent, but because of a special immunity based on a public policy. An example of a conspiracy claim failing for such a reason was provided where a person claimed that two policemen had conspired to make false statements about him to the Director of Public Prosecutions and to give false evidence both in court and before the masters of his Inn of Court, such proceedings being privileged and allowing for no civil action.[544] The tort of conspiracy differs from the crime of conspiracy in that to establish the tort it is necessary for the claimant to prove the overt acts which were the cause of his damage.[545] By contrast while it has been held that a conspiracy to commit a tort, such as trespass, became a crime only when it invaded the public domain or caused more than nominal damage, that limitation does not apply to civil conspiracy.[546] 24-101

[538] The position was summarised in *JSC BTA Bank v Ablyazov (No 14)* [2018] UKSC 19; [2018] 2 W.L.R. 1125 at [12]: in *Revenue & Customs Commissioners v Total Network SL* [2008] UKHL 19; [2008] 1 A.C. 1174 "the House declined to apply to unlawful means conspiracies the condition which it had held in *OBG Ltd v Allan* [2008] 1 A.C. 1 to apply to the tort of intentionally harming the claimant by unlawful acts against third parties, namely that those acts should be actionable at the suit of the third party. They held that the means were unlawful for the purpose of founding an action in conspiracy, whether they were actionable or not." Cf. *Pro-Sys Consultants Ltd v Microsoft Corp* 2014 BCSC 1280; (2014) 376 D.L.R. (4th) 302 at [38]–[45] where the submission that the Supreme Court decision in *Bram Enterprises Ltd v A.I. Enterprises Ltd* 2014 SCC 12; (2014) 366 D.L.R. (4th) 573 had changed the law on what constituted unlawful means for the purposes of unlawful means conspiracy was rejected. In *Bram* Cromwell J had held that it was not necessary to seek identical treatment for "unlawful means" for all the torts where it was a requirement and he expressly limited his reasoning to the unlawful means tort and distinguished the approach to unlawful means in the torts of conspiracy and intimidation; see *Pro-Sys v Microsoft* at [67] and [69]. In *Reisinger v J.C. Akin Architect Ltd* 2017 SKCA 11; (2017) 411

D.L.R. (4th) 687 it was noted that in *Bram Enterprises Ltd v A.I. Enterprises Ltd* 2014 SCC 12; (2014) 266 D.L.R. (4th) 573 the Canadian Supreme Court had observed that unlawful means conspiracy might require a broader definition of unlawful means than that which was appropriate for the unlawful means tort because of the existence of "the so-called predominant purpose conspiracy tort." It was not necessary for the unlawful means or acts required for conspiracy to be actionable torts if they were otherwise unlawful.

[539] *Crofter* [1942 A.C. 435 at 462, per Lord Wright; *Sorrell v Smith* [1925] A.C. 700 at 723, 729–730, per Lord Dunedin and at 712 and 714, per Viscount Cave LC.

[540] *Rookes v Barnard* [1964] A.C. 1129. See also *Messenger Group Newspapers Ltd v NGA* [1984] I.R.L.R. 397 (intimidation, nuisance and other torts).

[541] *Stratford & Son Ltd v Lindley* [1965] A.C. 269 HL; *Pritchard v Briggs* [1980] Ch. 338 at 410–418, per Goff LJ; *Norbrook Laboratories Ltd v King* [1984] I.R.L.R.200 CA (NI) (interference with contract by unlawful means as well as nuisance and trespass). The suggestion made by Porter J in *De Jetley Marks v Greenwood* [1936] 1 All E.R. 863 at 872, that a conspiracy to induce a breach of contract is actionable only after the breach has been effected, does not seem to have survived the modern cases.

[542] *Crofter* [1942] A.C. 435 at 462, per Lord Wright; *Metall und Rohstoff AG v Donaldson, Lufkin & Jenrette Inc* [1990] 1 Q.B. 391 CA at 481.

[543] Especially where directors are in breach of their fiduciary duties or in breach of statutory prohibitions: see *Belmont Finance Corp v Williams Furniture Ltd (No.2)* [1980] 1 All E.R. 393 CA; the Companies Act 2006 ss.188–225 and *Gower & Davies: Principles of Modern Company Law*, 10th edn (2016), Ch.16. In *Keymed (Medical & Industrial Equipment) Ltd v Hillman* [2019] EWHC 485 (Ch) at [122], Marcus Smith J accepted that a director's breach of fiduciary duty could constitute unlawful means for the purposes of the conspiracy tort, and in *Iranian Offshore Engineering & Construction Co v Dean Investment Holdings SA* [2019] EWHC 472 (Ch), Butcher J held several defendants liable for an unlawful means conspiracy where the unlawful means were breaches of fiduciary duty, dishonestly assisting such breaches, and knowing receipt (at [172]). In *Recovery Partners GP Ltd v Rukhadze* [2018] EWHC 2918 (Comm); [2019] Bus.L.R. 1166 at [442], Cockerill J reported: "It was (rightly) not in issue that if liability is established in breach of fiduciary duty or breach of confidence those torts would be sufficient to establish the unlawful means, if the other requirements of the tort [of unlawful means conspiracy] were made out."

[544] This was the explanation provided in *JSC BTA Bank v Ablyazov (No 14)* [2018] UKSC 19; [2018] 2 W.L.R. 1125 at [23] for the decision in *Marrinan v Vibart* [1963] 1 Q.B. 234; affirmed [1963] 1 Q.B. 528 CA; *Hargreaves v Bretherton* [1959] 1 Q.B. 45.

[545] *Crofter* [1942] A.C. 435 at 440, per Viscount Simon LC; *Midland Bank Trust Co Ltd v Green (No.3)* [1979] Ch. 496 at 520–524; [1982] Ch. 529 CA; *Qatar Petroleum Co v Thomson* [1959] 2 Lloyd's Rep. 405 CA; *Kuwait Oil Tanker Co SAK v Al-Bader* [2000] 2 All E.R. (Comm) 271 at 312. Cf. *The Dolphina* [2011] SGHC 273; [2012] 1 Lloyd's Rep. 304 at [269]: unlawful means could be effected by omission on the basis of the Singapore Interpretation Act provision that "act" could mean "omission" where the context so required.

[546] *Sharston Engineering Ltd v Evans* (1972) 12 K.I.R. 409 (sit-in strike). On the criminal law see the Criminal Law Act 1977 ss.1 and 5 and the Criminal Justice and Public Order Act 1994 ss.61, 63, 68, 70, and 73. Compare the position in Scotland: *Plessey Ltd v Wilson* [1982] I.R.L.R. 198; (see Miller (1982) 11 I.L.J. 115); *Phestos Shipping Co v Kurmiawan*, 1983 S.L.T. 389 (see Brodie (1983) 12 I.L.J. 170); *Shell (UK) v McGillivray*, 1991 S.L.T. 667 (OH).

Replace paragraph with:

24-104 Further consideration was given to the extent of "unlawful means" in this form of the conspiracy tort in *Wagner v Gill*.[556] In that case the New Zealand Court of Appeal held that where a company director acted in breach of fiduciary duty by moving assets between companies under his control, that did not constitute unlawful means for the purposes of an unlawful means action by an affected creditor.[557] While accepting that in principle breach of fiduciary duty might qualify as unlawful means, there were strong reasons why it should not do so in a case like this where, on the facts, the defendant's action was subject to statutory regulation which made it actionable only by the company while providing the plaintiff with the right to apply for a court order that the defendant as a director repay funds which had been acquired in breach of duty to the company. By contrast in *JSC BTA Bank v Ablyazov (No 14)*[558] the UK Supreme Court held that contempt of court could also amount to unlawful means for the purposes of this form of the tort of conspiracy, at least where the claimant was a bank and the contempt involved breaches of a freezing order and receivership order that had been made on the application of the bank. The single judgment of Lord Sumption and Lord Lloyd-Jones provided further general guidance:

> "Conspiracy being a tort of primary liability, the question what constitute unlawful means cannot depend on whether their use would give rise to a different cause of action independent of conspiracy. The real test is whether there is a just cause or excuse for combining to use unlawful means. That depends on (i) the nature of the unlawfulness, and (ii) its relationship with the resultant damage of the claimant."[559]

The suggestion that whether acts constitute "unlawful means" depends on an evaluation of the conspirators' reasons for combining to use those means ("just cause or excuse") is not straightforward. In *Palmer Birch (a partnership) v Lloyd*[559A] HHJ Russen QC took the quoted passage to mean that "there may be categories of unlawfulness which a combiner may be excused from agreeing to perpetrate either because of the classification of the unlawful act (identified by reference to the purpose or duty which it subverts) or because it is too incidental to the claimant's position to be actionable." In line with this, it is submitted that acts are more likely to be regarded as sufficient to constitute "unlawful means" where: (i) there is a strong link between the reasons why the acts are categorised as unlawful and protection of the the claimant's interests, and (ii) the effectiveness of the conspirators' scheme is linked to them having used the unlawful acts rather than similar, but lawful, methods.

[556] [2014] NZCA 336; [2015] 3 N.Z.L.R. 157. See Carty (2015) 74 C.L.J. 261.

[557] [2014] NZCA 336; [2015] 3 N.Z.L.R. 157 at [87]; see generally [53]–[88].

[558] [2018] UKSC 19; [2018] 2 W.L.R. 1125.

[559] [2018] UKSC 19; [2018] 2 W.L.R. 1125 at [11].

[559A] 572 [2018] EWHC 2316 (TCC); [2018] 4 W.L.R. 164 at [189].

Breach of statute

Replace paragraph with:

Some earlier authorities suggested that breach of a criminal statute (or other crime) must amount to unlawful means for the purposes of tort liability for conspiracy.[560] Subsequent to the *Total Network* and *JSC BTA Bank* cases, it is clear that this was too bold, and whether a claim can be based on a particular statutory crime will depend on application of the general approach outlined in the previous paragraph. In the *JSC BTA Bank* case the Supreme Court stated that whether, or when, breach of a civil statutory duty would constitute "unlawful means" was "liable to raise more complex problems": "Their relevance may depend on the purpose of the relevant statutory provision, which may or may not be consistent with its deployment as an element in the tort of conspiracy."[561] It has already been noted in relation to the unlawful interference tort that the House of Lords decision in *Lonrho v Shell* limited the circumstances in which a claimant could rely on breach of statute as unlawful means to cases where on its proper "construction" either the relevant statutory obligation was imposed for the benefit of a particular class of individuals which included the claimant, or, where a "public right" was infringed, the claimant suffered special damage over and above that incurred generally.[562] Since the general position is that conspiracy can accommodate a broader field of "unlawful means" than the unlawful interference tort, because of the intrinsic wrongfulness 24-105 of combining with the intention of causing harm, it would be surprising if acts that were sufficient for the purposes of the interference tort were insufficient for conspiracy. But within unlawful means conspiracy a broader range of breaches of non-criminal statutes may be sufficient.[563] If, on the "construction" approach the statute does allow for an action, but only one of the two defendant conspirators breaks the statute in a way that gives the claimant a cause of action in tort against that party alone, the question may arise whether the second party is liable for conspiracy or whether the two parties are liable as joint tortfeasors by reason of their concerted action.[564] If they are liable as joint tortfeasors, denial of liability for conspiracy would seem to have little point. If they are not liable as joint tortfeasors, however, the denial of an action for conspiracy might deprive the claimant of advantages even if one of the defendants is liable individually.[565] Similar principles to those applicable in deciding when breach of statute can constitute unlawful means apply to determine when breach of directly applicable provisions of European Community law can amount to the use of unlawful means.[566]

[560] *Sorrell v Smith* [1925] A.C. 700 at 714, per Viscount Cave LC and 719, per Lord Dunedin; and per Lord Wright in *Crofter* [1942] A.C. 435 at 461–462, including breach of s.7 of the Conspiracy and Protection of Property Act 1875 (now TULRCA 1992 s.241), but after the careful analysis of Scott J in *Thomas v NUM (South Wales Area)* [1986] Ch. 20 at 54–65, no independent tort liability can be based on that section. In *Rookes v Barnard* [1964] A.C. 1129 at 1206, Lord Devlin took it not to be disputed that a threat to commit a crime *simpliciter* was a threat to use unlawful means.

[561] *JSC BTA Bank v Ablyazov (No 14)* [2018] UKSC 19; [2018] 2 W.L.R. 1125 at [15].

[562] *Lonrho Ltd v Shell Petroleum Co Ltd (No.2)* [1982] A.C. 173 HL; see too *Gouriet v Union of Post Office Workers* [1978] A.C. 435. See para.24-83.

[563] For example, *Brent LBC v Davies* [2018] EWHC 2214 (Ch) raises the question whether a conspiracy of public officials to cause harm to a public authority by acting in ways that were contrary to the statutes that governed their powers might be actionable; in the actual case Zacaroli J did not have to confront such questions since he found that there had not been a pre-conceived plan to harm the claimant, and the conspirators were unaware that their actions were unlawful.

[564] On liability as joint tortfeasors see Ch.4.

[565] On the acts of some conspirators being attributed to others see para.24-113. For a disinclination to use joint tortfeasorship see *Williams v Natural Health Foods* [1998] 1 W.L.R. 830 at 838–839. In *Michaels v Taylor Woodrow Developments Ltd* [2001] Ch. 493 at 516, Laddie J acknowledged that it is possible to sue for wrongful means conspiracy where some but not all of the conspirators would be liable individually for the wrongful act. In this respect the tort of conspiracy "dovetails with, or overlaps, the law of joint tortfeasance". But the courts could suppress the pleading of conspiracy where the same allegation could be expressed in terms of joint tortfeasance.

[566] *Garden Cottage Food Ltd v Milk Marketing Board* [1984] A.C. 130 HL; *Barretts & Baird (Wholesale) Ltd v IPCS* [1987] I.R.L.R. 3; *R. v Secretary of State for Transport Ex p. Factortame* [2001] 1 W.L.R. 942; *Three Rivers DC v Bank of England (No.3)* [2003] 2 A.C. 1; Fox [2001] C.L.J. 33.

Other forms of unlawful means

Replace paragraph with:

24-106 The *Total Network* and *JSC BTA Bank* cases have expanded the scope of "unlawful means" in the context of conspiracy, but have not gone so far as to re-instate the former "general" approach, which found unlawful means whenever defendants had done acts which they were not at liberty to commit.[567] Such an approach would risk "tortifying" too many forms of behaviour that are prohibited for reasons very different from those that should determine the scope of protection in the economic sphere, would undercut the high requirement for a "predominant purpose" of causing injury that is a condition of liability for "simple conspiracy" (without unlawful means), and would further magnify the contentious difference between the scope of the tortious liability of individuals acting alone and in combination with others.

[567] *Torquay Hotel Co Ltd v Cousins* [1969] 2 Ch. 106 at 139, per Lord Denning MR, an approach approved in *Associated British Ports v TGWU* [1989] 1 W.L.R. 939 CA (reversed on other grounds [1989] 1 W.L.R. 939 HL).

Breach of contract

Replace paragraph with:

Further difficulty arises in relation to a combination to effect a breach of contract as a form of unlawful means conspiracy. Where there is no threat of breach, this would not be conspiracy to intimidate such as was found to have occurred by the House of Lords in *Rookes v Barnard*. But since in that case the House of Lords held that a breach of contract was an "illegal act" for the purposes of the tort of intimidation there would not seem to be any reason for excluding it from the scope of illegal or unlawful means for the purposes of the tort of unlawful means conspiracy.[575] Yet Lord Devlin (alone of the Law Lords in *Rookes v Barnard*) went out of his way to leave this point open.[576] Notwithstanding this reservation, in several cases it has been acknowledged, albeit only in obiter dicta, that a person could be liable for conspiracy to break a contract to which he was not party where he merely combined, with a common design, together with the party or parties committing the breach.[577] **24-107**

[575] The "Donovan" *Report of the Royal Commission on Trade Unions* (1968) Cmnd.3623 accepted the need to protect against this liability in trade disputes, see para.854, and the Trade Union and Labour Relations Act 1974 s.13(3) did so until its repeal by the Employment Act 1980 s.17(8).

[576] [1964] A.C. 1129 at 1210: "I am not saying that a conspiracy to commit a breach of contract amounts to the tort of conspiracy; that point remains to be decided."

[577] *Barretts & Baird (Wholesale) Ltd v IPCS* [1987] I.R.L.R. 3 at 8–10, per Henry J; and see Lord Denning MR in *Midland Bank Trust Co Ltd v Green (No.3)* [1982] Ch.529 at 539. This is also consonant with the reasoning of the Court of Appeal in *Associated British Ports v TGWU* [1989] 1 W.L.R. 939 CA (reversed on other grounds, [1989] 1 W.L.R. 939 CA).

Add new paragraph:

Justification The question whether a defendant can rely on a defence of justification to avoid liability for combining to use unlawful means with the intention of causing harm is not straightforward. Two obstacles face the submission that such a defence should be recognised: it would only have logical space to operate in cases where whatever justification the defendant invoked had not been sufficient to prevent the means being categorised as unlawful and had also been insufficient to prevent a finding that the defendant had the intention of harming the claimant. In *Palmer Birch (a partnership) v Lloyd*[577A] HHJ Russen QC expressly rejected the possibility of justification being a defence "to an otherwise established unlawful means conspiracy". However, an apparently contrary position was adopted in *Meretz Investments NV v ACP Ltd* where the three alleged conspirators had acted so as to: (i) lawfully exercise a power of sale of a lease, granted as security for the loan of money to carry out property development, which (ii) prevented the borrower from performing its contractual promise to leaseback the premises to the claimant. Despite the fact that the transaction brought about a breach of contract by the borrower, Toulson LJ reasoned that because the purchaser of the lease "had a perfectly legitimate reason for acting as he did [i]t would therefore be wrong to classify such conduct as founding an action for unlawful means conspiracy".[577B] It is submitted that the *Meretz* case reveals that where a claim alleges a conspiracy to breach a contract it may be appropriate to recognise a defence of justification of the scope necessary to parallel the potential defence of justification for procuring **24-107A**

a breach of contract.[577C] Otherwise, a party who could rely on his "equal or superior right" as a justification for procuring a breach of contract could nonetheless end up liable—as a conspirator—for having combined with the party in breach to cause loss to the claimant by means of the breach.

577A 594 [2018] EWHC 2316 (TCC); [2018] 4 W.L.R. 164 at [193].

577B [2007] EWCA Civ 1303; [2008] Ch. 244 at [170], per Toulson LJ.

577C See paras 24-55 to 24-58.

(c) Conspiracy to injure

Damage

Replace paragraph with:

24-115 Damage is an essential element of the tort of conspiracy,[621] the gist of the cause of action.[622] It has been held that the damage constituted by the expense incurred by claimants in exposing and resisting the wrongful activities of the defendants can be awarded to them as damage directly caused by the conspiracy.[623] Damages for injury to feelings or to reputation, however, cannot be recovered in an action based upon a "lawful means" conspiracy to injure.[624] The special limitations surrounding the granting of injunctions against publication of allegedly defamatory material may, however, be displaced if a conspiracy to injure is proved.[625]

621 *Crofter* [1942] A.C 435 at 440, per Viscount Simon LC Cf. *Ward v Lewis* [1955] 1 W.L.R. 9; *Lonrho Ltd v Shell Petroleum Co Ltd (No.2)* [1982] A.C. 173 HL; *Lonrho Plc v Fayed (No.5)* [1993] 1 W.L.R. 1489 CA at 1501, per Stuart-Smith LJ. For the question whether there is a defence of justification available in a case of unlawful means conspiracy, see para.24-107A.

622 *Crofter* [1942] A.C. 435 at 461, per Lord Wright; per Lord Diplock in *Lonrho v Shell* [1982] A.C. 173 at 188; per Oliver J. in *Midland Bank Trust Co Ltd v Green (No.3)* [1979] Ch. 496 at 524; cf. Holdsworth, *History of English Law*, 2nd edn (1937), Vol.VIII, pp.393-394.

623 *British Motor Trade Association v Salvadori* [1949] Ch. 556. Damages appear to be at large: Edelman, *McGregor on Damages*, 20th edn (2017), para.48-020. On the remedy of interim (interlocutory) injunction see paras 24-166 to 24-169.

624 *Lonrho Plc v Fayed (No.5)* [1993] 1 W.L.R. 1489 CA, at least in the absence of proof of pecuniary loss, since that would allow the claimant "to circumvent the requirements of a defamation action ... without the defendants being able to plead justification", per Dillon LJ at 1493. As to the place of such a claim for damages "parasitically", or as part of damages at large, see the differing formulations of Dillon LJ, [1993] 1 W.L.R. 1489 CA at 1494–1497, Stuart-Smith LJ at 1501 and 1504–1505, and Evans LJ at 1509. Cf. *Joyce v Sengupta* [1993] 1 W.L.R. 337 CA (malicious falsehood and damage to reputation).

625 See *Gulf Oil (GB) Ltd v Page* [1987] Ch. 327 CA, limiting the practice based upon *Bonnard v Perryman* [1891] 2 Ch. 269 CA.

6. Trade Disputes

(a) General

Trade disputes and the economic torts

Replace footnote 627 with:

24-116 627 For detailed consideration see Sir O. Kahn-Freund, *Labour and the Law*, 3rd edn (1983), Davies and Freedland (eds), Ch.8; S. Deakin and G.M. Morris, *Labour Law*, 6th edn (2012), Ch.11; G. Morris and T.J. Archer, *Collective Labour Law* (2000), Ch.6; C. Barrow, *Industrial Relations Law*, 2nd edn (2002), Chs 13–17; K.W. Wedderburn, *The Worker and the Law*, 3rd edn (1986), Chs 7 and 8, and (1989) 18 I.L.J. 1; Smith, Baker and Warnock, *Smith & Wood's, Employment Law*, 14th edn (2019), Ch.10; K.W. Wedderburn, *Employment Rights in Britain and Europe* (1991) and *Labour Law and Freedom* (1995),

Chs 2 and 4; Simpson (1991) 54 M.L.R. 418; Carty (1991) 20 I.L.J. 1; Morris (1993) 22 I.L.J. 194; Simpson (1993) 22 I.L.J. 287.

(d) Specific limitations on the protection against liability

Action to extend negotiation or union membership

Replace footnote 767 with:

[767] TULRCA 1992 s.222(1)(b). Discrimination arises if the employer engages in conduct, in relation to persons employed by him, or who apply or are considered for employment, or in relation to provision of employment generally, which is different in some or all cases according to whether persons are not members of a union (or a particular union, etc.), and that conduct is more favourable to those who are members: s.222(2). In *Birmingham CC v Unite the Union* [2019] EWHC 478 (QB); [2019] I.R.L.R. 423, Freedman J held that the union did not lose its immunity under s.222(1)(b) where it was seeking parity for its members, rather than advantageous treatment. Acts done in furtherance of a trade dispute to induce the employer to hire or favour non-union workers appear to retain protection; but see the restrictions in s.137 (hiring), ss.145A and 145B (inducements), s.146 (detriment) and s.152 (dismissal). Sections 145A and 145B were inserted by the ERA 2004 and s.146 was amended by the ERA 1999 and ERA 2004 to counter the effects of *Associated British Ports v Palmer and Associated Newspapers Ltd v Wilson* [1995] 2 A.C. 454 HL, and to remedy the failure of the law to comply with art.11 of the ECHR identified by the European Court of Human Rights in *Wilson v UK* [2002] I.R.L.R. 568. See Wedderburn (2000) 29 I.L.J. 1, 18–20; Ewing (2003) 32 I.L.J. 1, 5–15. **24-134**

(h) Trade disputes and ballots

Replace footnote 861 with:

[861] On the correct approach to construction of the provisions on industrial action ballots in TULRCA ss.226 to 235 see *P v NASUWT* [2003] UKHL 8; [2003] 2 A.C.663 per Lord Bingham at [7]: "The House must attempt to give the provisions a likely and workable construction." See too Elias LJ in *London & Birmingham Railway Ltd v ASLEF* [2011] EWCA Civ 226; [2011] I.C.R. 848 at [9]: "the legislation should simply be construed in the normal way without presumptions one way or the other", with Lord Bingham's "likely and workable construction" as the starting point. In *Balfour Beatty Engineering Services Ltd v Unite* [2012] EWHC 267 (QB); [2012] I.C.R. 822 at [8] Eady J added to these two approaches recognition "since the advent of the Human Rights Act 1998 at least that it is appropriate to construe the relevant statutory provisions in a way that is compatible with rights enshrined in the European Convention on Human Rights and Fundamental Freedoms ... the approach at Strasbourg has been to recognise the right to strike as part and parcel of the right to freedom of association conferred under Article 11(1)". The *Code of Practice* (Industrial Action Ballots and Notice to Employers: revised in 2017) is taken into account for interpretation: s.207(3); but it "puts a gloss on the law", warning unions they are "at risk of legal action" even where it would not be "successful": per Lord Inglewood, Parl. Deb. HL, 29 June 1995, col.914: Simpson (1993) 22 I.L.J. 297. On the 2005 revision of the *Code of Practice* see Simpson (2005) 34 I.L.J. 331. A revised version of the Code which takes account of the changes made to the law by the Trade Union Act 2016 was issued in March 2017. **24-148**

Postal ballots

Replace paragraph with:

Since 1993, the ballot has been required to be fully postal. So far as is reasonably practicable, a voting paper must be sent to the member's home address giving him a convenient opportunity to vote by post.[863] The courts had earlier acknowledged that changes of address and the like will often make it impossible for a union to guarantee to reach each relevant member by post.[864] In response to pressures to permit electronic voting, in particular to facilitate the union's meeting the requirement for a minimum to 50 per cent of the members balloted to actually vote in a ballot, s.4 of the Trade Union Act 2016 required the Secretary of State to commission an independent review of the delivery of secure methods of electronic voting in industrial action ballots.[865] The obligation to hold such a ballot now arises whether the members to be induced to take action are employees or persons under a contract by virtue of which they personally perform services for another.[866] **24-149**

[863] TULRCA 1992 s.230(2) as substituted by TURERA 1993 s.17. Under s.230(2A)–(2C) as further substituted by ERA 1999 Sch.3 para.7, merchant seaman may be permitted to vote on board ship, or at a place where the ship is, if that is reasonably practicable.

[864] *British Railways Board v NUR* [1989] I.C.R. 678 CA at 684, per Lord Donaldson MR; but see now s.232A, para.24-150. In *Balfour Beatty Engineering Services Ltd v Unite* [2012] EWHC 267 (QB); [2012] I.C.R. 822 at [12] Eady J cited Lord Walker in *P v NASUWT* [2003] UKHL8; [2003] 2 A.C.663 at [65]: "it is a fact of life that no trade union of any size can keep completely full and accurate records of the names and addresses of its ever changing body of members, still less their current places of work, trade categories and pay grades" as highlighting the need to make due allowance for these realities in deciding whether the union had conducted the ballot in accordance with s.230.

[865] Such a review was conducted by Sir Ken Knight, and reported in December 2017. It recommended that e-balloting be tested in the context of non-statutory balloting over a reasonable period—to be decided by the Secretary of State—to examine its reliability, in particular its capacity to withstand attack by those motivated by a desire to disrupt.

[866] TULRCA 1992 s.235; this seems to include even those who provide professional services and therefore fall outside the definition of worker in s.296, which applies for the purposes of the definition of a trade dispute in s.244; see para.24-150.

Separate workplace ballots

Replace footnote 881 with:

24-151 [881] See para.30 of the 2017 revision of the *Code of Practice* on Industrial Action Ballots and Notices to Employers which notes that it is possible for a union to hold more than one ballot on a dispute at a single workplace and that some of these ballots may include members at other workplaces. cf. *Partington v NALGO* [1981] I.R.L.R. 537 (union not allowed to apply rules on discipline where agreement made with employers not to call out safety workers). See now on "unjustifiable discipline" of members who refuse to join in industrial action, TULRCA s.64, but that wrong cannot amount to unlawful means in tort: s.64(4). Where, as is common, a union intends that safety personnel should carry out essential services during industrial action, s.228 would seem to be satisfied if it calls upon all the relevant workers to take part but then suspends the action by safety personnel at various workplaces for limited periods for safety work, making it clear that these suspensions are not terminations of their action: *Post Office v UCW* [1990] I.C.R. 258 CA, distinguishing *Monsanto Plc v TGWU* [1987] I.C.R. 269 CA.

Appointment of scrutineer

Replace footnote 882 with:

24-152 [882] TULRCA 1992 s.226C; the *Code of Practice* 2005 states that where 50 or fewer members are entitled to vote, the union may want to consider whether the appointment of a scrutineer would still be of benefit in enabling the union to demonstrate compliance with the statutory requirements more easily (para.13). See now para.13 of the 2017 *Code of Practice* to the same effect; para.12 of this Code suggests that giving the scrutineer additional functions relating to the production and distribution of voting papers, being the person to whom the ballot papers are returned and retaining custody of the ballot papers after the ballot result, "might help to ensure that adequate standards for the conduct of the ballot or simplify the balloting process".

Content of the ballot paper

Replace paragraph with:

24-154 Difficulty has arisen about the nexus between the ballot paper, associated statements and the scope of action protected. This prompted two approaches. It has been held that the union must show that the members have not been asked to participate in a ballot "by reference to issues other than a trade dispute".[896] In *University College Hospital NHS Trust v Unison*,[897] it was even declared that, inspecting the "different strands of the ballot paper", the court found that references to the terms of employment of staff who might be employed many years in the future, made it "impossible to identify the motives of those who voted in favour of strike action ... it follows that this nullifies the ballot which took place. In addition the ballot paper is very persuasive evidence as to what is the proposed purpose of the strike."

The terms of the ballot paper showed that it "was for many purposes, one of which is clearly flawed".[898] Alternatively, it has been pointed out that "no express requirement to this effect is to be found in the statute"; it is, of course, necessary to "identify the strike which is called with the strike which was voted for. But that is a matter of evidence."[899] That the latter view is correct is suggested by the fact that the same ballot can suffice under these provisions and also under those affording a member a right to apply to the court, where no issue arises on trade disputes.[900] The union will of course become liable to an injunction if it is calling action which is not in contemplation or furtherance of a trade dispute, but that is not a reason to hold that the requisite ballot support was not obtained.[901] The paper must include one or both of the permitted questions (however framed): one asking if the members are prepared to take part in a strike, the other if they are prepared to take part in action short of a strike.[902] The two questions must be put and answered separately; no "rolled up" question is allowed.[903] In view of the difficulties surrounding the definition of "strike" and "industrial action short of a strike",[904] trade unions appear in practice to need to put both questions in many situations to be sure they are covered in subsequent events. Where both questions are put and one (for example for a strike) receives a majority, but the other (for action short of a strike) does not, that is nevertheless enough to support the strike as each question must be considered separately.[905]Section 5 of the Trade Union Act 2016 has made three significant additions to the provisions in TULRCA s.229 on the content of the ballot paper. First, it must contain a summary of the matter(s) in issue in the trade dispute to which the proposed industrial action relates.[905A] Second, where it contains a question on action short of a strike, the type or types of action must be specified; third, it must state the period or periods within which each type of action is expected to take place.[906] It is unclear whether these additions will have the effect of limiting the union's protection against economic tort liability to the specified action short of dismissal and to strike or other action within the period or periods stated as the times when the action is expected to take place. The voting must be by marking a paper, as far as reasonably practicable in secret and without any costs to the voters[907]; members must be allowed to vote without interference or constraint imposed by the union, its members, officials or employees.[908] The union must ensure that votes are honestly and accurately counted[909]; and as soon as reasonably practicable it must provide those entitled to vote with what is now detailed information about the result.[910] The extent of the obligations now imposed on a trade union in drafting the ballot paper will depend on the courts' interpretation of the additional requirements introduced by the 2016 Act. Two central issues are raised by these amendments. The first is the legal effect of the way in which the ballot paper identifies the substance of the trade dispute; it is not clear whether a general reference to, for example, "pay", "working time" or "overtime working" will be sufficient. Second, it is especially unclear whether a statement of intended action such as "a ban on overtime working at weekends" would limit the legality of a union's call for action such that a call for a ban on overtime working on other days or for other action short of a strike, would lack the required support of a ballot notwithstanding a majority vote and compliance with all the other conditions in the ballot in support of action short of a strike.

[896] *London Underground Ltd v NUR (No.1)* [1989] I.R.L.R. 341 at 343, per Simon Brown J (four issues mentioned on the ballot paper; only one clearly within the definition of trade dispute); cf. *London Underground Ltd v NUR (No.2)* [1989] I.R.L.R. 343.

897 [1999] I.C.R. 204 CA. The feature in the ballot unacceptable to the Court of Appeal was the demand by the union that the employers should guarantee the conditions for employees of employers who were at that time unknown, but who would come into the scheme perhaps 30 years in the future. On the question whether this was furtherance of a trade dispute under TULRCA 1992 s.244, see para.24-176.

898 [1999] I.C.R. 204 CA per Lord Woolf MR at 215. The terms of the ballot paper may well be evidence as to the nature and purpose of the threat to strike; but it is submitted that this had little or nothing to do with the "motives" of those involved, nor is that a matter the court is called upon to investigate in regard to the "furtherance" of the trade dispute.

899 *Associated British Ports v TGWU* [1989] I.R.L.R. 291 at 301, per Millett J (affirmed on other grounds [1989] 1 W.L.R. 939 HL): "What matters is that a majority supported strike action; it does not matter why they did so." The nature of the dispute may be revealed through the question on the ballot paper: *Wandsworth LBC v NAS/UWT* [1994] I.C.R. 81 at 96, per Neill LJ. If there is no trade dispute the union will, of course, have little chance of avoiding an injunction against its inducement of the action.

900 See TULRCA 1992 s.62(9). Also, a ballot may "relate" (s.233(3)(a)) to future industrial action by workers without "relating" to others already called on to take action: *Newham LBC v NALGO* [1993] I.C.R. 189 CA.

901 It is suggested that Woolf LJ went no further than this in *Newham LBC v NALGO* [1993] I.C.R. 189 at 198-200, in saying that the continuance of a "live dispute" on issues presented on the ballot paper depended on a party having an honest and genuine belief that the dispute continued; see the overlapping test of "furtherance" of a dispute, paras 24-181 to 24-182; see *Express Newspapers Ltd v McShane* [1980] A.C. 672 HL.

902 TULRCA 1992 s.229(2); on the definition of "strike" in s.246, and lack of definition of industrial action, para.24-148. See further on the lack of precision about the nature of industrial action the special provision designating overtime and call-out bans as action short of a strike: TULRCA 1992 s.229(2A) inserted by ERA 1999 Sch.3 para.6 (reversing the decision in *Connex SE v RMT* [1999] I.R.L.R. 249 CA).

903 *Post Office v UCW* [1990] I.C.R. 258 CA.

904 See para.24-148; a stoppage for five minutes every hour can be seen as a "concerted stoppage of work", but in ordinary language it would be called action short of a strike: Wedderburn, *Employment Rights in Britain and Europe* (1991), Ch.10. But a ballot on strike action alone was not invalidated by the inaccurate statement in accompanying information that in law all action was regarded as strike action: *British Telecommunications Plc v Communication Workers Union* [2003] EWHC 937 (QB); [2004] I.R.L.R. 58.

905 *West Midlands Travel Ltd v TGWU* [1994] I.C.R. 978 CA (reversing Schiemann J; 1256 for a strike, against 1225; but 1059 for and 1156 against action short of a strike); TULRCA 1992 s.226(2)(a)(iii), "the majority voting in the ballot" had "answered 'yes' to the question applicable".

905A In *Argos Ltd v Unite the Union* [2017] EWHC 1959 (QB), in refusing to grant an interim injunction, Dingemans J held that the claimants were not likely to be able to prove at trial that a summary on the ballot paper was inadequate: he held that the meaning of the summary should be assessed by reference to a hypothetical reasonable member of the union receiving the ballot paper: at [33].

906 TULRCA 1992 s.229(2B)–(2D). In *Thomas Cook Airlines Ltd v British Airline Pilots Association* [2017] EWHC 2253 (QB); [2017] I.R.L.R. 1137, in refusing an interim injunction against a strike, Lavender J expressed the view that a court was not more likely than not to interpret s.229(2D) as requiring more detail about the expected period of industrial action than "discontinuous industrial action in the form of strike action on dates to be announced over the period from 8th September 2017 to 18th February 2018."

907 The cost of postage may fall to be borne both ways by the union: cf. *Paul v NALGO* [1987] I.R.L.R. 83 CA (union internal election). The scheme for refunding union costs of secret postal ballots for certain purposes (TULRCA 1992 s.115) ceased in 1996.

908 This does not mean that the union is prohibited from being "partisan" in the campaign for the ballot: *Newham LBC v NALGO* [1993] I.C.R. 189. No express ban is put on interference or constraint by others (e.g. the employer); but it is submitted any such interference would be a wrongful interference with statutory rights. Dissemination of false information might be interference, albeit innocent: *RJB Mining v NUM* [1997] I.R.L.R. 621 at 623 (but not prohibited if the employer is the guilty party).

909 Accidental inaccuracies are disregarded if they cannot affect the result: TULRCA 1992 s.230(4).

910 TULRCA 1992 s.231; as amended by s.6 of the Trade Union Act 2016 this information must now include the number of persons entitled to vote; whether or not the number of votes cast was at least 50 per cent of those entitled to vote, thus satisfying the minimum turnout requirement in s.226(2)(a)(iia) (inserted by s.2 of the 2016 Act) and, where the support of at least 40 per cent of those entitled to vote is required under the amendments made by s.3 of the 2016 Act, whether or not it has been achieved.

Notices to employers

Replace footnote 915 with:

[915] *London & Birmingham Railway Ltd v ASLEF* [2011] EWCA Civ 226; [2011] I.C.R. 848 per Elias LJ at [60]–[77]; both the limitation of the duty by reference to information in possession of the union and the fact that unions would normally have this information available supported limiting the duty to provide figures from information actually held by the union at the time they were provided. This approach was followed in *United Closures & Plastics Ltd v Unite* [2011] CSOH 114; 2011 S.L.T. 1105 at [46]-[47]; cf. *EDF Energy Powerlink Ltd v RMT* [2009] EWHC 2852 (QB); [2010] I.R.L.R. 114, which seems to be inconsistent with this construction and *Metroline Travel Ltd v Unite* [2012] EWHC 1778 (QB); [2012] I.R.L.R. 749 where the information provided was held to be inadequate to enable the employer to "readily deduce" the numbers, categories and workplaces of those concerned as s.226A(2C) requires. cf. para.24 of the 2017 revision of the *Code of Practice* which suggests that "in order to reduce the likelihood of a dispute" the union "might wish to invite an opinion from the relevant employer" whether its conclusion on entitlement to vote complies with these statutory requirements; *sed quaere*. **24-155**

Duration of ballot protection

Replace paragraph with:

Under the provisions on industrial action ballots as originally enacted in 1984, a favourable ballot ceased to be effective at the end of four weeks beginning with the date of the ballot.[930] During the passage of the 1990 Bill, the issue arose of cases where a union was subjected to interim injunctions while litigation extended, especially in appeals, beyond the four week period, which meant that even if it won in court, the union would need to reballot its members.[931] The 1990 Act therefore amended the law so that where during the four weeks period a court order prohibited the union from calling for industrial action but the order subsequently lapsed or was discharged, recalled or set aside, the union could apply to the court for an order that the period during which the earlier order prohibited the calling of industrial action should not count towards the four week period within which a call for industrial action could be made.[932] A further amendment in 1999 enabled the period within which the ballot remained effective to be extended from four weeks to up to eight weeks by agreement between the union and the employer.[933] Section 9 of the Trade Union Act 2016 has further extended the period for which a ballot remains effective to six months or a longer period up to nine months by agreement between the union and the employer.[934] This extension of the period for which a union can rely on the support of a ballot is likely to cover most cases in which a court order prohibiting the union from calling for industrial action is reversed on appeal. The right of a union to apply for an order that the period during which an earlier court order prohibiting the union from calling for industrial action was in force, shall not count towards these new longer periods for which a ballot remains effective, is however retained.[935] So too is the provision forbidding the court from making an order if it appears likely that either the result of the ballot no longer represents the views of the members or an event is likely to occur as a result of which these members would be likely to vote against industrial action if another ballot were to be held.[936] **24-158**

[930] Trade Union Act 1984 s.10(3)(c), consolidated in TULRCA s.234(1). On the date of the ballot see now TULRCA 1992 s.246.

[931] As in *Associated British Ports v TGWU* [1989] I.R.L.R.291 at 301, Millet J and [1989] 1 W.L.R. 939 CA and HL (union successful at first instance, not in the Court of Appeal but successful in the House of Lords; new ballot required for national dock strike); see also *Barretts & Baird (Wholesale) Ltd v IPCS* [1987] I.R.L.R. 3 (delay before inter partes hearing after ex parte injunction).

[932] Employment Act 1990 s.8, consolidated in TULRCA 1992 s.234(2).

933 TULRCA 1992 s.234(1), as substituted by the Employment Relations Act 1999 s.4, Sch.3 paras 1 and 10.

934 TULRCA 1992 s.234(1A), as substituted by the Trade Union Act 2016 s.9(1).

935 TULRCA 1992 s.234(2).

936 TULRCA 1992 s.234(4). It is submitted that the courts would require objective evidence that such a change or event is reasonably probable.

(j) Picketing and trade disputes

Replace footnote 951 with:

24-161 951 There is no statutory definition of "picketing". It is generally considered to be attendance in the course of an industrial dispute seeking to persuade workers not to work: see *Code of Practice on Picketing* (2017), para.10. The Code was revised in 2017 to take account of the amendments made to the law by the Trade Union Act 2016 which came into force in March 2017. This persuasion is sometimes assumed to induce them to break their contracts, even if no words are said: *Union Traffic Ltd v TGWU* [1989] I.C.R. 98 CA at 106, per Bingham LJ ("presence alone at the site" of the pickets was enough). Further on definitions of "picketing": Bercusson (1977) 40 M.L.R. 265 at 271.

Pickets and obstructions

Replace footnote 969 with:

24-163 969 [1974] A.C. 587 HL. The statutory protection here was the Industrial Relations Act 1971, s.134; but the same reasoning would apply to TULRCA 1992 s.220. That section (which expressly referred to acts being neither a crime under s.7 of the 1875 Act nor a tort) was taken to give some protection for pickets against criminal liability; per Lord Salmon at 603, and see, per Viscount Dilhorne at 600. Contrast the *Code of Practice on Picketing* (2017) paras 46–49.

Replace paragraph with:

24-164 Thus, the traditional protection of "peaceful picketing" has never been one of any great width.[975] Under the current law, incorporating the new limitations introduced in 1980, in order to obtain protection against the causes of action mentioned in s.219(1) and (2), the picket acting in furtherance of a trade dispute must (unless he is within an exception or is a trade union official) attend only "at or near his own place of work".[976] The "place of work" does not move merely because the employer unilaterally moves the work to a new place, without moving the workers; it is a "geographical location" where the worker actually works under his employment contract.[977] The exception relates to a person who "works or normally works otherwise than at any one place",[978] or where it is "impracticable"[979] to attend for the purpose of picketing. A person within the exception may attend at or near "any premises of his employer from which he works or from which his work is administered". The Code of Practice (2017) recommends (as did earlier versions) that "in general" the number of pickets at any entrance should not exceed six, a provision of which the courts (and the police) have made extensive use.[980] Further, persons who are unemployed but who attend near the place where their employment was terminated in connection with a trade dispute or where that termination was one of the circumstances giving rise to the dispute, may attend near that place.[981] But where drivers dismissed as redundant picketed depots other than their main depot (which had been closed down) they were not protected, even though those other depots had been "ports of call" and it was now futile to picket the closed depot.[982]

975 Where threatening behaviour or violence occurs a variety of criminal liabilities may arise, e.g. "intimidation" or other crimes of public order; see *Moss v McLachlan* [1985] I.R.L.R. 76; Public Order Act 1986 ss.2 (violent disorder), 5 and 6 (harassment), Pt II (processions and assemblies), Sch.2, para.1 (amending s.7 of the 1875 Act, now TULRCA 1992 s.241); see also Morris (1985) 14 I.L.J. 149. With

the enactment of the Criminal Justice and Public Order Act 1994 attendance at, near or on land or premises encounters new criminal liabilities in certain situations, e.g. ss.61 (removal of trespassers), 68 (aggravated trespass), 70, 71 (trespassory assemblies: new ss.14A, 14B, 14C of the Public Order Act 1986), 73 (squatters), 77 (residing in vehicles), although it is not anticipated that s.63 (raves) will normally be relevant to pickets. But see the liberal approaches of the majority in *DPP v Jones* [1999] 2 A.C. 240 HL.

[976] TULRCA 1992 ss.220 and 219(3). For the definition of "official": s.119. See *Code of Practice on Picketing* (2017) paras 21–23: "attendance at, or near, an entrance to or exit from the factory, site or office at which the picket works" (para.22); "even if those working at another place of work are employed by the same employer or are covered by the same collective bargaining agreements as the picket" (para.23).

[977] *News Group Newspapers Ltd v SOGAT (No.2)* [1987] I.C.R. 181 at 213; compare the definition of "place of work" for the purpose of separate strike ballots in TULRCA 1992 s.228(4).

[978] TULRCA 1992 s.220(2)(a).

[979] TULRCA 1992 s.220(2)(b); semble including workers who work at a place where it would be contrary to an enactment, or dangerous to picket (e.g. some building sites or an oil rig) or possibly a workplace many miles into a private estate.

[980] See *Code of Practice on Picketing* (2017) para.56, retaining the wording of earlier versions of the code. *Thomas v NUM (South Wales Area)* [1986] Ch. 20 at 70-72; *News Group Newspapers Ltd v SOGAT (No.2)* [1987] I.C.R. 181 at 231; see generally Lewis (ed.), *Labour Law in Britain* (1986), Ch.7; Wedderburn, *The Worker and the Law*, 3rd edn (1986), pp.540-553. Cf. Canadian doctrines on picketing "quasi-public" places: S. Robinson (1999) Jo. Can. Lab. E.L.J. 391 (with texts) and see the important decision of the Canadian Supreme Court in *Pepsi-Cola Beverages (West) Ltd v Retail, Wholesale and Development Store Union Local 558* [2002] 1 S.C.R. 156 that "secondary picketing", that is picketing by persons other than workers at their own place of work, is not per se unlawful, but is lawful unless it involves conduct that is independently criminal or tortious. The decision was expressly intended to align the law with the fundamental freedoms of association and expression set out in the Canadian Charter of Rights and Freedoms.

[981] TULRCA 1992 s.220(3). The last category is generally said to include only workers who are not in employment, that is not those who have taken jobs at another place of work: Code of Practice, para.20; *sed quaere* whether a part-time job or entering a training scheme where the worker technically became an "employee", would always have this effect?

[982] *Union Traffic Ltd v TGWU* [1989] I.C.R. 98 CA; but a dismissed worker may picket only his last (main) place of work: ibid. In such cases, when the employer has transferred the business to another person, the dismissed worker may find also that he is unable to show that he is acting in furtherance of a trade dispute by picketing at that place: *Kenny v TGWU, The Times,* 15 June 1989. On trade disputes, see TULRCA 1992 s.244, and para.24-170 onwards.

Trade union officials

Replace footnote 985 with:

[985] TULRCA 1992 s.220(4) and *Code of Practice*, paras 27–28. Thus "a branch official" may attend "only where members of his branch are lawfully picketing" (para.28); "he must represent and be responsible for them in the normal course of his union duties". *Quaere*: the meaning of being "responsible" for members in this context. *Quaere*: where members of two trade unions elect an official, directly or indirectly, to act for them, e.g. a convenor of shop stewards? **24-165**

(k) Contemplation or furtherance of a trade dispute

Labour injunctions

Replace footnote 1009 with:

[1009] The greater the likelihood of establishing a trade dispute defence, the greater the weight attached to it: per Lord Diplock in *Hadmor Productions Ltd v Hamilton* [1983] 2 A.C. 191 at 224. See too *Balfour Beatty Engineering Services Ltd v Unite* [2012] EWHC 267 (QB); [2012] I.C.R. 822 at [3]–[4] per Eady J: while a defendant trade union's establishing the likelihood of it having a trade dispute defence did not conclude the interim injunction issue in its favour, it would be exceptional for a court having reached that conclusion to grant relief; to similar effect, *Birmingham CC v Unite the Union* [2019] EWHC 478 (QB); [2019] I.R.L.R. 423. **24-168**

[illegible]

the enactment of the Criminal Law [illegible] and [illegible] Act [illegible] [illegible] [illegible]

[illegible] 1992 ss. [illegible] and 21 [illegible] [illegible]

[illegible]

[illegible] above, [illegible]

[illegible]

[illegible]

[illegible]

[illegible]

Trade Union Officials

[illegible]

[illegible]

(B) Contemplation or Furtherance of a Trade Dispute

Labour Injunctions

[illegible]

[illegible]

CHAPTER 25

STATUTORY AND EU INTELLECTUAL PROPERTY RIGHTS

TABLE OF CONTENTS

1. INTRODUCTION

European influence on intellectual property rights

Replace paragraph with:

Each intellectual property right described below has been subject to the influ- **25-03** ence of EU legislation to a greater or lesser extent.[7] There has also been a partial approximation of the enforcement of intellectual property rights with the aim of establishing a high level of protection for the rights.[8] Copyright, rights in databases and rights in performances have been the subject of approximation of national laws by means of a series of Directives adopted over the period since 1986.[9] There is no EU copyright code to replace national laws, but the Court of Justice of the European Union ("CJEU") has steadily built up a European copyright jurisprudence on the interpretation of the Directives.[10] Moral rights have not been the subject of EU legislation. By contrast, designs and trade marks have been almost entirely harmonised within the E and EU-wide rights are available in addition to or in substitution for national trade marks and designs (although UK unregistered design right[11] remains in place).[12] Both Community Trade Marks ("CTMs") and Community Registered Designs ("CRDs") are administered at the European Intellectual Property Office ("EUIPO"), located at Alicante, Spain.[13] Until very recently, there has been no EU instrument governing patent law, which has instead been a matter of national law and/or the provisions of the European Patent Convention. However, following 30 years of negotiation and an international agreement adopted in 2013, the EU stands on the brink of a unitary patent administered by a Unified Patents Court.[14]

[7] For a brief summary of possible outcomes in the event of Brexit, see para.25-03A.

[8] See Directive 2004/48/EC of 24 April 2004, on the Enforcement of Intellectual Property Rights and in particular Recital 10. This Directive has been implemented but few of its provisions were thought to require changes to the law. Specifically in relation to copyright, see also Directive 2001/29/EC of 22 May 2001, on the harmonisation of certain aspects of copyright and related rights in the information society, art.8. The most significant change resulting from these provisions has been the introduction of injunctions against service providers whose services have been used for infringement. See below para.25-48.

[9] The Directives, some of which are codified replacements of earlier Directives as amended, are as follows: Council Directive 87/54/EEC of 16 December 1986, on the legal protection of topographies of semiconductor products; Council Directive 93/83/EEC of 27 September 1993, on the coordination of certain rules concerning copyright and rights related to copyright applicable to satellite broadcasting and cable retransmission; Directive 96/9/EC of 11 March 1996, on the legal protection of databases; Directive 2001/29/EC of 22 May 2001, on the harmonisation of certain aspects of copyright and related rights in the information society; Directive 2001/84/EC of 27 September 2001, on the resale right for the benefit of the author of an original work of art; Directive 2006/115/EC of 12 December 2006, on rental right and lending right and on certain rights related to copyright in the field of intellectual property; Directive 2006/116/EC of 12 December 2006, on the term of protection of copyright and certain related rights (which was amended by Directive 2011/77/EU of 27 September 2011); Directive 2009/24/EC of 23 April 2009 on the legal protection of computer programs; Directive 2012/28/EU of 25 October 2012 on certain permitted uses of orphan works; and Directive 2014/26/EU of 26 February 2014 on collective management of copyright and related rights and multi-territorial licensing of rights in musical works for online use in the internal market; and Directive 2017/1564 EU of 13 September 2017 on permitted uses for the print disabled.

[10] This case law is binding on national courts. In the course of answering specific questions the CJEU has laid down important principles of interpretation. Thus, for example, it has held that concepts embodied in the Directives on copyright and related rights must be interpreted in a manner consistent with relevant international conventions: the Berne Convention, the WIPO Copyright Treaty ("WCT"), the WIPO Performances and Phonograms Treaty ("WPPT") and the TRIPs Agreement. Another principle is that terms of a provision of EU law must be given an autonomous and uniform interpretation throughout the EU, in the interest of uniform application of EU law and the principle of equality. See, e.g. *Football Association Premier League Ltd v QC Leisure* (C-403/08) [2012] E.C.D.R. 8; *Stichting de Thuiskopie v Opus Supplies Deutschland GmbH* (C-462/09) [2011] E.C.D.R. 18.

[11] Conferred by CDPA 1988 Pt III.

[12] There is a significant EU jurisprudence on designs and an immense EU jurisprudence on trade marks with decisions being made both by CJEU and by the General Court.

[13] The relevant EU legislation in respect of designs comprises Directive 98/71/EC of 13 October 1998 on the legal protection of designs and Council Regulation 6/2002 of 12 December 2001 on community designs. For trade marks, see Council Regulation 40/94/EEC, codified by Council Regulation (EC) 207/2009 and now amended by Regulation (EU) 2015/2424. The latest harmonising directive is Directive 2015/2436/EC.

[14] See para.25-121.

Add new paragraph:

Brexit At the time of writing it is not clear whether, when or on what terms the UK may leave the EU. The Withdrawal Agreement between the UK and the EU dated 14 November 2018 contains express provisions in respect of designs, databases, trade marks (but not patents) and exhaustion of rights. In the absence of a withdrawal agreement, as matters stand, the position on exit will be governed by the European Union (Withdrawal) Act 2018 ("the Withdrawal Act") and statutory instruments made under it. In broad terms, the effect of the Withdrawal Act will be to incorporate existing EU derived legislation and case law into UK law. Various statutory instruments are intended to address failures of retained EU law to operate effectively and other deficiencies arising from Brexit. So far as copyright and related rights are concerned, there are amendments in respect of satellite broadcasts, term of protection, disability permitted acts, the orphan works scheme, qualification for protection, extended collective licensing, cross-border portability, databases, and artist's resale right.[14A] In the field of designs and trade marks there is provision for continuity of protection.[14B] Patents are dealt with by a separate statutory instrument.[14C] Finally, provision is made in relation to exhaustion of rights.[14D] **25-03A**

[14A] The Intellectual Property (Copyright and Related Rights)(Amendment) (EU Exit) Regulations 2019 (SI 2019/605).

[14B] The Designs and International Trade Marks (Amendment etc.) (EU Exit) Regulations 2019 (SI 2019/638).

[14C] The Patents (Amendment) (EU Exit) Regulations 2019 (SI 2019/801).

[14D] By the Intellectual Property (Exhaustion of Rights) (EU Exit) Regulations 2019 (SI 2019/265).

2. Copyright, Artist's Resale Right and Database Right

(a) Scope of protection

(i) Copyright

Replace footnote 15:

Copyright, Designs and Patents Act 1988 **25-04**

[15] Since the Copyright Act 1988 entered into force it has been amended frequently, mainly to implement the EU Directives referred to in para.25-03. Other substantial amendments were made by the Broadcasting Acts 1990 and 1996. In addition, the Copyright Act 1988 has been amended to make provision for so-called "orphan works" and "extended collective licensing", to regulate "collective management organisations" and to modify and extend the acts which may be done without infringing ("permitted acts" or "exceptions"). On copyright, see generally *Copinger and Skone James on Copyright*, various editors, 17th edn (London: Sweet & Maxwell, 2016) and Laddie, Prescott and Vitoria, *The Modern Law of Copyright and Designs*, various editors, 5th edn (London: LexisNexis, 2018).

Scope and term of copyright protection: general

Replace paragraph with:

25-05 There is no copyright in an "idea" as such, however original. What may be protected is the expression of an idea in a "work" if it is sufficiently original.[24] No clear principle is or could be laid down in the cases in order to tell whether what is sought to be protected is on the ideas side of the dividing line, or on the expression side.[25] However, it is clear that copyright does not extend to procedures, methods of operation or mathematical concepts as such.[26] Nor does it extend to clothing information, facts, ideas, theories and themes with exclusive property rights, so as to enable a claimant to monopolise historical research or knowledge and prevent the legitimate use of historical and biographical material, theories propounded, general arguments deployed, or general hypotheses suggested (whether they are sound or not) or general themes written about.[27] The period of copyright in a literary, dramatic, musical or artistic work is 70 years from the year of the death of the author or, if the work is of unknown authorship, from first publication or similar disclosure.[28]

[24] See most recently *Levola Hengelo BV v Smilde Foods BV* (C-310/17) [2018] Bus. L.R. 2442; [2019] E.C.D.R. 2 at [39]. "It is a cliché of copyright law that copyright does not protect ideas: it protects the expression of ideas. But the utility of the cliché depends on how ideas are defined": *SAS Institute v World Programming Ltd* [2013] EWCA Civ 1482; [2015] E.C.D.R. 17; [2014] R.P.C. 8 at [20]. See the specialist texts. See also *Ladbroke (Football) Ltd v William Hill (Football) Ltd* [1980] R.P.C. 539 at 546, per Lord Denning MR; [1964] 1 W.L.R. 273 HL; *LB Plastics Ltd v Swish Products Ltd* [1979] R.P.C. 611 HL; *Elanco Products Ltd v Mandops (Agrochemical Specialists) Ltd* [1980] R.P.C. 213; cf. *Bauman v Fussell* [1978] R.P.C. 485; *Kleeneze Ltd v DRG (UK) Ltd* [1984] F.S.R. 399; *Designers' Guild Ltd v Russell Williams (Textiles) Ltd* [2000] 1 W.L.R. 2416; *Baigent and Leigh v The Random House Group Ltd* [2007] EWCA Civ 247; [2008] E.M.L.R. 7.

[25] *Baigent and Leigh v The Random House Group Ltd* [2007] EWCA Civ 247; [2008] E.M.L.R. 7 at [5], [147], [101].

[26] *SAS Institute v World Programming Ltd* [2013] EWCA Civ 1482; [2015] E.C.D.R. 17; [2014] R.P.C. 8 at [20]; *Levola Hengelo BV v Smilde Foods BV* (C-310/17) [2018] Bus. L.R. 2442; [2019] E.C.D.R. 2 at [39].

[27] *Baigent and Leigh v The Random House Group Ltd* [2007] EWCA Civ 247; [2008] E.M.L.R. 7 at [156], [101].

[28] CDPA 1988 s.12. Directive 93/98 (now codified as Directive 2006/116/EC as amended) required Member States to enact legislation extending the term of copyright in literary and artistic works to 70 years from the end of the calendar year in which the author died. The previous term was 50 years and there are transitional provisions relating to revived copyright, etc. There are special rules for works of "co-authorship" (i.e. collaborative musical compositions with words—see CDPA 1988 s.10A) and joint authorship (see CDPA 1988 s.12(8)). As an author allows each part of a text to move on from one stage to the next he or she creates a new work in which copyright subsists. Earlier drafts can be separate copyright works: *Sweeney v Macmillan Publishers Ltd* [2002] R.P.C. 35.

Subjects of copyright

Replace paragraph with:

25-06 Copyright is afforded by Pt I of the Copyright Act 1988 to "works" of various types[29]: original[30] literary, dramatic, musical and artistic works; sound recordings; films; broadcasts; and the typographical arrangement of published editions. However, these categories now need to be treated with caution. The CJEU has recently held that a "work" is an autonomous EU concept. It follows[30A] that creations that do not fall within the categories laid down by the Copyright Act 1988 may be protected provided they satisfy the criteria laid down in the EU case law, namely that they are expressions rather than ideas[30B]; that they are original[30C]; and that they are identified with sufficient precision and objectivity.[31] Returning to the Copyright

Act 1988, for each type of work, the Act proscribes certain acts as being restricted by the copyright in the work in question. Infringement of copyright[32] involves doing, without the licence of the copyright owner, one or more of the acts restricted by the copyright. For each type of work, certain exceptions to the rules as to infringement are provided.[33] Acts restricted by the copyright include acts done directly or indirectly in relation to a substantial part of the work as well as acts done to the whole work; and in the case of literary, dramatic and musical works they include acts done to an adaptation of the work.[34]

[29] CDPA 1988 s.1.

[30] As to originality, see para.25-20.

[30A] Subject to how a UK court would apply the principle in *Marleasing SA v La Comercial Internacional de Alimentation SA* (C-106/89) [1993] B.C.C. 421.

[30B] See para.25-05.

[30C] See para.25-20.

[31] *Levola Hengelo BV v Smilde Foods BV (C-310/17)* [2018] Bus. L.R. 2442; [2019] E.C.D.R. 2 at [35]–[44] holding that the taste of a food product did not qualify because it was insufficiently identifiable.

[32] See para.25-29.

[33] These, where not noted under the separate kinds of "works", below, are considered in para.25-43.

[34] CDPA 1988 ss.16(3) and 21. As to the meaning of "adaptation", see below, under the various types of work.

"Works" and subsistence of copyright

Replace paragraph with:

The different types of work in which copyright may subsist under the Copyright Act 1988[34A] are summarised below. Frequently, more than one copyright will subsist in a particular work. As a result, a particular act restricted by copyright may be governed by several copyrights, which may have different owners. For example, playing a CD of music in public is an act restricted by the copyright both in the recording, of which the producer is the author, and in the original music, of which the composer is the author. The performers of the music may also have relevant rights which would be infringed by acts of that kind. Similarly, unauthorised reproduction of a magazine may involve infringement of copyright in both text and photographs—which copyright may be owned by different people. **25-07**

[34A] But see para.25-06.

Compilations and databases

Replace footnote 40 with:

[40] See the definition in Directive 96/9/EC art.1(2). Recent examples of databases can be found in *Forensic Telecommunications Services Ltd v Chief Constable of West Yorkshire Police* [2011] EWHC 2892 (Ch); [2012] F.S.R. 15; *Technomed Ltd v Bluecrest Health Screening Ltd* [2017] EWHC 2142 (Ch), [2018] F.S.R. 8; *Freistaat Bayern v Verlag Esterbauer GmbH* (C-490/14) [2015] Bus. L.R. 1428, [2016] E.C.D.R. 6 (topographic map); and *Keystone Healthcare Ltd v Parr* [2017] EWHC 309 (Ch). **25-09**

Computer programs

Replace footnote 48 with:

[48] See *Bezpecnostni Softwarová Asociace* (C-393/09) [2011] E.C.D.R. 3 at [35]. The expression "computer program" includes preparatory design work leading to the development of a program if that work is such that a program can result from it at a later stage: Recital 8 to the Directive. **25-10**

Dramatic works

Replace paragraph with:

25-11 The expression "dramatic work" includes a work of dance or mime if written or otherwise recorded.[51] It includes films,[52] although films considered as first fixations are also dealt with separately, but not scenic effects by themselves.[53] Where a musical work requires action and scenery for its proper performance the music may be protected as a musical work and the whole as a dramatic work.[54] It is at least arguable as a matter of concept that the format of a television game or quiz show can be protected as a dramatic work. Such protection will not subsist unless at least (i) there are a number of clearly identified features which, taken together, distinguish the show from other shows, and (ii) those features are connected with each other in a coherent framework which can be repeatedly applied so as to enable the show to be reproduced in recognisable form.[54A]

[51] CDPA 1988 s.3.

[52] See *Norowzian v Arks Ltd (No.2)* [2000] F.S.R. 363.

[53] *Tate v Thomas* [1921] 2 Ch. 503. See also *Martin v Kogan* [2017] EWHC 2927 (IPEC); [2018] F.S.R. 9 at [42].

[54] *Fuller v Blackpool Winter Gardens* [1895] 2 Q.B. 429.

[54A] *Banner Universal Motion Pictures Ltd v Endemol Shine Group Ltd* [2017] EWHC 2600 (Ch); [2018] E.C.D.R. 2 at [43]–[44].

Films

Replace paragraph with:

25-15 A film is defined as a recording on any medium from which a moving image may by any means be produced.[67] The sound track accompanying a film is treated as part of the film. The period of copyright is 70 years from the end of the year of death of the last to die of the principal director, screenplay author, dialogue author or film music composer.[68]

[67] CDPA 1988 s.5B. The definition excludes a copy taken from a previous film. For consideration of the exact nature of film copyright, see *Dramatico Entertainment Ltd v British Sky Broadcasting Ltd* [2012] EWHC 268 (Ch); [2012] E.C.D.R. 14 at [63] and *Football Association Premier League Ltd v QC Leisure* [2012] EWHC 108 (Ch); [2012] F.S.R. 12 at [69]; *England and Wales Cricket Board Ltd v Tixdaq Ltd* [2016] EWHC 575 (Ch); [2017] E.C.D.R. 2 at [58].

[68] CDPA 1988 s.13B.

Broadcasts

Replace footnote 69 with:

25-16 [69] CDPA 1988 s.6(1). It only covers encrypted transmissions if decoding equipment has been made available by or with the authority of the person making the transmission or providing the contents of the transmission: s.6(2). See *England and Wales Cricket Board Ltd v Tixdaq Ltd* [2016] EWHC 575 (Ch); [2017] E.C.D.R. 2 at [96].

(b) Subsistence, authorship and ownership

(i) Copyright

Originality

Replace footnote 86 with:

25-20 [86] *Infopaq International A/S v Danske Dagblades Forening* (C-5/08) [2009] E.C.D.R. 16; *Levola Hengelo BV v Smilde Foods BV* (C-310/17) [2018] Bus. L.R. 2442, [2019] E.C.D.R. 2 at [36].

Authorship

Replace paragraph with:

Authorship plays an important role in the law of copyright, both in relation to qualification for protection and because, in general, the author is the first owner of the copyright in the work. The author of a copyright work is the person who creates it.[89] A work will be one of joint authorship where the contribution of each author is not distinct from that of the other author or authors.[90] **25-21**

[89] CDPA 1988 s.9(1).

[90] CDPA 1988 s.10. It includes broadcasts made by more than one person. For a summary of what is necessary to establish joint authorship, see *Martin v Kogan* [2017] EWHC 2927 (IPEC); [2018] F.S.R. 9 at [54]. There must be a contribution of ideas is not enough: see *Wiseman v George Weidenfeld & Nicolson Ltd* [1985] F.S.R. 525; *Robin Ray v Classic FM Plc* [1998] F.S.R. 622; *Fylde Microsystems Ltd v Key Radio Systems Ltd* [1998] F.S.R. 449 (testing and debugging software does not give rise to joint authorship); *Brighton v Jones* [2004] EWHC 1157 (Ch); [2005] F.S.R. 16 ("significant" contribution required for joint authorship). Compare *Sawkins v Hyperion Records Ltd* [2005] EWCA 565; [2005] 1 W.L.R. 3281 where the Court of Appeal held that a skilled editor of an out of copyright piece of music was entitled to a new (sole) copyright in the performing score as a result of his skill and labour in producing it. There is no requirement that the parties intended the other to be a joint author in order for the work to be of joint authorship. Authors who reached the threshold of a significant and original contribution in furtherance of a common design to produce the work were co-authors: *Beckingham v Hodgens* [2002] EWHC 2143 (Ch); [2003] F.S.R. 14 (composer of violin part for "Young at Heart" held to be co-author). See also *Brown v Mcasso Music Production Ltd*, (PCC) Patents County Court [2006] E.M.L.R. 3 and *Fisher v Brooker* [2009] UKHL 41; [2009] 1 W.L.R. 1764.

Ownership of copyright

Replace paragraph with:

As indicated in the previous paragraph, the general rule is that the author of a work is the first owner of copyright in it, but there are important exceptions, particularly for works made by employees.[91] Although a person commissioning a copyright work will not usually be entitled to the legal title to the copyright in it (absent agreement), in many circumstances the court will be prepared to imply terms to the effect that the person commissioning the work will be treated as the equitable owner of the copyright in it with the right to call for an assignment of the copyright.[92] For particular kinds of works, the position as regards first ownership of copyright is as follows: **25-22**

(a) *Literary, dramatic, musical and artistic works.* The copyright in these works belongs originally to the author, unless the work is made by an employee in the course of his or her employment when, in the absence of an agreement to the contrary, the first owner is the employer.[93]
(b) *Sound recordings.* In the case of a sound recording, the author is taken to be the producer, that is the person by whom the arrangements necessary for the making of the sound recording are undertaken.[94]
(c) *Films.* In the case of a film, the author is taken to be the producer and the principal director.[95] The producer is the person by whom the arrangements necessary for the making of the film are undertaken.[96]
(d) *Broadcasts.* In the case of a broadcast, the person making the broadcast is taken to be the author or in the case of a broadcast which relays another broadcast by reception and immediate retransmission, the person making that other broadcast is the author.[97]

(e) *Typographical arrangements.* In the case of a typographical arrangement of a published edition, the publisher is taken to be the author.[98]

There are special provisions governing Crown Copyright and Parliamentary Copyright and copyright vesting in certain international organisations.[99]

[91] See also the previous paragraph for the circumstances in which a person may be a joint author and therefore a joint first owner of the copyright.

[92] Such situations include, for example, where an advertising agency makes a work on behalf of a client and it is clear that the client was to have title to the copyright in the work, even though that was not expressly provided for in the contract between them: see *Griggs Group Ltd v Evans* [2005] EWCA Civ 11; [2005] F.S.R. 31, which outlines the main principles. By contrast, in *Clearsprings Management Ltd v Businesslinx Ltd* [2005] EWHC 1487 (Ch); [2006] F.S.R. 3, the court held that there was no need to imply anything more than a perpetual licence in a contract for the design of bespoke property management software.

[93] CDPA 1988 s.11. For pre-1988 works the position is somewhat different, see Copyright Act 1956 ss.4, 12(4), Sch.VII para.28(2)(b), Sch.VIII para.1, and previous editions of this work. For when a work will be considered to have been created in the course of employment, see *Mei Fields Designs Ltd v Saffron Cards and Gifts Ltd* [2018] EWHC 1332 (IPEC); [2018] F.S.R. 33 at [36]–[42]. If the work is computer-generated, the author is the person who undertakes the arrangements necessary for its creation: CDPA 1988 s.9(4). For the effect on ownership of extended and revived copyright see SI 1995/3297 regs 18–20.

[94] CDPA 1988 s.9(2)(aa),178. The focus is on the person directly responsible for the "arrangements", particularly in the financial sense: *Re FG (Films) Ltd* [1953] 1 W.L.R. 483. See also *A&M Records Ltd v Video Collection International Ltd* [1995] E.M.L.R. 349. For pre-1988 works, the first owner is (broadly) the person who commissioned the recording or (if there was no commission), the person who owned the first record embodying the recording at the time the recording was made: Copyright Act 1956 s.12(4), (8).

[95] CDPA 1988 s.9(2)(ab).

[96] CDPA 1988, s.178. In respect of pre-1 July, 1994 films, the first owner was the producer who was defined in the same way: see the previous version of CDPA 1988 s.9(2) and Copyright Act 1956 s.13(4), (10).

[97] CDPA 1988 s.9(b). See also s.6(3) for the definition of "the person making the broadcast".

[98] CDPA 1988 s.9(2)(d).

[99] CDPA 1988 ss.163–168.

(iii) Database right

Qualification for protection

Replace footnote 110 with:

25-27 [110] Copyright and Rights in Databases Regulations 1997 (SI 1997/3032) reg.13(1). The Regulations implement Council Directive No.96/9/EC on the legal protection of databases. As to the kind of evidence which will satisfy a court that investment has been "substantial", see *Health & Case Management Ltd v The Physiotherapy Networks Ltd* [2018] EWHC 869 (QB) at [90]–[93].

(c) Infringement of copyright and database right

(i) Copyright

General

Replace footnote 116 with:

25-29 [116] No formality is required to grant a licence but the defendant must establish the existence and extent of the alleged licence: *Noah v Shuba* [1991] F.S.R. 14. See generally as to the criteria for implication of a licence: *Robin Ray v Classic FM Plc* [1998] F.S.R. 622; *Griggs Group v Evans* [2005] EWCA Civ 11; [2005] F.S.R. 31. The test of whether a licence was granted is objective: *Redwood Music Ltd v Chap-*

pell [1982] R.P.C. 109. Where an architect only charges a nominal fee for preparing plans for obtaining planning permission, there is no implied licence to use the plans for the erection of the building; *Stovin-Bradford v Volpoint Properties Ltd* [1971] Ch. 1007; cf. *Blair v Tomkins* [1971] 2 Q.B. 78. While the courts will only imply a licence to manufacture spare parts in infringement of copyright in appropriate cases, they will not permit the manufacturer of goods to derogate from his grant by preventing the manufacture of spare parts: *British Leyland Motor Corp Ltd v Armstrong Patents Co Ltd* [1986] A.C. 577. Cf. *Cannon Kabushiki Kaisha v Green Cartridge Co* [1997] A.C. 728. Such cases will depend on their facts: thus a licence has been implied where the repair of a mechanical device involved the reproduction of copyright drawings owned by the supplier (*Solar Thomson Engineering Co Ltd v Barton* [1977] R.P.C. 537) but not to establish a right to copy file layouts for a file transfer program (*Ibcos Computers Ltd v Barclays Mercantile Finance Ltd* [1994] F.S.R. 275). See also *Dyson Ltd v Qualtex (UK) Ltd* [2004] EWHC 2981 (Ch); [2005] R.P.C. 19. It is possible that the effect of *Soulier v Premier minister* (C-301/15) [2017] 2 C.M.L.R. 9; [2017] E.C.D.R. 23 is that the conditions for the existence of an implied licence are a matter of EU law involving stricter requirements than those laid down in the UK case law.

Other primary infringements

Replace footnote 148 with:

[148] Recent CJEU decisions on the "distribution right" provided for in the Information Society Directive have accorded the term "distribution" a much wider meaning which encompasses activities which in UK law would be considered to be secondary infringements (e.g. offering for sale) and thus require proof of knowledge or reason to believe as a condition of liability. See *Peek & Cloppenburg AG v Cassina SpA* (C-456/06) [2009] E.C.D.R. 9; *Donner* (C-5/11) [2015] E.C.D.R. 22; *Blomqvist v Rolex SA* (C-98/13) [2014] E.C.D.R. 10; and *Dimensione Direct Sales Srl v Knoll International SpA* (C-516/13) [2015] E.C.D.R. 12; and *Syed* (C-572/17) [2019] E.C.D.R. 4. It seems unlikely that these activities are now primary infringements within the meaning of CDPA 1988 s.18 such that knowledge or reason to believe no longer needs to be proved. **25-37**

Communication to the public

Replace paragraph with:

In the UK, the expression "communication to the public" means "communication to the public by electronic transmission" and includes both broadcasting and the making available of a work to the public by electronic transmission in such a way that members of the public may access it from a place and at a time individually chosen by them.[151] In deciding whether there has been a communication to the public, the court must take account of several complementary criteria.[152] There must be an act of "communication" to a "public". A "communication" is any act of making available, irrespective of the technical means or process used and irrespective of whether the work is actually accessed.[152A] As a rule every transmission which uses a specific technical means must be individually authorised.[153] The mere provision of physical facilities for making or receiving a communication is not itself a communication.[154] A "public" is an indeterminate but fairly large number of persons.[155] It is relevant to know how many persons have access at the same time as well as in succession.[156] The public must be "new", that is a public which was not taken into account by the rightholder when he or she authorised the original communication.[157] If the public is not "new" in this sense, there will still be a communication to the public if the transmission is by a different technical means to that adopted by the rightholder for the original communication.[158] It is necessary that the alleged infringer should have intervened, in full knowledge of the consequences of his or her action, to give access to the copyright work to his or her customers where they would not otherwise be able to access it.[159] It is relevant to consider whether the communication is of a profit-making nature (although this is not determinative).[160] **25-38**

[151] CDPA 1988 s.20.

[152] *Reha Training Gesellschaft v GEMA* (C-117/15) [2017] E.C.D.R. 1 at [35]; *Stichting Brein v Ziggo BV* (C-610/15) at [25].

152A *SGAE v Rafael Hoteles SL* (C-306/05) [2007] Bus. L.R. 521; [2007] E.C.D.R. 2.

153 *Reha Training Gesellschaft v GEMA* (C-117/15) [2017] E.C.D.R. 1 at [38]–[39].

154 Recital 27 to Directive 2001/29; *Stichting Brein v Wullems* (C-527/15) at [41]; *Stichting Brein v Ziggo BV* (C-610/15) at [38].

155 *Reha Training Gesellschaft v GEMA* (C-117/15) [2017] E.C.D.R. 1 at [41]. "Indeterminate" connotes "persons in general" as opposed to specific individuals belonging to a private group while the requirement of a "fairly large number" excludes groups of persons which are too small, or insignificant: *Reha Training Gesellschaft v GEMA* (C-117/15) [2017] E.C.D.R. 1 at [43]. See also *Stichting Brein v Ziggo BV* (C-610/15) at [41].

156 *Reha Training Gesellschaft v GEMA* (C-117/15) [2017] E.C.D.R. 1 at [44]; *Stichting Brein v Ziggo BV* (C-610/15) at [41].

157 *Reha Training Gesellschaft v GEMA* (C-117/15) [2017] E.C.D.R. 1 at [45]; Case C-610/15 *Stichting Brein v Ziggo BV* at [44].

158 *GS Media BV v Sanoma Media Netherlands BV* [2016] E.C.D.R. 25 at [37]. However, there was no mention of this requirement in *AKM v Zürs.net Betriebs GmbH* (C-138/16).

159 *Reha Training Gesellschaft v GEMA* (C-117/15) [2017] E.C.D.R. 1 at [46]; *Stichting Brein v Ziggo BV* (C-610/15) at [34].

160 *GS Media BV v Sanoma Media Netherlands BV* (C-160/15) [2016] E.C.D.R. 25; *Reha Training Gesellschaft v GEMA* (C-117/15) [2017] E.C.D.R. 1 at [49]; *Stichting Brein v Ziggo BV* (C-610/15) at [46].

Examples of communication to the public

Replace paragraph with:

25-39 The law is developing rapidly but the following activities have been held to amount to a communication to the public: the presentation by a publican of broadcasts on a television screen in a public house;[161] the reception of a broadcast signal by a hotel operator and its transmission to the rooms and common parts of the hotel;[162] the provision of hyperlinks to unlicensed content by a person who knows or ought to know that the content is unlicensed;[163] and the operation of a website which indexed, categorised and kept up to date Torrent files identifying unlicensed copies for "sharing"[164]; the operation of various forms of streaming services[164A]; the sale of media players containing links to infringing material[164B]; and making available on a website a photograph which had been copied from another freely available website.[164C] The operator of a service which recorded terrestrial television programmes pursuant to users' online requests and transmitted the recordings to cloud storage was communicating the broadcasts to the public. The process involved a transmission by a different means to the broadcasts and required to be individually authorised.[164D] Acts which do not amount to communication to the public include a public performance by live performers;[165] the playing of sound recordings at a dentist's whose patient list is small;[166] and the provision of hyperlinks to lawfully available content.[167] UK law, which (permissibly[168]) goes beyond what is required by EU law, provides for a general communication to the public right for broadcasters, which includes the simultaneous retransmission of a terrestrial broadcast.[169]

161 *Football Association Premier League Ltd v QC Leisure* (C-403/08) [2012] E.C.D.R. 8. There is an overlap with the public performance right in this respect.

162 *SGAE v Rafael Hoteles SL* (C-306/05) [2007] E.C.D.R. 2; *Phonographic Performance (Ireland) Ltd v Ireland* (C-162/10) [2012] E.C.D.R. 15. The same applied to the provision of television facilities to users of a spa (*OSA v Lecebne lazne Marianske Lazne as* (C-351/12) [2014] E.C.D.R. 25) and a rehabilitation centre (*Reha Training Gesellschaft v GEMA* (C-117/15) [2017] E.C.D.R. 1).

163 *GS Media BV v Sanoma Media Netherlands BV* (C-160/15) [2016] E.C.D.R. 25. A commercial operator will be presumed to have the relevant state of mind; by contrast a non-commercial operator will not. The sale of media players with embedded hyperlinks linking to unlicensed streaming sites was held to be a communication to the public in *Stichting Brein v Wullems* (C-527/15).

[164] *Stichting Brein v Ziggo BV* (C-610/15).

[164A] 176 *ITV Broadcasting Ltd v TV Catchup Ltd* [2011] EWHC 1874 (Pat); *Football Association Premier League v QC Leisure* (C-607/11) [2012] F.S.R. 1; *Football Association Premier League v British Telecommunications Plc* [2017] EWHC 480, [2017] E.C.C. 17; *Union Associations Européenes de Football v British Telecommunications Plc* [2017] EWHC 3414 (Ch).

[164B] *Stichting Brein v Wullems* (C-527/15) [2017] Bus. L.R. 1816; [2017] E.C.D.R. 14.

[164C] *Land Nordrhein-Westfalen v Renckhoff* (C-161/17) [2018] Bus. L.R. 1815; [2018] E.C.D.R. 21.

[164D] *VCast Ltd v RTI SpA* (C-256/16) [2018] E.C.D.R. 8.

[165] *Circul Globus Bucaresti* (C-283/10) [2011] E.C.R. I-12031.

[166] *SCF v Del Corso* (C-1235/10) [2012] E.C.D.R. 16. The patients were a determinate circle, the use was unlikely to affect the dentist's income and the patients were exposed to the music without exercising any choice in the matter. See the analysis of this case in *Reha Training Gesellschaft v GEMA* (C-117/15) [2017] E.C.D.R. 1 at [48], [50], [52].

[167] *Svensson v Retriever Sverige AB* (C-466/12) [2014] E.C.D.R. 9 (same technical means and no new public).

[168] See *C More Entertainment AB v Sandberg* (C-279/13) [2015] E.C.D.R. 15.

[169] CDPA 1988 s.20(1)(c). See *ITV Broadcasting Ltd v TV Catchup Ltd* [2011] EWHC 1874 (Pat); [2011] F.S.R. 40 at [49], [79]; *ITV Broadcasting Ltd v TVCatchup Ltd* (C-607/11) [2013] E.C.D.R. 9.

Reason to believe

Replace footnote 177 with:

[177] *Linpac Mouldings Ltd v Eagleton Direct Export Ltd* [1994] F.S.R. 545 CA and *LA Gear Inc v Hi-Tec Sports Ltd* [1992] F.S.R. 121. In *Cantel Medical (UK) Ltd v ARC Medical Design Ltd* [2018] EWHC 345 (Pat) at [246]–[252] the defendant was held not to have reason to believe where he knew nothing of the existence of the (design) rights in question. It is unclear whether this decision is correct. The case law was reviewed in *F.B.T. Productions, LLC v Let Them Eat Vinyl Distribution Ltd* [2019] EWHC 829 (IPEC) at [35]–[41]. **25-42**

Exceptions to infringement: general

Replace "(f)" with:

(f) The making and certain uses of "accessible copies" for the personal use of disabled persons.[191] The Act permits the making in the prescribed circumstances of copies both by a disabled person and by an "authorised body", that is an educational establishment or a body which is not conducted for profit.[192] **25-43**

[191] CDPA 1988 ss.31A–31F.

[192] "Educational establishment" is defined in CDPA 1988 s.174.

Replace footnote 222: **25-47**

(d) Remedies for infringement of copyright and database right

[222] Remedies for infringement of copyright are set out in CDPA 1988 Ch.VI ss.96–115. Sections 96 to 102 are applied to database right by reg.23 of the Copyright and Rights in Databases Regulations (SI 1997/3032). For the EU principles, in relation to enforcement see *Hollister Inc v Medik Ostomy Supplies Ltd* [2012] EWCA Civ 1419; [2013] Bus. L.R. 428; [2013] F.S.R. 24 and *Merck KGaA v Merck Sharp & Doehme Corp* [2017] EWCA Civ 1834; [2018] E.T.M.R. 10.

Civil remedies

After "copyright and database", add:

right **25-47**

Injunction

Replace footnote 246 with:

[246] See most recently *Twentieth Century Fox Film Corp v SKY UK Ltd* [2015] EWHC 1082 and *Football* **25-48**

Association Premier League Ltd v British Telecommunications Plc [2017] EWHC 480 (Ch); [2017] E.C.C. 17 (streaming servers). An innocent ISP will normally be entitled to be indemnified against the costs of complying with such an order by the rightholder: *Cartier International AG v British Telecommunications Plc* [2018] UKSC 28; [2018] 1 W.L.R. 3259. For the CJEU's jurisprudence, see *UPC Telekabel Wien GmbH v Constantin Film Verleih GmbH, Wega Filmproduktionsesellschaft mbH* (C-314/12) [2014] E.C.D.R. 12. See also *McFadden v Sony Music Entertainment Germany GmbH* (C-484/14) [2016] E.C.D.R. 26: it may be permissible for a court to require an operator of a public wireless network which has been used to download infringing copies to require users to identify themselves as a condition of getting access.

Damages or account of profits

Replace paragraph with:

25-49 A successful claimant is entitled to an inquiry as to damages[247] or, in the alternative, may choose an account of an infringer's profits.[248] As to damages, where a defendant competes with the claimant, the claimant will be entitled to his loss of profit on sales which would have been made by him but where the claimant exploits the work by licensing, he will be entitled to recover a royalty based on what a willing licensor and willing licensee would have agreed.[249] Loss of profits must be proved and it will not necessarily be assumed that every sale made by a defendant would have been made by the claimant.[250] In cases in which the claimant does not exploit the work, the court will be left to make a crude estimate of a reasonable royalty or lump sum.[250A] Damages will sometimes be based on the diminished value of the copyright in the claimant's hands.[251] There is a general discretion to award "additional" damages. The discretion is unfettered but relevant considerations are whether the infringement is flagrant and any benefit accruing to the defendant from it.[252] Where copyright is subject to an exclusive licence, the terms of the licence are taken into account in assessing damages and there is provision for securing that the copyright owner and exclusive licensee do not between them recover double damages.[253] Damages must be attributable to the infringement so where the damage is caused by the use of the ideas in a copied work rather than the text of the work itself, substantial damages will not arise. However, a fairly substantial sum may be awarded for the right to use the work.[254] There is no provision in the Copyright Act to provide a remedy in respect of groundless threats to bring legal proceedings for copyright infringement.[255]

[247] *Glyn v Weston Feature Film Co* [1916] 1 Ch. 261. The tort test of remoteness applies to damages for copyright infringement: *Claydon Architectural Metalwork Ltd v D.J. Higgins & Sons Ltd* [1997] F.S.R. 475. See also Enforcement Directive (2004/48/EC) art.13. As matters stand, the only real change wrought by this provision is to provide that damages may include "unfair profits" and that there can be recovery for "moral prejudice", in each case where there is knowledge or reason to believe. "Unfair profits" were discussed in *Ghias v Grill'O Express Ltd* [2018] EWHC 3445 (IPEC). The meaning of "moral prejudice" is not clear. See *Liffers v Producciones Mandarina SL* (C-99/15) [2016] E.C.D.R. 22 and *Henderson v All Around the World Recordings Ltd* [2014] EWHC 3087 (IPEC).

[248] *Pike v Nicholas* (1870) L.R. 5 Ch. 251 at 260. See also *Potton Ltd v Yorkclose Ltd* [1990] F.S.R. 11. For when the infringer can deduct general overheads, see *OOO Abbott v Design and Display Ltd* [2016] EWCA Civ 98; [2016] F.S.R. 27; *Jack Wills Ltd v House of Fraser (Stores) Ltd* [2016] EWHC 626 (Ch). The claimant is entitled to sufficient information to make an informed choice between damages and profits before electing: *Island Records Inc v Tring International Plc* [1996] 1 W.L.R. 1256; *Brugger v Medicaid Ltd* [1996] F.S.R. 362.

[249] *General Tire and Rubber Co v Firestone Tyre and Rubber Co* [1975] 1 W.L.R. 819.

[250] *Columbia Pictures v Robinson* [1988] F.S.R. 531. The court will not require certainty of proof and will often adopt the maxim omnia praesumuntur contra spoliatorem ("all things are presumed against a wrongdoer"): see *Infabrics Ltd v Jaytex Ltd* [1985] F.S.R. 75.

[250A] For a review of the case law on notional licence fees, see *Reformation Publishing Company Ltd v Cruiseco Ltd* [2018] EWHC 2761(Ch); [2019] Bus. L.R. 78.

[251] For discussion see *Sutherland Publishing Co Ltd v Caxton Publishing Co Ltd* [1936] Ch. 323; *Fenning Film Service v Wolverhampton, etc. Cinemas* [1914] 3 K.B. 1171; *Birn Bros Ltd v Keene & Co Ltd* [1918] 2 Ch. 281; *Ash v Dickie* [1936] Ch. 655.

[252] CDPA 1988 s.97(2). Such a claim must be pleaded and grounds given. The following points arise from *Phonographic Performance Ltd v Ellis* [2018] EWCA Civ 2812, [2019] F.S.R. 15: additional damages may be partly or wholly punitive (at [37]); they are consistent with the Enforcement Directive but having regard to the CJEU"s decision in *OTK v SPF* (C-367/15) [2017] E.C.D.R. 16 a particularly egregious award of exemplary damages may be an abuse of rights (at [42]); an infringement which is also a contempt of court will usually be flagrant (at [60]); flagrancy implies scandalous conduct or deceit (at [61]). Additional damages can be important where compensatory damages are small, as in *Nottinghamshire Healthcare NHS Trust v News Group Newspapers Ltd* [2002] EWHC 409 (Ch); [2002] E.M.L.R. 33. Often a "mark up" on ordinary damages is awarded: see, e.g. *Peninsular Business Service Ltd v Citation plc* [2004] F.S.R. 17 (100% mark up). Insulting behaviour may well give rise to additional damages under the section. *Beloff v Pressdram Ltd* [1973] 1 All E.R. 241. So will deceitful and treacherous conduct; *Nichols Advanced Vehicle Systems Inc v Rees* [1979] R.P.C. 127; *ZYX Music v King* [1995] 3 All E.R. 1; cf. *Ravenscroft v Herbert* [1980] R.P.C. 193. There can be no claim for additional damages where the claimant has elected an account of profits: *Redrow Homes Ltd v Betts Brothers Plc* [1999] 1 A.C. 197 HL.

[253] CDPA 1988 s.102(4).

[254] *USP Plc v London General Holdings Ltd* [2005] EWCA Civ 931; [2006] F.S.R. 6.

[255] There is, however, provision for threats actions in respect of unregistered UK design right: s.253. Nor was there any provision under the 1956 Act but nevertheless an interlocutory injunction was granted in *Jaybeam Ltd v Abru Aluminium Ltd* [1976] R.P.C. 308. However, an action claiming damages for inducing a breach of contract by threats of bringing a copyright infringement action was struck out: *Granby Marketing Services Ltd v Interlego AG* [1984] R.P.C. 209.

Prohibition of importation of copies—customs powers

Replace footnote 262 with:

[262] CDPA 1988 s.111(3A). See Customs Notice 34 para.8.1. **25-51**

Criminal sanctions

Replace footnote 263 with:

[263] CDPA 1988 s.107. Criminal proceedings are not as widely employed as the civil remedies but the criminal courts treat counterfeiting in particular as a serious offence of dishonesty meriting custodial sentences. See, e.g. *R. v Carter* (1992) 13 Cr. App. R. (S.) 576, [1993] F.S.R. 303; *R. v Evans* [2017] EWCA Crim 139, [2017] 1 Cr. App. R. (S.) 56. **25-52**

3. Moral Rights

Right to object to derogatory treatment of work

Replace footnote 290 with:

[290] The following are excluded from "treatment": translation of a literary or dramatic work or an arrangement or transposition of a musical work involving no more than a change in key or register: CDPA 1988 s.80(2)(a). But such "treatments" may infringe copyright. As to what may constitute derogatory treatment, see: *Morrison Leahy Music Ltd v Lightbond Ltd* [1993] E.M.L.R. 144. For examples from other jurisdictions see Laddie, Prescott and Vitoria, *The Modern Law of Copyright*, 5th edn (London: LexisNexis, 2018), para.38.39; Adeney, *The Moral Rights of Authors and Performers—An International and Comparative Analysis* (Oxford: OUP, 2006); Davies and Garnett, *Moral Rights*, 2nd edn (London: Sweet & Maxwell, 2016). **25-56**

4. Collective Management, Control of Licensing and Competition

Collective management of copyright

Replace footnote 309 with:

[309] The Copyright and Rights in Performances (Licensing of Orphan Works) Regulations 2014 (SI 2014/2863). A "work" is defined as an orphan work where the right owner or right owners cannot be identified or located. Take up so far has been limited. Libraries, museums and similar organisations can benefit from the EU orphan works scheme: CDPA 1988 Sch. ZA1. **25-60**

Copyright Tribunal—control of licensing and competition

Replace paragraph with:

25-62 The Copyright Tribunal[316] is a statutory tribunal consisting of a legally qualified chairman and two deputy chairmen appointed by the Lord Chancellor and up to eight ordinary members appointed by the Secretary of State. Its principal role is to exercise competition law constraints on certain types of copyright licensing in the media and entertainment industries,[317] and persons requiring licences under those rights, but it extends to licensing schemes for the rental of films or computer programs; reprographic copying; recordings made for educational purposes; licences relating to sound recordings, films or broadcasts, which include any entertainment or other event; payments in respect of retransmission; applications to settle royalties payable in respect of the rental of sound recordings, films and computer programs; applications for settling licences of right; and other minor rights.[318] References to the Tribunal are mainly of three sorts: those concerned with the reasonableness or otherwise of licence schemes maintained by the licensing bodies; claims for a licence by persons refused licences under a scheme; and claims for licences, or for more favourable licences, by persons outside any existing scheme.[319] Participation in a licensing scheme avoids infringement.[320] The Tribunal has determined numerous issues in relation to licensing schemes.[321] An appeal from the Tribunal lies to the High Court but only on a point of law.[322]

[316] CDPA 1988 s.145.

[317] CPDA 1988 ss.145–146 and s.152 (on appeals from the tribunal). See the standard copyright texts for further details.

[318] CPDA 1988 ss.130, 131, 132, 133, 134, 135A to 135H, 142, 144, 144A and 149. The Broadcasting Act 1990 expanded the jurisdiction of the Copyright Tribunal to settle terms of payment for the right to reproduce programme listing information: see *News Group Newspapers Ltd v Independent Television Publications Ltd* [1993] R.P.C. 178. The Tribunal has the power to rule on the terms on which acts restricted by non-UK copyrights are licensed if the licensing scheme treats such acts as commercially indivisible from acts restricted by UK copyrights: *British Broadcasting Corp v Sky UK Ltd* [2018] EWHC 2931 (Ch) at [105]–[115].

[319] The Copyright Tribunal has jurisdiction in other special cases: e.g. educational use (CDPA 1988 s.139).

[320] CDPA 1988 ss.123(2), (5), 128(1) and 136.

[321] See its website *https://www.gov.uk/government/publications/copyright-tribunal-decisions-and-orders* [Accessed 23 April 2019].

[322] CDPA 1988 s.152.

Competition law

Replace paragraph with:

25-63 Refusals to grant licences under a copyright (or indeed any of the rights considered in this Chapter) can, in very special circumstances, be contrary to competition law, especially applying art.102 of the Treaty on the Functioning of the European Union (TFEU) or the Competition Act 1998.[323] Conduct by CMOs may also engage art.102.[323A] Agreements between right holders and other practices may be prohibited by art.101 TFEU or under the Competition Act 1998. Readers are referred to specialist texts for details.[324]

[323] See *Volvo v Veng* [1989] 4 C.M.L.R. 122; *CIRCA v Renault* [1990] 4 C.M.L.R. 265; *RTE v EC Commission* [1995] I-E.C.R. 743; *Chiron Corp v Murex Diagnostics Ltd (No.2)* [1994] F.S.R. 187; *IMS Health GmbH v NDC Health GmbH & Co KG* [2004] C.M.L.R. 28, CJEU.

[323A] See *Autortiesibu un Komunicesanas Konsultaciju Agentura-Latvijas Autoru Apvieniba v Konkurences Padome* (C-177/16) [2018] E.C.D.R. 11 (alleged abusive pricing).

[324] See the standard copyright texts.

Replace footnote 373: **25-70**

6. UNREGISTERED DESIGNS

[373] See: *Russell-Clarke and Howe on Industrial Designs*, 9th edn (2016); Stone, *European Union Design Law*, 2nd edn (2016); *Copinger and Skone James on Copyright*, 17th edn (2016), Ch.13.

(b) UK unregistered design right

Background

Replace footnote 384 with:

[384] With effect from 28 July 2016 with a transitional period until 28 January 2017: Enterprise and Regulatory Reform Act 2013 (Commencement No.10 and Saving Provisions) Order 2016 (SI 2016/593). See the Government's Guidance at*https://assets.publishing.service.gov.uk/government/uploads/system/uploads/attachment_data/file/606207/160408_guidance_s52_final_web_accessible.pdf* [Accessed 21 September 2018]. **25-71**

UK unregistered design right

Replace footnote 385 with:

[385] Prior to 1 October 2014 the words "any aspect of" appeared between "the design of" and "the shape or configuration". The change, which applies to acts of infringement which are alleged to have been committed on or after 1 October 2014, precludes claims in respect of disembodied features, arbitrarily selected, which are not, in design terms, parts of the design: *Neptune (Europe) Ltd v Devol Kitchens Ltd* [2017] EWHC 2172 (Pat); [2017] E.C.D.R. 25 at [33], [42]. See *DKH Retail Ltd v H. Young (Operations) Ltd* [2014] EWHC 4034 (IPEC); [2015] F.S.R. 21 at [10]; *Whitby Specialist Vehicles Ltd v Yorkshire Specialist Vehicles Ltd* [2014] EWHC 4242 (Pat); [2015] E.C.D.R. 11 at [41]; *Action Storage Systems Ltd v G-Force Europe.Com Ltd* [2016] EWHC 3151 (IPEC); [2017] F.S.R. 18 at [12]–[16]. **25-72**

Jurisdiction of the Comptroller and the court

Replace footnote 427 with:

[427] CDPA 1988 ss.253–253D. **25-80**

Change title of paragraph: **25-81**

Unjustified groundless threats of legal proceedings

Replace paragraph with:

A remedy exists, as with patents and registered designs, where unjustified threats of legal proceedings are made in respect of the alleged infringement of a design right.[428] **25-81**

[428] CDPA 1988 ss.253–253A. For examples of cases involving an earlier version of s.253, see *Landor & Hawa International Ltd v Azure Designs Ltd* [2006] EWCA Civ 1285; [2007] F.S.R. 9, and *Grimme Landmaschinenfabrik GmbH & Co KG v Scott* [2010] EWCA Civ 1110; [2011] F.S.R. 7.

(c) Unregistered Community design

Scope of protection

Replace paragraph with:

An unregistered Community design[429] protects a design for the appearance of a product or part of a product resulting from "the features of, in particular, the lines, contours, colours, shape, texture or materials of the product itself and/or its **25-82** ornamentation".[430] A Community design may not subsist in features of appearance dictated solely by their technical function[431] or which permit the article to be connected to or placed around, in or against another product so that either may perform its function.[432] Protection does not extend to component parts which are not visible during normal use of the product.[433] To qualify for protection, a design must be "new" and have "individual character".[434] The scope of and conditions for protection for registered Community designs are by and large the same (apart from the requirement for registration). Accordingly, registered design cases are referred to in the following paragraphs.

[429] See the summary of the law in the Community registered designs context in *Whitby Specialist Vehicles Ltd v Yorkshire Specialist Vehicles Ltd* [2014] EWHC 4242 (Pat); [2015] E.C.D.R. 11 at [20]–[30].

[430] Regulation 6/2002/EC art.3(a). Appearance is the decisive factor for a design: *DOCERAM GmbH v CeramTec GmbH* (C-395/16) [2018] E.C.D.R. 13 at [25].

[431] The meaning of this difficult expression has finally been resolved by the CJEU. Protection is excluded where the need to fulfil a technical function is the only factor determining the choice of a feature and considerations of another nature, in particular those related to the product's visual aspect, have not played a role: *DOCERAM GmbH v CeramTec GmbH ("Doceram")* (C-395/16) [2018] E.C.D.R. 13 at [26]. Protection will be excluded even if other designs fulfilling the same function exist: *Doceram* at [31]. In determining whether the technical function exclusion applies, the court must take account of all relevant objective circumstances which may be indicative of the reasons which dictated the choice of the feature in issue together with information on the use of the product concerned and the existence of alternative designs which fulfil the same technical function. There is no need to base the decision on the perception of an "objective observer": *Doceram* at [35]–[38].

[432] Regulation 6/2002/EC art.8(2). See for example *Camatic Pty Ltd v Bluecube Ltd* [2012] E.C.D.R. 12, in which a Community registered design was held invalid under this so-called "must-fit" exception. Designs "serving the purpose of allowing the multiple assembly or connection of mutually interchangeable products within a modular system" are not excepted: art.8(3).

[433] Regulation 6/2002/EC art.4(1) and Recital (12); *Groupe Nivelles v OHIM* (T-15/13) [2016] E.C.D.R. 11 at [37].

[434] Regulation 6/2002/EC art.4. Prior art can include products which have a similar appearance to the registered design but which were designed for a different purpose: *Gimex International Groupe Import Export v Chill Bag Co Ltd* [2012] EWPCC 31; [2012] E.C.D.R. 25. A design applied to or incorporated in a product which becomes a component part in a complex product is only to be considered new or of individual character if it remains visible during normal use by the end user, and to the extent that the visible parts of that product are new and have individual character. See, e.g. *Kwang Yang Motor Co Ltd v OHIM* [2012] E.C.D.R. 2, General Court.

Novelty

Replace paragraph with:

25-83 The test for novelty is whether the design differs "only in immaterial details" from designs made available to the public before the design itself was first made available to the public.[435] A design is made available if it is published, exhibited, used in trade or otherwise disclosed except where these events could not reasonably have become known in the normal course of business to the circles specialised in the sector concerned, operating within the Community.[436]

[435] Regulation 6/2002/EC art.5.

[436] art.7(1). Disclosures only made in confidence are ignored (art.7(1)). The question whether the events could reasonably have become known (etc.) is one of fact in each case and events occurring outside the Community are not excluded from consideration if they could reasonably have become known etc.: *Senz Technologies BV v OHIM* (T-22/13 and 23/13) [2015] E.C.D.R. 19 at [27]. The "sector concerned" is that of the prior design: *Green Lane Products Ltd v PMS International Group Ltd* [2008] EWCA Civ 358; [2008] E.C.D.R. 15. Prior designs for any type of product can be taken into account: *Easy Sanitary Solutions v Group Nivelles* (C-361/15 P) [2018] E.C.D.R. 4 at [104], [135]. However, there is no requirement to prove that the informed user would know the product in which the earlier design is incorporated

or to which it is applied: [134]. See also *L'Oréal Société Anonyme v RN Ventures Ltd* [2018] EWHC 173 (Pat); [2018] F.S.R. 20 at [151]–[152].

Individual character: general

Replace footnote 437 with:

[437] *Karen Millen Fashions Ltd v Dunnes Stores* (C-345/13) [2016] E.C.D.R. 13; *Whitby Specialist Vehicles Ltd v Yorkshire Specialist Vehicles Ltd* [2014] EWHC 4242 (Pat); [2015] E.C.D.R. 11 at [25]. See also *Pulseon OY v Garmin (Europe) Ltd* [2019] EWCA Civ 138; [2019] E.C.D.R. 8 at [19]–[21]. Prior designs for any type of product can be taken into account: *Easy Sanitary Solutions v Group Nivelles* (C-361/15 P) [2018] E.C.D.R. 4. **25-84**

The "informed user"

Replace footnote 441 with:

[441] *Samsung Electronics (UK) Ltd v Apple Inc* [2012] EWHC 1882 (Pat); [2013] E.C.D.R. 1, summarising the EU case law, especially *PepsiCo, Inc v Grupo Promer Mon Graphic SA* (C-281/10) [2012] F.S.R. 5 at [53]–[59]. This summary was approved on appeal ([2012] EWCA Civ 1339; [2013] F.S.R. 9) and adopted in *Pulseon OY v Garmin (Europe) Ltd* [2019] EWCA Civ 138; [2019] E.C.D.R. 8 at [16]. **25-85**

Relevant factors

Replace footnote 450 with:

[450] *Shenzhen Taiden Industrial Co Ltd v OHIM* (T-153/08) at [58]; *Pulseon OY v Garmin (Europe) Ltd* [2019] EWCA Civ 138; [2019] E.C.D.R. 8 at [22]–[23]. **25-86**

Infringement

Replace paragraph with:

The proprietor has the exclusive right to "use" the design for products whose overall impression on the informed user does not differ from the design. However, there can be no infringement of an unregistered Community design without copying. If that is established, infringement involves very much the same questions as arise in connection with whether the design relied on has individual character. All other things being equal, a design should receive a broader scope of protection where the designer had a greater degree of freedom and vice versa;[452] while a design which is markedly different from the design corpus should receive a broader scope of protection than one which differs only slightly from the design corpus.[453] "Using" the design includes the making, offering, putting on the market, importing, exporting or using of a product, or stocking a product for those purposes.[454] **25-88**

[452] *Whitby Specialist Vehicles Ltd v Yorkshire Specialist Vehicles Ltd* [2014] EWHC 4242 (Pat); [2015] E.C.D.R. 11 at [26]: (applying art.9(2) of the Designs Directive, which is in the same terms as art.10(2) of Regulation 6/2002/EC). However this does not apply where the striking elements of the design are those where there is little design freedom, in particular because of technical requirements: see at [29].

[453] *Whitby Specialist Vehicles Ltd v Yorkshire Specialist Vehicles Ltd* [2014] EWHC 4242 (Pat); [2015] E.C.D.R. 11 at [27]–[28]: (referring to Recital (13) to the Designs Directive, which is in the same terms as Recital (14) to Regulation 6/2002/EC). However this does not apply where the striking elements of the design are those where there is little design freedom, in particular because of technical requirements: see at [29]. See also *L'Oréal Société Anonyme v RN Ventures Ltd* [2018] EWHC 173 (Pat); [2018] F.S.R. 20 at [155].

[454] Regulation 6/2002/EC art.19.

Defence

Replace paragraph with:

Article 110 of Regulation 6/2002 excludes protection for designs which constitute **25-89** a component part of a complex product used for the purpose of the repair of that complex product so as to restore its original appearance. It is not necessary in order for the defence to operate that the protected design should be dependent on the appearance of the complex product.[455] However, the replacement part must have an identical visual appearance to that of the part which was originally incorporated into the complex product when it was placed on the market.[455A] Moreover, in order to come within the defence, the manufacturer or seller of the allegedly infringing part is under a duty of diligence as regards compliance by downstream users with the conditions laid down in art.110. This duty is onerous.[455B] Additional defences are provided for in art.20 for acts done privately and for non-commercial purposes, acts done for experimental purposes and acts for the purpose of making citations or teaching. The citation and teaching defences apply in a commercial context and are capable of extending to the display of images of a product protected by a design in advertisements for other products intended to be used as accessories. However, art.20(c) makes clear that the defence only applies if the display is compatible with fair trade practice, does not unduly prejudice the normal exploitation of the design and mentions the source.[455C]

[455] *Acacia Srl v Pneusgarda Srl ("Acacia")* (C-397/16 and 435/16) [2018] Bus. L.R. 927 at [29]–[54].

[455A] See *Acacia* at [55]–[78].

[455B] See *Acacia* at [85]–[88].

[455C] See *Nintendo Co Ltd v Bigben Interactive GmbH* (C-24/16) [2018] E.C.D.R. 3 at [77]–[85].

Remedies

Replace paragraph with:

25-91 The proprietor of a design which has been found to be infringed is entitled to substantially the same relief as is given to the proprietor of any other intellectual property right in similar circumstances. Injunctive relief in respect of Community designs can be far-reaching—for example, a Community-wide injunction was obtained by Apple Inc against Samsung Electronics in the Düsseldorf District Court in Germany in August 2011, in respect of tablet computers said to infringe Apple's iPad registered design.[457] Unjustified threats of infringement are actionable.[457A]

[457] For an example of an interim injunction see *Utopia Tableware Ltd v BBP Marketing Ltd* [2013] EWPCC 15. The court can order publication of a finding of infringement where necessary to deter further infringement and to contribute to the awareness of the public at large. It can also order publication of a finding that a product does not infringe if there is a real need to dispel commercial uncertainty: *Samsung Electronics (UK) Ltd v Apple Inc* [2012] EWCA Civ 1339; [2013] F.S.R. 9 at [71], [75]. For some of the jurisdiction issues which may arise in infringement proceedings, see *Bayerische Motoren Werke AG v Acacia Srl* (C-433/16) [2017] E.C.D.R. 18 and *Nintendo Co Ltd v Bigben Interactive GmbH* (C-24/16) [2018] E.C.D.R. 3.

[457A] Community Design Regulations 2005 (SI 2005/2339) regs 2–2F.

7. Registered Designs

Registration

Replace paragraph with:

25-93 The registrar of UK registered designs is the Comptroller-General of Patents, and the register is kept at the Intellectual Property Office. Registered Community designs are registered at the European Intellectual Property Office (formerly OHIM). Both registers may be searched online.[460] The date for considering whether a design is novel or has individual character is the date of filing of the application for registration or the date of priority if priority is claimed.[461] Disclosures by the designer, his successor in title or a third person as a result of information provided or action taken by the designer or his successor in title during the 12-month period prior to the date of filing or the date of priority are ignored.[462] Provision is made for registered designs to be invalidated if they do not satisfy the requirements for registration and on certain other grounds.[463] A registered design expires five years after registration unless renewed. Renewal may take place for up to four further five-year periods.[464]

[460] See *https://euipo.europa.eu/ohimportal/en/databases* [Accessed 23 April 2019] and *https://www.gov.uk/search-registered-design* [Accessed 23 April 2019].

[461] Council Regulation 6/2002/EC art.5(1)(b); 6(1)(b); RDA 1949 s.1B(2), (3), (7). Priority may be claimed where an application for a design right or utility model has been filed in or for any State Party to the Paris Convention for the Protection of Industrial Property or the Agreement establishing the World Trade Organisation or certain other States: Council Regulation 6/2002 art.41(1), (5); RDA 1949 s.14. Article 44 of the Council regulation provides for exhibition priority.

[462] Council Regulation 6/2002/EC art.7(2); RDA 1949 s.1B(5)(b), (6)(c)–(e).

[463] Council Regulation 6/2002/EC arts 24–26; RDA ss.11ZA–11ZF.

[464] Council Regulation 6/2002/EC art.12. RDA 1949 s.8.

The scope of the registration

Replace paragraph with:

The extent of the protection afforded by a particular registered design ultimately depends on the proper interpretation of the registration in issue and in particular of the images included in that registration.[465] The applicant is entitled to choose the level of generality at which the design is to be considered. If the applicant chooses too general a level, the design may be invalidated by the prior art. If the applicant chooses too specific a level, he or she may not be protected against similar designs.[466] EUIPO has issued guidance as to the manner in which designs should be represented and the conventions to be used, for example to indicate what is and is not part of the design.[467] In general, where a design is shown in colours, the colours are claimed; if it is shown in monochrome, it covers all colours.[468] However, a monochrome CAD drawing depicting a shape part of which is in grey and part of which is in black has been held to amount to a claim for a shape in two contrasting colours.[469] It seems that absence of decoration can be a feature of a registered design if that is what the images, properly interpreted, show.[470] **25-94**

[465] *Magmatic Ltd v PMS International Ltd* [2016] UKSC 12; [2016] 4 All E.R. 1027 at [30]. For the importance of clear representations, see *Mast-Jägermeister SE v EUIPO* (C-217/17 P) [2018] E.C.D.R. 20 at [55].

[466] See per Lewison J in *Procter & Gamble Co v Reckitt Benckiser (UK) Ltd* [2006] EWHC 3154 (Ch); [2007] E.C.D.R. 4 at [48], referred to with approval in *Magmatic Ltd v PMS International Ltd* [2016] UKSC 12; [2016] 4 All E.R. 1027 at [30].

[467] See *https://www.gov.uk/government/publications/designs-practice-notice-dpn-116/dpn-116-guidance-on-use-of-representations-when-filing-registered-design-applications* [Accessed 21 September 2018] and *https://euipo.europa.eu/ohimportal/en/design-guidelines* [Accessed 21 September 2018]. See also Schlötelburg *The Community Design: First Experience with Registrations* [2003] E.I.P.R. 383, which was relied on by the Supreme Court in *Magmatic Ltd v PMS International Ltd* [2016] UKSC 12; [2016] 4 All E.R. 1027 at [31].

[468] *Magmatic Ltd v PMS International Ltd* [2016] UKSC 12; [2016] 4 All E.R. 1027 at [34].

[469] *Magmatic Ltd v PMS International Ltd* [2016] UKSC 12; [2016] 4 All E.R. 1027 at [53].

[470] *Magmatic Ltd v PMS International Ltd* [2016] UKSC 12; [2016] 4 All E.R. 1027 at [40]–[50] (obiter).

Infringement

Replace paragraph with:

The same acts amount to infringement of a registered design as amount to **25-97** infringement of an unregistered Community design.[473] In this case, however, it is not necessary to show copying. A central issue in many infringement cases is the scope of the design as evidenced by the representations filed.[474] There is a defence of "prior use".[475]

[473] See para.25-88. For guidance as to the conduct of infringement proceedings, see *Spin Master Ltd v PMS International Group* [2017] EWHC 1477 (Pat); [2017] F.S.R. 44. For the sequence in which the issues should be determined, see *Pulseon OY v Garmin (Europe) Ltd* [2018] EWHC 47 (Ch) at [17]. For the correct approach to comparing a registered Community design with an alleged infringement, see *Cantel Medical (UK) Limited v ARC Medical Design Ltd* [2018] EWHC 345 (Pat) at [181]–[182].

[474] See para.25-94.

[475] RDA 1949 s.7B; Council Regulation 6/2002 art.22.

25-101 *Change title of paragraph:*

Unjustified groundless threats of legal proceedings

Replace paragraph with:

25-101 A remedy exists, as with patents and design rights, where unjustified threats of legal proceedings are made in respect of alleged infringements of registered designs.[480]

[480] RDA 1949 ss.26–26F.

8. REGISTERED TRADE MARKS

(a) Introduction

Trade mark infringement and passing off

Replace footnote 482 with:

25-102 [482] *R. (on the application of British American Tobacco UK Ltd) v Secretary of State for Health* [2016] EWCA Civ 1182; [2018] Q.B. 149 (plain packaging for cigarettes).

Replace footnote 483:

The Trade Marks Act 1994[483]

25-103 [483] See Mellor, et al., *Kerly's Law of Trade Marks and Trade Names*, 15th edn (Sweet & Maxwell, 2011) and Morcom, et al., *The Modern Law of Trade Marks*, 5th edn (Butterworth, 2016). There is only scope in this work to provide a short outline of the law and reference to the leading cases. Note that there is a parallel system of EU Trade Marks, established by Council Regulation 40/94/EEC, which was codified by Council Regulation (EC) 207/2009 and has now been amended by Regulation (EU) 2015/2424 (see fn.625) to which similar principles apply thanks to harmonising directives, the latest of which is Directive 2015/2436/EC (see fn.627). Such EUTMs have effect throughout the EU, and may be obtained by application to the European Intellectual Property Office (formerly the Office for the Harmonization of the Internal Market ("OHIM")) in Alicante, Spain. The EUIPO website contains comprehensive explanations of the types of intellectual property protection available: *https://euipo.europa.eu/ohimportal/en/home* [Accessed 2 May 2019]. Further discussion of this and international applications are beyond the scope of this work. For procedure generally, see Trade Marks Rules 2008 and CPR Pt 63 PD—Intellectual Property Claims, and the trade marks section of the UKIPO's website: *https://www.gov.uk/topic/intellectual-property/trade-marks* [Accessed 2 May 2019].

The meaning of "trade mark"

Replace paragraph with:

25-104 In the 1994 Act, a "trade mark" is widely defined as any sign capable of being represented graphically which is capable of distinguishing goods or services of one undertaking from those of other undertakings.[491] A trade mark may, in particular, consist of words (including personal names), designs, letters, numerals or the shape of goods or their packaging. It may also consist of smells or sounds.[492]

[491] TMA 1994 s.1(1). There are special provisions governing "collective marks" (s.49), "certification marks" (s.50) and European Union Trade Marks (ss.51 and 52). The requirement that the mark be capable of graphical representation is removed by the new Regulation with effect from 1 October 2017. The Court of Justice has held that the representation of the layout of a retail store (such as an Apple "flagship" store) may be registered as a trade mark, provided that it is capable of distinguishing the goods and services of one undertaking from another: *Apple Inc v Deutsches Patent und Markenamt* (C-421/13) [2014] Bus. L.R. 962; [2014] E.T.M.R. 48.

[492] In *L'Oréal SA v Bellure* [2007] EWCA Civ 968; [2008] E.T.M.R. 1 at [127] Jacob LJ, obiter, doubted whether a fragrance can be registered as a trade mark. A chocolate company was not entitled to register a shade of purple as "the predominant colour applied to the whole of the visible surface ... of the packaging of the goods", since the proposed "sign" in fact lacked clarity, precision, self-containment, durability and objectivity: *Société Des Produits Nestlé SA v Cadbury UK Ltd* [2013] EWCA Civ 1174; [2014] 1 All E.R. 1079, and the offending wording was not allowed to be deleted from the registration, since it was a single mark rather than a series mark, and so the mark as a whole was invalid: *Cadbury UK Ltd v Comptroller General of Patents Designs and Trade Marks* [2016] EWHC 796 (Ch); [2017] F.S.R. 2; appeal dismissed: [2018] EWCA Civ 2715, [2019] F.S.R. 7. The same principles were applied in finding a trade mark for purple inhalers invalid in *Glaxo Wellcome UK Ltd (t/a Allen & Hanburys) v Sandoz Ltd* [2017] EWCA Civ 335; [2017] F.S.R. 33. Likewise in *Red Bull GmbH/Marques v EUIPO/Optimum Mark sp. z o.o., (General Court)* (T-101/15 and T-102/15) [2011] E.T.M.R. 11, in which protection was claimed "for the colours blue (RAL 5002) and silver (RAL 9006). The ratio of the colours is approximately 50%–50%."

(b) Registration

Registration of trade marks and applications for registration of trade marks

Replace paragraph with:

An application for registration of a trade mark is made to the registrar[493] who examines whether the application for registration of a trade mark satisfies the requirements of the Act.[494] **25-105**

(a) *Distinctiveness.* The chief purpose of a registered trade mark is to identify the goods on which it is used with its proprietor. It must therefore be distinctive. Of the restrictions on registrability, the most important relate to the distinctiveness of the proposed mark.[495] Marks which are not capable of distinguishing or which are "devoid of any distinctive character" may not be registered. The same applies to signs which are descriptive of the goods or services for which they are sought to be registered.[496] Signs which consist exclusively of the shape which results from the nature of the goods themselves or the shape of the goods which is necessary to obtain a technical result or the shape which gives substantial value to the goods are also not capable of registration.[497] Marks may acquire distinctive character through use.[498]

(b) *Other restrictions on registration.* There are other restrictions on registrability where the trade mark is of such a nature as to deceive the public or is contrary to public policy or accepted principles of morality.[499] Certain protected emblems (such as Royal Arms) may only be registered in special circumstances.[500] A trade mark may not be registered if or to the extent that the application is made in bad faith.[501]

(c) *Earlier rights.* There are provisions to prevent registration of trade marks which conflict with earlier trade marks and earlier rights, with exceptions in the case of honest concurrent use[502] and consent. Marks may be registered subject to disclaimer or limitations with correspondingly limited effect.[503]

[493] TMA 1994 s.32, which sets out the requirements of an application. The website of the UK Intellectual Property Office is helpful: *https://www.gov.uk/topic/intellectual-property/trade-marks*. There are provisions in the Act concerning claims to priority from applications for protection of a trade mark in a Convention country and other overseas applications (CDPA 1988 ss.35 and 36). As to the meaning of "Convention country", see TMA 1994 s.55(1)(b).

[494] TMA 1994 s.37. The registrar must permit the applicant to amend the application if it appears that the requirements for registrations are not met. Sections 62 to 74 of the Act govern the registrar and the Trade Marks Rules 2008 (as amended) govern procedure before the registrar. Appeals from the registrar lie either to an appointed person or to the court: s.76(1). In *Koninklije Philips Electronics NV v Remington Consumer Products Ltd* [2006] EWCA Civ 16; [2006] F.S.R. 30, the Court of Appeal upheld Rimer J's finding of invalidity of shape marks on the grounds that they consisted exclusively of the shape which was necessary to obtain a technical result but, reversing the judge, held that certain logo marks depicting the shape were distinctive and not excluded from registration. Applicants must identify the goods and services for which the protection of a trade mark is sought with sufficient clarity and precision to enable the competent authorities and economic operators to determine the extent of the protection conferred by the trade mark: *Chartered Institute of Patent Attorneys v Registrar of Trade Marks* (C-307/10) [2013] R.P.C. 11, Grand Chamber.

[495] TMA 1994 s.3(1). Reference should be made to the section for the precise grounds for refusal. There is extensive jurisprudence both from the UK courts and from the Court of First Instance on the requirements for distinctiveness. See for general guidance: *Philips Electronics NV v Remington Consumer Products Ltd* [1999] R.P.C. 809 CA and the judgment of the CJEU Case C-299/99 *Philips Electronics NV v Remington Consumer Products Ltd* [2003] Ch. 159. See also *32Red Plc v WHG (International) Ltd* [2011] EWHC 62 (Ch); [2011] E.T.M.R. 21, with this point upheld on appeal: [2012] EWCA Civ 19; [2012] E.T.M.R. 14. In *JW Spear & Sons Ltd v Zynga Inc* [2012] EWHC 3345 (Ch); [2013] F.S.R. 28 (affirmed: [2013] EWCA Civ 1175; [2014] 1 All E.R. 1093) the claimant's "tile mark" was found to encompass an infinite number of permutations and combinations of letters and numbers on a tile, and was held to lack distinctive character. The mark "NOW TV" in *Starbucks (HK) Ltd v British Sky Broadcasting Group Plc* [2012] EWHC 3074 (Ch); [2013] F.S.R. 29 (affirmed: [2013] EWCA Civ 1465; [2014] F.S.R. 20) was held to be either a characteristic of the television service in question, or else devoid of distinctive character. As to distinctiveness in the case of unusual trade marks such as shapes of goods, see the discussion in *Bongrain SA's TM Application* [2004] EWCA Civ 1690; [2005] R.P.C. 14 (shape of cheese—mark refused). See also *Coca-Cola Co v Office for Harmonisation in the Internal Market (Trade Marks and Designs) (OHIM)* (T-411/14) [2016] E.T.M.R. 25, in which the shape of a bottle without fluting was held to lack distinctive character; *London Taxi Corp Ltd (t/a London Taxi Co) v Fraser-Nash Research Ltd* [2016] EWHC 52 (Ch); [2016] E.T.M.R. 18—shape marks for models of taxi cab lacked distinctive character. This was upheld on appeal: see [2017] EWCA Civ 1729; [2018] F.S.R. 7. The new Regulation and Directive use the broader form of words "shape or another characteristic" in setting out the exclusions corresponding to s.3(2) of the TMA 1994; this change has effect as of 23 March 2016. Distinctiveness and shape marks were discussed in *Mondelez UK Holdings & Services Ltd v EUIPO / Société des produits Nestlé SA* (T-112/13) (General Court) [2017] E.T.M.R. 13.

[496] A mark having a single descriptive meaning is taken to be descriptive even if there are other, non-descriptive, meanings of the mark: *OHIM v Wm Wrigley Jnr Co ("DOUBLEMINT")* (C-191/01) [2004] 1 W.L.R. 1728. The CJEU has ruled that the exclusion for descriptiveness applies to a word mark which comprises the juxtaposition of a descriptive word combination plus a letter sequence which is not in itself descriptive, but which the public will readily perceive as being an abbreviation consisting simply of the first letters of the word combination—see *Alfred Strigl* (Joined cases C-90/11 and C-91/11). The marks in question were "Multi Markets Fund MMF" and "NAI—der Natur-Aktien-Index". In *Fine & Country Ltd v Okotoks Ltd* [2013] EWCA Civ 672; [2014] F.S.R. 11 the mark "FINE AND COUNTRY" was held to be not merely laudatory or descriptive. Contrast *British Shorinji Kempo Federation's Trade Mark Application* [2014] EWHC 285 (Ch), in which the words "shorinji kempo" were held to be generic identifiers of a particular martial art. The prohibition on descriptiveness also extends to indications of geographical origin. Contrast *Luen Fat Metal and Plastic Manufactory Ltd v Jacobs and Turner Ltd (t/a Trespass)* [2019] EWHC 118 (IPEC) in which it was said that the question was whether there was a sufficiently direct and specific link between the sign in issue and the goods, to enable the average consumer immediately to perceive, without further thought, a description of those goods or of one of their characteristics. In *Moreno Marin v Abadia Retuerta SA* (C-139/16) EU:C:2017:518; [2018] Bus. L.R. 431, the sign "*la Milla de Oro*" did not constitute an indication of geographical origin, since it was not accompanied by a geographical name designating the actual physical location where the product could be found—contrast *J Portugal Ramos Vinhos SA v Adega Cooperativa de Borba CRL* (C-629/17) [2019] E.T.M.R. 14. A similar challenge to the validity of the mark "Sivec" for quarried marble failed in *Mermeren Kombinat AD v Fox Marble Holdings Plc* [2017] EWHC 1408 (IPEC); [2018] F.S.R. 1. The mark had acquired distinctiveness as a trade mark by the time of its registration, whereas its parallel status as the name of a geographical location was too obscure to invalidate the registration.

[497] TMA 1994 s.3(2). See *Philips Electronics NV v Remington Consumer Products Ltd* [1999] R.P.C. 809 CA, which resulted in a reference to the CJEU. Subsequently in *Koninklijke Philips NV v Remington Consumer Products Ltd* [2006] EWCA Civ 16; [2006] F.S.R. 30, the Court of Appeal upheld Rimer J's finding of invalidity of shape marks on the grounds that they consisted exclusively of the shape which was necessary to obtain a technical result but, reversing the judge, held that certain logo marks depicting the shape were distinctive and not excluded from registration. In relation to the technical result exclusion, see *Lego Juris A/S v Office for Harmonisation in the Internal Market (Trade Marks and Designs) (OHIM)* (C-48/09 P) [2010] E.T.M.R. 63 CJEU (Grand Chamber). "Technical result" must be interpreted as referring only to the manner in which the goods function, not the way they are manufactured: *Société*

des Produits Nestlé SA v Cadbury UK Ltd (C-215/14) [2015] E.T.M.R. 50; [2016] F.S.R. 8. See also *Simba Toys GmbH & Co KG v EUIPO* (C-30/15 P) [2007] E.T.M.R. 6 (shape of Rubik's cube). The General Court in *Novartis AG v EUIPO* EU:T:2018:48 (T-44/16) upheld EUIPO's decision to declare Novartis' device mark in the shape of a plaster invalid on the ground that it was composed of a sign consisting exclusively of the shape of the product necessary to obtain a technical result. The shape of cigarette lighter fell foul of technical result exclusion in *Flamagas SA v EUIPO* (T-580/15), EU:T:2017:433; [2017] E.T.M.R. 33. The shape of London taxi cabs was held to add substantial value to the goods in *London Taxi Corp Ltd (t/a London Taxi Co) v Frazer-Nash Research Ltd* [2017] EWCA Civ 1729; [2018] F.S.R. 7. The issue of whether the notion of "shape" is limited to the three-dimensional properties of the goods, such as their contours, measurements and volume, or whether it can include other, non-three dimensional properties of the goods such as their colour (in particular red soles for luxury shoes), was referred to the CJEU in *Louboutin v Van Haren Schoenen BV*(C-163/16); the Court held such a sign does not consist exclusively of a shape and as such could not fall foul of the exclusion: EU:C:2018:423, [2018] E.T.M.R. 31.

498 The High Court referred certain questions to the CJEU on the issue of acquired distinctiveness in relation to the shape of the Kit-Kat four-finger chocolate bar—see *Société des Produits Nestlé SA v Cadbury UK Ltd* [2014] EWHC 16 (Ch); [2014] E.T.M.R. 17. Reflecting the CJEU's ruling, the Court held that in order to demonstrate acquired distinctiveness, it is necessary to show that a significant proportion of the relevant consumers perceive the goods or services as originating from a particular undertaking because of the shape in question, not just that they recognised the shape and associated it with the undertaking: *Société des Produits Nestlé SA v Cadbury UK Ltd* [2016] EWHC 50 (Ch); [2016] 4 All E.R. 1081 (an appeal against this was dismissed: [2017] EWCA Civ 358; [2018] 2 All E.R. 39). See now the latest ruling in *Mondelez UK Holdings & Services Ltd v EUIPO / Société des produits Nestlé SA* (T-112/13) (General Court) [2017] E.T.M.R. 13 (a shape mark may acquire distinctiveness even if used in combination with a word or figurative mark)—upheld on appeal to the CJEU, (C-84/17 P) [2018] Bus. L.R. 1848; [2019] F.S.R. 6. The same principles were applied in upholding a finding of no acquired distinctiveness in the shapes of London taxi cabs: *London Taxi Corp Ltd (t/a London Taxi Co) v Frazer-Nash Research Ltd* [2017] EWCA Civ 1729; [2018] F.S.R. 7. A longstanding shape mark for Tic Tac boxes was held to have only weak distinctive character in *BMB sp z oo v European Union Intellectual Property Office (EUIPO)* (T-695/15) (General Court), EU:T:2017:684; [2018] E.T.M.R. 2.

499 TMA 1994 s.3(3). See on likely to deceive: *"Swiss Miss" TM* [1998] R.P.C. 889. An application for the mark "Canary Wharf" was refused because it was held to designate geographical origin: *Canary Wharf Group Plc v Comptroller General of Patents, Designs and Trade Marks* [2015] EWHC 1588 (Ch); [2015] F.S.R. 34.

500 TMA 1994 ss.3(3), 3(4) and 4.

501 TMA 1994 s.3(6). "Bad faith" is hard to define but includes dishonesty and some dealings which fall short of the standards of acceptable commercial behaviour observed by reasonable and experienced men. This has been described as whether the applicant knew his behaviour was unacceptable by the standards of reasonable men of business, i.e. it contains a significant objective component. See *Gromax Plasticulture Ltd v Don & Low Nonwovens Ltd* [1999] R.P.C. 367; *Ajit Weekly TM* [2006] R.P.C. 25; and *Hotel Cipriani Srl v Cipriani (Grosvenor Street) Ltd* [2010] EWCA Civ 110; [2010] R.P.C. 16. In *Chocoladefabriken Lindt & Sprungli v Franz Hauswirth* (C-529/07) [2009] E.T.M.R. 56 the Court held that consideration *must* be given to the applicant's subjective intention identifying similar relevant types of knowledge that would be relevant as the English courts had identified in the cases referred to earlier. This principle was applied by Henderson J, finding bad faith, in *32Red Plc v WHG (International) Ltd* [2011] EWHC 62 (Ch); [2011] E.T.M.R. 21 (and not doubted on appeal: [2012] EWCA Civ 19; [2012] E.T.M.R. 14). Additional general guidance has been provided by Henry Carr J in *Trump International Ltd v DTTM Operations LLC* [2019] EWHC 769 (Ch).The CJEU has ruled that applying for a mark with no intention of using it, but with the intention of using the mark as a basis for obtaining a top-level .eu domain name could amount to bad faith within the meaning of the relevant domain name regulation (Regulation 874/2004): *Internetportal und Marketing GmbH v Schlicht* (C-569/08) [2011] Bus. L.R. 726; [2010] E.T.M.R. 48, CJEU (Second chamber). The CJEU has confirmed that bad faith is an autonomous concept of EU law which should have uniform interpretation across the Community: *Malaysia Dairy Industries Pte Ltd v Ankenaevnet for Patenter og Varemaerker* (C-320/12) [2013] E.T.M.R. 36; that case also held that a finding of bad faith does not follow simply because an applicant was aware of an earlier registration of the same mark in a foreign country. There is no requirement in the EU Trade Mark Regulation that the applicant must intend to use the mark, thus the lack of such intention does not on its own amount to bad faith (at least in respect of EU trade marks): *Jaguar Land Rover Ltd v Bombardier Recreational Products Inc* [2016] EWHC 3266 (Ch); [2017] F.S.R. 20. However, the court in *Sky Plc v Skykick UK Ltd* [2018] EWHC 943 (Ch); [2018] R.P.C. 12 has now referred to the CJEU the question of whether it can constitute bad faith to apply to register a trade mark without any intention to use it in relation to the specified goods or services, and if so whether such an application might be held to have been made partly in good faith and partly in bad faith, depending on the intention (or not) to use the trade mark in relation to each of the specified goods or services.

502 TMA 1994 ss.5–8. Note that the holder of the earlier mark may be required to prove genuine use—see para.25-108 and fn.651. See, on the right to prevent registration under s.5(4) where use of the mark

applied for would constitute passing off: *"Wild Child" TM* [1998] R.P.C. 455. Unregistered rights were held to invalidate a registration in *Frost Products Ltd v FC Frost Ltd* [2013] EWPCC 34; [2013] E.T.M.R. 44. National rights in "extended form" passing off were also applicable in this context in *Tilda Riceland Private Ltd v OHIM* (T-304/09) [2012] E.T.M.R. 15, General Court, concerning the term "basmati". The Court of Appeal considered the effect of Trade Marks Act s.5(4)(a) and earlier unregistered rights in *Caspian Pizza Ltd v Shah* [2017] EWCA Civ 1874; [2018] F.S.R. 12. The defendant's earlier rights, although in a different geographical area to that in which the claimant operated, were sufficient basis to invalidate a national trade mark registration. There was no equivalent to TMA 1994 ss.47(5) and (6) allowing for a declaration of only partial validity on the basis of a geographically limited earlier right. See Ch.26 for further discussion of extended passing off. A rice-related trade mark was also invalid against earlier unregistered UK rights in *Tresplain Investments Ltd v OHIM* (C-76/11 P) [2012] E.T.M.R. 22. The CJEU has given its views on the notion of "honest concurrent use" in *Budejovicky Budvar Narodni Podnik v Anheuser-Busch Inc* (C-482/09) [2012] E.T.M.R. 2. It ruled that the provisions of the Directive 2008/95/EC and Regulation (EC) 207/2009 do not allow a trade mark proprietor to prevent the use of an identical mark where there has been long concurrent use such that there is not likely to be any damage to the "essential function" of the earlier mark. Note that the case turned on its specific and rather unusual facts. The Court also ruled on the meaning of "acquiescence" as a concept of Community law. In *IPC Media Ltd v Media 10 Ltd* [2014] EWCA Civ 1439; [2015] F.S.R. 12 (in which the mark in dispute was "Ideal Home") the Court of Appeal again found that the long period of honest concurrent use meant that the lower court was entitled to dismiss a claim for infringement. Honest concurrent use was also found in *Supreme Petfoods Ltd v Henry Bell & Co (Grantham) Ltd* [2015] EWHC 256 (Ch); [2015] E.T.M.R. 20. However, consensual use does not altogether preclude a trade mark owner from subsequently withdrawing consent and enforcing its rights against a former co-user of the mark: *Martin y Paz Diffusion SA v David Depuydt, Fabriek van Maroqinerie Gauquie NV* (C-661/11) [2014] E.T.M.R. 6. The CJEU has held that the peaceful co-existence of marks in two Member States need not rule out a likelihood of confusion in other Member States of the EU: *Ornua Co-operative Ltd v Tindale & Stanton Ltd Espana SL* (C-93/16) EU:C:2017:571; [2017] E.T.M.R. 37. For an examination of the effects of a coexistence agreement on later trade mark use, see *Merck KGaA v Merck Sharp & Dohme Corp* [2017] EWCA Civ 1834; [2018] E.T.M.R. 10.

[503] TMA 1994 s.13. See *Paton Calvert Cordon Bleu TM* [1996] R.P.C. 94.

Revocation for non-use, etc. and invalidity of registration

Replace paragraph with:

25-108 The registration of a trade mark may be revoked on the grounds of non-use or suspension of use for five years without proper reason or because, by reason of the acts or inactivity of the proprietor, the mark has become the common name in the trade for the product or service for which it is registered or that, in consequence of the use made of it by the proprietor or with his consent, it is liable to mislead the public.[508] In addition, the registration of a trade mark may be declared invalid on the ground that the trade mark was not a registrable mark at the date of registration but if, in consequence of use made of it after registration, the mark has acquired a distinctive character, it will not be declared invalid.[509] The registration of a trade mark may also be declared invalid on the ground that it conflicts with an earlier mark or right.[510] An application for revocation or a declaration of invalidity may be made by any person[511] and there is provision for partial revocation or declaration of invalidity in relation to only some of the goods or services in respect of which the trade mark is registered.[512] Where the registration of a trade mark is declared invalid to any extent, the registration shall to that extent be deemed never to have been made.[513] There are provisions concerning rectification and correction of the register of trade marks and the procedure and evidence before the registrar of trade marks.[514] A registered trade mark may be surrendered.[515] As to the question of whether a mark has become a common name, this must be assessed by reference to the perception of both trade users and end consumers, although it is the perception of the end consumer that will generally be decisive.[516] The court in *Sky Plc v Skykick UK Ltd*[516A] has referred to the CJEU the question of whether an EU trade mark or a national trade mark registered in a Member State can be declared wholly or partially invalid on the ground that some or all of the terms in the specification of goods and services are lacking in sufficient clarity and precision to enable the competent authorities and third parties to determine on the basis of those terms alone the extent of the protection conferred by the trade mark. This issue arises following the ruling of the CJEU in *Chartered Institute of Patent Attorneys v Registrar of Trade Marks*.[516B]

[508] TMA 1994 s.46. See also the "use conditions" introduced into TMA 1994 ss.6A and 47 by the Trade Marks (Proof of Use) Regulations 2004 (SI 2004/946). See s.46(2),(3) as to what constitutes "use" for the purpose of s.46. As to the type of evidence required to show "use" see *Moo Juice Trade Mark* [2005] EWHC 2584; [2006] R.P.C. 18. The CJEU has handed down a detailed decision on "use": see *Anheuser-Busch Inc v Budejovicky Budvar Narodni Podnik* (C-96/09 P) [2011] E.T.M.R. 31. Article 15(1) of Regulation 207/2009 requires that the territorial borders of the Member States of the Community be disregarded for the purposes of assessing whether a trade mark has been put to genuine use—*Leno Merken BV v Hagelkruis Beheer BV* (C-149/11) [2013] E.T.M.R. 16, CJEU. Provisions of national law are irrelevant to the operation and scope of Regulation 207/2009 in relation to genuine use: *Rivella International AG v OHIM* (T-170/11) [2013] E.T.M.R. 4; General Court, appeal dismissed: [2014] E.T.M.R. 20. Genuine use may be satisfied for a registered trade mark which has become distinctive as a result of use as part of a composite mark with other elements, even where it has only ever been used as part of that composite: *Colloseum Holding AG v Levi Strauss & Co* (C-12/12) [2013] E.T.M.R. 34; cf. *Fruit of the Loom Inc v OHIM* (T-514/10) [2012] E.T.M.R. 44, General Court. A wordless EUTM may be genuinely used even where it has been used only in conjunction with another word EUTM superimposed over it and the combination of those two marks was itself registered as an EUTM: *Specsavers International Healthcare Ltd v Asda Stores Ltd* (C-252/12) [2014] F.S.R. 4, CJEU; the Court of Appeal consequently allowed the claimant's appeal: [2014] EWCA Civ 1294; [2015] F.S.R. 8. For an example of an appeal against revocation for lack of genuine use, see *Galileo International Technology LLC v European Union (formerly European Community)* [2011] EWHC 35 (Ch); [2011] E.T.M.R. 22. The appeal was dismissed. For recent discussion on proof of use see *Property Renaissance Ltd (t/a Titanic Spa) v Stanley Dock Hotel Ltd (t/a Titanic Hotel)* [2016] EWHC 3103 (Ch); [2017] E.T.M.R. 12. In *Redd Solicitors LLP v Red Legal Ltd* [2012] EWPCC 54; [2013] E.T.M.R. 13, the court held that even though the claimant used the mark primarily only in relation to intellectual property law, that did not mean that it would be fair to restrict the mark to that sphere of legal practice. Use of marks on cruise ships that had entered UK territorial waters and docked at Southampton was held to be insufficient in *Johnny Rockets Licensing Corp v Eddie Rockets (Ireland) Ltd* [2016] E.T.M.R. 37; [2017] F.S.R. 9.

[509] TMA 1994 s.47(1).

[510] TMA 1994 s.47(2).

[511] There is a special exception in the case of five years' acquiescence by the proprietor of an earlier trade mark or other earlier right, TMA 1994 s.48(1). Questions have been referred to the CJEU about the scope of this acquiescence provision: see *Budejovicky Budvar Narodni Podnik v Anheuser-Busch Inc* [2009] EWCA Civ 1022; [2010] R.P.C. 7.

[512] TMA 1994 ss.46(4) and 46(5) as well as ss.47(4) and 47(5). See for example the partial revocation in *Comic Enterprises Ltd v Twentieth Century Fox Film Corp* [2014] EWHC 185 (Ch); [2014] F.S.R. 35 ("Glee Club") (not disturbed on appeal: [2016] EWCA Civ 41; [2016] E.T.M.R. 22).

[513] TMA 1994 s.47(6). This does not affect transactions past and closed.

[514] TMA 1994 ss.64 (rectification or correction of the register), 66 (forms), 68 (costs), 69 (evidence), 76 (appeals from the registrar). Application may be made to the UK Intellectual Property Office or to the High Court. As to the latter, see CPR Pt 63. If the former procedure is used, cause of action and/or issue estoppel may operate if the party seeking revocation attempts to run the same arguments in subsequent court proceedings: *Evans v Focal Point Fires Plc* [2009] EWHC 2784 (Ch); [2010] R.P.C. 15. This case is to be contrasted with the Court of Appeal decision in *Special Effects Ltd v L'Oréal SA* [2007] EWCA Civ 1; [2007] R.P.C. 15.

[515] TMA 1994 s.45.

[516] *Backaldrin Österreich the Kornspitz Co v Pfahnl Backmittel* (C-409/12) [2014] Bus. L.R. 320; [2014] E.T.M.R. 30.

[516A] [2018] EWHC 943 (Ch); [2018] R.P.C. 12.

[516B] (C-307/10) as to which see fn.494.

(c) Infringement of trade mark

Infringement of registered trade mark

Replace paragraph with:

There are three ways in which a registered trade mark may be infringed, and there **25-110** are also ancillary torts relating to the affixation of trade marks in certain circumstances without consent.

(a) A person infringes a registered trade mark under s.10(1) if he uses[527] in the course of trade a sign which is identical with[528] the trade mark in relation to goods or services which are identical with those for which it is registered.[529]
(b) A person infringes a registered trade mark under s.10(2) if he uses in the course of trade a sign where because (i) the sign is identical with the trade mark and is used in relation to goods or services similar to those for which the trade mark is registered, or (ii) the sign is similar to the trade mark and is used in relation to goods or services identical with or similar to those for which the trade mark is registered, there exists a likelihood of confusion on the part of the public, which includes the likelihood of association with the trade mark.[530]
(c) It is also an infringement of a registered trade mark under s.10(3) if a person uses in the course of trade a sign which is identical with or similar to the trade mark and is used in relation to goods or services which are not similar to those for which the trade mark is registered where the trade mark has a reputation in the UK and the use of the sign, being without due cause, takes unfair advantage of or is detrimental to the distinctive character or the repute of the trade mark. The High Court considered the principles applicable to identifying the extent of a mark's reputation within the EU in *Burgerista Operations GmbH v Burgista Bros Ltd.*[530A] This can include for example "cybersquatting".[531] The CJEU has ruled in *Intel Corp Inc v CPM UK Ltd*[532] that detriment to distinctive character requires proof of at least a serious likelihood of change in the economic behaviour of the consumer. In a more recent decision, the CJEU in *L'Oréal v Bellure*[533] held that taking unfair advantage of a trade mark's reputation does not require confusion or a likelihood of detriment to the distinctive character of the mark but rather only that the advantage to the infringer is one taken unfairly such that they seek to "ride on the coat tails" of the mark's reputation so as to benefit from its power of attraction. The principles are drawn together by the Court of Appeal in *Whirlpool Corp v Kenwood Ltd*[534] and further discussed in *Daimler AG v Sany Group Co Ltd.*[535]
(d) A person who applies a registered trade mark to material intended to be used for labelling or packaging goods, as a business paper, or for advertising goods or services, is treated as a party to any use of the material which infringes the registered trade mark, if when he applied the mark he knew or had reason to believe that the application of the mark was not duly authorised by the proprietor or a licensee.[536]

[527] A person uses a sign if, in particular, he:

(a) affixes it to goods or the packaging thereof;
(b) offers or exposes goods for sale, puts them on the market or stocks them for those purposes under the sign, or offers or supplies services under the sign;
(c) imports or exports goods under the sign; of; and
(d) uses the sign on business papers or in advertising: see TMA 1994 s.10(4).

Use "in the course of trade" may include use by a non-profit organisation such as an NHS trust: *APT Training and Consultancy Ltd v Birmingham and Solihull Mental Health NHS Trust* [2019] EWHC 19 (IPEC); [2019] E.T.M.R. 22.

[528] Identity is assessed strictly: see *Koninklijke Philips NV v Remington Consumer Products Ltd* [2004] EWHC 2327 (Ch); [2005] F.S.R. 17 and *LTJ Diffusion SA v Sadas Vertbaudet SA* (C-291/00) [2002]

E.T.M.R. 40. An earlier black and white mark later used in colour is not identical to the same mark in colour unless the differences in colour are insignificant. An earlier mark in greyscale is not identical to the same mark in colour or in black and white unless the differences in colour or in contrast of shades are insignificant: see European Trade Mark and Design Network, *Common Communication on the Common Practice of the Scope of Protection of Black and White ("B&W") Marks*, 15 April 2014, p.2. "Insignificant" means a difference that only a reasonably observant consumer will perceive on a side-by-side comparison of the marks.

[529] TMA 1994 s.10(1). As to the meaning of "use in relation to goods", see *Trebor Bassett Ltd v The Football Association* [1997] F.S.R. 211 (use of England logo on shirts of players photographed for football cards, not use in relation to the cards).

[530] TMA 1994 s.10(2). See para.25-113.

[530A] [2018] EWHC 35 (IPEC); [2018] E.T.M.R. 16.

[531] TMA 1994 s.10(3). On this concept see, *British Telecommunications Plc v One in a Million* [1999] 1 W.L.R. 903 where the Court of Appeal suggested obiter that, in an action based on s.10(3), it is not necessary to prove that the use complained of be trade mark use nor that it be confusing use. See also *Global Projects Management Ltd v Citigroup Inc* [2005] EWHC 2663 (Ch); [2006] F.S.R. 39. *One in a Million* held it to be infringement of trade marks and passing off to register Internet domain names incorporating the trade marks of famous companies and threaten to use them or sell them to others. The law was surveyed more recently in *Victoria Plum Ltd (t/a Victoria Plumb) v Victorian Plumbing Ltd* [2016] EWHC 2911 (Ch); [2017] F.S.R. 17. The principles are equally applicable to company names: *Bayerische Motoren Werke AG v BMW Telecommunications Ltd* [2019] EWHC 411 (IPEC). See also on the effect of s.10(3), *Pfizer Ltd v Eurofood Link (UK) Ltd* [2000] E.T.M.R. 896; [2001] F.S.R. 3 (VIAGRA registered for anti-impotence tablets could prevent use of VIAGRENE for aphrodisiac drink under s.10(2) or s.10(3) as an alternative); *General Motors Corp v Yplon* [2000] R.P.C. 572. The scope of a s.10(3) claim extends to the situation where the goods are similar: *Adidas-Salomon AG v Fitnessworld Trading Ltd* (C-408/01) [2004] Ch. 120.

[532] [2009] E.T.M.R. 13. The relevant principles were considered and applied in *Maier v ASOS* [2013] EWHC 2831 (Ch); [2014] F.S.R. 16 at [126]–[135], although the conclusion reached by the judge on the facts of the case was reversed by the Court of Appeal: [2015] EWCA Civ 220; [2016] 2 All E.R. 738.

[533] (C-487/07) [2009] E.T.M.R. 55. See also the Court of Appeal's judgment following the CJEU verdict: [2010] EWCA Civ 535; [2010] E.T.M.R. 47. Unfair advantage was also considered in depth in *Red Bull GmbH v Sun Mark Ltd* [2012] EWHC 1929 (Ch); [2013] E.T.M.R. 53, in which Arnold J held that the strapline "NO BULL IN THIS CAN" infringed the claimant's "RED BULL" mark for energy drinks. See also the discussion of unfair advantage in *Jack Wills Ltd v House of Fraser (Stores) Ltd* [2014] EWHC 110; [2014] E.T.M.R. 28; *Hearst Holdings Inc v AVELA Inc* [2014] EWHC 439 (Ch) (IPEC); and the successful appeal against a finding of no unfair advantage in *Lonsdale Sports Ltd v Erol* [2013] EWHC 2956 (Pat); [2013] E.C.C. 33.

[534] [2009] EWCA Civ 753; [2010] E.T.M.R. 7.

[535] [2009] EWHC 2581 (Ch). See also *Thomas Pink Ltd v Victoria's Secret UK Ltd* [2014] EWHC 2631 (Ch); [2014] F.S.R. 40 at [183]–[208].

[536] TMA 1994 s.10(5).

Likelihood of confusion

Replace footnote 547 with:

[547] *Och-Ziff Management Europe Ltd v Och Capital LLP* [2010] EWHC 2599 (Ch); [2011] E.T.M.R. 1; [2011] F.S.R. 11 at [72] et seq. For discussions of issues surrounding infringement, see *32Red Plc v WHG (International) Ltd* [2011] EWHC 62 (Ch); [2011] E.T.M.R. 21; and on appeal [2012] EWCA Civ 19; [2012] E.T.M.R. 14; *Kingspan Group Plc v Rockwool Ltd* [2011] EWHC 250 (Ch); *Samuel Smith Old Brewery (Tadcaster) v Lee (t/a Cropton Brewery)* [2011] EWHC 1879 (Ch); [2012] F.S.R. 7; *Maier v ASOS Plc* [2015] EWCA Civ 220; [2016] 2 All E.R. 738; and *JW Spear & Sons Ltd v Zynga Inc* [2013] EWHC 3348 (Ch); [2014] F.S.R. 19 (SCRABBLE / SCRAMBLE—no infringement, upheld on appeal: [2015] EWCA Civ 290; [2016] 1 All E.R. 226). For contrasting decisions about whether re-using a trade-marked product can give rise to infringement see *Schutz (UK) Ltd v Delta Containers Ltd* [2011] EWHC 1712 (Ch) (in which infringement was found) and *Viking Gas A/S v Kosan Gas A/S* (C-46/10) [2011] E.T.M.R. 58 (no infringement, on the basis of exhaustion—see para.25-114(d)). Use of abbreviations on social media (e.g. LDNR for Londoner) was considered in *Frank Industries Pty Ltd v Nike Retail BV* [2018] EWHC 1893 (Ch); [2018] F.S.R. 35. 25-113

Limitations on the effect of a registered trade mark

Replace list with:

25-114 (a) *Reference to the proprietor's own goods—comparative advertising.* The 1994 Act does not prevent the use of a registered trade mark by any person for the purpose of identifying goods or services as those of the proprietor or of a licensee, but any such use otherwise than in accordance with honest practices in industrial or commercial matters[551] is treated as infringing the registered trade mark if the use without due cause takes unfair advantage of, or is detrimental to, the distinctive character or repute of the trade mark. Honest comparative advertising is thereby permitted.[552] The Court of Appeal referred questions to the CJEU on whether the defendant's indicative use of the claimant's registered trade mark may constitute infringement in the cases of *L'Oréal SA v Bellure*[553] and *O2 Holdings Ltd v Hutchison 3G UK Ltd.*[554] In *O2 Holdings Ltd*[555] the CJEU confined its judgment to Council Directive 89/104 art.5(1)(b) (TMA 1994 s.10(2)). However, in *L'Oréal*[556] the CJEU stated that where a defendant used a claimant's mark and explicitly states that his product is an imitation of the claimant's, the advantage so gained must be considered to be one taken unfairly of the mark's reputation within the meaning of art.3a(1)(g) of Directive 2006/114/EC on comparative advertising.

(b) *Descriptive use, use of own name, ancillary use, etc.* There is no infringement by:

- (i) the use by a person of his own name or address[557];
- (ii) the use of indications concerning the kind, quality, quantity, intended purpose, value, geographical origin, the time of production of goods or of rendering of services or other characteristics of goods or services; or
- (iii) the use of the trade mark where it is necessary to indicate the intended purpose of a product or service (in particular, as accessories or spare parts) provided the use is in accordance with honest practices in industrial or commercial matters.[558]

(c) *Other exceptions to infringement.* There are a number of other exceptions to infringement, including situations where there are earlier rights.[559]

(d) *Exhaustion of rights.* A registered trade mark is not infringed by the use of the trade mark in relation to goods which have been put on the market in the European Economic Area (EEA) under that trade mark by the proprietor or with his consent[560] except where there are legitimate reasons for the proprietor to oppose further dealings in the goods.[561] The conditions set by the CJEU for parallel importers who repackaged or re-labelled trade marked goods in *Bristol Myers Squibb Co v Paranova A/S*,[562] were subsequently elaborated upon by the CJEU in its second reference for *Boehringer Ingelheim KG v Swingward Ltd.*[563] This was then applied by the Court of Appeal in *Boehringer Ingelheim KG v Swingward Ltd*[564] in its resumed hearing. The Court of Appeal held that though the CJEU in its second reference had said that partial de-branding in principle damaged the trade mark, it was a question of fact. Co-branding did not automatically lead to the damage and de-branding was not an infringement of the trade mark. A registered trade mark owner's rights are not exhausted by placing the goods on the market outside the EEA[565]; only express consent to subsequent marketing in the EEA is likely to suffice to exhaust the proprietor's registered trade mark rights. In *Oracle v M-Tech*, the way in which the claimant marketed its goods was designed to make it difficult to tell if goods had first been marketed within the EEA; the Court of Appeal held that it was arguable that this was contrary to Community law on free movement of goods, but this was reversed by the Supreme Court.[566] The rights of a trade mark proprietor also appear to extend to preventing third parties from first marketing in the EEA goods that the proprietor has already sold under the mark outside the EEA but from which the proprietor's marks have been stripped prior to EEA marketing by the third party.[566A] Damage done to the reputation of the trade mark is a legitimate reason for objecting to further commercialisation within the meaning of s.12. However, where a proprietor uses a trade mark for bringing the public's attention to the further commercialisation of the goods, the proprietor must show that the use of the trade mark for this purpose seriously damages the reputation of the trade mark.[567] Similarly, if a licensee acts in contravention of the terms of its licence, but where the proprietor is taken to have given permission for the goods to be placed on the market, sale of the goods can only be prevented where the sale damages the reputation of the mark (e.g. its reputation for luxury).[568] The CJEU held in *Viking Gas v Kosan Gas* that the proprietor of a shape mark for gas canisters had exhausted its rights in that mark by placing the product on the market in the EEA, and could not prevent customers exchanging empty canisters for ones refilled by a third party, absent any proper reason for objecting under art.7(2) of Directive (EC) 207/2009.[569]

[551] In *Barclays Bank Plc v RBS Advanta* [1996] R.P.C. 307, Laddie J said that the test was objective and depended on whether the use would be considered honest by members of a reasonable audience.

[552] TMA 1994 s.10(6). See *Barclays Bank Plc v RBS Advanta* [1996] R.P.C. 307. There are several decisions on the application of s.10(6) to comparative advertising. Their effect is summarised by Jacob J in *Cable & Wireless Plc v British Telecommunications Plc* [1998] F.S.R. 383. See also *O2 Holdings Ltd v Hutchison 3G Ltd* [2006] EWCA Civ 1656; [2007] 2 C.M.L.R. 15; [2007] R.P.C. 16. As long as the use of the competitor's mark is honest, it will be permitted. The test is objective: would a reasonable reader be likely to say, upon being given the full facts, that the advertisement was not honest? A significantly misleading advertisement will fail that test. The provisions of s.10(6) are independent of the provisions of the Comparative Advertising Directive 2006/114/EC. Vulgar abuse making use of a trade mark, is protected by s.10(6) and is not actionable: *British Airways Plc v Ryanair Ltd* [2001] F.S.R. 32 ("Expensive BA ______ DS" with price comparison: claim failed). Section 10(6) falls to be interpreted narrowly and restricted to cases in which the use of the mark is not on the proprietor's own goods: *Levi Strauss & Co v Tesco Stores Ltd* [2002] EWHC 1625 (Ch); [2002] 3 C.M.L.R. 11; [2003] R.P.C. 18. Where a competitor uses a trade mark proprietor's product numbers, that may constitute comparative advertising, but the competitor will only be liable for trade mark infringement, if the effect of the reference to them is to create in the mind of the persons at whom the advertising is directed an association between the manufacturer whose products are identified and the competing supplier: *Toshiba Europe GmbH v Katun Germany GmbH* (C-112/99) [2002] F.S.R. 39, CJEU. Sometimes an action for malicious falsehood can be more effective than reliance on trade mark rights. See, e.g. *DSG Retail v Comet Group Plc* [2002] EWHC 116 (QB); [2002] F.S.R. 58; but contrast the decision in *Kingspan Group Plc v Rockwool Ltd* [2011] EWHC 250 (Ch), in which a claim for malicious falsehood failed, while the claim for infringement based on comparative advertising succeeded. The court will not grant an interlocutory injunction in a comparative advertising case where the defendant has an arguable case and to do so would interfere with the right to free speech: *Macmillan Magazines Ltd v RCN Publishing Co Ltd* [1998] F.S.R. 9. See also *Boehringer Ingelheim Ltd v Vetplus* [2007] EWCA Civ 583; [2007] F.S.R. 29 (no interim injunction was granted to prevent comparative advertising). Section 10(6) does not only protect comparative advertising but prevents a claim arising from other kinds of genuine reference to the claimant's goods or services: *Wolters Kluwer (UK) Ltd v Reed Elsevier (UK) Ltd* [2005] EWHC 2053 (Ch); [2006] F.S.R. 28. The CJEU has ruled that the definition of "advertising" in the Directive extends to the use of a domain name and metatags, but not to the mere registration of a domain name: *Belgian Electronic Sorting Technology NV v Peelaers* (C-657/11) [2013] E.T.M.R. 45.

[553] [2007] EWCA Civ 968; [2008] E.T.M.R. 1.

[554] [2006] EWCA Civ 1656; [2007] 2 C.M.L.R. 15.

[555] (C-533/06) [2008] 3 C.M.L.R. 14.

[556] *L'Oréal v Bellure* (C-487/07) [2009] E.T.M.R. 55.

[557] s.11(2). However honest a defendant's subjective intentions were, any use of his own name which

amounted to passing off would not be in accordance with honest practices in industrial or commercial matters and the "own name" defence would not apply in such circumstances: *Asprey and Garrard Ltd v WRA (Guns) Ltd* [2001] EWCA Civ 1499; [2002] F.S.R. 31. It is possible to rely on the defence unless significant deception is shown to result: *Reed Executive Plc v Reed Business Information Ltd* [2004] EWCA Civ 159; [2004] E.T.M.R. 56. In relation to Community trade marks (Regulation 207/2009), a company may rely on its trading name as well as its corporate name, depending on the circumstances: *Hotel Cipriani Srl v Cipriani (Grosvenor Street) Ltd* [2010] EWCA Civ 110; [2010] R.P.C. 16; it is submitted that the same would apply in relation to s.11(2). For an example of a defendant choosing its company name with no good reason (and thereby having no defence to infringement) see *Smithkline Beecham Ltd v GSKline Ltd* [2011] EWHC 169 (Ch). The own-name defence was upheld in *Stichting BDO v BDO Unibank Inc* [2013] EWHC 418 (Ch); [2013] E.T.M.R. 31, and also in *A&E Television Networks LLC v Discovery Communications Europe Ltd* [2013] EWHC 109 (Ch); [2013] E.T.M.R. 32, in which "DISCOVERY HISTORY" did not infringe "THE HISTORY CHANNEL". An own-name defence failed as regards past acts but was upheld in relation to ongoing dealings in *Property Renaissance Ltd (t/a Titanic Spa) v Stanley Dock Hotel Ltd (t/a Titanic Hotel)* [2016] EWHC 3103 (Ch); [2017] E.T.M.R. 12.

558 TMA 1994 s.11(2). In *Hearst Holdings Inc v AVELA* [2014] EWHC 439 (Ch); [2014] F.S.R. 36 the court rejected the argument that the defendant was simply using pictures of the cartoon character "Betty Boop" in a descriptive manner (see [179]–[189]). The "repair clause" found in art.14 of the Design Directive 98/71/EC does not afford a defence to trade mark infringement: *Ford Motor Company v Wheeltrims srl* (C-500/14) [2016] E.C.D.R. 14 (marketing of spare-part wheel covers for cars). For use held not to be an honest indication of the kind of goods, see *Hasbro Inc v 123 Nahrmittel GmbH* [2011] EWHC 199 (Ch); [2011] E.T.M.R. 25 (product described as "play-dough"; claimant owned registered trade mark "PLAY-DOH"). The "indication of kind" defence was also rejected in *Bayerische Motoren Werke AG v Round & Metal Ltd* [2012] EWHC 2099; [2013] F.S.R. 18.

559 TMA 1994 s.11(3). Note that in general, estoppel and/or acquiescence cannot be relied on to provide a defence to trade mark infringement: *Coreix Ltd v Coretx Holdings Plc* [2017] EWHC 1695 (IPEC); [2018] F.S.R. 6.

560 The CJEU has given a restrictive interpretation of the concept of "consent" for the purpose of exhaustion of rights holding that consent to goods being placed on the market in the EEA could not be inferred from the fact that the proprietor has not communicated the opposition to marketing, that no warning was given or that no contractual reservations were made at the time of sale—see joined *Zino Davidoff SA v A Imports Ltd* (C-414/99 to C-416/99) [2002] Ch. 109; [2002] E.T.M.R. 9. The CJEU in *Schweppes SA v Red Paralela SL* (C-291/16) [2018] E.T.M.R. 13 has ruled that the proprietor of a mark is to be prohibited from opposing the import of identical goods bearing the same mark originating in another Member State when that mark initially belonged to the proprietor and was assigned to a third party with whom the proprietor remains economically linked or continues to coordinate its trade mark strategy in order to exercise joint control over the trade mark.

561 In particular, where the condition of the goods has been changed or impaired after they have been put on the market: TMA 1994 s.12. This section gives effect to the principle of exhaustion of rights within the EEA. The principles are reviewed in *Bristol Myers Squibb v Paranova* (C-427/93, C-429/93 and C-436/93) [2003] Ch. 75; [1997] F.S.R. 102. See also *Mastercigars Direct Ltd v Hunters & Frankau Ltd* [2007] EWCA Civ 176; [2007] R.P.C. 24. For an example of a successful opposition to such remarketing, concerning disassembled components for charm bracelets, see *Nomination Di Antonio e Paolo Gensini snc v Brealey (t/a JSC Jewellery)* [2019] EWHC 599 (IPEC). See also *Junek Europ-Vertrieb GmbH v Lohmann & Rauscher International GmbH & Co KG* (C-642/16) ECLI EU:C:2018:32 (no legitimate reasons for opposing), distinguished by Birss J in *Dansac A/S v Salts Healthcare Ltd* [2019] EWHC 104 (Ch); [2019] E.T.M.R. 25. The onus is on the defendant in an infringement action to put forward a defence of exhaustion: *Honda Motor Co Ltd v David Silver Spares Ltd* [2010] EWHC 1973 (Ch); [2010] F.S.R. 40.

562 [2003] Ch. 75.

563 (C-348/04) [2007] E.T.M.R. 71.

564 [2008] EWCA Civ 83; [2008] E.T.M.R. 55; [2008] E.T.M.R. 36. In *Speciality European Pharma Ltd v Doncaster Pharmaceuticals Group Ltd* [2015] EWCA Civ 54; [2015] 3 All E.R. 504 the Court of Appeal held that rebranding by a parallel importer went no further than was necessary to overcome artificial barriers to effective market access. The use of a small-print disclaimer to state that the parallel-imported goods are not made or marketed by the entity which owns the trade mark is not a defence to infringement: *Flynn Pharma Ltd v Drugsrus Ltd* [2015] EWHC 2759 (Ch); [2016] E.T.M.R. 4 (appeal subsequently dismissed: [2017] EWCA Civ 226; [2017] E.T.M.R. 25).

565 *Silhouette International Schmied GmbH & Co KG v Handelsgesellschaft mbH* (C-355/96) [1999] Ch. 77; [1998] F.S.R. 729. See also *Coty Prestige Lancaster Group GmbH v Simex Trading AG* (C-127/09) [2010] E.T.M.R. 41, following *Makro Zelkbedeiningsgroothandel CV v Diesel SpA* (C-324/08) [2010] Bus. L.R. 608.

566 *Oracle America Inc v M-Tech Data Ltd* [2010] EWCA Civ 997; [2010] E.T.M.R. 64; Supreme Court: [2012] UKSC 27; [2012] 1 W.L.R. 2026.

[566A] *Mitsubishi Shoji Kaisha Ltd v Duma Forklifts NV* (C-129/17) [2018] E.T.M.R. 37; [2019] F.S.R. 4.

[567] *Parfums Christian Dior SA v Evora BV* [1998] R.P.C. 166, CJEU.

[568] *Copad SA v Christian Dior Couture SA* (C-59/08) [2009] E.T.M.R. 40; [2009] F.S.R. 22.

[569] *Viking Gas A/S v Kosan Gas A/S* (C-46/10) [2011] E.T.M.R. 58.

(d) Proceedings

Proceedings for trade mark infringement and remedies

Replace paragraph with:

Infringement of registered trade mark is actionable by the proprietor of the trade mark.[571] All such relief by way of damages injunctions, accounts or otherwise is available to him as is available in respect of the infringement of any other proprietary right[572] and orders may be made for the erasure, removal or obliteration of offending signs or the destruction of infringing goods, and blocking injunctions are available against internet service providers in respect of websites selling infringing goods.[573] Damages may include any loss of trade actually suffered by the claimant either directly from the acts complained of or properly attributable to the injury to the claimant's reputation, business or goodwill, including the cost of corrective advertisements.[574] In some cases it may be appropriate to award a somewhat arbitrary capital sum to reflect the expropriation against the claimant's wishes of the monopoly right to use the mark.[575] There is no presumption that the claimant would have made the sales made by the defendant.[576] When conducting an account of profits it is not appropriate simply to allocate a proportion of the infringer's general overheads to the infringing activity; the infringer must show what costs are properly attributable to the infringements[577]. Orders may also be made for delivery up or disposal of infringing material goods or articles.[578] Interlocutory injunctions are granted on the usual principles.[579] Trade mark infringement can be amenable to summary judgment.[580] 25-115

[571] TMA 1994 s.14. In certain circumstances, infringement may be actionable at the suit of a licensee: see ss.30 and 31. No infringement proceedings may be begun before the date on which the trade mark is in fact registered: s.9(3). The fact that the mark alleged to infringe is itself registered is no bar to a finding of infringement, and the proprietor of the earlier mark need not first obtain a finding of invalidity against the later mark: *Fédération Cynologique Internationale v Federación Canina Internacional de Perros de Pura Raza* (C-561/11) [2013] E.T.M.R. 23, CJEU. This presents an apparent conflict with s.11(1) TMA 1994, which may have to be resolved in due course.

[572] TMA 1994 s.14(2). There are limitations on the right of persons who have not registered relevant transactions in due time: see s.25, and blocking injunctions are available against internet service providers in respect of websites selling infringing goods. Proof of infringement entitles a claimant to nominal damages but the burden is on the claimant to prove any actual damage. For a detailed consideration of the deduction and offset of overheads in calculating an account of profits, see *Jack Wills Ltd v House of Fraser (Stores) Ltd* [2016] EWHC 626 (Ch). The High Court (approved by the Court of Appeal) has established the availability of "blocking injunctions" to require internet service providers to block subscriber access to websites that are advertising and selling counterfeit goods: *Cartier International AG v British Sky Broadcasting Ltd* [2016] EWCA Civ 658; [2017] 1 All E.R. 700. An appeal to the Supreme Court overturned the Court of Appeal's view that the ISPs should bear the costs of implementing such blocks ([2018] UKSC 28; [2018] 1 W.L.R. 3259). See also *Cartier International Ltd v British Telecommunications Plc* [2016] EWHC 339 (Ch); [2016] E.T.M.R. 20. The "user" principle of applying a royalty was considered and applied in *32Red Plc v WHG (International) Ltd* [2013] EWHC 815 (Ch). An account of profits was assessed in *Woolley v UP Global Sourcing UK Ltd* [2014] EWHC 493 (Ch); [2014] F.S.R. 37; loss of profits was used to quantify damages in *Link Up Mitaka Ltd v Language Empire Ltd* [2018] EWHC 2633 (IPEC). On the approach to summary assessment of damages in a case in which there was user of a trade mark on a website, resulting in some benefit to the claimant see *Roadtech Computer Systems Ltd v Mandata Ltd* [2000] E.T.M.R. 970. Innocence is no defence to damages (*Gillette UK Ltd v Edenwest Ltd* [1994] R.P.C. 279) but may be a defence to an account of profits.

[573] TMA 1994 ss.14(2) and 15. For discussion of blocking injunctions see *Cartier International v Brit-*

ish Telecommunications Plc [2018] UKSC 28, [2018] 1 W.L.R. 3259, which held that trade mark owners must indemnify ISPs against the cost of complying with such injunctions.

[574] *Spalding v Gamage* (1918) 35 R.P.C. 101; *Manus v Fullwood* (1954) 71 R.P.C. 243.

[575] *Duracell v Ever Ready* [1989] 1 F.S.R. 71.

[576] *Draper v Trist* (1939) 56 R.P.C. 429; *Leather Cloth v Hirschfield* (1865) L.R. 1 Eq. 299.

[577] *Hollister Inc v Medik Ostomy Supplies Ltd* [2012] EWCA Civ 1419; [2013] F.S.R. 24. For another example of account of profits see *Champagne Louis Roederer (CLR) v J. Garcia Carrion S.A.* [2017] EWHC 289 (Ch).

[578] TMA 1994 ss.16 and 19. See s.17 for the meaning of "infringing goods", "infringing material" and "infringing articles". There are time limits after which the remedy of delivery up is not available: s.18.

[579] *American Cyanamid Co v Ethicon Ltd* [1975] A.C. 386; *Series 5 Software Ltd v Clarke* [1996] 1 All E.R. 853. Something more is needed than a case that will avoid being struck out as frivolous or vexatious: *Mothercare Ltd v Robson Books Ltd* [1979] F.S.R. 466 (a passing off case). A factor to be taken into account in deciding whether to grant an interim injunction is that the defendant's proposed operations might "swamp" the claimant's goodwill: *Elan Digital Systems Ltd v Elan Computer Ltd* [1984] F.S.R. 373 at 385. Often, an order for a speedy trial will be more appropriate. Trade mark infringement (and passing off) proceedings present a special difficulty: a defendant who has been enjoined and adopted a new mark as a result will often be unable to return to the mark in issue. In such a case, the interlocutory injunction application will, in practice, determine the whole action. On the whole the courts have been sensitive to this concern: *BBC v Talbot Motor Co Ltd* [1981] F.S.R. 228; cf. *Elan Digital Systems Ltd v Elan Computers Ltd* [1984] F.S.R. 373 at 386. For a detailed decision concerning calculation of damages resulting from a cross-undertaking in the context of a trade mark claim see *Lilly Icos LLC v 8PM Chemists Ltd* [2009] EWHC 1905 (Ch); [2010] F.S.R. 4. An injunction was refused in *Cowshed Products Ltd v Island Origins Ltd* [2010] EWHC 3357 (Ch); [2011] E.T.M.R. 42, after a detailed evaluation based on that same set of principles. The court likewise refused an injunction in *Surtec International GmbH v A-Tech Chemicals UK Ltd* [2013] EWHC 2942 (Ch), since the claimant would be protected by interim undertakings offered by the defendant. Note that an injunction against infringement of an EUTM will, as a rule, extend to the entire EU: *DHL Express France SAS v Chronopost SA* (C-235/09) [2011] E.T.M.R. 33. An injunction was also refused in *Protomed Ltd v Medication Systems Ltd* [2012] EWHC 3726 (Ch), where it was held that the claimant did not have a good arguable case on infringement; affirmed on appeal: [2013] EWCA Civ 1205. The principles relating to prohibitory and mandatory injunctions were considered in detail by the Court of Appeal in *Frank Industries Pty UK v Nike Retail BV* [2018] EWCA Civ 497; [2018] F.S.R. 24.

[580] *British Sky Broadcasting Group Plc v Digital Satellite Warranty Cover Ltd (In Liquidation)* [2011] EWHC 2662 (Ch); [2012] F.S.R. 14. That case concerned s.10(1). Arnold J also considered database right and passing off. For summary judgment on s.10(2) infringement see *Lewis v Client Connection Ltd* [2011] EWHC 1627 (Ch); [2012] E.T.M.R. 6, and *United Airlines Inc v United Airways Ltd* [2011] EWHC 2411 (Ch).

Criminal offences and customs powers

Replace paragraph with:

25-116 There are criminal sanctions for the unauthorised use of trade marks in relation to goods.[581] Offences include falsification of the register,[582] and falsely representing trade marks as registered.[583] The proprietor of a registered trade mark or a licensee may give notice in writing to the Commissioners of Customs and Excise requesting the Commissioners to treat infringing goods, material or article as prohibited goods. Where such a notice is in force, the importation of the goods to which the notice relates is prohibited, otherwise than by a person for his private and domestic use.[584]

[581] TMA 1994 s.92. The House of Lords addressed criminal liability under s.92 in *R. v Johnstone* [2003] UKHL 28; [2003] 1 W.L.R. 1736. A criminal defendant should only be liable where his actions would have amounted to a civil infringement of the trade mark. The court may make a confiscation order under the Proceeds of Crime Act 2002 in relation to trade mark offences: *R. v Ghori* [2012] EWCA Crim 1115. In a separate decision the Court of Appeal rejected arguments that such an order was oppressive: *R. v Beazley* [2013] EWCA Crim 567; [2013] 1 W.L.R. 3331. Offences under the Trade Marks Act 1994 s.92(1) apply not only to counterfeit goods but also to "grey goods" – i.e. ones manufactured with the permission of the trade mark proprietor but not authorised for sale: *R. v C, R. v T, R. v M* [2017] UKSC 58; [2017] 1 W.L.R. 3006.

[582] TMA 1994 s.94.

[583] TMA 1994 s.95. It is also an offence to make unauthorised use of Royal arms, etc. s.99.

[584] TMA 1994 s.89. As to the meaning of "counterfeit" in this context, Kitchin J held in *Nokia Corp v Revenue and Customs Commissioners* [2009] EWHC 1903 (Ch); [2009] E.T.M.R. 59 that the goods in question had to infringe someone's trade marks in the relevant territory. The CJEU has ruled that goods brought into the EU customs area under a suspensive procedure (rather than being actually sold or advertised) cannot be classified as counterfeit or pirated goods: *Koninklijke Philips Electronics NV v Lucheng Meijing Industrial Co Ltd* (C-446/09), [2012] E.T.M.R. 13. Contrast *Blomqvist v Rolex SA* (C-98/13) [2014] E.T.M.R. 25, in which the CJEU held that mere acquisition of goods through an online sales website was enough to justify seizure under the customs Regulation, even without an offer for sale or advertisement targeting consumers in the State where the seizure took place. As to what constitutes targeting UK consumers on the internet, see *Argos Ltd v Argos Systems Inc* [2018] EWCA Civ 2211; [2019] F.S.R. 3.

Change title of paragraph: **25-118**

Unjustified threats of trade mark infringement proceedings

Replace paragraph with:

It is an actionable wrong to threaten any person with proceedings for trade mark infringement unless the threat can be justified, other than in respect of: **25-118**

(a) applying, or causing another person to apply, a sign to goods or their packaging;
(b) importing, for disposal, goods to which, or to the packaging of which, a sign has been applied; or
(c) supplying services under a mark.[585A]

"Any person" aggrieved may bring proceedings for a declaration that the threats are unjustifiable, an injunction against the continuance of the threats and damages in respect of any loss sustained by the threats.[586] The test is whether a reasonable person in the position of a recipient would understand from the communication that the patent exists, and a person intends to bring infringement proceedings against another person in respect of acts done (or to be done) in the UK.[587] Merely giving notice that a trade mark exists is one of the "permitted acts" under s.21B, i.e. it is not actionable. This is a similar provision to that relating to patents, where the principles are well-established (see below). It is a defence to an action for threats to prove that "the acts in respect of which proceedings were threatened constitutes (or if done would constitute) an infringement of the trade mark".[587A]

[585A] TMA 1994 ss.21–21E; as with patents (see para.25-141), the unjustified threats provisions in respect of trade marks were amended by the Intellectual Property (Unjustified Threats) Act 2017, replacing the old TMA 1994 s.21. Various detailed exceptions and conditions apply to the new provisions (such as for permitted communications, and professional advisers), and the reader is advised to consult the statute.

[586] TMA 1994 s.21C(1).

[587] TMA 1994 s.21(1). Under the old s.21 implied threats were actionable: *Scandecor Development AB v Scandecor Marketing AB* [1999] F.S.R. 26 CA as were "veiled and muffled" threats: *L'Oréal (UK) Ltd v Johnson & Johnson* [2000] F.S.R. 686. Cf. *Nvidia Corp v Hardware Labs Performance Systems Inc* [2016] EWHC 3135 (Ch); [2017] Bus. L.R. 549. A Community-wide mark could found an action for threats of infringement proceedings under the old provisions, but only if the threat was in relation to proceedings within the UK: *Best Buy Co Inc v Worldwide Sales Corp España SL* [2011] EWCA Civ 618; [2011] F.S.R. 30. See also *Data Marketing & Secretarial Ltd v S & S Enterprises Ltd* [2014] EWHC 1499 (IPEC); [2015] F.S.R. 1.

[587A] TMA 1994 s.21C(2).

9. PATENTS

(a) Introduction

Patents—scope of section

Replace footnote 588 with:

25-119 [588] See R. Miller, G. Burkhill, C. Birss and D. Campbell, *Terrell on the Law of Patents*, 18th edn (Sweet & Maxwell, 2016); P. Cole et al., *CIPA Guide to the Patents Acts*, 8th edn (Sweet & Maxwell, 2016); F. Clark, R. Jacob, W. Cornish, G. Hamer and T. Moody-Stuart, *Encyclopedia of United Kingdom and European Patent Law* (Sweet & Maxwell, last release April 2017). *Halsbury's Laws*, 5th edn, Vol. 19(2A) Intellectual Property, (London: LexisNexis 2010). For procedure in infringement, etc. before the courts, including the England and Wales Intellectual Property Enterprise Court ("IPEC") (formerly the Patents County Court ("PCC")) see Civil Procedure (Amendment No.2) Rules ("CPR") Pt.63, "Patents and Other Intellectual Property Claims", as amended to 1 October 2012. Note that routes of appeal in Pt. 63 have been amended by the Civil Procedure Rules (Amendment No.3) Rules (CPR) (SI 2016/788). Detailed information on the work of IPEC is set out in the Intellectual Property Enterprise Court Guide (updated to 2 August 2016) and the associated Intellectual Property Enterprise Court: A Guide to Small Claims, published 10 July 2014. The small claims track is for low value intellectual property disputes, with a value capped at £10,000. The PCC was renamed with effect from 1 October 2013, to clarify its jurisdiction, which covers all areas of intellectual property, not just patents. For procedure before the Intellectual Property Office (IPO, formerly the Patent Office), see the Patents Rules 2007 (SI 2007/3291), and Patent (Fees) Rules 2007 (SI 2007/3292), as amended to 30 September 2016, and *The Manual of Patent Practice* (updated to 29 March 2019). All the above documents are available at *http://www.gov.uk/topic/intellectual-property/patents* [Accessed 2 May 2019].

Introduction—the statutory framework

Replace paragraph with:

25-120 Patents are purely statutory. The principal Act is the Patents Act 1977 ("PA 1977"), which brought UK law in line with the European Patent Convention 1973 (revised 2000) ("EPC"). Until the coming into force of that Act, somewhat different rules applied to the validity of patents under the Patents Act 1949—in particular that patents could be challenged on somewhat wider grounds. Some of the principles from the older cases are still of importance. Later laws, including the Copyright, Designs and Patents Act 1988, the Regulatory Reform (Patents Act) Order 2004, the Patent Act 2004, the Intellectual Property Act 2014 and the Intellectual Property (Unjustified Threats) Act 2017 have changed the 1977 Act.[589]

[589] An unofficial consolidation of the Patents Act 1977 (as amended up to and including 25 July 2018) is available on the Intellectual Property Office website: *https://www.gov.uk/government/publications/the-patents-act-1977* [Accessed 2 May 2019]. See also the Patents (Convention Countries) Order 2007 (SI 2007/276), (as amended by the Patents (Convention Countries) (Amendment) Order 2013 (SI 2013/538)) for the protection afforded to foreign nationals pursuant to the international obligations of the UK as a member of the EPC, PCT, Paris Convention for the Protection of Industrial Property and the World Trade Organisation (WTO).

The Unified Patents Court

Replace paragraph with:

25-121 Until very recently, there has been no EU instrument governing patent law, although certain connected rights, such as Supplementary Protection Certificates, are governed by EU law.[590] Following an agreement reached in December 2012 by the European Parliament and 25 EU Member States (all Member States except Croatia (which subsequently joined the Union) Italy and Spain) concluding more than 30 years of negotiations, a patent package consisting of two Regulations and an international Agreement were adopted early in 2013, laying the foundations for the creation of unitary patent protection in the EU. The Regulations implement enhanced co-operation in the area of unitary patent protection and the applicable translation requirements for such protection respectively. The Regulations entered into force on 20 January 2013. The third instrument, the Agreement on a Unified Patent Court, which will have exclusive jurisdiction relating to litigation concerning unitary patents, was signed by all Member States except Poland and Spain on 19 February 2013. These three instruments apply once the international Agreement enters into force following ratification by 13 contracting states (now exceeded, but see below), including France, Germany and the UK.[591] Following the UK referendum vote in June 2016 there has been a degree of uncertainty about the future of the Unified Patent Court, given the UK's intended role as a key signatory and one of the host countries for the court; however, in November 2016 the UK government confirmed that it was proceeding with preparations to ratify the Unified Patent Court Agreement, and ratified the Agreement on 26 April 2018. The Unified Patent Court has now received 16 ratifications of the Protocol on Provisional Application, but is awaiting the resolution of a complaint before the Constitutional Court in Germany before it can begin the period of provisional operations, which will include the commencement of the "sunrise" period in which unitary patents will become available, but with an opt-out for applicants for European patents.[592]

[590] The new unitary patent system does not provide for unitary Supplementary Protection Certificates ("SPCs"). The current EU SPC Regulation would allow national SPCs to be granted based on a unitary patent. The Commission is currently considering the creation of a unitary SPC. On SPCs generally, see para.25-125.

[591] Regulation (EU) No. 1257/2012 of the European Parliament and of the Council of 17 December 2012, implementing enhanced cooperation in the area of the creation of unitary patent protection; Council regulation (EU) No. 1260/2012 of 17 December 2012, implementing enhanced cooperation in the area of the creation of unitary patent protection with regard to the applicable translation arrangements. The Agreement on a Unified Patent Court ("UPC") was signed on 19 February 2013. This instrument is an international agreement concluded outside the EU institutional framework. Part 2 of the Intellectual Property Act 2014 implements a number of changes to patent law, including provisions enabling the UK to bring the Unitary Patent and Unified Patent Court into effect. More detailed amendments to PA 1977 are contained in the Patents (European Patent with Unitary Effect and Unified Patent Court) Order 2016 (SI 2016/388), which will give effect to the legislation on the unitary patent and UPC; the order comes into force on the date of entry into force of the Agreement on a Unified Patent Court: see art.1(2).

[592] For full details, including agreements, substantive law and updates, see the website of the Unified Patent Court at *https://www.unified-patent-court.org* [Accessed 2 May 2019].

European Patent Convention 1973

Replace footnote 594 with:

[594] The EPO's website may be viewed at *http://www.epo.org* [Accessed 2 May 2019]. **25-122**

Application for a patent—priority date

Replace footnote 599 with:

[599] There is also the possibility of filing an international application with effect in several states under the Patent Cooperation Treaty ("PCT") 1970, which is administered by the World Intellectual Property Organization ("WIPO"), in Geneva. The PCT provides a unified procedure for obtaining patent protection in 148 countries worldwide on the basis of a single application. National patents may be obtained in PCT Contracting States as well as regional patents such as those granted by the EPO. The international PCT phase includes a formalities check, an international search and the option of a preliminary examination. Readers are referred to the above-mentioned specialist works for details and the WIPO website (*www.wipo.int/pct/en* [Accessed 2 May 2019]). **25-124**

Term of patent

Replace footnote 604 with:

25-125 [604] See PA 1977 s.128B to which the EU Regulations 1768/92 (medicinal products) and 1610/96 (plant protection products) are scheduled. The CJEU handed down three judgments on SPCs in 2011. Two established the principle that an application for a SPC must relate to a medicament (human or veterinary) "product" that: is protected by a patent; has been subject to an administrative authorisation procedure; and has not been placed on the market anywhere in the EEA as a medicinal product prior to being subject to safety and efficacy testing and a regulatory review (see *Generics (UK) Ltd v Synaptech Inc* (C-427/09) [2012] 1 C.M.L.R. 4; [2012] R.P.C. 4 and *Synthon BV v Merz Pharma GmbH & Co KGaA* (C-195/09) [2012] R.P.C. 3). In the third case, the CJEU held that the competent industrial property office of a Member State is precluded from granting a supplementary protection certificate relating to active ingredients which are not specified in the wording of the claims of the basic patent relied on. A certificate may be granted, however, for a combination of two active ingredients where the medicinal product in question contains not only that combination but also other active ingredients (*Medeva BV v Comptroller General of Patents, Designs and Trade Marks* (C-322/10) [2012] R.P.C. 25). See also the subsequent decision of the Court of Appeal [2012] EWCA Civ 523; [2012] 3 C.M.L.R. 9. Supplementary protection is only available when the marketing authorisation granted for the product is the first for that product. However, the CJEU in *Neurim Pharmaceuticals (1991) Ltd v Comptroller-General of Patents* (C-130/11) [2013] R.P.C. 23 held that the mere existence of an earlier marketing authorisation obtained for a veterinary medicinal product does not preclude the grant of a Supplementary Protection Certificate for a different application of the same product for human use for which a marketing authorisation has been granted. Thus, products relating to additional or second medical uses of an active ingredient are now eligible for supplementary protection. Arnold J has referred a question to the CJEU on whether the Regulation precludes the grant of a SPC to a patent proprietor in respect of a product which was the subject of a marketing authorisation held by a third party without that party's consent—see *Eli Lilly and Co v Genentech Inc* [2019] EWHC 388 (Pat); [2019] 3 WLUK 4.

The specification—description and claims

Replace paragraph with:

25-127 Patent specifications fall into two parts: the description of the invention and the claims. The claims must define the matter for which the applicant seeks protection, be clear and concise, be supported by the description and must relate to one invention or to a group of inventions which are so linked as to form a single inventive concept.[614] The court is often asked to construe the claims of a patent, mainly for the purpose of determining whether there is infringement and whether prior art anticipates any given claim. An invention is taken to be that specified in the claims, as interpreted by the description and any drawings contained in the specification.[615] The Protocol on the Interpretation of art.69 of the European Patent Convention applies to the construction of 1977 Act patents. This provides that:

> "Article 69 should not be interpreted as meaning that the extent of the protection conferred by a European patent is to be understood as that defined by the strict, literal meaning of the wording used in the claims, the description and drawings being employed only for the purpose of resolving an ambiguity found in the claims. Nor should it be taken to mean that the claims serve only as a guideline and that the actual protection conferred may extend to what, from a consideration of the description and drawings by a person skilled in the art, the patent proprietor has contemplated. On the contrary, it is to be interpreted as defining a position between these extremes which combines a fair protection for the patent proprietor with a reasonable degree of legal certainty for third parties."

Guidance has been provided by the English courts on the approach to construction, especially in the context of infringement actions in numerous cases. The law was comprehensively reviewed by the House of Lords in *Kirin-Amgen Inc v Hoechst-Marion Roussel Ltd*, and later by the Court of Appeal in *Virgin Atlantic Airways Ltd v Premium Aircraft Interiors Group*[616]; however, those authorities are now to be read in light of the guidance of the Supreme Court in *Actavis UK Ltd v Eli Lilly & Co*. The Supreme Court in *Actavis* considered the proper approach to the interpretation of claims, and in particular the requirement of the European Patent Convention 2000 to take account of "equivalents" to what is covered by the literal meaning of the claims. It concluded that the court must ask not just what is the "normal interpretation" of the claims, but also whether the alleged infringements represent variants on the claimed invention that differ only in an "immaterial" way. In order to answer that second question, the court reformulated the so-called *Improver* questions; this new approach to the "doctrine of equivalents" is discussed at para.25-134. As to the "normal interpretation" of the claims, it appears that this is simply the same as the "purposive" (as opposed to rigidly literal) construction well known from the older authorities.[616A]

[614] PA 1977 s.14(5).

[615] PA 1977 s.125.

[616] *Actavis UK Ltd v Eli Lilly & Co* [2017] UKSC 48; [2018] 1 All E.R. 171; [2017] R.P.C. 21; *Kirin-Amgen Inc v Hoechst-Marion Roussel Ltd* [2004] UKHL 46; [2005] 1 All E.R. 667; [2005] R.P.C. 9 at [71]; *Virgin Atlantic Airways Ltd v Premium Aircraft Interiors Group* [2009] EWCA Civ 1062; [2010] R.P.C. 8 at [5]–[22]. *Virgin Atlantic* also makes clear that when reading the patent, the skilled addressee is assumed to have some knowledge of patent law in order to understand the relevance of different parts of the patent. See also on the approach to construction: *Improver Corp v Remington Consumer Products Ltd* [1989] R.P.C. 69. The court often applies the *Catnic* test when considering the ambit of a patent claim under the 1977 Act, although as noted in *Kirin Amgen Inc v Hoechst Marion Roussel Ltd* [2004] UKHL 46; [2005] 1 All E.R. 667 the formulations in the *Improver* case of the *Catnic* principles are only guidelines. The Supreme Court in *Actavis* has indicated that there are only limited circumstances in which it will be relevant to refer to the prosecution history of a patent for the purposes of assisting with construction.

[616A] See Arnold J's interpretation of *Actavis* in *Generics (UK) Ltd (t/a Mylan) v Yeda Research and Development Co Ltd* [2017] EWHC 2629 (Pat); [2018[R.P.C. 2.

(b) Validity

Validity

Replace paragraph with:

The validity of a patent may be challenged on a number of grounds, the most important of which is that the patent does not claim a patentable invention.[617] This is a compendious term. An invention is only a patentable invention under the 1977 Act if it satisfies all the following conditions: **25-128**

(a) *Novelty.* The invention must be new.[618]
(b) *Not obvious.* The invention must involve an inventive step (i.e. it must not be obvious to a person skilled in the art).[619]
(c) *Capable of industrial application.* The invention must be capable of industrial application.[620]
(d) *Not specifically excluded.* None of the special reasons in ss.1(2) and 1(3) of the Patents Act 1977 for excluding patentability apply. Section 1(2) provides that the following (amongst other things) are not inventions for the purpose of the Patents Act 1977, namely, anything which consists of:
    (a) a discovery, scientific theory or mathematical method;
    (b) a literary, dramatic, musical or artistic work or any other aesthetic creation whatsoever;
    (c) a scheme, rule or method of performing a mental act, playing a game or doing business, or a programme for a computer;[621] or
    (d) the presentation of information.

Section 1(3) excludes the grant of a patent for an invention the commercial exploitation of which would be contrary to public policy or morality.[622] If a patent does not claim a patentable invention, it may be revoked by the court or the comptroller on the application of any person.[623] In practice, lack of novelty and obviousness are the most frequently invoked bases for challenging a patent.

[617] Note what is claimed must be an "invention". Thus it may be an objection to validity that the patent does not claim an invention at all: see *Genentech's Patent* [1989] R.P.C. 147.

[618] An invention is taken to be novel if it does not form part of the state of the art which comprises all matter which has been made available to the public whether in the UK or elsewhere before the priority date of the invention: PA 1977 s.2(2). The court in *Unwired Planet International Ltd v Huawei Technologies Co Ltd* [2015] EWHC 3366 (Pat); [2016] Bus. L.R. 435 held that "before the priority date" is to be judged by reference to the time zone in which the filing took place, i.e. the 24-hour period beginning at midnight in that time zone; this was upheld on appeal: [2017] EWCA Civ 266. Anticipation requires prior disclosure of subject matter which, if performed, must necessarily infringe the patent: *Synthon BV v Smithkline Beecham Plc* [2005] UKHL 59; [2006] 1 All E.R. 685, per Lord Hoffmann. The disclosure must also be enabling (ibid). Where the disclosure is in a document, the antecedent statement must be such that a person of ordinary knowledge of the subject would at once perceive and understand and be practically able to apply the discovery without the necessity of making further experiments and the information given by the prior publication must, for the purposes of practical utility, be equal to that given by the patent: *Hill v Evans* (1860) 31 L.J. Ch. 457. To anticipate the patentee's claim, the prior publication must contain clear and unmistakable directions to do what the patentee claims to have invented—it must "plant the flag" in the invention: *General Tire & Rubber Co v Firestone Tyre & Rubber Co Ltd* [1972] R.P.C. 457, but it is not essential that the disclosure be express, as long as the skilled person would inevitably infer the relevant teaching: *Edwards Lifesciences LLC v Boston Scientific Scimed Inc* [2017] EWHC 405 (Pat), affirmed on appeal: [2018] EWCA Civ 673; [2018] F.S.R. 29. Where a number of options are presented in a piece of prior art, each of these will generally be capable of anticipating. Description of the same invention in a prior art document using different words may be sufficient to render the invention non-novel: *Belvac Production Machinery Inc v Carnaudmetalbox Engineering Ltd* [2009] EWHC 292 (Ch). Where there has been prior use of a product, the question is what the disclosure of the product was and whether it had made the product available to the public (see *Merrell Dow Pharmaceuticals Inc v Norton & Co Ltd* [1995] R.P.C. 233. The appeal to the House of Lords was dismissed [1996] R.P.C. 76). The information must have been made available to at least one member of the public who was free in law and equity to use it. Prior secret user will not render a patent invalid for lack of novelty under the 1977 Act. Disclosures in breach of confidence or at international exhibitions are disregarded if made within six months before the date of filing the application for the patent and there are other special exceptions (PA 1977 s.2(4)(c)) and there are provisions for including in the state of the art anticipatory patent applications published after the priority date (PA 1977 s.2(3)). Since *Actavis* (see para.25-127), Arnold J has indicated in *Generics (UK) Ltd (t/a Mylan) v Yeda Research and Development Co Ltd* [2017] EWHC 2629 (Pat); [2018] R.P.C. 2 that it is no longer the law that a claim will lack novelty if the prior art discloses subject matter that, if performed, would necessarily infringe the claim, since the potential scope of infringement has been broadened by *Actavis*. Arnold J held that a claim would only lack novelty if the prior art disclosed subject matter that fell within the claim on its "proper interpretation"—that is, the narrower scope of the purposive construction of the claim – it is not sufficient that the subject matter would infringe the claim applying the doctrine of equivalents.

[619] PA 1977 s.3. In order to identify whether the invention is obvious the court will often adopt the "*Pozzoli*" approach, formulated by the Court of Appeal in *Pozzoli SpA v BDMO SA* [2007] EWCA Civ 588; [2007] F.S.R. 37. First, the court identifies: (a) the notional "person skilled in the art"; and (b) the relevant common general knowledge of that person; next it identifies the inventive concept of the claim in question or if that cannot readily be done, it construes it; third, the court identifies what, if any, differences exist between the matter cited as forming part of the "state of the art" and the inventive concept of the claim or the claim as construed; and finally, it decides whether viewed without any knowledge of the alleged invention as claimed, those differences constitute steps which would have been obvious to the person skilled in the art or whether they require any degree of invention. An ex post facto analysis is to be avoided: *Non-drip Measure Co Ltd v Strangers Ltd* (1943) 60 R.P.C. 135. In *Conor Medsystems Inc v Angiotech Pharmaceuticals Inc* [2008] UKHL 49; [2008] 4 All E.R. 621; [2008] R.P.C. 28, Lord Hoffmann held that the inventive concept should be determined by reference to the claim and not to some vague paraphrase based on the disclosure in the description (see particularly at [19]). A patent might be obvious due to being "obvious to try" if there is a "fair expectation of success" (ibid.)—often this occurs when a product has been selected from a previously disclosed class of products. See also on "obvious to try" *Medimmune Ltd v Novartis Pharmaceuticals UK Ltd* [2012] EWCA Civ 1234; [2013] R.P.C. 27 and *Hospira UK Ltd v Genentech Inc* [2016] EWCA Civ 1185. Findings on obviousness are rarely overturned on appeal—see *Biogen v Medeva* [1997] R.P.C. 1 45 HL. For a helpful review of the contemporary approach to obviousness, see *Generics (UK) Ltd v Daiichi Pharmaceuticals Co Ltd* [2009] EWCA Civ 646; [2009] R.P.C. 23 and IPEC case *VPG Systems UK Ltd v Air-Weigh Europe Ltd* [2015] EWHC 1862; [2016] F.S.R. 4. For guidance on what constitutes common general knowledge, see *General Tire & Rubber Co v Firestone Tyre & Rubber Co Ltd* [1972] R.P.C. 457 at 482–483 and *Beloit Technologies Inc v Valmet Paper Machinery Inc* [1997] R.P.C. 489 at 494–495. The approach to permission to appeal in patent cases was recently revised in *Teva UK Ltd v Boehringer Ingelheim Pharma GmbH & Co KG* [2016] EWCA Civ 1296.

[620] By which is meant that it can be made or used in any kind of industry including agriculture: PA 1977 s.4. See *Chiron Corp v Murex Diagnostics* [1996] F.S.R. 153. A method of treatment of the human or

animal body by surgery or therapy or of diagnosis practised on the human or animal body shall not be taken to be capable of industrial application but that does not prevent a substance or composition being capable of industrial application merely because it is invented for use in any such method (PA 1977 s.4A). See as to second medical use of pharmaceutical substances: *Wyeth's Application* [1985] R.P.C. 545. For claims which do not accord with generally accepted scientific principles, see *Blacklight Power Inc v Comptroller-General of Patents* [2008] EWHC 2763 (Pat); [2009] R.P.C. 6. A helpful summary of the law relating to industrial applicability is provided by Kitchin J in *Eli Lilly & Co v Human Genome Sciences Inc* [2008] EWHC 1903 (Pat); [2008] R.P.C. 29 at [178]–[227] and by Jacob LJ on appeal in the same case: [2010] EWCA Civ 33; [2010] R.P.C. 14; (2010) 112 B.M.L.R. 161 at [50]–[112]. See also the decision of the Supreme Court in *Human Genome Sciences Inc v Eli Lilly & Co* [2011] UKSC 51; [2012] 1 All E.R. 1154.

[621] IPO practice on the patentability of mental acts is set out in a Practice Notice dated 17 October 2011. Its practice on patenting computer-implemented inventions (software patents) is based on *Aerotel Ltd v Telco Holdings and Macrossan's Application* [2006] EWCA Civ 1371; [2007] 1 All E.R. 225, and *Symbian Ltd's Application* [2008] EWCA Civ 1066; [2009] R.P.C. 1 (see Practice Notice of 8 December 2008, which should be read with Practice Notices dated 2 November 2006 and 7 February 2008 on patentable subject-matter. For EPO practice on this subject, see the EPO Enlarged Board of Appeal decision, G3/08 of 12 May 2010 (OJ EPO 1/2011, 10). Note that the provision prevents anything from being treated as an invention for the purposes of the Act only to the extent that a patent or application for a patent relates to that thing as such (as to which see *Gale's Patent Application* [1991] R.P.C. 305). As to the test for patentability, the UK approach is that this is determined by the technical contribution of the invention (see *Aerotel Ltd v Telco Holdings Ltd* [2006] EWCA Civ 1371; [2007] 1 All E.R. 225; [2007] R.P.C. 7 and the interpretation of *Aerotel* in *Symbian Ltd v Comptroller General of Patents* [2008] EWCA Civ 1066; [2009] R.P.C. 1. See also, *HTC Europe Co Ltd v Apple Inc* [2013] EWCA Civ 451; [2013] R.P.C. 30 (*Symbian* followed); and *Lantana Ltd v Comptroller-General of Patents* [2014] EWCA Civ 1463; [2015] R.P.C. 16.

[622] PA 1977 also prevents the grant of patents for inventions the publication or exploitation of which would be generally expected to encourage offensive, immoral or anti-social behaviour. Plant and animal varieties and essentially biological processes (not being microbiological processes or the products thereof) are excluded, PA 1977 s.1(3). A patent may also not be granted for methods of treatment or diagnosis, PA 1977 s.4A. European Directive 98/44/EC on the patentability of biotechnological inventions has been implemented into UK law by amendment to the PA 1977 s.76A and Sch.A2. Paragraph 3 of the Schedule provides that the following also are not patentable inventions: the human body, at the various stages of its formation and development, and the simple discovery of one of its elements, including the sequence or partial sequence of a gene; processes for cloning human beings; processes for modifying germ line genetic identity of human beings; uses of human embryos for industrial or commercial purposes and processes for modifying the genetic identity of animals which are likely to cause them suffering without any substantial medical benefit to man or animal, and animals resulting from such processes. In 2011 the CJEU delivered a judgment on the definition of the term "human embryo", *Brüstle v Greenpeace eV* (C-34/10) [2012] All E.R. (EC) 809; [2012] 1 C.M.L.R. 41. A new reference to the CJEU for a preliminary ruling on the definition of human embryos and seeking clarification of the CJEU's decision in *Brüstle* was made by the Patent Court in *International Stem Cell Corp v Comptroller General of Patents* (C-364/13) [2015] Bus. L.R. 98; [2015] 2 C.M.L.R. 26. The CJEU ruled that "an unfertilised human ovum whose division and further development have been stimulated by parthenogenesis does not constitute a 'human embryo'". Following that decision, on 25 March 2015, the IPO published statutory guidance on inventions involving human embryonic stem cells replacing and updating previous practice notices on the subject.

[623] PA 1977 s.72. It is not an abuse of process to claim for revocation of a patent even if the claimant has no commercial interest in the patent: *TNS Group Holdings Ltd v Nielsen Media Research Inc* [2009] EWHC 1160 (Pat); [2009] F.S.R. 23.

Other grounds upon which a patent may be revoked

Replace paragraph with:

As well as the objection that the invention is not a patentable invention,[624] a patent may be revoked on any of the following grounds, of which in practice (after lack of novelty and obviousness) insufficiency and added matter are the most frequently invoked. **25-129**

(a) *Not entitled to the patent.* The patent was granted to person who was not entitled to be granted that patent.[625]
(b) *Insufficiency.* The specification does not disclose the invention clearly enough and completely enough for it to be performed by a person skilled

in the art.[626] This attack is at its most powerful where the patentee has failed to give adequate guidance as to how to make or perform the claimed subject-matter of the patent but in *Biogen Inc v Medeva Plc*,[627] the House of Lords gave guidance as to the scope for challenge to a patent under this head where the claims of the patent were over-broad, exceeding the patentee's technical contribution to the art. The House of Lords in *Generics (UK) Ltd v H Lundbeck A/S*[628] has clarified the law on sufficiency in the situation where a product is claimed as the result of an inventive process. Provided at least one method of making the product is adequately described in the specification the product claim is not insufficient. In *Conor Medsystems Inc v Angiotech Pharmaceuticals Inc*[629] Lord Hoffmann held that where the description exceeds the threshold of making the invention plausible it need not offer further explanation as to how or why the invention works provided that it will work as described.[630]

(c) *Added matter.* The matter disclosed in the specification of the patent extends beyond that disclosed in the application as filed.[631] The nub of the objection under this head is that the patentee has added a significant technical disclosure after he filed the patent.

(d) *Wrongful extension of protection by amendment.* The protection conferred by the patent has been extended by an amendment which should not have been allowed.[632]

624 See para.25-128 for a discussion on the objections to validity.

625 PA 1977 s.72(1)(b). An application on this ground may only be made by a person entitled to be granted that patent or to be granted a patent for part of the matter comprised in the specification of the patent sought to be revoked and there are limits on the time in which such an application may be made: PA 1977 s.72(2).

626 PA 1977 s.72(1)(c). The Court of Appeal has summarised the principles relating to insufficiency in *Regeneron Pharmaceuticals Inc v Kymab Ltd* [2018] EWCA Civ 671; [2018] R.P.C. 14. Disclosure of an invention does not have to be complete in every detail so that anyone, whether skilled or not, can perform it. Since the specification is addressed to the skilled man it is sufficient if the addressee can understand the invention as described and can then perform it. The hypothetical addressee is not a person of exceptional skill and he is not expected to exercise any invention or any prolonged research, inquiry or experiment. In *Glaxo Group Ltd v Vectura Ltd* [2018] EWHC 3414 (Pat) five European patents were held invalid for insufficiency, since their specifications did not enable the skilled person, without undue effort, to determine whether a process or product was within the scope of the claims. The skilled person must, however, be prepared to display a reasonable degree of skill and common knowledge of the art in making trials and to correct obvious errors in the specification, if a means of correcting them can readily be found: *Mentor Corp v Hollister Inc* [1993] R.P.C. 7. The disclosure must be sufficient to enable the whole width of the claimed invention to be performed. What will suffice to satisfy this criterion will vary depending upon the nature of the claim that has been made: *Biogen Inc v Medeva Plc* [1997] R.P.C. 1. See also *Kirin-Amgen Inc v Hoechst Marion Roussel Ltd* [2004] UKHL 46; [2005] 1 All E.R. 667 where the House of Lords emphasised the need to analyse what the invention was before determining whether the specification of the patent enabled it. Older cases on the test of sufficiency continue to be of relevance. See for example: *R. v Arkwright* (1785) 1 W.P.C. 64; *Edison and Swan Electric Co v Holland* (1889) 6 R.P.C. 243; *Gold Ore v Golden Horseshoe* (1919) 36 R.P.C. 95; *IG Farbenindustrie AG's Patents* (1930) 47 R.P.C. 289 (sufficiency of selection patent); *British Thomson-Houston Co Ltd v Corona Lamp Works Ltd* (1922) 39 R.P.C. 49; *No-Fume v Pitchford & Co* (1935) 52 R.P.C. 231; *Valensi v British Radio Corp* [1973] R.P.C. 337; *Genentech's Patent* [1989] R.P.C. 147. The question of sufficiency of the specification of a patent under the 1977 Act must be addressed by reference to the state of the art at the date of the application: *Biogen Inc v Medeva Plc* [1997] R.P.C. 1. The Court of Appeal has emphasised that the assertion that an invention must work across the scope of the claim must be plausible and credible: *Generics (UK) Ltd (t/a Mylan) v Warner-Lambert Co LLC* [2016] EWCA Civ 1006; [2017] R.P.C. 1; an appeal to the Supreme Court on the issue of insufficiency was dismissed (Lords Hodge and Mance dissenting): [2018] UKSC 56; [2019] Bus. L.R. 360. The Court of Appeal has summarised the principles relating to insufficiency in *Regeneron Pharmaceuticals Inc v Kymab Ltd* [2018] EWCA Civ 671; [2018] R.P.C. 14.

627 [1997] R.P.C. 1.

628 [2009] UKHL 12; [2009] 2 All E.R. 955; [2009] R.P.C. 13.

[629] [2008] UKHL 49; [2008] 4 All E.R. 621; [2008] R.P.C. 28, see particularly at [37]–[39]. See also *Regeneron Pharmaceuticals Inc v Genentech Inc* [2013] EWCA Civ 93; [2013] R.P.C. 28.

[630] See also *Regeneron Pharmaceuticals Inc v Genentech Inc* [2013] EWCA Civ 93; [2013] R.P.C. 28 and *Actavis Group PTC EHF v Eli Lilly & Co* [2015] EWHC 3294 (Pat); [2016] R.P.C. 12. Some reason must be disclosed for regarding an assertion of efficacy as plausible: *Generics (UK) Ltd (t/a Mylan) v Warner-Lambert Co LLC* [2018] UKSC 56; [2019] Bus. L.R. 360.

[631] Or in certain earlier applications: PA 1977 s.72(1)(d). The decision as to whether there is an extension of disclosure must be made by a comparison of the two documents (application as filed and patent as granted) read through the eyes of a skilled addressee. The task of the court is threefold:

(a) to ascertain through the eyes of the skilled addressee what is disclosed, both explicitly and implicitly in the application;
(b) to do the same in respect of the patent as granted; and
(c) to compare the two disclosures and decide whether any subject-matter relevant to the invention has been added whether by deletion or addition.

The comparison is strict in the sense that subject-matter will be added unless such subject-matter is clearly and unambiguously disclosed in the application, either explicitly or implicitly: *Bonzel (T) v Intervention (No.3)* [1991] R.P.C. 553; *Molnlycke AB v Proctor & Gamble Ltd (No.5)* [1994] R.P.C. 49; *A.P. Racing Ltd v Alcon Components Ltd* [2014] EWCA Civ 40; [2014] R.P.C. 27. The authorities on added matter were reviewed in *Nicocigs Ltd v Fontem Holdings 1 BV* [2016] EWHC 2161 (Pat). Amending a claim to include variations on embodiments that do not affect the way the invention works may avoid an added matter objection: *IPCOM GmbH and Co KG v HTC Europe Co Ltd* [2017] EWCA Civ 90.

[632] PA 1977 s.72(1)(e). See para.25-131, "Amendment" on what amendments are allowable.

(c) Infringement

Acts not constituting infringement

Replace footnote 654 with:

[654] *United Wire Ltd v Screen Repart Services (Scotland) Ltd* [2000] 4 All E.R. 353; [2001] F.S.R. 24 HL; *Schutz (UK) Ltd v Werit (UK) Ltd* [2013] UKSC 16; [2013] R.P.C. 16, applied in *Parainen Pearl Shipping Ltd v Kristian Gerhard Jebsen Skipsrederi AS* [2018] EWHC 2628 (Pat). **25-133**

Variants on the claimed invention

Replace paragraph with:

It is often the case that an action is brought in respect of a product not falling squarely within the wording of the claims but which is a variant on the claimed invention, delivering the same or similar benefits. The correct approach to the application of the so-called "doctrine of equivalents" has now been clarified by the Supreme Court in *Actavis UK Ltd v Eli Lilly & Co*.[656] The first step when considering infringement is to ask whether the accused product or process falls within the claim as a matter of "normal interpretation", i.e. the usual "purposive" construction of the claim—see para.25-127. If the answer to that first question is "no", then the court must ask whether the variant differs from the subject matter of the claim in only an immaterial way. As to what is "immaterial", the Supreme Court said that it is appropriate to answer this by reference to a slightly reformulated version of the three-step test set out in *Improver* (and as before treating it as a guide, not a strict rule).[657] The updated set of questions is as follows: **25-134**

(1) Notwithstanding that it is not within the literal meaning of the relevant claim(s) of the patent, does the variant achieve substantially the same result in substantially the same way as the invention?
(2) Would it be obvious to the person skilled in the art, reading the patent at the priority date, but knowing that the variant achieved substantially the same result as the invention, that it did so in substantially the same way as the invention?

(3) Would such a reader of the patent have concluded that the patentee nonetheless intended that strict compliance with the literal meaning of the relevant claim(s) of the patent was an essential requirement of the invention?

If the answers to those questions are "yes", "yes" and "no", then the alleged infringement is likely to be an immaterial variant that thus falls within the scope of protection of the claim. A German defence to infringement by equivalents, known as the *Formstein* defence, was raised in *Technetix BV v Teleste Ltd*,[657A] whereby if the equivalent would have lacked novelty or inventive step as at the priority date, it would be held to fall outside the claim; the judge noted that the defence did not exist in English law, but did not rule out the possibility that it might be introduced.

[656] [2017] UKSC 48; [2018] 1 All E.R. 171; [2017] R.P.C. 21. The *Actavis* principles have since been analysed in detail by Kitchin LJ in *Icescape Ltd v Ice-world International BV* [2018] EWCA Civ 2219; [2019] F.S.R. 5. The inventive concept or core of the invention was characterised in *Regen Lab SA v Estar Medical Ltd* [2019] EWHC 63 (Pat) as "the new technical insight conveyed by the invention—the clever bit—as would be perceived by the skilled person".

[657] Prior to *Actavis*, the courts' approach to alleged infringing variants was often based on the principles outlined in *Catnic Components Ltd v Hill Smith Ltd* [1983] F.S.R. 512 and the three-step test formulated in *Improver Corp v Remington Consumer Products* [1990] F.S.R. 181, per Hoffmann J, often known as the "*Improver* questions". Earlier cases must be read in light of *Actavis* but may still have some relevance: see *Daily v Établissements Fernand Berchet* [1993] R.P.C. 357; *Lux Traffic v Pike Signals* [1993] R.P.C. 107; *Société Technique de Pulverisation Step v Emson Europe Ltd*[1993] R.P.C. 513 (despite the purposive construction, an integer cannot be treated as struck out despite the fact that it does not appear to make any difference to the inventive concept); *Rockwater Ltd v Technip France SA* [2004] EWCA Civ 381; [2004] R.P.C. 46.

[657A] [2019] EWHC 126 (IPEC).

Defences

Replace paragraph with:

25-136 The following are the most common defences to a claim for infringement[661]:

(a) *Act is not an infringing act.* What are and are not infringing acts are discussed at paras 25-132 and 25-133.

(b) *Product is outside the claims.* On the true construction of the claims, the product or process is not within them. See paras 25-127 and 25-134.

(c) *Licence (express or implied) or exhaustion of rights.* It is only infringement to do the specified acts without the consent of the proprietor of the patent. If a person is licensed, expressly or impliedly, there will be no infringement.[662] Where an article protected by a patent is manufactured or sold by or with the consent of the patentee, a purchaser of that article is entitled, in the absence of notice to the contrary,[663] to exercise in relation to that article all the rights of an owner, including that of reselling the article and of passing with it the same right to deal with it.[664] Once a patented article has been put on the market in any EC country by the patentee or a licensee, the doctrine of "exhaustion of rights" applies and the patent in any country may not be used to prevent goods entering another Member State.[665] The implied licence extends to "fair repair" of the article concerned, but not to the production of a new article under the cloak of making a repair.[666]

(d) *Patent invalid.* See para.25-128 onwards. This is a very common defence. If the patent is invalid, there can be no infringement[667] but relief may be granted for infringement of a partially valid patent.[668]

(e) *Prior user.* There is provision to allow persons who in good faith were doing (or making serious and effective preparations to do) acts before the priority date of the patent which would have infringed the patent had it been in force to continue to do such acts, such acts not constituting infringement.[669]

(f) *Competition law defences.* It was formerly a defence to proceedings for infringement to prove that at the time of the infringement there was in force a contract made by or with the consent of the patentee containing a term which is rendered void by the Patents Act s.44, but this has been removed by the Competition Act 1998.[670] In exceptional circumstances, the enforcement of a patent may constitute an abuse of dominant position, contrary to art.102 on the Functioning of the European Union ("TFEU") (formerly art.82 of the Treaty of Rome).[671] Related to this area are what are known as "FRAND" defences; patentees in certain fields of industry (notably mobile telecommunications) will often undertake to license their patents on FRAND (fair, reasonable and non-discriminatory) terms as part of a quid pro quo for the invention in the patent being incorporated into an important industry standard. The idea is to prevent patentees from blocking others from working the standard. Such FRAND obligations by the patentee may then give rise to a defence to any claim for an injunction, i.e. the defendant will try to negotiate a FRAND licence instead.[671A]

(g) *No defence of innocence.* It is not a defence that a defendant did not know he was infringing (but innocence may affect the claim for damages: see below).

661 In addition, there are special defences to certain types of relief claimed—these are discussed in para.25-137. Note also that the Supreme Court has held that the grant of a patent gives rise to private rights, the infringement of which does not engage the public interest so as to give rise to the ex turpi causa defence. The paradigm case of turpitude is a criminal act but includes quasi-criminal acts (*Les Laboratoires Servier v Apotex Inc* [2014] UKSC 55; [2015] A.C. 430). A more rarely pleaded defence is experimental use: see s.60(5)(b) PA 1977 and *British Gas Trading Ltd v Vanclare SE LLC* [2016] EWHC 2278 (Pat).

662 The general defences of acquiescence and estoppel are available in actions for infringement: see, for the principle, *Habib Bank Ltd v Habib Bank AG* [1981] 1 W.L.R. 1265 (a passing off case).

663 *Gilette v Bernstein* (1941) 58 R.P.C. 271 at 282; *Roussel Uclaf SA v Hockley International Ltd* [1996] R.P.C. 441.

664 *Betts v Wilmott* (1871) L.R. 6 Ch. 239 at 244.

665 This is a well-established principle of EU law: *Centrafarm v Sterling Drug* [1974] E.C.R. 1147. See for a comprehensive review of EU exhaustion principles: *Merck & Co Inc v Primecrown Ltd* (C-267/95 and C-268/95) [1997] F.S.R. 237, CJEU.

666 *Sirdar Rubber Co Ltd v Wallington, Weston & Co* (1907) 24 R.P.C. 539 at 543; *British Leyland Motor Corp v Armstrong Patents Co* [1986] A.C. 577; *Dellareed Ltd v Delkin Developments* [1988] F.S.R. 329.

667 A convenient short cut in an infringement action is the so-called "Gillette Defence" (from *Gillette Safety Razor Co v Anglo-American Trading Ltd* (1913) 30 R.P.C. 465); if the alleged infringement was itself an obvious thing to do or to make at the priority date of the relevant claims, then the claims must be bad as covering something obvious. This defence must be strictly proved: *Hickman v Andrews* [1983] R.P.C. 147.

668 PA 1977 s.63.

669 PA 1977 s.64. They may not licence others to do such acts. The defence applies where a person was making "effective and serious preparations": see *Helitune Ltd v Stewart Hughes Ltd* [1991] F.S.R. 171 and *Lubrizol Corp v Esso Petroleum Corp Ltd* [1998] R.P.C. 727.

670 PA 1977 s.44 (repealed).

671 See *Parke Davis v Probel* [1968] E.C.R. 55, CJEU; *Volvo v Erik Veng* [1988] E.C.R. 6211; [1989] 4 C.M.L.R. 122, CJEU; *Pitney-Bowes v Francotyp-Postlia GmbH* [1991] F.S.R. 72 (authorities reviewed); *Chiron Corp v Murex Diagnostics Ltd* [1994] F.S.R. 187; [1996] F.S.R. 153 CA. The mere fact of securing the benefit of an exclusive right is not an abuse. Nor is it an abuse to refuse to licence as such. The exercise of a patent right may be prohibited if it gives rise to abusive conduct such as an arbitrary refusal to supply repairers: *Philips Electronics NV v Ingman Ltd* [1999] F.S.R. 112. See for a case where a competition law defence was not struck out and the court contemplated an inquiry into the patentee's licensing practices: *Intel Corp v Via Technologies Inc* [2002] EWCA Civ 1905; [2003] F.S.R. 33.

[671A] The Court determined the scope and terms of the FRAND licences to be taken by a losing defendant in *Unwired Planet International Ltd v Huawei Technologies Co Ltd* [2017] EWHC 711 (Pat); [2019] 4 C.M.L.R. 7 (affirmed on appeal: [2018] EWCA Civ 2344; [2018] R.P.C. 20) and *Unwired Planet International Ltd v Huawei Technologies Co Ltd* [2017] EWHC 2988 (Pat); [2017] R.P.C. 19.

Action for infringement, relief and remedies

Replace footnote 677 with:

25-137 [677] *American Cyanamid v Ethicon* [1975] A.C. 396; [1975] R.P.C. 513; *Series 5 Software Ltd v Clarke* [1996] 1 All E.R. 853; [1996] F.S.R. 273. Interlocutory relief will be refused if, for example, the claimant can be adequately compensated in damages: *Polaroid Corp v Eastman Kodak* [1977] R.P.C. 379. See for a helpful review of some of the factors commonly taken into account: *Quantel Ltd v Shima Seiki Europe Ltd* [1990] R.P.C. 436. There has been a trend for there to be orders for speedy trials in addition to or instead of interim injunctions. See, e.g. *SmithKline Beecham Plc v Apotex Europe Ltd* [2003] EWCA Civ 137; [2003] F.S.R. 31. *Wake Forest University Health Sciences v Smith & Nephew Plc* [2009] EWHC 45 (Pat); [2009] F.S.R. 11 provides a further example. *Les Laboratoires Servier v Apotex Inc* [2008] EWHC 2347 (Ch); [2009] F.S.R. 3 provides an example of the risk in obtaining an interim injunction: the defendant was awarded £17.5 million for lost sales and market share during the period before the interim injunction was discharged. More recently, see *Boston Scientific Scimed inc v Edwards Lifesciences SA* [2018] EWHC 3738 (Pat) (interim injunction refused).

25-140 *Change title of paragraph:*

Declaratory relief

Replace paragraph with:

25-140 A person doing or proposing to do an act may seek a declaration from the court that the act is not or would not be an infringement of a patent.[688] The person must have applied in writing to the patentee for an acknowledgement that the act does not or would not infringe and must have furnished the patentee with full particulars in writing of the act in question. Only after the patentee has refused or failed to give such acknowledgement may such a declaration be made. It is also possible to obtain similar protection by seeking a declaration that a particular act would be anticipated and/or obvious as at a particular date, so that to the extent the act or product may be alleged to be patented, the patent too would be anticipated and/or obvious to the same extent.[689] Relief may also be granted in the form of an "*Arrow* declaration", named after *Arrow Generics Ltd v Merck & Co Inc*.[689A] This takes the form of a declaration that a product or process was not novel, or was obvious, as at a particular date. It is typically sought where a defendant's case is that its product or process was either not new at the priority date of the patent or else that it was so close to the prior art that if the patent is broad enough to catch the product or process, then the patent must be invalid for lack of novelty or obviousness. The principles governing the grant of *Arrow* declarations were considered in detail in *Glaxo Group Ltd v Vectura Ltd*[689B] and *Fujifilm Kyowa Kirin Biologics Co Ltd v Abbvie Biotechnology Ltd*.[689C]

[688] PA 1977 s.71. A person may also seek a declaration under the inherent jurisdiction of the court provided that the patentee has asserted his right.

[689] See, e.g. *Fujifilm Kyowa Kirin Biologics Co Ltd v Abbvie Biotechnology Ltd* [2017] EWHC 395 (Pat); [2018] R.P.C. 1.

[689A] [2007] EWHC 1900 (Pat); [2008] Bus. L.R. 487.

[689B] [2018] EWCA Civ 1496; [2019] Bus. L.R. 648. Arrow declarations were also granted in *Glaxo Group Ltd v Vectura Ltd* [2018] EWHC 3414 (Pat).

[689C] [2017] EWHC 395 (Pat); [2018] R.P.C. 1.

Change title of paragraph: **25-141**

Unjustified threats of infringement proceedings

Replace paragraph with:

It is an actionable wrong to threaten any person (other than in respect of the manufacture of goods, or the import of goods for disposal, or the use of a process, and subject to certain other excepted acts and "permitted communications" under ss.70A and 70B of the 1977 Act) with proceedings for infringement of patents unless the threat can be justified.[690] There are also exceptions for professional advisers under s.70D. "Any person" aggrieved by such a threat may sue the person making it for a declaration that the threat is unjustified, for an injunction to restrain repetition of the threat and for damages,[691] so a person may be aggrieved although the threat is not against him. Indeed, the form of threat that is most damaging to a manufacturer is a threat against his customers, which may cause them to take their custom elsewhere, or a communication to a third party in the hope of so influencing customers.[692] Under the old s.70, the essence of a threat was an intimation that someone has patent rights and intends to enforce them against another;[693] the statutory test is now whether a reasonable person in the position of a recipient would understand from the communication that the patent exists, and a person intends to bring infringement proceedings against another person in respect of acts done (or to be done) in the UK. Merely giving notice that a patent exists is a permitted act, i.e. not actionable.[694] It is a defence to an action for threats to prove that "the acts in respect of which proceedings were threatened constitutes (or, if done, would constitute) an infringement of a patent".[695] **25-141**

[690] PA 1977 ss.70–70E, as amended by the Intellectual Property (Unjustified Threats) Act 2017. The old s.70 was considered by the Court of Appeal in *Icescape Ltd v Ice-world International BV* [2018] EWCA Civ 2219; [2019] F.S.R. 5. It is suggested that the older cases referred to later in this paragraph will remain relevant to the application of the amended provisions.

[691] PA 1977 s.70C. Loss of business is recoverable as damages: *Skinner v Perry* (1894) 11 R.P.C. 406; [1894] 2 Ch. 581.

[692] See *Olin Mathieson Chemical Corp v Biorex Laboratories Ltd* [1970] R.P.C. 157.

[693] See *Luna Advertising Co v Burnham* (1928) 45 R.P.C. 258; *Bowden Controls v Acco Cable Controls Ltd* [1990] R.P.C. 427 (threat can be veiled or implied just as much as it can be explicit).

[694] PA 1977 s.70B(2)(a).

[695] PA 1977 s.70C(3). Under the old s.70 see *FNM Corp Ltd v Drammock International Ltd* [2009] EWHC 1294 (Pat), per Arnold J.

Reform of patent litigation procedure

Add to end of paragraph:

For up to date guidance on patent litigation see Pt 63 of the Civil Procedure Rules and the Patents Court Guide.[698A] **25-142**

[698A] *https://www.gov.uk/government/publications/patents-court-guide* [Accessed 2 May 2019].

CHAPTER 26

PASSING OFF

TABLE OF CONTENTS

1. GENERAL PRINCIPLES

Instruments of deception

Replace footnote 22 with:

[22] [1999] 1 W.L.R. 903. See also *EasyJet Co Ltd v Dainty* [2002] F.S.R. 6; *Phones4u Ltd v phone4u.co.uk* [2005] EWHC 334 (Ch); *SmithKline Beecham Ltd v GSKline Ltd* [2011] EWHC 169 (Ch) at [23] Arnold J. In *Vertical Leisure Ltd v Poleplus* [2014] EWHC 2077 (IPEC) HH Judge Hacon stated that the law set out in *British Telecommunications Plc v One In A Million* [1999] 1 W.L.R. 903 remains good law with regard to passing off and instruments of deception where domain name registration is concerned. Cf. on the facts, *Argos Ltd v Argos Systems Inc* [2017] EWHC 231 (Ch); [2017] E.T.M.R. 19, Richard Spearman QC, sitting as Deputy Judge. **26-04**

2. REQUIREMENTS

(a) Goodwill

Goodwill

Replace paragraph with:

The tort of passing off does not protect the mark, get-up, etc. as such. A passing off action protects a proprietary interest in goodwill.[25] Goodwill has been defined as[26] "the benefit and advantage of the good name, reputation[27] and connection of a business. It is the attractive force which brings in custom". The goodwill, however, need not be extensive.[28] A small business is as much entitled to protection as is a large one.[29] Goodwill in the sense of reputation may be acquired by famous personalities who trade on their reputation by commercialising their image and that valuable reputation will be protected by the tort against unlicensed use by other parties.[30] The damage that must be shown (as actual or prospective) is damage to the integrity of the claimant's goodwill.[31] **26-05**

[25] "A passing off action is a remedy for the invasion of a right of property not in the mark, name or get-up improperly used but in the business or goodwill likely to be injured by the misrepresentation …", per Lord Diplock in *Star Industrial Co Ltd v Yap Kwee Kor* [1976] F.S.R. 256. And see Sir John Mummery in *Starbucks (HK) Ltd v British Sky Broadcasting Group Plc* [2013] EWCA Civ 1465; [2014] F.S.R. 20 at [102]. In *Nuanti Ltd v Google Inc* [2019] E.T.M.R. 5, Phillip Johnson, Appointed Person,

held that an open source project (where software developers give up their time without payment) can attract goodwill. The goodwill is in relation to attracting the provision of software developer services.

[26] Lord Macnaghten in *IRC v Muller* [1901] A.C. 217 at 223–224.

[27] Though reputation is referred to by Nourse LJ in *Consorzio del Prosciutto di Parma v Marks and Spencer Plc* [1991] R.P.C. 351 CA, reputation alone is not sufficient: goodwill means actual customer connection or experience. See *Anheuser-Busch Inc v Budejovicky Budvar NP (the Budweiser case)* [1984] F.S.R. 413; and see para.26-07.

[28] *Knight v Beyond Properties Pty Ltd* [2007] EWHC 1251 (Ch); [2007] F.S.R. 34, per David Richards J. Reputation on a small scale could attract the protection of the tort of passing off but the size of goodwill had to be more than a reasonable person would consider to be trivial.

[29] *Chelsea Man Menswear Ltd v Chelsea Girl Ltd* [1985] F.S.R. 567; [1987] R.P.C. 189 CA. In *Student Union Lettings Ltd v Essex Student Lets Ltd* [2018] EWHC 419 (IPEC); [2018] E.T.M.R. 21 at [50]–[53] Miss Recorder Amanda Michaels discusses nationwide versus localised goodwill (in the context of Trade Marks Act 1994 s.11(3)).

[30] In *Irvine v Talksport Ltd* [2002] EWHC 367 (Ch); [2002] 1 W.L.R. 2355, Laddie J stressed the "substantial reputation" of the claimant who had a property right in his goodwill which he could protect from unlicensed appropriation consisting of a false claim or suggestion of endorsement of a third party's goods or business; and see *Fenty v Arcadia Group Brands Ltd* [2015] EWCA Civ 3; [2015] 1 W.L.R. 3291 where it was held that unauthorised merchandising of the celebrity image may deceive the public into believing it is approved merchandise.

[31] Acts done abroad may damage the claimant's UK goodwill: *Mecklermedia Corp v DC Congress Gesellschaft mbH* [1998] Ch. 40; [1997] F.S.R. 627.

Goodwill and foreign undertakings

Replace paragraph with:

26-07 In *Starbucks (HK) Ltd v British Sky Broadcasting Group Plc*[41] the Supreme Court reiterated that goodwill is territorial in nature, it must exist within the jurisdiction; mere reputation within the jurisdiction is insufficient. However the Supreme Court also accepted that it was not necessary for a claimant to have an office/establishment in the jurisdiction. Foreign undertakings[42] have sometimes been held to possess sufficient goodwill in the UK to maintain an action for passing off.[43] The question is whether the claimant has generated goodwill within the jurisdiction: "does the claimant have customers here",[44] as opposed to "people in the jurisdiction who happen to be customers elsewhere",[45] (as was the case on the facts of *Starbucks (HK) Ltd v British Sky Broadcasting Group Plc* itself).[46] The Supreme Court in *Starbucks (HK) Ltd v British Sky Broadcasting Group Plc* considered the position of a foreign service business and approved the decision of the Court of Appeal in *Hotel Cipriani SRL v Cipriani (Grosvenor Street) Ltd*. Here the claimant's business was located in Italy, but goodwill was present in the UK. Though the service was provided overseas, the Court of Appeal held that goodwill existed given "it had a substantial reputation in England and a substantial body of customers from England…".[47] The Court of Appeal discussed generally the issue of whether an overseas service had to be booked by customers from within this jurisdiction in order for there to be the requisite goodwill.[48] Lloyd LJ noted that: "in the circumstances of the present day, with many establishments worldwide featuring on their own or shared websites, through which their services and facilities can be booked directly (or their goods can be ordered directly) from anywhere in the world, the test of direct bookings may be increasingly outmoded. It would be salutary for the test to be reviewed in an appropriate case."[49] However, in view of the Court of Appeal decision in *Anheuser-Busch Inc v Budejovicky Budvar NP*,[50] where goodwill in *goods* rather than services was concerned, there was no goodwill here if the claimant's goods are not available for sale to the public here, at least where the goods are "ordinary retail goods for domestic consumption".[51] However, Lloyd LJ noted that *Anheuser-Busch* had been the subject of criticism by commentators and judges in some other common law jurisdictions.[52] In *Yell Ltd v Giboin*[53] the defendant was the owner and controller of a website outside the UK but the services he advertised could be purchased in the UK. The alleged passing off was within the jurisdiction of the court. However, in *Plentyoffish Media Inc v Plenty More LLP* the claimant had a foreign-based dating website which had attracted visits or "hits" from UK visitors, but there was no evidence any of them had become members. The concept of customers in the jurisdiction required more than visiting a website; nor could the claimant equate visitors with customers simply because the "hits" generated revenue from advertisers.[54] In *Banner Universal Motion Pictures Ltd v Endemol Shine Group Ltd*,[54A] Snowden J held that it is not sufficient to establish goodwill in the jurisdiction that the claimant's website is accessed here, applying *Starbucks (HK) Ltd v British Sky Broadcasting Group Plc*.[54B]

[41] [2015] UKSC 31; [2015] 1 W.L.R. 2628.

[42] Note that under the Trade Marks Act 1994 s.56 a proprietor of a trade mark which is entitled to protection under the Paris Convention as a well-known trade mark is entitled to restrain by injunction the use in the UK of a trade mark which or the essential part of which is identical or similar to his mark, in relation to identical or similar goods or services, where the use is likely to cause confusion, whether or not that person carries on business or has any goodwill in the UK. See para.25-89.

[43] *SA des Anciens Etablissements Panhard et Levassor v Panhard Levassor Motor Co* [1901] 2 Ch. 513 (England one of claimant's markets).

[44] *Athletes Foot Associates v Cobra Sports Ltd* [1980] R.P.C. 343 at 357, per Walton J. The claimant may have licensed the use of his name or mark on products which are sold here: *Globelegance v Sarkissian* [1974] R.P.C. 603. In *Jian Tools Inc v Roderick Manhattan Group Ltd* [1995] F.S.R. 924, Knox J, sales from the American claimant to a small number of English customers "transatlantically inspired" by magazines and recommendations by foreign residents were sufficient to create goodwill. The Supreme Court of Ireland in *C&A Modes Ltd v C&A Waterford Ltd* [1978] F.S.R. 126, held that there may be customers in the jurisdiction, though they travel abroad to obtain the claimant's goods or services. (*Alain Bernadin Cie v Pavilion Properties Ltd* [1967] R.P.C. 581 appeared to demand that the claimant have a trading base within the jurisdiction).

[45] *Starbucks (HK) Ltd v British Sky Broadcasting Group Plc* [2015] UKSC 31; [2015] 1 W.L.R. 2628 (Lord Neuberger at [52])

[46] *Starbucks (HK) Ltd v British Sky Broadcasting Group Plc* [2015] UKSC 31; [2015] 1 W.L.R. 2628 at [52]. The claimant had substantial goodwill in Hong Kong for its internet subscription service. Chinese speaking English residents could gain free access to some of this service via the internet. Merely accessing a foreign service on the internet did not make people in this jurisdiction "customers" within the UK. In the Court of Appeal ([2013] EWCA Civ 1465; [2014] F.S.R. 20 at [104]), Sir John Mummery stated: "generating a goodwill for service delivery generally involves making, or at least attempting to make, some kind of connection with customers in the market with a view to transacting business and repeat business with them", adding that the claimant's customers are those who at the very least are targeted for projected business transactions.

[47] [2010] EWCA Civ 110; [2010] R.P.C. 16, per Lloyd LJ at [118]; Sir Stanley Burnton LJ at [126]. See also *Sheraton Corp of America v Sheraton Motels Ltd* [1964] R.P.C. 202; *Alain Bernardin et Cie v Pavilion Properties Ltd* [1967] R.P.C. 581.

[48] Citing the discussion in C. Wadlow, *The Law of Passing Off: Unfair Competition by Misrepresentation*, 3rd edn (London: Sweet & Maxwell, 2004), para.3-80 that service businesses were of several different kinds so that the same test may not be appropriate for each kind of service, e.g. with hotels the service will be provided at the premises of the supplier, whereas other services may be supplied at the customer's premises, and others simply at a suitable location (now see Wadlow, 5th edn (2016), para.3–99 to 3–100).

[49] [2010] EWCA Civ 110; [2010] R.P.C. 16 at [124]. In the lower court, obiter, Arnold J [2008] EWHC 3032 (Ch); [2009] R.P.C. 9, at [215]–[221] agreed with the view of Browne-Wilkinson VC in *Pete Waterman Ltd v CBS UK Ltd* [1993] E.M.L.R. 27 that it would be sufficient to find goodwill if the foreign service provider had customers here. In *Starbucks (HK) Ltd v British Sky Broadcasting Group Plc* [2015] UKSC 31; [2015] 1 W.L.R. 2628 Lord Neuberger noted that it could be enough if the claimant could show that there were people in the jurisdiction who by booking with or purchasing from an entity in this country obtained a right to receive the claimant's service abroad. Such an entity would not have to be part of the claimant; someone acting for/on behalf of the claimant would be sufficient.

50 [1984] F.S.R. 413.

51 [2010] EWCA Civ 110; [2010] R.P.C. 16 at [38]; "customers among the general public in the UK for those products" at [106], per Lloyd LJ. See Wadlow, 5th edn (2016), para.3–98: "there may be goodwill in England if there are customers here prepared to take whatever trouble is necessary to obtain the claimant's goods from abroad".

52 [2010] EWCA Civ 110; [2010] R.P.C. 16 at [107].

53 [2011] EWPCC 9, HHJ Birss QC.

54 [2011] EWHC 2568 (Ch); [2012] R.P.C. 5, HHJ Birss QC (sitting as a judge of the High Court).

54A [2017] EWHC 2600; [2018] E.C.C. 4 at [81]–[85].

54B [2015] UKSC 31; [2015] 1 W.L.R. 2628.

(b) Misrepresentation

Misrepresentation

Replace paragraph with:

26-16 There must be a misrepresentation,[100] which is a question of fact.[101] In *British Telecommunications Plc v One in a Million Ltd*[102] Aldous LJ held that the mere registration of a domain name containing a well-known name or mark was in itself a misrepresentation (to persons who consult the register of domain names). The misrepresentation must be likely to damage the claimant's goodwill.[103] Passing off may involve misrepresentations made only to suppliers.[104] It is no defence to say that the description used is literally true if, in fact, it misleads. The false representation may be made expressly[105] or impliedly.[106] Since the cause of action depends upon the defendant making a misrepresentation, a trader who uses another's trade mark, but in conjunction with additional matter making it clear to all concerned that the goods are not those of the owner of the mark, will not pass off thereby although if the mark is a registered trade mark he may infringe. Making the distinction clear is not always possible, however; in particular, if the public know the claimant's goods but not his name.[107] A disclaimer is not appropriate where it is unlikely to come to the attention of the reader or may confuse him more if it does.[108] "[T]he qualification must be 'up front' and must be perfectly clear and unambiguous. There may be cases where it is impossible to disclaim adequately."[109] It is sometimes stated that for the tort of passing off, deception, rather than "mere confusion", is required.[110] However, in *Phones 4U Ltd v Phone4U.co.uk Internet Ltd*,[111] Jacob LJ reiterated his view that this distinction can be "elusive". Rather than focusing on the "causative effect", "a more complete test would be whether what is said to be deception rather than mere confusion is really likely to be damaging to the claimant's goodwill or divert trade from him."

100 Stressed by Jacob LJ in *Boehringer Ingelheim KG v Swingward Ltd* [2004] EWCA Civ 129; [2004] 3 C.M.L.R. 3. A defendant may use a mark so as to denote that his goods are suitable for use with the claimant's goods without thereby representing that the defendants' goods are of the claimant's manufacture, e.g. in *Gledhill v British Perforated Toilet Paper Co* (1911) 28 R.P.C. 714, the term "Gledhill coil" had come to mean "coils suitable for use with Gledhill till" and not "coils manufactured by Gledhill". See also *Cellular Clothing v White* (1953) 70 R.P.C. 9; *Singer v Wilson* (1875) 2 Ch D. 434; 3 App. Cas. 376; *Singer Manufacturing Co v Loog* (1880) L.R. 18 Ch D. 395; affirmed at (1882–83) L.R. 8 App. Cas. 15 HL. In *National Guild of Removers & Storers Ltd v Bee Moved Ltd* [2018] EWCA Civ 1302 the defendant had formerly been a member of the claimant trade association. On ceasing membership, the defendant deleted reference to his former membership of that trade association from a house moving website. However, due to IT difficulties involving that website reference to the membership of the trade association was re-instated without the knowledge of the defendant. Held, the defendant had not "made" the misrepresentation (concerning membership) of which the claimant complained.

101 Where goods are sold in specialised markets, evidence of persons accustomed to dealing in those markets as to the likelihood of confusion and deception is essential: *International Business Machines*

Corp v Phoenix International (Computers) Ltd [1994] R.P.C. 251, citing *GE Trade Mark* [1972] 1 W.L.R. 729 HL.

102 [1999] 1 W.L.R. 903. By analogy Patten J in *Reality Group Ltd v Chance* [2002] F.S.R. 13 refused to strike out the claim that the defendant's application to register the name "Reality" as a CTM was in itself passing off. *Bayerische Motoren Werke AG v BMW Telecommunications Ltd* [2019] EWHC 411 (IPEC), HH Judge Hacon. The principle applying to domain name registration is also applicable to company name registration.

103 *Schulke Mayr UK v Alkapharm UK Ltd* [1999] F.S.R. 161 (misrepresentation did not refer to claimant).

104 *Woolworth (FW) & Co v Woolworths (Australasia) Ltd* (1930) 47 R.P.C. 337; *Waterford Wedgewood Plc v David Nagli Ltd* [1998] F.S.R. 92.

105 Or some such act as supplying another's goods in response to an order for the claimant's.

106 *Mornay Ltd v Ball & Rogers (1975) Ltd* [1978] F.S.R. 91, per Goulding J: the defendants marketed a gift package containing the claimants' bathfoam and an unidentified scent, not of the claimants' manufacture. The court accepted that there was arguably a representation that the claimant had authorised the (inferior) scent to be sold in conjunction with its product. See *British Sky Broadcasting Group Plc v Sky Home Services Ltd* [2006] EWHC 3165 (Ch); [2007] 3 All E.R. 1066; [2007] F.S.R. 14, Briggs J, where the misrepresentation was held to be, inter alia, that during telemarketing the defendant's employees failed to correct customer confusion as to the approval of the claimant.

107 As in the "Yorkshire Relish" case, *Birmingham Vinegar Brewery Co v Powell* [1897] A.C. 710. See, on the difficulties of adequate disclaimer in such cases, *Parker-Knoll v Knoll International* [1962] R.P.C. 243 and [1962] R.P.C. 265 HL.

108 *Associated Newspapers v Insert Media* [1991] 1 W.L.R. 571; need to be "massive and omnipresent": *Asprey & Garrard v WRA (Guns) Ltd* [2002] F.S.R. 30, Jacob J. On appeal in *Asprey & Garrard* Gibson LJ noted that: " ... the judge was entitled to draw on his considerable experience in this field to say that such disclaimers hardly ever work": [2001] EWCA Civ 1499; [2002] E.T.M.R. 47; [2002] F.S.R. 31 at [37].

109 Jacob LJ in *IN Newman Ltd v Adlem* [2005] EWCA Civ 741; [2006] F.S.R. 16 at [44]–[45].

110 *Barnsley Brewery Co Ltd v RBNB* [1997] F.S.R. 462 at 467, per Robert Walker J; *Fine & Country Ltd v Okotoks Ltd* [2013] EWCA Civ 672; [2014] F.S.R. 11 at [55] per Lewison LJ: " ... the essence of the action is not confusion, but misrepresentation". Indeed, the Court of Appeal in *Bristol Conservatories Ltd v Conservatories Custom Built Ltd* [1989] R.P.C. 455 noted that there may be passing off without confusion. In *Comic Enterprises Ltd v Twentieth Century Fox Film Corp* [2016] EWCA Civ 41; [2016] E.T.M.R. 22 evidence of customer confusion did not necessarily establish an actionable misrepresentation on the part of the defendant. Kitchin LJ said "the scope of protection conferred by the law of passing off is not the same as that afforded by a registered trade mark" (at [159]).

111 [2006] EWCA Civ 244; [2007] R.P.C. 5 at [16], [19], Jacob LJ. See HH Judge Hacon in *Bayerische Motoren Werke AG v Technosport London Ltd* [2016] EWHC 797 (IPEC) at [46]. And see *Henry Martinez (trading as Prick) v Prick Me Baby One More Time Ltd (trading as Prick)* [2018] EWHC 776 (IPEC); [2018] E.T.M.R. 27, Judge Melissa Clarke, at [22]–[24].

Misrepresentations actionable as passing off

Replace paragraph with:

The general rule is that any misrepresentation[112] calculated to harm the goodwill **26-17** of another will suffice. The classic case of passing off is that of the defendant misrepresenting goods to be those of the claimant. A misrepresentation by the defendant that his and the claimant's business or goods are in some way connected[113] may also be an actionable passing off. So a trader may be restrained from falsely representing that he is a manufacturer's authorised dealer.[114] Persons selling unauthorised character merchandise have been restrained on the basis that members of the public would believe the defendant's goods to be authorised by those responsible for creating the characters.[115] False celebrity endorsement has been held to be an actionable misrepresentation. In *Irvine v Talksport Ltd*[116] the defendant's advertising brochure included a photograph of the claimant, the famous Formula One driver. This photograph had been manipulated to remove the mobile phone that the claimant had in his hand and replace it with the image of a portable radio to which the name of the defendant radio station had been added. Laddie J held that there was an implicit representation of endorsement and that this false representation rendered the defendant liable in passing off. Though Laddie J was keen to distinguish between endorsement cases and "mere" merchandising cases, where the famous image is on memorabilia rather than as recommendation/endorsement of the product, in *Fenty v Arcadia Group Brands Ltd* the Court of Appeal held that unauthorised merchandising of the celebrity image may deceive the public into believing it is approved merchandise and that false belief would be material to their decision to buy the product.[117] It is also passing off to misrepresent inferior lines of goods as higher quality goods of the same manufacturer,[118] or to misrepresent second-hand, altered or deteriorated goods as new.[119] It would also appear to be passing off for the defendant to claim that the claimant's goods are his goods or that the claimant's quality (as evidenced by samples, commendations or testimonials)[120] is his quality.[121] This has been termed "inverse passing off".[122] If the defendant supplies a competing product when the customer had requested the claimant's product, there is passing off.[123] Initial interest confusion may result from a misrepresentation but involves customers not remaining confused at the time of any sale. It is not established whether such initial interest confusion may be sufficient to constitute passing off.[124] However, Wadlow contends that "switch selling"—often by advertising the claimant's goods so as to attract customers in order to persuade them to purchase other goods—may be capable of constituting actionable passing off.[125] Courts in this country have rejected claims based on post-sale confusion as improbable.[126] In *Jadebay Ltd v Clarke-Coles Ltd (t/a Feel Good UK)*,[126A] the claimants had a registered trade mark, Design Element. The defendants used the claimants' Amazon listing for flagpoles – which included the words "by DesignElements" to sell its own flagpoles. The Amazon listings procedure allows multiple sellers to sell the same product on that listing; the default seller is selected by Amazon usually on the basis of the lowest price. The defendants by undercutting the price of the claimants' product had become the default seller. It was held that the defendants' use of the claimants' listing was a misrepresentation.

[112] How the courts will allow the tort to develop is unclear. In *Matthew Gloag & Son Ltd v Welsh Distillers Ltd* [1998] F.S.R. 718, Laddie J refused to strike out an action where Scotch whisky was flavoured with herbs and sold by the defendants as "Welsh Whisky". The claimants, as scotch whisky producers, alleged that this was some sort of actionable product misdescription and the harm alleged was that the defendants were "diluting" the reputation of scotch whisky by using its quality to sell their own product.

[113] The exact nature of the mis-connection that must be shown by the claimant is not clear. In *Harrods Ltd v Harrodian School* [1996] R.P.C. 697, Millett LJ held that the relevant connection must be one by which the claimants would be taken by the public to have made themselves responsible for the quality of the defendants' goods or services (cited by Briggs J in *British Sky Broadcasting Group Plc v Sky Home Services Ltd* [2006] EWHC 3165 (Ch); [2007] 3 All E.R. 1066, and by Birss J in *Fenty v Arcadia Group Brands Ltd* [2013] EWHC 2310 (Ch); [2014] F.S.R. 5). However, Sir Michael Kerr in *Harrods Ltd*, dissenting, took a much wider view: provided the public assumed that the claimants were somehow "mixed up" with the defendants' business or goods that would be sufficient (echoing *Ewing v Buttercup Margarine Co Ltd* [1917] 2 Ch. 1). See also Proudman J in *Future Publishing Ltd v Edge Interactive Media Inc* [2011] EWHC 1489 (Ch); [2011] E.T.M.R. 50 at [71]: statements leading the public to believe the defendant's product "in some way approved or authorised" by the claimant. See *Victoria Plum (t/a Victoria Plumb) v Victorian Plumbing Ltd* [2016] EWHC 2911; [2017] E.T.M.R. 8 (Ch), Henry Carr J with regard to passing off and keyword advertising.

[114] *Sony KK v Saray Electronics (London) Ltd* [1983] F.S.R. 302. *International Scientific v Pattison* [1979] F.S.R. 429; *Kimberley-Clark Ltd v Fort Sterling Ltd* [1997] F.S.R. 877; *Musical Fidelity Ltd v Vickers* [2002] EWCA Civ 1989; [2003] F.S.R. 50. And see *Primark Stores Ltd v Lollypop Clothing Ltd* [2001] F.S.R. 37, identical clothes but manufactured without authorisation.

[115] *Mirage Studios v Counter-Feat Clothing Co Ltd* [1991] F.S.R.; *Hearst Holdings Inc v AVELA Inc* [2014] EWHC 439 (Ch); [2014] E.T.M.R. 34, Birss J, especially at [107]. However, compare the views of Laddie J and the Court of Appeal in *Elvis Presley Trade Mark* [1997] R.P.C. 543 at 554 and [1999] R.P.C. 567; and *BBC Worldwide Ltd v Pally Screen Printing Ltd* [1998] F.S.R. 665 at 674.

116 [2002] EWHC 367; [2002] 1 W.L.R. 2355, per Laddie J. (The Court of Appeal upheld Laddie J's judgment on passing off but overruled him on quantum: [2003] EWCA Civ 423; [2003] 2 All E.R. 881). *McCulloch v Lewis A May* [1947] 2 All E.R. 845 rejected; *Henderson v Radio Corp Pty Ltd* [1969] R.P.C. 218 (a decision of the High Court of New South Wales, sitting in its appellate jurisdiction) preferred. Note the false brand endorsement claim in *Unilever Plc v Griffin* [2010] EWHC 899 (Ch); [2010] F.S.R. 33, Arnold J.

117 [2015] EWCA Civ 3; [2015] 1 W.L.R. 3291. It was accepted that mere sales of T-shirts with the celebrity image would not per se be passing off.

118 *Spalding (AG) & Bros v AW Gamage Ltd* (1915) 84 L.J. Ch. 449; 32 R.P.C. 273; *Colgate-Palmolive v Markwell Finance Ltd* [1989] R.P.C. 497 and cases cited there.

119 *Standard Motor Co v Grantchester Garage* [1960] R.P.C. 211 and cases cited there; *Wilts United Dairies v Robinson* [1953] R.P.C. 94 (also malicious falsehood); *International Business Machines Corp v Phoenix International (Computers) Ltd* [1994] R.P.C. 251.

120 *Bristol Conservatories Ltd v Conservatories Custom Built Ltd* [1989] R.P.C. 455—defendant misrepresented that the claimant's goods/services were the defendant's, thereby appropriating the goodwill of the claimant; *Tallerman v Dowsing* [1900] 1 Ch. 1; *Copydex Ltd v Noso Products Ltd* (1952) 69 R.P.C. 38. In *Orvec International Ltd v Linfoots Ltd* [2014] EWHC 1970 (IPEC) HH Judge Hacon at [36] commented on inverse passing off: "the courts have not since disagreed with the principle expressed in *Bristol Conservatories* and it has become accepted that where a defendant represents the claimant's article as being the product of his own effort and skill, this may be an actionable misrepresentation."

121 Cf. cases involving "product equivalence" misrepresentations, where the defendants are liable for incorrectly alleging that their goods are "equivalent to" or "the same as" the claimants: *Masson Seeley & Co v Embossotype Mfg Co* (1924) 41 R.P.C. 160, per Tomlin J; *Combe International Ltd v Scholl (UK) Ltd* [1980] R.P.C. 1, per Fox J.

122 In *Matthew Gloag & Son Ltd v Welsh Distillers Ltd* [1998] F.S.R. 718, Laddie J accepted the legitimacy of an allegation of inverse passing off as did the Court of Appeal of the Republic of Singapore in *John Robert Powers School Inc v Denyse Bernadette Tessensohn* [1995] F.S.R. 947. In *Doosan Power Systems Ltd v Babcock International Group Plc* [2013] EWHC 1364 (Ch); [2013] E.T.M.R. 40 at [174] Henderson J held there to be a "subtle" misrepresentation that the claimant's expertise was that of the defendant (rather than a source misrepresentation). However in *Woolley v Ultimate Products Ltd* [2012] EWCA Civ 1038 Arden LJ at [6] rejects "reverse passing off" in the sense of a misrepresentation that confuses the public into thinking that the goods of the claimant are the goods of the defendant.

123 *Bovril v Bodega* (1916) 33 R.P.C. 153.

124 Wadlow, 5th edn (2016), para.7-53 onwards contends that *Doosan Power Systems Ltd v Babcock International Group Plc* [2013] EWHC 1364 (Ch); [2013] E.T.M.R. 40, where at [178] per Henderson J stated:

> "it matters not that the truth is subsequently discovered by the purchaser. From the point of view of the claimant, the damage has already been done and the distinctiveness of the goodwill has been eroded"

was in fact a case of inverse passing off and that *Och-Ziff Management Europe Ltd v Och Capital LLP* [2010] EWHC 2599 (Ch); [2011] F.S.R. 11 (where Arnold J appeared to accept initial interest confusion at [155]–[157]) was an "ordinary" case of passing off in which damage was inferred. See also HH Judge Hacon in *Moroccanoil Israel Ltd v Aldi Stores Ltd* [2014] EWHC 1686 (IPEC) at [21]–[28] and *Argos Ltd v Argos Systems Inc* [2017] EWHC 231 (Ch); [2017] E.T.M.R. 19, Richard Spearman QC, sitting as Deputy Judge, at [356].

125 See Wadlow, 5th edn (2016) at para.7–53 onwards.

126 *Bostick Tld v Sellotape GB Ltd* [1994] R.P.C. 556; *Hodgkinson & Corby Ltd v Wards Mobility Ltd* [1994] 1 W.L.R. 1564 at 1577 (Jacob J); cf. NZ: *Levi Strauss & Co v Kimbyr Investments Ltd* [1994] F.S.R. 335.

126A [2017] EWHC 1400 (IPEC); [2017] E.T.M.R. 34.

"Extended passing off": product misdescription

Replace footnote 128 with:

128 Lord Diplock in *Advocaat* [1979] A.C. 731 at 747: "if one can define with reasonable precision the type of product that has acquired the reputation, one can identify the members of the class entitled to share in the goodwill"; Laddie J in *Chocosuisse Union des Fabricants Suisses de Chocolat v Cadbury Ltd* [1998] R.P.C. 117: there must be a "defined class of goods with a distinctive reputation" (appeal on **26-18**

passing off dismissed: [1999] R.P.C. 826 CA). Designation of origin or geographical indications for agricultural products/foodstuffs may be covered by Reg (EU) 1151/2012. In *Fage UK Ltd v Chobani UK* [2014] EWCA Civ 5; [2014] E.T.M.R. 26 the defendant claimed that in light of this Regulation the court had no power to grant injunctive relief otherwise than in conformity with the provisions of that Regulation. However it was held that the EU law does not preclude the application of national rules for the protection of geographical denomination which do not fall within the scope of the 2012 Regulation (see Kitchin LJ at [88]). In *Military Mutual Ltd v Police Mutual Assurance Society Ltd* [2018] EWHC 1575 (IPEC); [2018] E.T.M.R. 33 at [67], HH Judge Hacon noted, obiter, that though previous "extended passing off" cases have involved a name associated with a type of product, there was no reason why the tort should not similarly protect goodwill associated with the name of a type of service or perhaps goodwill associated with a name given to a type of organisation.

(c) Damage

Damage

Replace paragraph with:

26-20 Once a claimant has established that there has been a misrepresentation, it is usually easy to show that damage to goodwill will result. Some damage will often be assumed once it has been established that there is a misrepresentation so proof of actual damage is not essential to establishing liability.[151] Commonly damage in this tort involves diversion of sales or the risk of devaluation of reputation/injurious association.[152] Lost licensing fees may be recovered if licensing is part of the claimant's goodwill[153] and loss of reputation control may also be recoverable (as in *Fenty v Arcadia Group Brands Ltd*).[154] Dilution (loss of distinctiveness) is also a head of recoverable damage.[155] In *Woolley v Ultimate Products Ltd*[156] Arden LJ noted that the heads of damage for the tort include "an erosion or diminution in the value of goodwill". But no cause of action arises for mere dilution of goodwill where there is no relevant misrepresentation that causes it. In *Student Union Lettings Ltd v Essex Student Lets Ltd*[156A] there was no direct loss of sales caused by the defendants' misrepresentation. However harm could potentially arise through inadequacies in the defendants' services and the restriction of the claimants' intended expansion of its activities.

[151] *Procea v Evans* (1951) 68 R.P.C. 210. In *British Sky Broadcasting Group Plc v Microsoft Corp* [2013] EWHC 1826 (Ch) at [250], Asplin J noted "damage is inherently likely where frequently the customers of a business wrongly connect it to another".

[152] As to loss of sales, see *Draper v Trist* [1939] 3 All E.R. 513; (1939) 56 R.P.C. 429 CA. With regard to injurious association see, e.g. *Annabel's (Berkeley Square) Ltd v Schock (Trading as Annabel's Escort Agency)* [1972] F.S.R. 261 CA. In *Associated Newspapers Ltd v Express Newspapers* [2003] EWHC 1322 (Ch); [2003] F.S.R. 51, Laddie J, the defendants were restrained from using a similar title for their newspaper to that used by the claimants' paper as there was a likelihood that the claimants would "lose control of its personality". The defendants' newspapers included adverts for adult chat lines and massage parlours, services which would not be acceptable in the claimants' papers. And see *Unilever Plc v Griffin* [2010] EWHC 899 (Ch); [2010] F.S.R. 33, Arnold J.

[153] *Fine & Country Ltd v Okotoks Ltd* [2013] EWCA Civ 672; [2014] F.S.R. 11. In relation to harm to expansion potential see *Alfred Dunhill Ltd v Sunoptic SA* [1979] F.S.R. 337 CA.

[154] *Fenty v Arcadia Group Brands Ltd (t/a Topshop)* [2015] EWCA Civ 3; [2015] 1 W.L.R. 3291. In *Comptroller-General of Patents Designs and Trade Marks v Intellectual Property Agency Ltd* [2015] EWHC 3256 (IPEC) HH Judge Hacon, the defendants were involved in a renewal scam on IP right holders, requesting higher fees than those they ultimately passed on to the claimant, the UK IPO. Though the claimant did in fact receive the appropriate renewal fees, inactivity on the part of the claimant in preventing the scam would be likely to harm its reputation; passing off was established. See also *Ukelele Orchestra of Great Britain v Clausen* [2015] EWHC 1772 (IPEC); [2015] E.T.M.R. 40, HH Judge Hacon: the use by the defendants of a confusingly similar trade name caused damage to the claimant's goodwill by their loss of control over their reputation as performers.

[155] Especially in cases of extended passing off, see, e.g. *Fage UK Ltd v Chobani UK Ltd* [2014] EWCA Civ 5; [2014] E.T.M.R. 26 at [67], per Kitchin LJ. On dilution and substitution see: *Och–Ziff Manage-*

ment Europe Ltd v Och Capital LLP [2010] EWHC 2599 (Ch); [2011] F.S.R. 11, Arnold J at [158]–[160].

156 [2012] EWCA Civ 1038 at [7].

156A [2018] EWHC 419 (IPEC), Miss Recorder Amanda Michaels.

4. DEFENCES

Unconscionability

Replace paragraph with:

No relief will be granted if it would be unconscionable to do so on the grounds that the claimant has acquiesced in the use complained of. The defendant must show that he has altered his position on the basis of an act, omission or representation of the claimant.[174] Delay alone will not bar the right but may have an effect on, for example, whether an injunction will be granted.[175] The courts give limited effect to the clean hands doctrine. Thus, no one can claim to be protected in the use of a trade mark, name, or description, which is a fraud on the right of another trader, or a deception on the public, or used as an instrument of dishonest trading. EU law has had little impact on the law of passing off.[176] This is chiefly because of the difficulty in persuading any English court that any part of the Treaty on the Functioning of the EU permits a person to mislead likely purchasers as to the nature or quality of his goods.[177] The defendants in *Fage UK Ltd v Chobani UK Ltd*[178] argued that in a case involving cross-border trade the relevant test to apply in deciding whether there was deception was whether the "average consumer" would be deceived, rather than the traditional passing off test of confusion/deception of a substantial part of the public, in order to ensure that there was a sufficiently serious risk of misleading consumers. The Court of Appeal held the point could not be taken as it had not been advanced before the trial judge, but Kitchin LJ noted that as the law of passing off operates to prevent confusion and deception of the public, it operated compliantly with arts 34–36 of the Treaty of the Functioning of the EU.[179] In *Coreix Ltd v Coretx Holdings Plc*[179A] Recorder Douglas Campbell QC concluded that estoppel/acquiescence can be relied upon to provide a defence in a passing off action (though on the facts the defences failed). There is a clear distinction in case law between mere acquiescence/inaction and the encouragement or creation of expectation.[179B] **26-24**

174 See *Habib Bank Ltd v Habib Bank AG Zurich* [1981] 1 W.L.R. 1265 (claimant assisted defendant in setting up in business).

175 Peter Smith J noted in *A&E Television Networks LLC v Discovery Communications Europe Ltd* [2013] EWHC 109 (Ch); [2013] E.T.M.R. 32 that the lack of complaint for seven years was strong evidence for the defendant.

176 See, e.g. Wadlow, *The Law of Passing-Off: Unfair Competition by Misrepresentation*, 5th edn (2016) for a full discussion. There is, of course, a large body of EC jurisprudence dealing with registered trade marks.

177 Accordingly, although they are sometimes raised, defences to passing off actions based on EC law, whether arts 28 and 30 or 81 and 82 of the Treaty of Rome, have yet to succeed (now arts 34 and 36; 101 and 102 respectively of the Treaty on the Functioning of the EU). The fairness of commercial transactions and the defence of the consumer are "mandatory requirements" giving rise to a derogation from art.30 of the Treaty of Rome: *Cassis de Dijon* (120/78) [1979] E.C.R. 649; [1979] 3 C.M.L.R. 494. It is no defence that the goods in question could lawfully be sold in other EC countries: *Löwenbräu München v Grunhalle Lager International Ltd* [1974] R.P.C. 492. Where goodwill has been assigned to different trading entities so as to divide up the European Community, an argument based on art.101 TFEU may have some chance of success: see *Sirena SRL v Eda SRL* [1971] E.C.R. 69; [1971] C.M.L.R. 260; *IHT Internationale Heitztechnik GmbH v Ideal Standard GmbH* [1995] F.S.R. 59; [1994] 3 C.M.L.R. 857.

[178] [2014] EWCA Civ 5; [2014] E.T.M.R. 26.

[179] [2014] EWCA Civ 5; [2014] E.T.M.R. 26 at [110]; and see Lewison LJ at [173].

[179A] [2017] EWHC 1695 (IPEC); [2018] F.S.R. 6.

[179B] [2017] EWHC 1695 (IPEC); [2018] F.S.R. 6 at [88]. On estoppel see at [89].

5. RELATIONSHIP TO OTHER RIGHTS

Relationship to Trade Marks Act 1994[180]

Replace footnote 180 with:

26-25 The Trade Marks Act 1994 does not affect the law relating to passing off: Trade Marks Act 1994 s.2(2). By s.5(4)(a) of the Trade Marks Act 1994, a trade mark shall not be registered if its use in the UK is liable to be prevented, inter alia, by the law of passing off. The issue of passing off should be assessed at the date upon which the application for registration was made *Dixy Fried Chickens (Euro) Ltd v Dixy Fried Chickens (Stratford) Ltd* [2003] EWHC 2902 (Ch), per Laddie J. In *Maier v ASOS Plc* [2015] EWCA Civ 220; [2015] F.S.R. 20 [165], with reference to art.8(4) of Regulation 207/2009 CTMR, the CTM equivalent of s.5(4)(a), Kitchin LJ discussed the relevant date for determining whether a claimant has established the necessary reputation or goodwill. *Tilda Riceland Private Ltd v OHIM* [2016] E.T.M.R. 5, General Court of the European Union: in opposition proceedings (under art.8(4) Regulation 207/2009) to a community trade mark application, where the opponent relied on the UK action for passing off, the extended form of that action was applicable. On the relationship to CTM registration see: *Pinterest Inc v Premium Interest Ltd* [2015] EWHC 738 (Ch); [2015] F.S.R. 27 Arnold J (registration of a CTM did not provide a defence to a claim for passing off). In *Caspian Pizza Ltd v Shah* [2017] EWCA Civ 1874; [2018] E.T.M.R. 8 in opposition proceedings under the Trade Marks Act 1994, s.5(4)(a) it was held that the opponent could rely on local goodwill to invalidate the claimant's trade mark. Patten LJ said, at [23]: "goodwill which is established in a particular locality will be capable of preventing registration of a countrywide mark".

Chapter 27

BREACH OF CONFIDENCE AND PRIVACY

Table of Contents

1. General introduction

Modern developments and the protection of privacy

Replace footnote 9 with:

[9] See paras 27-29, 27-37, 27-39. In *Fearn v Board of Trustees of the Tate Gallery* [2019] EWHC 246 (Ch) Mann J held that art.8 rights might also be protected by the tort of nuisance: "external prying into a home would contravene the privacy protected by Article 8" (at [171]) and to give effect to that courts can develop, inter alia, the tort of nuisance. **27-02**

2. Action for breach of confidence

Parties

Replace paragraph with:

Only the party to whom the duty of confidence is owed has a right of action to protect it.[49] The claimant is usually the owner[50] of the confidential material or one whose confidential communications are otherwise protected by the law. However, the majority of the House of Lords in *OBG Ltd v Allan*[51] determined that on the facts an obligation of confidence was also owed to an exclusive licensee of the information concerned. This case involved Hello! magazine's publication of unauthorised photographs of Michael Douglas and Catherine Zeta-Jones's wedding reception. The celebrity magazine *OK!* had contracted with the couple for "exclusive" rights over approved wedding photographs. The photographs were taken on a private occasion where there had been an express prohibition by the couple on unauthorised photography. In the Court of Appeal the Douglases' breach of confidence claim **27-08** (which contained both privacy and commercial aspects) succeeded[52] but OK!'s claims failed. OK!'s appeal to the House of Lords was based inter alia on the alleged duty of confidence owed to them in the photographic images of the wedding. Unlike the Court of Appeal, the majority of the House of Lords—Lords Hoffmann, Brown and Baroness Hale—held that the obligation of confidence extended to OK!, as exclusive licensee, because "everyone knew that the obligation of confidence was imposed for the benefit of OK! as well as the Douglases" and "they paid or the benefit of the obligation of confidence imposed on all those present".[53] The minority—Lords Nicholls and Walker—found no duty owed to OK! in respect of the unauthorised pictures.[54] As far as defendants are concerned, the position of those receiving information innocently is considered below, as is the position of indirect recipients and those on whom it is sought to impose secondary liability.[55] In *Warwickshire CC v Matalia*[55A] the claimant county council had commissioned test papers from a university (which retained copyright) for use in local schools. The same paper was to be used for different sittings of the test. After the first sitting the defendant published details of the test—obtained from pupils who had sat the test—on his website. The county council had locus standi to bring a claim for breach of confidence: "As the provider and administrator of the tests the Council had a substantial and legitimate interest in the maintenance of confidentiality".[55B] The defendant owed a duty of confidence to the claimant. The confidential character of the information was obvious to the defendant "whether or not the children who supplied the information to him were themselves under any duty of confidence".[55C]

[49] *Fraser v Evans* [1969] 1 Q.B. 349 ("the party complaining must be the person who is entitled to the confidence and to have it respected"). In *Jones v IOS (RUK) Ltd* [2012] EWHC 348 (Ch) (HH Judge Hodge QC) it was held that the claimant had to have "sufficient interest in the information" (see [40]). And see *Abbey v Gilligan* [2012] EWHC 3217 (QB); [2013] E.M.L.R. 12 Tugendhat J at [40]–[41].

[50] It is common to speak of the "owner" of the information but, because the courts have not held that information is property as traditionally conceived, use of the term "person to whom the duty is owed" is perhaps less controversial.

[51] [2007] UKHL 21; [2008] 1 A.C. 1.

[52] *Douglas v Hello (No.3)* [2005] EWCA Civ 595; [2006] Q.B. 125.

[53] Lord Hoffmann in *OBG Ltd v Allan* [2007] UKHL 21; [2008] 1 A.C. 1 at [114] and [117].

[54] Lord Walker contended that "OK! no more had a monopoly in any possible photographs of the spectacle than it had in the spectacle itself": [2007] UKHL 21; [2008] 1 A.C. 1 at [296], citing the High Court of Australia in *Victoria Park Racing and Recreation Grounds Ltd v Taylor* (1937) 58 C.L.R. 479 in support.

[55] Lord Griffiths, *Att Gen v Guardian Newspapers (No.2)* [1990] 1 A.C. 109 at 268: "the duty of confidence is, as a general rule, also imposed on a third party who is in possession of information which he knows is subject to an obligation of confidence." See generally paras 27-17 to 27-18. As for vicarious liability, see Lord Neuberger in *Vestergaard Fransden S/A v Bestnet Europe Ltd* [2013] UKSC 31; [2013] 1 W.L.R. 1556.

[55A] [2017] EWCA Civ 991; [2017] E.C.C. 25.

[55B] [2017] EWCA Civ 991; [2017] E.C.C. 25 at [30] per David Richards LJ.

[55C] See the discussion [2017] EWCA Civ 991; [2017] E.C.C. 25 at [46]–[47].

(a) Information in respect of which an action for breach of confidence may arise

Need for identification of the confidential information

Replace footnote 79 with:

27-11 [79] *Ocular Sciences Ltd v Aspect Vision Care Ltd* [1997] R.P.C. 289. Applied, *Bains v Moore* [2017] EWHC 242 (QB); [2017] E.M.L.R. 20, Tugendhat J.

(b) Where an obligation of confidence arises

Rights against ex-employees

Replace footnote 135 with:

[135] *Balston Ltd v Headline Filters Ltd* [1987] F.S.R. 330, per Scott J In *Force India Formula One Team Ltd v 1 Malaysia Racing Team Sdn Bhd* [2013] EWCA Civ 780; [2013] R.P.C. 36 at [60] Lewison LJ agreed with Scott J in declining to read Faccenda as holding that confidential information not protected by the implied term could not be protected by an express term. (See also *Lancashire Fires Ltd v SA Lyons & Co Ltd* [1997] I.R.L.R. 113). *Invista Textiles UK Ltd v Botes* [2019] EWHC 58 (Ch) Birss J contains a useful review of case law on restrictive covenants [46]–[48]. **27-15**

Secondary or accessory liability

Replace footnote 153 with:

[153] [2013] UKSC 31; [2013] 1 W.L.R. 1556 at [34]. (And see *Marathon Asset Management LLP v Seddon* [2017] EWHC 300 (Comm); [2017] I.C.R. 791 Leggatt J, at [132]). *Unilever Plc v Gillette Ltd* [1989] R.P.C. 583 CA, a patent case, was distinguished as not applying to confidential information and involving possible strict liability, see [36]–[37]; cf. *Lancashire Fires Ltd v SA Lyons & Co* [1996] F.S.R. 629 where it had been conceded that the principle in *Unilever* applied to confidential information cases. See Lord Neuberger in *Vestergaard* [2013] UKSC 31; [2013] 1 W.L.R. 1556 at [38]–[39]. **27-18**

Statutory obligations/public bodies

Replace footnote 154 with:

[154] The principal general statute regulating the use of personal data—some of which is not necessarily confidential—is the Data Protection Act 2018, see further para.27-54. **27-19**

(c) Breach

Use and disclosure

Delete footnote 163. Replace footnote 166 with:

[166] [2010] EWCA Civ 908; [2011] Fam. 116 at [69] and [72]. And see *Primary Group (UK) Ltd v The Royal Bank of Scotland Plc* [2014] EWHC 1082 (Ch); [2014] R.P.C. 26 at [243] per Arnold J. See also *Warwickshire CC v Matalia* [2018] EWHC 1340 (Ch), HH Judge Simon Barker QC (for the background facts see para.27-08): the defendant by continuing to seek to obtain and actually obtaining the confidential information without authority was in breach of confidence, even without the dissemination or publication of that information (citing *Tchenguiz v Imerman* [2010] EWCA Civ 908; [2011] Fam. 116). **27-20**

Involuntary or accidental use

Replace footnote 167 with:

[167] *Seager v Copydex* [1967] 1 W.L.R. 923. *Paymaster (Jamaica) Ltd v Grace Kennedy Remittance Services Ltd* [2017] UKPC 40 (PC); [2018] Bus. L.R. 492 at [41]: conscious plagiarism not a necessary component for a claim for breach of confidence. **27-21**

Replace footnote 175: **27-24**

Use by regulatory authorities[175] and for legal proceedings

[175] As to regulatory authorities, see para.27-30. Under the Investigatory Powers Act 2016 UK intelligence/law enforcement agencies were granted new powers to intercept communications and powers of bulk communications data acquisition. In *R. (on the application of NCCL) v Secretary of State for the Home Dept* [2018] EWHC 975 (Admin); [2018] 3 W.L.R. 1435 the Investigatory Powers Act 2016, Pt 4 (on the retention of data) was held to be incompatible with fundamental rights in EU law. To

be amended by 1 November 2018. In *Big Brother Watch v UK (58170/13)* [2018] 9 WLUK 157, ECtHR, the right to intercept internet communications in bulk under s.8(4) of the Regulation of Investigatory Powers Act 2000 was held to have breached art.8.

(d) Defences

(ii) Public interest

Disclosure of matters of real public concern

Replace paragraph with:

27-28 There is a clearly established defence of disclosure of matters of public interest in the action for breach of confidence. The much quoted dictum: "The true doctrine is that there is no equity in the disclosure of iniquity"[192] is merely an example of the broader principle that the disclosure of confidential information will not be restrained when there is a just cause or excuse for disclosing it.[193] The defence of public interest certainly covers "matters carried out or contemplated in breach of the country's security, or in breach of the law, including statutory duty, fraud, or otherwise destructive of the country or its people, including matters medically dangerous to the public: and doubtless other misdeeds of similar gravity"[194] but it is not limited to these categories.[195] The general principle is that disclosure should be made to one who has a proper interest in receiving the information.[196] The question is whether the information is such that it ought to be disclosed to a competent authority,[197] or whether it ought to be made available to the public at large through the media.[198] In the following cases (all prior to the Human Rights Act 1998) the information concerned was of "real public concern" and disclosure permitted: unreliability of intoximeters used in the course of testing the breath of drivers, disclosed by employees to newspaper[199]; medical practices alleged to be dangerous[200]; accountants disclosing information about their client, a collapsed bank, to a Bank of England inquiry.[201] In all these cases there is a conflict between two public interests: that of maintaining confidentiality and that of making matters or public interest known to those with a proper interest. A balancing act has to be performed.[202] It has been the case in the past that in undertaking this balancing act the courts have acknowledged the relevance of freedom of expression. However, this consideration is now enhanced by the Human Rights Act 1998.[203] This should be borne in mind when reviewing cases on the public interest defence that predate the Human Rights Act 1998.[204] In *Brevan Howard Asset Management LLP v Reuters Ltd*[204A] the defendant claimed that the public interest applied. The judge, with whom the Court of Appeal agreed, held that *HRH Prince of Wales v Associated Newspapers Ltd*[204B] applied in a commercial confidence case. There is an important public interest in the observance of duties of confidence; it is not enough to justify publication that the information is a matter of public interest. Sir Terence Etherton MR said, at [62], that "the fact that information relates to information received in confidence is a factor that art.10(2) recognises as of itself justifying restrictions on freedom of expression".[204C] There was nothing inconsistent between the application of the *Prince of Wales* case and the jurisprudence of the ECtHR.[204D]

[192] *Gartside v Outram* (1857) 26 L.J. Ch. 113.

[193] It does not extend only to the detection or prevention of wrongdoing: *Lion Laboratories Ltd v Evans* [1985] Q.B. 526. The burden lies on the defendant to justify the defence: see *Att Gen v Guardian Newspapers (No.2)* [1990] 1 A.C. 109.

194 See *Beloff v Pressdram Ltd* [1973] 1 All E.R. 241; *British Steel v Granada Television Ltd* [1981] A.C. 1096.

195 See *Lion Laboratories Ltd v Evans* [1985] Q.B. 526, per Stephenson LJ. See also the categories of information mentioned in the Public Interest Disclosure Act 1998, para.27-32, though the House of Lords made clear in *Cream Holdings Ltd v Banerjee* [2004] UKHL 44; [2005] 1 A.C. 253 that these "whistleblower" provisions added protection to employees; they were not intended to cut down the circumstances where public interest might apply to the publication of private information. There is a public interest in correcting misleading public statements: *Viagogo Ltd v Myles* [2012] EWHC 433 (Ch), Hildyard J.

196 See, e.g. *Initial Services v Putterill* [1968] 1 Q.B. 396; *Francome v Mirror Group Newspapers Ltd* [1984] 1 W.L.R. 892 (only limited disclosure required).

197 *A Company's Application, Re* [1989] Ch. 477 (no injunction granted to prohibit disclosure of financial affairs to regulatory body).

198 *Initial Services Ltd v Putterill* [1968] 1 Q.B. 396; *Hubbard v Vosper* [1972] 2 Q.B. 84; *Lion Laboratories Ltd v Evans* [1985] Q.B. 526.

199 *Lion Laboratories Ltd v Evans* [1985] Q.B. 526.

200 *Hubbard v Vosper* [1972] 2 Q.B. 84.

201 *Price Waterhouse v BCCI Holdings (Luxembourg) SA* [1992] B.C.L.C. 583, principles reviewed and restated by Millett J.

202 *Lion Laboratories Ltd v Evans* [1985] Q.B. 526; *Att Gen v Guardian Newspapers (No.2)* [1990] 1 A.C. 109.

203 The issue of public interest/art.10 and privacy is discussed in para.27-49.

204 For cases post-Human Rights Act 1998 see *London Regional Transport v Mayor of London* [2001] EWCA Civ 1491; [2003] E.M.L.R. 4; *Jockey Club v Buffham* [2002] EWHC 1866 (QB); [2003] Q.B. 462.

204A [2017] EWCA Civ 950; [2017] E.M.L.R. 28.

204B [2006] EWCA Civ 1776; [2008] Ch. 57.

204C [2017] EWCA Civ 950; [2017] E.M.L.R. 28 at [62].

204D [2017] EWCA Civ 950; [2017] E.M.L.R. 28 at [66]. The difference in outcomes in *London Regional Transport v Mayor of London* [2001] EWCA Civ 1491; [2003] E.M.L.R. 4 and *Northern Rock Plc v The Financial Times Ltd* [2007] EWHC 2677 (QB) was explained (at [71]–[72]). Non-disclosure agreements and the public interest were discussed in *ABC v Telegraph Media Group Ltd* [2018] EWCA Civ 2329; [2019] E.M.L.R. 5. The Court of Appeal stressed the public interest in upholding contractual bargains (see *Mionis v Democratic Press SA* [2017] EWCA Civ 1194; [2018] Q.B. 662). See also *Linklaters LLP v Mellish* [2019] EWHC 177 (QB), Warby J.

3. THE ACTION FOR MISUSE OF PRIVATE INFORMATION/PRIVACY

The action for misuse of private information acknowledged

Replace paragraph with:

In recent years the action for breach of confidence has been developed to protect privacy interests.[258] This has been influenced by the incorporation of the ECHR by the Human Rights Act 1998 and, in particular, the Convention right to respect for private life, contained in art.8. This provides: **27-37**

> "(1) Everyone has the right to respect for his private and family life, his home and his correspondence.
>
> (2) There shall be no interference by a public authority with the exercise of this right except such as is in accordance with the law and is necessary in a democratic society in the interests of national security, public safety or the economic well-being of the country, for the prevention of disorder or crime, for the protection of health or morals, or for the protection of the rights or freedoms of others."[259]

An important landmark in this process is the House of Lords' decision in *Campbell v MGN Ltd.*[260] Here Lord Hoffmann noted that "English law has adapted the action for breach of confidence to provide a remedy for the unauthorised disclosure of personal information … this development has been mediated by the analogy of the right to disentitle them to a reasonable expectation of privacy article 8 of the European Convention on Human Rights".[261] In that case the defendant newspaper published the fact of the claimant's drug addiction and treatment. It also published details of that treatment, together with a covertly taken photograph of the claimant attending for treatment. The claimant, a celebrity model, accepted that as she had lied about her addiction, the truth about her addiction and the fact of seeking treatment was not protected. The majority of the House of Lords (Baroness Hale, Lords Hope and Carswell) however held that the *details* of the treatment and the accompanying photograph linked to the treatment went too far. This was private information, over and above setting the record straight, the disclosure of which was distressing and put the treatment at risk. On the facts the claimant's art.8 right outweighed the defendant newspaper's right to freedom of expression, under art.10 of the ECHR. The House of Lords acknowledged that art.8 of the ECHR has reshaped the action for breach of confidence so that it now protects against the "misuse of private information".[262] In *Secretary of State for the Home Department v TLU*[262A] Gross LJ referred to "evolving legal policy in this area" citing *R. (on the application of Catt) v Association of Chief Police Officers*[262B] and Lord Sumption JSC's "illuminating thumbnail sketch of the development of the Law's protection of privacy". In the case itself there had been an accidental publication on the government website of the personal data of a failed asylum seeker: liability for misuse of private information also extended to unnamed family members, given that their identity and location could be inferred.

[258] See for example, Sedley LJ in *Douglas v Hello! Ltd* [2001] Q.B. 967 at 1002: "the law has to protect not only those people whose trust has been abused but those who simply find themselves subjected to an unwanted intrusion into their personal lives." Tugendhat J in *Goodwin v News Group Newspapers Ltd* [2011] EWHC 1437 (QB); [2011] E.M.L.R. 27 at [85] analysed what the right to respect for private life involved. Citing Warby, Moreham and Christie (eds), *Law of Privacy and the Media*, 2nd edn (Oxford: OUP, 2011) he notes the two core components are confidentiality and intrusion. (He further noted, at [116], that protection against intrusion was also provided by the Protection from Harassment Act 1997—see para.27–55). There is a statutory right to privacy in photographs taken for private or domestic purposes: s.85 of the Copyright, Designs and Patents Act 1988.

[259] The notion of necessity implies that an interference corresponds to a pressing social need and that it is proportionate to the legitimate aim pursued: *Olsson v Sweden* (1988) 11 E.H.R.R. 259. Article 10, freedom of expression, may also afford privacy protection as certain kinds of surveillance may interfere with rights of freedom of expression under art.10: see *Halford v UK* (1997) 24 E.H.R.R. 523; [1997] I.R.L.R. 471, where the point was argued but not decided in the light of the finding of a violation of art.8.

[260] [2004] UKHL 22; [2004] 2 A.C. 457.

[261] [2004] UKHL 22; [2004] 2 A.C. 457 at [118].

[262] Lord Nicholls at [14]: "information about an individual's private life would not, in ordinary usage, be called 'confidential'. The more natural description today is that such information is private. The essence of the tort is better encapsulated now as misuse of private information." As to what constitutes "misuse" see Lord Neuberger in *Tchenguiz v Imerman* [2010] EWCA Civ 908; [2011] Fam. 116 at [69].

[262A] [2018] EWCA Civ 2217; [2018] 4 W.L.R. 101 at [29].

[262B] [2015] UKSC 9; [2015] A.C. 1065.

The correct approach

Replace footnote 282 with:

27-40 [282] That the reasonable expectation test is a question of fact was confirmed by the Court of Appeal in *Murray v Express Newspapers Plc* [2008] EWCA Civ 446; [2009] Ch. 481 at [41]. *Napier v Pressdram Ltd* [2009] EWCA Civ 443; [2009] E.M.L.R. 21 at [42], affirmed that the test for privacy is objective.

See the analysis by N.A. Moreham "Unpacking the reasonable expectation of privacy test" (2018) 134 L.Q.R. 651.

(a) The reasonable expectation of privacy

The reasonable expectation of privacy

Replace paragraph with:

"[I]nstead of the cause of action being based on the duty of good faith applicable to confidential personal information and trade secrets alike, it focuses on the protection of human autonomy and dignity—the right to control the dissemination of information about one's private life and the right to the esteem and respect of other people".[291] Certain information is obviously private[292]: information about health[293]; personal relationships[294] and finances. Where the information does not fall within such categories of obviously private, the test suggested in *Campbell*[295] is whether "in respect of the disclosed facts the person in question had a reasonable expectation of privacy".[296] The question is what a reasonable person of ordinary sensibilities[297] would feel if [s]he was placed in the same position as the claimant and faced with the same publicity.[298] In *Re JR38's Application for Judicial Review*, Lord Clarke noted: "the concept of reasonable expectation is a broad objective concept and the court is not concerned with the subjective expectations of the person concerned ...".[299] In *Axon v Ministry of Defence* Nicol J noted that "the notion of 'private life' is not limitless".[300] In *Richard v BBC*[300A] Mann J held that a police suspect prima facie (though not invariably) has a reasonable expectation of privacy in relation to a police investigation and police search; that expectation is not lost merely because the information has reached the media. **27-42**

[291] Lord Hoffmann in *Campbell v MGN Ltd* [2004] UKHL 22; [2004] 2 A.C. 457 at [51]. It is worth noting that the NZ Court of Appeal in *Hosking v Runting* [2004] NZCA 34; [2005] 1 N.Z.L.R. 1 (referred to by the House of Lords in *Campbell*) disliked the English approach: they preferred the development of two distinct heads of liability, the one to protect confidentiality, the other a tort of wrongful publicity given to private lives.

[292] See Baroness Hale in *Campbell v MGN Ltd* [2004] UKHL 22; [2004] 2 A.C. 457 at [136], drawing on the speech of Gleeson CJ in *ABC v Lenah Game Meats Pty Ltd* (2001) 185 A.L.R. 1. And see *Tchenguiz v Imerman* [2010] EWCA Civ 908; [2011] Fam. 116 at [76] per Lord Neuberger MR.

[293] e.g. details of medical condition, medical treatment or indeed non-medical therapy as in *Campbell* itself. See also *Z v Finland* (1997) 25 E.H.R.R. 371 (medical data).

[294] See para.27-48 and *Dudgeon v UK* (1981) 4 E.H.R.R. 149 (information relating to sexuality). The court may have to consider the extent to which the relationship in question has been conducted in secrecy. In *Ntuli v Donald* [2010] EWCA Civ 1276; [2011] 1 W.L.R. 294 the claimant had been unable to demonstrate that the relationship had not been conducted openly. And note *Ferdinand v MGN Ltd* [2011] EWHC 2454 (QB) at [58] where Nicol J commented "it is not necessary to consider whether in an extreme case there would be some merit in the argument that widespread and extensive discussion by the person of similar aspects of their private life would disentitle them to a reasonable expectation of privacy".

[295] [2004] UKHL 22; [2004] 2 A.C. 457. Lord Nicholls and Baroness Hale rejected the phrase "highly offensive" contained in the privacy provision of the *Restatement (Second) of Torts*, para.652D (referred to in the judgment of Gleeson CJ in the High Court of Australia decision, *ABC Corp v Lenah Game Meats Pty Ltd* (2002) 185 A.L.R. 1) as this suggested a stricter test of private information; Lord Hope, however, did refer to this test where the nature of the information was unclear. Consideration of whether the publication was "highly offensive" may or may not be relevant to the consideration of the balance to be struck between arts 8 and 10 (the NZ Court of Appeal case of *Hosking v Runting* [2004] NZCA 34; [2005] 1 N.Z.L.R. 1 applied the "highly offensive" test to the first stage. And see *X v Persons Unknown* [2006] EWHC 2783 (QB); [2007] E.M.L.R. 10, per Eady J).

[296] [2004] UKHL 22; [2004] 2 A.C. 457 at [21], per Lord Nicholls. Baroness Hale at [134] said that it arises where "the person publishing the information knows or ought to know that there is a reasonable expectation that the information in question will be kept confidential" (echoing Lord Woolf CJ in *A v B Plc* [2002] EWCA Civ 337; [2003] Q.B. 195 at [11](ix)). The standard to be set is based not on the recipient of the disclosure but on the reasonable person whose private information is threatened: *Campbell v MGN Ltd* [2004] UKHL 22; [2004] 2 A.C. 457.

[297] Lord Hope [2004] UKHL 22; [2004] 2 A.C. 457 at [94]: "the law of privacy is not intended for the protection of the unduly sensitive."

[298] Lord Hope [2004] UKHL 22; [2004] 2 A.C. 457 at [99]. In *Von Hannover v Germany* (2005) 40 E.H.R.R. 1; [2004] E.M.L.R. 21 the European Court of Human Rights appeared to set a lower threshold for determining whether information was to be deemed private. There, publication of photographs of Princess Caroline of Monaco in her daily life were held to fall within the scope of her private life.

[299] [2015] UKSC 42; [2016] A.C. 1131 at [109]. The majority of the Supreme Court held that a reasonable expectation of privacy was the touchstone for an allegation of art.8 violation. However, Lords Kerr and Wilson dissented, Lord Kerr supporting a "more nuanced approach", at [55]–[66]. Lord Clarke suggested, at [110], that in the light of the present state of Strasbourg jurisprudence he would not go so far as to say that it was impossible that absent a reasonable expectation of privacy there was no relevant interference with personal autonomy. In *R. (Catt) v Association of Chief Officers of Police of England, Wales and Northern Ireland* [2015] UKSC 9; [2015] A.C. 1065 at [4] Lord Sumption JSC. said the test must extend to "every occasion on which a person has a reasonable expectation that there will be no interference with the broader right of personal autonomy recognised in the case law of the Strasbourg Court".

[300] [2016] EWHC 787 (QB); [2016] E.M.L.R. 20 at [41] (reviewing the case law at [41]–[49]) and at [64] Nicol J stated: "misconduct is not just relevant to the balance of interests under Articles 8 and 10 ... but is also material as to whether the claimant has a reasonable expectation of privacy in the information about that conduct".

[300A] [2018] EWHC 1837 (Ch); [2019] Ch. 169. And see *ZXC v BloombergLP* [2019] EWHC 970, QB, Nicklin J: reasonable expectation of privacy in information relating to a criminal investigation into claimant's activities.

Factors indicating a reasonable expectation of privacy

Replace paragraph with:

27-43 In *Murray v Express Newspapers Plc*[301] Sir Anthony Clarke MR noted that the question of a presence of a reasonable expectation of privacy was an objective question with a need to consider all the circumstances of the case, including " he attributes of the claimant, the nature of the activity in which the claimant was engaged, the place at which it was happening, the nature and purpose of the intrusion, the absence of consent and whether it was known or could be inferred, the effect on the claimant and the circumstances in which and the purposes for which the information came into the hands of the publisher."[302] Lord Walker in *M v Secretary of State for Work and Pensions*[303] noted that the interference with private life had to be of some seriousness before art.8 was engaged. In *HRH Prince of Wales v Associated Newspapers Ltd*,[304] the Court of Appeal held that the information in the Prince of Wales' journal divulged by one of his employees to a newspaper was obviously of a private nature, it being particularly relevant that the disclosure by the employee had been in breach of a confidential relationship.[305] Even if the information had previously been available to the public there may be a good reason, based on privacy, to prevent further publicity or dissemination.[306] As for information posted on the internet, in *CC v AB*[307] some comments on the secret adulterous relationship between the claimant and the defendant's wife had been posted on the internet by the defendant but it was held that the information had not become generally accessible. In *WXY v Gewanter*[308] Slade J commented that even where there has been publication in one forum, publication in another forum can be restrained, noting the difference between internet websites and the print media. In *Weller v Associated Newspapers Ltd*[309] the photographs, though published in England had been taken in California, where such activity was lawful. However, this was not determinative of the issue whether there was a reasonable expectation of privacy. In *Ali v Channel 5 Broadcast Ltd*,[309A] Arnold J, the defendant broadcast scenes of the claimant and his wife being evicted from their home. On the facts there was a reasonable expectation of privacy: inter alia the broadcast showed them in a state of distress and it was foreseeable that the broadcast would have an adverse effect on their children.[309B] The mere fact that some of the events took place in the street did not mean there was no reasonable expectation of privacy.[309C] In *Arthurs v News Group Newspapers*[309D] the claimant (who was 18 at the time) had taken part in a television talent show. The defendant newspaper disclosed that his father was a convicted IRA terrorist. It was held that there was no reasonable expectation of privacy: he had voluntarily put himself in the public eye and the father's convictions were in the public domain.

[301] [2008] EWCA Civ 446; [2009] Ch. 481.

[302] [2008] EWCA Civ 446; [2009] Ch. 481 at [36]. No reasonable expectation of privacy in *Mahmood v Galloway* [2006] EWHC 1286 (QB); [2006] E.M.L.R. 26. *Murray* was considered in *Weller v Associated Newspapers Ltd* [2014] EWHC 1163 (QB); [2014] E.M.L.R. 24.

[303] [2006] UKHL 11; [2006] 2 A.C. 91 at [83].

[304] [2006] EWCA Civ 1776; [2008] Ch. 57.

[305] [2006] EWCA Civ 1776; [2008] Ch. 57 at [69]: "the nature of the relationship that gives rise to the duty of confidence may be important." And see *McKennitt v Ash* [2006] EWCA Civ 1714; [2008] Q.B. 73, nature of the pre-existing relationship between the parties; *Browne v Associated Newspapers Ltd* [2007] EWCA Civ 295; [2008] Q.B. 103 at [33].

[306] See also *Mills v News Group Newspapers Ltd* [2001] E.M.L.R. 41, at [25] per Lawrence Collins J: the information could still be confidential even if "it has previously been very widely available… . In such cases restraining further dissemination of the confidential material may be justified to prevent harm." And see *Douglas v Hello! Ltd (No.3)* [2005] EWCA Civ 595; [2006] Q.B. 125 at [84], [105]–[106].

[307] [2006] EWHC 3083 (QB); [2007] E.M.L.R. 11.

[308] [2012] EWHC 1601 (QB). She also noted, at [95], that "There is utility in restraining the publishing of information which, even if once known is likely to have faded from memory because of the passage of time". And see the discussion at para.27-56 of the Supreme Court decision *PJS v News Group Newspapers Ltd* [2016] UKSC 26; [2016] A.C. 1081.

[309] [2015] EWCA Civ 1176; [2016] 1 W.L.R. 1541 ([70]–[71]).

[309A] [2018] EWHC 298 (Ch); [2018] E.M.L.R. 17, Arnold J; on appeal the finding of a reasonable expectation of privacy was not challenged: [2019] EWCA Civ 677.

[309B] [2018] EWHC 298 (Ch); [2018] E.M.L.R. 17 at [169].

[309C] See also para.27-47, and *Peck v UK* (2003) 36 E.H.R.R. 41; [2003] E.M.L.R. 15).

[309D] [2017] NICA 70; [2018] E.M.L.R. 11.

Public figures and the reasonable expectation of privacy

Replace paragraph with:

As for public figures, Buxton LJ in *McKennitt v Ash*[325] commented that the European Court of Human Rights had in *Von Hannover v Germany*[326] "restated" what previously was thought to be the rights and expectations of public figures in respect of their private lives, and he noted that Lord Woolf's views in *A v B Plc*[327] on public figures and role models were not to be read as any sort of binding authority on arts 8 and 10. Eady J in *X v Persons Unknown*[328] noted that well-known people were entitled to a private life. In *HRH Prince of Wales v Associated Newspapers Ltd* it was noted that the fact that the claimant was an important public figure meant that disclosure "can be particularly intrusive".[329] However, if the claimant was a "public figure" there may be a public interest involved in disclosing the private information.[330] In *Richard v BBC*[330A] Mann J stated: "A public figure is not, by virtue of that quality, necessarily deprived of his or her legitimate expectations of privacy… it may be that a given public figure waives at least a degree of privacy by courting publicity, or adopting a public stance which would be at odds with the privacy rights claimed…".[330B] **27-46**

[325] [2006] EWCA Civ 1714; [2008] Q.B. 73 at [64]. In *Axon v Ministry of Defence* [2016] EWHC 787

(QB); [2016] E.M.L.R. 20, Nicol J, the claimant, a commanding officer of a Royal Naval ship, had no reasonable expectation of privacy in relation to the details concerning his removal from command (despite the security markings on the relevant documents).

326 (2005) 40 E.H.R.R. 1; [2004] E.M.L.R. 21 where at [69] the European Court of Human Rights noted that "anyone, even if they are known to the general public, must be able to enjoy a 'legitimate expectation' of protection and respect for private life" (the German courts had rejected her claim partly because she was a "figure of contemporary society par excellence").

327 [2002] EWCA Civ 337; [2003] Q.B. 195.

328 [2006] EWHC 2783 (QB); [2007] E.M.L.R. 10 at [27].

329 [2006] EWCA Civ 1776; [2008] Ch. 57 at [70].

330 See the discussion at para.27–51. In *Goodwin v News Group Newspapers Ltd* [2011] EWHC 1437 (QB); [2011] E.M.L.R. 27 at [64] Tugendhat J noted "in the law of privacy there has been some recognition in the authorities of the concept of a public figure, defined as those who exercise public or official functions". In the case itself, the chief executive of one of the largest publicly quoted companies was a public figure. At [103] Tugendhat J noted sportsmen and celebrities do not come within that definition "but even in the case of sportsmen, there may be a public interest if the sexual relationship gives rise to conflicts with professional interests or duties, for example to his team".

330A [2018] EWHC 1837 (Ch); [2019] Ch. 169.

330B [2018] EWHC 1837 (Ch); [2019] Ch. 169 at [256]. See also the discussion at [284]–[287].

Family and personal relationships

Replace paragraph with:

27-48 A pre-existing relationship between the parties will be relevant to whether there is a reasonable expectation of privacy.[344] In particular the courts will restrain the disclosure of information imparted in confidence between spouses[345] and, as the Court of Appeal acknowledged in *A v B Plc*[346] the courts will also recognise the extensive range of relationships beyond marriage that now exist, in order to restrain the disclosure of details of a sexual relationship.[347] The more stable the relationship the greater will be the significance attached to it by the court. However, though in some "kiss and tell" cases (where newspapers obtain intimate details from the other party in a transient sexual relationship) the courts had been reluctant to restrain the disclosure of intimate details, acknowledging the art.10 rights of the discloser,[348] this has been criticised as a "less generous view" than that which would be applied by the European Court of Human Rights.[349] In *CC v AB*, Eady J held that even an adulterous relationship could attract a legitimate expectation of privacy, noting: "it may yet be the case hat a fleeting one-night encounter will attract less protection, if any, than a long-term relationship. This is an uncertain area, because it is by no means fully determined how appropriate it is for individual judges to apply moral evaluations to such encounters".[350] In *YXB v TNO*[351] Warby J held that, given a relationship that did not involve any form of intimacy other than sexual, the interference with privacy that the publication involved was correspondingly limited. In *Mosley v News Group Newspapers Ltd*, he doubted whether the concept of "no confidence in iniquity" can be applied to sexual activity between consensual adults in private, noting that the modern approach to privacy and sexual preferences and practices was "very different from that of past generations.[352] In *AXB v BXA*,[352A] Sir David Eady commented that: "the mere fact that a person wishes to publish an account of her own life … does not provide a sufficient entitlement where to do so would engage the Article 8 rights of some other person(s) whose consent is not forthcoming".

344 *McKennitt v Ash* [2006] EWCA Civ 1714; [2008] Q.B. 73 at [15] and [24].

345 *Argyll v Argyll* [1967] Ch. 302.

346 [2002] EWCA Civ 337; [2003] Q.B. 195.

[347] *Stevens v Avery* [1988] Ch. 449; *Barrymore v News Group Newspapers Ltd* [1997] F.S.R. 600.

[348] See *Theakston v MGN Ltd* [2002] EWHC 137 (QB); [2002] E.M.L.R. 22, per Ouseley J; *A v B Plc* [2002] EWCA Civ 337; [2003] Q.B. 195.

[349] *Douglas v Hello! Ltd (No.3)* [2005] EWCA Civ 595; [2006] Q.B. 125, per Lord Phillips MR at [73].

[350] [2006] EWHC 3083 (QB); [2007] E.M.L.R. 11 at [22].

[351] [2015] EWHC 826 (QB) (see at [61] for the factors taken into account).

[352] [2008] EWHC 1777 (QB); [2008] E.M.L.R. 20 at [125]. However, note *AVB v TDD* [2014] EWHC 1442 (QB), Tugendhat J. See para.27-51 with regard to "kiss and tell" scenarios.

[352A] [2018] EWHC 588 (QB) at [56].

(b) Competing interests

Balancing art.8 and art.10

Replace footnote 353 with:

[353] See the earlier discussion at para.27-40. See *PNM v Times Newspapers Ltd* [2014] EWCA Civ 1132; [2014] E.M.L.R. 30 (information of claimant's arrest already extensively referred to in other court proceedings) and *ZXC v Bloomberg LP* [2017] EWHC 328 (QB); [2017] E.M.L.R. 21, Garnham J (information concerning law enforcement agency's investigation of claimant) where legitimate journalistic decisions to publish were held to be justified. Reference in *PNM* was made to the 2013 *College of Policing Guidance on Relations with the Media.* **27-49**

Relevant considerations in the balancing process

Replace paragraph with:

Relevant considerations in this process include: how the information was obtained[358]; the potential of the disclosure to cause harm and distress[359]; the extent of the intrusiveness[360]; the purpose of the disclosure;[361] the impact on the claimant's family life;[362] and indeed the nature of the information at issue.[363] An evaluation of the use to which the defendant has put or intends to put his freedom of expression is relevant. Relief is more readily granted in respect of intrusive photographs (especially if covert).[364] A relationship of confidence was held to be a significant factor by Lord Phillips in *HRH Prince of Wales v Associated Newspapers Ltd,*[365] and it was held arguable in *Campbell v Frisbee* that an express contractual duty of confidence may carry more weight than a duty not so based when weighed against the right to freedom of expression.[366] Earlier public interest defence cases may still have relevance in this context,[367] though as Lord Nicholls warned in *Campbell v MGN Ltd*, arts 8 and 10 "call for a more explicit analysis of competing considerations."[368] In *Ali v Channel 5 Broadcast Ltd*[368A] Arnold J held that though the broadcast did contribute to a debate of public interest, it went beyond what was justified for that purpose. On appeal it was held that this assessment could not be said to be wrong, though Irwin LJ noted that "where there was a rational view by which public interest can justify publication, particularly giving full weight to editorial knowledge and discretion, then the court should be slow to interfere".[368B] In *Richard v BBC*[368C] Mann J held the BBC liable to the celebrity claimant for infringement of his privacy. They had broadcast the fact that he was the subject of a police investigation and that his property had been searched. The claimant was never arrested or charged. The criteria provided in the *Axel Springer*[368D] case were discussed, including: whether the disclosure contributed to a debate of public interest; the public status of the claimant; the method of obtaining the information; the content, form and consequences of the publication. The judge noted that the BBC decided on an invasion of the claimant's privacy rights "in a big way"[368E] and that the relevant privacy code for s.12(4)(b) was the BBC's own editorial guidelines. It was **27-50** noted that a journalist's right of freedom of expression was subject to the proviso, inter alia, that the journalist be acting in good faith.[368F]

[358] The use of unlawful means to obtain the information could well be a "compelling factor": per Lord Woolf in *A v B Plc* [2002] EWCA Civ 337; [2003] Q.B. 195 (however, it must be confidential information that is involved: see *ABC v Lenah Game Meats Pty Ltd* (2001) 185 A.L.R. 1) or indeed the use of covert or surreptitious means: see *Campbell v MGN Ltd* [2004] UKHL 22; [2004] 2 A.C. 457.

[359] In *Campbell v MGN Ltd* [2004] UKHL 22; [2004] 2 A.C. 457 at [153] Baroness Hale noted the sense of betrayal likely and the potential to undermine the claimant's therapy was also noted.

[360] The fact that the claimant is not a public figure may well be relevant: *A v Newham LBC* (2001), Garland J unreported, available Westlaw (photograph of child used without consent by defendant in their Aids and crime leaflets).

[361] See *Von Hannover v Germany* (2005) 40 E.H.R.R. 1; [2004] E.M.L.R. 21; *Green Corns Ltd v Claverley Group Ltd* [2005] EWHC 958(QB); [2005] E.M.L.R. 31. However, in *Ferdinand v MGN Ltd* [2011] EWHC 2454 (QB) at [84] Nicol J stated that though the article was a "kiss and tell story" "stories may be in the public interest even if the reasons behind the informant providing the information are less than noble". In *CC v AB* [2006] EWHC 3083 (QB); [2007] E.M.L.R. 11 it was noted that the purpose for which the defendant sought to exercise his freedom of speech might be relevant (here, profit and revenge seemed to be the motivation).

[362] *CC v AB* [2006] EWHC 3083 (QB); [2007] E.M.L.R. 11; *ETK v News Group Newspapers Ltd* [2011] EWCA Civ 439; [2011] 1 W.L.R. 1827; *SKA v CRH* [2012] EWHC 766 (QB) at [24], Tugendhat J: the court must have regard to the art.8 rights of non-parties but he noted "such persons should, if practicable, speak for themselves"; and see *Hutcheson (formerly KGM) v News Group Newspapers Ltd* [2011] EWCA Civ 808; [2012] E.M.L.R. 2 at [26].

[363] Baroness Hale notes in *Campbell v MGN Ltd* [2004] UKHL 22; [2004] 2 A.C. 457 at [148] that there are different types of speech "some of which are more deserving of protection in a democratic society than others", highlighting the importance of political speech, intellectual and educational speech and artistic speech (and note the views of the European Court of Human Rights in *Von Hannover v Germany* (2005) 40 E.H.R.R. 1; [2004] E.M.L.R. 21). In *LNS v Persons Unknown* [2010] EWHC 119 (QB); [2010] E.M.L.R. 16 at [99] Tugendhat J rejected the submission that the conduct of the claimant in private must be unlawful before the defendant was permitted to criticise it in public.

[364] *Theakston v MGN Ltd* [2002] EWHC 137 (QB); [2002] E.M.L.R. 22; *Campbell v MGN Ltd* [2004] UKHL 22; [2004] 2 A.C. 457. In *Douglas v Hello! Ltd* [2001] Q.B. 967 (unauthorised pictures of wedding taken surreptitiously) the defendant had argued that the guests lawfully there could have relayed the same information subsequently by word (or drawing). However, Keene LJ at 1011 observed that "a picture is worth a thousand words". And note also *D v L* [2003] EWCA Civ 1169; [2004] E.M.L.R. 1 (secret recordings of private conversations could have more impact and cause more distress than an account of the conversations themselves). In *Von Hannover* (2005) 40 E.H.R.R. 1; [2004] E.M.L.R. 21 it was noted (at [59]) that the publication of photographs was an area where the protection of the rights of others was of particular importance. Lord Walker in *OBG v Allan* [2007] UKHL 21; [2008] 1 A.C. 1 at [288] commented that "if a photograph is a blatant and obviously unjustifiable invasion of personal privacy, its publication by the perpetrator will not give him a 'public domain' defence for further publication". And see *Mosley v News Group Newspapers Ltd* [2008] EWHC 1777 (QB); [2008] E.M.L.R. 20, Eady J at [15]–[16].

[365] [2006] EWCA Civ 1776; [2008] Ch. 57.

[366] [2002] EWCA Civ 1374; [2003] I.C.R. 141 at [22]. Cf. observations of Walker LJ in *London Regional Transport v Mayor of London* [2001] EWCA Civ 1491; [2003] E.M.L.R. 4 at [46].

[367] So, e.g. earlier cases on medical confidentiality might still be useful, e.g. *X v Y* [1988] 2 All E.R. 648; cf. *W v Egdell* [1990] Ch. 359. See also *Secretary of State for the Home Department v Central Broadcasting Ltd* [1993] E.M.L.R. 253; *R. v Chief Constable of the North Wales Police Ex p. AB* [1999] Q.B. 396 (criminal record of paedophilia disclosable if "pressing need" and, if possible, after providing opportunity to comment).

[368] *Campbell v MGN Ltd* [2004] UKHL 22; [2004] 2 A.C. 457 at [19].

[368A] [2018] EWHC 298 (Ch); [2018] E.M.L.R. 17 (see para.27-43).

[368B] [2019] EWCA Civ 677 at [83].

[368C] [2018] EWHC 1837 (Ch); [2019] Ch. 169.

[368D] *Axel Springer AG v Germany* (39954/08) [2012] E.M.L.R. 15 (ECtHR).

[368E] [2018] EWHC 1837 (Ch); [2019] Ch. 169 at [301].

[368F] [2018] EWHC 1837 (Ch); [2019] Ch. 169 at [288].

Human Rights Act 1998 s.12(4)

Replace footnote 384 with:

[384] The newspaper industry has established a new press regulator, the Independent Press Standards Organisation. However, note also the Royal Charter on the self-regulation of the press: so far the only approved regulator is IMPRESS. On s.12 generally see *Middleton v Persons Unknown* [2016] EWHC 2354 (QB), Whipple J. And see *ABC v Telegraph Media Group Ltd* [2018] EWCA Civ 2329; [2019] E.M.L.R. 5. 27-53

(c) Relevant statutory provisions

Replace title and paragraph: 27-54

Data Protection Act 2018 Personal information is also protected by data protection law. Previously the principal general statute regulating the use of personal data was the Data Protection Act 1998. This implemented Directive 95/46/EEC. The EU adopted a directly effective General Data Protection Regulation (EU 2016/679) which came into force on 25 May 2018 (this applies if the data controller, data processor or data subject is based in the EU: see art.3). This overhauls and harmonises the law on data protection and replaces the 1995 Directive. Personal data may include pseudonymised personal data. The GDPR (art.2) does not apply to the processing of personal data by an individual "in the course of a purely personal or household activity". The Regulation (art.5) sets out seven key principles relating to the processing of personal data: "Lawfulness, fairness and transparency"; "Purpose limitation"; "Data minimisation"; "Accuracy"; "Storage limitation"; "Integrity and confidentiality"; and "Accountability". Processing is only lawful if it complies with the requirements of the regulation (see art.6; there are also "special categories" of personal data under art.9: these attract additional requirements). Chapter 3 contains the rights of the data subject including (in art.17) a right to erasure (the "right to be forgotten"). Responsibilities/obligations of data controllers and data processors are contained in Chapter 4. The Data Protection Act 2018 came into force on 25 May 2018. This replaced the Data Protection Act 1998. It enacts the GDPR into UK law and also adds to and tailors its provisions. The general processing regime is contained in Pt 2 c.1 s.4(2)(b) stating: this chapter "supplements, and must be read with, the GDPR". (Part 2 c.3 adds an equivalent regime to certain processing to which the GDPR does not apply.) As before, there are exemptions to the right afforded.

(d) Remedies

Privacy injunctions and open justice

Replace footnote 440 with:

[440] *POI v Lina* [2011] EWHC 25 (QB) Tugendhat J at [8]; *N v Ryan* [2013] EWHC 637 (QB) Sharp J. But Tugendhat J in *SKA v CRH* [2012] EWHC 766 (QB) at [74] did not accept that the alleged blackmailer forfeited his art.10 rights, it remaining necessary for the court "to consider the value of the speech that would be made if the defendants were permitted to make the disclosure they threaten to make". *PML v Persons Unknown* [2018] EWHC 838 (QB) Nicklin J (blackmail threat from hacker to publish data stolen from claimant; interim non-disclosure order without notice on the defendant); *LJY v Persons Unknown* [2017] EWHC 3230 (QB) at [29], Warby J (blackmail allegation: "... blackmail represents a misuse of free speech rights. Such conduct will considerably reduce the weight to be attached to free speech and correspondingly increase the weight of the argument in favour of restraint"). See also *NPV v QEL* [2018] EWHC 703 (QB); [2018] E.M.L.R. 20, Nicklin J. 27-57

Damages

Replace paragraph with:

Damages for injury to a claimant's feelings or mental distress may be awarded 27-59 (including aggravated damages).[452] In *Mosley v News Group Newspapers Ltd*[453] Eady J debated the nature of compensatory damages in privacy cases, noting that the law is concerned to protect such matters as personal dignity, autonomy and integrity although unlike the tort of defamation it was not as such concerned with injury to reputation.[454] It was reasonable to suppose that damages for an intrusion into a person's sexual tastes would include distress, hurt feelings and loss of dignity.[455] The Court of Appeal in *Gulati v MGN Ltd*[456] accepted that awards in privacy cases are not limited to damages for distress. According to Arden LJ "the essential principle is that, by misusing their private information ... [the appellants] ... deprived the respondents of their right to control the use of private information". Such damages were not the same as vindicatory damages. However, it was accepted that the assessment of compensation may be affected if the information would have become public knowledge anyway.[457] It has been said that such damages should be kept to a modest level, well below the level of general damages for serious physical or psychological injury.[458] However, in *Spelman v Express Newspapers*[459] Tugendhat J, discussing damages in relation to intrusion, commented: "if a remedy in damages is to be an effective remedy, then the amount that the court may award must not be subject to too severe a limitation." The approach of Mann J in *Gulati v MGN Ltd*[459A] was followed by Arnold J in *Ali v Channel 5 Broadcast Ltd.*[459B] On appeal the Court of Appeal upheld the level of damages awarded, commenting "it is important that an appeal court should be slow to interfere with an assessment of damage in such a case as this, where the measure of damage is necessarily general and cannot be calculated mathematically".[459C]

[452] On damages see: *Cornelius v De Taranto* [2001] E.M.L.R. 12 (not appealed on this point; though a contractual duty was involved in that case; Morland J held that the proper protection of the art.8 right had to be given). In *A v Newham LBC* unreported 2001, a settlement of £5,000 was agreed. The European Court of Human Rights in *Wainwright v UK* (2007) 44 E.H.R.R. 40 awarded £3,000 to each applicant. In *WXY v Gewanter* [2013] EWHC 589 (QB); [2013] Info. T.L.R. 281 aggravated damages of £5,000 were awarded given that the defendant's threats were to put pressure on the claimant for financial gain. On aggravated damages see Crime and Courts Act 2013 s.39.

[453] [2008] EWHC 1777 (QB); [2008] E.M.L.R. 20.

[454] Though note Mann J in *Hannon v News Group Newspapers* [2014] EWHC 1580 (Ch); [2015] E.M.L.R. 1 at [70]–[71].

[455] [2008] EWHC 1777 (QB); [2008] E.M.L.R. 20 at [212]–[231]. He noted that it may be appropriate to take into account aggravating conduct. He awarded £60,000 to Mosley.

[456] [2015] EWCA Civ 1291; [2017] Q.B. 149.

[457] [2015] EWCA Civ 1291; [2017] Q.B. 149 at [45].

[458] *Archer v Williams* [2003] EWHC 1670 (QB); [2003] E.M.L.R. 38, per Jackson J. And see *Lloyd v Google* [2018] EWHC 2599 (QB); [2019] 1 W.L.R. 1265 at [66] where Warby J noted, obiter: "I do not read *Gulati*'s case as authority for a rule or principle that substantial damages are invariably recoverable and must always be awarded for misuse of private information ... and regardless of the nature of the wrong and its impact on the individual claimant". The facts in *Gulati* were that the defendants' conduct had adversely affected the claimants' ability to exercise control over their personal information.

[459] [2012] EWHC 355 (QB) at [114].

[459A] [2015] EWHC 1482; [2016] F.S.R. 12. See para.27-60.

[459B] [2018] EWHC 298 (Ch); [2018] E.M.L.R. 17.

[459C] [2019] EWCA Civ 677 at [118], Irwin LJ. See also *Richard v BBC* [2018] EWHC 1837 (Ch); [2019] Ch. 169, per Mann J at [343], holding that damage to reputation is recoverable in a privacy claim: "the preponderance of speeches" in *Khuja v Times Newspapers Ltd* [2017] UKSC 49; [2019] A.C. 161 "acknowledged that the protection of reputation was part of the function of the law of privacy". In *Richard v BBC* Mann J awarded aggravated damages, given that the BBC had submitted the offending broadcast for an award.

Guidance on the measure of damages

Replace footnote 465 with:

27-60 [465] [2015] EWCA Civ 1291; [2017] Q.B. 149 at [62]). Note *TLT v Secretary of State for the Home*

Department [2016] EWHC 2217 (QB), Mitting J. Assessment of damages where the Home Office accidentally published asylum applicants' personal data: given that they were shocked and put in fear the cases were closer to those involving psychiatric injury. Liability (which was upheld) but not damages award appealed: [2018] EWCA Civ 2217; [2018] 4 W.L.R. 101.

CHAPTER 28

DAMAGES

TABLE OF CONTENTS

1. INTRODUCTION

Scope of chapter

Replace paragraph with:

28-01 This chapter is primarily concerned with the principles governing the types of loss, or heads of damage, for which compensatory damages are payable and the method of assessing such damages.[1] As such it assumes that the logically prior question of the defendant's liability in tort has already been determined. This distinction between "liability" principles and "quantification" principles is a convenient one and it is also necessary for certain procedural[2] rules, but is not entirely free from difficulty as there are certain matters which may be classified under either category. This is particularly true of causation and remoteness of damage. Typically the courts have formulated the relevant principles in the context of liability issues, notably within the law of negligence, and for this reason, save for a brief account of their relevance to the assessment process,[3] they have been dealt with in an earlier chapter.[4] What follows is an account of the general law of damages.[5] Some earlier chapters have dealt with the damages relevant to the tort or torts in question. So in this chapter, there will be no specific consideration of, for example, damages for defamation,[6] trespass to land[7] and trespass to the person,[8] malicious prosecution,[9] misrepresentation,[10] pure economic loss caused by negligence,[11] economic torts,[12] and interference with rights in chattels.[13] Damages for breach by a public authority of a victim's convention right under the Human Rights Act 1998 have also been considered in an earlier chapter.[14]

[1] For specialist works see: Edelman, *McGregor on Damages*, 20th edn (2017); Burrows, *Remedies for Torts, Breach of Contract and Equitable Wrongs*, 4th edn (2019), Chs 2–18; Tettenborn, Wilby and Bennett, *The Law of Damages*, 2nd edn (2010).

[2] e.g. under CPR rr.14.7, 25.7. The distinction used to be relevant to the conflict of laws (the measure of damages was regarded as procedural and governed by the *lex fori*, while liability issues were regarded as substantive and governed by the *lex causae*: see, e.g. *Harding v Wealands* [2006] UKHL 32; [2007] 2 A.C. 1; *Cox v Ergo Versicherung AG* [2014] UKSC 22; [2014] A.C. 1379. But in the context of the applicable law for a tort, the effect of the Private International Law (Miscellaneous Provisions) Act 1995 s.15A is that that distinction is no longer important.

[3] See para.28-08.

[4] Ch.2.

[5] The general principles considered must be read subject to the fact that the parties themselves may have validly limited damages (whether by contract or non-contractual notice) or exceptionally there may be a statutory provision limiting damages, e.g. s.185 of the Merchant Shipping Act 1995.

[6] See paras 22-188, 22-225 onwards.

[7] See para.19-66 onwards.

[8] See para.15-139 onwards.

[9] See para.16-06 onwards. But for consideration of costs as damages, see paras 28-125 to 28-126.

[10] See para.18-39 onwards.

[11] See para.2-178 onwards and 10-147, 10-185, 10-209, 10-228, 10-249. That includes the particularly important decision in *South Australia Asset Management Corp v York Montague Ltd* [1997] A.C. 191 HL; for detailed criticism of the reasoning in that case see Burrows, *Remedies for Torts, Breach of Contract and Equitable Wrongs*, 4th edn (2019), pp.117–127.

[12] See Ch.24.

[13] See para.17-93 onwards. We also do not discuss in this chapter "loss of management time", on which see, e.g. *Admiral Management Services Ltd v Para-Protect Ltd* [2002] EWHC 233 (Ch.); [2002] 1 W.L.R. 2722 (loss of revenue and damages for management time); *Aerospace Publishing Ltd v Thames Water Utilities Ltd* [2007] EWCA Civ 3; [2007] N.P.C. 5 (damages recoverable for payments made to staff to deal with the consequences of a flood caused by the defendant's breach of statutory duty).

[14] See para.14-114 onwards. See also *Damages under the Human Rights Act 1998*, Law Commission No.266 (2000); *R. (on the application of KB) v Mental Health Review Tribunal* [2003] EWHC 193 (Admin); [2004] Q.B. 936; *Anufrijeva v London Borough of Southwark* [2003] EWCA Civ 1406; [2004] Q.B. 1124; *R. v Secretary of State for the Home Department Ex p. Greenfield* [2005] UKHL 14; [2005] 1 W.L.R. 673; *Van Colle v Hertfordshire Police* [2007] EWCA Civ 325; [2007] 1 W.L.R. 1821 (overturned on liability without discussing damages by the House of Lords [2008] UKHL 50; [2009] 1 A.C. 225); *Rabone v Pennine Care NHS Foundation Trust* [2012] UKSC 2; [2012] 2 A.C. 72; *R. (on the application of Faulkner) v Secretary of State for Justice* [2013] UKSC 23; [2013] 2 A.C. 254; *DSD v Commissioner of Police for the Metropolis* [2014] EWHC 2493 (QB); [2015] 1 W.L.R. 1833; *Alseran v Ministry of Defence* [2017] EWHC 3289 (QB); [2018] 3 W.L.R. 95 (this enlightened decision of Leggatt J turns the approach of *Greenfield* on its head by treating the domestic scale for non-pecuniary loss as being of primary importance and relegating the Strasbourg level to being a secondary cross-check). For criticism of the *Greenfield* case, see Burrows, "Damages and Rights" in Nolan and Robertson (eds), *Rights and Private Law* (Oxford: Hart Publishing, 2012), pp.275, 290–303.

2. GENERAL PRINCIPLES

(b) General and special damages

Replace footnote 28 with:

[28] *Ratcliffe v Evans* [1892] 2 Q.B. 524 at 528, per Bowen LJ; *Stroms Bruks Aktie Bolag v John and Peter Hutchison* [1905] A.C. 515 at 525, per Lord Macnaghten. SeeStreet, *Principles of the Law of Damages*, pp.18-22; Edelman, *McGregor on Damages*, 20th edn (2017), paras 3-001 to 3-006, 52-010 to 52-018; Jolowicz, "The Changing Use of 'Special Damage' and its Effect on the Law" [1960] C.L.J. 214. **28-05**

(c) General principle of compensation

Replace footnote 45 with:

[45] See paras 28-149 to 28-150. Nominal damages may be awarded for torts actionable per se; see Edelman, *McGregor on Damages*, 20th edn (2017), Ch.12; Burrows, *Remedies for Torts, Breach of Contract and Equitable Wrongs*, 4th edn, Ch.25. See, e.g. *R. (Lumba) v Secretary of State for the Home Department* [2011] UKSC 12; [2012] 1 A.C. 245 (false imprisonment but would have been imprisoned in any **28-07**

event had correct procedures been followed). In *Grobbelaar v News Group Newspapers Ltd* [2002] UKHL 40; [2002] 1 W.L.R. 3024 (where damages of £1 were awarded and were described as nominal but are probably better viewed as contemptuous in that they recognised that the claimant's rights had been infringed while admonishing the claimant for his own conduct).

(e) Mitigation

Replace footnote 58 with:

28-09 [58] *Roper v Johnson* (1873) L.R. 8 C. & P. 167; *Yetton v Eastwoods Froy* [1967] 1 W.L.R. 104 at 115; *Garnac Grain Co Inc v Faure & Fairclough Ltd* [1968] A.C. 1130; *London and South of England Building Society v Stone* [1983] 1 W.L.R. 1242 CA; *Gebrüder Metelmann GmbH & Co KG v NBR (London) Ltd* [1984] 1 Lloyd's Rep. 614; *Geest Plc v Lansiquot* [2002] 1 W.L.R. 3111 PC (disapproving *Selvanayagam v University of West Indies* [1983] 1 W.L.R. 585); *LE Jones (Insurance Brokers) Ltd v Portsmouth City Council* [2002] EWCA Civ 1723; [2003] 1 W.L.R. 427 at [26].

(f) Certainty

Replace paragraph with:

28-12 There remains to consider the extent to which the losses pleaded must be certain and how account is taken of future contingencies.[75] A distinction must first be drawn between the question of the degree of proof required in relation to the losses pleaded in the statement of case and the question whether losses which depend on future contingencies may be pleaded and how they are to be assessed. With regard to the former, the general principle was stated by Bowen LJ in *Ratcliffe v Evans*[76]: "the character of the acts themselves which produce the damage, and the circumstances under which these acts are done must regulate the degree of certainty and particularity with which the damage done ought to be stated and proved. As much certainty and particularity must be insisted on … as is reasonable, having regard to the circumstances and to the nature of the acts themselves by which the damage is done." Clearly, special damages such as expenses and the loss on particular contracts must be pleaded and proved exactly.[77] Some elements in general damages, particularly non-pecuniary losses such as pain and suffering, are inferred or presumed and little is required by way of evidence.[78] Financial elements in the general damages will not normally be presumed,[79] and thus should be supported by evidence. In personal injury claims, the claimant must attach to his particulars of claim a schedule of details of any past and future expenses and losses which he claims.[80]

[75] Edelman, *McGregor on Damages*, 20th edn (2017), Ch.10; Burrows, *Remedies for Torts and Breach of Contract and Equitable Wrongs*, 4th edn (2019), Ch.5.

[76] [1892] 2 Q.B. 525 at 532–533.

[77] See paras 28-05 to 28-06.

[78] Edelman, *McGregor on Damages*, 20th edn (2017), para.52-008.

[79] *Domsalla v Barr* [1969] 1 W.L.R. 630. The same is true of business losses at least where the loss is consequent on a physical injury to property: e.g. *The Risoluto* (1883) 8 P. & D. 109 and see para.28-121. Where however the tort constitutes a direct invasion of a business interest (e.g. passing off, injurious falsehood, inducement of breach of contract) loss of profits is generally presumed: *Goldsoll v Goldman* [1914] 2 Ch. 603 at 615; *Draper v Trist* [1939] 3 All E.R. 513 at 526. Even so, it is often advisable to produce evidence of the loss, as the amount presumed might be small or even nominal: cf. *Hayward v Hayward* (1887) 34 Ch D. 198.

[80] See para.28-06.

Replace paragraph with:

28-18 This area of the law was reviewed by the House of Lords in the difficult case of *Gregg v Scott*.[95] A doctor negligently diagnosed a lump under the claimant's left arm as benign when it was in fact cancerous. This led to a delay of nine months in the claimant receiving proper treatment. It was found that, on the balance of probabilities, the claimant would not have been "cured" of cancer (with "cure" meaning surviving for more than 10 years) even if there had been no delay. It was also found that the delay had reduced the claimant's chances of cure from 42 per cent to 25 per cent. The majority of the House of Lords (Lord Hoffmann, Lord Phillips and Baroness Hale) refused to award the claimant damages for the reduction in the chances of cure. Despite this, it remains to be seen whether a loss of chance approach can ever be appropriate in medical negligence cases, where the negligence has reduced the claimant's chances of cure.[96] The case has also left some other difficulties unresolved. Two linked uncertainties are particularly troubling. The first is that no clear justification was given for why a loss of the chance approach is thought appropriate—as many past cases have established that it is[97]—for professional negligence cases causing pure economic loss but not for medical negligence. The second is that, while receiving some apparent support from Lord Hoffmann[98] (and from Lord Nicholls dissenting),[99] the precise status of Stuart-Smith LJ's influential judgment in *Allied Maples Group Ltd v Simmons & Simmons*[100] is left unclear. Stuart-Smith LJ had there attempted to rationalise the law on hypothetical events by laying down that a loss of chance approach was appropriate where the uncertainty was as to the hypothetical conduct of third parties, but not the hypothetical conduct of the claimant who could be expected to prove, on the balance of probabilities, one way or the other, what he would have done had there been no breach of duty by the defendant. However, that particular uncertainty has subsequently been resolved by the support of the Supreme Court in *Perry v Raleys Solicitors*[100A] for the distinction drawn in the *Allied Maples* case.

[95] [2005] UKHL 2; [2005] 2 A.C. 176. See paras 2-86 to 2-96.

[96] See paras 2-93 to 2-96.

[97] See para.28-14, fn.85.

[98] [2005] UKHL 2 at [82]–[83].

[99] [2005] UKHL 2 at [19].

[100] [1995] 1 W.L.R. 1602.

[100A] [2019] UKSC 5; [2019] 2 W.L.R. 636.

3. DAMAGES FOR PERSONAL INJURIES

(a) Itemisation of awards

Replace footnote 122 with:

[122] [1980] A.C. 192. See also *Damages for Personal Injury: Non-Pecuniary Loss*, Law Commission Report No.257 (1999), paras 2.65-2.68; Edelman, *McGregor on Damages*, 20th edn (2017), paras 40-059 to 40-061. 28-22

(b) Medical and other expenses

Replace paragraph with:

The claimant may recover any medical or related expenses, such as hospital, nursing or special accommodation costs,[123] that he has reasonably[124] incurred or will reasonably incur[125] as a result of his injury.[126] He cannot recover as damages the capital cost of acquiring special accommodation for he retains the capital in question in the form of the accommodation[127]; but he may recover a sum for the cost of the capital.[128] Where the claimant has been deprived of her womb because of the 28-23 defendant's negligence and therefore cannot have children, the costs of surrogacy may be recoverable, whether or not the child would not be genetically linked to the claimant (i.e. even if neither the baby nor the pregnancy would be hers).[129] The Law Reform (Personal Injuries) Act 1948 s.2(4), lays down that the possibility of avoiding expenses or part of them by making use of the facilities of the National Health Service is to be disregarded. However, if advantage is in fact taken of those facilities the claimant is not entitled to recover what he would have had to pay if he had contracted for them privately.[130] Similarly, if it appears to the court to be likely that the claimant will be unable to obtain privately all the nursing services he will need, so that he will eventually have to enter a National Health Hospital, an appropriate deduction shall be made.[131] Account should also be taken of the fact that a person who is dependent on institutional care saves on domestic expenses which otherwise would have been incurred: so, in the case of private care, a deduction will be made from the damages awarded for the cost of care,[132] while by the Administration of Justice Act 1982 s.5, "any saving which is attributable to his maintenance wholly or partly at public expense in a hospital, nursing home or other institution shall be set off against any income lost by him as a result of his injuries".[133]

[123] *Shearman v Folland* [1950] 2 K.B. 43; *Cutts v Chumley* [1967] 1 W.L.R. 742; *George v Pinnock* [1973] 1 W.L.R. 118.

[124] *Winkworth v Hubbard* [1960] 1 Lloyd's Rep. 150 (medical treatment in New York held reasonable); *Rialas v Mitchell* (1984) 128 S.J. 704 CA (reasonable to be treated at home even if care in a private institution would be substantially cheaper); *Sowden v Lodge* [2004] EWCA Civ 1370; [2005] 1 W.L.R. 2129 (test is one of reasonableness not one of what is in the claimant's best interests: but, even if unreasonable for the claimant to live in her own home, rather than in local authority residential accommodation, it might be workable and reasonable to have extra services in such accommodation thereby requiring a "top-up-fee" paid for by the defendant); *Godbold v Mahmood* [2005] EWHC 1002; [2006] P.I.Q.R. Q5 (defendant had not shown that the claimant's proposed option of a privately-funded care home was unreasonable). In *Peters v East Midlands SHA* [2009] EWCA Civ 145; [2010] Q.B. 48 the disabled claimant would, on the balance of probabilities, be cared for and accommodated by a local authority in a residential home. It was held that she was entitled as of right to damages for the cost of self-funding that residential care even though the local authority would provide it for free if she did not self-fund. It was decided-with respect, controversially-that the duty to mitigate had no role to play here but that, even if it did, the claimant's preference to be self-funded, and not to be reliant on the state, was reasonable. It was thought that there was here no risk of double recovery (i.e. being awarded damages for self-funding and then being provided with free residential care) because the claimant's affairs were controlled by the Court of Protection. *R. (on the application of Tinsley) v Manchester CC* [2017] EWCA Civ 1704; [2018] 2 W.L.R. 973 concerned a claimant who had been so severely injured in a road accident caused by another's negligence that he had been compulsorily detained in hospital under the Mental Health Act 1983. The relevant local authority refused to fund post-detention care services for the claimant on the ground that he had been awarded tort damages for future care and could therefore afford to pay for the care out of the damages. In judicial review proceedings, this refusal was held to be unlawful: the statute required such after-care services to be provided free of charge.

[125] As with future loss of earnings, future expenses are generally calculated using a "multiplier" method, and there will normally be no adjustment for a higher rate of tax payable on the income from investing the damages. See paras 28-29 to 28-35.

[126] See, generally, *Damages for Personal Injury: Medical, Nursing and Other Expenses; Collateral Benefits*, Law Commission Report No.262 (1999), s.A.

[127] *George v Pinnock* [1973] 1 W.L.R. 118; *Cunningham v Harrison* [1973] Q.B. 942; *Roberts v Johnstone* [1989] Q.B. 878.

[128] In *Wells v Wells* [1999] 1 A.C. 345 HL, it was laid down, inter alia, that the discount rate used in calculating the cost of the capital, for the purposes of applying *Roberts v Johnstone*, is the interest rate on index-linked government stock (ILGS), which was for the time being treated as being three per cent. However, the appropriate discount rate in assessing future pecuniary loss has subsequently been reduced to minus 0.75% by the Lord Chancellor, acting under the powers conferred by the Damages Act 1996 s.1: see para.28-33. The effect of this negative discount rate on a *Roberts v Johnstone* award for the cost of the capital is unclear but it can be powerfully argued that the logical consequence is that there should now be no sum payable as the cost of the capital under *Roberts v Johnstone*. On the question of whether there should be a deduction for betterment, see *Roberts v Johnstone* [1989] Q.B. 878 at 893.

[129] *XX v Whittington Hospital NHS Trust* [2018] EWCA Civ 2831; [2019] Med L.R. 99, declining to follow *Briody v St Helens and Knowsley HA* [2001] EWCA Civ 1010; [2002] Q.B. 856 on the ground that public policy in relation to surrogacy had moved on since that decision.

[130] *Harris v Brights Asphalt Contractors Ltd* [1953] 1 Q.B. 617 at 635, per Slade J; *Cunningham v Harrison* [1973] Q.B. 942 at 957, per Lawton LJ; *Lim Poh Choo v Camden and Islington AHA* [1980] A.C. 174 at 188, per Lord Scarman; *Woodrup v Nicol* [1993] P.I.Q.R. Q104 at Q114, per Russell LJ.

[131] *Cunningham v Harrison* [1973] Q.B. 942; *Lim Poh Choo v Camden and Islington AHA* [1980] A.C. 174; *Woodrup v Nicol* [1993] P.I.Q.R. Q104 CA; *Eagle v Chambers* [2004] EWCA Civ 1033; [2004] 1 W.L.R. 3081 (the same factual test should be applied to services provided by social services as to services provided by the NHS; and where a private care regime is needed, the burden of proving that services will be provided by the NHS or social services lies on the defendant); *Walton v Calderdale Healthcare NHS Trust* [2005] EWHC 1053 (QB); [2006] P.I.Q.R. Q3; *Freeman v Lockett* [2006] EWHC 102 (QB); [2006] Lloyd's Rep. Med. 151. Applying the basic principle that benefits should be deducted from damages (see *Hodgson v Trapp* [1989] A.C. 807; see para.28-40) where a court finds that a claimant will receive direct payments from a local authority for care, they must be taken into account (i.e. deducted) in assessing damages for the cost of care: *Crofton v NHS Litigation Authority* [2007] EWCA Civ 71; [2007] 1 W.L.R. 923.

[132] *Shearman v Folland* [1950] 2 K.B. 43; *Lim Poh Choo v Camden and Islington AHA* [1980] A.C. 174.

[133] This provision overruled *Daish v Wauton* [1972] 2 Q.B. 262 on this point. The claimant will be left overcompensated to the extent that he has suffered no loss of income or a loss of income lower than the expense saved. In *O'Brien v Independent Assessor* [2007] UKHL 10; [2007] 2 A.C. 312 the same approach was applied in the different context of the statutory compensation scheme for those whose conviction has been quashed for a miscarriage of justice: the saved cost of food, clothing and accommodation while in prison was held to be deductible from the compensation for loss of earnings.

(c) Loss of earnings

(i) The "multiplier method"

Replace footnote 162 with:

[162] Edelman, *McGregor on Damages*, 20th edn (2017), paras 40-066 to 40-148; Burrows, *Remedies for Torts, Breach of Contract and Equitable Wrongs*, 4th edn (2019), pp.244–247. **28-29**

(iii) The "discount" rate

Replace footnote 184 with:

[184] *Actuarial Tables for Use in Personal Injury and Fatal Accident Cases*, 3rd edn (1998); (now 7th edn, 2011). See also (Ogden) Supplementary Tables (March 2017) (accessible at *https://www.gov.uk/government/publications/ogden-tables-actuarial-compensation-tables-for-injury-and-death* [Accessed 25 September 2018]). **28-32**

Replace paragraph with:

28-33 But while *Wells v Wells* set out the relevant principles applied by the courts in fixing the discount rate, it has been superseded by the Lord Chancellor fixing the discount rate under the powers conferred by s.1(1) of the Damages Act 1996. That subsection provides that: "in determining the return to be expected from the investment of a sum awarded as damages for future pecuniary loss ... the court shall ... take into account such rate of return (if any) as may from time to time be prescribed by an order made by the Lord Chancellor". By the Damages (Personal Injury) Order 2017[187] the Lord Chancellor set a discount rate of minus 0.75 per cent as from 20 March 2017.[188] The courts are bound by the rate set unless, applying s.A1(2) of the Damages Act 1996,[188A] any party to the proceedings shows that a different rate of interest is "more appropriate in the case in question". The important issue has therefore now turned to the scope of s.1(2). In *Warriner v Warriner*[189] it was said that, in the interests of certainty, a departure from the rate set would probably be rare. In the instant case, there was nothing unusual justifying a lower rate than that set by the Lord Chancellor (which at that time was 2.5 per cent). In *Cooke v United*

Bristol Health Care[190] the Court of Appeal rejected a different line of attack by the claimant on the conventional method for assessing future pecuniary loss. The claimants wanted to adduce evidence that the cost of care, and indeed earnings, had increased, and could be expected to increase, at a substantially higher rate than the retail prices index. Claimants, it was argued, are therefore being under-compensated by the conventional method, especially where there are high future costs of care. The claimants sought to argue that, to prevent such under-compensation, there should be adjustments to the multiplicands. But the Court of Appeal refused to allow such evidence to be adduced on the basis that, in reality, the claimants were arguing for a departure from the discount rate for multipliers set by the Lord Chancellor; and in line with *Warriner v Warriner* such a departure was thought to be unjustified. Although not mentioned by the Court of Appeal, it is perhaps worth adding, as a further reason for rejecting the claimants' arguments that, in adopting the ILGS rate in *Wells v Wells*, the House of Lords assumed that it is the retail prices index that is the correct measure of inflation and this is also the index used for updating awards for non-pecuniary loss in personal injury cases.

[187] SI 2017/206.

[188] In *Simon v Helmot* [2012] UKPC 5; [2012] Med. L.R. 394, on an appeal from Guernsey, where there is no legislation governing the discount rate so that the courts must decide that rate, it was held that on the then present economic evidence a "negative discount rate" of minus 1.5 per cent should be applied in assessing damages for loss of future earnings (i.e. in calculating the multiplier, there should be an addition to, rather than a deduction from, the number of years during which the loss would be suffered).

[188A] Inserted by the Civil Liability Act 2018 s.10.

[189] [2002] EWCA Civ 81; [2002] 1 W.L.R. 1703.

[190] [2003] EWCA Civ 1370; [2004] 1 W.L.R. 251.

Add new paragraph:

28-33A There continues to be considerable controversy as to whether the ILGS rates are the best way of assessing the discount rate and hence arriving at the correct amount of compensation. Those representing the interests of defendant insurers argued that the negative discount rate of minus 0.75 per cent over-compensates claimants because they can readily invest to obtain higher returns. Those representing personal injury victims counter-argued that one should not be treating personal injury victims as normal investors and that, in any event, empirical historical evidence shows that personal injury victims have certainly not been overcompensated. The Ministry of Justice, following a consultation exercise, proposed[190A] that, while full compensation should remain the aim of damages, the discount rate should not be set on what it considers to be the unrealistic basis that claimants will invest in ILGS. Rather it should be assumed that, while claimants are low-risk investors, they will invest (and would be professionally advised to invest) in a mixed portfolio which will enable them to achieve higher rates of return. It also proposed that, while the Lord Chancellor should set the rate, they should be advised by an independent expert panel; and that there should be a review of the discount rate at least once every three years. These proposals (but substituting five years for three years) have been carried through into the Civil Liability Act 2018 (inserting a new Sch.A1 into the Damages Act 1996).[190B]

[190A] The Personal Injury Discount Rate: How it should be set in Future (Draft Legislation, Ministry of Justice, September 2017, Cm 9500).

[190B] Damages (Personal Injury) Order 2019 (SI 2019/1126).

Ogden Tables

Replace footnote 193 with:

[193] *Actuarial Tables for Use in Personal Injury and Fatal Accident Cases*, 7th edn (2011). See also (Ogden) Supplementary Tables (March 2017) *https://www.gov.uk/government/publications/ogden-tables-actuarial-compensation-tables-for-injury-and-death* [Accessed 25 September 2018]. **28-35**

(v) Effect of taxation

Replace footnote 204 with:

[204] [1956] A.C. 185. See, generally, Edelman, *McGregor on Damages*, 20th edn (2017), Ch.18; Bishop and Kay, "Taxation and Damages: The Rule in Gourley's case" (1987) 104 L.Q.R. 211, advocating legislation making all damages awards taxable; Dawes, "Tax and Damages" (1998) 148 N.L.J. 337; Maugham and Peacock, "Taxing Damages Awards" (2000) 150 N.L.J. 1153. *Gourley* has not been followed in Canada or New Zealand: *R. v Jennings* (1966) 57 D.L.R. (2d) 644; *North Island Wholesale Groceries Ltd v Hewin* [1982] 2 N.Z.L.R. 176. In Australia, *Atlas Tiles v Briers* (1978) 144 C.L.R. 202, which had rejected *Gourley*, was overturned by *Cullen v Trappell* (1980) 146 C.L.R. 1. **28-37**

Replace footnote 211 with:

[211] It is for this reason that the courts have generally not taken account of capital gains tax liability: Edelman, *McGregor on Damages*, 20th edn, (2017), paras 18-063 to 18-071. For an example of damages being subject to tax, see *Deeny v Gooda Walker Ltd (No.2)* [1996] 1 W.L.R. 426 HL. **28-39**

(vii) Other collateral benefits

Replace footnote 236 with:

[236] See generally Edelman, *McGregor on Damages*, 20th edn, (2017), paras 40-149 to 40-182; *Damages for Personal Injury: Medical, Nursing and Other Expenses; Collateral Benefits*, Law Commission Report No.262 (1999), s.B. **28-44**

(d) Non-pecuniary loss

(ii) Loss of faculty and loss of amenity

Replace paragraph with:

Usually the judges make a single award to cover pain and suffering and loss of amenities. It seems clear, however, that the major element in this is the compensation to represent the injury itself (often called the loss of faculty[290]) and the consequences that injury has on the claimant's way of life and therefore for his loss of happiness.[291] In the majority of cases, and especially when the injury is serious, it is unnecessary to distinguish between the consequences of the injury and the injury itself. Damages are awarded so as to cover both and, in any case, as Lord Reid has pointed out,[292] the normal man is usually more concerned about the dislocation of his life than about his actual physical injury. Nevertheless, it may be appropriate to consider the physical injury itself independently for two reasons. First, a minor but permanent impairment of bodily integrity may have no substantial effect on the claimant's enjoyment of life but he may recover a sum simply for the injury itself.[293] Secondly, and perhaps more importantly, the judges in assessing damages for loss of amenities tend to proceed according to the gravity of the physical disability.[294] In other words, they attribute an assumed loss of enjoyment of life to flow from different categories of injury. As will be seen, this prima facie figure may then be revised to take account of the special features of the claimant's case, but it necessarily provides a starting point which is convenient both because it obviates too close an investigation on such subjective matters as the claimant's inner feelings,[295] and because it renders damages awards more uniform and therefore **28-56** predictable.[296] The conventional sums awarded for different types of injury are derived from the general experience of judges as manifested in previous comparable cases,[297] and represent the judiciary's perception of what is fair, just and reasonable compensation.[298] The figures emerging are not, of course, fixed for all time: it has been stressed that in having regard to them the judges should take account of changes in the retail prices index.[299] Moreover, in *Heil v Rankin*,[300] acting on the recommendation of the Law Commission, the Court of Appeal increased damages for non-pecuniary loss because awards had fallen behind what was regarded as "fair, just and reasonable". In an attempt to produce greater consistency in awards, the Judicial Studies Board in 1992 produced a report entitled *Guidelines for the Assessment of General Damages in Personal Injury Cases* which sets out the brackets for various injuries based on, but without mentioning the names of, cases.[301] The fourteenth edition of the *Guidelines for the Assessment of General Damages in Personal Injury Cases* was published in 2017 and was updated to the end of May 2017.[301A] From 1 April 2013, when the legislative changes to the costs regime recommended by Sir Rupert Jackson came into force, damages for pain, suffering and loss of amenity (and indeed all awards of damages for non-pecuniary loss) were increased by 10 per cent. This uplift was essentially designed to compensate claimants, who are funding litigation under a conditional fee agreement, for the loss of their right to recover the success fee from the defendant so that the uplift does not apply where such a success fee is ordered under s.44(6) of the Legal Aid, Sentencing and Punishment of Offenders Act 2012).[302]

[290] Cf. *Andrews v Freeborough* [1967] 1 Q.B. 1 at 18, per Davies LJ.

[291] Cf. *H West & Son Ltd v Shephard* [1964] A.C. 326 at 355, per Lord Devlin.

[292] *H West & Son Ltd v Shephard* [1964] A.C. 326 at 341.

[293] e.g. *Forster v Pugh* [1955] C.L.Y. 741 (loss of spleen), *Dryden v Johnson Matthey Plc* [2018] UKSC 18; [2018] 2 W.L.R. 1109 (platinum sensitisation); but cf. *Hamilton v Burdon* [1962] C.L.Y. 859; *Grieves v FT Everard & Sons* [2007] UKHL 39; [2008] 1 A.C. 281 (pleural plaques).

[294] *Wise v Kaye* [1962] 1 Q.B. 638 at 652, per Sellers LJ; *H West & Son Ltd v Shephard* [1964] A.C. 326, per Lord Pearce at 366; *Fletcher v Autocar and Transporters Ltd* [1968] 2 Q.B. 322 at 340, per Diplock LJ.

[295] *Wise v Kaye* [1962] 1 Q.B. 638, per Sellers LJ at 649; *H West & Son v Shephard* [1964] A.C. 326, per Lord Pearce at 368–369.

[296] *Ward v James* [1966] 1 Q.B. 273 at 300, per Lord Denning MR. See also *Hennell v Ranaboldo* [1963] 1 W.L.R. 1391.

[297] Collections of personal injury awards are available in Kemp and Kemp, *The Quantum of Damages; Current Law* and Halsbury, *Laws of England: Monthly Review*. On the other hand there are some kinds of injury for which there is no established pattern of awards. See *Hawkins v New Mendip Engineering Ltd* [1966] 1 W.L.R. 1341 and *Parry v English Electric Co Ltd* [1971] 1 W.L.R. 664. This was the justification given in *Hodges v Harland and Wolff Ltd* [1965] 1 W.L.R. 523, for the exceptional ordering of a jury trial. For an approach to multiple injuries, see *Dureau v Evans* [1996] P.I.Q.R. Q18.

[298] See para.28-07.

[299] *Walker v McLean (John) & Sons* [1979] 1 W.L.R. 760; *Wright v British Railways Board* [1983] 2 A.C. 773; *Heil v Rankin* [2001] Q.B. 272 CA.

[300] [2001] Q.B. 272 CA.

[301] The status of the Judicial Studies Board's Guidelines was considered in *Arafa v Potter* [1994] P.I.Q.R. Q73 and *Reed v Sunderland HA*, *The Times*, 16 October 1998.

[301A] The Civil Liability Act 2018 Pt 1 (not yet in force) allows for regulations imposing a low fixed tariff of damages for pain, suffering and loss of amenity in respect of whiplash injuries, with a duration of up to two years, caused by negligent driving. The purpose of this is to crack down on fraudulent whiplash claims thereby reducing motor insurance premiums.

[302] *Simmons v Castle* [2012] EWCA 1039; [2012] EWCA Civ 1288; [2013] 1 W.L.R. 1239.

Replace paragraph with:

If such subjective factors are relevant to increase the sum awarded, it might seem logical to reduce the prima facie figure where the claimant is rendered unconscious or is unable to appreciate the loss. However, in *Wise v Kaye*,[310] the Court of Appeal held by a majority that though this fact justified making no award for pain and suffering, it had no bearing on the damages for loss of amenities. Two years later this decision was confirmed by the majority of the House of Lords in the similar case of *H West & Son Ltd v Shephard*,[311] which itself was followed by the House of Lords in *Lim Poh Choo v Camden and Islington AHA*.[312] So although the High Court of Australia has declined to follow *West v Shephard* on this point,[313] and while there has occasionally been a reluctance to do so by English judges,[314] it is settled that so far as English law is concerned it is the objective loss of amenities in respect of which damages are awarded. As Lord Morris said: "The fact of unconsciousness is ... relevant in respect of and will eliminate those heads or elements of damage which can exist only by being felt or thought or experienced. The fact of unconsciousness does not, however, eliminate the actuality of the deprivations of the ordinary experiences and amenities of life which may be the inevitable result of some physical injury."[315] There can be no separate award, over and above damages for pain, suffering and loss of amenity, for "loss of autonomy" where there has been medical negligence comprising a failure to obtain the patient's consent.[315A] **28-58**

[310] [1962] 1 Q.B. 638 (Diplock LJ dissenting).

[311] [1964] A.C. 326 (Lords Reid and Devlin dissenting).

[312] [1980] A.C. 174.

[313] *Skelton v Collins* (1966) 39 A.L.J. 480.

[314] *Andrews v Freeborough* [1967] 1 Q.B. 1, per Willmer LJ at 12, per Davies LJ at 18, per Winn LJ at 20.

[315] [1964] A.C. 326 at 349.

[315A] *Shaw v Kovac* [2017] EWCA Civ 1028; [2017] 1 W.L.R. 4773.

(e) Damages for wrongful birth

McFarlane v Tayside Health Board

Replace paragraph with:

Two main matters were left unresolved by *McFarlane*. The first was what the position would be if the parents could sue for breach of contract. Lord Steyn expressly confined his views to claims in delict or tort; and certainly in respect of breach of contract one could not regard the issue as going to liability rather than the extent of liability.[325] But the same basic policy approach to wrongful birth claims should apply whether the claim is brought in tort or for breach of contract. That point has subsequently been strongly affirmed in the context of the breach of a strict contractual obligation in *ARB v IVF Hammersmith*.[325A] A private IVF clinic acted in breach of its contract with the claimant by thawing and implanting embryos, created with the claimant's gametes, into his ex-girlfriend without his consent. This ultimately resulted in the birth of a healthy daughter. The claimant sought damages for that breach of contract to cover the costs of bringing up the daughter. It was held by the Court of Appeal that, applying *McFarlane*, such damages were not recoverable on policy grounds and that it did not matter that the claim was for breach of contract (comprising the breach of a strict duty) rather than the tort of negligence. The second unresolved issue from *McFarlane* was whether the posi- **28-61** tion would be any different if the unwanted child was disabled. The previously leading case of *Emeh v Kensington AHA*[325B] concerned a child with congenital abnormalities. That decision was not expressly overruled and Lord Steyn specifically left open what the position would be in such a case.

[325] In *McFarlane* Lord Slynn commented that if a client wants to be able to recover the economic costs of raising a healthy child, they must do so by "an appropriate contract", but he did not specify what an appropriate contract might consist of: [2000] 2 A.C. 59 at 76. Patients treated under the NHS do not enter into a contractual relationship with their doctor. See also *Reynolds v The Health First Medical Group* [2000] Lloyd's Rep. Med. 240 (county court) where the claimant's attempt to put a failed sterilisation claim on a contractual basis in order to avoid the effect of *McFarlane* was rejected.

[325A] [2018] EWCA Civ 2803; [2019] Med. L.R. 119.

[325B] [1985] Q.B. 1012 CA: para.28-59.

Parkinson v St James and Seacroft University Hospital NHS Trust

Replace footnote 326 with:

28-62 [326] [2001] EWCA Civ 530; [2002] Q.B. 266. See also *Rand v East Dorset HA* (2000) 50 B.M.L.R. 39; *Hardman v Amin* [2000] Lloyd's Med. Rep. 448; *Lee v Taunton and Somerset NHS Trust* [2001] 1 F.L.R. 419; *Groom v Selby* [2001] EWCA Civ 1522; [2002] P.I.Q.R. P18; Quick, "Damages for Wrongful Conception" [2002] Tort L. Rev. 5. In *Khan v Meadows* [2019] EWCA Civ 152; [2019] 4 W.L.R. 3 the claimant would have had an abortion had she received the proper advice from the defendant about the risks of her child being born with haemophilia. As it was, her child was born and suffered from both haemophilia and autism. Controversially, it was held that, applying the difficult decision of *South Australia Asset Management Corp v York Montague Ltd* [1997] A.C. 191, only the extra costs of bringing up a child with haemophilia—and not the extra costs of bringing up a child with autism—were recoverable.

5. DEATH AS A CAUSE OF ACTION

(b) Dependants

28-87 *Replace footnote 445 with:*

[445] Including a child *en ventre sa mère*: *The George and Richard* (1871) L.R. 3 A. & E. 466; *Lindley v Sharp* (1974) 4 Fam. Law 90; Edelman, *McGregor on Damages*, 20th edn (2017), para.41–006. Adopted children are treated as the children of their adoptive parents and no one else; Adoption Act 1976 s.39.

(d) Damages for bereavement

28-92 *Replace footnote 472 with:*

[472] s.1A(2). In *Rabone v Pennine Care NHS Foundation Trust* [2012] UKSC 2; [2012] 2 A.C. 72 the claimant parents of a deceased adult, who had committed suicide while on home release from hospital, were held to be entitled to damages, and were awarded £5,000, under the Human Rights Act 1998 as victims of the infringement of the right to life under art.2 of the ECHR. In this respect, a claim under the Human Rights Act 1998 may be regarded as outflanking the Fatal Accidents Act 1976 because the parents would have had no claim for bereavement damages under the 1976 Act: see A. Tettenborn, "Wrongful Death, Human Rights and the Fatal Accidents Act" (2012) 128 L.Q.R. 327. But, in answering a slightly different question, it was held by the Court of Appeal in a bold judgment in *Smith v Lancashire Teaching Hospitals NHS Foundation Trust* [2017] EWCA Civ 1916; [2018] 2 W.L.R. 1063, that the exclusion from the limited list of those who can claim bereavement damages, under the 1976 Act, s.1A(2)(a), of a cohabitee who had been living with the deceased for two years as his wife (and the same reasoning applies to a cohabitee living as the deceased's husband or civil partner) infringed the cohabitee's art.8 and art.14 convention rights under the Human Rights Act 1998. A declaration of incompatibility was made under the 1998 Act, s.4.

6. DESTRUCTION OF OR DAMAGE TO GOODS

(b) Damage to goods

Replace footnote 592 with:

28-119 [592] *Burdis v Livsey* [2002] EWCA Civ 510; [2003] Q.B. 36. For criticism of this decision, not least for being inconsistent with the denial of hire costs in *Dimond v Lovell* [2002] 1 A.C. 384 HL, see Burrows, *Remedies for Torts, Breach of Contract and Equitable Wrongs*, 4th edn (2019) pp.212–214.

7. RECOVERY OF COSTS OF ACTION

Replace footnote 624 with:

[624] Edelman, *McGregor on Damages*, 20th edn (2017), para.21-003: "It would make nonsense of the rules about costs if the successful party in an action who has been awarded costs could claim in a further action by way of damages the amount by which the costs awarded him fell short of the costs actually incurred by him." **28-125**

8. EQUITABLE DAMAGES

Measure of damages

Replace paragraph with:

It has been stated by Lord Wilberforce, with the concurrence of other members of the House of Lords, that, apart from cases "where damages could not be claimed at all at common law, there is sound authority for the proposition that the Act does not provide for the assessment of damages on any new basis".[662] The implication of this is that the common law principles of assessment[663] apply to those losses which have already been sustained,[664] while an analogous compensatory approach should be adopted with regard to future acts which the injunction, had it been granted, would have covered. As at common law, equitable damages for a tort may alternatively be assessed on a restitutionary basis.[665] However, this must now be read subject to *Morris-Garner v One Step (Support) Ltd*[665A] which has rejected a restitutionary analysis of what have often been called "*Wrotham Park* damages". **28-132**

[662] *Johnson v Agnew* [1980] A.C. 367 at 400. See also *Surrey CC v Bredero Homes Ltd* [1993] 1 W.L.R. 1361; *Jaggard v Sawyer* [1995] 1 W.L.R. 269.

[663] See paras 28-02 to 28-19.

[664] e.g. *Kine v Jolly* [1905] 1 Ch. 480; *Griffith v Richard Clay & Sons Ltd* [1912] 2 Ch. 291; *Wills v May* [1923] 1 Ch. 317.

[665] *Bracewell v Appleby* [1975] Ch. 408 at 419–420; *Carr-Saunders v Dick McNeil Associates Ltd* [1986] 1 W.L.R. 922 at 932, per Millett J; *Jones v Ruth* [2011] EWCA Civ 804; [2012] 1 W.L.R. 1495 at [36]–[41]; see generally paras 28-149 to 28-150. In *Coventry v Lawrence* [2014] UKSC 13; [2014] A.C. 822 the Supreme Court left open the possibility of there being an award of "gain-based damages" in lieu of an injunction for the tort of private nuisance. See also *Wrotham Park Estate Co Ltd v Parkside Houses Ltd* [1974] 1 W.L.R. 798 at 815 (equitable damages for breach of a restrictive covenant); *Att Gen v Blake* [2001] 1 A.C. 268 HL (account of profits for breach of contract). In *Tamares (Vincent Square) Ltd v Fairpoint* [2007] EWHC 212 (Ch); [2007] 1 W.L.R. 2167, damages for infringing a right to light granted in lieu of a mandatory restorative injunction were rationalised as "compensating" for the lost opportunity of obtaining an injunction.

[665A] [2018] UKSC 20; [2018] 2 W.L.R. 1353. See paras 28-149 to 28-150A.

9. EXEMPLARY DAMAGES

(a) Distinguished from aggravated damages

Replace footnote 668 with:

[668] See, e.g. *Westwood v Hardy* [1964] C.L.Y. 994; *Ansell v Thomas* [1974] Crim. L.R. 31 CA; *W v Meah* [1986] 1 All E.R. 935; *Appleton v Garrett* [1996] P.I.Q.R. P1; *JXL v Britton* [2014] EWHC 2571 (QB) (assault and battery); *Bracegirdle v Orford* (1813) 2 M. & S. 77; *McMillan v Singh* (1985) 17 H.L.R. 120 CA (trespass to land); *Archer v Brown* [1985] Q.B. 401 (deceit); *Thompson v Commissioner of Police for the Metropolis* [1998] Q.B. 498 CA (false imprisonment and malicious prosecution); *Alexander v Home Office* [1988] 1 W.L.R. 968; *Deane v Ealing LBC* [1993] I.C.R. 329; *Gbaja-Biamila v DHL International (UK) Ltd* [2000] I.C.R. 730; *Armitage, Marsden and HM Prison Service* **28-133**

v Johnson [1997] I.C.R. 275 (racial discrimination); *Vento v Chief Constable of West Yorkshire Police (No.2)* [2002] EWCA Civ 1871; [2003] I.R.L.R. 102; *Zaiwalla & Co v Walia* [2002] I.R.L.R. 697 (sex discrimination); *Campbell v MGN Ltd* [2004] UKHL 22; [2004] 2 A.C 457 (breach of confidence); *Mosley v News Group Newspapers Ltd* [2008] EWHC 1777 (QB); [2008] E.M.L.R. 20 (breach of privacy/confidence); *Richard v BBC* [2018] EWHC 1837 (Ch); [2019] Ch. 169 (breach of privacy). But aggravated damages were held to be irrecoverable for the tort of negligence in *Kralj v McGrath* [1986] 1 All E.R. 54 at 61. For general consideration of damages for mental distress for torts see Burrows, *Remedies for Torts, Breach of Contract and Equitable Wrongs*, 4th edn (2019), pp.281–292; Murphy, "The Nature and Domain of Aggravated Damages" [2010] C.L.J. 353.

(b) Scope of exemplary damages

(i) Oppressive, arbitrary or unconstitutional action by the servants of the government

Replace footnote 706 with:

28-138 [706] [2011] UKSC 12; [2012] 1 A.C. 245. See also *Bostridge v Oxleas NHS Foundation Trust* [2015] EWCA Civ 79; [2015] Med. L.R. 113; *Parker v Chief Constable of Essex* [2018] EWCA Civ 2788, [2019] 1 W.L.R. 2238.

(ii) Defendant's conduct has been calculated by him to make a profit which may well exceed the compensation payable

Replace paragraph with:

28-139 This category has fallen to be considered in a number of actions for defamation,[708] including *Broome v Cassell & Co Ltd* itself.[709] But the main use of this category has been in actions by tenants against landlords for wrongful harassment or eviction founded on the torts of trespass or nuisance.[709A] For example, in *Drane v Evangelou*,[710] in which a landlord had forcefully entered premises of which the claimant was the tenant and had taken various steps to evict him, an award of £1,000 exemplary damages for the trespass involved was upheld by the Court of Appeal as coming within the second category, though both Lawton and Goff LJJ considered that it could have been justified as aggravated damages. Similarly, in *Guppys (Bridport) Ltd v Brookling and James*,[711] two tenants were awarded exemplary damages for the tort of nuisance where their landlord, in an attempt to evict them, had (during building work) removed all the internal sanitary and washing facilities, discontinued the supply of water to the external toilets and cut off the electricity. Again in *Design Progression Ltd v Thurloe Properties Ltd*[712] exemplary damages were awarded to a tenant for breach by a landlord of its statutory duty under s.1(3) of the Landlord and Tenant Act 1988. Occasionally exemplary damages have also been awarded under the second category for tortious interference with the claimant's business.[713] In *Borders (UK) Ltd v Commissioner of Police of the Metropolis*[714] the Court of Appeal held that exemplary damages were appropriate in a case where "tens, possibly hundreds, of thousands of new books" had been stolen from the claimants by shoplifters and sold by the defendant from his market stalls. A recent trend has been for exemplary damages to be awarded for insurance fraud.[714A] A good example was *AXA Insurance UK Plc v Financial Claims Solutions Ltd*[714B] where fictitious motor accident claims, alleged to involve insureds of AXA, were brought and initially succeeded but were ultimately thwarted when the sophisticated fraud was exposed. Punitive damages of £20,000 (in addition to compensatory damages) were awarded within Lord Devlin's second category for the tort of deceit and unlawful means conspiracy. Finally, in *AT v Dulghieru*[715] exemplary damages were awarded under this category for the torts of unlawful conspiracy, false imprisonment and assault by forcing several women from Moldova to work as prostitutes.

[708] e.g. *McCarey v Associated Newspapers Ltd (No.2)* [1965] 2 Q.B. 86; *Broadway Approvals Ltd v Odhams Press Ltd (No.2)* [1965] 1 W.L.R. 805; *Manson v Associated Newspapers Ltd* [1965] 1 W.L.R. 1038; *Riches v News Group Newspapers Ltd* [1986] Q.B. 256; *John v MGN Ltd* [1997] Q.B. 586 CA.

[709] [1972] A.C. 1027.

[709A] See J. Goudkamp and E. Katsampouka, "An Empirical Study of Punitive Damages" (2018) 38 O.J.L.S. 90. They studied every electronically accessible judgment in England, Wales and Northern Ireland between January 2000 and December 2015 in which punitive damages were sought (146 claims). Most claims were made for "interference with property" (35.6%) and punitive damages were awarded in 53.8% of those claims. In contrast, for example, there were very few such claims for defamation and privacy (5.5%) and there were no awards of punitive damages in respect of those claims.

[710] [1978] 1 W.L.R. 455.

[711] (1984) 14 H.L.R. 1. See also, e.g. *McMillan v Singh* (1985) 17 H.L.R. 120 CA; *Millington v Duffy* (1984) 17 H.L.R. 232 CA; *Asghar v Ahmed* (1985) 17 H.L.R. 25; *Ramdath v Daley* (1993) 25 H.L.R. 273 (also illustrating the point that there can be no exemplary damages under this category where the defendant is acting for another's benefit); *Ramzan v Brookwide Ltd* [2011] EWCA Civ 985; [2012] 1 All E.R. 903 (exemplary damages awarded for the tort of trespass to land).

[712] [2004] EWHC 324 (Ch); [2005] 1 W.L.R. 1; para.28-143.

[713] *Bell v Midland Ry Co* (1861) 10 C.B. (N.S.) 287; *Messenger Newspaper Group Ltd v National Graphical Association* [1984] I.C.R. 345.

[714] [2005] EWCA Civ 197; *The Times*, 15 April 2005.

[714A] The study by J. Goudkamp and E. Katsampouka, "An Empirical Study of Punitive Damages" (2018) 38 O.J.L.S. 90 shows that, where sought, exemplary damages are very commonly awarded in respect of insurance fraud (for the tort of deceit). As they say, at 114, "The award of punitive damages for insurance fraud, which has been possible only since the demise of the cause-of-action test, constitutes a new trend in the case law."

[714B] [2018] EWCA Civ 1330; [2019] R.T.R. 1.

[715] [2009] EWHC 225 (QB).

(c) Rejection of the "cause of action test"

Replace footnote 726 with:

[726] In *Mosley v News Group Newspapers Ltd* [2008] EWHC 1777 (QB); [2008] E.M.L.R. 20, it was held that exemplary damages could not be given for breach of the equitable wrong of breach of confidence/privacy as this would require a development of the law that was not justified in terms of necessity and proportionality. For general consideration of the question of whether exemplary damages can be awarded for equitable wrongs, see Burrows, *Remedies for Torts, Breach of Contract and Equitable Wrongs*, 4th edn (2019), pp.536–537. **28-142**

10. RESTITUTIONARY DAMAGES

Replace footnote 754 with:

[754] See, e.g. Birks, *An Introduction to the Law of Restitution*, Ch.X; Burrows, *The Law of Restitution*, 3rd edn (Oxford: OUP, 2011), Ch.24; Birks, *Civil Wrongs: A New World* (Butterworth Lectures, 1990-91); Beatson, *The Use and Abuse of Unjust Enrichment*, pp.206–243; Edelman, *McGregor on Damages*, 20th edn (2017), Chs 14 and 15; Edelman, *Gain-Based Damages* (2002); Jackman [1989] C.L.J. 302. **28-150**

Add new paragraph:

Paragraphs 28-149–28-150 must now be read in the light of *Morris-Garner v One Step (Support) Ltd.*[756A] Although the case concerned a breach of contract, the Supreme Court also discussed tort cases in seeking to clarify the purpose and scope of what have often been called "*Wrotham Park* damages" or "hypothetical release damages" (i.e. damages assessed according to what the claimant could reasonably have charged the defendant for releasing the defendant from the duty that has been broken had the defendant approached the claimant immediately before commit- **28-150A** ting that breach). Several important points emerge from the leading and controversial judgement given by Lord Reed (with whom Lady Hale, Lord Wilson and Lord Carnwath agreed). (i) The preferred terminology for these damages is "negotiating damages"; (ii) The purpose of these damages is to compensate for a loss (albeit not a loss in the ordinary sense) and not to remove gains from the defendant; (iii) Such damages will be apt where one is concerned with the infringement of a proprietary right (or, it would seem, analogously, where the right infringed was designed to protect an asset of the claimant); and (iv) It is possible that such damages may be awarded more widely in equity in lieu of an injunction under the Senior Courts Act 1981 s.50. On the facts in question, where there had been the breach of a contractual non-compete clause, such damages were not available (although a court might use a hypothetical bargain as an evidential tool in assessing the claimant's ordinary loss). This was because there had been no infringement of a proprietary right and the damages were not being sought or awarded in lieu of an injunction.

[756A] [2018] UKSC 20; [2018] 2 W.L.R. 1353.

Replace footnote 757:

11. Appeals on quantum of damages[757]

28-151 [757] Generally, see Edelman, *McGregor on Damages*, 20th edn (2017), Ch.53.

Appeals from jury

Replace footnote 758 with:

28-151 [758] Senior Courts Act 1981, s 69; County Courts Act 1984, s.66. The right to a jury trial in defamation cases was removed by the Defamation Act 2013, s.11. When there were juries in defamation cases, deference was shown to their awards and levels of awards for non-pecuniary loss in personal injury cases were cited to them: see, generally, *John v MGN Ltd* [1997] Q.B. 586 and *Kiam v MGN Ltd* [2002] EWCA Civ 43; [2003] Q.B. 281. But in the former case, the Court of Appeal did substitute a figure of £35,000 compensatory damages for the "excessive" £75,000 damages awarded by the jury; and substituted a figure of £50,000 exemplary damages for the "manifestly excessive" £275,000 awarded by the jury.

CHAPTER 29

INJUNCTIONS

TABLE OF CONTENTS

1. INTRODUCTION

Change footnote 1 in title of paragraph:

Principle on which injunction granted[1]

[1] D. Bean, *Injunctions*, 12th edn (2015); A. Burrows, *Remedies for Torts, Breach of Contract and Equitable Wrongs*, 4th edn (2019), Ch.23; R. Sharpe, *Injunctions and Specific Performance*, 4th edn (2012), Pt I; I. Spry, *Equitable Remedies*, 9th edn (2013), Ch.4. See generally J. Murphy, "Rethinking injunctions in Tort Law" (2007) 27 O.J.L.S. 509. **29-01**

Torts of all kinds may be restrained by injunction where "just or convenient"

Replace paragraph with:

29-02 The power to grant an injunction is now possessed by all divisions of the High Court and also by the county court in cases falling within its jurisdiction.[2] Injunctions may be granted in all cases in which it appears to the court to be "just or convenient" to do so, but these words do not confer an arbitrary discretion on the court. Their effect is to enable the court to grant such injunctions as could formerly have been granted by a court of equity.[3] In an appropriate case, therefore, an injunction may be granted in relation to any form of tortious conduct.[4] The breach of statutory obligations which are supported by criminal sanctions does not give rise to a tortious claim unless the court considers that such was the intention of Parliament[5]; where no such inference is drawn (and no other private wrong is made out) the court may not grant an injunction to a private individual in respect of the breach.[6] In *Burris v Azadani*[7] the Court of Appeal upheld an injunction imposing an "exclusion zone" on the defendant to prevent repetition of his tortious harassment of the claimant. It was acknowledged that the effect of the order was to forbid certain lawful actions on the part of the defendant, namely his use of the highway. But it was held that an injunction can be granted restraining conduct that is not itself tortious (or otherwise unlawful), if such an order is necessary to prevent a tort. Although under the general law of tort no injunction can be granted in the absence of the infringement of some tortious right in the claimant,[8] it is now clear that the infringement of the claimant's human rights can give adequate ground for an injunction even if not otherwise wrongful.[9] Most of the decisions tend to concern art.8 (the right to privacy)[10] or art.2 (the right to life).[11] In *Cartier International AG v British Sky Broadcasting Ltd*[11A] injunctions were ordered against internet service providers requiring them to block access by their customers to certain websites which were advertising and selling counterfeit copies of the claimant's goods. This was so even though the service providers were not themselves committing any wrong/tort (such as breach of copyright or infringement of a trade mark).

[2] Senior Courts Act 1981 s.37(1); County Courts Act 1984 s.38. By the County Court Remedies Regulations 2014 (SI 2014/982) the county court generally has no jurisdiction to grant a search (*Anton Piller*) order but does now have jurisdiction to make a freezing (*Mareva*) injunction.

[3] *North London Railway v Great Northern Ry* (1883) 11 Q.B.D. 30; *South Carolina Insurance Co v Assurantie Maatschappij de Zeven Provincien NV* [1987] A.C. 24 HL; *UL v BK* [2013] EWHC 1735 (Fam); [2014] Fam. 35 at [14].

[4] See, e.g. *Saxby v Easterbrook* (1878) 3 C.P.D. 339 (defamation); *Egan v Egan* [1975] Ch. 218 (assault); *Erven Warnink BV v J Townend & Sons (Hull) Ltd* [1979] A.C. 731 (passing-off); *X v Y* [1988] 2 All E.R. 648 (breach of confidence); *Coflexip SA v Scott Comex Seaway MS Ltd* [2001] 1 All E.R. 952 (Note) (patent infringement); *Secretary of State for Environment, Food and Rural Affairs v Meier* [2009] UKSC 11; [2009] 1 W.L.R. 2780; *London (Mayor) v Hall* [2010] EWCA Civ 817; [2011] 1 W.L.R. 504 (trespass to land); *Brand v Berki* [2014] EWHC 2979 (QB) (tort of harassment under the Protection from Harassment Act 1997). In *Bird v O'Neal* [1960] A.C. 907 an injunction was granted to restrain picketing which was being carried on with threats of intimidation. In *Miller v Jackson* [1977] Q.B. 966 at 980, Lord Denning MR said that he did not know of a case where an injunction had been granted to stop a negligent action.

[5] Ch.9. For an example of an injunction being granted to restrain the tort of breach of statutory duty, see *Warder v Cooper* [1970] 1 Ch. 495; cf. *McCall v Abelesz* [1976] Q.B. 585.

[6] *Thorne v British Broadcasting Corp* [1967] 1 W.L.R. 1104; *Gouriet v Union of Post Office Workers* [1978] A.C. 435; *Lonhro Ltd v Shell Petroleum Co Ltd* [1982] A.C. 173; *RCA Corp v Pollard* [1983] 1 Ch. 135. The Attorney General, however, has locus standi, either on his own initiative or in a relator action, to seek an injunction to uphold the public interest: *Gouriet v Union of Post Office Workers*, above, and (e.g.) *Att-Gen v Harris* [1961] 1 Q.B. 74. Local authorities, in pursuance of particular statutory enforcement powers, may also apply for an injunction: e.g. *Stafford BC v Elkenford Co* [1977] 1 W.L.R.

324 (trading standards); *Hammersmith LBC v Magnum Automated Forecourts Ltd* [1978] 1 W.L.R. 50 (noise pollution). They also have power under s.222 of the Local Government Act 1972 to take proceedings, including injunctive proceedings, for the benefit of the locality: e.g. *Stoke-on-Trent BC v B & Q (Retail) Ltd* [1984] A.C. 754; *Runnymede BC v Ball* [1986] 1 W.L.R. 353; *Birmingham CC v Shafi* [2008] EWCA Civ 1186; [2009] 1 W.L.R. 1961. Public authorities may where appropriate obtain injunctions to support them in their performance of their statutory duties: e.g. *Broadmoor Hospital Authority v R.* [2000] Q.B. 775 CA (injunction granted to hospital authority to support performance of its statutory duty). So too with other office-holders: e.g. *Re Oriental Credit Ltd* [1988] Ch. 204 (company liquidator).

[7] [1995] 1 W.L.R. 1372.

[8] See, e.g. *Day v Brownrigg* (1878) 10 Ch D. 294 (naming suburban villa identically with grander neighbouring property, with concomitant confusion and injury to *amour propre*: no injunction, since no right infringed).

[9] *Venables v News Group Newspapers Ltd* [2001] Fam. 430 put the point beyond doubt (child murderer granted new identity, with attendant injunctions, on the basis of the right to life under art.2).

[10] *Re KT* [2004] EWHC 3428 (Fam) (allegations in open court of pederasty); *Re Guardian News & Media Ltd* [2010] UKSC 1; [2010] 2 A.C. 697 (non-secret allegations of terrorist involvement: would harm subject's engagement with community).

[11] As in *Venables v News Group Newspapers Ltd* [2001] Fam. 430, above; also *Venables v News Group Newspapers Ltd*, unreported, 30 July 2010 QBD (same person allowed to suppress information about (new) name under which convicted in open court on child pornography charges after release). Cf. *Mills v News Group Newspapers Ltd* [2001] E.M.L.R. 41 (no sufficient threat shown to prevent disclosure of Heather Mills' address).

[11A] [2016] EWCA Civ 658; [2017] 1 All E.R. 700.

Injunction against whom?

Replace footnote 13 with:

[13] [2003] EWHC 1205; [2003] 1 W.L.R. 1633 (unknown persons threatening to publish pirated versions of Harry Potter book). The power is particularly useful against anonymous groups of trespassers: e.g. *Hampshire Waste Services Ltd v Persons Intending to Trespass and/or Trespassing upon Chineham Incinerator Site* [2003] EWHC 1738 (Ch); [2004] Env. L.R. 9; *Secretary of State for Environment, Food and Rural Affairs v Meier* [2009] UKSC 11; [2009] 1 W.L.R. 2780; *Boyd v Ineos Upstream Ltd* [2019] EWCA Civ 515. There is no injustice to anyone in making such an order provided the description is sufficiently certain to identify those included and those who are not. See generally J. Seymour, "Injunctions Enjoining Non-Parties: Distinction without Difference" [2007] C.L.J. 605. **29-03**

2. PROHIBITORY INJUNCTIONS

Claimant's conduct

After "complete list of", replace "'special circumstances' depriving the claimant of his prima facie right to a prohibitory injunction" with:

relevant factors **29-06**

Trivial harm

Replace paragraph with:

29-07 Another ground upon which the issue of an injunction was refused in *Armstrong v Sheppard & Short Ltd* was the triviality of the harm caused to the claimant by the passage of effluent through the sewer under the surface of his land.[35] That the triviality of the harm suffered by the claimant[36] is in itself a ground for the refusal of an injunction has been affirmed on more than one occasion,[37] but it has also been held several times that for the claimant to be entitled to an injunction it is not necessary that the harm caused by the repetition or continuance of the wrong should be substantial.[38] It has, indeed, been said that: "the very fact that no harm is done is a reason for rather than against the granting of an injunction: for if there is no damage done the damage recovered in the action will be nominal and if the injunction is refused the result will be no more nor less than a licence to continue the tort ... in return for a nominal payment."[39] It is difficult to see how the authorities on this matter can be reconciled,[40] and it is suggested, especially after *Coventry v Lawrence*,[41] that the better view is that triviality of harm does tend to preclude a prohibitory injunction.

[35] [1959] 2 Q.B. at 396–397, per Lord Evershed MR. His Lordship indicated that an award of damages under Lord Cairns' Act (paras 28-127 to 28-132) might have been appropriate, but no claim for such damages was made.

[36] The court should also take account of the risks of harm which have not yet materialised: see, e.g. *Miller v Jackson* [1977] Q.B. 966 at 986, where in his dissenting judgment Geoffrey Lane LJ took account of the fact that the playing of cricket by the defendants had not only caused physical harm to the claimant's property but had also created a risk of personal injury. Lord Denning MR and Cumming-Bruce LJ, however, thought that it was not unreasonable to expect the claimant and her family to keep out of the garden while cricket was being played (respectively, at 981 and 989).

[37] *Goldsmid v Tunbridge Wells Improvement Commissioners* (1866) L.R. 1 Ch. 349 at 354–355, per Turner LJ; *Llandudno Urban DC v Woods* [1899] 2 Ch. 705; *Behrens v Richards* [1905] 2 Ch. 614.

[38] *John Trenberth Ltd v National Westminster Bank Ltd* (1979) 39 P. & C.R. 104; *Patel v WH Smith (Eziot) Ltd* [1987] 1 W.L.R. 853; *Anchor Brewhouse Developments Ltd v Berkley House (Docklands Developments) Ltd* (1987) 38 B.L.R. 82.

[39] *Woollerton & Wilson Ltd v Richard Costain Ltd* [1970] 1 W.L.R. 411 at 413, per Stamp J cited with approval in *Patel v WH Smith (Eziot) Ltd* [1987] 1 W.L.R. 853 at 860, per Balcombe LJ. The learned judge nevertheless suspended the operation of the injunction which was to restrain the defendants from allowing the jib of their crane to enter the claimant's air space, for long enough to enable them to complete their building operations. In *Charrington v Simons & Co Ltd* [1971] 1 W.L.R. 598 the Court of Appeal expressed its reservations on this aspect of Stamp J.'s decision and in *John Trenberth Ltd v National Westminster Bank Ltd* (1979) 39 P. & C.R. 104 and in *Jaggard v Sawyer* [1995] 1 W.L.R. 269 CA, it was treated as wrong.

[40] The suggestion that the triviality of the harm caused is a reason for not granting an injunction except where the consequences of the wrongful act, however slight, will endure indefinitely (see, e.g. *Att Gen v Sheffield Gas Consumer Co* (1852) 3 De G.M. & G. 304 at 314–315, per Lord Cranworth LJ) is inconsistent with, e.g. *Armstrong v Sheppard & Short Ltd* above and *Woollerton & Wilson Ltd v Richard Costain Ltd* above.

[41] [2014] UKSC 13; [2014] A.C. 822.

5. INTERIM INJUNCTIONS

(a) American Cyanamid

Replace footnote 98 with:

29-22 [98] [1975] A.C. 396 at 408. For a clearer setting out of the principles, see *Fellowes & Son v Fisher* [1976] Q.B. 122, per Browne LJ at 137–138. For a clear and thorough application of the *American Cyanamid* principles resulting in the lifting of an interim injunction ordered in the context of a statutory procurement process, see *Alstom Transport UK Ltd v London Underground Ltd* [2017] EWHC 1521 (TCC); (2017) 174 Con. L.R. 194. Sir John Donaldson MR in *Francome v Mirror Group Newspapers Ltd* [1984] 1 W.L.R. 892 at 899 expressed preference for the term "balance of justice" as against "balance of convenience". See also *Cayne v Global Natural Resources Plc* [1984] 1 All E.R. 225 at 237, per May LJ. For an interpretation of *American Cyanamid*, according to which the courts can always take into account any clear view they have reached as to the relative strengths of the parties' cases (albeit that they should rarely attempt to resolve complex issues of disputed fact or law), see *Series 5 Software Ltd v Clarke* [1996] 1 All E.R. 853.

(b) Exceptional situations

Freedom of speech

Replace footnote 132 with:

29-28 [132] [2007] EWCA Civ 295; [2008] Q.B. 103. *Banerjee* was also applied to the claim for breach of confidence in *Donald v Ntuli* [2010] EWCA Civ 1276, [2011] 1 WLR 294. It was also applied in *PJS v*

News Group Newspapers [2016] UKSC 26; [2016] A.C. 1081 (but there it was made clear that the claim was for the tort of privacy, which was distinguished from breach of confidence, and that privacy (one might say, like reputation in the context of defamation) should be accorded greater protection because it merits protection even where the information is known to some of the public, whereas confidential information, once known about, does not merit further protection). See also *ABC v Telegraph Media Group Ltd* [2018] EWCA Civ 2329; [2019] E.M.L.R. 5 (where an interim injunction was ordered to restrain an alleged breach of confidence comprising breach of a non-disclosure settlement agreement).

(f) Freezing injunctions

After "over other creditors.", add new footnote 216a:

[216a] It follows that payment out to a secured creditor is not prohibited by a freezing injunction so that the secured creditor does not need to seek a variation of the freezing injunction to allow such payment out although if, out of an abundance of caution, such a variation was sought, it would not be refused: *Taylor v Van Dutch Marine Holding Ltd* [2017] EWHC 636 (Ch); [2017] 1 W.L.R. 2571. **29-45**

(ii) Real risk of defendant's assets being disposed of

Replace footnote 231 with:

[231] *Third Chandris Shipping Corp v Unimarine SA* [1979] Q.B. 645; *Z. Ltd v A-Z* [1982] Q.B. 558; *Ninemia Maritime Corp v Trave Schiffahrtsgesellschaft GmbH (The Niedersachsen)* [1983] 1 W.L.R. 1412; *Montecchi v Shimco (UK) Ltd* [1979] 1 W.L.R. 1180; *Establissement Esefka International Anstalt v Central Bank of Nigeria* [1979] 1 Lloyd's Rep. 445 CA. In the latter two cases there was no such risk. In *Polly Peck International Plc v Nadir (No.2)* [1992] 4 All E.R. 769 it was explained that the circumstances would have to be unusual for a freezing injunction to be granted against a bank. On the appointment of an administrative receiver, a freezing injunction against a company should normally be varied or discharged because there is no longer a risk of dissipation of the assets to frustrate a judgment; *Capital Cameras Ltd v Harold Lines Ltd* [1991] 1 W.L.R. 54. In *Mobil Cerro Negro Ltd v Petroleos de Venezuala SA* [2008] EWHC 532 (Comm); [2008] 2 All E.R. (Comm) 1034 it was held that, to be relevant, the dissipation of assets must be by conduct that is unjustifiable. The same test (that there must be a real risk of disposal) applies also to that form of freezing order that is referred to as a "notification order", i.e. an injunction that the defendant should not dispose of assets without informing the claimant: *Holyoake v Candy* [2017] EWCA Civ 92; [2018] Ch. 297. **29-47**

(iii) Undertaking in damages

Replace footnote 238 with:

[238] *Third Chandris Shipping Corp v Unimarine SA* [1979] Q.B. 645. The court should generally be sure that the defendant is good for the undertaking and may insist on security; *Ashtiani v Kashi* [1987] Q.B. 888. See Sch.B(2) of the standard forms annexed to the *Practice Direction*. Cf. *Allen v Jambo Holdings Ltd* [1980] 1 W.L.R. 1252. For consideration of whether there should be fortification of a party's undertaking in damages in support of a freezing injunction, see *Energy Venture Partners Ltd v Malabu Oil and Gas Ltd* [2014] EWCA Civ 1295; [2015] 1 W.L.R. 2309. But if security was not insisted on at the time the freezing injunction was granted it should not be ordered when the injunction has been discharged: *Commodity Ocean Transport Corp v Basford Unicorn Industries Ltd (The Mito)* [1987] 2 Lloyd's Rep. 197. For the approach to claims for damages enforcing the undertaking see *Cheltenham & Gloucester Building Society v Ricketts* [1993] 1 W.L.R. 1545; *Fiona Trust & Holding Corporation v Privalov (No 2)* [2016] EWHC 2163 (Comm); [2017] 2 All E.R. 570. But a cross-undertaking may not be required of a public authority that seeks a freezing injunction in exercise of its law enforcement function: *Securities & Investment Board v Lloyd-Wright* [1993] 4 All E.R. 210; *United States Securities & Exchange Commission v Manterfield* [2009] EWCA Civ 27; [2010] 1 W.L.R. 172. For the award of damages under the undertaking, see *Al-Rawas v Pegasus Energy Ltd* [2008] EWHC 617 (QB); [2009] 1 All E.R. 346 at para.29-42. **29-48**

[illegible] which was [illegible] that there was [illegible] was [illegible] [illegible] which [illegible] and that [illegible] [illegible]

(i) [illegible]

[illegible]

[illegible] 29–43

(j) [illegible] of defendant's assets [illegible]

[illegible]

[illegible] 29–47

[illegible]

[illegible]

[illegible] 29–48

[illegible]

CHAPTER 31

DISCHARGE OF TORTS

TABLE OF CONTENTS

2. WAIVER: ELECTION

"Waiver of tort"

Replace footnote 2 with:

[2] For the law on restitution for a tort see Birks, *An Introduction to the Law of Restitution*, Ch.X: Burrows, *Remedies for Torts, Breach of Contract, and Equitable Wrongs*, 4th edn (2019), Ch.19; Edelman, *Gain-Based Damages* (2002); Edelman, *McGregor on Damages*, 20th edn (2017) Chs 15–16; Beatson, *The Use and Abuse of Unjust Enrichment* (1991), pp.206-243; Winfield, *Province of the Law of Tort* (1931), pp.168-176. See also Lord Wright, "United Australia v Barclays Bank Ltd" (1941) 57 L.Q.R. 184; Fridman, "Waiver of Tort" (1955) 18 M.L.R. 1; Hedley, "The Myth of Waiver of Tort" (1984) 100 L.Q.R. 653. See also paras 28-149 to 28-150. **31-02**

6. RES JUDICATA

(a) Principle of res judicata

Replace paragraph with:

Under the principle of res judicata, even if no judgment has been recovered in the same action against the same party,[111] a litigant in a civil action may be estopped from denying what has previously been finally decided by a competent court.[112] Res judicata is not a technical doctrine, and the principle applies whether or not the previous judgment was given by a court of record or a court of limited jurisdiction.[113] It is a rule of public policy based on the desirability that litigation should not drag on indefinitely and that a defendant should not be oppressed by suc- **31-24** cessive actions when one would do.[114] Moreover, in what may be referred to as the "wider principle of *Henderson v Henderson*", the courts have an inherent jurisdiction to strike out as vexatious a claim or defence which not only has been already decided in previous proceedings against the party raising it, but also which might have been raised in previous proceedings in which the facts necessary to raise it have been decided against him.[115] The law relating to res judicata was helpfully summarised by Lord Sumption in *Virgin Atlantic Airways Ltd v Zodiac Seats UK Ltd*,[116] who noted that "res judicata" is in fact a "portmanteau term which is used to describe a number of different legal principles with different juridical origins".[117]

[111] See paras 31-14 to 31-23. This may be labelled "cause of action estoppel" and precludes a party from re-litigating the same cause of action unless fraud or collusion is alleged so as to justify setting aside the earlier judgment.

[112] This may be labelled "issue estoppel". See generally *Henderson v Henderson* (1843) Hare 100 at 115, per Wigram VC; *Hoystead v Taxation Commissioner* [1926] A.C. 155; *New Brunswick Rail Co v British and French Trust Corp* [1939] A.C. 1; *Blair v Curran* (1939) 62 C.L.R. 464 at 531 onwards, per Dixon J; *Thoday v Thoday* [1964] P. 181; *Fidelitas Shipping Co Ltd v V/O Exportchleb* [1966] 1 Q.B. 630; *Carl-Zeiss-Stiftung v Rayner & Keeler Ltd (No.3)* [1967] 1 A.C. 853; *Mills v Cooper* [1967] 2 Q.B. 459, per Diplock LJ; *SCF v Masri (No.3)* [1987] Q.B. 1028; *Bobolas v Economist Newspaper Ltd* [1987] 1 W.L.R. 1101; *Norway's State Application (No.2), Re* [1990] 1 A.C. 723; *Thrasyvoulou v Secretary of State for Environment* [1990] 2 A.C. 273; *Arnold v Westminster Bank Plc* [1991] 2 A.C. 93; *Hines v Birkbeck College (No.2)* [1992] Ch. 33; *Republic of India v India Steamship Co Ltd* [1993] A.C. 410; *Desert Sun Loan Corp v Hill* [1996] 2 All E.R. 847 CA; *Buehler AG v Chronos Richardson Ltd* [1998] 2 All E.R. 960 CA; *Friend v Civil Aviation Authority (No.2)* [2001] EWCA Civ 1204; [2001] 4 All E.R. 385; *Hormel Foods Corp v Antilles Landscape Investments NV* [2005] EWHC 13; [2005] E.T.M.R. 54 (dealing with infringement of patents and trade-marks); *Special Effects Ltd v L'Oréal SA* [2007] EWCA Civ 1; [2007] R.P.C. 15 (no issue estoppel or abuse of process in reopening in court matters decided by the Trade Marks Registry in opposition proceedings); *Naraji v Shelbourne* [2011] EWHC 3298 (QB); *Price v Nunn* [2013] EWCA Civ 1002; *Clark v In Focus Asset Management and Tax Solutions Ltd* [2014] EWCA Civ 118; [2014] 1 W.L.R. 2502 (cause of action in the courts barred by res judicata where the claimant had been awarded compensation by the Financial Services Ombudsman under the Financial Services and Markets Act 2000); *Nayif v High Commission of Brunei Darussalam* [2014] EWCA Civ 1521; [2015] 4 All E.R. 159. Spencer-Bower, Turner and Handley, *The Doctrine of Res Judicata*, 4th edn (2009), Pt I; Munday, *Cross and Tapper on Evidence*, 13th edn (2018), pp.88–100.

[113] *May, Re* (1885) 28 Ch D. 516 at 518. The principle of res judicata also extends to successive proceedings before non-statutory disciplinary or regulatory tribunals: *R (on the application of Coke-Wallis) v Institute of Chartered Accountants in England and Wales* [2011] UKSC 1; [2011] 2 A.C. 146 (commented on by Handley (2011) 127 L.Q.R. 343). For acceptance that a consent order can give rise to an estoppel by res judicata, see *Zurich Insurance Co Plc v Hayward* [2011] EWCA Civ 641; [2011] C.P. Rep. 39, but note also *Spicer v Tuli* [2012] EWCA Civ 845; [2012] 1 W.L.R. 3088.

[114] *Barrow v Bankside Members Agency Ltd* [1996] 1 W.L.R. 257 at 260, per Sir Thomas Bingham MR. The policy that underpins this rule is relevant to successive pre-trial applications for the same relief, but should be applied less strictly than in relation to a final decision of the court: *Woodhouse v Consignia Plc* [2002] EWCA Civ 275; [2002] 1 W.L.R. 2558 at [56].

[115] This may also be labelled "issue estoppel in the wider sense". In "the wider principle of *Henderson v Henderson*". In addition to several of the cases cited in fn.112, especially *Henderson v Henderson* (1843) 3 Hare 100 at 115, see *Macdougall v Knight* (1890) 25 Q.B.D. 1; *Stephenson v Garnett* [1898] 1 Q.B. 677; *Mackenzie-Kennedy v Air Council* [1927] 2 K.B. 517, per Scrutton LJ at 528; *Greenhalgh v Mallard* [1947] 2 All E.R. 255; *Wright v Bennett (No.2)* [1948] W.N. 62; *Hunter v Chief Constable of the West Midlands* [1982] A.C. 529; *Yat Tung Investment Co Ltd v Dao Heng Bank Ltd* [1975] A.C. 581; *Brisbane CC v Att Gen of Queensland* [1979] A.C. 411; *North West Water Authority v Binnie and Partners* [1990] 3 All E.R. 547; *Talbot v Berkshire CC* [1994] Q.B. 290 (wider principle of *Henderson v Henderson* applies to personal injury actions); *Barrow v Bankside Agency Ltd* [1996] 1 W.L.R. 257 CA; *C (A Minor) v Hackney LBC* [1996] 1 W.L.R. 789 CA; *Johnson v Gore Wood & Co* [2001] 2 A.C. 1 HL; *Woodhouse v Consigna plc* [2002] EWCA Civ 275; [2002] 1 W.L.R. 2558 at [56].

[116] [2013] UKSC 46; [2014] 1 A.C 160 at [17]–[26] (with the full agreement of the Court). For further clarification, in the context of setting aside a judgment for fraud, see *Takhar v Gracefield Developments Ltd* [2019] UKSC 13; [2019] 2 W.L.R. 984. Lord Sumption made clear at [61]–[62] that setting aside a judgment for fraud involves neither cause of action estoppel nor issue estoppel but it is concerned with an abuse of process and therefore falls within the wider principle of *Henderson v Henderson* (1843) Hare 100 at 115.

[117] [2013] UKSC 46 at [17].

Replace footnote 118 with:

[118] [2002] 2 A.C. 1; commented on by Handley (2002) 118 L.Q.R. 397; Watt (2001) 20 C.J.Q. 90. The principles laid down in *Johnson v Gore Wood & Co* were applied by the Court of Appeal in *Playboy Club London Ltd v Banca Nazionale Del Lavoro SpA* [2018] EWCA Civ 2025 in deciding that it was not an abuse of process for the claimant to bring a deceit claim even though it had failed in its earlier negligence claim. **31-25**

Chapter 32

LIMITATION

Table of Contents

1. GENERAL

(e) Starting the limitation period

(ii) The problem of latent damage

Replace paragraph with:

32-13 In *Forster v Outred & Co*[57] solicitors had negligently failed to advise the claimant that what she thought was only temporary security for bridging finance to her son was in fact a permanent mortgage of her farm to cover all her son's present and future debts to a company. It was held that damage occurred, and hence time started to run, from when she executed the mortgage thereby diminishing the value of her land, even though the actual demand for her to repay her son's debts did not arise until two years later. Similarly, it has been held that a claimant suffered damage as soon as he took a lease of property in reliance on a surveyor's negligently prepared report,[58] or as soon as he executed a contract in reliance on the negligent advice of a solicitor.[59] On the other hand, *Forster v Outred & Co* has been distinguished in other cases in which the claimant was regarded as suffering damage at a date later than when he acted in reliance on negligent advice[60]; and in *Law Society v Sephton & Co*[61] the House of Lords drew a distinction between a contingent liability that may depress the value of other property, as in *Forster*, and a contingent liability that stands alone which, until the contingency occurs, is not as such damage for the purposes of the accrual of a cause of action in negligence.

[57] [1982] 1 W.L.R. 86.

[58] *Secretary of State for the Environment v Essex, Goodman and Suggitt* [1986] 1 W.L.R. 1432. See also *Kitney v Jones Lang Wootton* (1988) 20 E.G. 88; *Lee v Thompson* (1989) 40 E.G. 89 CA; *Iron Trades Mutual Insurance Co Ltd v JK Buckenham Ltd* [1990] 1 All E.R. 808; *Islander Trucking Ltd v Hogg Robinson Gardner Mountain (Marine) Ltd* [1990] 1 All E.R. 826; *Bell v Peter Browne & Co* [1990] 2 Q.B. 495; *Knapp v Ecclesiastical Insurance Group Plc* [1998] P.N.L.R. 172; *Byrne v Hall Pain & Foster* [1999] 1 W.L.R. 1849; *Shore v Sedgwick Financial Services Ltd* [2008] EWCA Civ 863; [2008] P.N.L.R. 37; *Pegasus Management Holdings SCA v Ernst & Young* [2010] EWCA Civ 181; [2010] 3 All E.R. 297; *Axa Insurance Ltd v Akther and Darby Solicitors* [2009] EWCA Civ 1166; [2010] 1 W.L.R. 1662; *Halsall v Champion Consulting Ltd* [2017] EWHC 1079 (QB); [2017] P.N.L.R. 32.

[59] *DW Moore & Co Ltd v Ferrier* [1988] 1 W.L.R. 267. See also *McCarroll v Statham Gill Davies* [2002] EWCA Civ 425; [2003] P.N.L.R. 25; *Nouri v Marvi* [2010] EWCA Civ 1107; [2011] P.N.L.R. 7; *Green v Eadie* [2011] EWHC B24 (Ch); [2012] Ch. 363; *Boycott v Perrins Guy Williams* [2011] EWHC 2969 (Ch); [2012] P.N.L.R. 25; *Lane v Cullens Solicitors* [2011] EWCA Civ 547; [2012] Q.B. 693 (in a claim

by the administrator of an estate against his solicitor for negligent failure to advise him not to distribute the estate it was held that the claimant's loss was suffered when he distributed the estate); *Osborne v Follett Stock* [2017] EWHC 1811 (QB); [2017] P.N.L.R. 35.

60 In *UBAF Ltd v European American Banking Corp* [1984] Q.B. 713 an allegedly negligent defendant had induced the claimant to lend money to an insolvent company outside the limitation period and inside the limitation period it had defaulted on the loan. The Court of Appeal held that time ran from the default on the loan. In *Mathew v Maughold Life Assurance Co, The Times,* 23 January 1985, it was held that time ran against a negligent accountant from when financial loss eventually resulted from the advice and not from when the advice was originally acted upon (the decision was overturned on a different point by the Court of Appeal: [1955–95] P.N.L.R. 309, *The Times,* 19 February 1987). See also *First National Commercial Bank v Humberts* [1995] 2 All E.R. 673 CA. In *Berney v Saul* [2013] EWCA Civ 640; [2013 P.N.L.R. 26 it was held that the cause of action against the defendant solicitor accrued when the solicitor settled the claimant's action against a third party and not before.

61 [2006] UKHL 22; [2006] 2 A.C. 543.

2. New claims in pending actions

Replace footnote 84 with:

84 At first sight, there appears to be an exception for "an original set-off or counterclaim" (defined as "a claim made by way of set-off or ... by way of counterclaim by a party who has not previously made any claim in the action"): Limitation Act 1980 s.35(3). But it was controversially decided, as a matter of statutory interpretation, in *Al-Rawas v Hassan Khan and Co* [2017] EWCA Civ 42; [2017] 1 W.L.R. 2301 that this does not permit an original set-off or counterclaim to be brought where already time-barred at the time of the action. Rather an original set-off or counterclaim was regarded as being merely an exception to the restrictions on adding or substituting a new cause of action or party in s.35(5). For earlier cases, see *Lloyd's Bank v Wojcik, The Independent,* 19 January 1998, CA; and *Law Society v Wemyss* [2008] EWHC 2515 (Ch); [2009] 1 W.L.R. 2254 (in which it was held that although the counterclaim fell within s.35(3) of the Limitation Act 1980 as an original counterclaim, the amendment to the claim form needed to bring that counterclaim should be refused under CPR r.17.4(2)). 32-19

3. Persons under a disability

Replace paragraph with:

A person is under a disability while he is an infant (i.e. he is under the age of 18) or lacks capacity (within the meaning of the Mental Capacity Act 2005) to conduct legal proceedings.[97] If a person to whom a right of action accrues is, at the date of the accrual, under a disability the action may be brought within six years[98] from when he ceases to be under the disability or dies, whichever event first occurs.[99] Thus, an infant has an indefeasible right to bring an action for personal injuries at any time before the age of 21[100]; and where a claimant is under a permanent disability there is effectively no limitation period.[101] To this rule there are, however, two provisos: (i) the rule does not apply where the right of action first accrued to some person (not under a disability) through whom the person under the disability claims[102]; and (ii) where a right of action which has accrued to a person under a disability accrues to another person under a disability, no further extension of time is allowed by reason of the disability of the second person.[103] It was also said obiter dicta in *Toropdar v D*[104] that a person could be granted a negative declaration that he was not liable to the injured party even though the limitation period had not run out (because the injured party was under 18) and might never run out (if he had suffered permanent brain damage). If the claimant had capacity when the action accrued, but subsequently lacks capacity, this does not prevent time running.[105] Where a person lacked capacity when he acquired knowledge for the purposes of the latent damage limitation period laid down in s.14A(4)(b) of the Limitation Act 1980, but did not lack capacity when the cause of action accrued, an action may be brought within three years from when he ceased to lack capacity or died (whichever first occurred).[106] 32-21

[97] Limitation Act 1980 s.38(2) (as amended by the Mental Capacity Act 2005). For the previous law on "unsoundness of mind" see the 20th edn of this work at para.32-22.

[98] For personal injury and death actions the period is three years: s.28(6); for claims for contribution the period is two years: s.28(5); for defamation actions the period is one year: s.28(4A). For actions under the Consumer Protection Act 1987 the period is three years, but the 10-year long-stop cannot be overridden: s.28(7); see para.32-82.

[99] Limitation Act 1980 s.28(1).

[100] *Tolley v Morris* [1979] 1 W.L.R. 592.

[101] *Headford v Bristol and District HA* [1995] 6 Med. L.R. 1.

[102] Limitation Act 1980 s.28(2). And see s.38(5).

[103] Limitation Act 1980 s.28(3).

[104] [2009] EWHC 567 (QB); [2010] Lloyd's Rep. I.R. 358. For criticism of this reasoning, see Patten, "When is a Limitation Period not a Limitation Period?" [2010] C.J.Q. 284.

[105] *Purnell v Roche* [1927] 2 Ch. 142. In a personal injuries action this rule can be mitigated by the exercise of the court's discretion: Limitation Act 1980 s.33(3)(d) (see para.32-63); see also *Kirby v Leather* [1965] 2 Q.B. 367: where the tort causes immediate lack of capacity, time does not run.

[106] Limitation Act 1980 s.28A(1); but the 15-year long-stop cannot be overridden: s.28A(2). See para.32-70 onwards.

7. ACTIONS FOR PERSONAL INJURIES AND DEATH

(c) The court's discretion

Add new paragraph:

32-55A Paragraphs 32-54 and 32-55 must now be read in the light of the summary of general principles applicable to s.33 set out by Sir Terence Etherton MR in *Chief Constable of Greater Manchester v Carroll.*[228A] He said that there were the following thirteen general principles:

"1. Section 33 is not confined to a 'residual class of cases'. It is unfettered and requires the judge to look at the matter broadly: *Donovan v Gwentoys Ltd* [1990] 1 WLR 472 at 477E; *Horton v Sadler* [2006] UKHL 27; [2007] 1 AC 307, at [9] (approving the Court of Appeal judgments in *Finch v Francis* (unreported) 21 July 1977); *A v Hoare* [2008] UKHL 6, [2008] AC 844, at [45], [49], [68] and [84]; *Sayers v Lord Chelwood* [2012] EWCA Civ 1715, [2013] 1 WLR 1695, at [55].

2. The matters specified in section 33(3) are not intended to place a fetter on the discretion given by section 33(1), as is made plain by the opening words 'the court shall have regard to all the circumstances of the case', but to focus the attention of the court on matters which past experience has shown are likely to call for evaluation in the exercise of the discretion and must be taken into a consideration by the judge: *Donovan*'s case, at 477H–478A.

3. The essence of the proper exercise of the judicial discretion under section 33 is that the test is a balance of prejudice and the burden is on the claimant to show that his or her prejudice would outweigh that to the defendant: *Donovan*'s case, at 477E; *Adams v Bracknell Forest Borough Council* [2005] 1 AC 76, at [55], approving observations in *Robinson v St Helens Metropolitan Borough Council* [2003] PIQR P128 at [32] and [33]; *McGhie v British Telecommunications plc* [2005] EWCA Civ 48, (2005) 149 SJLB 114, at [45]. Refusing to exercise the discretion in favour of a claimant who brings the claim outside the primary limitation period will necessarily prejudice the claimant, who thereby loses the chance of establishing the claim.

4. The burden on the claimant under section 33 is not necessarily a heavy one. How heavy or easy it is for the claimant to discharge the burden will depend on the facts of the particular case: *Sayers*'s case at [55].

5. Furthermore, while the ultimate burden is on a claimant to show that it would be

inequitable to disapply the statute, the evidential burden of showing that the evidence adduced, or likely to be adduced, by the defendant is, or is likely to be, less cogent because of the delay is on the defendant: *Burgin v Sheffield City Council* [2005] EWCA Civ 482 at [23]. If relevant or potentially relevant documentation has been destroyed or lost by the defendant irresponsibly, that is a factor which may weigh against the defendant: *Hammond v West Lancashire Health Authority* [1998] Lloyd's Rep Med 146.

6. The prospects of a fair trial are important: *A v Hoare* at [60]. The Limitation Acts are designed to protect defendants from the injustice of having to fight stale claims, especially when any witnesses the defendant might have been able to rely on are not available or have no recollection and there are no documents to assist the court in deciding what was done or not done and why: *Donovan*'s case, at 479A; *Robinson*'s case at [32]; *Adams*' case at [55]. It is, therefore, particularly relevant whether, and to what extent, the defendant's ability to defend the claim has been prejudiced by the lapse of time because of the absence of relevant witnesses and documents: *Robinson*'s case at [33]; *Adams*' case at [55]; and *A v Hoare* at [50].
7. Subject to considerations of proportionality (as outlined in (11) below), the defendant only deserves to have the obligation to pay due damages removed if the passage of time has significantly diminished the opportunity to defend the claim on liability or amount: *Cain v Francis* [2008] EWCA Civ 1451, [2009] QB 754 at [69].
8. It is the period after the expiry of the limitation period which is referred to in subsubsections 33(3)(a) and (b) and carries particular weight: *Donovan*'s case at 478G. The court may also, however, have regard to the period of delay from the time at which section 14(2) was satisfied until the claim was first notified: *Donovan*'s case at 478H and 479H–480C; Cain's case at [74]. The disappearance of evidence and the loss of cogency of evidence even before the limitation clock starts to tick is also relevant, although to a lesser degree: *Collins v Secretary of State for Business Innovation and Skills* [2014] EWCA Civ 717, [2014] PIQR P19 at [65].
9. The reason for delay is relevant and may affect the balancing exercise. If it has arisen for an excusable reason, it may be fair and just that the action should proceed despite some unfairness to the defendant due to the delay. If, on the other hand, the reasons for the delay or its length are not good ones, that may tip the balance in the other direction: *Cain*'s case at [73]. I consider that the latter may be better expressed by saying that, if there are no good reasons for the delay or its length, there is nothing to qualify or temper the prejudice which has been caused to the defendant by the effect of the delay on the defendant's ability to defend the claim.
10. Delay caused by the conduct of the claimant's advisers rather than by the claimant may be excusable in this context: *Corbin v Penfold Metallising Co Ltd* [2000] Lloyd's Rep Med 247.
11. In the context of reasons for delay, it is relevant to consider under subsection 33(3)(a) whether knowledge or information was reasonably suppressed by the claimant which, if not suppressed, would have led to the proceedings being issued earlier, even though the explanation is irrelevant for meeting the objective standard or test in section 14(2) and (3) and so insufficient to prevent the commencement of the limitation period: *A v Hoare* at [44]–[45] and [70].
12. Proportionality is material to the exercise of the discretion: *Robinson*'s case at [32] and [33]; *Adams*'s case at [54]–[55]. In that context, it may be relevant that the claim has only a thin prospect of success (*McGhie*'s case at [48]), that the claim is modest in financial terms so as to give rise to disproportionate legal costs (*Robinson*'s case at [33]; *Adams*'s case at [55]); *McGhie*'s case at [48]), that the claimant would have a clear case against his or her solicitors (*Donovan*'s case at 479F), and, in a personal injury case, the extent and degree of damage to the claimant's health, enjoyment of life and employability (*Robinson*'s case at [33]; *Adams*'s case at [55]).
13. An appeal court will only interfere with the exercise of the judge's discretion under section 33, as in other cases of judicial discretion, where the judge has made an er-

ror of principle, such as taking into account irrelevant matters or failing to take into account relevant matters, or has made a decision which is wrong, that is to say the judge has exceeded the generous ambit within which a reasonable disagreement is possible: *KR v Bryn Alyn Community (Holdings) Ltd* [2003] EWCA Civ 783, [2003] QB 1441 at [69]; *Burgin*'s case at [16]."

228A [2017] EWCA Civ 1992; [2018] 4 W.L.R. 32 at [42].

(i) The balance of prejudice

Replace footnote 231 with:

32-56 231 See *Dale v British Coal Corp* [1992] P.I.Q.R. 373 at 380; *Forbes v Wandsworth HA* [1997] Q.B. 402 at 417. In *JL v Bowen* [2017] EWCA Civ 82; [2017] P.I.Q.R. P11 a trial judge's decision to disapply the limitation period in a case of alleged historic sexual abuse (continuing into adulthood) was overturned because, inter alia, the judge had artificially ignored his adverse findings against the claimant when considering the limitation question.

(ii) The six listed factors

(1) s.33(3)(a) The length of and the reasons for the delay on the part of the plaintiff.

Extent to which the evidence is less cogent

Replace footnote 254 with:

32-61 254 *Rowe v Kingston-Upon-Hull CC* [2003] EWCA Civ 1281; [2004] P.I.Q.R. P16; *A v Trustees of the Watchtower Bible and Tract Society* [2015] EWHC 1722 (QB) at [58] per Globe J (the facts concerned historic sexual abuse). Cf. *Catholic Child Welfare Society v CD* [2018] EWCA Civ 2342; [2019] E.L.R. 1 (limitation period in sexual abuse case not disapplied under s.33 because, in particular, the long delay meant that relevant witnesses on behalf of the defendant could not now be called). In *Brookes v J & P Coats (UK) Ltd* [1984] I.C.R. 158, s.11 was disapplied after a 12-year delay. While it was accepted that the cogency of the defendant's evidence was impaired it was thought that a clear enough picture could be presented for a fair trial. The system of work was in issue which was easier to recall than the sequence of events comprising a single incident. See also *Ashe Construction Ltd v Burke* [2003] EWCA Civ 717; [2004] P.I.Q.R. P11, which also involved an allegation of an unsafe system of work, where it was possible to have a "respectably fair trial" despite the considerable delay.

8. NEGLIGENCE ACTIONS FOR LATENT DAMAGE (OTHER THAN PERSONAL INJURY)

Claimant's knowledge

Replace footnote 307 with:

32-74 307 [2006] UKHL 9; [2006] 1 W.L.R. 682. The test for "knowledge" under s.14A has been examined in a number of other cases: see, e.g. *Felton v Gaskill Osborne & Co* [1993] 43 E.G. 118; *Spencer-Ward v Humberts* [1995] 1 E.G.L.R. 123 CA; *Hallam-Eames v Merrett Syndicates Ltd* [1996] 7 Med. L.R. 122; *Abbey National Plc v Sayer Moore* [1999] E.G.C.S. 114; *Birmingham Midshires Building Society v Wrethin* [1999] P.N.L.R. 685; [1999] Lloyd's Rep. P.N. 133; *Mortgage Corp Plc v Lambert & Co* [1999] Lloyd's Rep. P.N. 947; *Webster v Cooper Burritt* [2000] Lloyd's Rep. P.N. 167; *Oakes v Hopcroft* [2000] Lloyd's Rep. Med. 394 CA; *Bowie v Southorns* [2002] EWHC 1389 (QB); [2003] P.N.L.R. 7; *McCarroll v Statham Gill Davies* [2003] EWCA Civ 425; [2003] P.N.L.R. 25; *Gravgaard v Aldridge & Brownlee* [2004] EWCA Civ 1529; [2005] P.N.L.R. 19; *Shore v Sedgwick Financial Services Ltd* [2008] EWCA Civ 863; [2008] P.N.L.R. 37. In *Graham v Entec Europe Ltd* [2003] EWCA Civ 1177; [2003] 4 All E.R. 1345, it was held that, where an insurer is bringing a subrogated action in the insured's name, the insurer's knowledge—including the knowledge of its loss adjuster—is relevant under s.14A. See (subsequent to *Haward v Fawcetts*) *Harris Springs Ltd v Howes* [2007] EWHC 3271 (TCC); [2008] B.L.R. 229; *Boycott v Perrins Guy Williams* [2011] EWHC 2969 (Ch); [2012] P.N.L.R. 25; *Integral Memory Plc v Haines Watt* [2012] EWHC 342 (Ch); [2012] S.T.I. 1385; *Roger Ward Associates Ltd v Britannia Assets (UK) Ltd* [2013] EWHC 1653 (QB); *Jacobs v Sesame Ltd* [2014] EWCA Civ 1410; [2015] P.N.L.R. 6; *Schumann v Veale Wasbrough* [2015] EWCA Civ 441; [2015] P.N.L.R. 25; *Halsall v Champion Consulting Ltd* [2017] EWHC 1079 (QB); [2017] P.N.L.R. 32.

9. Other special periods of limitation

(a) Merchant Shipping Act 1995

Replace footnote 318 with:

[318] See *Norfolk v My Travel Group* [2004] 1 Lloyd's Rep. 106 (county court); *Michael v Musgrove, The Sea Eagle* [2011] EWHC 1438 (Admlty); [2012] 2 Lloyd's Rep. 37. But in *Feest v South West Strategic Health Authority* [2015] EWCA Civ 708; [2016] Q.B. 503 it was held that the two-year limitation period under the Athens Convention does not bar a claim by an alleged tortfeasor for contribution against the carrier, under the Civil Liability (Contribution) Act 1978, in respect of personal injury to a passenger. Article 16(3) of Sch.6 extends the two-years, up to a long-stop of three years, where there is domestic legislation providing for "suspension" or "interruption" of the limitation period: this provision was held to include the domestic law's postponement of the limitation period for disability (by reason of age) in the Scottish case of *Warner v Scapa Flow Charters* [2018] UKSC 52; [2018] 1 W.L.R. 4974. **32-78**

(f) Human Rights Act 1998

Replace paragraph with:

By s.7(5) of the Human Rights Act 1998, proceedings for breach by a public authority of a person's Convention rights under the Human Rights Act 1998 must be brought within one year from the date on which the act complained of took place or such longer period as the court considers equitable having regard to all the circumstances. The discretion under s.7(5) is analogous to that under s.33 of the Limitation Act 1980 so that the court should have regard to all the circumstances of the claimant, including the circumstances of the group in a group action.[354] In *O'Connor v Bar Standards Board*[354A] it was held that the conduct of the Bar Standards Board in bringing and pursuing disciplinary proceedings against the claimant was, for the purposes of s.7(5), a single continuing act which continued until the Visitors to the Inns of Court allowed the claimant's appeal: i.e. the limitation period of one year did not start to run until the single continuing act had ceased. The claimant's action under the Human Rights Act 1998 was therefore commenced within a year of the date on which the act complained of took place and was not time-barred. **32-83**

[354] *Dobson v Thames Water Utilities Ltd* [2007] EWHC 2021 (TCC); [2008] 2 All E.R. 362 (partly reversed on a different point at [2009] EWCA Civ 28; [2009] 3 All E.R. 319). *M v Ministry of Justice* [2009] EWCA Civ 419; (2009) 159 N.L.J. 860.

[354A] [2017] UKSC 78; [2017] 1 W.L.R. 4833.

(h) Contribution between tortfeasors

Replace paragraph with:

Section 6 of the Law Reform (Married Women and Tortfeasors) Act 1935, which provided for claims to contribution between tortfeasors,[357] made no provision for the limitation of such claims and so, probably, they had to be brought within six years of their accrual. This was changed by s.4 of the Limitation Act 1963, which reduced that period to two years from the date when the right to contribution accrued. This date was defined as the date of the judgment or award against the tortfeasor claiming contribution, if he had been held liable, and if he had admitted liability to the person injured by his tort, the time when the amount to be paid by him in discharge of his liability had been agreed. This section was deficient because it left unclear the position where a person settled a claim against him under a *denial*[358] of liability. In 1978,[359] s.4 of the Limitation Act 1963 was recast as what is now s.10 of the Limitation Act 1980.[360] By s.10(3), where the tortfeasor seeking contribution is held liable by a judge or arbitrator, the cause of action accrues when **32-85** the judgment or award is given.[361] The judgment or award referred to is a judgment or award which ascertains the quantum, and not merely the existence of the tortfeasor's liability so that, where there are separate judgments or awards in relation to liability and quantum, the two-year limitation period runs from the judgment or award on quantum.[362] By s.10(4), if the claim is settled, with or without an admission of liability, the cause of action accrues when the amount to be paid is agreed. In *Knight v Rochdale Healthcare NHS Trust*[363] it was held that time ran from the date of the agreement even though that agreement was later embodied in a consent order; that is, that s.10(4) of the Limitation Act applied, not s.10(3). The agreement referred to in s.10(4) means a binding contract as to the amount to be paid and not a preliminary non-binding agreement[364].

357 See now the Civil Liability (Contribution) Act 1978. See para.4-12 onwards.

358 See *Stott v West Yorkshire Road Car Co Ltd* [1971] 2 Q.B. 651.

359 Civil Liability (Contribution) Act 1978 Sch.1 para.6.

360 By s.28(5) the disability provision—s.28(1)—applies with two years substituted for six. See para.32-21.

361 s.10(3) goes on to clarify that no account is to be taken of any judgment or award given on appeal in so far as it varies the amount of damages awarded against the tortfeasor.

362 *Aer Lingus Plc v Gildercroft Ltd* [2006] EWCA Civ 4; [2006] 1 W.L.R. 1173. Similarly, an interim payment does not start the two-year limitation period running: *Jellett v Brooke* [2016] EWHC 2828 (QB); [2017] 1 W.L.R. 1177.

363 [2003] EWHC 1831 (QB); [2004] 1 W.L.R. 371. This was approved in *Chief Constable of Hampshire v Southampton CC* [2014] EWCA Civ 1541; [2015] P.I.Q.R. P5.

364 *RG Carter Building Ltd v Kerr Business Services Ltd* [2018] EWHC 729 (TCC); [2018] 1 W.L.R. 4598.